The Handbook of Portuguese Linguistics

Blackwell Handbooks in Linguistics

This outstanding multi-volume series covers all the major subdisciplines within linguistics today and, when complete, will offer a comprehensive survey of linguistics as a whole.

The most recent publications in the series can be found below. To see the full list of titles available in the series, please visit www.wiley.com/go/linguistics-handbooks

The Handbook of Portuguese Linguistics

Edited by

W. Leo Wetzels, João Costa,
and Sergio Menuzzi

WILEY Blackwell

Registered Office
John Wiley & Sons, Inc., 111 River Street, Hoboken, NJ 07030, USA

Editorial Office
The Atrium, Southern Gate, Chichester, West Sussex, PO19 8SQ, UK

For details of our global editorial offices, customer services, and more information about Wiley products visit us at www.wiley.com.

Wiley also publishes its books in a variety of electronic formats and by print-on-demand. Some content that appears in standard print versions of this book may not be available in other formats.

Library of Congress Cataloging-in-Publication Data

Names: Wetzels, Leo, editor. | Costa, João, editor. | Menuzzi, Sergio, 1964– editor.
Title: The handbook of Portuguese linguistics / edited by W. Leo Wetzels, João Costa, and Sergio Menuzzi.
Description: Chichester, West Sussex [England] ; Malden, MA : Wiley Blackwell, 2016. | Series: Blackwell handbooks in linguistics | Includes bibliographical references and index.
Identifiers: LCCN 2016011572 (print) | LCCN 2016002912 (ebook) | ISBN 9781118791950 (hardback) | ISBN 9781119096764 (paper) | ISBN 9781118791745 (Adobe PDF) | ISBN 9781118791851 (epub)
Subjects: LCSH: Portuguese language–Grammar–Handbooks, manuals, etc. | Portuguese language–Usage–Handbooks, manuals, etc. | Portuguese language–Handbooks, manuals, etc. | BISAC: LANGUAGE ARTS & DISCIPLINES / Linguistics / General.
Classification: LCC PC5067.3 H36 2016 (ebook) | LCC PC5067.3 (print) | DDC 469/.82421–dc23
LC record available at https://lccn.loc.gov/2016011572

Cover image: © clivewa/Shutterstock
Cover design by Wiley

Set in 9.5/11.5pt Palatino by SPi Global, Pondicherry, India
Printed and bound in Singapore by Markono Print Media Pte Ltd

10 9 8 7 6 5 4 3 2 1

Contents

Notes on Contributors

Renato Miguel Basso is Professor of Linguistics at the Universidade Federal de São Carlos (UFSCar, São Carlos SP, Brazil). He is co-author of *O Português da Gente* (with Rodolfo Ilari, 2006), *História Concisa da Língua Portuguesa* (with Rodrigo Tadeu Gonçalves, 2014). He has also published articles in several academic journals in Brazil. His current research interests include natural language semantics and pragmatics, indexicals, the history of Brazilian Portuguese, and natural language syntax.

Leda Bisol received her MA and PhD in Linguistics from the Federal University of Rio de Janeiro (UFRJ). She spent a postdoctoral year at Stanford University. She currently acts as a Professor at the Faculty of Humanities of PUCRS, Porto Alegre, Brazil and is a researcher of the National Council for Scientific and Technological Development (CNPQ). Her research focus is on the phonology of Brazilian Portuguese.

Ana Maria Brito (PhD in Linguistics, 1998) is Professor at the Faculdade de Letras of the University of Porto, Portugal, where she has been responsible for the MA and PhD programs since 2007. She is one of the authors of the *Gramática da Língua Portuguesa*, Caminho, Lisboa, 2003, and the author of over 70 papers on different aspects of Portuguese syntax. She was the president of the Portuguese Linguistics Association from 2008 to 2010.

Maria Teresa Brocardo is Associate Professor of Linguistics at the Universidade Nova de Lisboa. Her current research topics include the diachrony of Portuguese verb forms and constructions, analogy, and grammaticalization. Her recent publications include *Tópicos de História da Língua Portuguesa* (2014).

Luiz Carlos Cagliari holds his MA from UNICAMP and his PhD from the University of Edinburgh. He is a retired Professor of phonetics from UNICAMP (State University of São Paulo, Campinas). Presently, he is a lecturer at UNESP (Universidade Estadual Paulista Júlio de Mesquita Filho), Araraquara, Brazil. His main field of research is phonetics.

Márcia Cançado is Professor at the Universidade Federal de Minas Gerais. She works on the syntax–lexical semantics interface, focusing on verb classes, verb alternations, and Brazilian Portuguese syntactic and semantic description.

Ana Maria Carvalho is Professor at the University of Arizona. She has published multiple articles on the sociolinguistics of language contact situations, and is the editor of *Português em Contato* (Vervuert, 2009), co-editor of *The Romance Linguistics Continuum: Crossing Boundaries and Linguistic Categories* (John Benjamins, 2011), *Portuguese-Spanish Interfaces* (John

Benjamins, 2014), *Subject Pronouns in Spanish* (Georgetown University Press, 2015), and associate editor of *Studies in Hispanic and Lusophone Linguistics*.

Gisela Collischonn graduated in Portuguese and English in 1987. She holds a masters degree in Language (1993) from the Federal University of Rio Grande do Sul (UFRGS) and a PhD in Applied Linguistics from the Catholic University of Rio Grande do Sul (1997). She is currently Professor at the Institute of Languages at UFRGS. Her research areas include phonological theory, stress and syllable structure in Portuguese, and phonological variation in southern Brazilian Portuguese.

Clara Nunes Correia is Assistant Professor at the Linguistics Department of the Universidade Nova de Lisboa, where she also received her PhD in semantics. She is responsible for undergraduate and postgraduate semantics courses. Her main areas of research include nominal determiners, tense, and aspect in Portuguese.

João Costa is Professor of Linguistcs at the Faculdade de Ciências Sociais e Humanas, Universidade Nova de Lisboa, Portugal. He served as Secretary of State of Education in the Portuguese Government (2015–2019).

Sonia Cyrino is Associate Professor at the University of Campinas. She has been a Visiting Scholar at the University of Maryland at College Park (USA), at Cambridge University, and at Stony Brook University (USA). She is interested in syntactic theory and diachronic change in Brazilian Portuguese. She has contributed chapters to books published by Mouton de Gruyter, John Benjamins, Oxford University Press, and articles in *the Journal of Portuguese Linguistics, the Iberia-International Journal on Theoretical Linguistics*, and *Natural Language & Linguistic Theory*.

Inês Duarte is Professor of Linguistics at the Department of General and Romance Linguistics (Faculty of Arts) at the University of Lisbon, and researcher at CLUL. Her main research domains are syntactic theory and comparative syntax, with special reference to Portuguese.

Maria Eugenia Lammoglia Duarte is Professor of the Universidade Federal do Rio de Janeiro (UFRJ, Brazil) and holds a research grant from CNPq. She studies syntactic change in Brazilian Portuguese from the perspective of the Theory of Principles and Parameters. Some of her main publications are "The loss of the 'Avoid Pronoun' Principle in Brazilian Portuguese" (In Kato and Negrão, eds., *Brazilian Portuguese and the Null Subject Parameter*, 2000) and "Null Subjects in European and Brazilian Portuguese", co-authored by Pilar Barbosa and Mary Kato (*Journal of Portuguese Linguistics*, 2005).

Marcelo Barra Ferreira is Professor in the Department of Linguistics at the University of São Paulo. He received his PhD from the Massachusetts Institute of Technology in 2005. His research area is formal semantics and its interfaces with syntax and pragmatics.

Giovana Ferreira-Gonçalves is Professor at the Federal University of Pelotas, Brazil, and a researcher of the Emergence of Oral Language Laboratory of the same University (LELO/UFPEL). Her work focuses on phonological acquisition and phonological theory.

Maria Cristina Figueiredo Silva is Associate Professor in the Linguistics Department at the Universidade Federal do Paraná (UFPR, Brazil), working mainly on Brazilian Portuguese syntax and morphology.

Maria João Freitas is Associate Professor at Lisbon University and carries out her research in the Centro de Linguística of the same University. She is mainly active in the area of language acquisition (primarily phonological acquisition). In recent years she also has been working on clinical and educational linguistics.

Sónia Frota is Associate Professor at the University of Lisbon and Director of the Laboratório de Fonética and the Lisbon Baby Lab. She is also editor of *the Journal of Portuguese Linguistics*. Her research focuses on prosody in language, comprising phrasing, intonation, and rhythm, and the acquisition and development of prosody. She is the author of *Prosody and Focus in European Portuguese. Phonological phrasing and intonation* (Routledge), and has recently co-edited *Intonation in Romance* (Oxford University Press).

Charlotte Galves is Professor of syntax and diachronic syntax at the Universidade de Campinas (Campinas, Brazil). Her research interests include comparative diachronic studies of the syntax of Portuguese, including Classical Portuguese, and Brazilian and European Portuguese; collection and annotation of electronic corpora; probabilistic modelling of language change. She has published many articles on the syntax and history of Brazilian Portuguese, and is one of the editors of *Parameter Theory and Linguistic Change* (Oxford: Oxford University Press, 2012).

Anabela Gonçalves is Professor at the University of Lisbon, where she carrries out her research in the Centro de Linguística. She works in the area of syntax, mainly on verbs and sentence structure. Over the last few years, she has also worked on the acquisition of syntax and on educational linguistics.

Carlos Alexandre Gonçalves is Professor at the Federal University of Rio de Janeiro (UFRJ) since 1993. He is a researcher of CNPq since 1999. His research interests are in morphology and the phonology–morphology interface. He is the author of several books and papers.

D. Eric Holt is Associate Professor of Spanish and Linguistics in the Department of Languages, Literatures, and Cultures and the Linguistics Program at the University of South Carolina. His scholarly interests include Hispanic linguistics, historical phonology, dialectology and phonological theory, as well as second-language phonology.

Dermeval da Hora holds his doctorate in Applied Linguistics from the Pontifícia Universidade Católica do Rio Grande do Sul (1990). He was a post-doctoral student at the Vrije Universiteit, Amsterdam. He is Associate Professor IV at the Universidade Federal da Paraíba and holds a productivity grant from CNPq. His main research focus is on phonological variation, style, attitude, and perception.

Rodolfo Ilari is Professor of Linguistics. He retired after 30 years from the Universidade Estadual de Campinas (Brazil), where he belonged to the team that started the first Graduate Program in Linguistics (1971) and the first Linguistics Department in Brazil (1975). His main teaching and research subjects are the history of the Romance languages, semantic and pragmatic theory, and Brazilian Portuguese grammar, with a focus on verb semantics. He has also translated many important works in the field of General Linguistics and Semantics.

Georg A. Kaiser is Professor of Romance at the University of Konstanz. His research focus is on Romance syntax and historical linguistics, as well as language contact and language conflict. He has published on pronominal clitics, word order, and question-formation in

French, Portuguese, Spanish, Raeto-Romance, and Occitan. He recently published an introduction to diachronic Romance linguistics.

Mary Aizawa Kato is retired volunteer Professor at the State University of Campinas. Her research in comparative and historical syntax covers topics such as word order, *wh*-constructions, and null arguments.

Anthony Kroch is Professor of syntax and the history of English at the University of Pennsylvania. His research interests include the formal analysis of natural language syntax and the study of historical syntax and parametric change through the analysis of corpus data. He has published many articles on the syntax of English, syntactic changes in English, and on resources for electronic historical corpora. He is the author of the chapter "Syntactic Change" in the *Handbook of Contemporary Syntactic Theory* (Oxford: Blackwell, 1991).

Maria Lobo is Assistant Professor in the Faculdade de Ciências Sociais e Humanas at the Universidade Nova de Lisboa and researcher at the Centro de Linguística da Universidade Nova de Lisboa. Her research covers language acquisition and language variation, including topics such as clitics and pronouns, relative clauses, clefts, and adverbial clauses, among other topics.

Ana Cristina Macário Lopes is Associate Professor of Portuguese Linguistics at Coimbra University and a member of CELGA, a research center funded by the FCT (Fundação para a Ciência e Tecnologia). Her research and publications are on Portuguese Semantics and Pragmatics. Her current main research interests are discourse connectives, discourse relations, and grammaticalization.

Célia Regina dos Santos Lopes is Professor at the Federal University of Rio de Janeiro (Brazil). Her teaching and research interests are historical sociolinguistics and grammaticalization in the pronominal system of Brazilian Portuguese. Her recent publications include *Las formas de tratamiento en español y en portugués* (co-edited with Letícia Couto).

Ruth E. V. Lopes is Associate Professor of Linguistics at the University of Campinas. She was a visiting researcher at the University of Maryland at College Park, the University of Massachusetts at Amherst, and the University of Chicago. Her research interests include language acquisition and the syntax–semantics interface. She co-edited *Parameter Theory and Linguistic Change* (Oxford, 2012) and co-organized the 45th Linguistics Symposium on Romance Languages, hosted at the University of Campinas, Brazil.

Dante Lucchesi is Professor of Portuguese at the Federal University of Bahia and a researcher of CNPq (National Council for Research). He is the author and organizer of *Português Afro-Brasileiro* (EDUFBA, 2009) and the author of *Sistema Mudança e Linguagem* (Parábola Editorial, 2004) and *Língua e Sociedade Partidas* (Contexto, 2015).

Ana R. Luís is Assistant Professor at the Faculty of Arts at the University of Coimbra. Her research focuses on Portuguese inflectional morphology and cliticization, with a special interest in the morphology of Portuguese contact varieties. She has published both as a single author and as a co-author on the morphology–syntax interaction, Portuguese inflectional morphology, the morphology of creole languages, and cliticization.

Ana Madeira is Assistant Professor in the Linguistics Department and a researcher in the Linguistics Research Center at the Universidade Nova de Lisboa (FCSH/NOVA). Her current research focuses on the second language acquisition of Portuguese (morphosyntax, semantics and discourse) and on Portuguese syntax (synchrony and diachrony).

José Magalhães is Associate Professor at the Federal University of Uberlândia, Brazil. He holds his doctorate in linguistics from the Pontifícia Universidade Católica do Rio Grande do Sul (2004). In his dissertation he studied the stress system of non-verbs in Brazilian Portuguese. His recent research focuses on the history of unstressed vowels in eighteenth- and nineteenth-century Brazilian Portuguese.

Rui Marques is Assistant Professor in the Faculdade de Letras at the Universidade de Lisboa, where he has been teaching Semantics, Pragmatics, and Text Linguistics, and a researcher at CLUL (http://www.clul.ul.pt/en/researcher/96-rui-marques). His main research interests are propositional attitudes, mood, and modality.

Ana Maria Martins is Professor at the University of Lisbon. Her research in comparative and historical syntax covers topics such as word-order, clitics, negation, emphatic polarity, and infinitives.

Gladis Massini-Cagliari holds her PhD in Linguistics (1995) from UNICAMP (State University of São Paulo, Campinas). She was a postdoctoral student from 2002 to 2003 at Oxford University. Since 1996 she is a lecturer at UNESP (Universidade Estadual Paulista Júlio de Mesquita Filho), Araraquara, Brazil. She is the author of several monographs on historical linguistics and phonology, with special emphasis on Medieval Portuguese.

Gabriela Matos is Associate Professor with "Agregação" in the Faculdade de Letras at the University of Lisbon and a researcher in the Centro de Linguística at the same University. She works on Portuguese syntax from a comparative perspective. Her main research interests are ellipsis, coordination vs. subordination, parenthetical clauses, negation, and clitics. She also participates in work on the acquisition and processing of Portuguese.

Sergio Menuzzi is Professor at the Department of Classical and Vernacular Letters, Federal University of Rio Grande do Sul (UFRGS), Porto Alegre, Brazil. He is also the current director of the Faculty of Letters in the same university, and has been a researcher of the National Council of Research (CNPq) since 2004.

Carlos Mioto was Professor at the Universidade Federal de Santa Catarina (Florianópolis, Brazil) from 1994 to 2012. Currently, he is a visiting Professor at the Universidade Federal da Fronteira Sul (Chapecó, Brazil). His main area of research is the syntax of Brazilian Portuguese, with a particular emphasis on the syntax of *wh*-constructions and the left periphery of the sentence.

João Antônio de Moraes is Professor of Portuguese at the Federal University of Rio de Janeiro, and a researcher of the Brazilian Research Council of Science and Technology. His research interests are the phonetics and phonology of Brazilian Portuguese, especially intonation, prosody, nasality, and experimental phonology. His recent publications include *Estudos de Fonética e Fonologia Experimentais* (ed.) and *Illocution, Attitudes and Prosody: A Multimodal Analysis* (with Albert Rilliard).

Jairo Nunes is Professor of Linguistics at the Universidade de São Paulo. He is the author of *Linearization of Chains and Sideward Movement* (MIT Press, 2004), co-author of *Understanding Minimalism* (Cambridge University Press, 2005) and *Control as Movement* (Cambridge University Press, 2010), and editor of *Minimalist Essays on Brazilian Portuguese Syntax* (John Benjamins, 2009).

Maria Fátima Oliveira is Professor of Portuguese Linguistics at the University of Porto (Porto, Portugal). She has published many papers on formal semantics, dealing mainly with the semantics of verbs, especially topics such as tense, aspect, and modality. She is also interested in the semantics of anaphora, questions, and reference. She is the author of the chapters on tense and aspect, mood and modality, and nominal reference in *the Gramática de Língua Portuguesa* (Mateus et al., 2003). Her most recent article is "Activities with culmination" (co-authored by A. Leal, *Oslo Studies in Language*, 2015).

Roberta Pires de Oliveira is a Researcher of the Brazilian National Council for Research (CNPq), working at the Universidade Federal do Paraná and the Universidade Federal de Santa Catarina. Her main area of research is natural language semantics and pragmatics. She is also interested in logics and philosophy of language. Recently, she has been developing experiments as a means to test theoretical proposals in semantics.

Wayne J. Redenbarger is Professor Emeritus at the Ohio State University. BA Indiana University, MA, PhD Harvard University. Formerly Assistant Dean and director of the OSU doctoral program in Romance Linguistics, his research is on the lexical phonology and morphology of Latin, and their evolution into Hispano-Romance and Portuguese.

Celeste Rodrigues holds her PhD in Portuguese Linguistics from the University of Lisbon in (2001). She is currently an Assistant Professor at the University of Lisbon, Portugal.

Raquel S. Santos is Associate Professor at the University of São Paulo (USP), Brazil. She has her MA and her PhD from the Universidade Estadual de Campinas. Her work focuses on the phonology of Portuguese, the syntax-phonology interface, and the acquisition of L1 phonology.

Maria Marta Pereira Scherre is a Senior Visiting Professor at the Universidade Federal do Espírito Santo (UFES, Vitória, Brazil) and holds a research grant from CNPq. Her research focuses on variation and change in Brazilian Portuguese since the 1970s. Recent publications include "Remodeling the age variable: number concord in Brazilian Portuguese" and "Sociolinguistic correlates of negative evaluation: variable concord in Rio de Janeiro" (*Language Variation and Change*, 2013–2014).

Scott A. Schwenter is Professor of Hispanic and Lusophone Linguistics at the Ohio State University. His research focuses on morphosyntactic phenomena in Spanish and Portuguese. He is the author of *Pragmatics of Conditional Marking* and articles in *Language Variation and Change, Lingua, Linguistics, Journal of Linguistics,* and *Studies in Language.*

Luiz Carlos Schwindt is Associate Professor in the Department of Linguistics, Philology and Literary Theory at the Federal University of Rio Grande do Sul (UFRGS) and a researcher of the National Council for Scientific and Technological Development, in Brazil. His main areas of interest are the phonology–morphology interface, language variation and change, and the architecture of grammar.

João Veloso is Professor of Portuguese Phonology at the University of Porto, Portugal. His main research focuses on syllable structure, phonological wordhood constraints, prosodic constituency, and phonological processes of Portuguese.

Marina Vigário is Associate Professor in the Faculty of Arts and Humanities at Lisbon University and a member of the Laboratory of Phonetics and the Lisbon Baby Lab (University of Lisbon). Her research interests include Portuguese prosodic phonology from a cross-linguistic perspective, the frequency of phonological objects and patterns, and prosody in early language development.

Alina Villalva is Professor at Lisbon University since 1984 and a member of the Centro de Linguística of the Universidade de Lisboa (CLUL) since 2008. Her research is on the morphology and the lexicon, especially of European Portuguese. She is the author of several books and papers.

W. Leo Wetzels is Professor Emeritus of the VU University Amsterdam, The Netherlands, where he held the chair of Romance languages and Amazon languages until July 2017. Since September 2017 he acts as a visiting Professor at the Federal University of Ceará in Fortaleza, Brazil and, since January 2019, as an invited researcher at the EHESS in Paris, France. He is Editor-in-Chief of *Probus, International Journal of Romance Linguistics*.

1 History and Current Setting

MARIA TERESA BROCARDO AND CÉLIA REGINA DOS SANTOS LOPES

1. From Latin to Portuguese—Main Linguistic changes and conditioning factors

The development of Portuguese can be traced back to Latin, whose establishment in the Iberian Peninsula was a consequence of the Roman conquest, initiated in 218 BCE, but completed only about 200 years later. In the early fifth century CE the peninsula was invaded by several Germanic tribes, among which was the Suebi, the only tribe that resisted after the arrival of another group of Germanic invaders, the Visigoths. The Visigoths, who eventually conquered the entire peninsula, were already Latin-speaking before they arrived. Of major importance for the linguistic history of the Ibero-Romance area is the Moorish conquest of the Iberian Peninsula, starting in 711 CE. The northern territories of the peninsula were the refuge of the surviving Christian kingdoms, which would later expand southwards. The varieties of Latin spoken in those areas, where the Arabic influence was naturally more superficial, are at the origin of the Ibero-Romance languages.

Portuguese originally emerged in the northwest of the Iberian Peninsula and later expanded southwards with the Christian Reconquest. This "initial" or "primitive" area of Portuguese roughly comprises what corresponds today to Galiza and part of northern Portugal (see Castro 2006: 64–67). Thus, the designation "Galician-Portuguese" is sometimes used in the literature to refer to this original language unity.

In the following description of the language-formation process, we discuss the linguistic features characteristic of the most ancient periods of Portuguese, signaling the most relevant differences within the Romance context, in particular those that are distinctive to the Ibero-Romance area, for which we take Castilian (Cast.) as our point of reference.

As a Romance language, Portuguese both continues Latin and diverges from it, which means that we can identify features that are diachronically characterizable as more conservative while others are of a more innovative nature. This type of contrast, recurrent in traditional approaches but also considered crucial for diachronic analyses in modern approaches (see Maiden, Smith, and Ledgeway 2011 who oppose "innovation" and "persistence" in their *History of the Romance Languages*), will serve as a guideline for our description.

Several vocalic features of Portuguese evidence tendencies of persistence. Among these features is the continuation of the Latin diphthong /aw/ as /ow/, while more generally in Romance it emerges as a monophthong (*ouro* "gold" < *auru-*, Cast. *oro*). This diphthong was preserved in Portuguese even in unstressed syllables (*ousar* "dare," *outono* "autumn").

The Handbook of Portuguese Linguistics, First Edition. Edited by W. Leo Wetzels, João Costa, and Sergio Menuzzi.
© 2016 John Wiley & Sons, Inc. Published 2020 by John Wiley & Sons, Inc.

Exceptions are limited to a few forms with earlier monophtonghization (*orelha* "ear" < *auric(u)la–*, *pobre* "poor" < *paupere–*), sometimes already attested in (Vulgar) Latin. It should be noted that Portuguese /ow/ also originated from secondary */aw/, formed through distinct processes (*amou* "(he/she) loved" < *amauit*, *soube* "(he/she) knew" < *sapuit*, *outro* "other" < *alteru–*). Portuguese also preserves /ej/, a diphthong formed in Latin in cases where /j/ became adjacent to /ɛ/ or /a/ including cases where /j/ derived from a consonant, usually /k/ in coda position, also in contrast with the more innovative Cast. result (*madeira* "wood" < *materia–*, Cast. *madera*, *leite* "milk" < *lacte–*, Cast. *leche*).

The lack of diphthongization of the Latin vowels /ɛ/ < Ĕ and /ɔ/ < Ŏ also contrasts with their Castilian reflexes (*erva* "grass" < *hĕrba*, Cast. *hierba*, *morte* "death" < *mŏrte–*, cast. *muerte*) and is different from the other Romance areas, in which diphthongization occurred in several phonological contexts. This feature is particularly relevant for the individualization of Portuguese, since it is indicative of a linguistic borderline between Portuguese and non-Portuguese varieties, including Castilian and some varieties of Leonese (Cintra 1983: 140). The Portuguese vowel system as it appears in stressed syllables is still identical to the one that emerged consequent to the loss of the Latin quantity oppositions, already attested in Latin sources, a system defined as "Proto-Western-Romance" (Vincent 1988: 32): /i/, /e/, /ɛ/, /a/, /ɔ/, /o/, /u/. Other phonological changes affected consonants, such as the evolution of the medial sequences /jt/, /lj/ and /jl/, where Portuguese preserved the sequence /jt/ and where /lj/ and /jl/ developed into /ʎ/, which contrast with the more innovative Castilian reflexes: *oito* "eight" < *octo*, Cast. *ocho*, *folha* "leaf" < *folia*, Cast. *hoja*, *olho* "eye" < *oc(u)lu–*, Cast. *ojo*.

Conservative tendencies are also manifest at other levels. If we assume that the personal infinitive is the continuation of the Latin imperfect subjunctive (Martins 2001), its formal preservation would represent a particularly conservative feature, since the Latin imperfect subjunctive survives elsewhere only in Sardinian (Vincent 1988: 47). The Latin pluperfect indicative is equally preserved in Portuguese (*mostrara* "(I) had shown" < *monstrara(m)*), as in Castilian, in contrast with the other Romance areas. In past stages of Castilian and Portuguese, pluperfect forms conveyed modal as well as temporal values, depending on the context of use, which later split to become a temporal category in contemporary Portuguese while functioning as a modal category in Spanish. Only later in the history of Portuguese would fully grammaticalized compound forms emerge from periphrastic constructions with *habere* and later *tenere* (imperfect) + past participle (*havia/tinha mostrado*) for the expression of the "past in the past" temporal value. The tmesis of clitic pronouns in future and conditional forms (*mostrar-lhe-ei*, *mostrar-lhe-ia* "(I) will / would show him / her") is often also considered a conservative feature of Portuguese. Although tmesis was already optional in past stages of the language, it persists in contemporary European Portuguese in more formal styles, whereas in Brazilian Portuguese it is restricted to the written register.

Regarding the Latin inherited lexicon, Portuguese and Castilian share a number of etyma that configure lexical contrasts with other Romance areas: *comer* "eat" < *comedere* (cf. Italian / French *manger* / *mangiare* < *manducare*); *falar* / *hablar* "speak" < *fabulare* (cf. *parler* / *parlare* < *parabolare*); *medo* / *miedo* "fear" < *metu–* (cf. *peur* / *paura* < *pavore*, **pauura*); *pássaro* / *pájaro* "bird" < **passaru–* (cf. *oiseau* / *ucello* < *auicellu–*). Forms of this type would indicate a common Hispanic origin (Piel 1989: 12) of a more conservative nature. In other cases, however, the shared lexicon of Portuguese and Castilian is somewhat more innovative: *irmão* / *hermano* "brother" < (*frater*) *germanu–* (cf. French *frère* < *frater*); *cabeça* / *cabeza* "head" < **capitia* (French *chef* < *caput*); *coração* / *corazón* "heart" < **coratione–* (cf. French *coeur* < *cor*). The conservative character of some rare examples of Portuguese specific lexical types (*colmo* "straw" < *culmu–*, *adro* "atrium" < *atriu–*, *gume* "cutting edge" < *acumen*) could be explained by the peripherality of the Portuguese area (Piel 1989: 12).

Some traditional interpretative approaches (Baldinger 1972: 104–124) explained conservative tendencies as a consequence of the manner in which linguistic Romanization took place and the specific location of the Portuguese primitive area, by pointing out that Latin expanded to this area from the south (*Hispania Baetica*), where Romanization had occurred much earlier. The variety of Latin that expanded from the south to the northwest of the Iberian Peninsula was supposedly more "cultivated" and thus linguistically conservative. The peripheral location of the Portuguese primitive area, as well as the fact that it was kept in relative isolation by the Suebi kingdom during the first phase of the German occupation (early fifth to early eighth centuries), would also have contributed to linguistic conservatism (Baldinger 1972: 166, Castro 2006: 58–59).

The decisive phonological changes that set apart Portuguese from the other romance languages—the loss of intervocalic *–n–* and *–l–*—occurred later, after the Arab invasions of the peninsula, and clearly are innovative. The exact dating of the loss of *-n-* remains controversial. Regressive nasalization (*manu–* > /mãno/) must have occurred first (Baldinger 1972: 165, 221) and *–n–* loss (/mãno/ > /mão/ "hand," with a hiatus in Old Portuguese) may have been initiated during the tenth century (Sampson 1999: 184). Nasality is preserved in many forms (*lana* > *lãa* (*lã* "wool"), *bonu–* > *bõo* (*bom* "good"), *unu–* > *ũu* (*um* "one")), although in a number of other cases it was later lost (*luna–* > *lũa* (*lua* "moon"), *ponere* > *põer* (*pôr* "put"); *tenere* > *têer* (*ter* "have")). The loss of *–n–* must be related to the more general process of nasalization, which distinctively characterizes Portuguese in the Romance context (French excepted), and by which oral vowels were nasalized when followed by a syllable-final nasal consonant (*non* > Old Portuguese *n*[õ] (*não* "no"), *grande–* > *gr*[ã]*de* "big," verbal endings *–an(t)* and *–un(t)* > Old Portuguese *–*[ã] and *–*[õ]).

During approximately the same period (the tenth century, according to Baldinger 1972 and Teyssier 1982: 15) intervocalic *–l–* was also lost after a hypothetical intermediate stage of velarization: *salire* > **sa*[ł]*ir* > *sair* "leave"; *colore* > Old Portuguese *coor* > *cor* "colour." Intervocalic *–l–* and *–n–* occur, of course, in many non-inherited words (or words derived from Latin stems, cf. *mão* / *manual* "manual," *dor* "pain" / *doloroso* "painful") and also in words later reshaped according to the Latin model, e.g., Old Portuguese *mẽos* "less" (< *minus*) was later replaced by *menos*, while *pena* and *pẽa* "punishment" (< *poena–*) both occur in ancient texts. The consequences of *–n–* and *–l–* deletion are noticeable in the peculiar forms of the Portuguese indefinite and definite articles (and of the accusative personal pronouns, descendants of the same Latin forms). The Latin masculine numeral *unu-* "one" became Old Portuguese /ũu/ and coalesced to /ũ/ probably by the end of the same period, while the result of the feminine form *una–* > /ũa/ still persists in Middle Portuguese and suffered epenthesis of *–m–* only later (written *um, uma, uns, umas* in Modern Portuguese). As for the definite articles, which represent the Latin accusative forms *illu–, illa–* (from the demonstrative *ille* "that, near to it / him / her"), the *l–* of the intermediary forms, *lo/a(s)*, was preserved only in contexts of assimilation to another consonant (*pelo* < *per* "by" + *lo*), besides several other forms in past stages (Old Portuguese *todolos* < *todos* + *los* "all the," alternative to *todos os*) and also in pronoun cognate forms (*mostramo-lo* "(we) show it" < *mostramos* + *lo*). Otherwise, *l-* loss was systematic, probably because the article and pronoun occurred frequently in intervocalic position in sentence contexts, thus the forms *o, a, os, as*.

The merger to the affricate /tʃ/ of the Latin initial clusters *pl–, fl–, cl–* is another innovative change relevant to the differentiation of Portuguese. The merger also occurs in Castilian, where it became /ʎ/, suggesting a more complex change for the Portuguese result: *plenu–* > Old Portuguese *chēo* > *cheio* "full," Cast. *lleno; flamma* > *chama* "flame," Cast. *llama; clave–* > *chave* "key," Cast. *llave*. Note that this merger does not occur in other Romance areas (cf. French and Italian *plein/pieno, flamme/fiamma, clef/chiave*). The outcome of this change resulted in a contrast between the new affricate /tʃ/ and the fricative /ʃ/, originated by a distinct (earlier) palatalization process (roughly Latin /s/ influenced by /j/), and the testimonies of Old and Middle Portuguese show a systematic distinction— /tʃ/ written as <ch> and /ʃ/ as <x>. The two consonants would later merge into /ʃ/, except in a dialectally restricted area of European Portuguese (Cintra 1983: 143). Many doublets evidence distinct diachronic paths (*cheio / pleno* "full," *chamar / clamar* "call"), and a few words show a less radical change, manifested only in the evolution of *–l* to [ɾ] (*prazer* (verb and noun) "please, pleasure" < *placere, fraco* "weak" < *flaccu-, cravo* "nail" < *clavu-*).

The outcome of the linguistic changes that originated in the northwest of the Iberian Peninsula expanded toward the south as a consequence of repopulation movements subsequent to the Christian Reconquest of the territories that had remained longer under Arabic influence (Castro 2006: 68–69). This migration was the decisive factor in the making of the European Portuguese linguistic area. Portuguese preserves only a few vestiges, mainly in toponyms, of Romance varieties originally spoken in southern areas, generically referred as *moçárabe* (Mozarabic) (Castro 2006: 62–64). These *moçarabismos* (e.g. *Fontanela*) are clearly identifiable in contrast with (Galician-)Portuguese forms precisely because they preserve intervocalic *–l–* and *–n–*.

2. Old and Middle Portuguese

2.1. Periodization issues

If we take as a reference the approximate date of the phonological innovations discussed in Section 1, we would propose the tenth century as the period of the "birth" of Portuguese (Castro 2006: 75). Although the relatively late appearance of written records of the Portuguese language, similar to the other Romance areas, results in a considerable gap between the estimated date of the emergence of the language and that of the beginning of its attested history, this intermediate period must not be considered entirely non-attested. It is indirectly attested through extant Latin (or Latin-Portuguese) written texts, the most ancient Latin text of the Portuguese area dating from 882. Currently, there is no absolute consensus about the identification of the most ancient text written in Portuguese. In the mid-twentieth century, the results of the research on this subject undertaken by several scholars (see Martins 1999 for references), had converged to the identification of two texts as the earliest preserved Portuguese written records, the *Testamento de Afonso II* (The Will of King Afonso II), dated 1214, and the *Notícia de Torto*, a undated private document probably written around the same date. However, the results of Martins' (1999) research have reopened the debate. According to this author, among other manuscripts from the late twelfth and early thirteenth centuries, the *Notícia de Fiadores*, dated 1175, is the oldest Portuguese written text. Because it is a very short document with some superficially Latinate forms and constructions, the discussion about how to characterize its writing, and the writing of other documents from about the same period, as Portuguese, Latin or Latin-Portuguese is not closed. The importance of such texts is, of course, undeniable for the documentation of the complex transitional process from Latin to Portuguese writing.

For the periodization of Portuguese history, different proposals have been put forward, some diverging only in detail, while others differ more significantly, especially regarding the evaluation of the relevant linguistic features and the adequate methodologies. Of major importance in this debate is the type of criteria used for establishing the distinct periods. While one would agree that, at least ideally, the proper periodization should be sustained by both linguistic and external facts, more recent proposals tend to emphasize the relevance of linguistic criteria. Here, we will propose a distinction between two medieval periods (following the unpublished proposal of Lindley Cintra, adopted by many): Old Portuguese, comprising broadly the thirteenth and fourteenth centuries, and Middle Portuguese, dating from the beginning of the fifteenth century to the middle of the sixteenth century. Other proposals consider a broader period, usually referred to as *Português Arcaico* "Archaic Portuguese," covering the whole of the two periods distinguished above.

The main argument for proposing two distinct medieval periods is that several changes, with relevant linguistic consequences, occurred in the transitional period between them, even though they did not all happen at exactly the same time. In the following section we shall briefly describe these changes, concentrating mainly on their consequences for nominal and verbal inflexion.

2.2. *Contrasting features and linguistic changes*

The analysis of the spelling of written Old Portuguese shows a predominant distinction between nasal endings in *–ã* and *–õ*, consistent with the etymology, as exemplified in Table 1.1.

Texts from the late fourteenth century and in particular from the fifteenth century show that these endings were no longer distinguished. The types of non-etymological spellings include confusion between the two endings (*falõ* "(they) talk," *razã* "reason") and, especially in later testimonies within the Middle Portuguese period, "phonetic" spellings (*razão* "reason," *são* "(I) am" or "(they) are," *andavão* "(they) were walking," *ordenarão* "(they) ordered"), which clearly attest the merger of the two endings to a nasal diphthong. The merger also included the sequence *–ão*, from Latin *–anu–* (*mão* "hand," *irmão* "brother"), corresponding to a hiatus in Old Portuguese, but one which had also evolved into a diphthong as the result of disyllabification of the second element. In the words of Sampson (1999: 195), "The details of the merger of the final vowels [-ã], [-õ] and [-ão] of thirteenth century Portuguese as [-ɐ̃w] and the precise factors which it brought are still uncertain and hence controversial." A patent phonological consequence of this merger was the loss of uniformity of nasal realizations in different contexts (contrast Old Portuguese *red*[õ]*do* "round" / *raz*[õ], *gr*[ã]*de* "big" / *p*[ã] "bread" with *red*[õ]*do* / *raz*[ɐ̃w], *gr*[ã]*de* / *p*[ɐ̃w] in later stages), but we shall concentrate here on the consequences of this change on other levels. In the nominal inflexion of forms with original *–ã* or *–õ* endings, the merger resulted in increased paradigmatic irregularity, and, thus, synchronically less predictable plurals: *pã / pães > pão / pães* and *razõ / razões > razão / razões* (besides *mão* (*<–manu*) */ mãos*). The change also has consequences in verb inflexion, namely the syncretism of the 3rd person plural of the simple perfect, originally in *–õ*, and the pluperfect, originally in *–ã*. This syncretism may have contributed to the disuse of this particular pluperfect form and maybe of the entire paradigm, at least in non-formal registers, and to the increased frequency of the periphrastic pluperfect. It should be noted

Table 1.1   Examples of the evolution of Old Portuguese nasal endings *–ã* and *–õ*.

Old Portuguese		Latin
–ã	**Nominal forms**	
	pã "bread," *cã* "dog"	*–an(e)*
	Third person plural verb forms	
	amã "love" (present), *amavã* (imperfect), *amarã* (pluperfect)	*–an(t)*
–õ	**Nominal (and other)forms**	
	razõ "reason," *oraçõ* "prayer," *nõ* "no," *cõ* "with"	*–on(e), –on, –um*
	Third person plural verb forms	
	Preterite	
	ganharõ "won," *fezerõ* "made," *partirõ* "left"	*–un(t)*
	Present of *ser* **"be"**	
	sõ "(I) am" or "(they) are"	*–um, –un(t)*

that, although the simple pluperfect is fully preserved in Contemporary Portuguese in more formal registers, it is in practice a defective paradigm, since the 3rd person plural forms are uninterpretable. Unlike other forms (*dissera* "(he/she) had said," *fizera* "had made," *saíra* "had left"), the 3rd person plural forms (*disseram, fizeram, saíram*) are always interpreted as the simple perfect. Note that in the plural counterpart of a sentence like *O ministro reafirmou o que **dissera** antes* "The minister reaffirmed what he had said before," *Os ministros reafirmaram o que ?disseram/tinham dito antes*, the form *disseram* would not be interpreted as the pluperfect. The only available pluperfect forms are, in this case, the periphrastic ones (*tinham dito / feito / saído*), even if this is usually not signaled in Portuguese descriptive grammars.

Another feature that distinguishes Old and Middle Portuguese is the predominance, in the earlier period, of past participle endings in *–ud–* (varying in gender / number *–udo/a/s*) for 2nd conjugation verbs (with thematic vowel *e*). In the later period, they appear to be only residual and are eventually entirely replaced by *–id–*, causing a merger with the 3rd conjugation (with thematic vowel *i*) endings, for example *perdudo > perdido, vençudo > vencido*, past participles of *perder* "lose" and *vencer* "win," like *partido*, past participle of *partir* "leave." The change is usually described as a result of analogy, triggered by the lack of "structural support" for *–u–* (Câmara 1975: 159) in other forms of the verb class. We may assume that both the inter-paradigmatic factors (the influence of the past participle *–id–* endings of the 3rd conjugation verbs) and the intra-paradigmatic factors (the influence of *–i–* endings that already occurred in the 2nd conjugation verbs in the simple perfect and imperfect (*venci, vencia* "(I) won, was winning") concurred for the loss of the *–ud–* endings in past participles. We would then have a change characterizable as either analogical extension or analogical (paradigmatic) leveling, although there may be an additional argument to support the former. The 2nd conjugation lost to the 3rd conjugation a number of verbs, e.g., *caer > cair* "fall," *finger > fingir* "pretend," *confonder > confundir* "confuse" at approximately the same period (Maia 1986: 726–731). This prevalence of the *i*-theme paradigms could favor the hypothesis of analogical extension in the case of the change *–ud– > –id–*, as part of a more general trend for a partial merger of the 2nd and 3rd conjugations since the loss of *–ud–* endings reduced the number of contrasting forms. It should be noted, however, that the systematic character of the change, with no residual verb endings in *–ud–*, is somewhat atypical of analogical changes, which tend to apply only to a subset of the potential "candidate" forms. The exceptionless character of the change would, thus, point to a combination of extension and leveling factors, a combination that may be related to more regular analogical changes (Hock 1991: 179).

Another distinguishing feature between Old and Middle Portuguese, also concerning verb inflexion, is the realization of the 2nd person plural suffixes. The almost uniform realizations *–de / –des* (imperative/other inflected forms), with only the exception of the simple perfect (*–stes*), predominant in the former stage, contrast with the variation observable in Middle Portuguese, which demonstrates the loss of intervocalic *–d–*.

As can be observed in Table 1.2, the increased allomorphy in person/number marking resulted not only from divergent realizations that emerged as a consequence of *–d–* loss in the various conjugations (diphthong or vowel through *–i + i*-reduction) but also from the preservation of *–d–* in non-intervocalic contexts and after a nasal. Moreover *–d–* was preserved intervocalically in a set of "exceptional" forms. This was explained by scholars on the basis of different factors, phonological (Williams 1975: §155, 4) as well as morphological (Piel 1989: 218). In Middle and Classic Portuguese, there are attestations of variation in both intervocalic (*ides/is*) and non-intervocalic contexts (*fazerdes/fazeres*) that could indicate that *–d–* loss may have been somewhat less restricted initially.

Note that while in contemporary European Portuguese 2nd person plural forms (with or without expressed *vós* "you-plural") are used only in the northern and in some central dialects with a plural addressee, they occurred regularly, as in other Romance areas, also to

Table 1.2   Examples of the evolution of second person plural verb suffixes.

Verbs	Old Portuguese (pres. indicative and inflected infinitive)	Results of intervocalic –d– loss	Preserved –d–	
			after –r–/nasal	*intervocalic*
amar "love"	*amades*	*amais*		
	amardes		*amardes*	
fazer "do"	*fazedes*	*fazeis*		
	fazerdes		*fazerdes*	
ter "have"	*tendes*		*tendes*	
crer "believe"	*credes*			*credes*
partir "leave"	*partides*	*partis*		
	partirdes		*partirdes*	
ir "go"	*ides*			*ides*

address a singular interlocutor (a use that persisted until the late eighteenth / early nineteenth century), thus contrasting with 2nd person singular (*tu* "you-singular"), in distinct pragmatic contexts. The disuse of these forms has been related diachronically to the emergence of honorifics in the late fifteenth/ early sixteenth century (*Vossa Mercê, Vossa Alteza*). These were used with 3rd person verb forms (Cintra 1986: 18), expanding later to other contexts. We can only hypothesize that the increased allomorphy in the person / number verb inflexion that resulted from –d– deletion may also have contributed to the tendency towards the disuse of the 2nd person plural forms, complementing Cintra (1986: 31) who suggests that the disuse of *vós* may have been favored by a tendency to "simplify" the verb inflexion.

3. The historical dimension of Brazilian Portuguese

An overview of the historical evolution of Portuguese from the medieval period to the period of Brazilian Portuguese will be based on a periodization already argued for in the literature by other scholars (see Ramos and Venâncio 2006 and references cited there). The dynamics of the societal formation of Brazil, which, from the onset, involved contact between Portuguese speakers and peoples who spoke non-Indoeuropean languages, may be held responsible for the differentiation between European Portuguese (henceforth EP) and Brazilian Portuguese (henceforth BP).

In the remainder of this section we will attempt to put the creation of the linguistic diversity in Brazil in the context of the country's complex social history. This will also help us to understand the actual differences between BP and EP and the different variational aspects of the two varieties.

3.1. *The historical origins: Brazilian Portuguese*

The social history of Brazil is profoundly marked by the contact established among at least three historical agents: the Portuguese who arrived on the coast of Brazil as of 1500, the indigenous populations, and the African slaves brought to Brazil until late in the nineteenth century (Mattos e Silva 2004b). We distinguish three different periods: 1) the first period of colonization during the sixteenth century, when the Portuguese language was transplanted, though only to a limited degree, to the Brazilian territory; 2) the particular language setting in the eighteenth century; and 3) the linguistic diversification that took place in the nineteenth century.

The first period represents the beginning of the colonization of Brazil by Portugal in 1532. In the so-called "colonial period" (Teyssier 1982), settlers established themselves on the Atlantic coast. The earliest texts written in Brazil, such as travel stories, historical or geographical writings, treaties, and letters, were mainly descriptive and produced by the newly arrived Portuguese, who were astonished by the nature and the native people of the new world. European settlers represented a minority in Brazil until the eighteenth century. According to Mussa (1991), the Portuguese and their descendants comprised less than 30 percent of the population in the seventeenth century. The indigenous presence was very large; at the beginning of colonization the region's population was almost five million. Some authors (Lobo 2003, Mattos e Silva 2004a) characterize first three centuries of the social history of Brazil as one of "generalized multilingualism." Such a designation accounts for the fact that Portuguese was in contact with a large number of indigenous languages, mainly belonging to the Macro-Jê linguistic stock and, on a smaller scale, to the Tupi-Guarani language family. Communication between the Portuguese and the natives was through the "língua geral" (widely spoken language) (Rodrigues 1996). The term "língua geral" is used to designate two different languages: 1) "língua geral paulista," a Tupi-based language that was spoken in São Paulo and used by the Portuguese explorers, who penetrated the Brazilian hinterlands in search of especially gold and silver or Indians for enslavement, and taken to the central part and south of the country (Goiás, Mato Grosso and the north of Paraná); 2) "língua geral amazônica," a Tupinambá-based language, spoken in the north–northeast (Pará and Maranhão) and taken to Amazonia. Before the arrival of the Portuguese, the Tupi and Tupinambá languages were spoken over a large geographical area. For this reason, they were used for the evangelization of the indigenous populations by the Jesuits during the sixteenth and seventeenth century and became the contact languages used between Portuguese and Indians of different tribes. The linguistic contact between the "língua geral" and EP in colonial Brazil constitutes the social-historical basis of BP.

In addition to the contact with indigenous languages, the "generalized multilingualism" of the first period of Brazil was affected by the presence of African languages. Almost five million slaves with distinct languages from different regions of Africa were brought to Brazil in this first period. The Africans and their descendants were the main diffusing agents of BP in its popular variety (Mattos e Silva 2004b). In demographic terms, the African slaves outnumbered the Portuguese settlers by around 60 percent in the seventeenth century (Mussa 1991). The African slaves needed to adopt the settlers' language in their daily life, learning it as their 2nd language. Their influence was decisive in the linguistic restructuring of non-Standard Portuguese and its diffusion throughout the Brazilian territory (Lobo 2013: 23).

The transition between the seventeenth and eighteenth century was characterized by an increased influence of the African and Portuguese populations on the indigenous peoples and the restriction of the use of the "língua geral" as a means of communication with the Indians. Other factors that contributed to the growing importance of Portuguese as the sole language of communication were the accelerated growth of the Portuguese population in Brazil in the eighteenth century (reaching 800,000) and Pombal's linguistic policy, which imposed the use of Portuguese in official documents. Up to this period, the texts written in Brazil did not present any striking differences as compared with EP. For this reason, it is referred to as "Common Portuguese" as it was spoken in Lisbon.

The nineteenth century effectively gave birth to a new period with important social changes in the first and second halves of the century. It was the period of the "re-lusitanization" of Brazil (Teyssier 1982), which started when the royal family arrived in Rio de Janeiro in 1808 and, later, when many Portuguese immigrants arrived in Brazil in the 1950s. In the twentieth century, Brazil gradually ceased to be a rural colony due to the urbanization of the coastal cities, the migration of the rural elites to Rio de Janeiro, capital of the kingdom, and the demographic and economic rise of the urban working class. During that period, European and Asian immigrants started to do the work previously done by slaves and favored the spreading of Portuguese, especially in its popular variety. Indeed, the acquisition of Portuguese as a second language by the newcomers took place in the rural areas with foremen, laborers, and descendants of slaves. Since immigrants from different regions of the world settled in different areas of Brazil, this immigration flow laid the basis for the regional linguistic diversity of BP (Lucchesi 1998).

To sum up, the social dynamics that characterized the colonial period in Brazil set up a "crossbreed Portuguese" that took on features foreign to EP due to the confluence of different languages: EP, indigenous and African languages. In the next section, we intend to provide evidence showing that the regional and social heterogeneity of BP is a result of the Brazilian social-historical formation.

3.2. *Linguistic settings in Brazilian Portuguese*

The complexity of the historical formation of BP is evidenced by: (1) the contact established between the Portuguese colonizers, natives, and Africans; (2) the Jesuit evangelization of Indians, allowing intercommunication on the coast with the explorers from São Paulo; (3) the diffusion of popular Portuguese carried out by people of African descent (internal traffic); (4) European and Asian immigration; and 5) the internal migration from rural areas to the cities in the twentieth century. These factors produced dialectal heterogeneity at the horizontal and vertical levels, most of all in terms of phonetic–phonological phenomena.

Although there are polarized norms (standard and vernacular) in current BP, some phonetic–phonological phenomena may evidence linguistic differences and similarities between BP and EP. On one side, BP preserves features from the colonial times, while, on the other, it presents specific innovations.

4. European Portuguese and Brazilian Portuguese: main contrasting features and changes

4.1. *Some phonetic–phonological distinctions*

As in its origins, when Portuguese distanced itself from Castilian through its vocalism, the modern EP vowel system presents innovations that do not appear in BP and vice-versa. According to Mateus and d'Andrade (2000: 2), "The most obvious differences between these two varieties are located in the unstressed vowel system—the vowels are more audible in BP than in EP." In final position, for example, the unstressed mid vowels /e/ and /o/ became high vowels around 1800 in EP: [e] > [i] and [o] > [u]. Word-final unstressed [i] almost became silent: bat[e] > bat[i] > bat[i]/bat "beat" (Teyssier 1982). Except after palatalized coronal stops, word-final /i/ does not generally delete in BP, which is considered by some a conservative feature of this variant. Equally, unstressed /a/ in word-final position does not seem as reduced in BP as it is in EP.

While EP has a strong tendency to reduce and delete vowels in unstressed positions, in BP unstressed vowels are generally maintained. However, different from EP, BP shows a tendency towards consonantal weakening and loss in the syllable coda, where the consonants /l, r, s/ suffer vocalization or even total deletion. The behavior of the consonants in coda position distinguishes the two varieties and evidences a phonetic-phonological aspect with morpho-syntactic consequences: the change of a CVC type syllable structure to a CV type.

The deletion of / r/ in word-final position, for example, which occurs only in BP, has a greater incidence in verbs, where this consonant is the infinitive marker: *cantar* > *cantá* "to sing." In the other lexical categories, the deletion rate of / r/ remains below 40 percent: *colar* > *colá(r)* "necklace" (Callou, Leite, and Moraes 2002). The deletion of /s/, when it occurs word-finally, interferes with nominal agreement and the expression of plurality. In BP, nominal agreement corresponds to a variable rule with a tendency to mark agreement only in the first constituent of a noun phrase, whereas EP expresses the plural affix *–s* on every constituent of the NP that can receive inflection: *os meninos pequenos* (EP) *vs. o̱s meninoØ pequenoØ* (BP) "the little boys" (Scherre 1988; Brandão 2013). This difference in behavior can be associated to the historical formation of BP, since many African languages that came to Brazil, as well as the Tupi languages, did not present a closed syllable (CVC) such as occurs in EP which tends to preserve the consonants in the syllable coda. Although a correlation between external and internal history can be overly reductive, it is undeniable that the complex social-historical formation of BP has set up conditions such that (1) heterogeneity emerged, and (2) the implementation of certain changes propagated more quickly in the new territory.

4.2. *Some morphosyntactic aspects*

The differentiation between BP and EP is less clear-cut in the morphosyntax than it is in the phonology. Existing written documents provide some evidence of different directions of change that have operated probably since the eighteenth century in both areas.

The use of the gerund (*escrevendo* "writing"), nowadays generalized in Brazil, was a recurring strategy to indicate the progressive aspect until the sixteenth or seventeenth century. In EP, the innovative strategy (called the *gerundial infinitive*) formed by combining the preposition *a* "to" with the *infinitive* (*a escrever* "to write") started to be used from the eighteenth century on (Barbosa 2008) in variation with the gerund (*escrevendo* "writing"), although the first occurrences of this construction can already be found as early as the fifteenth century. In the eighteenth century, no clear differences in the use of this construction can be observed in BP and in EP. The use of the *gerundial infinitive* starts to increase in Portugal at the beginning of the twentieth century, combined with the auxiliary verbs *estar* "be," *andar* "walk," *ficar* "stay" and *continuar* "continue" (Mothé 2007). Studies show different frequency levels depending on the type of text.

The behavior of *haver* and *ter* "have" in existential constructions also shows differences between the two varieties of Portuguese. In terms of its Latin origin, the form *habere* had as its first meaning "to have in one's possession," "to store," while the verb *tenere* meant "to hold in one's hand," "to obtain." Over time, *habere* underwent an extension of its semantic content and assumed the figurative meaning of "to have in one's hand." In the first Portuguese documents of the thirteenth century, the verb *haver* used to be more productive for any semantic value of possession as a full verb (Mattos e Silva 1997). The verb *haver* was also used in variation with *ter* for the more concrete meaning of material possession: *haver/ter pan, casa* "to have bread, a house." In contexts of immaterial possession, when the value of possession was more abstract, the use of the verb *ter* was less productive. As an example, if the possessed object presented "immaterial acquirable properties" the use of *ter* was rare in the thirteenth century (*haver/ter fé* "to have faith"), but, in contexts of "the possessor's inherent properties," the verb *haver* was categorical in this period: *haver enfermidade, cegui-dade* "to have an illness, blindness" (Mattos e Silva 2002). There is some evidence that, until the fourteenth century, the two verbs could convey distinct values with *haver* marking an inherent relation or strict possession (in cases of material possession) and *ter* a non-inherent relation, or, in cases of material possession, a temporary possession.

Gradually, until the middle of the sixteenth century, the verb *ter* took the place of *haver* for all the possession types mentioned, while *haver* had specialized its meaning in existential constructions and eliminated the etymological form *ser* (verb "be" meaning existence). The generalization of *haver* as an impersonal verb was also favored by the fact that this verb assumed inanimate subjects consisting of place names from the time of Latin: ARCA NOE HABUIT HOMINES "Noah's ark had men" (Bourciez 1956: 252). These constructions made an existential interpretation possible due to the reanalysis of the subject as a locative complement introduced by the preposition "in": IN ARCA NOE HABUIT HOMINES "There were men in Noah's ark."

In BP, the verb *ter* assumed an existential meaning replacing the verb *haver* in this context probably from the nineteenth century on. However, this replacement only occurs in written texts in the first half of the twentieth century, as shown by Marins (2013). According to Callou and Avelar (2007), the emergence of the verb *ter* as an existential construction may be associated with other linguistic changes in BP. The weakening of the verbal agreement and the inability to interpret a sentence in which the verb *ter* occurs with a null subject as a possessive construction favored its reanalysis as an existential construction. For instance, a sentence such as *Tem várias maçãs na geladeira* "Have several apples in the fridge" is interpreted as *"There are* several apples in the fridge" in BP, while its interpretation is *"He/She has* several apples in the fridge" in EP.

The postverbal (V-Cl) or preverbal (Cl-V) pronominal clitic placement is another aspect recurrently mentioned to distinguish between EP and BP. Martins (2005) argues that medieval Portuguese presents variation between enclisis and proclisis in contexts that are ungrammatical in modern Portuguese. This variable behavior—preverbal in (1) or postverbal in (2)—occurred in affirmative main clauses without triggers of proclisis (negative items, *wh*-phrases, quantifiers, etc.), that is, in the "unmarked main clauses":

(1) Sobrinho, eu *vos* rogo que fiquedes aqui
    Nephew, I *you*-pl-dat beg that stay here
    "Nephew, I beg you to stay here."

(2) Rogo-*vos* que nom vaades em esta demanda
    I-beg-*you*-pl-dat that not go in this demand
    "I beg you not to make this demand."
    (Fifteenth century *A Demanda do Santo Graal*)

Written texts in the medieval and early Renaissance period show a progressive increase in the use of clitic–verb order. In the thirteenth century, enclisis was predominant in the unmarked main clause; in the sixteenth century, however, proclisis became more frequent than enclisis. Although the verb–clitic order was infrequent during the sixteenth century, it was grammatically possible, mainly in neutral sentences. Martins (2005) argues that proclisis was emphatic and semantically motivated in EP in the period extending from the thirteenth to the sixteenth century, while enclisis was interpreted as neutral and non-emphatic. From the seventeenth century on, the verb–clitic order replaced the sequence clitic–verb, just as in modern EP.

Thus, it is possible to say that the Portuguese settlers had brought this variation in the preverbal and postverbal placement of clitic elements in main clauses to Brazil. In BP, however, the clitic–verb order became dominant in contexts where enclisis is obligatory in EP. For instance, we can see proclisis in BP in the first absolute position as in (3), the co-occurrence of clitics with past participle in (4) and gerunds in (5) in verbal periphrastic constructions:

(3) *Me*lembro muito de você com muitas saudades
    Me-dat-remember.pres.1sg very much of you with very miss-noun
    "I remember you very much and miss you so much."
    (Missive written by Barbara Ottoni, nineteenth century. In Lopes, 2005: 215)

(4) ... verificar   que   tens   **te**   adiantado
    ... to verify   that   you-have-NOM you-acc   attempted
    "... to verify that you have attempted yourself"
    (Missive written by Barbara Ottoni, nineteenth century. In Lopes 2005: 127)

(5) estou sempre   *me*lembrando   de que você   sempre queria
    I-am   always   *me*-refl-remembering   of that you   always wanted.2sg
    me ajudar
    me-acc-help.inf
    "I always remember that you always wanted to help me."
    (Missive written by Barbara Ottoni, nineteenth century. In Lopes 2005: 215)

The facts, as described above, reconstructed on the basis of the remaining BP documentation, show that, in BP, clitic placement is sensitive to external factors, such as the type of text, adoption of standard EP, social prestige, etc. In addition, Brazilian texts of the nineteenth century contain some examples of clitic–verb orders very common nowadays in spoken BP.

5. Conclusions

The preceding sections provide a diachronic overview of the Portuguese language. We have briefly reviewed some of the more salient tendencies, both conservative and innovative, which determine the Portuguese differentiation within the Ibero-Romance context. This perspective has also guided the description of the phonetic-phonological and morphosyntactic phenomena which contributed to distinguish BP from EP. As shown, the differences between these two varieties are more obvious and outstanding in the phonology than in the morphosyntax. The most striking discrepancy is probably to be found in the vocalism, especially the unstressed vowel system, which is subject to different neutralization strategies in EP and BP. From the seventeenth century on, BP texts do not show significant morphosyntactic differences as compared with EP, which is due to the fact that a very small literate group was responsible for writing the extant texts. Nevertheless, it could be shown that, regarding the phenomena selected here, as from the eighteenth and the nineteenth century, EP and BP took separate paths. Detailed analyses of the synchronic differences between BP and EP phonology, morphology, and syntax can be found in other chapters of this volume.

REFERENCES

Baldinger, K. (1972). *La formación de los domínios lingüísticos en la Península Ibérica*, 2nd edn. Madrid: Gredos.

Barbosa, A. G. (2008). Fontes escritas e história da língua portuguesa no Brasil: as cartas de comércio no século XVIII. In I. Lima and L. do Carmo (eds.), *História social da língua nacional*. Rio de Janeiro: Edições Casa de Rui Barbosa, pp. 181–214.

Bourciez, E. (1956). *Elements de Linguistigue Romane*, 4th edn. Paris: Librairie C. Klincksieck.

Brandão, S. F. (2013). Patterns of agreement within the noun phrase. *Journal of Portuguese Linguistics*, 12 (2), pp. 51–100.

Callou, D. and Avelar, J. (2007). Sobre a emergência do verbo possessivo em contextos existenciais no português brasileiro. In A. Castilho et al. (eds.), *Descrição, História e Aquisição do português brasileiro*. São Paulo: Pontes/FAPESP, pp. 375–402.

Callou, D., Leite, Y., and Moraes, J. (2002). Processo(s) de enfraquecimento consonantal no português do Brasil. In M. B. Abaurre and A. Rodrigues (eds.), *Gramática do português falado VIII: novos estudos descritivos*. Campinas: UNICAMP/FAPESP, pp. 537–555.

Câmara, J. M. (1975). *História e estrutura da língua portuguesa*, 2nd edn. Rio de Janeiro: Padrão.

Castro, I. (2006). *Introdução à história do português*, 2nd edn. Lisboa: Colibri.

Cintra, L. F. L. (1983). *Estudos de Dialectologia Portuguesa*. Lisboa: Sá da Costa.

Cintra, L. F. L. (1986). *Sobre "formas de tratamento" na língua portuguesa*, 2nd edn. Lisboa: Livros Horizonte.

Hock, H. H. (1991). *Principles of Historical Linguistics*, 2nd edn. Berlin: Mouton de Gruyter.

Lobo, T. (2003). A questão da periodização da história linguística do Brasil. In I. Castro and I. Duarte (eds.), *Razões e emoção. Miscelânea de estudos em homenagem a Maria Helena Mira Mateus*, Vol. 2. Lisboa: Imprensa Nacional-Casa da Moeda, pp. 395–411.

Lobo, T. (2013). Rosa Virgínia Mattos e Silva e a sócio-história do português brasileiro. http://www.usc.es/revistas/index.php/elg/article/view/2314/2861, accessed October 10, 2015. DOI: http://dx.doi.org/10.15304/elg.7.2314

Lopes, C. R. S. (2005). *A Norma brasileira em construção: fatos linguísticos em cartas pessoais do século XIX*. Rio de Janeiro: FAPERJ/PPGLEV.

Lucchesi, D. (1998). A constituição histórica do português brasileiro como um processo bipolarizado: tendências atuais de mudança nas normas culta e popular. In S. Große and K. Zimmermann (eds.), *"Substandard" e mudança no português do Brasil*. Frankfurt am Main: Teo Ferrer de Mesquita (TFM), pp. 73–100.

Maia, C. A. (1986). *História do galego-português: Estado linguístico da Galiza e do Noroeste de Portugal do século XIII ao século XVI*. Coimbra: INIC.

Maiden, M., Smith, J. C., and Ledgeway, A. (eds.). (2011). *The Cambridge History of the Romance Languages*, Vol. I *Structures*. Cambridge: Cambridge University Press.

Marins, J. E. (2013). As repercussões da remarcação do Parâmetro do Sujeito Nulo: um estudo diacrônico das sentenças existenciais com *ter* e *haver* no PB e no PE. Rio de Janeiro: Federal University of Rio de Janeiro (PhD Thesis).

Martins, A. M. (1999). Ainda "os mais antigos textos escritos em português": Documentos de 1175 a 1252. In I. H. Faria (ed.), *Lindley Cintra:*

Homenagem ao Homem, ao Mestre e ao Cidadão. Lisboa: Cosmos / FLL, pp. 491–534.

Martins, A. M. (2001). On the origin of the Portuguese inflected infinitive: A new perspective on an enduring debate. In L. J. Brinton (ed.), *Historical Linguistics 1999: Selected Papers from the 14th Conference on Historical Linguistics*. Amsterdam: John Benjamins, pp. 207–222.

Martins, A. M. (2005). Clitic placement, VP-ellipsis and scrambling in romance. In M. Batllori *et al.* (eds.) *Grammaticalization and Parametric Change*. Oxford: Oxford University Press, pp. 175–193.

Mateus, M. H. M. and d'Andrade, E. (2000). *The Phonology of Portuguese*. Oxford: Oxford University Press.

Mattos e Silva, R. V. (1997). Observações sobre a variação no uso dos verbos *ser, estar, haver, ter* no galego-português ducentista. *Estudos lingüísticos e literários*, 19, pp. 253–285.

Mattos e Silva, R. V. (2002). Vitórias de *ter* sobre *haver* nos meados do século XVI: usos e teorias em João de Barros. In R. V. Mattos e Silva and A. Venâncio Filho (eds.), *O Português Quinhentista—Estudos Lingüísticos*. Salvador: EDUFBA/UEFS, pp. 121–142.

Mattos e Silva, R. V. (2004a). *Ensaios para uma Sócio-História do Português Brasileiro*. São Paulo: Parábola Editorial.

Mattos e Silva, R. V. (2004b). O português brasileiro: sua formação na complexidade multilinguística do Brasil colonial e pós-colonial. In S. B. B. Costa, A. Machado Filho, and A. V. Lopes (eds.), *Do português arcaico ao português brasileiro*. Salvador: EDUFBA.

Mothé, N. G. M. (2007). *Variação e mudança aquém e além mar: gerúndio versus infinitivo gerundivo no português dos séculos XIX e XX*. Rio de Janeiro: UFRJ (MA thesis).

Mussa, A. B. N. (1991). *O papel das línguas africanas na história do português do Brasil*. Rio de Janeiro: UFRJ (MA thesis).

Piel, J. M. (1989). *Estudos de Linguística Histórica Galego-Portuguesa*. Lisboa: IN-CM, pp. 213–244.

Ramos, J. M. and Venâncio, R. P. (2006). Por uma cronologia do português escrito no Brasil. In T. Lobo et al. (eds.), *Para a História do Português Brasileiro*. Salvador: EDUFBA, pp. 575–595.

Rodrigues, A. (1996). As línguas gerais sul-americanas. *Papia*, 4 (2), pp. 6–18.

Sampson, R. (1999). Ibero-Romance II: Galician-Portuguese. In *Nasal vowel evolution in*

Romance. Oxford: Oxford University Press, pp. 175–218.

Scherre, M. P. (1988). *Reanálise da concordância de número em português.* Rio de Janeiro: UFRJ (PhD thesis).

Teyssier, P. (1982). *História da Língua Portuguesa.* Lisboa: Sá da Costa.

Vincent, N. (1988). Latin. In M. Harris and N. Vincent (eds.), *The Romance Languages.* London: Routledge, pp. 26–78.

Williams, E. B. (1975). *Do latim ao português. Fonologia e morfologia históricas da língua portuguesa,* 3rd edn. Rio de Janeiro: Tempo Brasileiro.

2 European Portuguese and Brazilian Portuguese: An Overview on Word Order

MARY AIZAWA KATO[1] AND ANA MARIA MARTINS[2]

1. Introduction

The most widely studied varieties of Portuguese are European Portuguese (EP) and Brazilian Portuguese (BP), the official languages of Portugal and Brazil. With the advent of the Principles and Parameters theory and the revival of historical and comparative grammar in Portugal and in Brazil, linguists have started to reveal parametric differences between the two varieties, and not merely phonological and lexical distinctions that would define the two varieties as merely two dialects of the same language.

According to Tarallo (1983, 1990) the main changes that gave rise to Brazilian Portuguese started to appear clearly by the end of the nineteenth century in written language, but had probably been in the spoken modality since the end of the eighteenth century, when social and historical factors were favorable to the changes.

This chapter will present a comparative description of word order in the two varieties, starting in Section 2 with the surface similarities that underlie most of the mutual comprehension between the Portuguese and the Brazilians. Section 3 will describe a major difference in the grammar of the two varieties, namely the placement of clitic pronouns. Section 4 will describe the particularities of word order in declarative sentences. Section 5 will deal with word order differences in *wh*-questions and contrastive focus structures. We will finish with some conclusions.

2. Surface similarities between the two varieties

When exposed to the first pages of a manual of Portuguese as a second language, the learner may not distinguish between EP and BP examples. In the two varieties, the unmarked order for simple declarative sentences is SV(O):

The Handbook of Portuguese Linguistics, First Edition. Edited by W. Leo Wetzels, João Costa, and Sergio Menuzzi.
© 2016 John Wiley & Sons, Inc. Published 2020 by John Wiley & Sons, Inc.

(1) a. *O   gato   comeu   o   passarinho.*   (EP BP)
      the   cat   ate   the   bird
      "The cat ate the bird."
  b. *O   dólar   subiu.*   (EP BP)
      the   dollar   went-up
      "The dollar went up."
  c. *A   Maria   recebeu   flores   do   Pedro.*   (EP BP)
      the   Maria   received   flowers   from-the   Pedro
      "Maria received flowers from Pedro."

Negative sentences are equally identical in EP and BP, and so is the negative concord phenomenon:

(2) a. *O   gato   **não**   comeu   **nada.***   (EP BP)
      the   cat   not   ate   nothing
      "The cat didn't eat anything."
  b. *O   dólar   **não**   subiu   **nada.***   (EP BP)
      the   dollar   not   went-up   nothing
      "The dollar didn't go up a cent."
  c. *A   Maria   **não**   recebeu   **nada**   do   Pedro.*   (EP BP)
      the   Maria   not   received   nothing   from-the   Pedro
      "Maria didn't receive anything from Pedro."

In many languages *Yes/no* questions are either marked by a particle, like the Japanese *-ka* and the Bulgarian *-li*, or by a syntactic order distinct from the declarative one, as the English Aux-to-C pattern. In the two varieties of Portuguese, the distinction is, at least superficially, purely prosodic: while declaratives typically have a falling intonation (\), interrogatives typically have a rising one (/).

(3) a. *O   gato   comeu   o   passarinho.* \   (EP BP)
      the   cat   ate   the   bird
      "The cat ate the bird."
  a.' *O   gato   comeu   o   passarinho?* /   (EP BP)
      the   cat   ate   the   bird
      "Did the cat eat the bird?"
  b. *O   dólar   subiu.* \   (EP BP)
      the   dollar   went-up
      "The dollar went up."
  b.' *O   dólar   subiu?* /   (EP BP)
      the   dollar   went-up
      "Did the dollar go up?"

EP and BP also share a common *wh*-question pattern, with the sentential word order SV(X):

(4) a. *Quem   foi   que   o   Garfield   viu?*   (EP BP)
      who   was   that   the   Garfield   saw
      "Who did Garfield see?"
  b. *O   que   é   que   eles   bebem?*   (EP BP)
      the   what   is   that   they   drink
      "What do they drink?"

Despite the similarities seen above, deep structural differences underlie the grammars of EP and BP, some of which will be seen in detail below.

3. Two systems of clitic placement in Portuguese

Clitic placement offers a case of striking contrast in word order between BP and EP. Whereas BP displays generalized proclisis, EP displays enclisis and proclisis in both finite and non-finite domains. Other differences between BP and EP relative to clitic pronouns are also very clear: for example, the fact that clitics cannot cluster in BP and the 3rd person accusative clitic is not part of the (colloquial) BP grammar, or the fact that dative clitics are easily replaced by prepositional phrases with non-clitic pronouns in BP. This strategy is also used to avoid a 3rd person accusative clitic, or else BP resorts to a null element. These differences between BP and EP are illustrated in (5) and (6) below, but in the remainder of this section we will concentrate on clitic placement since the main focus of this chapter is word order.

(5) a. *O* *livro,* *eu* *já* **lho** *dei.* (EP *BP) *clitic cluster: dative + accusative*
the book I already him-it gave

b. *O* *livro,* *eu* *já* **lhe** *dei.* (EP BP) *null 3rd person accusative*
the book I already him gave

c. *O* *livro,* *eu* *já* *dei* **pra** **ele** (*EP BP) *non-clitic 3rd person pronoun*
the book I already gave for he
"The book, I have already given it to him."

(6) a. *Essa* *menina,* *eu* *não* **a** *conheço.* (EP *BP) *3rd person accusative clitic*
that girl I not her know

b. *Essa* *menina,* *eu* *não* *conheço.* (EP BP) *null 3rd person accusative*
that girl I not know

c. *Essa* *menina,* *eu* *não* *conheço* **ela.** (*EP BP) *non-clitic 3rd person pronoun*
that girl I not know she
"That girl, I don't know her."

A distinct property of clitic placement in Portuguese, in comparison to the other Romance languages, is its independence with respect to verbal morphology. In fact, the opposition [± finite] does not lie behind the split between proclitic and enclitic placement, in contrast with Spanish, Catalan and Italian, nor does the opposition [± imperative], in contrast with French.

But while proclisis is general and exceptionless in Brazilian Portuguese, in European Portuguese enclisis and proclisis surface both in finite and non-finite domains, with a contextual distribution governed by grammatical factors that are quite complex.[3]

A detailed description of the distribution of proclisis and enclisis in EP is not our purpose here (see Chapter 12, this volume, and Martins 2013), but we will underscore a few descriptive observations that indicate the particularity of EP among the Romance languages.[4] We will then suggest that the complexity of the EP system may have prompted the change that resulted in the generalized proclitic pattern that characterizes BP and is unique among the Romance languages.

The five characteristic features of the EP system identified below contribute to what Costa, Fiéis, and Lobo (2014) refer to as "input variability" and show to result in clitic misplacement and late acquisition of the adult grammar by Portuguese children.

(i)   In EP there is a correlation between sentential polarity and clitic placement. The dichotomy affirmation/negation brings about the opposition enclisis/proclisis:

(7) a. *Hoje   ele   falou-me.*
       today   he   spoke-me
       "Today he spoke to me."
    b. *Hoje   ele   não   me   falou.*
       today   he   not   me   spoke
       "Today he didn't speak to me."

(ii) In EP the dichotomy between root and subordinate finite clauses gives rise to the opposition between enclisis and proclisis, which applies to all types of finite subordinate clauses:

(8) a. *Evidentemente   o   coronel   suicidou-se*
       evidently   the   colonel   killed-himself
       "Evidently the colonel killed himself."
    b. *Dizem   que   o   coronel   se   suicidou.*
       say-3pl   that   the   colonel   himself   killed
       "People say that the colonel killed himself."

(iii) In EP some syntactic contexts allow variation between enclisis and proclisis. The variable pattern of clitic placement exhibited by the prepositional infinitival clauses in (9) is part of both standard and dialectal EP.

(9) a. *Pensou   em   suicidar-se.*
       thought-3sg   in   kill-himself
    b. *Pensou   em   se   suicidar.*
       thought-3sg   in   himself   kill
       "He thought about killing himself."

(iv) In sharp contrast with Spanish, Catalan and Italian, the opposition finite/non-finite does not govern the alternation between proclisis and enclisis in EP. As exemplified in (10) both enclisis and proclisis can be found in finite and non-finite domains. In (10b) and (10d), it is the presence of the adverb *também* that induces proclisis.

(10) a. *Ele   aposentou-se   cedo,*
        he   retired-himself   early
        "He retired early."
     b. *Ele   também   se   aposentou   cedo.*
        he   also   himself   retired   early
        "He also retired early."
     c. *Esperava   aposentar-se   cedo.*
        wished   retire-infin-himself   early
        "He wished to retire early."
     d. *Esperava   também   se   aposentar   cedo.*
        wished   also   himself   retire-infin   early
        "He wished to also retire early."

(v) The concept of "proclisis trigger" is descriptively useful to handle clitic placement in EP, but not in BP, Spanish, Catalan, Italian or French. Only in EP, proclisis in affirmative root sentences depends on the presence in preverbal position of one of a set of apparently heterogeneous elements, not easily reducible to a class or type (independently of the chosen ontology). A few examples are given in (11b–e), which instantiate respectively the aspectual adverb *já*, the quantifier *todos*, the *wh-* phrase *onde* and the fronted focalized phrase *de notícias* as proclisis triggers.[5]

(11) a. *Ele   casou-se.*
         he   married-*himself*
         "He got married."
      b. *Ele   já   se   casou.*
         he   already   himself   married
         "He has got married already."
      c. *Todos   se   casaram.*
         all   themselves   married
         "All of them got married."
      d. *Onde   se   casaram?*
         where   themselves   married
         "Where did they get married?"
      e. *De   notícias   se   faz   o   nosso   mundo.* (TV channel slogan)
         of   news   itself   makes   the   our   world
         "It's news that makes up our world."

The complexity of the EP system of clitic placement leads not only to late acquisition, as mentioned above, but also to a residual amount of marginal variability in the adult grammar, across geolinguistic varieties and across time (cf. Martins 2011). This is shown in (12)–(13) with examples that represent literary/journalistic EP, EP dialects and the African varieties of Portuguese, which all share with EP the same pattern of clitic placement. Because examples of enclisis in proclitic contexts have been largely referred in the literature (e.g. Duarte and Matos 2000), we give here instead an illustration of the opposite situation, with proclisis emerging in enclitic contexts. All the sentences below have a correlate with enclisis in the same dialect or Portuguese variety, which represents the ordinary pattern.

(12) a. *Isto   que   digo,   Miguel Torga   o   disse,   a   seu   modo,   antes   de   mim.*
         this   that   say-3sg   Miguel Torga   it   said   in   his   way   before   of   me
         "What I am saying, Miguel Toga has said before, in his own way."
         (António Lobo Antunes, *Visão* magazine)
      b. **Me**   *enganaste?!*
         me   tricked
         "Did you trick me?!"
         (CORDIAL-SIN: Melides, Alentejo)
      c. *Às   vezes   **me**   junto   com   os   meus   amigos*
         at   times   me   gather   with   the   my   friends
         "Sometimes I get together with my friends."
         (CORDIAL-SIN: Santo André, Vila Real)
      d. *Homem,   tu   o   viste   no   outro   dia*
         man   you   him   saw   in-the   other   day
         "Man, you saw him the other day."
         (CORDIAL-SIN: Pico, Azores)

e. *Eles   se   encontram   marginalizados.*
   they themselves   find   marginalized
   "They find themselves marginalized."
   (Portuguese of Mozambique. Mapasse 2005: 67)

f. *Mano,   ela   me   cansou.*
   brother she   me   tired
   "Brother, I got tired of her."
   (Portuguese of Mozambique. Justino 2010)

g. *Me   disseste que   era   segredo, não meterias a   foto   dele   no*
   me   said   that was   secret   not would-put the photo of-him in-the
   Facebook, *me   mentiste*
   Facebook   me   lied
   "You told me that it was a secret, that you would not post his photo in Facebook,
   you lied to me."
   (Portuguese of Angola. Domingos 2010)

(13) a. *Não quero me   gabar,   mas li   todo o   Ulysses do   Joyce*
        not want   myself praise-infin but read all   the Ulysses of-the Joyce
        "I don't wish to praise myself, but I have read the whole of *Ulysses* by Joyce."
        (*Público* newspaper. In Rodygina 2009: 71)

     b. *Não sei   porquê. Não posso então lhe   explicar.*
        not know   why   not can   then   you   explain-infin
        "I don't know why. So I can't explain to you."
        (CORDIAL-SIN: Pico, Azores)

     c. *Não querendo se   dedicar   aos   estudos*
        not wanting   themselves apply-infin to-the studies
        "Not wishing to apply themselves to study…"
        (Portuguese of Mozambique. Mapasse 2005: 74)

Interestingly, written BP (in contrast to colloquial BP) also displays variation between proclisis and enclisis in the same syntactic configurations, as illustrated in (14), with finite verbs,
and (15), with infinitives.[6]

(14) a. *O   jesuíta se   acomodou   num   caixote de   vinhos.*
        the Jesuit   himself   accommodated in-a box   of   wines
        "The Jesuit sat on a box of wine bottles."
        (Pessotti 1997: 20)

     b. *O   padre   apresentou-se.*
        the priest introduced-himself
        "The priest introduced himself."
        (Pessotti 1997: 17)

(15) a. *Pode me   chamar   por   meu   nome.*
        can   me   call-infin by   my   name
        "Please, call me by my first name."
        (Pessotti 1997: 16)

     b. *Resolvi   render-me.*
        decided-1sg   surrender-infin-myself
        "I decided to surrender."
        (Pessotti 1997: 22)

So, maybe written BP is not merely an artificial system (as has been usually thought of) but an elaboration of some earlier stage of historical development that precedes the emergence of generalized proclisis (cf. Pagotto 1992; Carneiro 2005).[7] In fact, the stable low level of variability that seems to be intrinsic to the EP system could have risen significantly in a historical situation favoring incomplete acquisition due to particular social conditions and broad language contact (see Chapter 3, of this volume). The rise of "input variability" beyond a certain threshold for learnability would then prompt the emergence of a new system of clitic placement. This is not the place to follow or explore this line of reasoning, but it suggests an avenue for further inquiry. We will now focus on the description of clitic placement in (colloquial) Brazilian Portuguese.

In BP object clitics are proclitic to the verb selecting them, irrespective of verbal morphology and type of clause:

(16) a. *(Maria,)*   ***me***   *dá*   *um*   *beijo.*
     Maria,   me   give   a   kiss
     "(Maria,) give me a kiss."
  b. *A*   *Maria*   ***me***   *viu.*
     the   Maria   me   saw
     "Maria saw me."
  c. *A*   *Maria*   *pode/quer*   *sempre*   ***me***   *ver.*
     the   Maria   can/wants   always   me   see-infin
     "Maria can always see me./Maria always wants to see me."
  d. *A*   *Maria*   *está*   *sempre*   ***me***   *olhando.*
     The   Maria   is   always   me   looking
     "Maria is always looking at me."
  e. *Você*   *já*   *tinha*   ***me***   *dado*   *um*   *beijo.*
     you   already   had   me   given   a   kiss
     "You had kissed me already."

As shown in (16), Brazilian Portuguese clitics show no restrictions with respect to being initial or to cliticizing to nominal forms of the verb, including infinitival complements of restructuring verbs, gerunds and past participles. In fact, clitic climbing associated with restructuring verbal complexes, which is a grammatical option in EP, is not allowed in BP, where proclisis to the thematic verb is general:

(17) a. *Você*   *não*   *pode*   ***me***   *despedir.*   (*EP BP)
     you   not   can   me   fire-infin
  b. *Você*   *não*   ***me***   *pode*   *despedir.*   (EP *BP)
     you   not   me   can   fire-infin
     "You can't fire me."

(18) a. *Ele*   *está*   ***me***   *provocando.*   (*EP BP)
     he   is   me   provoking
  b. *Ele*   ***me***   *está*   *provocando.*   (EP *BP)
     he   me   is   provoking
     "He is provoking me."

(19) a. *Você*   *não*   *tinha*   *ainda*   ***me***   *contado.*   (*EP BP)
     you   not   had   yet   me   told
  b. *Você*   *não*   ***me***   *tinha*   *ainda*   *contado.*   (EP *BP)
     you   not   me   had   yet   told
     "You hadn't told me that yet."

Clitic placement is thus invariant in BP. Object clitics behave as elements akin to verbal pre-fixes, as far as they always occur at the left edge of the thematic verb.[8] But the relevant comparison to establish seems to be with stressed prefixes. In this respect it is worth noting the similarity between the distribution of BP clitics and the distribution of the prefix *recém*. Both left-adjoin to the verb and cannot precede an auxiliary except in passives, possibly because in passives the past participle can incorporate into the auxiliary (cf. Campos 1999):

(20) a. *Nós*   *(recém)*   *casamos*   *(*recém).*
        we   just   married   just
        "We have just married."
     b. *Nós*   *(*recém)*   *tinhamos*   *(recém)*   *casado.*
        we   just   had   just   married
        "We had just married."

(21) a. *Ele foi   recém contratado.*
        he   was   just   hired/elected
        (Google search)
     b. *Ele recém foi   contratado. (idem)*
        he   just   was   hired/elected
        "He had just been hired/elected."

(22) a. *Ele foi   me   apresentado. (idem)*
        he   was   me   introduced
     b. *Ele me   foi   apresentado. (idem)*
        he   me   was   introduced
        "He was introduced to me."

Stressed prefixes are modifiers that left-adjoin to a word (not to the verbal root), giving rise to a complex prosodic word (Villalva 2000; Vigário 2003; Newell 2005). Adjunct modifiers are non-category-changing entities as they do not project category features. If clitics in BP are like stressed prefixes in being non-category-changing entities that left adjoin to the verbal head, we expect that clitics and the prefix *recém* can alternate in their relative positions. This is in fact so:

(23) a. *Recém nos   conhecemos.*
        just   us   know
        (Luís Fernando Veríssimo)[9]
     b. *Nós   nos   recém conhecemos.*
        we   us   just   know
        "We only recently know/met each other."

Although stressed prefixes have a certain degree of independence in EP as well, there are no cases of the kind of word order variation attested in (23), which signals that clitics are entities of a different nature in Brazilian and European Portuguese.[10]

4. Divergences in the word order of declarative sentences[11]

4.1. The "categorical" and "thetic" distinction[12]

Sentences can express a "categorical" judgment, namely they can attribute a property to an entity, which may be codified as **the subject** or **the topic** of a sentence. In the two varieties, the unmarked order for simple declarative sentences of the *categorical*, or predicational type, is SV(X):[13]

(24) a. **O**   **Santos**   *venceu*   *o*   *Corinthians.*   (EP BP)
    the   Santos   beat   the   Corinthians
    "Santos has beaten Corinthians."

  b. **O**   **dólar**   *subiu.*   (EP BP)
    the   dollar   went-up
    "The dollar went up."

A "thetic" sentence, on the other hand, describes a situation in which no single entity is assigned a topic status. In the two varieties the unmarked order **can** be VS (X):

(25) a. *Chegou   a   primavera.*   (EP BP)
    arrived   the   Spring
    "Spring arrived."

  b. *Há   prédios   lindos   em   São Paulo.*   (EP BP)
    have   buildings   beautiful   in   São Paulo
    "There are beautiful buildings in São Paulo."

  c. *Desapareceu   o   iPhone   da   minha   bolsa.*   (EP BP)
    disappeared   the   iPhone   from   my   purse
    "My iPhone disappeared from my purse."

  d. *Passaram   poucos   alunos   no   exame.*   (EP BP)
    passed   few   students   in-the   exam
    "Few students passed the exam."

  e. *Viajou   comigo   um   cantor   de   rock.*   (EP BP)
    traveled   with-me   a   singer   of   rock
    "A rock singer traveled with me."

In EP, the unmarked pattern for categorical sentences is SV(X) as exemplified above, with the subject being assigned a property of the predicate. In BP spoken language a common pattern is a construction like (26b) and (27b) where the subject pronoun doubles the topic, constituting a left dislocation pattern. This variety has also a categorical sentence with what is called a topic-subject,[14] where a noun argument raises to the subject position, as in (28c), which is not possible in EP:

(26) a. **O**   *Paulo   chega   hoje.*   (EP BP)
    the   Paulo   arrives   today
    "Paulo arrives today."

  b. **O**   *Paulo,   ele   chega   hoje.*   (*EP BP)
    the   Paulo   he   arrives   today
    "Paulo, (he) arrives today.

(27) a. **O**   *meu   carro   está   na   oficina.*   (EP BP)
    the   my   car   is   at-the   mechanic
    "My car is at the mechanic.

  b. **O**   *meu   carro,   ele   está   na   oficina.*   (*EP BP)
    the   my   car   it   is   at-the   mechanic
    "My car is at the mechanic's."

(28) a. **O**   telhado   da   casa   caiu.   (EP BP)
    the   roof   of-the   house   fell
    "The roof of the house collapsed."

  b. **A**   casa   caiu   o   telhado.   (*EP BP)
    the   house   fell   the   roof
    "The roof of the house collapsed."

As for thetic sentences, EP is less restrictive than BP in the availability of the order VS with verbs that are not of the monoargumental type, in which case BP generally resorts to the unmarked order SV(X), as in (29) to (31). EP disallows VSO with direct transitive verbs. But VSO is permitted when the verb is accompanied by an auxiliary, as in (32), the verb selects an indirect or oblique object, as in (33) and (34), or if the complement is a dative clitic, as in (34) and (35):

(29) a. *Chega   o   Paulo   hoje.*   (EP BP)
arrives the Paulo today
"Paul arrives today."
b. *O   Paulo   chega   hoje.*   (#EP BP)
the   Paulo   arrives today
"Paul arrives today."
(categorical reading of (29b) favored in EP; descriptive reading in BP)

(30) a. *Moram   muitos   imigrantes   na   periferia   de   São Paulo.* (EP BP
                                                                                written)
live   many   immigrants in-the outskirts of   São Paulo
b. *Muitos   imigrantes   moram   na   periferia   de   São Paulo.* (#EP BP)
Many   immigrants live   in-the outskirts of   São Paulo
"Many immigrants live on the outskirts of São Paulo"
(categorical reading of (30b) favored in EP)

(31) *Correram   100   atletas   a   maratona,*   (EP *BP)
ran   100   athletes   the   marathon
"There were 100 athletes running the marathon."

(32) a. *Está   um   gato   a   dormir   no   jardim.*   (EP *BP)
is   a   cat   to   sleep   in-the   garden
"There is a cat sleeping in the garden."
b. *Um   gato   está   a   dormir/dormindo   no   jardim.*   (#EP BP)
a   cat   is   to   sleep/sleeping   in-the   garden.
"There is a cat sleeping in the garden."
(categorical reading of (32b) favored in EP)

(33) *Chama   uma   ambulância.   Picou   uma   abelha   ao   João   e   ele*   (EP *BP)
call   an   ambulance. stung   a   bee   to-the   João   and   he
é   alérgico
is   allergic
"Call an ambulance. João was stung by a bee and he is allergic."

(34) a. *Mordeu   um   cão   ao   gato.*   (?EP *BP)
bit   a   dog   to-the   cat
"A dog bit the cat.
(intonation is relevant for acceptability in EP)
b. *Mordeu-lhe   um   cão.*   (EP *BP)
Bit-it a   dog
c. *Um   cão   mordeu   ele.*   (*EP BP)
a   dog   bit   he
"A dog bit him."
(Cf. Section 3. above: EP excludes the non-clitic pronoun *ele* in object position)

(35) *Picou-lhe   uma   abelha   na   cara.*   (EP *PB)
Stung-him   a   bee   in-the   face
"A bee stung him in his face."

4.2. *Word order and focus*

Another relevant notion for word order issues is the notion of "focus." Here we distinguish two types of focus: information focus and contrastive (or emphatic) focus. In this section we will deal only with information focus. Contrastive focus will be dealt with in Section 5.

Information focus can be better understood in contrast to the notion of *presupposition* or *background*. If a sentence is an answer to a question like (36Q) or (37Q), which provides the discourse context of the answer, it has a part that is presupposed and one which is the information focus (in bold):

(36)   Q: *Who does John love?*
     A: *He loves* **Mary**.

(37)   Q: *Where did John arrive yesterday?*
     A: *Yesterday, he arrived* **in Paris**.

In (36A) the presupposition part is *John loves x*, and the information focus is *Mary*. In (37A) the presupposed part is *John arrived yesterday at x*, and the information focus is *in Paris*.

Information focus has always the nuclear stress of the sentence, which is sentence-final in English. In Portuguese, in the two varieties, the nuclear stress is also sentence-final. This predicts that answers like (38A) and (39A) in Portuguese will have similar syntactic patterns, and also be similar to English:

(38)   A: *Ele   ama   a   **Maria.***
         he   loves   the   Maria
         "He loves Maria."

(39)   A: *Ontem,   ele chegou   **em/a   Paris.***[15]
         yesterday   he arrived   in/to   Paris
         "Yesterday he arrived in Paris."

However, the same word-order pattern can have a distinct presuppositional part, and consequently a distinct focus depending on the context. A similar answer can be given to different questions, but depending on the question the focus is a different portion of the answer (in bold):

(40)   Q: *O   que   foi   que   a   Maria   cozinhou?*   (EP BP)
         the   what   was   that   the   Maria   cooked
         "What did Maria cook?"
     A: *(Ela)   cozinhou   **batatas.***
         she   cooked   potatoes
         "She cooked potatoes."

(41)   Q: *O   que   foi   que   a   Maria   fez?*   (EP BP)
         the   what   was   that   the   Maria   did
         "What did Maria do?"
     A: *(Ela)   **cozinhou   batatas***   (EP BP)
         she   cooked   potatoes
         "She cooked potatoes."

(42) Q: *Quem foi   que   cozinhou   batatas?*   (EP BP)
         who   was   that   cooked   potatoes
         "Who cooked potatoes?"

     A: *Foi   a   Maria.*   (EP BP)
         (was) the   Maria
         "It was Maria."

(43) Q: *Quem cozinhou batatas?*   (EP BP)
         who   cooked   potatoes
         "Who cooked potatoes?"

     A: *Cozinhou (batatas)   a   Maria.*   (EP *BP)
         cooked   potatoes   the   Maria
         "Maria cooked potatoes."

When the *wh*-question focuses on the subject, EP has the order V(X)S so that the nuclear stress falls on the subject. As BP has strong restrictions regarding the type of verb to license this type of word order, what we find in BP is an answer adjusted to the cleft-type of question (cf. (42Q)). Here the copula can be deleted as will be seen in Section 5. Otherwise, BP may block VS, as in (43). However, if the verb is of the unaccusative type the answer using the order VS is perfectly natural in BP, as the contrast between (44) with the unaccusative verb *cair* and (45) with the transitive *ver* shows:

(44) Q: *Quem caiu?*   (EP BP)
          who   fell
          "Who fell?"

     A1: *Caiu   uma   criança.*   (EP BP)
          fell   a   child
          "A child fell."

(45) Q: *Quem foi   que   viu   um   gato?*   (EP BP)
          who   was   that   saw   a   cat?
          "Who saw a cat?"

     A1: *Viu   uma   criança.*   (EP *BP)
          saw   a   child

     A2: *(Foi) uma   criança.*   (EP BP)
          was   a   child
          "It was a child."

On the other hand, there is no restriction as to the length of the predicate that is preposed to the subject in EP, though inversion is more easily found when one or more complements exhibit clitic forms:

(46) Q: *Quem   encontrou   ontem   a   Maria   no   shopping?*   (EP BP)
          who   met   yesterday   the   Maria   in-the   mall
          "Who met Maria yesterday at the mall?

     A1: *Encontrou   ontem   a   Maria   no   shopping a   Joana.*   (EP *BP)
          met   yesterday   the   Maria   in-the   mall   the   Joana

     A2: *Encontrou(-a)   (ontem   no   shopping) a   Joana.*   (EP *BP)
          met-her   yesterday   in-the   mall   the   Joana
          "It was Joana who met Maria in the mall."

(47) Q: *Quem foi que deu um iPod à/para a Maria?*[16]   (EP BP)
         who was that gave an iPod to/for the Maria
         "Who gave an iPod to Maria?"

    A1: *Deu(-lho) o Pedro.*   (EP *BP)
         gave-her-it the Pedro
         "Pedro gave it to her."
         (cf. Section 3: BP also excludes clitic clusters)

    A2: *Foi o Pedro.*   (EP BP)
         was the Pedro
         "It was Pedro."

Information focus does not have to single out a constituent of a sentence, in which case we would have a *narrow* focus. It can be the whole sentence, a case often referred to as *wide/broad* focus interpretation.

(48) Q: *O que se passa?*
         the what se happens
         "What is the matter?"

    A: *A Maria está a cozinhar/cozinhando batatas.*   (EP BP)
         the Maria is to cook/cooking   potatoes
         "Maria is cooking potatoes."

Notice that the answer in (48A) is a thetic sentence, as the answer describes a situation. In conclusion, we can say that thetic sentences have always wide focus interpretation and allow both VS and SV orders (with VS order subject to the constraints described above). Categorical sentences on the other hand are always SV. Hence word order (concretely, the subject position) can be used as a discourse strategy to disambiguate between a categorical/predicative interpretation and a thetic/presentative interpretation. EP uses this strategy more extensively than BP because the latter imposes stronger restrictions to subject–verb inversion, which will be further confirmed in the next sections. For further scrutiny of the interplay between VS order and (different types of) focus in EP and BP, see Costa and Figueiredo Silva (2006), which is in line with other authors that relate the scarcer availability of VS in BP with the loss of pro-drop (Nascimento 1984; Berlinck 1996; Britto, 2000; Kato and Tarallo 2003).

4.3. Word order and agreement

Though both EP and BP can have the order VS in thetic and subject-focus sentences when the verb is of the monoargumental type (and the verb is unaccusative or existential), there is a further difference where agreement with the subject is involved. In EP agreement with the postposed subject is the norm (but see Costa 2001, Carrilho 2003, who describe dialectal EP varieties without agreement), while in spoken BP the structure merges a null expletive, and the agreement is with the 3rd person, like with the existential verb *haver*. In the written style of BP, however, agreement is found in both orders.

(49) a. *Os ovos chegaram.*   (EP BP)
         the eggs arrived-3pl

     b. *Chegaram os ovos.*   (*EP BP spoken; also dialectal EP)
         arrived-3pl the eggs

     c. *Chegou os ovos.*   (*EP BP spoken; also dialectal EP)
         arrived-3sg the eggs
         "The eggs arrived."

(50) a. *Alguns   clientes   telefonaram.*   (EP BP)
         some   clients   called-3pl
     b. *Telefonaram   alguns   clientes.*   (EP BP written)
         called-3pl   some   clients
     c. *Telefonou   uns   clientes.*   (*EP BP spoken)
         called-3sg   some   clients
         "Some clients called."

4.4. *Favorable exceptional contexts for subject–verb inversion*

Though the availability of VS order in BP is limited, as discussed in Sections 4.1 and 4.2, it has been noted that there are certain contexts where such order is favored.

Pinto (1997) discovered that Italian has also restrictions with regard to VS order, but inversion is favored if the verb selects a locative which appears sentence-initially.[17]

(51) a. *In   questo   albergo   hanno   lavorato   molte   donne   straniere.*
         in   this   hotel   have   worked   many   women   foreign
         "In this hotel, there have worked many foreign women."
     b. *In   questa   casa   ha   abitato   Beatrice,*
         in   this   house   have lived   Beatrice
         "Beatrice has lived in this house."

BP can also have locative inversion with verbs that are not unaccusative:

(52) a. *Nesta   casa   morou   o   Jobin.*   (EP BP)
         in-this house   lived   the Jobin
         "Jobin lived in this house."
     b. *Nesta   obra   trabalham   imigrantes   de toda   a   America Latina.* (EP BP)
         in-this construction   work   immigrants   of all   the America Latin
         "Immigrants from all over Latin America work on this construction."

With transitive bridge verbs, in the narrative style, inversion is common in both varieties, but while in EP subject–verb inversion is obligatory, BP allows both orders:

(53) a. *Estou   exausto,   disse   o   Pedro.*   (EP BP)
         am   exhausted   said   the   Pedro
     b. *Estou   exausto,   o   Pedro   disse.*   (*EP BP)
         am   exhausted   the Pedro   said
         "I am exhausted, Pedro said."

(54) a. *Ela   já   vem,   respondeu   a   mãe.*   (EP BP)
         she   already   comes   answered   the   mother
     b. *Ela   já   vem,   a   mãe   respondeu.*   (*EP BP)
         she   already   comes   the mother   answered
         "She is coming, the mother answered."

For Belletti (2001: 70–71), though Italian has restrictions similar to BP, V(X)S can be easily found in particular registers, as in TV soccer reports, where the predicate describes a predictable situation:

(55)   *Mette   la   palla   sul   dischetto   del   rigore   Ronaldo.*   (Italian)
       puts   the   ball   on-the   point   of-the   penalty   Ronaldo
       "Ronaldo puts the ball on the penalty spot."

Pilati (2006, 2008) shows that BP has sentences similar to the Italian ones, which she calls "concomitant narrative" sentences, but she analyzes them using Pinto's frame. According to the latter author, deictic locatives can trigger inversion even when they are covert. Thus, in the contrast below, the inverted type is interpreted as having a deictic locative *here*, or a deictic temporal *now*, while in the non-inverted sentence the locative has indefinite interpretation.

(56)   a.   *È   entrato   Dante.*   (Italian)
            is   entered   Dante (here)
       b.   *Dante   è   entrato.*   (Italian)
            Dante   is   entered (somewhere)
            "Dante entered."

Actually, in many examples given by Pilati, the deictic expression seems to be the temporal *agora*.

(57)   a.   *(Agora)   Tem   a   palavra   a   senadora   Heloísa   Helena.*   (EP BP)
            now   has   the   say   the   senator   Heloisa   Helena
            "The senator Heloísa Helena has the floor."
       b.   *(Agora)   Abre   o   placar   o   time   do   Palmeiras.*   (EP BP)
            Now   opens   the   score   the   team   of-the   Palmeiras.
            "The Palmeiras team opens the scoring."
       c.   *(Agora)   Ergue   o   braço   o   juiz.*   (EP BP)
            now   raises   the   arm   the   referee
            "The referee raises his arm."

The generalization seems to be that inversion is possible in the two varieties if some XP precedes the verb in wide focus thetic sentences, even if this XP is a covert deictic expression. Still this grammatical option is subject to certain constrains in BP that are not found in EP. Verb type/class, discourse context and syntactic conditions such as the need to fill in the canonical subject position in BP seem to be relevant factors.

5. Word order in contrastive (or emphatic) focus constructions

5.1. Stress in information focus and in contrastive focus[18]

As was seen above, information focus is the constituent that receives the nuclear stress in a sentence and this is the reason why in Romance languages that dispose of subject-inversion, like EP and Spanish, the order V(X)S obtains when the subject is the focus of the sentence:[19]

(58)   Q: a.   *Quem   levou   o   meu   laptop?*   A: a.   *Levou   [$_F$ O LADRÃO]*   (EP *BP)
                 who   took   the   my   lap-top   took-it   the thief
            b.   *Quién   llevó   mi   laptop?*   b.   *Lo   llevó   [$_F$ EL LADRÓN]*   Spanish
                 who   took   my   lap-top   it   took   the thief
                 "Who took my lap-top?"   "The *thief* took it."

BP, on the other hand, is often similar to English when the information focus is the subject. While in the case of non-subjects, it is always the rightmost element that receives the nuclear stress, here the primary stress can be on the subject in preverbal position, the leftmost element in TP. According to Zubizarreta (1998: 20), this is due to the way English, French and German, and we can add BP, assign the nuclear stress. In these languages, defocalized and functional categories are (or can be) "metrically invisible" in the application of the nuclear stress rule (NSR), while in other Romance languages, like Spanish and EP, all phonologically specified elements are "metrically visible."

(59) Q: a. *Who*   took   my   laptop?   A: a. [$_F$ THE THIEF] took   it.   English
        b. <u>*Quem*</u> *levou* *o meu* *laptop?*   b. [$_F$ O LADRÃO] *levou* *ele.* (*EP BP)

Contrary to what happens in English and BP, when the stress falls on the preverbal subject in EP and Spanish, the interpretation is that of a contrastive focus. This is also true in BP and English. This means that in English and in BP, without a clear context, focalization on the subject can be ambiguous between information focus and contrastive focus. (60) provides "a corrective context,"[20] which makes the sentence unambiguous, with O LADRÃO a contrastive focus.

(60) a. *O* *LADRÃO* *levou* *o* *seu* *laptop,* *e* *não* *o* *seu* *vizinho.* (EP BP)
         the thief   took the your laptop and not the your neighbor
         "The THIEF took your laptop, and not your neighbor."
     b. *O* *MIGUEL* *adormeceu* *no* *carro,* *e* *não* *o* *Lucas.*   (EP BP)
         the Miguel   fell-asleep in-the car and not the Lucas
         "Miguel fell asleep in the car, not Lucas."

5.2. *Focus movement and prosodic prominence*

While in the previous subsection we saw cases of prosodic prominence alone to mark contrastive focus, in this section we are going to see cases of movement of a constituent to the left periphery of the sentence, a position where the focus also obtains prosodic prominence in both EP and BP.[21]

With regard to the position of the subject, EP has obligatorily the order VS, except in cases like (64), where a negative element is part of the focus, and when the fronted constituent includes a focus marker like *só* "only" or *até* "even."[22] In BP, on the other hand, VS can occur optionally with contrastive focus-movement.

(61) a. *DE* *NOTÍCIAS* *se* *faz* *o* *nosso* *mundo.* (EP BP)
         of news   SE makes the our world
     b. **DE* *NOTÍCIAS* *o* *nosso* *mundo* *se* *faz.* (*EP BP)
         of news   the our world SE makes
         "It's news that makes up our world."

(62) a. *UMA* *MELANCIA* *INTEIRA* *me* *comeu* *aquele* *bruto.* (EP BP)
         a   watermelon entire me-dat ate that brute
     b. *UMA* *MELANCIA* *INTEIRA* *aquele* *bruto* *me* *comeu.* (*EP BP)
         a   watermelon entire that brute me-dat ate
         "A whole watermelon, that's what that beast ate!"

(63) a. *UMA*   *FORTUNA*   *faturou*   *a*   *nossa*   *barraca.*   (EP BP)
      a   fortune   made   the   our   stand
   b. *UMA*   *FORTUNA*   *a*   *nossa*   *barraca*   *faturou.*   (*EP BP)
      a   fortune   the   our   stand   made
      "Our microbusiness earned us a fortune."

(64) a. *NEM*   *SEMPRE*   *ganha*   *o*   *favorito.*   (EP BP)
      not   always   wins   the   favorite
   b. *NEM*   *SEMPRE*   *o*   *favorito*   *ganha.*   (EP BP)
      not   always   the   favorite   wins
      "The favorite doesn't always win."

5.3. Cleft sentences: a multi-functional strategy to codify focus[23]

There is a strategy in Portuguese, and in other Romance languages,[24] which marks the focus syntactically, through the copula, namely the so-called cleft (or *that*-cleft) constructions and pseudo-cleft (or *wh*-clefts) constructions. Both types can convey information focus and contrastive focus.

5.3.1. Information focus

(65) Q: *O*   *que*   *é*   *que*   *o*   *ladrão*   *levou?*
      the   what   is   that   the   thief   took
      "What did the thief take?
   A1: *O*   *ladrão*   *levou*   [$_{FP}$ *O MEU LAPTOP*].   (EP BP)
      the   thief   took   the my laptop
      "The thief took my lap-top."
   A2: **O**   *que*   *o*   *ladrão*   *levou*   *foi*   [$_{F}$ *O MEU LAPTOP*]. (*wh*-cleft)   (EP BP)
      the   **what**   the   thief   took   was   the my laptop
      "What the thief took was my lap-top. "
   A3: *Foi*   [$_{F}$ *O MEU LAPTOP*]   **que**   *o*   *ladrão*   *levou.* (*that*-cleft)   (EP BP)
      was   the my laptop   **that**   the   thief   took
      "It was my laptop that the thief took."

5.3.2. Contrastive focus

(66) a. *Foi* [$_{F}$ *O MEU LAPTOP*] *o*   **que**   *o*   *ladrão*   *levou, não o*   *teu.* (*wh*-cleft)
      was   the my laptop   **the what**   the   thief   took   not the   yours   (EP BP)
      "It was my laptop that the thief took, not yours.
   b. *Foi* [$_{F}$ *O JOÃO*] **quem** *falou, não o*   *Pedro.* (*wh*-cleft) (EP BP)
      was   the João   **who**   spoke   not   the   Pedro
      "It was João who spoke, not Pedro."

(67) a. *Foi*   [$_{F}$ *O MEU LAPTOP*] **que** *o*   *ladrão levou, não o teu.* (*that*-cleft) (EP BP)
      was   the my laptop   **that** the   thief   took   not the yours
      "It was my laptop that the thief took, not yours."
   b. *Foi*   [$_{F}$ *O JOÃO*] **que** *falou, não o*   *Pedro.* (*that*- cleft) (EP BP)
      was   the João   **that**   spoke   not   the   Pedro
      "It was João who spoke, not Pedro."

In the examples above, the copula is always in initial position, but we can also have other positions for the copula. With *wh*-clefts, we can have: a) the copula in initial position, b) the copula in second position preceded by the focus and c) the copula in second position preceded by the *wh*-clause. With *that*-clefts we can have: a) the copula in initial position and b) the copula in second position preceded by the focalized element.

(68) a. **Sou** [$_F$ *EU*] *quem* *mais* *trabalha* *na* *empresa.*   (EP BP)
     am   I   who   more   works   in-the   company
  b. [$_F$ *EU*] **sou** *quem* *mais* *trabalha* *na* *empresa.*   (EP BP)
     I   am   who   more   works   in-the   company
     "I am the one who works the most in the company."
  c. *Quem* *mais* *trabalha* *nesta* *empresa* **sou** [$_F$ *EU*].   (EP BP)
     who   more   works   in-this   company   am   I
     "The one who works the most in the company is me."

(69) a. **Sou** [$_F$ *EU*] *que* *trabalho* *mais* *nesta* *empresa.*   (EP BP)
     am   I   that   work   more   in-this   company
  b. [$_F$ *EU*] **é** *que* *trabalho* *mais* *nesta* *empresa.*   (EP BP)
     I   is   that   work   more   in-this   company
  c. **É**   [$_F$ *EU*] *que* *trabalho* *mais* *nesta* *empresa.*   (*EP BP)
     is   I   that   work   more   in-this   company
     "It is me that works the most in this company."

While the copula agrees with the focus in all varieties of *wh*-clefts, with *that*-clefts, there is agreement with the focus only in structures like (69a), but not in structures like (69b), which illustrates an inverse cleft. In fact, inverse clefts, like (69b), display the invariable 3rd person singular copula in both EP and BP. On the other hand, (69c) shows that agreement is optional in non-inverted clefts in BP but not in EP (which is related to the non-agreeing pattern of postverbal subjects commented on in Section 4.3).

Form (69c) is an innovation in BP. The copula underwent grammaticalization in all *that*-clefts, not only in person agreement, but also in tense agreement (*consecutio temporum*). This is further followed by the deletion of the copula, as a new step in grammaticalization, as in (70c).

(70) a. *Foram* [OS MENINOS] *que* *sairam.*   (EP BP)
     were   the   boys   that   left-3pl
  b. **É** [OS MENINOS] *que* *sairam.*   (*EP BP)
     is   the   boys   that   left-3pl
  c. [OS MENINOS] *que* *sairam.*   (*EP BP)
     the   boys   that   left-3pl
     "[THE BOYS] left."

6. Word Order in *wh*-questions

6.1. *The* wh-*parameter*

The first issue concerning word order in *wh*-questions is the so-called *wh*-parameter, proposed in Huang (1982), according to which languages are of two types: a) those that move the *wh*-word or expression to the sentential periphery (e.g. English), and those that leave the *wh*-element *in-situ* (e.g. Japanese). Cheng and Rooryck (2000) show, however, that there are languages with optional *wh*-movement like French, and Kato (2013) shows that *wh*-movement in BP is also optional.

What is important here is to point out that BP has been showing a great increase in cases of *wh in-situ* since the nineteenth century,[25] and, contrary to French, it is free of restrictions.

The description of cases of *wh in-situ* in BP will be left out of the present chapter, and we refer the reader to Kato (2013), in which she proposes that the apparent *wh-in-situ* constructions do have actual *wh-movement* of a short type. See also Chapter 15, this volume.

6.2. *Main assumption of this section and the data*

It is a strong assumption in this chapter that *wh*-questions are contrastive focalization structures, with the *wh*-constituent the focus of the sentence, and should, thus, exhibit a parallel behavior with declarative contrastive focalization sentences.[26]

We will show, indeed, that what we saw about word order in declarative sentences in the previous sections is mirrored in the word order of *wh*-questions in contemporary EP and BP:[27]

a. unambiguous VSX order with fronted *wh*- is found productively in EP (cf. (71a and b)), but not in BP;
b. WhV(X)S with inergatives and transitives are found only in EP (cf. (72a and b));
c. WhVS order with unaccusative verbs or the copula is found in both varieties (cf. (73a–d));
d. strict SV is found only in BP (cf (74a and b)).[28]

(71) a. *Que   trouxe   **ele** de   novo para a   construção   romanesca?*   (EP)
what brought he of new for the construction novel
"How did he innovate in the novel genre?"

b. *Como consegue **ele** isto?*   (EP)
how obtains he this
"How is he able to do/get this?"

(72) a. *De   que   ri   o   **Diamantino?***   (EP)
of what laughs the Diamantino
"What does Diamantino laugh at?"

b. *O   que   fará   o   terceiro?*   (EP)
the what will-do-3sg the third
"What will the third one do?"

(73) a. *Onde   morreram   as   esperanças   e   as   ilusões?*   (EP)
where died the hopes and the illusions
"Where have the hopes and the illusions died?"

b. *Onde   estariam   **forma** e   teoria?*   (EP)
where would-be-3pl form and theory
"Where would form and theory be?"

c. *Com   quem   surgiu   esse   conceito?*   (BP)
with whom appeared this concept
"With whom did this concept appear?"

d. *Quando entra   o   **Real?***   (BP)
when enters the Real
"When does the Real enter?"

(74) a. *Com   quem   ele   governará?*   (BP)
        with   whom   he   will-govern
        "Whom will he govern with?"
     b. *Em   quem   eu   devo   acreditar?*   (BP)
        in   whom   I   should   believe
        "Whom should I believe in?"

6.3. Wh-*questions from cleft structures*

In the same way that focalization can be obtained by complex cleft structures, *wh*-questions have been able to be derived as cleft sentences[29] in both varieties since the beginning of the nineteenth century.[30]

(75) a. *Quando   é   que   falas   comigo?*   (EP nineteenth century)
        when   is   that   speaks   with-me
        "When is it that you speak with me?"
     b. *O   que   é   que   tu   fizeste?*   (EP twentieth century)
        the   what   is   that   you   did
        "What is it that you did?"

(76) a. *Onde   foi   que   ouvi   este   nome?*   (BP nineteenth century)
        where   was   that   heard-1sg   this   name?
        "Where is it that I heard this name?"
     b. *Como   é   que   chama   isso?*   (BP twentieth century)
        how   is   that   call   this
        "How is this called?"

With the copula in initial position, as in declarative clauses, *wh*-questions are found only in BP children's speech and in motherese:

(77) a. *É   quem   que   ta   tocano   o   violão?*   (Luana 2; 3.22)
        is   who   that   is   playing   the   guitar?
        "Who is playing the guitar?"
     b. *É   quem   que   tá   tomano   banho?*   (motherese)
        is   who   that   is   taking   bath
        "Who is taking a bath?"

The *wh*-questions in (75) and (76), however, when converted to (78), with the copula in initial position, and with necessary pronominal adjustments, are easily accepted by adult Brazilians,[31] but not by European speakers.

(78) a. *É   quando   que   você   fala   comigo?*   (*?EP BP)
        is   when   that   you   speak   with-me
        "When is it that you speak with me?"
     b. *É   o   que   que   você   fez?*   (*EP BP)
        is   the   what   that   you   did
        "What is it that you did?"
     c. *Foi   onde   que   ouvi   este   nome?*   (*?EP BP)
        was   where   that   heard-1sg   this   name?
        "Where did I hear that name?"
     d. *É   como   que   chama   isso?*   (*EP BP)
        is   how   that   call   this
        "How is this called?"

Finally, we will claim, that a pattern like (79b), and those in (80), without the copula, are in fact *"in-situ"* clefts, an idea defended by Noonan (1992) for Quebec French. We just have to add that the (78) examples, which are canonic clefts, undergo copula deletion, a common phenomenon in Brazilian Portuguese when the copula is in initial position.[32]

(79) a. *(C'ést)* *où* *que* *t'ás* *mis* *les* *oranges?*   Quebec French
   it is   where that you have put the   oranges
 b. *Où* *que* *t'á* *mis* *les* *oranges?"*   (Noonan 1992) Quebec French
   where that you have put the oranges
   "Where did you put the oranges?"

(80) a. *(É)* *quando* *que* *você* *fala* *comigo?*   (*EP BP)
   is   when   that you speak with-me
   "When is it that you speak with me?"
 b. *(É)* *o* *que* *que* *você* *fez?*   (*EP BP)
   is   the what that you did
   "What is it that you did?"
 c. *(Foi)* *onde* *que* *eu* *ouvi* *este* *nome?*   (*EP BP)
   was   where that I heard this name?
   "Where did I hear this name?"
 d. *(É)* *como* *que* *chama* *isso?*   (*EP BP)
   is   how   that call this
   "How is this called?"

7. Conclusion

In this chapter we have chosen constituent order to illustrate important differences between EP and BP, as word order is central to grammatical systems. We have shown that the two varieties of Portuguese may radically diverge in word order as is the case with clitic placement. In other instances, both varieties use the alternation between unmarked (SVO) and marked constituent orders as a means to signal semantic or pragmatic distinctions (predicative/descriptive sentences; narrow/wide focus; information/contrastive focus). But BP is more restrictive than EP as for the availability of subject–verb inversion (VS) and may use instead strategies that are compatible with the unmarked SVO order. Some of these strategies are innovations that are presumably parametrically related and put BP in a diverging path from EP.

NOTES

1   The first author had the support of CNPq (Grant n. 305515/2011-2017).
2   The second author had the support of FCT—*Fundação para a Ciência e a Tecnologia*, under the project WOChWEL (PTDC/CLE-LIN/121707/2010).
3   Verbal morphology plays a role in European Portuguese only with respect to *mesoclisis*, which surfaces in enclitic contexts when the verb is inflected in the future or conditional forms. Mesoclisis is the placement of the clitic pronoun before the sequence formed by the tense

morpheme (present or past) plus the agreement morpheme, as exemplified in (i) below. In this chapter we will put aside mesoclisis, which is nowadays restricted to formal EP.

(i) Eu   pagá-*lo*-ei.
    I   pay-it-acc-will-[T(present)+Agr morphemes]
    "I will pay for it."

4   Only Galician (cf. Álvarez and Xove 2002) and Astur-Leonese (cf. González i Planas 2007; Fernández-Rubiera 2006, 2009) pattern with EP in clitic placement.
5   A detailed identification and description of the different elements that trigger proclisis in EP affirmative root sentences is provided in Martins (2013).
6   The examples are taken from the late twentieth-century novel by Isaias Pessotti, *A Lua da Verdade* (São Paulo: Editora 34. 1997). Similar examples could easily be extracted from newspapers.
7   We are not implying that variation between proclisis and enclisis as displayed in current written BP can be purely aleatory. Tendencies dependent on textual types or individual preferences can certainly be devised by quantitative analyses. We are not aware, however, of any published investigation on this topic (except for some occasional observations based on limited data).
8   On the prefixal properties of PB clitics, see Nunes (2007: 28). The author shows that BP allows nouns to be derived from a string of proclitic and verb (respectively, *se* and *toca/manca* in (i)a below), as shown in (i)b and c, where the nouns in italics are derived from the idiomatic verbal expressions in (i)a, that include the reflexive clitic *se*.

(i) a. O   João   não   **se**   toca   **se**   *manca.*
        the   João   not   SE   touch/ SE   see
        "João is not aware of how inconvenient he is."
   b. O   João   precisa   de   um   **setocômetro.**
        the   João   needs   of   a   *setocômetro*
        "João needs an instrument to measure how inconvenient he is."
   c. O   João   tá   precisando   tomar   **semancol.**
        the   João   is   needing   to-take   *semancol*
        "João needs to take medicine against being inconvenient."

9   Luís Fernando Veríssimo, *Novas Comédias da Vida Privada*. Porto Alegre: L&PM. 1997 [13th edn.]. p. 176.
10   This is so even for the EP dialects that allow interpolation, which Magro (2007) analyzes as *metathesis*, in the sense of Harris and Halle 2005.
11   On word order in European Portuguese, see Duarte (1987, 1997), Ambar (1992), Martins (1994, 2010), Barbosa (1995, 2006, 2009), Costa (1998, 2001, 2004), among others; for Brazilian Portuguese, see Berlink (2000), Kato (2000), Kato and Tarallo (2003), Viotti (2007), Pilati (2007), among others.
12   These notions are borrowed from Kuroda (1965, 1972), who uses them to distinguish between the morphemes *-wa* and *-ga* in Japanese.
13   Cf. Martins (1994) on the categorical and thetic distinction in EP, and Kato (1989) and Britto (1998) on the same distinction in BP.
14   See Kato (1989), Lunguinho (2006), Duarte and Kato (2013), among others, on these constructions.
15   BP and EP display different prepositions in the locative complement, namely *em* "in" in BP and *a* "to" in EP.
16   EP displays preposition *a*, BP preposition *para*.
17   Locative inversion is not restricted to Romance languages, as can be seen in English and in Chichewa (Cf. Bresnan and Kanerva 1989).

   (i) *Among the guests sat my friend Rose.*
   (ii) *Ku mu-dzi ku-li chi-tsime.*
       "In the city is a well."

18   For contrastive focus in EP see Costa and Martins (2011) and for BP see Kato and Ribeiro (2009).

19   Examples taken from Kato and Ribeiro (2009).

20   For Bianchi, Bocci, and Cruschina (2013) contrastive focus involves different notions depending on the context: (a) corrective context, (b) mirative context (unexpected or surprising), (c) contrastive context.

21   Examples taken from Costa and Martins (2011), except (63a), which is taken from Naro and Votre (1999).

22   See details in Costa and Martins (2011).

23   Examples based on Kato and Ribeiro (2009). See also Modesto (2001), Mioto (2006, 2008) and Resenes (2009) on clefts in Brazilian Portuguese.

24   *Wh*-clefts are more widely found in languages than *it*-clefts (cf. Lambrecht 2001).

25   See Lopes-Rossi (1996) and Kato and Mioto (2008) for quantitative data.

26   This hypothesis was raised and confirmed in Kato and Ribeiro (2009) through diachronic facts.

27   The empirical description and the examples on contemporary EP and BP are from Kato and Mioto (2008), who used for EP the corpora http://acdc.linguateca.pt/acesso/, the subcorpus Natura-Público, and for BP the NILC-São Carlos. See also Ambar (1992) for an exhaustive description of EP.

28   Ambar (1992) predicts, however, that d-linked *wh*-expressions may have SV order.

29   Lopes-Rossi (1996) and Kato and Ribeiro (2009) show that *wh*-clefts as *wh*-questions are older, and that *that*-clefts appear only in the late eighteenth century, and are part of the vernacular in both varieties today.

30   The diachronic facts and examples are from Duarte (1987), Lopes-Rossi (1996), Kato and Duarte (2002) and Kato and Ribeiro (2009). The contemporary facts on EP are confirmed in Ambar (1988), Ambar and Veloso (2001), and Barbosa (2001).

31   Such patterns are not found in the written corpus used by Kato and Mioto (2008). They may be present, however, in more recent spoken corpora.

32   See, for instance, (i) and (ii), apud Kato (2007):

(i)   (É)   lindo   o   seu   cabelo.
      is   beautiful   the   your   hair
      "Your hair is beautiful."

(ii)   (É)   um   gênio   o   seu   filho.
      is   a   genius   the   your   son
      "Your son is a genius."

REFERENCES

Álvarez, Rosario and Xosé Xove (2002). *Gramática da Lingua Galega*. Vigo: Galaxia.

Ambar, Manuela (1992). *Para uma Sintaxe da Inversão Sujeito-Verbo em Português*. Lisboa: Edições Colibri.

Ambar, Manuela and Rita Veloso (2001). On the nature of *wh*-phrases, word order and *wh*-in-situ: Evidence from Portuguese, French, Hungarian and Tetum. In Y. D'hulst, Johan Rooryck and Jan Schroten (eds.), *Romance languages and linguistic theory 1999: Selected papers from "Going Romance" 1999, Leiden, 9–11 December 1999*. Amsterdam: John Benjamins, pp. 1–38.

Barbosa, Pilar (1995). Null Subjects. Ph.D. dissertation, MIT.

Barbosa, Pilar (2001). On inversion in wh-questions in Romance. In Aafke Hulk and Jean-Yves Pollock (eds.), *Subject inversion in Romance and the theory of universal grammar*. Oxford: Oxford University Press, pp. 20–59.

Barbosa, Pilar (2006). Ainda a questão dos sujeitos pré-verbais em Português Europeu: uma resposta a Costa (2001). *D.E.L.T.A.*, 22 (2), pp. 345–402.

Barbosa, Pilar (2009). Two kinds of subject pro. *Studia Linguistica*, 63 (1), pp. 2–58.

Belletti, Adriana (2001). "Inversion" as focalization. In: Aafke Hulk and Jean-Yves Pollock (eds.), *Subject inversion in Romance and the theory of universal grammar*. Oxford: Oxford University Press, pp. 60–90.

Berlinck, Rosane Andrade (1996). La Position du sujet en Portugais: etude dichronique des varietés brésilienne et européene. Ph.D. dissertation, Leuven, Katholiecke Universiteit.

Bianchi, Valentina, G. Bocci, and S. Cruschina (2013). Focus fronting and its implicatures. Paper presented at Going Romance 2013, University of Amsterdam.

Bresnan, Joan and Jonni M. Kanerva (1989). Locative inversion in Chichewa: A case study of factorization in grammar. *Linguistic Inquiry*, 20 (1), pp. 1–50.

Britto, Helena (2000). Syntactic codification of categorical and thetic judgments in Brazilian Portuguese. In Mary A. Kato and Esmeralda V. Negrão (eds.), *Brazilian Portuguese and the null subject parameter*. Frankfurt: Vervuert: Iberoamericana, pp. 195–222.

Campos, Héctor (1999). Passive constructions and partitive case checking in Spanish. In Jon A. Franco Alazne Landa, and Juan Martín (eds.), *Grammatical analyses in Basque and Romance linguistics: Papers in honor of Mario Saltarelli*. Amsterdam: John Benjamins, pp. 23–34.

Carneiro, Zenaide (2005). Cartas da Bahia: Um Estudo Lingüístico-filológico. Ph.D. dissertation, University of Campinas, São Paulo.

Carrilho, Ernestina (2003). Ainda a "unidade e diversidade da língua portuguesa": a sintaxe. In Ivo Castro and Inês Duarte (eds.), *Razões e Emoção: Miscelânea de estudos em homenagem a Maria Helena Mira Mateus*. Lisboa: INCM, pp. 163–178.

Cheng, Lisa L.S. and Johan Rooryck (2000). Licensing *wh*-in-situ. *Syntax*, 3 (1), pp.1–19.

CORDIAL-SIN: *Syntax-oriented corpus of Portuguese Dialects*. http://www.clul.ul.pt .

Costa, João (1998). *Word order variation: A constraint-based approach*. The Hague: Holland Academic Graphics.

Costa, João (2001). Postverbal subjects and agreement in accusative contexts in European Portuguese. *Linguistic Review*, 18, pp. 1–17.

Costa, João (2004). *Subject positions and the interfaces: The case of European Portuguese*. Berlin: Mouton de Gruyter.

Costa, João and M. Cristina Figueiredo Silva (2006). On the (in)dependence relations between syntax and pragmatics. In Valéria Molnar and Susanne Winkler (eds.), *The architecture of focus*. Berlin: Mouton de Gruyter, pp. 83–104.

Costa, João and Ana Maria Martins (2011). On focus movement in European Portuguese. *Probus*, 23 (2), pp. 217–245.

Costa, João, Alexandra Fiéis and Maria Lobo (2014). Input variability and late acquisition: clitic misplacement in European Portuguese. *Lingua*, 161, pp. 10–26.

Domingos, Manuel (2010). A colocação dos pronomes clíticos no português (oral) de Angola (POA). Trabalho do seminário de Linguística Comparada: Tópicos de Gramática do Português numa perspectiva comparativa. Unpublished manuscript. Faculdade de Letras da Universidade de Lisboa.

Duarte, Inês (1987). A Construção de Topicalização na Gramática do Português. Ph.D. dissertation, University of Lisbon.

Duarte, Inês (1997). Ordem de palavras: sintaxe e estrutura discursiva. In A. M. Brito, A.M., F. Oliveira, I. Pires de Lima and R. M. Martelo (eds.), *Sentido que a Vida Faz: Estudos para Óscar Lopes*. Porto: Campo das Letras, pp. 581–592.

Duarte, Inês and Gabriela Matos (2000). Romance clitics and the minimalist program. In Costa, João (ed.), *Portuguese syntax: New comparative studies*. Oxford: Oxford University Press, pp. 116–142.

Duarte, M. Eugenia and Mary A. Kato (2013). The lack of lexical expletives in Brazilian Portuguese. Paper presented at the GTTG/ANPOLL Meeting, University of São Paulo.

Fernández-Rubiera, Francisco J. (2006). Clitic placement in Asturian: Evidence for a syntactic FocusP interaction. *Georgetown University Working Papers in Linguistics 2006*, pp. 89–126.

Fernández-Rubiera, Francisco J. (2009). Clitics at the Edge: Clitic Placement in Western Iberian Languages. Ph.D.Dissertation, Georgetown University.

González i Planas, Francesc (2007). Sintaxis de los clíticos pronominales en asturleonés. *Ianua Revista Philologica Romanica 7*, pp.15–35.

Harris, James and Morris Halle (2005). Unexpected plural inflections in Spanish: Reduplication and metathesis. *Linguistic Inquiry*, 36 (2), pp. 195–22.

Huang, C. T. James (1982). Move WH in a language without WH movement. *The Linguistic Review 1*, pp. 369–416.

Justino, Víctor Mércia (2010). Estudo Comparativo dos Padrões de Colocação dos Pronomes Clíticos nos Discursos Oral e Escrito do Português de Moçambique. MS. University of Lisbon.

Kato, Mary A. (1989). Sujeito e Tópico: duas categorias em sintaxe? *Cadernos de Estudos Linguísticos*, 17, pp. 109–132.

Kato, Mary A. (2000). The partial pro-drop nature and the restricted VS order in Brazilian Portuguese. In M. A. Kato and E. V. Negrão (eds.), *Brazilian Portuguese and the null subject parameter*. Frankfurt: Vervuert/ IberoAmericana, pp. 223–258.

Kato, Mary A. (2007). Free and dependent small clauses in Brazilian Portuguese. *DELTA*, 23, pp. 85–111.

Kato, Mary A. (2013). Deriving "wh-in-situ" through movement in Brazilian Portuguese. In V. A. Camacho-Taboada, A. Gimenez-Fernancez, J. Martin-Gonzales, and M. Reyes-Tejedor (eds.), *Information structure and agreement*. Amsterdam: John Benjamins, pp. 175–191.

Kato, Mary A. and Carlos Mioto (2008). A multi-evidence study of European and Brazilian Portuguese *wh*-questions. In S. Kepser and M. Reis (eds), *Linguistic evidence: Empirical, theoretical, and computational perspectives*. Berlin: Mouton de Gruyter, pp. 307–328.

Kato, Mary A. and Ilza Ribeiro (2009). Cleft sentences from Old Portuguese to Modern Brazilian Portuguese. In A. Dufter and D. Jacob (eds.), *Focus and background in Romance languages*. Amsterdam: John Benjamins, pp. 123–154.

Kato, Mary A. and Fernando Tarallo (2003). The loss of VS syntax in Brazilian Portuguese. In B. Schliebe Lange, I. Koch and K. Jungbluth (eds.), *Dialogue between schools: Sociolinguistics, conversational analysis and generative theory in Brazil*. Münster: Nodus Publicationen, Klaus D. Ditz, pp. 101–129.

Lambrecht, Knud (2001). A frame for the analysis of cleft constructions. *Linguistics*, 39 (3), pp. 463–516.

Lopes-Rossi, M. Aparecida (1996). A Sintaxe Diacrônica das Interrogativas-Q do Português. Ph.D. dissertation, University of Campinas.

Lunguinho, Marcus V. (2006). Partição de constituintes no português brasileiro: características sintáticas. In Denise Silva (ed.), *Língua, gramática e discurso*. Goiânia: Cânone Editorial, pp.133–150.

Magro, Catarina (2007). Clíticos: Variações sobre o tema. Ph.D. dissertation, University of Lisbon.

Mapasse, Ermelinda Lúcia Atanasio (2005). Clíticos Pronominais em Português de Moçambique. M.A. thesis, University of Lisbon.

Martins, Ana Maria (1994). Clíticos na História do Português. Ph.D. dissertation, University of Lisbon.

Martins, Ana Maria (2010). Constituent order in simple declarative clauses Relatório do seminário de Linguística Comparada: Tópicos de Gramática do Português numa perspectiva comparativa, apresentado a provas públicas para obtenção do título académicos de agregado no ramo de Linguística. Unpublished Report. University of Lisbon, pp. 103–125.

Martins, Ana Maria (2011). Clíticos na história do português à luz do teatro vicentino. *Estudos de Lingüística Galega*, 3, pp. 55–83.

Martins, Ana Maria (2013). A posição dos pronomes pessoais clíticos. In E. Paiva Raposo, M. F. Bacelar do Nascimento, M. A. Mota, L. Segura, and A. Mendes (eds) *Gramática do Português*. Lisboa: Fundação Calouste Gulbenkian, pp. 2231–2302.

Mioto, Carlos (2006). Focus and clefting. Paper presented at the Workshop on Formal Linguistics. University of Florianópolis.

Mioto, Carlos (2008). Pseudo-clivadas reduzidas em espanhol caribenho e em português brasileiro. Paper presented at the IIIrd Workshop on Romania Nova. Montevideo.

Modesto, Marcello (2001). *As construções clivadas no português do Brasil: relações entre interpretação focal, movimento sintático e prosódia*. São Paulo: Humanitas.

Naro, Anthony and Sebastião Votre (1999). Discourse motivations for linguistic regularities: verb / subject order in spoken Brazilian Portuguese. *Probus*, 11, pp. 76–100.

Nascimento, M. 1984. Sur la posposition du sujet dans le Portugais du Brésil. Ph.D. dissertation, Université de Paris VIII.

Newell, Heather (2005). A late adjunction solution to bracketing paradoxes. Proceedings of the 35th annual meeting of the North East Linguistic Society (NELS).

Noonan, Maire (1992). *Case and syntactic geometry*. Ph.D. dissertation, McGill University.

Nunes, Jairo (2007). Triangulismos e a sintaxe do português brasileiro. In Ataliba T. de Castilho, M. Aparecida Torres-Morais, Ruth E. Vasconcellos Lopes, and Sônia M. Lazzarini Cyrino (eds.) *Descrição, História e Aquisição do Português Brasileiro*. São Paulo: Pontes/ FAPESP, pp. 25–33.

Pagotto, Emílio G. (1992). A Posição dos Clíticos em Português: Um Estudo Diacrônico. M.A. thesis, University of Campinas.

Pessotti, Isaias (1997). *A Lua da Verdade*. São Paulo: Editora 34.

Pilati, Eloisa (2006). Aspectos sintáticos e semânticos das orações com ordem verbo-sujeito no português do Brasil. Ph.D. dissertation. University of Brasília.

Pilati, Eloisa (2008). *Aspectos sintáticos e semânticos das orações com ordem Verbo-Sujeito no Português do Brasil: o percurso de uma pesquisa*. Brasília: Ceell.

Pinto, Manuela (1997). *Licensing and interpretation of inverted subjects in Italian*. Ph.D. dissertation, University of Utrecht.

Resenes, Mariana S. (2009). Sentenças pseudo-clivadas do português brasileiro. M.A. thesis, University of Florianópolis.

Ribeiro, Ilza and Mary A. Kato (2009). Focalização de predicados no português arcaico e moderno. In V. Aguilera (ed.), *Para a História do Português Brasileiro, Tomo I: Vozes, Veredas, Voragens*. Londrina: Eduel, pp. 369–392.

Rodygina, Olga Vadimovna (2009). Colocação dos pronomes átonos nas orações infinitivas no Português Europeu. M.A. thesis, University of Minho.

Tarallo, Fernando (1983). Relativization Strategies in Brazilian Portuguese. Ph.D. dissertation. University of Pennsylvania.

Tarallo, Fernando (1990). *Tempos Lingüísticos. Itinerário Histórico da Língua Portuguesa*. São Paulo: Ática.

Vigário, Marina (2003). *The prosodic word in European Portuguese*. Berlin: Mouton de Gruyter.

Villalva, Alina (2000). *Estruturas Morfológicas: Unidades e Hierarquias nas Palavras do Português*. Lisboa: Fundação Calouste Gulbenkian/ Ministério da Ciência e Tecnologia.

Zubizarreta, M. Luiza (1998). *Prosody, focus and word order*. Cambridge, MA: MIT Press.

3   Portuguese in Contact

ANA MARIA CARVALHO AND
DANTE LUCCHESI[1]

1. Introduction

Portuguese is the sixth most spoken language in the world and the official language of eight countries: Brazil, Portugal, Angola, Mozambique, Guinea-Bissau, Sao Tome and Principe, Cape Verde, and East Timor, with more than 200 million native speakers. The distribution of the Portuguese language in the world today reflects the development of Portuguese colonial control from the sixteenth to the twentieth century and migration trends. Throughout its 500 years of expansion, the Portuguese language came into contact with hundreds of very different languages, in equally diverse situations. From these diverse contact conditions, profound changes resulted, such as those that brought about the Portuguese creoles of Africa and Asia. As a less radical result of linguistic contact, the popular varieties of Brazilian Portuguese have developed. In addition, a wide range of contact situations involving Portuguese gave rise to the emergence of varieties of Portuguese spoken as L2 in Africa and Asia, in addition to bilingual varieties in communities on the borders of Portuguese and Spanish-speaking countries, both in South America and in Europe. This chapter provides an overview of the multiplicity of contact situations involving Portuguese and their linguistic consequences.[2]

2. The emergence of pidgin and creole languages and the process of irregular language transmission

In most cases, the effects of language contact are observed mainly in lexical borrowings, without direct effects on the grammar of the languages involved. However, massive and abrupt language contact sometimes gives rise to entirely new languages, called *pidgins* and *creoles*. The majority of such languages known today were formed during European colonial expansion, in specific sociological contexts such as (1) agricultural export activities employing slave or forced labor, that were established in America, Africa, Asia and Oceania; (2) communities of runaway slaves, called *quilombos*, *palenques*, or *maroons* in Africa and America; (3) trading posts in European strongholds in Africa, Asia and Oceania. Typically, the process of pidginization and creolization occurred in asymmetric situations, wherein a dominant European minority imposed its language upon a majority of speakers of different and mutually unintelligible languages.

The Handbook of Portuguese Linguistics, First Edition. Edited by W. Leo Wetzels, João Costa, and Sergio Menuzzi.
© 2016 John Wiley & Sons, Inc. Published 2020 by John Wiley & Sons, Inc.

There is extensive discussion as to whether pidgins and creoles have a special status among human languages.[3] While most languages have evolved gradually over many generations, the formation of pidgins and creoles may occur within two or three generations. In the initial contact situation, this process involves the functional expansion and grammaticalization of a small vocabulary from the dominant language (the lexifier language) to form a second language code of interethnic communication. From this process, a number of typical structural features emerge. A creole speech community forms when children develop their native language from the model of L2 (pre-pidgin or pidgin) spoken by adults. Depending on the sociohistorical context, the result of this process of language development may be more, or less, radical. In the next section, we present a theoretical perspective which contemplates both types, and which captures the nature of historical language contact in Brazil.

2.1. *Irregular language transmission*

The notion of irregular language transmission (ILT) as a gradual process seeks to develop a broader model for linguistic change induced by language contact (Lucchesi 2008, 2012). Whereas massive contact between languages can lead to the formation of a creole language, with a qualitatively different grammar from that of the target language, it can also result in the formation of varieties of the dominant language with only some of the structural features of creole languages, characterizing a light type of irregular language transmission.[4]

In both cases, there is a need for the restoration of grammatical structures lost in the initial contact situation, resulting from incomplete language acquisition of the lexifier language by adult speakers of the dominated groups. Hence, it is the intensity of erosion of the dominant language grammar that determines the degree of grammatical restructuring of the emergent linguistic variety. In typical creolization situations, communication happens through a restricted vocabulary from the dominant language, virtually devoid of grammatical structure, called a pre-pidgin (Siegel 2008). Where the dominated groups speak mutually unintelligible languages, the pre-pidgin becomes used in communicative functions beyond the restricted relationship between dominators and dominated. This functional expansion triggers grammatical restructuring engendering the pidgin language. As speakers of the dominated groups have very limited access to grammatical models of the dominant language, they resort to grammatical structures of their native languages to grammaticalize the pre-pidgin, a process called relexification (Lefebvre 1998) or substrate transfer (Siegel 2008). To the extent that children born in the contact circumstances are acquiring pre-pidgin or pidgin as their first language, creolization (nativization) occurs.

The grammatical restructuring that distinguishes the formation of pidgins and creoles occurred in very specific sociohistorical situations of language contact. Nonetheless, the conditions fostered by European colonialism in America, Africa, Asia and Oceania varied greatly with respect to their social, ethnic, and demographic variables. Thus, in many situations of massive language contact, pidgins and creoles did not develop, yet this does not mean that the varieties of English, Portuguese, and Spanish that developed are devoid of structural changes resulting from the imposition of colonial languages upon millions of speakers of other languages.

What differentiates light ILT from the cases considered typical of creolization is the greater access of the speakers of the dominated groups to models of the target language. This *greater access* inhibits the embryonic processes of grammaticalization and transfer of the substrate, essential for development of a pidgin or creole grammar. However, the process that is shared with pidginization and creolization is the morphological simplification affecting primarily the grammatical mechanisms that either have no informational value or have a more abstract semantic value. Hence, the difference between the two cases resulting from contact is merely quantitative. In radical ILT yielding pidginization/creolization those mechanisms would be virtually excluded, whereas lighter irregular language transmission would yield a broad complex of variation in the use of these mechanisms, without their exclusion.

3. Brazil

The first effective Portuguese colonization of Brazil occurred in the region of São Paulo, in 1532, and was based on the enslavement of local indigenous people. The small contingent of settlers, overwhelmingly men, gave rise to an extensive process of miscegenation, which resulted in the formation of a Mameluco mestizo society,[5] characterized by the predominant use of a *restructured* variety of Tupi, called *língua geral*. The diglossia between the *língua geral* and the Portuguese of the colonists, typical of São Paulo Society in the sixteenth and seventeenth centuries, can be seen as the initial manifestation of the sociolinguistic polarization of Brazil.

Following the expulsion of the French from São Luís, in 1615, a variety of Tupinambá, known as *Nheengatu* ("good language"), came to predominate in the Portuguese colonial society established initially in Maranhão. Subsequently, the Portuguese settlers spread this language to the Amazon in their search for spices and indigenous slaves, and Nheengatu was adopted by Amazonian indigenous people who spoke quite distinct languages, such as the Arawak and Carib languages. Nheengatu nativized among these peoples and has survived as the mother tongue in some Upper Amazon localities. In the more dynamic regions of Portuguese America in the sixteenth and seventeenth centuries – such as the areas surrounding the towns of Olinda and Salvador, in northeastern Brazil – the indigenous population was quickly decimated and replaced by large contingents of African slaves.

Between the sixteenth and nineteenth centuries, the slave trade introduced some ten million Africans to the Americas. On the linguistic level, the African contribution is highlighted by the emergence of more than thirty creole languages, including Haitian (French-lexified), Palenquero (Colombia, Spanish-lexified), and Saramaccan and Sranan (Suriname, English-lexified). It is estimated that Brazil was the destination of almost 40 percent of the Atlantic slave trade, amounting to some four million individuals. Until the mid-nineteenth century, approximately 70 percent of Brazil's population consisted of Indians, Africans, and their descendants—that is, only one-third of Brazilian society were native speakers of Portuguese born from parents with the same mother tongue. As of the seventeenth century, the presence of Africans and their descendants grew significantly, constituting the workforce of three principal activities: sugar-cane, tobacco and cotton plantations in the northeast of Brazil between the seventeenth and nineteenth centuries; mining of gold and precious stones in Minas Gerais in the eighteenth century; and coffee plantations of southeast Brazil in the nineteenth century. By 1850, Africans and their offspring represented approximately 65 percent of Brazil's total population. Although the slave trade ended in 1850, slavery was abolished only in 1888. Until the early twentieth century, the vast majority of people of African origin lived in the countryside and was illiterate (Lucchesi 2009).

In the face of these facts, there is strong evidence for the influence of language contact in the formation of the variety of Portuguese spoken by blacks and mulattos who dominated the base of the Brazilian social pyramid (Mattos and Silva 2004). Historic records (especially literary texts) of the speech of Africans and *crioulos* in the nineteenth century reveal traits of morphological simplification characteristic of pidgin and creole languages, notably the lack of articles, verbal inflection, nominal number, gender agreement, and pronominal case inflection (Alkmim 2008). Consequently, one may conclude that the historical predecessor of present Popular Brazilian Portuguese underwent a process of ILT of a light type, as described in the previous section.[6]

Throughout the twentieth century, a significant part of the rural population of African descent migrated to the large cities, entering the consumer market and the world of literacy, albeit precariously. Thus, the population of Brazilian cities multiplied, highways were constructed throughout the country and a wide network of public schools was established. This produced significant sociolinguistic changes: the speech of the ruling classes began to distance itself from the model of Portugal, being influenced by linguistic changes from below, whereas the speech of the great mass of descendants of African slaves (or of Brazilian Indians, depending on the region) became increasingly influenced by linguistic changes from above. Thus, a linguistic leveling occurred with an increasing influence from the so-called Brazilian educated urban standard (*norma culta*) in all regions of the country. In addition to the socioeconomic factors cited here, the rapid growth of the mass media acted decisively in implementing this linguistic leveling (Lucchesi 2001 and 2009).

This entire process alleviated the ethnic character of the linguistic differences between the upper and lower classes, weakening the effects of changes triggered by historical language contact. However, the effects of those changes still divide the Brazilian sociolinguistic scene. The most notable reflex of this partition is the massive variation that affects the rules of nominal and verbal agreement in popular speech (eg, *meus filho chegou cedo* "my (pl) son (sing) arrived (sing) early" instead of *meus filhos chegaram cedo* "my (pl) children (pl) arrived (pl) early)." The current maintenance of these characteristics resulting from language contact is due to the dependent and late character of capitalist development in Brazil and the extensive exploitation of the working classes. As such, these characteristics of popular speech constitute strong social stigma, and lack of morphosyntactic agreement is a linguistic feature, which is used to discriminate against individuals from the lower Brazilian socioeconomic classes.

4. Africa

Unlike Brazil, in Africa the indigenous languages were preserved. Only a minority speak Portuguese, mostly as an L2, concentrated in urban centers. In contrast, the island countries Cape Verde and São Tomé and Príncipe were populated by a minority of Portuguese colonists and a majority of enslaved Africans. In this close contact, creolized varieties of Portuguese became the native languages of increasingly mixed local populations. A mixed scenario originated in Guinea-Bissau, with the preservation of native African languages and the emergence of a creole which acts as a lingua franca in the cities.

4.1. *African varieties of Portuguese*

The presence of the Portuguese and the dissemination of the Portuguese language in Angola was very limited, even after 1576, when the Portuguese ruled Luanda and extended their domain into the interior. Until the mid-eighteenth century, the African-Portuguese administrative elite used Portuguese only as their L2. Even though, in the second half of the eighteenth century, Portugal sought to hinder the Africanization of the local elite, the situation changed little, until the first decades of the twentieth century (Vansina 2001). It was only during the Salazar dictatorship (1928–1974) that the Portuguese presence in Angola increased, with the new policy requiring that Angolans be fully fluent in Portuguese in order to participate in public life. The effect was minimal. The proportion of settlers within the entire Angolan population was less than 1 per cent by 1940, increasing to some 5 percent in the 1970s (Bender 2004: 71). With political independence in 1975, this number dropped dramatically.

Currently, only a very small sector of the Angolan elite speaks Portuguese as its mother tongue, in a variety very similar to that of Portugal. Over 90 percent of the population is native in one of the approximately forty Bantu languages spoken in the country, the main ones being Kimbundo, Kikongo, and Umbundo. Some 20 to 30 percent of the population, mostly young people living in coastal cities, uses Portuguese as a second language. This *Vernacular Angolan Portuguese* displays alterations due to the influence of the Bantu substrate (Inverno 2009). Some of these characteristics are common to popular Brazilian Portuguese, such as variable nominal and verbal agreement and loss of pronominal case inflection (e.g., *encontrou eu ontem* "((s)he) met I yesterday" instead of *encontrou-me ontem* "((s)he) met me yesterday"). However, unlike Brazilian Portuguese, Angolan Portuguese also displays variable gender agreement in the noun phrase (*um pessoa* "a (MASC) person (FEM)" instead of *uma pessoa* "a (FEM) person (FEM)") and variable verbal agreement with the 1st person singular (e.g., *eu trabalha* "I (p1) work (p3)" for *eu trabalho* "I (p1) work (p1)").

The history of the diffusion of Portuguese in Mozambique is very similar to that of Angola. Until the twentieth century, the presence of the Portuguese was minimal. Despite the arrival of some 140,000 settlers in the 1950s and 1960s, the proportion of Portuguese within the Mozambican population has always been less than 2 percent (Ribeiro 1981: 390). Nevertheless, as in Angola, Portuguese was retained as an official language and the language of national unity after the independence in 1975. With the expansion of public education and Portuguese being the language of instruction, the proportion of native Portuguese speakers rose from 1.2 percent in 1980 to 6.5 percent in 1997. The vast majority of the population is composed of native speakers of one of the more than twenty Bantu languages spoken in the country, such as Makua, spoken by roughly 26 percent of the population, and Xangana, spoken by about 11 percent. Portuguese is the L2 of almost 40 percent of the population, 75 percent of which is urban (Gonçalves 2010). In addition to the morphological simplification resulting from imperfect L2 acquisition similar to that observed in Angola, Mozambique Portuguese (MP) displays a clear Bantu influence, notably in the argument structure of the verb (Gonçalves 2010: 46–55):

1. Intransitive verbs in European Portuguese (EP) receive two arguments: *Ela nasceu dois filhos na Suazilândia* (MP) "(lit.) She was born two children in Swaziland" instead of *Dois filhos dela nasceram na Suazilândia* (EP) "Two of her children were born in Swaziland."
2. Suppression of prepositions governing the verbal complement in EP: *O detetive desconfiou um indivíduo* (PM) "The detective suspected an individual" rather than *O detetive desconfiou de um indivíduo* (EP) "(lit.)The detective suspected of an individual."
3. Double object constructions instead of a prepositional dative: *entregou o emissário a carta* (MP) "(S)he handed the emissary the letter" rather than *entregou a carta ao emissário* (EP) "(S)he handed the letter to the emissary."
4. Passive constructions unacceptable in EP: *A aldeia foi evoluída por aquele rapaz* (MP) Literally "The village was evolved by that boy."

A growing number of studies compare the morphosyntactic aspects common to popular Brazilian Portuguese, Angolan Portuguese, and Mozambican Portuguese, aiming to define more precisely how language contact has affected the grammar of Portuguese, in situations other than those of creolization on the west coast of Africa.

4.2. *Portuguese creoles in Africa*

In Africa, contact situations involving Portuguese resulted in creolization in the Cape Verde archipelago and the islands of São Tomé, Príncipe, and Anobom. On the continent, creolization occurred in Guinea-Bissau, which may be explained in part by the close relationship between this country and Cape Verde until their independence in 1975. Some scholars assign a common origin to Cape Verdean creole and the creole of Guinea-Bissau (Kihm 1994: 3–8).

Cape Verdean creole, comprising two major varieties, *barlavento* "windward" and *sotavento* "leeward," and the creole of Guinea-Bissau can be considered lighter creoles, due to the lack of grammatical restructuring they display relative to Portuguese. Grammatical restructuring that characterizes the Atlantic creoles, such as verb serialization, generally did not take place. The light creolization of these languages is also evident in the retention, although with a different semantics, of the verbal suffix *–va*, expressing habitual past in Portuguese, in addition to the typical preverbal tense / mood / aspect (TMA) particles, which these creoles also exhibit. At the same time, Cape Verdean and Guinea-Bissau creoles do not display subject–verb agreement inflection as well as gender and number agreement in noun phrases, a commonly observed feature of creoles.

A more radical creolization occurred on the island of São Tomé, yielding a creole which later branched into four creoles (Ferraz 1979; Hagemeijer 2009), namely: Santomé (or Forro), which developed among the mestizo population of São Tomé; Angolar, which evolved from the original creole among the maroons who took refuge in the southern part of the island; Lung'ie (or Principense), which developed from Santomé transplanted to Principe island; and Fa d'Ambo, a variety which also developed from Santomé, transplanted to the island of Annobón, which came under Spanish rule in 1778.

The initial creole was formed roughly between 1493 and 1520. During this period, slaves were mainly imported from Benin, where Edo (a Kwa language) was, and still is, spoken. Among the African substrate languages, Edo has influenced most of the grammar of the Portuguese creoles of the Gulf of Guinea (Hagemeijer 2009: 1–3). Although as of 1520 the islands of São Tome and Principe received an enormous contingent of Bantu-speaking slaves from Congo and Angola, the Bantu languages had little influence on the development of the Santome grammar (Ferraz 1979).

The above-mentioned creoles went through a more radical process of grammatical restructuring (Ferraz 1979: 60–89; Hagemeijer 2009: 10–17). The following examples are taken from Santomé, except for the example in (6), which is from Angolar:

1. All Portuguese verbal inflection was eliminated and replaced by preverbal TMA particles, such as the particle *tava*, expressing the past anterior (*e **tava** ba shinema* "he had gone to the cinema").
2. As a consequence of the loss of inflection, these creoles, unlike Portuguese, do not allow null referential subjects, and require subject pronoun clitics, as in French.
3. Pronominal case inflection was lost, leaving uninflected pronouns for all syntactic functions.
4. The Edo pronominal form *inen* functions as a third person plural pronoun (***inen** sebe* "they know") and as a nominal pluralizer (***inen** mina* "the children").
5. An indeterminate subject pronoun, probably from Edo origin, was created (*a pó fé kwa sé* "one can do that") (Ferraz 1979: 66).
6. The Edo noun for "body" grammaticalized as a reflexive pronoun (*Ê mata ôngê rê* "he killed himself").
7. Double negation construction *na… fa* was created (*Sun **na** bila lembla ngê ku sa mosu **fa*** "you did not remember who was the boy").
8. Development of verb serialization, in which verbs gramaticalize into other functions, as, for example, the verb "give" functions as a dative preposition (e.g. *complá sapé **da** mu* "buy hat to me").

5. Asia

Bartolomeu Dias rounded the Cape of Good Hope in 1487, opening maritime routes to India for the first time. By 1518, the Portuguese had reached Goa, Daman, and Diu in India, Malacca in Malaysia, Macao in China, East Timor in Southeast Asia, and today's Sri Lanka.

The Portuguese presence in Asia gave rise to diverse Portuguese-based language varieties, including several Portuguese-lexified pidgins and creoles. Cardoso (2009) illustrates the presence of a number of Portuguese-lexified contact languages spread across South Asia, shown in Figure 3.1.

Clements (1996) proposes four subgroups for the Portuguese-based creoles in Asia, summarized in Table 3.1.

Some of these Portuguese-lexified contact languages are still spoken in Diu, Daman, and Korlai, but only to a limited extent (Cardoso 2009: 7), and they are nearly extinct in Macao and Malacca. Moreover, varieties of Portuguese as a first or second language are still found in Goa, Macao, and East Timor.

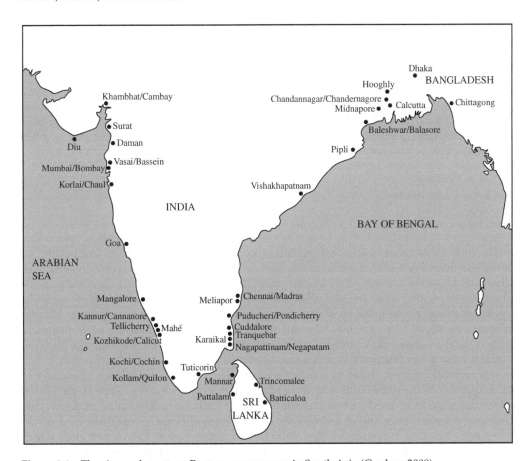

Figure 3.1 The sixteenth-century Portuguese presence in South Asia (Cardoso 2009).

Table 3.1 Portuguese-based creoles in Asia (based on Clements 1996: 1).

Subgroups	Languages
Gauro-Portuguese	Diu, Daman, Norteiro (Bombay and Korlai)
Dravido-Portuguese	Mangalore, Camanore, Mahé, Cochin, Nagappattinam, Sri Lanka
Malayo-Portuguese	Malacca, East Timor, Singapore, Batavia
Sino-Portuguese	Macao, Hong Kong

5.1. *Portuguese-based varieties in India*

In West India, one finds Portuguese-lexified creoles in Diu, Daman, and Korlai. It is estimated that there are 200 Portuguese speakers in Diu and 4000 in Daman, while approximately 700 are believed to still speak Portuguese in Korlai (Holm 1989; Cardoso 2009).

According to Cardoso (2009), the use of Portuguese in Diu is currently related to
Catholicism, education, economic prosperity, and nostalgia for the colonial area. Local varieties of Portuguese vary along the Standard Portuguese and Diu Indo-Portuguese continuum, as variable verbal and nominal agreement illustrates. The examples (1 a and b), also
from Cardoso (2009, 21), show the difference between a local form (1 a) and the Standard
European form (1 b) produced by the same speaker, when saying "I don't know":

(1) a. *yo nã sab* (Diu Indo-Portuguese)
     b. *yo nã sey* (Standard Portuguese)

Portuguese varieties spoken in Daman and in Diu are mutually understandable, because both
originated from the contact with Gujarati, the regional language, and because there are frequent
interpersonal contacts between their inhabitants. Among some of the differences, Daman
speakers use constructions with auxiliary and gerundive verb forms to express progressive
aspect, as example (2) illustrates for the verb *cantar* ("to sing") with the gerund suffix -*n*, while
Diu speakers prefer progressive with the infinitive (3), as illustrated in Cardoso (2009: 23).

(2) *Joyce   te kanta-n agor*
     "Joyce is singing now."
(3) *Leslie   ta kãt-a*
     "Leslie is singing."

The differences between these varieties are mostly quantitative and point to a perception
in the communities that Diu speakers incorporate more Standard Portuguese in their varieties than Damans. Compared to Daman and Diu, Korlai creole, which is spoken in the
Chau–Korlai region, is also an old creole that survived due to its geographic isolation. Unlike
Daman and Diu, Korlai grew apart from Standard Portuguese showing increasing Marathi
influence as attested by the shift from the SVO order prevalent until the early twentieth
century to the current SOV order (Clements 1990). Nowadays, the Portuguese origin of
Korlai is most noticeable in the core lexicon (Clements 1996).

A somewhat different situation is found in Goa, where Portuguese replaced the creole in
the beginning of the nineteenth century (Holm, 1989). Portuguese was kept as the appropriate language to be used in this important Roman Catholic ecclesiastical center, among
civil servants and clerics, and in the military. Beyond these circles, the vast majority used the
indigenous Konkani language as their primary language, except for a small elite, which
continued to speak Portuguese (Rodrigues, 2000). After Goa's independence, English gradually became the language of prestige, although there is still some schooling, written media,
and a few interest groups in Portuguese.

5.2. *Portuguese-based varieties in Southeast Asia*

In Southeast Asia, Portuguese is spoken to a limited extent as a first or second language in
Macao and East Timor, while Kristang (Malacca) and Maquista (Macao) are in clear decline.
Since the foundation of Macao in 1557, the contact between Chinese, Portuguese, and other
languages spoken by Indians, Malayans, and Africans, resulted in the use of Portuguese as a
first and as a second language, in addition to the development of Portuguese-based pidgins
and creoles (Baxter 2009). In 1999, when Macao became a Special Administrative Region of

Figure 3.2 Public sign in Macao, China.

the People's Republic of China, Chinese was declared the co-official language along with Portuguese. Baxter estimates that Macao counts 4000 individuals who speak Portuguese as their first language, in addition to 2500 speakers of Portuguese as a second language.

The linguistic landscape of Macao is clearly bilingual due to the current language policy that enforces bilingual public signage, as illustrated by the picture in Figure 3.2.[7]

Baxter (2009: 296) lists a series of Macao Portuguese features resulting from contact with Chinese that show parallels with the former creoles of Macao and Malacca, such as the lack of nasal vowels and rhotic distinctions. In addition, Baxter discusses features in Macao Portuguese that show parallels in other Portuguese vernaculars, including variable nominal agreement with prenominal elements favoring the plural marker, also attested in Brazil and Africa (see Sections 3 and 4 above). More direct cases of contact-induced changes in local Macao Portuguese are variable gender agreement, absence of articles and verbal tense marking, and other features claimed to be either reminiscent of Macao creole or more directly influenced by Chinese (Baxter 2009).

In East Timor, as in Macao, Portuguese was mainly used in the central administration, in the army, and among missionaries. Currently the co-official language along with Tetum, Portuguese existed before the independence and during the occupation by Indonesia (1975–1999) as the lingua franca of the educated elites. Since Timor's independence, Portuguese is estimated to be spoken by 5 percent to 35 percent of the population, mainly among the elderly (Albuquerque 2011: 68). Unlike the situation in the former African colonies, where Portuguese was maintained as the lingua franca after independence, Tetum is the language preferred in East Timor as a common means of communication among the speakers of one of the 16 different indigenous languages.

In Albuquerque's (2011) study of Portuguese varieties currently used in East Timor, the author shows features that fluctuate between standard Portuguese and local dialects, which include features found in other Portuguese monolingual varieties and others clearly resulting from substratum interference, such as prosodic patterns, absence of prepositions, and differential agreement marking. The author also finds similarities among East Timorese Portuguese and other Portuguese-based creoles in the region, such as from Malacca and Macao.

Contact with Portuguese gave rise to creoles in Southeast Asia as well, but most have undergone language shift. Kristang, spoken by a small community in Malacca, is the last variety of the East and Southeast Asian Portuguese creoles, but it is currently under pressure from Malay and English and showing clear signs of language shift. Baxter (2005) shows that Kristang is in the process of being lost, as witnessed by the replacement of Kristang lexical items with Malay and English equivalents in addition to signs of structural borrowing from English. According to Baxter, only through the immediate implementation of language revitalization measures can Kristang be saved from extinction.

In Macao, pidginized varieties of Portuguese also evolved from contact that took place among traders and missionaries. As claimed by Baxter (2005), Makista originated from both Portuguese-based pidgins and creoles from other Portuguese colonies brought to Macao. In the nineteenth century, Makista started to lose ground to Portuguese due to the increasing presence of schooling in Portuguese. By the twentieth century the process of decreolization was completed. Currently, the variety is believed to be nearly extinct, surviving only in local artistic performances (Baxter 2009).

Connections between Portuguese-based varieties in West and East Asia have been the subject of great scholarly attention. Baxter (2009: 286) identifies morphosyntactic structures and lexical items shared by Kristang and Makista due to historical connections between the regions in the sixteenth century. For example, he claims that the presence of *ja* as the perfective particle and the SVO order illustrate, among others features, the result of intense contact between different substratum languages with the Portuguese superstrate.[8]

6. Portuguese in contact with Spanish

Unlike the contact situations discussed previously that resulted from Portuguese expansion overseas, the contact between Portuguese and Spanish arises from the geographic contiguity of Portuguese- and Spanish-speaking countries in South America and in the Iberian Peninsula, where political and linguistic borders do not coincide. This particular setting posits different analytical challenges, since sorting out shared inheritance from contact-induced changes is difficult. Furthermore, it is commonly assumed that cognate languages facilitate contact-induced phenomena. The contact of Portuguese with Spanish in contexts of language acquisition, transnational communication across borders, and bilingualism, presents an ideal platform for testing such a hypothesis. In this section, we will focus our attention on Portuguese–Spanish contact during which societal and prolonged bilingualism has given rise to stable varieties, as in northern Uruguay in South America and Miranda do Minho and Barranco in Europe.

6.1. *Uruguay*

The presence of Portuguese in Uruguay is the result of the region's colonial history. From the earliest European presence in the Southern Cone, Spaniards and Portuguese battled over Uruguayan territory. The presence of the Portuguese army in what is nowadays Uruguay is attested to by the foundation of the city of Colonia do Sacramento in 1680 and the complete control of the "Cisplatine Province" from 1815 until 1825. In northern Uruguay, Portuguese was spoken until the nineteenth century, when the Uruguayan government promoted the establishment of Hispanic culture and language in the border communities as a nation-building strategy. By the early twentieth century, Spanish had indeed penetrated the Portuguese-speaking north. However, despite several Spanish-only language policies, Portuguese has survived in that area, including in the border towns of Rivera, Artigas, and Aceguá, where bilingualism is widespread. With Spanish being the language of education and public life and Portuguese being used as a vernacular for in-group interaction, the linguistic situation can be defined as semi-diglossic.

Uruguayan Portuguese has clear origins in rural, non-standard Brazilian Portuguese (BP) spoken in adjacent areas of southern Brazil, as attested by the presence of words such as *inté* (*até* "until"), *ansin* (*assim* "this way"), the proclictic address form *nhá* (*senhora*), in addition to *lh*-gliding, variable verbal and nominal agreement, and presence of the -*emo* verbal suffix for first-person plural in -*ar* verbs (*e.g., cantemo* for *cantamos*, "we sing") (Elizaincín et al. 1987). In addition, it presents several features borrowed from Spanish, such as lexical items as illustrated in (4), where *padre* is used for BP *pai* ("father") , lexicalized NPs as in (5), where *fideo con tuco* is used for BP *macarrão com molho* ("spaguetti and sauce"), in addition to lexical calques, as illustrated in (6) where *povo*, cf. Sp. *pueblo*, "village" is used for BP *vila*, and syntactic calques, as in (7), where *um* (cf. Sp. *uno* "one") is used as the subject of an indeterminate construction.

(4) *Olha, quando meu* padre *não tá passo o dia todo olhando televisão.*
     "Look, when my 'father' is not [around] I spend the whole day watching television."
(5) *Acho que é* fideo con tuco, *porque todo mundo adora um* fideo con tuco.
     "I think it is 'spaghetti with sauce', because everyone loves 'spaghetti with sauce'."
(6) *Eu passava numa quinta de eucalipto que tava bem ao lado do povo.*
     "I used to pass by a Eucalyptus plantation that was next to the village."
(7) *É a realidade da vida. Aunque um não queira as vez se dar conta.*
     "That is the reality of life. Although one doesn't want to face it sometimes."

In addition, other contact features are present, such as phonetic transfers, amply discussed in Douglas (2004) and Meireles (2009), as well as code-switching (Douglas 2004; Carvalho 2014). In fact, the presence of contact features in these border dialects led Lipski (2009, among others) to argue that the contact of Portuguese with Spanish in Uruguay gave rise to a new hybrid language the so-called *Portuñol*. Others find clear continuities between border varieties and monolingual counterparts spoken in adjacent areas that contradict the notion of "a new language" (Carvalho 2003, 2004, 2014; Pacheco, 2014). Studies based on data collected on both sides of the border fail to see clear isoglosses separating Brazilian from Uruguayan varieties of Portuguese (Meirelles 2009; Pacheco 2014). While highly hybrid constructions are indeed abundant in unmonitored speech, the diglossic dynamics that render the separation of codes socially significant in addition to the normative pressure which national varieties exert on border dialects give rise to multidialectal and bilingual repertoires that are stylistically and socially stratified, thus defying the monolectal perspective of a single and unified mixed code (Carvalho 2014). Dialectal leveling of Uruguayan Portuguese towards urban varieties of Brazilian Portuguese is evidenced by the incorporation of features such as pronominal *a gente* "we" (Pacheco 2014) and the palatalization of dental stops (*di*) and (*ti*) (Carvalho 2004; Catañeda Molla 2011), and may signal dialect shift in the long term, unless more focused varieties of Uruguayan Portuguese continue to be used as a border identity marker, alongside Spanish and increasingly standardized versions of Portuguese.

6.2. *Portugal*

Two areas in Portugal present cases of dialects that coexist with Spanish which depart substantially from the surrounding monolingual varieties of Portuguese: Miranda do Douro and Barranco. Mirandese, spoken in northeastern Portugal is a structurally transitional variety along the Portuguese–Mirandese–Spanish continuum (Martins 2014). Directly derived from Asturo-Leonese, Mirandese has developed into a variety with features that either coincide with Portuguese or Spanish, or features that are not encountered in either language. For example, while Mirandese has the nasal vowels and diphthongs from the Portuguese vowel system, it shows the maintenance of intervocalic /l/ in *pila* as in Spanish (Portuguese *pia*, "sink") (Martins 2014). One of the few features that are unique to Mirandese is the use of *-e* as a theme vowel for regular *-ar* verbs and a verbal morphology that shares features with both Portuguese and Spanish, thus demonstrating its transitional character.

Martins' comparison of census data, language choice surveys, and interviews carried out in Miranda do Douro show that the vitality of Mirandese is very low due to a process of gradual language shift towards Portuguese. This trend is confirmed by a series of proficiency tests that show children having higher proficiency in Portuguese than in Mirandese. The children were also submitted to a perception test where they had to discern Mirandese and Portuguese features, in which they demonstrated the ability to perceive both varieties as different entities (Martins 2014).

Barranquenho is another Portuguese-based variety in contact with Spanish found in Portugal. Spoken in Barrancos within an area of Spanish–Portuguese bilingualism, it is heavily influenced by Spanish. According to Clements, Amaral, and Luís (2011), this dialect represents a mixed language that has developed and survived because of its strong relation with the local identity. In this region, Portuguese has coexisted alongside Spanish since the sixteenth century due to constant territory disputes between the two countries. Nowadays, frequent travels to Spain for shopping and medical assistance, in addition to the higher prestige attributed to Spanish, motivate border dwellers to acquire Spanish, while the community's official language remains Portuguese, and Barranquenho is reserved for in-group interactions (Clements et al. 2011). The description of Barrenquenho by Clements et al. (2011) shows several traits illustrating its affiliation with Portuguese, such as the seven oral vowel system and the /s–z/ contrast. Other elements presented as typical of Barranquenho are also present in monolingual varieties of Portuguese, such as the lack of the /b–v/ distinction, the deletion of word-final consonants, and variable clitic placement. Clear evidence of changes induced by the contact with Spanish includes indirect object doubling with full NPs, as illustrated in Clements et al. (2011) and reproduced in (8).

(8) *Le conté a meu pai.*
     Standard Portuguese *Contei ao meu pai.*
     Standard Spanish *Le conté a mi padre.*
     "I told my father."

Also typical is the use of the Spanish discourse marker *bueno*, a commonly borrowed word in Uruguayan and Southern Brazilian Portuguese as well. In addition, the authors document the variable use of the Spanish construction involving the "gustar-type" verbs with the experiencer coded as the indirect object and the corresponding Portuguese construction where the experiencer is coded as the subject. For Clements et al. (2011), these direct interferences from Spanish are numerous and categorical enough to justify the classification of Barranquenho as a new language. Barranquenho presents an ideal context for variationist analysis that would disambiguate contact features from internal changes, and account for the social and stylistic distribution of these features in the community.

In sum, the analyses of Uruguayan Portuguese, Mirandese, and Barranquenho reveal contexts where cognate languages such as Portuguese and Spanish maintain their structural differences while allowing the emergence of local and unique varieties in the bilingual repertoire. Despite typological similarities, which in theory are believed to give rise to mixed varieties that replace the source languages, the presence of social pressure, identity issues, and diglossic dynamics allow for the preservation of cross-linguistic differences in these bilingual dialects.

7. Conclusion

In this chapter, it has been suggested that Brazilian Portuguese is affected, to a greater or lesser extent, by the contact of Portuguese with Brazilian indigenous languages and African languages that were taken to Brazil. In addition, situations of language contact in Africa, Asia, and Oceania were surveyed, including both contexts that gave rise to the emergence of creole languages and situations where varieties of Portuguese are spoken as a second language by millions of speakers. Finally, the contact between Portuguese and Spanish along national borders in Brazil and Portugal was discussed, shedding light on issues of permeability of cognate languages in contact situations.

In addition to their political and cultural relevance, situations involving contact between Portuguese and other languages constitute valuable and promising fields of linguistic research whose findings can contribute to our understanding of important issues, such as the origin of human language, patterns of language variation and change in contact situations, and issues related to first and second language acquisition. As such, language contact constitutes a phenomenon of significant historical, social, and linguistic dimensions within the Lusophone world.

NOTES

1   Dante Lucchesi thanks Alan Baxter for comments and suggestions regarding Sections 2–4. Any errors are the responsibility of the author.
2   Numerous other contexts illustrate situations where Portuguese is in contact with other languages, including bilingual varieties of Portuguese spoken by immigrants and the indigenous population in Brazil, and Portuguese-speaking migrants in America, Asia and Europe. A discussion of these other situations is outside the scope of this chapter due to space limitations.
3   Bakker et al. (2011) propose that creoles constitute a special language typology, while others defend the opposite view (DeGraff 2001).
4   For a similar proposal, see Holm (2004).
5   The term *mameluco* is used traditionally to refer to the mestizo offspring of European colonizers and indigenous women.
6   Naro and Scherre (2007) present an alternative view according to which the current characteristics of Popular Brazilian Portuguese would have originated through natural language-internal evolution, based on the concept of drift proposed by Sapir (1921). However, they also refer to a "confluence of causes", including language contact and pidginization of Portuguese in Brazil, which would have intensified and accelerated the changes that were foreseen in the structure of the language.
7   Photo by Ana M. Carvalho, 2013.
8   For a comprehensive overview of the relationships among Portuguese-based creoles in Asia, see Cardoso, Baxter, and Nunes 2012.

REFERENCES

Albuquerque, D. B. (2011). O Português no Timor Leste: Contribuições para o estudo de uma variedade emergente. *PAPIA*, 21 (1), pp. 65–82.

Alkmim, T. (2008). Falas e cores: Um estudo sobre o português de negros e escravos no Brasil do século XIX. In I. S. Lima and L. do Carmo (eds.), *História Social da Língua Nacional*. Rio de Janeiro: Casa de Rui Barbosa, pp. 247–264.

Bakker, P., A. Daval-Markussen, M. Parkvall, and I. Plag (2011). Creoles are typologically distinct from non-creoles. *Journal of Pidgin and Creole Languages*, 26 (1), pp. 5–42.

Baxter, A. (2005). Kristang (Malacca Creole Portuguese): A long-time survivor seriously endangered. *Sociolinguistic Studies*, 6 (1), pp. 1–37.

Baxter, A. (2009). O Português de Macau. In A. M. Carvalho (ed.), *Português em Contato*, Madrid: Iberoamericana:Verviert Verlag, pp. 277–312.

Bender, G. J. (2004). *Angola sob o domínio português: mito e realidade*. Luanda: Editorial Nzila.

Cardoso, H. (2009). *The Indo-Portuguese Language of Diu*. Uthrecht: LOT.

Cardoso, H., A. N. Baxter, and M. P. Nunes (eds.) (2012). *Ibero-Asian Creoles: Comparative Perspectives*. Amsterdam: John Benjamins.

Carvalho, A. M. (2003). Rumo a uma definição do português uruguaio. *Revista Internacional de Lingüística Iberoamericana*, 2, pp. 125–150.

Carvalho, A. M. (2004). "I speak like the guys on TV": Palatalization and the urbanization of Uruguayan Portuguese. *Language Variation and Change*, 16 (2), pp. 127–151.

Carvalho, A. M. (2014). Sociolinguistic continuities in language contact situations: the case of Portuguese in contact with Spanish along the Uruguayan–Brazilian border. In P. Amaral and A. M. Carvalho (eds.), *Portuguese–Spanish Interfaces*. Amsterdam: John Benjamins, pp. 263–294.

Catañeda Molla, R. M. (2011). *Linguistic variation in a border town: Palatalization of dental stops and vowel nasalization in Rivera*. Ph.D. dissertation, University of Florida.

Clements, C. (1990). Deletion as an indicator of SVO–SOV shift. *Language Variation and Change*, 2, pp. 103–133.

Clements, J. C. (1996). *The Genesis of a Language: The Formation and Development of Korlai Portuguese*. Amsterdam: John Benjamins.

Clements, J. C., P. Amaral, and A. Luís (2011). Spanish in contact with Portuguese: The case of Barranquenho. In M. Díaz-Campos (ed.), *The Handbook of Hispanic Sociolinguistics*. Oxford: Wiley-Blackwell, pp. 395–417.

DeGraff, M. (2001). On the origin of creoles: A Cartesian critique of "neo"–Darwinian linguistics. *Linguistic Typology*, 203, pp. 213–310.

Douglas, K. L. (2004). *Uruguayan Portuguese in Artigas: Tri-dimensionality of transitional local varieties in contact with Spanish and Portuguese standards*. Ph.D. dissertation, University of Wisconsin, Madison, WI.

Elizaincín, A., L. Behares, and G. Barrios (1987). *Nós falemo Brasileiro. Dialectos portugueses del Uruguay*. Montevideo: Amesur.

Ferraz, L. I. (1979). *The Creole of São Tomé*. Johannesburg: Witwatersrand University Press.

Gonçalves, P. (2010). *A gênese do português de Moçambique*. Lisboa: Imprensa Nacional.

Hagemeijer, T. (2009). As Línguas de S. Tomé e Príncipe. *Revista de Crioulos de Base Lexical Portuguesa e Espanhola*, 1 (1), pp. 1–27.

Holm, J. (1989). *Pidgins and Creoles: Volume 2*. Cambridge: Cambridge University Press.

Holm, J. (2004). *Languages in Contact: The Partial Restructuring of Vernaculars*. Cambridge: Cambridge University Press.

Inverno, L. (2009). A transição de Angola para o português vernáculo: um estudo morfossintático do sintagma nominal. In A. Carvalho (ed.), *Português em Contato*. Madrid: Iberoamericana, pp. 87–106.

Kihm, A. (1994). *Kriyol Syntax – The Portuguese-based creole language of Guinea-Bissau*. Amsterdam: John Benjamins.

Lefebvre, C. (1998). *Creole Genesis and the Acquisition of Grammar: The Case of Haitian Creole*. Cambridge: Cambridge University Press.

Lipski, J. (2009). Searching for the origins of Uruguayan Fronterizo dialects: Radical codemixing as "fluent dysfluency". *JPL*, 8 (1), pp. 3–44.

Lucchesi, D. (2001). As duas grandes vertentes da história sociolingüística do Brasil. *DELTA*, 17 (1), pp. 97–130.

Lucchesi, D. (2008). Aspectos gramaticais do português brasileiro afetados pelo contato entre línguas: uma visão de conjunto. In C. Roncarati and J. Abraçado (eds.), *Português brasileiro II: contato linguístico, heterogeneidade e história*. Niterói: EDUFF, pp. 366–390.

Lucchesi, D. (2009). História do Contato entre Línguas no Brasil. In D. Lucchesi, A. Baxter, and I. Ribeiro (eds.), *O Português Afro-Brasileiro*. Salvador: Edufba, pp. 41–73.

Lucchesi, D. (2012). A diferenciação da língua portuguesa no Brasil e o contato entre línguas. *Estudos de Lingüística Galega*, 4, pp. 45–65.

Martins, C. (2014). Mirandese in contact with Portuguese and Spanish. In P. Amaral and A. M. Carvalho (eds.), *Portuguese–Spanish Interfaces*. Amsterdam: John Benjamins, pp. 295–315.

Mattos e Silva, R. V. (2004). *Ensaios para uma sócio-história do português brasileiro*. São Paulo: Parábola.

Meirelles, V. A. G. (2009). O portugués da frontera Uruguai–Brasil. In A. M. Carvalho (ed.), *Português em Contato*. Madrid: Iberoamericana, pp. 257–275.

Naro, A. and M. Scherre (2007). *Origens do Português Brasileiro*. São Paulo: Parábola.

Pacheco, C. (2014). *Alternância "nós" e "a gente" no português brasileiro e português uruguaio na fronteira Brasil–Uruguai*. Ph.D. dissertation, University of Brasília.

Ribeiro, O. (1981). *A colonização de Angola e seu fracasso*. Lisboa: Imprensa Nacional.

Rickford, J. and S. Romaine (eds.) (1999). *Creole Genesis, Attitudes and Discourse*. Amsterdam: John Benjamins.

Rodrigues, M. B. C. (2000). The status of Portuguese language and some cultural aspects in Goa. In *Lusotopie 2000. Lusophonies asiatiques, Asiatiques en lusophonies*. Paris: Karthala, pp. 597–609.

Sapir, E. (1921). *Language: An Introduction to the Study of Speech*. New York: Harcourt, Brace.

Siegel, J. (2008). *The Emergence of Pidgin and Creole Languages*. Oxford: Oxford University Press.

Vansina, J. (2001). Portuguese vs Kimbundu: Language use in the colony of Angola (1575–c.1845). *Bulletin dês Sèances Academie Royale des Sciences d'Outre-Mer*, 47, pp. 267–281.

4 A Comparative Study of the Sounds of European and Brazilian Portuguese: Phonemes and Allophones

GLADIS MASSINI-CAGLIARI, LUIZ CARLOS CAGLIARI, AND WAYNE J. REDENBARGER

From a phonological point of view, the segment inventory of most dialects of European Portuguese (EP) and Brazilian Portuguese (BP) is very similar.[1] Some of the differences between dialects are due to innovations in Brazil and Portugal after 1500, for example, final unstressed [i] > [i] in Portugal and [ti, di] > [ʧi, ʤi] in Rio de Janeiro. Other processes have been seen as the result of neutralization processes, as in the structuralist analysis of Câmara Jr., 1970, or in the generative analysis of Mateus and et al. 1990. In this chapter, we will focus on the sounds of BP with special attention given to the Paulista (São Paulo State) dialect. When EP presents noticeable differences from BP we will provide appropriate comments and examples. Other dialectal differences will be noted when considered useful.

1. Consonants

BP has 21 consonantal phonemes, which are represented in Table 4.1.

All these consonants appear in the word-initial syllable onsets, except the palatals [ɲ], [ʎ] and tap [ɾ], which are found only word-internally.[2]

pato	[ˈpa.tu]	"duck"	*fato*	[ˈfa.tu]	"fact"
bato	[ˈba.tu]	"I beat"	*vasto*	[ˈvas.tu]	"vast"
tato	[ˈta.tu]	"tact"	*sapo*	[ˈsa.pu]	"toad"
dato	[ˈda.tu]	"I date"	*zaga*	[ˈza.ga]	"Fullback"
cato	[ˈka.tu]	"I gather"	*chato*	[ˈʃa.tu]	"boring"
gato	[ˈga.tu]	"cat"	*jato*	[ˈʒa.tu]	"jet"
mato	[ˈma.tu]	"bush"	*lato*	[ˈla.tu]	"broad"
nato	[ˈna.tu]	"born"	*palha*	[ˈpa.ʎa]	"straw"
banho	[ˈbẽ.ɲu]	"bath"	*rato*	[ˈha.tu]	"rat"
			caro	[ˈka.ɾu]	"dear"

The Handbook of Portuguese Linguistics, First Edition. Edited by W. Leo Wetzels, João Costa, and Sergio Menuzzi.
© 2016 John Wiley & Sons, Inc. Published 2020 by John Wiley & Sons, Inc.

Table 4.1 BP consonantal phonemes.

	Stops	*Fricatives*	*Nasals*	*Laterals*	*Rhotics*
Labial	p b	f v	m		
Coronal	t d	s z	n	l	ɾ
Palatal		ʃ ʒ	ɲ	ʎ	
Dorsal	k g				
Dorsal & Round	kʷ gʷ				
Glottal		h			

At the phonetic level, other consonants appear, as a result of the application of various phonetic processes.

1.1. *Affricates*

In BP, palatalization converts the stops [t] and [d] to [ʧ] and [ʤ] whenever they precede a high front [i] vowel. The affricates [ʧ] or [ʤ] behave as a single segment in BP. This affrication of coronal stops occurs in many dialects of BP, including the Paulista and Carioca (Rio de Janeiro) varieties.

tia	[ˈʧi.a]	"aunt"
dia	[ˈʤi.a]	"day"
parte	[ˈpah.ʧi]	"part"
advogado	[a.ʤi.vo.ˈga.du]	"lawyer" [3]

This process does not apply in EP.

In a few varieties in the Northeast and Central regions of Brazil, affricates occur following a high front tense vowel [i] or a palatal glide [j]: *rito* [ˈhi.ʧu] "cult"; *prefeito* [pɾe.ˈfej.ʧu] "mayor"; *vida* [ˈvi.ʤa] "life"; *doido* [ˈdoj.ʤu] "crazy."

1.2. *Nasals*

Both in BP and EP, an underlying nasal consonant in the syllable coda assimilates to the place of articulation of the following onset stop in citation forms: *bambo* [ˈbĕm.bu] "loose"; *bando* [ˈbĕn.du] "band"; *banco* [ˈbĕŋ.ku] "bench." In normal speed speech, the nasal in coda position is usually not pronounced: *bambo* [ˈbĕ.bu] "loose," *bando* [ˈbĕ.du] "band," *banco* [ˈbĕ.ku] "bench." Before fricatives, liquids or rhotics, no nasal consonant occurs in BP or EP: *infeliz* [ĩ.fe.ˈlis], *[in.fe.ˈlis] "unhappy"; *enlatado* [ẽ.la.ˈta.du] / [ẽj.la.ˈta.du], *[en.la.ˈta.du] "canned"; *honra* [ˈõ.ha], *[ˈon.ha] "honor." In BP and EP, the velar nasal [ŋ] also occurs following a back vowel, resulting from a progressive assimilation of the articulator feature of the preceding vowel: *som* [ˈsõŋ] "sound"; *lã* [ˈlẽŋ] "wool" (Cagliari, 1977).

1.3. *Laterals*

Exclusively in BP, in coda position, a lateral consonant is frequently realized as a labial glide [w]: *mal* [ˈmɑw] / [ˈmaw] "evil." The velarized consonant [ɫ] is the typical European Portuguese pronunciation in this environment: *sol* [ˈsɔɫ] "sun"; *Brasil* [bɾa.ˈziɫ] "Brazil."

Nowadays [ɫ] is rare in BP and it occurs principally in the South of Brazil. Tasca (2002) observes that, besides the velarized [ɫ] and the vocalized [w], the coronal lateral [l] also occurs as a coda variant of /l/ in Rio Grande do Sul.

1.4. Palatal sonorants

In Wetzels (2000: 6), it is proposed that /ɲ, ʎ/ are phonological geminates in BP. But we can also apply Wetzels' arguments to EP. One of the author's arguments relates to the systematic nasalization of a preceding unstressed vowel before /ɲ/. The allophonic nasalization of a vowel in the context of a following nasal onset consonant is variable in BP, but obligatory only for stressed vowels: *cana* ['kẽ.na] "sugarcane," but *caneta* [ka.'ne.ta] "pen." However, in the case of palatal nasal /ɲ/, nasalization is consistent in both stressed and unstressed position:

Unstressed nasal vowels before /ɲ/:

<blockquote>

Nasal vowel in pretonic position
dinheiro   [dĩ.'ɲej.ɾu]   "money"
senhor   [sẽ.'ɲoɾ]   "sir"

Nasal vowel in tonic position:
cozinha   [ko.'zĩ.ɲa]   "kitchen"
aranha   [a.'ɾẽ.ɲa]   "spider"

</blockquote>

Another observation is that syllable rhymes which precede [ɲ, ʎ] are always light. If palatal sonorants are geminates, this would follow from the BP rhyme constraint, which allows only two segments in a syllable rhyme, the last of which would be occupied by the first part of the geminate (Wetzels 1997). Also, since falling diphthongs are not allowed before [ɲ, ʎ], the natural syllabification for the sequence "vowel + high vowel + [ɲ, ʎ]" would be to maintain hiatus: *rainha* [ha.'ĩ.ɲa] "queen"; *faulha* [fa.'u.ʎa] "spark."[4] Under this analysis, the sequence "vowel + high vowel" before a sonorant [m, n, l, ɾ], is obligatorily syllabified as a VG falling diphthong: *queima* ['kej.ma] "it burns"; *reino* ['hej.nu] "kingdom"; *baile* ['baj.li] "ball"; *Laura* ['law.ɾa] "Laura." The geminate hypothesis also correctly predicts that main stress could never be on the third syllable from the right word-edge in words which have [ɲ, ʎ] in the onset of the word-final syllable, as in *alcunha* [aw.'kũ.ɲa] "nickname," or *cozinha* [ko.'zĩ.ɲa] "kitchen," since main stress can never skip a prefinal heavy syllable in BP.[5]

For many Brazilians, but not for EP speakers, there is no phonetic difference in the pronunciation of the palatal lateral [ʎ] and a sequence of an alveolar lateral plus a palatal glide [lj]: *família* [fa.'mi.ʎa] / [fa.'mi.lja] "family." In the lower-income sociolect of Brazil, the palatal lateral is usually realized as a palatal glide [j]: *palhaço* [pa.'ʎa.su] > [pa.'ja.su] "clown" (Cagliari, 1999: 70–72).

1.5. Fricatives

In EP, the coronal fricatives [s, z] palatalize in coda position to [ʃ, ʒ]: *deste* ['deʃ.tɨ] "of/from this", *desde* ['dez.di] "since". With the exception of the dialect of Rio de Janeiro (carioca) and in few other regions, BP dialects do not palatalize coda fricatives. In all varieties of BP and EP, word-final [s] fails to palatalize when it syllabifies as the onset of the initial syllable of a following word, in which case is it always realized as [z].

The distribution of the voiced or unvoiced variants is shown in Table 4.2.

Table 4.2 Variation of coronal fricatives.

Rio de Janeiro & EP	Examples		
[ʃ] / ___ [–voice]	*desta*	[ˈdɛʃ.ta]	"of this (fem.)"
___ ##	*mês*	[ˈmeʃ]	"month"
[ʒ] / ___ [+voice]	*vesgo*	[ˈveʒ.gu]	"squint-eyed"
[z] / ___ # V	*casas amarelas*	[ˈka.za.za.maˈɾɛ.laʃ]	"yellow houses"
[ʃ]; [ʒ] ___ # C	*os filhos*	[uʃ fi.ʎuʃ]	"the sons"
	os velhos	[uʒˈvɛ.ʎuʃ]	"the old ones"
Other BP varieties	Examples		
[s] / ___ [–voice]	*desta*	[ˈdɛs.ta]	"of this (fem.)"
___ ##	*mês*	[ˈmes]	"month"
[z] / ___ [+voice]	*vesgo*	[ˈvez.gu]	"squint-eyed"
[z] / ___ # V	*casas amarelas*	[ˈka.za.za.maˈɾɛˋ.las]	"yellow houses"
[s]; [z] ___ # C	*os filhos*	[us.fiˈʎus]	"the sons"
	os velhos	[uzˈvɛ.ʎus]	"the old ones"

1.6. Rhotics in BP

BP has two variants of the rhotic sound: "strong r" [h, x] and "weak r" [ɾ], which are contrastive only in intervocalic position and which are in complementary distribution elsewhere. The intervocalic contrast is reflected in the orthography by the use of single <r>, representing /ɾ/, as opposed to double <rr>, representing /h, x/: *caro* "dear" versus *carro* "car." Strong r occurs word-initially (*roda* "wheel") and syllable-initially after a non-vocoid segment (*Israel* "Israel"). In BP, weak r is typically pronounced as the tap [ɾ] between vocoid sounds and when a second member of a complex onset (*prato* "dish"). In EP, syllable-finally (*porta* "door", *estudar* "study"), the common pronunciation of the rhotic is [ɾ].

In BP, strong r can be phonetically realized by several allophones, including certain fricatives. In fact, the fricatives [h] and [x] are currently the most frequent realizations of strong r in the majority of BP dialects. In communities of German immigrant descendants, strong r can be realized also as the uvular trill [ʀ]. The alveolar trill [r] is common in the South of Brazil and in Italian immigrant communities.

roda [ˈhɔ.da] / [ˈxɔ.da] / [ˈrɔ.da] / [ˈʀɔ.da] "wheel"

Cagliari (2007: 44) summarizes the vast variation concerning the phonetic realization of rhotic consonants in BP. For instance, strong r can be pronounced in the beginning of words as [x, h, r]. When intervocalic, the rhotics [x] and [h] may be voiced [ɣ] and [ɦ]: *barriga* [ba.ˈxi. ga], [ba.ˈhi.ga]; [ba.ˈɣi.ga], [ba.ˈɦi.ga] "belly." When before [i], the variant [x] may assimilate the palatal quality, becoming a palatal fricative [ç] or [ʝ]: *Rita* [ˈçi,ta], [ˈʝi.ta] "Rita."

In BP, the range of phonetic realizations of the rhotic in the syllable coda is very large and different across dialects: typical strong r variants [h, x, r] are found, which are voiced or voiceless, depending on the voice specification of the following segment, but also the variants [ɾ, ɹ, ɻ] can be heard, which are usually associated with the weak r. In the Carioca dialect, the strong r variant [x] is favored in the syllable ending, whereas in the Paulista dialect the weak r realizations predominate in that position. Retroflexed realizations are found in the Caipira dialect of Brazil, mainly in the interior of the States of São Paulo and Paraná, which have more recently also spread to other regions of the country. There are two retroflex rhotic sounds: one anterior [ɹ], the other posterior [ɻ]. In the speech of the elderly speakers of the Standard Paulista dialect, a voiceless trill [r̥] or even a cluster composed of a tap plus a voiceless apical retroflex [ɻ̊] can be heard: *porta* [ˈpoɾɻ̊.ta] "door"; *mar* [ˈmaɾɻ̊] "sea." A voiceless trill [r̥] may be found in the more formal registers before pause among the speakers who use the trill typically in that environment. In Minas Gerais, the most frequent realization of the coda rhotic is the laryngeal fricative [h].

> *porta* [ˈpoɾ.ta] / [ˈpoɹ.ta] / [ˈpoɻ.ta] / [ˈpox.ta] / [ˈpoh.ta]   "door"
> *mar* [ˈmaɾ] / [ˈmaɹ] / [ˈmaɻ] / [ˈmax] / [ˈmah]   "sea"

There are a number of analytical problems involved in the proper phonological definition of the contrasting rhotics of BP, related to the fact that the sounds that contrast in the intervocalic context are in complementary distribution elsewhere: how exactly must the phonological contrast be defined and which phoneme of the contrastive pair represents the rhotics in the contexts in which they exclude each other?

Câmara (1970: 38) proposed that the existence of a contrast in intervocalic context (*caro* [ˈkaɾu] "dear" *vs. carro* [ˈkahu] "car") between the strong r [h / x] and the weak r [ɾ] should be interpreted as a difference between different types of vibrants (*vibrante forte* "strong vibrant" vs. *vibrante branda* "weak vibrant"). In an earlier interpretation of this contrast, Câmara (1953) considered the possibility of a single rhotic phoneme in BP, in which the intervocalic strong r was represented as a sequence of two taps [ɾɾ]. Evidence for the interpretation of strong r as a sequence of (identical) consonants [ɾɾ] is the fact that after nasal vowels, interpreted as phonological /VN/ sequences, as well as after coda consonants only strong r occurs (*genro* [ˈʒẽ.xu]/ [ˈʒẽ.hu]/ [ˈʒẽ.ɣu] "son in law") and the fact that after diphthongs only [ɾ] is possible (*ouro* [ˈow.ɾu] "gold"; *beira* [ˈbej.ɾa] "margin"; *Maira* [ˈmaj.ɾa] "Maira."). The main problem with this interpretation is how one must explain that some version of the strong r instead of the tap occurs word-initially (in the way it occurs in Italian), if its phonetic realization is identical with the phonological geminate in the middle of words? Another problem is that the phonetic realization of both the single and the geminate rhotic is that of a simple onset consonant. Similar questions can be raised with respect to Monaretto (1997), who follows Câmara Jr.'s (1953) interpretation. In turn, the analysis that considers the opposition to be between two types of vibrants (h / x vs. ɾ) cannot explain why /ɾ/ occurs only in the intervocalic context and in the second position of onset clusters (C_V). Most importantly, it cannot explain why /ɾ/ does not occur word-initially. Abaurre and Sândalo (2003) argue in favor of an underlying fricative sound which contrasts in intervocalic position with its geminate counterpart. The tap [ɾ] is a weakened realization of the single fricative between vocoids (*caro* [ˈkaɾu] "dear") and in the second position of a consonantal cluster (*prato* [ˈpɾatu] "plate"). Notice that this interpretation does not explain the cases of retroflex [ɹ]. At this moment, an agreement about the phonological definition of the rhotics has not been reached.

1.7. Rhotics in EP

Several of the BP rhotic realizations described above: [x], [h], etc. are exclusively found in BP and do not occur in EP.

Mateus and d'Andrade (2000) and others codify the distribution of rhotics in European Portuguese by positing the tap /ɾ/ as the underlying rhotic segment and deriving the EP trilled version by rule. The EP tap trills by rule in word-initial position and after a coronal continuant. Between vowels, where it is spelled <rr>, the trill derives from an underlying geminate /ɾɾ/.

Phonetically, the trill is still a coronal trill [r] in Portuguese Africa – the original historical pronunciation; in continental EP a few areas still have the coronal trill as well. However, in most dialects of continental EP, including Lisbon, the coronal trill became a uvular trill [ʀ], an allophone heard today primarily in citation forms. Since the uvular trill is challenging to produce, in EP the [ʀ] trill typically doesn't trill and thus becomes the rhotic fricative [ʁ].

2. Vowels

2.1. *Stressed vowels*

Portuguese has a system of seven underlying vowels: /i, e, ɛ, a, ɔ, o, u/. See Table 4.3.[6]

Examples:
[i]	*vi*	['vi]	"I saw"
[e]	*vê*	['ve]	"you see"
[ɛ]	*fé*	['fɛ]	"faith"
[a]	*vá*	['va]	"go"
[ɔ]	*avó*	[a.'vɔ]	"grandmother"
[o]	*avô*	[a.'vo]	"grandfather"
[u]	*tu*	['tu]	"you"

The tense/lax contrast [e, ɛ] and [o, ɔ] performs important functions in Portuguese. It salients third singulars from first singulars in the second conjugation:

devo	['de.vu]	"I should"
deve	['dɛ.vi]	"he should"

and it is a major result of Portuguese vowel harmony. When a verb's theme vowel is deleted in first person singular present tense forms, often the only clue as to conjugation membership is the harmonized stressed vowel:

moro	['mɔ.ɾu]	First Conjugation – "I reside"
movo	['mo.vu]	Second Conjugation – "I move"

Tense/lax mid-vowels also help distinguish words that belong to different lexical classes, particularly verbs and nouns, such as:

bolo (N)	['bo.lu]	"cake"
bolo (V)	['bɔ.lu]	"I prepare"
meta (N)	['mɛ.ta]	"goal"
meta (V)	['me.ta]	"put in (Imperative)"

Table 4.3   Vowel phonemes.

	i	*e*	*ɛ*	*a*	*u*	*o*	*ɔ*
High	+	−	−	−	+	−	−
Tense	+	+	−	−	+	+	−
Back	−	−	−	−	+	+	+
Round	−	−	−	−	+	+	+
Low	−	−	−	+	−	−	−

As was shown by instrumental studies in Redenbarger (2005), even those EP dialects which have begun to neutralize some tense / lax contrasts carefully maintain the tense / lax distinctions produced by vowel harmony in verbs.

Wetzels (1997; 2011) reveals that the distribution of stressed upper and lower mid-vowels in BP is to a large extent predictable, on the basis of phonological, prosodic, or morphological conditionings.

In BP, the phoneme /a/ is commonly realized as a back low vowel [ɑ] when followed by the back glide /w/ in diphthongs: *calma* [ˈkɑw.ma] "calm"; *saudade* [sɑw'da.dʒi] "nostalgia" (Cagliari, 1999: 106; 2007: 69–71). In unstressed EP syllables the usual realization of [a] is [ɐ]: *saudade* [sɐw.'da.di] "nostalgia," but before velar [ɫ] EP also has [ɑ] *caldo* [ˈkɑɫ.du] "crock."

One of the salient features of the EP vowel system as compared to BP is the occurrence of [ɐ] and [ɨ] from underlying [a] and [i] in unstressed syllables,

EP: *casa* /ˈka.za/ [ˈka.zɐ] "house"
     deve /ˈdɛ.ve/ [ˈdɛ́.vi] "he should"

BP: *casa* /ˈka.za/ [ˈka.za] "house"
     deve /ˈdɛ.vi/ [ˈdɛ́.vi] "he should"

The articulatory basis of the EP vowels was studied in Redenbarger (1982). He posits that tensing, i.e. genio-glossus contraction, is common to both [ɐ] and [ɨ], allowing for a unification of the unstressed tensing of [a] → [ɐ] with the [i] → [ɨ] process. One advantage of that analysis is that it explains why BP which does not tense unstressed [a] also does not have unstressed [ɨ]. This high [ɨ] vowel is worthy of much further instrumental and myoelectric investigation.

Another striking feature of EP when compared with BP is the greater occurrence of voiceless vowels. In BP, voiceless vowels are only found in word-final position before pause, and not always then. In EP they are regularly found in that and other contexts. EP voiceless vowels may also be deleted when they occur in unstressed syllables. Vowel loss often occurs when there is a liquid consonant in the syllable which can become syllabic. This vowel deletion has substantial impact on the intercomprehensibility between speakers of BP and of EP.

EP: *verdade* [veɾ.'da.dɨ] / [veɾ.'da.dɨ̥] / [vɾ̩'da.dɨ̥] "truth"
     pote [ˈpɔ.tɨ] / [ˈpɔ.tɨ̥] / [ˈpɔt] "pot"
     Portugal [poɾ.tu.'gɑɫ], puɾ.tu.'gɑɫ], [pu̥ɾ.tu.'gɑɫ] "Portugal"

BP: *verdade* [veɾ.'da.dʒi], [veɾ.'da.dʒi̥], "truth"
     pote [ˈpɔ.tʃi], [ˈpɔ.tʃi̥], "pot"

In the Lisbon variety of EP, the pronunciation of [ɐj] instead of [ej] is characterisic, as in *primeiro* [pɾi'mej.ɾu] / [pɾi'mɐj.ɾu] "first." In colloquial Lisbon speech, this pronunciation typically extends to all prepalatal contexts: *espelho*: [iʃ 'pe.ʎu] / [iʃ 'pɐ.ʎu] "mirror"; *tenho* [ˈte.ɲu] / [ˈtɐ.ɲu] "I have." This innovation is one of the most salient features distinguishing the Lisbon dialect from the other EP prestige dialects, such as the one spoken in Coimbra, where this Lisbon innovation was not adopted.

In dialects of the Azores archipelago front rounded vowels appear, e.g. [ø] associated with the spelling <ou> is found in verbs forms like *falou* [fɐˈlow] / [fɐˈlø] "he said."

2.2. *Nasal vowels, nasalized vowels*

Portuguese has five (surface) distinctive nasal vowels: [ĩ, ẽ, ɐ̃, õ, ũ].

> Examples:
> | | | |
> |---|---|---|
> | *sinto* | [ˈsĩ.tu] | "I feel" |
> | *tempo* | [ˈtẽ.pu] | "time" |
> | *amplo* | [ˈɐ̃.plu] | "ample" |
> | *pombo* | [ˈpõ.bu] | "dove" |
> | *cumpro* | [ˈkũ.pɾu] | "I fulfill" |

Portuguese vowels tense before a nasal consonant[7]:

> | | | | | | | |
> |---|---|---|---|---|---|---|
> | *move* | [ˈmɔ.vi] | "he moves" | vs. | *come* | [ˈko.mi] | "he eats" |
> | *cara* | [ˈka.ɾa] | "face" | vs. | *cama* | [ˈkɐ.ma] | "bed" |

In addition to tensing, they nasalize when the following nasal closes their syllable.

> | | | | | | | |
> |---|---|---|---|---|---|---|
> | *come* | [ˈko.mi] | "he eats" | vs. | *compre* | [ˈkõ.pɾi] | "he buys" |
> | *teme* | [ˈte.mi] | "he fears" | vs. | *tempo* | [ˈtẽ.pu] | "time" |

This generates the singularly Portuguese phonetic distribution [a], [ɐ], and [ɐ̃], where [a] is lax but [ɐ] and [ɐ̃] are tense:

> | | | |
> |---|---|---|
> | *cara* | [ˈka.ɾa] | "face" |
> | *cama* | [ˈkɐ.ma] | "bed" |
> | *canta* | [ˈkɐ̃.ta] | "he sings" |

In BP, in addition to this phonological tensing and nasalization, there is (almost) obligatory phonetic nasalization of a stressed vowel preceding a nasal onset consonant:

Nasal vowels (nasal in coda):

> | | | | | | | |
> |---|---|---|---|---|---|---|
> | *junta* | [ˈʒũ.ta] | "he gathers" | vs. | *juta* | [ˈʒu.ta] | "jute" |
> | *cinto* | [ˈsĩ.tu] | "belt" | vs. | *sito* | [ˈsi.tu] | "placed" |
> | *lenda* | [ˈlẽ.da] | "legend" | vs. | *Leda* | [ˈle.da] | "Leda" |

Nasalized vowels (nasal in onset):

> | | | |
> |---|---|---|
> | *ano* | [ˈɐ̃.nu] / [ˈɐ.nu] | "year" |
> | *cima* | [ˈsĩ.ma] / [ˈsi.ma] | "top" |

Since [ɐ] is always the realization of /a/ in a nasal environment, it cannot be considered a different phoneme, at least in BP. In EP, there is a limited contrast between [a] and [ɐ] in verb forms like *cantamos* [kɐ̃ˈta.mus] "we sang" (past perfect) vs. *cantamos* [kɐ̃ˈtɐ̃.mus] "we sing" (present). In BP, the pronunciation [kɐ̃ˈtɐ̃.mus] is used for both the present and the past perfect, as regularly follows from the productive rules of nasalization in this variant.

2.3. *Unstressed vowels*

In standard Paulista BP, the pretonic vowels are: /i, e, a, o, u/.

Although there is no contrast between mid-vowels in unstressed position, unstressed lower mid-vowels [ɛ, ɔ] do occur at the phonetic level in BP. This variation is geographical; in the north and northeast of Brazil, in pretonic position the variation comprises [ɛ, e, i]: *Recife* [heˈsi.fi] / [hiˈsi.fi] / [hɛˈsi.fi] "Recife" (city). The same happens to back vowels [ɔ, o, u]: *boneca* [boˈnɛ.ka] / [buˈnɛ.ka] / [bɔˈnɛ.ka] "doll." This phenomenon extends to Minas Gerais and Espírito Santo, in the southeast.[8] Southern dialects tend to use closed vowels [e/i], [o/u]. Sociolinguistic studies on the realization of pretonic vowels in BP show that this variation is quite widespread. Indeed, there are words in which three different vowels can occur in pretonic position within the same speech community: lower mid- [ɛ, ɔ], upper mid- [e, o] or high [i, u] vowels.[9]

Unlike BP, in normal speed EP the unstressed vowels which occur in pretonic position are [ɐ, ɨ, u]: *café* [kɐˈfɛ] "coffee"; *poder* [puˈdeɾ] "power"; *dever* [dɨˈveɾ] "duty."

In both BP and EP, in word-final unstressed positions, the vowel system is reduced to three vowels.

Word-finally in BP, the back rounded vowel /u/ is phonetically realized as a vowel with a somewhat lower and slightly more centralized quality [ʊ]: *porto* /ˈpoɾ.tu/ [ˈpoɾ.tʊ] "port." In the same context, the high front vowel is realized as [ɪ] (See Note 3).

[ʊ]	*tudo*	[ˈtu.dʊ]	"all"
[ɪ]	*risque*	[ˈxis.kɪ]	"scratch out"

In unstressed word-final syllables of EP, we find the three unstressed vowels [ɐ, ɨ, u] plus the unstressed [i] in a few words: *casa* [ˈka.zɐ] "house"; *pote* [ˈpɔ.tɨ] "pot"; *rito* [ˈʀi.tu] "ritual"; *júri* [ˈʒu.ɾi] "jury" (Emiliano, 2009).

In summary, one of the most salient differences between BP and EP is the occurrence in EP of the unstressed tense vowel [ɐ], where BP uses the lax vowel [a]. The vowel [ɐ] is observed in BP only in rapid speech: *casa* [ˈka.za] / [ˈka.zɐ] "house" and is even then not the tense [ɐ] of EP.

2.4. *Glides*

Both BP and EP present falling and rising phonetic diphthongs. Falling diphthongs are:

		BP	EP	
/aj/	*vai*	[ˈvaj]	[ˈvaj]	"goes"
/ej/	*reitor*	[hejˈtoɾ]	[ʀejˈtoɾ]	"University Principal"
/ɔj/	*mói*	[ˈmɔj]	[ˈmɔj]	"grinds"
/oj/	*boi*	[ˈboj]	[ˈboj]	"ox"
/uj/	*fui*	[ˈfuj]	[ˈfuj]	"I went"
/aw/	*pau*	[ˈpɑw]	[ˈpɑw]	"stick"
	saudade	[sɑw.ˈda.dʒi]	[sɑw.ˈda.dɨ]	"nostalgia"
/ew/	*seu*	[ˈsew]	[ˈsew]	"your"
/ɛw/	*véu*	[ˈvɛw]	[ˈvɛw]	"veil"
/ow/	*vou*	[ˈvow]	[ˈvow]	"I go"
/iw/	*viu*	[ˈviw]	[ˈviw]	"you saw"

Scholars distinguish traditionally for both BP and EP between true and false diphthongs (Bisol, 1989; Mateus and d'Andrade, 2000).

True diphthongs are irreducible falling diphthongs, i.e., formed by a vowel plus a glide: *pai* ['paj] "father"; *pau* ['pɑw] "stick," *reitor* [hej.'toɾ] (BP) / [ɾɐj.'toɾ] (EP) "University Principal." In BP, the diphthongs [ɔw] and [ɛw] appear as the result of the l-vocalization in the syllable coda.

sol	/ˈsɔl/	[ˈsɔw]	"sun"
mel	/ˈmɛl/	[ˈmɛw]	"honey"

[ɛj] also appears in the plural ending of words of which the singular ends in /el/:

pincel	[pĩ.ˈsɛw]	"brush"
pincéis	[pĩ.ˈsɛjs]	"brushes" (plural)

False diphthongs are reducible diphthongs, which can be phonetically realized as monophthongs or diphthongs, depending on the phonetic context. In BP, the presence of [ʃ] or [ɾ] in the onset of a following syllable creates a context that favors the alternation between diphthongs and monophthongs.

peixe	[ˈpej.ʃi] / [ˈpe.ʃi]	"fish"
caixa	[ˈkaj.ʃa] / [ˈka.ʃa]	"box"
ouro	[ˈow.ɾu] / [ˈo.ɾu]	"gold"

In EP, the diphthongs /ej/ and /aj/ become [ɐj] and the diphthong /ow/ may vary with the sound [oj]: *peixe* [ˈpɐj.ʃi] "fish"; *caixa* [ˈkɐj.ʃa] "box"; *ouro* [ˈow.ɾu] / [ˈoj.ɾu] "gold."

Both in BP and EP, rising diphthongs are more appropriately interpreted as a sequence of vowels (hiatus), which are variably realized as rising diphthongs (Bisol, 1994; Mateus and d'Andrade, 2000): *quiabo* [ki'a.bu] / [ˈkja.bu] "okra"; [su'aɾ] / [ˈswaɾ] *suar* "to sweat."

There are also rising diphthongs which never alternate with vowel sequences. Those diphthongs are typically found after a velar stop, such as in *líquido* [ˈli.kwi.du] / *[ˈli.ku.i.du] "liquid," *água* [ˈa.gwa] / *[ˈa.gu.a] "water," *qualidade* [kwa.li.ˈda.ʤi] / *[ku.a.li.ˈda.ʤi] "quality," *aguentar* [a.gwẽn.ˈtaɾ] / *[a.gu.ẽn.ˈtaɾ] "to put up with." In a few rare cases, in BP, the phonetic diphthong may alternate with a single consonant: *líquido* [ˈli.kwi.du]/ [ˈli.ki.du] "liquid," *quota* [ˈkwɔ.ta]/ [ˈkɔ.ta] "share."

The formation of possible triphthongs occurs only as the realization of sequences of / kw, gw/ followed by a falling diphthong (which could be derived from an underlying sequence of vowel plus alveolar lateral):

qual	[ˈkwɑw]	"which – sing."
quais	[ˈkwajs]	"which – pl."

2.5. *Nasal diphthongs*

Nasal diphthongs may be the phonetic realization of an underlying VN sequence in the syllable rhyme in BP, both word-internally and word-finally. In EP, nasal diphthongs may not be followed by the nasal consonant.

	BP	EP	
pente	['pẽn.ʧi] / ['pẽjn.ʧi] / ['pẽj.ʧi]	['pẽ.ti]	"comb"
penca	['pẽŋ.ka] / ['pẽjŋ.ka] / ['pẽj.ka]	['pẽ.kɐ]	"bunch"
conto	['kõn.tu] / ['kõw̃n.tu] / ['kõw̃.tu]	['kõ.tu]	"short story"
bomba	['bõm.ba] / ['bõw̃m.ba] / ['bõw̃.ba]	['bõ.bɐ]	"bomb"

In word-medial position, a stressed vowel is commonly pronounced as a nasal diphthong before a palatal nasal consonant in the following onset. In EP, instead of [e]/[ej] we find [ɐ] and [ɐj], before a palatal, which are usually not nasalized. In some varieties of BP, the palatal nasal may drop: *banha* ['bɐ̃j.a] "lard." In this case, the nasal glide is ambisyllabic, occupying at the same time the coda of the previous syllable and the onset of the following: *banha* ['bɐ̃j.ja] "lard."

	BP	EP	
banha	['bɐ̃.ɲa] / ['bɐ̃j.ɲa]	['bɐ.ɲɐ]	"lard"
venha	['vẽ.ɲa] / ['vẽj.ɲa]	['vɐ.ɲɐ]	"come"
fronha	['frõ.ɲa] / ['frõj.ɲa]	['fro.ɲɐ]	"pillow case"
unha	['ũ.ɲa] / ['ũj.ɲa]	['u.ɲɐ]	"nail"
linha	['lĩ.ɲa] / ['lĩj.ɲa]	['li.ɲɐ]	"line"

There are also nasal diphthongs which occur in derived inflected forms for both BP and EP:

	Singular		Plural	
cão	[kɐ̃w̃]	*cães*	[kɐ̃js]	"dog"
limão	[li.'mɐ̃w̃]	*limões*	[li.'mõjs]	"lemon"
cidadão	[si.da.'dɐ̃w̃]	*cidadãos*	[si.da.'dɐ̃w̃s]	"citizen"
mão	[mɐ̃w̃]	*mãos*	[mɐ̃w̃s]	"hand"

In several dialects in BP, but typically in São Paulo state, a few words have an underlying falling diphthong with an anterior glide that may be nasalized or not when followed by a nasal in the following syllable.

teima	['tej.ma] / ['tẽj.ma]	"stubbornness"
reino	['hej.nu] / ['hẽj.nu]	"kingdom"
Roraima	[ho.'raj.ma] / [ho.'rẽj.ma]	"Roraima" (a state of Brazil)

Falling diphthong with a posterior glide followed by a nasal consonant in the onset of the subsequent syllable are usually not nasalized: *trauma* ['traw.ma] "trauma"; *fauna* ['faw.na] "fauna."

The word *cãibra* "cramp" has a very rare phonological structure with an underlying nasal diphthong which cannot be reduced to a monophthong or vary with an oral diphthong—BP: ['kɐ̃j.bra]; EP: ['kɐ̃j.brɐ].

In word-final position, nasal diphthongs vary with a sequence of a nasal vowel plus a nasal consonant, most typically in BP.

vem	['vẽj] / ['vẽn]	"he comes"
fim	['fĩj] / ['fĩɲ]	"end"
bom	['bõw̃] / ['bõŋ]	"good"

NOTES

1 See also Chapters 2, 30, and 31.
2 There is some disagreement among phoneticians and phonologists working on BP about how unstressed word-final high vowels should be represented, frequently used transcriptions being [ɪ, ʊ] and [i, u]. From a phonetic point of view, word-final unstressed high vowels are underachieved vowels which are slightly centralized and slightly lowered which would suggest a transcription using the IPA symbols [ɪ, ʊ]. For reasons of homogeneity, we have adopted here the transcription [i, u] for all unstressed high vowels in BP.
3 There is a controversy about whether in words like *advogado* the high front vowel is epenthetic or lexical (phonologically /e/, following Cagliari, 2002, 2007; Massini-Cagliari, 2005. See also Cagliari, 1997: 75–78; Collischonn, 2002).
4 Examples adapted from Wetzels (2000).
5 See Chapter 7.
6 Different feature systems have been proposed by different phonologists studying Portuguese vowels. For reasons of expository coherence we use here the system based on Redenbarger (1982), who uses the feature [tense] to distinguish two series of mid vowels. For the use of ATR, see Wetzels (1997); for arguments in favour of a 4-height system for BP see Wetzels (2011). Different proposals opposing the features ATR, tense, open, etc. to define the BP vocalic system have been discussed by Wetzels (1997: 299–301). Cagliari (2007) uses a more phonetic approach to the problem.
7 There is variation before nasal consonants between upper and lower mid-vowels in a few words, such as *fome* ['fɔ.mi]/ ['fɔ̃.mi] / ['fo.mi]/ ['fõ.mi] "hunger" and *treme* ['trɛ.mi] / ['trɛ̃.mi]/ ['tre.mi]/ ['trẽ.mi] "he trembles" (Cagliari, 2007, p. 86).
8 Carmo (2013) compared a number of studies for the quality of pretonic vowels in BP showing that variation among the upper and lower mid qualities is widespread. Lee and Oliveira (2003) show that there is unpredictable variation in the production of a single person relating to different words, which suggests a lexical conditioning.
9 See Chapters 5 and 30.

REFERENCES

Abaurre, M. B. M. and M. F. S. Sandalo (2003). Os róticos revisitados. In D. Hora and G. Collischonn (eds.), *Teoria Lingüística: Fonologia e outros temas*. João Pessoa-PB: Editora Universitária, pp. 144–180.

Bisol, L. (1989). O ditongo na perspectiva da fonologia atual. *D.E.L.T.A.*, 5 (2), pp. 185–224.

Bisol, L. (1994). Ditongos derivados. *D.E.L.T.A.*, 10, pp. 121–140.

Cagliari, L. C. (1977). *An experimental study of nasality with particular reference to Brazilian Portuguese*. Ph.D. thesis, University of Edinburgh.

Cagliari, L. C. (1997). *Fonologia do português: análise pela geometria de traços*. Campinas: Edição do Autor.

Cagliari, L. C. (1999). *Fonologia do português: análise pela geometria de traços e pela fonologia lexical*. Campinas: Edição do Autor.

Cagliari, L. C. (2002). *Análise fonológica: introdução à teoria e à prática, com especial destaque para o modelo fonêmico*. Campinas: Mercado de Letras.

Cagliari, L. C. (2007). *Elementos de fonética do português brasileiro*. São Paulo: Ed. Paulistana.

Câmara Jr., J. M. (1953). *Para o estudo da fonêmica portuguesa*. Rio de Janeiro: Organizações Simões.

Câmara Jr., J. M. (1970). *Estrutura da língua portuguesa*. Petrópolis: Editora Vozes.

Carmo, M. C. (2013). *As vogais médias pretônicas na variedade do interior paulista*. São José do Rio Preto: UNESP. Ph.D. thesis.

Collischonn, G. (2002) A epêntese vocálica no português do Sul do Brasil. In L. Bisol and C. Brescancini (eds.), *Fonologia e Variação: recortes do Português Brasileiro*. Porto Alegre: EDIPURS, pp. 205–230.

Emiliano, A. (2009) *Fonética do Português Europeu: Descrição e Transcrição*. Lisbon: Guimarães.

Lee, S.-H. and M. A. Oliveira (2003). Variação inter- e intra-dialetal no Português Brasileiro: um problema para a teoria fonológica. In D. Hora and G. Collischonn (eds.), *Teoria linguística: fonologia e outros temas*. João Pessoa: Editora Universitária. pp. 67–91.

Massini-Cagliari, G. (2005). *A música da fala dos trovadores: Estudos de prosódia do Português Arcaico, a partir das cantigas profanas e religiosas.* Thesis (Livre-Docência em Fonologia), Universidade Estadual Paulista.

Mateus, M. H. M., A. A. Andrade, M. C. Viana, and A. Villalva (1990). *Fonética, Fonologia e Morfologia do Português*. Lisbon: Universidade Aberta.

Mateus, M. H. and E. d'Andrade (2000). *The Phonology of Portuguese*. Oxford: Oxford University Press.

Monaretto, V. N. O. (1997). *Um reestudo da vibrante: análise variacionista e fonológica.* Ph.D. thesis, Porto Alegre PUC-RS.

Redenbarger, W. J. (1982). *Articulator Features and Portuguese Vowel Height*. Cambridge, MA: Harvard University Press.

Redenbarger, W. J. (2005). Pre nasal laxing in European Portuguese. In D. Eddington (ed.), *Selected Proceedings of the Seventh Hispanic Linguistics Symposium*. Somerville: Cascadilla.

Tasca, M. (2002). Variação e mudança do segmento lateral na coda silábica. In L. Bisol and C. Brescancini (eds.), *Fonologia e Variação: recortes do Português Brasileiro*. Porto Alegre: EDIPURS, pp. 303–312.

Wetzels, W. L. (1997). The lexical representation of nasality in Brazilian Portuguese, *Probus*, 9 (2), pp. 203–232.

Wetzels, W. L. (2000). Consoantes palatais como geminadas fonológicas no português brasileiro. *Revista de Estudos da Linguagem*, 9 (2), pp. 5–15.

Wetzels, W. L. (2011) Aperture features and the representation of vowel neutralization in Brazilian Portuguese. In E. Hume, J. Goldsmith, and W. L. Wetzels (eds.), *Tones and Features*. Berlin: de Gruyter, pp. 331–359.

5 Phonological Processes Affecting Vowels: Neutralization, Harmony, and Nasalization

LEDA BISOL AND JOÃO VELOSO

1. Introduction

In this chapter, we discuss the processes of Vowel Neutralization (VNeu), Mid-Vowel Harmony (MVH), and Vowel Nasalization (VNas). Of these processes, VNeu and VNas are active in the vowel systems of both European (EP) and Brazilian (BP) Portuguese, whereas MVH is only found in BP. We will propose a rule-based analysis of these processes, modeled in the framework of Feature Geometry.

VNeu in Portuguese may affect both unstressed and stressed mid-vowels. Although our focus will be on Unstressed Vowel Neutralization (UVNeu), Stressed Mid-Vowel neutralization will be briefly discussed also. We will analyze unstressed as well as stressed VNeu in both varieties as a mechanism of feature deletion followed by respecification with the unmarked features. Particularly with regard to UVNeu we show that in BP contrastive aperture features are progressively deleted, whereas in EP the set of neutralizable segments are merged in a single operation.

MVH is a variable rule of all regional variants of BP. It applies in the part of the word that precedes the main stress and only affects mid-vowels. In contemporary EP, this process is inoperative.

EP and BP possess a set of contrastive nasal vowels and nasal diphthongs. The ongoing debate among phonologists is whether the oral vs. nasal contrast in vowels and diphthongs is phonological or phonetic. We will follow here the mainstream analysis for BP and EP nasal vowels, which derives these sounds from an underlying /VN/ sequence. For the nasal diphthongs, we will propose a representation in which the nasal feature is associated with the syllable rhyme.

2. Unstressed vowel neutralization

UVNeu is a process that reduces the set of contrastive vowel features under specific prosodic conditions. In BP, UVNeu applies gradiently in the sense that it progressively reduces the

The Handbook of Portuguese Linguistics, First Edition. Edited by W. Leo Wetzels, João Costa, and Sergio Menuzzi.
© 2016 John Wiley & Sons, Inc. Published 2020 by John Wiley & Sons, Inc.

number of height distinctions in the vowel system. In EP, UVNeu results from two different operations, one is neutralization, the other centralization. In this study, we will conceive of neutralization as a process by which contrastive features are removed from the representation of vowel segments in specific prosodic positions.

According to the typology of neutralization processes proposed by Trubetzkoy (1967: 77, 82–87), UVNeu in EP and BP belong to different types. Trubetzkoy distinguishes four types of neutralization, of which the first and third types are relevant for the variants of Portuguese under discussion here.

For the *first* neutralization type, the representative of the neutralizable opposition that appears in the neutralization context does not coincide with either term of the opposition. Instead, it corresponds to:

Trubetzkoy Type 1

(a) an intermediary sound, phonetically related to both terms of the opposition; or
(b) a sound which, in addition to the features shared by both segments, has specific features of its own.

The third neutralization type is *internally conditioned*, that is to say, the choice of one of the terms of the opposition as the outcome of the neutralization process only relates to the segments of the neutralized set, without being dependent on contiguous segments. This neutralization type can involve two kinds of phonological oppositions—privative and gradient.

Trubetzkoy Type 3

(a) In privative oppositions involving a marked and an unmarked term, the marked feature[+F] is neutralized in favour of unmarked [–F];
(b) in gradient oppositions, as in the aperture contrasts between vowels, the extreme term of the opposition appears in the neutralization context.

From the perspective of Trubetzkoys typology of neutralization processes, UVNeu in EP is somewhat ambiguous. The neutralized front vowels /i, e, ɛ/ are represented by a central vowel, the precise phonetic definition of which is a matter of debate among phoneticians (see below). At least superficially, this part of the process could be interpreted as a (1b) type of neutralization. On the other hand, the neutralization of the set of labial vowels /u, o, ɔ/, which is phonetically represented by /u/, belongs to Trubetzkoy's type (3b). As for BP, we will argue that UVNeu involves two steps in a process of progressive neutralization that affects a binary opposition between a marked and an unmarked feature in different contexts, i.e. type (3a) in Trubetzkoy's typology. Furthermore, although the neutralization of front vowels in EP yields a central vowel that is not included in the set of neutralizable vowels, we will argue that UVNeu in EP is best interpreted as the neutralization of the gradient opposition between lower-mid, upper-mid, and high vowels, representing an instance of case (3b) in Trubetzkoy's typology.

2.1. *Unstressed vowel neutralization in Brazilian Portuguese*

Neutralization of BP unstressed vowels has been explained by different authors[1] pertaining to different theoretical backgrounds by way of three rules, each one applying in a different environment: pretonic neutralization (cf. (1a) below), non-final post-tonic neutralization (cf. (1b)), and word-final neutralization (cf. (1c)).

(1) a. Pretonic
      'b[ɛ]lo ~ b[e]'leza   "handsome" ~ "beauty"
      'k[ɔ]lo ~ k[o]'lar   "I glue" ~ "to glue"
   b. Non-final post-tonic:
      'fosf[o]ro ~ 'fosf[u]ro   "match"
   c. Word-final:
      'verd[e] ~ 'verd[i]   "green"
      'kol[o] ~ 'kol[u]   "I glue"

Just as in pretonic syllables, lower mid-vowels do not occur in post-tonic syllables. According to Câmara Jr. (1970), in prefinal post-tonic syllables there is a tendency for dorsal upper-mid vowels to be realized as high vowels (cf. (1b)). In this chapter, we will not be concerned with this phenomenon, since evidence has been advanced suggesting that, in the southern varieties of BP, this process is better described as variable mid-vowel raising, which also involves /e/ (Vieira, 1994).

Consider the words below, which show the productivity of mid-vowel neutralization in pretonic syllables (2a) as well as the neutralization of the contrast between the three series of non-low vowels word-finally (2c).

(2) a. Neutralization of the contrast between upper- and lower-mid vowels in pretonic syllables
      'b[ɛ]la ~ b[e]'leza   "beautiful (fem)" ~ "beauty"
      'm[ɔ]le ~ m[o]'leza   "soft" ~ "softness"
      'm[ɛ]scla ~ m[e]s'clado   "mixture" ~ "mixed"
      'm[ɔ]rte ~ m[o]r'tal   "death" ~ "deadly"
      m[ɛ]l ~ m[e]'lado   "honey" ~ "molasses"
      s[ɔ]l ~ s[o]'laço   "sun" ~ "great good sun"
   b. Exceptions
      'b[ɔ]la ~ b[ɔ]'linha   "ball" ~ "little ball"   *b[o]linha
      'f[ɔ]rte ~ f[ɔ]r'tissimo   "strong" ~ "very strong"   *f[or]rtíssimo
      m[ɛ]l ~ m[ɛ]l'zinho   "honey" ~ "delicious honey"   *m[e]lzinho
      'f[ɔ]rte ~ f[ɔ]rte'mente   "strong" ~ "strongly"   *f[o]rtement[e]
   c. Neutralization of non-low vowels word-finally in unstressed open syllables and in syllables closed by /s/.
      com[e]mos ~ com[i]   "eat-1pl. pr. ind." ~ "eat-3si. pr. ind."
      abat[e]dor ~ bat[i]   "butcher" ~ "beat-3si. pr. ind."
      lev[e]zinho ~ lev[i]   "very light" ~ "light"
      camp[o]nês ~ camp[u]   "countryman" ~ "field"
      mat[o]rral ~ mat[u]   "dense bush" ~ "bush"
      pov[o]ar ~ pov[u]   "populate" ~ "people"
      Londr[e]s ~ Londr[i]s   "London"

Because of neutralization, BP realizes three different vowel systems in different prosodic contexts through a progressive reduction of the aperture distinctions: /a, ɛ, e, i, u, o, ɔ/—/a, e, i, u, o/—/ a, i, u/. As a consequence of the neutralization of the mid-vowel contrast, the set of seven vowels that occurs in stressed syllables is reduced to a five-vowel system with a single mid-vowel series in unstressed syllables. The further neutralization of the remaining mid-vowel series and the corresponding high vowels creates the basic three-vowel system found in word-final unstressed open syllables.

With regard to pretonic UVNeu, a set of systematic exceptions is found, involving the suffixes, -*(z)inho*, -*mente*, and –*íssimo*, exemplified in (2)b. To explain the exceptional behavior of these words, two different hypotheses have been considered:

(a) The suffixes -*mente* (adverbial), -*(z)inho* (evaluative), and -*íssimo* (superlative) are prosodic words, so words like *s[ɔ]lzinho* "agreeable sun" e *f[ɔ]rtemente* "stongly" must be interpreted as compounds. This analysis is defended in Leite (1974), Menuzzi (1993), and Schwindt (2013).
(b) The mentioned suffixes are a special set of suffixes, being attached at a level in the grammar in which pretonic neutralization no longer applies. This proposal is worked out in different ways by different scholars in various versions of lexical phonology. See, for example, Villalva (2000), Mateus and d'Andrade (2000), Bisol (2010). Here we just want to have mentioned this class of systematic exceptions, without taking position with regard to the explanation of their deviant behavior.

The progressive loss of mid-vowels is caused by the neutralization of aperture distinctions in weak prosodic positions. In Table 5.1, we distinguish the four aperture degrees relevant for Portuguese stressed vowels by the multiple use of a binary [± open] feature, following Clements (1991).

The first [open] feature divides the aperture space in [+open] and [−open]. The [−open$_1$] space is divided into [−open$_2$] and [+open$_2$] giving way to a series of mid-vowels, in addition to the low and high vowels. Finally, the [+open$_2$] space is further divided into [−open$_3$] and [+open$_3$], creating a contrast between two series of mid-vowels, one upper-mid, the other lower-mid.

Adopting Wetzels' (1992, 2011) modelling of obligatory unstressed vowel neutralization in BP, we propose the rule in (3).

(3) a. Neutralization of the lower- and upper-mid vowel series in BP:
      Delete [+open$_3$] in unstressed syllables
      Domain: Phonological Word

      Root [+vocoid]

      |

      Aperture

      ǂ

      [+open$_3$] ($\longrightarrow$ [−open$_3$])

As a first step in the neutralization process of upper- and lower-mid vowels, the marked (positive) [+open$_3$] feature is dissociated from the aperture node in unstressed nuclei, where it is automatically substituted by the negative (unmarked) [-open3] feature. The process applies to all unstressed syllables, pretonic as well as post-tonic, as a consequence of which the lower-mid vowels /ɛ, ɔ/ only occur under main stress.

Table 5.1   Aperture distinctions in Portuguese stressed syllables.

	i/u	e/o	ɛ/ɔ	a
open$_1$	−	−	−	+
open$_2$	−	+	+	+
open$_3$	−	−	+	+

(3) b. Neutralization of the mid-vowel and high-vowel series in unstressed word-final syllables which are open or closed by /s/ in BP:

Delete [+open$_2$]/__(s)##

Root [+vocoid]

Aperture

[+open$_2$] ($\longrightarrow$ [–open$_2$])

The rule in (3b) deletes the marked [+open$_2$] feature form unstressed word-final syllables that are either open or closed by /s/. This rule is obligatory and categorical in most varieties of BP. Nevertheless, due to bilingualism or in areas along the Brazilian border with Spanish-speaking countries, word-final neutralization can be variable or optional: *bol*[o] ~ *bol*[u] "cake," *val*[e] ~ *val*[i] "valley."

UVNeu in BP is a prosodically conditioned rule targeting a gradient opposition of aperture degrees which are successively eliminated to create three different vowel subsystems: the most elaborate seven-vowel system appears in the strongest prosodic position, i.e. under main stress; a five vowel system occurs in the prosodically weaker unstressed syllables; the smallest three-vowel system functions in the weakest prosodic position, which is the unstressed word-final open syllable.

The figure (4) below shows the progressive neutralization of the contrastive aperture features through the successive substitution of the marked values of the [± open] feature by the unmarked negative values on the [open$_3$] and [open$_2$] tiers:

(4)

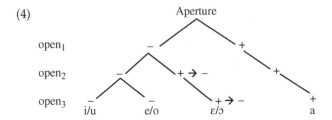

2.2. *Unstressed vowel neutralization in European Portuguese*

In EP, UVNeu acts differently upon coronal and labial vowels. While labial vowels merge into /u/, the coronal vowels are represented by a central vowel, different from any vowel that belongs to the neutralized set. Gonçalves Viana (1973 [1892]), Mateus (1982), Mateus and Delgado-Martins (1982) and Delgado-Martins (1996), among others, transcribe the central vowel as [ə], whereas in more recent studies it is transcribed as [ɨ] (Mateus and d'Andrade 2000; Vigário 2001; Veloso 2010).

UVNeu in EP applies to derived and underived words alike. It affects all unstressed vowels, regardless of their position in the word, except word-initially, where [ɨ] is not allowed. The following alternations show the productivity of the raising/centralization process. Examples were taken from Mateus and d'Andrade (2000: 18) and Mateus (1982: 29).

(5) a. Pre-tonic, underived words

    morar m[u]rar "to live in"
    murar m[u]rar "to build a wall"
    pagar p[ɐ]gar "to pay"
    pegar p[i]gar "to take"

b. Pre-tonic, derived words

    f[ɛ]sta ´party" ~ f[i]stinha "small party"
    f[o]go "fire" ~ f[u]geira "fireplace"
    m[ɛ]l "honey" ~ m[i]lado "molasses"
    p[ɔ]rta "door" ~ p[u]rteiro "doorman"

c. Non-final post-tonic

    pérola per[u]la "pearl"
    báculo bac[u]lo "staff"
    ágape ag[ɐ]pe "agape"

d. Final unstressed

    júri jur[i] "jury"
    jure jur[i] "he/she swears-subj"
    juro jur[u] "I swear- ind."

Some unsystematic exceptions to word-final centralization exist, as exemplified in (5d) by the word *júri* "jury," providing evidence that neutralization takes precedence over centralization in front vowels. Nonetheless, unstressed word-final [i] is very rare in EP. In the northern dialects it is usually centralized: *júr*[ɨ], *táx*[ɨ], etc.

One may interpret the EP variant of UVNeu as a two-step process. As a first step, the contrast between high, upper-mid, and lower-mid vowels is neutralized in favor of the corresponding high vowels. Subsequently, the coronal high vowel, together with the low vowel, are centralized. The differential behavior of the features [coronal], which is lost in the neutralization process, and [labial], which is preserved (Veloso 2013), in addition to the historical evidence showing that neutralization and centralization began to act in different stages of the history of the language (Marquilhas 2003; Mattos and Silva 2008; Paiva 2008, 2009; Maia 2013) suggest that two different rules, neutralization and centralization, are active in EP, as earlier proposed by Veloso (2013).

In present-day EP, there is no evidence for a two-step BP-like neutralization process with progressive neutralization of the [±open₃] and [±open₂] aperture contrasts. Unstressed mid-vowels are found mainly as unsystematic exceptions, most of them as a remnant from past stages of the language. In present-day EP, vowel reduction is a single lexical rule of neutralization with a considerable number of exceptions.[2]

As an instance of Trubetzkoy's type (3b) neutralization, both upper- and lower-mid vowels are replaced by the corresponding high vowels. This implies the deletion of the relevant aperture features and their subsequent replacement by the unmarked feature values, which, for unstressed vowels, are the negative values.

(6) Neutralization of high, upper-mid, and lower-mid contrasts in EP

    Delete [+open₃,₂]/unstressed syllables
    Domain: Phonological Word

    Root [+vocoid]

    Aperture

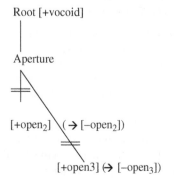

    [+open₂] (→ [−open₂])

        [+open3] (→ [−open₃])

As before, we assume that after the removal of the contrastive features from the relevant tiers, the unmarked negative specifications are automatically provided, i.e. all mid-vowels surface as high vowels.

Instead of treating neutralization for labial vowels and centralization of coronal vowels as two different processes, we opt here for a global process of neutralization creating high vowels, with centralization of the high and the low vowels taken care of by a separate rule. The rule-ordering that we propose is shown in the following derivation:

(7)

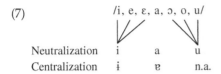

/i, e, ɛ, a, ɔ, o, u/

Neutralization	i	a	u
Centralization	ɨ	ɐ	n.a.

The precise phonetic definition of the central vowel is a thorny issue. As was observed by Veloso: "central vowels can be characterized as highly variable, unstable, ill-defined vocoids" (2010: 199).

Within the perspective of the above-proposed analysis, one may suggest that the neutralization rule is phonological, while centralization is a rule of allophony, active at the level of the phonological word. The centralization rules concede some exceptions in the standard language, which are not tolerated in non-standard dialects of EP.

2.3. *Mid-vowel neutralization in stressed syllables in EP and BP*

An interesting case of mid-vowel neutralization occurs in stressed syllables in both varieties of Portuguese, as observed in Wetzels (1992). Different from unstressed neutralization, the vowel representing the neutralized mid-vowel contrast in stressed syllables is always lower-mid.[3] The process affects words with proparoxytonic stress and words with prefinal stress that end in a heavy syllable. The examples in (8) show the productivity of the process, called Dactylic Lowering by the author, in derived and underived proparoxytonic words.[4]

(8) Dactylic Lowering

  (a) Underived words

m[ɛ]dico	"physician"	ab[ɔ]bora	"pumpkin"
h[ɛ]lice	"propeller"	c[ɔ]digo	"code"
c[ɛ]rebro	"brain"	l[ɔ]bulo	"lobule"
r[ɛ]dea	"bridle"	[ɔ]sseo	"bony"

  (b) Derived words

esquel[é]to	"skeleton"	esquel[ɛ]tico	"skeletal"
visig[ó]do	"visigoth"	visig[ɔ]tico	"visigothic"
n[o]do'ar	"to stain"	n[ɔ]doa	"stain"
ásp[e]ro	"rough"	asp[ɛ]rrimo	"very rough"

(9) Dactylic Lowering

    (ó σ σ)ω   Domain: phonological word (non-verbs)

    |

    Aperture

    ╫

    [open₃]

In (9) above, neutralization is obtained by the deletion of the contrastive [open₃] feature. However, since Dactylic Lowering applies in stressed syllables and given the preference of stressed syllables for sonorant nuclei, Wetzels (1992) proposes that the unmarked value for the [± open₃] feature is the positive value in stressed syllables.

A similar process, called Spondaic Lowering, applies in paroxytonic words with a final heavy syllable. Some examples follow.

(10) Spondaic Lowering

m[ɔ]vel	"mobile"	C[ɛ]sar	"Caesar"
c[ɔ]dex	"codex"	indel[ɛ]vel	"unerasable"
d[ɔ]lar	"dollar"	est[ɛ]ril	"sterile"
m[ɔ]rmon	"Mormon"	el[ɛ]tron	"electron"
c[ɔ]smos	"cosmos"	w[ɛ]stern	"western"

Both lowering rules are exceptionless in derived environments and near-exceptionless in underived words. Loan words with the appropriate structure undergo lowering: d[ɔ]ping "doping," d[ɔ]lar, "dollar," W[ɛ]ber "Weber." As the names given to the rules suggest, according to Wetzels (1992), these rules are conditioned by their specific rhythmical patterns.

3. Pretonic Mid-Vowel Harmony in BP

Mid-Vowel Harmony (MVH) is a variable phonological process which is part of the history of BP, but completely absent in contemporary EP. MVH can be defined as a process of regressive assimilation of pretonic mid-vowels to a following high vowel within the domain of the phonological word. Its variability is stable, without signs of the process becoming obligatory. MVH has been widely documented with Labovian type sociolinguistic studies in all regions of Brazil, as in Bisol (1981); Callou and Leite (1986); Maia (1986); Viegas (1987), (2001); Barbosa da Silva (1989); Castro (1990); Bortoni, Gomes, and Malvar (1992); Schwindt (1995); Casagrande (2004); Nascimento Silva (2009).

Factors that influence its application concern the distance between trigger and target, the quality of the target and trigger vowels, as well as a number of non-linguistic factors, as one usually encounters for variable rules.

In the previous section it was shown that in the dialects of south and southwest Brazil the sequence of syllables preceding the main stress realizes a five-vowel system. In (11) below, we repeat the way in which aperture distinctions for vowels are represented in the Clements (1991) system of aperture contrasts. The full system in (11) represents the stressed vowel system of BP. In pretonic syllables the aperture feature definitions for the mid-vowels in the southern dialects are those given for /e, o/, while in the northern and northeastern dialects, the lower mid-vowels /ε, ɔ/ prevail in that position.

(11) Aperture distinctions for vowel phonemes

Aperture	i/u	e/o	ε/ɔ	a
open₁	−	−	−	+
open₂	−	+	+	+
open₃	−	−	+	+

The following words, taken from the studies cited above, illustrate the effect of MVH in nouns and verbs.

(12) Nouns

		Verbs	
b[o]nita ~ b[u]nita	"pretty"	b[e]bia ~ b[i]bia	"(s)he drank"
c[o]stura ~ c[u]stura	"sewing"	c[o]rri ~ c[u]rri	"(I) ran"
f[e]liz ~ f[i]liz	"happy"	m[o]via ~ m[u]via	"(I) moved"
m[e]nino ~ m[i]nino	"boy"	m[e]ntirei ~ m[i]ntirei	"(I) will lie"
pr[e]guiça ~ pr[i]guiça	"laziness"	f[e]rido ~ f[i]rido	"hurt"

As the examples show, mid-vowels become high before a high vowel in an immediately following syllable. The low vowel /a/ does not trigger low harmony and acts as a blocker: *m[e]lancia* "watermelon" does not become **m[i]lancia*, despite the presence of a stressed high vowel following /a/. Similarly, in the exceptional cases in which unstressed lower-mid vowels appear in the pretonic context (cf. the suffixes in (2b) above), raising does not take place: *b[ε]líssimo, *b[e]líssimo* or **b[i]líssimo; b[ɔ]linha,* not **b[o]linha* or **b[u]linha.*

While in the southern dialects lower-mid vowels are absent from the part of the word that precedes the main stress, the northern and northeastern dialects have a preference for lower-mid vowels in this context. However, upper-mid vowels emerge before a syllable with a high nucleus, creating a considerable number of exceptions to the generalization that in these dialects only pretonic lower-mid vowels occur: *f[ε]liz ~ f[e]liz* "happy," *al[ε]gria ~ al[e]gria* "happiness," *f[ɔ]rtuna-f[o]rtuna* "fortune" (see Barbosa da Silva (1989), Nascimento Silva (2009), and others). As in the southern dialects, mid-vowels are raised one degree on the aperture scale. In this respect the processes are identical, but the result of their application is different: in the variants with pretonic upper-mid vowels total assimilation is obtained whereas assimilation is only partial in dialects with pretonic lower-mid vowels. The processes are exemplified in (13a) and (13b), respectively.

(13)   a. Total assimilation   b. Partial assimilation

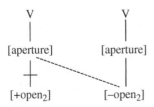
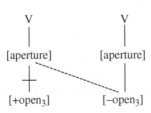

In the southern dialects, where pretonic mid-vowels are defined as [−open₁, +open₂, −open₃] spreading of the [−open₂] feature of the high vowel creates high vowels out of upper-mid

vowels, while in the northern dialects the spreading of the [−open₃] feature to the lower-mid vowels, defined as [−open₁, +open₂, +open₃], yields upper mid-vowels. The following examples, taken from Nascimento Silva (2009: 193) enable one to compare the outcome of MVH for the two dialect areas:

(14) South   North and northeast
  al[e]gria ~ al[i]gria   al[ɛ]gria ~ al[e]gria   "happiness"
  b[e]bida ~ b[i]bida   b[ɛ]bida ~ b[e]bida   "drink"
  f[e]liz ~ f[i]liz   f[ɛ]liz ~ f[e]liz   "happy"
  f[o]rtuna ~ f[u]rtuna   f[ɔ]rtuna ~ f[o]rtuna   "fortune"
  p[o]ssível ~ p[u]ssível   p[ɔ]ssível ~ possível   "possible"
  pr[e]sidente ~ pr[i]sidente   pr[ɛ]sidente ~ pr[e]sidente   "president"
  pr[o]cissao ~ pr[u]cissao   pr[ɔ]cissão ~ pr[o]cissão   "procession"
  n[o]vidade ~ n[u]vidada   n[ɔ]vidade ~ n[o]vidade   "novelty"

In both variants of BP, MVH has the effect of raising the pretonic mid-vowels one degree on the aperture scale. This much has been established beyond doubt. For the northern and northeastern dialects some researchers have claimed that complete assimilation is also possible, as in the word *al[ɛ]gria ~ al[e]gria ~ al[i]gria* (cf. Barbosa da Silva, 1989; Nascimento Silva. 2009).

According to Baković (2007), regressive assimilation can involve contiguous or non-contiguous targets, although usually, contiguity is a necessary condition for this process. In BP, the assimilating feature may spread long distances. Long-distance spreading can be observed in both nouns and verbs, although in the latter category spreading may involve non-contiguous syllables. Examples are provided below.

(15) Long distance MVH

  a. Nouns

    m[e]r[e]cimento   "merit"   m[e]r[i]cimento ~ m[i]r[i]cimento   *m[i]r[e]c[i]mento

    n[e]c[e]ssidade   "need"   n[e]c[i]ssidade ~ n[i]c[i]ssidade   *n[i]c[e]ssidade

    p[e]r[e]grino   "pilgrim"   p[e]r[i]grino ~ p[i]r[i]grino   *p[i]r[e]grino

    r[e]p[e]tição   "repetition"   r[e]p[i]tição ~ r[i]p[i]tição   *r[i]p[e]tição

  b. Verbs

    b[e]beria "drink, 3sg cond."   b[e]b[e]ria ~ b[e]b[i]ria ~ b[i]b[i]ria ~ b[i]b[e]ria

    c[o]rreria "run, 3sg cond."   c[o]rr[e]ria ~ c[o]rr[i]ria ~ c[u]rr[i]ria ~ c[u]rr[e]ria

    p[o]deria "be able, 3sg cond." p[o]d[e]ria ~ p[o]d[i]ria ~ p[u]d[i]ria ~ p[u]d[e]ria

    s[o]freria "suffer, 3sg cond." s[o]fr[e]ria ~ s[o]fr[i]ria ~ s[u]fr[i]ria ~ s[u]fr[e]ria

Whereas spreading in nouns always affects contiguous syllables, in verbs syllables can be skipped apparently. This is particularly visible in the class of /e/-conjugation verbs, when more than one mid-vowel precedes an /i/-initial suffix. Besides the cases of continuous harmony, one often finds a corresponding form in which the theme-vowel remains unaffected by MVH, as in the right column of the verbs in (15b). However, also in verb forms of other conjugations we observe the presence of high vowels, as in *c[o]nseguir* "succeed" ~ *c[u]nseguir* "I succeed," where /e/ is part of the root. At the same time, the sequence *c[u]nsigo* "I succeed" is found as the 1si. present indicative form of the same verb, which could be interpreted as the regular outcome of MVH. One might consequently think that, to explain the high vowel in the first syllable of the infinitive *c*[u]*nseguir* "succeed," some paradigmatic force is at work. However, reality is more complex, as is shown by the verb forms *g*[o]*verno* ~ *g*[u]*verno* "I govern" or *g*[o]*vernaria* ~ *g*[u]*vernaria* "I would govern." Notice that the alternation in the latter form cannot be explained by the high vowel of the suffix, since we have seen above that /a/ is a blocker. Matters clear up if we consider alternations between mid-vowels and high vowels in nouns: *b*[o]*neca* ~ *b*[u]*neca* "doll," *t*[o]*mate* ~ *t*[u]*mate* "tomato," *g*[o]*verno* ~ *g*[u]*verno* "government," where there is no trigger for MVH. As it appears, MVH co-exists with a variable process of mid-vowel raising (MVR) in pretonic syllables.[5] We may consequently explain the cases of apparent non-contiguous MVH in verbs as prosodically conditioned raising, similar to what happens in post-tonic and, particularly, in unstressed word-final open syllables in BP, where mid-vowels are realized as high vowels.

(16)		MVR		MVH		
c[o]mer	~	c[u]mer	"eat"	c[u]m[e]ria	~ c[u]m[i]ria	"I would eat"
c[o]rrer	~	c[u]rrer	"run"	c[u]rr[e]ria	~ c[u]rr[i]ria	"I would run"
p[o]der	~	p[u]der	"be able"	p[u]d[e]ria	~ p[u]d[i]ria	"I would be able"
g[o]verno	~	g[u]verno	"govern"	g[u]v[e]rnaria	~ g[o]v[e]rnaria	"I would govern"

As for the verb forms categorized as resulting from MVH in the right-hand column of (16), it would be possible in principle to consider them as the result of long-distance MVH or as the conjoint effect of local MVH and mid-vowel raising.

Another interesting aspect of MVH concerns the different triggering potential of the two high vowels /i, u/. It was repeatedly observed in studies dealing with MVH that /i/ more frequently triggers assimilation than /u/. In particular, unlike /u/, /i/ has the same raising effect on either one of the mid-vowels, whether it be /e, ɛ/ or /o, ɔ/. On the other hand, the labial high vowel has a greater effect on /o, ɔ/ than on /e, ɛ/.

Comparing the height of the two high vowels within the phonetic space of the BP vowel system, one observes that /i/ is the highest vowel, with /u/ being considerably lower, only slightly higher than /e/. Consequently, the high labial vowel has a weaker raising potential with regard to /e/, which, in order to be raised to /i/, becomes phonetically higher than the trigger vowel /u/ itself. This may account for the preservation of the mid-vowel in such words as *l*[e]*gume* "vegetable," *p*[e]*rgunta* "question," *p*[e]*rfume* "perfume," in which MVH is unattested (see Bisol, 1981).

A final remark concerns the prosodic strength of the trigger vowel. The triggers for MVH can be both stressed and unstressed vowels, as in *f*[e]*liz* ~ *f*[i]*liz* "happy" with stressed word-final /i/, as compared with *pr*[o]*cissão* ~ *pr*[u]*cissão* "procession," with stress on the nasal diphthong, although harmony more frequently happens when the trigger vowel is stressed.

4. Nasal vowels and nasal diphthongs

4.1. *Nasal vowels*

In both variants of Portuguese, the contrast between upper- and lower-mid vowels is neutralized for nasal vowels in favor of the upper-mid quality. At the phonetic surface, oral and nasal vowels are contrastive, as illustrated with the words in (17):

(17) | s[ẽ]da | "path" | *seda* | "silk" |
|---|---|---|---|
| l[ĩ]do | "beautiful" | *lido* | "read" |
| t[ũ]ba | "tomb" | *tuba* | "tuba" |
| l[õ]bo | "loin" | *lobo* | "wolf" |

Surface contrastive nasal vowels have at least three different phonetic realizations: [ˈvẽndɐ], [ˈvẽjdɐ], [vẽdɐ] for *venda* "sale." Whereas in BP all three pronunciations occur, in EP the third possibility is the most frequent, as argued by Mateus and d'Andrade (2000). When a consonant is present phonetically, its place features are identical with those of the following stop. Before a fricative onset or word-finally, the consonantal element may share its place features with the preceding vowel or surface as a falling diphthong: *bem* [bẽj/ɲ] "well" or *bom* [bõw̃/ŋ] "good."

Since the time of structural linguistics, two views about Portuguese nasal vowels are competing. Whereas one group of scholars maintains that nasality is contrastive in vowels (/Ṽ/ vs. /V/), as, for example, defended in Hall (1943a,b), the other group argues in favor of a biphonemic representation consisting of an oral vowel followed by a tautosyllabic nasal consonant /VN/, as in Nobeling (1903) and many others after this author's early publication. Clearly, the controversy originates from the fact that the nasal vowel often surfaces without or with only a short nasal constriction in BP, while in EP the consonantal constriction usually does not appear.

The biphonemic interpretation of the nasal vowel becomes prevailing with Câmara Jr. (1953, 1970) in Brazil and with Barbosa (1965) in Portugal. Câmara Jr. (1970) includes his analysis of nasal vowels in the chapter on syllabification, arguing that nasal vowels are phonologically closed syllables.

Here we adopt the biphonemic way of representing nasal vowels, for which we summarize the evidence as given in Câmara Jr. (1953, 1970), Barbosa (1965), and Mateus and d'Andrade (2000).

- In Portuguese, weak /R/ and strong /R/ contrast intervocalically, as in *caro* "expensive" and *carro* "car," respectively. Elsewhere, these sounds are in complementary distribution, with strong /R/ systematically following the nasal vowel: *hon*/R/*a* "honor," *ten*/R/*o* "tender," *gen*/R/*o* "son-in-law." Since strong /R/ is also obligatory syllable-initially after a consonantal coda: *is*/R/*ael* "Israel," *guel*/R/*a* "gill," etc., the biphonemic representation readily explains the ban on weak /R/ following a phonological /VN/ sequence.
- Branching rhymes make heavy syllables. Nasal vowels show solidarity with branching rhymes as regards generalizations that refer to syllable weight. For example, words with antepenultimate stress are relatively frequent in Portuguese. However, the proparoxytonic stress pattern is only allowed in words with a prefinal light syllable. Typically, words with prefinal nasal vowels never show proparoxytonic stress: *rápido* "fast," **rápindo*, **rápildo*, **rápirdo*, etc.
- In morphological derivations before vowel-initial suffixes, the underlying /VN/ sequence often surfaces as an oral vowel followed by a nasal consonant: *afeg*[ɐ̃] "Afghan (fem.)" ~ *Afeg*[ɐ̃n]*istão* "Afghanistan," *r*[ɐ̃] "frog" ~ *r*[ɐ̃n]*ário* "frog farm," *pat*[ĩ] "skate"~ *pat*[in]*agem* "skating," etc. The same is true for productive prefixes like *–in*, which surface with a nasal vowel when prefixed to a consonant-initial root, as in [ĩ] *possível* "impossible," but with an oral vowel when the nasal consonant is syllabified as the onset of the root: [in]*útil*, "useless."

The view of nasal vowels representing underlying /VN/ sequences was tested in a perception test done by Moraes (2013: 109–110), who describes the experiment as below.

> In a word like *mando* [ˈmẽⁿdu], the sound [d] was electronically erased. Depending on the perceptual prominence of the nasal appendix [n], the resulting word should be perceived as either *mão* [mẽw̃] or *mano* [mẽnu]. The first alternative would support the hypothesis of a mere transition, not phonological, of this consonantal segment (homosyllabic interpretation).

The second alternative ([n] perceived as heterosyllabic) means that the original appendix in the syllable coda resyllabifies and becomes a full consonant in the syllable onset, in which case the biphonemic hypothesis would be preferred.

As it turned out, the second alternative—*mano*—was chosen by most participants, confirming the phonological status of the nasal consonant as part of the underlying /VN/ sequence.

4.2. Nasal diphthongs

Besides the phonetic nasal diphthongs derived from underlying /VN/, Portuguese also has lexical nasal diphthongs. In lexical nasal diphthongs, the nuclear vowel is either /a/ or /o/.[6] The following words show a nasal diphthong in the singular and the corresponding plural. The phonetic transcription reflects the BP pronunciation.

(18) Singular   Plural

	Singular			Plural	
a.	*irmão*	[ixmẽw̃]	"brother"	*irmãos*	[ixmẽw̃s]
	mão	[mẽw̃]	"hand"	*mãos*	[mẽw̃s]
	cidadão	[sidadẽw̃]	"citizen"	*cidadãos*	[sidadẽw̃s]
b.	*cão*	[kẽw̃]	"dog"	*cães*	[kẽjs]
	capitão	[kapitẽw̃]	"captain"	*capitães*	[kapitẽjs]
	pão	[pẽw̃]	"bread"	*pães*	[pẽjs]
c.	*verão*	[verẽw̃]	"summer"	*verões*	[verõjs]
	limão	[limẽw̃]	"lemon"	*limões*	[limõjs]
	feijão	[fejʒẽw̃]	"bean"	*feijões*	[fejʒõjs]

The apparent irregularity of the plural forms, [ãjs], [õjs] corresponding with the singular [ẽw̃] has been much debated in the literature. To account for these alternations in the synchronic grammar of Portuguese, Câmara Jr. (1970: 85) explains the different plural forms as the consequence of different underlying nominal class markers, as shown with the plural examples in (19b).

(19) a. Singular   b. Plural

a. Singular			b. Plural		
[irmẽw̃]	/irmaN-o/	"brother"	[irmẽw̃s]	/irmaN+o+S/	
[kapitẽw̃]	/kapitaN-e/	"captain"	[kẽpitẽjs]	/kapitaN+e+S/	
[verẽw̃]	/veroN-e/	"summer"	[verõjs]	/veroN+e+S/	

Similar proposals can be found in Morales-Front and Holt (1997), Mateus and d'Andrade (2000), Veloso (2005), Bisol (2013) and others. In Wetzels (1997) it is argued that words ending in nasal diphthongs are athematic and lexically represented with a nasal glide.[7]

    The words in (18a), which preserve [ãw̃] in the plural form, are very limited in number. Some examples are: *irmãos* "brothers," *pagãos* "pagans," *grãos* "grains," *mãos* "hands," *órfãos* "orphans," *órgãos* "organs." Even less frequent is the class in (b) in which the vowel /a/ is present in both the singular and plural forms: *capitães* "captains," *pães* "loaves (of bread)," and *cães* "dogs." By far the most frequent are the words in (c), which show a [ẽw̃] ~ [õj̃] alternation. As it appears, Portuguese nominal roots surfacing with a nasal diphthong either end in /aN/ or in /oN/ lexically. The class of root-final /oN/ nouns are the most numerous class.

We have just seen that Câmara Jr. (1970: 85) proposes for the word *irmão* "brother" the representation /aN+o/, i.e. as being thematic. In a different study he establishes a parallel between, on the one hand, the representation of oral and nasal vowels as a contrast between /V/ vs. /VN/ and, on the other hand, the nasal diphthong as an oral diphthong followed by /N/ (1971: 33). Here we will adopt the view that word-final nasal diphthongs are derived from underlying /VN+V/, where /+V/ is a class marker. A morphologically conditioned rule deletes the nasal consonant, while its nasal feature remains in the representation /V[nasal]+V/. Since we assume that words surfacing with a nasal diphthong derive from thematic words, in accordance with Câmara Jr (1970), Mateus and d'Andrade (2000), and Bisol (2013), the theme vowel must be changed into a glide, which assimilates the coronal features of the plural morpheme /S/: /V[nasal]jS/. Finally, to account for the fact that phonological sequences of the type /veroN+o/ surface with word-final [ẽw̃], we must posit a lexical rule which neutralizes the contrast between [ẽw̃] and [õw̃], probably by dissimilation. Obviously, the few words in which the labial glide does not become coronal must be marked as exceptional to the lexical rule that turns /u/ to /i/ before /S/.

5. Conclusion

EP and BP both have a neutralization rule which reduces the seven-vowel system that exists in stressed syllables to the three-vowel system /i, u, a/ in atonic syllables. This basic system is attested in all positions in EP, but only word-finally in BP. The distinction that must be made in BP between unstressed vowel neutralization and word-final unstressed vowel neutralization has motivated our decision to derive the neutralization facts in this variety of Portuguese as a two-step process. No such evidence exists in EP, for which the global reduction of the seven-vowel system to the three-vowel system is derived as a single process. By separating neutralization and centralization in EP, we were able to show that the neutralization rules in BP and EP are very similar and only different in scope. As regards the rules of stressed mid-vowel neutralization, both rules are productive in EP and PB.

In BP, neutralization is not the only rule that is active in pretonic syllables. Within the five-vowel system created by UVNeu, two variable processes are simultaneously eliminating the mid-vowels in the southern dialects. One is a rule of regressive MVH triggered by the high vowels /i, u/, in which /i/ is more forceful as a trigger than /u/. The other one is a prosodically conditioned rule which raises /e, o/ to /i, u/. The combined effect of these rules suggests a future for these dialects in which the basic three-vowel system /i, a, u/ extends to all unstressed syllables, generalizing the pattern that already exists in word-final unstressed open syllables. In the dialects of the north(east), which show a preference for lower-mid vowels in pretonic syllables, VH raises /ɛ, ɔ/ to /e, o/, recreating a seven-vowel system as it exists under stress.

The phonological analysis of nasal vowels and nasal diphthongs is without doubt the part of the Portuguese vocalism where scholars disagree the most. Here we have presented the traditional view of the lexical presentation of these sounds, conscious of the fact that the discussion will surely continue.

NOTES

1   See, among others, Câmara Jr. 1970, Lopez 1979, Wetzels 1992, Lee 1995.
2   Vigário (2001) identifies the most relevant of such exceptions.
3   Unless neutralization is the result of assimilation, in which case the resulting vowel may be either upper or lower mid.
4   The examples in (9–10) are taken from Wetzels 2011.
5   Vowel raising is not observed for all nouns, as those given in (15a). For vowel raising in words without a high vowel, see Klunck 2007, Cruz 2010, Correa da Silva 2014.
6   Nasal diphthongs are almost always word-final and almost exceptionally attract word-stress. A few exceptions exist: (1) Few words have a word-internal nasal diphthong, such as in *cãimbra* "cramp" or *zãimbro* "one-eyed"; (2) in a small set of words stress is prefinal, as in *órfão* "orphan," *órgão* "organ," and *bênção* "blessing."
7   See also Chapter 6 on the syllable and Chapter 11 on the morphology and phonology of inflection.

REFERENCES

Baković, E. (2007). Local assimilation and constraint interaction. In P. de Lacy (ed.), *The Cambridge Handbook of Phonology*. Cambridge: Cambridge University Press, pp. 335–351.

Barbosa, J. M. (1965). *Études de Phonologie Portugaise*. Lisbon: Junta de Investigações Científicas do Ultramar.

Barbosa da Silva, M. (1989). *As Pretônicas no Falar Baiano: a Variedade Culta de Salvador*. Ph.D. thesis, UFRJ, Rio de Janeiro.

Bisol, L. (1981). *Harmonização Vocálica*. Ph.D. thesis, UFRJ, Rio de Janeiro.

Bisol, L. (2010). O Diminutivo e suas demandas. *D.E.L.T.A.*, 26, pp. 59–83.

Bisol, L. (2013). Fonologia da Nasalização. In A. Castilho et al. (eds.). *Gramática do Português Falado*, vol. VII. São Paulo: Editora Contexto/FAPESP, pp. 113–140.

Bortoni, S. M., E. Gomes, and C. Malvar (1992). A variação das vogais pretônicas no Português de Brasília: Um Fenômeno Neogramático ou de Difusão Lexical. *Estudos Lingüísticos*, 1, pp. 9–29.

Callou, D. and Y. Leite (1986). Variação das Vogais Pretônicas. *Simpósio-Diversidade Lingüística no Brasil*. Salvador: UFBA, pp. 157–169.

Câmara, J. M. (1953). *Para o Estudo da Fonêmica Portuguesa*. Rio de Janeiro: Livraria Padrão.

Câmara, J. M. (1970). *Estrutura da Língua Portuguesa*. Rio de Janeiro: Editora Vozes.

Casagrande, G. P. B. (2004). *Harmonização Vocálica: Análise Variacionista em Tempo Real*. MA thesis, PUCRS, Porto Alegre, Brazil.

Castro, E. C. (1990). *As Pretônicas na Variedade Mineira de Juiz de Fora*. MA thesis, UFRJ, Rio de Janeiro, Brazil.

Clements, G. N. (1991). Vowel height assimilation in Bantu languages. *Working Papers of the Cornell Phonetics Laboratory*, 5, pp. 37–76.

Correa da Silva, A. P. (2014). *Elevação sem Motivação Aparente das Vogais Médias Pretônicas entre os Jovens Porto-Alegrenses*. MA thesis, PUCRS, Porto Alegre.

Cruz, M. (2010). *As Vogais Médias Pretônicas em Porto Alegre -RS: um Estudo sobre o Alçamento sem Motivação Aparente*. MA thesis, PUCR, Porto Alegre.

Delgado-Martins, M. R. (1996). Relação fonética/fonologia: A propósito do sistema vocálico do português. *Congresso Internacional sobre o Português*. Actas, vol. I. Lisbon: Colibri, pp. 311–325.

Gonçalves Viana, A. R. (1973[1892]). *Estudos de Fonética Portuguesa*. Lisbon: Imprensa Nacional—Casa da Moeda.

Hall Jr., R. (1943a). The unit phonemes of Brazilian Portuguese. *Studies in Linguistics*, 1 (15), pp. 1–6.

Hall Jr., R. (1943b). Occurrence and orthographical representation of phonemes in Brazilian Portuguese. *Studies in Linguistics*, 2 (1), pp. 6–13.

Klunck, P. (2007). *Alçamento das Vogais Médias Pretônicas sem Motivação Aparente*. MA thesis, PUCRS, Porto Alegre.

Lee, S. H. (1995). *Morfologia e Fonologia Lexical do Português Brasileiro*. Ph.D. thesis, UNICAMP, Brazil.

Leite, Y. (1974). *Portuguese stress and related rules*. Ph.D. dissertation, University of Texas.

Lopez, B. (1979). The sound pattern of Brazilian Portuguese (cariocan dialect). Ph.D. dissertation, University of California.

Maia, C. de A. (2013). O Vocalismo Átono na História do Português: Contributos para a Cronologia das Mudanças. In R. Alvarez et al. (eds.), *Ao Sabor do Texto: Estudos dedicados a Ivo Castro*. Santiago de Compostela: Universidade de Santiago de Compostela, pp. 335–354.

Maia, V. L. M. (1986). As Pretônicas Médias na Fala de Natal. *Estudos Lingüísticos e Literários*. 5, pp. 209–225.

Marquilhas, R. (2003). Mudança Analógica e Elevação das Vogais Pretónicas. In I. Castro and I. Duarte (eds.), *Miscelânea de Estudos em Homenagem a Maria Helena Mira Mateus*, vol. II. Lisbon: Imprensa Nacional—Casa da Moeda, pp. 7–18.

Mateus, M. H. (1982). *Aspectos da Fonologia Portuguesa*. Lisbon: INIC (Textos de Linguística, 6) [Lisbon: Centro de Estudos Filológicos 1975].

Mateus, M. H. and E. d'Andrade (2000). *The Phonology of Portuguese*. Oxford: Oxford University Press.

Mateus, M. H. M. and M. R. Delgado-Martins (1982). Contribuição para o estudo das vogais átonas [ə] e [u] no português europeu. *Biblos*, LVIII, pp. 111–125.

Mattos e Silva, R. V. (2008). *O Português Arcaico*. Lisbon: Imprensa Nacional—Casa da Moeda.

Menuzzi, S. (1993). *On The Prosody of the Diminutive Alternation -inho/-zinho in Brazilian Portuguese*. Manuscript, HIL/University of Leiden.

Moraes, J. A. de. (2013). Produção e Percepção das Vogais Nasais. In A. Castilho et al. (eds.), *Gramática do Português Falado*, vol. VII. São Paulo: Editora Contexto/FAPESP, pp. 95–112.

Morales-Front, A. and E. Holt (1997). The interplay of morphology, prosody and faithfulness in Portuguese pluralization. In F. Martínez-Gil and A. Morales-Front (eds.), *Issues in the Phonology and Morphology of the Major Iberian Languages*. Washington, DC: Georgetown University Press, pp. 359–437.

Nascimento Silva, A. (2009). *As Pretônicas no Falar Teresinense*. Ph.D. thesis, PUCRS, Porto Alegre.

Nobeling, O. (1903). Die Nasalvokale im Portugiesischen. *Die Neueren Sprache*, 11, pp. 129–153.

Paiva, M. H. (2008). A Descrição do Vocalismo Átono Quinhentista: Linhas e Entrelinhas nos Textos Metalinguísticos Coevos. *Linguística*, 3, pp. 197–221.

Paiva, M. H. (2009). Variação e Mudança no Vocalismo Átono Quinhentista: Práticas Escriturais e Juízos Normativos. *Linguística*, 4, pp. 85–110.

Schwindt, L. C. (1995). *Harmonia Vocálica em Dialetos do Sul do País*. MA thesis, PUCRS, Porto Alegre, Brazil.

Schwindt, L. C. (2013). Neutralização da Vogal Pretônica e Formação de Palavras em Português Brasileiro. *Organon*, 28 (54), pp. 137–154.

Trubetzkoy, N. S. (1967). *Principes de Phonologie*. Paris: Éditions Klincksieck.

Veloso, J. (2005). Estrutura Interna e Flexão de Número dos Nomes Terminados em "-ão": Onde Reside a "Irregularidade"? In G. M. Rio-Torto, O. M. Figueiredo, and F. Silva (eds.), *Estudos em Homenagem ao Professor Doutor Mário Vilela*, vol. I. Porto: Faculdade de Letras da Universidade do Porto, pp. 325–338.

Veloso, J. (2010). Central, epenthetic, unmarked vowels, and schwas: A brief outline of some essential differences. *Linguística*, 5 (1), pp. 193–213.

Veloso, J. (2013). Redução do Vocalismo Átono do Português Europeu Contemporâneo: Assimetria dos Elementos de Tonalidade e Interação entre Diversos Tipos de Redução Vocálica. In F. Silva, I. Falé, and I. Pereira (eds.), *Textos Selecionados do XXVIII Encontro Nacional da Associação Portuguesa de Linguística*. Coimbra: Associação Portuguesa de Linguística, pp. 655–672.

Viegas, M. C. (1987). *Alçamento de Vogais Médias Pretônicas: uma Abordagem Sociolingüística*. MA thesis, UFMG, Belo Horizonte.

Viegas, M. C. (2001). O Alçamento das Vogais Pretônicas e os Itens Lexicais. Ph.D. thesis, UFMG, Belo Horizonte.

Vieira, M. J. (1994). *Neutralização das Vogais Médias Postônicas*. MA thesis, PUCRS, Porto Alegre.

Vigário, M. (2001). *The prosodic word in European Portuguese*. Ph.D. thesis, Universidade de Lisboa, Lisbon.

Villalva, A. (2000). *Estruturas Morfológicas. Unidades e Hierarquias nas Palavras do Português*. Lisbon: Fundação Calouste Gulbenkian/ Fundação para a Ciência e a Tecnologia.

Wetzels, W. L. (1992). Mid vowel neutralization in Brazilian Portuguese. *Cadernos de Estudos Linguísticos*, 23, pp. 19–55.

Wetzels, W. L. (1997). The lexical representation of nasality in Brazilian Portuguese. *Probus*, 9 (2), pp. 203–232.

Wetzels, W. L. (2011). Aperture Features and the representation of vowel neutralization in Brazilian Portuguese. In E. Hume, J. Goldsmith, and W. L. Wetzels (eds.), *Tones and Features*. Berlin: de Gruyter, pp. 331–359.

6 Syllable Structure

GISELA COLLISCHONN AND W. LEO WETZELS

1. Introduction

The syllable and its constituents play an important role in describing and explaining restrictions on the co-occurrence of segments and the distribution of individual segments and their allophones. Syllables as domains, but also their edges constitute recurrent environments that condition phonological processes across languages. As part of a hierarchy of prosodic domains, the way in which syllables are joined into larger domains such as the foot and the prosodic word shows how word-accent and rhythm emerge and gives a notion of what a possible word-prosodic system is or how restrictions on syllable structure may be loosened at the edges of phonological words. At a relatively young age, children are able to count the number of syllables in a word and have clear intuitions about the locus of syllable boundaries when they map syllables to tunes in lyrics and easily learn to manipulate syllables and their constituents in word games.[1] In both European and Brazilian Portuguese, a number of generalizations must be expressed by reference to syllable edges, such as the velarization (EP and BP) and vocalization (BP) of /l/ in the syllable coda, as in *sal* [saɫ/w] "salt" and *salta* ['saɫ/w.ta] "jump-3sg.pr.ind.," or the distribution of the allophones of the rhotic /R/. Syllables can be targeted in word-formation, such as hypocoristic reduplication. In this chapter we will not be concerned primarily with phonological or morphological processes that relate to the syllable,[2] but focus on justifying the structure of the Portuguese syllable and its constituents.

We will not distinguish between the syllable structure of European (EP) and Brazilian Portuguese (BP), despite the fact that, at first impression, these two variants sound very different, most evidently due to the frequent loss of unstressed vowels in PE. Instead, we will focus on the structure of the BP syllable, where the facts are somewhat more straightforward, and subsequently introduce the complexities typical of EP, following the analysis by Mateus and d'Andrade (2000). These authors propose that the EP syllable structure is, at some shallow level of abstraction, if not identical, at least very similar to that of BP.

Although we assume that the structure of the Portuguese syllable outlined in this chapter is valid for the normative speech variants of both Brazil and Portugal, the phonetic realization of vowels and consonants is sometimes subject to dialectal variation within these broad areas. Illustrations for BP will be taken from the cultivated speech typical of the southern states (São Paulo, Santa Catarina, Paraná, and Rio Grande do Sul), whereas the Lisbon variant is our point of reference for EP.

The Handbook of Portuguese Linguistics, First Edition. Edited by W. Leo Wetzels, João Costa, and Sergio Menuzzi.
© 2016 John Wiley & Sons, Inc. Published 2020 by John Wiley & Sons, Inc.

2. The structure of the Portuguese syllable

The purpose of this section is to characterize the structure of the Portuguese syllable against the background of a general theory of syllable structure. We will justify the global syllable constituency as represented in (1) below, which distinguishes between an onset and a rhyme constituent, the latter subdivided into a nucleus node and a coda node.

(1)

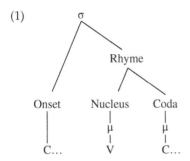

The terminal structural nodes in (1) dominate the segments of Portuguese directly (onset) or indirectly via the mora constituents (nucleus, coda).

In Portuguese, the syllable nucleus is obligatorily filled with a vowel. Stressed syllables may contain any of the seven vowels /i, e, ɛ, a, ɔ, o, u/ which constitute the full vowel system of this language, whereas in BP unstressed syllables may contain one of the vowels /i, e, a, o, u/, a set which is word-finally further reduced to [i, a, u] in BP. In EP, only [ɐ, ɨ, u] occur in all unstressed syllables.[3] The syllable onset and coda may remain empty. Empty onsets occur word-initially and word-internally: *a.ve* "bird, *ru.a* "street," *ca.otico* "chaotic," although various processes exist that militate against vowel sequences. Given an allowed maximum of two consonants in the onset (Obstruent + Liquid) and in the coda (Sonorant + /S/), the following syllable types are predicted to occur in Portuguese, presented in the order of decreasing frequency: CV, CVC, V, VC, CCV, CCVC, CVCC, CCVCC, VCC.

The CV type is by far the most frequent, accounting for 60 percent of the total number of syllables occurring in the Houaiss dictionary, which comprises 150,875 words, whereas the last three types each account for less than 1 percent (Viaro and Guimarães Filho, 2007, for BP[4]). The relative frequency of the syllable types corresponds roughly with the relative complexity of their onsets and codas. Not surprisingly, the relative complexity of the syllable margins is mirrored in the acquisition process, during which children acquire the simpler syllable types before the more complex ones. The following stages are observed in the learning of syllable types for Brazilian children by Lamprecht (2004):

Earliest	CV, V	*sa*.po "frog," *á*.gua "water"
	CVC, VC	*fes*.ta "party," *es*.pelho "mirror"
	CCV, CCVC	*prato* "dish," *flor* "flower"
Latest	CVCC, VCC, CCVCC	*mons*.tro "monster," *ins*.trumento "instrument"
		trans.porte "transportation"

The *Sonority Sequencing Principle* (SSP) is widely accepted as a principle to explain the phonotactic organization of the segments that make up a syllable in terms of their inherent sonority.[5] According to the SSP, the nucleus constitutes the sonority peak of a syllable. Consonant sequences located in the syllable margins (onset and coda) are ordered in such a way that their sonority values rise in function of their proximity to the nucleus. The sonority value of vowels and consonants are determined by a sonority scale, for which a number of variants are found in the literature. For describing the global structure of the Portuguese syllable, the sonority scale proposed by Clements (2009) suffices, which distinguishes five degrees of sonority, corresponding to what are traditionally referred to as the major classes of segments. Clements proposes, moreover, that the sonority value for a given segment is obtained by adding up the positive specifications of the binary major class features that together define the major sound classe to which the segment belongs, as shown below:

Sonority scale for major sound classes

	Obstruents p, t, k, b, d, g, f, s, ʃ, v, z, ʒ	Nasal Cons. m, n, ɲ	Liquids l, ʎ, R	Glides j, w	Vowels i, e, ɛ, a, ɔ, o, u
"syllabic"[6]	–	–	–	–	+
vocoid	–	–	–	+	+
approximant	–	–	+	+	+
sonorant	–	+	+	+	+
relative sonority	0	1	2	3	4

According to the classification above, vowels are most sonorant (= 4), then glides (= 3), liquids (= 2), nasals (= 1), and the obstruents (= 0) are least sonorant. The SSP interacts with language-specific restrictions to define the phonotactic structure of a given language. As in most languages, in Portuguese, segment sequences with the same sonority value (sonority plateaus) are not allowed inside the same syllable constituent. Consequently, in BP, borrowings such as *pterodátilo* "pterodactyl" or *mnemônico* "mnemonic," are adapted to comply with the syllable structure of the language by the creation of a supplementary syllable peak realized as [i]: *p*[i]*terodátilo*, *m*[i]*nemônico*.

2.1. *The structure of the onset*

In Portuguese, most consonantal segments and glides may be onsets. Some restrictions exist on the occurrence of word-initial consonants and glides. For example, the contrast between "weak R" and "strong R" only exist intervocalically in Portuguese (ca[ɾ]o "expensive," ca[x]o "car"). Word-initially, only "strong R" is found: ['xa.tu] "rat." Word-initial palatal lateral and nasal consonants /ʎ, ɲ/ are extremely rare, some examples being *nhô, nhá*, which are reduced forms of *sinhô, sinhá* "master," "mistress," regionally and in popular variants pronounced as [jõ], [jã], or the clitic pronoun *lhe*, "him/her," typically pronounced as [li]. Word-initially, high vowels usually maintain their status as a syllable nucleus (*hiato* [i.'atu] "hiatus"), whereas between vowels word-internally they are syllabified as onsets: *tuiuiu* [tuju'ju], *cauauá* [kawa'wa] "black-necked stork" (both).

There are severe restrictions on the way segments are combined to form complex onsets. A complex onset may consist of maximally two segments, of which the second can only be one of the liquids /l/ or /ɾ/.[7] A further restriction requires that the first segment be a member of the obstruent class, either a plosive or a labiodental fricative. The voiced labiodental fricative /v/ only, and rarely, occurs in complex onsets inside the word and only allows /ɾ/ in second position.[8] The sequence /dl/ is disallowed as a complex onset, while /tl/ is very sporadic, occurring in the words *atlas* "atlas," *atleta* "athlete" and their derivatives, among few others. Less rare but not very frequent is the onset /dr/.[9] Complex onsets are often subject to simplification in popular speech, as in ['kwa.tu] *quatro* "four," ['pɔ.bi], *pobre* "poor," *exemplo* [e'zẽᵐpu]. Deletion of the sonorant consonant happens more often in unstressed than in stressed syllables, which may be related to the higher prosodic prominence of the latter.

In terms of the sonority scale presented in the table above, we may define grammatical onsets in Portuguese as combinations of segments belonging to the sonority classes 0 and 2, in that order.

In addition to fixing the width of the sonority intervals between elements of complex onsets and codas, languages may impose phonotactic restrictions of a different nature. For reasons of articulation or perception, some sequences are more frequent than others across languages. Portuguese shares with many languages the dislike for /dl/ and /tl/ clusters, which have identical place and manner features, [coronal] and [– continuant]. In BP, coronal fricatives /s, z, ʃ, ʒ/ may not function as the first member of a complex onset. This general ban on /sC/[10] onsets can be explained taking into account that /sObstruent/ represents a sonority plateau, /sNasal/ does not respect the sonority interval required between members of a complex onset, and the /sLiquid/ clusters share [coronal] place in /sl/ and [coronal] and [+continuant] in /sr/.

Words borrowed into BP that start with an /sC/ cluster in the original language are repaired by epenthesis, as in [is.'pa] Eng. "spa," [is'mɔkĩ] Eng. "smoking jacket, tuxedo." In some cases, two variants can be heard: /is.'lajd/ or /si.'lajd/ Eng. "slide" (Freitas, 1992). If we sidestep the fact that /tl/ and /vr/ exist word-internally in a few words and ignore the very rare instances of /vl/, we can define the grammatical onsets of Portuguese globally as in (2a) below.[11]

(2)

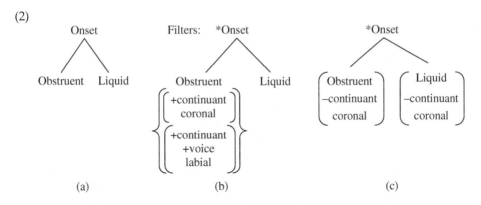

      (a)   (b)   (c)

The special filter (2b) disqualifies complex onsets that have either a coronal fricative /z, s, ʒ, ʃ/ or a labiodental voiced fricative as their left member, leaving /fr/ and /fl/ as the only grammatical fricative-initial complex onsets of Portuguese. Additionally, the filter (2c) excepts /dl/ and /tl/ from the set of possible complex onsets.

2.2. The structure of the rhyme

The Portuguese syllable rhyme contains no more than two positions, except for /S/, which can be added as a third element. We will refer to this as the Maximal Rhyme Constraint (MRC). Besides the vowels that occupy the nuclear position, the segments that may integrate the rhyme are the sonorant consonants /ɾ/, /l/, /N/ and the glides [j, w].[12] There is a consensus among phonologists of Portuguese that a consonant belonging to the syllable rhyme is located in the coda, as opposed to the nucleus. In Portuguese, vowels combine freely with glides to form falling diphthongs: *pai* (['paj] "father," *peito* ['pej.tu] "chest," *pau* ['paw] "stick," *feudo* ['few.du] "feud," etc.[13] Phonologists disagree about whether a falling diphthong must be modeled as a complex nucleus or whether the glide is located in the syllable coda. Below, we will argue in favor of the latter position.

In the structure of the syllable proposed in (1) it was assumed that segments that are located in the syllable rhyme are dominated by the nucleus and coda nodes through an intermediate mora constituent. Moras are weight units, which provide a formal expression for the notion of syllable weight (Hyman 1985, Hayes 1989). Many languages make a distinction between heavy (two moras) and light (one mora) syllables for the sake of main stress allocation. In these languages heavy syllables attract stress, whereas light syllables do not. In the great majority of cases, onset consonants do not contribute to syllable weight, which is the reason why they are not moraic. It has been claimed by many that only languages with a durational contrast in vowels can have weight-sensitive stress. Latin is a well-known example. In Latin, vowel length is contrastive (*mălum* "misfortune" vs. *mālum* "apple"). Syllables with long vowels, diphthongs, or closed syllables are heavy. The penultimate syllable receives the main stress if it is heavy, otherwise stress goes on the antepenult syllable. Stress is never on a word-final syllable, which does not count for the sake of stress assignment and is called "extrametrical." The following words illustrate the Latin Stress rule. In the first two words, the prefinal syllable is light, hence stress is on the antepenult. In the last two words, the prefinal syllable carries the word stress for being heavy.

(3) 'anĭma   "soul"
     'arbŏrem   "tree-acc."
     pe'dester   "on foot"
     for'tūna   "fortune"

Despite the recurrent claim that phonological vowel length is a necessary condition for weight-sensitive stress, it appears that a considerable number of languages that distinguish between light and heavy syllables do not have a length contrast for vowels (cf. Goedemans, 2010, p. 659). For the stress rule of Portuguese, a language without contrastive vowel length, diphthongs and syllables closed by a consonant count as heavy, while open syllables are light, as is by now believed by most scholars, at least for BP (Wetzels, 1992, 2007: Bisol, 1992; Magalhães, 2004; Massini-Cagliari, 2005). For most lexical words that are not verbs, word-final heavy syllables attract stress, otherwise stress goes on the prefinal syllable: ca'nal "canal" vs. bo'nito "pretty." Newly created non-derived words follow this rule (cf. Hermans and Wetzels, 2012). The main stress rule of Modern BP thus functions similar to the Latin stress rule, without generalized final extrametricality.

The distinction between light and heavy syllables is also crucial for a rule known as Spondaic Lowering, which neutralizes the contrast between upper and lower mid-vowels in prefinal stressed syllables in words with final heavy syllables:

(4) Vl#   'm[ɔ]vel   "mobile"   pro'j[ɛ]til   "projectile"
     Vr#   'd[ɔ]lar   "dollar"   'C[ɛ]sar   "Caesar"
     Vs#   'D[ɔ]ris   "Doris"   'f[ɛ]zes   "feces"
     VG#   'j[ɔ]quei   "jockey"   'j[ɛ]rsei   "jersey"
     ṼG#   's[ɔ]tão   "loft"   'm[ɛ]dão   "sand dune"
     VN#   '[ɔ]rfã   "orphan girl"   e'l[ɛ]tron   "electron"

Observe that the mid-vowel opposition is not neutralized in words with prefinal stress that end in a light syllable: 'r[ɛ]to "straight," 'c[e]do "early," 'm[ɛ]ta "aim," 'm[e]sa "table," 'c[ɔ]sta "coast" 'm[o]sca "housefly," 'f[ɛ]sta "party," 'b[e]sta "beast."

For EP, the question whether main stress assignment is conditioned by syllable weight is subject to disagreement.[14]

A particular problem related to the structure of the rhyme concerns the phonotactic distribution of the palatal sonorants /ɲ, ʎ/. It appears that palatal sonorants tolerate only light nuclei to their left. Observe that in the examples given in (5), heavy rhymes freely occur to the left of /m, n, l/, but not before /ɲ, ʎ/:

(5) ar.ma   "weapon"   ador.no   "ornament"   *Vr.ñV
     abis.mo   "abyss"   cis.ne   "swan"   *Vs.ñV
     tei.moso   "stubborn"   rei.no   "kingdom"   *ei.ñV

     or.la   "border"   *Vr.ʎV
     es.linga   "sling"   *Vs.ʎV
     lei.lão   "auction"   *ei.ʎV

The sequences marked as ungrammatical in (5) above, not only do not occur in Portuguese, they also sound odd to native speakers. To account for the asymmetry in the distribution of plain and palatal sonorants, it was proposed in Wetzels (1997, 2000b) that palatal sonorants add weight to the preceding syllable, i.e. they are moraic. It was also suggested that the ambisyllabic nature of palatal sonorants is due to their complex articulation, realizing a consonantal and a vocalic place node[15] represented as in (6) below, in line with Clements and Hume (1995).[16]

(6)

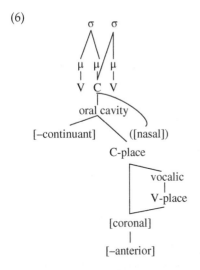

In (6), palatal sonorants are represented as ambisyllabic consonants that add weight to the left syllable. This being the case, these consonants occupy the only non-nuclear rhyme position available in that syllable, which explains the non-occurrence of heavy rhymes before this consonant type.

The hypothesis that palatal sonorants are moraic not only explains why a preceding rhyme cannot be heavy, but also why there are no words of the type 'VCV{ʎ,ɲ}V (type *máconha "marihuana") with antepenult stress,[17] or why palatal sonorants only occur intervocalically, and, crucially, why words that contain a sequence V[V+high] preceding {ʎ,ɲ} must be syllabified with an obligatory hiatus: ra.'inha "queen," mo.'inho "mill," fa.'ulha "fine dust." Since the Portuguese rhyme has only two positions available, it cannot integrate a sequence V[V+high] into the rhyme that already contains part of a palatal sonorant.

Whereas palatal sonorants disallow heavy rhymes to their left, nasal vowels[18] differ from oral vowels for not allowing tautosyllabic consonants to their right, except /S/. This fact strongly suggests that nasal vowels occupy two positions in the rhyme. Indeed, nasal vowels behave like heavy syllables with regard to the rules of the grammar that distinguish between light and heavy syllables. Word-finally, nasal vowels usually attract word stress: *cupim* [kuˈpĩ(ɲ)] "termite," *jejum* [ʒeˈʒũ] "fasting," *armazém*[19] [axmaˈzẽ(j̃)] "storeroom," *cupom* [kuˈpõ(w)] "coupon," *maçã* [maˈsẽ] "apple." Also, newly created words ending in a nasal vowel are stress-final: acronyms *ABRALIN, PROCOM*; fantasy first names like *Edum, Froin*; brand names for industrial products *Fenaren, Ponstan*.[20] Words with a nasal vowel in the prefinal syllable never have stress on the antepenultimate syllable. Words ending in a nasal vowel that are exceptions to the stress rule are subjected to Spondaic Lowering, including loans: ˈpr[ɔ]ton "proton," ˈ[ɔ]rfã "orphan girl," ˈd[ɔ]ping, "doping," etc. Expectedly, sequences of an oral vowel and a nasal vowel are always analyzed as heterosyllabic sequences, also when the nasal vowel is high, as in *amendo.ˈim* "peanut" *pa.ˈinço* "variety of millet," *a.ˈinda* "still," whereas similar sequences of oral vowels are realized as mono-syllabic diphthongs: *doi* [dɔj] "hurts-3sg.pr.ind.," *pai(s)* [paj(s)] "father/parents."

Portuguese has a limited number of nasal diphthongs. Only three occur in the non-derived vocabulary: [ẽw̃, ẽj̃, ũj̃]. Of these, only [ẽw̃] is relatively frequent, but only word-finally. A unique instance of the high diphthong [ũj̃] is found in the word *muito* "much." Word-finally, [ẽj̃] occurs exclusively in *mãe* "mother." A handful of words show word-internal [ẽj̃]:

(7) cãimbra   [kẽj̃bra]   "cramp"
     cãibro   [kẽj̃bru]   "pair of corn cobs"
     zãibo   [zẽj̃bu]   "squint-eyed"

Words which end in a nasal diphthong usually have stress on their final syllable, demonstrating that nasal diphthongs represent heavy syllables. As expected, nasal diphthongs do not occur in syllables closed by a consonant other than /S/: *pães* "loaves (of bread)." Very few words ending in [ẽw̃] show irregular penultimate stress, some of which are given in (8) below.

(8) *órfão*   "orphan boy"   *médão*   "dune"
     lódão   "lotus"   *orégão*   "oregano"
     acórdão "sentence"   *cédrão*   "cedar-tree"
     sótão   "attic"   *zângão*   "bumblebee"

As expected, the words in (8) undergo Spondaic Lowering, when applicable.

The phonological representation of nasal diphthongs is a thorny issue, especially against the background of the prevailing opinion that nasal vowels are derived from tautosyllabic VN sequences. This hypothesis entails that nasality is not contrastive for vowels at the lexical level. In accordance with this hypothesis, Câmara Jr. (1971: 33) proposed that nasal diphthongs derive from an oral diphthong followed by a nasal archiphoneme: /muiNto/ "much." Despite its uniform way of representing the source of surface nasality for vowels and diphthongs, the proposal is problematic, considering the fact that the Portuguese rhyme is bipositional. Regular syllabification would create a sequence of an oral vowel followed by a nasal vowel from underlying /ViN/, as shown above. The grammar consequently cannot distinguish between words like *ruim* [xu.ˈĩ] "bad," *ainda* [a.ˈĩda] "still," etc. with a nasal vowel, and *muito* [ˈmũj̃.tu] "much," *cãimbra* [ˈkẽj̃.bra] "cramp," etc. with a nasal diphthong. Without the use of some arbitrary lexical marking, both structures cannot be derived from the lexical sequence /ViN/. Foreign names like *Brown* [brawn] and *Einstein* [ˈæjn.stæjn], which are pronounced by native speakers of BP as [bɾaw] and [ajs.ˈtaj] with the nasal consonant being deleted, testify to the fact that /N/, when part of a sequence /VGlideN/, cannot be integrated into the Portuguese rhyme. For these and other reasons it was proposed in Wetzels (1997) that invariable nasal diphthongs[21] derive from a lexical sequence of an oral vowel followed by a high nasal vowel: *muito* / muĩto/ "much" or *irmão* / irmaũ/ "brother," the latter being consequently classified as athematic.[22]

2.3. The structure of the coda

Above we have seen examples of how clusters are broken up in illicit BP onsets: *pneu* [piˈnew] "tire," *mnemônico* [mineˈmõniku] "mnemonic," *psicologia* [ˌpisiˌkoloˈʒia] "psychology." In BP, the same strategy of vowel epenthesis is used to parse consonants as onsets that are not allowed or do not fit in the syllable coda. Word-internal examples are: *ob[i]ter* "obtain," *cap[i] tar* "pick up, *compac[i]to* "compact," *ob[i]séquio* "favor," *fic[i]ção* "fiction," *hip[i]nose* "hypnosis," *at[i]mosfera* "atmosphere," *pig[i]meu* "pygmy," *af[i]ta* "cold sore." Word-finally, epenthesis is also productive[23] when the postnuclear coda segment of the source language does not belong to the set of licensed codas in Portuguese, as can be seen in borrowings: Eng. "top" [ˈtɔpi], Eng. "staff" [isˈtɛfi], Eng. "club" [ˈklubi], or when the rhyme in the source language comprises three segments of which the third segment is not /S/: Eng. "surf" [ˈsuxfi], Eng. "sport" [isˈpɔxtʃi], Eng. "clown" [ˈklawni], Eng. "drink" [ˈdɾĩki], but Dutch "Hans, proper name" [ɛ̃s]. Words ending in obstruent stop plus /S/ are treated similarly: *tórax* [ˈtɔrakʲs], *hélix*, [ˈɛlikʲs], *índex* [ˈĩdekʲs]. Epenthesis occurs variably in all speech styles, although in formal registers the epenthetic vowel maybe very short and is more often absent. When the newly created syllable immediately follows the stress, the epenthetic vowel is usually more perceptible: *duplex* [duˈplɛkis] "duplex," *inox* [iˈnɔkis] "inox," *plets* [ˈplɛtʃis] "chewing gum, brand," but even here, it may not be realized. Words with three postnuclear segments, like *aids* either contain the epenthetic [i], or, without [i], /s/ functions as the syllable nucleus: [ˈaj.dʒis] ~ [ˈaj.dʒs].

When the epenthetic vowel is not realized itself, it may show its (intended) presence indirectly, by blocking or triggering phonological processes. For example, assimilatory coda devoicing does not occur in words like *observa*: [o.biˈ.sɛɾ.va] or [ob.ˈsɛɾ.va], not *[ob̪.ˈsɛrva] "observe-3sg.pr.ind.," where at least partial devoicing is expected. Palatalization of /t,d/ before /i/ is a productive process in large areas of Brazil and also affects coronal stops before epenthetic [i]: *étnico* [ˈɛ.tʃ⁽ⁱ⁾.ni.ku] "ethnic," *advogado* [a.dʒ⁽ⁱ⁾.vo.ˈga.du] "lawyer." In these words, palatalization is obligatory, although the epenthetic vowel may not be audible. The epenthetic vowel is not recorded in the official spelling, but spelling mistakes are regularly encountered, as in *seguimento* for *segmento* "segment," *obituração* for *obturação* "obturation," *adivogado* for *advogado* "lawyer," etc.

Although the Portuguese rhyme may comprise up to three positions, three-segment rhymes are rather infrequent. They mostly consist of a diphthong followed by /S/: *fausto* "luxury," *pães* "loaves (of bread)," *cais* "dock." Syllables with a nasal or a liquid followed by /S/ in the coda are restricted to a very small set of words. In BP colloquial speech, complex codas consisting of the rhotic followed by /S/ tend to be simplified by deletion of one of the consonants: *perspectiva* [pes.pe.ki.ˈtʃi.va] "perspective, *superstição* [su.pex.tʃi.ˈsẽw] "superstition." The intolerance for this cluster can be explained by the fact that the rhotic is often realized as a velar or uvular fricative and thus forms a sonority plateau with /s/, in violation of the SSP.

We have seen that sonorant and nonsonorant consonants behave very differently as regards their affiliation to the rhyme constituent. One clearly must distinguish between sonorant segments and /S/, which are obligatorily syllabified in the syllable coda, and nonsonorant consonants, which are only reluctantly tolerated as codas, and with a clear preference for the onset position. Different ways of accounting for this divergent behavior can be envisioned, depending on the theoretical framework adopted.[24] We will here take the position that nonsonorant consonants that are either word-final or the first member of an intervocalic cluster that is not allowed to function as an onset, are optionally syllabified either as codas or as onsets of a newly created syllable. On the other hand, the MRC is always respected: independently of the major class membership of a given phoneme, there are only two positions available in the rhyme, with the proviso that a third position is available exclusively for /S/.

In the structure provided in (9), the consonants that are obligatorily integrated in the syllable rhyme are associated with the coda node by means of a solid association line, whereas the non-sonorants stops and /f/, which are only optionally integrated, are associated with a dotted association line.

(9)

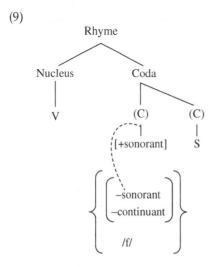

In this representation, we have opted for a representation of the rhyme with a non-complex nucleus. This means that sonorant consonants and /S/, but also glides, are considered coda segments. Our reasons are that falling diphthongs and syllables closed by a consonant act together as a conditioning context for generalizations that refer to the difference between light and heavy syllables, because they are united in allowing only /S/ as a third element in the rhyme, and because otherwise no difference in the behavior between glides and permissible coda consonants was found that would suggest a different syllable affiliation for these sound classes.

Besides /s/, the set of segments that is obligatorily syllabified in the syllable coda are sonorants: glides and sonorant consonants. For the latter class, the place of articulation can be predicted from their major category and manner features, which allows a partially specified representation of these sounds before consonants and morpheme-finally. We will see below that this may be the right representation for nasal consonants. The only non-sonorant consonant is the coronal fricative /S/, which realizes the unmarked place feature [coronal]. For oral and nasal diphthongs, the place specification of the glide is contrastive: *pai* "father," *mau* "bad," *pão* "stick," *mãe* "mother."

(10)　/l/:　[–vocoid, +approximant, **+ sonorant**, – continuant]
　　　/R/:　[–vocoid, +approximant, **+sonorant**, + continuant]
　　　/N/:　[–vocoid, – approximant, **+sonorant**, +nasal]
　　　/S/:　[–vocoid, – approximant, **– sonorant**, + continuant]

Particularly for EP speakers, the lexically distinctive features of the final segments in the words below remain unaltered in their surface representation, except for /N/, which most frequently surfaces as a vocoid.[25] In Brazil, a great amount of variation exists for all the non-vocoid codas, regionally, but also within a given speech community and within the speech of a single individual, as is illustrated for word-final stressed syllables with the following examples:

(11)

			Brazil	Portugal
ane/l/	"ring"		[ɫ] (Southern states) [**w**]	[ɫ]
ma/R/	"see"	→	[ɾ], [x], [**h**], [**ø**] Brazil	[ɾ]
marf/iN/	"ivory"	→	[ĩ], [ĩj̃], [ĩɲ]	
jej/uN/	"fasting"	→	[ũ], [ũw̃],[ũŋ]	
armaz/eN/	"storehouse"	→	[ẽ], [ẽj̃], [ẽɲ]	
edred/oN/	"eider quilt"	→	[õ], [õw̃], [õŋ]	
irm/aN/	"sister	→	[ã], [ãŋ]	
rapa/S/	"boy"	→	[s], [ⁱs], [ʃ], [**h**], [**ø**]	[ʃ]

Despite the great variation in the way underlying /VN/ sequences are pronounced, their phonetic realization is always predictable. When the phonetic output of the /VN/ sequence ends in an approximant or a consonantal constriction, the place features are always parasitic on the place features of the preceding vowel.[26] The impossibility of realizing an independent place feature for coda /N/ can also be observed in the process of borrowing. In loans containing a syllable-final [VN], normally the original place features are lost and, depending on the quality of the preceding vowel, the [VN] sequence is realized as in (11) above. For the original place features to be preserved, the nasal consonant of the borrowed word must be parsed as an onset: Eng. "Kremlin" ˈ*Krem*[i]*lin*, Eng. "dancing" [ˈdẽsĩ] or [ˈdẽsĩ⁽ⁱ⁾gi], Eng. "doping" [ˈdɔpĩ], Eng. *gin* [ʒĩ], Eng. "Ben, proper name" [bẽ]. When the nasal consonant is the third element in the rhyme in the source language ([VCN]), it is usually preserved as an onset, as in Eng. "clown" [ˈklawni], Eng. "film" [ˈfiwmi], Eng. "western" [uˈɛstex] or [uˈɛstexni].[27] Since epenthesis seems to be the preferred option to integrate word-final [VCN] sequences in BP phonotactics, the alternative form [uˈɛstex] next to [uˈɛstexni] may be explained by the fact that [x.n] makes a bad syllable contact (see Section (2.4) below).

In (11) above the "weakest" BP realizations of the underlying coda consonants are printed in boldface. The realization of coda /l/ as [w] is almost general in Brazil and syllable-final debuccalization ([h]) or full deletion are widespread realizations of syllable-final/R/. Syllable-final /S/ is more resistant, especially when word-final, probably because of its semantic function as the exponent of plurality. Yet, in popular varieties, final [h], zero, or [j] (through intermediate [ⁱs], as in *rapaz* [xaˈpaⁱs] > [xaˈpaj] "boy") are often encountered. If the view that the popular variants of a language represent its future norm is correct, the conclusion is justified that the BP variant of Portuguese is developing towards an almost C(L)V language, with glides as the only possible codas, which are, at the same time, the ideal codas from the point of view of the SSP.

2.4. How EP is different

The systematic resort to vowel epenthesis to avoid illicit onsets and codas is typical for the BP variant of Portuguese. In EP, onset clusters that do not respect the minimal sonority difference established above for BP, including sonority plateaus, are not unusual. Similarly, word-internal sequences occur that do not fit with the canonical syllable structure previously established for BP. In general, while a large part of the phonology of BP conspires to create open syllables, in EP closed syllables are more tolerated. Also, relatively large consonant sequences can be created through the deletion of unstressed vowels. The examples below, as well as all others presented in this section, are from Mateus and d'Andrade (2000).

(12a) Non-alternating consonant clusters

[ps]icologia	"psychology	a[bs]urdo	"absurd"
[pt]ério	"pterion"	a[dk]uirir	"acquire"
[pn]eu	"tire"	a[pn]eia	"apnea"
[gn]omo	"gnome"	dia[gn]ose	"diagnosis"

(12b) Consonant clusters created by variable vowel deletion

pequeno	[pkénu]	"small"
decifrar	[dsifráɾ]	"decipher"
meter	[mteɾ]	"put"
devedor	[dvdóɾ]	"debtor"
despregar	[dʃpɾgáɾ]	"unfasten"
empedernir	[ẽpdɾnír]	"petrify"

The prosthetic vowel that is obligatory in word-initial ##sC clusters in BP is dispensed with in EP:

(13) | *espaço* | [ʃpásu] | "space" |
|---|---|---|
| *esfinge* | [ʃfĩʒ] | "sphynx" |
| *esbirro* | [ʒbiʁu] | "constable" |
| *esmagar* | [ʒmɐgáɾ] | "crush" |

In their account of these facts, Mateus and d'Andrade (2000) distinguish between the words in (12a) and (13), in which evidence for an underlying vowel is lacking, and the ones in (12b), for which such evidence exists. The authors hypothesize that "base syllabification" (2000: 46) in EP is identical with the one established above for BP, except that, where BP inserts an epenthetic vowel to avoid illicit affiliations of consonants with subsyllabic constituents, EP creates an empty syllable. On the other hand, the consonant clusters in (12b) are derived by rules of unstressed vowel deletion which create surface exceptions to the constraints of core syllabification.

According to Mateus and d'Andrade, a number of observations are indicative for the existence of empty nuclei in EP: 1. EP speakers hesitate between hetero- and tautosyllabic parsing of intervocalic consonant clusters (*a-dmirar* vs. *ad-mirar* "admire"), 2. Portuguese children apply the BP strategy to insert an epenthetic vowel (*p[ɨ]neu* "tire," *af[ɨ]ta* "aphtha"), 3. except for preconsonantal /s/, voice assimilation between consonants in intervocalic clusters does not occur (*a[bs]urdo* "absurd"), 4. The empty vowels created in EP correspond with the epenthetic vowels of BP.

The fact that there is variation in the way EP speakers treat intervocalic consonants clusters shows that there is an aversion to the affiliation of non-sonorant consonants with the syllable coda also in this variant. This provides evidence for the same distinction made between obligatory and optional coda affiliation for BP in (9) above. However, instead of positing empty nuclei,[28] it would be possible to assume that unsyllabifiable segments remain unaffiliated until a point in the grammar where the constraints of core syllabification are loosened. In BP, the choices available for the syllabification of word-internal nonsonorant consonants is either as an onset (if necessary through the creation of a new syllable and in compliance with the established core syllabification principles) or as a coda (against the constraints of core syllabification). In EP, both available strategies go against the constraints of core syllabification, one of which is the creation of an illicit coda and the other of which involves a complex onset that violates the maximal distance requirement for onsets. It is not made explicit in Matues and d'Andrade (2000) for which type of intervocalic clusters more than one syllabification option is available in EP.

2.5. *Syllable contact*

The role of sonority can also be seen in heterosyllabic segment sequences. As was observed by Hooper (1976: 220), heterosyllabic segment sequences $s_1)_{\sigma\sigma}(s_2$ are preferred cross-linguistically in proportion to the extent that s_1 has a higher sonority degree than s_2 (Syllable Contact Law). The higher the difference in the degree of sonority between the first and the second segment, the more harmonic is the syllable transition. In Portuguese, with a preponderance of sonorant codas, the following syllable contacts are theoretically possible:

(14) Glide. Glide/Liquid/Nasal/Obstruent

*aw.ja, *aj.wa				$s_1\text{-}s_2 = 0$
bai.lar	"dance"	penei.rar	"sift"	$s_1\text{-}s_2 = 1$
fleu.ma	"apathy"	boi.na	"beret"	$s_1\text{-}s_2 = 2$
pei.to	"breast"	pou.co	"little"	$s_1\text{-}s_2 = 3$

(15) Liquid. Glide/Liquid/Nasal/Obstruent

*al.ja, *al.wa, *ar.ja, *ar.wa				$s_1\text{-}s_2 = -1$
or.la		"border"	guel.ra "gill"	$s_1\text{-}s_2 = 0$
ol.mo		"elm"	car.ne "meat"	$s_1\text{-}s_2 = 1$
or.dem		"order"	al.to "high"	$s_1\text{-}s_2 = 2$

(16) Nasal. Glide/Liquid/Nasal/Obstruent

*an.ja, *an.wa				$s_1\text{-}s_2 = -2$
Fin.landia	"Finland"	hon.ra	"honor"	$s_1\text{-}s_2 = -1$
*an.ma, *am.na				$s_1\text{-}s_2 = 0$
on.da	"wave"	on.ça	"snake"	$s_1\text{-}s_2 = 1$

(17) /S/. Glide/Liquid/Nasal/Obstruent

*as.ja, *as.wa				$s_1\text{-}s_2 = -3$
legis.lar	"legislate"	Is.rael	"Israel"	$s_1\text{-}s_2 = -2$
as.no	"donkey"	cos.mo	"cosmos"	$s_1\text{-}s_2 = -1$
as.tro	"star"	es.belto	"slender	$s_1\text{-}s_2 = 0$

The optional syllabification of non-sonorant coda consonants set aside, almost all the logically possible syllable contacts are attested in Portuguese. In addition to the heterosyllabic sequence of nasal consonants, the only sequences that are systematically absent are the ones in which s_2 represents a glide. In a sequence of a consonant plus a high vowel, the high vowel tends to be syllabified as a nucleus (*tapi.'oca* , **tap.'joca* "tapioca") or, in more rapid speech, it may function as the second member of a complex onset (*ta.'[pj]oca*). In sequences of high vowels the creation of word-internal codas is avoided: *tuiuiu* "bird spec." is pronounced [tuju'ju], not *[tuj.'wiw] or *[tuj.wi'u].[29] Of the remaining syllable transitions, which are all attested in the native vocabulary, there is a very significant difference in the frequency of occurrence between bad and good syllable contacts in the way predicted by the Syllable Contact Law. If the coda contains a sonorant segment, only the syllable contacts for which s_1 minus $s_2 \geq 1$ are frequent. If the coda is /S/, the more frequent transitions obey the requirement that s_1 minus $s_2 \geq -1$.

Heterosyllabic sequences that are not allowed or are infrequent may be created by processes of word formation. In Portuguese, especially prefixation and compounding may produce syllable transitions that are otherwise disfavored in the language: *enredar* "entangle" (en–$_{Prefix}$ + red$_{Stem}$ + –ar$_{Suffix}$), *enlouquecer* "to go mad" (en–$_{Prefix}$ + louqu$_{Stem}$ + –ecer$_{Suffix}$), *bem-remunerado* "well paid." This points to the fact that the syllable contact requirements only hold inside the phonological word (cf. Schwindt, 2004).

3. Syllable structure and syllabification

With the recognition of the syllable as a unit of prosodic structure, the question of how languages parse sequences of phonological segments into syllables becomes important. The general absence of cross-linguistic syllabification contrasts combined with the generative grammar view of the lexicon as the depository of morphemes devoid of their predictable properties has motivated the decision that syllable structure is not encoded in the lexical representation of morphemes. Consequently, interpretive theories must make explicit how the underlying phonological sequences are syllabified. In the recent history of phonological theory three main views on how syllable structure is derived can be distinguished: (1) syllable structure is built by ordered rules (Kahn, 1976; Clements and Keyser, 1983; Harris 1983, among others), (2) syllable structure is assigned to a string by a mapping procedure which obeys universal principles and language particular conditions (Selkirk, 1982; Ito, 1986, among others), and (3) different syllable structures result from different typologies that emerge from language-particular rankings of universal but violable constraints.

Studies which have sought to determine the principles of syllabification for Portuguese in a derivational model are Mateus and d'Andrade (2000) and Bisol (1999), among others. Collischonn (1997) deals with the syllable structure of BP following Ito's templatic approach. Lee (1999) provides a preliminary analysis of Portuguese syllabification based on universal constraints within Optimality Theory (OT). Keller and Alves (2010) discuss from a more general perspective the advantages of the way OT accounts for syllable structure cross-linguistically, with an eye on Portuguese. In the following we provide a broad outline of how the different approaches account for the basic syllable structure of Portuguese and how the Brazilian variety resolves illicit phonotactic structures through epenthesis.

In Bisol (1999), a set of ordered rules is proposed by which sequences of segments are parsed into syllables. The first rule designates vowels as the syllable nuclei. Subsequently, by virtue of the Onset First Principle (OFP), consonants to the left of a nucleus are turned into onsets in accordance with the *Basic Syllable Template* (BST) of Portuguese, similar to the template-cum-filters model proposed in (9) above. Finally, the remaining segments are integrated as codas, again in conformity with the BST, which, in Bisol's proposal, provides for a single coda position. When /s/ remains unparsed after onsets and codas are syllabified, a separate

/s/-adjunction rule associates this consonant as a second coda segment. The procedure is illustrated below with the word *claustro* ['klaws.tru] "cloister."

(18)

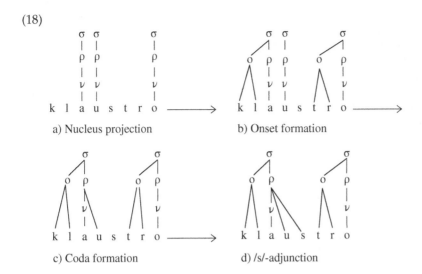

In (18a) every vowel projects a nucleus, which automatically involves the projection of the rhyme and syllable nodes. Subsequently, consonants to the left of the nucleus are integrated iteratively into the syllable as onsets to the extent allowed by the BST. In Bisol (1999), every vowel present in the string is identified initially as a syllable nucleus. Since high vowels are allowed in the syllable coda, they lose their status as a nucleus in the process of coda formation, as is illustrated in (18c). Finally, in (18d), /s/-adjunction takes place.

In Bisol's proposal, syllabification obeys the Principle of Prosodic Licensing (PPL), formulated by Ito (1986), which requires all prosodic units of a given level to be parsed as constituents of the immediately dominating prosodic category. Consequently, all segments must be syllabified, or, when syllabification of some segment is not allowed by the rules of the language, some proviso must be made for the segment string to comply with the PPL. If the stray segment is in the word-periphery, it can be given the status of an extrametrical segment, which may become integrated into the syllable structure in the course of word-formation (or postlexically, depending on the language). Other options involve the deletion of the unsyllabifiable segment or the creation of a new syllable nucleus with which the stray segment can be affiliated. It is equally possible, especially in models that allow different lexical strata or distinguish between a lexical and a postlexical stratum, to enlarge the set of segments that can be affiliated with a specific syllable constituent at a later level.

To conclude, in Bisol's proposal, the rules that construct syllable structure are governed by general principles, such as the OFP and the PPL, and language-specific rules and filters. These mechanisms have a dual function: they constrain the number and nature of syllable types in a given language and also call for repair mechanisms to deal with segments which the regular syllabification rules are not allowed to parse (at least at some early level of representation).

According to the view introduced in Selkirk (1982), syllabification is not constructed by ordered rules, but is an automatic process which complies with a number of general conditions. This idea is further elaborated in Ito (1986) within a "Principles and Parameters" perspective, in which syllable-building rules give way to generalizations of a more universal character. Ito proposes a model of syllabification as continuous template matching, governed by universal and language-specific syllable well-formedness conditions and a directionality parameter. The syllable template defines the global syllable pattern of a given language, whereas the directionality parameter establishes the direction (left-to right or right-to-left) in which the template is mapped upon the segmental string.

Inspired by Ito's proposal, Collischonn (1997) proposes for Portuguese the syllable template [CCVCC]. Each time a string of segments matches the template, a syllable is built. Segments that do not fit the syllabic template are left without a syllable affiliation. In a second scan, consonants that do not match with the syllabic template, as for example the word-internal /k/ in *cacto* "cactus" /$_\sigma$(ka)$_\sigma$k.$_\sigma$(to)$_\sigma$/, have an empty nucleus inserted at their right, thus allowing syllabic affiliation of these stray consonants as the onset of the newly created syllable. The empty nucleus is subsequently filled with a high front vowel: ['ka.ki.tu]. No specific epenthesis rule is needed. Below, the procedure is exemplified with the words *pneu* [pinew] "tire" and *escola* [eskɔla] "school," which show different epenthesis sites in BP.

(19)

In (19), the subscripts to the syllable symbols indicate the order in which the syllables are constructed. Since the directionality parameter is set as R→ L, segments are linked with the rightmost matching C and V positions of the template. When a syllable is built, the template shifts to the left and the procedure is repeated until the phoneme sequence is syllabified. This scanning of the phoneme sequence yields the parses $p_\sigma(neu)_\sigma$ and $s_\sigma(kɔ)_{\sigma\sigma}(la)_\sigma$.

In principle, the epenthesis site follows from the directionality parameter setting. In a R→ L setting, when the template encounters a consonant that has remained unsyllabified after the first scan, a nucleus is created to the left of the stray consonant, with which the latter forms a new syllable. This is illustrated with the word *escola*, in which the syllable 6_3 is the result of nucleus formation.[30] However, in the case of *pneu*, the empty nucleus is inserted to the right of the stray consonant, contrary to expectation. Collischonn accounts for this by observing that, as /p/ is not a possible coda consonant, a sequence *[ipneu] would not be a well-formed word in BP. Therefore, the template creates a nucleus to the right of the stray /p/.

As was shown in Selkirk's (1982) and Ito's (1986) approaches, syllabification can be achieved without language-specific rules, although (partly) language-specific templates and language specific filters or constraints remain necessary. As it turns out, filters and constraints that seem language-specific at first sight, turn out to be very similar cross-linguistically, such as the requirement on minimal sonority differences between members of complex onsets and complex codas, the avoidance of sequences with identical place and/or manner features, the relatively high sonority of coda consonants in languages in which not all consonants are permissible codas, etc. For these reasons, alongside the well-known fact that syllabification is at least partially governed by universal principles, it doesn't come as a surprise that Optimality Theory (OT) is rather successful in accounting for syllabification cross-linguistically. In OT, language-specific rules do not exist. Instead, universal markedness and faithfulness constraints interact to account for the surface shape of lexical morphemes in a given language. Faithfulness constraints militate for the preservation of a strict correspondence between bases and outputs, while markedness constraints enforce changes of the input representations in favor of unmarked segmental or phonotactic structures. Differences between languages are accounted for by different rankings of the universal constraints.

In OT, the focus changes from the procedures that generate syllable structure to the evaluation of competing syllable parsings of a given string. As any other adequate theory of syllabification, OT must account for what the syllable patterns of Portuguese are and what segments may occupy which positions. The basic syllable patterns of Portuguese are CV, CVC, V, VC, CCV, VCC, CCVC, CVCC, and CCVCC, where the postvocalic C represents a consonant or a glide. This means that syllables may or may not have onsets or codas, and onsets and codas may be complex. In OT these patterns can be derived by the interaction of the following constraints, of which (20 a, b) are markedness constraints and (20c, d) are faithfulness constraints:

(20) a. ONSET: Syllables must start with an onset
    b. *CODA: Syllables must end in a vowel
    c. *DEL(ETION) (MAX-IO): Input segments must have output correspondents
    d. *EP(ENTHESIS) (DEP-IO): Output segments must have input correspondents

Portuguese allows for syllables without onsets word-initially and word-internally. ONSET and *CODA require intervocalic consonants to be parsed as onsets, everything else being equal. However, to satisfy ONSET, at least in the partial grammar given in Table 6.1, in which *DEL and *EP are ranked above ONSET,[31] no segments may be added or deleted to avoid syllables without onsets.

The relation between the input sequence /atras/ and the output candidates (a–f) is determined by the functions GEN, which generates for every input an unlimited list of output candidates and EVAL, which evaluates the candidate set for the given constraint ranking. The optimal candidate is the most harmonic one, i.e. the one that violates the constraints minimally. Table 6.1 shows the relevant constraints at work to determine that, among the (limited) set of candidates considered here as outputs for the underlying sequence /atras/, the most harmonic candidate from the point of view of syllable structure is [a.tras].

In Portuguese, only two-consonant sequences can be analyzed as complex onsets. Moreover, of all the possible two-consonant sequences only a small subset qualifies as well-formed. Also, while only sonorant consonants and /s/ are acceptable in the syllable coda, the only possible complex coda is a sequence of a sonorant consonant followed by /s/. To account for these restrictions, the grammar must assign segments with specific properties to specific syllable constituents. One way of achieving this is to have constraints that relate syllable positions with major sound classes or their corresponding sonority values, as exposed in (9) above.

We have seen that two-consonant onsets maintain between their constituting members a minimal sonority distance of 2 on the sonority scale. The requirement of a minimal sonority distance of two grades on the sonority scale between the segments of a complex onset would at the same time account for the non-existence of three-consonant onsets in Portuguese, since

Table 6.1 Portuguese syllable structure (partial)

/atras/ "behind"	*DEL	*EP	Onset	*CODA
a. a.tras ☞			*	*
b. ta.tras		*!		*
c. tras	*!			*
d. a.tra	*!		*	
e. atr.as			**!	**
f. at.ras			*	**!

no sequence of consonants $C_1C_2C_3$ could be rising in sonority and at the same time maintain a sonority distance of minimally 2 between C_1C_2 and between C_2C_3. We therefore propose the constraint[32]

(21)   Minimum Sonority Distance$_{onset}$ (MSD$_{onset}$): in an onset sequence $C_1...C_n$, for every pair of contiguous consonants C_xC_y, the sonority value of C_y minus the sonority value of $C_x \geq 2$

In terms of the constraint (21) the sequence /pn/ in /pnew/ will have a sonority distance 1, whereas /fl/ as in /flor/ has a sonority distance 2. A sequence /rn/ has a sonority distance of -1. Consequently, of the examples given, only /fl/ is a well-formed onset of Portuguese.

We have seen earlier that when BP borrows words from another language with syllable patterns that are ill-formed from the perspective of BP, segments are not deleted in the borrowing process. Instead, new syllables are created through the epenthesis of a high vowel: [i]smith "Smith," p[i]sicologia "psychology," cap[i]tar "capture," club[i] "club." In the first three words, the sequences broken up by epenthesis are ill-formed onsets in Portuguese. Also, except for [i]smith, in none of the examples cited, the consonant that functions as the onset of the epenthesized nucleus would qualify as a well-formed coda. For this reason, the only way to bring a word like psicologia in line with BP phonotactics without deleting segments is to break up the cluster the way it is done, since the alternative [i]psicologia would contain an illicit coda. As it turns out, the epenthesis site can be predicted by the interaction of the MSD constraint, which disqualifies /ps, pt, sm, etc./ as grammatical onsets and a constraint that disallows obstruents in the syllable coda, except /s/. The constraint in (22) bans obstruents from the syllable coda:

(22)   *Obstruent$_{coda}$: Obstruents are not allowed in the syllable coda

The constraint above defines /s/ as a member of the set of illicit codas. Yet, we have seen that in Portuguese, sonorant consonants, glides and /s/ may close a syllable. Indeed, the inclusion of /s/ in the set of permissible codas is surprising, because /s/ does not constitute a natural class with glides and sonorant consonants in terms of its major category features. The coronal fricative is moreover exceptional for being the only segment allowed to form a complex coda. Considering the way a word-initial ##sC sequence is resolved, it is again surprising to see that it is different from the way other sequences with an identical sonority profile are treated, for example ##ps or ##pt. After all, Smith could be adapted as s[i]mith instead of [i]smith. Several ways are proposed in the literature to account for the deviant behavior of /s/, one of which is to separate /s/ from the class of obstruents and assign it a different place on the sonority scale. Here, we prefer to maintain the relative simplicity of the sonority scale provided above, which is fully adequate to account for Portuguese syllable structure, including the fact that ##sC clusters are treated as ill-formed onsets on a par with any combination of segments of the obstruent class, which fact suggests that /sC/ constitutes a sonority plateau. We propose instead the constraint below,[33] which gives /s/ the special status it appears to have:

(23)   Licence /s/$_{coda}$ (Lic/s/): /s/ must be syllabified in the syllable coda

As all constraints, Lic/s/ is violable and therefore /s/ can be forced into the syllable onset by a higher ranked constraint, such as ONSET. This is shown in Table 6.2, which also contains MSD:

In Table 6.2, a relevant candidate set corresponding with the underlying sequences is evaluated for the proposed constraint ranking. The high ranking of *DEL assures that deletion is not an option to enforce ONSET satisfaction, while the low ranking of *EP[34] turns this

Table 6.2

	MSD	*DEL	ONSET	Lic/s/	*Obstr_coda	*EP
/kasaR/ "hunt"						
a. ka.sar ☞				*		
b. kas.ar			*!		*	
/smis/ "Smith"						
a. is.mis ☞					* *	*
b. si.mis				*!	*	*
c. smis	*!			*	*	
d. mis		*!				
/kɔbra/ "snake"						
a. kɔ.bra ☞						
b. kɔb.ra					*!	
/psikoloʒia/ "psychology"						
a. pi.si.k... ☞				*		*
b. ip.si.k...				*	*!	*
c. psi.k...	*!			*		
d. si.k...		*!		*		
/kaptaR/ "capture"						
a. ka.pi.tar ☞					*	*
b. kap.tar					*!*	
c. ka.tar		*!			*	
d. ka.ptar	*!				*	
/klub/ "club"						
a. klu.bi ☞						*
b. klub					*!	
c. klu		*!				

constraint inefficient in the selection of the optimal candidate. Consequently, in order to satisfy the higher-ranked constraints, *EP is violated when necessary. The ranking ONSET >> Lic/s />> *Obstr_coda accounts for the typical behavior of /s/, which is syllabified as an onset only between vowels. Elsewhere /s/ will be affiliated to the syllable as a coda.

4. Conclusion

In this chapter we have characterized the Portuguese syllable focusing on the structures shared by both the EP and BP variants. We have shown that, for both variants, a major part of the syllable structure is identical and obligatory, which obeys the SSP as well as a number of specific constraints that account for the association of certain segment classes with specific syllable constituents. In both EP and BP, the MRC makes only two positions available in the rhyme, with /S/ being the only segment that can be added as a third element. Another part of the syllable structure is less categorical and offers options to the speakers, which are partially different for EP and BP. While for BP one of the options complies with the constraints of core syllabification, in EP both options violate the principles of core syllabification in different ways. Moreover, in EP, large scale unstressed vowel deletion creates strings of consonants allowing segments other than vowels, such as liquids and fricatives, to shift to the nuclear position giving way to a (partial) resyllabification of the segmental string at the phonetic level. Future research will likely reveal that this process follows in its own way the general preference of syllables for relatively high sonorant nuclei and for syllable margins to respect the sonority slopes as required by the SSP with reference to a more elaborate sonority scale than the one necessary for the core syllabification.

NOTES

1   Such as the *língua do pê* "p-language," very popular among youngsters in Brazil, which consists in adding the syllable [pe] before each syllable of a word. For example, *gato* "cat" becomes [pe.₍ga.pe.₍to].

2   See Chapters 4, A Comparative Study of the Sounds of European and Brazilian Portuguese: Phonemes and Allophones, and 28, Main Current Processes of Phonological Variation.

3   But see Chapter 5, Phonological Processes Affecting Vowels: Neutralization, Harmony, and Nasalization.

4   Similar findings for PE are reported in Vigário, Martins, and Frota (2006).

5   Or "resonance," according to Clements (2009): "The most resonant speech sounds are […] those with a prominent, relatively undamped formant structure. Sounds having this property include not only vowels, the resonants par excellence, but also semivowels, liquids and nasals…"

6   We leave open the question of how exactly the difference between the nuclear and the marginal position of high vowels is to be expressed theoretically.

7   The palatal lateral /ʎ/ does not appear in any kind of cluster, whether tautosyllabic or heterosyllabic.

8   There are some exceptions in proper nouns, such as Vladimir, which is moreover a loan.

9   The prohibition on /dl/ onsets and the rarity of /tl/ and /dr/ onsets are inherited from Latin (Cf. Marotta, 1999).

10   Here and below, /s/ in /sC/ represents the set of coronal fricatives.

11   The words we use to refer to the major sound classes in (2) are shorthand notations for their feature definitions provided in the sonority scale above.

12   The symbols /S/ and /N/ represent the coronal fricative and nasal consonant non-specified for voice and place of articulation when occurring in the syllable coda. In most dialects of BP, /l/ is vocalized syllable-finally. However, /l/ is nevertheless part of lexical representations to account [w] ~[l] alternations: *ane*[w] "ring," *anelar* "to curl," *anelão* "big ring," *aneleira* "ring case."

13   See Chapter 4 for details.

14   See Chapter 7 for details.

15   The representation in (6) represents a palatalized consonant rather than a palatal consonant. In his palatographic study on BP palatal consonants Cagliari (1974) observes: "Portuguese /ʎ/ is characterized by being central, very often tending towards [lʲj]," where [lʲj] represents a palatalized lateral followed by a coronal glide.

16   C in (6) represents a consonantal root node characterized by the appropriate major class specifications for the nasal and the liquid, as in the sonority scale above.

17   In Portuguese, a considerable number of words exists with antepenultimate stress, but only when the prefinal syllable is light.

18   BP has (surface) contrastive nasal vowels (*lombo* [lõbu] "sirloin" vs. *lobo* "wolf") and nasalized vowels *pino* [pĩnu] "pin." Here we refer to the former category. See also Chapters 4 and 5.

19   Although there are quite a few exceptions, especially among words ending in /eN/, many of which have a doublet without final /N/: *abdómen*/*abdome* "abdomen."

20   See Hermans and Wetzels (2012) for lists of acronyms, fantasy first names, and brand names.

21   There also exist phonetic nasal diphthongs, derived from nasal vowels, especially word-final /eN/ and /oN/, which can be realized optionally as [ẽj̃] and [õw̃], respectively.

22   Chapter 5 presents a different proposal for the underlying structure of (part of) BP nasal diphthongs.

23   Most of the following examples are taken from Freitas (1992).

24   See the discussion in Sections 2.4 and 3 for how non-sonorant coda consonants may be dealt with in different theories of the syllable.

25   See also Chapter 5.

26   In word-internal /VN/ sequences, the consonantal point of articulation can also be homorganic with the following consonant. See Chapter 4 for more details.

27   English loans are taken from Freitas (1992).

28   On the assumption that there is no alternation in EP between an empty nucleus and an epenthetic vowel in adult speech.

29   Heterosyllabic sequences of glides are occasionally found in the non-native vocabulary, as in Taiwan, or Wajwaj "Indigenous group."

30   Interestingly, as Collischonn (1997: 164, footnote 20) points out, when loans are borrowed into BP that start with a palatal fricative /ʃ/, the epenthetic vowel is inserted to the right, as in the names *Schmidt* and *Schneider*, from German origin: [ʃi]*midt*, [ʃi]*neider*, while similar words from English origin, such as *Smith* are adapted as [is.]*mith*. In almost all dialects of Portuguese the contrast between alveolar and palatal fricatives is neutralized in the syllable coda. Therefore, the contrast [is.]*mith* and [iʃ.]*midt* in the original words cannot be expressed in the coda in Portuguese. Consequently, the different syllable integration of /ʃ/ as compared to /s/ could be considered a loan strategy, through which speakers manage to maintain the contrast between /s, ʃ/, syllabifying /ʃ/ as an onset.

31   The limited set of data discussed here contain no evidence that *DEL and *EP are ranked with regard to each other. This is indicated by the dotted lines in the tableau, as opposed to the solid lines, which indicate crucial rankings. Below it will be shown that *DEL must be crucially ranked above *EP.

32   We assume that the constraint in (21) is part of a family of MSD constraints for which the value for n varies in Cx – Cy ≥ n.

33   A formulation more in line with OT would be: "assign a violation mark * for every /s/ not associated with the syllable coda," which would leave open the possibility for other ways of satisfying the constraint, such as /s/-deletion.

34   *EP should be understood as "No vowel epenthesis," since a higher ranked *EP/consonant should avoid that *psicólogo* surfaces as *p*[i]s[t]*icólogo* in order to bring /s/ in line with Lic/s/.

REFERENCES

Alves, U. K. and T. Keller (2010). Sílaba. In L. Bisol and L. C. Schwindt (eds.), *Teoria da Otimidade*. São Paulo: Pontes, pp. 57–92.

Bisol, L. (1998). A Nasalidade, um Velho Tema. *DELTA*, 14, São Paulo, pp. 27–46.

Bisol, L. (1999). A Sílaba e Seus Constituintes. In M. H. de Moura Neves (ed.), *Gramática do Português Falado*, VII. Campinas: UNICAMP/FAPESP, pp. 701–742.

Camara Jr, J. M. (1971). Problemas de lingüística descritiva 4th edition, Editora Vozes Limitada, Petrópolis, RJ. Brazil.

Cagliari, L. C. (1974). *A palatalização em Português: Uma investigação palatográfica*.

Unpublished MA thesis. Universidade Estadual de Campinas, Campinas. Brazil.

Clements, G. N. (2009). Does sonority have a phonetic basis? In E. Raimy and C. E. Cairns (eds.), *Contemporary Views on Architecture and Representations in Phonology*. Cambridge, MA: MIT Press, pp. 165–176.

Clements, G. N. and S. J. Keyser (1983). CV Phonology: a Generative Theory of the Syllable (Linguistic Inquiry Monograph 9). MIT Press Cambridge, Ma.

Clements, G. N. and E. Hume (1995). The internal organization of speech sounds. In J. Goldsmith (ed.), *The Handbook of Phonological*

Theory. Cambridge, MA: Blackwell, pp. 245–317.

Freitas, M. A. (1992). Empréstimos, Teoria Auto-segmental e Abertura Vocálica. *Cadernos de Estudos Linguisticos. Número Especial, Fonologia do Português*, 23, pp. 71–81.

Freitas, M. J. (2001). Sons de ataque: Segmentos complexos, grupos segmentais e representações fonológicas na aquisição do Português Europeu. *Letras de Hoje*, 36 (3), pp. 67–84.

Goedemans, R. W. N. (2010). A typology of stress patterns. In H. G. van der Hulst, R. W. N. Goedemans, and E. A. van Zanten (eds.), A Survey of Word Accentual Patterns in the Languages of the World. Berlin: Mouton de Gruyter, pp. 647–666.

Gonçalves, C. A. V. (2009). *Introdução à Morfologia Não-Linear*. Rio de Janeiro: Publit.

Harris, J. (1983). *Syllable Structure and Stress in Spanish: a Nonlinear Analysis*. Cambridge, MA: MIT Press.

Hayes, B. (1989). Compensatory lengthening in moraic phonology. *Linguistic Inquiry*, 20 (2), pp. 253–306.

Hermans, B. and W. L. Wetzels (2012). Productive and unproductive stress patterns in Brazilian Portuguese. *Revista Letras & Letras*, 28, pp. 77–115.

Hooper, J. (1976). *An Introduction to Natural Generative Phonology*. New York: Academic Press.

Hyman, L. M. (1985). *A Theory of Phonological Weight*. Dordrecht: Foris.

Ito, J. (1986). Syllable Theory in Prosodic Phonology. Ph.D. dissertation, University of Massachusetts, Amherst.

Kahn, D. (1976). *Syllable-based Generalisations in English Phonology*. Ph.D. dissertation, MIT, Cambridge, MA, USA.

Lamprecht, R. R. (2004). Aquisição fonológica do Português. In R. R. Lamprecht (ed.), *Aquisição Fonológica do Português. Perfil de Desenvolvimento e Subsídios para Terapia*. Porto Alegre: Artmed.

Lee, S. H. (1999). Teoria da Otimalidade e Silabificação do PB. In V. Benn-Ibler, E. A. de Mendonça Mendes, and P. M. Oliveira (eds.), *Revisitações – Edição Comemorativa dos 30 anos da FALE/UFMG*. Belo Horizonte: UFMG, pp. 43–156.

Magalhães, J. (2004). *O Plano Multidimensional do Acento na Teoria da Otimidade*. MA thesis, PUCRS, Porto Alegre, Brazil.

Marotta, G. (1999). The Latin syllable. In H. van der Hulst and N. A. Ritter (eds.). *The Syllable:*

Views and Facts. De Gruyter, Berlin. pp. 285–310.

Massini-Cagliari, G. (2005). *A musica da fala dos trovadores: Estudos de prosódia do Portugues Arcaico, a partir das cantigas profanas e religiosas*, Livre-Docencia em Fonologia, Universidade Estadual Paulista Araraquara, Brazil.

Mateus, M. H. and E. d'Andrade (2000). *The Phonology of Portuguese*. Oxford: Oxford University Press.

Murray, R. W. and T. Vennemann (1983). Sound change and syllable structure in Germanic phonology. *Language*, 59, pp. 514–528.

Selkirk, E. (1982). The syllable. In H. Van der Hulst and N. Smith (eds.), *The Structure of Phonological Representations*, volume 2. Dordrecht: Foris, pp. 337–383.

Schwindt, L. C. (2004). Produtividade, Transparência e Estatuto Prosódico de Palavras Derivadas por Prefixação em Português Brasileiro e Espanhol Peninsular. *Organon* (UFRGS), *Porto Alegre*, 18 (36), pp. 131–137.

Viaro, M. E. and Z. O. Guimarães Filho (2007). *Análise Quantitativa da Freqüência dos Fonemas e Estruturas Silábicas Portuguesas. Estudos Lingüísticos*, São Paulo, XXXVI, pp. 28–36.

Vigário, M., F. Martins, and S. Frota (2006). A Ferramenta FreP e a Frequência de Tipos Silábicos e Classes de Segmentos no Português. In F. Oliveira and J. Barbosa (eds.), *XXI Encontro da Associação Portuguesa de Linguística. Textos Seleccionados*. Lisbon: APL, pp. 675–687.

Wetzels, W. L. (1997). The lexical representation of nasality in Brazilian Portuguese. *Probus*, 9 (2), pp. 203–232.

Wetzels, W. L. (2000a). Comentários Sobre a Estrutura Fonológica dos Ditongos Nasais no Português do Brasil. *Revista de Letras*, 22 (1/2), pp. 25–30.

Wetzels, W. L. (2000b). Consoantes Palatais como Geminadas Fonológicas no Português Brasileiro. *Revista de Estudos da Linguagem*, 9, pp. 5–15.

Wetzels, W. L. (2006/7). Primary stress in Brazilian Portuguese and the quantity parameter. In G. Elordieta and M. Vigário (eds.), *Journal of Portuguese Linguistics Vol 5/6, Special Issue on the Prosody of the Iberian Languages*, pp. 9–58.

Wetzels, W. L. (2007). A Silabificação das Vogais Altas no Português Brasileiro. Paper presented at the *III Seminário Internacional de Fonologia*, Pontifícia Universidade Católica de Rio Grande do Sul, Porto Alegre.

7 Main Stress and Secondary Stress in Brazilian and European Portuguese

JOSÉ MAGALHÃES[1]

1. Introduction

Vulgar Latin and Medieval Portuguese had a quite simple stress pattern, with primary stress falling on the second syllable counting from the right side of the word or on the final syllable if it was closed (Williams 1975; Massini-Cagliari 1994). At least for primary stress, this pattern has remained characteristic of the language currently spoken in Brazil and Portugal. However, sound changes and borrowings created words with stress on a final open syllable, while at various moments in the history of Portuguese, especially since the fifteenth century, words with proparoxytonic stress have become integrated into the language.

In this chapter, we will discuss the regular and irregular stress patterns of Portuguese, which, as we assume, are basically identical for the Brazilian and European varieties. We will also provide an overview of the different theoretical accounts that have been proposed for Portuguese stress, which reveal profound differences of opinion about what exactly the explanatory principles are underlying the regular stress patterns. Whereas scholars working on Brazilian Portuguese, such as Bisol (1994), Wetzels (2003, 2006), and Magalhães (2004, 2008), are strong advocates of the role of heavy syllables as stress attractors, others, especially specialists in European Portuguese, reject the relevance of syllable weight, arguing instead for a morphology-based analysis of main stress (d'Andrade and Laks (1992); Pereira (1999); Mateus and d'Andrade (2000). Another point of disagreement concerns the question whether the stress principles apply cross-categorically or whether verbs and non-verbs represent different subsystems, which must consequently be described separately.

While there are no noteworthy differences relative to the location of primary stress in the European and Brazilian varieties of Portuguese, secondary stress shows some differences in connected speech, which will also be addressed.

2. A note on the history of Portuguese stress

The regular stress pattern of contemporary Portuguese continues a centuries-old pattern which goes back to Vulgar Latin, with stress being located on one of the two word-final syllables.

The Handbook of Portuguese Linguistics, First Edition. Edited by W. Leo Wetzels, João Costa, and Sergio Menuzzi.
© 2016 John Wiley & Sons, Inc. Published 2020 by John Wiley & Sons, Inc.

Vulgar Latin is different from Classical Latin in two major respects. First, the durational contrast for vowels that existed in Classical Latin disappeared in Vulgar Latin, as exemplified with the words in (1). (Here and henceforth, stressed syllables are bold).

(1) Classical Latin　Vulgar Latin
　　acētum　　　　acétu　　　　"sour"
　　sudōrem　　　　sudóre　　　　"sweat"

Furthermore, in Vulgar Latin, a small number of words had changed from proparoxytonic to paroxytonic through a number of processes. In words with a / Cr / cluster in the onset of the final syllable stress shifted one syllable to the right (2). Other processes had altered the segmental structure of the Classical Latin word, such as syncope (3), or the fusion between a consonant and a following prevocalic coronal high vowel (4).

(2) Classical Latin　Vulgar Latin
　　íntegrum　　　　intégru　　　"entire"
　　cólubra　　　　colóbra　　　"snake"

(3) vernáculus　　　vernáclus　　"vernacular"
　　Artículus　　　artíclus　　"article"

(4) **bá**.ni.u　　　　**bá**.n^{y}u　　"bath"
　　pá.li.a　　　　**pá**.l^{y}a　　"straw"
　　lán.ci.a　　　**lán**.c^{y}a　"spear"

By the beginning of the archaic period, around the thirteenth century, words with stress on the antepenultimate syllable have become rare (Massini-Cagliari, 1995, 1999). On the other hand, at this stage of the language, words with final stress, unknown during the Latin period, have become very frequent, due to the historical processes of vowel and consonant deletion (cf. Vasconcelloz, 1900; Nunes, 1975; Williams, 1975).

(5) Vulgar Latim　　Old Portuguese
　　a.**mó**.re　　　*a.**mór***　　　"love"
　　fi.**dé**.le　　　*fi.**él***　　　"faithful"
　　do.**ló**.re　　　*do.**ór***　　"pain"
　　fe.**lí**.ce　　　*fe.**líz***　　"happy"

The entrance of words with proparoxytonic stress into the Portuguese lexicon happened mainly in the fifteenth and sixteenth century, generally through borrowings from Greek and Latin (Araújo et al, 2007). All these stress patterns are carried over into Modern Portuguese.

For a global assessment of the stress patterns of Modern Portuguese, consider the words in (6):

(6) a. *vá.le*　　　"valley"　　　　b. *ca.**fé***　　"coffee"
　　pór.ta　　　"door"　　　　　　*so.**fá***　　"couch"
　　*pa.**lí**.to*　"stick"　　　　　*pa.le.**tó***　"suit"
　　c. *fu.**níl***　"funnel"　　　　d. *fá.cil*　　"easy"
　　*tam.**bór***　"drum"　　　　　*lí.der*　　"leader"
　　*co.ro.**nél***　"colonel"　　　*mó.vel*　　"furniture"
　　e. *ma.te.**má**.ti.ca*　"mathematics"
　　prá.ti.co　　"practical"
　　có.mo.do　　"comfortable"

The words in (6a) show the trochaic pattern, which is considered the unmarked pattern by most scholars. For those seeking a phonology-based description of Portuguese stress, the words in (6c) are integrated into the regular pattern by defining the trochaic foot over pairs of moras instead of syllables. Researchers who argue in favor of a morphology-based account locate regular stress on the last vowel of the root. From their perspective, this explains why the words in (6a) have stress on the prefinal syllable, since the last syllable contains the theme vowel as a nucleus, which is skipped by the stress rule. On the other hand, stress falls regularly on the last syllables in athematic nouns, exemplified in (6b) and (6c).

The words in (6b), (6d), and (6e) are qualified as exceptions by weight-based analysis, whereas the words in (6d) and (6e) cannot be explained by morphology-based accounts. Most scholars agree that syllable weight does not play an explicative role in the determination of stress in verbs, a fact which is presented by the proponents of the morphology-based theory as a strong point in favor of a generalized morphology-based account of Portuguese stress.

3. Primary stress: the data

Experimental studies by Major (1981) and Massini-Cagliari (1992) have shown that the acoustic correlates of main stress in Brazilian Portuguese (henceforth BP) are duration, fundamental frequency (F0), and intensity, where the given order mirrors their decreasing importance. Duration and energy were found to be the main phonetic correlate of main stress in European Portuguese (henceforth EP) in a study by Delgado Martins (1986, apud Pereira 1999), who found, moreover, that these properties can be established instrumentally for final and antepenultimate stress, but much less systematically for stress on the penultimate syllable.

3.1. Stress in verbs

Whereas scholars disagree about the conditioning factors that account for the distribution of main stress in non-verbs, there is agreement that stress in verbs interacts with morphology, as described by Wetzels (2006) for BP and Mateus (1990) or Mateus and d'Andrade (2000) for EP. In the following, we present Wetzels' account of verbal stress, which at the same time serves as an introduction to the relevant empirical data, leaving the discussion of alternative accounts for a later section.

Generalizing over the three existing verb conjugations identified on the basis of their theme vowel (TV), Wetzels (2006) defends the idea that verb stress in Portuguese enhances the existing tense distinctions distinguished in the Portuguese verb: present, past, and future.

The past tense forms, which include the perfect past, imperfect past, pluperfect past, and the imperfect past of the subjunctive mood, receive stress on the theme vowel, as stated in (7):

(7) $XVC_0]_{root}\acute{V}]_{theme}Y_0]_{past}$

Past tense forms are accented on the last vowel of the verbal theme (adapted from Wetzels, 2006: 40.)

The generalization in (7) is illustrated below with the verbs *falar* "speak" (*a*-theme, first conjugation), *bater* "beat" (*e*-theme, second conjugation), and *partir* "leave" (*i*-theme, third conjugation). The different forms are given in the traditional order, from top to bottom: 1sg, 2sg, 3sg, 1pl, 2pl, 3pl.

(8) Stress in past tense forms
Indicative imperfect

fal]_{root}*a*]_{theme}va	bat]_{root}*i*]_{theme}a	part]_{root}*i*]_{theme}a

fal]$_{root}$*a*]$_{theme}$va bat]$_{root}$*i*]$_{theme}$a part]$_{root}$*i*]$_{theme}$a
fal]$_{root}$*a*]$_{theme}$vas bat]$_{root}$*i*]$_{theme}$as part]$_{root}$*i*]$_{theme}$as
fal]$_{root}$*a*]$_{theme}$va bat]$_{root}$*i*]$_{theme}$a part]$_{root}$*i*]$_{theme}$a
fal]$_{root}$*a*]$_{theme}$vamos bat]$_{root}$*i*]$_{theme}$amos part]$_{root}$*i*]$_{theme}$amos
fal]$_{root}$*a*]$_{theme}$veis bat]$_{root}$*i*]$_{theme}$eis part]$_{root}$*i*]$_{theme}$eis
fal]$_{root}$*a*]$_{theme}$vaũ bat]$_{root}$*i*]$_{theme}$aũ part]$_{root}$*i*]$_{theme}$aũ

Indicative perfect

fal]$_{root}$*e*]$_{theme}$i bat]$_{root}$*e*]$_{theme}$i part]$_{root}$*i*]$_{theme}$i
fal]$_{root}$*a*]$_{theme}$ste bat]$_{root}$*e*]$_{theme}$ste part]$_{root}$*i*]$_{theme}$ste
fal]$_{root}$*o*]$_{theme}$u bat]$_{root}$*e*]$_{theme}$u part]$_{root}$*i*]$_{theme}$u
fal]$_{root}$*a*]$_{theme}$mos bat]$_{root}$*e*]$_{theme}$mos part]$_{root}$*i*]$_{theme}$mos
fal]$_{root}$*a*]$_{theme}$stes bat]$_{root}$*e*]$_{theme}$stes part]$_{root}$*i*]$_{theme}$stes
fal]$_{root}$*a*]$_{theme}$raũ bat]$_{root}$*e*]$_{theme}$raũ part]$_{root}$*i*]$_{theme}$raũ

Indicative pluperfect

fal]$_{root}$*a*]$_{theme}$ra bat]$_{root}$*e*]$_{theme}$ra part]$_{root}$*i*]$_{theme}$ra
fal]$_{root}$*a*]$_{theme}$ras bat]$_{root}$*e*]$_{theme}$ras part]$_{root}$*i*]$_{theme}$ras
fal]$_{root}$*a*]$_{theme}$ra bat]$_{root}$*e*]$_{theme}$ra part]$_{root}$*i*]$_{theme}$ra
fal]$_{root}$*a*]$_{theme}$ramos bat]$_{root}$*e*]$_{theme}$ramos part]$_{root}$*i*]$_{theme}$ramos
fal]$_{root}$*a*]$_{theme}$reis bat]$_{root}$*e*]$_{theme}$reis part]$_{root}$*i*]$_{theme}$reis
fal]$_{root}$*a*]$_{theme}$raũ bat]$_{root}$*e*]$_{theme}$raũ part]$_{root}$*i*]$_{theme}$raũ

Subjunctive imperfect

fal]$_{root}$*a*]$_{theme}$se bat]$_{root}$*e*]$_{theme}$se part]$_{root}$*i*]$_{theme}$se
fal]$_{root}$*a*]$_{theme}$ses bat]$_{root}$*e*]$_{theme}$ses part]$_{root}$*i*]$_{theme}$ses
fal]$_{root}$*a*]$_{theme}$se bat]$_{root}$*e*]$_{theme}$se part]$_{root}$*i*]$_{theme}$se
fal]$_{root}$*a*]$_{theme}$semos bat]$_{root}$*e*]$_{theme}$semos part]$_{root}$*i*]$_{theme}$semos
fal]$_{root}$*a*]$_{theme}$seis bat]$_{root}$*e*]$_{theme}$seis part]$_{root}$*i*]$_{theme}$seis
fal]$_{root}$*a*]$_{theme}$seĩ bat]$_{root}$*e*]$_{theme}$seĩ part]$_{root}$*i*]$_{theme}$seĩ

Future tense forms are stressed on the syllable containing the TAM morpheme.

(9) X]$_{theme}$r$\acute{V}$ Y$_0$]$_{future}$

Future tense forms are accented on the syllable containing the future (or conditional) suffix (Wetzels, 2006: 41)

(10) Stress in future tense or conditional forms

Indicative

fal]$_{root}$a]$_{theme}$*rei* bat]$_{root}$e]$_{theme}$*rei* part]$_{root}$i]$_{theme}$*rei*
fal]$_{root}$a]$_{theme}$*ras* bat]$_{root}$e]$_{theme}$*ras* part]$_{root}$i]$_{theme}$*ras*
fal]$_{root}$a]$_{theme}$*ra* bat]$_{root}$e]$_{theme}$*ra* part]$_{root}$i]$_{theme}$*ra*
fal]$_{root}$a]$_{theme}$*remos* bat]$_{root}$e]$_{theme}$*remos* part]$_{root}$i]$_{theme}$*remos*
fal]$_{root}$a]$_{theme}$*reis* bat]$_{root}$e]$_{theme}$*reis* part]$_{root}$i]$_{theme}$*reis*
fal]$_{root}$a]$_{theme}$*raũ* bat]$_{root}$e]$_{theme}$*raũ* part]$_{root}$i]$_{theme}$*raũ*

Conditional

fal]$_{root}$a]$_{theme}$*ria* bat]$_{root}$e]$_{theme}$*ria* part]$_{root}$i]$_{theme}$*ria*
fal]$_{root}$a]$_{theme}$*rias* bat]$_{root}$e]$_{theme}$*rias* part]$_{root}$i]$_{theme}$*rias*
fal]$_{root}$a]$_{theme}$*ria* bat]$_{root}$e]$_{theme}$*ria* part]$_{root}$i]$_{theme}$*ria*
fal]$_{root}$a]$_{theme}$*riamos* bat]$_{root}$e]$_{theme}$*riamos* part]$_{root}$i]$_{theme}$*riamos*
fal]$_{root}$a]$_{theme}$*rieis* bat]$_{root}$e]$_{theme}$*rieis* part]$_{root}$i]$_{theme}$*rieis*
fal]$_{root}$a]$_{theme}$*riaũ* bat]$_{root}$e]$_{theme}$*riaũ* part]$_{root}$i]$_{theme}$*riaũ*

To account for stress in the present tense, a special rule is proposed for the forms of the 1pl and 2pl, in which stress falls on the thematic vowel, different from the remaining verb forms, which are stressed on the last vowel of the root. There are, then, two separate rules to account for stress in the present tense:

(11) a. special case $\quad$ $\text{XVC}_0]_{\text{root}} \acute{\text{V}}]_{\text{theme}}]_{\text{present 1,2pl}}$

$\quad$ b. elsewhere case $\quad$ $\text{X}\acute{\text{V}}\text{C}_0]_{\text{root}} \text{Y}]_{\text{present}}$

(12) Stress in present tense forms

Present indicative

$\text{fal}]_{\text{root}}\text{o}$	$\text{bat}]_{\text{root}}\text{o}$	$\text{part}]_{\text{root}}\text{o}$
$\text{fal}]_{\text{root}}\text{as}$	$\text{bat}]_{\text{root}}\text{es}$	$\text{part}]_{\text{root}}\text{is}$
$\text{fal}]_{\text{root}}\text{a}$	$\text{bat}]_{\text{root}}\text{e}$	$\text{part}]_{\text{root}}\text{i}$
$\text{fal}]_{\text{root}}\acute{a}\text{mos}$	$\text{bat}]_{\text{root}}\acute{e}\text{mos}$	$\text{part}]_{\text{root}}\acute{i}\text{mos}$
$\text{fal}]_{\text{root}}\acute{a}\text{is}$	$\text{bat}]_{\text{root}}\acute{e}\text{is}$	$\text{part}]_{\text{root}}\acute{i}\text{s}$
$\text{fal}]_{\text{root}}\text{aũ}$	$\text{bat}]_{\text{root}}\text{eĩ}$	$\text{part}]_{\text{root}}\text{eĩ}$

Present subjunctive

$\text{fal}]_{\text{root}}\text{e}$	$\text{bat}]_{\text{root}}\text{a}$	$\text{part}]_{\text{root}}\text{a}$
$\text{fal}]_{\text{root}}\text{es}$	$\text{bat}]_{\text{root}}\text{as}$	$\text{part}]_{\text{root}}\text{as}$
$\text{fal}]_{\text{root}}\text{e}$	$\text{bat}]_{\text{root}}\text{a}$	$\text{part}]_{\text{root}}\text{a}$
$\text{fal}]_{\text{root}}\text{emos}$	$\text{bat}]_{\text{root}}\acute{a}\text{mos}$	$\text{part}]_{\text{root}}\acute{a}\text{mos}$
$\text{fal}]_{\text{root}}\text{eis}$	$\text{bat}]_{\text{root}}\acute{a}\text{is}$	$\text{part}]_{\text{root}}\acute{a}\text{is}$
$\text{fal}]_{\text{root}}\text{eĩ}$	$\text{bat}]_{\text{root}}\text{aũ}$	$\text{part}]_{\text{root}}\text{aũ}$

As was illustrated, in verbs the different stress patterns correspond with different tense categories.

3.2. Stress in non-verbs

Stress in non-verbs is predominantly prefinal in words ending in a vowel. When the word-final syllable ends in a diphthong or a syllable closed by a consonant, final stress is the normal case.

(13) *pá.to* $\qquad$ "duck" $\qquad$ *fre.gués* $\quad$ "customer"

$\quad$ *ca.sá.co* $\qquad$ "jacket" $\qquad$ *po.már* $\quad$ "orchard"

$\quad$ *pós.te* $\qquad$ "pole" $\qquad$ *fu.níl* $\qquad$ "funnel"

$\quad$ *as.fál.to* $\qquad$ "asphalt" $\qquad$ *re.fém* $\quad$ "hostage"

Derived words usually comply with these generalizations, giving rise to alternations in the location of stress between derived words and their base. Exceptions are bi-moraic suffixes that are pre-accenting, like *–ico*, or *-vel*, as in *atléta* "athlete" ~ *atlético* "athletic," and *movér* "move" ~ *móvel* "mobile," or neoclassical compounds based on bound stems of Greek or Latin origin (*quilômetro* "kilometer," *carnívoro* "carnivorous," etc.), which also can combine with native words to create hybrid formations (*camelódromo* "place to shelter street vendors," *sambódromo* "sambadrome," etc.). Furthermore, the plural suffix only rarely alters the position of the main stress as it appears in the corresponding singular form (*pátos* "ducks," *freguéses* "costumers," *pormáres* "ochards," *funis* "funnels," etc). The words in (14a) show alternating stress in words derived with derivational suffixes and their bases, whereas the words in (14b) show lack of alternation between the singular and the corresponding plural forms.

(14) a.

belo	*beleza*	"beautiful" / "beauty"
bola	*bolada*	"ball" / "hit with a ball."
topete	*topetudo*	"tuft" / "tufty"
inferno	*infernal*	"hell" / "infernal"
calor	*caloroso*	"heat" / "warm"
fuzil	*fuzilado*	"rifle" / "shot with a rifle"

b.

bola	*bolas*	"ball" / "balls"
topete	*topetes*	"tuft" / "tufts"
infernal	*infernais*	"infernal" / "infernal-pl"
calor	*calores*	"heat" / "heat waves"

Paroxytonic words ending in consonants, as well as words with antepenultimate stress are generally classified as irregular. As for the latter stress pattern, there is one subclass of proparoxytonic words that appears to be productive, which contains words that end in a sequence of a high vowel followed by another vowel, such as *mis.té.rio* "mystery," *lín.gu.a* "tongue," *sá.bi.o* "wise" (Magalhães 2004; Hermans and Wetzels 2012). Examples of irregular prefinal stress are given in (15).

(15)

lí.der	"leader"	*hí.fen*	"hyphen"
ní.vel	"level"	*jó.vem*	"young"
lá.pis	"pencil"	*jó.quei*	"jockey"

The following words illustrate antepenultimate stress

(16)

fô.le.go	"breath"
ár.vo.re	"tree"
fós.fo.ro	"match"

Among the words with antepenultimate stress, examples with a branching rhyme in the penultimate syllable are almost completely lacking. The few exceptions to this generalization are either of foreign origin or are rarely used. In popular variants, these words are often modified to fit the regular pattern, at least in BP. For example, relatively frequent words such as *recorde* "record," or *pênalti* "penalty" are pronounced by many as [xe.**kɔr**] or [xe.**kɔr**.dʒɪ] and [pe.**náw**]. Moreover, while words with a prefinal falling diphthong such as *ca.déi.ra* "chair," *di.no.ssáu.ro* "dinosaur," *te.sóu.ro* "treasure," etc., represent a frequent word pattern in Portuguese, words of the type **có.pei.ro,* di.nó.ssau.ro, *té.sou.ro*, with stress on the syllable preceding a prefinal falling diphthong, do not exist.

Proparoxytonic words with a final branching rhyme are also rare, limited to items such as *Lú.ci.fer* "Lucifer," *jú.ni.or* "junior," *jú.pi.ter* "Jupiter," *sí.fi.lis* "syphilis," and *ín.te.rim* "interim." Proper nouns, such as *Washington* and *William* are normally pronounced without the last consonant: [u**ɔ**.ʃɪ.tʊ] and [u.**í**.lja], respectively. In other borrowings with antepenultimate stress in the source language, stress often falls on one of the two final syllables in Portuguese: *Manchester* [mã.**ʃɛs**.tex], *Rotterdam* [xo.tex.**dã**]. This way of integrating borrowed words supports the view that the proparoxytonic pattern is marked in Portuguese.

In addition to the exceptional patterns considered so far, there is a significant number of words with stress on a final open syllable:

(17) *fu.bá*   "corn meal"
    ca.fé   "coffee"
    a.ba.ca.xí "pineapple"
    a.vó   "grandmother"
    u.ru.bú   "vulture"

Most words with stress on a final open syllable are borrowed from other romance languages, especially French and English, from African languages brought into Brazil during colonial times, as well as from indigenous languages, especially Tupi.

4. The formal modeling of primary stress

In defense of the claim that Portuguese stress is sensitive to the weight of the word-final syllable, Bisol (1992/2013) points out that 78 percent of non-verbs ending in a consonant have word-final stress. To this statistical argument one may add the fact that newly created words, such as acronyms, proper names, and brand names for new industrial products which end in a consonant almost exceptionally receive final stress. The following examples are from a survey by Hermans and Wetzels (2012):

(18)
a. Acronyms	b. Proper names	c. Brand names (pharmaceutics)
JO'CUM	Fro'in	Aro'tin
FE'BEM	Jurupi'tan	Fena'ren
FU'NAI	Harpa'lus	De'press
SU'SAU	Yo'pros	Dor'less
BE'NES	Na'bor	Efe'xor
REI'PLAS	Hepila'zir	Pame'lor
U'FIR	Zarifebar'bar	Bese'rol
PRO'ER	Baru'el	Tra'mal
VAR'SUL	Idela'zil	Le'gil
AN'POL	Avo'al	Pax'trat(i)
FA'PESP([i])	Galeno'gal	Mir'tax(i)
VAL'MET([i])	Fran'cel	Nisu'lid(i)

To account for the surface representation of the irregular patterns, Bisol (1992/2013, 1994) postulates consonant and syllable extrametricality, which renders the final consonant of paroxytones and the final syllable of proparoxytones invisible to the stress algorithm. Since words that are lexically marked for extrametrical consonants or syllables are subjected to the general stress rules, they are stressed on the last syllable of the "metrical" sequence if that syllable is heavy, otherwise on the prefinal syllable. Lexical extrametrical elements are exclusively allowed in the periphery of the stress domain. It is canceled in lexical items to which suffixes are added in the process of word formation. As is shown by the words in (19), when derivational suffixes are added to a base with exceptional stress, the derived forms follow the regular stress pattern.

(19) a.   *móve*<l> – *moveleiro*   "furniture" / "furnisher"
       líde<r>   – *liderança*   "leader" / "leadership"
       açúca<r> – *açucarado*   "sugar" / "sugary"
       árvo<re> – *arvoredo*   "tree" / "grove"
       músi<k>   – *musical*   "music" / "musical"
    b. *móve*<l>   – *móveis*   "furniture" / "furniture-pl"
       líde<r>   – *líderes*   "leader" / "leader-pl"
       açúca<r> – *açúcares*   "sugar" / "sugar-pl"
       júnio<r> – *juniores*   "junior" / "junior-pl"

Bisol reacts to the problem of words stressed on a final open syllable by hypothesizing that these end in an abstract consonant lexically (catalexis). This consonant shows up in derived words with suffixes that are usually vowel-initial, as shown in (20) below

(20) *pé > ped+al*   "foot" / "pedal"
     café > cafez+al   "coffee" / "coffee plantation"
     chá > chal+eira   "tea" / "tea kettle"

Also, the choice of the consonant-initial allomorph of the diminutive suffix is considered by Bisol as independent evidence for a final lexical consonant in these words: *café* "coffee," *jacaré* "cayman," *garí* "street-sweeper," etc. take *–zinho* instead of *–inho* as the diminutive suffix, which is regular for words ending in a consonant: *pomar > pomarzinho* "orchard" / "little orchard," *canal > canalzinho* "canal" / "small canal," and also *café > cafezinho* "coffee" / "small cup of coffee," *jacaré > jacarezinho* "cayman" / "small cayman," *gari > garizinho* "street-sweeper" / "little street-sweeper," never **cafeinho,*jacareinho,*gariinho*, etc. Similarly, the diminutive form of vowel-final monosyllables is derived with *–zinho: pá+zinho* "small shovel," *nó+zinho* "little knot," *nu+zinho* "naked."

Bisol (1992/2013, 1994), who adopts the framework developed by Halle and Vergnaud (1987), proposes the same mechanisms to account for stress in verbs and non-verbs. The stress rules apply for all lexical categories at the level of the phonological word.

In non-verbs, the stress rule assigns an asterisk on line 1 for word-final syllables ending in a consonant, as in (21a). In words ending in a vowel, a left-headed binary constituent is built on the right word edge, as in (21b). To deal with irregular stresses, lexical extrametricality exempts final syllables (cf. 22a) or consonants (cf. 22b) from the metrical sequence, giving rise to words with antepenultimate stress or with prefinal stress despite the presence of a final heavy syllable.

(21) Regular stress in non-verbs
        (*)   (*)   (*)
   a. *po.**mar*** "orchard" *tro.**féu*** "trophy" *co.ro.**nel*** "colonel"
   b. (*   .)   (*   .)   (*   .)
      *ca.**sa*** "house"   *pa.**re**.de* "wall"   *bor.bo.**le**.ta* "butterfly"

(22) Irregular stress in non-verbs
      (*   .)   (*   .)
   a. *fos.**fo**<ro>* "match"   *ar.**vo**<re>* "tree"
   b. (* .)   (* .)
      *u.**ti** <l>* "useful"   *vi.**si**.ve<l>* "visible"

Stress in verbs is derived in the same way as in non-verbs. The difference is in the nature of extrametricality, which is applied in verbs by a general rule, not idiosyncratically on a word by word basis. Extrametricality in verbs affects the final syllable in the 1,2pl forms of the indicative and subjunctive imperfect, as in (23a), as well as all the final consonants representing a suffix, as in (23b), where final / s / represents the 2sg suffix and / N / the nasal mora that denotes the 3pl suffix.

(23) Stress in verbs
    a. Subjunctive imperfect b. Indicative imperfect
       (* .)   (* .)
       fa.la.sse<mos>   *fa.la.va.<mos>* 1pl "talk"
       ba.te.sse<is>   *ba.ti. e <is>* 2pl "hit"
    c. Present Ind. d. Present subj. e. Infinitive
       (* .)   (* .)   (*)
       fa.la<s>   *fa.le<N>*   *fa.lar* "talk"
       ba.te<s>   *ba.te<N>*   *ba.ter* "hit"

Some authors have criticized Bisol's proposal for a number of reasons: for its abundant use of extrametricality, for the assumed relevance of syllable weight, and for the unified way of accounting for stress in verbs and non-verbs. For example, Lee (1995), in line with Mateus (1983), d'Andrade and Laks (1992), and Pereira (1999) argues that stress is not sensitive to the weight of the syllable and is not assigned at the level of the phonological word. Lee's alternative account follows the model proposed by Hayes (1991) combined with the assumptions of Derivational Lexical Phonology, which distinguishes between lexical and postlexical modules, and which posits, within the lexical component, different levels for the interaction between morphology and phonology. Lee distinguishes two lexical levels: on the first level, which he calls the α level, derivational morphology takes place, on the second level, the β level, inflection is accounted for.

(24) Stress rules for non-verbs: α level (derivational root)
    a. Parameter settings for regular stress: foot binarity, foot is right-headed, right to left footing, non-iterative footing (cf. a).
    b. Parameter settings for irregular stress: foot binarity, foot is left-headed, right to left footing, non-iterative footing (cf. b).

Stress is assigned to the derivational root. Words with irregular stress are lexically marked for the applicable parametrical choices.

(25) a. [almoço] "lunch" [kafɛ] "coffee" [abobor]a "pumpkin"
      (. *)   (. *)   —   (24a)
                                     (* .) (24b)
      —   —

In normal derivation, stress assigned at a previous cycle is erased, as in *brasíl / brasiléiro* "Brazil" / "Brazilian."

    b. 1st cycle   [brazil]   Prosodic Constituent Formation (PCF)
                 [brazíl]   Stress Rule
       2nd cycle [brazil] eir] o   Suffixation and PCF
                 [brazíleir] o   Stress Erasure Convention
                 [braziléir] o   Stress Rule

Since plural formation takes place at level β, at which non-verbal stress is no longer active, it is predicted that pluralization does not interfere with the stress determined at level α.

For verbs, the stress rules apply at level β, which is also the level at which verbal inflectional suffixes are added.

(26) Stress rules for verbs: β level (word)
  a. Parameter settings for regular stress: foot binarity, foot is leftheaded, right to left footing, non-iterative footing.
  b. Parameter settings for irregular stress: foot binarity, foot is rightheaded, right to left footing, non-iterative footing.

/*computo*/ "compute"	/*falamos*/ "talk"	/*batera*/ "hit"	
(* .)	(* .)	—	(26a)
—	—	(. *)	(26b)

Lee also admits a limited use of extrametricality, which is applied to the 1pl suffix -*mos* in the imperfect, pluperfect and future conditional indicative, as well as in the past subjunctive.

(27) *falava*<mos>   *falaria*<mos>   *falasse*<mos>
    (* .)   (* .)   (* .)

While Lee's proposal reduces considerably the resort to extrametricality, the overall description of main stress increases in complexity.

As in Lee's account, the relevance of syllable weight is denied in the interpretation of Portuguese stress by Mateus (1983, 1990), Pereira (1999), and Mateus and d'Andrade (2000), who propose a treatment conditioned by morphology for all lexical categories. Their approach differs from Lee's account with regard to the definition of the morphological constituents that function as the domains for the stress rule. For non-verbs, the domain is the root, whereas for verbs it is the verbal theme.

Portuguese non-verbs are traditionally divided in two classes, thematic and athematic. Thematic nouns end in one of the theme vowels –*a*, -*o*, -*e*, adjectives in either –*a* or –*o*, as in *canet-a* "pen," *cab-o* "cable," *carn-e* "meat." Athematic words lack a thematic vowel and come in two types: words ending in a consonant *gentil* "friendly," *calor* "heat," or in a stressed vowel: *urubú* "vulture," *guichê* "information counter." As we have shown in Section 3.1, Portuguese verbs also come in three classes, *a*-themes, *e*-themes, and *i*-themes. With this in mind, consider the stress rules in (28), as proposed by Mateus (1990: 355):

(28) In verbs, stress is on the last vowel of the theme
    In non-verbs, stress is on the last vowel of the root

The following examples illustrate the application of the rule:

(29) Stress in Verbs

cant+á]$_{theme}$+*r*	*cant+á*]$_{theme}$ +*va*	*cant+á*]$_{theme}$+*va+mos*	"sing"
infinitive	3-sg imperfect	1-pl imperfect	
comé]$_{theme}$ +*u*	*comé*]$_{theme}$ +*ra*	*comé*]$_{theme}$ +*ra+mos*	"eat"
3-sg perfect	3-sg pluperfect	3-pl pluperfect	
part+í]$_{theme}$ +*u*	*part+í*]$_{theme}$ +*sse*	*part+í*]$_{theme}$+*r+mos*	"leave"
3-sg perfect	1-/3-sg past subjunctive	1-pl future subjunctive	

(30) Non-verbs

modél-o	"model"
escád-a	"stairs"
románc-e	"romance"
hospitál-ø	"hospital"
café-ø	"coffee"
pó-ø	"powder"

Since a considerable number of verb forms does not comply with the generalization that stress is on the theme vowel, special rules are necessary to account for the exceptional forms, which typically correspond with present and future tense forms, as illustrated in (31) for the present tense with the verb *falar* "speak."

(31)

		Present Ind.	Present Subj.	Imperative
a. 1-sg		*fál-o*	e. *fále*	
b. 2-sg		*fála-s*	f. *fále-s*	i. *fála*
c. 3-sg		*fála*	g. *fále*	
d. 3-pl		*fála-m*	h. *fále-m*	

When the theme vowel does not appear in the surface form, as in (31a) and (31e-h), when it is word-final (31c, 31i), or when it is followed by the person/number morpheme/+s/or/+m / (31b, 31d), stress is on the last vowel of the root. Stress is also exceptional in the 1/2pl of the present subjunctive, in which forms stress is located on the vowel representing the TAM morpheme.

(32) a. 1-pl *falémos* compare with regular present indicative *falámos*
     b. 2-pl *faléis* compare with regular present indicative *faláis*

For the future tense and conditional forms, the special rule proposed by Mateus is similar to that one in Wetzels (2006) discussed in section 3.1.

As for the distribution of stress in verbs, the major difference between the proposal by Mateus (1990) and the one by Wetzels (2006) is that in the latter account, stress on the theme vowel is not considered the general rule, but one of three different rules that distribute stress with reference to the tense categories *present*, *past*, and *future*. Indeed, in the verb forms in (31), which are present tense forms, stress falls systematically on the last vowel of the root.

Turning to the non-verbal lexical categories, in the account by Mateus (1990), consonant-final athematic nouns with prefinal stress are considered exceptional: *útil* "useful," *dólar* "dollar," *lápis* "pencil," etc. Proparoxytonic stress also cannot be accounted for: *médico* "physician," *abóbora* "pumpkin," *fôlego* "breath." The same stress patterns are considered exceptional in the weight-based account. On the other hand, in the morphology-based analysis, words ending in a stressed vowel are classified as athematic and their final stress is consequently accounted for by the general stress rule for non-verbs. In the weight-based account vowel-final words are predicted to have prefinal stress, which means that *café* "coffee," *guichê* "counter," *jacaré* "cayman," etc. must be listed as exceptions. This fact is often interpreted as evidence for the morphological analysis of non-verbal stress. However, it remains to be seen whether the characterization of this word class as regular is correct, especially since stress on word-final open syllables rarely shows up in newly created words.

5. The syllable weight controversy

Although a number of scholars have worked out a uniform cross-categorical analysis of Portuguese stress, there appears to be a growing consensus that there are differences in the principles regulating the stress patterns of verbs and non-verbs, with stress in verbs clearly being conditioned by morphology. In the discussion so far, it has become evident that probably the most controversial issue in the definition of main stress in Portuguese concerns the relevance of syllable weight for non-verbs. We will therefore address this issue in some more detail, assessing the arguments that are presented in the literature in favor and against the role of syllable weight.

Among the arguments contesting the role of syllable weight in the phonology of Portuguese, some are typological, such as the claim attributed by many to Trubetzkoy (1939/1969) according to which only languages with contrastive vowel length can have a quantity-sensitive stress system. Mateus and d'Andrade (2000: 118) directly refer to this allegedly universal law, stating:

> if some phonologists wish to consider an alternation between long and short vowels, they must recognize that, when a vowel is long, then it is systematically stressed. Therefore, there is general agreement that duration is a by-product of stressing. If so, length cannot be assigned the role of an explanatory principle of stress location.

In other words, vowel length in Portuguese is phonetic, not phonological, and therefore this language cannot have a weight-sensitive stress system. However, Wetzels (2003, 2006) presents empirical data from various languages which have a stress rule referring to the distinction between branching and non-branching rhymes without the presence in their vowel system of a length contrast, thereby refuting the validity of the above-mentioned law, which he moreover attributes not to Trubetzkoy, but to the Polish linguist Kurylowicz (Wetzels, 2006: 3). In the same study, Wetzels shows that a further claim made by Mateus and d'Andrade (2000:117) according to which, as a general rule, languages reject the differential treatment of verbs and non-verbs for the sake of stress allocation is not supported by cross-linguistic evidence either.

Some arguments against the relevance of syllable weight refer to the history of the language. Here, the claim is that what looks like a synchronic generalization is in reality the effect of some specific historical change, which has given rise to a regular pattern that is not as such part of the internalized grammar of the native speakers of Modern Portuguese. One such generalization concerns the fact that proparoxytonic stress is not attested in words with a prefinal branching rhyme: *cadéira* "chair" (*cádeira), **lâm**pada "light bulb" (*lámpanda). As it appears, the prefinal heavy syllable acts as a barrier for the stress rule, which cannot reach the penultimate syllable. Opponents to the weight sensitivity hypothesis argue that the reason why stress cannot be antepenultimate in such words must be sought in the Latin ancestor of Portuguese (Pereira 1999; Mateus and d'Andrade 2000). In Latin, the penultimate syllable systematically bears the accent if it is heavy.[2] Since the penultimate heavy syllable blocked the emergence of proparoxytonic words in Latin, this stress pattern could only exist in words with a light penult.

As was pointed out earlier, words with antepenultimate stress were in decline towards the thirteenth century (Williams, 1975; Câmara 1976; Collishonn 2005; Massini-Cagliari, 1999). However, many new proparoxytones were directly borrowed from Latin after this date. Consequently, the proparoxytonic stress pattern which was reintroduced into the language was again typical for words with a prefinal light syllable. This being the case, and given that all productive generalizations have their history, the question remains whether or not speakers of Portuguese are capable of grasping the condition that the antepenultimate stress type is restricted to words with the given characteristic. That this probably is the case can be concluded from the way in which proparoxytonic proper nouns, especially toponymes from foreign origin, are borrowed into Portuguese by shifting their stress to the right (see Section 3.1 for examples and discussion).

Independently of the question of the syllable make up of proparoxytonic words, studies by Fernandes (2007) for EP, and Aguilera (2008) for BP, show that there is a tendency, especially in popular variants, for this stress pattern to be eliminated through syncope. The markedness of antepenultimate stress is often seen as a causal factor for the elimination of this pattern in both EP and BP. Most typically, proparoxytones are realized as paroxytones in everyday speech through the deletion of the vowel following the stressed syllable. The following examples are illustrative of this process:

(33) Syncope in proparoxytonic words

árvore	[áɣ.vo.ɾɪ]	>	[áɣ.vrɪ]	~	[áx.vɪ]	"tree"
fósforo	[fɔ́s.fo.ɾʊ]	>	[fɔ́s.frʊ]	~	[fɔ́.fʊ]	"match"
abóbora	[a.bɔ́.bo.ɾɐ]	>	[a.bɔ́.brɐ]	~	[a.bɔ́.bɐ]	"pumpkin"
pássaro	[pá.sa.ɾʊ]	>	[pá.sʊ]			"bird"
cócegas	[kɔ́.se.gɐs]	>	[kɔ́s.kɐs][3]			"tickle"
música	[mú.zi.kɐ]	>	[múz.gɐ]			"music"

More evidence for the quantity sensitivity hypothesis for Portuguese stress comes from the observation that there are no proparoxytonic words in which the onset of the last syllable is a palatal sonorant or a velar fricative (or uvular vibrant in EP), as in the examples below:

(34) *abelha* [a.bé.ʎɐ]　　　cf. *[á.be.ʎɐ]　"bee"
　　desenho [de.zé.ɲʊ]　　cf. *[dé.zẽ.ɲʊ]　"design"
　　cachorro [ka.ʃó.xʊ] ~ [ka.ʃó.ʀʊ] cf. *[ká.ʃo.xʊ] "dog"

In the case of the velar fricative or uvular vibrant, usually referred to as "strong R," Câmara (1953) analyses this segment as a phonological geminate in intervocalic position. On the other hand, Wetzels (2006) provides a number of arguments which lead him to conclude that palatal sonorants add weight to the preceding syllable: the non-existence of complex rhymes before palatal sonorants, the creation of a prosthetic vowel in loans from Indigenous languages or from other Romance languages that begin with a palatal sonorant, the non-existence of palatal sonorants word-finally, the obligatory bisyllabic syllabification of V+highV sequences before palatal sonorants (cf. *raínha* "queen," *faúlha* "spark"), among others. Obviously, the hypothesis that "strong R" and palatal sonorants add weight to the preceding syllable predicts that the prefinal syllable in words with a palatal sonorant in the onset of the final syllable acts as heavy, which fact explains at the same time why stress in the antepenultimate syllable cannot occur.[4]

6. Stress in compounds

The stress pattern of compounds is identical for EP and BP. Each element of the compound receives its own main stress, of which the final stress is the most prominent, as shown by Collischonn (1993) and Lee (1995) for BP and by Vigário (2003) for EP. The same pattern extends to the adverbs derived with the *–mente* suffix as well as words derived by the group of so-called z-evaluative suffixes *-zinho*, *-zito*, which behave as independent prosodic words. In cases of stress clash, the left stress is shifted or erased.

(35) *guárda + chúva*   >   *guàrda-chúva*   "umbrella"
      ítalo + brasiléiro >   *ìtalo-brasiléiro* "Italian Brazilian"
      marróm-cláro   >   *màrron-cláro*   "light brown"
      médico-chéfe   >   *médico-chéfe*   "chief physician"
      cérta-ménte   >   *cèrtaménte*   "surely"
      café + zínho   >   *càfezínho*   "small cup of coffee"
      iguál-ménte   >   *ìgualménte*   "likewise"

7. Secondary stress

While the location of primary stress in BP and EP shows no significant differences, the properties of secondary stress are less clear, especially in the European variety, for which some disagreement exists about its precise nature, at the word level and above. The following characteristics are shared by EP and BP: 1) the domain for secondary stress is the sequence of syllables to the left of the primary stress, 2) secondary stress is insensitive to the internal morphological structure of words, and 3) secondary stress is variable, as shown by Collischonn (1993, 1994).

Collischonn (1993, 1994) describes secondary stress in BP in a number of word types: non-derived words, words derived by suffixes, words derived by prefixes, and compounds. The author convincingly shows that for all these word types secondary stress follows a left-headed binary rhythm, resulting from a right-to-left scansion of the string of pretonic syllables. This alternating rhythm between strong and weak syllables is easily identified in words with an even number of pretonic syllables (secondary stresses are underlined):

(36) <u>cò</u>.*li.***brí**   "humming-bird"
      <u>prò</u>.*ba.*<u>bì</u>.*li.***dá**.*de*   "probability"
      <u>ìr</u>.*res.*<u>pòn</u>.*sa.*<u>bì</u>.*li.***dá**.*de*   "irresponsibility"

In words with an uneven number of pretonic syllables, the place of the secondary stress is variable. One option consists in building a dactyl at the beginning of the word, followed by alternating stresses, if applicable. The other option is the right-to-left scansion with the word-initial syllable remaining stressless.

(37) <u>tèm</u>.*pe.ra.***tú**.*ra*   *tem.*<u>pè</u>.*ra.***tú**.*ra*   "temperature"
      <u>ìn</u>.*co.mu.*<u>nì</u>.*ca.*<u>bì</u>.*li.***dá**.*de* *in.*<u>cò</u>.*mu.*<u>nì</u>.*ca.*<u>bì</u>.*li.***dá**.*de* "incommunicability"

A lapse of two unstressed syllables can only occur after the word-initial stress, which means that patterns like *<u>ìn</u>.*co.*<u>mù</u>.*ni.*<u>cà</u>.*bi.li.***dá**.*de* are ungrammatical. Another factor which, in BP, contributes to the binary rhythm is the frequent erasure of one of the pretonic vowels in words with an uneven number of syllables preceding the main stress, although the same phenomenon has also been observed in words with an even number of syllables to the left of the primary stress (Abaurre et al., 2006).

(38) <u>sà</u>.*tis.fa.***tó**.*ria*   >   <u>sàts</u>.*fa.***tó**.*ria*   "satisfactory"
      <u>mò</u>.*der.ní.za.çāo*   >   <u>mò</u>.*dern.za.* **çã̂o**   "modernization"

In an instrumental analysis of secondary stress in BP, Moraes (2003) shows that there is a preference in current speech for a single secondary stress per word, which is on the initial syllable. Moraes constructs two different sentence frames in which words of varying length are inserted, such as *regular* "regular," *regularizo* "I regularize," *regularizar* "regularize," *regularização* "regularization" (Moraes 2003:149). In one frame, these words appear at the edge of the intonational phrase I, the "strong" context, in which position phrasal stress occurs. In the other frame, the same words are positioned in a weak position inside the intonational phrase, as illustrated below (Moraes 2003: 150):

(39) [*Ele disse_____*]I [*de novo*]I   (strong context) "He said ____ again"
      [*Ele disse_____ hoje*]I [*de novo*]I (weak context)   "He said:___ today again"

Moraes' findings reveal a tendency towards a single secondary stress in words with two to five pretonic syllables: *règulár, règularízo, règularizár, règularização*. However, the author also found secondary stresses alternating with unstressed syllables throughout the word. Another important outcome of Moraes' experiment is that the prosodic (weak vs. strong) position in the carrier sentence had no influence on the secondary stress patterns observed for the set of words that were used in the test.

Secondary stress in BP is variable, somewhat different for words pronounced in isolation or when part of longer sequences in current speech, but have in common the possibility of a word-initial secondary stress varying with a binary rhythmic stress in the way reported above. For EP, the characteristics of secondary stress are still subject to controversy among specialists. D'Andrade and Viana (1989) established the existence of a binary rhythm in EP with stress on every even syllable counting from the main stress, resulting in a pattern equivalent to the one described by Collischonn (1993, 1994) for BP. The same conclusion was reached in Pereira (1999) and in Castelo (2006). On the other hand, Carvalho (1988, 1989) claims that secondary stress characteristically shows a ternary pattern, while Frota (1998) and Vigário (1998) found that secondary stress is optional and, when it occurs, tends to be unbounded.

In a more recent study of secondary stress in EP, Abaurre et al. (2006) challenge the binary rhythm hypothesis for this language. In an experiment based on a corpus of 20 sentences, read three times by three native speakers of EP, and by two native speakers of BP, these authors conclude that, while BP mainly applies a binary rhythm, EP shows unbounded footing. Another important result of this study, confirming similar findings by Frota and Vigário (2000), is that function words may be integrated into the domain within which secondary stress applies and may carry stress in EP. This possibility does not exist in BP, where function words can only be stressed in emphatic pronunciation. The examples in (38) taken from Abaurre et al. (2006), show the variation existing in the location of secondary stress as found for EP:

(40) *ò investigadór ~ o ìnvestigadór*   "the investigator/masc"
      à catalogadóra ~ a cátalogadóra   "the cataloguer/fem"

8. Conclusion

The position of main stress in BP and EP verbs and non-verbs is identical, even though scholars of both varieties have accounted for the facts in very different ways. While most scholars agree that stress in verbs interacts with morphology, there is no consensus on exactly how this interaction takes place. One trend is to mark flectional elements as extrametrical in those forms that escape what is considered the general rule, another one is to refer directly to inflectional categories to determine the different stress locations in verb forms.

Without doubt, the most controversial issue in the discussion of Portuguese stress concerns the relevance of syllable weight for the distribution of stress in non-verbs, which globally divides scholars working on BP and EP in different camps. Possibly the two stress systems do function differently, which fact could be related to other differences between the two languages, such as their different rhythms. Frota and Vigário (2000) have shown that some rhythmic measures distinguish EP from BP, with BP sharing properties with mora-timed languages like Japanese.

The problems related to establishing the principles that account for secondary stress are of an empirical nature, maybe due to the difficulty of detecting secondary stresses, especially in running speech, and to their variable and optional realization. There is agreement at least with regard to the fact that there is more than one way in which secondary stress is manifested in both varieties. It appears that, for BP, it is relatively clear how exactly secondary stress may vary. In EP, this topic needs to be investigated further in order for a consensus to be reached among scholars.

NOTES

1   I am grateful to Gisela Collischonn for comments. I especially thank Leo Wetzels for his comments on an earlier draft of this chapter.
2   See Chapter 6 on syllable structure for the Latin stress rule.
3   In cases such as *"cócegas"* and *"música,"* the deletion of the non-final post-tonic vowel causes progressive assimilation of the [+ / −voice] feature triggered by / s,z / (cf. Magalhães, 2014).
4   Other arguments to sustain the relevance of syllable weight in the phonology of Portuguese, not related to the stress rules, are presented in Wetzels (2003, 2006). An interesting case presented by the author is a rule of "spondaic lowering," by which a stressed mid-vowel in the prefinal syllable becomes lower mid, when the last syllable is heavy: *móvel* [mɔ.vew] "piece of furniture," *elétron* [ɛ.lɛ́.trõ], "electron," etc. See also Chapter 5.

REFERENCES

Abaurre, M. B. M., F. Sandalo, A. Mandel, and C. Galves (2006). Secondary stress in two varieties of Portuguese and the Sotaq optimality based computer program. *Probus* 18, pp. 97–125.

Aguilera, V. A. (2008). Arcaização, mudança e resistência lexicais em atlas lingüísticos brasileiros: o rural e o urbano. In Maria Inês Pagliarini Cox (ed.), *Que português é esse? Vozes em conflito*. Cuiabá: EdUFMT, pp. 83–98.

Araújo, G. A., Z. O. Guimaraes-Filho, L. Oliveira, and M. E. Viaro (2007). As proparoxítonas e o sistema acentual do português. In G. A. Araújo (ed.), *O acento em português: abordagens fonológicas*. São Paulo: Parábola, pp. 37–60.

Bisol, L. (1994). O acento e o pé binário. *Letras de Hoje*, 29, pp. 25–36.

Bisol, L. (1992/2013). O acento: duas alternativas de análise. In *Organon*, vol. 28, no. 54. Porto Alegre: UFRGS.

Camara Jr., J. M. (1953). *Para o Estudo da Fonêmica Portuguesa*. Rio de Janeiro: Padrão.

Camara Jr., J. M. (1976). *História e estrutura da língua portuguesa*. Rio de Janeiro: Padrão.

Carvalho, J. B. (1988). Réduction vocalique, quantité et accentuation: pour une explication structurale de la divergence entre portugais lusitanien et portugais brésilien. *Boletim de Filologia*, 32, pp. 5–26.

Carvalho, J. B. (1989). Phonological conditions on Portuguese clitic placement: On syntactic evidence for stress and rhythmical patterns. *Linguistics*, 27, pp. 405–436.

Castelo, A. (2006). A proeminência secundária rítmica no Português Europeu: uma proposta. In *XXI Encontro Nacional da Associação Portuguesa de Linguística*. Lisbon: APL, pp. 261–272.

Collischonn, G. (1993). *Um estudo do acento secundário em português*. Master dissertation, Universidade Federal do Rio Grande do Sul.

Collischonn, G. (1994). Acento secundário em português brasileiro. *Letras de Hoje*, 29, pp. 43–53.

Collischonn, G. (2005). O acento em português. In L. Bisol (ed.), *Introdução a Estudos de Fonologia do Português Brasileiro*. Porto Alegre: EDIPUCRS, pp. 135–170.

d'Andrade, E. and B. Laks (1992). Na crista da onda: o acento de palavra em português. In *Actas do IV Encontro Nacional da Associação Portuguesa de Linguística*. Lisbon: APL/Colibri, pp. 15–26.

d'Andrade, E. and M. C. Viana (1989). Ainda sobre o acento e o ritmo em português. In *Actas do IV Encontro Nacional da Associação Portuguesa de Linguística*. Lisbon: APL, pp. 3–15. *Delgado Martins, M. R. (1986). Sept Etudes Sur la Perception. Lisbon: Instituto Nacional de Investigação Científica.*

Fernandes, A. C. G. (2007). *Apagamento de Vogais Átonas em Trissílabos Proparoxítonos: um Contributo para a Compreensão da Supressão Vocálica em português Europeu*. MA thesis, Universidade do Porto.

Frota, S. (1998). *Prosody and focus in European Portuguese*. Ph.D. dissertation, Universidade de Lisboa.

Frota, S. and M. Vigário (2000). Aspectos de prosódia comparada: ritmo e entoação no PE e no PB. In R. V. Castro and P. Barbosa (eds.), *Actas do XV Encontro da Associação Portuguesa de Linguística*, Vol.1. Coimbra: APL, pp. 533–555.

Halle, M. and J. R. Vergnaud (1987). *An Essay on Stress*. Cambridge, MA: MIT Press.

Hayes, B. (1991). *Metrical stress theory – principles and case studies*. Manuscript, UCLA.

Hermans, B. and L. Wetzels (2012). Productive and unproductive stress patterns in Brazilian Portuguese. *Revista Letras*, 28, pp. 77–115.

Lee, S.-H. (1995). *Morfologia e Fonologia Lexical do Português*. Ph.D. dissertation, UNICAMP.

Magalhães, J. (2004). *O Plano Multidimensional do Acento na Teoria da Otimidade*. MA thesis, PUCRS.

Magalhães, J. (2008). The stress in non-verbs in Brazilian Portuguese in the multidimensional metrical plane. In L. Bisol and C. R. Brescancini (eds.), *Contemporary Phonology in Brazil*. Newcastle: Cambridge Scholars Publishing, pp. 22–53.

Major, R. C. (1981). Stress-timing in Brazilian Portuguese. *Journal of Phonetics*, 9, pp. 343–351.

Massini-Cagliari, G. (1992). *Acento e ritmo*. São Paulo: Editora Contexto.

Massini-Cagliari, G. (1994). Em busca dos parâmetros do ritmo do Português Arcaico. *Letras de Hoje*, 29 (4), pp. 101–112.

Massini-Cagliari, G. (1995). Cantigas de amigo: do ritmo poético ao lingüístico: um estudo do percurso histórico da acentuação em português. MA thesis, UNICAMP.

Massini-Cagliari, G. (1999). *Do poético ao lingüístico no ritmo dos trovadores: três momentos da história do acento*. Araraquara: Cultura Acadêmica.

Mateus, M. H. M. (1983). O acento de palavra em português: uma nova proposta. *Boletim de Filologia*, XXVIII (Lisbon), pp. 211–229.

Mateus, M. H. M. (1990). *Fonética, Fonologia e Morfologia do Português*. Lisbon: Universidade Aberta.

Mateus, M. H. M. and E.d'Andrade (2000). *The Phonology of Portuguese*. Oxford: Oxford University Press.

Moraes, J. A. (2003). Secondary stress in Brazilian Portuguese: perceptual and acoustical evidence. *Proceedings of the 15th ICPhS*, Barcelona, Spain, pp. 2063–2066.

Nunes, J. J. (1975). *Compêndio de Gramática Histórica Portuguesa: Fonética e Morfologia*, 8th edn. Lisbon: Livraria Clássica Editora.

Pereira, I. (1999). *O acento de palavra em Português – uma análise métrica*. MA thesis, Universidade de Coimbra.

Trubetzkoy, N. (1939/1969). *Principles of Phonology*. Translated by C. A. Baltaxe. Berkeley, CA: University of California Press.

Vasconcélloz, A. G. R. de. (1900). *Grammática Histórica da Língua Portuguesa*. Paris: Typ. Aillaud, Alves ét Cia.

Vigário, M. (1998). Cliticização no português europeu: uma operação pós-lexical. *XIV National Meeting of the Portuguese National Association of Linguistics*, Aveiro, Portugal.

Vigário, M. (2003). *The Prosodic Word in European Portuguese*. Berlin: Mouton de Gruyter.

Wetzels, W. L. (2003). On the weight issue in Portuguese: A typological investigation. *Letras de Hoje*, 134, pp. 107–133.

Wetzels, W. L. (2006). Primary word stress in Brazilian Portuguese and the weight parameter. *Journal of Portuguese Linguistics*, 5/6, pp. 59–90.

Williams, E. B. (1975). *From Latin to Portuguese. Historical Phonology and Morphology of the Portuguese Language*, 3rd edn. Translated by Antônio Houaiss from *Do Latim ao Português. Fonologia e Morfologia Históricas da Língua Portuguesa*. Rio de Janeiro: Tempo Brasileiro.

8 The Phonology–Syntax Interface

RAQUEL S. SANTOS AND MARINA VIGÁRIO[1]

1. Introduction

Since the early 1970s it has been acknowledged that (1) phonological phenomena often apply with reference to domains that do not necessarily coincide with morphological or syntactic constituents, and (2) the interaction between the phonological and syntactic components is limited and principled. These observations have led to the construction of the theory of Prosodic Phonology (Selkirk 1984, Nespor and Vogel 1986). This chapter provides an overview of the work on prosodic phonology and the syntax–phonology interface in Brazilian and European Portuguese (BP and EP, respectively). Section 2 focuses on the evidence available for prosodic domains above the foot-level. The construction of prosodic domains and the interaction between phonology and other components of the grammar are surveyed in Section 3. We conclude in Section 4 with some final remarks.

2. Evidence for prosodic structure from Portuguese

In this section we review some of the phonological evidence for prosodic constituents in Portuguese, a topic that has received great attention since the seminal work by Bisol (1992) on BP and Frota (1995) on EP, both of which articulated within the framework of Prosodic Phonology developed in Nespor and Vogel (1986). As phonologists disagree on whether the lowest prosodic domain that interacts with syntax is the clitic group or the (post-lexical) prosodic word, we start looking at the available evidence for the prosodic word level in both varieties of Portuguese (Section 2.1) and discuss the prosodic status of clitics and the internal prosodic structure of compounds (Section 2.2). We then consider the phonological properties of higher levels of the prosodic hierarchy, namely, the phonological phrase (Section 2.3) and the intonational phrase (Section 2.4).

2.1. The prosodic word

Early insights regarding the distinction between morphosyntactic and prosodic words may be traced back to Morais Barbosa (1965) and Mattoso Câmara (1972). Acknowledging the mismatch between these two types of grammatical constructs, recent work has mainly focused on (1) identifying phonological diagnostics for the prosodic word (henceforth, PW)

The Handbook of Portuguese Linguistics, First Edition. Edited by W. Leo Wetzels, João Costa, and Sergio Menuzzi.
© 2016 John Wiley & Sons, Inc. Published 2020 by John Wiley & Sons, Inc.

and (2) defining the prosodic organization of morphosyntactic units at this level. In this subsection we will focus on the former.

In both varieties of Portuguese, the presence of word stress and the (non-)application of phonological rules that are sensitive to it provide the major cues for the identification of the PW.[2] Examples include various processes that target unstressed vowels, such as neutralizations in BP involving pretonic (/ɛ/ > [e]; /ɔ/ > [o]; cf. (1a)) and post-tonic final vowels (/e/ > [i]; /o/ > [u]), the so-called process of vowel reduction in EP (/e, ɛ/ > [i]; /o, ɔ/ > [u]; /a/ > [ɐ]; cf. (1b)), and the optional processes of prevocalic glide formation (cf. (1c)) and vowel deletion to break a hiatus in both varieties.[3]

(1) a. p[o]rteira   "gate"   vs. p[ɔ]rta   (porta)$_{PW}$ (BP)
       (porteira)$_{PW}$ "door"
    b. p[u]rteira   "door keeper$_{fem}$" vs. p[ɔ]rta   (porta)$_{PW}$ (EP)
       (porteira)$_{PW}$ "door"
    c. ad[j]ar   "to delay"   vs. ad[í]o   (adio)$_{PW}$ (EP, BP)
       (adiar)$_{PW}$ "(I) delay"

Both varieties also have a number of assimilation rules that are circumscribed to the PW, as illustrated in (2). These include vowel harmony (cf. (2a)) and nasalization of vowels preceding a nasal onset consonant in BP (this process occurs in all dialects if the target vowel is stressed, as in (2b), and in some dialects also if it is unstressed, as in the first syllable of *banana* (2b)); stressless *e*-deletion in EP, which is (almost) obligatory in PW final position (cf. (2c)); and the optional processes of vowel deletion (cf. (2d)), glide formation (cf. (2e)), and syllable degemination (cf. (2f)) at the right edge of the PW in both varieties.

(2) a. p[e]PIno ~ p[i]PIno "cucumber"
    b. baN[ẽ]na ~ b[ẽ]N[ẽ]na *baN[á]na "banana" vs. *VEl[ẽ] NOva "new candle" and
       *RApid[ẽ]MENte (rapida)$_{PW}$(mente)$_{PW}$ "rapidly"
    c. *bebe água* > beb água   "(he) drinks water"
    d. *bela organização* (bela)$_{PW}$ (organização)$_{PW}$ > bel[o]rganização "nice organization" and
       ultra-ocupado (ultra)$_{PW}$ (ocupado)$_{PW}$ > ultr[o]cupado "extra busy" vs. *maometano*
       >*m[o]metano "Mohammedan"
    e. *iogurte* > [j]ogurte "yogurt"
    f. *gato temeroso* > ga temeroso "scared cat"

Nonsegmental phenomena may also cue the PW.[4] Prominence related phenomena such as initial stress, emphatic stress, and pitch accent, for instance, signal the presence of PW, as initial and emphatic stress are assigned to PW initial syllables and, at least in EP, pitch accents can only be associated with syllables bearing primary word stress. Furthermore, some deletion processes, such as deletion under identity (as we will see in Section 3.5) and word clipping or truncation in EP target the prosodic word. For example, in this variety clipping consists of the deletion of a PW and thus cannot target only part of a PW, as illustrated by the contrast in (3) below.[5]

(3) a. TEleMÓvel (tele)$_{PW}$ (móvel)$_{PW}$ > *móvel*   "mobile phone"
    b. teleFOne (telefone)$_{PW}$ > *fone, *tele "telephone"

Finally, there are several phonotactic restrictions that apply to PWs in both varieties. For example, no PW starts in [ɾ, ɲ, ʎ], while these segments may be syllable initial inside words, as in a[ɾ]a[ɾ]a *arara* "macaw," se[ɲ]or *senhor* "sir," ca[ʎ]a *calha* "roof rack").

2.2. *Clitic–host combinations and compound-like groupings*

As in many other languages, a number of functional words in Portuguese do not bear word stress. Which words are clitics and which ones have the status of PWs is to a certain extent language-specific. Processes that apply in unstressed environments in Portuguese, such as stressless vowel neutralization, glide formation, and deletion, as well as violations of pho-notactic restrictions imposed on PWs (cf. (4)), show that weak personal pronouns, many monosyllabic prepositions and complementizers, and definite articles are clitics (Bisol 2000, Vigário 2003).

(4) p[u]r tela "by screen"   vs. p[o]rtela   "Portela (proper name)"   (BP)
    de [di]~ [d], da [dɐ] "of," "of + the$_{fem}$"   vs. dê [dé], dá [dá] "give$_{imp.}$," "give$_{pres}$ 3p -sg"   (EP)
    no alto [nua]~[nwa] "in the$_{masc}$ high"   vs. nu artístico [nua]/*[nwa] "artistic nude"   (BP, EP)
    lhe [ʎi]   pronoun DAT-3p-sg   vs. *lhado   *non-word*   (BP, EP)

Clitics display specific phonological behavior in each variety of Portuguese, depending on the particular prosodic organization they establish with their hosts, which depends on their position relative to the host (this issue is adressed in Section 3).

Unlike simplex words and most morphologically complex words, transparent com-pounds, and some derived words are formed by more than one PW. The PW status of the internal components of the latter category of words is shown, among other facts, by their behavior with respect to processes that refer to the PW domain, such as word stress (cf. (5a)), the impossibility for glide formation to affect stressed vowels (cf. (5b)), deletion under identity (cf. (5c)), or resyllabification (cf. (5d)) (data from Bisol 2000, Schwindt 2000, and Vigário 2003).

(5) a. PÓS-acentuAL "post-stressed," agraDAvelMENte "pleasantly," PORta-banDEIras
        "flag-bearer," FMI (Efe-Eme-I) "IMF"
      vs. posPÔR "postpone," visionaMENto "viewing," portaGEIro "toll collector,"
      efemiNAdo[6] "effeminate"
   b. b[í]-anuAL "biannual," b[í]o-degraDÁvel "biodegradable"
      vs. r[i]organizar or r[j]organizar "to reorganize," b[i]ologia or b[j]ologia "biology"
   c. aLEgreMENte ou TRIsteMENte> aLEgre ou TRIsteMENte "happily or sadly"
   d. sub+locar [sub.lo]car ~ [su.bi.lo]car (BP) *[su.blo]car "sublease"
      vs. sublime [su.bli]me * [sub.li]me *[su.bi.li]me "sublime"

Depending on the intrinsic properties of the morphemes or words involved and the type of morphosyntactic construction they integrate, compound-like internal elements may behave phonologically in different ways. The prosodic organization displayed by this sort of words when formed by more than one PW is discussed in Section 3.

2.3. *The phonological phrase*

The phonological phrase (PhP) is the next higher level in the prosodic hierarchy. Like other domains, PhP also has a prominent element, which in neutral utterances corresponds to its rightmost PW. Both stress clash resolution phenomena and tone distribution are constrained by PhP-level prominence. For example, optional vowel deletion processes across words may be blocked under certain stress conditions, as illustrated in (6), taken from Frota (2000). In

(6a) deletion is not possible because V2 bears PhP prominence. As for (6b), deletion is possible because although V2 has word-level stress, it is not the head of its PhP. Similar data are available for BP as well, as illustrated in (7) (from Bisol 2003).

(6) a. O dançaRIno̲ A̲ma a bailarina russa   ˚dançarin[a]ma
        "The dancer loves the Russian chorus girl"
    b. O bailaRIno̲ A̲Nda sempre de limousine   ᴼᴷbailarin[an]da
        preta
        "The dancer always drives a black limousine"

(7) a. ele masTIga Ervas   *mastig[ɛr]vas
        "He chews herbs"
    b. ele masTIga Ervas amargas   ᴼᴷmastig[ɛr]vas
        "He chews bitter herbs"

Vowel deletion and semivocalization are affected by stress clash configurations, although the specific strategy employed to resolve stress clashes varies depending on the prosodic configuration and the language variety (Tenani 2002). According to Frota (2000), in EP, when the clashing sequence is part of the same PhP, the first syllable of the clashing pair is lengthened (cf. (8a)), but there is no lengthening when a PhP boundary intervenes between the clashing syllables (cf. (8b)).

(8) a. (O caFÉ: LUso)ɸ contém cevada de boa qualidade
        "The Lusitanian coffee contains barley of good quality"
    b. (O caFÉ)ɸ (LUta)ɸ pelo prémio do produto mais qualificado
        "The coffee contends for the award for the best product"

In BP, different prosodic domains also show different means to resolve internal stress clashes. Within the PhP, (optional) stress shift is applied, as in (9a) vs. (9b) (Abousalah 1997). When the stress clash occurs between PhPs, as in (9b), one clash-avoiding strategy consists in inserting a pause between the clashing syllables (Gravina and Fernandes-Svartman 2013).[7] The fact that stress shift is the preferred option not only in sentences such as (9a), but also in (9c), where the adjective follows the nominal head, provides evidence for the possibility of reestructuring non-branching phonological phrases with the preceding PhP in this variety.

(9) a. (dezeSSEIS HOmens)ɸ   DEzesseis HOmens   "sixteen men"
    b. (o daVI)ɸ (GOSta)ɸ   * o DAvi GOSta   "Davi likes"
    c. (caFÉ)ɸ (QUENte)ɸ   CAfé QUENte   "hot coffee"

The different strategies employed to resolve clashes reflect different prosodic mappings for the clashing stressed syllables. For instance, since optional stress shift only takes place within PhPs in BP, it always prompts the reading in (10a) below. By contrast, the insertion of a pause or the association of a pitch accent with each word involved in the clash prompts the reading given in (10b), as these are processes that apply between PhPs (Gravina and Fernandes-Svartman, 2013; example taken from Guimarães, 1998).

(10)   *o professor de balé russo*   "The Russian ballet teacher"
    a. Russian ballet: (o professor)ɸ (de baLÉ RUsso)ɸ   BAlé RUsso   ~ baLÉ RUsso
    b. Russian teacher: (o professor de baLÉ)ɸ (RUsso)ɸ   *BAlé RUsso

Tonal marking also makes reference to PhP in both varieties, although in different ways. In BP, a phrasal accent (L-) optionally marks a PhP boundary after a focalized element (Fernandes 2007). In EP, pitch accents are optional in non-nuclear positions and when they occur in this position, they are usually only associated with the prominent element of the PhP (Frota 2014).

2.4. *The intonational phrase*

The intonational phrase (IP) defines the domain of intonational contours (minimally formed by a nuclear pitch accent and a boundary tone) and of final lengthening, and constitutes the loci for pause insertion (see Chapter 9, this volume). Like all other levels mentioned in this chapter, IP neutral prominence is rightmost, a fact that is corroborated by the obligatory presence of a pitch accent associated with the head of the IP, the final PhP, as well as stress clash effects on vowel hiatus resolution (Frota 2000, Tenani 2002).

The IP is also the domain of an array of sandhi phenomena involving resyllabification in both varieties of Portuguese. These include optional word-final deletion, vowel degemination[8], and prevocalic gliding as ways of breaking a hiatus, syllable-final fricative voicing, and syllable degemination (cf. (11a-e), respectively) (Bisol 1992, et seq., Tenani 2002, for BP; Frota 2000, for EP).

(11) a. belo amigo   "great friend, masc"
     b. bel[a]miga   "great friend, fem"
     c. bel[w]amigo   "great friend, masc"
     d. boa[z] avaliações   "good marks"
     e. A gente tocou.   "people played"

Besides their different sensitivity to stress clash configurations, EP and BP differ with regard to the domain of sandhi phenomena and resyllabification.[9] While in EP the domain is clearly the IP (Frota 2014), in BP it appears that these phenomena are prosodically unbound. The example in (12) below, taken from Tenani (2002), illustrates diphtongation and resyllabification across semantically unrelated utterances in BP, which are not allowed in EP.

(12) *O Pedro comprou pêssego. Alegaram falta de provas.* >> pesseg[wa]legaram
     "Pedro bought peaches. (They) alleged lack of proofs."

3. Construction of prosodic domains and the syntax–phonology interface

Within Prosodic Phonology, domains at the PW-level and above are built with reference to syntactic information. Nevertheless, it is generally assumed that phonological domains are distinct from syntactic ones in a number of fundamental ways: they are composed of a limited number of constituents that occupy a fixed position within a prosodic hierarchy and are organized in a way such that higher domains always contain one or more domains of the immediate lower level (except for the syllable). The organizational principles which account for the wellformedness of prosodic trees are known as the *Strict Layer Hypothesis* (Nespor and Vogel 1986; Selkirk 1996). Work on Portuguese phonology provides strong evidence for this type of prosodic organization. Nevertheless, a number of questions regarding the precise interaction between phonology and other components of the grammar remain controversial: To what extent is syntactic structure relevant for the specific organization of word and sentence prosody? What are the phonological conditions imposed on the formation of prosodic constituents? Exactly which domains compose the prosodic hierarchy and which tree configurations are (im)possible? In the following subsections, we address these questions.

3.1. Syntax–phonology mapping and the construction of prosodic domains

In this section we present the main features that have been proposed to account for the construction of prosodic domains in Portuguese.

3.1.1. Prosodic structure between the prosodic word and the phonological phrase

Usually a morphosyntactic word in Portuguese forms a PW (*fé* "faith," *belo* "beautiful$_{masc}$," *adorou* "loved 3p-sg."). However, some morphosyntactic words, namely clitics (among which complementizers, prepositions, and the weak personal pronouns), are prosodically dependent in the sense that they do not form PWs by themselves. In other words, clitics are syntactic words that occupy syntactic terminal nodes, but which are defectively prosodized, since they do not form autonomous PWs. Conversely, some morphological words may include more than one PW, as in the case of compounds and certain derived words (e.g. *sócio-cultural* "sociocultural," *guarda-chuva* "umbrella," *pós-guerra* "post-war," *sinceramente* "sincerely," *sozinho* "alone"). It is worth observing that (1) words belonging to open classes always form (at least) one PW; (2) clitics always belong to closed classes, are highly frequent, and have at most two syllables; and (3) some affixes are assigned lexical stress and may form a PW independent from their bases. In what follows, we will focus on the (postlexical) prosodization of clitics and the prosodization of syntactic words containing more than one PW.

Because of the phonological properties of clitic–host combinations, it has been proposed that clitics combine with their hosts to form a postlexical PW or, in some accounts, a clitic group (CG). While in some studies the postlexical PW and CG coincide (Bisol 2000, Brisolara 2008), in others the CG is explicitly rejected, based on arguments against clitics being parsed within a fixed domain of the prosodic hierarchy (Vigário 2003, Simioni 2008).

In EP, evidence points fairly clearly to the prosodic adjunction of proclitics to the host PW and the incorporation of enclitics into the host PW, as depicted in (13a–b), respectively (Vigário 2003).

(13)

    a. Proclitics: b. Enclitics:

    Prosodic adjunction to PW   Prosodic incorporation into PW

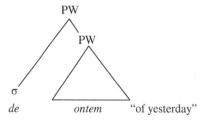

The process of front vowel deletion—a rule that applies (nearly always) at the right-edge of the PW in intonational phrase internal position—illustrates the main facts (see 14). The process of *e*-deletion applies in (14a–c) but not in (14d–e), because only in the former the non-back vowel is in PW-final position. Notice that in (14c) and (14e) the weak pronoun incorporates into the host PW, meaning that in (14c) the clitic final vowel becomes PW final and deletes, and in (14e) the host final vowel is nolonger PW final, and therefore cannot delete. In turn, *e*-deletion is not mandatory in (14f), indicating that the clitic by itself does not pattern like a PW and is not enclitic to the previous PW (this and other facts argue in favor of the proclitic nature of preverbal weak pronouns); here deletion may optionally occur due to a reduction process typically found in highly frequent words. In the examples below "ˣ" signals very infrequent, marked realizations; bold signals the target vowel.

(14) a. DEv**e**   0/ˣ[i]   "(he) owes"
      b. DEv**e** aconteCER   0/ ˣ[j]/ ˣ[i]   "(it) must happen"
      c. DEv**e**-te aconteCER 0/ ˣ[j]/ ˣ[i]   "(it) must happen to you"
      d. realiZAR   *0/[i]/[j]   "(to) accomplish"
      e. DEv**e**-a   *0/[j]   "owes it 3p-sg"
      f. JÁ t**e** aconteCEU   0/[j]/ ˣ[i]   "(it) has already happened to you"

Importantly, proclitics as well as the initial elements of their host behave like PW initial and unlike PW non-initial syllables in that they may bear emphatic stress and allow variable realization of stressless vowels, as in *ou organizações* "or organizations." Hence, these EP data are only compatible with an analysis in which proclitics adjoin to the PW, instead of attaching to a higher prosodic level (as in 15a, and unlike 15b).

(15)

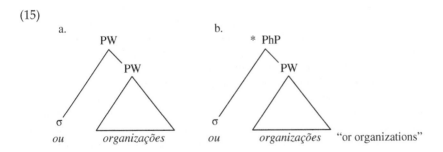

For BP, all studies agree that proclitics and enclitics behave alike, but the evidence for where and how clitics are prosodically structured is less clear. Bisol (2000), for instance, claims that clitics (whether proclitic or enclitic) do not integrate the PW host, but rather adjoin to it in an extended prosodic word (postlexical prosodic word) or a clitic group, based on the fact that many clitics (e.g. *de* "of," *me* "to me" or *por* "by") optionally exhibit a high vowel ([i, u]) regardless of their position (as in m[e] fala ~ m[i] fala and fala-m[e] ~ fala-m[i] "talk to me"), just like final weak syllables in lexical PWs (e.g. *fale* fal[e] ~ fal[i] "speak, imp"; *árabe* arab[e] ~ arab[i] "Arabic").[10] In addition, vowel elision can occur between a clitic and its host (e.g. *uma hotelaria* > um[o]telaria "hotel management," *da hotelaria* d[o]telaria "of the_fem hotel management"), while elision does not occur inside the PW (e.g. *maometano > m[o]metano "Mahomedan"). The fact that palatalization of plosives followed by [i, j] applies to clitics, but not across PWs (e.g. *da historia* ᴼᴷ[dʒ]istória "of the history," but *carta importante* *car[tʃ] i]mportante "important letter") is seen as evidence that clitics are not adjoined to the PhP.

In turn, Toneli (2009) defends the view that clitics adjoin to the PW in BP, based on the fact that proclitics, like in EP, may bear PW initial stress, which is assigned to stressless syllables in PW initial position. Toneli also claims that when clitics are under focus, they form independent PWs.

That clitics are inert with respect to stress location (e.g. *víamos-te*/*viamós-te* "we used to see you") and may violate phonotactic restrictions on PWs is usually assumed to follow from the view that stress assignment and phonotactic restrictions operate in the lexical phonology only (Bisol 2000, Vigário 2003). Alternatively, Simioni (2008) suggests that BP clitics attach directly to the PhP, and therefore do not interact with word-stress and are not subject to the phonotactic restrictions imposed on PWs (e.g. they may start in [ʎ]). We may note that this analysis cannot account for the fact that proclitics pattern like PW initial, at least in EP, nor can it be extended to EP enclitics, which behave like PW internal syllables with respect to the postlexical phonology (although they are also inert with respect to primary word stress location in the host).

The exact mechanism responsible for the prosodic organization of clitics with their hosts has been investigated in Vigário (2003) for EP and Simioni (2008) for BP. In the former, the mapping between lexical and postlexical PW boundaries plays an important role: it is proposed that the lowest syntactic Lex° is mapped onto a PW and that only the left edge of the lexical PW is projected postlexically; this is meant to account for the fact that in EP only the left, but not the right boundary of lexical PWs is reflected postlexically (recall that in EP the phonological evidence indicates that proclitics adjoin to the PW and enclitics incorporate into the host PW). In turn, Simioni develops an OT analysis à la Selkirk (1996), with a particular constraint ranking accounting for the attachment of both proclitics and enclitics directly to the PhP.

Like clitics, compound-like constructs also occupy terminal nodes of syntactic structures. The prosodization of this type of expression has been subject to controversy, too. Admitting that some recursion is allowed in prosody, Guimarães (1998), Schwindt (2008), among many others, assume that the organization of compounds and other types of PW combinations involves recursive prosodic words (e.g. $((porta)_{PW}(bandeiras)_{PW})_{PW}$ "standardbearer"). Departing from previous work, Vigário (2010) claims that the constituents of these prosodic groupings form distinct domains instead of recursive prosodic words. It is argued that this type of constructions forms an independent domain, distinct from both the PW and the PhP (see Section 3.3 below), which is referred to as the prosodic word group (PWG) (instead of CG, as in previous accounts within prosodic phonology).[11] Evidence for the PWG in Portuguese includes segmental and suprasegmental phenomena, briefly illustrated below.

As we have seen above, vowel deletion processes are possible across words as a means for hiatus resolution, but are blocked under stress clash. Within compounds, PW-final deletion in EP is obligatorily blocked if V2 bears PWG prominence (corresponding to the rightmost PW within PWG). This is exemplified in (16): in (16a) V2 bears PWG (but not PhP) prominence, and PW-final vowel deletion is blocked (in the case of *e*, it typically surfaces as [j] in this context); in (16b), by contrast, V2 is not the head of the PWG and V1 may delete.

(16) a. SN (ess*e*-ene) complexo   [ɛsj ɛn]   JS (jot*a*-esse) envelhecida   [ʒɔtɐ ɛs]
         "complex NP (nominal phrase)"   "aged JS (youth party organization)"
     b. FMI (ef*e*-eme-i)   [ɛf ɛmj í]   JSD (jot*a*-esse-dê)   [ʒɔt ɛs dé]
         "IMF (International Monetary Fund)"   "JSD (youth party organization)"

According to Vigário and Fernandes-Svartman (2010), the PWG is a crucial domain for pitch accent assignment in BP, because pitch accents are obligatory on the rightmost PW of complex words containing more than one PW, whereas non-final PWs only have to be pitch-accented if they are long.

The coincidence most often observed between the edges of syntactic terminal nodes (specifically, lexical X^0) and the edges of the PWG is attributed to the role played by alignment constraints (McCarthy and Prince 1994) requiring that the right and left edges of a lexical X^0 coincide with the right and left edges of the PWG, respectively. Under Vigário's (2010) approach, every syntactic lexical terminal node forms a PWG, even if it is formed of a single PW (e.g. *brinquedo* "toy"). This constituent is also subject to size conditions, which are purely phonological (see Section 3.2. below).

3.1.2. The phonological phrase

We next consider the formation of the phonological phrase. The majority of studies on both varieties of Portuguese adopt (or adapt) Nespor and Vogel's (1986) basic algorithm for PhP formation. According to Frota (2000), for instance, the phonological phrase in EP includes the material within the maximal projection of a lexical syntactic head (Lex^{max}), namely the lexical head (Lex^0) and the elements on the head's nonrecursive side within Lex^{max}. Non-branching phrases are grouped within the PhP that contains the previous lexical head. Although this seems to be a phonological requirement, it is also constrained by syntactic information, since only complements or modifiers of the previous lexical head may be parsed within the PhP containing that head. Guimarães (1998) takes a somewhat different approach to the construction of prosodic domains, by making use of some aspects of the minimalist program in the syntax–phonology mapping he proposes. In his reanalysis, there are two linearization algorithms: one that applies to lexical items and generates unordered chains of lexical items (π chains) and another one that linearizes the π chains. In both Nespor and Vogel's system and Guimarães' reanalysis, heads and specifiers are parsed into different PhPs. However, such parsing encounters a number of problems with respect to BP. Santos (1997), for instance, observes that stress shift is possible in a sentence like *de leite, o DAvi GOsta* "**Milk**, Davi likes" in which *o Davi* cannot be restructured with *gosta* (compare this sentence with *o daVI GOSta de leite* "Davi likes milk," in which stress shift is not allowed). In addition, Guimarães (1998) shows that stress shift may also take place when the subject is a pronoun (as in *voCÊ JOga futebol* "You play football," which can be produced as *VOcê JOga futebol*).

3.1.3. The intonational phrase

Let us now consider the syntax–phonology mapping at the level of IP (Frota 2000, Tenani 2002, Fernandes 2007). The IP includes all adjacent PhPs within a root sentence. PhPs in a string not structurally attached to the sentence tree (e.g. parenthetical phrases, explicative clauses, vocatives, topics) form IPs on their own, and so does any remaining sequence of adjacent PhPs attached to the sentence tree. In an SVO sentence with a parenthetical intervening between S and VO, for instance, both S and VO form an IP. Long IPs are constrained by phonological conditions, which may be responsible for the formation of shorter IPs, as we will see in the next subsection. Importantly, however, these shorter IP must be obtained in compliance with a further syntactic requirement: head–complement and modifier–modifyee relations should not be broken.

Whereas in Standard European Portuguese (SEP) SVO sentences tend to be phrased as a single IP, unless the subject is long, in the variety spoken in Braga, in the north of Portugal (NEP), subjects very often form an IP irrespective of length considerations. Elordieta, Frota, and Vigário (2005) propose that this difference follows from a difference in the syntax of subjects. Specifically, it is suggested that in NEP (as in Spanish) subjects may syntactically attach higher in the sentence than in SEP, being base-generated as adjuncts to InflP or CP, instead of being internal to InflP (or the Extended VP projection), as in SEP. Being more external in the sentence, subjects in NEP tend therefore to form their own intonational phrase, like topics, for instance, unlike in SEP.

3.2. *Purely phonological constraints on prosodic phrasing at different levels (PWG, PhP, IP)*

The prosodic constituents from the PWG-level up are constrained by purely phonological requirements, such as maximal or minimal weight or size.[12]

In EP, PWGs seem to be maximally composed of three PWs. Evidence for this includes prominence and deletion processes (Vigário 2010). As we have seen above, PW-final *e*-deletion is obligatorily blocked only when V2 bears PWG prominence. The examples in (16) above show that PWGs formed of two or three PWs only block *e*-deletion once. However, as soon as a compound contains four PWs, pairs of PWs are grouped into two PWGs, each of which with the prominent PW on the right. Once V2 bears PWG prominence, V1 deletion is blocked.[13] Notice that, if the four PWs were grouped into a single PWG, there would be no explanation for V1 resisting deletion, like in other internal positions where V2 is not the PWG head. Besides that, prominence relations are also perceived. The example in (17) below, show the prominence relations at the PW and PWG level.

(17)   *w*   *s*   *w* *s*   PWG-level prominence
                                        s   *s*   *s* *s*   PW-level prominence
            MRPP (Em*e*-Erre-PÊ-PÊ) (Em[j]-Erre)$_{PWG}$-(PÊ-PÊ)$_{PWG}$

At the PhP level one also observes minimality conditions on its size. When a lexical phrase is a non-branching modifier or a non-branching complement of the previous Lex, it is grouped with the PhP containing the previous Lex. Evidence from EP includes stress clash-resolution strategies as well as prominence and pitch accent assignment (Frota 2000). For example, it was shown in Section 2.3 that lengthening is a strategy for stress clash resolution within a PhP, but not across PhPs, as exemplified in (8). (8b) further shows that a PhP may contain just one PW, which led Frota (2000) to propose that a PhP should contain more material than a PW if possible. According to Sândalo and Truckenbrodt (2002), this requirement is overruled in BP by the *Principle of Uniformity*, which favors PhPs of equal length. According to these authors, the construction of PhPs in BP takes into consideration not only syntactic information, but also focus, eurythmic, and length effects. Length effects are taken into account for explaining why stress shift is more acceptable in *o caFÉ QUENte queima a boca* "hot coffee burns the mouth," whose PhPs are of the same size, than in *o caFÉ QUENte queima*, whose PhPs sizes are imbalanced. In the latter case, if each lexical word is the head of its own PhP, this creates more balanced phrases, but it also entails that stress shift, which is a strategy available only inside PhP, may no longer apply.

IPs are also subject to phonological conditions: long IPs tend to be divided and IP phrasing favors balanced phrases or else longer phrases at the rightmost position (Frota 2014). There is evidence for a maximal optimal IP size in EP. According to Elordieta, Frota, and Vigário (2005), while short SVO sentences usually form a single IP, subjects containing more than 8 syllables tend to form an IP on their own. Furthermore, Frota's (2000) findings suggest that when syntax–phonology mapping requirements yield short IPs (e.g. when a parenthetical is short), these IPs are not avoided, but a compound domain may be formed instead, grouping a short IP with an adjacent IP, as in [[*as alunas*]$_I$ [*até onde sabemos*]$_I$]$_I$ [*obtiveram boas avaliações*]$_I$ "The students, as far as we know, have got good marks." We return to IP compounding in Section 3.3. below.

As in other languages, speech rate may also be responsible for mismatches between syntactic structure and prosodic structure, as the same sentence may be phrased differently, depending on speech rate.

3.3. *On the geometry of prosodic trees*

Among the most controversial issues in the syntax–phonology interface is the status of recursivity. While recursivity is clearly a property of syntactic structures, phonology has been considered to be non-recursive since the early days of prosodic phonology (Selkirk 1984, Nespor and Vogel 1986). This was seen as one of the major differences between the two structures, the former being deeper, with (potentially) unlimited depth, and the latter being flatter and composed of a fixed number of levels, as defined by the Strict Layer Hypothesis (SLH). In more recent work within optimality theory, the SLH has been reinterpreted as a set of constraints, some of which are violable (Selkirk 1996). This has given way to proposals in which adjunction and compound structures violating *Recursion may surface. As we have seen in previous sections, these structures involve proclitics (often argued to be adjunct to PW—as in *a alma* (a (alma)$_{PW}$)$_{PW}$ "the soul"), compound-like elements with internal PWs (frequently claimed to be grouped into a recursive PW—as in (*ultra-calmo* (ultra)$_{PW}$-(calmo)$_{PW}$)$_{PW}$ "extra calm"), and short IPs inside longer sentences, under particular conditions.

As was argued earlier, the prosodization of clitics is usually taken to allow prosodic configurations that violate restrictions otherwise respected in the construction of prosodic domains, even in proposals where the CG is adopted, as in Bisol (2005). In the case of compounding, often analyzed as involving balanced recursion such that the higher node dominates two or more constituents of the same level, the possibility of PW recursion has been explicitly argued against, as by Vigário (2010), who argues in favor of an additional PWG domain. This author shows that several types of categorical phonological phenomena from EP and other languages make reference to this domain, and that the PWG is subject to size conditions that are not imposed on PWs. Another piece of evidence is especially telling in showing that the relevant constituent does not correspond to a recursive PW. In languages like Turkish and Dutch, the main rule for word stress refers to the *right* edge of the PW, whereas within compounds, stress is assigned with reference to the *left* edge of the higher node. Such different stress patterns would be unexpected in recursive PWs.

Unlike compound-like groupings, the topmost node that includes compound IPs (IP^{max}) appears to display exactly the same kind of phonology as the internal IPs, although with more salient traits. For example, IP^{max} may display pause insertion, its preboundary final lengthening is stronger, and its pitch range at the right-edge is larger (see Frota 2012). Importantly, prosodic rules circumscribed to the IP domain (e.g. resyllabification) apply not only inside the internal IP but also across internal IPs, within IP^{max}, as expected if the higher node is also an IP.

The phonology of PWGs and of compound IPs has been argued to point to the existence of two distinct types of prosodic organizations. According to Frota (2012), there is a difference between prosodic constituents and levels of phrasing. The former are defined by syntax-to-phonology mapping relations and are cued by a particular set of phonological and phonetic properties, whereas the latter involve recursion and groupings of the same prosodic category and are cued by gradient differences in the strength of the same set of phonological and phonetic properties.

3.4. *Phonological phenomena and the organization of grammar*

In addition to syntax, phonology seems to relate to other grammatical components. For instance, lexical phonology, unlike postlexical phonology, may refer to morphological, as well as lexical information (e.g. exceptions to rules must be lexically listed). In turn, postlexical processes may be sensitive to combinations of words and are often optional and only make reference to phonological information. As we have seen earlier, the division between lexical and postlexical phonology is in fact crucial for most proposals on the prosodic organization of clitics and compounds in Portuguese. For example, phonological phenomena in EP indicate a similar prosodization of enclitics and suffixes, on the one hand, and proclitics and prefixes, on the other; however, enclitics and proclitics differ from suffixes and prefixes in not interacting with lexical phonological phenomena (see Vigário 2003).

Phrasal prosody alone may also signal meaning, that is, in some cases information that is required for sentence interpretation comes from prosody alone. In languages like Portuguese, contrastive focus may be signaled solely by prosodic means. This happens, for example, when H*+L is assigned to a focused element, which becomes the head of IP, and tonal compression follows. Here phonology marking appears not to be just a reflection of syntactic structure, as in the case of topics, for example. Similarly, phonology alone may also signal sentence types by means of particular tunes.[14]

3.5. Other (non-trivial) interactions between syntax and prosody

While in general the relation between syntax and phonology seems largely confined to the point in the grammar where prosodic domains are built, in a number of specific constructions the two components seem to interact further. In coordinated structures in Portuguese, for example, a PW may be deleted under conditions of phonological identiy (Vigário and Frota 2002). The fact that deletion under identity targets PWs is shown by contrasts like those in (18a); in turn, the relevance of coordination is demonstrated by examples like (18b), which do not involve syntactic coordination and where deletion is impossible under the same prosodic conditions.

(18) a. $(alegre)_{PW}$ ~~(mente)~~$_{PW}$ ou $(triste)_{PW}$ $(mente)_{PW}$ vs. *$(acampa$~~mento~~$)_{PW}$
            ou $(acantonamento)_{PW}$
            "happily or sadly"   "camping or sheltering"
            $(mono)_{PW}$~~(gâmico)~~$_{PW}$ e $(poli)_{PW}$$(gâmico)_{PW}$ vs. *$(mono$~~grafia~~$)_{PW}$ e $(biografia)_{PW}$
            "monogamic and polygamic"   "monography and biography"
      b. *$(certa)_{PW}$~~(mente)~~$_{PW}$ $(inteligente)_{PW}$$(mente)_{PW}$ "certainly intelligently"

Another case of non-trivial syntax–phonology interaction involves word-order preferences under prosodic conditions related to weight (size of prosodic constituents and prominence), as illustrated in (19) below. Some particular syntactic constructions (e.g. topicalization, parenthetical insertion, and heavy NP shift) suggest that the preference for a particular word order on the basis of phonological weight is restricted to *late* syntactic operations (stylistic or discourse related), still available when the syntax–phonology mapping takes place (Frota and Vigário 2002).

(19) ??*A Ana comprou o quadro do vencedor do concurso ao Pedro*
       A Ana comprou ao Pedro o quadro do vencedor do concurso.
       "Ana bought from Pedro the painting by the winner of the contest"

Yet another case of complex interactions is illustrated by "syllabified intonation" in BP (Nunes 2000). This phenomenon involves a specific change in the speech rate triggered by certain determiners, which is used to signal an evaluative reading, as in *O João dançou com*

U-MA-me-ni-na-no-ba-ile "João danced with a girl at the ball" (meaning a very beautiful girl). Interestingly, such "syllabified intonation" must be maintained as far as the end of the IP. According to Nunes (2000), the domain of application of this process is to be defined in syntactic terms, namely, Spell Out domains.

Finally, it is worth mentioning the interesting issue of whether empty syntactic categories can be computed by phonology. Nespor and Vogel (1986) and others argue against the idea of empty syntactic categories playing a role in prosodic computations. However, Nunes and Santos (2009) show that stress shift in BP cannot apply blindly across any type of empty syntactic category. Specifically, traces of syntactic movement do not block stress retraction, but a null pronominal (*pro*) does (regardless of the Case properties of the null elements), as illustrated in (19) below. Assuming Chomsky's (1995) copy theory of movement, according to which traces are deleted copies, the authors argue that the data in (20) can be accounted for if copy deletion takes place before stress clash computation. In other words, traces have already been deleted at the point where stress shift applies, whereas *pro* is still present and is computed for adjacency purposes.

(20) a. [nem   a   unha]$_i$ a   Maria CORtou t_i HOje
      "not even the fingernail, Maria cut today"
   b. [a carta da Maria]$_i$ CHEgou t_i Ontem
      "Maria's letter arrived yesterday"
   c. # [esse bolo]   a   Maria passou mal [$_{island}$ depois que COmeu *pro* HOje]
      "this cake, Maria felt sick after she ate today"
   d. # esse bebê, a babá   CUIdou   *pro* ontem.
      "this baby the nanny took care of yesterday"

4. Concluding remarks

Issues related to the syntax–phonology interface in Portuguese have been extensively studied in the past two decades, mainly within the framework of prosodic phonology. In general, the focus has been on the description of Portuguese from a cross-linguistic perspective. The major contribution of Portuguese-oriented studies has been their adding to the cumulating evidence in favor of the model of prosodic phonology and the view that the relation between phonology and other components of grammar is limited and principled.

Since prosody provides a structure for the organization of speech and establishes a principled interface with syntax and morphology, it plays a crucial role both in language acquisition and in speech processing by children and adults. Owing to space limitations, we have not addressed these issues in the present chapter. However, it is worth mentioning some of the matters that have attracted the attention of researchers working on Portuguese in these domains: the role of prosody in early word segmentation and word categorization; the effect of morphosyntactic information and the position within prosodic domains on the emergence and development of coda segments; the grammatical status of filler sounds in early speech; the role of prosodic information in speech processing and syntactic disambiguation.

Finally, we would like to point out that there is very little research on the prosody of varieties of Portuguese other than those spoken in Brazil and Portugal. Nevertheless, we believe that work on other varieties will provide fruitful grounds for future research and contribute to deepening our understanding of Portuguese grammar(s) and the possible sources of variation in prosodic organization.

NOTES

1   This work has been partially supported by the Interactive Atlas of the Prosody of Portuguese Project (PTDC/CLE-LIN/119787/2010, Fundação para a Ciência e Tecnologia) and FAPESP (process 2012/23900-4). We are grateful to Leo Wetzels and Jairo Nunes for very helpful comments in several stages of this work.

2   For details and relevant discussion, see among others, Wetzels (1992), Bisol (2000), Schwindt (2000), and Vigário (2003).

3   When relevant, syllables bearing word stress will be represented with capital letters.

4   See a.o. Vigário (2003), Fernandes (2007), Toneli (2014).

5   Vowel Reduction and deletion provide evidence that in (3a) there are two PWs, while in (3b) there is only one: in *telefone* all letters <*e*> are either pronounced as schwas or deleted, which means that they do not bear stress. In turn, in *telemóvel* the first <*e* > is low, and stress is perceptible in the first syllable. EP differs from many other languages, including BP, in that clipping targets the whole PW.

6   The underlined vowels undergo neutralization in stressless position in both varieties, the process being obligatory in EP and optional in BP.

7   According to Tenani (2002), furthermore, in addition to stress shift, BP also uses beat insertion as a strategy for hiatus resolution when the central vowels (*a a*) are involved, within and across PhPs, unlike in EP.

8   In EP, syllable degemination is characterized as involving fusion between two vowels (cf. Frota 2000)—in (11b), for instance, the two medium central vowels merge into a low central vowel. In BP, on the other hand, linguists disagree on the actual process that takes place, as the vowel does not change in quality. For Bisol (1992), for example, the process deletes the first vowel, whereas for Tenani (2002) there is fusion and optional shortening of the vowel.

9   BP and EP also seem to differ with respect to the possibility of V2 semivocalization: while *camisa usada* > *camisa*[w]*sada* "used shirt" is possible in BP, it has been described as marginal in EP (cf. Bisol 1992 and Vigário 2003, respectively).

10   See also Brisolara (2008), who shows that vowel height alternations in pronominal clitics do not result from Vowel Harmony, but from the neutralization of stressless vowels.

11   A fundamental difference distinguishes the Prosodic Word Group from the Clitic Group (Nespor and Vogel 1986) and the Composite Group (Vogel 2009): the former, unlike the latter two, is assumed to have no special status with respect to the prosodization of clitics.

12   In many languages the PW is subject to minimality conditions (e.g. it cannot be shorter than a binary foot). However, this is not the case in Portuguese, as words like *li* "(I) read" or *nu* "naked" are relatively frequent (Bisol 2000).

13   In the examples, "*s*" represents heads; "*w*" signals non-heads.

14   See Chapter 9, Intonation in European and Brazilian Portuguese.

REFERENCES

Abousalah, E. (1997). *Resoluções de choque de acento no português brasileiro: elementos para uma reflexão sobre a interface fonologiasintaxe.* MA thesis, Universidade Estadual de Campinas.

Bisol, L. (1992). Sândi Vocálico Externo: Degeminação e Elisão. Cadernos de Estudos Lingüísticos, 23, pp. 83–101.

Bisol, L. (2000). O clítico e seu status prosódico. *Revista de Estudos da Linguagem*, 9 (1), pp. 5–30.

Bisol, L. (2003). Sandhi in Brazilian Portuguese. *Probus*, 15, pp. 117–200.

Bisol, L. (2005). O clítico e seu hospedeiro. *Letras de Hoje*, 40 (3), pp. 163–184.

Brisolara, L. (2008). *Os clíticos pronominais do Português Brasileiro e sua prosodização.* Ph.D. dissertation, Pontifícia Universidade Católica do Rio Grande do Sul.

Chomsky, N. (1995). *The Minimalist Program.* Cambridge, MA: MIT Press.

Elordieta, G., S. Frota, and M. Vigário (2005). Subjects, objects and intonational phrasing in Spanish and Portuguese. *Studia Linguistica*, 59 (2–3), pp. 110–143.

Fernandes, F. R. (2007). *Ordem, focalização e preenchimento em português: sintaxe e prosódia*. Ph.D. dissertation, Universidade Estadual de Campinas.

Frota, S. (1995). Clashes and Prosodic Domains in EP. *Proceedings 19. Institute of Phonetic Sciences*, University of Amsterdam, pp. 93–107.

Frota, S. (2000). *Prosody and Focus in European Portuguese. Phonological Phrasing and Intonation*. New York: Garland.

Frota, S. (2012). Prosodic structure, constituents and their representations. In A. Cohn, C. Fougeron, and M. Huffman (eds.), *The Oxford Handbook of Laboratory Phonology*. Oxford. Oxford University Press, pp. 255–265.

Frota, S. (2014). The intonational phonology of European Portuguese. In Sun-Ah Jun (ed.), *Prosodic Typology II*. Oxford: Oxford University Press, pp. 6–42.

Frota, S. and M. Vigário (2002). Efeitos de peso no Português Europeu. In M. H. Mateus and C. N. Correia (eds.), *Saberes no Tempo. Homenagem a Maria Henriqueta Costa Campos*. Lisbon: Colibri, pp. 315–333.

Gravina, A. P. and F. R. Fernandes-Svartman (2013). Interface sintaxe-fonologia: desambiguação pela estrutura prosódica no português brasileiro. *Alfa: Revista de Linguística* (UNESP. Online), 57, pp. 639–668.

Guimarães, M. (1998) *Repensando a Interface Sintaxe-Fonologia a partir do Axioma de Correspondência Linear*. MA thesis, Universidade Estadual de Campinas.

Mattoso Câmara, J. Jr. (1972). *The Portuguese Language*. Chicago: University of Chicago Press.

McCarthy, J. J. and A. Prince (1994). Generalized alignment. In G. Booij and J. van Marle (eds.), *Yearbook of Morphology 1993*. Dordrecht: Kluwer Academic, pp. 79–153.

Morais Barbosa, J. (1965). *Etudes de phonologie portugaise*. Lisbon: Junta de Investigações do Utramar [2nd edn., Évora: Universidade de Évora, 1983].

Nespor, M. and I. Vogel (1986). *Prosodic phonology*. Dordrecht: Foris. Republished 2007 by Mouton de Gruyter, Berlin.

Nunes, J. (2000). Entonação silabada no português: uma análise minimalista. Paper presented at 48th Meeting of the SBPC

(Sociedade Brasileira para o Progresso da Ciência). Universidade de Brasília, July 14, 2000.

Nunes, J. and R. S. Santos (2009). Stress shift as a diagnosis for identifying empty categories in Brazilian Portuguese. In J. Nunes (ed.), *Minimalist Essays in Brazilian Portuguese Syntax*. Amsterdam: John Benjamins, pp. 121–136.

Sândalo, F. and H. Truckenbrodt (2002). Some notes on phonological phrasing in Brazilian Portuguese. *Delta*, 18, pp. 1–30.

Santos, R. (1997). A fonologia fornecendo pistas sobre a sintaxe: o caso dos objetos nulos. *Cadernos de Estudos Linguisticos*, 34, pp 169–179.

Schwindt, L. C. (2000). *O prefixo no português brasileiro: análise morfofonológica*. Ph.D. dissertation, Pontifícia Universidade Católica do Rio Grande do Sul.

Schwindt, L. C. (2008). Revisitando o estatuto prosódico e morfológico de palavras prefixadas do PB em uma perspectiva de restrições. *Alfa*, 52 (2), pp. 391–404.

Selkirk, E. (1984). *Phonology and Syntax. The Relation Between Sound and Structure*. Cambridge, MA: MIT Press.

Selkirk, E. (1996). The prosodic structure of function words. In J. L. Morgan and K. Demuth (eds.), *Signal to Syntax: Bootstrapping from Speech to Grammar in Early Acquisition*. Mahwah, NJ: Lawrence Erlbaum, pp. 187–213.

Simioni, T. (2008). O clítico e seu lugar na hierarquia prosódica em português brasileiro. *Alfa*, 52 (2), pp. 431–446.

Tenani, L. (2002). *Domínios prosódicos no Português*. Ph.D. dissertation, Universidade Estadual de Campinas.

Toneli, Priscila (2009). *A palavra prosódica no Português Brasileiro: o estatuto prosódico das palavras funcionais*. MA thesis, Universidade Estadual de Campinas.

Toneli, Priscila (2014). *A palavra prosódica no Português Brasileiro*. Ph.D. dissertation, Universidade Estadual de Campinas.

Vigário, M. (2003). *The Prosodic Word in European Portuguese*. Berlin: Mouton de Gruyter.

Vigário, M. (2010). Prosodic structure between the prosodic word and the phonological phrase: recursive nodes or an independent domain? *The Linguistic Review*, 27 (4), pp. 485–530.

Vigário, M. and F. Fernandes-Svartman (2010). A atribuição tonal em compostos no Português do Brasil. In A. M. Brito, F. Silva, J. Veloso, and

A. Fiéis (eds.), *XXV Encontro Nacional da Associação Portuguesa de Linguística. Textos seleccionados*. Porto: Associação Portuguesa de Linguística, pp. 769–786.

Vigário, M. and S. Frota (2002). Prosodic word deletion in coordinate structures. *Journal of Portuguese Linguistics*, 1 (2), pp. 241–264.

Vogel, I. (2009). The status of the clitic group. In J. Grijzenhout and B. Kabak (eds.), *Phonological Domains. Universals and Deviations*. Berlin: Mouton de Gruyter, pp. 15–46.

Wetzels, L. (1992) Mid vowel neutralization in Brazilian Portuguese. *Cadernos de Estudos Lingüísticos*, 23, pp. 19–55.

9 Intonation in European and Brazilian Portuguese

SÓNIA FROTA AND JOÃO ANTÔNIO DE MORAES

1. Introduction: Intonation and its functions in Portuguese

Intonation is the use of phonetic features, namely pitch, to express phrase-level meanings in ways that are linguistically structured (Gussenhoven 2007; Ladd 2008). The roles played by intonation in language have long been described in terms of three main functions of intonation (e.g. Halliday 1967): demarcation, that is the chunking or phrasing of the speech stream into intonation-based units; highlighting, that is the placement of prominence within an utterance; and the distinction of utterance types, i.e. statements, questions, imperatives, vocatives. Grammaticalizations of all or some of these functions may be found in different languages, with different realizations, and define the language-specific phonology of intonation. In this chapter, we describe the intonation system of Portuguese, concentrating on the analysis of the three main functions of intonation. The framework adopted is the autosegmental metrical theory of intonational phonology (e.g., Gussenhoven 2004; Jun 2005, 2014; Ladd 2008), along the lines of previous descriptions of the intonation of Brazilian and European Portuguese (Viana 1987; Frota 1997, 2000, 2002a, 2014; Mata 1999; Frota and Vigário 2000, 2007; Tenani 2002; Fernandes 2007a, b; Moraes 2008; Serra 2009, inter alia).[1]

We begin by considering the chunking function of intonation in Section 2, where intonational phrasing in Portuguese is described. Tonal marking of intonational phrases is discussed, as well as the distribution of tonal events within the intonational phrase. Other levels of prosodic phrasing that are intonationally relevant are also discussed.

Section 3 addresses the highlighting function of intonation in Portuguese, namely the strategies used to mark focus prosodically. Several strategies are discussed, like pitch accent placement, pitch accent type, phrasing markers, expanded pitch range for the focal accent, prefocal and postfocal deaccenting or pitch range compression.

Section 4 is devoted to the contribution of intonation to sentence type distinctions. The nuclear contours of four main sentence types are described: statements, questions (*wh*-questions and yes–no questions), imperatives (commands and requests), and vocatives (greeting call and insistent call). Together with a basic intonational inventory of pitch accents and boundary tones, other key features of the intonation system of Portuguese are discussed, namely the ways the language explores tonal alignment to convey meaning distinctions and the preferred tune–text accommodation strategies.

Unless otherwise stated, the present chapter is based on the description of a single variety: the Lisbon variety for European Portuguese (hereafter EP), and the Rio de Janeiro variety for Brazilian Portuguese (hereafter BP). In Section 5, we provide a summary description of the

The Handbook of Portuguese Linguistics, First Edition. Edited by W. Leo Wetzels, João Costa, and Sergio Menuzzi.
© 2016 John Wiley & Sons, Inc. Published 2020 by John Wiley & Sons, Inc.

main dimensions of variation across varieties of Portuguese, covering the data available for different European and Brazilian varieties.

Finally, Section 6 discusses the intonation of Portuguese within the Romance space, from a typological perspective.

2. Intonation and phrasing

One of the key functions of intonation is the division of the speech stream into prosodic units. Intonation is one of the ways in which the prosodic structure of an utterance manifests itself (together with timing patterns and variations in segmental variation), and thus provides relevant cues to the grouping/demarcation of the prosodic units that characterize spoken utterances. Importantly, the organizational structure of spoken utterances is not entirely predictable from their syntactic structure, depending on the phonological grammar of the language and the particular choices made by the speaker among the possibilities available for a given utterance (Nespor and Vogel 2007; Wagner and Watson 2010). In this section, we describe the language-particular preferences in intonational grouping that characterize European and Brazilian Portuguese, the size of intonational phrases, the distribution of tonal events within the intonational phrase and the ways in which intonational boundaries are realized. Although the intonational phrase is the prosodic unit under analysis, other levels of prosodic phrasing that are intonationally relevant in Portuguese are also discussed.

The intonational phrase (IP) is the prosodic constituent that constitutes the domain for the intonation contour (Nespor and Vogel 2007), in other words it necessarily contains one and only one nuclear contour. In stress languages like English and Portuguese, the nuclear contour is the melody on the nuclear syllable and subsequent post-tonic syllable(s). In most Romance languages nuclear prominence is rightmost within the IP (Nespor and Vogel 2007; Ladd 2008). Beyond this general definition of the IP, which fully applies to Portuguese, European and Brazilian Portuguese differ in important ways with respect to intonational phrases.

One of the main differences between EP and BP concerns the intonational characterization of the IP. In EP, only the head of the IP needs to be pitch accented and only the right-edge of the IP requires tonal boundary marking (Frota 2000, 2014). In BP, almost every prosodic word is pitch accented (Frota and Vigário 2000; Tenani 2002; Fernandes 2007b; Tenani and Fernandes-Svartman 2008; Vigário and Fernandes-Svartman 2010). This is illustrated by the sparse pitch accentuation of the rendition of the five prosodic word utterance in Figure 9.1 by an EP speaker in contrast with the rich pitch accentuation of a similar utterance produced by a BP speaker.

Thus, in EP tonal events, pitch accents included, mostly occur near the edges of intonational phrases, and phrase-internal prosodic words are frequently unaccented. Tonal events have therefore a demarcative function signalling intonational phrasing. In BP, by contrast, tonal events tend to characterize prosodic words and cue prominent syllables. However, in EP as in BP intonational phrase boundaries are usually signalled by a continuation rise contour (a rising accent LH followed by a high boundary tone) if utterance-internal, although a low boundary tone can also be found (Frota 2000; Tenani 2002; Frota, d'Imperio, Elordieta, Prieto, and Vigário 2007; Serra 2009).

The division of utterances into intonational phrases has been extensively studied for EP on the basis of neutral declarative sentences containing a subject, a verb and an object, in that linear order (Elordieta, Frota, and Vigário 2005; Frota and Vigário 2007). It was found that the intonational phrasing of SVO in a single IP prevails, yielding relatively long phrases containing four or more prosodic words. Although parallel studies are not yet available for BP, recent data from the Interactive Atlas of the Prosody of Portuguese Project (Frota 2012–2015) suggest that phrasing preferences in BP promote shorter phrases in equivalent contexts, as shown in Figure 9.2.

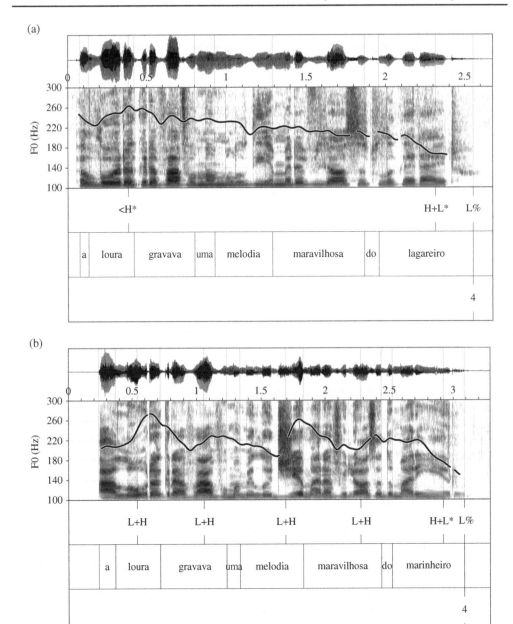

Figure 9.1 F0 contour of the utterance *A loura gravava uma melodia maravilhosa do lagareiro/ marinheiro* ('The blond girl recorded a wonderful song from the olive-pressman/sailor'), produced by an EP speaker (panel a) and a BP speaker (panel b).

Portuguese has been described has having only one level of prosodic phrasing relevant for intonational structure: the intonational phrase. This means that prosodic phrases smaller than the intonational phrase do not exhibit tonal boundary marking (Frota 2000, 2002a; Tenani 2002; Moraes 2008). However, unlike in EP, in some descriptions of BP (São Paulo variety) narrow focus may be manifested by the presence of a low phrase boundary

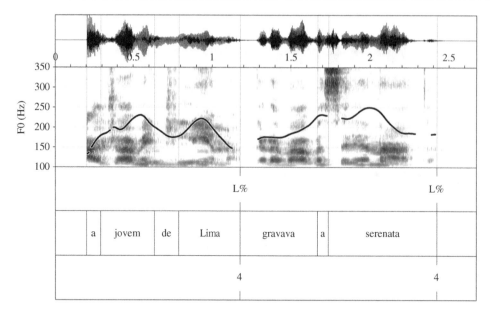

Figure 9.2   F0 contour of the utterance *A jovem de Lima gravava a serenata* ('The young woman from Lima recorded a serenate'), produced by a BP speaker.

associated to the right edge of the phonological phrase that contains the focused element (Fernandes 2007a; Tenani and Fernandes-Svartman 2008). In this pragmatic context, tonal boundary marking may function as a demarcation cue in BP, signaling a level of prosodic phrasing lower than the intonational phrase. Prosodic focus in Portuguese is the topic of the following section.

3. Intonation and focus

It is known that languages with word stress tend to have postlexical pitch accents (Jun 2005). This generalization could be extended to include the likelihood of stress languages to grammaticalize the highlighting function of intonation. In these languages, prominence at the intonational phrase level tends to be realized culminatively by means of a pitch accent, which is the nuclear pitch accent within the prosodic phrase, and nuclear pitch accent location reflects the intended focus of the utterance. Portuguese is a stress language that uses intonation as a device to express focus.

Focus is here understood as the most important part of an utterance. There are several theories of focus and various definitions of types of focus (e.g., Ladd 2008; Wagner and Watson 2010). Two types of focus are usually distinguished: (1) narrow focus, which indicates the contribution, in terms of new (or more relevant) information made in the utterance, and (2) contrastive focus, which explicitly contradicts a previous assertion or presupposition. In the former, focus identifies the part of the answer that corresponds to the *wh*-part of a question; in the latter, focus leads to a corrective interpretation of a previous proposition. The domain or size of the focus constituent may also vary, distinguishing narrow and contrastive focus from broad focus. In the narrow and contrastive focus cases the domain is typically a single word or a short constituent. In broad focus cases a larger constituent or the whole utterance is the focus.

In Portuguese, focus can be implemented by syntactic, morphological or prosodic devices, or by a combination of them. For example, the inversion of the canonical word order can be used as a mechanism to express contrastiveness, as in *Elegante está você* (canonical order *Você está elegante*), rendered in English by a cleft sentence "It is you that is stylish." Cleft structures can also be used in Portuguese, as in the expression *Eu é que agradeço* ("I am the one that is grateful," implying *me*, not *you*). The same interpretation can be achieved by the assignment of prosodic prominence to the utterance's subject "*Eu*," as in *EU agradeço* ("*I* thank you"). In this section, we describe the strategies used in Portuguese to mark focus prosodically, concentrating on utterances with narrow and contrastive focus. For the intonational analysis of Portuguese, and along the lines of previous work on EP and BP (Frota 2000, 2002b, 2014; Frota and Vigário 2000; Tenani 2002; Fernandes 2007a, b; Moraes 2008; Frota et al. 2015), we recognize two main types of tonal events: pitch accents, which may be simple or complex (i.e., monotonal like L* or bitonal like L*+H), and boundary tones, peripherally associated to intonational phrase edges and that may also be simple or complex events (e.g., L% or LH%).

3.1. Focus in statements

Previous work on prosodic focus in statements shows that pitch accent placement is a robust strategy to signal focus in Portuguese, but the choice of pitch accent may differ in EP and BP.

In EP, narrow focus, whether contrastive or not, is expressed by similar pitch contours: a falling pitch accent with the peak on the stressed syllable of the focalized element immediately followed by a fall (Frota 1997, 2000, 2002b, 2014; Vigário 1998; Fernandes 2007b; Frota et al. 2015). Figure 9.3 illustrates the focus contour in narrow and contrastive focus contexts (panel a and panel b versus panel c), and in late and early focus position in the sentence (panel a versus panel b and panel c).

The focus contour has been analyzed as showing an H*+L pitch accent, which contrasts with the nuclear fall that characterizes neutral (broad focus) statements where the peak is located in the pre-nuclear syllable (H+L*, see Section 4). Importantly, narrow/contrastive focus is also signaled by lengthening, whereas peak height was not found to be a robust cue of focus across speakers (Frota 2000). The systematic contrast between H*+L and H+L* revealed in production data was also found to play a role in perception. Frota (2012) provides experimental evidence that the difference in the alignment pattern of HL is enough to trigger a perceptual change between a neutral and a narrow/contrastive focus interpretation.

Besides the presence of a special pitch accent as a strategy to signal focus, pitch range compression is also a focus marker in statements with an early focus. The postnuclear stretch shows a compressed pitch range, which enhances the nuclear prominence of the focused element, as illustrated in Figure 9.3 (panels b and c). However, there is no deaccenting in the postnuclear contour. A postnuclear accent on the last stressed syllable of the IP is usually found, but with reduced range, as shown in Figure 9.3 (Frota 2000, 2002a, 2014). Prefocal pitch range compression, unlike postfocal one, has not been documented in EP. The presence of a narrow or contrastive focus in an utterance was also not found to impact on the prosodic and intonational phrasing of that utterance that remains similar to its neutral counterpart (Frota 2000, 2002b).

In BP, there seems not to be a single pitch accent type associated with the expression of focus. In addition, some studies have reported that narrow and contrastive focus are conveyed by similar pitch contours (Truckenbrodt, Sândalo, and Abaurre 2009), while other reported differences between the two types of foci (Moraes 2006).

Differently from EP, narrow focus in final position presents a low fall nuclear contour, characterized by a F0 peak on the syllable preceding the final stressed syllable of the utterance (belonging or not to the same word) and a fall on the stressed syllable (Moraes 2008, Truckenbrodt et al. 2009). This contour, illustrated in Figure 9.4 (panel a), is analysed as a

(a)

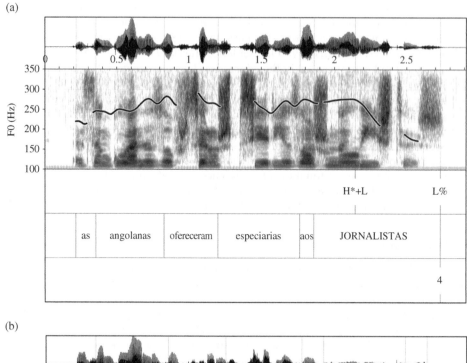

(b)

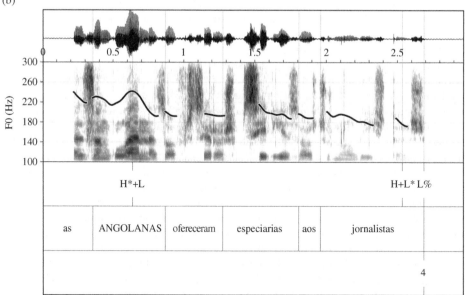

Figure 9.3   F0 contour of the utterance *As angolanas ofereceram especiarias aos jornalistas*
('The Angolan girls offered spices to the journalists'), with a narrow focus on '*aos jornalistas*'
(in response to 'Whom did they give spices to?'), in the panel a, and with a narrow focus on '*as
angolanas*' (in response to 'Who offered spices to the journalists?'), in the panel b. F0 contour of
the utterance *O pintor cantou uma manhã angelical*, with a contrastive focus on '*manhã*' (in
response to 'Was it an angelic night that the artist sang?'), in the panel c.

(c)

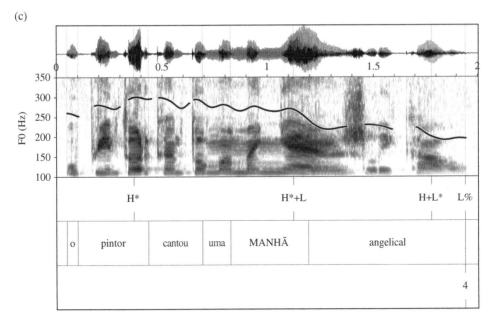

Figure 9.3   (Continued)

H+L* pitch accent and does not differentiate a statement with a late narrow focus from a neutral statement, which also has H+L* as the nuclear accent (see Section 4). If the final focus is contrastive, the H+L* pitch accent can show expanded pitch range, as in Figure 9.4 (panel b). The contrastive focus pattern is thus characterized by a rise to an extra-high level on the prenuclear syllable and a fall to a low level on the stressed syllable of the focused word. The focused word also presents an increase in duration and in intensity, mainly in the stressed syllable, features which play an important role in the identification of this pattern (Moraes 2008).

Unlike in Moraes (2008), where the Rio de Janeiro variety is described, in the description by Truckenbrodt et al. (2009) of the São Paulo variety no F0 height differences are reported between late narrow and contrastive focus, which are expressed by the H+L* nuclear accent. These findings may suggest regional differences in the implementation of the contrastive focus pattern, but further research is needed to clarify this point.

Multiple strategies are used in BP when the focus is early in the utterance. In early narrow-focus cases, both falling and rising accents have been reported. Truckenbrodt et al. (2009) describe the presence of H+L*, L* H and H*+L, with inter-speaker differences. In Fernandes (2007b), two main strategies are described (H*+L and L*+H L–) with inter- and intra-speaker variation. Similar findings are reported in Tenani and Fernandes-Svartman (2008), also on the basis of data from the São Paulo variety. In early contrastive focus cases, several pitch accents have also been reported. Moraes (2008) describes two variants used in Rio de Janeiro that are differentiated by the presence of the peak on the prenuclear (H+L*) or the nuclear syllable (H*+L). The second variant is illustrated in Figure 9.4 (panel c). It can be argued that, at the pragmatic level, there is, in the Rio de Janeiro variety, a difference in meaning between these two variants, with the prenuclear peak correlating with a "colder" or "professorial" correction effect, while the peak in the stressed syllable signals a greater involvement of the speaker.

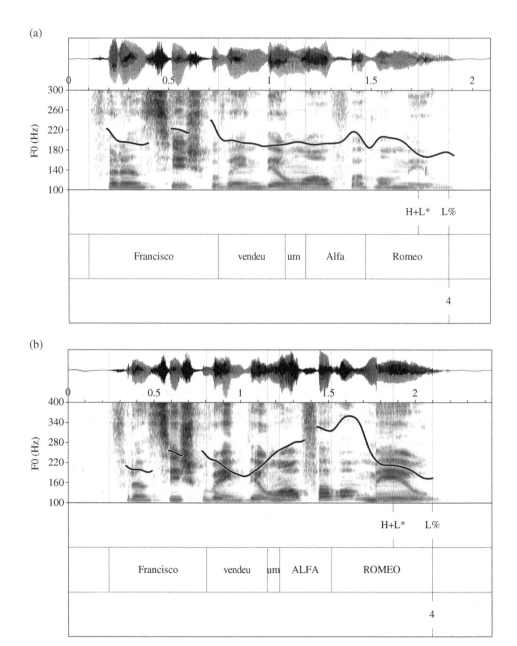

Figure 9.4 F0 contour of the utterance *Francisco vendeu um Alfa Romeo* ('Francisco sold an Alfa Romeo'), with narrow focus on '*Alfa Romeu*' (in response to 'What car Francisco sold yesterday?'), in the panel a, and with contrastive focus on '*Alfa Romeu*' (in response to the previous utterance 'Francisco sold a Porsche'), in the panel b. The utterance *O América venceu o Vasco* ('América has beaten Vasco'), with contrastive focus on '*América*' (in response to the previous utterance 'Fluminense (a soccer team) has beaten Vasco'), in the panel c.

(c)

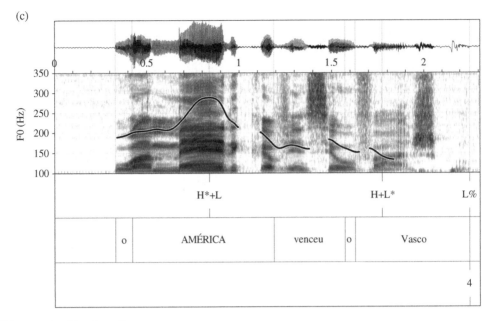

Figure 9.4 (Continued)

By and large, unlike in EP, in BP pitch accent type is not a robust strategy to signal focus. BP uses the EP focus accent H*+L, together with the neutral declarative accent H+L* and with rising accents. In addition, expanded pitch range of H+L* and the presence of a low tonal boundary marking the right edge of the phonological phrase that contains the focused element have also been described. However, in BP as in EP, pitch range compression is a focus marker in statements with an early focus, yielding the reduction of the final pitch accent in postnuclear position (Fernandes 2007a, b; Truckenbrodt et al. 2009). Postfocal pitch range compression is illustrated in Figure 9.4 (panel c).

In summary, pitch accent placement and postfocal pitch range compression are the common prosodic strategies to signal focus in Portuguese. Besides these shared properties, EP consistently uses a special pitch accent type, whereas BP is characterized by the use of multiple prosodic strategies.

3.2. Focus in questions

Prosodic focus in questions has been less studied than prosodic focus in statements. In yes–no questions, a non-neutral form of interrogation may arise when some information is already shared by speaker and listener, and the speaker challenges, doubts, or asks about the information that is shared. The piece of information that is challenged is the focus of the question. For example, in the yes–no question *Os rapazes compraram lâminas?* ("Did the boys buy slides?"), a focus on *lâminas* would express the meaning "I would like to know if they have bought slides and not something different."

In EP, the nuclear contour of yes–no questions with focus on a particular constituent shows a pitch accent different from the one found in neutral yes–no questions: in focused questions the nuclear syllable shows low-rising pitch, and not the nuclear fall of neutral yes–no questions (H+L*—see Section 4.2). The nuclear accent of focused questions has been described as L*+H, and this particular accent occurs on the focused element irrespective of its early or late position in the sentence. If the focus is final, a boundary fall follows; if the

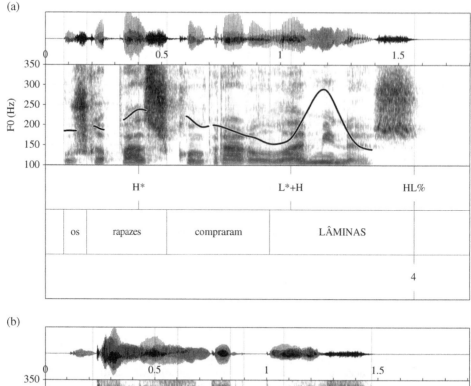

Figure 9.5   F0 contour of the focused yes–no question *Os rapazes compraram lâminas?* ('Did the boys buy slides'?), with the focus on '*lâminas*', produced by an EP speaker (panel a); F0 contour of the focused yes–no question *O galã anda de Porsche?* ('Does the hero drive a Porsche?'), with the focus on *galã*, produced by an EP speaker.

focus is early, a boundary rise marks the right-edge of the question (Frota 2002a, 2014). Figure 9.5 illustrates both a late and an early focus case.

Similarly to focus in statements, there is no deaccenting in the postnuclear contour in yes–no questions with an early focus, as shown in Figure 9.5 (panel b).

In BP, and differently from EP, the same nuclear melody is found in neutral yes–no questions and yes–no questions with focus on a particular constituent: an LHL melody. Figure 9.6 shows examples of focused yes–no questions with a late and an early nucleus. Although there is a general agreement that the nuclear pitch accent is rising, different authors have proposed different analyses for the accentual rise, namely L+H* (Moraes 2008 for the Rio variety; Truckenbrodt et al. 2009 for the São Paulo variety) and L*+H (Crespo-Sendra et al. 2014) for several BP varieties. The different analyses, however, may result from differences in speech style, in additional pragmatic meanings, or in phonological interpretation of the data. The accentual rise is followed by a fall, analyzed as an L% boundary. If the focus is early, the LHL occurs on the nuclear element and at the edge of the utterance (Figure 9.6, panel b). This suggests that the early nuclear rise is also followed by a low boundary tone, similarly to one of the possible strategies of prosodic marking of early focus in statements (see Section 3.1). Finally, the presence of the LHL melody postnuclearly indicates that, as in EP, there is no deaccenting in yes–no questions with an early focus.

Despite important differences in the melodies of focused yes–no questions, the two varieties of Portuguese employ accentual rises to signal focus and show no postnuclear deaccenting.

4. Intonation and utterance types

The distinction between utterance types is among the phrase-level meanings conveyed by intonation. Besides the demarcative function of chunking the speech stream into prosodic units and the culminative function of highlighting important information, the melody of speech can contrast paradigmatically to signal different sentence types. In Portuguese, these contrasts are usually achieved by means of the nuclear contour, that is the pitch accent associated with the nuclear syllable and any tonal events on subsequent post-tonic syllable(s). In this section, we describe the nuclear contours that characterize statements, questions (*wh*-questions and yes–no questions), imperatives (commands and requests), and vocatives (initial call and insistent call). Together with a basic intonational inventory of pitch accents and boundary tones, other key features of the intonation system of Portuguese are discussed, namely the ways the language explores tonal alignment to convey meaning distinctions and the preferred tune-text accommodation strategies when the segmental string, by virtue of not being long enough, imposes pressure on the realization of the tune.

4.1. Statements

In Portuguese, broad focus or neutral statements are characterized by a final fall through the stressed syllable of the nuclear word, which is represented by an accentual low target immediately preceded by a peak (H+L*). The accentual fall is followed by low pitch at the bottom of the speaker's range, or in other words by a low boundary tone (L%). The tune H+L* L% is thus the nuclear contour of declarative intonation in Portuguese, as illustrated in Figure 9.7 (and also in Figures 9.1 and 9.2 above).

If the nuclear contour does not distinguish between European and Brazilian Portuguese declarative intonation, the prenuclear stretch sets the two varieties of Portuguese apart. The difference is clearly seen in longer utterances, and is due to the sparse pitch accentuation that characterizes EP versus the rich pitch accentuation that characterizes BP already described in Section 2 above. In EP, as shown in Figure 9.1, the prenuclear contour contains an initial high tone and an accentless stretch up to the nuclear fall. In BP, by contrast, the prenuclear contour shows a pitch accent per prosodic word. Non-final stressed syllables typically exhibit a rising melody, that has been described either as an L*+H or an L+H* accent (Tenani 2002; Fernandes

(a)

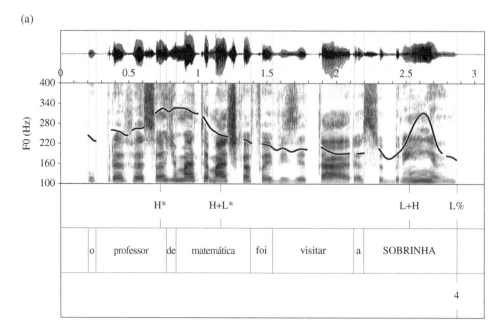

(b)

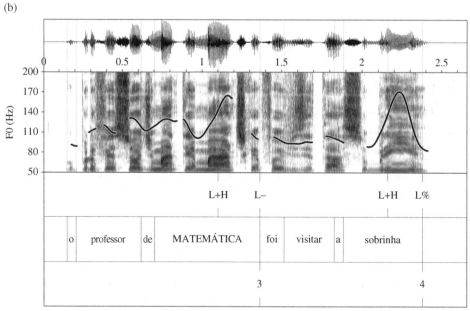

Figure 9.6   F0 contour of the focused yes–no question *O professor de matemática foi visitar a sobrinha?* ('Has the mathematics teacher visited her nephew?', produced by a BP speaker with the focus on '*sobrinha*' (panel a), and with the focus on '*de matemática*' (panel b).

2007a, b; Moraes 2008). Considering the variability in melodic shape of the prenuclear stressed syllables, across and within speakers of the same variety (at least for Rio de Janeiro and São Paulo), it seems more adequate in the present stage to leave the rising pitch accent unspecified as to the starred tone (L+H). Further research is needed to clarify the format of

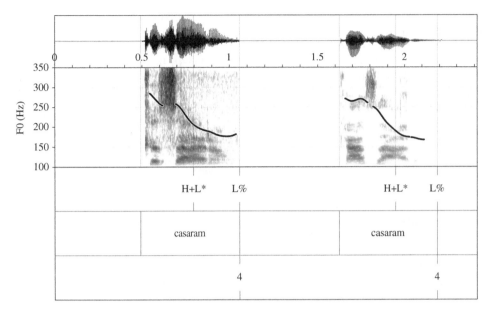

Figure 9.7 F0 contour of the neutral statement *Casaram* ('(They got) married", as in an answer to "What about John and Mary?"), produced by an EP speaker (left) and a BP speaker (right).

the prenuclear rising accent in BP. Importantly, BP conforms to the generalization that languages with a dense pitch accent distribution tend to show the same type of prenuclear pitch accent (as suggested in Jun 2005). Another feature that distinguishes between BP and EP is the presence of accentual-like tonal events in pre-tonic syllables in BP. These tonal events, usually in the form of high or rising pitch, have been described in statements (whether neutral or focalized) and other sentence types (Frota and Vigário 2000; Tenani 2002; Moraes 2003; Vigário and Fernandes-Svartman 2010; Frota et al. 2015). The number of syllables to the left of the stressed syllable and the presence of secondary stress are among the conditions that may govern the distribution of such accentual tones, but further research is required.

4.2. Questions

In this section, the intonation of two major types of questions is described: *wh*-questions and yes–no questions, as types of pragmatically neutral information-seeking questions. In Portuguese, *wh*-questions are syntactically and lexically marked. The presence of a question word identifies the utterance as a question. Question words typically appear at the beginning of the sentence (although *wh*-questions with in-situ *wh*-words are also possible). Here we will only be concerned with the intonation of *wh*-questions with the question word in sentence initial position. Unlike *wh*-questions, yes–no questions have the same surface syntactic properties as declarative sentences and contain no lexical marker. Thus, Portuguese is one among the large group of languages that signals the distinction between statements and yes–no questions only by prosodic means.

4.2.1. Wh-*questions*

Descriptions of *wh*-question intonation have pointed to similarities between *wh*-questions and statements. In Portuguese, both sentence types show the nuclear contour H+L* L%. In the case of European Portuguese, the prenuclear contour shows a high plateau similar to that found in statements, as illustrated in Figure 9.8 (panel a). The presence of a higher initial pitch in questions relative to statements seems to be an optional feature. Another optional feature is the presence of a final rise after the nuclear pitch accent H+L*, which seems to add additional politeness to the question (Frota 2002a, 2014). In Brazilian Portuguese, unlike in European Portuguese, the prenuclear contour seems to distinguish *wh*-questions from statements: *wh*-questions are characterized by an extra-high pitch in the *wh*-word and a gradual fall over the following syllables, until the last stressed syllable, as shown in Figure 9.8 (panel b).

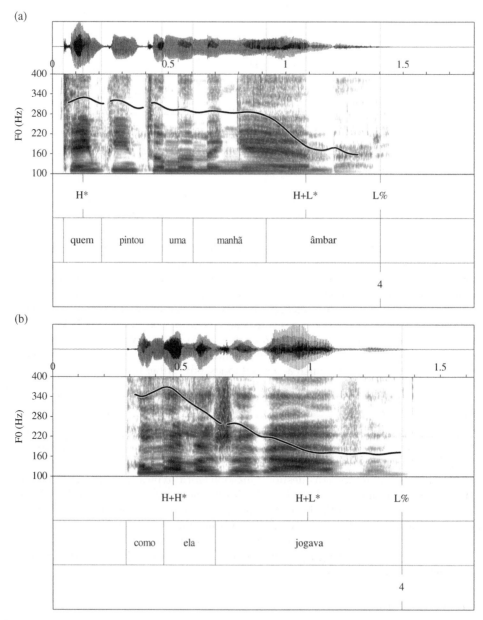

Figure 9.8　Panel a: F0 contour of the *wh*-question *Quem pintou uma manhã âmbar?* ('Who painted an amber morning?'), in EP; Panel b: F0 contour of the *wh*-question *Como ela jogava?* ('How did she (use to) play?'), in BP.

This prenuclear accent contrasts with the default rising accent found in statements, and has been represented as H+H* (Moraes 2008).

Given the high beginning of *wh*-questions in BP and the following gradual fall, the pitch level in the nuclear accent is usually lower than in statements. However, perceptual tests with resynthesized stimuli in which the nuclear pitch contour of the statement was replaced by that of the *wh*-question and vice-versa showed that this phonetic difference is not perceptually relevant for sentence type identification (Moraes 2008).

4.2.2. Yes–no questions

Contrary to *wh*-questions, the nuclear contour clearly distinguishes yes–no questions from statements in Portuguese. Besides this common feature, the distinction is conveyed differently in EP and BP: in EP, interrogation is signaled by the boundary tone; in BP, it is conveyed by a pitch accent contrast. Illustrative examples of neutral yes–no questions are provided in Figure 9.9.

In EP, yes–no questions show an obligatory final rise as the distinctive feature that sets them apart from statement and *wh*-question intonation (Frota 2002a, 2014). The properties of the final fall-rise of the yes–no question tune show that it consists of an accentual fall (H+L*) and a boundary rise (LH%), as exemplified in Figure 9.9 (panel a). In BP, by contrast, the distinctive feature is the nuclear accent, which shows a rise through the final stressed syllable with a late alignment of the F0 peak (Moraes 2008). In BP yes–no questions end with a rise–fall contour that comprises an accentual rise (L+H) and a L% boundary (Figure 9.9 (panel b)). The accentual rise as been analyzed both as an L+H* accent (Moraes 2008) or an L*+H accent (Crespo-Sendra et al. 2014, Frota et al. 2015). The two varieties of Portuguese thus explore different intonational markers to signal interrogation.

Yes–no question intonation provides a fruitful ground to examine tune-text accommodation strategies in Portuguese. Given the complex fall–rise (EP) or rise–fall (BP) nuclear contours, in an utterance that ends in a word with final stress the segmental string has only one syllable available for the realization of the complex tune. Languages are usually divided into compression languages, i.e., those that compress the tune to fit the segmental string, and truncation languages, i.e., those that truncate the tune to fit the segmental string (Ladd 2008). In EP, the fall–rise contour is fully realized due to the extension of the segmental string to cope with tonal realization (Frota 2000, 2014). This is achieved by extended lengthening of the nuclear vowel or by insertion of an epenthetic vowel, as in Figure 9.10 (panel a). Therefore, EP is neither a compression nor a truncation language.

BP seems to show tune–text accommodation strategies different from EP, allowing truncation of the low boundary tone (Moraes and Colamarco 2008; Frota et al. 2015), as illustrated in Figure 9.10 (panel b). In yes–no questions in BP, unlike in EP, it is the tune that gets accommodated to the text.

4.3. Imperatives

In Portuguese, as in most (if not all) Romance languages, imperative sentences are characterized by morphosyntactic markers that distinguish them from statements (namely, verb initial position, use of the second person and imperative mood). In this section, the intonation of imperative sentences that convey commands and requests is described.

4.3.1. Commands

The intonation of commands exhibits different features in EP and BP. In EP, commands typically show the nuclear accent of narrow focus declaratives (whether the nucleus is on the

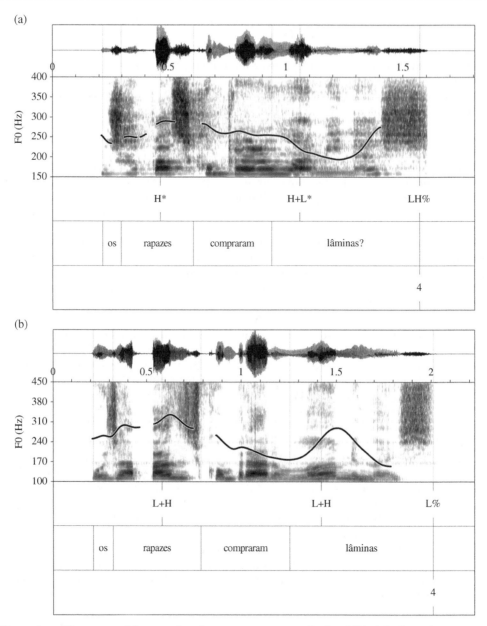

Figure 9.9 F0 contour of the question *Os rapazes compraram lâminas?* ('Did the boys buy slides?'), produced by an EP speaker (panel a) and a BP speaker (panel b).

verb or on the object) or of focalized yes–no questions (if the nucleus is on the verb), followed by a low boundary tone. In other words, commands are characterized by the use of focus accents (H*+L or L*+H), but crucially not of the H+L* nuclear accent found in neutral statements (Frota 2014). Differently, in BP the nuclear configuration of commands is the same of neutral statements, that is H+L* L% (Moraes 2008). The typical EP and BP patterns are illustrated in Figure 9.11. Given that the most frequent nuclear configurations for commands in Romance languages are either the broad-focus or the narrow-focus statements contours (Frota and Prieto 2015), BP and EP respectively exemplify these two common trends. In the

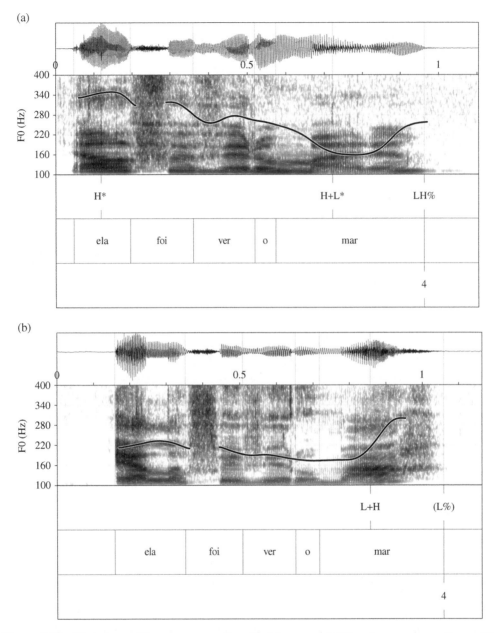

Figure 9.10 F0 contour of the yes–no question *Ela foi ver o mar?* ('Has she gone to see the sea?'), produced by an EP speaker (panel a), and a BP speaker (panel b).

prenuclear stretch, commands are characterized by a high tone on the first stressed syllable of the utterance.

The intonational properties of commands in Portuguese seem not to distinguish this sentence-type from statements or *wh*-questions (some phonetic traits like peak height could act as possible clues, but their consistency and efficacy has not been demonstrated). It is the combination of the particular morphosyntax of these utterances with the intonational features just described that may unambiguously signal the utterance as a command.

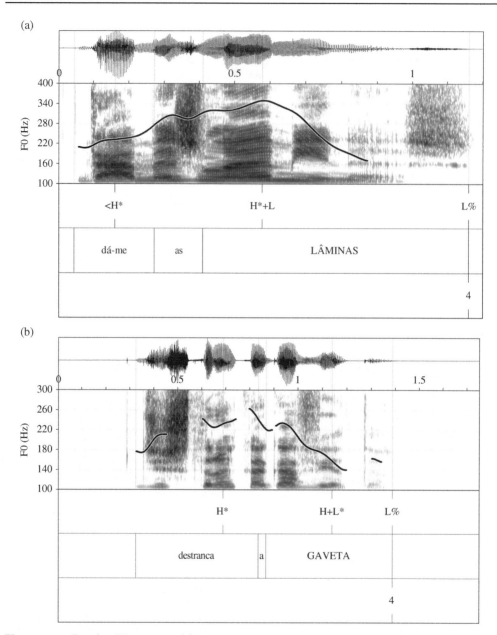

Figure 9.11   Panel a: F0 contour of the utterance *Dá-me as lâminas* ('Give me the slides'), produced as a command by an EP speaker; Panel b: F0 contour of the utterance *Destranca a gaveta* ('Unlock the drawer'), produced as a command by a BP speaker.

4.3.2. Requests

As in commands, European and Brazilian Portuguese also display different intonational patterns in imperative sentences expressing requests. In EP, the presence of a low nuclear contour (L* L%) characterizes a request, contrasting sharply with the falling (or rising, in the case of an early nucleus) pattern found in commands. The prenuclear contour shows an initial high tone on the first stressed syllable or at the left-edge of the utterance if no stressed syllable is available (cf. Frota 2014). An example of the intonation contour of requests in EP is provided in Figure 9.12 (panel a).

In BP, requests show a rise-fall nuclear configuration that has been analyzed as L+H* L% (Moraes 2008; Moraes and Colamarco 2008). This circumflex contour, illustrated in Figure 9.12

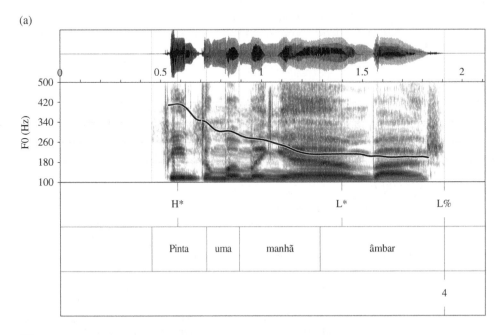

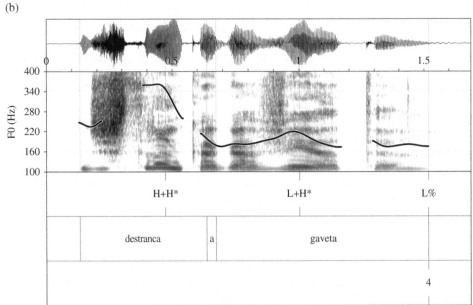

Figure 9.12 Panel a: F0 contour of the utterance *Pinta uma manhã âmbar* ('Paint an amber morning'), produced as a request by an EP speaker; Panel b: F0 contour of the utterance *Destranca a gaveta* ('Unlock the drawer'), produced as a request by a BP speaker.

(panel b), contrasts with the nuclear fall (H+L* L%) found in commands. The first stressed syllable displays a prenuclear accentual peak that is usually realized with particularly high pitch.

The distinction between commands and requests in Portuguese is thus mainly conveyed by the nuclear pitch accent (falling vs. low nucleus in EP; falling vs. rising nucleus in BP). Another trait that is common to EP and BP is the lengthening of the nuclear syllable in the request contour. Importantly, perception experiments have shown that native EP and BP speakers are able to reliably identify commands and requests on the basis of their prosody (Frota 2014; Moraes and Rilliard 2014).

4.4. Vocatives

Like in many European languages, calling contours in Portuguese show two main variants: the vocative chant or sustained-pitch variant and the low-call variant (Ladd 2008; Moraes and Silva 2011; Frota 2014; Frota and Prieto 2015). Interestingly, however, EP and BP use different variants of the calling contour to express similar pragmatic meanings.

4.4.1. Vocative chant

The typical vocative chant, characterized by high pitch on the nuclear syllable followed by a step down into the first postnuclear syllable after which the pitch level is sustained, is illustrated in Figure 9.13. This contour has been analyzed as consisting of an L+H* !H% melody, where the leading tone may show variable realization (Frota 2014; Frota et al. 2015). The chanted melody is accompanied by a characteristic duration pattern whereby the nuclear syllable, and especially the final syllable, are lengthened.

The prosodic features of the vocative chant block vowel-reduction patterns that otherwise are present in the language. In EP, post-tonic phonetic vowel reduction (or even vowel deletion, as in the case of a word-final [u]) is blocked and thus the final unstressed vowel is fully realized, as shown in Figure 9.13 (see also Frota 2014). In BP, post-tonic final mid vowels are realized as high vowels. This change in vowel quality is blocked in the vocative chant, and the final vowel is realized as a mid vowel (i.e., [o] does not become [u], as shown in Figure 9.13). Furthermore, to comply with both the chanted melody and the lengthening requirements, the nuclear syllable gets split up when there is no post-tonic material, as in João (['ʒwẽ.ẽw̃]) and Zé (['zɛ.ɛ] "Zé") shown in Figure 9.14.

It can thus be concluded that the vocative chant contour is part of the intonation system of Portuguese and is realized with very similar properties in EP and BP. However, the most common pragmatic uses of this calling contour seem to distinguish between EP and BP. In European Portuguese, the vocative chant is the calling contour that is typically used in the context of a greeting call or an initial call. In Brazilian Portuguese, by contrast, the vocative chant tends to be used in the context of an insistent call or when the person called is far away and not paying attention. Overall, this pattern in BP is rare and felt as more marked (at least, in the Rio de Janeiro variety). The most common calling contour in BP is the low call.

4.4.2. Low call

The low-call pattern is characterized by a nuclear rise immediately followed by falling pitch, as shown in Figure 9.15. The difference between the low call and the vocative chant lies on the boundary tone, and thus the low call melody is analyzed as L+H* L%, again with variable realization of the leading low tone (e.g., Frota 2014, Frota et al. 2015). Furthermore, unlike in the vocative chant, in the low call the boundary syllable is not lengthened, the reduction of the final vowel is not blocked (Figure 9.15, panel a), and there is no split up of the nuclear syllable in the absence of post-tonic material (Figure 9.15, panel b).

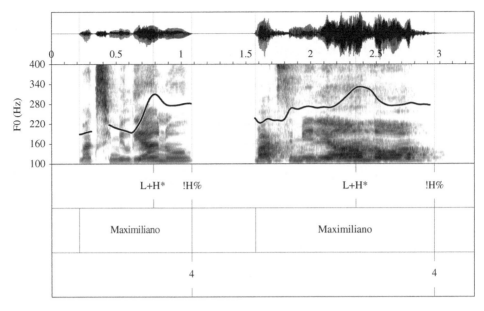

Figure 9.13 F0 contour of the utterance *Maximiliano* ('Maximiliano') produced by an EP speaker (left) and a BP speaker (right), illustrating the vocative chant.

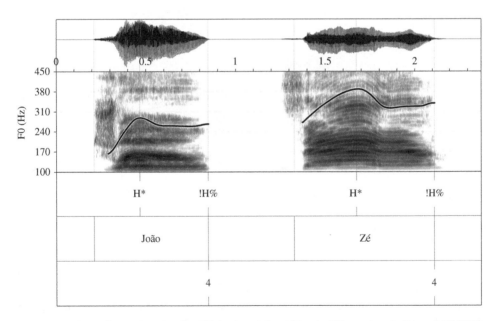

Figure 9.14 The calling contours *João* ('John'), produced by an EP speaker (left), and *Zé* ('Zé'), produced by a BP speaker (right), illustrating the vocative chant.

Although the formal properties of the low call are strikingly similar in EP and BP, the functional use of this contour differs: in EP, the low call conveys an insistent and impatient call; in BP, it is the most frequent calling contour and is commonly used either as a greeting call or an insistent call (with wider pitch range and higher intensity in the latter case).

(a)

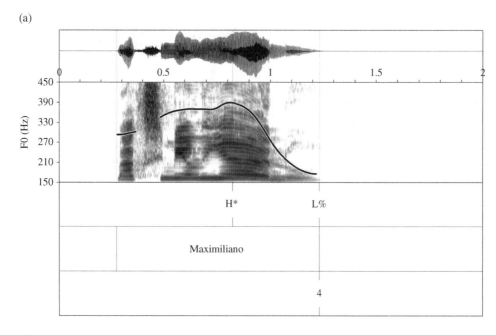

(b)

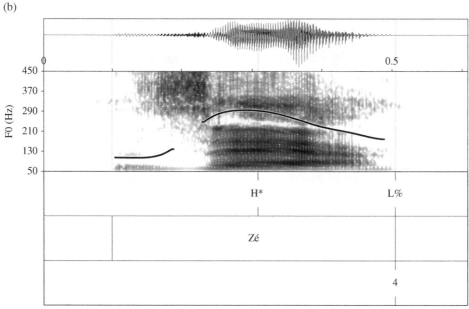

Figure 9.15 The calling contours *Maximiliano* ('Maximiliano'), produced by an EP speaker (panel a), and *Zé* ('Zé'), produced by a BP speaker (panel b), illustrating the low call.

5. Intonation across varieties of Portuguese

Studies of intonational variation within Portuguese, using a comparable and theoretically informed framework of analysis, are recent developments in the field of the intonational phonology of Portuguese (Vigário and Frota 2003; Frota and Vigário 2007; Fernandes 2007b;

Vigário and Fernandes-Svartman 2010; Cruz 2013; Cruz and Frota 2013; Crespo-Sendra et al. 2014; Frota et al. 2015).

A systematic comparison between varieties of European Portuguese and varieties of Brazilian Portuguese was conducted in Frota et al. (2015). Three main dimensions of variation were highlighted: the inventory of nuclear contours, intonational phrasing, and pitch accent distribution. Variation in the intonational inventory revealed important systemic and semantic differences across varieties. For example, yes–no questions, as described in Section 4.2 above, have different contours in the Lisbon variety of European Portuguese and the Rio de Janeiro variety of Brazilian Portuguese, the two varieties on which the present chapter is based. Furthermore, the contour of yes–no questions may also differ across varieties of EP (with southern varieties showing an all-rising configuration instead of the fall–rise found in the Lisbon variety) and across varieties of BP (with northern varieties showing a high tonal boundary that contrasts with the low boundary found in Rio de Janeiro and other central-southern varieties). Variation is not only achieved through the presence and/or use of different contours across varieties. It is also the case that the same contour may be used with different meanings. A prominent example of this sort of difference are the meanings expressed by the two variants of the calling contours, described in Section 4.4.

A second dimension of variation concerns intonational phrasing. As noted in Section 3, in BP a low tonal boundary may mark the right edge of a prosodic domain smaller than the intonational phrase in utterances with an early focus, whereas in EP only the intonational phrase shows tonal boundary marking.

The third dimension of variation results from the ways pitch accents are distributed within utterances. Besides the contrast between the sparse pitch accentuation that characterizes the Lisbon variety of EP and the rich pitch accentuation that characterizes the Rio de Janeiro variety of BP (described in Section 2), within EP and BP the distribution of tonal events may also differ. Within BP, southern varieties tend to show a denser distribution of tonal events. Within EP, it is the standard (Lisbon) variety that shows a sparser distribution than other EP varieties.

Alongside the variation, a basic set of properties that characterize the intonational system of Portuguese were identified in Frota et al. (2015): right-headed prosodic phrases, absence of postnuclear deaccenting (see also Section 3 above), and two main types of tonal events, namely pitch accents and boundary tones, with the prevalence of bitonal accents and simple boundaries.

6. Portuguese intonation within Romance

A typological look at the intonation of Portuguese within the Romance space concludes this chapter. In Portuguese, as in Romance languages in general, forms of grammaticalization of the three main functions of intonation are found: demarcation or phrasing, highlighting or prominence, and signaling different utterance types.

Portuguese is similar to most Romance languages in showing intonationally defined constituents that are highly ranked in prosodic structure, namely the intonational phrase (the exceptions are French and Occitan, which make also use of a lower-level unit in their phrasing patterns, the accentual phrase— cf. Frota and Prieto 2015). However, as described in Section 2, Brazilian and European Portuguese (the standard variety) crucially differ in the domain for the distribution of pitch events: BP is like most other Romance languages in having a low domain for pitch accentuation (in BP nearly every prosodic word gets a pitch accent), whereas the standard variety of EP is an exception within Romance languages with the intonational phrase as the domain for pitch accent distribution. Consequently, in BP as in most Romance languages, but unlike in EP, the prenuclear contour shows a dense distribution of pitch events that consists of a regular alternating tonal pattern (Jun 2014; Frota and Prieto 2015). In EP, by contrast, tonal events occur essentially at the edges of intonational phrases, which underscores their demarcative function.

In most Romance languages, nuclear prominence is rightmost and Portuguese is no exception to this general pattern. Portuguese, though, is a language that uses intonation as a device to highlight important information, together with syntactic or morphological means (see Section 3). Thus, changes in the placement of the nuclear accent, pitch accent type, extended pitch range in the focal element, and postfocal pitch range compression can be used as means to express focus in Portuguese (perhaps in a stronger and more flexible way in EP than in BP), like in some Romance languages or West Germanic languages.

Intonational marking of sentence types and pragmatic meanings is commonly achieved by the use of different nuclear configurations in Romance languages (Frota and Prieto 2015). In Portuguese, this role is mainly taken by pitch accent contrasts, since both EP and BP make a more restricted use of contrastive tonal boundaries, when compared to languages like Catalan, Spanish, or Italian (Moraes 2008; Frota et al. 2015). In Portuguese, as in most Romance languages, bitonal pitch accents are more productive in nuclear configurations than monotonal accents.

On the one hand, it can be concluded that the intonation system of Portuguese exhibits the main features that characterize the intonation of Romance languages. On the other hand, it seems clear that Brazilian Portuguese intonation is more typically Romance-like than (Standard) European Portuguese intonation.

Acknowledgements

We are grateful to the research team of the InAPoP project, for preparing the figures in this chapter. A set of the examples presented here were selected from the InAPoP speech database. The preparation of this chapter was partially funded by the grant PTDC/CLE-LIN/119787/2010 (FCT/MEC, Portugal), awarded to the first author.

NOTE

1   Other work on the intonation of Portuguese within different frameworks of analysis includes Cruz-Ferreira 1998, Moraes 1998, and Lucente 2012.

REFERENCES

Crespo-Sendra, V., M. Cruz, J. Silva, and S. Frota (2014). Asking questions across Portuguese varieties. Talk given at the 6th International Conference on Tone and Intonation in Europe. Netherlands: University of Utrecht. http://labfon.letras.ulisboa.pt/files/Crespo-Sendraetal_TIE6.pdf, accessed November 2, 2015.

Cruz-Ferreira, M. (1998). Intonation in European Portuguese. In D. Hirst and A. Di Cristo (eds.), *Intonation Systems. A Survey of Twenty Languages*. Cambridge: Cambridge University Press, pp. 167–178.

Cruz, M. (2013). Prosodic variation in EP: phrasing, intonation and rhythm in central-southern varieties. Ph.D. dissertation, Universidade de Lisboa.

Cruz, M. and S. Frota (2013). On the relation between intonational phrasing and pitch accent distribution. Evidence from European

Portuguese varieties. *Proceedings of the 14th Annual Conference of the International Speech Communication Association (ISCA) – Interspeech 2013*, pp. 300–304.

Elordieta, G., S. Frota, and M. Vigário (2005). Subjects, objects and intonational phrasing in Spanish and Portuguese. *Studia Linguistica*, 59 (2/3), pp. 110–143.

Fernandes, F. (2007a). Tonal association in neutral and subject-narrow-focus sentences of Brazilian Portuguese: a comparison with European Portuguese. *Journal of Portuguese Linguistics*, 5/6 (Special Issue Prosody in Ibero-Romance and related languages, ed. by G. Elordieta and M. Vigário), pp. 91–115.

Fernandes, F. (2007b). *Ordem, focalização e preenchimento em Português: sintaxe e prosódia*. Ph.D. dissertation, State University of Campinas, Brazil.

Frota, S. (1997). Association, alignment, and meaning: the tonal sequence HL and focus in European Portuguese. In A. Botinis, G. Kouroupetroglou, and G. Carayiannis (eds.), *Intonation: Theory, Models and Applications – Proceedings of an ESCA Workshop*. Athens: ESCA/University of Athens, pp. 127–130.

Frota, S. (2000). *Prosody and Focus in European Portuguese. Phonological Phrasing and Intonation*. New York: Garland/Routledge.

Frota, S. (2002a). Nuclear falls and rises in European Portuguese: a phonological analysis of declarative and question intonation. *Probus*, 14 (Special issue Intonation in Romance, ed. by J. Ignacio Hualde), pp. 113–146.

Frota, S. (2002b). Tonal association and target alignment in European Portuguese nuclear falls. In C. Gussenhoven and N. Warner (eds.), *Laboratory Phonology 7*. Berlin: Mouton de Gruyter, pp. 387–418.

Frota, S. (2012). A focus intonational morpheme in European Portuguese: production and perception. In G. Elordieta and P. Prieto (eds.), *Prosody and Meaning*. Berlin: Mouton de Gruyter, pp. 163–196.

Frota, S. (coord.) (2012–2015). *InAPoP - Interactive Atlas of the Prosody of Portuguese* (Funded by FCT, PTDC/CLE-LIN/119787/2010). http://labfon.letras.ulisboa.pt/InAPoP/, accessed November 2, 2015.

Frota, S. (2014). The intonational phonology of European Portuguese. In S.-A. Jun (ed.), *Prosodic Typology II. The Phonology of Intonation and Phrasing*. Oxford: Oxford University Press, pp. 6–42.

Frota, S., M. Cruz, F. Fernandes-Svartman, G. Collischonn, A. Fonseca, C. Serra, P. Oliveira,

and M. Vigário (2015). Intonational variation in Portuguese: European and Brazilian varieties. In S. Frota and P. Prieto (eds.), *Intonation in Romance*. Oxford: Oxford University Press, pp. 235–283.

Frota, S., M. D'Imperio, G. Elordieta, P. Prieto, and M. Vigário (2007). The phonetics and phonology of intonational phrasing in Romance. In P. Prieto, J. Mascaró, and M.-J. Solé (eds.), *Prosodic and Segmental Issues in (Romance) Phonology*. Amsterdam: John Benjamins, pp. 131–153.

Frota, S. and P. Prieto (2015). Intonation in romance: systemic similarities and differences. In S. Frota and P. Prieto (eds.), *Intonation in Romance*. Oxford: Oxford University Press, pp. 392–418.

Frota, S. and M. Vigário (2000). Aspectos de prosódia comparada: ritmo e entoação no PE e no PB. In R. V. Castro and P. Barbosa (eds.), *Actas do XV Encontro da Associação Portuguesa de Linguística*, Vol. I. Coimbra: APL, pp. 533–555.

Frota, S. and M. Vigário (2007). Intonational phrasing in two varieties of European Portuguese. In T. Riad and C. Gussenhoven (eds.), *Tones and Tunes*, Vol. I. Berlin: Mouton de Gruyter, pp. 265–291.

Gussenhoven, C. (2004). *The Phonology of Tone and Intonation*. Cambridge: Cambridge University Press.

Gussenhoven, C. (2007). Intonation. In P. de Lacy (ed.), *The Cambridge Handbook of Phonology*. Cambridge: Cambridge University Press, pp. 253–280.

Halliday, M. A. K. (1967). *Intonation and Grammar in British English*. The Hague: Mouton.

Jun, S.-A. (ed.) (2005). *Prosodic Typology. The Phonology of Intonation and Phrasing*. Oxford: Oxford University Press.

Jun, S.-A. (ed.) (2014). *Prosodic Typology II. The Phonology of Intonation and Phrasing*. Oxford: Oxford University Press.

Ladd, D. R. (2008). *Intonational Phonology*. 2nd edn. Cambridge: Cambridge University Press.

Lucente, L. (2012). Aspectos Dinâmicos da Fala e da Entoação no Português Brasileiro. Ph.D. dissertation, Universidade de Campinas.

Mata, A. I. (1999). Para o estudo da entoação em fala espontânea e preparada no Português Europeu. Ph.D. dissertation, University of Lisbon.

Moraes, J. A. (1998). Intonation in Brazilian Portuguese. In D. Hirst and A. Di Cristo (eds.), *Intonation Systems: a Survey of Twenty Languages*. Cambridge: Cambridge University Press, pp. 179–194.

Moraes, J. A. (2003). Secondary stress in Brazilian Portuguese: perceptual and acoustical evidence. *Proceedings of the XV International Congress of Phonetic Sciences*, Barcelona, pp. 2063–2066.

Moraes, J. A. (2006). Variações em torno de tema e rema. *Cadernos do CNLF [Cadernos do IX Congresso Nacional de Lingüística e Filologia]*, IX (17), pp. 279–289.

Moraes, J. A. (2008). The pitch accents in Brazilian Portuguese: analysis by synthesis. In P. Barbosa, S. Madureira, and C. Reis (eds.), *Speech Prosody 2008: Fourth Conference on Speech Prosody*, pp. 389–397.

Moraes, J. A. and M. Colamarco (2008). Accommodation of intonational patterns in Brazilian Portuguese short utterances: compression or truncation? In L. Bisol and C. Brescancini (eds.), *Contemporary Phonology in Brazil*. Cambridge: Cambridge Scholars, pp. 2–21.

Moraes, J. A. and A. Rilliard (2014). Illocution, attitudes and prosody: A multimodal analysis. In T. Raso and H. Mello (eds.), *Spoken Corpora and Linguistic Studies*. Amsterdam: John Benjamins, pp. 233–270.

Moraes, J. A. and H. Silva (2011). A entoação de vocativos e apostos no Português do Brasil. In L. Couto and C. R. Lopes (eds.), *As Formas de Tratamento em Português e em Espanhol; variação, mudança e funções conversacionais*. Niterói: Editora da Universidade Federal Fluminense, pp. 103–124.

Nespor, M. and I. Vogel (2007). *Prosodic Phonology*, 2nd edn. Berlin: Mouton de Gruyter.

Serra, C. (2009). Realização e percepção de fronteiras prosódicas no Português do Brasil: Fala espontânea e leitura. Ph.D. dissertation, Federal University of Rio de Janeiro.

Tenani, L. E. (2002). Domínios prosódicos no Português do Brasil: implicações para a prosódia e para a aplicação de processos fonológicos. Ph.D. dissertation, State University of Campinas.

Tenani, L. E. and F. Fernandes-Svartman (2008). Prosodic phrasing and intonation in neutral and subject-narrow-focus sentences of Brazilian Portuguese. *Speech Prosody 2008: Fourth Conference on Speech Prosody*, pp. 445–448.

Truckenbrodt, H., F. Sandalo, and M. B. Abaurre (2009). Elements of Brazilian Portuguese intonation. *Journal of Portuguese Linguistics*, 8, pp. 75–114.

Viana, M. C. (1987). Para a síntese da entoação do Português. Assistant researcher dissertation, CLUL-INIC.

Vigário, M. (1998). *Aspectos da Prosódia do Português Europeu: estruturas com advérbio de exclusão e negação frásica*. Braga: CEHUM.

Vigário, M. and F. Fernandes-Svartman (2010). A atribuição de acentos tonais em compostos no Português do Brasil. In A. M. Brito, F. Silva, J. Veloso, and A. Fiéis (eds.), *Textos Seleccionados – XXV Encontro da Associação Portuguesa de Linguística*, Porto: Associação Portuguesa de Linguística, pp. 769–786.

Vigário, M. and S. Frota (2003). The intonation of Standard and Northern European Portuguese: a comparative intonational phonology approach. *Journal of Portuguese Linguistics*, 2 (2) (Special issue Portuguese Phonology ed. by Wetzels), pp. 115–137.

Wagner, M. and D. Watson (2010). Experimental and theoretical advances in prosody: A review. *Language and Cognitive Processes*, 25 (7/8/9), pp. 905–945.

10 The Phonology and Morphology of Word Formation

ALINA VILLALVA AND CARLOS ALEXANDRE GONÇALVES

Portuguese shares many morphological features with other Romance languages, such as Castilian, Italian, or French, but it also displays properties that set it apart from the other members of the Romance family. In this chapter, we will privilege the latter aspects. The resemblance with other romance languages and, at the same time, the specificity of Portuguese morphology further echoes in the comparison of different national varieties, such as the European (henceforth EP) and Brazilian Portuguese (henceforth BP) subsystems.

Affixation and compounding are the main word-formation processes in Portuguese.[1] We will present an overview of their main morphological and phonological properties and also some border issues, indicating, when appropriate, contrasts between EP and BP (with reference to the dialects of Lisbon and southern Brazilian variants). In addition, we will discuss some types of word formation not addressed by the grammatical tradition. While influential traditional studies such as Mattoso Câmara (1971) and Basílio (1987), for BP, or Carvalho (1967) and Rio-Torto (1998), for EP, are discussed where appropriate, the discussion in this chapter is especially based on Villalva (1994), Gonçalves (2004), Gonçalves (2012), and Villalva and Silvestre (2014).

In our exposition of the Portuguese word-formation processes, we assume that words (W), as morphological structures, are projections of the root (R), which is morphologically specified by a thematic constituent[2] (TC) that generates a stem (S). The stem is then morpho-syntactically (MSS) specified.[3] This is the underlying morphological structure of all simple words:

(1) $[[[X]_R \ [Y]_{TC}]_S \ [Z]_{MSS}]_W$

Roots are lexical units, specified for a large number of features (their phonological representation and morphological, syntactic and semantic features, among others). One of these features concerns the thematic class to which they belong. Verbs are assigned to a conjugation class (first, second or third), a distinction that has no syntactic or semantic consequences—it is relevant merely for inflection (the phonetics are of the EP variant):

(2)		1st C	2nd C	3rd C
	infinitive	*can'**t**[a]r* "to sing"	*be'**b**[e]r* "to drink"	*fu'**g**[i]r* "to run away"
	pres.ind. 3rds.	*'cant*[ɐ]	*'beb*[i]	*'fog*[i]
	pres.subj.1st/3rd s.	*'cant*[i]	*'beb*[ɐ]	*'fuj*[ɐ]
	past participle	*can'**t**[a]do*	*be'**b**[i]do*	*fu'**g**[i]do*

The Handbook of Portuguese Linguistics, First Edition. Edited by W. Leo Wetzels, João Costa, and Sergio Menuzzi.
© 2016 John Wiley & Sons, Inc. Published 2020 by John Wiley & Sons, Inc.

Although this lexically determined distinction is not much more than a remnant of the Latin conjugation system, derivation is still sensitive to it. Deverbal suffixes that select verb stems specify a subclass of stems: infinitive stem (IST), present stem (PRST) and past stem (PTST). First conjugation verbs neutralize this distinction, but the thematic vowel of second and third conjugation inflected forms has different phonetic outputs:

(3)   1st C   2nd C   3rd C

IST   *apresen'␣t[a]r* "to present"   *absol'␣v[e]r* "to absolve"   *defi'␣n[i]r* "to define"

PRST   *apre'sent[ɐ]* "it presents"   *ab'solv[i]* "it absolves"   *de'fin[i]* "it defines"

PTST   *apresen'␣t[a]do* "presented"   *absol'␣v[i]do* "absolved"   *defi'␣n[i]do* "defined"

Deverbal suffixes are sensitive to this subclass feature:

(4)   1st C   2nd C   3rd C

IST   *ado'ç[ɐ]nte* "sweetener"   *reque'r[e]nte* "petitioner"   *pe'd[i]nte* "beggar"

PRST   *igno'r[ɐ]ncia* "ignorance"   *inci'd[e]ncia* "incidence"   *emer'g[e]ncia* "emergency"

PTST   *dedic[ɐ]'ção* "dedication"   *absolv[i]'ção* "absolving"   *defin[i]'ção* "definition"

Nouns and adjectives split over a larger number of classes, also lexically determined, which are related to the nature of the thematic vowel and to the gender value.[4] Even though final –*o*([u]) and final –*a*([ɐ]) have long been identified as gender morphemes, it is easy to conclude that they do not have that status: –*o* ending words are typically masculine, but masculine nouns may have many other endings. The same occurs with –*a* ending words and feminine. In the following table, all possibilities are registered for nouns:

(5)   Masculine   Feminine   Non-Specified
-*o*([u])   *ca'val[u](s)* "horse(s)"   *'trib[u](s)* "tribe(s)"   *sol'dad[u](s)* "soldier(s)"
-*a* ([ɐ])   *pro'fet[ɐ](s)* "prophet(s)"   *'vac[ɐ](s)* "cow(s)"   *a'tlet[ɐ](s)* "athlete(s)"
-*e*([i, I])   EP: *'pent[i](s)*   EP: *'pel[i](s)*   EP: *a'gent[i](s)*
                        BP: *'pent[I](s)* "comb(s)"   BP: *'pel[I](s)* "skin(s)"   BP: *a'gent[I](s)* "agent(s)"
-Ø ([]/[i, I])   EP: *tra'tor[]([i]s)*   EP: *'paz[]([i]s)*   *fis'ca[l]([j]s)*
                        BP: *trato'r[]([I]s)* "tractor(s)"   BP: *'paz[](I]s)* "peace(s)"   *fis'ca[w]([j]s)* "supervisor(s)"
athematic (⊤) *'pau(s)* "stick(s)"   *'pá(s)* "shovel(s)"   *refém(s)* "hostage(s)"

The difference between -*o* stems and -*a* stems is quite obvious: there is a final [u] and a final [ɐ], respectively in the words where they are present. The class of –*e* stems features the thematic index [i] in EP, [I] in BP. The class of –Ø stems features a thematic index that triggers a high vowel ([i] in EP, [I] in BP) with no phonetic realization in final position (singular), except for [l] ending roots. These two classes are very similar and they might be considered as one if all [l], [r] or [s] ending roots were –Ø stems, but this is not the case (*'pele/pa'pel* "skin/paper"; *fol'clore/'flor* "folklore/flower"; *'gás/'gaze* "gas/gauze").In EP, the endings of words such as *'pele* and *pa'pel* are phonetically very similar in the singular ([ˈpɛl]/ [pɐˈpɛl]), but they differ in the plural ([ˈpɛliʃ]/[pɐˈpɛjʃ]). The difference is easier to understand if these two words are assigned to different thematic classes. If their underlying representation is /pɛl+i/ and /pɐpɛl+/, then the plural of /pɐpɛl+/ can be obtained by semi-vocalization of the final consonant of the root, but only if it is a –Ø root. Notice that orthography is irrelevant: the majority of –*e* roots ends in a graphic <e>, but words such as *aval* (pl. *avales*) "approval" or *fel* (pl. *feles*) "gall" are also –*e* stems. Athematic stems are easier to recognize: they have neither a thematic index nor a trace of one.

The status of thematic classes is quite peculiar. They have no syntactic or semantic relevance, and, from a phonological point of view, thematic indices (i.e. -*a*, -*o*, -*e*) are uninteresting elements, since they are always unstressed vowels that show up at the right border of the word. Yet, thematic classes are morphologically relevant, both for inflection[5] and for word formation. As we will see below, the choice of roots, stems (including subtypes of stems for deverbal derivation) or words is part of the selectional constraints of affixes.

Complex words expand the structure in (1). In Portuguese, most word-formation processes occur in the root domain, and they may involve a root and an affix or several roots. Processes involving a single root usually attach an affix, which can be a morphological predicator (commonly known as derivational suffix) or a morphological modifier (a prefix or an evaluative suffix). Those involving more than one root are morphological compounding processes. This structural distinction requires a neat demarcation of roots and affixes. It also requires the identification of the grammatical roles for word constituents.

1. Affixation

Affixation is traditionally described as involving suffixation (which is predominant in Portuguese), or prefixation,[6] but this topological description needs to be complemented by a grammatical analysis. In fact, word-formation affixes can be predicators, which means that they are the head of the structure they generate, or modifiers. In Portuguese, all predicators are suffixes (= derivational suffixes), all prefixes are modifiers, and some suffixes (= evaluative suffixes) are modifiers.

1.1. Derivational suffixation

In Portuguese, derived words are generated on the basis of derivational suffixes according to their selectional and inherent properties. Selectional properties are the set of constraints involving the base form. Base forms can be roots (adjective roots, as in (6a); noun roots, as in (6b); verb roots, as in (6c)), stems (only verb stems are available, as in (6d–f)) or words (just adjectives, as in (6g)). Inherent properties define the features of the output, which is always a root that will be projected into a stem, first, and then to a word: derived forms can be adjective, adverb, noun, or verb roots:

(6) a. $[humanist]_{ADJR} \rightarrow$ $[[[huma'nístic]_{ADJR}o]_{ADJS}]_{ADJ}$ "humanist→humanistic"
         $[ingenu]_{ADJR} \rightarrow$ $[[[ingenui'dad]_{NR}e]_{NS}]_{N}$ "naïve→naiveté"
         $[fragil]_{ADJR} \rightarrow$ $[[[fragili'z]_{VR}a]_{VS}r]_{V}$ "fragile→to weaken"
     b. $[gost]_{NR} \rightarrow$ $[[[gos'tos]_{ADJR}o]_{ADJS}]_{ADJ}$ "taste→tasty"
         $[arroz]_{NR} \rightarrow$ $[[[arro'zal]_{NR}]_{NS}]_{N}$ "rice→rice field"
         $[frut]_{NR} \rightarrow$ $[[[frutifi'c]_{VR}a]_{VS}r]_{V}$ "fruit→to fructify"
     c. $[mand]_{VR} \rightarrow$ $[[[man'dão]_{NR}]_{NS}]_{N}/[[[man'don]_{NR}]a_{NS}]_{N}$ "to boss→bossy"
     d. $[dança]_{VSINF} \rightarrow$ $[[[dan'çant]_{ADJR}e]_{ADJS}]_{ADJ}$ "to dance→dancing"
         $[grava]_{VSINF} \rightarrow$ $[[[grava'dor]_{NR}]_{NS}]_{N}$ "to engrave→engraver"
     e. $[concorda]_{VSPRES} \rightarrow$ $[[[concor'dânci]_{NR}a]_{NS}]_{N}$ "to agree→agreement"
     f. $[procura]_{VSPAST} \rightarrow$ $[[[procu'rável]_{ADJR}]_{ADJS}]_{ADJ}$ "to search→searchable"
         $[separa]_{VSPAST} \rightarrow$ $[[[separa'ção]_{NR}]_{NS}]_{N}$ "to separate→separation"
     g. $[urgente]_{ADJ} \rightarrow$ $[[[ur'gente'ment]_{ADVR}e]_{ADVS}]_{ADV}$ "urgent→urgently"

Selectional properties vary from suffix to suffix. They can make use of, at least, phonological/prosodic properties of the base (see below the allomorphy of –ez ~ –eza, for instance), syntactic properties (especially for deverbal suffixes that require information on the argument structure of the base verb) and semantic properties (the collective noun forming suffix -agem selects the root of count nouns: 'folha→fo'lhagem "leaf→foliage".

Besides defining the syntactic category of the output, derivational suffixes also participate in broad semantic categories. The existence of competing suffixes occurs inside these categories:

(7) causative verbs:
$[[escur]_{ADJR}e'c]_{VR}er]_V$ "to darken"
$[[agil]_{ADJR}i'z]_{VR}ar]_V$ "to hasten"
$[[solid]_{ADJR}ifi'c]_{VR}ar]_V$ "to solidify"

action nouns:
$[[apresenta]_{VS}'ção]_{NR}$ "presentation"
$[[esqueci]_{VS}'ment]_{NR}o$ "forgetfulness"
$[[tole'râ]_{VS}nci]_{NR}a$ "tolerance"

subject nouns:
$[[apresenta]_{VS}'dor]_{NR}$ "presenter"
$[[represen'ta]_{VS}nt]_{NR}e$ "representative"

Derivational processes available in EP and BP are virtually identical: they share the same set of suffixes, and their behavior is quite similar. There is, however, a margin of contrasts that is worth noting. It is quite common to find different suffixes competing within the same morphosemantic category:

(8) EP: *desenha'dor*/BP: *dese'nhista*   "designer"
     EP: *fuma'dor*/BP: *fu'mante*   "smoker"

Thus, derived words in EP and BP are derived autonomously, yielding different results within a given morphosemantic category. Another distinction is set by the mutation of some affixes—for instance, in BP, the suffix *–d(a)*, in the expression X–*da* ((*dar uma*) *olhada* "to take a quick look"), forms brief action nouns. No such suffix exists in EP, although there is a semantically equivalent suffix, which is *–dela* ((*dar uma*) *olhadela*), not used in BP.

1.2. Parasynthesis

Parasynthesis is a particular case of derivation, usually defined as a process of simultaneous prefixation and suffixation. However, considering that sometimes no suffix intervenes and that the prefix is an expletive element, this type of derivation shows a striking resemblance with suffixation or conversion, except for the fact that it requires the presence of the expletive prefix:

(9) a. $[prefix[[ADJR]suffix]_{VR}]_{VR}$
        $[[[a[[mol]_{ADJR}e'c]_{VR}]_{VR}[e]]_{VS}[r]]_V$ "to soften"
        $[[[en[[rouqu]_{ADJR}e'c]_{VR}]_{VR}[e]]_{VS}[r]]_V$ "to hoarsen"
        $[prefix[[ADJR]]_{VR}]_{VR}$
        $[[[a[[cele'r]_{ADJR}]_{VR}]_{VR}[a]]_{VS}[r]]_V$ "to accelerate"
        $[[[en[[ri'j]_{ADJR}]_{VR}]_{VR}[a]]_{VS}[r]]_V$ "to harden"
     b. $[prefix[[NR]suffix]_{VR}]_{VR}$
        $[[[a[[pedr]_{NR}e'j]_{VR}]_{VR}[a]]_{VS}[r]]_V$ "to stone"
        $[[[en[[raiv]_{NR}e'c]_{VR}]_{VR}[e]]_{VS}[r]]_V$ "to enrage"
        $[prefix[[NR]]_{VR}]_{VR}$
        $[[[a[[carici]_{NR}]_{VR}]_{VR}['a]]_{VS}[r]]_V$ "to caress"
        $[[[en[[garra'f]_{NR}]_{VR}]_{VR}[a]]_{VS}[r]]_V$ "to bottle"

Most parasynthetic forms are deadjectival (10a) or denominal verbs (10b). There are some parasynthetic adjectives too (10c):

(10) a. *es[[clar]*_{ADJR}*e'c]*_{VR}*er*   "to clarify"
      b. *a[[cam'p]*_{NR}*]*_{VR}*ar*   "to camp"
      c. *a[[laran'j]*_{NR}*ad]*_{ADJR}*o*   "orangy"

1.3. Conversion

Cases traditionally treated as back-formation and "improper" derivation fit in this category, since they both involve the recategorization of a base, without the intervention of affixes. Conversion processes are not typical morphological processes, although they have several features in common with derivational suffixation. We will mention three:

Conversion can operate on different morphological categories, namely roots (11a) and fully inflected words (11b):

(11) a. *[ata'c]*_{VR}*ar*→   *[a'taqu]*_{NR}*e*   "to attack→attack"
      b. *[[[o'lh]*_{VR}*a]*_{VS}*r]*_{VINF→}   *[o'lhar]*_{NR}*(es)*   "to see→look"

Conversion generates words that belong to the same morphosemantic classes as those that are formed by derivation (cf. (7), above):

(12) causative verbs: *[lim'p]*_{ADJR}*]*_{VR}*ar*   "to clean"
      action nouns: *[a'taqu]*_{VR}*]*_{NR}*e*   "attack"
      subject nouns: *[pe'netra]*_{VPI3RDSG}*]*_{NS}   "intruder"

Conversion and derivation are usually in complementary distribution:[7]

(13) *mis'tura* vs. **mistura'ção*   "mix"
      *'grava vs. *grava'ção*   "recording"
      melho'rar vs. **melhorifi'car*   "to improve"
      *pu'rar vs. *purifi'car*   "to purify"

2. Modification

Many affixation processes are of a modification kind. Morphological modifiers are adjuncts that copy grammatical features from the base they are added to and they just change its semantic value. This category includes all evaluative suffixation and all prefixation.

2.1. Evaluative suffixation

Evaluative suffixation is one of the most interesting domains in Portuguese word formation. Since it is a resource primarily used in spoken language, it is quite superficially studied in schools and no standardization is available in reference grammars. Therefore, we can see the true dynamics of these word-formation processes.

Evaluative modifiers change the base they are added to according to a range of semantic features related to different value judgments, the true content of which depends on pragmatic circumstances.[8] Evaluative modification applies almost unrestrictedly: these suffixes can adjoin to all kinds of bases, either adjectival (14a), nominal (14b), adverbial bases (14c), or even to interjections (14d):

(14) a. [[[ma'gr]inh]o/a]   "thin+EVAL"
      b. [[[profe'ssor]'zinh]o]   "teacher+EVAL"
      c. [[['ced]inh]o]   "early+EVAL"
      d. [[[adeu's]inh]o]   "goodbye+EVAL"

Among the existing evaluative suffixes, the linguistic variants under consideration prefer –*inho*(*a*) and –*zinho*(*a*).[9] In EP, –*inho* and –*zinho* are not allomorphs of a single suffix—they belong to two different series, with distinctive features: vowel-initial suffixes (henceforth V-evaluatives) are adjoined to roots; [z]-initial suffixes (henceforth Z-evaluatives) are adjoined to words. The distribution of these two sets of competing suffixes is dialect-specific and it is also prone to speaker's preference, but some grammatical constraints also apply.[10]

In the two varieties, the most obvious constraint is the impossibility to adjoin V-evaluative suffixes to athematic bases (i.e. roots that have identical forms for the root, the stem and the singular word ([[[*café*]$_{NR}$[]$_{TI}$]$_{NS}$[]$_{MSS}$]$_N$ "coffee"). Athematic roots only allow for Z-evaluative suffixation, displaying, in the suffix, the unmarked thematic index (=TI) that agrees with the gender of the base (15a). This is also the case for athematic roots with a stressless final vowel (15b):

(15) a. [[[ca'fé]$_{MSC}$'zinh][o]$_{TI}$]$_{MSC}$ *cafe'inho   "coffee+EVAL"
          [[[ir'mã]$_{FEM}$'zinh][a]$_{TI}$]$_{FEM}$ *irmã'inha   "sister+EVAL"
      b. [[['táxi]$_{MSC}$'zinh][o]$_{TI}$]$_{MSC}$ *tá'xinho   "taxi+EVAL"

In some dialects of BP, '*mãe*'*zinha* ("mother+EVAL") may co-occur with *mã*'*inha* (or '*pai*'*zinho* and *pa*'*inho* "father+EVAL+"), for instance. This may indicate that the constraint that holds for EP does not hold for some dialects of BP. In southern dialects of PB, these instances are felt as typical northeastern formations.

–∅ roots also show a speaker's preference for Z-evaluative suffixation (16a), which seems to indicate that there is a large proximity between –∅ roots and athematic roots. This proximity is eventually higher in BP than in EP (16b), which suggests that [l]-final roots in BP have become athematic.

(16) a. [['dor]'zinha]   */?[[do'r]inha]   "pain+EVAL"
          [['sal]'zinho]   */?[[sa'l]inho]   "salt+EVAL"
      b. BP: *[[ane'l]inho]/[[a'nel]'zinho]   "ring+EVAL"
          EP: [[ane'l]inho]/[[a'nel]'zinho]

In EP, we often find cases of –∅ roots in free variation, which clearly illustrate that V-evaluative and Z-evaluative suffixes attach to different bases: V-evaluatives select a root; Z-evaluatives select a word. Notice that the stressed vowel of the base gets two different phonetic realizations depending on the choice of the suffix:[11]

(17) *caraco*'*linho*/*cara*'*col*'*zinho*   "snail+EVAL"
      casa'*linho*/*ca*'*sal*'*zinho*   "couple+EVAL"

In the case of the –*e* roots, chances for an equivalent distribution are even higher. It is possible to find more instances of V-evaluative and Z-evaluative suffixation that select the same bases, in both varieties of Portuguese, as it is possible to find cases of apparently random acceptance, or non-acceptance of both, or just of one of them:

(18) bi'finho   'bife'zinho   "steak+EVAL"
     pei'xinho   'peixe'zinho   "fish+EVAL"
     cha'vinha   'chave'zinha   "key+EVAL"

In -*a* and –*o* roots, distribution is also varied. Although it is not possible to find strict criteria, data show that the preference for V-evaluative suffixes lies in shorter highly frequent bases; the preference for Z-evaluative suffixes comes from longer and less frequent bases (which include most proparoxytonic words):

(19) a. bo'quinha   ros'tinho
         'boca'zinha   'rosto'zinho
         "mouth+EVAL"   "face+EVAL"
         ca'rinha   de'dinho
         ?'cara'zinha   ?'dedo'zinho
         "face+EVAL"   "finger+EVAL"
    b. ?'pupi'linha   pesco'cinho
         pu'pila'zinha   ?pes'coço'zinho
         "pupil+EVAL"   "neck+EVAL"
    c. ?sobrance'lhinha   ?crocodi'linho
         sobran'celha'zinha   croco'dilo'zinho
         "eyebrow+EVAL"   "crocodile+EVAL"
    d. ?medi'quinho   ?celu'linha
         'medico'zinho   'celula'zinha
         "doctor+EVAL"   "cell+EVAL"

Preference for Z-evaluative suffixation[12] may be explained by the fact that Z-evaluative suffixes facilitate the recognition of the base to which they associate. Notice that Z-evaluative suffixation triggers gender and number agreement between the evaluative word and the base word, which can be clearly demonstrated when the base word has allomorphic variation for number inflection (20a). When the base is an –*a* stem masculine root, or an -*o* stem feminine root, Z-evaluative suffixation triggers agreement in gender with the base and exhibits the unmarked thematic vowel for gender: –*o* for the masculine and –*a* for the feminine. V-evaluative suffixation keeps the thematic vowel of the base (20b). Consequently, when the base is an -*a* stem root non-specified for gender, Z-evaluatives disambiguate the gender value, whereas V-evaluatives do not (20c):

(20) a. $[[[[cara'col]_{SG}'zinh]o]]_{SG}$
      $[[[[cara'coi]_{PL}'zinh]o]s]_{PL}$
      $[[[['cão]_{SG}'zinh]o]]_{SG}$
      $[[[['cãe]_{PL}'zinh]o]s]_{PL}$
    b. $[[[sis'tema]_{MSC}'zinh]o]_{MSC}$ $[[[siste'm]_{MSC}inh]a]_{MSC}$ "system+EVAL"
      $[[['tribo]_{FEM}'zinh]a]_{FEM}$ $[[[tri'b]_{FEM}inh]o]_{FEM}$ "tribe+EVAL"
    c. $[[[ar'tista]_{MSC/FEM}'zinh]o]_{MSC}$ $[[[artis't]_{MSC/FEM}inh]a]_{MSC/FEM}$ "artist+EVAL"
      $[[[ar'tista]_{MSC/FEM}'zinh]a]_{FEM}$

2.2. Clipping

Clipping (or truncation) is quite productive in BP. It is a mechanism by which a word is shortened without its lexical meaning being affected, but with frequent stylistic or pragmatic nuances, which is why it is treated as a case of modification. It eliminates phonological material at the right periphery of the base. Clippings may (21a) or may not (21b, 21c) affect morphological constituents:

(21) a. *prole'tário*   >>   *pro'leta*   "proletarian"
          comu'nista   *co'muna*   "communist"
      b. *vaga'bunda*   *va'gaba*   "slut"
          cer'veja   *'cerva*   "beer"
      c. *bijute'ria*   *bi'ju*   "jewelry"
          refrige'rante   *re'fri*   "soft drink"

The patterns exemplified above require access to morphological and prosodic information. In (21a), we find words formed by a root base and the thematic index –*a*, a constituent unrelated to the gender of the base. In (21b), the base root is not fully present in the truncated form, but, as in (21a), the clippings are stressed on the penultimate syllable, always forming a trochee at the right edge of the shortened form. In these two groups, the affixation of the thematic index (–*a*) always takes place, but not in (21c). Here, the two first syllables of the base are kept, which form an iambic foot.

Bauer (1988: 33) questions the morphological status of such clippings because the excluded parts are not clearly morphological. According to Fandrych (2008: 116), clipping is unquestionably a process of word formation: the shortening "changes records or styles compared to their complete counterparts." This is indeed what is observed in the examples (21a–b), the most common cases. This pattern of clipping can also affect compounds:[13]

(22) *'São Gon'ç(alo)a*   "a district of Rio de Janeiro"
      'grã-'f(ino)a   "snobbish"
      'free-'l(ancer)a   "freelancer"

2.3. Prefixation

Like evaluative suffixes, modifiers that are left-adjoined to a head do not interfere with the grammatical properties of the words in which they occur:

(23) *'apto*_   [*i'n*]*apto*   "fit→unfit"
      *fa'zer*_   [*des*]*fa'zer*   "do→undo"
      *ma'rido*_ [*ex*]*ma'rido*   "husband→ex-husband"

The range of semantic values expressed by prefixes is wider than for evaluative suffixes. Prefixation can also be evaluative ([*'super*]*interes'sante* "super-interesting," [*'micro*]*computa'dor* "microcomputer"), but there are prefixes of negation ([*in*]*e'quívoco* "unequivocal"), opposition ([*des*]*mon'tar* "dismount"), repetition ([*re*]*encon'trar* "meet again") and spatial ([*'sub*]*'solo* "subsoil") or temporal location ([*'pós*]*opera'tório* "post-surgery").

Regardless of the semantic diversity found amongst prefixes, it is important to remark that the set of units usually called prefixes may have very different properties. The heterogeneity of these units can be analyzed according to a number of criteria showing that some behave like typical affixes, while others look like independent roots.[14]

The first criterion is related to the category of the base to which they may attach: some prefixes attach exclusively to roots or stems (24a), while others, especially those that can be coordinated with other prefixes, attach to words or even to phrases (24b).

(24) a. [[[*in*][*apt*]]*i*'*dão*]   "inaptitude"
          [[[*des*][*arm*]*a*]]'*mento*]   "disarmament"
          [[[*re*][*aprecia*]]'*ção*]   "re-appreciation"
     b. [['*pré*][*cam*'*panha*]]   "pre-campaign"
          [['*pré*][*cam*'*panha eleito*'*ral*]]   "pre-electoral campaign"
          [['*pré e* '*pós*][*cam*'*panha (eleito*'*ral*)]] "pre- and post-(electoral) campaign"

Prefixes that attach to roots or stems (typically *in–*, *des–* and *re–*) are unstressed units; those that adjoin to words or syntactic expressions (such as *pós–*, *pré–*, *ex–*, and *sub–*) are independent prosodic words (cf. Schwindt 2000). The latter type is formed by paroxytones with two syllables ('*contra–*, *an*'*ti–*, '*mega–*, and '*super–*) or stressed monosyllables ('*pró–*, '*ex–*, and '*pré–*).

One issue that must be raised in relation to this distinction concerns prefixes that have stressed and unstressed variants, like '*pré–/pre–* or '*pós–/pos–*. For instance, in (25a) the prefix is unstressed ([pri] in EP, [pre] in BP); in (25b) the prefix is stressed ([ˈprɛ] in both varieties):

(25) a. [[*pre*][ˈ*texto*]]   "excuse"
          [[*pre*][*s*ˈ*sentir*]]   "to sense"
     b. [[ˈ*pré*][*pro*ˈ*jeto*]]   "pre-project"
          [[ˈ*pré*][*da*ˈ*tar*]]   "to predate"

There is an obvious difference of formal and semantic transparency between words in (25a) and those in (25b): the former are opaque and can be seen as genuine cases of lexicalization—*pre*ˈ*texto*, for example, means "excuse," which is not related to *texto* ("text") nor to a temporal location value of the prefix. Thus, stressed prefixes become unstressed when the words get lexicalized: either for semantic reasons (*pres*ˈ*sentir* "to sense") or for structural reasons, when the prefix is adjoined to a neoclassical bound root (*prema*ˈ*turo* "premature").

A second criterion that is relevant to isolate prefixes concerns their (in)existence as autonomous words. Many of these forms are derived from Greek or Latin prepositions and adverbs, which have undergone a process of grammaticalization already in the old languages. In some cases, these prefixes only occur in lexicalized words ([*a*]*ssu*ˈ*mir* "to assume," [*con*]*su*ˈ*mir* "to consume," [*pre*]*su*ˈ*mir* "to presume," [*re*]*su*ˈ*mir*, "to summarize") and therefore their historical origin is irrelevant for their synchronic classification.

However, Portuguese follows the model of the classical languages by using prepositions and adverbs to build modified words:

(26) [[ˈ*ante*][ˈ*câmara*]]   "antechamber"
     [[*sem*][*a*ˈ*brigo*]]/[[*sem*][ˈ*teto*]]   "homeless"
     [[ˈ*não*][*agres*ˈ*são*]]   "non-aggression"

Also available for this type of modification are neoclassical forms, which may have served as prefixes in old languages, and which are again available in contemporary Portuguese (as in many other modern languages):

(27) a. [[ˈ*hiper*][*a*ˈ*tivo*]]   "hyperactive"
          [[ˈ*sobre*][*do*ˈ*tado*]]   "overly gifted"
     b. [[ˈ*hemi*][*atro*ˈ*fia*]]   "semi-atrophy"
          [[ˈ*meio*][*ir*ˈ*mão*]]   "half-brother"

The third criterion distinguishes forms that can only occur as left adjuncts from those that can themselves be the head of a complex word. The first class are prefixes (28a), the second one are roots (28b):

(28) a. [['*mega*][*manifesta*'*ção*]]   "huge demonstration"
      b. [[[*pat*][[*o*][*lo*'*g*]]]*ia*]   "pathology"
          [[[*cardi*][[*o*][*pa*'*t*]]]*ia*]   "heart disease"

Thus, both unstressed forms adjoined to roots or stems and stressed forms adjoined to words or phrases have a similar behavior, which raises the question of whether it is possible to find independent grammatical evidence for their different categorization.

2.4. *Productive phonology in affixation*

Root- and stem-based derived and modified words behave like simple words with respect to stress assignment: they always form a single stress domain. Consequently, in these cases, there is an isomorphism between morphological and prosodic words. Looking at the effects of unstressed vowel reduction processes in EP and BP helps to sustain this claim:

In EP, all low and mid vowels, before and after stressed syllables, undergo reduction and centralization:

(29) '*v*[ɛ]*la*   *v*[i]'*leiro*   "sail/sailboat"
      '*b*[e]*rço*   *b*[i]*r*'*çário*   "cradle/nursery"
      '*b*[a]*rco*   *b*[ɐ]*r*'*queiro*   "boat/boatman"
      '*s*[ɔ]*l*   *s*[u]'*lar*   "sun/solar"

In BP, only mid vowels are concerned: lower mid vowels of the base alternate with their corresponding upper mid vowels when they occur in a pre-stress position:

(30) '*p*[ɔ]*rta*   *p*[o]*r*'*teiro*/*p*[o]*rta*'*ria*   "door/doorman/hallway"
      '*v*[ɛ]*la*   *v*[e]'*leiro*/*v*[e]*le*'*jar*   "sail/sailboat/to sail"

Root based evaluative words behave differently. In EP, mid vowels and low central vowels are always reduced (31a); palatal and velar low vowels are preferably not reduced, although reduction may occur (31b):

(31) a. '*d*[e]*do*   **d*[e]'*dinho*/   *d*[i]'*dinho*   "finger(+EVAL)"
          '*b*[o]*llo* **b*[o]'*linho*/   *b*[u]'*linho*   "cake(+EVAL)"
          '*c*[a]*sa*   **c*[a]'*sinha*   *c*[ɐ]'*sinha*   "house(+EVAL)"
      b. '*fl*[ɛ]*sta* *fl*[ɛ]*s*'*tinha* *fl*[i]*s*'*tinha* "party(+EVAL)"
          '*b*[ɔ]*la*   *b*[ɔ]'*linha*   ᵗ*b*[u]'*linha* "ball(+EVAL)"

In evaluative words all vowels keep their underlying quality in BP. Compare the mid vowel quality of the examples below with their correspondents in derived words:

(32) '*p*[ɔ]*rta*   *p*[ɔ]*r*'*tinha*   "door(+EVAL)"
                      p[o]*r*'*teiro*/*p*[o]*rta*'*ria* "doorman/hallway"
      '*v*[ɛ]*la*   *v*[ɛ]'*linha*   "sail(+EVAL)"
                      v[e]'*leiro*/*v*[e]*le*'*jar*   "sailboat/to sail"

Word-based suffixed words form two stress domains, which means that the isomorphism between morphological and prosodic words is broken: one morphological word projects into two prosodic words. In derivation, only the adverb-forming suffix *–mente* has this capacity: it is added to an adjective (in the singular form, and it must be feminine if variable for gender). In EP, two vowels keep their underlying quality: the stressed vowel of the base and the stressed vowel of the suffix:

(33) ˈc[ɛ]rta   ˈc[ɛ]rtaˈmente   c[i]rˈteza
     "certain"   "certainly"   "certainty"
     aˈm[a]vel   aˈm[a]velˈmente am[ɐ]biliˈdade
     "kind"   "kindly"   "kindness"
     veˈl[ɔ]z   veˈl[ɔ]zˈmente   vel[u]ciˈdade
     "speedy"   "speedily"   "speed"

In BP, mid vowels in the first prosodic word keep their underlying lower mid quality (34a, b) and phonetic nasal vowels, which typically only emerge under primary stress in the southern Brazilian dialects, maintain their nasality (34c):

(34) a. aˈl[ɛ]gre   aˈl[ɛ]greˈmente   al[e]ˈgria
        "happy"   "happily"   "happiness"
     b. ˈf[ɔ]rte   ˈf[ɔ]rteˈmente   f[o]rtaleˈcer
        "strong"   "strongly"   "strengthen"
     c. uˈn[ẽ]nime   uˈn[ẽ]nimeˈmente   un[a]nimiˈdade
        "unanimous" "unanimously"   "unanimity"

Word-based evaluatives behave like derived-word-based words. These suffixes also project an independent prosodic word. In EP, the base stressed vowel keeps its underlying quality:

(35) proˈbl[e]ma   proˈbl[e]maˈzinho   "problem(+EVAL)"
             probl[i]ˈmático   "problematic"
     coˈlh[ɛ]r   coˈlh[ɛ]rˈzinha   "spoon(+EVAL)"
             colh[i]ˈrada   "spoonful"

In BP, phonetic nasal vowels, which typically only emerge under primary stress in the southern Brazilian dialects, also maintain their nasality:

(36) ˈch[ẽ]ma   ˈch[ẽ]maˈzinha   "flame(+EVAL)"
         ch[a]musˈcar   "to scorch"

Prefixation does not interfere with stress assignment, but the quality of prefix vowels presents some specificities. In EP, unstressed vowels in some prefixes are reduced, like all other unstressed vowels:

(37) a. d[i]sfaˈzer   "to undo"
        d[i]sˈcrer   "to disbelieve"
     b. r[i]liˈgar   "to reconnect"
        r[i]ˈver   "to see again"

Reduction fails to apply with prefixes such as n[ɛ]o-(ˈneo-naˈzista "neo-Nazi"), pr[ɛ]- (ˈpré-condiˈção "pre-condition") or p[ɔ]s- (ˈpós-operaˈtório "post-surgery").[15] This contrast can be related to different properties of the prefix: prefixes such as d[i]s- or r[i]- do not project an independent prosodic word, whereas prefixes such as n[ɛ]o-, pr[ɛ]- or p[ɔ]s- do. Alternatively, we claim that this behavior follows from a selectional property of the prefixes, which may also attach to roots or to words: when they attach to roots they expand the prosodic word of the base (*d*[i]*s–*, *r*[i]); when they attach to words they project a new prosodic word (n[ɛ]o–, pr[ɛ]–, p[ɔ]s–).

Notice that, in BP, *re–* and *pre–*, unlike *des–*, do not undergo vowel harmony. It leads to the raising of unstressed mid vowels, under the influence of a following stressed high vowel, similar to what happens with unprefixed forms such as *pe'pino* ("cucumber"), *pre'guiça* ("laziness") or *sen'tir* ("to feel")—they may be pronounced with [i] in the initial syllable (see Bisol and Veloso, Chapter 5 in this volume, for details). For instance, in BP, phonetic forms such as **r*[i]*vi'sita* ("revisit"), **r*[i]*'tinto* ("re-dye") and **r*[i]*'visto* ("revised") do not occur, nor do **pr*[i]*'ver* ("to preview") e **pr*[i]*s'sinto* ("I sense"), which suggests the existence of some morphological conditioning for the application of this phonological rule. Moreover, the raising of the stressed vowel does not occur in hiatus (**r*[i]*abaste'cer* "to refill";**r*[i]*u'sar* "to reuse"), and the vowels in these prefixes are less likely to deletion when the following vowel is identical (r[e]-[e]*xpli'car* "re-explain," r[e]-[e]*labo'rar* "re-elaborate").[16] Despite being unstressed, this prefix has a high degree of morphological integrity, since it resists several processes that affect the unstressed vocalism.

Finally, we mention the neutralization of mid vowels in stressed syllables. Suffixes like *–ico* and *–il* form dactylic (38a) and spondaic feet (38b), respectively. Stressed mid vowels in these derivatives always display lower mid qualities ([ɛ, ɔ]), which is also the pattern for non-derived words with the same prosodic structure (38c). The productivity of the process is shown by the fact that loans adapt to these models ('W[ɔ]*shington;* 'sh[ɔ]*pping*). These facts prove that lowering is a phonological rule in Portuguese (cf.Wetzels (1992).

(38) a. esque'*l*[e]*to*   esque'*l*[ɛ]*tico*   ca'*l*[o]*r*   ca'*l*[ɔ]*rico*
           "skeleton"   "skeletal"   "heat"   "caloric"
           'núm[e]ro   nu'm[ɛ]rico   BP:me'táf[o]ra   meta'f[ɔ]rico
           'núm[i]ro   nu'm[ɛ]rico   EP: me'táf[u]ra   meta'f[ɔ]rico
           "number"   "numerical"   "metaphor"   "metaphorical"
      b. BP: proj[e]'tar   pro'j[ɛ]til   'd[o]ce   'd[ɔ]cil
           EP: proj[ɛ]'tar   pro'j[ɛ]til   "sweet"   "docile"
           "to project"   "projectile"
      c. 'p[ɛ]tala   'f[ɔ]sforo   'r[ɛ]plica   'c[ɔ]cegas
           "petal"   "match"   "replica"   "tickles"

2.5. *Affixal allomorphy*

Some derivational suffixes have one or more allomorphs. In some cases, like *–al* ~ *–ar*, for instance, it was inherited from Latin: *–ar* occurs due to a dissimilation when the nominal base contains /l/:[17]

(39) a. [[aciden'*t*]*al*]   "accidental"
           [[horizon'*t*]*al*]   "horizontal"
      b. [[celu'*l*]*ar*]   "cellular"
           [[molecu'*l*]*ar*]   "molecular"
      c. [[elemen'*t*]*ar*]   "basic"
           [[nucle]'*ar*]   "core"

Another case of allomorphy (which does not have a Latin origin) concerns the suffix *–ez* ~ *–eza*,[18] that forms deadjectival quality nouns:

(40) 'velh(o)   ve'lhice ~ ve'lhez   "old/old age"

Contemporary formation of quality nouns prefers another suffix (i.e. *–idade*), which means that *–ez ~ –eza* is not used to form new words. Nevertheless, available data indicate that their distribution has a prosodic basis, which is related to their thematic status: *–ez* forms *–Ø* stem nouns, such as *timi'dez* "shyness," *–eza* forms *-a* stem nouns, like *ma'greza* "slimness." The allomorph distribution is sensitive to the number of syllables in the base:[19] *–eza* selects shorter bases (typically monosyllable roots) such as *fri'eza*("coldness"), and *-ez* selects longer bases (roots with two or more syllables), like *aci'dez*("acidity").

Prefixes can also have allomorphic variation. The prefix *in–*, for instance, has three allomorphs: [i.n], [i] e [ĩ]:

(41) [i]*le'gal* "illegal"   [ĩ]*pos'sível* "impossible"   [i.'**n**]*apto* "unfit"
     [i]*mo'ral* "immoral"   [ĩ]'*certo* "uncertain"   [i.n]*experi'ente* "inexperienced"
     [i]*rre'al* "unreal"   [ĩ]'*justo* "unfair"   [i.'**n**]*útil* "useless"

These alternations are the same in EP and BP: [i] occurs before sonorant consonants, [ĩ] is chosen before a base-initial non-sonorant, whereas the sequence [in] is found before a vowel-initial base.

Some derivational suffixes trigger the application of morphophonological rules that affect the phonetic shape of the output, such as the lenition of velars (42a) or haplology[20] (42b):

(42) a. *fi'lólo*[g]*o*   *filolo'*[ʒ]*ia*   "philologist/philology"
        his'tóri[k]*o*   *histori'*[s]*ismo*   "historic/historicism"
     b. *cari'dade*   *cari(da)'doso*   "charity/charitable"
        '*mínima*   *se(mi)'(mî)nima*   "half note/quarter note"

In the first case (cf. Lee 1995), velar plosives become fricatives before suffixes initiated by the vowel /i/, like *–ia*, *–ista*, and *–ismo*. In morphological haplology, two identical or phonetically similar syllables are reduced to one, usually the right one (cf. Gonçalves 2011).

3. Compounding

Affixation requires the presence of an affix, compounding combines roots or words: the combination of roots yields a morphological structure (a morphological compound); the combination of words yields lexical units that have a hybrid morphosyntactic structure (morphosyntactic compounds) or they are lexicalized phrases (syntactic compounds).

We have just seen that the difference between compounding and affixation suggests that there is a clear-cut distinction between affixes and roots (or even words), which, in fact, does not exist. We will nevertheless present a characterization of roots that helps to set them apart from affixes.

3.1. Roots

In Portuguese, some roots occur in simple and in complex words, as [*metr*] in ['*metr*]*o* "meter," [[['*métr*]*ic*]*o*] "metric" and [[[*me'tr*][*ónom*]]*o*] "metronome"; other roots only occur in complex words, as ([*fratr*] in [[[*fratr*][*i*]['*cid*]]*a*] "fratricide"). Derivational suffixes (like *-ção*) and modifier affixes (like *des-*) can only occur in complex words (*liga'ção* "connection"; *desli'gar* "to disconnect"). Thus, it is easy to distinguish roots (that may occur in both simple and complex words) from affixes (that cannot occur as simple words); it is harder to set apart roots that occur only in complex words, like affixes.

Roots that are present in simple word are roots by definition. Simple words make their inherent properties (such as word-class and subcategories (43a)) visible. These roots can also occur in words formed by derivation or modification (43b):

(43) a. $[[['bol]_{NR-A,\,FEM}a]_{NS}]_N$ "ball"
   $[[['bol]_{NR-O,\,MSC}o]_{NS}]_N$ "cake"
   $[[[ge'r]_{c1\,VR}a]_{VS}r]_V$ "to generate"
   $[[[ge'r]_{c3\,VR}i]_{VS}r]_V$ "to manage"
  b. $[[[[bo'l]_{NR}ad]_{NR}a]_{NS}]_N$ "hit with a ball"
   $[[[[bo'l]_{NR}inh]_{NR}o]_{NS}]_N$ "small cake"
   $[[[[ger]_{VR}a'dor]_{NR}]_{NS}]_N$ "manager"
   $[[[[ge'r]_{VR}ent]_{NR}e]_{NS}]_N$ "manager"

Roots that cannot occur in simple words are generally loans from classical languages that are particularly productive to form technical terms. These roots occur mainly in morphological compounds (44a), but they can also be selected by neoclassical suffixes (44b). Usually, they have an imprecise meaning, and they are underspecified for word-class and thematic membership. They depend on other constituents to become a member of a word-class (44c):

(44) a. $[[[top][o][lo'g]]ia]$ "topology"
  b. $[[['tóp][ic]]o]$ "topic"
  c. $[[[bi][o][lo'g]]ia]_N$ "biology"
   $[[[bi][o]['lóg]]ico]_{ADJ}$ "biologic"

Many of these roots can take any of the available positions (45a), but there are roots that can only be in the initial position (45b) and others that can only occur in final position (45c):

(45) a. $[antro'p]ólogo$ "anthropologist"
   $fil[an'trop]o$ "philanthropist"
  b. $[hom]o'nímia$ "homonymy"
  c. $herbi['cid]a$ "herbicide"

In the previous section, we established that roots that occur only as initial constituents, like *hom–* (a loan from Greek, meaning "equal") and prefixes are better described, indistinctly, as modifiers. The classification of units like *antrop* (a loan from Greek, meaning "man") as roots, rather than affixes, derives from their availability in both initial and final position. Finally, roots that can only occur in the final position of morphological compounds, such as *–cid* (a loan from Latin, meaning "kill") are different from derivational suffixes, because they do not define the word-class of their output,[21] and they are different from evaluative suffixes because they are heads.

3.2. Morphological compounds

Morphological compounds may have a modification or a coordination structure. Modification structures are the result of left adjunction of a root (the modifier) to another root (the head):

(46) $[[pat]_{MODIFIER}o[lo'g]_{HEAD}]ia$ "pathology"
   $[[en'cefal]_{MODIFIER}o[pa't]_{HEAD}]ia$ "encephalopathy"

In coordination structures, both roots are heads:

(47) [['*crani*]o[*ence*'*fál*]]*ico*   "cranioencephalic"

Usually, the boundary between roots is marked by the binding vowel –*o*–, unless it precedes a member of a (lexically determined) small set of Latinate roots, and only in modification structures. In this case, the binding vowel is -*i*-:

(48) *hom*[i]'*cida*   "homicide"
     frut[i]*cul*'*tura* "fruit production"
     ver'*m*[i]*fugo*   "vermifuge"
     ampl[i]'*forme*   "ampliform"
     car'*n*[i]*voro*   "carnivore"

The binding vowel may be absent in modification structures (not in coordination structures). This absence occurs when the right-hand root begins with a vowel:[22]

(49) *dem*[]*ago*'*gia*   "demagogy"
     '*sul*[]*ameri*'*cano*   "South American"

From a morphological point of view, these compounds are tripartite structures (root-binding vowel-root). Since the choice of the binding vowel is sensitive to the kind of structure (modification vs. coordination) and to a lexical feature of the right-hand root, the binding vowel is a morphological specifier of the right-hand root. From a phonological/prosodic point of view, morphological compounds project two prosodic words and the binding vowel is the final vowel of the first prosodic word.

The phonetic realization of the binding vowel is quite interesting in itself and it is also quite revealing. Binding vowels are usually in an unstressed position—that changes whenever the right-hand root's only vowel cannot be stressed and no derivational suffix is present: In BP the stressed mid vowel is lower mid in these words(dactylic lowering):

(50) *au*'*t*[*ó*]*grafo*   "autograph"
     bibli'[*ó*]*filo*   "bibliophile"
     psi'*c*[*ó*]*logo*   "psychologist"
     ver'*m*[*í*]*fugo*   "vermifuge"

These cases are irrelevant for the analysis of the quality of the binding vowel. On the contrary, the quality of the binding vowel -*o*- when it is in a non-stressed position is worth a note. In EP, this vowel resists to unstressed vowel reduction, surfacing as [ɔ] (51a), unless the word is lexicalized, which means that it becomes a single prosodic word (51b). In BP, the binding vowel tends to be surfacing as [u] (55a). In lexicalized instances, the binding vowel also surfaces as a different vowel ([o]): (looks as if the underlying value is lower mid in EP and upper mid in BP).

(51)   EP: BP:
     a. *p*'*sic*[ɔ]*lin*'*guística*   *p*'*sic*[u]*lin*'*guística*   "psycholinguistics"
        '*aut*[ɔ]*susten*'*tável*   '*aut*[u]*susten*'*tável*   "self-sustained"
        '*micr*[ɔ]'*clima*   '*micr*[u]'*clima*   "microclimate"
     b. *fil*[u]*so*'*fia*   *fil*[o]*so*'*fia*   "philosophy"
        aut[u]*gra*'*far*   *aut*[o]*gra*'*far*   "to autograph"
        micr[u]*s*'*cópio*   *micr*[o]*s*'*cópio*   "microscope"

Some morphological compounds use clips from other morphological compounds. As neoclassical loans, they convey their original meaning (52a), but as clips they bring the overall meaning of the compounds from where they originated (52b):

(52) a.   'fotos'síntese   "photosynthesis"
            fotogra'fia   "photography"
            'autorre'trato   "self portrait"
            auto'móvel   "car"
            biogra'fia   "biography"
            biolo'gia   "biology"
            econo'mia   "economy"
            ecolo'gia   "ecology"
      b.   foto('grafia)+jorna'lista   "photo+journalist"
            'fotojorna'lista   "photographic journalist"
            auto('móvel)+es'trada   "car+road"
            'autoes'trada   "freeway"
            bio(lo'gia)+degra'dável   "biology+degradable"
            'biodegra'dável   "biodegradable"
            eco(lo'gia)+tu'rismo   "ecology+tourism"
            'ecotu'rismo   "ecological tourism"

Clips such as *agro–*, *bio–*, *eco–*, *eletro–*, or *foto–* become new roots by merging the binding vowel with the neoclassical root. Consequently, they have a different behavior: for instance, when they precede a vowel-initial root, the final *–o* is not deleted:

(53) foto(gra'fia)+aven'tura   "photo+adventure"
       'fotoaven'tura   "photographic adventure"
       eco(lo'gia)+al'deia   "ecology+village"
       'ecoal'deia   "ecological village"

Clips often become words. That is the case of *foto* ("photo") and *micro* ("microphone"). BP has many more examples:

(54) Meus irmãos são 'héteros. (='hetero[ssexu'ai]s)
      "My brothers are heterosexuals"

3.3. *Morphosyntactic compounds*

Morphosyntactic compounds result from the right adjunction of a noun to a noun (55a), the coordination of nouns (55b) or, less frequently, of adjectives (55c) or even of verbs (55d), and the reanalysis of a verb phrase (55e):

(55) a.   'mãe-co'ruja   "doting mother"
      b.   lei'tor-grava'dor   "player-recorder"
      c.   'surdo-'mudo   "deaf-mute"
      d.   'leva-e-'traz   "gossiper"
      e.   'quebra-'nozes   "nutcracker"

Modification structures like those in (55a) and (56) are head-initial: the head noun determines the gender and the number of the compound. The modifier noun remains invariable:

(56) a.   [[ca'fé(s)]$_{N\_MSC\_SG/PL}$con'certo]$_{N\_MSC\_SG}$ "coffee concert = cabaret(s)"
      b.   [[es'cola(s)]$_{N\_FEM\_SG/PL}$mo'delo]$_{N\_FEM\_SG}$ "school model = model school(s)"

These compounds are interpreted as modification structures: the compound is a hyponym of its head: *ca'fé-con'certo* is a "type of coffee house"; *es'cola mo'delo* is a "type of school."

In coordination structures like (57b) and (57c), both constituents are heads. Therefore, they both inflect in number (57a). For animated nouns (57b) or adjectives (57c), gender agreement is also required. In the case of coordination of inanimate nouns with discordant values of gender, the gender is masculine (57d), which is the unmarked value:

(57) a. [*lei'tor(es)*]$_{\text{N\_MSC\_SG}}$[*grava'dor(es)*]$_{\text{N\_MSC\_SG}}$ "player-recorder(s)"
　　 b. [*nada'dor/a(s)*]$_{\text{N\_MSC/FEM\_SG/PL}}$[*salva'dor/a(s)*]$_{\text{N\_MSC/FEM\_SG/PL}}$ "lifeguard(s)"
　　 c. [*'doce(s)*]$_{\text{ADJ\_SG}}$[*a'margo/a(s)*]$_{\text{ADJ\_MSC\_SG}}$ "bittersweet"
　　 d. [*'bar(es)*]$_{\text{N\_MSC\_SG}}$[*disco'teca(s)*]$_{\text{N\_FEM\_SG}}$]$_{\text{N\_MSC\_SG}}$ "disco-bar(s)"

The meaning of coordinated compounds is not always easy to establish, since it may be additive (58a), sequential (58b), or reciprocal (58c):

(58) a. *lei'tor-grava'dor*　　"reader-recorder = device that plays and records"
　　 b. *ou'tono-in'verno*　　"autumn-winter"
　　 c. *a'luno-profes'sor*　　"student-teacher = relationship between student and teacher"

Note that the line between modification structure and coordination structure may be difficult to draw: in some cases they may be interpreted as reciprocal modification (59a). This difficulty is noticeable in the hesitation of speakers regarding number inflection (59b):

(59) a. *so'fá-'cama*　　　　　　　"sofa-bed" = sofa that serves as a bed or a sofa that serves as a bed and a bed that serves as a sofa

　　 b. *so'fás-'camas* vs. *so'fás-'cama*

Another type of morphosyntactic compounding is based on structures very similar to VPs. They are formed by the third-person singular indicative present form of a (typically) transitive verb; and by a (generally) plural noun, which is the head of the direct object of that verb. Usually, this compounding process generates a masculine subject-noun:

(60) *'guarda-'costas*　　'guards-back = bodyguard'
　　 'quebra-ca'beça(s)　　'breaks-heads = puzzle'

A final type of morphosyntactic compounding combines two verbs to form, again, a masculine noun. Two subtypes must be distinguished. The first corresponds to the coordination of two different verb forms (V_iV_j). Usually, these compounds occur only in the singular form and their meaning is quite transparent:

(61) BP:　　　　*'bate-en'tope*　　'hits-clogs = hit-clog'
　　 EP　　　　 *'sobe-e-'desce*　　'goes up-and-comes down = see saw'
　　 BP/EP:　　*'leva-e-'traz*　　'takes-and-brings = intriguer'

The second subtype, much more common in BP than in EP, involves reduplication of the verb to form a V_iV_i compound. These forms can convey two meanings: an action (62a) or an object (62b). In some cases, both meanings can be observed in the same word (62c):

(62) a. *'corre-'corre*　　'run-run'
　　 b. *'pisca-'pisca*　　'blinks-blinks = blinker'
　　 c. *'pula-'pula*　　'jumps-jumps =act of jumping repeatedly/a toy in the playground"

The bases of V_iV_i compounds are generally disyllabic. There are also a few cases like *a'garra-a'garra* ("grabs-grabs"), with three syllables that always start with an onsetless syllable. Since the reduplication of the verb base is governed by prosodic conditions, the final syllables are always open, except when the verb is monosyllabic (*'sai-'sai* "leaves-leaves" = "one goes out"). Finally, the main morphological characteristic of this type of formation is the selection of the third-person singular indicative present: we assume that this is the unmarked form of the verb paradigm, which allows the reinterpretation of the verb as a noun.

3.4. Syntactic compounds

Syntactic compounding is not a morphological word formation process—it is a process of lexicalization of phrases. Reference grammars usually list a number of different cases, such as the following:

(63) N-P-N $[[N][_P[N]_{NP}]_{PP}]_{NP}$ *ca'minho de 'ferro*   "road-of-iron = railroad"
      N-ADJ $[[N][ADJ]_{ADJP}]_{NP}$ *'cofre 'forte*   "safe-strong = safe"
      ADJ-N $[[ADJ]_{ADJP}[N]]_{NP}$ *'alta tempo'rada*   "high season"

These word sequences display typical syntactic properties, regarding number inflection (64a) and gender contrasts, when available (64b):

(64) a. *ca'minho(s) de'ferro*   "railroad(s)"
          'cofre(s) 'forte(s)   "safe(s)"
      b. *arqui'teto/a de interi'ores*   "interior (m/f) designer"
          pri'meiro/a mi'nistro/a   "prime minister (m/f)"

What motivates the treatment of these sequences as lexical units is their semantics, which is not compositional. Another property that distinguishes these lexicalized phrases from genuine syntactic phrases is the fact that the extraction of a single constituent is ungrammatical:

(65) **caminhos de [ferro velho]*   "[old iron] roads"
      *esse é um [cofre quê]?   "this is a [safe what]?"
      *[primeiro e único] ministro   "prime and only minister"
      *dos dois[caminhos_i []_i], prefiro o [[]_i [de ferro]_i]   "of both ways, I prefer the iron one"

3.5. Other types of compounding?

A non-concatenative morphological process often associated with compounding is blending. Although there are two words that serve as input for a third form (as in compounding), blends are different, because they are produced by the intersection of bases instead of concatenation, as in *cren'tino* (*'crente+cre'tino*, "religious+fool" = "false religious") and *lixera'tura* (*'lixo+litera'tura*, "garbage+literature" = "shoddy literature"). The deleted material is not predictable.

From a phonological perspective, blends are single prosodic words. The output form preserves the largest possible number of identical segments of the input forms, as in *aperta'mento* "small apartment" (*a'perto+aparta'tamento* "clench+apartment"). As a result, the transition of the first of the input forms to the second coincides with an identical segment or syllable (*'saco+pico'lé* "bag+popsicle" = *saco'lé* "popsicle in a bag"; *'pai+'mãe* "father+mother"=*'pãe* "caring father").

3.6. *Emergence of new morphological constituents*

The emergence of a new productive word-formation process may happen when speakers start using a loan to make new words, or because speakers reinterpret an existing morpheme or part of a morpheme with a new meaning. In the first case, the use of formatives such as *cyber–*, *wiki–*, and *e–*, which, combined with native bases, form words like 'cyber-a'*vó* ("cyber-grandmother"), '*wiki*-'*aves* ("wiki-birds") and *e-profes*'*sor* ("e-professor"). In the second case, the phenomenon can be seen as a kind of folk etymology: words without any internal structure may be reinterpreted as compounds or affixing forms that consist of two parts, like ma'*drasta* ("stepmother") and *patro*'*cínio* ("sponsorship"). They are intentionally misanalyzed as *má* ("bad") plus *drasta* to form a new meaning: "a bad stepmother"[23] and '*pa*(i) ("father") plus *trocínio*("sponsored by the father"). This strategy gives rise to forms such as:

(66) a. '*sogra*'*drasta*   "stepmother-in-law"
          ir'*mã*'*drasta*   "step-sister"
      b. '*tiotro*'*cínio*   "sponsored by an uncle"
          '*mãetro*'*cínio*   "sponsored by the mother"

These particles are usually called splinters, which are elements that occur at the edge of the word, the same way affixes do, but, because of their meanings, they correspond to roots. Therefore, splinters form a separate class, situated somewhere between roots and affixes. Thus, clipping and blending play an important role in the morphology of Portuguese, as they can produce splinters, not being, therefore, interpreted as exclusively non-morphemically.

4. Conclusion

The study of Portuguese morphology largely benefits from the fact that (at least) two subsystems can be easily compared: contrasts between EP and BP often offer the possibility to consolidate analyses independently outlined or, inversely, show how closely related languages may be different and ask for different analyses for certain subsystems of the grammar.

The vowel system in EP, which facilitates the identification of unstressed reduced vowels, is particularly relevant to establish that suffixes may attach to roots, stems or words, and it is also required to understand the structure of morphological compounds.

The description of processes that involve non-concatenative morphology or structural mutations clearly benefit from the livelihood they have in BP. In this variety, process like reduplication, blending and clipping are most commonly employed, which enables us to say that this is one of the main aspects that differentiate the two varieties described here.

NOTES

1   We will discuss the formation of nouns, adjectives and verbs and *–mente* adverbs. In all examples, the stress mark (') precedes the stressed syllable. Moreover, these syllables are written in bold.
2   Thematic constituents (thematic vowels for verbs and thematic indexes for all other classes) are morphological specifiers.
3   Morphosyntactic specifiers (= MSS) are inflectional suffixes.

4   Alongside masculine (= MSC) and feminine (= FEM), we will consider a third value (non-specified) that is assigned to bases that will be syntactically specified:

a'*tletas*$_{SUB}$ "athletes"
os$_{MSC}$ a'*tletas*$_{MSC}$
as$_{FEM}$ a'*tletas*$_{FEM}$

5   Consider, for instance, the above-mentioned inflection of '*pele* ("skin") and pa'*pel* ("paper"). The relevance of thematic classes for inflection is also obvious in the phonetic outputs of words ending in the diphthong [aw]. In BP, words ending in <l>, as ca'*nal* ("channel"), are pronounced the same way as words ending in <u>, as de'*grau* ("step"). In the plural, however, they differ considerably, since the plural of the latter, which is a projection of an athematic root, is obtained by the adjunction of the suffix –*s* (de'*graus*, "steps"), while the plural of the former is obtained by semi-vocalization of the final consonant of the –Ø root, /l/, to receive the plural suffix (ca'*nais* "channels").

6   Traditional accounts do not usually mention infixation.

7   There is a limited number of pairs of words formed by conversion and derivation from a same base, but generally they are not semantically equivalent ('*perda* "loss" and perdi'*ção* "perdition"; cele'*brar* "to celebrate" and celebri'*zar* "to make famous").

8   The examples presented in this section are usually called diminutive suffixes. Their semantic role may be related to size, but it may also convey other meanings: ca'*sinha* (the 'diminutive' from '*casa* "house") may refer a "small house", a "lovely house", a "cherished house", an "old house" an "ugly house", or other, depending on pragmatics. It may even be used as a rhetoric resource. This is why the tag 'evaluative' (including augmentative and superlative as well) seems more appropriate—it includes morphological devices that allow the speaker to convey an opinion about a lexical unit, from its inside.

9   Portuguese southern dialects prefer -*it*(o/a) (li'*vrito* "book+EVAL"), and –*zit*(o/a) ('*cão*'*zito* "dog+EVAL").

10   Other analyses are available, (see Bisol 2010, for instance, which considers –*inho* and –*zinho* allomorphs of the same morpheme). We follow the proposal of Villalva (1994, 2008, 2009).

11   In BP,–Ø roots that may combine with –*inho* are those ending in <r>, although few examples are found: colhe'*rinha*/colher'*zinha* "spoon+EVAL", devaga'*rinho*/devagar'*zinho* "slowly". Other instances are lexicalized words (cola'*rinho* "collar"+EVAL = foam *of* beer').

12   This preference has been demonstrated by the results of usage surveys (Villalva 2009).

13   In EP, there are cases of truncation, like a'*narca* ("anarchist"), which have a clear pejorative or derogatory value, but their prevalence in EP is smaller than in BP. Evidently, this is because in EP word-shortening is generally obtained by reducing unstressed vowels.

14   Most authors (e.g. Basílio 1987, Sandmann 1989) consider prefixation a derivational process. Some others (e.g. Mattoso Câmara 1971, Macambira 1978) argue that there are no substantial differences between prefixed and compound words; other still (e.g. Villalva 1994, Gonçalves 2012) argue that prefixation is midway between derivation and compounding. Our claim here is that prefixation is neither derivation nor compounding—it is a process of morphological modification that can make use of prefixes or roots.

15   In words such as n[j]olo'*gismo* ("neologism"), pr[i]ssenti'*mento* ("feeling"), or p[u]s'*por*("to postpone"), the prefix vowel is reduced as a result of lexicalization.

16   In EP, these hiatus are avoided by glide formation (r[j]labaste'*cer* "to refill", r[j]u'*sar* "to re-use"), and the vowels in these prefixes are less likely to deletion when the following vowel is identical (r[j]-[ɐ]xpli'*car* "to re-explain", r[j]-[e]labo'*rar* 'to re-elaborate').

17   Words such as colegi'*al* ("collegial"), coloni'*al* ("colonial") and coloqui'*al* ("colloquial") do not respect the –*ar* ~ –*al* allomorphy. This is probably due to the fact that they are Latinate words recently introduced in the Portuguese lexicon.

18   This suffix is etymologically related to the suffixes –*ice* (doi'*dice* "insanity"), and –*ície* (imun'*dicie* "filth"), but these behave as different suffixes, not as allomorphs, in Portuguese.

19   This suffix is no longer productive. Consequently, all the derivatives tend to be lexicalized. Therefore, we find the same base with both allomorphs (du'*rez*, du'*reza* "hardiness"), although usually only one of them is currently used. Some counter-examples, such as ru'*dez* ("rudeness") or aspe'*reza* ("roughness"), can also be found.

20   Haplology cases are quite rare and most of them are quite old.
21   The word-class of *herbi'cida* (adjective/noun) is a property of the structure.
22   The binding vowel is not deleted when the first root ends in a vowel (*bi+log* "life+knowledge" = *bi[o]logia* "biology"; *ge+graf* "earth+write" = *ge[ó]grafo* "geographer"). There is a considerable number of morphological compounds that do not fit in the above-described pattern. Either because of a preference for the most usual binding vowel (*parc[ó]metro* 'parkmeter') or for different reasons, which may be etymological, in some cases, contrastive, in some other, since most of these words are loans that can be found in many European languages.
23   In BP, a loving stepmother is named *mãe'drastra* ('*mãe*+*ma'drastra* "mother+stepmother"), another lexical blend.

REFERENCES

Basílio, M. (1987). *Teoria Lexical*. São Paulo: Ática.

Bauer, L. (1988). *Introducing Linguistic Morphology*. Edinburgh: Edinburgh University Press.

Bisol, L. (2010). O diminutivo e suas demandas. *DELTA*, 26 (1), pp. 59–85.

Carvalho, H. de (1967). *Teoria da Linguagem. Natureza do Fenómeno Linguístico e Análise das Línguas*. Coimbra: Atlântida.

Fandrych, I. (2008). Submorphemic elements in the formation of acronyms, blends and clippings. *Lexis – E-Journal in English Lexicology*, 2.

Gonçalves, C. A. V. (2004). Usos morfológicos: os processos marginais de formação de palavras em português. *Gragoatá*, 21, pp. 219–242.

Gonçalves, C. A. V. (2011). *Iniciação aos Estudos Morfológicos*. São Paulo: Contexto.

Gonçalves, C. A. V. (2012). Atuais tendências em formação de palavras no português brasileiro. *Signum. Estudos de Linguagem*, 15, pp. 169–199.

Lee, S. H. (1995). *Fonologia e Morfologia Lexical do Português*. Ph.D. dissertation, UNICAMP.

Macambira, J. R. (1978). *Português Estrutural*, 2nd edn. São Paulo: Pioneira.

Mattoso Câmara Jr., J. (1971). *Problemas de Linguística Descritiva*. Petrópolis: Vozes.

Rio-Torto, G. (1998). *Morfologia Derivacional. Teoria e Aplicação ao Português*. Porto: Porto Editora.

Sandmann, A. J. (1989). *Morfologia Geral*. São Paulo: Contexto.

Schwindt, L. C. (2000). *O Prefixo no Português Brasileiro: Análise Morfofonológica*. Ph.D. dissertation, Pontifícia Universidade Católica do Rio Grande do Sul.

Villalva, A. (1994). *Estruturas Morfológicas. Unidades e Hierarquias nas Palavras do Português*. Lisbon: FCG-FCT.

Villalva, A. (2008). *Morfologia do Português*. Lisbon: Universidade Aberta.

Villalva, A. (2009). Sobre a formação dos chamados diminutivos em Português Europeu. In *Actas do 25° Encontro da Associação Portuguesa de Linguística*, pp. 787–793.

Villalva, A. and J. P. Silvestre (2014). *Introdução ao Estudo do Léxico. Descrição e Análise do Português*. Petrópolis: Vozes.

Wetzels, W. L. (1992). Mid vowel neutralization in Brazilian Portuguese. *Cadernos de Estudos Linguísticos*, 23, pp. 19–55.

11 The Morphology and Phonology of Inflection

LUIZ CARLOS SCHWINDT AND W. LEO WETZELS

In this chapter we describe the morphology of nominal and verbal inflection of Portuguese and the way it interacts with phonology. Considering the regularity characteristic of inflectional processes, one does not expect to find significant differences between Brazilian and European Portuguese in this area. Nevertheless, our account of this topic provides an overview of some relevant studies produced by authors of the two varieties. Where relevant, the aspects that differentiate between them will be discussed.

1. Nominal inflection

Among the non-verbs of Portuguese, articles, nouns, adjectives, numerals, and pronouns represent the categories that can be inflected. For reasons of limited space we will focus in this chapter on the inflection of nouns and verbs.

Portuguese nouns belong to one of two grammatical gender classes, masculine or feminine, of which the feminine is considered the marked class. Nouns are also subject to pluralization with the –s suffix. Unlike adjectives and determiners, inflection for nouns is not the product of agreement; they trigger agreement by transferring their gender and number features to adjectives and determiners under conditions established by syntax.

(1) a. [[o]$_{\text{article masc. sg}}$ [menino]$_{\text{noun masc. sg}}$ [esperto]$_{\text{adjective masc. sg}}$]NP
         "the smart boy"
     b. [[as]$_{\text{article fem. pl}}$ [meninas]$_{\text{noun fem. pl}}$ [espertas]$_{\text{adjective fem. pl}}$]NP
         "the smart girls"

A suffix –a can be added to nominal stems to mark them as feminine nouns, while the –s suffix marks them for plurality. This seemingly simple inflectional system, however, has some significant phonological repercussions, which is the subject of this section.

1.1. Gender

Portuguese nouns divide into two grammatical gender classes, masculine and feminine, not necessarily associated with biological gender, not even in the case of animate referents, as is shown by the example *O agente de viagens foi atencioso* "The travel agent was courteous," where *agente* can refer to a man or a woman, but requires masculine agreement with the adjective.[1]

The Handbook of Portuguese Linguistics, First Edition. Edited by W. Leo Wetzels, João Costa, and Sergio Menuzzi.
© 2016 John Wiley & Sons, Inc. Published 2020 by John Wiley & Sons, Inc.

With regard to gender marking, nouns can be classified in three groups: marked variable gender (2), unmarked variable gender (3), and invariable gender (4).

(2) a. *menino/menina*   "boy"/"girl"
    b. *leão/leoa*   "lion"/"lioness"
    c. *presidente/presidenta*   "president (male)"/"president (female)"

(3) a. *dentista*   masc/fem   "dentist"
    b. *cliente*   masc/fem   "customer"
    c. *soprano*   masc/fem   "soprano"

(4) a. *problema*   masc   "problem"
    b. *tribo*   fem   "tribe"
    c. *dente*   masc   "tooth"
    d. *lente*   fem   "lens"

The words in (2) represent the most productive pattern of biological gender inflection in Portuguese. Most speakers, including children during language acquisition, associate nouns with animate referents that end in –*a* with females and those ending in –*o* with males.[2] Câmara Jr.(1970) interpreted this opposition privatively, with the feminine marker –*a* in opposition with ø in the masculine, the latter representing the unmarked gender. Although the examples in (2a, b) suggest an equipollent opposition, the linguistic tradition rejected the equipollent analysis with the following arguments: (i) –*a* contrasts with both –*o* and –*e*, as shown in (2c); (ii) –*e* attaches also to invariable gender nouns, masculine or feminine, as can be seen in (4c, d). The nouns in (3) have the same form for both the masculine and the feminine but are realized with two different genders, as is revealed by the agreement process in sentences like *a/o dentista esperta/o* "the smart dentist fem/masc." As for nouns ending in –*e*, while most of them allow the formation of a corresponding feminine form ending in –*a*, such as *a presidenta* "the president fem," some are more recalcitrant, such as *cliente* "customer" (3b), for which the form *clienta* sounds strange for most BP speakers. While nouns with variable gender ending in –*e* are capable of referring to both the masculine or the feminine, when the suffix –*a* is added, reference is exclusively to the feminine gender, showing the existence of an independent feminine marker. Examples such as (3c), which are two-gendered nouns ending in –*o*, are very rare; when they occur, they often show de-adjectival properties, i.e. the sentence *ela é uma soprano* "she is a soprano" can be paraphrased by means of a structure like *ela é uma cantora do tipo soprano* "she is a singer of the soprano type." This favors the strong association of –*o* with the masculine gender.

The nouns in (4), although they carry gender information transmitted by agreement, do not admit any change of gender. Unlike the examples in (2) and (3), these nouns have no association with biological gender, but refer to objects or abstract entities. They also have an unpredictable class marker, as they can end in –*a*, –*o*, or –*e*, and there is no systematic relation between grammatical gender and the class marker. Whereas the great majority of the *a*-final words in this class have feminine gender, some are masculine. Interestingly, in this category, examples of words with feminine gender ending in –*o* are also extremely rare.

1.1.1. Other mechanisms for forming feminine nouns

Although the addition of the suffix –*a* is the main expedient for biological gender inflection in Portuguese, the language also makes use of other strategies, which often involve the modification of the base to which the feminine suffix attaches, resulting in root allomorphy, as in (5a, b) below, or in the addition of a derivational extension before the feminine marker, as in (5c, d). These extensions are not synchronously transparent for native speakers, making this type of biological gender expression very restricted.

(5) Masculine/Feminine with root allomorphy
    a. *frei/freira*   "friar"/"nun"
    b. *judeu/judia*   "Jew"/"Jewess"
    c. *rei/rainha*   "king"/"queen"
    d. *príncipe/princesa* "prince"/ "princess"

The fact that these changes in the nominal root happen only from the masculine to the feminine supports the hypothesis of the masculine being unmarked in the language.

    Finally, Portuguese equally has noun pairs with opposite biological gender involving suppletion (cf. *homem/mulher* "man"/"woman"; *genro/nora* "son-in-law"/ "daughter-in-law").

1.1.2. *Formal class markers –e, –o, –a and their relation to gender*

Like other Romance languages, such as Spanish and Italian, for example, Portuguese non-verbs preferably end in vowels. There has been some discussion about whether this property finds its main motivation in morphology or in phonology, since this vowel, although traditionally described as a morpheme, acts at the same time to prevent illegal codas in the language. Câmara Jr. (1970) classified these final vowels as thematic vowels because of their relation with gender, separating them into three classes: Class 1, nouns ending in *–a*, class 2, nouns ending in *–o*, and class 3 nouns ending in *–e*. Mateus and d'Andrade (2000: 68), on the other hand, use the term "thematic vowels" only for verbs, referring to the final vowels in nouns and adjectives as "class markers," for different reasons, including the fact that the choice for one of them as the final segment in nouns is not obligatory, because consonant-final words also exist. As a matter of fact, Portuguese nouns may be classified in three groups: (1) nouns ending in an unstressed vowel or nasal diphthong, usually /a/, /o/, /e/, or /aũ/; (2) nouns ending in one of the consonants /l, R, S/[3] (the latter spelled <s> or <z>); or (3) nouns ending in any of the seven vowels that make up the stressed vowel system or in an oral diphthong.

(6) Gender in nouns and its relation to word endings
    Group I: Nouns ending in an unstressed vowel or nasal diphthong
    a. *menina*   fem   "girl"
    b. *casa*   fem   "house"
    c. *menino*   masc "boy"
    d. *muro*   masc "wall"
    e. *irmão*   masc "brother"
    f. *ponte*   fem   "bridge"
    Group II: Nouns ending in a consonant
    g. *animal*   masc "animal"
    h. *mar*   masc "sea"
    i. *luz*   fem   "light"
    Group III: Nouns ending in a stressed vowel or oral diphthong (athematic)
    j. *javali*   masc "wild boar"
    k. *urubu*   masc "vulture"
    l. *guichê*   masc "booth"
    m. *camelô*   masc "street vendor"
    n. *cipó*   masc "liana"
    o. *café*   masc "coffee"
    p. *alvará*   masc "business license"
    q. *mingau*   masc "porridge"

Let us consider the classification proposed in (6) and discuss its implications for gender formation.

(i)   The words of Group I receive a class marker *–a*, *–o*, or *–e*, which attaches to the nominal root, preparing it to receive the gender and number inflections. When the feminine suffix *–a* is added to the nominal theme to create feminine gender, the phonological process of vowel deletion in hiatus is applied (e.g. /menino+a/ → [me'nĩna]; /presidente+a/ → [presi'dẽⁿta], /turista+a/ → [tu'rista]). The lexical representation of nouns ending in a nasal diphthong represents a more controversial analytical issue. The classic hypothesis considers that words like *irmão* [iɾmãw̃] "brother" have an underlying form /irmaN+o/, which would also explain the appearance of /o/ (> [w]) in the plural form *irmãos*, for example. Such an analysis assigns these words to the class of thematic nouns, which, at some abstract level of representation, end in one of the class markers. These words mostly realize their feminine correspondent with the *–a* suffix, generally nasalized and attaching directly to the root (*irmão* "brother" ~ *irmã* "sister"). In some cases, however, the feminine suffix is oral and preceded by /o/ (*patrão* "master" ~ *patroa* "mistress").

(ii) Words of Group II generally have a single gender, mostly masculine. When these words allow gender switching, the simple addition of *–a* occurs, as in *professor* ~ *professora* "teacher masc/fem." Traditionally, most of the Group II words were also analyzed as thematic, with an underlying vowel final *–e* (cf. /animale/ "animal"). This analysis explains the surfacing of the plural form with a [js] ending (cf. *animais* "animals"). Below, when we discuss number inflection, we will challenge the classification of *irmão* and *animal* type nouns as members of the thematic class.

(iii) The words of the third group are athematic, i.e. the stressed final vowels as well as the oral diphthongs are considered part of the root. They usually belong to the masculine gender class, although a small number of feminine words exist. An athematic noun can only rarely have two genders, as the word *o/a xará* "the namesake-masc/fem." Words ending in stressed vowels are usually of indigenous origin, mostly Tupi, or African, or they are Gallicisms, bypassing the general trochaic accent pattern of Portuguese non-verbs.

The discussion so far permits the conclusion that Portuguese nouns generally end in a class marker. We have also seen that, at the surface, there exists homophony with respect to the final vowel *–a*, which can represent a class marker, as in *casa* "house" or a feminine suffix, as in *menina* "girl" (</menino+a/). Other authors would admit the same homophony for word-final unstressed *–o*, treating it as an exponent of a class marker (*muro* "wall") merged with the masculine suffix (/menin+o,a/).[4]

1.2. Number

Portuguese nouns may receive plural inflection. As with gender, plural inflection is subject to agreement under the appropriate syntactic conditions. There are some words with collective meaning with singular inflection expressing the notion of plurality (e.g. *o povo* "the people").

The opposite also exists: there is a small number of words that always realize the plural suffix while referring to a unitary semantic concept (e.g. *as férias* "the vacation").

Unlike gender, the inflectional nature of number is unchallenged, although the phonology involved to account for the correspondence between singular and plural forms is in some cases more intricate, without general agreement among specialists regarding the precise way in which they are phonologically related. In the words in (7), the adjunction of the plural suffix to words ending in a stressed or unstressed vowel is straightforward: the *–s* suffix is added to the final vowel, which may represent the class marker, the feminine suffix, or the final segment of the root.

(7) Plural nouns ending in simple vowel (atonic and tonic)
     a. *crianç+a+s*   "children"   g. *tricô+s*   "knittings"
     b. *menin+a+s*   "girls"   h. *bebê+s*   "babies"
     c. *livr+o+s*   "books"   i. *urubú+s*   "vultures"
     d. *garot+o+s*   "boys"   j. *colibri+s*   "hummingbirds"
     e. *agent+e+s*   "agents"
     f. *president+e+s*   "presidents"

The words ending in the stressed nasal diphthong [ãw̃] are less regular in the way they form their plurals. There is a small group that just adds –*s*, following the general pattern, as shown in (8b) below. This is also the way in which the rare words with an unstressed word-final nasal diphthong form their plural *órgão* ~ *órgãos* "organ." Another set, also few in number, realize their plural ending as [ãj̃s], as shown in (8c). In most cases, this sequence is the synchronic remnant of the Latin forms ending in –*anem* The majority of words ending in stressed [ãw̃], however, realizes their plural ending as [õj̃s], shown in (8a). This alternation, prevalent in words historically derived from Latin nouns ending in –*onem*, is the most widespread, including also words historically derived from Latin nouns with different endings.

(8) Pluralization of words ending in [ãw̃]
     singular   plural
     a. *leão*   *leões*   "lion(s)"
     b. *mão*   *mãos*   "hand(s)"
     c. *cão*   *cães*   "dog(s)"

The literature presents different analyses for this pattern. As we have seen, the traditional approach posits an underlying class marker in these words, as is /leoN+e/ "lion." The singular and plural forms are derived by a set of rules illustrated with the following derivation (adapted from the discussion in Wetzels (1997) and Bisol (1998)).

(9) Singular [ãw̃] ~ plural [õj̃s]: traditional analysis
     a. accent   león+e   león+e+s
     b. nasalization   leõn+e   leõn+e+s
     c. deletion of the nasal consonant   leõ+e   leõ+e
     d. deletion of the class marker   leõ   n.a.
     e. glide insertion   leõw   n.a.
     f. delabialization of /o/   leãw   n.a.
     g. glide formation   n.a.   leõjs
     h. spreading of the nasal feature   leãw̃   leõj̃s

One of the arguments commonly advanced in favor of the hypothesis of an underlying nasal consonant is the fact that /n/ often emerges when a derivational suffix is attached to words with a final nasal vowel, as in *leão* "lion" ~ *leonino* "leonine." Nevertheless, Wetzels (1997) questions this argument, in view of the significant number of Portuguese words that contain the word final sequence Vn{o,a,e}# in which this consonant does not delete in the forms of the singular (compare *leão* with *panetone* *[pane'tãw̃] "panettone," *irmão* with *decano* *[de'kãw̃] "dean," *irmã* with *banana* *[ba'nã]) as predicted by the derivation (9c) or, for *irmão* and *irmã*, some variant thereof. In addition, the hypothesis of an underlying class marker that subsequently must be deleted as well as the insertion of the labial glide in the singular forms lack independent motivation.

There are several possibilities to account for the surface alternation [ãw̃] ~ [õj̃s] more directly. A phonological solution could involve assimilation by way of a double flop affecting the place features of the last two segments, in which process the [coronal] feature of the suffix /–S/ spreads to the preceding /ũ/, which in turn passes its [labial] feature to the preceding /a/:

(10)   /a   ũ⁵   S/

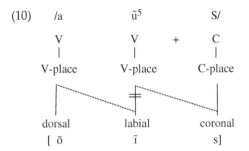

            V   V   +   C
            | | |
        V-place   V-place   C-place

        dorsal   labial   coronal
        [õ   ĩ   s]

   This analysis faces the problem of marking the (few) words of the type (8b, c) as exceptional with regard to the second spreading operation (*cão/cães* "dog(s)"), or both operations (*mão(s)* "hand(s)"). An alternative analysis, with the same set of exceptions, could perhaps relate the change /aũ/ > [õw̃] to a similar process of assimilation that occurs in verb-final diphthongs (cf. the perfective paradigm of the verb *falar* "speak": *falei, falaste, falou, falamos, falastes, falaram*). It is equally possible to posit different underlying structures for *cão* and *leão*: /kaũ+s/ and /leoũ+s/. To derive the plural forms, only coronal place assimilation would be sufficient: /kaĩ+s/ and /leoĩ+s/. Moreover, the feminine *leoa* "lioness" could easily be derived by truncation /leoũ+a/ > /leoa/. A rule of neutralization: /oũ/ > /aũ/ would account for the singular *leão* [leãw̃], since at the surface there is no contrast between [ãw̃] and [õw̃] representing lexical nasal diphthongs.[6] The very few words like *mão* that form their plural in *–ãos* remain exceptional with regard to the coronal assimilation rule. Obviously, a more radical solution, although not necessarily the best one given the relatively high productivity of the [ãũ] ~ [õj̃s] pattern,[7] would involve the lexicalization of the /aũ/ ~ /oĩ/ or /aũ/ ~ /aĩ/ allomorphs, subcategorized for number. Clearly, in order to decide between the available alternatives more in-depth knowledge of the overall phonological grammar of Portuguese is necessary, which would also involve the relation between the lexical base and derived words like *leão* "lion" ~ *leonino* "leonine," *caminhão* "truck" ~ *caminhoneiro* "truck driver," etc.
   The words ending in one of the consonants /R, S, l/ also deserve special attention. Words ending in R and S in stressed syllables necessarily require the presence of a vowel between the root and the plural suffix.

(11)   Plural of final-stressed nouns ending in R and S
       a. *ator ~ atores*   "actor(s)"
       b. *rapaz ~ rapazes*   "boy(s)"

   Regardless of the morphological status given to this vowel, be it an abstract class marker or part of a plural allomorph, –S/–eS, the main motivation for its emergence seems to be phonological. That is, it serves to prevent the emergence of ill formed coda clusters in Portuguese *rs,[8] *ss.[9] In the few nouns ending in unstressed /VR/ or /VS/, alternative strategies are available: in the case of *rs, although epenthesis remains the default repair (cf. *revólver* > *revólveres* "revolver(s)"), it is not uncommon to hear *revólvers* in BP; in the case of *ss, degemination, instead of epenthesis, is obligatory (cf. *dois lápis/*lápises* "two pencils").

Words closed by /l/ have a plural correspondent in which –S is preceded by an oral diphthong [Vjs], as in (12a–c). When V represents stressed [í], the sequence [ís] surfaces, as shown in (12d).

(12) Plural of nouns ending in /l/
      a. *móvel ~ móveis*   "furniture(s)"
      b. *anel ~ anéis*   "ring(s)"
      c. *réptil ~ répteis*   "reptile(s)"
      d. *funil ~ funis*   "funnel(s)"

To account for the [l] ~ [j] alternation several analyses have been proposed. One is similar to the treatment of words ending in R and S, such that an epenthetic vowel is added between underlying /l/ and the plural suffix. Another analysis is suggested by Mateus and d'Andrade (2000), who propose the semivocalization of the lateral consonant, which is moved to occupy the final position in the nucleus of a newly added syllable triggered by the addition of –S (cf. footnote 9). The situation is somewhat more complex in those dialects of BP where syllable-final /l/ is subject to semivocalization independently of plural formation: *ane*[w] ~ *ane*[js] "ring(s)."[10] In these dialects, which represent the great majority of BP speakers, the necessity for the projection of an empty nucleus is unmotivated for this word type. Instead, the plural form can be derived by a general rule of coda vocalization and assimilation of the glide to the coronal place of the plural suffix /anɛl/ > /anɛw/ > /anɛj+s/, which echoes the discussion of the [ãw̃]/[õj̃s] alternation discussed above.

1.3. *Labial mid-vowel alternations and noun inflection*

In a large group of nouns containing a stressed labial mid-vowel, when inflected with the feminine or the plural suffix, an alternation exists between an upper and a lower mid vowel, as in (13 c, f) below. In nouns showing this alternation, the upper mid-vowel appears in the masculine singular form, the lower mid-vowel in the feminine and plural forms. Other nouns maintain their underlying value throughout, as in (13 a, b, d, e).

(13) Gender and number with umlaut in the root
      a. l[o]bo ~ l[o]ba   "wolf male/female" $[o]_{masc} \sim [o]_{fem}$
      b. c[ɔ]po ~ c[ɔ]pa   "cup"/"glass"[11] $[ɔ]_{masc} \sim [ɔ]_{fem}$
      c. p[o]rco ~ p[ɔ]rca   "pig male/female" $[o]_{masc} \sim [ɔ]_{fem}$
      d. m[o]ço ~ m[o]ços "young man/men" $[o]_{sg} \sim [o]_{pl}$
      e. v[ɔ]to ~ v[ɔ]tos   "vote(s)" $[ɔ]_{sg} \sim [ɔ]_{pl}$
      f. [o]sso ~ [ɔ]ssos   "bone(s)" $[o]_{sg} \sim [ɔ]_{pl}$

In discussing this phenomenon, Câmara Jr. (1970) noted that the lower mid variants of the alternating nouns manifest the synchronic reflex of Latin short ŏ, as in Lt. *pŏrcum* "pig." This led him to propose an analysis considering the lower mid-vowel of the plural (and feminine) as basic (in his words the "theoretic" form) for the alternating forms, qualifying the alternating vowel quality as a submorphemic phenomenon, because redundant with the gender and number markers. Such an analysis is supported synchronically by the fact that the pattern $[ɔ]_{masc,sg} \rightarrow [o]_{fem., pl.}$ is not attested. From a generative perspective, Miranda (2000) proposes that the underlying vowel in words such as (13 b, c, e, f) is /ɔ/, which allows the formulation of an assimilation rule that raises the lower mid-vowel to upper-mid in the masculine singular form, which ends in /o/. Independent of the analysis adopted, there seems to be no strong reason for considering the feminine or plural suffix as triggers for this vowel shift in modern Portuguese.

1.4. Evaluative suffixes

Portuguese words can vary in degree, as expressed by the use of diminutive and augmentative suffixes, such as *–inho/–zinho* and *–ão*, to cite the most common ones.[12]

(14)

		diminutive	augmentative
a. *prato*	"dish"	*pratinho*	*pratão*
b. *livro*	"book"	*livrinho*	*livrão*
c. *tela*	"screen"	*telinha*	*telão*
d. *bola*	"ball"	*bolinha*	*bolão*

Words with evaluative affixes not always express an evaluative meaning, but can be used in a euphemistic sense (*gordinho* "a little fat," which could also refer to someone obese). Diminutives and augmentatives may lexicalize with a pejorative meaning, as one observes in the word *mulherzinha*, literally "small woman," meaning "insignificant woman," or *sapatão*, literally *sapato grande* "big shoe," meaning "lesbian" in BP. For this reason, and for not exercising some contextual effect on surrounding words in syntax, evaluative suffixation is traditionally treated as derivation. However, different from other derivational processes, evaluative suffixation is very productive, without any obvious gaps, and in this respect looks more like inflection. Also, especially in the case of -*(z)inho*, when there are competing suffixes, an alternative form with this suffix is always possible (e.g. *tabuleta ~ tabuinha/tabuazinha* "small wooden board").

This ambiguous behavior of evaluative suffixation in Portuguese, even if it is an insufficient reason to treat it as inflection, provides some evidence for an approach that distinguishes contextual inflection from inherent inflection (cf. Booij, 1993, 1996), or which conceives of different types of affixation as a continuum from prototypical derivational to prototypical inflectional (see Hooper,1976; Stephany, 1982).

2. Verbal inflection

2.1. Morphological structure of the verb

The morphology of the Portuguese verb is somewhat less transparent and the corresponding phonology more intricate than what we have seen for the noun.[13] Most scholars adopt the morphological structure in (15) below, proposed by Câmara Jr., as underlying the verbal paradigm of Portuguese.

(15) Morphological structure of Portuguese finite verb forms
    [Root + Theme]Stem + Tense/Aspect/Mood/+ Person/Number

Portuguese distinguishes three theme classes, subclassified with reference to their different theme vowels: /a, e, i/. The language expresses three different moods, of which the indicative and subjunctive combine with tense and aspect categories in the way shown below.

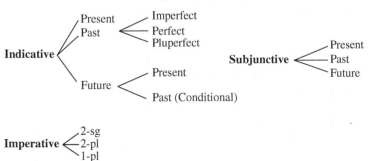

Tense, aspect, and mood (TAM), as well as person and number (PN) are usually expressed as part of a single suffix. Inflectional suffixes can have zero realizations. The existence of six different PN categories are part of the linguistic conscience of most native speakers (1/2/3-sg, 1/2/3-pl), although the 2-pl form has become non-standard in EP and BP, being replaced by the 3-pl form: *vós falais > vocês falam* "you-pl speak." Moreover, in BP, the 2-sg form is replaced by the 3-sg form in most parts of Brazil: *tu falas > você fala* "you-sg speak." Below, the complete set of inflected verb forms are illustrated for the three conjugation classes with the verbs *falar* "speak," *bater* "hit," and *partir* "leave," with comments when useful.

(16)　Morphology of the verb
　　　a. Indicative Mood
　　　a.1. Present

a-theme

$\text{fal}]_{root} \text{a}]_{theme} + \text{ø}]_{tam} + \text{o}]_{pn}$
$\text{fal}]_{root} \text{a}]_{theme} + \text{ø}]_{tam} + \text{s}]_{pn}$
$\text{fal}]_{root} \text{a}]_{theme} + \text{ø}]_{tam} + \text{ø}]_{pn}$
$\text{fal}]_{root} \text{a}]_{theme} + \text{ø}]_{tam} + \text{mos}]_{pn}$
$\text{fal}]_{root} \text{a}]_{theme} + \text{ø}]_{tam} + \text{is}]_{pn}$
$\text{fal}]_{root} \text{a}]_{theme} + \text{ø}]_{tam} + \tilde{\text{u}}^{14}]_{pn}$

e-theme

$\text{bat}]_{root} \text{e}]_{theme} + \text{ø}]_{tam} + \text{o}]_{pn}$
$\text{bat}]_{root} \text{e}]_{theme} + \text{ø}]_{tam} + \text{s}]_{pn}$
...
...
...
...

i-theme

$\text{part}]_{root} \text{i}]_{theme} + \text{ø}]_{tam} + \text{o}]_{pn}$
$\text{part}]_{root} \text{i}]_{theme} + \text{ø}]_{tam} + \text{s}]_{pn}$
...
...
...
...

The present indicative forms are unmarked for TAM, while the 3-sg is unmarked for PN. Theme vowels are assumed to be part of the underlying representation of all verb forms, although they do not always appear at the surface. Before non-high vowels, as in the 1-sg forms of the present indicative and in all the forms of the present subjunctive (see below), theme vowels do not surface, but are deleted by a truncation process that will be discussed in Section 2.2.

a.2. Past imperfect

$\text{fal}]_{root} \text{a}]_{theme} \text{va}]_{tam} + \text{ø}]_{pn}$ 　$\text{bat}]_{root} \text{i}]_{theme} \text{a}]_{tam} + \text{ø}]_{pn}$ 　$\text{part}]_{root} \text{i}]_{theme} \text{a}]_{tam} + \text{ø}]_{pn}$
$\text{fal}]_{root} \text{a}]_{theme} \text{va}]_{tam} + \text{s}]_{pn}$ 　...　...
$\text{fal}]_{root} \text{a}]_{theme} \text{va}]_{tam} + \text{ø}]_{pn}$ 　...　...
$\text{fal}]_{root} \text{a}]_{theme} \text{va}]_{tam} + \text{mos}]_{pn}$ 　...　...
$\text{fal}]_{root} \text{a}]_{theme} \text{ve}]_{tam} + \text{is}]_{pn}$ 　$\text{bat}]_{root} \text{i}]_{theme} \text{e}]_{tam} + \text{is}]_{pn}$ 　$\text{part}]_{root} \text{i}]_{theme} \text{e}]_{tam} + \text{is}]_{pn}$
$\text{fal}]_{root} \text{a}]_{theme} \text{va}]_{tam} + \tilde{\text{u}}]_{pn}$ 　...　...

The distinction between the /e/ and /i/ class markers is neutralized in the imperfect.[15] The past imperfect TAM suffix varies according to the different theme classes: /va/ vs. /a/, as illustrated. Alternatively, one may represent the TAM allomorph /a/ as /ia/, assuming a phonological rule which merges the high vowel of the suffix with the theme vowel, as proposed by Câmara Jr. (1970) and Mateus and d'Andrade (2000). The variant /(v)e/ in the 2-pl is recurring and can be described by a morphologically conditioned rule which raises /a/ to /e/ before tautosyllabic /i/. The 1/3-sg forms have no person marker.

a.3. Past Perfect

$\text{fal}]_{root} \text{e}]_{theme} + \text{ø}]_{tam} + \text{i}]_{pn}$ 　$\text{bat}]_{root} \text{i}]_{theme} + \text{ø}]_{tam} + \text{i}]_{pn}$ 　$\text{part}]_{root} \text{i}]_{theme} + \text{ø}]_{tam} + \text{i}]_{pn}$
$\text{fal}]_{root} \text{a}]_{theme} + \text{ø}]_{tam} + \text{ste}]_{p} + \text{ø}]_{sg}$ 　$\text{bat}]_{root} \text{e}]_{theme} + \text{ø}]_{tam} + \text{ste}]_{p} + \text{ø}]_{sg}$
$\text{fal}]_{root} \text{o}]_{theme} + \text{ø}]_{tam} + \text{u}]_{pn}$
$\text{fal}]_{root} \text{a}]_{theme} + \text{ø}]_{tam} + \text{mos}]_{pn}$
$\text{fal}]_{root} \text{a}]_{theme} + \text{ø}]_{tam} + \text{ste}]_{p} + \text{s}]_{pl}$
$\text{fal}]_{root} \text{a}]_{theme} + \text{ra}]_{tam} + \tilde{\text{u}}]_{pn}$

The past perfect is unmarked for TAM, except for the 3-pl form, in all three conjugations.[16] It contains the only instance in which person and number can be analyzed as separate morphemes, but only for the second person, with the 2-sg being unmarked. The merger of the themes /e/ and /i/ occurs in the 1sg. In the same form, a PN suffix /i/ is assumed, motivated by the overt presence of that suffix in the *a*-class. Consequently, a rule of merger must be posited, reducing /ii/ to /i/. In the first conjugation, the theme /a/ assimilates to the tautosyllabic glides /i/ in the 1sg, surfacing as /e/ in BP ([faléj]), as [ɐ] in EP ([falɐ̃ɐj]) and to /o/ in the 3-sg, which merges with the PN suffix in EP [faló], but BP [falów].

a.4. Past Pluperfect

$$\text{fal}]_{\text{root}} \text{a}]_{\text{theme}} + \text{ra}]_{\text{tam}} + \text{ø}]_{\text{pn}} \qquad \text{bat}]_{\text{root}} \text{e}]_{\text{theme}} \text{ra}]_{\text{tam}} + \text{ø}]_{\text{pn}} \qquad \text{part}]_{\text{root}} \text{i}]_{\text{theme}} \text{ra}]_{\text{tam}} + \text{ø}]_{\text{pn}}$$

$$\text{fal}]_{\text{root}} \text{a}]_{\text{theme}} + \text{ra}]_{\text{tam}} + \text{s}]_{\text{pn}} \qquad \dots \qquad \dots$$

$$\text{fal}]_{\text{root}} \text{a}]_{\text{theme}} + \text{ra}]_{\text{tam}} + \text{ø}]_{\text{pn}} \qquad \dots \qquad \dots$$

$$\text{fal}]_{\text{root}} \text{a}]_{\text{theme}} + \text{ra}]_{\text{tam}} + \text{mos}]_{\text{pn}} \qquad \dots \qquad \dots$$

$$\text{fal}]_{\text{root}} \text{a}]_{\text{theme}} + \text{re}]_{\text{tam}} + \text{is}]_{\text{pn}} \qquad \dots \qquad \text{re}]_{\text{tam}} \qquad \dots \qquad \text{re}]_{\text{tam}}$$

$$\text{fal}]_{\text{root}} \text{a}]_{\text{theme}} + \text{ra}]_{\text{tam}} + \tilde{\text{u}}]_{\text{pn}} \qquad \dots \qquad \dots$$

The simple forms of the past pluperfect are not used in spoken BP. Instead, they are replaced by the equivalent compound forms: *tinha falado* "I had said," *tinhas falado* "you had said," etc. Similar to the imperfect, 1/3-sg forms are unmarked for PN in the pluperfect. The TAM morpheme /ra/ has a variant /re/ in the three theme classes, which is accounted for by the now familiar raising rule.

a.5. Present Future

$$\text{fal}]_{\text{root}} \text{a}]_{\text{theme}} + \text{re}]_{\text{tam}} + \text{i}]_{\text{pn}} \qquad \text{bat}]_{\text{root}} \text{e}]_{\text{theme}} + \text{re}]_{\text{tam}} + \text{i}]_{\text{pn}} \qquad \text{part}]_{\text{root}} \text{i}]_{\text{theme}} \text{re}]_{\text{tam}} + \text{i}]_{\text{pn}}$$

$$\text{fal}]_{\text{root}} \text{a}]_{\text{theme}} + \text{ra}]_{\text{tam}} + \text{s}]_{\text{pn}} \qquad \dots \qquad \dots$$

$$\text{fal}]_{\text{root}} \text{a}]_{\text{theme}} + \text{ra}]_{\text{tam}} + \text{ø}]_{\text{pn}} \qquad \dots \qquad \dots$$

$$\text{fal}]_{\text{root}} \text{a}]_{\text{theme}} + \text{re}]_{\text{tam}} + \text{mos}]_{\text{pn}} \qquad \dots \qquad \dots$$

$$\text{fal}]_{\text{root}} \text{a}]_{\text{theme}} + \text{re}]_{\text{tam}} + \text{is}]_{\text{pn}} \qquad \dots \qquad \dots$$

$$\text{fal}]_{\text{root}} \text{a}]_{\text{theme}} + \text{ra}]_{\text{tam}} + \tilde{\text{u}}]_{\text{pn}} \qquad \dots \qquad \dots$$

The pluperfect and present future forms are distinguished by stress, which is located on the theme in the pluperfect, while it occurs on the TAM morpheme in the future. The 3-sg form is unmarked. The /re/ variant of the TAM suffix not only occurs in syllables closed by /i/, but also in the 1-pl form.

a.6. Past Future

$$\text{fal}]_{\text{root}} \text{a}]_{\text{theme}} + \text{ria}]_{\text{tam}} + \text{ø}]_{\text{pn}} \qquad \text{bat}]_{\text{root}} \text{e}]_{\text{theme}} \text{ria}]_{\text{tam}} \text{ø}]_{\text{pn}} \qquad \text{part}]_{\text{root}} \text{i}]_{\text{theme}} \quad \text{ria}]_{\text{tam}} \text{ø}]_{\text{pn}}$$

$$\text{fal}]_{\text{root}} \text{a}]_{\text{theme}} + \text{ria}]_{\text{tam}} + \text{s}]_{\text{pn}} \qquad \dots \qquad \dots$$

$$\text{fal}]_{\text{root}} \text{a}]_{\text{theme}} + \text{ria}]_{\text{tam}} + \text{ø}]_{\text{pn}} \qquad \dots \qquad \dots$$

$$\text{fal}]_{\text{root}} \text{a}]_{\text{theme}} + \text{ria}]_{\text{tam}} + \text{mos}]_{\text{pn}} \qquad \dots \qquad \dots$$

$$\text{fal}]_{\text{root}} \text{a}]_{\text{theme}} + \text{rie}]_{\text{tam}} + \text{is}]_{\text{pn}} \qquad \dots \qquad \dots$$

$$\text{fal}]_{\text{root}} \text{a}]_{\text{theme}} + \text{ria}]_{\text{tam}} + \tilde{\text{u}}]_{\text{pn}} \qquad \dots \qquad \dots$$

The 1/3-sg forms are unmarked. The /rie/ variant of the TAM suffix is due to raising. In EP, but not in BP, the forms of the future can be affected by what is called "mesóclisis," a process by which clitic object pronouns are inserted in the sequence $\dots]_{\text{theme}}\ \text{r}\_\_\text{V}$, i.e. to the left of the main stress: *falar-te-'emos* "we will speak to you," *falar-nos-'ia* "3-sg would speak to us." This process shows that the internal structure proposed above for the future tenses could be different in EP, with a supplementary word boundary following /r/: $\text{fal}]_{\text{root}} \text{a}]_{\text{theme}} + \text{r} \# \text{ia}]_{\text{tam}} + \text{ø}]_{\text{pn}}$, as proposed by Mateus and d'Andrade, (2000: 81).

(17) Subjunctive Mood

a.1. Present

$$fal]_{root} \, a]_{theme} + e]_{tam} + \emptyset]_{pn} \qquad bat]_{root} \, e]_{theme} + a]_{tam} + \emptyset]_{pn} \qquad part]_{root} \, i]_{theme} + a]_{tam} + \emptyset]_{pn}$$
$$fal]_{root} \, a \,]_{theme} + e]_{tam} + s]_{pn} \qquad ... \qquad ...$$
$$fal]_{root} \, a]_{theme} + e]_{tam} + \emptyset]_{pn} \qquad ... \qquad ...$$
$$fal]_{root} \, a]_{theme} + e]_{tam} + mos]_{pn} \qquad ... \qquad ...$$
$$fal]_{root} \, a]_{theme} + e]_{tam} + is]_{pn} \qquad ... \qquad ...$$
$$fal]_{root} \, a]_{theme} + e]_{tam} + ũ]_{pn} \qquad ...$$

The 1/3-sg forms are unmarked for PN in all the forms of the subjunctive mood, present, past, and future. The present subjunctive is the only paradigm in which the theme vowel is lacking for all persons. Arguments for its underlying presence will be given below. Unexpectedly, no raising happens in the 2-pl forms of the /e/ and /i/ themes: *batais*, *partais*.

a.2. Past

$$fal]_{root} \, a]_{theme} + se]_{tam} + \emptyset]_{pn} \qquad bat]_{root} \, e]_{theme} + se]_{tam} + \emptyset]_{pn} \qquad part]_{root} \, i]_{theme} + se]_{tam} + \emptyset]_{pn}$$
$$fal]_{root} \, a]_{theme} + se]_{tam} + s]_{pn} \qquad ... \qquad ...$$
$$fal]_{root} \, a]_{theme} + se]_{tam} + \emptyset]_{pn} \qquad ... \qquad ...$$
$$fal]_{root} \, a]_{theme} + se]_{tam} + mos]_{pn} \qquad ... \qquad ...$$
$$fal]_{root} \, a]_{theme} + se]_{tam} + is]_{pn} \qquad ... \qquad ...$$
$$fal]_{root} \, a]_{theme} + se]_{tam} + ũ]_{pn} \qquad ...$$

The forms of the future subjunctive are identical with those of the impersonal infinitive: *falar*–1-sg, *falares*–2-sg, *falar*–3-sg, *falarmos*–1-pl, *falardes*–2-pl, *falarem*–3-pl, and similarly for the /e/ and /i/ conjugations.

(18) Imperative Mood

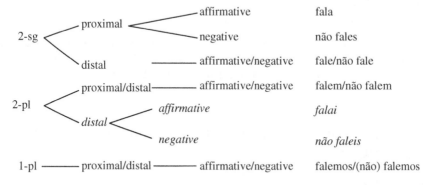

The distinction between proximal and distal 2-sg imperative forms is made systematically only in Portugal.[17] In Brazil, the use of the affirmative imperative associated with the indicative (*fala*) or the subjunctive (*fale*) form appears to depend mainly on non-linguistic parameters like geographical region (northeast vs. south, southeast, and center-west) and, within a given region, "state capital" vs. "interior." Moreover, a complex of other factors, syntactic and pragmatic, intervene in the use of the indicative or subjunctive forms, also in dialects with a predominant use of either one of the alternative forms. For example, it was shown that the indicative form is used preferentially with some verbs in all variants of BP and that the usage of the indicative vs. subjunctive forms relates to the dialogue vs. non-dialogue discourse, among other factors. In negative sentences with preverbal negation, the use of the imperative associated with the subjunctive form is more frequent, without a direct relation with the type of pronoun (*tu* vs. *você*) in use, contrary to what is traditionally assumed (see Scherre, 2007 and 2012, for extensive discussion).

In some dialects of northern Portugal, 2-pl imperative forms are used, printed in italic in (18), that are elsewhere only found in literary and liturgical texts, in Portugal and in Brazil.

2.2. *The Phonology of inflected verbs*

As for the phonology of verb inflection, the problem that has received most attention in the recent literature concerns the alternations involving root-final mid-vowels, analyzed in Harris (1974), Mateus (1975), Lopez (1979), Redenbarger (1981), and Quicoli (1990), amongst others. The verbs below containing root-final mid-vowels illustrate the alternations under discussion (when stress is not marked on the root vowel, it falls on the thematic vowel).

(19)	*secar*	*morar*	*beber*	*mover*	*seguir*	*cobrir*
	"dry"	"live"	"drink"	"move"	"follow"	"cover"
PrInd						
	s[ɛ]co	m[ɔ]ro	b[é]bo	m[ó]vo	s[í]go	c[ú]bro
	s[ɛ]cas	m[ɔ]ras	b[ɛ]bes	m[ɔ]ves	s[ɛ]ges	c[ɔ]bres
	s[ɛ]ca	m[ɔ]ra	b[ɛ]be	m[ɔ]ve	s[ɛ]ge	c[ɔ]bre
	s[e]camos	m[o]ramos	b[e]bemos	m[o]vemos	s[e]gimos	c[o]brimos
	s[e]cais	m[o]rais	b[e]beis	m[o]veis	s[e]gis	c[o]bris
	s[ɛ]cam	m[ɔ]ram	b[ɛ]bem	m[ɔ]vem	s[ɛ]gem	c[ɔ]brem
PrSub						
	s[ɛ]que	m[ɔ]re	b[é]ba	m[ó]va	s[í]ga	c[ú]bra
	s[ɛ]ques	m[ɔ]res	b[é]bas	m[ó]vas	s[í]gas	c[ú]bras
	s[ɛ]que	m[ɔ]re	b[é]ba	m[ó]va	s[í]ga	c[ú]bra
	s[e]quemos	m[o]remos	b[e]bamos	m[o]vamos	s[i]gamos	c[u]bramos
	s[e]cais	m[o]reis	b[e]bais	m[o]vais	s[i]gais	c[u]brais
	s[ɛ]quem	m[ɔ]rem	b[é]bam	m[ó]vam	s[í]gam	c[ú]bram

In (20) the underlying and derived vowel qualities are illustrated with the 1 sg pres. ind. forms for the verbs in (19).[18]

(20)	ε + a > ε	/sɛk+a+o/	[séku]	*seco*
	ɔ + a > ɔ	/mɔr+a+o/	[mɔ́ru]	*moro*
	ε + e > e	/bɛb+e+o/	[bébu]	*bebo*
	ɔ + e > o	/mɔv+e+o/	[móvu]	*movo*
	ε + i > i	/sɛg+i+o/	[sígu]	*sigo*
	ɔ + i > u	/kɔbr+i+o/	[kúbru]	*cubro*

Most authors dealing with the phonology of mid-vowels in the Portuguese verb agree that their varying surface shape can be predicted by three generalizations that apply in complementary contexts. One general rule predicts that non-final unstressed mid-vowels are upper-mid, which accounts for the systematic occurrence of [e, o] in unstressed syllables, marked in grey in (19). Another rule requires that stressed mid-vowels are lower-mid in verbs (henceforth MiVoLo), unless overruled by a rule of Vowel Harmony (VH) by which the aperture features of the theme vowel are transferred to the preceding mid-vowel in those forms where the theme-vowel is itself deleted.

To see the effect of MiVoLo, compare the words given in (21a) with those in (21b) (all verbs represent 3 sg present indicative forms):

(21) a. Noun   b. Verb
    dem[ɔ]ra   "delay"   dem[ɔ]ra   "delay"
    esc[ó]va   "brush"   esc[ɔ]va   "brush"
    conv[é]rsa "conversation"   conv[ɛ]rsa "talk"
    ap[é]lo   "appeal"   ap[ɛ]la   "appeal"

Whereas in non-verbs upper and lower mid-vowels are contrastive under stress, in verbs, only lower mid-vowels occur in stressed syllables.

In the process of VH, the aperture features of the theme vowel are spread to a root-final mid-vowel, when the former is followed by a non-high vowel. The underlying sequences that trigger VH in verbs are given in (22).

(22) Triggering environment for VH

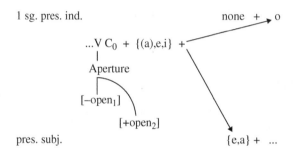

The [±open$_x$] features in (22) refer to a modeling of vowel height distinctions as proposed in Clements (1991)

(23)
    aperture: i/u   e/o   ɛ/ɔ   a

    open$_1$ −   −   −   +
    open$_2$ −   +   +   +
    open$_3$ −   −   +   +

In the system given in (23), the class of mid-vowels is defined as [−open$_1$, +open$_2$] and further differentiated on the [open3] tier as either upper-mid [−open$_3$] or lower-mid [+open$_3$]. While VH targets the class of mid-vowels, it applies only in the subset of the verb forms in which the theme vowel is followed by a non-high vowel: either the 1 sg present indicative suffix −o, or one of the subjunctive morphemes −e (1st conjugation), or −a (2nd and 3rd conjugations). Interestingly, the triggering environment for VH is identical to the one in which Vowel Truncation (VoTr) applies. It is precisely because of this duplication of contexts, that VH was accounted for indirectly in Wetzels (1992, 1995) as a stability effect of the aperture node with concomitant deletion of its host, i.e. the theme vowel. This phenomenon of feature stability under deletion is common in tone languages, when tones remain stable under deletion of the tone-bearing segment, or in languages like French, where the nasal feature is stable under deletion of the nasal consonant (compare masc. *bon* [bõ] with fem. *bonne* [bɔn] "good"). Similarly, in the case of Portuguese, the deleted theme vowel leaves its aperture features behind, so that they may be realized on the preceding mid-vowel.

While the target for VH is clearly the class of mid-vowels, it is less obvious whether all the theme vowels function as triggers. While the upper-mid quality of unstressed mid-vowels is independently explained by a general constraint that disallows lower mid-vowels in atonic positions, all the stressed forms of the first conjugation verbs *secar* and *morar* in (19) contain lower mid-vowels, including the forms for which the corresponding ones in the 2nd and 3rd conjugation verbs undergo VH. On the assumption that the lower-mid quality represents the default value for stressed mid-vowels in verbs, the lower mid-vowels in first conjugation verbs can be explained either as the combined result of VH and MiVoLo or by MiVoLo alone. Confronted with these alternatives, different scholars made different choices. Harris (1974) derives all the lower-mid vowels in first conjugation verbs with MiVoLo. Wetzels (1995), Mateus and d'Andrade (2000), and Carvalho (2004) opt for a generalized VH rule. Wetzels (1992) defines the class of theme vowels triggering VH as [-open$_3$], i.e. only –*e*, –*i*, trigger VH, while following Harris (1974) in explaining all the first conjugation lower mid-vowels as the result of MiVoLo. A number of arguments support the lowering option. First, this hypothesis dispenses with the need to refer to structure preservation to explain why VH triggered by /a/ does not create low coronal or low labio-dorsal vowels. Furthermore, the fact that all cases of non-assimilatory neutralization of stressed mid-vowels yield lower mid-vowels suggests the lower- mid value as the unmarked one for stressed mid-vowels in general, as discussed in Wetzels (1992, 2010). Finally, VH in the 2/3 conjugations have some unexpected exceptions, especially in words that are rarely used, such as the defective verbs[19] *explodir* "explode," *emergir* "emerge," etc., in which the root mid-vowel is often not raised to [i,u], or in the verb *querer* "want," with a lower mid-vowel in the 1 sg present indicative: *qu*[ɛ]*ro* "I want." On the other hand, exceptions to MiVoLo can always be explained by productive rules of phonology, such as mid-vowel raising before nasal consonants, which, for many, but not all, Brazilian speakers takes precedence over MiVoLo: *t*[õ]*ma* "(s)he takes," *engr*[ẽ]*na* "it engages." Another rule raises mid-vowels in diphthongs (*l*[ów]*vo* "I praise") and yet another one bans lower mid-vowels in hiatus: *cor*[ó]*o* "I crown." Interestingly, for some speakers of BP, MiVoLo takes precedence over PreNasal Raising and, again for some speakers, monophthongization of [ej] > [e] and [ow] > [o] feeds MiVoLo: *r*[ɔ]*ba* "(s)he steals" from the verb *roubar*, or *pen*[ɛ]*ra* "(s)he sifts" from *peneirar*, while the mid-vowel remains upper mid in the corresponding nouns, also when monophthongized *r*[ó(w)]*bo* "theft," *pen*[é(j)]*ra* "sift." Despite being restricted to verbs, MiVoLo appears to be a productive rule of Portuguese phonology.[20] The hypothesis that all lower mid-vowels are derived by MiVoLo can explain the asymmetry in the absence vs. presence of unsystematic exceptions to VH in the *a*-class as compared to the *e*- and *i*-classes.

It was observed earlier that VH only applies to root-final mid-vowels in those verb forms in which the theme vowel is truncated before a nuclear vowel, which is either the 1 sg PN suffix –*o* in the present indicative or one of the present subjunctive TAM suffixes {*e, a*} (cf. 22). The rule in (24) is adapted from Wetzels (1995).

(24) Truncation-cum-Aperture Stability

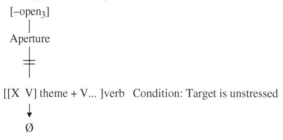

[[X V] theme + V...]verb   Condition: Target is unstressed

The right vowel, which triggers truncation, is not specified as non-high, since it is assumed that VoTr interacts with falling diphthong formation in such forms as the 2-pl. present indicative *meteis*/mete+is/ > [metéjs] or the 3-sg perfect *meteu*/mete+u/ > [metéw], of the verb *meter* "put" (Wetzels 1995, endnotes 2, 3).[21] While there are reasons to believe that VoTr is not restricted to verbs, the fact that the dissociation of the aperture node is specific for the verbal domain makes it necessary to restrict the scope of rule (24) accordingly. Notice also that the vowel triggering VoTr does not need to refer to any specific morpheme. While the theme vowel is truncated, the aperture node of the /e/ and /i/ themes is left behind and is subsequently associated with a root-final mid-vowel by VH.

In Wetzels (1995) the ordering between MiVoLo, VoTr, and VH was obtained by assuming that the different phonological rules follow the morphological built up of the verb. MiVoLo applies to verbal themes and VoTr-cum-VH applies as soon as inflectional suffixes are added. VH associates the aperture node set afloat by VoTr with a mid-vowel to its left, independently of that vowel surfacing as stressed, as in [síga] (</segi+a/)"(that) he follows" or unstressed, as in [sigámos] (</segi+a+mos) "(that) we follow."

A different approach to the surface variation of underlying mid-vowels in verbs is taken by Carvalho (2004). This author proposes a templatic representation for Portuguese verbs, the last two syllables of which have the structure in (25) below, adapted from Carvalho (2004: 23):

(25)

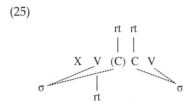

In (25), "rt" stands for the root node as part of the feature representation of the lexically specified segments, while the left σ represents the last syllable of the verbal root, which may be light or heavy. The right syllable is light and has its nucleus unspecified. The empty nucleus is either filled by one of the theme vowels /a, e, i/ or by a vowel of the set /–o, –a, –e/, of which /–o/ is the 1sg present indicative suffix and /–e/ (1st conjugation) or /-a/ (2/3 conjugations) the present subjunctive markers. The theme vowels, the 1sg present indicative suffix, and the present subjunctive suffixes are floating, i.e. they are lexically represented without a skeletal anchor. Since, presumably, each verbal theme is lexicalized with one of the floating theme vowels, if the 1 sg suffix or one of the subjunctive markers is inserted at the melodic tier, the type of structure is created as illustrated in (26), with the verbs *comprometer* "guarantee" and *dormir* "sleep" (for clarity, theme vowels are in boldface):

(26)

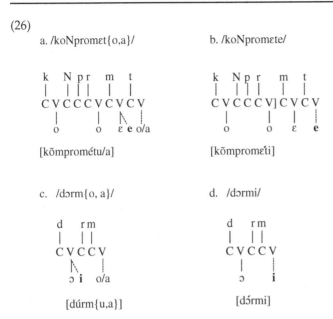

a. /koNpromɛt{o,a}/   b. /koNpromɛte/

[kõmprométu/a]   [kõmpromɛ́ti]

c. /dɔrm{o, a}/   d. /dɔrmi/

[dúrm{u,a}]   [dɔ́rmi]

The forms *comprometo/comprometa* in (26a) represent the 1sg present indicative and the 1/3sg present subjunctive, respectively. Both forms comprise a floating vowel morpheme, which is linked to the rightmost V-position of the template via a directionality parameter that maps floating vowels onto their skeletal anchors from right to left, as indicated by the dotted association line. The same parameter links the theme vowel to the empty V position in the 3sg present indicative *compromete* in (26b). In (26a,c), after {o, a} association has taken place, there is no empty V-position left to accommodate the theme vowel, which is therefore associated with the last vowel of the root. However, as the output forms in (26a,c) show, the theme vowel does not substitute the root vowel, since assimilation exclusively involves the aperture features. Therefore, depending on whether or not the theme vowel can be attached to an empty skeletal slot, it is represented at the melodic tier either as a fully specified vowel segment or by its corresponding aperture features alone. According to Carvalho, this must be so because "… there are no front rounded vowels in EP, … only the theme vowel's height feature is compatible with both root vowels" (2004: 25). In other words, in order to avoid ungrammatical *[dýrmu/a] instead of [dúrmu/a] for the verb *dormir* "sleep" or *[móvu/a] instead of [móvu/a] for *mover* "move," when the morphological structure contains one of the floating vowel morphemes to the right of the theme vowel, the latter is represented only by its aperture features. According to Carvalho (2004) the templatic approach to VH should be preferred for its greater explanatory power over the derivational analysis proposed by Wetzels (1995).

Although a proper assessment of Carvalho's proposal, which is not worked out in great detail, is difficult to achieve, a number of problems of the templatic approach are apparent. Independent evidence for templatic morphology is lacking in Portuguese, a language in which the vocalic, consonantal, and skeletal tiers have no independent lexical or morphosyntactic meanings, as they do in the Semitic languages. Also, the proposed association parameter must be considered language-specific, because its directionality is marked and because it functions not only as a mechanism mapping segments to empty skeletal positions, but also as a linking device attaching floating aperture nodes to underlyingly specified positions. Moreover, VH exclusively targets final mid-vowel in verb roots. Although this target condition is not expressed in the structures in (26) above to which the association parameter applies, it must be there, since, for example, /vive+o/ (compare *viver* "live") does not become *[vévu] "I live," but [vívu]. One must furthermore raise the question of how the grammar decides whether the theme vowel is represented by its fully specified root segment or by its aperture features alone. As Carvalho claims, this choice can be derived from structure preservation, but it is hard to see how: why do /kompromɛte+{o,a}/ and /dɔrmi+{o, a}/ not become [kompromét{o,a}] and [dórm{o, a}], both with an upper mid-vowel, as a consequence of the spreading of the [−open₃] feature alone?[22] Or why do these forms not surface as [kompromét{o,a}] and [dírm{o, a}], with the theme vowel substituting the mid-vowel? Both these operations are structure preserving, besides the one that actually occurs, which involves the spreading of the aperture node. Obviously, the grammar must contain an explicit statement expressing that in the relevant forms all and only the aperture features of the theme vowel are transferred to the root-final mid-vowel.

Carvalho's skepticism regarding the analysis in Wetzels (1995) concerns the use of morphological categories in the statement of rule (24) and the fact that the trigger vowels of VoTr are non-high, while the target must be unstressed, which restrictions make the rule even more stipulative. In Wetzels (1992: 134) it was proposed for Portuguese non-verbs that roots are lexicalized with their theme vowels, which hypothesis would entail the existence of a rule which deletes unstressed vowels in hiatus outside of the verb domain: *facada* "knifing" from *faca* "knife" /faka+ada/ > [fakáda][23]. Notice also that, even if the proposed lexicalization of non-verbal themes, which is controversial, turns out to be incorrect, MiVoLo in verbs shows that productive rules can be limited to a specific lexical category. Furthermore, the fact that VoTr interacts with diphthongization could easily be seen as independent plausibility for the existence of VoTr, which together with diphthongization militates against hiatus in complementary contexts. Finally, the fact that VoTr targets unstressed vowels is almost a predictable characteristic of truncation rules cross-linguistically.[24]

A number of proposals describing the changes that underlying mid-vowels undergo in verbs were proposed in the framework of Optimality Theory (OT). One OT account of these facts is proposed by Lee (2003). Within the OT tradition, which explains phonological patterns with recourse to a language-specific ranking of universal constraints, Lee accounts for what is traditionally treated as truncation by a high ranking of the Onset constraint which requires syllables to have onsets. Strategies used by languages to repair illicit vowel sequences involve truncation, C-epenthesis, diphthongization, or coalescence. According to Lee, the vowel alternations in the Portuguese verb are best understood as a case of vowel coalescence, in which two underlying vowels /V_1V_2/ are represented by a single surface vowel [$V_{1,2}$] containing elements of both /V_1V_2/. Lee's proposal can be globally described by the figure in (27) below:

(27)

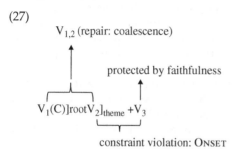

High-ranked Onset forces the elimination of the hiatus between the theme vowel V_2 and the relevant 1 sg present indicative and the present subjunctive suffixes represented by V_3. Another active constraint accounts for the fact that an underlying suffix surfaces unaltered, assuring that vowel coalescence affects V_1 and V_2. A Max[F] constraint protects the features

[+atr] and [+high] of the theme vowels *–i, –e* from deletion: /dɔ₁rmi₂+o/ →[dú₁,₂rmo] (→[dúrmu] by word-final vowel neutralization).

One unexpected aspect of Lee's analysis is the idea that coalescence may involve vowels that are not immediately adjacent. This view of the phenomenon requires some principled mechanism to avoid the surfacing of the aperture features of the theme vowel on a different vowel than the final root vowel. Expectedly, other instances of coalescence in Portuguese involve strictly adjacent vowels such as, for example, the one discussed above for the past perfect form *bati* "I hit" from /bat]$_{root}$ i]$_{theme}$+ø]$_{tam}$+i]$_{pn}$/ or /bat]$_{root}$ e]$_{theme}$+ø]$_{tam}$+i]$_{pn}$/ (see (16.a.3) above). In these forms, coalescence involves strictly adjacent /ii/ or /ei/.

A rather different explanation of the vowel alternations under discussion is proposed in Schwindt (2007). In Schwindt's analysis a general AGREE constraint requires the last vowel of the verb root to agree in height with the underlying theme vowel. This constraint competes with two conjoined constraints: Low&TRUNC]$_{theme}$ requires verb forms to surface without a theme vowel when their last root vowel is low, while STRESSROOT&IDENT-IO]$_{stem}$ penalizes unstressed verb roots that change the lexical specification of the root vowel, expressing the generalization that MiVoLo and VH are restricted to accented vowels. The conjoined constraints are unordered and together dominate AGREE, as shown below. To facilitate easy reading, we have in (28) indicated partial, and therefore irrelevant, violation of conjoined constraints between parentheses.

(28)

/beb+e+o/ 1sg.pr.ind.	STRESS-ROOT&IDENT-IO]$_{stem}$	Low&TRUNC]$_{theme}$	AGREE
a. bébo ☺		(*Low)	
b. bɛ́bo	(*IO)		*!
/beb+e+ø/ 1sg.pres.ind.			
c. bébe		*!	
d. bɛ́be ☺	(*IO)	(*Trunc)	*
/seg+i+o/ 1sg.pres.ind.			
e. sígo ☺	(*IO)	(*Low)	
f. ségo		(*Low)	*!
g. sɛ́go	(*IO)		*!
/seg+i+mos/ 1pl.pres.ind.			
h. segímos ☺	(*Str-Rt)	*	*
i. sigímos	*!	*	

The constraint STRESS-ROOT&IDENT-IO]$_{stem}$ penalizes in unstressed roots the surface occurrence of features or feature values without an identical underlying correspondent, where the underlying specification of the mid-vowel is assumed to be upper-mid, such as it appears in the unstressed root vowel of the infinitive (*beber* "drink," *seguir* "follow"). This can be observed in the (fatally) penalized candidate (28i), in which the root vowel is not upper-mid on top of being stressless. The activity of the constraint Low&TRUNC]$_{theme}$ can be seen by comparing the forms in (28c–d), both surfacing with the theme vowel, of which it eliminates the one with the upper-mid root vowel. All the forms that do not violate the conjoined constraints are passed on to AGREE, which favors the candidates in which the root vowel agrees in height with the underlying theme vowel (28a, c, e, i). In order to account for VH and truncation in the forms of the subjunctive, Schwindt posits a higher ranked Output–Output constraint (cf. Benua, 1997) which requires the root of all the forms of the present subjunctive to be identical with the root of the corresponding 1sg present indicative form. As Schwindt (2007) himself points out, the choice of the 1sg present indicative as the base for explaining the sound structure of the subjunctive forms awaits independent confirmation.

3. Discussion

As we have tried to show in this chapter, the discussion concerning the phonology and morphology of inflection in Portuguese involves the traditional issues and controversies concerning the nature of phonological rules or constraints and whether, or to what extent, these are allowed to refer to morphological categories. Answers to these questions change with successive paradigms and among the proponents of a specific paradigm little agreement exists. With regard to the singular/plural alternations in nouns ending in a nasal diphthong and the vowel alternations in the verb, an equally fundamental question concerns the way in which the observed variation should be interpreted in terms of the architecture of the grammar, as lexically specified allomorphy or as rules or constraints. We have shown that the relation between singular nouns ending in a nasal diphthong and their corresponding plurals is not completely predictable. Scholars tend to agree that MiVoLo is productive as a morphologically conditioned rule of Portuguese, but it remains unclear how exactly it is represented in the speakers'mind. As for VH, an experimental study by Schwindt and Quadros (2009) showed inconclusive results with regard to its productivity. In an oral and a written production test, students were asked to deliver, for a given infinitive nonce verb with an /i/ or /e/ theme, a number of inflected forms, including the ones without a theme vowel, in order to check for the productivity of VH in the latter forms. In another test, students were asked to provide the corresponding infinitive for inflected forms in which VH had applied. No conclusive evidence for a productive rule of VH was found in the results of the first two tests. However, the third test showed that most students had no problem relating the harmonized vowel to the appropriate theme vowel in the infinitive. If one is allowed to interpret these contradicting results as proof for the low productivity of VH, an allomorphic lexical representation stating the identity in aperture degree between harmonizing root vowels and the /i/, /e/ theme vowels could be modeled as in (29), in which the shared aperture node in the special case contains the aperture features of the –*i*, or –*e* thematic vowel:

(29)

$$[...\text{V C}_0 \text{ V]}_{\text{theme}} \sim [...\text{V C}_0 \text{ V]}_{\text{theme}} \text{ /1 sg pres. ind., pres. subj}$$

In (29), the left allomorph represents the default case, while the right allomorph represents the special case, in which the prefinal vowel shares its aperture specification with that of the theme vowel as it appears in the default form. The lexicalization of the effect of VH, of course, eliminates VH as a productive rule of Portuguese but still implies the necessity of VoTr. Future studies will hopefully provide additional evidence disambiguating which part of the alternations under discussion in this chapter is fully productive and which part is not, with the ensuing consequences for the architecture of the phonological grammar.

NOTES

1   Some authors question the inflectional character of gender in Portuguese, given its unsystematic correspondence with sex and because of its somewhat irregular distribution. Villalva (2008), while recognizing that nouns must have a specified value for gender, prefers to call it gender variance, rather than inflection. We consider this less relevant from the point of view of this chapter, since our main focus is on the interaction of the morphological process with phonology, regardless of the precise morphological status of what we have called the gender marker.

2   Only a small part of Portuguese nouns, around five percent, refer to animate concepts, and of those not all are overtly marked (cf. Rocha 1994). Nevertheless, the opposition "*o/a*" for animate nouns is so strongly associated with the male/female dichotomy that is not uncommon to hear children producing non-existing forms like *o crianço* "the (boy) child," shaped after the noun *criança* meaning "child," wrongly interpreted as "girl child."

3   The phonological representation of the sibilant and rhotic consonants is a recurrent issue in Portuguese phonology. We use capitals for avoiding the suggestion of taking position with regard to their precise lexical representation. See Chapter 4 for more detailed discussion.

4   Schwindt (2011), in a optimalistic approach of realizational morphology (cf. Wolf, 2008), assumes that the Portuguese class markers $-a$ and $-o$, and their respective homophonous gender markers, are merged at the surface (eg. menin+a$_{CL1}$+a$_F$ → menina $_{CL1,F}$/menino$_{CL2}$+o$_M$ → menino $_{CL2,M}$). Words ending in [e], on the other hand, realize only the class marker (a lent+e$_{CL3}$+ø$_F$/ o pent+e$_{CL3}$+øM). This priority scale is determined by the ranking MAX-M(CL3) >> MAX-M(FEM) >> MAX-M(CL2) >> MAX-M(CL1) >> MAX-M(MASC).

5   See Wetzels (1997) for arguments that support the underlying representation of nasal diphthongs as oral vowels followed by a high nasal vowel.

6   One does find surface [õw̃] as the optional realization of word-final nasal vowel [õ] in both EP and BP, usually represented lexically as /oN/. In a descriptive model allowing for phonological levels, neutralization of the /oũ/ ~ /aũ/ contrast and the variable realization of /oN/ as [õw̃] could be assigned to different levels.

7   One may hear *capitões* for *capitães* "captains," *alemões* for *alemães* "Germans," etc.

8   The cluster /rs/ in internal coda is found in a few words in Portuguese (e.g. *perspectiva* "perspective" or *perspicaz* "perspicacious") all of which are formed by the Latin prefix *per*, which suggests that the constraint prohibiting this sequence is inoperative in structures of the type (pseudo-) prefix+base.

9   Mateus and d'Andrade (2000) propose, in an autosegmental analysis, that the final consonant of the stem be associated with a new syllable when the plural suffix is added, of which the empty nucleus is filled by an epenthetic vowel. This vowel, in turn, spreads its voicing feature to the preceding consonant (e.g. *france*[s]*es* → *france*[z]*es* "French pl").

10 In EP and in a small part of southern Brazil, the velarized pronunciation [ɫ] of the lateral is also found in the syllable coda. The coronal variant, [l], however, can still be observed among the descendants of Italian immigrants and, more generally, in fixed expressions across word-boundaries (e.g. *ma*[l]*educado* "impolite") and in suffixal derivation (e.g. *mal* > *maléfico* "maleficent"). This would define a synchronic rule /l/ → [w] in BP as the result of rule telescoping, as described in Tasca (2000), which process historically goes from the coronal [l], passing through the velarized variant [ɫ], to the glide /w/.

11 We observe here a derivational case of gender change, with both words having a different meaning. We choose this example for lack of an alternative involving an inflectional gender change showing the non-occurrence of the alternation [ɔ]$_{masc}$ ~ [o]$_{fem}$.

12　See Chapter 10 for a more comprehensive discussion of evaluative suffixes.

13　Since space does not allow to discuss irregular verbs, we restrict ourselves to the regular inflection. We will also not discuss the compound tenses (*tenho falado* "I have said/have been saying," *tinha falado* "I had said/had been saying," *teria falado* "I would have said," etc.), which do not involve any different morphology or phonology.

14　By representing the 3pl as a nasal labial vowel, instead of a nasal consonant /N/, as most scholars propose, we assume a rule that turns this vowel into a coronal high vowel after /e/, as in *batem* [batẽj] "they hit," but also in *partem* [ẽj] "they leave". In traditional analyses, the 2/3sg. and 3pl. pres. ind. forms of the 3rd conjugation verbs, as in *partes, parte, partem* are considered to contain an /e/ allomorph. Given the general rule of unstressed word-final /e/ raising, we consider that, except for some parts of Brazil, especially in the South, where /e/-raising is variable, /i/ is underlying in all forms of the 3rd conjugation verbs, except for *partem*. In EP, the derived diphthong [ẽj] is pronounced [ẽj] (cf. Mateus and d'Andrade 2000: 47).

15　Also compare the past participles *partido* and *batido*.

16　In Mateus and d'Andrade (2000), the sequence /raũ/, or rather /rãũ/, is considered a PN suffix, which allows for a uniform zero-representation of the TAM suffix in the past perfect. Here we opt for a uniform representation of the 3 pl suffix as /ũ/.

17　Thanks to Marta Scherre for useful discussion.

18　We assume that underlying mid-vowels are lower-mid, defined as [-open$_3$] in the system in (23) below. However, an underlying representation unspecified for the [open$_3$] feature, or one in which underlying mid-vowels are specified as [-open$_3$] would not interfere with the analysis proposed.

19　This means that some verbs that are classified as defective by some grammarians are not so in reality, since the "missing" forms are sometimes produced spontaneously by native speakers. See also Nevins, Freitas, and Demulakis (2015).

20　Surprisingly, for some speakers, MiLoVe is blocked for coronal mid-vowels in verbs derived from nouns that contain a stressed upper mid-vowel followed by a palatal consonant. Compare *ele inv[ɛ]ja* "he envies" from *inv[ɛ]ja* "envy" with *ele (se) averm[é]lha* "he reddens" from *verm[é]lho* "red." For discussion, see Wetzels (1992: 49). The only non-derived 1st conjugation verb that, according to the norm, is pronounced with an upper mid-vowel is *fechar* "close," which in BP is usually pronounced with the lower mid-vowel, as in *ele f[ɛ]cha* "he closes."

21　Below, we return briefly to this topic as well as to the requirement for the deleted theme vowel to be unstressed.

22　This would mean that the low theme vowel /a/ does not participate as a trigger for VH, a fact which remains without empirical consequences, since, as we have seen, stressed mid-vowels not targeted by VH generally surface as lower-mid, as is also admitted by Carvalho (2004).

23　A similar hypothesis, based on different arguments, was proposed by Bermúdez-Otero (2013) for Spanish.

24　As was extensively discussed in Wetzels (1992: 25–30).

REFERENCES

Benua, Laura. 1997. *Transderivational Identity Phonological Relation between Words*. PhD. University of Massachusetts at Amherst.

Bermúdez-Otero, Ricardo. 2013. The Spanish Lexicon Stores Stems with Theme Vowels, not Roots with Inflectional Class Features. *Probus* 25,1, 3–103.

Bisol, Leda. 1998. A Nasalidade, um Velho Tema. *D.E.L.T.A.* 14, 27–46.

Booij, Geert. 1993. Against Split Morphology. In Booij, Geert and Jaap van Marle (eds), *Yearbook of Morphology*. 1993. Dordrecht: Kluwer, 27–49.

Booij, Geert. 1996. Inherent Versus Contextual Inflection and the Split Morphology Hypothesis. In Booij, Geert and Jaap van Marle (eds), *Yearbook of morphology 1995*. Dordrecht: Kluwer, 1–16.

Câmara Jr. Joaquim. M. 1970. *Estrutura da Língua Portuguesa*. Petrópolis, Vozes.

Carvalho, Joaquim, B. 2004. Templatic Morphology in the Portuguese Verb. *Nouveaux Départs en Phonologie*. Trudel Meisenburg and Maria Selig (eds.), Tübigen, Gunter Narr Verlag, 13–32.

Clements, G. Nick. 1991. Vowel Height Assimilation in Bantu Languages. *Working Papers of the Cornell Phonetics Laboratory* 5, 37–76

Harris, James. 1974. Evidence from Portuguese for the 'Elsewhere Condition' in Phonology. *Linguistic Inquiry.* 5, 61–80.

Hooper, Joan Bybee. 1976. *An Introduction to Natural Generative Phonology*. New York, Academic Press.

Lee, Seung-Hwa. 2003. Mid Vowel Alternation in Verbal Stems in Brazilian Portuguese. *Journal of Portuguese Linguistics*, 2,2, 87–100.

Lopez, Barbara. 1979. *The Sound Pattern of Brazilian Portuguese*. PhD. UCLA.

Mateus, Maria Helena, M. 1975. *Aspectos da Fonologia do Português*. Lisboa: Instituto Nacional de Investigação Científica.

Mateus, Maria Helena, M. and Ernesto d'Andrade. 2000. *The Phonology of Portuguese*. Oxford University Press.

Miranda, Ana Ruth, M. 2000. *A Metafonia Nominal (Português do Brasil)*. PhD. Porto Alegre: Pontifícia Universidade Católica do Rio Grande do Sul.

Nevins, Andrew, Freitas, Maria Luisa, and Gean Damulakis. 2015. *Defective Verbs in Portuguese: Where Phonology Steers the Learner*. Paper presented at the 2015 Linguistic Symposium on Romance Languages. Campinas, Brazil.

Quicoli, A. Carlos. 1990. Harmony, Lowering, and Nasalization in Brazilian Portuguese. *Lingua*, 80, 295–331.

Redenbarger, Wayne. J. 1981. *Articulator Features and Portuguese Vowel Height*. Cambridge. Harvard University.

Rocha, L. C. A. 1994. Flexão e Derivação no português. *Cadernos de Pesquisa*. NAPq, Belo Horizonte, FALE/UFMG 19.

Schwindt, Luiz Carlos; Quadros, Emanuel Souza de. (2009) A Harmonia Vocálica Verbal no Léxico Dicionarizado do PB. *Letrônica*, v. 2,

p. 58-70. [http://revistaseletronicas.pucrs.br/ojs/index.php/letronica/index]

Scherre, Maria Marta P. 2007. Aspectos sincrônicos e diacrônicos do imperativo gramatical no português brasileiro. *Alfa*, 51(1), p. 189–222.

Scherre, Maria Marta P. 2012. Padrões sociolinguísticos do português brasileiro: a importância da pesquisa variacionista. *Tabuleiro de Letras, Revista do Programa de Pós-Graduação em Estudos de Linguagens*. Universidade do Estado da Bahia.

Schwindt, Luiz Carlos. 2007. Paradigmatic correspondences in the Brazilian Portuguese Verbal Vowel System. *Acta Linguistica Hungarica*, v. 54, p. 35–50.

Schwindt, Luiz Carlos. 2011, Zeros na Morfologia Nominal Portuguesa à Luz da Optimal Interleaving Theory. *ReVEL*. 5, 264–276. [www.revel.inf.br].

Stephany, Ursula. 1982. Inflectional and Lexical Morphology: a Linguistic Continuum. *Glossologia* 1: 27–55.

Tasca, Maria. 2000. A Preservação da Lateral Alveolar na Coda: uma Explicação Possível. *Letras de Hoje* 35, 1. Porto Alegre: EDIPUCRS. 331–354.

Villalva, Alina. 2008. *Morfologia do Português*. Lisboa: Universidade Aberta.

Wetzels, W. Leo. 1992. Mid Vowel Neutralization in Brazilian Portuguese, B. Abaurre and W. L. Wetzels (eds.), *Fonologia do Português*, Número Especial dos Cadernos de Estudos Lingüísticos. IEL/ UNICAMP: 19–55.

Wetzels, W. Leo. 1995. Mid-Vowel Alternations in the Brazilian Portuguese Verb, *Phonology* 12, 281–304

Wetzels, W. Leo. 1997. The Lexical Representation of Nasality in Brazilian Portuguese. *Probus* 9, 203–232.

Wetzels, W. Leo. 2010. Aperture Features and the Representation of Vowel Neutralization in Brazilian Portuguese. Elisabeth Hume, John Goldsmith, and W. Leo Wetzels (eds.), *Tones and Features*. De Gruyter, Berlin, 331-359.

Wolf, Matthew. 2008. *Optimal Interleaving: Serial Phonology-Morphology Interaction in a Constraint-Based Model*. PhD University of Massachusetts, Amherst. ROA- 996.

12 Clitic Pronouns: Phonology, Morphology, and Syntax

ANA R. LUÍS AND GEORG A. KAISER[1]

1. Introduction

In the transition from vulgar Latin to the Romance languages, one of the most important innovations is the development of clitic pronouns: while vulgar Latin had only one series of personal pronouns, the Romance languages introduce a striking morphological separation of strong and weak pronouns. In all Romance languages, these weak pronouns became clitic elements, mainly with an object function, sometimes also with a subject function (Wanner 2001). Given their phonological deficiency and their highly idiosyncratic syntax, clitic pronouns exhibit properties which are typical neither of words nor of affixes. They therefore constitute a challenge to phonology, morphology and syntax.

This paper describes and investigates the phonological, morphological and syntactic properties of clitic pronouns in Modern European Portuguese (EP) and Brazilian Portuguese (BP). It will be shown that the clitic systems of both languages are quite distinct from each other. While in EP object clitic pronouns may occur both in preverbal and postverbal position and show crucial morphophonological differences according to their position with respect to the verb, in BP clitic pronouns are mostly restricted to the preverbal position and show a tendency to be replaced by strong pronouns or to be omitted. In addition, BP differs from EP by the emergence of weak forms of subject pronouns which show some typical characteristics of clitic elements.

The chapter is organized as follows: Section 2 offers an overview of the inventory of object clitic pronouns in Portuguese and describes typical properties. Section 3 focuses on clitic pronouns in EP, discussing the asymmetry between preverbal and postverbal clitic pronouns as evidenced in phonology, morphology and syntax. Section 4 deals with BP and looks in detail at BP-specific properties, such as preverbal placement, loss of object clitic pronouns and emergence of subject clitic pronouns. Section 5 offers a brief summary.

2. Survey

2.1. Inventory of pronominal clitic forms

The full paradigm of object and reflexive clitics in EP and BP is shown in Table 12.1.[2]

Both Portuguese varieties encode identical morphosyntactic distinctions with respect to case, number and gender. There are three case distinctions for 3rd person pronouns (i.e., accusative, dative and reflexive). For 1st and 2nd person pronouns, there is only a two-case distinction, due to the syncretism between accusative and dative forms. Gender

The Handbook of Portuguese Linguistics, First Edition. Edited by W. Leo Wetzels, João Costa, and Sergio Menuzzi.
© 2016 John Wiley & Sons, Inc. Published 2020 by John Wiley & Sons, Inc.

Table 12.1 Clitic forms for object and reflexive pronouns.

	Direct	*Indirect*	*Reflexive*
1sg	*me* EP [mə]/BP [me]		
2sg	*te* EP [tə]/BP [te]		
3sg.masc	*o* BP/EP [u]	*lhe* EP [ʎə]/	*se* EP [sə]/
3sg.fem	*a* EP [ɐ]/BP [a]	BP [ʎe]	BP [se]
1pl	*nos* EP [nuʃ]/BP [nus]		
2pl	*vos* EP [vuʃ]		
3pl.masc	*os* EP [uʃ]/BP[us]	*lhes*	*se*
3pl.fem	*as* EP [ɐʃ]/BP[as]	EP [ʎəʃ]/BP [ʎes]	EP [sə]/ BP [se]

distinctions are only found in the singular and plural forms, but more will be said about 3 sg/pl accusative forms in BP.

There are also important differences. In spoken BP, *vos* (2pl) is being replaced by the full pronoun *vocês* "you.pl"; *te* (2sg) can be replaced by *você* "you.sg," and *o(s)/a(s)* (3sg/pl acc) by *ele(s)/ela(s)* "he/she/it/they." In addition, *lhe* (3sg dat) has developed syncretism, since it can be used as a 2sg or 3sg accusative clitic. BP also differs from EP due to the emergence of weak subject pronouns, which exhibit some typical properties of clitics.

2.2. Pronominal clitic clusters

The clitic forms in Table 12.1 can combine into clusters, but only in EP. In BP, verbs are not allowed to express their arguments by more than one clitic. This section will therefore be essentially surveying properties from EP.

2.2.1. Clitic sequences

Clusters in EP have at most two clitic elements. One common pattern is given in (1), with the clitic *se* followed by a dative clitic:

(1) a. *Dá-se-lhe o remédio…*   (EP)
   give.3sg-se-dat.3sg the medicine
   "You give him/her the medicine ..."
   b. *Passou-se-me!*
   passed-se-dat.1sg
   "I forgot!"

Clitic clusters usually exhibit morphophonological alternations, as happens when 3rd person accusative pronouns are preceded by 1st or 2nd person plural dative pronouns. This feature combination triggers "reciprocal" allomorphy inside the cluster, given that both clitics undergo shape alternations (Crysmann 2002, Spencer and Luís 2005).

Table 12.2   Clitic clusters in EP.

	3sg.masc.acc	3sg.fem.acc	3pl.masc.acc	3pl.masc.acc
1pl.dat	no-lo	no-la	no-los	no-las
	(*nos-o)	(*nos-a)	(*nos-os)	(*nos-as)
2pl.dat	vo-lo	vo-la	vo-los	vo-las
	(*vos-o)	(*vos-a)	(*vos-os)	(*vos-as)

(2) a. *Deu-no-lo.* (*nos-o)   (EP)
     gave-dat.1pl-acc.3sg.masc
     "S/he gave it to us."

   b. *Ninguém vo-lo deu.* (*vos-o)
     no one dat.2pl-acc.3sg.masc gave
     "No one gave it to them."

Table 12.2 illustrates the complete inventory of clitic clusters displaying cluster internal reciprocal allomorphy.

The order in which clitics can appear is seriously restricted and does not reflect the order of nominal phrases bearing the same functions. In EP, indirect object NPs can either precede direct object NPs (3a) or follow them (3b), but with clitic pronouns accusative clitics must always follow dative, as in (3c) and (3d).

(3) a. *A criança deu o livro ao vizinho.* (acc > dat)   (EP)
     the child gave the book to-the neighbor
     "The child gave the book to the neighbor."

   b. *A criança deu ao vizinho o livro.* (dat > acc)
     the child gave to-the neighbor the book
     "The child gave the neighbor the book."

   c. *A criança deu-lho.* (dat > acc)
     the child gave-dat.3sg-acc.3pl.masc
     "The child gave it to him."

   d. **A criança deu o lhe.* (acc > dat)
     the child gave-acc.3pl.masc-dat.3sg
     "The child gave it to him."

Clitic clusters are subject not only to linearization constraints, but also to feature co-occurrence restrictions, given that not all logical person-number combinations are possible within the dat > acc sequence. For example, 1st and 2nd person clitics cannot co-occur (i.e., *I/II-I/II):

(4) *O João entregou-me-te.* (*1/2)   (EP)
     the João handed over-dat.1sg-acc.2sg
     "João handed you over to me."

Again, there appears to be no syntactic or semantic motivation for this restriction, since 2nd person accusative clitics can combine freely with a strong pronoun:

(5) *O João entregou-te a mim.*   (EP)
     the João handed-acc.2sg to me
     "João handed you over to me."

2.2.2. *Portmanteau forms*

Clitic clusters may also express two clitic pronouns as one portmanteau form. These clusters always involve the dative clitics *me*, *te* and *lhe/s* followed by any 3rd person accusative clitic:

(6) *A Maria ofereceu-ma.* (**me-a*)   (EP)
    the Maria offered-dat.1sg&acc.3sg.fem
    "Maria gave it to me."

All possible portmanteau clusters in EP are illustrated in Table 12.3.

Some portmanteau clusters also exhibit syncretism: when 3rd person dative clitics combine with 3rd person accusative clitics, the number features of the dative clitic neutralize. Hence, *lho* can mean either "it to him/her" or to "it to them":

(7) *Compra-lho!* (**lhe-o*)   (EP)
    buy.imp-dat.3&acc.3sg.masc
    "Buy it for him/her/them!"

The complete set of syncretic clusters in EP is illustrated in Table 12.4.

2.2.3. *Clitic sequences with portmanteau forms*

Finally, clusters may also comprise a portmanteau clitic preceded by impersonal *se*, realizing three distinct sets of morphosyntactic clitic features:

(8) a. *pagam-se-lhas*   (EP)
       pay.3pl-se-dat.3/acc.3pl.fem
       "you pay them to him/her/them"
    b. *dão-se-lhos*
       give.3pl-se-dat.3/acc.3pl.masc
       "you give them to him/her/them"

Summing up, then, clitic clusters in EP exhibit a number of morphophonological properties that are typical of affixes.

Table 12.3 Portmanteau forms with 1st and 2nd person dative clitics in EP.

	3sg.masc.acc	*3sg.fem.acc*	*3pl.masc.acc*	*3pl.fem.acc*
1sg.dat	*mo* (**me-o*)	*ma* (**me-a*)	*mos* (**me-os*)	*mas* (**me-as*)
2sg.dat	*to* (**te-o*)	*ta* (**te-a*)	*tos* (**te-os*)	*tas* (**te-as*)

Table 12.4 Portmanteau clusters.

	3sg.masc.acc	*3sg.fem.acc*	*3pl.masc.acc*	*3pl.fem.acc*
3sg.dat/3pl.dat	*lho*	*lha*	*lhos*	*lhas*

2.3. *Typical properties of clitic pronouns in EP and BP*

Pronominal clitics in both BP and EP exhibit typical properties that are common to other Romance clitics (Kayne 1975, Zwicky and Pullum 1983). One typical phonological property is their prosodic deficiency, which constitutes one of the hallmarks of clitics (Nespor and Vogel 2007, Spencer and Luís 2012).

Due to this deficiency clitic pronouns cannot stand alone nor can they be contrastively stressed, as illustrated with data from EP:

(9) a. *Quem (é) que o João viu? *ME.*   (BP/EP)
         who (is) that the João saw yesterday? acc.1sg
         "Who did João see yesterday? Me."
     b. *Querem *TE* pedir *ou querem ME pedir*?   (BP/EP)
         want-acc.2sg or want-acc.1sg
         "Do they want to ask me or do they want to ask you?"

In addition, clitic pronouns can neither be topicalized nor coordinated:

(10) a. *Foi A que ele convidou para a festa.*   (BP/EP)
         was acc.3sg.fem that he invited for the party
         "It was her that he invited to the party."
     b. *Não sei se o Filipe TE e ME convida para a festa.*
         not know if the Filipe acc.2sg and acc.1sg invite for the party
         "I don't know if Filipe invited you and me to the party."

One further property is the fact that they must combine with a stressed lexical item with which they form a prosodic word. This item, which is generally the thematic verb, serves as the host to which clitics attach postverbally or preverbally.[3]

(11) a. *O João chamou=me ontem?*   (EP)
         the João called acc.1sg yesterday
         "Did João call me yesterday?"
     b. *Você não me=chamou ontem?*   (BP/BP)
         you.sg not acc.1sg called yesterday
         "Didn't you call me yesterday?"

Phonologically, EP/BP object clitics are positioned outside the "three-syllable window" and, therefore, do not affect the stress pattern of the verb. In (12), lexical stress falls on the antepenultimate syllable in the presence or absence of a postverbal clitic:

(12) a. *com.prÁ.va.mos*   (BP/BP)
         "we bought"
     b. *comprÁ.va.mos-lhe*   (BP/BP)
         bought.1pl-dat.3sg
         "we bought him/her"

3. Clitic pronouns in European Portuguese

3.1. *Introduction*

In this section we examine the placement (3.2), the phonology (3.3) and the morphology (3.4) of EP clitic pronouns. The EP clitic system stands out from the other Romance languages for two reasons: on the one hand, because preverbal and postverbal placement is determined entirely by specific syntactic contexts rather than by the finiteness of the verb; on the other, because the default placement of clitic pronouns is postverbal, rather than preverbal. Our evidence also shows that preverbal and postverbal clitics differ from each other in a number of ways: preverbal clitics are i) dependent on the presence of proclitic triggers, ii) can be separated from the verb and iii) take wide scope over coordination, while postverbal clitics are adjacent to the verb and exhibit allomorphic alternations. Similarly, enclitics show lexical phonology, whereas proclitics attach postlexically.

3.2. The positioning of object clitic pronouns

3.2.1. Postverbal placement: the default position

Preverbal clitic pronouns in EP are excluded from first position in affirmative imperatives:

(13) a. **Me chama!*   (EP)
              acc.1sg call.imp
     b. *Chama-me!*
              call.imp acc.1sg
              "Call me!"

This behavior also holds for contexts such as declarative clauses or yes–no interrogative clauses:

(14) a. **Me chama.*   (EP)
              acc.1sg call.prs.3sg
     b. *Chama-me.*
              call.prs.3sg acc.1sg
              "(S)he calls me."

(15) a. **Me chamaste?*   (EP)
              acc.1sg called.2sg
     b. *Chamaste-me?*
              called.2sg-acc.1sg
              "Did you call me?"

In "normal" declarative clauses, the clitic pronoun always appears postverbally:

(16) a. **Ontem me chamou.*   (EP)
              yesterday acc.1sg called
     b. *Ontem chamou-me.*
              yesterday called-acc.1sg
              "(S)he called me yesterday."

(17) a. **A médica me chamou.*   (EP)
              the doctor acc.1sg called
     b. *A médica chamou-me.*
              the doctor called-acc.1sg
              "The (woman) doctor called me."

In declarative clauses that contain complex tenses with a participle or a gerund verb form, the clitic pronoun occurs after the finite auxiliary.

(18) a.   *O João tem-me chamado.*   (EP)
          the João has-acc.1sg called
      b.   **O João tem chamado-me.*
          the João has called-acc.1sg
      c.   **O João me tem chamado.*
          the João acc.1sg has called
          "He has called me."

(19) a.   *O professor foi-lhe dando alguns conselhos.*   (EP)
          the teacher was-dat.3sg giving some advices
      b.   *?O professor foi dando-lhe alguns conselhos.*
          the teacher was giving-dat.3sg some advices
      c.   **O professor lhe foi dando alguns conselhos.*
          the teacher dat.3sg was giving some advices
          "The teacher was giving him/her some advice."

But if the auxiliary is in the gerund and the main verb is in the participle, then the clitic must attach to the auxiliary:

(20) *Tendo-lhe perguntado se estava em casa, ela respondeu que sim.*   (EP)
      having-dat.3sg asked if was at home she answered that yes
      "Having asked her if she was at home, she replied 'Yes'."

With complex predicates, the clitic pronoun occurs after the non-finite thematic verb or "climbs" to the finite auxiliary and attaches after it. In either position, the clitic is postverbal and enclitic.

(21) a.   *A minha mãe quer batizar=me.*   (EP)
          the my mother wants baptize=acc.1sg
      b.   *A minha mãe quer=me batizar.*
          the my mother wants=acc.1sg baptize
          "My mother wants to baptize me."

An adverb can separate the clitic from the thematic verb, showing that it is effectively enclitic to the auxiliary.

(22) a.   *Querem=me sempre chamar.*   (EP)
          want.3pl=acc.1sg always call
          "He wants always to call me."
      b.   *Tem=me sempre chamado.*
          have.3pl=acc.1sg always called
          "He has always called me."

Clitics may also occur inside the verb, before the future and conditional ending:

(23) a.   *Quando eu tiver um filho, dar-lhe-ei muito amor.*   (EP)
          when I have-sbjv.fut a child I-dat.3sg-fut.3sg much love
          "When I have a child, I will give him/her much love."
      b.   *Se eu tivesse dinheiro, da-lo-ía aos pobres.*
          if I had money give-acc.3sg-cond.1sg to-the poor
          "If I had money, I would give it to the poor."

This phenomenon is known as mesoclisis and has sometimes been taken as an argument to analyze these clitics as inflectional markers (Spencer and Luís 2005).

3.2.2. *Preverbal placement*

Preverbal positioning in EP is only possible under certain morphosyntactic conditions (Duarte, Matos, and Faria 1995, Luís and Otoguro 2011): after a quantifier (24a), a monosyllabic adverb (24b) or a negation marker (24c). Note that in these cases the postverbal occurrence of the clitic pronoun is excluded:[4]

(24) a. *Todos me chamaram.* (EP)
          all acc.1sg called
          "Everyone called me."
      b. *Já me chamou.*
          already acc.1sg called
          "(S/he) already called me."
      c. *Ela não me chamou.* (EP)
          she not acc.1sg called
          "She didn't call me."

Preverbal ordering is also triggered by embedded clauses and by main clauses introduced by interrogative items:

(25) a. *Acho que me chamou.* (EP)
          think.1sg that acc.1sg called
          "I think he called me."
      b. *Porque me chamou?*
          why acc.1sg called
          "Why did you call me?"

In complex tenses containing a participle verb form, clitic pronouns must occur before the finite auxiliary (26a).

(26) a. *Acho que me tinha chamado.* (EP)
          think.1sg that acc.1sg had.3sg called
      b. **Acho que tinha chamado-me.*
          think.1sg that had called-acc.1sg
      c. **Acho que tinha me chamado.*
          think.1sg that had acc.1sg called
          "I think that (s)he had called me."

With complex predicates, the clitic pronoun may either attach postverbally to the lexical verb like an enclitic (27a) and (28a), or it may "climb" to the finite auxiliary verb and occur in preverbal position (27b) and (28b). However, it cannot appear between the auxiliary and the non-finite thematic verb (27c) and (27c).

(27) a. *Todos querem chamar-me.* (EP)
          all want call-acc.sg
      b. *Todos me querem chamar.*
          all acc.sg want call
      c. **Todos querem me chamar.*
          all want acc.sg call
          "They all want to call me."

(28) a. *Porque querem chamar-me?* (EP)
          why want call-acc.sg
      b. *Porque me querem chamar?*
          why acc.sg want call
      c. **Porque querem me chamar?*
          why want acc.sg call
          "Why do they want to call me?"

Clitic pronouns in preverbal —but not in postverbal —position may appear separated from the finite verb by an intervening (i.e., interpolated) element, in particular by the negation marker *não*, but also by monosyllabic adverbial particles and non-clitic pronouns:[5]

(29) a. *Se me não engano, ela faz anos a 21 de janeiro.*   (EP)
           if acc.1sg not mistake, she does years at 21 of January
           "If I'm not mistaken, her birthday is on January 21."
       b. *O electricista bem me cá veio arranjar a TV, mas …*
           the electrician good acc.1sg here came repair the TV, but …
           "The electrician did come and repair the TV, but …"
       c. *Paciência já a tu tens!*
           patience already acc.3sg.fem you.sg have
           "Patience, you already have!"

Preverbal clitics also have the ability to take wide scope over coordinated phrases (Crysmann 2002, Luís and Otoguro 2011) and be shared by conjoined verbs or verb phrases (30). Enclitics, on the contrary, must always be repeated on each conjunct (31):

(30) a. *Apenas a minha mãe me [ajudou e incentivou].*   (EP)
           only the my mother acc.1sg helped and encouraged
           "Only my mother helped me and encouraged me."
       b. *Acho que lhes [leram uma história e deram um livro].*
           think that dat.3pl read.pst a story and gave a book
           "I think that they read them a story and gave them a book."

(31) a. *Comprei-os ontem e usei-os hoje.*   (EP)
           bought-acc.3pl.masc yesterday and used-acc.3pl.masc today
       b. **Comprei ontem e usei-os hoje.*
           bought yesterday and used-acc.3pl.masc today
           "I bought them yesterday and used them today."

3.3. Phonological properties

In the research literature, one common question about clitic pronouns is the nature of their prosodization to the host, that is, whether they attach lexically or postlexically. In this section, we survey phonological rules which effectively suggest different prosodization patterns for preverbal and postverbal clitics in EP. In particular, it will be shown that proclitics attach postlexically whereas enclitics attach lexically. In section 3.4, morphological evidence will be provided to further support the divide between enclitics and proclitics.

3.3.1. Glide insertion

A crucial piece of phonological evidence indicating that enclitics and proclitics attach at different levels of grammar stems from their behavior with respect to the rule of glide insertion which takes place between [ə] and a following vowel (Vigário 2003). As shown below, this rule of hiatus resolution is compulsory with postverbal clitics and prefixes, as in (32), but optional with preverbal clitics and prepositions, as in (33).

(32) a. *bebe-o* *[ɐ]/[j]   (EP)
      drinks-acc.3sg.masc
      "drinks it"
  b. *re-organizar* *[ɐ]/[j]
      "reorganize"

(33) a. *te ofereci* [ɐ]/[j]   (EP)
      acc.2sg offered
      "offered to you"
  b. *de assunto* [ɐ]/[j]
      "of matter"

Optionality of glide insertion appears, indeed, to be a property of phrasal phonology, as shown by two adjacent lexical items, which can only optionally trigger glide insertion:

(34) *bebe agora* [ɐ]/[j]   (EP)
    "drinks now"

Such evidence strongly suggests that preverbal clitics undergo phrasal (or postlexical) phonology like function words (Bermúdez-Otero and Luís 2009). As to enclitics, the fact that the non-optionality of glide insertion in (32) is shared by both prefixed words and the verb-enclitic strongly suggests that enclitics are prosodified within the lexical domain.

Throughout Section 3, the idea that proclitics and enclitics attach at different levels of grammar finds support in syntactic, phonological and morphological evidence. Section 3.4.2, in particular, will focus on the morphological properties of the verb-enclitic combination and show that the phrasal behavior of proclitics is in marked contrast with the lexical behavior of enclitics.

In what follows, we will refine the claim that enclitics attach lexically to the verb by discussing the prosodic structure of the verb-enclitic combination. The main goal will be to provide phonological evidence which shows that enclitic suffixes are prosodically attached as outer layers of inflections. Based on two rules of lexical phonology, namely nasal diphthongization and mid-vowel centralization, it will be argued that enclitic suffixes are adjoined to the prosodic word.

3.3.2. Nasal diphthongization

Nasal diphthongization is typically a word-final rule in standard EP (35a) (Mateus and d'Andrade 2000: 47). It is never attested word-internally in standard EP, except at the boundary between the verb and the enclitic, as in (35b).

(35) a. *diz<u>em</u>* [diz<u>ẽj̃</u>]   (EP)
      say.3pl
      "they say"
  b. *diz<u>em</u>-lhe* [diz<u>ẽj̃</u>ʎə]   (EP)
      say.2pl-dat.3sg
      "they say to him/her"

Rather than ruling out the lexical status of enclitics, on the grounds that they violate the word-final status of nasal diphthongization, as argued in Vigário (2003), Luís (2004) instead accounts for (35b) by assuming that the enclitic suffix is prosodically outside the domain within which the rule of nasalization applies. Under this view, the occurrence of the enclitic suffix after a nasal diphthong follows out naturally.[6]

3.3.3. Mid-vowel centralization

Another lexical rule that shows that enclitic suffixes are prosodified outside the inner prosodic is mid-vowel centralization. This rule applies when mid vowels are followed by palatals, as in (36a-b), but is blocked by the verb-enclitic sequence in (36c) (Vigário 2003).

(36) a. *telha* [tɐ.ʎɐ]/*[te.ʎɐ])   (EP)
          "tile"
      b. *veículo* [vɐ.i.ku.lu]/*[ve.i.ku.lu]   (EP)
          "vehicle"
      c. *dê-lhe* [de. ʎə]/*[dɐ. ʎə]   (EP)
          give.imp-dat.3sg
          "give to him/her"

As in 3.3.2, the data in (36) can be accounted for by assuming that the lexical domain of mid-vowel centralization is the inner prosodic word. Under this assumption, the non-application of the rule in (36c) results from the prosodic boundary that exists between verb and enclitic.

Overall, then, the evidence provided by the rules of nasal diphthongization and mid-vowel centralization suggests the prosodic structure in (37), in which the enclitic suffix is adjoined to a prosodic word (Bermúdez-Otero and Luís 2009, Luís 2009).

(37)   Pwd

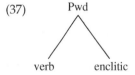

verb   enclitic

Summing up, this section has shown that there is phonological evidence suggesting that enclitics, but not proclitics, undergo rules of lexical phonology. It has further been argued that enclitic suffixes behave phonologically like outer layers of suffixes and that they are best analyzed as prosodically adjoined to the inner prosodic word.

In the following section we will examine in more detail the grammatical status of clitic pronouns in EP, and provide morphological evidence supporting the distinction between postverbal clitics and preverbal clitics.

3.4. Morphological properties

In this section we present data to show that postverbal clitics interact morphologically with the verb in ways strongly suggesting that they have developed into inflectional suffixes, while preverbal clitics exhibit phrasal properties such as interpolation and coordination (Luís 2004, 2009, 2014).

3.4.1. Selectivity and adjacency

Postverbal clitic pronouns only attach to verbs and must always be in strict adjacency to them:

(38) a. *Levas-nos agora?*   (EP)
        take.2sg-acc.2pl now
     b. **Levas agora nos?*
        take.2sg now acc.2pl
        "Do you take us now?"

Postverbal clitics may also surface in verb-internal position. In future or conditional verb forms, they can appear inside the verb before tense and agreement suffixes:

(39) a. *dar-lhes-ão (*darão-lhes)*   (EP)
        give-dat.3pl-fut
        "they will give them"
     b. *visitar-nos-iam (*visitariam-nos)*
        visit-acc.2pl-cond
        "they would visit us"

3.4.2. *Morphophonological alternations*

Morphosyntactically conditioned allomorphy is restricted to the verb-clitic sequence. Stem-allomorphy takes place between 1pl verb forms and the enclitics *nos* "us" and *vos* "you.pl":

(40) a. *Vêmo-nos amanhã. (*vêmos-nos)*   (EP)
        see.2pl-acc.1pl tomorrow
        "We (will) see us tomorrow."
     b. *Queremo-vos em casa cedo. (*queremos-vos)*
        want.2pl-acc.2pl in house early
        "We want you home early."

If *nos* and *vos* follow any other consonant-final verb, the allomorphy is not triggered:

(41) *Vendes-nos a casa? (*vende-nos)*   (EP)
     sell.2sg-acc.2pl the house
     "Would you sell the house?"

Enclitics also undergo allomorphic variation: when *o/os* or *a/as* is preceded by 3rd plural verb forms, an *n*-allomorph surfaces:

(42) a. *As enfermeiras levam-no. (*lavam-o)*   (EP)
        the nurses take-acc.3sg.masc
        "The nurses take him."
     b. *As mulheres tinham-nas visto. (*tinham-as)*
        the women had-acc.3pl.fem seen
        "The women had seen them."

While it may seem that the *n*-allomorph is triggered by the verb-final nasal diphthong, closer inspection shows that before any other nasal-final verb forms, such as 3rd singular present indicative forms, allomorphy is blocked.

(43) *O professor tem-os visitado. (*tem-nos)*   (EP)
     the teacher has-acc.3pl.masc visited
     "The teacher has been visiting them."

Allomorphy is reciprocal when both the stem and the clitic undergo variation. This happens when 3sg/pl accusative clitics precede a consonant-final verb (ending in -*s*, -*z* or -*r*), which triggers an *l*-initial allomorph and verb-final consonant deletion:

(44)   *Procuramo-lo todo o dia.* (**procuramos-o*)   (EP)
       look-for.1pl acc.3sg.masc all the day
       "We looked for him all day long."

This phenomenon can also be found verb-internally in mesoclitic verb forms, when a 3sg/pl accusative clitic is placed between the *r*-final verb stem and the future and conditional agreement markers:

(45)   *cantá-lo-ei* (**cantar-o-ei*)   (EP)
       sing-acc.3sg.masc-fut.1sg
       "I will sing it"

In sum, postverbal clitics trigger stem-allomorphy and undergo stem-induced allomorphy. The observed allomorphic alternations are determined by highly restricted contexts, such as the morphosyntactic properties of the verb or the morphosyntactic properties of both the verb and the enclitic.

3.4.3. Cluster-internal allomorphy

We have so far shown that preverbal and postverbal clitics differ with respect to their morphological interaction with the verb. In this section, however, we have provided evidence to show that despite such differences, morphophonological alternations can be found within the clitic cluster, regardless of whether it appears before or after the verb.

As already alluded to in Sections 2.2.1 and 2.2.2, one can have at most two elements which very rarely preserve their form as single clitics. The morphophonological changes observed within the cluster are of two kinds: (1) fusion, with or without syncretism; and (2) reciprocal allomorphy (affecting both clitics).

Fusion takes place when one single formative expresses morphosyntactic features that are usually expressed separately by distinct formatives. In the case of EP clitics, dative and accusative clitics features are expressed by one monosyllabic portmanteau form. Such forms always involve a dative clitic with a 3sg/pl accusative pronouns (see Table 12.3).

Clusters that realize amalgamated dative and accusative clitics may also exhibit syncretism, given that the fused clusters containing 3sg/pl dative forms neutralize the number distinction of the dative forms (see Table 12.4).

Finally, clitic sequences also exhibit morphological alternations as observed between the verb and the enclitic. Whenever the dative clitics *nos* and *vos* combine with 3sg/pl accusative pronouns, both the dative and the accusative clitic forms undergo allomorphy. While the dative pronoun loses its final consonant, the vowel initial accusative clitic surfaces as an *l*-initial allomorph.

To sum up, our morphological survey reveals a number of clear-cut inflectional properties within the clitic sequence and between the enclitic and the verb (Spencer and Luís 2005, 2012). Evidence also shows that clitics in preverbal position exhibit phrasal behavior (Crysmann 2002, Luís and Otoguro 2011, Luís 2014).

4. Clitic pronouns in Brazilian Portuguese

4.1. Introduction

In this section we turn to the clitic system of BP. Our survey starts with object clitics and provides an overview of the placement patterns (4.2).[7] We then examine their morphology (4.3) and phonology (4.4). Evidence will highlight differences between preverbal and postverbal clitics that resemble some of the differences previously observed in EP. We then look briefly at an important development in the grammar of clitic pronouns, namely the emergence of subject clitics (4.5).

4.2. *The positioning of object clitic pronouns*

4.2.1. *Preverbal placement: the default position*

BP clitic pronouns tend to occur mostly in preverbal position. This is the case in absolute V1 contexts, where the preverbal occurrence of clitic pronouns is considered to be one of the main innovations of BP syntax (Galves, Moraes, and Ribeiro 2005):

(46) a. *Me chamo Maria.* (BP)
    acc.1sg call Maria
  b. **Chamo-me Maria.*
    call-acc.1sg Maria
    "My name's Maria."

This is also the case with root affirmative clauses, which in EP would dictate postverbal placement. Compare (47) with the corresponding sentence in EP (cf. (17)).

(47) *A médica me chamou.* (BP)
    the doctor acc.1sg called
    "The (woman) doctor called me."

Given that clitic placement in BP is entirely independent of the presence of proclitic triggers, sentences such as (48) look exactly like their EP counterparts:

(48) *O médico não/já/nunca me chamou.* (BP/EP)
    the doctor not/already/never acc.1sg called
    "The doctor didn't call/already called/never called me."

In BP, preverbal placement is also compulsory with the imperative. In this context, BP differs not only from EP but also from most other Romance languages where clitics attach postverbally with affirmative imperatives (Rooryck 2000):

(49) a. *Me chama!* (BP)
    acc.1sg call.imp
  b. **Chama-me!*
    call.imp acc.1sg
    "Call me!"

In "Aux V" structures (i.e., analytic and periphrastic structures with an inflected "Aux" and a non-finite "V"), the pronoun attaches as a proclitic to the thematic verb (Galves and Abaurre 1996, Galves, Moraes, and Ribeiro 2005):

(50) a. *A senhora poderia me dizer o seu nome?* (BP)
    the lady could acc.1sg tell the your name
    "Could you tell me your name?"
  b. *Você tinha me dito que ficava.*
    you.sg had acc.1sg told that stayed.2sg
    "You told me that you would stay."
  c. *Eu estou te levando …*
    I am acc.1sg taking
    "I am taking you …"

The claim that the clitics in (50) attach to the thematic verb, but not to the auxiliary, as happens in EP, is supported by the fact that the insertion of an adverb between pronoun and the main verb form is excluded in BP (Comrie 1982, Nunes 2011) (compare (51) with the corresponding EP structure in (22)).

(51) a. *Ele tem me (*sempre) chamado.*   (BP)
      he has acc.1sg (*always) called
      "He has (always) called me."
   b. *Ele quer me (*sempre) chamar.*
      he wants acc.1sg (*always) call
      "He wants (always) to call me."

The behavior of clitics in "Aux V" structures with a participle verb is therefore in marked contrast with the behavior of EP clitics, where clitic climbing would be mandatory (26).

(52) *Acho que a senhora já tinha me chamado.*   (BP)
     think.1sg that the lady already had acc.1sg called
     "I think that you had already called me."

In fact, attachment to participles (as in (52)) or to gerunds is a BP-specific innovation which is not allowed in Modern EP.

4.2.2. *BP object clitics in postverbal position*

Although we can state that, as a general rule, BP object clitics occur in preverbal position and attach to the following verb, there are also contexts where they may appear in postverbal position. An interesting observation by Galves and Abaurre (1996) is that there seem to be two types of enclisis: one involving the clitic *se* in root matrix clauses (53) and another one the 3rd person clitic *o/a* in "Aux V_{inf}" structures (54).

(53) a. *chegou-se à conclusão …*   (BP)
      came-refl.3sg to-the conclusion
      "One came to the conclusion …"
   b. *parte-se um ovo …*
      crack-refl.3sg an egg
      "You crack an egg …"

In (53), *se* is a *"se indeterminado"* ("indeterminate *se*"), which further shows that enclitic placement is effectively quite restricted. In the "Aux V_{inf}" structure, enclisis with *o/a* appears to be largely determined by the morphological form of the thematic verb, which is non-finite:

(54) a. *Não seria conveniente mudá-lo.*   (BP)
      not would-be convenient change-acc.3sg.masc
      "It would not be convenient to change it."
   b. *Você vai levá-lo a encontrar uma solução …*
      you will take-acc.3sg.masc to find a solution
      "You will take him with you to find a solution …"

In "Aux V" structures, other clitics may be enclitic to the thematic verb (Comrie 1982). Yet it has been pointed out that the occurrence of postverbal clitics in BP reflects the written norm learned at school or through special training.

Despite the patterns (53) and (54), it is worth noting that there is some degree of optionality between preverbal and postverbal placement in BP (Galves and Abaurre 1996, Vieira 2003, Galves, Moraes, and Ribeiro 2005). For example, with prepositional clauses which take a non-finite verb, BP allows both positions such as EP:

(55) a. *Estou aqui para te dizer que ...*   (BP/EP)
       be.prs.1sg here for dat.2.sg say that ...
     b. *Estou aqui para dizer-te que...*   (BP/EP)
       be.prs.1sg here for dat.2.sg say that ...
       "I am here to tell you that ..."

4.2.3. Other developments

Another syntactic peculiarity of BP clitic pronouns concerns their use. With 2nd and 3rd person pronouns there is a tendency in colloquial BP to use non-clitic forms instead of clitic ones (Galves, Moraes, and Ribeiro 2005):

(56) a. *Não te chamei.*   (BP/EP)
       not acc.2sg called
     b. *Não chamei você.*   (BP)
       not called-1sg you
       "I didn't call you."

(57) a. *O João não lhe perguntou.*   (BP/EP)
       the João not dat.3sg called
     b. *O João não perguntou a ela.*   (BP)
       the João not called prep her
       "João didn't call her."

The first person plural form *nós* "us" is often replaced in colloquial BP by *a gente* (literally "the people"):

(58) a. *A Maria viu-nos na praia.*   (EP)
       the Maria saw-us on the beach
     b. *A Maria viu a gente na praia.*   (BP)
       the Maria saw the people on the beach
       "Maria saw us yesterday on the beach."

In addition to a tendency in BP to avoid clitic pronouns (Cyrino, Duarte, and Kato 2000), 3rd clitic pronouns can also be completely omitted. Although in EP clitic pronouns also can be omitted (Raposo 1986), null clitics are more frequent and less constrained in BP than in EP (Farrel 1990, Galves, Moraes, and Ribeiro 2005):

(59) a. *Eu comprei quando eu fui para o Rio.*   (BP)
       I bought when I went to the Rio
       "I bought it when I went to Rio."
     b. *A Júlia sempre chora quando ponho no berço.*
       the Julia always cries when put.prs.1sg in-the cradle
       "Julia always cries when I put her in the cradle."

Finally, *lhe* can have an accusative meaning, carrying 2nd person features (60) or 3rd person features (61) (Galves, Moraes, and Ribeiro 2005):

(60) a. *Lá encontrarás um tesouro que te fará rico.*   (EP)
          there you find-fut a treasure which acc.3sg.masc make.fut rich
      b. *Lá você encontrará um tesouro que lhe fará rico.*   (BP)
          there you find-fut a treasure which dat.3 sg.masc make.fut rich
          "You will find there a treasure which will make you rich."

(61) a. *... mas aquilo deixou-o sobressaltado.*   (EP)
          ... but it left-acc.3sg startled
      b. *... mas aquilo lhe deixou sobressaltado.*   (BP)
          ... but it dat.3sg left startled
          "... but it still left him startled."

4.3. Phonological properties

We now draw on previous research on the phonology of BP clitic pronouns to argue that the phonological rules applying between proclitics (such as *me*, *te*, *se* and *lhe*) and the verb have postlexical status. With the exception of accusative *o/a* in postverbal position (see 4.3.2), the phonological rules that apply between proclitics (such as *me*, *te*, *se*, and *lhe*) and the verb also apply across word boundaries. We will, however, not be committing ourselves to specific prosodization patterns.

4.3.1. Mid-vowel neutralization

One phonological rule which applies to stressless mid vowels in word-final position is known as mid-vowel neutralization (Câmara Jr. 1970, Wetzels 1992, Bisol 2000, 2003). Neutralization also applies to clitic pronouns such as *-me* [me], *-te* [te], *-se* [se] and *-lhe* [ʎe], in which the final mid vowel is raised to [i]:

(62) a. *me* [me] *leve > mi* [mi] *levi*   (BP)
          acc.1sg take.imp
          "take me"
      b. *se* [se] *senti > si* [si] *senti*
          refl.3sg feels
          "(s)he feels"

Crucial here is the fact that neutralization of stressless mid vowels can also be observed in function words (63) and lexical words (64) that have a mid vowel in word-final position:

(63) a. *de ferro > di* [di] *ferro*   (BP)
          "of iron"
      b. *se você quiser > si* [si] *você quiser*
          "if you want"

(64) a. *leve > lev*[i]   (BP)
          "light"
      b. *sente > sent*[i]
          "((s)he) feels"

An interesting property of this rule is that it does not apply word-internally and therefore can be used to disambiguate the minimal pairs in (65):

(65) *sessenta* (**sissenta*)   (BP)
      "sixty"

Likewise, stressless prefixes or pretonic syllables within a lexical word do not undergo neutralization:

(66) a. *preconceber (*priconceber)*   (BP)
       "to plan ahead"
    b. *reanimar (*rianimar)*
       "to reanimate"

BP varieties in which neutralization takes place seem to block the rule in fixed multiword expressions, such as *de noite* "at night" and *cor-de-rosa* "pink," as a result of lexicalization. In these expressions, the function word *de* preserves its mid vowel (Bisol 2005).

4.3.2. Vowel degemination

Vowel degemination in BP takes place when two identical stressless vowels belonging to adjacent syllables are fused into one vowel forming one syllable. Examples of degemination involving the mid vowel [e] can take place between a vowel and a verb:

(67) a. *me esquece > m*[e]*squece*   (BP)
       refl.1sg forgets
       "(s)he forgets me"
    b. *te ensina > t*[ẽ]*nsina*
       acc.2sg teaches
       "(s)he teaches you"

But degemination can also be found across word boundaries, as in (68), word-internally, between morphological boundaries or not, as in (69):

(68) a. *vida amarga > vid*[a]*marga*   (BP)
       "bitter life"
    b. *menino honesto > menin*[o]*nesto*
       "honest boy"

(69) a. *reestabelecer > restabelecer*   (BP)
       "to reestablish"
    b. *coordenar > cordenar*
       "to coordinate"

Based on evidence which shows that degemination occurs both within and across word boundaries, Bisol (2000, 2003) takes the view that this rule is postlexical.

4.3.3. Diphthongization

Diphthongization takes place between two adjacent vowels, one of which must be (underlyingly) high or mid and stressless. It is an optional rule that can take place between proclitics and the verb (70), as well as across word boundaries, either between a function word and a lexical word (71) or between two lexical words (72).

(70) a. *me amou > m*[ja]*mou*   (BP)
       acc.1sg loved
       "(s)he loved me"
    b. *me acorda > m*[ja]*corda*
       acc.1sg wake-up
       "(s)he wakes me up"

(71) *do amor* > *d*[wa]*mor*   (BP)
      "of the love"

(72) a. *casaco azul* > *casac*[wa]*zul*   (BP)
          "blue coat"
      b. *verdade oculta* > *verdad*[jo]*culta*
          "hidden truth"

Overall, then, phonological evidence seems to indicate that there are no clitic-specific rules that apply exclusively at the boundary between the verb and the proclitics *me*, *te*, *se*, and *lhe*. Proclitics undergo a set of phonological rules that are neither category specific nor mandatory and which also apply across word boundaries.

4.4. Morphological properties

Adopting the Zwicky and Pullum (1983) criteria, this section shows that BP clitics exhibit a number of properties that are generally attributed to affixes, such as selectivity and adjacency to the verb (4.4.1), allomorphy (4.4.2), and paradigmatic gaps (4.4.3). While these properties are also present in EP, they occur in BP in ways that are quite distinct from EP. In Section 4.4.4, finally, our evidence indicates that proclitics exhibit predominately phrasal properties.

4.4.1. Selectivity and adjacency

Neither enclitics nor proclitics can be separated from the verb by interpolated forms, unlike proclitics in EP. In this respect, BP is more similar to languages like Modern Spanish or Modern Italian.

The adjacency requirement takes a more literal meaning in BP, given that the preferred option in this language is attachment to the thematic verb rather than to the auxiliary verb. In Aux V structures, this property produces a placement pattern according to which the clitic is proclitic to the main verb and not enclitic to the preceding auxiliary.

4.4.2. Morphonological alternations

Postverbal positioning may occur in restricted contexts, i.e., with 3rd accusative *o/a* after non-finite verb forms (Galves and Abaurre 1996, Vieira 2003), in which case *o/a* surfaces with an *l*-initial allomorph:

(73) a. *Não seria conveniente mudá-lo.* (not mudar-o)   (BP)
          not would-be convenient change-acc.3sg.masc
          "It would not be convenient to change it."
      b. *Você vai levá-lo a encontrar uma solução* .... (not levar-o)
          you will take-acc.3sg.masc to find a solution
          "You will take him with you to find a solution ..."

The fact that BP clitics also exhibit allmophic variation constitutes evidence in favor of the inflectional status of postverbal *o(s)/a(s)*. In EP, the same morphophonology is found in a wider range of verb–clitic sequences (cf. 3.4.2) and also within clitic clusters (cf. 3.4.3).

4.4.3. Paradigm gaps and syncretism

The clitic pronouns also show idiosyncratic gaps in their paradigm. In general, the allowed clitic inventory includes the clitics *me* 1sg, *te* 2sg, *lhe* 3sg, and *se* refl, (Nunes 1995, Cyrino, Duarte, and Kato 2000). Several forms are therefore excluded or quite rarely used.

In some cases, what appears to determine the exclusion of certain clitic forms is the finiteness of the verb (Galves and Abaurre 1996, Vieira 2003,). For example, 3rd accusative clitics rarely occur with finite verbs, being instead replaced by full pronouns or being omitted (see examples in Section 4.2.3).

Another example of a paradigmatic gap is the absence of the 2nd plural clitic form *vos* "2pl" (Galves, Moraes, and Ribeiro 2005) and also the plural form *lhes* "dat.3pl" which is more infrequent than its singular counterpart *lhe* "dat.3sg" It is difficult to see how such exclusions might be accounted for on general syntactic grounds, not the least because there appears to be no syntactic principle that would license one set of pronominal features over another. The exclusion of some forms may perhaps best be viewed as the result of morphological idiosyncrasies in BP. This is what defines defectiveness, namely the fact that not all morphosyntactic feature combinations correspond to an inflectional cell (Baerman and Corbett 2010).

Another type of form-meaning idiosyncrasy which is typical of inflectional affixes is known as syncretism (i.e., homophony between inflectional forms). In BP, syncretism can be observed in 1st and 2nd singular clitic forms *me* and *te*, which neutralize case, but also in a more recent development of syncretism with the clitic form *lhe*, which can be used as the 2sg and 3sg direct object of a transitive verb, with the meaning of *te* and *a/o*, as illustrated in (60) and (61).

4.4.4. Wide scope over coordination

We have seen above that proclitics in BP must be strictly adjacent to the verb and therefore seem to qualify as affixes. Surprisingly, however, they also take wide scope over conjoined verbs (Luís 2012) behaving like phrasal units:

(74) a. *O Gabriel simplesmente se lavou e vestiu.* (BP)
      the Gabriel simply ref.3sg washed and dressed
      "Gabriel simply washed himself and got dressed."
  b. *Depois de fugir, a polícia acabou por me encontrar e prender.*
      after fleeing the police stopped prep acc.1sg find at home and arrest
      "After escaping, the police finally caught me and arrested me."

Thus, the BP clitic system seems to share with EP the mixed grammatical status of its proclitics.[8]

Summing up, a number of morphological properties have been identified, such as adjacency, selectivity, enclitic allomorphy and gaps. Postverbal 3rd accusative clitics trigger and undergo allomorphy indicating lexical attachment. Preverbal clitics, despite adjacency, can take wide scope. Overall, then, preverbal and postverbal clitics seem to exhibit different degrees of morphologization.

4.5. The emergence of subject clitic pronouns

BP speakers often make use of reduced forms of subject pronouns in colloquial speech. Table 12.5 provides a list of the reduced forms which has been remarked in the literature (Ramos 1997, Kato 1999).

The existence of such reduced forms has been interpreted as evidence that a new series of subject pronouns with clitic forms is beginning to emerge. Indeed, some of the tests for clitic-hood, already discussed in Section 2.3, provide evidence for this

Table 12.5 Reduced subject pronoun forms in BP.

	Standard Form	*Reduced Form*
2sg	*você*	*cê*
3sg.masc	*ele*	*el*
	ela	*é*
2pl	*vocês*	*cês*
3pl.masc	*eles*	*es*

interpretation (Vitral 1996, Reich 2001, Petersen 2008, Othero 2013). For instance, the form *cê* is not allowed to occur in isolated position, nor can it receive contrastive stress, contrary to the full form *você*:

(75) a. *Quem chamou o João? – Você?/*Cê*   (BP)
 who called det João you
 "Who called João? You."
 b. *Quem chamou o João foi você/*cê!*   (BP)
 who called det João was you
 "YOU called João!"

However, with respect to other tests for clitic-hood, *cê* behaves like the full pronoun *você*: it may be separated from the verb (76) or coordinated with another pronoun (77) (Othero 2013, Kaiser and Alencar 2014):

(76) a. *Você mesmo vai comprar o livro?*   (BP)
 b. *Cê mesmo vai comprar o livro?*
 you yourself will buy the book
 "Will you buy yourself the book?"

(77) a. *Você e ela podem sair mais cedo, se preferirem.*   (BP)
 b. *Cê e ela podem sair mais cedo, se preferirem.*
 you and she can leave more early if want.inf.3pl
 "You and she can leave earlier, if you want."

In sum, we can state that reduced forms of subject pronouns in BP exhibit some, but not all typical properties of clitic elements. They (still) seem to occupy an intermediate position between independent and clitic elements. Further investigation of these elements is needed in order to determine their exact nature with respect to their status as clitics. In any case, we are dealing here with the beginning of a similar development that has been observed in the history of French and many northern Italian dialects, where a series of subject clitics pronouns has emerged (Petersen 2008).

5. Final remarks

In this chapter we have discussed the typical properties of clitic pronouns in European and Brazilian Portuguese. With respect to their use, the most salient differences between EP and BP reside in the fact that in EP their ordering is highly restricted by syntactic and semantic rules, while BP clitics almost always occur in preverbal position. In addition, BP only allows one argument to surface as a clitic, regardless of whether the thematic verb takes more arguments or not.

Then there are other differences, such as the morphophonological alternations. In BP, morphophonological alternations take place only when 3rd accusative clitics attach postverbally to a non-finite verb. Such allmorphy is also dependent on register and other sociolinguistic factors. In EP, clitic allomorphy is more extensive and can be found within the clitic cluster and also between the verb-enclitic unit. Given their specific morphophonological characteristics, postverbal pronouns in EP have sometimes been analyzed as stem-level inflections. Preverbal clitic pronouns in EP, however, do not allow this classification, since they do not necessarily attach to the verb.

Interestingly, there seems to be a general tendency in EP to replace preverbal clitic pronouns by postverbal clitic pronouns even in those contexts where postverbal clitic pronouns should be disallowed (Duarte, Matos, and Faria 1995). Examples of "misplaced" enclitics in colloquial speech are illustrated in (78):

(78) a. *Quer que eu ponha-o cá dentro?*   (EP)
        want.3sg that I put.sbjv-acc.3sg.masc inside
        "Do you want me to put it inside?"
     b. *Ainda não vi-o dormir mais do que duas horas.*
        yet not saw-acc.3sg.masc sleep more prep that two hours
        "I haven't seen him sleep more than two hours yet."

In BP, one can observe a general tendency to replace preverbal clitic pronouns by strong pronouns (in postverbal position) or even to omit them. In addition, there is a tendency to develop a series of clitic subject pronouns.

NOTES

1   We are grateful to Gabriel Araújo, Bruce Mayo and Leo Wetzels for useful comments and suggestions which helped improve this manuscript. Any faults that remain are our own.
2   Note that despite the orthographic similarities in Table 12.1, the IPA transcriptions reveal that there are substantial phonological differences between clitic pronouns in EP and BP. Some of these clitics also undergo phonological and morphological changes which affect their form (see Sections 3.3–3.4 and 4.3–4.4).
3   Following standard conventions, we use "=" to indicate attachment.
4   However see Section 6 on the expansion of enclisis to contexts where proclisis would be expected.
5   Interpolation is a residue of older stages of EP where preverbal clitics could be separated from the verb by large(r) words or whole phrases (Martins 1995, Barbosa 1996, Hinzelin 2010).
6   See, for example, *homemzinho* "little man" or *homemzarrão* "big man." In Luís (2004, 2009) and Bermúdez and Luís (2009), it is argued that diminutives and augmentatives should also be analyzed as lexical suffixes that adjoin prosodically to the base.
7   For reasons of space, we will only illustrate the more general tendencies of BP clitic placement. More detailed descriptions, taking account of both register and sociolinguistic variables, can be found in the references throughout this section.
8   Selectivity, on one hand, and wide scope, on the other, suggest that proclitics are phrasal affixes: while they constitute morphological units, they do not attach to stems (like stem-level affixes) but to phrasal hosts (see Luís 2012, 2014, Spencer and Luís 2012).

REFERENCES

Baerman, M. and G. Corbett (2010). Introduction: defectiveness: typology and diachrony. In M. Baerman, G. Corbett, and D. Brown (eds.), *Defective Paradigms: Missing Forms and What They Tell Us.* Oxford: Oxford Uuniversity Press, pp. 1–18.

Barbosa, P. (1996). Clitic placement in European Portuguese and the position of subjects. In A. Halpern and A. Zwicky (eds.), *Approaching Second. Second Position Clitics and Related Phenomena.* Stanford, CA: Centre for the Study of Language and Information, pp. 1–40.

Bermúdez-Otero, R. and A. R. Luís (2009). Cyclic domains and prosodic spans in European Portuguese encliticization. *Handout at the Old World Conference in Phonology (OCP6),* University of Edinburgh.

Bisol, L. (2000). O clítico e seu status prosódico. *Revista de Estudos de Linguagem,* 9, pp. 5–30.

Bisol, L. (2003). Neutralização das átonas. *Revista de Documentação de Estudos em Lingüística Teórica e Aplicada,* 19, pp. 267–276.

Bisol, L. (2005). O clítico e o seu hospedeiro. *Letras de Hoje,* 40, pp. 163–184.

Câmara Jr., M. (1970). *Estrutura da Língua Portuguesa.* Petrópolis: Vozes.

Comrie, B. (1982). Remarks on clitic-climbing in Brazilian Portuguese. *Lingua,* 58, pp. 243–265.

Crysmann, B. (2002). *Constraint-based coanalysis.* Ph.D. dissertation, Universität des Saarlandes & DFKI.

Cyrino, S., M. Duarte, and M. A. Kato (2000). Visible subjects and invisible clitics in Brazilian Portuguese. In M. Kato and E. Negrão (eds.), *Brazilian Portuguese and the Null Subject Parameter.* Frankfurt: Vervuert, pp. 55–74.

Duarte, I., G. Matos, and I. H. Faria (1995). Specificity of European Portuguese clitics in Romance. In I. H. Faria and M. J. Freitas (eds.), *Studies on the Acquisition of Portuguese.* Lisbon: APL/Edições Colibri, pp. 129–154.

Farrell, P. (1990). Null objects in Brazilian Portuguese. *Natural Language and Linguistic Theory,* 8, pp. 325–346.

Galves, C. and M. Abaurre (1996). Os clíticos no português brasileiro: elementos para uma abordagem sintático-fonológica. In A. Castilho et al. (eds.), *Gramática do Português Falado. Vol. IV.* Campinas: UNICAMP, pp. 267–312.

Galves, C., M. Moraes, and I. Ribeiro (2005). Syntax and morphology in the placement of clitics in European and Brazilian Portuguese. *Journal of Portuguese Linguistics,* 4, pp. 143–177.

Hinzelin, M.-O. (2010). L'interpolation dans les langues romanes: aspects diachroniques. In M. Iliescu, H. M. Siller-Runggaldier, and P. Danler (eds.), *Actes du XXVᵉ Congrès International de Linguistique et de Philologie Romanes. Innsbruck 2007. Tome II.* Berlin: Mouton de Gruyter, pp. 331–340.

Kaiser, G. and L. Alencar (forthcoming). Zwischen Aussprechen und Auslassen. Zur Verwendung der Subjektspronomina im brasilianischen Portugiesisch. In B. Meisnitzer and E. Pustka (eds.), *Zwischen Sprechen und Sprache.* Frankfurt: Peter Lang.

Kato, M. (1999). Strong and weak pronominals in the null subject parameter. *Probus,* 11, pp. 1–37.

Kayne, R. (1975). *French Syntax. The Transformational Cycle.* Cambridge, MA: MIT Press.

Luís, A. R. (2004). *Clitics as morphology.* Ph.D. dissertation, University of Essex.

Luís, A. R. (2009). Para uma (re)definição da sufixação no Português Europeu: a adjunção prosódica de enclíticos pronominais. *Biblos – Revista da Faculdade de Letras da Universidade de Coimbra,* 7, pp. 451–470.

Luís, A. R. (2012). Weak object pronouns in Brazilian Portuguese: An LFG analysis. In F. Perdigão, H. Caseli, A. Villavicencio, and A. Teixeira (eds.), *Computational Processing of the Portuguese Language.* Berlin: Springer-Verlag, pp. 139–145.

Luís, A. R. (2014). On clitic attachment in Ibero-Romance: Evidence from Portuguese and Spanish. In P. Amaral and A. Carvalho (eds.), *Portuguese–Spanish Interfaces.* Amsterdam: Benjamins, pp. 203–236.

Luís, A. R. and R. Otoguro (2011). Inflectional morphology and syntax in correspondence: Evidence from European Portuguese. In A. Galani, G. Hicks, and G. Tsoulas (eds.), *Morphology and Its Interfaces.* Amsterdam: Benjamins, pp. 187–225.

Martins, A. (1995). Clitic placement from Old to Modern European Portuguese. In H. Andersen (ed.), *Historical Linguistics 1993.* Amsterdam: Benjamins, pp. 295–307.

Mateus, M. H. and E. d'Andrade (2000). *The Phonology of Portuguese.* Oxford: Oxford University Press.

Nespor, M. and I. Vogel (2007). *Prosodic Phonology*. Berlin: Mouton de Gruyter.

Nunes, J. (1995). Ainda o famigerado SE. *Revista de documentação de estudos em lingüística teórica e aplicada*, 11, pp. 201–240.

Nunes, J. (2011). On the diachronic reanalysis of null subjects and null objects in Brazilian Portuguese. Triggers and consequences. In E. Rinke and T. Kupisch (eds.), *The Development of Grammar. Language Acquisition and Diachronic Change. In Honour of Jürgen M. Meisel*. Amsterdam: Benjamins, pp. 331–354.

Othero, G. (2013). Revisitando o *status* do pronome *cê* no português brasileiro. *Revista de Estudos da Linguagem*, 21, pp. 135–156.

Petersen, C. (2008). A tripartição pronominal e o estado das proformas *Cê, Ocê* e *Você*. *Revista de documentação de estudos em lingüística teórica e aplicada*, 24, pp. 283–308.

Ramos, J. (1997). O uso das formas *você, ocê* e *cê* no dialeto mineiro. In D. da Hora (ed.), *Diversidade lingüística no Brasil*. João Pessoa: Idéia, pp. 43–60.

Raposo, E. (1986). On the null object in European Portuguese. In O. Jaeggli and C. Silva-Corvalán (eds.), *Studies in Romance Linguistics*. Dordrecht: Foris, pp. 373–390.

Reich, U. (2001). Grammatikalisierungsprozesse im modernen brasilianischen Pronominalsystem. In B. Schäfer-Prieß, H. Klöden, and R. Kailuweit (eds.), *Grammatikalisierung in den iberoromanischen Sprachen*. Wilhelmsfeld: Egert, pp. 13–32.

Rooryck, J. (2000). Enclitic ordering in imperatives and infinitives. In J. Rooryck (ed.), *Configurations of Sentential Complementation. Perspectives from Romance Languages*. London: Routledge, pp. 115–143.

Spencer, A. and A. R. Luís (2005). Paradigm function account of "mesoclisis" in European Portuguese. In G. Booij and J. van Marle (eds.), *Yearbook of Morphology 2004*. Dordrecht: Kluwer, pp. 79–154.

Spencer, A. and A. R. Luís (2012). *Clitics*. Cambridge: Cambridge University Press.

Vieira, S. (2003). Colocação pronominal nas variedades europeia, brasileira e moçambicana: para a definição da natureza do clítico. In S. Brandão and M. Mota (eds.), *Análise contrastiva de variedades do Português*. Rio de Janeiro: In-Folio, pp. 37–60.

Vigário, M. (2003). *The Prosodic Word in European Portuguese*. Berlin: Mouton de Gruyter.

Vitral, L. (1996). A forma CÊ e a noção de gramaticalização. *Revista de Estudos da Linguagem* 5, pp. 115–124.

Wanner, D. (2001). From Latin to the Romance languages. In M. Haspelmath, E. König, W. Oesterreicher, and W. Raible (eds.), *Language Typology and Universals. An Internationales Handbook. Volume 2*. Berlin: Mouton de Gruyter, pp. 1691–1707.

Wetzels, L. (1992). Mid vowel neutralization in Brazilian Portuguese. *Cadernos de Estudos Lingüísticos*, 23, pp. 19–55.

Zwicky, A. M. and G. K. Pullum (1983). Cliticization vs. inflection: English *n't*. *Language*, 59, pp. 502–513.

13 The Null Subject Parameter and the Structure of the Sentence in European and Brazilian Portuguese

INÊS DUARTE AND MARIA CRISTINA FIGUEIREDO SILVA

1. Introduction

1.1. Empirical coverage

In this chapter, readers will find information concerning the licensing and interpretation of null subjects in finite clauses in European and in Brazilian Portuguese (henceforth, EP and BP respectively). Throughout the chapter, the empirical data to be accounted for come from the standard varieties spoken by educated Portuguese and Brazilian native speakers.

Due to the nature of this contribution, a couple of choices had to be made concerning the extension and the complexity of the empirical coverage. As a consequence, we decided to exclude from our account null subjects in non-finite clauses (infinitival—both uninflected and inflected—gerundive and participial ones). In what concerns finite clauses, we only considered declarative and *wh*– interrogative root clauses, thus excluding coordinate structures, as well as other clause types. Regarding embedded clauses, we just looked at complement, relative and adjunct clauses, leaving aside degree constructions.

1.2. The null subject parameter and the functional architecture of the clause

Following Roberts and Holmberg (2010), a.o., we assume that the properties subsumed under the so-called Null Subject Parameter (Perlmutter 1971, Rizzi 1982) lie in a series of options concerning the presence and the specification of uninterpretable features on probes—in particular, on T, in the case of EP and BP. The features at stake are φ-features, which are "rich" enough to allow for the absence of lexical subjects in consistent null subject languages like EP; however, in partial null subject languages like BP, φ-features on T are too impoverished to do so in general, barely licensing null subjects under rather restricted conditions. As we will argue below, the relevant difference concerns the Person feature on T.[1]

Two main approaches with respect to the effect of richness of the φ-features on T have been argued for in the last 40 years: (1) the one that goes back to Rizzi 1982 and Chomsky

The Handbook of Portuguese Linguistics, First Edition. Edited by W. Leo Wetzels, João Costa, and Sergio Menuzzi.
© 2016 John Wiley & Sons, Inc. Published 2020 by John Wiley & Sons, Inc.

1982, claiming that rich φ-features on T license an empty weak pronoun, *pro* (Rizzi 1986; Cardinaletti 1997, Holmberg 2005, Roberts 2010, a.o.); (2) the one with its origins in Borer 1986, arguing that rich φ-features on T act like a pronoun, hence they may bear θ-roles, check nominative Case and EPP, dispensing with the need of *pro* in *Spec*,TP (Barbosa 1995, Alexiadou and Anagnostopoulou 1998, Holmberg 2010, a.o.). Under the latter approach, preverbal subjects in consistent null subject languages are (clitic) left-dislocated.

However, empirical evidence against the claim that, in most EP unmarked declarative sentences, preverbal subjects have the behavior of other left-dislocated arguments has been provided by some authors (Costa and Duarte 2003, Costa and Galves 2002, Costa 2004). The relevant evidence concerns, namely, agreement facts, asymmetries related to minimality effects, contrasts between apparent hyper-raising contexts and regular SV clauses, reconstruction, the behavior of negative QPs, multiple fronting, C-less optative clauses. We will only recall the first three pieces of evidence presented in the literature referred to above.

As the contrast between (1b) and (2b) shows, number agreement with postverbal 3rd person subjects of unaccusative verbs is optional, whereas it is mandatory with preverbal subjects. This contrast is unexpected under the left-dislocated analysis of preverbal subjects.

(1) a. *Chegaram três pessoas.*
/arrived-3 pl three people/
   b. *Chegou três pessoas.*   (? EP; OK BP)
/arrived-3 sg three people/
"There arrived three people."

(2) a. *Três pessoas chegaram.*
/three people arrived-3 pl/
"Three people arrived."
   b. *Três pessoas chegou.*   (*EP, *BP)
/three people arrived-3 sg/

Asymmetries between preverbal subjects and other left-dislocated arguments with respect to minimality have been noticed by several authors (Duarte 1987, 1996, a.o.). As the paradigm in (3) shows, a preverbal subject may intervene between a *wh*-phrase and the verb; however, if the intervener is a (clitic) left-dislocated element, ungrammaticality arises. This contrast is straightforwardly accounted for if one assumes that only the latter occupies an A-bar position, yielding minimality effects, as expected.

(3) a. *Perguntei que livro o Pedro leu.*
/(I) asked which book the Pedro read/
"I asked which book Pedro read."
   b. *Perguntei que livro, à Maria, lhe deram.*
/(I) asked which book, to Maria, (they) her-dat gave/

Apparent cases of hyper-raising, as in (4), are constructions that involve clitic left-dislocation of the embedded subject, according to Barbosa (2000).

(4) a. *Os homens parece que viram um monstro.*
/the men seems that saw-3 pl a monster/
"The men, they seem to have seen a monster."
   b. *A bicicleta parece que está partida.*
/the bicycle seems that is broken-fem sg/
"The bicycle seems to be broken."

The fact that specific indefinites (see (5)) are ruled out of this construction, whereas both definite DPs (see (4)) and bare nouns (see (6)) are possible, corroborates the left-dislocation analysis proposed by Barbosa, since the latter qualify as left-dislocated topics, whereas the former do not.

(5) a. *Umas meninas parece que estão doentes.*
        /some girls seem-3 sg that are sick pl/
    b. *Apenas uma criança parece que ficou ferida.*
        /only one child seem-3 sg that was hurt-fem sg/

(6) a. *Perfumes franceses parece que se esgotaram.*
        /perfumes French seem-3 sg that cl-3 sold-out-3 pl/
        "French perfumes, they seem to be out of stock."
    b. *Cães raivosos parece que morderam uma criança.*
        /dogs enraged-3 pl seem-3 sg that bite-past-3 pl a child/
        "Dogs with rabies, it seems that they bit a child."

Now, if preverbal subjects in "regular" SV clauses were left-dislocated, we would expect the same type of effects to show up, that is, we would expect both definite DPs and bare nouns to be possible and specific indefinites to be ruled out. However, this prediction is not borne out: as (7) and (8) show, both definite DPs and specific indefinites give rise to grammatical sentences, whereas bare nouns yield ungrammatical ones.[2]

(7) a. *Os perfumes franceses esgotaram-se.*
        /the perfumes French sold-out-3 pl-cl-3/
        "The French perfumes sold out."
    b. *Uns perfumes franceses esgotaram-se.*
        /D-indef-pl perfumes French sold-out-3 pl-cl-3/
        "Some French perfumes sold out."
    c. *Perfumes franceses esgotaram-se.*
        /perfumes French sold-out-3 pl-cl-3/

(8) a. *As crianças ficaram feridas.*
        /the children are hurt-fem pl/
        "The children got hurt."
    b. *Umas crianças ficaram feridas.*
        /some children got hurt-fem pl/
        "Some children got hurt."
    c. *Apenas uma criança ficou ferida.*
        /only one child was hurt/
        "Only one child got hurt."
    d. *Criança ficou ferida.*
        /child got hurt/

Based on this kind of evidence, we conclude that in sentences like (2a), (3a), (7) and (8) the preverbal subject is in *Spec*, TP. Furthermore, the contrast between the (b) sentences of (1) and (2) strongly suggests that the rich φ-features on T do not behave like a pronoun, since the sensitivity of the number feature to the position of the subject DP would be difficult to account for under current minimalist assumptions. Instead, if both EP and BP have a strong EPP (or Edge) feature on T, the presence of an expletive *pro* in sentences with postverbal subjects follows. Thus, the contrast between the two agreement options shown in (1) could be attributed to the presence in the Numeration of an expletive *pro* with specified number features (like French "il" or English "it") in (1b) or of one without number specification (like English "there") in (1a).

Therefore, we will adopt the classic approach that takes rich φ-features on T not to behave like a pronoun, but instead to license an empty weak pronoun, *pro*.

2. Null Subjects: distribution and licensing

Let us start positing our working hypothesis. We will assume a version of Rizzi's 1986 insight which supposes that a null subject, to be grammatical in a given language, must be formally licensed and must also have its features identified.

Adopting the classification of Roberts and Holmberg (2010), it seems that consistent and partial null subject languages share the property of formally licensing its features (whatever the theoretical implementation of this idea might be).

Hence, the problem faced by partial null subject languages is the identification of the features of the null subject. Here, it is worth to remember the well-known Benveniste's generalization and notice that there is a crucial difference between 1st and 2nd person, on one hand, and 3rd person, on the other. The actual impact of this idea will become clear in a moment.

EP as well as BP display the number feature in the verbal paradigm—in other words, the difference between singular and plural is always marked. However, with respect to the person feature, these two varieties of Portuguese exhibit a very different behavior. EP clearly presents the three values of the person feature—1st, 2nd and 3rd—in its verbal paradigm, as shown in (9a) below, where it is possible to see the six different endings on the verb form (but see below). Adopting Galves' (2001:111) formulation of the problem, BP does not mark the semantic value of person, but just its syntactic value. This means that the opposition is not threefold in BP, but only twofold, allowing a representation simply as [+person] or [–person]. Observe in (9b) below how the different endings are distributed in the BP paradigm: the first persons have particular endings, but 2nd and 3rd persons systematically share the same morpheme, which is true also for other moods and tenses in the verbal paradigm:

(9) Verbal paradigm of a regular verb belonging to the first conjugation in the Indicative
    Present: *cantar* (to sing)

EP	BP	
a. *eu canto*	b. *eu canto*	(I sing)
tu cantas	*você canta*	(you sing)
ele canta	*ele canta*	(he sings)
nós cantamos	*nós cantamos*[3]	(we sing)
vós cantais	*vocês cantam*	(you sing)
eles cantam	*eles cantam*	(they sing)

Putting things in more theoretical terms, in BP, there is no person feature on T, which means that the three persons are identical concerning identification, and a pronominal form—like *eu, você, nós/a gente, vocês*—must co-occur with the verb form.

Hence, sentences in (10), which are perfect in EP, seldom occur with 1st and 2nd person pronominal subjects in BP corpora like NURC or VARSUL, even if the (educated) native speakers recognize the verb forms as 1st and 2nd person ones.

(10) a. *Compr-ei um bolo.*
   /bought-1st a cake/
   "I bought a cake."
   b. *Compr-aste um bolo.*
   /bought-2nd a cake/
   "You bought a cake."

In fact, M. E. Duarte (1993: 117) clearly shows that the occurrence of 1st and 2nd person null subjects in a *corpus* of plays declined very impressively during the nineteenth century and the beginnings of the twentieth century, being scarce in the second half of this century.

The same is true for main interrogative sentences: while in EP null subjects of 1st or 2nd person are perfect, as shown in (11), in BP their occurrence in *corpora* is almost nonexistent:

(11) *Onde   é que   compraste   o bolo?*[4]
   /where   is that   bought-2nd-sg   the cake?/
   "Where did you buy the cake?"

Let us now go back to the paradigm in (9a). In standard EP, speakers do no longer use the 2nd person plural form of the verb, although they understand it if they hear it.[5] Instead, they use the 3rd plural form, combined with the pronoun "vocês,"[6] as shown in (12):

(12) a. *Vocês   fizeram   uma   ótima   sopa.*
   /you-pl   made-3 pl   an   excellent   soup/
   "You cooked an excellent soup"
   b. *O que é que   vocês comeram?*
   /what is that   you-pl ate-3 pl/
   "What did you eat?"

It is also the case that the singular pronoun "você" alternates with "tu," the former being used as a polite form of address, whereas the latter is used when speaker and addressee know each other well and are engaged in an informal verbal interaction. Hence, in contemporary standard EP, the paradigm in (9a) must in fact be reformulated as in (13):

(13) *eu canto*   (I sing-1 sg)
   tu cantas   (you$_{sg}$ sing-2 sg : semantic 2nd person, syntactic 2nd person)
   você canta   (you$_{sg}$ sing-3 sg: semantic 2nd person, syntactic 3rd person)
   ele canta   (he sing-3 sg)
   nós cantamos   (we sing-1 pl)
   vocês cantam   (you$_{pl}$ sing-3 pl: semantic 2nd person, syntactic 3rd person)
   eles cantam   (they sing-3 pl)

As a consequence, out-of-the-blue declarative sentences with null subjects like the ones presented in (14) are systematically ambiguous:

(14) a. *Comeu a sopa toda.*
   a'. "You ate all the soup."
   a''. "He/She ate all the soup."
   b. *Comeram a sopa toda.*
   b'. "You ate all the soup."
   b''. "They ate all the soup."
   b'''. "People ate all the soup."[7]

Summarizing: in EP the Person feature on T is able to identify 1st and 2nd person forms with non-conflicting semantic and syntactic features, hence a pronominal form is not needed for this purpose; on the contrary, when there are conflicting features, the Person feature on T cannot identify the relevant feature of a null subject. In BP, the lack of a person feature on T forces the subject position to be filled with 1st and 2nd person pronouns.

Let us now focus on (semantic) 3rd person null subjects, a rather interesting topic of inquiry in EP and in BP, since in both varieties they surprisingly share the need of an accessible antecedent in order to be identified.

This accessible antecedent can be, in both languages, a DP in an A-bar position (a discourse topic) or a DP in an A-position, in which case the identification requirements are the same in BP and in EP.

Therefore, in out-of-the-blue declarative sentences, neither in EP nor in BP a null subject is possible; however, if there is a salient topic, as in question-answer pairs, the null subject becomes perfect in both languages:

(15) A: - *E o João$_i$?*   B: - *ec$_i$ viajou.*
          /and the João?/   /ec$_i$ travelled/
          "What about João?"   "He travelled"

The same facts are attested if the null subject is in an embedded sentence: in a question–answer pair, the discourse topic is the responsible for the identification of the null subject:

(16) a: - *E o João$_i$?*   b: - *A Maria disse que ec$_i$ viajou*
          /and the João?/   /the Maria said that ___ travelled/
          "What about João?"   "Maria said that he travelled"

In out-of-the-blue embedded contexts, the only possibility for a null embedded subject in BP is to take as antecedent a DP in A-position: this antecedent must be in an immediately higher sentence, it must c-command the null subject and split antecedents are not acceptable, as (17) shows—the examples were taken from Ferreira (2004)'s paper, but the same facts were noted by Moreira da Silva (1983) and Figueiredo Silva (1996):

(17) a. * *O João$_i$ disse que a Maria acha que ec$_i$ é esperto.*
           /the João said that the Maria finds that ___ is smart-masc./
      b. * *A mãe do João$_i$ acha que ec$_i$ é esperto.*
           /the mother of the João find that ___ is smart-masc./
      c. * *O João$_i$ disse que a Maria$_j$ acha que ec$_{i+j}$ são espertos:*
           /the João said that the Maria find that ___ are smart-masc.- pl./

Interestingly, the same judgments hold for (17) in EP, that is, the *ec* in embedded subject position cannot be co-referent with the co-indexed DPs in the higher clauses. But, crucially, and differently from BP, the *ec* can only be disjoint in reference from the closest higher subject if it refers to the hearer.

With respect to 3rd person definite subjects, very relevant differences between EP and BP appear when the fulfilling of the embedded subject position is concerned, whether the matrix subject is a referential or a quantified DP. These effects, known in generative literature respectively as "avoid pronoun" (see (18)) and "overt pronoun constraint" (see (19)), set apart EP from BP, as we see in the judgments given by Portuguese and Brazilian informants to (18) and (19) below:[8]

(18)   *O João disse que ele comprou o carro.*
       "João said that he bought a car."

       EP: * *o João$_i$/ele$_i$*
       BP: ✓ *o João$_i$/ele$_i$*

(19)   Cada professor *disse que a Maria acha que ele é inteligente.*
       "Each teacher said that Maria thinks that he is intelligent."

       EP: * *cada professor$_i$/ele$_i$*
       BP: ✓ *cada professor$_i$/ele$_i$*

The facts concerning *only* DPs and VP-ellipsis go in the same direction, with minor differences:

(20)   a.   *Só o João$_i$ acha que ele$_i$ vai ganhar a corrida*
            /only the João thinks that he will win the race/
            "Only João thinks that he will win the race."
       b.   *Só o João acha que ec vai ganhar a corrida*
            /only the João thinks that *ec* will win the race/
            "Only João thinks that he will win the race."

(21)   a.   *O João$_i$ acha que ele$_i$ vai ganhar a corrida e a Maria também.*
            /the João$_i$ thinks that he$_i$ will win the race and the Maria too/
            "João thinks that he will win the race and Maria does too."
       b.   *O João acha que ec vai ganhar a corrida e a Maria também.*
            /the João$_i$ thinks that *ec* will win the race and the Maria too/
            "João$_i$ thinks that he$_i$ will win the race and Maria does too."

In EP, only the b. sentences are possible with the co-reference reading and therefore they are ambiguous between the sloppy and the strict readings.

On the contrary, as observed by Ferreira (2004), BP accepts also the sentence in which the embedded subject position is filled by a lexical pronoun co-indexed with the matrix subject. Nevertheless, this sentence does not have the same interpretation as the sentence with an empty category in embedded subject position. In the case of *only*-sentences, the sentence with the co-indexed lexical pronoun (20a) has only the strict reading, meaning that João is the only person who believes in João's victory, which implies that the sentence is false when other people also believe in João's victory. On the contrary, the sentence with an empty category in subject position (20b) means that João is the only person who believes in his own victory, hence it will be false if there is another self-confident person.

The behavior of pseudo-stripping structures in PB is also different from the one observed for EP. Thus, (21a) is ambiguous between a strict and a sloppy reading, hence being interpreted as meaning that João thinks that he will win the race and that Maria also thinks that he, João, will win the race or as meaning that João thinks that he will win the race and that Maria thinks that she, Maria, will win the race. By contrast, (21b) has only the sloppy reading (i.e. João thinks that he will win the race and that Maria thinks that she, Maria, will win the race).[9]

The behavior of BP null subjects has also been examined inside (strong and weak) islands. It should be kept in mind that the percentage of such sentences in BP's *corpora* is very low, hence null subjects have little chance to show up. When we test data like those in (22)–(24), people are reluctant in their judgments, which suggests that the sentences are perfect but they are not part of the vernacular BP system—they seem to be part of the language learned at school. As expected, the sentences sound quite good in EP—(22) illustrates relative sentences, (23) exemplifies adjunct islands and (24) weak islands in Portuguese, like Complex NP complements and embedded interrogatives:

(22) a. *O João$_i$ gostou dos livros que ec$_i$ leu na escola.*
/the João$_i$ liked of+the books that ec$_i$ read at+the school/
"João$_i$ liked the books he$_i$ read at school."
    b. *O João$_i$ foi a um/num restaurante onde ec$_i$ comeu polvo*
/the João$_i$ went to a restaurant where ec$_i$ ate octopus/
"João$_i$ went to a restaurant where he$_i$ ate octopus."/
    c. *O João$_i$ disse que as meninas que ec$_i$ encontrou na rua eram estrangeiras.*
/the João$_i$ said that the girls that ec$_i$ met in the street were foreigners/
"João$_i$ said that the girls he$_i$ met in the street were foreigners."

(23) a. *O João comeu um pastel de carne quando ec$_i$ foi à/ na feira.*
/the João$_i$ ate a meat pie when ec$_i$ went to+the fair/
"João$_i$ ate a meat pie when he$_i$ went to the street market."
    b. *O João comprou o livro porque ec$_i$ ficou impressionado com o autor.*
/the João$_i$ bought the book because ec$_i$ remained impressed by the author/
"João$_i$ bought the book because he$_i$ was impressed by its author."
    c. *O João comprou o livro embora ec$_i$ tivesse pouco dinheiro*
/the João$_i$ bought the book although ec$_i$ had little money/
"João$_i$ bought the book although he$_i$ had little money."

(24) a. *A Maria negou o boato (de) que ec$_i$ recebeu dinheiro do Pedro.*
/the Maria$_i$ denied the rumor (of) that ec$_i$ received money from+the Pedro/
"Maria$_i$ denied the rumor that she$_i$ received money from Pedro."
    b. *O João não sabe que livro ec$_i$ leu na semana passada.*
/the João$_i$ not know what book ec$_i$ read at+the last week/
"João$_i$ does not know which book he$_i$ read last week."
    c. *O João não sabe a/pra quem ec$_i$ emprestou esse livro.*
/the João$_i$ not know to whom ec$_i$ lent this book/
"João$_i$ does not know to whom he$_i$ lent this book."

The discussion concerning ditransitive verbs with a DP/PP plus a sentential complement (like *autorizar* "authorize" or *proibir* "forbid") is beyond the scope of this chapter; they are control verbs in Portuguese and so we direct the reader to the chapter on control.[10]

Summarizing: the data above suggest that in what concerns 3rd person null subjects, both EP and BP behave alike with respect to their referential status: contrary to overt 3rd person pronouns, they must seek for an A- or A'- antecedent, or else, in EP, pick up the addressee as their referent.[11] However, they behave quite differently with respect to the "avoid pronoun" and the "overt pronoun constraint," EP forbidding co-reference between an embedded overt pronoun and the matrix subject, whereas BP allows it.

Let us now look at non-referential null subjects. It has long been observed that EP behaves like other Romance null subject languages: it resorts to null subjects to express non-specificity in both existential and generic sentences; as (25) shows, either a 3rd person plural *ec* is used or a clitic of the reflexive morphological paradigm, "se," co-occurs with a 3rd person singular verb form:

(25) a. *Dizem que o governo vai aumentar outra vez os impostos.*
          /say-3 pl that the government goes raise-inf again the taxes./
          "People say the government will raise taxes again."
      b. *Sabe-se há muito que a Terra é redonda.*
          /knows-cl-3 there-is much that the Earth is round/
          "Everyone knows for long that the Earth is round."

But in BP, while (25a) is quite natural, (25b) is scarce in the available corpora, due to the fact that clitic pronouns in general are undergoing a massive process of loss. Related to the progressive loss of sentences like (25b) in BP, the grammaticality of sentences like the ones in (26)—originally due to Galves (2001)—is considered by Holmberg (2010) a property of partial null subject languages:

(26) *Aqui vende sapato.*   (* EP; OK BP)
      /here sells shoe/
      "Shoes are sold here."

According to him, in (26), a null generic subject occurs in *Spec*, TP. However, an alternative analysis has been provided by Avelar (2009), Avelar and Galves (2011) and Munhoz and Naves (2012), who consider sentences like (26) cases of locative inversion structures, where the locative adverb fills the *Spec*,TP position. Raising of locatives and possessor phrases to subject position is a common property of the innovative sentential patterns of BP. Besides the locative inversion with an arbitrary subject in (26), Munhoz and Naves (2012) distinguish locative topic subject constructions and genitive topic subject constructions, illustrated in (27) and (28), respectively—these examples are originally due to Pontes (1987):

(27) *O carro furou o pneu.*
      /the car punctures the tyre/
      "The car's tyre punctured."

(28) *Essa casa bate sol.*
      /that house hits sun/
      "That house gets a lot of sun."

According to Naves, Pilati, and Salles (2014), whereas sentences like (26) are possible with transitive and unergative verbs, genitive topic subject constructions are typically restricted to monoargumental unaccusative verbs and locative topic subject constructions only occur with biargumental unaccusative predicates.

Sentences with raising of genitives to subject position, like (27), are not possible in EP. In fact, the corresponding grammatical sentence would involve raising of the whole DP "*o pneu do carro*" (the car's tyre) to subject position, as shown in (29).

(29) *O pneu do carro furou.*
      /the tyre of the car punctured/
      "The car's tyre punctured."

Similarly, a grammatical sentence of EP corresponding to (28) would involve fronting of the locative PP selected for by the verb, as shown in (30):

(30) *Nessa casa bate o sol.*
    /in+that house hits the sun/
    "In that house one gets a lot of sun."

In what concerns null subjects of weather and raising verbs, both varieties of Portuguese behave alike; as (31) shows, no expletive overt subjects are available in these contexts.[12]

(31) a.   *Choveu toda a noite.*
      /rained-3 sg all the night
      "It rained the whole night through."
    b.   *Parece que o professor vai chegar atrasado.*
      /seems that the teacher goes arrive-inf late-masc-sg/
      "It seems that the teacher will be late."

Summarizing: although both varieties of Portuguese behave as expected with respect to expletive subjects of weather and raising verbs, in what concerns non specific null subjects, it remains a matter of dispute to consider 3rd person singular verb forms preceded by locative adverbs as instances of generic null subjects. However, the high frequency of genitive and locative topic subject constructions in spontaneous speech suggests that, in BP, the locative adverb in sentences like (26) fills the *Spec*,TP position.

3. VS Order

The classical view of the Null Subject Parameter associated the property of null subjects with the possibility of free inversion, which means that null subject languages would also be languages with VS order as an option in the grammar. However, VS is not exactly free, in the sense that, even in consistent null subject languages, VS must meet certain conditions, both structural and pragmatic. In particular, discourse properties like information focus and contrast play a role in the appropriate use of VS.

First, it must be noticed that both in PE and in PB, the right dislocation of the subject is perfect, as shown by the examples in (32a) below, something impossible in languages like French or English; however, both varieties also accept (32b), with a lexical pronoun in subject position, associated to the right dislocated subject—a construction also known as "false inversion" (cf. Kato 1987):

(32) a.   *Comem muito chocolate, essas crianças.*
      /eat-3 pl much chocolate, these childen/
      "They eat a lot of chocolate, these children."
    b.   *Elas comem muito chocolate, essas crianças.*
      /they eat much chocolate, these children/
      "They eat a lot of chocolate, these children."

Sentences in (32) are adequate in a context in which "these children" is given information, presents the contour of a prosodic phrase and is typically deaccented.

Secondly, VS with unaccusative verbs is quite frequent in EP. With such verbs, the VS order encodes the meaning that the sentence expresses a thetic judgment, that is, that it is presentational or that the postverbal subject is the information focus.

(33) *Chegou o carteiro.*
    /arrived the postman/
    "The postman arrived."

In BP, VS with unaccusative verbs is restricted to presentational contexts. So, whereas in EP (33) is possible in the two contexts presented in (34), in BP it is only possible in the a. context:

(34) a. (*Eu sei o que se passou e vou contar-te.*) *Chegou o carteiro (e arranjou a campainha).*
          "(I know what happened and I am going to tell you) The postman arrived (and fixed the bell)."
      b. (*Quem chegou?*) *Chegou o carteiro.*
          "(Who arrived?) It was the postman."

In EP, VS is also possible with unergative verbs in presentational contexts or when the subject is information focus; but contrary to what happens with unaccusatives, this word order is typically restricted to indefinite subject DPs (see (35a)) or else to subject DPs which are "descriptive definite" (Pinto, 1997), that is, which denote a uniquely identifiable referent in a given discourse context (see (35b)):

(35) a. *Trabalham muitos operários naquela fábrica.*
          /work-3 pl many workers in that plant/
          "There work many workers in that plant."
      b. (*Quem telefonou?*) *Telefonou o João/o teu estudante italiano.*
          /(who phoned?) Phoned the João/the your Italian student/
          "(Who phoned?) It was João/your Italian student."

In BP, as already noted by Nascimento (1984), VS is still possible with unergative verbs in presentational contexts, where subjects are typically indefinite (see the a. examples of (34)–(35). In line with this author, Tarallo and Kato (1989) also observed that VS is still possible with some unergative verbs, provided the subject is indefinite. They illustrated this possibility with the sentences in (36):

(36) a. *Viajou um estranho comigo.* (Tarallo and Kato 1989: (26a))
          /travelled a stranger with.me/
          "A stranger travelled with me."
      b. *Telefonou um cliente.* (id: 26b)
          /phoned a customer/
          "A customer phoned."

However, VS is completely excluded when the subject is informational focus, hence the b. sentences of (34)–(35) above are felt as ill-formed by Brazilian speakers. In fact, it seems that for many Brazilian speakers the only perfectly grammatical VS sentences with unergative verbs are locative inversion structures, such as the one illustrated in (37)—the example is from Pilati (2006):

(37) *Ali dormem as crianças.*
      /there sleep-3 pl the children/
      "The children sleep there."

Getting back to EP, with transitive and ditransitive verbs, VS is restricted to contexts where the subject is information focus. If the complement is also new, as in answers to multiple *wh*-questions, the resulting word order will be VSO, as shown in (38a); if the complement is given information, the felicitous word order will be VOS, as illustrated in (38b):

(38) a. (*Quem testemunhou o quê?*) *Testemunhou esta senhora um rapto.*
/(who witnessed what?) witnessed this lady a kidnapping/
"(Who witnessed what?) THIS LADY witnessed A KIDNAPPING."

b. (*Quem testemunhou o rapto?*) *Testemunhou o rapto esta senhora.*
/(who witnessed the kidnapping? witnessed the kidnapping this lady/
"(Who witnessed the kidnapping?) It was this lady."

If the speaker chooses the answer in (38a), the clause has an exhaustive pair-list reading (see Costa 1998, 2004). So, the answer cannot be continued in either of the two following ways:

(39) a. **Testemunhou esta senhora um rapto, os outros não sei.*
/witnessed this lady a kidnapping, the others not know/
b. **Testemunhou esta senhora um rapto e este senhor também testemunhou.*
/witnessed this lady a kidnapping and this man also witnessed/

On the contrary, if the answer to the question in (38a) is a SVO clause, no exhaustivity is implied, and the answer can be felicitously continued, as shown in (40):

(40) (*Quem testemunhou o quê?*)
a. *Esta senhora testemunhou um rapto, os outros não sei.*
/this lady witnessed a kidnapping, the others not know/
"This lady witnessed a kidnapping, the others I do not know."
b. *Esta senhora testemunhou um rapto e este senhor também testemunhou.*
/this lady witnessed a kidnapping and this man also witnessed/
"This lady witnessed a kidnapping and this man did too."

Accepting the subject-in-situ generalization of Alexiadou and Agnastatopoulos (2001, 2007), in (38a) the subject was moved out of *v*P before Spell-Out, and so was the nominal object in (38b),[13] and speakers judge VSO and VOS as quite marked orders. So, although the answers in (38) are both grammatical and felicitous in EP, it should be stressed that, instead of full VSO or VOS clauses, speakers clearly prefer to produce fragment answers (see (41a, b)) or (pseudo)clefts (see (41c)):[14]

(41) a. (*Quem testemunhou o quê?*) *Esta senhora, um rapto.*
/(Who witnessed what?) This lady, a kidnapping/
b. (*Quem testemunhou o rapto?*) (*Testemunhou*) *Esta senhora.*
/(Who witnessed the kidnapping?(witnessed) This lady/
c. (*Quem testemunhou o rapto?*) *Quem testemunhou o rapto foi esta senhora.*
/(Who witnessed the kidnapping?) Who witnessed the kidnapping
was this lady/
"(Who witnessed the kidnapping?) Who witnessed the kidnapping
was this lady.

In contexts like the ones illustrated in (38), VSO and VOS are impossible in BP. However, Pilati (2006) observes that VOS is not completely excluded, in particular in sports reporting (see (42a)), although she also acknowledges that VOS sentences sound more natural when the subject is a heavy DP, as expected (see (42b)):

(42) a. ? *Aponta o centro do campo o árbitro.*
/point to the center of the field the referee/
"The referee points to the center of the field"
b. *Ganha o jogo quem completar o tabuleiro.*
/wins the game who complete the board/
"Who completes the board wins the game."

The different restrictions holding for EP and BP with respect to VS word orders have consequences for the way categorical and thetic judgments are expressed. In EP, as observed in Duarte (1987), the former are expressed through SV orders, whereas VS may express the latter. In what concerns BP, Britto (1998) suggests that categorical judgments are packaged in left dislocation structures (see (43)), while SV with the subject internal to TP expresses thetic judgments. In fact, SV in BP, much as in English, exhibits at least two different intonational patterns, one to express focalized subjects (an impossible interpretation for VS structures in BP) and another one to convey thetic judgments (see Figueiredo Silva and Seara 2009).

(43)   *A Maria, ela faz doce pra vender.*
        /the Maria, she makes sweets to sell/
        "As for Maria, she makes sweets to sell."

Costa, Duarte, and Silva (2006) suggest an alternative analysis for sentences like (43) in BP: they consider them instances of double subject constructions, and claim these have properties which distinguish them from Romance-like left dislocations. In particular, personal pronouns may double quantified NPs, something which is impossible in regular Romance left dislocations (see the contrast between (44a) and (44b)):

(44)   a.   *Toda criança ela aprende rápido a gostar de coca-cola.* (Costa, Duarte and Silva 2006:
            (1b))
            /each child she learns quickly to like of coca-cola/
            "Every child quickly learns to like coke."
        b.   *Tout enfant il aprend vite à aimer la coca-cola.

The authors argue that, in BP, the personal pronoun is the spelling of the person feature internal to the DP subject, a hypothesis in line with Galves' (1993) proposal that the person feature in T is devoid of semantic content in BP.

    Another context where VS occurs in EP is in Contrastive Focus Fronting structures, illustrated in example (45):

(45)   a.   *Estás cansada. Vai passar uns dias na praia.* (Costa and Martins 2011)
            /are-2 sg tired-fem sg. Go-2 sg spend some days on-the beach/
            "You are tired. Go and spend a few days on the beach."
        b.   *Isso queria eu.*
            /that would-like-1 sg I/
            "That is what I would like."

The fronted constituent in the B sentence of (45) is a demonstrative, D-linked with the propositional content of the preceding clause, which it resumes, and the sentence conveys a speaker's attitude that contrasts with the expectation the speaker assumes to be the state of the other participant in the discourse.[15] The fact that in Contrastive Focus Fronting structures VS is obligatory, combined with the fact that proclisis is also obligatory, strongly suggest that both the fronted D-linked constituent and the verb raise to some position in the left periphery.

    Finally, in EP, VS is also an option in root *wh*-interrogative clauses. In fact, the alternative to VS (see (46a)) is the innovative pattern dating from the eighteenth century, and consisting in the insertion of "*é que*" right-adjacent to the *wh*-constituent, as illustrated in (46b):

(46) a. *O que comeu o rapaz?*
     /the that ate the boy?/
     "What did the boy eat?"
   b. *O que é que o rapaz comeu?*
     /the that is that the boy ate?/
     "What did the boy eat?"

In VS root wh-interrogatives, V raises to C, as shown by Ambar (1992). In root *wh*-interrogatives like the one illustrated in (46b), the expression "*é que*," formed by the present of the verb "*ser*" (to be) and the complementizer "*que*," suffered a process of reanalysis which turned it into a single complex complementizer. This innovative pattern is expanding in EP.

According to Tarallo and Kato (1989) and many more after them, (46b) is the default pattern for *wh*-interrogatives in BP. Sentences with VS, in particular if long or cyclic *move* has taken place, are strongly rejected by native BP speakers, as illustrated in (47):[16]

(47) a. *O que perguntou o teu amigo onde encontraste?*   (✓EP; *BP)
     /what asked the your friend where found-2 sg/
     "What did your friend ask where you found?"
   b. O que disse o teu amigo que a mãe ofereceu aos meus tios?   (✓EP; *BP)
     /what said the your friend that the mother offered to+the my
        uncles?/
     "What did your friend say that his mother offered my uncles?"

The rejection of VS in root *wh*-interrogatives is expected under Ambar (1992)'s analysis of these sentences as involving V-to(-T-to)-C, a conservative property of Romance grammars already lost in BP.

Summarizing: VS has been historically associated with the null subject property, a hypothesis confirmed by the EP data presented above. However, even in a consistent null language like EP, VS is not free: in declarative sentences, it must meet some pragmatic conditions, and structural conditions such as monoargumentality affect the speakers' preference for its use. With respect to BP, we have seen that the distribution of VS is highly constrained. Brazilian speakers only consider VS natural in sentences with unaccusative verbs in presentational situations; in other contexts, VS is considered both a well formed structure and a felicitous one solely in cases of locative inversion. With transitive verbs, only in very special contexts, such as sports reporting is VOS available. Finally, VS in instances of Heavy NP Shift is found both in EP and in BP, an option not associated to null subject phenomenology, available also to English.

4. Concluding remarks

In this chapter we have surveyed a number of properties of EP and BP related to the structure of the clause and the null subject parameter, and also discussed a correlated property of null subject languages, namely what used to be called "free inversion."

Our work made use of a specific hypothesis about the null subject parameter, formulated in Roberts and Holmberg (2010). Following these authors, we have claimed that EP is a consistent null subject language, since it shows the cluster of properties Perlmutter (1971) and Rizzi (1982) associated with the Null Subject Parameter; these properties are summarized in (48).

(48) a. The possibility of a silent, referential, definite subject of finite clauses.
    b. "Free subject inversion."
    c. The apparent absence of complementiser-trace effects.
    d. Rich agreement inflection on finite verbs.

Roberts and Holmberg 2010: (22), 16

The properties listed in (48a, b and d) were abundantly illustrated in Sections 1 to 3 for EP. The sentence in (49) exemplifies the absence of complementizer-trace effects—the *wh*-constituent is extracted from the *Spec, vP* position, the verb raises to T and the complementizer *"que"* (that) is merged in the embedded C position, as usual in embedded clauses:

(49)   *Quem$_i$ é que ele disse que dormiu ec$_i$ na festa?*
    / who is that he said that slept in+the party?/
    "Who did he say slept in the party?"

As we observed in the preceding sections, the cluster of properties listed in (48) is not fully found in BP—in fact, only property (48c) is observed with no restrictions. The loss of verb morphology (see (9b) above)) probably entailed a "defective" person feature, with no semantic feature-value, as suggested by Galves (2001). Thus, free inversion is severely restricted and so is also the occurrence of referential null subjects.

    However, BP can not be considered a non-*pro* drop language like English or French, as the data presented so far show. Additional evidence for the significant difference between BP and these languages comes from the occurrence of referential null subjects in sequences of sentences, licensed by an accessible topic (see (50)):

(50)   "Holly (*nota Gabriel*): *O que é que o nosso anjo$_i$ tem hoje?*
                    /what is that our angel$_i$ has today?
                    "What is wrong with our angel$_i$ today?"
    Margareth: pro$_i$ Tá com essa cara desde que pro$_i$ chegou do ginásio. pro$_i$ Nem foi em casa almoçar.
        /*pro$_i$* Is with that face since that *pro$_i$* came from+the school. *pro$_i$* not+even went in
           house lunch.inf/
        "He is in this mood since he got back from school."
    Dona Irene: Com certeza pro$_i$ vai ficar novamente em segunda época. Desde que pro$_i$ chegou
        que pro$_i$ não pára de olhar a caderneta."
        /for sure *pro$_i$* will stay again in second period. Since that *pro$_i$* came that *pro$_i$* not
           stopped of look.inf at the school report booklet/
        "No doubt he will again be left behind for the second examination period. He has
           not stopped to look at his school report booklet since he got back."

M. E. Duarte 1993: (86), 118

So, most authors agree in considering BP a partial null subject language. In fact, in BP, one finds the set of properties Holmberg, Nayudy, and Sheehan (2009) claim to identify partial pro-drop languages. This set of properties is listed in (51) for root and in (52) for finite embedded clauses:

(51) a. Expletive null subjects (see (31))
    b. Generic null subjects (see (26))
    c. Subject–verb inversion in declarative sentences with unaccusative predicates (see
        (1) and (33))
    d. Impossibility of null referential subjects in root clauses (but see the discussion on
        example (15))

(52) a. Overt non-controlled "topic" subject pronouns (see (53) below)
      b. Null or overt controlled subjects (see (54), a partial repetition of (18))

(53) a. *Eu sei que você vai chegar atrasado.*
          /I know that you go arrive late/
          "I know you will be late."
      b. **Eu$_i$ sei que ec$_j$ vai chegar atrasado.*
          /I know that go-3 sg to arrive late/

(54) a. *João$_i$ disse que ele$_{i/j}$ comprou o carro.*
          /João said that he bought a car/
          "João said that he bought a car."
      b. *João$_i$ disse que ec$_i$ comprou um carro.*
          /João said that bought a car/

However, it is not completely clear whether the properties listed in (51) and (52) are defining ones, that is, whether every language must exhibit the whole set to deserve the label "partial null subject" language. The observation of BP suggests that this is not the case. In fact, as (50) and (15), repeated here as (55), show, null referential subjects in root clauses are possible in BP, provided an accessible topic identifies their content, which is a violation of the property in (51d):

(55) a. - *E o João$_i$?*   b. - *ec$_i$ viajou.*
          /and the João?/   /ec$_i$ travelled/
          "What about João?"   "He travelled"

So, it is possible that in the 'scale of liberality' of null subject language types proposed in Roberts and Holmberg (2010: (16), 12) reproduced in (56) below, (at least) the type "partial null subjects" identifies a continuum where one may find intermediate stages of 'partiality':

(56) expletive null subjects ⊃ partial null subjects ⊃ consistent null subjects ⊃ discourse pro-drop

NOTES

1 Following Chomsky (2000: 102), a.o., we adopt throughout a parsimonious functional architecture of the clause: namely, C (unselected or selected for by V) selecting for TP, T, selecting for *v*P, and *v* selecting for VP, the lexical category.
2 The grammaticality judgments of (7c) and (8d) concern declarative sentences and not titles, leads or other types of abbreviated speech.
3 Both in EP and in BP, a DP grammaticalized as a personal pronoun, "*a gente*," occurs in informal speech. This form, although semantically plural and always including the speaker in its denotation, determines verb agreement in 3rd person singular.
4 The most common strategy to form root *wh-*.interrogatives in contemporary EP is to insert the expression "*é que*" (is that) to the right of the fronted *wh*-phrase; this strategy avoids the cost of moving the verb to C, something considered a residue from V/2 (see Rizzi 1997). This is also a common strategy in BP, where either "*é que*" or just "*que*" occur right adjacent to the *wh*-phrase. So, the examples of *wh*-interrogatives given in this text are instances of this format.

5   This form is only productive in the northern dialects of EP.

6   *"Você"* and *"vocês"* originated in the polite form of address *"Vossa Mercê"* (Your Mercy), later grammaticalized as a personal pronoun. In popular dialects of EP an intermediate form in the grammaticalization path, *"vossemecê(s),"* is used instead of *"você(s)."*

7   A null subject co-occurring with a 3rd person plural verb form is one of the strategies available in EP and BP to express non-specific subjects in existential or generic sentences. See below.

8   Again, examples (18) and (19) were taken from Ferreira (2004)'s paper, but, as he himself noted, these facts have been remarked by other scholars, namely Moreira da Silva (1983), Viotti and Negrão (2000), Modesto (2000), a. o. The facts concerning specifically DP antecedents and the Avoid Pronoun Principle are presented by Duarte (1995).

9   Ferreira (2004) presents another context in which EP and BP would differ: raising constructions, or more precisely hyperraising constructions as (i) below, possible in BP but not in EP, according to him:

(1)   *As meninas parecem que compraram um carro novo*
      /The girls seem(3a. pl) that bought(3a. pl.) a new car/

We will leave this construction out of our discussion, because, as observed by Modesto (2009), it is not clear that the analysis of this type of sentence must necessarily take into account some particularity of the subject position (see Modesto 2009, and also Martins and Nunes 2005, Ferreira 2009). However, it should be noticed that hyper-raising is also attested in EP (Costa and Rooryck 1995, Costa 2011).

10   See Rodrigues 2004, Nunes 2008, Modesto 2010.

11   See Frascarelli (2007) for the idea that in a consistent null subject language a definite null subject seeks for an A-topic antecedent; see Holmberg (2010) for the idea that in this case alone the null subject pronoun is incorporated in T and the EPP is satisfied via incorporation.

12   See Carrilho (2005), who proposes that in some EP dialects an expletive *"ele"* (*he/it*) occurs in the left periphery of evaluative clauses.

13   Costa (2004) suggests that in VSO clauses like (38a) the subject remains in situ, contra the Subject-in-situ generalization, and that in VOS clauses like (38b) the object is scrambled.

14   Guerreiro (2004) conducted a production experiment with a sample of adult Portuguese speakers with a higher education degree. The subjects were told to produce appropriate answers to "simple" and multiple *wh*-questions asked about a given context. VS answers were produced only with monoargumental verbs. With two and three argument verbs, the subjects resorted to clefting or to fragment answers to produce felicitous wh-questions. These results suggest that the Restriction of Monoargumentality proposed in Tarallo and Kato (1989) as a grammar rule for BP is a preference rule in EP when both subject and object are DPs. These results and observations are in line with the results obtained by Abalada (2011) in a comprehension experiment involving a truth-value judgment task with pictures; 30 Portuguese adults were tested and only 54.03 percent correct answers were obtained in the VOS (Subject = information focus) condition.

15   Duarte (1997) called these structures D-linked presentations.

16   Grammatical counterparts of (47) in BP are (1) and (2) below, with *"é que"* right-adjacent to the higher *wh*-constituent and SV order in the root clause:

(1)   *O que é que o teu amigo perguntou onde o Pedro viu?*   (✓EP; ✓BP)
(2)   *O que é que o teu amigo disse que a mãe deu aos meus tios?*   (✓EP; ✓BP)

It is also the case that the grammaticalized *"é que"* constituent suffered further reduction in vernacular BP, and often occurs merely as *"que"* (that), the default finite complementizer. Hence, speakers of this variety produce sentences like *"O que que o rapaz comeu?"* instead of (46b).

REFERENCES

Abalada, S. (2011). Aquisição de Estruturas com Constituintes nas Periferias Esquerda e Direita da Frase em Português Europeu. Masters dissertation, Faculdade de Letras da Universidade de Lisboa.

Alexiadou, A. and E. Anagnostopoulou (1998). Parametrizing agr: word order, verb movement and EPP-checking. *Natural Language and Linguistic Theory*, 16 (3), pp. 491–539.

Alexiadou, A. and E. Anagnostopoulou (2001). The subject-in-situ generalization and the role of case in driving computations. *Linguistic Inquiry*, 36, pp. 193–231.

Alexiadou, A. and E. Anagnostopoulou (2007). The subject-in-situ generalization revisited. In U. Sauerland and H.-M. Gärtner (eds.), *Interfaces + Recursion = Language? Chomsky's Minimalism and the View from Syntax-Semantics*. Berlin: Mouton de Gruyter, pp. 31–60.

Ambar, M. (1992). *Para uma sintaxe da inversão sujeito-verbo em português*. Coleção Estudos Linguísticos. Lisbon: Edições Colibri.

Avelar, J. (2009). Inversão locativa e sintaxe de concordância no português brasileiro. *Matraga*, 16, pp. 232–252.

Avelar, J. and C. Galves (2011). Tópico e concordância em português brasileiro e português europeu. In A. Costa, I. Falé, and P. Barbosa (eds.), *Textos Seleccionados do XXVI Encontro Nacional da Associação Portuguesa de Linguística*. Porto: Associação Portuguesa de Linguística, pp. 49–65.

Barbosa, P. (1995). Null Subjects. Ph.D. dissertation, MIT.

Barbosa, P. (2000). Clitics: a window into the null subject property. In J. Costa (ed.), *Portuguese Syntax: Comparative Studies*. New York: Oxford University Press, pp. 31–93.

Benveniste, E. (1966). *Problèmes de linguistique générale I*. Paris: Gallimard.

Borer, H. (1986). *The Syntax of Pronominal Clitics*. Syntax and Semantics 19. Orlando: Academic Press.

Britto, H. (1998). Deslocamento à esquerda, Resumptivo-sujeito, Ordem SV e a Codificação Sintática de Juízos Categórico e Tético no Português do Brasil. Ph.D. dissertation, Unicamp.

Cardinaletti, A. (1997). Subjects and clause structure. In L. Haegemann (ed.), *The New Comparative Syntax*. London: Longman, pp. 33–63.

Carrilho, E. (2005). Expetive "ele" in European Portuguese dialects. Ph.D. dissertation, Universidade de Lisboa.

Chomsky, N. (1982). *Some Concepts and Consequences of the Theory of Government and Binding*. Cambridge, MA: MIT Press.

Chomsky, N. (2000). *New Horizons in the Study of Language and Mind*. Cambridge: Cambridge University Press.

Costa, J. (1998). *Word Order Variation. A Constraint-Based Approach*. The Hague: Holland Academic Graphics.

Costa, J. (2004). *Subject Positions and Interfaces. The Case of European Portuguese*. Berlin: Mouton de Gruyter.

Costa, J. (2011). Topic prominence is not a factor of variation between Brazilian and European Portuguese. In J. Berns, H. Jacobs, and T. Scheer (eds.), *Romance Languages and Linguistic Theory 2009*. Amsterdam: John Benjamins, pp. 71–88.

Costa, J. and I. Duarte (2003). Preverbal subjects in null subject languages are not necessarily dislocated. *Journal of Portuguese Linguistics*, 1 (2), pp. 159–175.

Costa, J., I. Duarte, and C. R. Silva (2006). Construçoes de redobro em português brasilero: sujetos tópicos vs soletração do traço pessoa. *Revista Leitura*, 33, 135–145.

Costa, J. and C. Galves (2002). External subjects in two varieties of Portuguese. In C. Beyssade, R. Bok-Bennema, F. Drijkoningen, and P. Monachesi (eds.), *Romance Languages and Linguistic Theory 2000: Selected papers from Going Romance 2000*. Amsterdam: John Benjamins, pp. 109–125.

Costa, J. and A. M. Martins (2011). "On focus movement in European Portuguese". *Probus*, 23(2), pp. 217–245.

Costa, J. and J. Rooryck (1995). On pseudo-raising in English and Portuguese. In L. Nash, G. Tsoulas, and A. Zribi-Hertz (eds.), *Proceedings of Langue et Grammaire 2, Paris VII, 1997*, pp. 48–58.

Duarte, I. (1987). A construção de topicalização na gramática do português: regência, ligação e condições sobre movimento. Ph.D. dissertation, University of Lisbon.

Duarte, I. (1997). Ordem de Palavras: Sintaxe e Estrutura Discursiva. In A. M. Brito, F. Oliveira, I. P. de Lima, and R. M. Martelo (eds.), *Sentido que a Vida Faz. Estudos para Óscar Lopes*. Porto: Campo das Letras, pp. 581–592.

Duarte, M. E. L. (1993). Do pronome nulo ao pronome pleno: a trajetória do sujeito no português do Brasil. In I. Roberts and M. Kato (eds.), *Português Brasileiro: Uma Viagem Diacrônica*. Campinas: Editora da Unicamp, pp. 107–128.

Duarte, M. E. L. (1995). A perda do princípio "Evite pronome" no português brasileiro. Ph.D. dissertation, Unicamp.

Ferreira, M. (2004). Hyperraising and null subjects in Brazilian Portuguese. In A. Castro, V. Hacquard, A. Salanova, and M. Ferreira (eds.), *Romance. Collected Papers on Romance Syntax*. Cambridge, MA: MIT Press, pp. 57–85.

Ferreira, M. (2009). Null subjects and finite control in Brazilian Portuguese. In J. Nunes (ed.), *Minimalist Essays on Brazilian Portuguese Syntax*. Amsterdam: John Benjamins, pp. 17–49.

Figueiredo Silva, M. C. (1996). *A Posição Sujeito no Português Brasileiro: Frases Finitas e Infinitivas*. Campinas: Editora da Unicamp.

Figueiredo Silva, M. C. and I. Seara (2009). Mais sobre a entoação de sentenças com a ordem SV. *Revista Letras (UFPR)*, 75/76, pp. 171–181.

Frascarelli, M. (2007). Subjects, topics and the interpretation of referential pro. An interface approach to the linking of (null) pronouns. *Natural Language and Linguistic Theory*, 25, pp. 691–734.

Galves, C. (1993). O enfraquecimento da concordância no português brasileiro. In I. Roberts and M. Kato (eds.), *Português Brasileiro: Uma Viagem Diacrônica*. Campinas: Editora da Unicamp, pp. 387–403.

Galves, C. (2001). *Ensaios Sobre as Gramáticas do Português*. Campinas: Editora da Unicamp.

Guerreiro, P. (2004). *Construções de inversão: Um Estudo de Comportamento Linguístico Provocado em Crianças e Adultos*. Masters dissertation, University of Lisbon.

Holmberg, A. (2005). Is there a little pro? Evidence from Finish. *Linguistic Inquiry*, 36, pp. 533–564.

Holmberg, A. (2010). Null subject parameters. In T. Biberauer, A. Holmberg, I. Roberts, and M. Sheehan (eds.), *Parametric Variation: Null Subjects in Minimalist Theory*. Cambridge: Cambridge University Press, pp. 88–124.

Holmberg, A., A. Nayudy, and M. Sheehan (2009). Three partial null-subject languages: a comparison of Brazilian Portuguese, Finnish and Marathi. *Studia Linguistica*, 63 (1), pp. 59–97.

Kato, M. A. (1987). Inversão da ordem SV em interrogativas no português: uma questão sintática ou estilística? *DELTA*, 3 (2), pp. 243–252.

Martins, A. M. and J. Nunes (2005). Raising issues in Brazilian and European Portuguese. *Journal of Portuguese Linguistics*, 4, pp. 53–77.

Modesto, M. (2000). Null subjects without "rich" agreement. In M. Kato and E. Negrão (eds.), *Brazilian Portuguese and the Null Subject Parameter*. Frankfurt: Vervuert-Iberoamerica, pp. 147–174.

Modesto, M. (2004). Sujeitos nulos em línguas de tópico proeminente. *Revista da Abralin*, 3, pp. 119–145.

Modesto, M. (2009). Null subjects in Brazilian Portuguese: a critique of two possible analysis. In M. A. Torres Morais and M. L. Andrade (eds.), *História do Português Paulista*, vol, 2. Campinas: IEL Publicações, pp. 99–123.

Modesto, M. (2010). What Brazilian Portuguese says about control: remarks on Boeckx & Hornstein. *Syntax*, 13 (1), pp. 78–96.

Moreira da Silva, S. (1983). Études sur l'asymétrie et l'asymétrie SUJET/OBJET dans le portugais du Brésil. Ph.D. dissertation, Université de Paris VIII.

Munhoz, A. T. and R. Naves (2012). Construções de tópico-sujeito: uma proposta em termos de estrutura argumental e de transferência de traços de C. *Signum: Estudos Linguísticos*, 15, pp. 245–265.

Nascimento, M. (1984). Sur la postposition du sujet dans le portugais du Brésil. Ph.D. dissertation, Université de Paris VIII.

Naves, R., E. Pilati, and H. Salles (2014). Consequences of the split of 3rd person morphology in the agreement system of Brazilian Portuguese. Poster presented at the CGG24 – Madrid, 2014.

Nunes, J. (2008). Inherent case as a licensing condition for A-movement: the case of hyper-raising constructions in Brazilian Portuguese. *Journal of Portuguese Linguistics*, 7(2), pp. 83–108.

Perlmutter, D. (1971). *Deep and Surface Structure Constraints in Syntax*. New York: Holt, Rinehart, & Winston.

Pilati, E. (2006) Aspectos sintáticos e semânticos da ordem verbo-sujeito no português. Ph.D. dissertation, University of Brasília.

Pinto, M. (1997). Licensing and interpretation of inverted subjects in Italian. Ph.D. dissertation, Utrecht University.

Pontes, E. (1987). *O tópico em português do Brasil*. Campinas: Pontes.

Rizzi, L. (1982). *Issues in Italian Syntax*. Dordrecht: Foris.

Rizzi, L. (1986). Null objects in Italian and the theory of pro. *Linguistic Inquiry*, 17 (3), pp. 501–557.

Rizzi, L. (1997). The fine structure of the left periphery. In L. Haegmann (ed.), *Elements of Grammar*. Dordrecht: Kluwer, pp. 281–387.

Roberts, I. (2010). A deletion analysis of null subjects. In T. Biberauer, A. Holmberg, I. Roberts, and M. Sheehan (eds.), *Parametric Variation: Null Subjects in Minimalist Theory*. Cambridge: Cambridge University Press, pp. 58–87.

Roberts, I. and A. Holmberg (2010). Introduction: parameters in minimalist theory. In T.

Biberauer, A. Holmberg, I. Roberts, and M. Sheehan (eds.), *Parametric Variation: Null Subjects in Minimalist Theory*. Cambridge: Cambridge University Press, pp. 1–57.

Rodrigues, C. (2004). Impoverished morphology and A-movement out of case domains. Ph.D. dissertation, University of Maryland.

Tarallo, F. and M. Kato (1989). *Harmonia trans-sistêmica: variação intra- e interlinguística. Preedição 5*. Campinas: Editora da Unicamp.

Viotti, E. and E. Negrão (2000). Brazilian Portuguese as a subject-oriented language. In M. Kato and E. Negrão (eds.), *Brazilian Portuguese and the Null Subject Parameter*. Frankfurt: Vervuert-Iberoamerica, pp. 105–125.

14 The Structure of DPs

ANA MARIA BRITO AND RUTH E. V. LOPES

1. Introduction

This chapter discusses several aspects of the syntax of European (EP) and Brazilian (BP) Portuguese noun phrases.[1] Noun Phrases (NP) are constructions headed by a noun and, according to the lexical nature of the noun, may contain arguments, *da cidade* "of the city," as in (1), and modifiers, as the adjective *recente* "recent," in (2):

(1) *o bombardeamento da cidade* [2]
    "the bombing of the city"

(2) *o recente bombardeamento da cidade*
    "the recent bombing of the city"

Entity/object nouns are often followed by Prepositional Phrases (PP) modifiers (3) and preceded by possessives (4):

(3) *a casa da Maria*
    the house of-the Maria
    "Maria's house"

(4) *a minha casa*
    the my house
    "my house"

NPs also co-occur with functional elements, which are their extended projections. For instance, in Portuguese and other Romance languages, NPs are usually preceded by determiners (see (1)–(4)), as well as other elements such as quantifiers, the reason why these determiner-preceded NPs are usually called Determiner Phrases (DP), a term we will employ from now on.

However, under certain conditions, Portuguese may exhibit bare nouns:

(5) *Vinho faz bem à saúde.*
    wine does good to-the health
    "Wine is good for one's health."

The Handbook of Portuguese Linguistics, First Edition. Edited by W. Leo Wetzels, João Costa, and Sergio Menuzzi.
© 2016 John Wiley & Sons, Inc. Published 2020 by John Wiley & Sons, Inc.

(6)   *Lulas vivem em média um ano.*
      squids live in average one year
      "Squids usually live for a year."

(5) and (6) illustrate the use of mass and plural bare nouns, but in BP even singular count nouns can be bare in argument positions, as in (7):

(7)   *Ontem eu comprei livro no shopping.* (*EP/OK BP)
      yesterday I bought book in-the shopping.
      "Yesterday I bought a book/books at the mall."

In terms of agreement, in EP agreement marks affect all the elements in the DP (8):

(8)   *todos*   *os*   *teus*   *amigos*
      all-masc pl   the-masc pl   your-masc pl   friends-masc pl
      "all your friends"

In spoken BP, on the other hand, number agreement may not be present in the nominal head (9) and other elements in the DP:

(9)   a.   *todos*   *os*   *teu(s)*   *amigo* (*EP, OK BP)
           all-masc pl   the-masc pl   your-masc pl   friend-masc
           "all your friends"
      b.   *O*   *teus*   *amigo* (*EP, OK BP)
           the-masc   your-masc pl   friend-masc

This chapter aims to discuss the syntax of these constructions, focusing on the specificity of Portuguese in both variants, EP and BP. It starts examining the argument structure of nouns, mainly those that are deverbal nominalizations (Section 2); PP modifiers and possessives with entity/object nouns will be presented in Section 3. Section 4 examines adjectives, their subclasses and positions. In Section 5, agreement relations and bare nouns will be analyzed from a syntactic point of view.

2. Deverbal nominalizations and the argument structure of nouns

Certain nouns are derived from verbs and, in most cases, inherit a similar argument structure from their verbal counterpart. Depending on the lexical nature of the head noun, some PPs will be arguments of the noun, while others will be modifiers.[3] In (10), the PP *da cidade* "of the town" is an argument of the noun, but *em 2012* "in 2012" is a modifier:[4]

(10)   *O bombardeamento da cidade em 2012 foi terrível.*
       "The bombing of the city in 2012 was terrible."

Besides the equivalent argument structure, deverbal nouns generally inherit the aspectual properties (representing states, activities, accomplishments or achievements) from the corresponding verbs:

(11)   *a corrida dos atletas* (activity)
       the run of the athletes
       "the athletes' jogging"

(12) *o temor de trovoadas de certas pessoas* (state)
      "the fear of thunder storms of certain people"

(13) *o bombardeamento da cidade pelo exército inimigo* (accomplishment)
      "the bombing of the city by the enemy army"

(14) *a chegada dos desportistas ao estádio* (achievement)
      "the arrival of the sportsmen at the stadium"

As the examples show, nominal arguments are never DPs in Portuguese, because nouns are not direct case assigners and therefore prepositions must be introduced as case assigners: *de* "of," *a* "to," *por* "by," *para* "for," "to," and others.

Deverbal nominalizations, especially those that are derived from accomplishment verbs, are ambiguous between, at least, an event and a result reading:

(15) *A tradução do livro (por/por parte de Graça Moura) levou dois anos.* (event)
      "The translation of the book (by Graça Moura) took two years."

(16) *A tradução (do livro) (do Graça Moura) foi publicada recentemente.* (result)
      "Graça Moura's translation (of the book) has been published recently."

(15) is an example of a "passive nominalization" (Picallo 1991), characterized by the following properties: (1) having an event reading; (2) the PP *do livro* "of the book" being interpreted as the theme; and (3) the agent, if present, being introduced by the preposition *por* "by" or *por parte de* (lit. "on the part of"). (16), on the other hand, presents a result reading, and the theme does not need to be present.

Noticing these characteristics, Grimshaw (1990: 49–54) related aspectual properties to the argument structure of a predicate: whereas process/event nouns take internal arguments (as in (15)), result nouns are like object/entity nouns and do not select arguments, as in (16). And since process/event nouns refer to situations, they are typically singular and determined by the definite article.

However, work on nominalizations in several languages has shown that Grimshaw's proposal may be too strong (Picallo 1991, Brito and Oliveira 1997, Sleeman and Brito 2010), leading to different generalizations:

(i)   Process/event nominals not always take internal arguments (17) and result nominals can optionally select one (18):

      (17) *A discussão durou duas horas.*
            "The discussion lasted two hours."

      (18) *A discussão dos dados veio publicada na revista.*
            "The discussion of the data was published in the journal."

(ii) Event nouns can pluralize in certain circumstances:

      (19) *Os representantes da ONU assistiram a vários ataques de cidades.*
            "The UN representatives watched several attacks on the towns."

(iii) Under certain conditions, the noun may be preceded by an indefinite (20) or a demonstrative determiner (21):

      (20) *Durante um ataque à cidade, muitas pessoas foram feridas.*
            "During an attack to the city, many people were injured."

(21) *Durante aquele ataque à cidade, muitas pessoas foram feridas.*
"During that attack to the city, many people were injured."

Until now we have seen PPs as complements or modifiers of deverbal nouns. But relational adjectives can also belong to the argument structure of these nouns (Bosque and Picallo 1996). Working on Spanish, these two authors showed that relational adjectives are of two types: thematic adjectives, which correspond to true arguments of the nouns, as in (22), and classifying adjectives, which are not true arguments in a strict sense, because they represent some type of external property of the entity denoted by the noun and are closer to adjuncts/modifiers, as in (23):

(22) *pesca bacolhoeira*
        fishing codfish-adj
        "codfish fishing"

(23) *parque jurássico*
        "Jurassic Park"

The interpretation of relational adjectives depends on the lexical nature of the adjective, the relation with the noun, and the coexistence of other relational adjectives. An isolated thematic adjective (expressing, for instance, nationality) with a nominal derived from an accomplishment verb, generally a transitive verb, is preferentially interpreted as the agent (24):

(24) *O bombardeamento sírio da cidade durou 24 horas.*
        "The Syrian bombing of the city lasted 24 hours."

A relational adjective may also express a theme argument, as in (25a, c), combined or not with another relational adjective acting as the agent (25b, c) (Miguel 2004):

(25) a. *a pesca bacalhoeira*
            "the codfish fishing"
        b. *a pesca portuguesa*
            "the Portuguese fishing"
        c. *a pesca bacalhoeira portuguesa*
            "the Portuguese codfish fishing"

If thematic adjectives basically occupy argument positions (internal, if they are themes, and external, if they are agents) how to explain the systematic postnominal position of these adjectives in Romance languages? Suppose that the (simplified) underlying structures of (25a, b, c) are the ones described in (26):

(26) a. $[_{DP} a [..... [_{NP} [_{N'} [_{N} pesca [bacalhoeira]]]]]]$
        b. $[_{DP} a [..... [_{NP} portuguesa [_{N'} [_{N} pesca]]]]]$
        c. $[_{DP} a [..... [_{NP} portuguesa [_{N'} [_{N} pesca [bacalhoeira]]]]]]$

In (25a) the thematic adjective stays in situ. In (25b) the final order N + relational ADJ may be explained by an N movement to a nominal functional category, XP, to be suggested below (Crisma 1993, Cinque 1994, Brito 1996).

What about (25c), where the sequence *pesca bacolhoeira* precedes the nationality adjective? How to explain that the head noun and its theme precede the nationality adjective that projects in spec of NP? One may consider that *pesca bacalhoeira* as a constituent, N', forms a compact unity and raises as a whole, deriving the appropriate linear word order observed in (25c). The movement of N' is justified by the fact that one cannot introduce any constituent between the N and the relational adjective.[5] Besides, as we will see in Section 4, the co-occurrence of relational adjectives with qualifying and evaluative adjectives confirms the view that not only N but also a phrasal constituent, such as N', moves in Romance languages.

The position of relational adjectives may therefore justify an analysis where the DP contains another functional element in between D and N. But what is the nature of this intermediate functional category?

Nouns may refer to one or more than one entity, therefore they have to be interpreted in terms of number; however, number is not an intrinsic part of a noun. Thus, assuming a number projection (NumP) as a functional category within the nominal domain seems to follow naturally, as proposed by Ritter (1991) for Hebrew, closely followed by Picallo (1991) and Bernstein (1993) for Romance languages.[6]

Sometimes the argument positions of event nominals may also be occupied by possessives, as internal or external arguments seen in (27) and (28):

(27)   *A cidade era linda; o seu bombardeamento foi um desastre!*
        "The city was beautiful; its bombing was a disaster."

(28)   *Quanto ao exército, o seu bombardeamento da cidade foi indesculpável.*
        "As for the army, its bombing of the city was unforgivable."

In (27), the possessive *seu* corresponds to the internal argument; in (28) *seu* corresponds to the external argument. In order to account for the possessive + N linear order in (27) it is assumed that the possessive has to move to a higher position. We will see in the next section that the syntax of DPs containing entity/object nouns and possessive determiners will help to determine their position.

3. Entity/object nouns, PP modifiers and possessive constructions

PPs that follow count nouns denoting entities are modifiers and occupy adjunct positions (Miguel 2004). They may be introduced by the preposition *de* "of" or other prepositions such as *para* "to"/"for," *com* "with," *a* "to"/"for," *entre* "between"/"among," *sem* "without," *sobre* "about"/"on," *sob* "under," *em* "in"/"on":

(29)   a.   *a casa da Maria*
            the house of-the Maria
            "Maria's house"
       b.   *o braço da Maria*
            the arm of-the Maria
            "Maria's arm"

(30)   a.   *um tecido para casaco*
            "a fabric for coats"
       b.   *uma criança com tranças*
            "a girl with braids"

As a form of expressing possession, entity/object nouns may be modified by possessive determiners:[7]

(31) *a/esta sua casa*
      the/this his/her house
      "his/her house"

Portuguese has two positions for these constituents: the prenominal one, mainly preceded by definite articles and demonstratives (31), and a postnominal position, usually with indefinites, interrogatives, and numerals (32) (Miguel 2004, Castro 2006, Brito 2007):[8]

(32) a. *uma casa sua*
          a house your
          "a house of yours"
      b. *três casas suas*
          three houses your
          "three houses of yours"
      c. *algumas casas suas*
          some houses his/her/them
          "some houses of him/hers/them"
      d. *Quantas casas suas ele conhece?*
          how-many houses his/her/their he knows
          "How many houses of him/hers/them does he know?"

The examples in (31) and (32) seem to justify two different positions for the possessives, constrained by definiteness. However, some questions remain: are possessives heads or phrasal? Is their nature the same in EP and BP? And what are their positions?

BP differs from EP in that respect, due to the fact that isolated possessives, not preceded by definite articles, are the most common option:

(33) *Nosso   final   de   semana   foi maravilhoso.*
      Our   end   of   week   was amazing.
      "Our weekend was amazing."

(34) *Dependemos   dos   automóveis   para realizar   nossas   atividades   cotidianas.*
      Depend-1pl   of-the   automobiles   to do   our   activities   daily
      "We depend on our cars to run our daily errands."

Giorgi and Longobardi (1991) proposed that in certain Romance languages, in particular Italian, possessives are adjectives, projected between D and N, differently from other languages where (prenominal) possessives are determiners (French, English, Spanish); but they never discuss the nature of the possessive form itself. Cardinaletti's (1998) work on Italian brought a new light on this matter. Despite the similar forms (*mia casa/una casa mia*), Cardinaletti shows that pre- and postnominal possessives behave differently in terms of focalization, coordination, modification by some adverbs, and human/non-human interpretation, taking her to propose a distinction between weak possessives (prenominal forms) and strong ones (postnominal forms). Castro and Costa (2003) adopted this distinction for Portuguese, proposing that the weak forms are heads while the strong ones display a phrasal nature.

Let us concentrate first on prenominal possessives in order to try to understand not only their category status but also their exact position in the DP.

In definite contexts, coordination of prenominal possessives is possible if the second member of the coordination is focalized (Castro and Costa 2003):

(35) ? *O meu e TEU artigo está aqui.*
      the my and YOUR paper is here
      "My paper and YOUR paper is here." (meaning there is one single paper)

Prenominal possessives may also be focalized in definite contexts:

(36) a. *O meu livro está esgotado.*
          the my book is out of print
          "My book is out of print."
      b. *O MEU livro está esgotado*
          the MY book is out of print
          "My book is out of print."
      c. *O MEU livro é que está esgotado.*
          the MY book is that is out of print
          "It is my book that is out of print."

This may show that prenominal possessives in Portuguese are not heads but some type of phrasal constituent. As for their position, they occupy a functional category between D and NumP. We will assume that Romance languages and Portuguese in particular have an AgrP in DP, where Agr is a high position for an N having person features at least; therefore the Spec of AgrP hosts prenominal possessives.[9]

Thus, *o meu livro* has the structure in (37):

(37) $[_{DP} \, o \, [_{AgrP} \, meu \, [_{Agr} \, livro_i \, [_{NUMP} \, t_i \, [_{NP} \, [_{N'} \, [_N \, t_i]]]]]]]$

Let us consider now possessives in indefinite contexts. We have already shown that in Portuguese it is usually the case that a postnominal possessive will be used when an indefinite article/numeral/interrogative is present; however, some speakers seem to accept prenominal possessives in such contexts as well, as in (38):

(38) *Uma minha amiga contou-me que vai haver mais um casamento…*
      a my friend told me that there will be another marriage
      "A friend of mine told me that there will be another marriage…"

These data favor the idea that Portuguese has at least two grammars for possessives, one more conservative, that accepts prenominal possessives with indefinites, and another one, more innovative, that only accepts prenominal possessives with definite determiners.

Focus on the prenominal possessive is an option in the grammar that accepts prenominal possessives with indefinites:

(39) *Uns MEUS amigos, não TEUS, vieram visitar-me.*
      some MY friends, not YOUR, came to visit me
      "My friends came to visit me, not yours."

In such a grammar, prenominal possessives are certainly not heads and may be focalized for being XPs, placed in Spec of AgrP.

In standard BP, possessives can be used without a determiner (see 33) and, thus, possessives could be taken to occupy a D position; but their co-occurance with a definite determiner is also possible, suggesting that their position may be similar to the one proposed for pre-nominal possessives in EP, albeit with a null determiner.

Let us now briefly discuss the position of postnominal possessives, as in (40):

(40) *um livro meu*
    a book my
    "a book of mine"

Their phrasal nature is uncontroversial (Castro and Costa 2003, Miguel 2004, Brito 2007). We will follow here a suggestion from Parodi (1994), for Spanish, according to whom the so-called "postnominal possessive" is in fact projected in an intermediate position, called PossP, above NumP but below AgrP, and the final linear order is derived from N moving to Spec of AgrP:[10, 11]

(41) $[_{DP}$ *um* $[_{AgrP}$ *livro*$_i$ $[_{PossP}$ *meu* $[_{NUMP}$ t$_i$ $[_{NP}$ $[_{N'}$ $[_N$ t$_i$]]]]]]]

Summing up, DPs have a lexical layer, formed by the N head and its argument structure, when it exists. Besides PPs, the argument structure of certain nouns may be expressed by relational adjectives and even by possessives. With the majority of entity/object nouns, PPs are modifiers, with many different interpretations. The syntax of pre-nominal possessives and of relational adjectives, in particular the agentive ones, justified the proposal of two functional categories, AgrP and NumP. Moreover, in order to justify the occurrence of postnominal possessives it was necessary to propose another functional category, above NumP but lower than AgrP. As we will see in Section 5, the functional layers of the DP in Portuguese are still a matter of controversy, mainly due to BP data.

4. Adjectives: classes and positions

Modification in nominal expressions may also be made through adjectives, as seen in the previous sections. Their position and nature depends on the different semantic classes to which they belong.

Qualifying adjectives (sometimes called "descriptive adjectives") express simple properties of entities, related to dimension, form, color, psychological or physical states (*pequeno* "small/short," *alto* "tall/high," *branco* "white," *quente* "hot," etc.); some authors distinguish them from evaluative adjectives (*carro fantástico* lit: car great, "great car"; *menina linda* lit: girl pretty, "pretty girl") because the latter denote subjective properties of entities (Brito and Raposo 2013: 1085–86).

Qualifying adjectives are gradable and they generally occupy the postnominal position:

(42) *as torres altas de Lisboa/* *as altas torres de Lisboa*
    the tower high of Lisbon/the high towers of Lisbon
    "the high towers of Lisbon"

As for evaluative adjectives, they may occupy pre- and postnominal positions; when affecting plural nouns and in postnominal position they may be ambiguous between a restrictive and a non-restrictive interpretation (see the readings (i) and (ii) in (43a)), while in prenominal position they are interpreted as non-restrictive (cf. (43b)):

(43) a. *os carros fantásticos do Pedro*
          the cars great of Pedro
          "Pedro's great cars"
          (i) some of Pedro's cars are great
          (ii) all Pedro's cars are great
      b. *os fantásticos carros do Pedro*
          the great cars of Pedro
          "Pedro's great cars"

When a qualifying adjective co-occurs with an evaluative one in postnominal position, the evaluative adjective usually occurs after the qualifying one:

(44) a. *uma casa baixa magnífica*
          a house small nice
          "a nice small house"
      b. *um vestido comprido lindo*
          a dress long gorgeous
          "a gorgeous long dress"

Because some qualifying adjectives may occupy both positions in the DP, they are associated with different interpretations. The postnominal position is related to their objective or denotative meaning (*uma mulher pobre* lit. a woman poor "a poor woman" = without resources); the prenominal position is related to a subjective, connotative or metaphorical meaning (*uma pobre mulher* lit. "a poor woman" = unlucky).

Other adjectives with similar behavior are: *velho* "old" (*um amigo velho* lit. a friend old = "a friend of a certain age"; *um velho amigo* "an old friend"); *rico* "rich" (*uma pessoa rica* lit. a person rich = "a rich person"; *uma rica pessoa* lit. a rich person = "a kind person"); *grande* "big" (*um homem grande* lit. a man big = "a tall or bulky person"; *um grande homem* lit. a big man = "a great person").

Being gradable, both qualifying and evaluative adjectives are phrasal, allowing degree adverbs to project (see (45a, b); the so called "lexical superlatives" like *fantástico, magnífico, maravilhoso,* and so forth (Brito and Raposo 2013: 1092) co-occur with difficulty with adverb modification in EP (45c), although they are accepted in BP (45d):

(45) a. *uma torre   muito alta*
          a tower   very high
          "a very high tower"
      b. *uma menina   muito linda*
          a child   very pretty
          "a very pretty child"
      c. ? *um carro   muito fantástico*
          a car very fantastic
          "a very fantastic car"
      d. *um   vestido   muito/super maravilhoso*
          a   dress   very/super gorgeous
          "a really gorgeous dress"

A different situation occurs with other classes of adjectives. Relational adjectives are non-gradable and are probably not phrasal. We have already seen that in Romance languages they always occupy the postnominal position. As some qualifying adjectives may occupy the two positions in the DP, when combined with a relational adjective the following orders may obtain: N ADJ ADJ (N + relational ADJ + qualifying ADJ) or ADJ N ADJ (qualifying ADJ + N + relational ADJ), as seen in the following examples:

(46) a. *uma produção   pesqueira   intensa/uma intensa produção pesqueira*
         a production   fishing   intense/an intense production fishing
         "an intense fishing production"
     b. *uma ordem   religiosa extinta/uma extinta   ordem religiosa*
         an order   religious extinct/an extinct   order religious
         "an extinct religious order"

There are also intensional adjectives (*principal* "main," *mero* "mere," *pleno* "absolute/full/high," *certo* "certain," *simples* "simple") and negative and conjectural adjectives (*falso* "false/untrue," *presumível* "probable/presumed," *alegado* "alleged") (Demonte (1999: 139–41) which are non-gradable, being most probably heads and always occupying a prenominal position:

(47) a. *um mero incidente/* um incidente mero*
         a mere incident/an incident mere
         "a mere incident"
     b. *o presumível ladrão/* o ladrão presumível*
         the presumed thief/the thief presumed
         "the presumed thief"

Other terms behave differently in pre and postnominal position: *outros* "other," *diversos* "several," *certos* "certain," *raros* "rare," *próprio* "real/appropriate," *qualquer* "any," *único* "only/unique." In prenominal position they are quantifiers, determiner-like, and it will be assumed here, for simplicity's sake, that they are projected as specifiers of NumP (48), whereas in postnominal position they are qualifying gradable adjectives (49):

(48) a. *Eu encontrei diversos livros.*
         "I found several books."
     b. *Só raras pessoas fazem isso.*
         "Only a few people do that."
(49) a. *Eu encontrei livros (muito) diversos.*
         I found books (very) different
         "I found quite different books."
     b. *Só pessoas (muito) raras fazem isso.*
         only people (very) rare do that
         "Only extraordinary people do that."

Due to the existence of such different classes of adjectives, it is possible to have several of them in the DP, as we have already seen above and as (50) illustrates:

(50) *uma   bela   pequena   redonda   maçã   vermelha   portuguesa*
      a   nice   small   round   apple   red   Portuguese
      "a nice round small Portuguese red apple"

Their order is not accidental and follows a hierarchy (Cinque 1994):

(51) quality > size > shape > color > origin/nationality

Deverbal nouns, as event or result nouns, examined in Section 2, are often modified by modal adjectives (*possível* "possible," *provável* "probable") and temporal–aspectual adjectives (*recente* "recent," *súbito* "sudden"), which may occupy pre- and postnominal positions in the DP:

(52) a. *uma possível descoberta/uma descoberta possível*
          a possible discovery/a discovery possible
          "a possible discovery"
      b. *o recente bombardeamento/o bombardeamento recente*
          the recent bombing/the bombing recent
          "the recent bombing"

Different classes of adjectives can also be combined (53):

(53) *vários devastadores recentes ataques inimigos*
      several devastating recent attacks enemy
      "several recent devastating enemy attacks"

For event nouns the order of adjectives is the following (Cinque 1994):

(54) subject oriented > time > manner > agentive/theme

After looking at these different possibilities of adjective placement inside a DP, many questions remain. Apart from thematic adjectives, considered here as arguments, the other classes were treated as modifiers, adjuncts to the DP, some of them projected in high, some in low positions. But if there are hierarchies among them, their combination constraints are to be explained. Cinque (1994) proposed that there are several functional categories in the DP, either above or below AgrP and NumP, housing specific adjectives in their spec positions. N movement would be the operation that results in the correct linear order.

Adjectives are also not homogeneous with respect to their head or phrasal nature: gradable adjectives are heads, modified by degree expressions; relational adjectives, both classificatory and thematic, seem to be maximal projections and do not admit degree expressions at their left. Some adjectives have different readings in pre- or postnominal position and there are restrictions on their combinations. Such scenario suggests that there is not a unified analysis for adjectives, even if only qualifying and evaluative adjectives are considered.

In order to capture this heterogeneity, and reviewing his old analysis, Cinque (2010) suggests that adjectives are projected in spec of functional categories but have a different origin: Some are direct modifiers (relational and qualifying) and are projected as spec of functional categories, according to an hierarchy; others, those that are always postnominal in Romance and have a predicative nature, are the result of the reduction of a relative clause and are projected in a high position; (55) represents the general structure proposed by the author:

(55) $[_{DP}... [_{FP_i}$ reduced relative $F^0 ... [_{FP_j}$ ADJP (mod.) $F^0 [_{FP_k}$ ADJP (mod.) $F^0 [_{NP}]]]]]$

A combination of an evaluative adjective with a relational one, as in (56), illustrates the proposal:

(56) *a pesca bacalhoeira corajosa*
    the fishing cod-adj courageous
    "the courageous cod-fishing"

In (56), the adjective *corajosa* is ambiguous between a restrictive and a non-restrictive interpretation. In the non-restrictive reading it is a modifier and is projected in a low-spec position of a functional category above NP; the movement of the phrasal constituent *pesca bacolheira* would originate in a structure like (57a); in the restrictive reading (one would be talking about the cod fishing that was courageous and only about that one), the adjective has a reduced relative origin, projected in a high position (57b):

(57) a. $[_{DP}$ a [..... [*pesca bacalhoeira* $]_i$ $[_{FPj}$ *corajosa* $t_i]]]]$
    b. $[_{DP}$ a [..... [*pesca bacalhoeira* $]_i$ $[_{FPi \text{ (reduced relative)}}$ *corajosa* F^0 $t_i]]]]$

So far, we have suggested that number morphology may be one of the triggers for N movement in Portuguese. As we will see below, number morphology is, under certain conditions, variable in BP; nevertheless, the position of adnominal adjectives is the same in both varieties. Thus the relationship between NumP and word order inside the DP may be subtler than expected.

5. DP-internal agreement and bare nouns

In EP, every element inside the DP which is able to inflect for gender and/or number will be morphologically marked as so. That applies to the nouns, but also to determiners, demonstratives, quantifiers, possessives and adjectives:

(58) *todos*   *os/esses*   *teus*   *bons*   *amigos*
    all-masc-pl   det/dem-masc-pl   poss-2p-masc-pl   good-masc-pl   friend-masc-pl
    "all your good friends"

Menuzzi (1994) refers to this kind of system as "uniform," as opposed to "non-uniform" systems in which the agreeing heads do not inflect for some feature uniformly.

    Number agreement is a non-uniform system in spoken BP. Scherre (1988) has shown that plural marking varies in spoken BP and that the plural drop is dependent on social factors, as well as structural properties of the nouns and the DP.[12] The author shows that years of schooling will determine how much of the plural markers will be dropped. Highly educated speakers will drop the agreement markers at very low rates—around 18 percent—when compared to less educated groups. She also shows that the overt morphological marking depends on the position of a particular element inside the DP, that is, elements to the left of the nominal head tend to bear the plural markers while the ones to the right of the nominal head tend to favor no markers. Thus, the following patterns can be found:

(59) *todos*   *os*   *teus*   *amigo*
    all-masc-pl   the-masc-pl   your-masc-pl   friend-masc
    "all your friends"

(60) *as   minha(s)   amiga*
      the-fem-pl   my-fem-(pl)   friend-fem
      "my (girl) friends"

(61) *as   amiga*
      the-fem-pl   friend-fem
      "the (girl) friends"

Costa and Figueiredo Silva (2006) disagree with the pattern presented in (60) when the possessive is uninflected, claiming that if only one of the elements preceding the noun is to be inflected, then it is the possessive and not the determiner that will bear the plural marker.[13] However, Simioni (2011) shows that this generalization may be strong, at least in certain contexts. According to the author, if such an agreement pattern is accepted by some speakers it should be a phonological phenomenon, since tests with ellipsis do not yield the predicted results (see Simioni 2011: 21, example (i), fn 10):

(62) a. *Eu vi os   meus   livro   e   os   teus.*
          I saw the-masc-pl my-masc-pl book-masc and the-masc-pl your-masc-pl
          "I saw my books and yours."
      b. *Eu vi os   meu livro   e   os   teu.*
          I saw the-masc-pl my-masc book-masc and the-masc-pl your-masc
          "I saw my books and yours."
      c. **Eu vi o   meus   livro   e   teus.*
          I saw the-masc my-masc-pl book-masc and the-masc your-masc-pl

Nevertheless, one has to bear in mind that the results in (62) could be a by-product of the nature of the possessive or, else, further evidence for the existence of different grammars in the language.

  As pointed out at the previous section, plural marking will be sensitive to adjectival positions with respect to the noun and whether or not it is inflected, as discussed by Menuzzi (1994: 130):

(63) a. *(os)   novos   aluno*
          (the-masc-pl) new-masc-pl pupil-masc
          the new pupils
      b. **os   novo   aluno*
          the-masc-pl   new-masc   pupil-masc

(64) a. *os   aluno   novo*
          the-masc-pl   pupil-masc   young-masc
          "the young pupils"
      b. **os   aluno   novos*
          the-masc-pl   pupil-masc   young-masc-pl
      c. **alunos   novo*
          pupil-masc-pl young-masc

Scherre and Naro (1991: 30) state that in spoken Brazilian Portuguese the "presence of preceding markers led preferentially to more markers, and absence of preceding markers similarly led to absence of markers."

There are a few generalizations that can be drawn here. If number is overtly specified only on the determiner, the DP will be grammatical; on the other hand, if number is only specified on a noun and its eventual modifiers, the DP will be ungrammatical if an overt determiner is present. Those facts have led some researchers (see Menuzzi 1994; Cyrino and Espinal 2015; a.o.) to propose that number is specified in D in spoken BP, under certain conditions. NumP is not necessarily assumed to be an independent head in the grammar then.[14]

A related matter has to do with bare nouns in natural languages. There are different forms to express generic and existential meanings in a language, Portuguese not being different. It could be done with the use of a definite or indefinite determiner, for instance:

(65) a. *A lula vive em média um ano.*
          the squid lives in average one year.
          "The squid usually lives for a year."
      b. *Uma lula vive em média um ano.*
          a squid lives in average one year.
          "A squid usually lives for a year."

But in some languages they can also be conveyed through bare nominals. Note the translation to English in (66) as well:

(66) *Lulas vivem em média um ano.*
       squids live in average one year
       "Squids usually live for a year."

Here we will call "bare nouns" (BNs) nominal elements that are not preceded by phonological material. It is generally assumed that BNs tend to be restricted to plural (66) and mass (67) nouns in argument position, unless they are proper names (see Longobardi 1994; among so many others):

(67) *Vinho faz bem à saúde.*
       wine does good to-the health
       "Wine is good for one's health."

In fact this restriction not only applies differently even to close languages but BNs will or will not be licensed in a specific syntactic position in a language depending on their interpretation.

According to Müller and Oliveira (2004), in EP bare plural nouns are not licensed in subject position unless they are modified (see (68) and (69)). However, even the modified ones are not allowed with kind predicates as in (70):[15]

(68) a. ?/* *Professores trabalham muito.*
          "Teachers work a lot."
      b. **Elefantes são inteligentes.*
          "Elephants are intelligent"

(69) a. *Professores de Coimbra trabalham muito.*
          "Teachers from Coimbra work a lot."

b. *Elefantes de grandes dimensões são inteligentes.*
    elephants of big dimensions are intelligent
    "Huge elephants are intelligent."

(70) a. **Elefantes estão extintos.*
        "Elephants are extinct."
    b. * *Elefantes de grandes dimensões estão extintos.*
        elephants of big dimensions are extinct.
        "Huge elephants are extinct."

They tend to occur more freely in object position, except with a kind reading, as in (72):

(71) a. *A Maria compra livros todos os dias.*
        the Maria buys books every the day
        "Maria buys books every day."
    b. *A Maria comprou livros ontem.*
        the Maria bought books yesterday.
        "Maria bought books yesterday."
    c. *A Maria lê livros.*
        the Maria reads books.
        "Maria reads books."
    d. *A Maria adora livros.*
        the Maria loves books.
        "Maria loves books."

(72) * *Graham Bell inventou telefone.*
      Graham Bell invented telephone
      "Graham Bell invented the telephone."

EP, however, would never license a singular count noun in a bare form in argument position. As a matter of fact, it is usually the case that only languages that lack plural morphology and a determiner system should license BNs more freely as arguments (see Longobardi 1994, a.o.). In this respect, BP is an interesting language to be examined, since, despite having plural morphology and definite and indefinite determiners which inflect for gender and number, as previously discussed, it allows bare singular count nouns in argument positions, bearing both generic (73) and existential (74) readings depending on the predicate they are associated with:

(73) a. Camarão *é crustáceo.*
        shrimp is crustacean
        "Shrimps are crustaceans."
    b. Elefante *come amendoim.*
        elephant eats peanut.
        "Elephants eat peanuts."
    c. Professor *trabalha muito.*
        teacher works a lot
        "Teachers work a lot"
    d. Criança *gosta de palhaço.*
        child likes of clown
        "Children love clowns."

(74) a. *Tem* carro *aí.*
        has car there
        "There is/are a car/cars over there."
    b. *Ontem eu comprei* livro *no shopping.*
        yesterday I bought book at the mall
        "Yesterday I bought books at the mall."
        lit. "Yesterday I bought one book or more than one book
            at the mall."
    c. **Amigo/*amigos/*amigos do Rio de Janeiro foram embora ontem.*
        "Friend/friends/friends from Rio de Janeiro left
            yesterday."

The examples in (73) and (74) show that generic singular count BNs are licensed both in pre- and postverbal positions, while the existential ones are only licensed in postverbal positions.

Given the number agreement patterns discussed previously for BP, it comes to mind that the singular count BNs are a consequence of plural marking. If plural may be marked only in the determiner, when it is dropped all that is left is the unmarked head noun, especially considering that, although plural BNs are used, the singular form is always the preferred one (see Lopes, 2007). Nevertheless, Schmitt and Munn (2002, a.o.) have convincingly shown that not to be the case.

According to Scherre (1988) educated speakers will never drop the plural marking in words in which there is a vowel alternation besides the plural morphology (such as in "*ovo*" [ovu]/"*ovos*" [ɔvus]—egg/eggs). However, Schmitt and Munn (2002: 190) show that singular BNs are possible in those cases:

(75) *Ele encontrou* ovo *de tartaruga naquela praia.*
    He found egg of turtle in-that beach.
    "He found turtle eggs in that beach."

Besides that, the authors (2002: 187, 189) also show that plural and singular BNs behave differently with respect to number interpretation:

(76) *Ele comprou* computadores/computador.
    "He bought computers/{a computer/computers}."

(77) Criança *briga uma com a outra.*
    Child fights one with the other
    "Children fight with each other."

In (76), the plural BN can only be interpreted as such, while the singular form is ambiguous between a singular and a plural interpretation. In (77) a reciprocal (*uma com a outra*) can be bound by the subject (*criança*), clearly showing that the latter cannot be interpreted as singular. These facts have led the authors, among others, to assume that in such cases there is no independent NumP in the nominal domain (but see Cyrino and Espinal, 2015, for a different analysis).

The next question, then, is to ask whether there is a DP layer or not over the BNs; in other words, whether these nominals are DPs or NPs. As discussed before, it is widely accepted that only DPs can function as arguments. On the other hand, we have seen that BNs in BP occur quite freely in argument positions.

Syntactic evidence that singular BNs are DPs and not NPs comes from tests with coordinated structures, among others. Let us take again examples from Schmitt and Munn (2002: 193):

(78) a. *Ele encontrou o amigo e parente no aeroporto.*
          He met the friend and relative at-the airport.
      b. *Ele encontrou os amigos e parentes no aeroporto.*
          He met the friends and relatives at-the airport.
      c. *Ele encontrou amigo e parente no aeroporto.*
          He met friend and relative at-the airport
          "He met friends and relatives at the airport."

In (78a) the two conjoined NPs, being conjoined under a single determiner, mean that somebody met a single individual who happens to be a friend and a relative. This is not the case in (78b), where the plural DP is ambiguous, meaning either that the persons met are both friends and relatives or that somebody met both friends and relatives, as distinct individuals or set of individuals, at the airport.

As the authors have pointed out, if the singular BNs were to behave as NPs, (78c) should only pattern with (78a), but it is not the case. It patterns with (78b) and is ambiguous between the conjoined NP reading and the separate individuals one.[16]

As a last point, claiming that there is a DP layer over the BNs can mean quite different approaches. For some, that means that D will accommodate a phonologically null expletive determiner. The reasoning comes from the fact that a definite determiner can vary with a BN in true kind predications and with proper names in BP (see Longobardi 1994; and Castro 2006; Lopes 2007, for BP):

(79) a. *A rosa é uma flor.*
          the rose is a flower
          "Roses are flowers."
      b. *Rosa é flor.*
          rose is flower.
          "Roses are flowers."

(80) a. *(A)   Maria foi   para   casa.*
          the_fem   Maria went   o+the-fem   house
          "Maria went home."

For others, it means that D will host a bundle of features responsible for the nominal interpretation. There is still another analysis according to which N moves to D if D is empty and bears certain features. Arguing for one of them is beyond the scope of this chapter.

To conclude, we will pinpoint the common properties found in both variants, as well as the differences we have mentioned along the chapter, starting with the ones that are shared between EP and BP:

- Portuguese contains articles and a varied system of determiners and quantifiers; in certain circumstances bare nouns which are plural or mass can also be found.
- Portuguese has prenominal and postnominal possessives.
- Besides certain uses of possessives and relational adjectives, arguments in nominal expressions are mainly expressed by PPs, due to case reasons.
- Relational adjectives exclusively occupy the postnominal position, which justifies the proposal of N movement (and even N′ movement) to an intermediate functional category.

- Evaluative and qualifying adjectives may, under certain circumstances, occupy prenominal and postnominal positions.
- DPs are marked by number morphology.

Although sharing the general properties above, there are some differences between EP and BP that were explored:

- While in EP prenominal possessives are generally used with definite articles, BP often allows isolated possessives, without any definite article.
- Number agreement is a non-uniform system in spoken BP, and elements to the left of the nominal head tend to bear the plural markers while the ones to the right of the nominal head tend to favor no markers.
- While EP freely accepts plural bare nouns in object position and, with some restrictions, in subject positions, and does not allow bare singular count nouns, BP allows bare singular count nouns in argument positions, bearing both generic and existential readings, depending on the predicate they are associated with.

Some of the analysis assumed here, such as the presence or not of NumP in BP, or the specific functional elements inside the DP in both variants, as well as the kind of movement they allow, are still open for discussion and further developments in the formal literature.

NOTES

1   We will mention the two variants when necessary; when the phenomena discussed are common to both of them we will simply refer to Portuguese.
2   Glosses will be provided when necessary; otherwise only the translation of the examples will be provided.
3   The notion "modifier" is complex and sometimes misleading. It will be used here to refer to non-arguments of the noun, although not to a unique position.
4   Arguments can be distinguished from modifiers in the DP in the following manners: (1) in the presence of both, the argument, not the modifier, follows the noun: *?? *o bombardeamento em 2012 da cidade* "the bombing in 2012 of the city"; (2) arguments and modifiers cannot be coordinated: * *o bombardeamento da cidade e em 2012* "the bombing of the city and in 2012"; (3) modifiers can appear in sequence: *o bombardeamento da cidade em 2012 que provocou muitos estragos* "the bombing of the city in 2012 that caused many damages (much damage)."
5   This compact unit N′ is a constituent, not a compound, as Bosque and Picallo (1996) show for Spanish, because gender and number may be present in the two forms (see in EP *os amigos americanos* (the-masc.pl. friend-masc.pl. American-masc.pl.) and because the head N may be empty, differently from what occurs in a compound: *os americanos* (the-masc.pl. American-masc.pl.).
6   But see Section 5 on BP.
7   Kinship nouns are frequently used without possessives in Portuguese, especially in EP, referring to a 3rd person but also to the speaker or to the addressee: (i) *Vi o pai/a mãe/a prima*, saw the father/the mother/the cousin "I saw my/your/his/her father/mother/cousin." In anaphoric contexts the null possessive is also a possibility: (ii) *A criança pegou a mochila*, the child took the backpack, "the child took/his/her backpack." There are some differences between EP and BP that we will not pursue here.
8   In a very formal register Portuguese still preserves the postnominal (focalized) possessive with the definite article, as in the Lord's prayer: (1) "*O pão nosso de cada dia nos dai hoje* (…)" (the bread our of every day give us today, "give us this day our daily bread"). In medieval texts examples like (2) can also be found: (2) *a calça sua* (*apud* Mattos e Silva 1989: 174) the trousers his, "your trousers."
9   Since Abney (1987) and Szabolcsi (1987), it is relatively consensual that DPs have an Agr element. The evidence comes from languages like Hungarian, Turkish, and Yupik (an Eskimo language),

at least, where agreement morphology in nominal expressions, in particular with possessives, is similar to the one which occurs in the sentential level. In Portuguese, the morphology of agreement in nominal expressions and sentences is different because in the former it is number (and also gender) that is shared by the elements in the DP and in the latter it is person and number that are shared by the DP subject and the V. Therefore, the presence of Agr in DP is not so evident as in the aforementioned languages. That is the reason why some authors prefer to assume a PossP and not an AgrP for possessives. Nevertheless, we will maintain here the classical analysis. A different approach is proposed by Castro (2006). Based on Longobardi's (1994) analysis, Castro assumes that in the presence of a prenominal possessive, only possible with the definite article, the definite article is an expletive. This idea is reinforced by BP data, where the definite article is often absent (*meu casaco está aqui*, "my coat is here"); therefore, Castro proposes that the definite article and the prenominal possessive occupy the same D head. In EP, however, this view is inadequate, due to the possible occurrence of some weak adverbs between the definite article and the noun: *o ainda meu marido* (the still my husband). See also Section 5 on BP.

10 The possibility of two positions for possessives in Portuguese is reinforced by the existence of examples with two possessives like *a minha fotografia tua* (lit. the my photo yours), where *minha* may be interpreted as agent/possessor and *tua* as theme; therefore two PossP could be proposed (see, among others, Coene and d'Hulst (2003: 9). See also the previous note for a terminological discussion.

11 The situation is more complex than described in the text, because some quantifiers like *outros* "other," projected in the spec of NumP, may precede and follow the possessives: (1) *os meus outros livros*, the my other books "my other books"; (2) *os outros meus livros*, the other my books, "my other books." In (1) AgrP precedes NumP and the head N is in Num; in (2) NumP precedes PossP, the head N being in Num.

12 The author also explores the role of phonological factors in number marking. We will not go into that in this chapter.

13 The authors discuss two different variants of spoken BP, dubbed BP1 and BP2. According to them, in BP2 there is no DP-internal agreement, therefore, the only element to bear a plural marking is the determiner.

14 As the examples (63) and (64) from Menuzzi (1994) show, in BP a prenominal adjective agrees with the determiner, but a postnominal adjective agrees with the noun, not inflecting for PL if the N does not. The fact that a postnominal (relational) adjective intervenes between the noun and its arguments (see (1) *alguns amigo americano do João* (some-pl friend-0 American-0 of the João) versus (2) * *alguns amigo do João americano* (some-pl friend-0 of the João American-0)) shows that the movement of N also occurs in BP. But the agreement phenomena in (63) and (64) indicate that the N does not land in the head of NumP as the first step of its movement, as suggested for EP. Therefore, Menuzzi proposes that this intermediate functional category may be gender, as also proposed by Picallo (1991) and Bernstein (1993) for Spanish. Although we agree with Menuzzi that N (or N′) movement does not necessarily operates to Num in BP and may occur in another intermediate functional category, we do not see advantages in considering that gender is this intermediate functional category, because Gender should be considered a lexical, not a syntactic, property of nouns. However, exploiting this point and its consequences is beyond the scope of this chapter.

15 For a discussion on the semantic behavior of BNs, see Chapter 19.

16 Assuming that the BNs in BP are not DPs, but rather NPs, could force an analysis that they will be in some left periphery position when preverbal and will be incorporated to the verb, when in a postverbal position. See Müller (2002), a.o., for a NP analysis. We will not explore that possibility here.

REFERENCES

Abney, Steven (1987) The English noun phrase and its sentential aspect. Ph.D. dissertation, MIT.

Bernstein, J. (1993). Topics in the syntax of nominal structure across romance. Ph.D. dissertation, City University of New York.

Bosque, I. and C. Picallo (1996). Postnominal adjectives in Spanish DPs. *Journal of Linguistics*, 32, pp. 349–385.

Brito, A. M. (1996). A ordem de palavras no Sintagma Nominal em Português numa perspectiva de sintaxe comparada – um caso particular: os Ns deverbais eventivos. In I. Duarte and I. Leiria (eds.), *Actas do Congresso Internacional do Português*. Lisbon: Colibri, pp. 81–106.

Brito, A. M. (2007). European Portuguese possessives and the structure of DP. *Cuadernos de Lingüística XIV 2007, Instituto Universitario de Investigación Ortega y Gasset*, pp. 21–50.

Brito, A. M. and F. Oliveira (1997). Nominalization, aspect and argument structure. In G. Matos, M. Miguel, I. Duarte, and I. Faria (eds.), *Interfaces in Linguistic Theory*. Lisbon: Linguistic Society of Portugal, pp. 57–80.

Brito, A. and E. P. Raposo (2013). Complementos, modificadores e adjuntos no sintagma nominal. In E. P. Raposo, F. B. Nascimento, M. A. Mota, L. Segura, and A. Mendes (eds.), *Gramática do Português*. Lisbon: Fundação Calouste Gulbenkian, pp. 1045–1113.

Cardinaletti, A. (1998). On the deficient/strong position in possessive systems. In A. Alexiadou and C. Wilder (eds.), *Possessors, Predicates and Movement in the Determiner Phrase*. Amsterdam: John Benjamins, pp. 17–53.

Castro, A. (2006). Possessives in European Portuguese. Ph.D. dissertation, Universidade Nova de Lisboa and Paris VIII-Saint Denis.

Castro, A. and J. Costa (2003). Weak forms as X°: prenominal possessives and preverbal adverbs in Portuguese. In A. T. Pérez-Leroux and Y. Roberge (eds.), *Romance Linguistics: Theory and Acquisition*. Amsterdam: John Benjamins, pp. 95–110.

Cinque, G. (1994). On the evidence for partial N-movement in the Romance DP. In G. Cinque, J. Roster, J.-Y. Pollock, L. Rizzi, and R. Zanuttini (eds.), *Paths towards Universal Grammar, Studies in honor of Richard Kayne*. Georgetown: Georgetown University Press, pp. 85–110.

Cinque, G. (2010). *The Syntax of Adjectives: A Comparative Study*. Cambridge, MA: MIT Press.

Coene, Martine and Yves D'Hulst (2003) *From NP to DP*. Vol. 2. Amsterdam: John Benjamins.

Costa, J. and M. C. Figueiredo Silva (2006). Nominal and verbal agreement in Portuguese: an argument for distributed morphology. In J. Costa and M. C. Figueiredo Silva (eds.), *Studies on Agreement*. Amsterdam: John Benjamins, pp. 25–46.

Crisma, P. (1993). On adjective placement in Romance and Germanic event nominals. In G. Giusti and L. Bruge (eds.), *Venice Working Papers in Linguistics*, 3 (2), pp. 81–106.

Cyrino, S. and M. T. Espinal (2015). Bare nominals in Brazilian Portuguese. More on the NP/DP analysis. *Natural Language and Linguistic Theory*, 33 (2), pp. 471–521.

Demonte, V. (1999). El adjectivo: clases y usos. La posición del adjectivo en el sintagma nominal. In I. Bosque and V. Demonte (eds.), *Gramática Descriptiva de la Lengua Española*. Madrid: Espasa, vol. I, pp. 129–215.

Giorgi, A. and G. Longobardi (1991). *The Syntax of Noun Phrases*. Cambridge: Cambridge University Press.

Grimshaw, J. (1990). *Argument Structure*. Cambridge, MA: MIT Press.

Longobardi, G. (1994). Proper names and the theory of N-movement in syntax and logical form. *Linguistic Inquiry*, 25, pp. 609–665.

Lopes, R. (2007). Against a unified analysis for bare nouns in Brazilian Portuguese. Paper presented at the *21st Going Romance*. Amsterdam: University of Amsterdam.

Mattos e Silva, R. V. (1989). *Estruturas Trecentistas. Elementos para uma gramática do Português Arcaico*. Lisbon: Imprensa Nacional-Casa da Moeda.

Menuzzi, S. (1994). Adjectival positions inside DP. In C. Cremers and R. Bok-Benema (eds.), *Linguistics in the Netherlands*, vol. 11. Amsterdam: John Benjamins, pp. 127–138.

Miguel, M. (2004). O Sintagma Nominal em Português Europeu. Posições de Sujeito. Ph.D. dissertation, University of Lisbon.

Müller, A. (2002). The semantics of generic quantification in Brazilian Portuguese. *Probus*, 14 (2), pp. 279–298.

Müller, A. and F. Oliveira (2004). Bare nominals and number in Brazilian and European Portuguese. *Journal of Portuguese Linguistics*, 3, pp. 9–36.

Parodi, C. (1994). On case and agreement in Spanish and English DPs. In M. L. Mazzola (ed.), *Issues and Theory in Romance Linguistics. Selected Papers from the Linguistic Symposium on Romance Languages 1993*. Washington, DC: Georgetown University Press.

Picallo, M. C. (1991). Nominals and nominalization in Catalan. *Probus*, 3, pp. 287–288.

Ritter, E. (1991). Two functional categories in noun phrases: evidence from modern Hebrew. *Syntax and Semantics*, 25, pp. 37–62.

Scherre, M. M. P. (1988). Reanálise da concordância nominal em português. Ph.D. dissertation, Federal University of Rio de Janeiro.

Scherre, M. M. P. and A. J. Naro (1991). Marking in discourse: "Birds of a feather." *Language Variation and Change*, 3, pp. 23–32.

Schmitt, C. and A. Munn (2002). The syntax and semantics of bare arguments in Brazilian Portuguese. *Linguistic Variation Yearbook*, 2, pp. 185–216.

Simioni, L. (2011). Concordância em construções passivas com argumentos pré e pós- verbais, e incorporação de nomes nus no PB. Ph.D. dissertation, University of São Paulo.

Sleeman, P. and A. M. Brito (2010). Nominalization, event, aspect and argument structure: a syntactic approach. In M. Duguine, S. Huidobro, and N. Madariaga (eds.), *Argument Structure from a Crosslinguistic Perspective*. Amsterdam: John Benjamins, pp. 113–129.

Szabolcsi, Anna (1987) Functional categories in the noun phrase. In István Kenesei (ed.), *Approaches to Hungarian 2*, Szeged: JATE, pp. 167–189.

15 *Wh*-movement: Interrogatives, Relatives and Clefts

CARLOS MIOTO AND MARIA LOBO

1. Introduction

Interrogatives, relatives and clefts are structures that have a common property: they may begin with a *wh*-expression (e.g. *quem* "who," *o que* "what") generally linked to an empty position in its clause. In generative approaches, as in Chomsky's classic article entitled "On *wh*-movement" (Chomsky 1977), this expression is assumed to have been moved from a clause internal position to a left peripheral position. In (1) we present an example of each construction.

(1) a. *De quem é que Joana desconfia?*   Interrogative
       Of whom is that Joana is.suspicious?
    b. *Conheço o homem [de quem Joana desconfia]*   Relative
       know-1p-sg the man of who Joana is.suspicious
    c. *[O que Joana comeu] foi o bolo.*   Pseudo-cleft
       What Joana ate was the cake.

The three structures differ, however, in their discourse properties, word order patterns and syntactic distribution.

In this chapter, we will consider these structures, pointing out their general properties, and relevant differences between European Portuguese (EP) and Brazilian Portuguese (BP), and we will review theoretical approaches to them.

2. Interrogatives

This section is dedicated to *wh*-interrogative sentences in Portuguese. They are attractive to syntax because of the richness of ways of making questions, the abundance of phenomena related to them, and for comparative reasons.

2.1. Wh-*in-situ*

Standard studies on *wh*-interrogatives (e.g. Rizzi, 1996) assume a parameter opposing languages with and without *wh*-movement in syntax. All languages have the same behavior at LF where *wh*-movement must occur: *wh*-expressions are operators and need to set up their

The Handbook of Portuguese Linguistics, First Edition. Edited by W. Leo Wetzels, João Costa, and Sergio Menuzzi.
© 2016 John Wiley & Sons, Inc. Published 2020 by John Wiley & Sons, Inc.

scope at LF, which is achieved by moving *wh*-expressions to a scope position. But languages differ with respect to the visibility of *wh*-movement: whereas in English it must be visible—that is, it must apply in SS—in Chinese it cannot be.

Significantly, Portuguese is problematic for this picture since it licenses both *wh*-in-situ and *wh*-movement in the overt syntax. We have the following paradigm:

(2) a. *Joana   comeu   o quê?*
       Joana   ate   what
       "What did Joana eat?"
   b. *O que comeu Joana?*   (EP^OK   BP*)
   c. *O que Joana comeu?*   (EP*   BP^OK)

(3) a. *Pedro   disse   que   Joana   comeu   o quê?*
       Pedro   said   that   Joana   ate   what
       "What did Pedro say that Joana ate?"
   b. *O que disse Pedro que Joana comeu?*   (EP^OK   BP^??)
   c. *O que Pedro disse que Joana comeu?*   (EP*   BP^OK)

(4) a. *Joana   chorou   quando   Pedro   cantou   o quê?*
       Joana   cried   when   Pedro   sang   what
   b. **O que   Joana chorou quando   Pedro cantou?*

Single *wh*-in-situ expressions are allowed in matrix sentences (2a), and in embedded contexts (3a), but they are obligatory when they are inside strong islands,[1] as in (4a).

The coexistence of *wh*-in-situ with *wh*-movement in a language raises serious problems since a priori optionality is usually banned from syntax (see Chomsky 1995). To avoid optionality, the approaches propose that a *wh*-in-situ question is pragmatically different from a *wh*-fronted question, and they follow at least two paths. The first one assumes that *wh*-in-situ simply results from no movement at all: the lack of *wh*-movement is morphologically or pragmatically conditioned. The second one assumes that the *wh*-expression is always moved and the final order results from moving other constituents: the burden of optionality is located in the way the presupposed material is treated.

Ambar (2003) provides an approach of the second type, claiming that (2a) and (3a) are derived by *wh*-movement to WhP before the movement of remnant IP to AssertiveP, à la Kayne (1994).[2] The final order is derived by treating the presupposed IP as a moved block. However, like every approach supposing overt *wh*-movement to CP, Ambar's account seems to have problems in dealing with the acceptability of (4a), given the impossibility of extracting from strong islands (4b), as Pires and Taylor (2007) point out.

Kato (2013) also provides an approach deriving *wh*-in-situ by movement. But her analysis assumes that the *wh*-expression moves clause-internally to the left periphery of vP, à la Belletti (2004). Since this is not a movement out of an island, it does not violate the Island Condition, and (4a) can naturally be derived.

The analyses supposing lack of movement in *wh*-in-situ constructions avoid the island problem. Some of them postulate the existence of an overt or covert *wh*-particle base-generated in C, and particular intonations associated to it that license *wh*-in-situ (Cheng and Rooryk 2000, Cheng 2003). Languages like Chinese, which have a *wh*-particle, tend to have no *wh*-movement (but see Bruening 2007). Extending this analysis to Portuguese, there would be a silent morpheme licensing *wh*-in-situ: the optionality of *wh*-in-situ would be due to presence or absence of the morpheme in the numeration (Kato 2013). Even assuming that BP has a "fake *wh*-in-situ" (because of *wh*-movement to FocusP in the left periphery of vP),

Kato (2013) still postulates a silent Q-operator (where "Q" stands for "Question"): for her, this operator would be responsible for the various intonation patterns of *wh*-in-situ in BP.

Pires and Taylor (2007) claim that no movement occurs in *wh*-in-situ questions, and they observe that their occurrence requires the satisfaction of specific discourse-pragmatic conditions, defined in terms of Common Ground (CG) (Stalnaker 2002). Besides echo questions, *wh*-in-situ is felicitous in what they call specific Qs (which request more specific information about something mentioned before), expected Qs (which occur when new information is expected) and reference Qs (which ask for a paraphrase or repetition of something mentioned before). The *wh*-expression remains in-situ because in the numeration there is a [+wh,+Q] Comp that does not trigger *wh*-movement. As a first approximation, we believe this is a good description of the different uses of *wh*-in-situ in Portuguese.

2.2. *Fronted* wh

It is in matrix interrogatives with fronted *wh* that we find the major differences between EP and BP. The first difference is observed in (5):

(5) a. *O que Joana leu?* (EP* BP^OK)
    What Joana read
  b. *O que leu Joana?* (EP^OK BP*)
    What read Joana
    "What did Joana read?"

In EP the subject cannot intervene between a *wh*-expression like *o que* "what" and the verb (referred as the WHVS order, versus the WHSV order), as in (5a), while in BP it can. In presence of a *wh*-expression like *que livro* "which book," the WHSV order is allowed in EP:

(6) *Que*   *livro Joana leu?* (EP^? BP^OK)
    Which   book Joana read

Another type of sentence with fronted WH is the cleft interrogative:

(7) a. *O que é/foi que Joana fez?*
    What is/was-perf that Joana did-perf
  b. *O que é/era que Joana fazia?*
    What is/was-imperf that Joana did-imperf
    "What did Joana do?"

These sentences have three characteristic properties. First, either the copula remains in the present form disagreeing with the verb *fez* "did," or it agrees with the main verb—hence, the perfective form *foi* "was" in (7a), and the imperfective *era* "was" in (7b). Second, the presence of cleaving material allows the subject to occur before the verb *fazer* "to do" in EP. Third, cleft interrogatives do not allow *wh*-in-situ (8a), nor in the focus position between the *é* "is" and *que* "that" (8b):

(8) a. **É/Foi que Joana fez o quê?*
  b. **É o que que Joana fez?*
  c. *?Foi que/o quê que Joana fez?* (non-echo)

If the *wh*-expression appears between *foi* "was" and *que* "that," the sentence is marked but acceptable (8c).

The cleft interrogative with the present form copula is the most natural *wh*-question in EP. But in BP it seems to be a sort of emphatic question. The most natural *wh*-question in BP shows a Doubly-Filled Comp, as in (9a); just like cleft interrogatives, in this structure *wh*-in-situ is ruled out, as shown in (9b):

(9) a. *O que que Joana comeu?*   (EP* BP^{OK})
         What that Joana ate
         "What did Joana eat?"
     b. **Que Joana comeu o quê?*

In BP, even when we have a cleft/emphatic question, we can have a Doubly-Filled Comp, as in (10); and again *wh*-in-situ is forbidden, as in (10b):

(10) a. *O que que é/foi que Joana comeu?*   (EP* BP^{OK})
         What that is/was that Joana ate
         "What is it that Joana ate?"
     b. **Que é/foi que Joana comeu o quê?*

We will discuss four properties concerning the *wh*-moved interrogatives: first, the position occupied by the fronted *wh* in (5) to (10) and by the finite verb in (5b); second, the property that triggers the *wh*-movement; third, the impossibility of *wh*-in-situ in questions with material (finite verb or *que* "that") in Comp and in cleft questions; and fourth, the derivation for each grammatical sentence in (5) to (10).

Barbosa (2001) claims that in (5b) the *wh*-expression is in Spec-TP and the finite verb in T. Thus there is no position to host the subject between the two. However, the extension of this analysis to BP seems to be complicated because of the free occurrence of the WHSV.

Ambar (1988), in her more traditional approach to EP, claims that the *wh*-expression is moved to SpecCP and the finite verb to C. The reason for these movements would be to create the proper configuration for the identification of an empty category (ec) that would characterize "simple" *wh*-expressions like *quem* "who," *o que* "what," *onde* "where," etc. In "complex" *wh*-expressions, such as *que livro* "which book" in (6), there would be no ec; hence, verb movement to C° becomes unnecessary. However, Ambar's solution cannot be applied to BP interrogatives.

Mioto (1994) and Mioto and Kato (2005) propose an analysis based on Rizzi's (1996) criterion system,[3] deriving the differences between EP and BP from the properties of Infl: EP has a [+wh] Infl, which must be in a Spec-head configuration with a [+wh] operator, while BP has a [–wh] Infl. In EP the configuration is achieved when the *wh*-expression is in SpecCP and Infl is in C°. This analysis does not account for the *wh*-in-situ in EP, since if Infl is defined as [+wh], *wh*-movement is obligatorily triggered to provide the Spec-head relation. Having Infl [–wh], BP can have *wh*-in-situ provided that a *wh*-in-situ is not an operator triggering a Spec-head relation at SS. To explain obligatory movement in cleft interrogatives and Doubly Filled Comp constructions such as (10), the authors claim that *que* "that" defines C° as a [+wh] head. Thus, every time we have phonological material in C°, like *que* "that" in BP and Infl in EP, *wh*-movement is required.

The fact that *wh*-expressions cannot naturally land between the copula and the complementizer in clefts (8b, c) is explained by Mioto (2011) by claiming that the *wh*-expression has a [+focus,+wh] feature geometry for checking with Focus° and the higher C°, as in (11a):

(11) a. $[O\ que_i\ que_{WH°}\ é/foi\ [t_i\ que_{Foc°}\ [Joana\ comeu\ t_i]]]$?
     b. $[O\ que\ [_{C°}\ é\ que]\ Joana\ comeu\ t_i]$?

The [+wh, +focus] geometry explains why the *wh*-expression can never remain in-situ in cleft interrogatives. Costa and Duarte (2001) and Costa and Lobo (2009), on the other hand, claim that the *wh*-expression cannot stay between the copula and the complementizer because *é-que* "is that" is an idiom, as in (11b).

2.3. Embedded wh-*questions*

Embedded interrogatives occur in selected contexts, generally as complements of verbs. They are headed either by the "conjunction" *se* "if," when the embedded sentence is a yes–no question, or by a *wh*-expression. The scope of their questioning is limited to the embedded sentence. The *wh*-expression must be fronted to the embedded CP:

(12) a. *João   perguntou   que livro Joana leu.*
        "João   asked   which book Joana read"
     b. **João   perguntou   se Joana leu que livro.*
        João   asked   if Joana read which book
        "João asked which book Joana read."
     c. **João   perguntou   (que) Joana leu que livro.*
        João   asked   (that) Joana read which book

However, if the *wh*-expression bears a subject or object function inside the embedded CP and has matrix scope, it can be either licensed in-situ or fronted to the matrix CP:

(13) a. *João   perguntou   se Joana leu que livro?*
        João   asked   if Joana read which book
     b. *Que livro João perguntou se Joana leu?*

Embedded clauses with fronted *wh*-expressions follow the same pattern of matrix interrogatives, except that the WHVS order is not required for most *wh*-phrases in EP:

(14) a. *João perguntou*   [*o que Joana leu*].   (EP[OK] BP[OK])
     b.   [*o que é que Joana leu*].   (EP[OK] BP[OK])
     c.   [*o que que Joana leu*].   (EP* BP[OK])

The WHVS order is only required in EP when the *wh*-expression is *que* "what":

(15) a. *João   perguntou   que leu Joana.*   (EP[OK] BP*)
        João   asked   what read Joana
        "João asked what Joana read."
     b. **João perguntou que Joana leu.*

With the other *wh*-expressions besides *que* "what" WHVS in subordinate interrogatives is said to be optional in EP.

Ambar (1988) attributes the possibility of the embedded WHSV order to the fact that the matrix verb identifies the ec of the embedded *wh*-expression. The WHVS order remains obligatory only with *que* "what" because in this case the matrix verb would be unable to identify its particular ec. But Mioto (2011) claims that *que* "what" has clitic properties that force it to be adjoined to the embedded verb. In cases other than *que* "what," he claims that the WHVS order in embedded sentences in EP is triggered by focusing on the embedded subject.

3. Relatives

In this section, we will discuss some properties of relative clauses in Portuguese. Relative clauses do not differ substantially in the two varieties of Portuguese, although non-standard strategies seem to be more accepted in the BP variety. Therefore, we will only distinguish the two varieties when there are relevant differences between them.

We will first consider headed relatives (HR), discussing briefly different kinds of analyses and standard and non-standard strategies (3.1); then we will discuss free relatives (FR) and their various constraints (3.2); finally, we will introduce some special properties of infinitival free relatives (IFR) (3.3).

3.1. *Headed relatives*

HRs are subordinate clauses introduced by a relativizer that establishes a relation with a noun in the main clause. The relativizer can be a *wh*-word or the complementizer *que* "that." In this case, it is generally assumed that an empty operator is filling the position of the *wh*-expression (e.g. Brito 1991). Differently from *wh*-questions, in relatives the *wh*-word is always in the initial position (e.g. Costa, Fiéis, and Lobo 2012). There are no in-situ relatives in Portuguese, although there are relativizing strategies that avoid overt movement.

In traditional analyses (Chomsky 1977; for Portuguese, Tarallo 1983; Brito 1991), it is assumed that, in standard Portuguese, HRs involve movement of a *wh*-phrase to the left periphery of the clause and adjunction of the relative clause to a nominal projection, as in (16):[4]

(16) *Esta é* [$_{NP}$ [$_{NP}$ *a cidade*] [$_{CP}$ [*onde*]$_i$ *eu nasci*   t$_i$]]
   This is the town where I was.born

Restrictive relatives are adjoined to a lower position than non-restrictive relatives, but in both cases we have an adjunction structure. Assuming the DP hypothesis, one can assume that restrictive relatives are adjoined to NP, while appositive relatives are adjoined to DP (Mioto, Figueiredo Silva, and Lopes 2013):

(17) a. [$_{DP}$ [$_D$ *os*] [$_{NP}$ [$_{NP}$ [$_N$ *alunos*]] [$_{CP}$ *que reprovaram*]]]
         the   students   that failed
    b. [$_{DP}$ [$_{DP}$ [$_D$ *os*] [$_{NP}$ [$_N$ *alunos*]]]   [$_{CP}$ *que reprovaram*]]
           the   students   that failed

More recently, analyses of HRs in Portuguese have followed Kayne's (1994) hypothesis that HRs involve head raising. That is, the so-called antecedent of the relative pronoun is taken to have been extracted from the relative clause, which itself is taken to be a complement of D (Kenedy 2002; Cardoso 2011):

(18) [$_{DP}$ [$_D$ *o*] [$_{CP}$ *livro*$_i$ *que* [$_{IP}$ *Camões escreveu* t$_i$]]]
       the   book   that   Camões wrote

Empirical evidence for this analysis, presented for different languages (Kayne 1994) and for BP by Kenedy 2002, comes from different phenomena, including binding, coordination, and restrictions on definite DPs, although some of these arguments are controversial. For example, an empirical argument presented by Kenedy (2002) comes from contrasts between contexts where definite DPs are allowed: a definite DP is allowed with the existential verb *"haver"* only when there is a relative clause. In a raising analysis this is taken as evidence for D selecting a CP:

(19) a. [$_{DP}$ *os* [$_{CP}$ *livros*$_i$ *que havia* t$_i$ *na biblioteca*]] *eram bons*
       The   books that there was in.the library were good
   b. * [$_{VP}$ *havia* [$_{DP}$ *os* [$_{NP}$ *livros bons*]] na biblioteca]
       there was the good books in the library

There still is some controversy concerning the derivation of HRs, as CPs adjoined to a nominal projection, in which a *wh*-word or a null operator establishes a relation with an antecedent, the standard and more widespread analysis, or as CPs selected by D, in which the antecedent is raised from inside IP, as assumed in analyses inspired by Kayne's proposal, since some of the arguments presented in favor of the raising analysis are not convincing (see for example, Alexandre, 2000).

Considering now differences between Portuguese and other languages, it is relevant to mention that, unlike English, Portuguese does not allow preposition stranding (as in 20b). When the *wh*-word is inserted in a PP, the only standard available strategy involves pied-piping of the preposition along with the *wh*-expression, as in (20a).

(20) a. *Encontrei o homem* [*de quem*] *o inspetor desconfia* ___.
       I found the man of whom the inspector is.suspicious
   b. *Encontrei o homem* [*quem*] *o inspetor desconfia de* ___.
       I found the man whom the inspector is.suspicious of

There are, however, non-standard strategies that are very common in colloquial speech, especially in BP (Tarallo 1983; Alexandre 2000). For PP-relatives, these may involve chopping the preposition, as in (21a), or filling the gap position with a resumptive pronoun (21b).

(21) a. *Encontrei o homem que o inspetor desconfia.*
       I found the man that the inspector is.suspicious
   b. *Encontrei o homem que o inspetor desconfia dele.*
       I found the man that the inspector is.suspicious of-him

In DP-relatives, the resumptive strategy can also be found in non-standard colloquial speech both in BP and in EP (Alexandre 2000; Braga, Kato, and Mioto 2009).

(22) a. *há certas coisas*$_i$ *que não as*$_i$ *compreendo* (EP, apud Alexandre 2000)
       there are certain things that I do not understand them
   b. *Temos lá, no meu ano,* rapazes$_i$ *que eles*$_i$ *parecem atrasados mentais* (EP, apud Alexandre 2000)
       We have, there, in my class, boys that they seem retarded
   c. *o homem*$_i$ *que eu vi ele*$_i$ ... (BP, apud Kenedy 2002)
       the man that I saw him ...
   d. *eu preferia deixar evidentemente essa questão a* um consultor jurídico$_i$ *que ele*$_i$ *poderia então lhe dar um resposta mais conclusiva...* (BP, adapted from Braga et al. 2009)
       I would rather leave that issue to a juridic consultant that he could then give you a more conclusive answer

In all these cases, the relativizer is always *que* "that." This may be explained if these strategies do not involve overt *wh*-movement, but only an operator-variable relation, the C position being occupied by the complementizer *que* "that" and the specifier by an empty operator (Brito 1991), base-generated in the specifier of CP, according to Tarallo (1983), or moved into that position, according to Brito (1991).

The nature of resumption (and consequently of resumptive relatives) and whether it involves movement or not is controversial (Rouveret 2011). Usually, resumption is viewed as a strategy that does not involve movement (Tarallo 1985, McCloskey 1990, Alexandre 2000). Instead, a pronoun is inserted in what would be the gap position and it establishes a relation with a null operator directly inserted in the specifier of CP. Some of the arguments for the absence of movement in resumptive structures include lack of subjacency (insensitivity to island conditions) and weak crossover effects (McCloskey 1990, Rouveret 2011).

(23) a. *Conheço um homem que os cães começam a ladrar quando se cruzam com ele.*
  b. **Conheço um homem com quem os cães começam a ladrar quando se cruzam.*
  I know a man that/*with whom the dogs start to bark when they cross with him/*__

(24) a. *O homem$_i$ que a sua$_i$ própria mulher o$_i$ matou*
  b. *??O homem$_i$ que a sua$_i$ própria mulher matou*
  The man that/??who his own wife killed him/??__

For many authors (Tarallo 1985, Rouveret 2011, among others) resumption is viewed as a rescuing strategy when movement is ruled out. However, in Portuguese data we can find resumptive relatives in contexts where there is no subjacency violation, alternating with gap strategies (Alexandre 2000). Although Portuguese resumptive relatives cannot be viewed only as a strategy of last resort, they do seem to be sensitive to gap distances and they are far more productive in prepositional relatives as a strategy to avoid pied-piping. Unlike Irish (McCloskey 1990), non-standard Portuguese may have resumptive subject relatives, as in (22b) and (22d). However, the more the distance between the gap and the antecedent, the more acceptable are resumptive relatives (Alexandre 2000).

The status of the resumptive pronoun is not very clear, since it seems to have properties of a syntactic variable: it licenses parasitic gaps and is sensitive to strong crossover effects (Alexandre 2000).

3.2. Finite free relatives

Let us now consider another type of relative clause, the so-called free relatives (FRs) or relatives without an overt antecedent. These clauses are similar to HRs and *wh*-questions in that they are introduced by a *wh*-word that binds a gap inside the relative clause. They differ, however, from HRs in that there is no overt antecedent (25b):

(25) a. *[Os alunos [que estudam]] têm boas notas.*
  The students that study have good marks
  b. *[Quem estuda] tem boas notas*
  Who studies has good marks

Besides the absence of an overt antecedent, FRs differ from HRs in several respects (Móia 1992; Marchesan 2012; Marchesan and Mioto 2012): they cannot be introduced by the complementizer *que* "that" and by some of the *wh*-pronouns (such as *cujo* "whose" or *o qual* "which"); they have a more limited distribution in the clause; and they are subject to matching requirements. Before discussing these properties, however, it is important to mention that FRs can be easily confused with embedded interrogatives, since they have a similar shape: they are both embedded clauses that begin with a *wh*-word and can occur in argument positions. However, embedded *wh*-interrogatives occur mainly as complements of a few classes of verbs, in particular epistemic verbs and verbs of inquiry, such as *perguntar* "ask" or *saber* "know," which also select unambiguous interrogative clauses introduced by *se* "if, whether." In standard varieties, they can be distinguished because only interrogatives may have the *é-que* "(it)-is-that" expression (Marchesan 2012), as in the contrast (26a) vs. (27a):

(26) a. *O professor elogiou quem (*é que) fez o trabalho.*
     The teacher praised who (is that) did the homework
   b. **O professor elogiou se o aluno fez o trabalho.*
     The teacher praised if the student did the homework

(27) a. *O professor sabe quem (é que) fez o trabalho.*
     The teacher knows who (is that) did the homework
   b. *O professor sabe se o aluno fez o trabalho.*
     The teacher knows if the student did the homework

Therefore, FRs have to be distinguished from embedded *wh*-questions.

Moreover, they must be distinguished from HRs, too. First of all, there are *wh*-expressions that can introduce both HRs and FRs, such as *onde* "where" and *como* "how," as in (28). However, HRs can also be introduced by the complementizer *that* "que," but FRs cannot, as shown in (29). Finally, some *wh*-expressions such as *quem* "who" and *o que* "what" (lit. "the that") cannot introduce HRs by themselves, but they can introduce FRs, as in (30) (Brito 1991, Móia 1992, Marchesan and Mioto 2012):

(28) a. *Eu morei (no lugar) onde ela mora.*
     "I lived (in the place) where she lives"
   b. *Eu detesto (o modo) como ele fala.*
     I hate (the way) how he speaks

(29) a. *Eu conheço *(o rapaz) que ela convidou.*
     "I know *(the boy) that she invited"
   b. *Eu detesto *(o livro) que ele comprou.*
     I hate *(the book) that he bought

(30) a. *Eu conheço (*o rapaz) quem ela convidou.*
     I know the boy who she invited
   b. *Eu detesto (*o livro) o que ele comprou.*
     I hate (*the book) what he bought

The status of the FR clause and of the constituent in which it is embedded is open to discussion. Some authors have considered FRs to be plain CPs. Others have considered that they are nominal structures—hence, embedded in some type of NP or DP. Brito (1991) and Móia (1992), following Harbert (1983) and Suñer (1984), argue that FRs are embedded in an NP that has an ec, *pro*.[5] Brito (1991) explains the unavailability of *que* in finite FRs by hypothesizing that *pro* is only licensed when the *wh* has phi-features. Móia (1992) supports this analysis by explaining the restrictions on the distribution of FRs according to Rizzi (1986)'s conditions on the licensing and identification of *pro*; he further proposes a morpho-phonological rule by which the relative pronoun incorporates the ec. This would explain the difference in the *wh*-words that introduce HRs and FRs, the restrictions on the presence of *wh*-words preceded by a preposition and the matching requirements that we will describe below. Considering the above restrictions on the expressions that introduce FRs, Marchesan (2012) and Marchesan and Mioto (2012) propose that FRs are introduced by a *wh*-word that incorporates a noun specified for different features: [+human] *quem* "who"; [+locative] *onde* "where"; [+time] *quando* "when"; [–human] *o que* "what"; [+quantity] *quanto* "how much"; [+manner] *como* "how."

However, the most distinctive characteristic of FRs is the fact that they are subject to mismatch restrictions (MRs). Since Grimshaw (1977), MRs on FRs have been widely discussed in the literature for different languages and also for EP and BP (Móia 1992, Negrão 1994, Marchesan 2012). Consider the following contrast:

(31) a. *O rapaz a quem telefonaste saiu.*
        the boy to whom you.phoned left
     b. **A quem telefonaste saiu.*
        To whom you.phoned left

(32) a. *Conheço o rapaz com quem ela casou.*
        I.know the boy with whom she married
     b. **Conheço com quem ela casou.*
        I.know with whom she married

Although there is no restriction on the position where HRs can occur, there are restrictions on the distribution of FRs. For example, in (31b) an FR introduced by a preposition cannot be the subject of the main clause, and in (32b) an FR introduced by the preposition *com* "with," selected by the verb *casou* "married," cannot occur as an internal argument of the transitive verb *conhecer* "know." These cases suggest that in Portuguese the *wh*-expression that introduces a FR must match the categorial requirements of the matrix position where the relative is embedded.

There are, however, some contexts where mismatches seem to be acceptable, though MRs do not have the same effects in the two varieties. In EP, a FR may be introduced by a preposition when the same preposition is selected by the main verb. According to Móia (1992), this is fully acceptable when the main verb is the same as in the embedded clause (33a), grammaticality judgments vary in the other cases (33b,c), but mismatch is ungrammatical (33d,e):

(33) a. *Eu confio em quem tu confias.* (Móia 1992: 89)
        I trust in whom you trust
     b. *Eu dei um livro a quem tu ofereceste uma bicicleta.* (Móia 1992: 89)
        I gave a book to whom you offered a bicycle
     c. *?Eu zanguei-me com quem tu conversaste.* (Móia 1992: 89)
        I got.angry with whom you talked
     d. **Eu vi ontem (de) quem tu gostas.* (EP, Brito 1991: 204)
        I saw yesterday (of) whom you like
     e. **Detesto (com) quem tu saíste.* (EP, Brito 1991: 204)
        I.hate (with) whom you went.out

In BP, however, prepositions can be deleted under some circumstances, and this makes room for structures that would, otherwise, result in mismatching. Specifically, if the preposition selected by the embedded predicate is deletable, and the matrix position selects for a DP, then mismatch is avoided and the sentence is possible, as in (34); if, for some reason, the preposition is not deletable, then mismatch cannot be avoided, and the sentence is excluded, as in (35) (cf. Negrão 1994, Marchesan 2012):

(34) a. *Eu só ajudo (*de) quem eu gosto.*
        I only help (*of) whom I am.fond
     b. *Eu comprei (*d)o que eu precisava.*
        I bought (*of) what I have.need

(35) a. **Eu conheço [quem a Maria casou com].*
     I know whom Maria married with
   b. **João detesta [quem o filho anda com].*
     João hates whom his son walks with
   c. **Eu convidei [quem você saiu com].*
     I invited whom you went.out with

Mismatches can also be found with FRs introduced by *quando* "when," *onde* "where," and *como* "how." In BP, they may occur in subject position and as direct objects, unlike WH PPs, although there is some variation in acceptability judgements:

(36) a. *[Quando o bebê dormir] vai ser um bom momento para conversarmos.*
     When the baby will.fall.asleep is a.good time (for us) to talk
   a'. *Adoro [quando estou de férias]*
     I.love when I.am on holiday
   b. *?[Onde os meus pais moram] é um sítio sossegado.*
     Where my parents live is a quiet place
   b'. *Encontrei [onde estava o telefone]*
     I.found where the telephone was.
   c. *?[Como ele se veste] pode chocar algumas pessoas.*
     How he dresses may shock some people
   c'. *Adoro [como ele se veste]*
     I.love how he dresses

In EP, these *wh*-words have a more limited distribution, but they may have a null antecedent and thus can function as DPs (Móia 1992, Marchesan and Mioto 2012).

3.3. Infinitival free relatives

A special type of FR are IFRs (Brito 1991; Móia 1992; Ferreira 2007; Marchesan 2012; Marchesan and Mioto 2012).[6] These FRs have a special behavior: they are infinitival clauses and they only occur as complements to a limited set of verbs, including mainly the existential verb *haver* "(there) to be" and the possessive verb *ter* "to have," but also more rarely verbs like *encontrar* "to find," *arranjar* "to get," or *trazer* "to bring" (Ferreira 2007):

(37) a. *Não há para onde fugir.*
     (There) not is to where to.escape
   b. *Ela não tem de que viver.*
     She (does) not have from what to.live
   c. *Não encontrei com quem desabafar.*
     (I did) not find with whom to.talk

IFRs do not allow the *wh*-expression to be the subject of the clause (39a,b):

(38) a. *Não tenho a quem telefonar.*
     (I).don't have to whom to.phone
   b. **Não tenho quem telefonar aos alunos.*
     (I).don't have who to.phone to.the students
   c. *Não tenho quem telefone aos alunos.*
     (I).don't have who phones to.the students

When the *wh*-expression is the subject, the verb of the relative takes the subjunctive form (38c). IFRs are weak islands to extraction, unlike other complement FRs (39) (Móia 1992; Marchesan and Mioto 2012):

(39) a. ?*Que livro é que ele não tem a quem dar?*
         Which book is that he does.not have to who give
     b. **Que livro é que ele elogiou quem leu?*
         Which book is that he praised who read

The analysis of IFRs is controversial. According to Brito (1991), IFRs are CPs embedded in an NP headed by a null category *pro* that acts as antecedent of the *wh*-expression and that receives an arbitrary feature from the matrix verb. This would explain the fact that they always have an indefinite reading and can only have an indefinite overt antecedent:

(40) a. *Não tenho ninguém a quem telefonar.*
         (I do) not have nobody to whom to.phone.
     b. *Não tenho (*os) meninos com quem brincar.*
         (I do) not have children with whom to.play

To explain the extraction phenomena (absence of subjacency in IFRs), Móia (1992) proposes that the selected constituent is a maximal CP (and not a CP embedded in a nominal projection) and *pro* occupies the highest specifier projection of maximal CP:

(41) $[_{V'}$ *ter* $[_{CPmax}$ *pro* $[_{CP}$ *[com quem]*$_i$ $[_{C'}$ PRO   *discutir o assunto* t$_i$]]]]
        have   pro   with whom   PRO   to.discuss the subject

Marchesan and Mioto (2012) consider that IFRs are weak islands for extraction because of the defective status of the non-finite IP.

4. Clefting

Portuguese is very rich in focusing processes, which share some properties with *wh*-questions. Without the clefting apparatus, the focused constituent can remain in-situ or be dislocated to the left, as for the *wh*-expression. With clefting, the focused constituent must be moved. We can understand this similarity if we consider that the behavior of cleft constituents can be reduced to *wh*-movement.

Despite the unique function of focusing a phrasal constituent, clefts and pseudo-clefts (PCL) have resisted a unified treatment, raising challenges since the end of the 1960s (see Akmajian 1970, Costa and Duarte 2001, among others). For that reason, we dedicate a specific section to each construction.

4.1. Clefts

In their full form, clefts (CL) are complex sentences with a matrix clause headed by the functional verb *ser* "be" and an embedded clause with the main predication, headed by the complementizer *que* "that." In the examples below, the focused constituents are underlined:

(42) a. *Foi João que pescou esse peixe.*
Was João that fished this fish
"It was João that fished this fish."
b. *João foi que pescou esse peixe.*   (EP* BP^OK)
c. *João é que pescou esse peixe.*
João is that fished this fish

(42a) is a standard CL, called "*it*-cleft"; (42b) is an inverted-CL with tense agreement between the copula and the lexical verb; (42c) is another type of inverted-CL, but with the copula in the present form. Other possible focusing structures arguably derived from clefts are the ones in (43):

(43) a. *João que pescou esse peixe.*   (EP* BP^OK)
João that fished this fish
"It was João that fished this fish."
b. *Foi João.*[7]
"It was João."

(43a) corresponds to a CL without copula, only available in BP, and (43b) is a *be*-fragment-CL, with the *que*-clause elided (e.g., when it is given in the previous discourse: (43b) could be an answer for *Quem foi que pescou esse peixe?* "Who was it that fished this fish?").

The first issue raised by CLs concerns the status of the *que*-clause in (42). Observe (44) (adapted from Mioto and Negrão 2007):

(44) a. *Foi o aluno que foi reprovado.*
Was the pupil that was reproved
"It was the pupil that was reproved."
b. *Quem foi reprovado?*
"Who was reproved?"
c. *Que aluno pediu cursos de revisão?*
"Which pupil asked for refresher courses?"

The focus in (44a) can be set up according to the questions in (44b and c). If (44a) is an answer to (44b), *o aluno* "the pupil" is the focus and it bears the main stress of the sentence, while the rest of the sentence is presupposed and receives a destressed intonation. But if (44a) is the answer to (44c), the focus and the main stress will lie on the *que*-clause. Is the *que*-sentence a relative in (44a)? Ambar (2005) and Mioto and Negrão (2007) claim that it is not when the sequence corresponds to a CL, that is, when answering to (44b).[8]

The second issue has to do with tense and person agreement. Tense agreement is easier to describe since the copula and the main verb have to agree in tense (45), except when the cleft is inverted, that is, when the focus precedes the copula (46):

(45) *Era esse peixe que João estava pescando.*   (EP^OK BP^OK)
Was-imperf that fish that João was-imperf fishing
"It was this fish that João was fishing."

(46) a. *Esse peixe é que João estava pescando.*   (EP^OK BP^OK)
b. *Esse peixe era que João estava pescando.*   (EP^OK BP^OK)

In BP, either there is tense agreement, or *ser* appears in its present form *é*; in EP the copula is always invariable in this case.

Although there can be tense agreement in BP between the copula and the main verb when the focus is fronted, there cannot be person agreement neither in BP nor in EP (47). However, there is person agreement between the copula and a focused pronominal that follows it, especially when it is the subject of the *que*-clause (48):

(47) a. *Eu é que pesquei esse peixe.*
　　　　I is that fished1-p-sg this fish
　　　　"It was me that fished this fish."
　　 b. * *Eu sou que pesquei esse peixe.*
　　　　I am that fished1-p-sg this fish.

(48) a. *Fui eu que pesquei esse peixe.*
　　　　Was-1p-sg I that fished-1p-sg this fish
　　　　"It was me that fished this fish."
　　 b. **Foi eu que pesquei esse peixe.*
　　　　Was-3p-sg I that fished-1p-sg this fish

Person and number agreement with the copula is widespread in *be*-fragments with a focused DP:

(49) a. – *Quem pescou esses peixes?*
　　　　"Who fished these fishes?"
　　　 – *Foram os meninos.*
　　　　Were-3p-pl the boys
　　　　"It was the boys."
　　　 – ? *Foi os meninos*
　　　　Was-3p-sg the boys
　　 b. – *O que é que os meninos pescaram?*
　　　　"What did the boys fish?"
　　　 – *Foram esses peixes.*
　　　　Were-3p-pl these fishes
　　　 – ? *Foi esses peixes.*
　　　　Was-3p-sg these fishes

The third property we will now consider is the kind of focus CLs can convey. For this purpose, assume that it is sufficient to distinguish mere new information (an answer to *wh*-question) from other types of focus (see Zubizarreta 1998). Non-informational (contrastive) focus can be conveyed by every type of CL (and by in-situ and dislocated constituents). But only *be*-fragment CLs unrestrictedly convey mere information focus (as well as in-situ focus). CLs without copula (43a) and standard *it*-CLs (42a) convey mere information focus only when the subject is focused (Guesser 2011, Quarezemin 2009).

As for the derivation of CLs, since Chomsky (1977) the *it*-CL in (43a) has been known to be derived by *wh*-movement. Under Chomsky's analysis, a *wh*-pronoun is moved to SpecCP and deleted later, as in *that*-relatives. Kiss (1998) postulates a FP category above CP where the focus is moved to when it can be moved, or where it is directly generated when the movement cannot occur. Mioto and Figueiredo Silva (1995), Modesto (2001), Lobo (2006), and Soares (2006) derive (42a) by moving the focus to the Spec position of the CP subcategorized by the copula.

The derivation of inverted CLs (42b, c) can be achieved in two ways. With the copula in present tense it can be assumed that *é-que* "is-that" is an idiom (see Casteleiro 1979, and

Costa and Duarte 2001), and that the focus movement targets the higher CP directly. Thus, the inverted CL is a monoclausal sentence with the focus in Spec-CP and *é-que* in C° (Lobo, Santos, and Soares-Jesel, 2015) or in a left periphery projection (Soares 2006). Where there is no idiom, either the focus stays between the copula and *that* (42a) or, as in BP clefts with *foi-que* "was-that," it is moved higher (42b) (see Guesser 2011).

The BP CL without copula (43a), which is also monoclausal, can be derived by moving the focus phrase to SpecCP (see Resenes 2009).

4.2. Pseudo-clefts

In their full form, pseudo-clefts (PC) are complex sentences. Their matrix clause contains *ser* "to-be" and the focus (underlined in (50)), and the embedded clause seems to be a FR, as in (50):

(50) a. *O que João pescou foi <u>esse peixe</u>.*
    What João fished was this fish.
  b. *Foi <u>esse peixe</u> o que João pescou.*
  c. *<u>Esse peixe</u> foi o que João pescou.*

In (50) we have examples of PCs, with *o que* "what" heading the FR: (50a) is a standard PC; (50b) is a PC with the FR extraposed; (50c) is a PC with inverted focus. Moreover, there are other focusing "PC" strategies available: consider (51), sometimes called reduced PC, where the *wh*-pronoun is absent:

(51) *João pescou foi <u>esse peixe</u>.*
    João fished was this fish
    "(What) João fished was this fish"

Akmajian (1970) points out that a sequence like (52a) is ambiguous in English:

(52) a. What Joana is is scandalous.
  b. Joana is scandalous.
  c. Joana is x and being x is scandalous.

(52a) can have a specificational reading (52b), or a predicational one, (52c). It is interesting to notice that the gender mark in biform adjectives in Portuguese helps us determine the status of a sequence that can be ambiguous in English:

(53) a. *O que Joana é é escandalosa.*
    What Joana is is scandalous-fem
  b. *O que Joana é é escandaloso.*
    What Joana is is scandalous-masc

The feminine mark triggers the specificational reading in (53a) (corresponding to (52b)) while the masculine mark triggers the predicational one in (53b) (corresponding to (52c)).

The gender agreement of the adjective not only contributes to solving the ambiguity, but it also sheds light on the syntactic structure of (53a and b). On the one hand, the FR is the argument of the predicate *escandaloso* "scandalous-masc" and the subject of the copular sentence; thus, the adjective takes the unmarked form (masculine) to agree with the FR. On the other hand, this shows that the syntactic structure of (53a) cannot be like the one of (53b), since the adjective agrees with Joana, taking the feminine form; hence, [*o que Joana é*] does not behave as a subject FR in (53a). We assume that a specificational PC must be a sentence with a meaningless grammatical apparatus (*wh*-pronoun and copula) to focus a constituent, *escandalosa* (scandalous-fem) in (53a).

It should be noticed that attempts to derive a PC from a small clause from which the FR is moved (as proposed by Costa and Duarte 2001, for example) must be prepared to explain the patterns of gender agreement just described.

The agreement problem meets the well-known "Connectivity Effects" (CE) of specificational pseudo-clefts, since both phenomena depend on the c-command configuration. Boskovic (1997) provides a solution for CE by recovering c-command at LF. Analyses such as those proposed by Boeckx (2007) and Kato and Mioto (2010) seek to solve agreement and the CE problems by restoring the subject-predicate relation in visible syntax, at the beginning of the derivation. For Boeckx, a sentence like (53a) starts up as (54a); for Kato and Mioto, as (54b):

(54) a. Boeckx (adapted):   *Joana é indigna de si mesma*
                                          Joana is unworthy-fem of herself
       b. Kato and Mioto: *Joana é [o que, indigna de si mesma]*[9]
                                          Joana is [what, unworthy-fem of herself]

After successive mergers and movements, PC is derived. By doing so, such analyses recover the required c-command configuration lost along the derivation.

As for the reduced PC, there are two different approaches. Wheeler (1982) and Toribio (1992) suppose that a reduced PC is simply a PC without the *wh*-pronoun. But, by pointing out several asymmetries in Caribbean Spanish, Bosque (1999) convincingly shows that the derivation of reduced PC cannot be so simple. Bosque (1999), Camacho (2006), Kato and Mioto (2010) and Mioto (2012) consider that the copula is taken to be a device to focus the constituents at the low IP area, including the whole VP.

5. Concluding remarks

In this chapter, we have shown that there are common properties to three different structures of Portuguese—interrogatives, relatives and clefts. However, we have also shown that these structures differ in many respects. We have described some of these similarities and differences; we have also tried to describe and explain some of the differences between EP and BP varieties. The nature of the cross-linguistic constraints on *wh*-movement structures is still open to discussion and further investigation will certainly bring new light on some of the issues we have briefly discussed here. However, we hope to have shown that the data from Portuguese, in particular the rich patterns of interrogatives and clefts, are extremely interesting for the understanding of the nature of abstract principles of grammar and of the syntax–discourse interface.

NOTES

1 Strong islands are sentential domains, like a relative sentence, from where a phrase cannot be extracted, as in:

(i) **O que, João viu o menino   [que   comeu t,]?*
    What   João saw the boy   that   ate

However, extraction from a weak island, like an interrogative, is possible in Portuguese:

(ii) *Que livro$_i$ João perguntou [se Joana leu t$_i$]?*
Which book João asked whether Joana read

2 Ambar's analysis supposes a multilayered CP hosting the *wh*-phrase and the remnant IP as presupposed information (Kayne 1994).

3 The *wh*-criterion requires a head endowed with the *wh*-feature to be in Spec-head configuration with a *wh*-operator (a *wh*-phrase) and vice-versa.

4 In traditional analyses, the relative clause is either adjoined to NP, the nominal maximal projection, or to N'. More recently, following the DP hypothesis (Abney 1987), one may consider that the relative clause may be adjoined to NP selected by D (restrictive relative) or to DP (appositive relative) (Demirdache 1991).

5 *Pro* is one of the empty categories postulated in the principles and parameters framework. It is a base-generated empty category, functioning as a null pronominal. First proposed for null subjects (Chomsky 1982), it was later extended to other contexts, including for example nominal ellipsis (Lobeck 1995) and some types of null objects (Rizzi 1986).

6 Other structures discussed in the literature are so-called "transparent free relatives" (Ferreira 2007; Marchesan 2012). Due to space limitations, we will not discuss them here.

7 Below we will discuss if the *be*-fragment can be a fragment of a cleft or a pseudo-cleft.

8 At least it does not correspond to a full cleft. (45a) can be considered a *be*-fragment cleft whose full form would be:
Foi o aluno que foi reprovado que pediu cursos de revisão.
was *the student that failed* that requested courses of revision

9 The bracketed constituent is conceived by Kato and Mioto as a complex constituent similar to those of clitic doubling postulated by Kayne (2002).

REFERENCES

Abney, S. P. (1987). The English noun phrase in its sentential aspect. Ph.D. thesis, Massachusetts Institute of Technology. MIT Working Papers in Linguistics, Cambridge, MA.

Alexandre, N. (2000). A Estratégia Resumptiva em Relativas Restritivas do Português Europeu. Masters dissertation, Faculdade de Letras da Universidade de Lisboa.

Akmajian, A. (1970). On deriving cleft sentences from pseudocleft sentences. *Linguistic Inquiry*, 1, pp. 149–168.

Ambar, M. (1988). *Para uma Sintaxe da Inversão Sujeito-Verbo em Português*. Ph.D. dissertation. Lisboa: Colibri (published 1992).

Ambar, M. (2003). WH asymmetries. In A. M. Di Sciullo (ed.), *Asymmetries in Grammar*. Amsterdam: John Benjamins, pp. 209–250.

Ambar, M. (2005). Clefts and tense asymmetries. In A. M. di Sciullo (ed.), *UG and External Systems*. Amsterdam: John Benjamins, pp. 95–129.

Barbosa, P. (2001). On inversion in wh-questions in romance. In A. Hulk and J.-Y. Pollock (eds.), *Subject Inversion in Romance and the Theory of*

Universal Grammar. New York: Oxford University Press, pp. 20–59.

Belletti, A. (2004). Aspects of the low IP area. In L. Rizzi (ed.), *The Structure of IP and CP. The Cartography of Syntactic Structures*, vol. 2. New York: Oxford University Press, pp. 16–51.

Boeckx, C. (2007). Pseudocleft: a fully derivational account. In J. Bayer, T. Bhattacharya, and M. T. Hany Babu (eds.), *Linguistic Theory and South Asian Languages: Essays in Honour of K. A. Jayaseelan*. Amsterdam: John Benjamins, pp. 29–40.

Bosque, I. (1999). On focus vs. wh-movement: the case of Caribbean Spanish. *Sophia Linguistica Working Papers in Linguistics*, 44/45, pp. 1–32.

Bošković, Ž (1997). Pseudoclefts, *Studia Linguistica*, 51(3), pp. 235–277.

Braga, M. L., M. A. Kato, and C. Mioto (2009). As Construções-Q no Português Brasileiro Falado. In: M. A. Kato and M. do Nascimento. (eds.), *Gramática do Português Culto Falado no Brasil: a Construção da Sentença*. Campinas: Editora da UNICAMP, Vol. 3, pp. 237–290.

Brito, A. (1991). A sintaxe das orações relativas em português: estrutura, mecanismos interpretativos e condições sobre a distribuição dos morfemas relativos. Ph.D. dissertation, Instituto Nacional Nacional de Investigação Científica.

Bruening, B. (2007). *Wh*-in-situ does not correlate with *wh*-indefinites or question particles. *Linguistic Inquiry*, 38 (1), pp. 139–166.

Camacho, J. (2006). In situ focus in Caribbean Spanish: towards a unified account of focus. In N. Sagarra and J. Toribio (eds.), *Hispanic Linguistics Symposium*. Somerville, MA: Cascadilla Press, pp. 13–23.

Cardoso, A. (2011). Orações relativas apositivas em português: entre a sincronia e a diacronia. *Estudos de Lingüística Galega*, 3, pp. 5–29.

Casteleiro, J. M. (1979). Sintaxe e semântica das construções enfáticas com "é que". *Boletim de Filologia*, XXV, pp. 97–166.

Cheng, L. L.-S. (2003). Wh-in-situ. *Glot International*, 7 (4), pp. 103–109.

Cheng, L. and J. Rooryk (2000). Licensing wh-in-situ. *Syntax*, 3, pp. 1–19.

Chomsky, N. (1977), On wh movement. In P. Culicover, T. Wasow, and A. Akmajian (eds.), *Formal Syntax*. New York: Academic Press, pp. 71–132.

Chomsky, N. (1982). *Some Concepts and Conequences of the Theory of Government and Binding*. Cambridge, MA: MIT Press.

Chomsky, N. (1995). *The Minimalist Program*. Cambridge, MA: MIT Press.

Costa, J. and I. Duarte (2001). Minimizando a estrutura: uma análise unificada das construções de clivagem em Português. In C. Correia and A. Gonçalves (eds.), *Actas do XVI ENAPL*. Lisbon: APL/Colibri, pp. 627–638.

Costa, J., A. Fiéis, and M. Lobo (2012). Pied-piping e movimento em estruturas adverbiais. *Textos Selecionados, XXVII Encontro Nacional da Associação Portuguesa de Linguística*. Lisbon: APL, pp. 185–195.

Costa, J. and M. Lobo (2009). Estruturas clivadas: evidência dos dados do português europeu não-*standard*. *Anais do Congresso Internacional da Abralin – João Pessoa – 2009*, vol. 2. João Pessoa: Universidade Federal Paraná, pp. 3800–3806.

Demirdache, H. (1991). Resumptive chains in restrictive relatives, appositives, and dislocation structures. Ph.D. dissertation, MIT.

Ferreira, S. A. (2007). Sobre a função e a forma de alguns subtipos especiais de orações relativas sem antecedente expresso do português. MA dissertation, Lisbon: FLUL.

Grimshaw, J. (1977). English Wh-Constructions and the Theory of Grammar. PhD Dissertation, University of Massachusetts, Amherst.

Guesser, S. (2011). La Sintassi delle frasi cleft in Portoghese Brasiliano. Ph.D. dissertation, Università di Siena.

Harbert, W. (1983). On the nature of the matching parameter. *The Linguistic Review*, 2 (3), pp. 237–284.

Kato, M. A. (2013). Deriving "wh-in-situ" through movement in Brazilian Portuguese. In V. Camacho-Taboada, Á. L. Jiménez-Fernández, J. Martín-González, and M. Reyes-Tejedor (eds.), *Information Structure and Agreement*. Amsterdam: John Benjamins, pp. 175–192.

Kato, M. A. and C. Mioto (2010). Pseudo-clefts and semi-clefts in Portuguese and Caribbean Spanish. Paper presented at Romania Nova, Campos do Jordão.

Kayne, R. (1994). *The Antisymmetry of Syntax*. Cambridge, MA: MIT Press.

Kayne, R. (2002). Pronouns and their antecedents. In S. Epstein and D. Seely (eds.), *Derivation and Explanation in the Minimalist Program*. Malden, MA: Blackwell, pp. 133–166.

Kenedy, E. (2002). Aspectos estruturais da relativização em português – uma análise baseada no modelo raising. Masters dissertation, Federal University of Rio de Janeiro.

Kiss, K. (1998). Identificational focus versus information focus. *Language* 74, pp. 245–273.

Lobeck, A. (1995). Ellipsis: functional heads, licensing and identification. *Language*, 72 (3), pp 634–637.

Lobo, M. (2006). Assimetrias em construções de clivagem do português: movimento vs. geração na base. *XXI Encontro Nacional da Associação Portuguesa de Linguística. Textos Seleccionados*, Lisbon: APL/Colibri, pp. 457–473.

Lobo, M., A. L. Santos, and C. Soares-Jesel (2015). Syntactic structure and information structure: the acquisition of Portuguese clefts and Be-fragments, *Language Acquisition*, DOI: 10.1080/10489223.2015.1067317

Marchesan, A. C. (2012). *As relativas livres no Português Brasileiro*. Masters dissertation, Federal University of Santa Catarina.

Marchesan, A. C. and C. Mioto (2012). As relativas livres infinitivas no PB. Manuscript.

McCloskey, J. (1990). Resumptive pronouns, Ā-binding and levels of representation in Irish. In R. Hendrick, ed. *The Syntax of the Modern Celtic Languages. Syntax and Semantics* Vol. 23,

San Diego: Academic Press, pp. 199–248. [Republished in Rouveret, A. (ed.) (2011). *Resumptive Pronouns at the Interfaces*.] Amsterdam/Philadelphia: John Benjamins.

Mioto, C. (1994). As interrogativas no português brasileiro e o critério-WH. *Letras de Hoje*, 96, pp. 19–33.

Mioto, C. (2011). Interrogativas WH no português europeu e no português brasileiro. In R. Pires de Oliveira and C. Mioto (eds.), *Percursos em Teoria da Gramática*. Florianópolis: Editora da UFSC, pp. 43–72.

Mioto, C. (2012). Reduced pseudoclefts in Caribbean Spanish and in Brazilian Portuguese. In V. Bianchi and C. Chesi. (eds.), *Enjoy Linguistics! Papers offered to Luigi Rizzi on the occasion of his 60th birthday*. Siena: CISCL Press, pp. 287–302.

Mioto, C. and M. C. Figueiredo Silva (1995). Wh que = Wh é que? *DELTA*,11(2), pp. 301–311.

Mioto, C. and M. A. Kato (2005). As interrogativas Q do português europeu e do português brasileiro atuais. *Revista da ABRALIN*, 4 (1), pp. 171–196.

Mioto, C. and E. V. Negrão (2007). As sentenças clivadas não contêm uma relativa. In A. T. de Castilho, M. A. Torres-Morais; R. E. V. Lopes, S. M. L. Cyrino (eds.), *Descrição, História e Aquisição do Português Brasileiro*. Campinas: Pontes, pp. 159–183.

Mioto, C., M. C. Figueiredo Silva and R. Lopes (2013). *Novo manual de sintaxe*. São Paulo: Editora Contexto.

Modesto, M. (2001). *As construções clivadas no português do Brasil: relações entre interpretação focal, movimento sintático e prosódia*. São Paulo: Humanitas/FFLCH/USP.

Móia, T. (1992). A sintaxe das orações relativas sem antecedente expresso do português. Masters dissertation, Faculdade de Letras da Universidade de Lisboa.

Negrão, E. V. (1994). As relativas livres no PB: efeito de conformidade categorial. *Estudos Linguísticos, Seminário do Gel*, XXIII, Ribeirão Preto. Anais, São Paulo, vol. 2, pp. 1036–1284.

Pires, A. and H. L. Taylor (2007). The syntax of wh-in-situ and common ground. *Proceedings from the Annual Meeting of the Chicago Linguistic Society 43*, 2, pp. 201–215.

Quarezemin, S. (2009). Estratégias de focalização no português brasileiro: uma abordagem cartográfica. Ph.D. dissertation, Universidade Federal de Santa Catarina.

Resenes, M. S. de (2009). Sentenças Pseudo-clivadas do Português Brasileiro. Masters dissertation, Universidade Federal de Santa Catarina.

Rizzi, L. (1986). Null objects in Italian and the theory of *pro*. *Linguistic Inquiry*, 17 (3), pp. 501–557.

Rizzi, L. (1996). Residual verb second and the wh criterion. In A. Belletti and L. Rizzi (eds.), *Parameters and Functional Heads: Essays in Comparative Syntax*. New York: Oxford University Press, pp. 64–90.

Rouveret, A. (2011). Some issues in the theory of resumption: A perspective on early and recent research. In A. Rouveret (ed.), *Resumptive Pronouns at the Interfaces*. Amsterdam/Philadephia: John Benjamins, pp. 1–62.

Soares, C. (2006). La syntaxe de la périphérie gauche en portugais européen et son acquisition. PhD dissertation. Paris: University of Paris 8.

Stalnaker, R. (2002). Common ground. *Linguistics and Philosophy*, 25, pp. 701–721.

Suñer, M. (1984). Free relatives and the matching parameter. *The Linguistic Review*, 3 (4), pp. 363–387.

Tarallo, F. (1983). Relativization strategies in Brazilian Portuguese. Ph.D. dissertation, University of Pennsylvania.

Tarallo, F. (1985). The filling of the gap: Pro-drop rules in Brazilian Portuguese. In L. King, L. And A. Maley (eds.), *Selected Papers from the XIIIth Linguistic Symposium on Romance Languages*. Amsterdam/Philadelphia: John Benjamins.

Toríbio, A. J. (1992). Proper government in Spanish subject relativization. *Probus*, 4, pp. 291–304.

Wheeler, D. (1982). Portuguese pseudo-clefts: evidence for free relatives. *Eighteenth Regional Meeting Chicago Linguistic Society*, pp. 507–520.

Zubizarreta, M. L. (1998). *Prosody, Focus, and Word Order, Linguistic Inquiry Monograph 33*. Cambridge, MA: MIT Press.

16 Null Objects and VP Ellipsis in European and Brazilian Portuguese

SONIA CYRINO AND GABRIELA MATOS

1. Introduction

Null Object and VP ellipsis share the property of involving the omission of the complement selected by the verb. Their occurrence across languages does not fully overlap. In Portuguese, both constructions coexist, some sentences being ambiguous between the two constructions. In this section we will outline the scope of our study, in Sections 2 and 3 we will respectively analyze the properties of Null Object and VP ellipsis in European and Brazilian Portuguese, (henceforth, EP and BP).

Null Object (henceforth, Null-Obj) designates the absence of the phonological expression of the necessary nominal internal complement of a verb, and corresponds to a silent DP that could be recovered from a situational or linguistic context.

This construction has been the topic of various studies since the 1980s, in the Principles and Parameters framework. The issue emerged in the discussion of empty categories and the Null Subject Parameter, from the observation that some languages allow the complement of transitive verbs to be phonologically null. The seminal work on Null-Obj was published by Huang (1984). It focuses on Chinese, a language that allows both subjects and objects to be null. In Chinese, null subjects can be pronominal or variables, but null objects are variables bound by a discourse topic.

Following that work, Null-Obj has been discussed in many languages, among them, EP (Raposo 1986, 2004, Duarte 1987, Duarte and Costa 2013), and BP (Galves 1989; Farrell 1990; Kato 1993; Cyrino 1997). Many kinds of omitted direct objects received attention in the literature, namely:

Deitic and situational Null-Obj: the referent of the null object is recovered from the situational context:

(1) *Envie__ por correio.*
    send   by mail
    "Send this/that by mail."

The Handbook of Portuguese Linguistics, First Edition. Edited by W. Leo Wetzels, João Costa, and Sergio Menuzzi.
© 2016 John Wiley & Sons, Inc. Published 2020 by John Wiley & Sons, Inc.

(2) [Situation: Someone sees a famous star in a restaurant and makes the comment:]
    Eu   viu   __   na   TV ontem.
    I   saw   on.the TV yesterday
    "I saw him on TV yesterday."

Cognate Null-Obj: the null object refers to an object easily recovered from the lexical content of the verb:

(3) *Durante as minhas férias,   quero sobretudo ler__.*
    during the my   vacation want mainly   read
    "During my vacation, I mainly want to read."

Arbitrary Null-Obj, where the missing object is understood as part of the lexical meaning of some verbs:

(4) *Isto   leva   à   seguinte   conclusão.*
    this leads to-the following conclusion
    "This leads (us/people) to the following conclusion."

Anaphoric Null-Obj: the null object has a linguistic antecedent.

(5) *Ele comprou o   casaco sem   experimentar__.*
    he bought   the coat   without try
    "He bought the coat without trying (it) on."

As shown in the examples (1) to (5), Portuguese allows different types of Null-Obj. In this work we will focus on definite anaphoric and situational null objects, i.e., the cases in (2) and (5).

VP ellipsis (henceforth, VPE) designates the lack of the phonological expression that includes the verbal complement of a verb or verbal sequence and optionally its adjunct(s). Early analyses on VP ellipsis focused on English. In this language VP ellipsis only occurs with auxiliary verbs, the infinitival marker *to* and the copulative verb "to be":

(6) Mary loves Peter and Ann does ___, too.

(7) Mary wants to buy an encyclopedia and I also want to ___.

(8) a. who is the best basketball player in the neighborhood?
    b. John is ___.

The study of predicate ellipsis has been extended to other languages, and a different strategy of VP ellipsis has been put forth, where the elliptical VP is licensed by a main verb. Goldberg (2005) called this "verb stranding VPE." Raposo (1986) was the first to claim the existence of this strategy in EP.

(9) a. *A   empregada   colocou os   livros   na   estante?*
      the housemaid put   the books on-the shelf
      "Did the housemaid put the books on the shelf?"
    b. *Sim, colocou ___.*
      Yes, put
      Yes, she did.

Within the Principles and Parameters framework, VPE analyses mainly focused on the licensing condition(s) on the elliptical constituent and the recovering strategy of ellipsis. We will retain these topics in the study of VPE in EP and BP.

2. Null-Obj in EP and BP

The recurring issues on Null-Obj in EP and BP are the determination of the omitted constituent and the [± animacy] status of its antecedent.

2.1. *The nature of the empty category*

Null-Obj was first characterized for EP by Raposo (1986). He showed that the content of the object gap could be recovered by the pragmatic (10a) or the linguistic (10b) context, and denoted entities with specific definite content, as attested by their capacity to alternate with definite clitic pronouns (11):

(10) a. *A   Joana   viu _   na   TV   ontem.*   (EP)
        the   Joana   saw _   on-the TV   yesterday
        "Joana saw (it/him/her/them) on TV yesterday."
     b. *A   Maria   pegou   nos   livros   e   guardou _ cuidadosamente   na*
        the Maria   pick up   in-the   books   and   put   carefully   in-the
        estante.
        shelf
        "Maria pick up the books and carefully put (them) on the shelf."

(11) a. *A   Joana   viu-o(s)/a(s)*   *na   TV   ontem.*   (EP)
        the Joana   saw-cl.3-masc/fem-sg/pl   on-the TV   yesterday
        "Joana saw them on TV yesterday."
     b. *A   Maria   pegou   nos   livros   e   guardou-os   cuidadosamente   na*
        the Maria   pick up   in-the   books   and   put-cl-3pl   carefully   in-the
        estante.
        shelf
        "Mary pick up the books and carefully put them in the shelf."

Raposo pointed out that the availability of definite Null-Obj distinguishes EP from other Romance languages, which require a definite overt pronoun (see (12) for Spanish and in (13) for French):

(12) *Maria   *(los)   vio   en   la   tele   ayer.*
     Maria   (cl.3-pl)   saw   on   the   TV   yesterday
     "Maria saw them on TV yesterday."

(13) *Marie   *(les)   a   vu   à   la   télé   hier.*
     Marie   (cl.3-pl)   has   seen   on   the   TV   yesterday
     "Marie has seen them on TV yesterday."

Raposo remarked that Null-Obj in EP and Chinese behave alike. In both languages they may be pragmatic controlled (10a) and the object gap functions as a variable. Thus, following

Huang (1984), he assumes that Null-Obj in EP involves a Topic position, whose meaning is recovered from the situational context:

(14) [Top -] [*a Joana viu _ na TV ontem*]

He also presents evidence that the omitted object is an A'-bound variable, contrasting the examples (15) and (16). In (15a) the object gap inside the embedded sentence may not co-refer with the subject of the embedding clause, in contrast with an overt pronoun in object position (15b). As shown in (16), the omitted object in Null-Obj behaves like a variable resulting from *wh*-movement—in both cases there is as a strong crossover violation, i.e., a Principle C effect, since the variable must be free within the scope domain of its A'-binder, the null operator in (15a), *quem* "who," in (16):

(15) a. **Ele$_i$ pensa   que   eu   recomendei$_{-i}$ ao   professor.*   (EP)
      he   thinks   that   I   recommended   to-the   professor
   b. *Ele   pensa   que   eu   o   recomendei   ao   professor.*   (EP)
      he   thinks   that   I   cl-masc-3-sg   recommended   to-the   professor.
      "He thinks that I recommended him to the professor."

(16) **Quem$_i$ é que   ele$_i$ pensa   que   eu   recomendei   __$_i$ ao   professor?*
      who   is_that   he   thinks   that   I   recommended   to-the   professor
      "Who does he thinks that I recommended to the professor."

However, departing from Huang, who directly relates the variable to the "zero topic," Raposo assumes that the null operator arises from movement of the omitted object to Comp in syntax. A rule of predication would relate Top and the null operator in Comp, establishing its content in a latter level of representation, sensitive to discourse/pragmatic information:

(17) [Top -]$_p$ [[$_C$ OP$_i$-]$_p$ [*a Joana viu*$_{-i}$ *na   TV ontem*]]

Raposo also shows that Null-Obj in EP involves A'-Movement in overt syntax, since it is excluded from islands, namely from the Complex-NP (18), the Sentential Subject (19) and the Sentential Adjunct (20):

(18) a. *O   rapaz   trouxe__   agora   mesmo   da   pastelaria.*   (EP)
      the   boy   brought   right   now   from-the   pastry shop.
   b. **O   rapaz   que   trouxe__   agora   mesmo   da   pastelaria   era   o*
      the   boy   who   brought   right   now   from-the   pastry shop   was   the
      teu   afilhado.   (EP)
      your   godson

(19) [context: talking about a new personal computer]
      *Que a   IBM   venda__   a   particulares   supreende-me.   (EP)
      that the   IBM   sell.subjunctive   to   private people   surprises-cl.acc-1-sg

(20) [context: talking about a treasure map]   (EP)
      *O   pirata   partiu   para   as   Caraíbas   depois de   ter   guardado__   no   cofre.
      the   pirate   left   to   the   Caraíbas   after of   has   kept   in-the   safe

Also, like other syntactic A′-movement variables, the object gap in EP may license parasitic gaps in adjunct adverbial sentences occurring after the Null-Obj clause. As shown in (21), the parasitic gap in this example is as acceptable as the anaphoric null object in (5), above:

(21) *Arrumei___   na   estante   sem   sequer   ler___pg .*   (EP)
       put   in-the   shelf   without   even   read

Since this analysis captures the core behavior of Null-Obj in EP, for the most part, it has been kept in later work, which mainly discussed the initial nature of the object gap and its final landing site in this language variety.

Raposo (1986) imputes the need of object movement to the original nature of the null object, which he claims to be PRO, a category that may not be governed. Thus, PRO must raise from object position to Comp, a non-thematic position. Assuming the configuration (17), Raposo abandons Huang's (1984) parametric criterion to distinguish languages with and without Null-Obj. According to Huang, discourse-oriented languages, like Chinese, accept a null R-expression A′-bound by a null topic, but sentence-oriented languages, like English, do not. For Raposo, the parametric variation between these types of languages relies on the application of the Predication rule: in Chinese and EP this rule may apply to a pragmatic topic, in English, French, or Spanish it cannot.

Duarte (1987) casts doubts on the derivational change of the null category, and proposes that it should be basically generated as a variable. She closely relates Null-Obj in EP to Topicalization, a specific topic construction that A′-moves a constituent that binds a variable:

(22) *Esse   jogo,   a   Joana   viu___   na   TV   ontem.*   (EP)
       that   match   the   Joana   saw   on-the TV   yesterday
       "That match, Joana saw (it) on TV yesterday."

Accepting that topicalization in EP involves adjunction to CP or IP, she presents an alternative configuration for Null-Obj, where the null topic in A′-position is included within the Comp domain:

(23) $[_{CP} [_{Top} -] [_{IP}$ *a Joana viu _ na TV ontem]* $]$

Accordingly, Duarte reviews Raposo's (1986) formulation of the Null-Obj parameter and reformulates it in terms much closer to those of Huang (1984):

(24) The content of a null (or overt) syntactic operator may/or may not be set in LF′ by an element of the discursive or situational context.

In turn, Raposo (2004) reexamines his previous analysis and relates Null-Obj in EP to Clitic Left Dislocation (CLLD), (25). He claims that the object gap is merged as a DP with a null definite determiner that selects $[_{NP}$ *pro*$]$, (26):

(25) *Esse   livro,   eu   só   o   encontrei   na   FNAC.*   (EP)
       that   book   I   only   cl-masc-3-sg   found   in-the   FNAC
       "That book, I only found it at FNAC."

(26) a. *Eu   só   encontrei _ na   FNAC.*   (EP)
         I   only   found   in-the   FNAC
         "I only found it at FNAC."
     b. *Eu   só   encontrei* $[_{DP}$ *Ø*$_{def}$ $[_{NP}$ *pro]] na FNAC*

Raposo argues that in the context of a definite null Det, *pro* is not adequately identified because vi lacks number and gender features. To be recovered, *pro* has to move to a position as close as possible of i-s antecedent, a topic or an argument in A-position. He claims that *pro* adjoins to the head F, a functional category in the sentence left periphery that codifies the interplay between LF with the semantic, discursive and pragmatic systems. In that position *pro* acts as an operator that A'-binds and identifies its copy, represented as "t" in (27):

(27) *(esse livro)*, [$_{FP}$ pro F [$_{TP}$ *eu só encontrei* [$_{DP}$ ₀ø [$_{NP}$t]] *na FNAC*.

Raposo's (2004) analysis allows him to assume that there is no change in the nature of the null category during the derivation, while maintaining the core ideas of his original proposal: the characterization of the object gap as a variable resulting from A'-Movement in syntax, and the indirect relation between the null operator (*pro* in F) and the Topic in CLLD. However, this CLLD approach is challenged by himself, since he denies the possibility of considering the D heading the null object DP as a clitic, given its lack of phonological features.

Turning now to BP, within the Government and Binding framework, Farrell (1990), Galves (1989) and Kato (1993) proposed *pro* for the empty category occurring in Null-Obj, based on the fact that this construction may appear in islands in BP, as shown by the acceptability of (28) in PB in contrast with its marginality in EP (cf. (18b)–(20)):

(28) a. *O   rapaz   que   trouxe__   agora mesmo   da   pastelaria   era   o   teu*
         the   boy   that brought   now just   of-the   pastry shop   was   the your
         afilhado.   (BP)
         godson
         "The boy that brought (it) just now from the pastry shop was your godson."

     b. *O   pirata   partiu   para   as   Caraíbas   depois   de   ter   guardado___*
         the   pirate   left   to   the   Caraibas   after   of   have   kept
         cuidadosamente   no   cofre.   (BP)
         carefully   in-the   safe.
         "The pirate left for the Caraibas after having kept (it) carefully in the safe."

Additionally, Farrell (1990) rejects the variable status of null object in BP because some sentences, which are unacceptable in some contexts and would be analyzed as Principle C effects (29a, c), become acceptable in other contexts (29b):

(29) a. **Ele$_i$ disse   que   Maria   não   beijou   ___$_i$*   (BP)
         He   said   that Maria   not   kissed
         "He$_i$ said that Maria didn't kiss (him$_i$)."

     b. *Todo   mundo   disse   que   Maria   beijou   Pedro$_i$ depois   do   baile.*
         All   world   said   that Maria   kissed   Pedro   after   of-the   dance.
         Mas   ele$_i$ disse   que   Maria   não   beijou ___$_i$.   (BP)
         But   he   said   that Maria   not   kissed
         "Everybody said that Maria kissed Pedro$_i$ after the dance. But he$_i$ said that Maria didn't kiss (him$_i$)."

     c. *OP$_i$ ele$_i$ disse   que   Maria   não   beijou ___$_i$.*   (BP)
              he   said   that Maria   not   kissed.

To account for the marginality of (29a), he claims that the antecedent of a null object in a complement clause cannot be the subject of the matrix sentence, but he assumes that this is possible in adjunct clauses in BP, on the basis of examples like (30a), which are rejected by several BP native speakers, unless they occur in an adequate discourse context (31b):

(30) a. (*)*A   Júlia$_i$ sempre   chora   quando   ponho* ___$_i$ *no   berço*   (BP)
       the   Júlia   always   cries   when   put   in-the cradle.
       "Julia$_i$ always cries when (I) put (her$_i$) in the cradle."

   b. *Eu   sempre   ponho   meus   filhos   no   berço   sem   problemas.* (BP)
       I   always   put-1-sg   my   children   in-the   cradle   without   problems.
       Mas   a   Júlia$_i$ sempre   chora   quando   ponho ___$_i$ *no   berço.*   (BP)
       But   the   Júlia   always   cries   when   put   in-the   cradle.
       "I always put my children in the cradle with no problems. But Julia$_i$ always cries when (I) put (her$_i$) in the cradle."

However, there is some disagreement regarding the licensing and identification of *pro* among the analyses that take this category as null object in BP.

Farrell (1990) considers that the omitted object is formally licensed by INFL or V, and intrinsically specified as 3rd person. But Kato (1993) remarks that, then, BP would have one kind of *pro* for subjects and another for objects.

Galves (1989) assumes that the object *pro* is a base-generated empty category bound to an external subject in BP, being a simultaneously free and bound empty category. In later work she claims that the object *pro* is licensed by V and identified by a *pro* in Spec-Agr, leaving, however unexplained the unacceptability of (29a), (30a).

Kato (1993) proposes that the null object in BP is an instance of *pro* which is identified as 3rd person and licensed by a null clitic, whose antecedent is always in an anti-c-command position.

Barra-Ferreira (2000) conceives the null object in BP as a *pro* without Case features, which is A′-bound by a null topic. According to him, sentences with topicalized elements may be obtained through movement to Top, or result from the insertion of a caseless *pro*. Thus the object position in (31) is ambiguous between a trace or a caseless *pro*:

(31) *Esse   livro$_{i'}$ a   Maria   conhece   o   cara   que   escreveu* ___$_i$.   (BP)
      This   book   the   Maria   know   the   guy   that   wrote
      "This book, Maria knows the person who wrote (it)."

Since traces of movement are excluded from islands, a sentence like (32) could only contain a *pro* in object position. It should be grammatical in BP, but marginal in EP, which is, in fact, considered degraded by most EP native speakers:

(32) *Esse   livro$_{i'}$ eu   ainda não   consegui   um   aluno   que   lesse pro$_i$.* (BP/*EP)
      that book   I   still   not   got   a   student   that   read
      "This book$_{i'}$ I still haven't got a student that read (it$_i$)."

Still, the proposal for the null object in BP as a *pro* is not uncontroversial, and does not explain why *pro* behaves differently from an overt an pronoun in sentences like (33):

(33) *O   Pedro$_i$ disse   que   ela   não   beijou {*___$_i$/$^\sqrt{}$ele$_i$}.*   (BP)
      the   Pedro   said   that   she   not   kissed___/him
      "Pedro$_i$ said that she didn't kiss (him$_i$)."

Furthermore, the null object cannot be *pro*, because it differs from *pro* in accepting both strict and sloppy readings:

(34) *De noite, João abriu   a   janela,   mas Pedro preferiu   fechar__.*   (BP)
     At night João opened   the   window but   Pedro preferred to-close
     "At night, João opened the window, but Pedro preferred to close it."
     __= João's window (*strict reading*)
     __= Pedro's window (*sloppy reading*)

Cyrino (1997) presents a different proposal. She claims that the null object in BP is the result of DP ellipsis, due to a diachronic process that related propositional ellipsis to the demise of 3rd person clitics in the language.

The proposal that the null object in BP is an instance of DP ellipsis is backed up by two facts that point to a similarity with the propositional ellipsis: the null object in BP requires an [-animate] antecedent and allows strict/sloppy readings.

2.2. *Animacy restrictions on Null-Obj antecedent*

Within the Principles and Parameters framework, several authors correlated the fact that the null object preferably has a [-animate] antecedent with the nature of the null object.

Contrasting sentences like (35) with (36), Bianchi and Figueiredo (1994) propose to split the analysis for the empty category into two, variables and *pro*, according to whether the antecedent is [+animate] or [-animate]:

(35) a. **O   José$_i$ impediu   a   esposa   de   matar __$_i$*   (BP)
       the   José   prevented   the   wife   of   kill
       "José$_i$ prevented his wife from killing (him$_i$)."
   b. **O   José$_i$ sabe   que   a   Maria   gostaria   de conhecer __$_i$*
       the   José   knows   that   the   Maria   likes   of know
       "José$_i$ knows that Maria would like to meet (him$_i$)."

(36) a. *Esse tipo   de   garrafa$_i$ impede   as   crianças   de   abrirem __$_i$ sozinhas.*   (BP)
       this kind   of   bottle prevents   the   children   of   open   alone.
       "This kind of bottle prevents children from opening (it) by themselves."
   b. *Esse prato$_i$ exige   que   o   cozinheiro acabe   de   preparar __$_i$ na mesa.*   (BP)
       this   dish   requires   that   the   cook   finish   of   prepare in-the table.
       "This dish requires that the cook finishes to prepare (it) at table."

For the [+animate] antecedent, the null object would be a variable, thus, not permitted in islands, (37); for the [-animate] antecedent, it would be a *pro*, hence allowed in island domains, (38)

(37) **O   José$_i$ conheceu   a   mulher   que   beijou __$_k$.*   (BP)
     the   José   knew   the   woman   that   kissed
     "José$_i$ knew the woman who kissed (him$_k$)."

(38) *O   José$_i$ conheceu   a   mulher   que   comprou __$_k$.*   (BP)
     the   José   knew   the   woman   that   bought.
     "José$_i$ knew the woman who bought (it)."

Cyrino (1997) remarks that the fact that the null object in BP has an [–animate] antecedent cannot be captured by the variable/*pro* analysis. In fact, sentence (39b), with a null object and an overt pronoun, shows that the only interpretation for the null object is the non-animate antecedent, *o rosto dele* "his face," while the overt pronoun may refer back either to *o rosto dele* or to *meu pai*, the latter an [+animate] antecedent:

(39) a. *Eu   nunca   vejo   o   [meu   pai]₁.   Nem   me lembro   d[o   rosto dele]ⱼ.* (BP)
I   never   see   the   my   father   not-even me remember of-the face   of-his
b. *Acho   que   já   esqueci {____ⱼ/eleᵢ.}*   (BP)
think   that   already   forgot {__/him/it}
"I never see my father. I don't even remember his face. I think I forgot (it)/him/it."

In order to explain the animacy restrictions in null objects (and full pronouns), Cyrino, Duarte, and Kato (2000) propose a Referentiality hierarchy, which stated that if a language has an empty category for a certain element, it will also have this empty category for other elements which are lower in referentiality.

(40) Referentiality hierarchy
non-arguments   propositions   [–animate]   [+animate]
3rd person   2nd person   1st person
[–specific]   [+specific]
[–referential] ←- -→ [+referential]

This hierarchy proposes that referentiality is highly relevant in pronominalization in several languages. Thus, [+N, +human] arguments are in the highest position in the hierarchy, and non-arguments, in the lowest. Regarding pronouns, the speaker (= I) and the hearer (= you), being inherently humans, are in the highest and the third person that refers to a proposition is in lowest, with the [-human] entity in the middle. The [± specific] features interact with all these features. Languages will vary in the spell out of the pronouns.

For the object, specifically, the authors predicted that if the input exhibits a pronoun or a clitic in a lower position of the hierarchy, the child in the acquisition process will consider it a weak pronoun in either a head or an argument position, and, therefore, all the higher positions will also be lexical pronouns or clitics (e.g. English, EP). However, if the input shows a null object for a referential entity, say, for a [–animate] entity as in BP, the child assumes that all lower positions can be null. Thus, for a language that has the internal option for full or empty categories, one of the factors that can influence the choice is the animacy status of the antecedent.

The referential hierarchy elucidates why the pronoun *ele*, which is used for [+animate] antecedents and sometimes also for [–animate] antecedents, is never used for propositional antecedents.

As for EP, Raposo (2004) claims that the animacy restrictions are not clear in this language, based on his acceptability judgments for the following sentences, which exhibit a null object with an [+animate] antecedent (41), and an [–animate] antecedent (42)

(41) a. *??O   polícia   que agrediu   [esse preso]ᵢ   levou ___ᵢ para o hospital.*   (EP)
the   cop   that hit   that prisoner took   to the hospital
b. *?O   polícia que agrediu[esse preso]ᵢ   acha   que é melhor levar ___ᵢ para o   hospital* (EP)
the cop   that hit   that prisoner thinks that is better to-take to   the hospital
"The cop that hit that prisoner thinks that it is better to take him to the hospital."

(42) a. ??*O aluno que tem [o teu artigo]*$_i$ *em casa devolve* ___$_i$ *ainda hoje.* (EP)
the student that keeps the your paper at home brings back still today

    b. *O aluno que tem [o teu artigo]*$_i$ *em casa decidiu que ia*
the student that keeps the your paper at home decided that will
devolver ___$_i$ *ainda hoje.* (EP)
bring back still today
"The student that keeps your paper at home decided that he will bring it back still today."

For him, (41a)–(42a) are both unacceptable because the A'-operator (*pro* in Comp) c-commands the antecedent that identifies it, since it moves to FP in the root sentence, (43). This does not happen in (41b)–(42b), since *pro* occurs in the FP of the embedded clause, (44):

(43) [$_{FP}$ pro F [$_{TP}$ [*O aluno que tem o* teu *artigo em casa*] [*devolve* [$_{DP}$ D pro] *ainda hoje*]]]

(44) [$_{TP}$ *O aluno que tem o* teu *artigo em casa decidiu* [$_{CP}$*que* [$_{FP}$ pro F [$_{TP}$ ia *devolver* [$_{DP}$ D pro] *ainda hoje*]]]

However, many EP native speakers consider all the examples in (41)–(42) degraded independently of the animacy effects, which suggests the null operator always raises to the root sentence in EP.

Duarte and Costa (2013) reconsider the animacy effect in EP, and remark that when the antecedent and the omitted object occur in the same sentence, an animacy restriction appears:

(45) ??*Quando encontro o Pedro*$_i$, *beijo* ___$_i$ *com ternura.* (EP)
when find the Pedro, kiss tenderly
"When I find Pedro, I kiss him tenderly."

(46) *Quando encontro uma gralha*$_i$, *corrijo* ___$_i$ *imediatamente.* (EP)
when find a flaw, correct immediately
"When I find a flaw, I correct it immediately."

However, when the referent is recovered from the situational context or has an antecedent external to the null object sentence, no animacy effect occurs:

(47) [Context: the speaker asks, looking at a picture of a boy on the hearer's desk]
*Conheceste*___ *na Itália?* (EP)
know in-the Italy
"Did you know him in Italy?"

(48) a. *E a Ana?* (EP)
and the Ana
"What about Ana?"

    b. *Encontrei*___ *ontem no concerto.*
Met yesterday in-the concert
"I met her in the concert yesterday."

These authors also notice that the information recovered by the null object must be accessible in the situational or linguistic discourse, as illustrated by the following contrast:

(49) a. O   Pedro   tirou   os   óculos₁   e   guardou__₁   na   gaveta.   (EP)
        the Pedro   took off the   glasses   and kept   in-the drawer
        "Pedro took off the glasses and kept them in the drawer."
     b. *O   Pedro   tirou   os   óculos₁. Ligou   a   TV   e   guardou__₁
        the Pedro   took off the   glasses. Turned on   the TV   and kept
        na   gaveta.   (EP)
        in-the drawer

Duarte and Costa relate this behavior to the need of the omitted object to be recovered by a null topic whose content is established by the prominent linguistic or situational context.

In sum, in Null-Obj in EP and BP, the object gap corresponds to two different categories. In EP it is a variable an A'-bound by a null constituent in Topic position. As for BP, although most researchers have characterized it as *pro*, it presents some properties that suggest that it should be conceived as an elided DP.

Both BP and EP present animacy restriction on null object antecedents, partially related to a referential hierarchy of overt and null pronouns. Yet, these restrictions disappear when the [+animate] antecedent occurs in the previous situational context or in the immediately precedent linguistic discourse.

3. VP ellipsis in EP and BP

Since the 1980s, VPE in EP has been extensively studied, and the properties that this construction displays in EP and BP carefully analyzed. In the literature on VPE in Portuguese (as for English) the main issues focused upon have been: the empirical domain of VPE; the categorial status of the gap; the ellipsis strategy and the licensing condition of the elliptical VP; and the structural conditions on the linguistic antecedent that legitimate the ellipsis. In this work we will mainly focus on the first three issues, since the last one is not specific to VPE and occurs in other kinds of ellipsis and anaphora (for an overview of this subject in EP, see Matos 1992, chapter 2).

EP and BP share the main features that characterize this construction. However, when the licensing of VPE is done by verbal sequences, there are divergences that result from independent factors in each of these language varieties. This fact is crucial to establish in a principled way an account for this construction in both varieties.

3.1. VPE, Null-Obj and NCA

Raposo (1986) was the first to mention the existence in EP of a construction akin to English VPE but involving main verbs. This construction differs from Null-VP by omitting all the complements of the verb (65b(i)), and optionally the VP modifiers (Matos 1992), (65b(ii)):

(50) a. Os miúdos puseram   os   brinquedos na   caixa   antes   do   jantar?
        the kids   put   the   toys   inside-the   box   before   of-the   dinner?
     b. (i) Puseram__.
             put
             "Yes, they did."
     b. (ii) Puseram__ apenas   depois   do   jantar.
             Put   just   after   of-the   dinner
             "Yes, they did, just after dinner."

Raposo remarks that this construction differs from Null-Obj in not recovering an antecedent from a situational context: (50b(i)) is pragmatically anomalous without the linguistic antecedent in (50a):

(51) [situation: The kinds are putting their toys inside a box. Someone entering the room says]:
#*Puseram___.*
(they) put.

He notices that VPE in EP is not sensitive to islands, as shown in (67), where the omitted material occurs inside a Complex DP with a relative clause.

(52) *A   Maria   entregou   o   dinheiro   ao Manel,   mas   eu   sei*
the   Maria   gave   the   money   to the Manel,   but   I   know
de   algumas   pessoas   que   nunca   teriam   entregue___.
of   some   people   that   never   have-condit-3pl   given
"Maria gave the money to Manel, but I know some people that would never have given."

However, the distinction between V-stranding VPE and Null-Obj is not always easy to establish. In fact, the island criterion is not available for BP, where Null-OBJ is insensitive to islands. Furthermore, as Raposo mentions, when the main verb only selects a direct object, the sentences are ambiguous between the two constructions:

(53) a. *Quem   é   que   viu   o   filme?*
who   is   that   saw   the   movie
b. *O   Manel viu___.*
the   Manel saw
Interpretations: (i) "Manel did."
                          (ii) "Manel saw it."

Accepting Raposo's proposals, Matos (1992) developed an analysis of for EP and presented additional facts that differentiate these constructions. She remarks that VPE in EP may be licensed not only by main verbs (50)–(53), but also by auxiliaries (which are obviously excluded from Null-Obj), as illustrated in (69b) and (70), where the perfect tense and the passive auxiliaries occur:

(54) a. *As   crianças   têm   estado   a   estudar?*
the   children   have   been   to   study
"Have the children been studying?"
b. *Sim,   têm ___.*
"Yes, (they)   have."

(55) *As   revistas   não   foram   guardadas   na   estante,   mas   os   livros*
the   journals   not   were   stored   in-the   shelf,   but   the   books
já   foram___
already   were
"The journals have not been stored in the shelf, but the books have been, already."

She additionally notices that the verbal identifier of the omitted material in VPE is subject to a lexical parallelism condition with some verb in the antecedent, (56)–(57b), a constraint not required in Null-Obj, (58):

(56) *Eu   pus   os   óculos   na   mesa   quando   ela   também pôs___   /*colocou_.*
I   put   the   glasses   on-the   table   when   she   also   put   /placed
"I put the glasses on the table when she did, too."

(57) a. *Não   sei   se   hei-de   comprar   esta   gramática.*
     not   know   if   should   buy   this   grammar
     "I don't know if I should buy this grammar."
   b: *Claro que   {hás-de__! /*tens__!}*
     of course   should   /has to
     "Of course you should!"

(58) *Ela   tirou   o   anel   do   dedo   e   guardou__ no   cofre.*
   she   took   the   ring   of-the   finger   and   put   in-the   safe
   "She took off the ring from her finger and put it in the safe."

Matos distinguishes V-stranding VPE from *Null Complement Anaphora* (henceforth NCA), a construction that involves the omission of a sentential complement of the main verb, e.g. *aprovar* "approve," (59a), and also occurs with restructuring verbs like *querer* "want," *dever* "ought," poder "be able to," the last two usually translated by the auxiliaries *shall, can/may* in English, (59b).

(59) a. *Ele   lê   o   jornal   todos os dias   e   eu   aprovo__.*
     he   reads   the   newspaper   every day   and   I   approve__
     "He reads the newspaper every day, and I approve."
   b. *Ele   não lê   o   jornal,   embora   devesse__.*
     he   not reads   the   newspaper   although   ought__
     "He does not read the newspaper, although he should."

As Null-Obj, NCA does not require parallelism between the verb identifying the omitted complement and a verbal antecedent (59a); as VPE, it is not sensitive to island contexts (59b). Yet, as expected, when the antecedent and clause with the complement gap exhibit the same verb, the sentences are ambiguous between NCA and VPE.

This characterization of VPE and NCA has been accepted in several works, and developed to account for EP and BP (see Matos and Cyrino 2001, Cyrino and Matos 2002, 2005, for VPE; Cyrino and Matos 2006, Gonçalves and Matos 2009, for NCA).

3.2. *The parallelism requirement*

Matos (1992) remarks that VPE in EP requires that the verb adjacent to the gap, independently of being an auxiliary or a main verb, be identical to a verb in the antecedent. Thus, (60a) is unacceptable, because in the antecedent only occurs the main verb, but the elliptical VP is locally identified by an auxiliary. In contrast, (60b) is well-formed, since the auxiliary appears in the antecedent and the elliptical sentence. The same lexical parallelism occurs in (60c), where the main verb occurs in both sentences.

(60) a. **Eu   não   compreendi   a   situação,   mas   ele   já   tinha_   há muito.*
     I   not   understood   the   situation,   *but*   he   already   had   since long
     "I did not understand the situation, but he already had since long."
   b. *Eu   não tinha compreendido   a   situação,   mas   ele   já   tinha_há muito.*
     I   not had   understood   the   situation,   *but*   he   already had   since long
   c. *Eu   não   compreendi   a   situação   imediatamente,   mas   ele   compreendeu _.*
     I   not   understood   the   situation   immediately,   *but*   he   understood
     "I did not understand the situation immediately, but he did."

This parallelism requirement becomes understandable when we consider that in Portuguese both auxiliary and main verbs raise out of the verbal phrase to a functional category, T, according to Matos (1992). Thus, in VPE the copy of the moved constituent is part of the ellipsis, as illustrated in (61) for (60b, c). In these representations "t" stands for the copy of the moved elements and the base-merged elliptical constituents are struck through.

(61) a. ...*mas* [$_{TP}$ *ele*$_i$ [$_T$ *tinha*$_j$] [$_{VPaux}$ t$_i$ [$_{vP}$ t$_j$ ~~*compreendido* [*há muito*]~~]
b. ...*mas* [$_{TP}$ *ele*$_i$ [$_T$ *compreendeu*$_j$] [$_{vP}$ t$_i$ t$_j$ ~~*comprendeu* [*imediatamente*]~~]

Accepting this analysis, we assume that VPE corresponds to an elliptical constituent with internal structure, and requires a lexical and structural identity condition for the recovering of the omitted vP/VP.

Still, Santos (2009), restricting her analysis to EP and focusing on main verbs, questions this verbal parallelism on VPE. She denies the NCA status of the omitted constituent selected by complementation restructuring verbs, like *dever* and *poder*, and takes (62) as a case of VPE. In doing so she excludes (the copy of) v from the elliptical constituent, implicitly assuming that VPE is not a verbal projection, but a CP/TP gap, the complement of the verb.

(62) *Ela   podia   ver   filmes   do   César Monteiro   e   tu   também   devias.*
      she   could   see   movies   of-the   César Monteiro   and   you   also   should

Santos also claims that two different non-complementation main verbs may occur in VPE, if they present an identical subcategorization frame:

(63) *O   João   vendeu   livros   à   Teresa   ontem   e   a   Ana   ofereceu*
      the   João   sold   books   to-the   Teresa   yesterday   and   the   Ana   offered
      [~~livros   à   Teresa   ontem~~]
      books   to-the   Teresa   yesterday
      "João sold books to Teresa yesterday and Anna offered them."

Yet, (63) is not an instance of VPE. As the author's translation of this example reveals, only the direct object is recovered. This suggests that in some way (63) involves Null-Obj. Corroborating this hypothesis, these examples become degraded in EP, when they occur in islands:

(64) ??/*Ele   ofereceu   livros   aos   amigos   ontem   porque   ninguém   vendeu__*
       he   offered   books   to-the   friends   yesterday   because   nobody   sold

This proposal is also supported by Costa and Duarte (2003), who extended de notion of null object to the all range of complements of the verb.

Additionally, Santos (2009) takes examples like (65), where the main verb plus the direct object are overt and some other complement is missing, as VPE, by claiming that they may occur in islands in EP:

(65) *A   Ana   entregou   as   chaves   ao   porteiro   quando   a   irmã   entregou*
      the   Ana   gave   the   keys   to-the   porter   when   the   sister   gave
      o   carro__.
      the   car
      "Ana gave the keys to the porter when her sister gave him the car."

Once again, the author's English translation of this example shows that a VPE interpretation is unavailable. Furthermore, this proposal is problematic, since it presupposes that the verb and the direct object form a complex verbal unit (a sort of light verb structure) able to locally identify the alleged elliptical verbal phrase, only constituted by the indirect object, complement of the verb.

Adopting these assumptions, Santos is unable to account for the contrasts in acceptability of (56), (57b) and (60a), and loses a unified explanation of VPE in languages like Portuguese.

So, in the current work we will stick to the traditional view that the local identifier of VPE is a verbal element. We also accept that a parallelism requirement on the verbal licensor of the ellipsis regarding its antecedent must be satisfied in a V-stranding VPE language, like Portuguese.

3.3. *Identity condition on ellipsis and licensing of VPE*

Assuming a derivational approach of grammar, the most plausible way to account for the internal structure of VPE is to assume that deletion has applied to a structure fully filled with lexical items. However, these may be conceived as feature bundles that must not be spelt out at the phonological interface level, in contrast with the non-elliptical constituents.

Thus, independently of adopting a deletion or an interpretative approach of ellipsis the same core properties must be met: the elliptical constituents to be deleted/interpreted must be recovered on the basis of the lexical and structural material of the antecedent.

As mentioned by several authors, the identity requirements on ellipsis must be better understood as a condition of lexical and structural non-distinctiveness. In fact, local restrictions imposed by the overt elements in the elliptical sentence may override strict identity. Thus, as shown in Matos (1992), there is no need of morphological coincidence in the mood or tense of the verb forms of the local identifier of VPE and its antecedent.

(66) Nós temos posto   o   carro na   garagem, embora   ele ainda não
     we have put-indicative the car in-the garage, although he yet   not
     tenha__.
     have-subjunctive
     "We have put the car in the garage, although he has not, yet."

(67) O   João tem   comido demasiado e   a   Ana disse que (ela)
     the João have-prs-3-sg eaten too much and the Ana said that she
     também tinha__
     also have-past.
     "João has been eating too much and Ana said that she did too."

In addition to the semantic and structural non-distinctiveness between VPE and its antecedent, it has been recognized that VPE is subject to a syntactic licensing condition. The contrasts in English between a VPE sentence in (68a) and the ungrammatical sequence with a main verb in (68b), shows that a necessary condition for VPE is that the licensing verb moves out the verbal phrase to a sentence functional projection:

(68) a. John was reading this book and Mary was__, too.
     b. *John started reading this book and Mary started__ too.

In fact, as is well known, the predicative main verbs in current English do not move out of the verbal phrase. The availability of VPE with main verbs in languages like EP, with generalized verb movement, is consistent with that licensing condition.

Although there is some consensus that the verbal licensor of VPE must occur in a functional category c-commanding vP/VP, divergent proposals have occasionally been advanced. Thus, Rouveret (2012), apparently ignoring the contrasts in (68) for English, claims that VPE across languages (including English and EP) is licensed by a verb heading vP. For him, the difference between the languages with and without VPE relies on the fact that only in the latter does the verb raise to Infl to complete its verbal morphology.

Even accepting that a verbal element must occur in a functional head to license VPE, the nature of this functional category in Portuguese and the implementation of the licensing strategy have varied, mostly in consequence of the adopted framework.

Working on late Government and Binding theory, Matos (1992), assumed that T was the host of the VPE licensor, and, proposed a version of Rizzi's (1986) Proper Head Government as licensing principle:

(69) VPE is licensed by a head with verbal predicative or temporal value that properly governs the elliptical VP.

Within the minimalist program, where government takes no place, alternative proposals have arisen. In early minimalism, mainly focusing VPE with main verbs in EP, Martins (1994) argues that the licensor of VPE is sigma (Σ), a functional category occurring above TP and VP, proposed by I. Laka to account for sentence polarity and preverbal focus:

(70) [CP [ΣP [AgrSP [TP ...[VP]]]]]

According to Martins, the licensing and identification of VPE is achieved by movement of the verb to Σ with strong-V features, and checking of the (truth value) features of the null VP, which raises to adjoin [Spec,ΣP] or ΣP. She also claims that there is a correlation between VPE and enclisis: Romance languages with enclisis as unmarked pattern of clitic placement in finite clauses present VPE, e.g. EP and Galician, as a consequence of V movement to Σ (enclisis would arise because the verb raises to Σ and the clitic stays in AgrS); in contrast, those languages that systematically exhibit proclisis in finite clauses lack VPE, e.g. Spanish and French, because the verb does not move to Σ.

Although attractive, this proposal is unable to account for VPE in EP in negative (71) and embedded sentences (72), or both (73):

(71) a. *As   crianças   têm   estudado ultimamente?*
          the   children   have   studied lately
          "Have the children studied lately?"
      b. *Não, não   têm__.*
          No, not   have
          "No, they haven't."

(72) *A Ana   não   tem   trabalhado   muito   embora   diga   que   tem __.*
       the Ana   not   has   worked   hard   although says   that has
       "Ana has not been working hard, although she says she has."

(73) *Tu   tens   estado a trabalhar   muito   ainda que   digas   que   não   tens ___.*
       You   have   been working   too much   although says   that   not   has
       "You did not work too much, although she says she did."

For Martins (1994:183), in negative sentences in EP, Neg occupies Σ° and the verb stays in AgrS; this would account for the clitic–verb order in these sentences in standard EP (74). However, accepting this assumption, the author must admit that the licenser of the elided VP in (71b) is AgrS. The same prediction for VPE (cf. (72) and (73)) arises from Martins' analysis of embedded sentences: to account for proclisis in EP these domains, she claims that Σ raises to C and the inflected verb occurs in AgrS (Martins 1994:202).

(74) a. *As   crianças   não   lhe   telefonaram.*
        the   children   not   him-cl   phoned
        "The children did not phone."
     b. [Σ_p *As crianças* [Σ *não*] [_AgrS *lhe*[_AgrS *telefonaram*] …]

This analysis faces another problem. As shown by BP, where proclisis is the predominant pattern, there is no direct correlation between VPE and enclisis, assuming, as usual, that in this variety of Portuguese clitics have not yet been grammaticalized as prefixes of the verb.

Within the minimalist program, reconsidering previous work (Matos and Cyrino 2001, Cyrino and Matos 2002, Cyrino and Matos 2005) propose that VPE is licensed in the following configuration:

(75) In VPE the elliptical verbal predicate is licensed under local c-command by the lexically filled functional head with V-features that merges with it.

The authors claim that the functional head differs in EP and BP and remark that (75) must be complemented with other provisos to account for VPE across languages.

3.4. VPE licensing in EP and BP

The main differences between EP and BP concern VPE with verbal sequences. In EP certain verbal sequences easily allow a VPE interpretation, but others do not favor this reading. In opposition, the VPE interpretation is always clearly preferred in BP.

Matos (1992) shows that in EP the auxiliary sequences in (76a)–(76b) and (77a)–(77b) allow a full recovering of the VPE content:

(76) *A   Ana   tem   estado   a   comprar   esses   livros   às   crianças*
      the   Ana   has   been   to   buy   those   books   to-the   children
      "Ana has been buying those books to her children."
     a. *e   a   Maria   também   tem__.*   (EP)
        and   the   Maria   also   has
        "and Maria has, too."
        Reading: [__=(has) been buying those books to the children]
     b. *e   a   Maria   também   tem   estado ___.*
        and   the   Maria   also   has   been   (EP)
        "and Maria has been, too."
        Reading: [__= (been) buying those books to the children]

(77) *As   revistas   não   têm   estado   a   ser   arrumadas   nas   estantes   pela*
      the   journals   not   have   been   to   be   stored   on-the   shelves   by-the
      bibliotecária
      librarian
      "The journals have not been being stored on the shelves by the librarian."
     a. *mas os livros têm__.*   (EP)
        but the books have
        Reading: [__ (have) been being stored on the shelves by the librarian]
     b. *mas os livros têm sido__.*   (EP)
        but the books have been
        Reading: [__(been) being stored on the shelves by the librarian]

But, when the verbal sequences include the main verb, the VPE reading is available or lost, depending on the auxiliary: while with the perfect tense auxiliary verb, *ter* "have," the VPE interpretation is retained (cf. (78)), with the progressive auxiliary, *estar –a – Vinf*, (79) or the passive auxiliary (80), the VPE reading is preferentially lost, despite the fact that it should be compelling when the main verb obligatorily requires its complements:

(78) a. *A   Ana tem lido poemas aos   alunos   e   a   Maria também tem lido.*
        the Ana has read poems to-the students and the Maria also   has read
        "Ana has read poems to her students and Maria has too."
   b. *Este ano temos ido   ao   teatro   regularmente porque   a   Maria*
        the Ana have gone   to-the theatre regularly   because the Maria
        também   tem ido.   (EP)
        also   has gone
        "This year we have gone to the theatre regularly because Maria has, too."
   c. *Ela não tem   posto   as suas economias nesse   banco,   mas têm amigos que*
        she not has put   the her savings   in-that bank,   but has friends that
        têm   posto.   (EP)
        has   put
        "She has not put her savings in that bank, but she has some friends who did."

(79) a. *A Ana está a ler   poemas aos   alunos   e   a   Maria*   (EP)
        the Ana is   to read poems to-the students and the Maria
        também está a ler.
        also is to read
        (i)   Preferred reading: "Ana is reading poems to her students and Maria is also reading."
        (ii) Unlikely reading: "Ana is reading poems to her students and Maria is too."
   b. *?? Este   ano   estamos a   ir   ao   teatro   regularmente porque   a*
          this   year   are   to   go   to-the theatre   regularly   because   the
          Maria   também está   a   ir.   (EP)
          Maria   also   was   to   going
          "This year we are going to the theatre regularly because Maria is (also going to the theatre regularly.)
   c. *? Ela   não   está a   pôr   as   suas   economias nesse   banco,   mas   tem*
         she   not   is   to   put the   her   savings   in-that bank,   but   has
         amigos   que   estão a pôr.   (EP)
         friend   that   are   to put
         "She is not putting her savings in that bank, but she has some friends that are putting (their savings in that bank)."

(80) *As   revistas   não   têm   estado   a   ser   arrumadas   nas   estantes   pela*
      the   journals not   have been   to   be   stored   on-the   shelves   by-the
      bibliotecária
      librarian
      "The journals have not been being stored on the shelves by the librarian."
   a. *# mas   os   livros   têm   estado   a   ser   arrumados.*   (EP)
        but   the   books   have been   to   be   stored
   b. *# mas   os   livros   foram   arrumados.*   (EP)
        but   the   books   were   stored

In (79a), the verb *ler* "read" allows two interpretations for the absence of complements of the verb: a cognate null object interpretation, which is preferential, and VPE reading, which is felt as much less natural by the speakers. In (79b) and (79c) the null object reading is not available in EP, even in the extended version of Costa and Duarte (2003) because the omitted constituents occur in island domains and the main verb obligatorily select their complements; nevertheless, the VPE interpretation of these examples is somewhat marginal in EP.[1] As for (80), the VP ellipsis is lost (as in (79a)): the reader knows that the books have been stored somewhere by someone, but the precise information about the person who stored the books and the place where they have been stored is lost.

Matos (1992) imputes this different behavior to the properties of the auxiliaries involved. The perfect tense auxiliary *ter* selects a past participle projection with active v-features (81) and may form with it a verbal unit, as evidenced by the possibility of these verbs to move together in T-to-C constructions in EP (82).

(81) $[ter \ [VP_{past\ part} ...[V_{past\ part} <+v>]... \ ] \ ] ...$

(82) a. *Que têm lido provavelmente os alunos?   Até posso adivinhar!*
          what have read probably   the students? (I) even may guess
          "What did probably the students read? I even may guess it!"
      b. $[_{CP} Que \ [C \ têm \ lido] \ [provavelmente \ os \ alunos] \ ]$

As for *estar*, she adopted Raposo's (1989) proposal that this verb selects a prepositional infinitival construction in EP, formed by a small clause headed by the prepositional marker "a" and a TP infinitival complement:

(83) $... estar[_{SC}DP[_{particle}a][_{TP}...V_{inf}...]] ...$

Matos shows that this construction optionally presents restructuring, based on the optionality of clitic climbing:

(84) a. *Ela está-lhe   a dar o livro.*
          She is-cl   to give the book
      b. *Ela está a dar-lhe   o   livro*
          she is to give-cl   the   book
          "She is giving him the book."

She also argues that restructuring in this construction is obligatory in EP in the context of VPE, mainly grounded on the position of *também*. This adverbial must have local scope over the verbal licensor of the elided VP. As shown in (85), *também* must precede and c-command the whole verbal sequence to produced full acceptable VPE interpretations:

(85) a. *A manteiga está a ser   posta no   frigorífico e   a   cerveja também*
          the butter   is   being put in-the fridge   and the beer   also
          está a   ser
          is   being
          "The butter is being put in the fridge and the beer is being too."
      b. *??A manteiga   está a ser   posta no   frigorífico e   a   cerveja está*
          the butter   is   being put in-the fridge   and the beer   is
          também   a ser
          also   being

Finally, to account for the impossibility of recovering the main verb complements in sequences involving the passive auxiliary plus the main verb (cf. (80)), Matos (1992) claims that the passive participle is unable to license VPE in EP due to its deficitary status as a verbal category.

Thus, Matos (1992) concludes that in EP the sequences formed by the aspectual *estar* plus the main verb in the infinitive, as well as those constituted by the passive auxiliary plus the main verb in the passive participle, do not participate in the verbal chain headed by the auxiliary in the finite T that licenses the elided VP, and allows its recovery.

This analysis has been refined and developed by Cyrino and Matos to account for the contrasts in VPE in BP and EP. In fact, in contrast with EP, in BP the VPE interpretation is clearly preferred in all types of verbal sequences, i.e. those that only exhibit auxiliaries and those that present auxiliaries plus the main verb. The authors imputed these contrasts to the different properties of the progressive and the passive auxiliaries in EP and BP and to the properties of the functional categories they select in these language varieties.

Cyrino and Matos (2002, 2005) proposed that in EP and English, the licenser for VPE is T, but, in BP, VPE can be licensed by other functional heads: T, Asp or passive participle. They based their proposal on the contrasts found in sequences of auxiliary verbs (progressive and passive) followed by the main verb when the adverb *também* "too/also" intervenes in the verbal sequence.

In a verbal sequence, when *também* is placed between an auxiliary and the last verb, it brakes this verbal sequence and forces the last verb to be the licensor of the elided constituent, as illustrated in (86) and in (87), which involve the progressive and the passive auxiliaries plus the main verb. These examples stress the different behavior of BP and EP in these contexts: in BP the VPE reading is available, in EP it is (almost) lost:

(86) a. *Ela   estava   a chegar   da   Inglaterra   e   nós   estávamos   também   a chegar.*
      she   was   to arrive   from   England   and   we   were   also   to arrive
      VPE reading: "She was arriving from England and we were too."
      (✓BP, ??EP)
      Non-VPE reading: "She was arriving from England and we were also arriving
      (from   somewhere)"
      (✓BP, ✓EP)
   b. *Ele   estava   {cantando/a cantar}   cantigas   às   crianças,   porque   eu estava*
      he   was   singing to sing   songs   to-the   children   since I   was
      também cantando/a   cantar.
      (i)   VPE reading: "He was singing songs to the children, since I was too."
          (✓BP, ??EP)
      (ii) Cognate null object reading: "He was singing songs to the children, because
          I was also singing."
          (✓BP, ✓EP)

The sentences involving cognate objects are particularly revealing, because in this case the intransitive reading is almost mandatory in EP, but optional in BP. Note that the fact that *estar* selects the gerund in BP, but the infinitive in standard EP does not change the preferred interpretations.

Likewise, in sentences with the passive auxiliary and the main verb, in BP, the elided constituent recovers all the non-moved arguments of the main verb, but in EP this does not happen:

(87) *Os brinquedos   foram dados   às   crianças e   os   livros   foram*
     the toys   were given   to-the   children and   the   books   were
     também   dados.
     also   given
     (i) VPE reading: "The toys were given to the children and the books were too" (✓BP)
     (ii) Non VPE reading: "The toys were given to the children and the books were
        also given (away)"   (✓EP)

In (86) and (87) the verbs with finite inflection raise to T, but the verbs in the progressive constructions in the gerund or in the expression "a_V$_{inf}$," as well the verbs in the passive participle occupy the head of a projection of their own, respectively Asp(P) and Pass(P), an instance of *Voice(P)*.

(88) a. (...) [$_{TP}$ *estava*   *também*   [$_{AspP}$ *cantando* [$_{vP}$ —]]]
              was   also   singing
      b. (...) [$_{TP}$ *estava*   *também*   [$_{AspP}$ a [$_{TP}$ *cantar* [$_{vP}$ —]]]
              was   also   to   sing
      c. (...) [$_{TP}$ *foram*   *também*   [$_{PassP}$ *dados* [$_{vP}$ —]]]
              were   also   given

In BP, the verbs in Asp and Pass may license the elided VP; the same does not happen in EP, where finite T is the licenser of VPE. This shows that, in BP, the verbs that participate in the VPE licensing sequences have a greater autonomy than in EP and, apparently, restructuring does not apply to verbal sequences in BP. Thus, Matos and Cyrino (2001) claim that in BP, the auxiliary verbs select non-defective functional projections, and exhibit another active T domain able to license elliptical constituents. Therefore, both the possibility of having the interposition of *também* and the possibility for the lower (main) verb to be able to license VPE is explained. In both cases the licenser of ellipsis in BP is the functional head that is lower in the structure:

(89) a. *A Ana está   lendo   os   livros às   crianças   e   a   Maria está*   (BP)
              the Ana is   reading   the books to-the children and the Maria is
          também   lendo.
          also   reading
          "Ana is reading the books to the children and Maria is too."
      b. ...*e a Maria* [$_{TP}$ [$_{T°}$ *está*] [$_{VauxP}$ t [$_{TP}$*também* [$_{T°<+active>}$ *lendo*] [$_{AspP}$ t [$_{vP}$-]]]]]

Additional evidence for a second TP (functional) projection comes from clitic placement in BP. In EP the modal *poder,* but not the auxiliary *ter* of compound tenses, selects TP—consequently, the following contrast is observed:

(90) a. *João podia* [$_{TP}$ *ler-lhe*   o   livro*].   (EP)
          João could   read-cl.dat-3 sg   the   book
          "João could read him/her the book."
      b. **Ele tem* [$_{VauxP}$ *lido-lhe*   o   livro*]
          He has   read-cl.dat-3 sg   the   book
      c. **Ele tinha* [$_{VauxP}$ *já*   lhe   lido   o   livro*]
          He has   already   cl.dat-3 sg   read   the book

On the contrary, in BP, the possibility for proclisis to the past participle and to the gerund in the constructions with auxiliaries confirms that these select TP active domains (91). As expected, in these domains, *também* can co-occur with the clitic (92).

(91) a. *João   tem* [te   lido   o   livro*]   (BP)
          João   has   cl.dat-3 sg   read   the book
          "João"
      b. *João está* [te   enviando o livro*]
          João is   cl.dat-3 sg   read   the book

(92) O Pedro está *te* enviando livros e João está *também te* enviando livros. (BP)

These data lead Cyrino and Matos (2005) to refine the VPE licensing condition proposed in (75), which stated that "VPE is licensed by a lexically filled functional head with v-features that locally c-commands the elliptical predicate." Although necessary, this condition is not sufficient, since it predicts that languages with generalized verb movement have VPE, a prediction that is not borne out by languages like Spanish, French or Italian.

The authors attributed the lack of VPE in those languages to a grammaticalization process of the auxiliary verbs. This grammaticalization produces the weakening of the aspectual value of auxiliaries and the loss of the temporal value of the tense affixes that affect the auxiliary verb. Thus, in the French and Spanish examples below, despite the fact that the auxiliary exhibits a present tense affix, the composed verbal form [$Aux_{Present}$ + Past Participle] is interpreted as past and can be used as the *Simple Past*:

(93) a. Jean a vu ses amis.
     b. Juan ha visto a suyos amigos.
        "Jean/Juan saw his friends."

Cyrino and Matos also claimed that in languages in which the complex verb forms are highly grammaticalized (e.g. Spanish and French), Asp is closely linked to tense and it is not interpreted as part of the vP predicate, (94):

(94) $[_{CP} C [_{TP} T [Asp ... [_{vP}]]]]$

In contrast, in the languages in which these complex verb forms keep their aspectual values (e.g. Portuguese and English), AspP is understood as an extended projection of the vP predicate forming a complex AsP_vP:

(95) $[_{CP} C [_{TP} T [_{AspP-vP} Asp-vP ... [_{vP}]]]]$

Adopting this analysis, Cyrino and Matos (2005) propose that the parametrical difference between generalized V-movement languages with and without VPE is the availability/unavailability of immediate command of the elided predicate by the potential licensor.

This happens in EP, since T merges with Asp-vP, as well as in BP, where the verbal licensor may occur in Asp(P) or Pass(P), since these categories may merge with vP, satisfying the immediate c-command requirement. However, it does not occur in French or Spanish, because Asp intervenes between T and vP.

Building on that work, Cyrino (2013) argues that BP has lost "long" verb movement and, because of that, null objects can be licensed as ellipsis (as seen above). On the same line of reasoning, and on the basis of the position of adverbs, Tescari Neto (2013) shows that VPE in BP is licensed by the verb in a very low functional projection.

Acknowledgements

This research has been funded by the following research grants: Brazilian CNPQ – Conselho Nacional para o Desenvolvimento Científico e Tecnológico (research grant 303742/2013-5) and FAPESP-Fundação de Amparo à Pesquisa do Estado de São Paulo (research grant 2012/06078-9), Portuguese FCT-Fundação para a Ciência e Tecnologia (project PEst-OE/LIN/UI0214/2013). We also thanks an anonymous reviewer for helpful comments on a previous version of this paper.

NOTE

1   Notice that although in standard EP the examples in (79c) are not fully acceptable, they tend to be more easily permitted by the young generation. A plausible explanation for this fact, is the increasing grammaticalization of progressive *estar* in their internal grammar.

REFERENCES

Barra-Ferreira, M. (2000). Argumentos Nulos em Português Brasileiro. Master dissertation, Unicamp, Campinas.

Bianchi, V. and M. C. Figueiredo (1994). On some properties of agreement-object in Italian and Brazilian Portuguese. In M. Mazzola (ed.), *Issues and Teory in Romance Linguistics*. Washington, DC: Georgetown University Press, pp. 181–197.

Costa, J. and I. Duarte (2003). Objectos Nulos em debate. In I. Castro and I. Duarte (eds.), *Razões e Emoção*. Lisbon: Imprensa Nacional – Casa da Moeda, pp. 249–260.

Cyrino, S. (1997). *O Objeto Nulo no Português Brasileiro: Um estudo sintático-diacrônico*. Londrina: Editora da UEL. [Published version of Cyrino's (1994) Ph.D. dissertation, Unicamp, Campinas].

Cyrino, S. (2013). On richness of tense and verb movement in Brazilian Portuguese. In M. V. Camacho-Taboada, A. Jiménez-Fernández, J. Martín-González, and M. Reyes-Tejedor (eds.), *Information Structure and Agreement*. Amsterdam: John Benjamins, pp. 297–317.

Cyrino, S. and G. Matos (2002). VPE in European and Brazilian Portuguese: A comparative analysis. *Journal of Portuguese Linguistics*, 1 (2), pp. 177–214.

Cyrino, S. and G. Matos (2005). Local licensers and recovering in VPE. *Journal of Portuguese Linguistics*, 4 (2), pp. 79–112.

Cyrino, S. and G. Matos (2006). Null complement anaphora in romance: deep or surface anaphora? In J. Doetjes and P. González (eds.), *Romance Languages and Linguistic Theory 2004*. Amsterdam: John Benjamins, pp. 95–120.

Cyrino, S., E. Duarte, and M. Kato (2000). Visible subjects and invisible clitics in Brazilian Portuguese. In M. Kato and E. Negrão (eds.), *Brazilian Portuguese and the Null Subject Parameter Frankfurt am Main*. Madrid: Iberoamericana, pp. 55–73.

Duarte, I. (1987) A construção de Topicalização na Gramática do Português: Regência, Ligação e condições sobre movimento. Ph.D. dissertation, Universidade de Lisboa.

Duarte, I. and J. Costa (2013). Objecto Nulo. In E. Raposo, M. F. Nascimento, M. A. Mota, L. Segura and A. Mendes (eds.), *Gramática do Português*, vol. II. Lisbon: Fundação Calouste Gulbenkian, pp. 2339–2348.

Farrell, P. (1990). Null objects in Brazilian Portuguese. *The Linguistic Review*, 8, pp. 325–346.

Galves, C. (1989b). Objet Nul et Structure de la Proposition en Portugais Brésilien. *Revue des Langues Romanes*, 93, pp. 305–336.

Goldberg, L. (2005). Verb-Stranding VPE: A Cross-Linguistic Study. Ph.D. dissertation, McGill University.

Gonçalves, A. and G. Matos (2009). Ellipsis and restructuring in European Portuguese. In E. Aboh, E. Linden, J. Queer, and P. Sleeman (eds.), *Romance Languages and Linguistic Theory*. Amsterdam: John Benjamins, 109–129.

Huang, C. T. J. (1984). On the distribution and reference of the empty categories. *Linguistic Inquiry*, 15, pp. 531–574.

Kato, M. (1993). The distribution of pronouns and null elements in object position in Brazilian Portuguese. In W. Ashby, M. Perissinotto, and E. Raposo (eds.), *Linguistic Perspectives on the Romance Languages*. Amsterdam: John Benjamins.

Martins, A. M. (1994). Enclisis, VP-deletion and the nature of Sigma. *Probus*, 6, pp. 173–205.

Matos, G. (1992). Construções de Elipse do Predicado em Português: SV Nulo e Despojamento. Ph.D. dissertation, Universidade de Lisboa.

Matos, G. and S. Cyrino (2001). Elipse de VP no Português Europeu e no Português Brasileiro. *Boletim da Abralin*, 26, número especial, pp. 386–390.

Raposo, E. (1986). On the null object in European Portuguese. In O. Jaeggli and C. Silva Corvalán (eds.), *Studies in Romance Linguistics.* Dordrecht: Foris, pp. 373–390.

Raposo, E. (1989). Prepositional infinitival construction in European Portuguese. In O. Jaeggli and K. Safir (eds.), *The Null Subject Parameter*. Dordrecht/Boston/London: Kluwer Academic Publishers, pp. 277–305.

Raposo, E. (2004). Objetos Nulos e CLLD: Uma teoria unificada. *Revista da ABRALIN*, 3 (1,2), pp. 41–73.

Rizzi, L. (1986). Null objects and the theory of pro. *Linguistic Inquiry*, 17, pp. 501–558.

Rouveret, A. (2012). VPE, phases and the syntax of morphology. *Natural Language and Linguistic Theory*, 30 (3), pp. 897–963.

Santos, A. L. (2009). *Minimal Answers: Ellipsis, Syntax and Discourse in the Acquisition of European Portuguese*. Amsterdam: John Benjamins.

Tescari-Neto, A. (2013). On Verb Movement in Brazilian Portuguese: A Cartographic Study. Ph.D. dissertation, Universitá Ca'Foscari, Venice.

17 Passives and *Se* Constructions

ANA MARIA MARTINS AND JAIRO NUNES

1. Introduction

In this chapter we discuss some of the main properties of constructions involving participial passives, passive *se*, and impersonal *se* in Portuguese, focusing on its two main varieties, European and Brazilian Portuguese (henceforth EP and BP, respectively).[1] When the two dialects differ, we will provide the relevant judgments each dialect assigns to the data under discussion by using the abbreviations EP and BP.

The chapter is organized in four sections. Section 2 deals with participial passives, distinguishing between adjectival and verbal passives and between the participial forms of passives and compound tenses. Section 3 focuses on passive *se* and impersonal *se* constructions, comparing them with verbal passives when appropriate. Section 4 concludes the paper.

2. Participial passive constructions

As one finds in many languages, passive constructions in Portuguese involve a reorganization of the argument structure of transitive verbs[2] associated with some specific morphology, which has several consequences for syntactic computations. Take the transitive verb *plantar* "plant," for instance. In an active construction such as (1a) below, for example, its external argument is realized as the syntactic subject, bearing nominative case and triggering verbal agreement, whereas the internal argument is realized as the syntactic object, bearing accusative case. In turn, in the passive version of (1a) given in (1b), the external argument is realized as an adjunct-like PP and the internal argument is the element that bears nominative case and triggers verbal agreement with an auxiliary verb (*ser* "be"). The passive form is obtained by adding participial morphology to the verb and the participial form also agrees with the internal argument.

(1) a. *Eu   plantei   as   flores.*
      I   planted.1sg   the   flowers
      "I planted the flowers."
  b. *As   flores   foram   planta-d-a-s   por   mim.*
      the flowers.fem.pl   were.3pl   plant-pple.fem.pl   by   me
      "The flowers were planted by me."

The Handbook of Portuguese Linguistics, First Edition. Edited by W. Leo Wetzels, João Costa, and Sergio Menuzzi.
© 2016 John Wiley & Sons, Inc. Published 2020 by John Wiley & Sons, Inc.

Each of the ingredients of passive constructions mentioned above independently interacts with other parts of the grammar. Consider the participial morphology, for instance. Besides being associated with passives, as seen in (1b), it may also encode perfectivity, as shown in (2a) below. (2b) further shows that the two uses of the participial morphology may in fact be found in the same clause. One difference between them, though, is that the passive participle may bear agreement morphology, as seen in (1b), but not the perfective participial, as seen in (2a), which displays default morphology (masculine singular). Thus, in the perfective passive in (2b), the perfective participle has default morphology, whereas the passive participle agrees in gender and number with the internal argument.

(2) a. *A   Maria   tinha   contrata-d-o   as   funcionárias.*
        the   Maria   had   hire-pple-masc.sg   the   employees.fem.pl
        "Maria had hired the employees."
    b. *As funcionárias   tinham si-d-o   contratad-a-s   pela   Maria.*
        the employees.fem.pl had   been-pple-masc.sg hire-pple-fem-pl   by.the Maria
        "The employees had been hired by Maria."

These two uses of the participle interact with clitic placement in an interesting way in the varieties of Portuguese analyzed here, as illustrated in (3) and (4):[3]

(3) a. **O   João tinha   enviado-me   as   revistas.*   (EP*; BP*)
        the   João had   sent-me   the   magazines
    b. *O   João tinha,   com toda a   certeza,   me enviado   as revistas.*   (EP*; BP^{oK})
        the   João had   with all the   certainty me sent   the magazines
    c. *O   João tinha-me, com toda a certeza,   enviado as   revistas.*   (EP^{oK}; BP*)
        the   João had-me   with all the certainty   sent   the   magazines
        "João had(, for sure,) sent me the magazines."

(4) a. **As   revistas   foram   enviadas-me   pelo   João.*   (EP*; BP*)
        the   magazines   were   sent-me   by-the   João
    b. **As   revistas   foram, com toda a certeza,   me enviadas pelo   João.* (EP*; BP*)
        the magazines   were   with all the certainty me sent   by-the João
    c. *As revistas foram-me, com toda a certeza, enviadas pelo João.*   (EP^{oK}; BP*)
        the magazines were-me with all the certainty sent by-the João
    d. *As   revistas   me foram enviadas pelo João.*   (EP*; BP^{oK})
        the   magazines   me were sent   by-the João
        "The magazines were (, for sure,) sent to me by João."

Let us first consider BP, which is essentially a proclitic system (but see Section 3.2 below for further discussion). Thus, the ungrammaticality of the sentences in (3a, c) and (4a, c) in this dialect directly follows from its general ban on enclisis. What about the contrast between (3b) and (4b), both involving proclisis to the participial form? A very plausible explanation is that the agreement in gender and number in the case of the passive participle in (4b) renders it close to adjectives and independently, an adjective cannot be a target for clitic attachment in either dialect, as illustrated in (5), where the clitic is an argument of the adjective.[4]

(5) a. **Eles sempre foram fiéis-me.*   (EP*; BP*)
     they always were faithful-me
  b. **Eles sempre foram, sem   dúvida alguma, me fiéis.*   (EP*; BP*)
     they aways were without doubt some   me faithful
  c. *Eles foram-me, sem   dúvida alguma, fiéis.*   (EP°K; BP*)
     they were-me without doubt some   faithful
  d. *Eles sempre me foram fiéis.*   (EP*; BP°K)
     they always me were faithful
     "(Undoubtedly,) they were always faithful to me."

As for EP, it is essentially an enclitic system, but proclisis must be enforced in the presence of certain specific syntactic triggers such as negation or focus, for instance. Thus, the unacceptability of (3b) and (4b) in this dialect falls under its general ban on proclisis to a nonfinite verb, whereas the unacceptability of (4d) is related to the lack of a proclisis trigger. Crucially, the ungrammaticality of (4a) may have the same source as the one seen in BP for (4b), namely, the presence of adjectival agreement morphology (gender and number) on the passive participle blocks clitic attachment.[5]

The connection between passive participles and adjectives has further implications. As mentioned above, the auxiliary employed with passives is *ser*. Interestingly, superficially similar participial constructions may resort to aspectual verbs like *estar* "be" (stative) or *ficar* "remain/become," as illustrated in (6).

(6) a. *As obras de arte foram destruídas (por vândalos).*
     the works of art were destroyed by vandals)
     "The artworks were destroyed by vandals."
  b. *As obras de arte estavam/   ficaram   destruídas (*por vândalos).*
     the works of art   were.stative/ became   destroyed   by vandals)
     "The artworks laid/became damaged (*by vandals)."

The participial form in (6b) is felt as passive in the sense that it says something about the internal argument. However, the external argument, which is optional in the case of a canonical passive and is realized as a PP (see (6a)), is not allowed in the case of the seemingly passive in (6b) with either of the aspectual verbs.

The contrast between (6a) and (6b) is reminiscent of Wasow's (1977) classical distinction between verbal and adjectival passives.[6] For Wasow, verbal passives are formed in the syntactic component, whereas adjectival passives are formed in the lexicon. Thus, while the former are pretty much regular, the latter include a considerable degree of idiosyncrasy, which is commonly found associated with specific lexical items. Take the realization of the external argument, for instance. If a verb allows a verbal passive, the external argument will always be optional and always introduced by the preposition *por* "by" (see (1b)) or its allomorph *per* when contracted with a definite article (see (2b)). Adjectival passives, on the other hand, display a much diversified pattern, depending on the specific lexical items involved. Thus, the realization of the external argument is impossible with the adjectival passive of *destruir* "destroy," as seen in (6b), but is obligatory in BP with the adjectival passive of *compor* "compose," as illustrated in (7) below. The preposition introducing the element that may correspond to the external argument in an active construction may also vary. The lexical passive of *cercar* "surround," for instance, allows both the preposition *por/per* and *de* "of," as illustrated in (8b). There are also cases like (9), which shows that the verb *entristecer* "sadden," like many psych-verbs, does not allow a verbal passive (see (9b)), but admits an adjectival passive (see (9c)).[7] Interestingly, the external argument is realized with the preposition *com* "with," which is the same preposition that occurs with the adjective *triste* "sad" (see (9d)).

(7) *Este trabalho está   composto *(por quatro seções).*   (BP)
    this work   is.stative composed by four   sections
    "This work comprises four sections."

(8) a. *Os soldados foram cercados   por/*de inimigos.*
        the soldiers were surrounded by/*of enemies
        "The soldiers were surrounded by the enemy."
    b. *A cidade estava   cercada   por/de montanhas.*
        the city was.stative surrounded by/of enemies
        "The city was surrounded by mountains."

(9) a. *Os boatos   entristeceram a   Maria.*
        the rumors saddened   the Maria
        "The rumors saddened Maria."
    b. **A Maria foi entristecida (pelos boatos).*
        the Maria was saddened (by.the rumors)
        "Maria was saddened by the rumors."
    c. *A Maria estava/ficou   entristecida (com os boatos)*
        the Maria was.stative/became saddened   with the rumors
        "Maria was/became saddened with the rumors."
    d. *A Maria estava/ficou   triste (com os boatos)*
        the Maria was.stative/became sad with the rumors
        "Maria was/became sad with the rumors."

Focusing now on verbal passives, we have seen that despite being verbal, their agreement morphology (gender and number) makes them similar to adjectival predicates with respect to clitic placement (see (4a, b) and (5a, b)). In fact, the similarities also involve the realization of the agreement morphology itself. This point is better seen in BP, which has been undergoing a weakening of its verbal and nominal agreement paradigms and displays a considerable degree of idiolectal variation in the realization of gender and number, subject to many interfering factors. Roughly speaking, BP differs from EP in that (for some speakers) passive constructions may allow lack of number agreement with pre-verbal subjects, as shown in (10), and lack of both gender and number agreement with postverbal subjects, as shown in (11).[8]

(10) a. *[Os   projeto]   foram arquivado.*   (%BP)
        the.masc.pl project.masc were filed.masc
        "The projects were filed."
    b. *[As   proposta]   foram aprovada.*   (%BP)
        the.fem.pl proposal.fem were approved.fem
        "The proposals were approved."

(11) a. *Foi dito   muitas   coisa   ofensiva.*   (%BP)
        was said.masc   many.fem.pl thing.fem offensive.fem
        "Many offensive things were said."
    b. *Não foi encontrado as   revista   que ele pediu.*   (%BP)
        not was found.masc the.fem.pl magazine.fem that he asked
        "The magazines that he asked for were not found."

The data in (10) and (11) display the same pattern independently found with adjectival predicates in BP, as illustrated in (12) and (13).

(12) a. *Os   cavalo   ficaram calmo.*   (%BP)
        the.masc.pl horse.masc   became calm.masc
        "The horses became calm."
    b. *As   menina   tavam muito cansada.*   (%BP)
        the.fem.pl girl.fem were very tired.fem
        "The girls were very tired."

(13) a. *Eu achei complicado   as   proposta   apresentada.*   (%BP)
        I found complicated.masc the.fem.pl proposal.fem presented.fem
        "I found the proposals that were presented difficult to understand."
    b. *O João   considerou inadequado   as   medida   tomada.*   (%BP)
        the João considered inadequate.masc the.fem.pl measure.fem taken.fem
        "João considered the measures taken to be inadequate"

The case properties of verbal passives are in turn more transparent in EP, for in BP there are too many independent confounding properties such as the loss of third person accusative clitics, homophony between nominative and accusative third person weak and strong pronouns, and the general weakening of agreement morphology just seen above. So, we will, accordingly, focus on EP data. The data in (14) below show that the internal argument of a verbal passive cannot be marked with accusative case (see (14b–c)), displaying nominative case, instead (see (14d–e)).

(14) EP:
    a. *Foram plantadas as   flores.*
        were   planted   the flowers
        "The flowers have been planted."
    b. **Foram plantadas-as.*
        were planted-3.fem.pl.acc
    c. **Foram-nas   plantadas.*
        were-3.fem.pl.acc planted
        "They have been planted."
    d. *Elas   foram plantadas, mas morreram.*
        3.fem.pl.nom were planted   but died
        "They were planted but didn't last."
    e. *Fomos   vistos tu   e   eu   a arrancar   as flores.*
        were.1.pl seen 2.sg.nom and 1.sg.nom to pluck   the flowers
        "You and I were seen plucking the flowers."

Notice that the ungrammaticality of (14b) cannot be simply due to the impossibility of enclisis to a passive in EP, as seen in (4a). Recall that if the (dative) clitic of (4a) undergoes climbing and attaches to the auxiliary verb, we obtain a grammatical output, as seen in (4c). However, as shown in (14c), clitic climbing does not rescue the grammatical failure in (14b), indicating that we are indeed dealing with a case issue.

Given the ungrammaticality of (14b) and (14c), on the one hand, and the availability of (14d-e) with nominative pronouns and the corresponding verbal agreement, on the other, the logical conclusion is that the internal argument in (14a) bears nominative case.

3. *Se* constructions

In Section 3.1 below we will compare the two types of *se* constructions commonly referred to as *passive se* and *impersonal se* constructions. The latter is available in both BP and EP, while the former was lost in the course of time in BP. We will also contrast *se* passives and verbal passives and consider differences between BP and EP with respect to impersonal *se*. In Section 3.2, we will describe some peculiarities of impersonal *se* structures regarding clitic placement and some co-occurrence restrictions with respect to other clitics.

3.1. *Passive se and impersonal se: agreement, word order, case, and interpretation*

Like other Romance languages, Portuguese may form impersonal constructions with a clitic that is homophonous to the third person reflexive clitic (*se* in this case). When transitive verbs are involved and the internal argument is a third person plural element, the verb may agree with the internal argument or surface with (default) third person singular morphology, as illustrated in (15) below.[9] Despite their close similarity in form and meaning, these constructions exhibit strikingly different properties, as we will see below. The agreement with the internal argument in (15a) brings this type closer to passive constructions and accordingly, its clitic is commonly referred to as *passive se*, as opposed to the clitic in the non-agreeing construction, generally referred to as *impersonal se*. For purposes of exposition, we will adopt this terminology in what follows.

(15) a. *Ouviram-se   muitas explosões   ontem.*   (EP°ᴷ; BP*)
        heard.3pl-*se* many explosions yesterday
        "Many explosions were heard yesterday."
    b. *Ouviu-se   muitas explosões   ontem.*   (EP*; BP*)
        heard.3sg-*se* many explosions yesterday
        "People heard many explosions yesterday."

Diachronically, the passive *se* construction is the older construction, which suggests that the impersonal *se* construction emerged as a reanalysis of the previously existing passive *se* construction (see e.g. Naro 1976, Nunes 1990, 1991). In EP the two constructions are stable in the system, whereas in BP the impersonal *se* construction has completely replaced the passive *se* construction. The surviving (infrequent) instances of passive *se* in present-day BP are generally restricted to written language and formal style and are arguably due to a prescriptivist tradition that condemns the use of impersonal *se* with transitive verbs (see e.g. Galves 1986, Nunes 1990, 1991). Significantly, BP speakers have no judgments on the contrasts between the two constructions that are reported below. Thus, the discussion of the differences between passive *se* and impersonal *se* will concentrate on EP.

Besides exhibiting agreement with the internal argument, passive *se* constructions also pattern like standard verbal passives and unlike impersonal *se* constructions in several properties. First, in passive *se* constructions, the internal argument can move to the subject position, as exemplified in (16a) to be contrasted with (16b).[10]

(16) a. *Os bolos   comeram-se ontem.*   (EP)
        the cookies ate.3pl-*se*   yesterday
        "The cookies were eaten yesterday."
    b. **Os bolos   comeu-se   ontem.*   (EP)
        the cookies ate.3sg-*se*   yesterday
        "Someone ate the cookies yesterday."

Second, like verbal passives (see (14)) and unlike impersonal *se* constructions, passive *se* constructions do not allow accusative case to be assigned to the internal argument. Before we examine the relevant data, we should first observe that there is an independent adjacency restriction in EP ruling out a clitic *se* followed by an accusative clitic, as shown in (17) below with reflexive *se*. Hence, for many speakers, neither passive *se* nor impersonal *se* is compatible with an accusative clitic, as illustrated in (18).

(17)   *O João   deu-se-o   (EP)
        the João gave-*se*-it.masc.acc
        "João gave it to himself."

(18)   a.   *Compraram-se-os   ontem.   (EP)
              bought.3pl-*se*-them.masc.acc   yesterday
              "They were bought yesterday."
        b   Comprou-se-os   ontem.   (%EP)
              bought.3sg-*se*-them.masc.acc   yesterday
              "People/we bought them yesterday."

However, it should be noted that whereas there are speakers who allow (18b) (including the first author of this paper), there are no speakers who accept (18a).[11] And, crucially, when the adjacency restriction is circumvented by placing each clitic on a different host, as in (19) below, all speakers agree with respect to the contrast. Similarly, the contrast also becomes clear if a dative clitic intervenes between *se* and the accusative clitic, as in (20) (from Martins 2013). This shows that only impersonal *se* constructions allow the internal argument to be assigned accusative case.

(19)   a.   *Podem-se comprá-los   amanhã.   (EP)
              can.3pl-*se* buy-them.masc.acc tomorrow
              "They can be bought tomorrow."
        b.   Pode-se   comprá-los   amanhã.   (EP)
              can.3sg-*se* buy-them.masc.acc tomorrow
              "One/we can buy them tomorrow."

(20)   a.   *Histórias de lobisomens,   ouviam-se-lhas   vezes sem conta.   (EP)
              stories   of werewolves heard.3pl-*se*-dat.them.fem.acc times without count
              "Werewolf stories could be heard from him again and again."
        b.   Histórias de lobisomens,   ouvia-se-lhas   vezes sem conta.   (EP)
              stories   of werewolves heard.3sg-*se*-dat.them.fem.acc times without count
              "Werewolf stories, you could hear them from him again and again."

The ungrammaticality of (18a), (19a) and (20a) may be taken to show that passive *se* behaves like the participial passive morphology in that it deactivates the verb's accusative case assigning property (see (14)).[12] As for impersonal *se*, we find the converse situation: it checks the nominative case available in the clause. Consider the data in (21), for instance.

(21)   [*Context: After a fire in the zoo, the animal keepers are checking on the animals and find the snakes unharmed*]
        a.   Como se salvaram   elas?   [*pointing to the snakes*]   (EP)
              how   *se* saved.3pl 3.fem.pl.nom
              "How were they saved?" or "How did they save themselves?"
        b.   *Como se puderam   salvá-las?   [*pointing to the snakes*]   (EP)
              how   *se* could.3pl save.3.fem.pl.acc
              "How was it possible to save them?" or "How did they manage to save themselves?"

c. *Como se pôde   salvá-las?*   [*pointing to the snakes*]   (EP)
how *se* could.3sg save.3.fem.pl.acc
"How was it possible to save them?" but not "How did they manage to save themselves?"

d. **Como se salvou   elas?*   [*pointing to the snakes*]   (EP)
how *se* saved.3sg 3.fem.pl.nom
"How did one saved them?" or "How did they save themselves?"

(21a) is ambiguous between a passive *se* interpretation and a reflexive reading. This ambiguity is partially due to the case specification of the pronoun *elas* "they.fem." As a nominative pronoun, it may be the internal argument in a passive *se* structure—as accusative case is unavailable in this type of structure—or the external argument in a reflexive structure, with the reflexive bearing the internal θ-role and accusative case. Accordingly, a sentence like (21b) leads to ungrammaticality regardless of the interpretation: under the passive *se* structure, there is no licenser for the accusative case specification of the clitic *as* "them.fem" and under the reflexive structure, the two clitics would be competing for the same case licensing. In turn, (21c) is grammatical, but only under the impersonal *se* interpretation, with *se* bearing nominative and the object clitic, accusative; again, the reflexive reading is excluded as the two clitics would be competing for accusative case. Finally, (21d) disallows the reflexive reading—because the putative subject (the pronoun *elas*) fails to trigger verbal agreement—and the impersonal *se* reading, as the two pronouns compete for nominative case.[13]

So far, we have seen that verbal passives and *se* passives share some properties. But there are also differences between them. For example, passive *se* constructions pattern like monoargumental unaccusative sentences and unlike verbal passives in that they easily allow postverbal definite subjects in out-of-the-blue (broad information focus) sentences, as shown in (22).

(22) a. *Apanharam-se estas maçãs todas sem   estarem   maduras.*   (EP)
picked.3pl-*se* these apples all without be.inf.3.pl ripe
"All these apples were picked while still green."

b. *Caíram estas maçãs todas sem   estarem   maduras.*   (EP)
fell   these apples all without be.inf.3.pl ripe
"All these apples fell off while still green."

c. **?Foram apanhadas estas maçãs todas sem   estarem   maduras.*   (EP)
were   picked   these apples all   without be.inf.3.pl ripe
"All these apples were picked while still green."

There are also differences with respect to the landing site for the movement of the internal argument. Both passive *se* and verbal passive constructions allow movement of the internal argument to a preverbal position, as shown in (23), with no need of a marked intonation (see foonote 10).

(23) a. *Estas maçãs   todas apanharam-se sem   estarem   maduras.*   (EP)
these apples all   picked.3pl-*se* without be.inf.3.pl ripe

b. *Estas maçãs todas foram apanhadas sem   estarem   maduras.*   (EP)
these apples all   were picked   without be.inf.3.pl ripe
"All these apples were picked while still green."

However, as proposed by Raposo and Uriagereka (1996), the preverbal DP of a passive *se* sentence like (23a) seems to occupy a topic position rather than the canonical subject position, for the passive *se* reading is blocked when there is no available topic position, as in the inflected infinitival clause in (24), for example (from Raposo and Uriagereka 1996).

(24) a. *Vai ser difícil*   *[os documentos serem*   *aceites]*   (EP)
      will be difficult the documents be.inf.3pl accepted
      "It will be difficult for the documents to be accepted."
   b. **Vai ser difícil*   *[os documentos aceitarem-se]*   (EP)
      will be difficult the documents accept.inf.3pl-*se*
      "It will be difficult for someone or other to accept the documents"

But the most salient difference between verbal passives and passive *se* constructions is that the external argument may be optionally expressed by means of a PP (the "*by*-phrase") in the case of verbal passives, but not in the case of *se* passives, as illustrated in (25).

(25) a. *Os bolos foram comidos (pelos meninos).*
      the cookies were eaten (by-the children)
      "The cookies were eaten (by the children)."
   b. *Comeram-se os bolos (*pelos meninos).*   (EP)
      ate.3pl-*se* the cookies (*by-the children)
   c. *Os bolos comeram-se (*pelos meninos).*   (EP)
      the cookies ate.3pl-*se* (*by-the children)
      "The cookies were eaten (*by the children)."

The lack of an overtly expressed external argument also leads to different interpretations. A passive sentence such as (26a) below is compatible with both a [+hum] or a [-hum] interpretation for the implicit external argument; that is, the houses may have been destroyed, say, by their owners or by the rain. By contrast, passive *se* constructions only allow a [+hum] interpretation for their external argument; thus, (26b) cannot be employed to describe the destruction of the houses by the rain, for example.

(26) a. *As casas*   *foram destruídas.*
      the houses were destroyed
   b. *Destruíram-se*   *as casas.*   (EP)
      destroyed.3pl-*se* the houses
      "The houses have been destroyed."

The impersonal *se* construction has inherited this restriction from the passive *se* construction. So, the sentence in (27) can only be interpreted as involving an indefinite [+hum] subject, which may or may not include the speaker.

(27) *Destruiu-se*   *as casas.*
    destroyed.3sg-*se* the houses
    "People/we destroyed the houses."

Interestingly, in some dialects of EP the impersonal clitic *se* can be doubled by a strong nominative pronoun, as illustrated in (28) below (see Martins 2009). In (28a) and (28b), *a gente* (lit. "the people"), which was grammaticalized as a first person plural pronoun, and *nós* "we" set an inclusive reading for *se*, whereas *eles* "they" in (28c) sets an exclusive reading.

(28) %EP:

    a. *Chama-se-lhe   a gente   espigas.*   (CORDIAL-SIN. AAL)
       call.3sg-*se*-it.dat the people spikes
       "We call it spikes."

    b. *Há   várias qualidades que até   ainda nós não se conhecemos.* (CORDIAL-SIN. ALV)
       has   several qualities that even still   we not *se* know.1pl
       "There are so many species (of fish) that even we (fishermen) do not know all of them yet."

    c. *Sei   é de real certeza   que isto era com   o que se eles   batiam   o centeio.*
       know.1sg is of real certainty that this was with what *se* they beated.3pl the rye
       "What I know for sure is that this was the thing that people used to husk the rye."
                                                       (CORDIAL-SIN. FLF)

The discussion above suggests that *se* is to be analyzed as a syntactic subject in impersonal *se* constructions, but not in passive *se* constructions. Arguably related to this distinction is the fact that only impersonal *se* licenses a subject-oriented secondary predicate, as illustrated in (29):

(29) a. **Criam-se avestruzes despreocupado.*   (EP)
         raise.3pl-*se* ostriches unpreoccupied
         "One raises ostriches unconcerned."

      b. *Cria-se avestruzes despreocupado.*   (EP)
         raise.3sg-*se* ostriches unpreoccupied
         "One raises ostriches unconcerned."

Given that verbal passives do not require the expression of the external argument, that passive *se* construction excludes it, and that impersonal *se* is a ([+hum]) indefinite subject, it is not difficult to find cases in EP where the three constructions are so similar in meaning that they may be used as optimal paraphrases of one another. This is illustrated by the sentences in (30), for instance.

(30) a. *Foram encontrados finalmente os destroços do   avião.*   (EP)
         were found   finally   the remains of-the plane
         "The wreckage of the plane was finally found."

      b. *Encontraram-se finalmente os destroços do   avião.*   (EP)
         found.3pl-*se* finally   the remains of-the plane
         "The wreckage of the plane was finally found."

      c. *Encontrou-se finalmente os destroços do   avião.*   (EP)
         found.3sg-*se* finally   the remains of-the plane
         "One finally found the wreckage of the plane."

In face of this general interchangeability, an intriguing contrast arises in EP when the three constructions are embedded under raising and control verbs. Take the data in (31) and (32) below, for example.[14] While all the sentences with the (modal) raising verb *dever* "ought" in (31) may alternate as good paraphrases of one another, the superficially parallel sentences in (32) with the control verb *querer* "want" show interpretive differences depending on the type of passive construction (i.e. participial passive *vs. se* passive).

(31) EP:

    a. *Deve-se encontrar os culpados.*
       ought.3sg-*se* find the culprits
       "One ought to find the culprits."

    b. *Devem encontrar-se os culpados.*
       ought.3pl find-*se* the culprits

    c. *Devem-se encontrar os culpados.*
      ought.3pl-*se* find the culprits
    d. *Devem ser encontrados os culpados.*
      ought.3pl be found the culprits
    e. *Os culpados devem ser encontrados.*
      the culprits ought.3pl be found
      "The culprits ought to be found."

(32) EP:
    a. *Quer-se   encontrar os culpados.*
      want.3sg-*se* find   the culprits
    b. *Querem encontrar-se os culpados.*
      want.3pl find-*se*   the culprits
    c. *Querem-se encontrar os culpados.*
      want.3pl-*se* find   the culprits
      "One wants to find the culprits"
    d. **Querem ser encontrados os culpados.*
      want.3pl be found   the culprits
      [No available interpretation]
    e. *Os culpados querem   ser encontrados.*
      the culprits want.3pl be found
      "The culprits want to be found."

The contrast between (31) and (32) can be accounted for once one takes into account the thematic properties of the embedding verb (*dever* "ought" does not assign an external θ-role, but *querer* "want" does) and the restructuring possibilities within the embedded clause. The agreement between *querer* and the plural DP in (32b) and the possibility of clitic climbing in (32c) indicate that *querer*, like *dever* in (31), can be a restructuring verb in EP and its infinitival complement is compatible with restructuring.[15] As restructuring creates a verbal complex whose case and θ-assignment are defined by the embedded verb, the verbal complex of (32b) and (32c) pattern like the embedded verb of (32a), rendering them very close in meaning. Hence, (32a–c) replicates the paraphrase possibilities found in (31a–c). By contrast, the ungrammaticality of (32d) shows that the passive participle resist restructuring. Thus, the sentence in (32e) requires a biclausal analysis, with the plural DP being the external argument of *querer*, and it cannot be a paraphrase of (32a–c), for the external argument is now referentially definite. The paradigm in (32) is interesting in that it shows that the passive *se* construction may, in some environments, pattern with the impersonal *se* construction and differently from the participial passive.

    Once impersonal *se* emerged out of a reanalysis of the passive *se* constructions as a syntactic subject, it ceased to be restricted to transitive verbs and came to be used with any type of verb, as illustrated in (33) below. However, as pointed out by Martins and Nunes (2005), the acceptability of impersonal *se* with specific raising verbs is subject to variation among EP speakers and is even more restricted in BP (see Nunes 1990, 1991). The sentence in (33f), for instance is allowed in EP, but not in BP.

(33) a. Transitive verbs with prepositional complements:
      Precisa-se   de funcionários.
      need.3sg-*se* of waiters
      "Waiters wanted."
    b. Unergative verbs:
      Trabalha-se muito nesta   cidade.
      work.3sg-*se* much in-this city
      "One works a lot in this city."

c. Unaccusative verbs:
   Chegava-se   cedo ao   trabalho.
   arrived.3sg-*se* early at-the work
   "One used to arrive early at work."

d. Passive verbs:
   Quando se é promovido, as coisas ficam   mais fáceis.
   when   *se* is promoted the things become more easy
   "When one is promoted, things become easier."

e. Copular verbs:
   Não se ficou   contente com a   nova situação.
   not *se* became.3sg happy   with the new situation
   "People did not become happy with the new situation."

f. Raising verbs:
   Parecia-se ir   ganhar o   jogo.   (EP°ᴷ; BP*)
   seemed-*se* go win   the game
   "It seemed that we would win the game."

We have seen that EP and BP behave differently with respect to *se* constructions involving transitive verbs with prepositionless complements. That is to say, while both impersonal *se* and passive *se* are allowed in EP, only impersonal *se* is admitted in BP. BP also departs from EP in being able to drop impersonal *se* in generic tenses (see e.g. Galves 1987, Nunes 1990, 1991), yielding an indefinite reading for a null third person singular subject, as illustrated in (34) below.

(34) a. *Não usa mais esse estilo de redação.*   (BP)
        not use more this style of writing
        "One doesn't use this writing style anymore."

   b. *Casava   muito cedo no   século passado.*   (BP)
      marry-imperf very   early in-the century passed
      "People used to get married very early in the last century."

   c. *No   futuro vai descobrir remédio   para tudo   quanto é doença.*   (BP)
      in-the future go discover medicine for everything which is sickness
      "In the future people will discover medicines for every kind of sickness."

Both of these peculiarities of BP conform with the generalization that it favors lack of overt verbal agreement morphology and use of bare verbal forms whenever possible. That being so, one wonders if the sentences in (34) do indeed result from deletion of impersonal *se* or if they simply constitute another instantiation of the weakening of third person plural morphology, which can convey an arbitrary reading (see Cinque 1988), as illustrated in (35).

(35) a. *Telefonaram para você.*
        called   to   you
        "There was a phone call for you."

   b. *Estão batendo   na   porta.*
      are knocking in-the door
      "Someone is knocking on the door."

One crucial difference between the sentences in (34), on the one hand, and (35), on the other, is that the indefinite subject necessarily excludes the speaker in (35), but not in (34). Recall that impersonal *se* constructions may or may not include the speaker and this may be even disambiguated in some EP dialects via doubling (see (28)). Based on the fact that the interpretation of (34) is actually closer to the one we finds in impersonal *se* constructions than the one found in constructions with arbitrary third person plural, Nunes (1990) argues that sentences such as (34) do result from deletion of the impersonal *se*. As Nunes (1990) further points out, this reasoning is also consistent with the diachronic facts of BP: constructions such as (34) emerged in the nineteenth century in BP, after the impersonal *se* construction started being the canonical impersonal construction, leading the passive *se* construction to their present-day obsolescence.

The final contrast between BP and EP we would like to mention here is related to their differences with respect to the availability of null subjects. As BP became a partial null subject language, it started favoring overtly expressed subjects in syntactic contexts where a null subject language of the Romance type chooses a null pronominal as the unmarked option. Accordingly, impersonal *se* came to be more frequently expressed within infinitival clauses in BP than in EP, as a strategy to support an arbitrary/generic interpretation for the infinitival subject. This contrast between BP and EP is especially clear in prepositioned infinitival clauses such as the ones in (36) and (37), in which EP noticeably disfavors, or even excludes, the presence of impersonal *se*, in the same way that it excludes other overt subjects.

(36) a. *O mar está perigoso   para nadar.*   (BP^{OK}; EP^{OK})
        the sea is dangerous for swim
        "The sea is currently dangerous for swimming."
    b. *O mar está perigoso   para se nadar.*   (BP^{OK}; EP:??)
        the sea is dangerous for *se* swim
        "The sea is currently dangerous for one to swim."

(37) a. *Nova Iorque e   Barcelona são cidades fáceis de gostar.*   (BP ?*; EP^{OK})
        New York and Barcelona are cities   easy of like
        "It is easy to like New York or Barcelona."
    b. *Nova Iorque e   Barcelona são cidades fáceis de se gostar.*   (BP^{OK}; EP*)
        New York and Barcelona are cities   easy of.se like
        "It's easy for one to like New York or Barcelona."
    c. *Nova Iorque e   Barcelona são cidades fáceis da gente gostar.*   (BP^{OK}; EP*)
        New York and Barcelona are cities   easy of.us   like
        "It's easy for us to like New York or Barcelona."

The discussion above has considered some of the "macroproperties" of constructions involving passive *se* and impersonal *se*. We will now examine some properties of *se* related to its status as a clitic, focusing on impersonal *se* in order to be able to make a comparison between BP and EP.

3.2. *Impersonal se: syntactic placement and co-occurrence restrictions*

The reader might have noticed that although we said that BP is essentially a proclitic system, the sentences in (33a–c), for instance, all involve enclisis and are acceptable in BP. In fact, the impersonal *se* is exceptional in BP in that in absence of proclisis triggers, it is in general enclitic and this has surprising consequences. In order to examine them, let us first consider the paradigm in (38) in BP, which involves clitics other than impersonal *se*.

(38) BP:

    a. *Me viram/*viram-me no   cinema.*
       me saw/*saw-me   in-the movies
       "People saw me at the movies."

    b. *Eles não te   criticaram/*criticaram-te.*
       they not you criticized/criticized-you
       "They didn't criticize you."

    c. *Você deve,   sem   sombra de dúvida, se inscrever na competição.*
       you should without shadow of doubt *se* register in-the competition
       "No doubt you should register for the competition."

    d. **Você se deve/deve-se,   sem   sombra de dúvida, inscrever na   competição.*
       you *se* should/should-*se* without shadow of doubt   register in-the competition
       "No doubt you should register for the competition."

    e. *Você não deve,   sem   conhecer as regras, se inscrever na   competição.*
       you not should without knowing the rules *se* register in-the competition
       "You shouldn't register for the competition without knowing the rules."

    f. **Você não se deve/deve-se,   sem   conhecer as regras,*
       you not *se* should/should-*se* without knowing the rules
       inscrever na   competição.
       register in-the competition
       "You shouldn't register for the competition without knowing the rules."

Example (38a) shows that proclisis is required even if the clitic ends up in sentence initial position. When auxiliaries are involved, the clitic procliticizes to the main verb, as shown by the contrast between (38c) and (38d); in other words, clitic climbing is not allowed. Interestingly, the presence of negation, which triggers proclisis in EP, does not alter the basic pattern in BP, as shown in (38e) and (38f). This could be interpreted as suggesting that once BP became a proclitic system, the old proclisis triggers became vacuous in the new system.

Surprisingly, this very plausible analysis makes incorrect predictions for impersonal *se*, as shown in (39).

(39) BP:

    a. *Contratou-se/*Se contratou um novo professor.*
       hired-*se*/*se* hired   a new teacher
       "One hired a new teacher."

    b. *Não se contratou/*contratou-se um novo professor.*
       not *se* hired/hired-*se*   a new teacher
       "One didn't hire a new teacher."

    c. **Deve, sem   sombra de dúvida, se contratar um novo professor.*
       should without shade of doubt *se* hire   a new teacher

    d. *Deve-se, sem   sombra de dúvida, contratar um novo professor.*
       should-*se* without shade of doubt hire   a new teacher
       "No doubt one should hire a new professor."

    e. **Não deve,   sem   haver justa causa, se despedir um professor.*
       not should without having just cause *se* fire   a teacher

    f. **Não deve-se,   sem   haver justa causa, despedir um professor.*
       not should-*se* without having just cause fire   a teacher

    g. *Não se deve,   sem   haver justa causa, despedir um professor.*
       not *se* should without having just cause fire   a teacher
       "One shall not fire a professor without just cause."

The paradigm in (39) shows that as opposed to the other clitics of BP, impersonal *se* must encliticize in absence of a proclisis trigger; hence the contrast between (39a) and (39b). Furthermore, when auxiliary verbs are involved, the clitic enclitizes to the finite auxiliary; hence the contrast between (39c) and (39d). When negation is added to the picture, it triggers proclisis to the finite auxiliary and not to the main verb (see (39e–g)). In other words, clitic climbing is allowed with impersonal *se* in environments where this is not possible with other clitics (cf. (38f)). In this regard, the positions occupied by the clitic in (38c–f), on the one hand, and (39e–g), on the other, are especially revealing, for the reflexive and the impersonal clitic are homophonous. This leads us to conclude that in BP, impersonal *se* has lexical specifications that set it apart from the other clitics of the language, including the third person reflexive clitic, which is also spelled out as *se*.

Let us hold this conclusion for a moment and turn our attention to EP. Like other Romance languages, EP does not allow impersonal *se* to co-occur with reflexive *se* within the same clause, as illustrated by the contrast between the monoclausal structures in (40) and the biclausal structure in (41).

(40) a. **Levanta-se-se   cedo neste país.*   (EP)
         rises-se_{IMP}-se_{REFL} early in-this country
         "One gets up early in this country."
     b. **Vai-se   levantar-se cedo amanhã.*   (EP)
         goes-se_{IMP} rise-se_{REFL} early tomorrow
         "People are going to get up early tomorrow."

(41) *Soube-se   ter-se   ele suicidado.*   (EP)
      knew-se_{IMP} have-se_{REFL} he committed-suicide
      "It was heard that he committed suicide."

Taking the contrast between (40) and (41) as a starting point, Martins and Nunes (2014a) examine control structures in EP where the controller is the impersonal clitic *se* and the controlled predicate has an instance of reflexive *se*. As shown in (42), the result they find is that control structures behave like monoclausal structures as far as the co-occurrence restriction on the two clitics is concerned, regardless of the surface distance between the two clitics.

(42) EP:
     a. **Quer-se   sentar-se (e   não se   pode).*
         wants-se_{IMP} sit se_{REFL} and not se_{IMP} can
         "One wants to sit down but can't."
     b. **Conseguiu-se evitar sentar-se na   última fila.*
         managed-se_{IMP} avoid sit-se_{REFL} in-the last   row
         "One managed to avoid sitting in the last row.'
     c. **Tentou-se conseguir evitar sentar-se na   última fila.*
         tried-se_{IMP} manage avoid sit- se_{REFL} in-the last   row
         "One tried to manage to avoid sitting in the last row."

Martins and Nunes argue that the contrast between (41) and (42) can be accounted for if one adopts the movement theory of control (see e.g. Hornstein 1999, 2001 and Boeckx, Hornstein, and Nunes 2010). Since (41) does not involve control, each clitic is generated and surfaces in a different clause. By contrast, from the perspective of the movement theory of control, the impersonal clitic *se* in (42) should be generated in the most embedded clause and then move to its surface position, leaving copies behind. That being so, we end having a copy of impersonal *se* and the reflexive *se* in the most embedded clause, which should then be ruled out by the co-occurrence restriction that excludes the sentences in (40).

Bearing this in mind, let us examine comparable data in BP. At first sight, (43) below seems to show that BP behaves like EP in disallowing impersonal *se* and reflexive *se* in a local domain.[16] However, when the data in (44) below are taken into account, we realize that the explanation cannot be as simple as that, for the two clitics are arguably within the same domain but the result is grammatical.[17]

(43) **Pode-se   se   sentar em qualquer lugar.*   (BP)
     can.3sg-se_{IMP} se_{REFL} sit   in any   place
     "One can sit anywhere."

(44) a. *Não se   pode se   divertir com um barulho desses.*   (BP)
        not se_{IMP} can se_{REFL} enjoy with a noise of-these
        "One can't have a good time with such a level of noise."
     b. *Não se   deve   se   levantar tarde.*
        not se_{IMP} should se_{REFL} raise   late
        "One shouldn't get up late."

Our proposal is that what matters in BP is simply adjacency. Thus, the sentences in (44) are well formed because the clitics are not adjacent to each other. In fact, sentences such as (43) may become grammatical if parenthetical material disrupts the adjacency between the two clitics, as illustrated in (45).

(45) *Pode-se, salvo engano, se   sentar em qualquer lugar.*   (BP)
     can-se_{IMP} saving mistake se_{REFL} sit   in any   place
     "I think one can sit in any place."

Similar considerations apply to BP control configurations analogous to (42), where the impersonal *se* is the controller and an embedded predicate contains the reflexive *se*. As illustrated in (46) below, an ill-formed results arises only if impersonal *se* and reflexive *se* are adjacent. If phonetic material or a pause intervenes between the two clitics, the co-occurrence restriction is circumvented, as shown in (47).[18]

(46) a. **Tentou-se se   livrar do   problema.*   (BP)
        tried-se_{IMP} se_{REFL} set.free of-the problem
        "One tried to get rid of the problem."
     b. **Esperava-se se   sentar na   primeira fila.*   (BP)
        expect-se_{IMP} se_{REFL} sit   in-the first   row
        "One expected to be able to sit in the front row."

(47) a. *Tentou-se de todas as formas se   livrar do   problema.* (BP)
        tried-se_{IMP} of all the forms se_{REFL} set.free of-the problem
        "One tried in every possible way to get rid of the problem."
     b. *Esperava-se conseguir se   sentar na   primeira fila.*   (BP)
        expect-se_{IMP} manage se_{REFL} sit   in-the first   row
        "One expected to be able to sit in the front row."

Assuming that something along these lines is on the right track, one wonders why EP and BP behave so differently with respect to the conditions they impose for the restriction on the co-occurrence of impersonal and reflexive *se*. Our conjecture is that this has to do with the exceptional properties of impersonal *se* in BP. In EP, the impersonal and the reflexive are not only phonologically identical, but are subject to the exact same conditions on syntactic clitic placement. By contrast, in BP only their phonetic spell-out is identical, for they go completely separate ways as far as syntactic clitic placement goes. Thus, this co-occurrence restriction is more syntactic in nature in EP as it makes reference to clausal domains but not to adjacency. By contrast, in BP the restriction is more phonological in nature, making crucial reference to adjacency.[19]

4. Conclusion

In this chapter we have described participial passives (in particular, verbal passives as opposed to adjectival passives) and passive *se* and impersonal se constructions in EP and BP with respect to their agreement, case, word order, and interpretive properties. By and large, we have seen that BP and EP essentially pattern similarly with respect to participial passives, except when distinct grammatical properties of each dialect interfere (e.g. agreement and clitic placement). However, the two dialects were shown to sharply split with respect to *se* constructions: First, only EP productively allows passive *se* constructions. And second, the contextual distribution of impersonal *se* in BP and EP is considerably different.

NOTES

"The first author had the support of FCT—Fundação para a Ciência e a Tecnologia, under the project WOChWEL (PTDC/CLE-LIN/121707/2010)". The second author has received support from CNPq (grant 309036/2011-9)

1　A discussion of other *se*-constructions (reflexive/reciprocal structures, middles, and anticausatives, for instance) falls outside the scope of this chapter.

2　As opposed to languages like German, for instance, which allows passives of unergative verbs, as illustrated in (i), this is not a possibility in Portuguese, as shown in (ii).

>　(i)　Es wurde getanzt.　　(*German*, Jaeggli 1986)
>　　　it was danced
>　　　"There was dancing."

>　(ii)　*Foi dançado.　　　(*Portuguese*)
>　　　was danced
>　　　"There was dancing."

3　Orthographic conventions dictate that there must be a hyphen between a clitic and the verb it attaches to in cases of enclisis, but not in cases of proclisis. In order to make the syntactic attachment visually clearer in cases where the clitic is sandwiched between two verbs, as in (3b, c) and (4b–c), for instance, some parenthetical material was added.

4　Participles may display irregular short forms in tandem with regular forms, as illustrated in (i) below. Significantly, passives require the short forms, which are more prone to be diachronically reanalyzed as adjectives; by contrast, perfective compound tenses require the regular (longer) forms.

>　(i)　a.　*O homicida　foi　preso /*prendido*.
>　　　　　the murderer was arrested/arrested
>　　　　　"The murderer was arrested."
>　　　b.　*A　polícia tinha prendido/*preso　o　homicida*.
>　　　　　the police　had arrested/arrested the murderer
>　　　　　"The police had arrested the murderer."

5　Once these sentences are independently explained away, the ungrammaticality of (3a) then shows that EP does not allow enclisis to a participle, regardless of whether or not it bears agreement morphology. It remains to be explained why a perfective participle may license proclisis (in a proclitic system; see (3b)), but not enclisis (in an enclitic system; see (3a)). In fact, when a proclisis trigger, like negation in (i) below, comes into play, procliticization to the participle becomes available also in EP:

(i) Eles têm sistematicamente não **me informado**. (EP)
they have systematically not me informed
"They have systematically kept back information unknown to me."

6 See also, among others, Levin and Rappaport 1986. On the distinction between two types of adjectival passives, namely, resultatives (with auxiliary *ficar* "stay") and statives (with auxiliaries *ser/estar* "be"), see e.g. Embick 2004, Alexiadou and Anagnostopoulou 2008, Duarte and Oliveira 2010, and Duarte 2013.

7 Verbal passives are typically formed with eventive verbs and exclude different types of stative transitive verbs, as illustrated in (i) below (from Duarte 2013).

(i) a. **A melhor nota da   turma foi tida pelo   João.*
the best grade of-the class was had by-the João
"João had the best grade in the class."
b. **Esses terrenos eram possuídos por um alemão.*
these lots   were owned by a German
"These lots were owned by a German."
c. **Cinquenta quilos eram pesados por mim no   ano passado.*
fifty   kilos were weighted by me in-the year past
"Last year I weighed fifty kilos."

8 See Simioni 2011 for relevant discussion.

9 For relevant discussion, see e.g. Naro 1976, Galves 1986, 1987, Cinque 1988, Nunes 1990, 1991, Raposo and Uriagereka 1996, and Cavalcante 2006.

10 The impersonal *se* construction in (16b) may in fact be judged as acceptable with a marked intonation, conventionally represented by a comma, as shown in (i). The non-neutral informational status of the internal argument in these cases indicates that it moves not to the subject position, but to a higher A′-position in the left periphery. Crucially, the passive *se* construction in (16a) does not require any special intonation in order to be licensed.

(i) *Os bolos, comeu-se ontem.*
the cookies ate.3sg-*se* yesterday
"Someone ate *the cookies* yesterday."

11 Sentences like (18b) are attested in the dialectal corpus CORDIAL-SIN, as illustrated below. Unfortunately, all the examples in the corpus display a third person *singular* accusative clitic.

(i) %EP:
a. *Deixa-se-a   crescer.*
let.3sg-*se*-it.acc grow   (CORDIAL-SIN, PST)
"We/people let it grow up."
b. *Pode-se-a   guardar na freezer.*
can.3sg-*se*-it.acc keep in-the freezer   (CORDIAL-SIN, STE)
"One can keep it in the refrigerator."
c. *Abre-se-o   de um metro de fundura e   um metro de largura.* (CORDIAL-SIN, ALC)
open.3sg-*se*-it.acc of one meter of deepness and one meter of wideness
"We/People open a hole one meter deep and one meter wide."
d. *Mas carregava-se-o   aí   às vezes também nos carros de bestas.* (CORDIAL-SIN, MLD)
but carried.3sg-*se*-it.acc there at times also   in-the cars of animals
"But sometimes people would also carry it in horse wagons."

12 See e.g. Jaeggli 1986 and Baker, Johnson and Roberts 1989.

13 (21d) is grammatical in BP under an impersonal reading due to the fact that *elas* may check accusative with the verb, as it is a syncretic form for nominative, accusative, dative, and oblique (Similar considerations apply to the other third person weak pronouns in BP).

14 (31b) and (32b) also allow an irrelevant reflexive reading if the DP *os culpados* "the culprits" has narrow focus.

15 For relevant discussion, see e.g. Gonçalves 1999 and Wurmbrand 2001.

16   Sentences without auxiliaries such as (40a), repeated below in (i), are also ungrammatical in BP. However, this is not very telling, for the reflexive is in an enclitic position and this is independently ruled out in BP, as seen in (38). (ib) controls for this noise (the reflexive *se* is proclitic and the impersonal *se*, enclitic), but the result is still unacceptable, presumably because movement of the reflexive across the impersonal *se* induces a minimality violation.

(i)   a. *Levanta-se-se*   *cedo*   *neste*   *país.*   (BP)
          rises-se$_{IMP}$-se$_{REFL}$ early   in-this   country
      b. *Se levanta-se*   *cedo*   *neste*   *país.*   (BP)
          se$_{REFL}$rises-se$_{IMP}$ early   in-this   country
          "One gets up early in this country."

17   Martins and Nunes (2014a, b) argue that (strong) phases, rather than clauses, constitute the relevant domain for computing the co-occurrence restriction involving indefinite and reflexive *se*. Thus, the two instances of *se* in the sentences of (43) and (44) may fall within the same strong phasal domain even if modals in BP are also to be analysed as raising verbs, for the light verb associated with raising verbs is assumed to be defective and not head a strong phase (see Chomsky 2001). For purposes of exposition, we will put this refinement aside, as it does not affect the reasoning to be presented below. See Martins and Nunes (2014a, b) for relevant discussion.

18   Pauses are more naturally inserted between a control verb and its infinitival complement than between an auxiliary and the main verb, as illustrated in (i) below. Accordingly, pauses are able to circumvent the co-occurrence restriction on two instances of *se* in (iia) in BP, but not in (iib).

(i)   a. *Alguém   tentou # sair   mais cedo.*   (BP)
          someone tried   leave more early
          "Someone tried to leave earlier."
      b. ??*Alguém vai # sair   mais cedo.*   (BP)
          someone goes leave more early
          "Someone is going to leave earlier."

(ii) a. *Tentou-se # se   levantar mais cedo.*   (BP)
          tried-se$_{IMP}$ se$_{REFL}$rise   more early
          "One tried to get up earlier."
      b. *Vai-se # se   levantar mais cedo.*   (BP)
          goes-se$_{IMP}$ se$_{REFL}$ rise   more early
          "One is going get up earlier."

19   Also consistent with the phonological nature of the restriction in BP is the fact that, as opposed to EP, it does not allow the complementizer *se* 'if' and impersonal *se* to be adjacent, as shown in (i). Thanks to Carolina França (p.c.) for bringing this point to our attention.

(i)   a. *Se se   contratar um novo professor, os problemas serão   resolvidos.*   (EP^{OK} **BP***)
          if se$_{IMP}$ hire   a   new teacher, the problems will.be solved
          "If a new teacher is hired, the problems will be solved."
      b. *Se não se   contratar um novo professor, os problemas não serão   resolvidos.*   (EP^{OK} BP^{OK})
          if not se$_{IMP}$ hire   a   new teacher, the problems not will.be solved
          "If a new teacher is not hired, the problems won't be solved."

REFERENCES

Alexiadou, A. and E. Anagnostopoulou (2008). Structuring participles. In C. B. Changa and H. J. Haynie (eds.), *Proceedings of the 26th West Coast Conference on Formal Linguistics*, pp. 33–41.

Baker, M., K. Johnson, and I. Roberts (1989). Passive arguments raised. *Linguistic Inquiry*, 20 (2), pp. 219–251.

Boeckx, C., N. Hornstein, and J. Nunes (2010). *Control as Movement*. Cambridge: Cambridge University Press.

Cavalcante, S. R. de O. (2006). O uso do *se* indefinido na história do português: Do português clássico ao português europeu e brasileiro modernos. Ph.D. dissertation, Unicamp.

Chomsky, N. (2001). Derivation by phase. In M. Kenstowicz (ed.), *Ken Hale: A Life in Language*. Cambridge, MA: MIT Press, pp. 1–52.

Cinque, G. (1988). On si constructions and the theory of arb. *Linguistic Inquiry*, 19, pp. 521–581.

CORDIAL-SIN: *Syntax-oriented Corpus of Portuguese Dialects*. http://www.clul.ul.pt/resources/212-cordial-sin-syntax-oriented-corpus-of-portuguese-dialects, accessed November 4, 2015.

Duarte, I. (2013). Construções ativas, passivas, incoativas e médias. In E. B. P. Raposo, M. F. Bacelar do Nascimento, M. A. C. da Mota, L. Segura, and A. Mendes (eds.), *Gramática do Português*, vol. 1. Lisbon: Fundação Calouste Gulbenkian, pp. 427–458.

Duarte, I. and F. Oliveira (2010). Particípios resultativos. In A. M. Brito, F. Oliveira, J. Veloso, and A. Fiéis (eds.), *Textos Selecionados do XXV Encontro Nacional da Associação Portuguesa de Linguística*. Porto: Associação Portuguesa de Linguística, pp. 397–408.

Embick, D. (2004). On the structure of resultative predicates in English. *Linguistic Inquiry*, 35 (3), pp. 355–392.

Galves, C. (1986). *Aluga-(se) casas: Um problema de sintaxe portuguesa na Teoria de Regência e Vinculação*. Campinas: Preedição 2.

Galves, C. (1987). A sintaxe do Português Brasileiro. *Ensaios de Linguística*, 13, pp. 31–50.

Gonçalves, A. (1999). Predicados complexos verbais em contextos de infinitivo não preposicionado do português europeu. Ph.D. dissertation, Universidade de Lisboa.

Hornstein, N. (1999). Movement and control. *Linguistic Inquiry*, 30, pp. 69–96.

Hornstein, N. (2001). *Move! A Minimalist Theory of Construal*. Oxford: Blackwell.

Jeaggli, O. (1986). Passive. *Linguistic Inquiry*, 17, pp. 587–633.

Levin, B. and M. Rappaport (1986). The formation of adjectival passives. *Linguistic Inquiry*, 17 (4), pp. 623–661.

Martins, A. M. (2013). Posição dos pronomes pessoais clíticos. In E. B. P. Raposo, M. F. Bacelar do Nascimento, M. A. C. da Mota, L. Segura, and A. Mendes (eds.), *Gramática do Português*, vol. 2. Lisbon: Fundação Calouste Gulbenkian, pp. 2229–2302.

Martins, A. M. (2009). Subject doubling in European Portuguese dialects: the role of impersonal *se*. In E. O. Aboh, E. van der Linden, J. Quer and P. Sleeman (eds.), *Romance Languages and Linguistic Theory. Selected papers from "Going Romance" Amsterdam 2007*. Amsterdam/Philadelphia: John Benjamins, pp. 179-200.

Martins, A. M. and J. Nunes (2005). Raising issues in Brazilian and European Portuguese. *Journal of Portuguese Linguistics*, 4, 53–77.

Martins, A. M. and J. Nunes (2014a). Co-occurrence restrictions on clitics in European Portuguese and minimalist approaches to control. Manuscript, Universidade de Lisboa and Universidade de São Paulo.

Martins, A. M. and J. Nunes (2014b). Identicalness avoidance effects in European Portuguese: a case study on phasal transfer. Manuscript, Universidade de Lisboa and Universidade de São Paulo.

Naro, A. (1976). The genesis of the reflexive impersonal in Portuguese: a study in syntactic change as a surface phenomenon. *Language*, 52, pp. 779–811.

Nunes, J. (1990). O famigerado se: Uma análise sincrónica e diacrónica das construções com *se* apassivador e indeterminador. Masters dissertation, Unicamp.

Nunes, J. (1991). *Se* apassivador e *se* indeterminador: o percurso diacrônico no português brasileiro. *Cadernos de Estudos Lingüísticos*, 20, pp. 33–58.

Raposo, E. and J. Uriagereka (1996). Indefinite *se*. *Linguistic Inquiry*, 14, pp. 749–810.

Simioni, L. (2011). Concordância em construções passivas com argumentos pré e posverbais e incorporação de nomes nus no PB. Ph.D. dissertation, Universidade de São Paulo.

Wasow, T. (1977). Transformations and the lexicon. In P. W. Culicover and A. Akmajian (eds.), *Formal Syntax*. New York: Academic Press, pp. 327–360.

Wurmbrand, S. (2001). *Infinitives: Restructuring and Clause Structure*. Berlin: Mouton de Gruyter.

18 Binding and Pronominal Forms in Portuguese

SERGIO MENUZZI AND MARIA LOBO

1. Introduction

In this chapter we discuss some of the properties of pronominal forms in the two main varieties of Portuguese—European Portuguese (EP) and Brazilian Portuguese (BP)—from the perspective of "Binding Theory" (BT).[1] Specifically, we focus on a few basic patterns of 3rd person anaphora bearing on some of BT's central issues, such as the nature of binding domains and of the complementary-like distribution of pronouns and other forms that compete for bound variable readings (like reflexives and null subjects). We start by summarizing the theoretical perspective of our discussion.

One of the main problems of standard BT was the arbitrariness of the definition of binding domain, involving notions such as "governing category", "accessible subject", etc. These notions were particular to BT, with no clear independent motivation; hence, much research was dedicated to relating BT principles to more "natural" notions of domain (see Menuzzi 1999, Reuland 2011, Safir 2004, 2013). Standard BT was also conceptually frail with respect to the nature of the DP types and their complementary-like distribution (Burzio 1991, Menuzzi 1999, Safir 2004). The typology remains a stipulation if DPs are simply lexically classified as "anaphor", "pronominal" and "R-expression"—that is, if their type is not derived from their independent properties. Hence, the need to relate binding principles explicitly to inherent properties of DPs, as in Reinhart and Reuland's (1993) framework (R&R, from now on).

Consider R&R's Principle B, reformulated as a condition on *reflexive predicates*:

(1) *Condition B* (R&R 1993):
 If a predicate is reflexive, it must be reflexive-marked.

Note that the domain of the condition is independently required (e.g. for argument selection). Now, complex anaphors containing a SELF form function as "reflexive-markers"; but pronouns and *se*-forms do not (R&R 1993, Safir 2004).[2] Thus, in the domain of a reflexive-predicate, a complex form, and not a *se*-form or a pronoun, will be required, as in Dutch:

(2) Jan haat {zichzelf/*zich/*hem}.
 Jan hates {*se-SELF* / *se* / him}
 "*Jan* hates *himself* / *him*."

The Handbook of Portuguese Linguistics, First Edition. Edited by W. Leo Wetzels, João Costa, and Sergio Menuzzi.
© 2016 John Wiley & Sons, Inc. Published 2020 by John Wiley & Sons, Inc.

Hence, part of the complementarity does relate to the morphosyntactic constitution of DPs—namely, if they may function as reflexive-markers or not. The strategy can be generalized. Consider "inherently reflexive" predicates, that is, predicates whose semantics-pragmatics is such that they are either necessarily or very often interpreted as reflexive (e.g., "behave" or "wash"). According to R&R, these predicates are "lexically marked" for reflexivity; hence, SELF forms are not required and, in principle, either a *se*-form or a pronoun will be available. But actually only the *se*-form is:

(3) <u>Max</u> wast {zich/*hem}
    Max washes {*se/him*}
    "Max washes (himself/*him)."

To account for this contrast, R&R invoke another type of constraint, operating on the domain of chains—that is, on anaphoric dependencies that fit the chain format:

(4) *Chain Condition* (R&R 1993):

    Only the head of a chain (the antecedent) must be [+R], that is, fully specified for φ-features (person, number, gender and case).

The effect of (4) is to impose a constraint we may call *chain economy*: the tail of an anaphoric chain must be [-R], i.e., not specified for φ-features. Now, *se*-anaphors are unspecified for many φ-features, and pronouns are specified for most; hence, in R&R's framework, the pronoun is excluded in (3). Note: the chain condition applies to an independently motivated grammatical domain (chains) and is sensitive to inherent properties of the DP (its φ-feature specification). In Section 3 we discuss Portuguese facts that seem to provide interesting evidence for this chains-and-reflexivity approach: there is an asymmetry in local binding in both EP and BP, bound pronouns being allowed only in PPs, and not in transitive-like structures.

If the distribution of DPs were to result only from the interaction of universal constraints and inherent properties of DPs, languages would develop specialized forms to satisfy all constraints. But this is not the case. For example, English has no *se*-anaphor, only pronouns and the corresponding reflexive-markers: *him/himself, her/herself*, etc. Hence, either the Chain Condition does not apply to English (hence, it is not universal), or we must claim that *himself* is [–R], like a *se*-form. Similar cases abound across anaphoric systems: in many languages pronouns can be locally bound because there are no corresponding reflexives (e.g. 1st and 2nd person pronouns in Romance); R-expressions can be bound if the language has no independent set of pronouns (see Lasnik 1989), etc. This aspect of binding systems has been incorporated in recent versions of BT, which assume bound forms "compete" for best-formation of anaphoric dependencies (Burzio 1991, Menuzzi 1999, Safir 2004). The idea is supported by many phenomena discussed in Sections 3 and 4: the availability of bound pronouns in transitive structures in some varieties of BP; the differences between EP and BP with respect to long-distance binding; the competition between pronouns and other forms with quantificational antecedents.

Finally, concerning the interpretive nature of the binding relation, it is widely accepted that the basic distinction to be made is that between *coreference* and *bound-variable* interpretations (cf. Reinhart 1983; Safir 2014 for recent discussion). Crucially, binding corresponds only to bound-variable relations: (a) DPs that cannot be interpreted as bound-variables cannot be bound (e.g. proper names); (b) canonical anaphors are interpreted as bound variables (e.g. the Portuguese reflexive *se*); (c) in general, bound-variable readings are dependent on c-command or similar relations. As we will see in section 4, φ-feature impoverished forms in Portuguese tend to be bound forms and to require local antecedents, and their availability seems to constrain bound readings for pronouns, in an effect similar to chain economy effects (like in (3)).

2. Pronominal forms in current Portuguese

Here we present just a brief summary of the pronominal systems of EP and BP, to give an impression of the different sets of oppositions—this will be relevant later on.[3] Table 18.1 below summarizes the EP system (underlined forms are those in which EP differs from standard Portuguese; forms between brackets are standard forms out of use in EP).

EP is considered a typical null subject language—hence, it has null subjects (*pro*) for all persons, and subject forms are used only under specific pragmatic demands (emphasis, contrast, etc.). Like Italian and Spanish, EP null subjects are licensed by a rich set of verb forms inflected for subject agreement: most tenses have four forms, and some have five. Still like other Romance languages, EP has a full system of "clitic pronouns" (signaled by hyphen), most of which are missing in current BP (see Table 18.2, in the next page). Side by side with clitics, EP also makes significant use of "null objects", an innovation it shares with BP. Because null objects seem to behave as R-expressions in both EP and BP, they are not discussed here (see Chapter 17, this volume).

An important aspect of the EP system is that the 2nd person form *você* "you" is *grammatically* 3rd person; though it has mixed with the old 2nd person series (Lara 2015), it also combines with many 3rd person forms. (For the history of *você*, see Chapter 31, this volume.) A peculiar consequence is that EP uses the reflexive *si* as the preposition-governed form for *você*, giving rise to ambiguous sentences:

(5) *Pedro$_i$ comprou esta cadeira para si$_{i/j}$.* (i = Pedro; j = listener)
  Pedro bought this chair for *se*
  "Pedro$_i$ has bought this chair for himself$_i$ / you$_j$"

This use is limited to singular 2nd person. And it is not found in BP.

With respect to the 3rd person possessives, normative grammars insist that the correct form is *seu* "his/her/their", but admit *dele* "of-him" in case *seu* leads to "ambiguity".

Table 18.1   System of pronominal forms of EP.

	Singular				Plural		
		2nd person					
	1st person	familiar	unfam.	3rd person	1st person	2nd person	3rd person
Subject	*Eu*	*tu*	*você*[a]	*ele*	*nós*	[*vós*] *vocês*	*eles*
	pro	*pro*	*pro*	*pro*	*pro*	*pro*	*pro*
Direct object	*-me*	*-te*	*-o*	*-o*	*-nos*	[*-os*]	*-os*
				<u>null</u>		<u>-vos</u>	<u>null</u>
Reflexive	*-me*	*-te*	*-se*	*-se*	*-nos*	*-se*	*-se*
Preposition-governed	*mim*	*ti*	<u>si</u> [*você*]	*ele*	*nós*	*vocês*	*eles*
Reflexive	*mim*	*ti*	*si*	*si*	*nós*	*vocês* [*si*]	*si*
Possessive	*meu*	*teu*	*seu*	*seu*	*nosso*	[*seu*]	*seu*
				dele		<u>vosso</u>	*dele*

Note
[a] Explicit use of *você* is a marked strategy in EP. Usually, one uses a null pronoun or a full DP corresponding to the proper noun of the addressee, his title or his kinship relation with the speaker.

Table 18.2 System of pronominal forms in BP.

| | Singular | | | | Plural | | |
| | 1st person | 2nd person | | 3rd person | 1st person | 2nd Person | 3rd person |
		equal	respect				
Subject	eu	você	o senhor	ele	a gente	vocês	eles
	[pro]	[pro]	[pro]	pro	[pro]	[pro]	[pro]
Direct object	me-	te-	o senhor	ele	a gente	vocês	eles
		você		null	[nos-]		null
Reflexive	me-	se-	se-	se-	se-	se-	se-
Preposition-governed	mim	você	o senhor	ele	a gente	vocês	eles
Reflexive	mim	você [si]	o senhor [si]	ele [si]	a gente [si]	vocês [si]	eles [si]
Possessive	meu	seu [teu]	seu	seu	nosso	seu	seu
				dele	da gente	de vocês	deles

However, both *seu* and *dele* are used in EP, though not with the same distribution; the same is true of BP (see below). Note that *seu* "his/her/their" is specified only for the grammatical person (3rd) of the antecedent, and not for its gender or number. In this, *seu* is similar to the reflexives *se* and *si*, and differs from the alternative series *dele/dela/deles/delas* "of-him/of-her/of-them(m)/of-them(f)".

The EP system preserves most of the forms of the system described by normative grammars. BP, on the other hand, has been affected by numerous changes, some still underway, resulting in a lot of variation. Table 18.2 above provides an approximate picture of the system (see Neves 2008, and Chapters 28 and 31, this volume; the forms in brackets are still available for some speakers, but likely to become obsolete).

We would like to call attention to three features of the above system.

First, Table 18. 2 shows that BP has many new forms: *você* has taken over the function of 2nd person pronouns (the *tu / te / ti* series remaining in some dialects); a new form, *o senhor* ("the gentleman"), has been generalized as a formal 2nd person; and *a gente* ("the people") has almost entirely taken over the space of old 1st person plural *nós*, with a few forms of this series still remaining.[4] Crucially, all new forms differ in *semantic* specification; *grammatically*, they are all 3rd person; as a consequence, Table 18.2 shows that old 3rd person forms like possessive *seu* and reflexive *se* are shared by many semantic persons. (On reflexive *si*, see 3.2 below.)

Second, related to this, the verb paradigm has also shrunk. In most tenses there are only two forms: grammatical 3rd person plural for *vocês* and *eles* vs. a unique form for other persons (corresponding to the old 3rd person singular form); in some tenses (e.g. simple present), there is an additional form (for 1st person singular). Probably as a consequence of this poor system of verb agreement, null subjects are quite restricted in BP, to the point that some claim BP is becoming a non-null subject language; only 3rd person null subjects are still frequent (see Barbosa, Duarte and Kato 2005 for overview).

Finally, another crucial change is the loss of most 3rd person clitics: the direct object forms *o(s)/a(s)* have disappeared altogether; the only surviving clitic is *se*, which is still in use as a reflexive, but is quickly shrinking in its other uses (e.g. as a marker of verb diathesis; see section 3.1). In the place of the direct object clitics, BP makes use either of the standard subject form *ele*, or of null objects.

3. Binding domains in Portuguese

3.1. *Binding in transitive structures*

EP follows the general pattern of Romance: pronominal clitics are excluded if the antecedent is the local subject, and a reflexive must be used (6a), and the reverse happens if the antecedent is non-local (6b) (Brito, Duarte and Matos 2003).

(6) a. *João não {<u>se</u>/*o} reconheceu naquela foto.*   (EP)
         João not {*se/him*} recognized in-that picture.
         "João did not recognize {*himself/*him*} in that picture."
     b. *João disse que tu não {<u>o</u>/*<u>se</u>} reconheceste naquela foto.*
         "João said that you did not recognize {*him/*himself*} in that picture."

In case reflexivity needs emphasis or contrast, EP resorts to a tonic form governed by the preposition *a* "to"; it can be either the reflexive *si* or a full 3rd person pronoun, and the construction may be clitic-doubled, but only with the reflexive clitic.

(7) *João não {<u>se</u>/*o} reconheceu a {<u>si</u>/<u>ele</u>} próprio naquela foto.*   (EP)
     João not {*se/him*} recognized to {*se/him*} own in-that picture.
     "João did not recognize *himself* in that picture."

These facts do not pose a challenge to current versions of BT. In particular, where the pronoun looks locally bound, it is "reinforced" by a SELF form (*próprio* ou *mesmo*)—so, it functions "like a reflexive-marker", satisfying R&R's version of Principle B.[5]

As for BP, recall it lost 3rd person accusative pronominal clitics, substituted by null objects and the full pronoun *ele*. Moreira da Silva (1983) claimed that, additionally, the 3rd person reflexive *se* form was lost as well: with inherently reflexive and similar verbs, it would have been substituted by zero (8a);[6] with non-inherently reflexive, truly biargumental verbs, by full pronouns—not necessarily modified by a SELF form (8b):

(8) a. Inherently reflexive verbs: (BP$_\emptyset$)
         *<u>Pedro</u> queixou/arrependeu/comportou {∅/*ele (mesmo)}.*
         Pedro complained/repented/behaved {∅/him (same)}
         "*Pedro* complained/repented/behaved (*himself*)."

     b. Non-inherently reflexive verbs:
         <u>Pedro</u> reconheceu/desenhou/criticou {ele / ele mesmo}.
         Pedro recognized/drew/criticized {him/him same}
         "*Pedro* has recognized/drawn/criticized *himself*."

Moreira da Silva's claim was addressed by subsequent literature, and a lot of variation was found; but the existence of dialects that have lost reflexives altogether was confirmed (hence, "BP$_\emptyset$"). Such dialects are found in the southeast region, especially in the states of Minas Gerais and São Paulo (d'Albuquerque 1984, Pereira 2007).

The tendency to drop reflexives with inherently reflexive-like verbs is also found in the main urban dialects, but with varying degrees of generalization—some verb classes actually resist reflexive dropping (Rodrigues and Pereira 2006, Pereira 2007). In such dialects, explicit reflexives, i.e. *se* and the form [pronoun + SELF], are preferred over zero with truly biargumental verbs; some claimed the unmodified pronoun *ele* can be used as well, but this is less clear. Thus, for such dialects, the pattern looks like:

(9) a. Inherently reflexive verbs: (BP_{se})

    Pedro {se/Ø} *queixou / arrependeu / comportou* {*ele (mesmo)}.

    Pedro {se/Ø} complained / repented / behaved {him (same)}

  b. Non-inherently reflexive verbs:

    Pedro {se} *reconheceu/desenhou/criticou* {*ele mesmo/??ele*}.

    Pedro recognized/drew/criticized {him same/him}

This pattern covers dialects that preserve the reflexive *se* to varying degrees (hence, "BP_{se}"), including educated urban dialects (Neves 2008; Menuzzi 1999).

The occurrence of a complex form [pronoun + SELF] in (9b) is not particularly problematic, but the use of an unmodified full pronoun would require some explanation, even for current BT (see below). Recent studies suggest, however, that the relevant occurrences are pragmatically motivated and include cases of "accidental coreference" (as suggested by Galves 1986; cf. Grolla and Bertolino 2012, Bertolino 2013).

Let us now turn to the analysis of the patterns presented, beginning with inherently reflexive verbs. These are marked in the lexicon for reflexive interpretation; hence, they need no independent reflexive marker, and complex forms [pronoun + SELF] are excluded, which is correct for all varieties. The variation is related to two parameters: (a) P1: whether the variety possesses forms that function as morphosyntactic markers for lexical operations like reflexive marking, verb diatheses, etc.; (b) P2: how generally the variety uses such markers. Of course, the relevant markers are the reflexive clitics in Portuguese (and in Romance in general).

P1 separates EP and BP_{se} from $BP_{\emptyset}$: $BP_{\emptyset}$ does *not* have clitics, and operations like lexical reflexivity etc. are not morphosyntactically signalled—hence, zero marking. P2 divides EP and BP_{se}. In EP, reflexives regularly mark lexical operations on verbs; only particular verbs may idiosyncratically dispense with such marking. For BP_{se}—perhaps as a result of the increasing restrictions on reflexives—we anticipate two cases (and maybe intermediate ones). In dialects closer to $BP_{\emptyset}$, clitics are not used to mark lexical operations systematically; only particular verbs still associate with *se* idiosyncratically. More conservative dialects make regular use of clitics for some lexical processes (e.g. lexical reflexivity) but not for others (e.g. some verb diatheses).

Now consider binding with non-inherently reflexive verbs. Some such verbs will favor a reflexive interpretation (e.g., naturally reflexive predicates like "wash") and will not require reflexive marking. Hence, complex forms [pronoun + SELF] are unnecessary (hence, disfavored); pronouns and clitic reflexives are left as options. Here comes in the condition requiring morphosyntactic economy of bound forms—in R&R's framework, the chain condition.

If this condition is categorical, it should exclude bound pronouns. This is correct for EP or BP_{se}: the pronoun is excluded, but *se* is not, as required. However, $BP_{\emptyset}$ will be a problem: it will be necessary to argue that pronouns in $BP_{\emptyset}$ do not violate chain economy. In R&R's framework, they will have to be [-R]; however, there is no relevant difference between full pronouns in $BP_{\emptyset}$ and BP_{se}. If economy is somehow relativized—e.g. by admitting that conditions are violable, and the best form is the one that violates less conditions—then $BP_{\emptyset}$ will follow: it does not have *se*, hence no form is more economical than full pronouns, which are allowed (as in Frisian; cf. Menuzzi 1999).

As for verbs that disfavor a reflexive interpretation, we might expect complex [pronoun + SELF] forms to be required, and non-reflexive markers excluded, including the clitic *se* (on a par with, say, *zich* in Dutch). But this is *not* the case: verbs like *criticar* "criticize", *agredir* "be agressive with, assault" can be used with *se* alone, without a SELF form. Apparently, the conclusion must be that clitic reflexives count as reflexive-markers both in EP and BP$_{se}$. This makes sense, since they are morphosyntactic markers of lexical operations (Reuland 1990, Baauw and Delfitto 2005).

3.2. *Binding into PPs*

Following Menuzzi (1999), binding of full pronouns inside PPs has received some attention both in EP (Estrela 2006) and in BP$_{se}$ (Bertolino 2013, Vieira 2014). The basic pattern described by Menuzzi was confirmed for both varieties: as first observed by Zribi-Hertz (1980) for French, acceptability of locally bound pronouns inside PPs depends on the pragmatics-semantics of the predicate; specifically, the more the predicate favors a reflexive interpretation, the more a pronoun is acceptable; and inversely for the complex form [pronoun + SELF]:

(10) a. reflexivity obligatory:
    João tem para {*ele* / *??ele mesmo*} *que Maria está grávida.*   (BP$_{se}$/EP)
        {*si* / *??si mesmo*}   (BP$_{se/si}$/EP)
    João has to {him (same) / *se* (same)} that Maria is pregnant
    "*João* tells to {*himself* / **him*} (=believes) that Maria is pregnant."
  b. reflexivity possible:
    Paulo só fala {*dele/dele mesmo*}.   (BP$_{se}$/EP)
        {*de si/de si mesmo*}   (BP$_{se/si}$/EP)
    "*Paulo* talks only about {*himself/*him*}."
  c. reflexivity unlikely:
    Maria luta contra {*ela mesma/??ela*}, *mas o vício é forte.*   (BP$_{se}$/EP)
        {*si mesma/?si*}   (BP$_{se/si}$/EP)
    "*Maria* fights against {*herself/*her*}, but the vice is strong."

Though EP and BP$_{se}$ are alike with respect to bound pronouns in PPs, it is unclear what the status of the preposition-governed reflexive *si* is in BP$_{se}$. Many authors put this form aside on the grounds that it is uncommon in spoken language (Bertolino 2013). Indeed, there is indirect evidence for its restricted use (Vieira 2014), but we are unaware of any deeper study. The form seems to be available for educated BP$_{se}$ speakers (Neves 2008), who may have incorporated it through intense contact with written language. We refer to this variety as BP$_{se/si}$. In EP, *si* is fully acceptable, on a par with full pronouns, and often preferred, especially when modified by *próprio* (Estrela 2006, Lobo 2013). For both BP$_{se/si}$ and EP, the distribution of SELF forms with *si* is similar to that with pronouns. As for BP$_{\emptyset}$, we presume the lack of *si* restricts the possible patterns to those containing pronouns in (10).

As regards the analysis of binding into PPs, the main question is: how to explain the possibility of locally bound pronouns in EP and BP$_{se}$, as opposed to their unavailability in transitive structures? The problem does not arise with BP$_{\emptyset}$: whatever is said for local binding of pronouns in transitive structures can be extended to binding into PPs. But EP and BP$_{se}$ (as well as other Romance languages) do pose a problem for standard BT: as Menuzzi (1999) argues, the notion of "governing category", being structurally defined, cannot distinguish the types of complement PPs that may or may not allow locally bound pronouns without *ad hoc* assumptions.

The chains-and-reflexivity framework, on the other hand, offers a natural explanation (Menuzzi 1999): there is no movement out of PPs in Portuguese, hence no chain is formed by binding pronouns across PPs; if no chain is formed, pronouns are not affected by the chain condition. Hence, the only active constraints are the reflexivity-marking conditions; a SELF form will be required only if the semantics/pragmatics of the predicate disfavors a reflexive interpretation. This correctly predicts the pattern first uncovered by Zribi-Hertz (1980). Note that nothing similar happens in transitive structures because direct objects do move (e.g. in passives)—hence, binding of pronouns in transitive structures does violate chain economy.

Recently, Grolla (2005) and Bertolino (2013) explored an approach based on Hornstein (2001)'s reinterpretation of BT in terms of movement. Crudely put, anaphors—e.g. reflexives in English—would be spell-outs of NP traces; and pronouns would be "elsewhere forms", that is, used when reflexives are excluded (because movement is excluded). This predicts the same basic distribution the chains-and-reflexivity analysis predicts: pronouns will be excluded in transitive structures and allowed within complement PPs. Still, where the two analyses differ, the chains-and-reflexiviy framework seems to do better.

First, the movement analysis has nothing to say about SELF modification and its correlation with the semantics-pragmatics of the predicate. That is, the movement analysis will need a reflexivity component anyway. Besides, it claims that pronouns are a kind of last resort device, available only when a reflexive is not. But, without further ado, this accounts only for languages where pronouns and reflexives are in neat complementary distribution. Bertolino (2013) claims this is the case of BP_{se}, which would not possess the reflexive *si*. Assume this is correct (ignoring $BP_{se/si}$). Still, there is EP, where full pronouns and the reflexive *si* are viable options within PPs. The chains-and-reflexivity analysis, on the other hand, accounts for the three varieties of Portuguese without *ad hoc* assumptions.

3.3. Long-distance binding of se

It is well-known that languages may allow long-distance binding—i.e. across a clause boundary—of *se*-forms (Koster and Reuland 1991). This was the case of Latin and it is known to be possible in Italian as well (Napoli 1979). The following example illustrates the possibility in EP (from Brito, Duarte and Matos 2003; see also Menuzzi 1996):

(11)   *Maria soube directamente do João [que alguém tinha falado mal de si].*   (EP)
       Maria knew directly from-the João that somebody had spoken ill of *se*
       "*Maria* heard directly from João [that somebody spoke ill of *her*]."

The example shows the main properties of long-distance bound *se* in Romance: it is subject-oriented (the antecedent must be *Maria*, and cannot be *João*), and it must be a non-clitic form—the clitic *se* is totally unacceptable in a similar context:

(12)   **Maria soube directamente do João que alguém se tinha difamado*   (EP)
       Maria knew directly from-the João that somebody *se* had maligned
       "*Maria* heard directly from João that somebody maligned *her*."

Crucially, long-distance binding of *se* indicates that EP *si* has a different status from BP *si*. Even $BP_{se/si}$ speakers do not accept sentences like (11). Some accept long-distance bound *si* under very favorable conditions, as in (13), where binding is across an infinitival clause boundary and the antecedent is "nobody", which strongly disfavors a full pronoun (14) (see section 4 below).

(13)   *Ninguém jamais me ouviu [falar mal {de si / ??dele}].*   ($BP_{se/si}$/EP)
       "*Nobody* ever heard [me speak ill of {*him* / *himself}]."

(14)   *Ninguém carrega dinheiro {consigo / ??com ele}.*   ($BP_{se/si}$/EP)
       "*Nobody* carries money with *himself*."

Note that the contrasts in (13) and (14) are also found in EP (Menuzzi 1996, Estrela 2006), from which we presume that the constraint disfavoring full pronouns with "nobody" antecedents is active in EP as well.

Summing up: long-distance binding of *si* is possible in EP under conditions similar to those found in languages like Latin and Italian; in BP, it may be available for educated speakers of $BP_{se/si}$, but only under very favorable conditions. (Of course, it is not available for $BP_{\emptyset}$ speakers.) Thus, there are basically two things to be explained: (a) the fact that clitic *se*, unlike preposition-governed *si*, does not enter long-distance dependencies; (b) the availability of long-distance binding of EP *si* vis-à-vis the restriction on *si* in BP, even for educated $BP_{se/si}$ speakers.

The unavailability of the clitic *se* for long-distance binding is no mystery; rather, it is a well-known restriction on clitic *se*-reflexives in general, long established in the literature (Napoli 1979, Reuland 1990). Most proposals see this restriction as further evidence that the clitic reflexive, rather than a free syntactic argument, is a morphosyntactic marker for lexical operations, which of course ensures local binding (Reuland 1990, Baauw and Delfitto 2005).

As for the difference between EP and educated $BP_{se/si}$, we need to consider which sources of variation would be plausible. Approaches to long-distance binding of *se*-forms based on abstract head movement will have to look for plausible constraints on *se* movement in $BP_{se/si}$, and absence of these constraints in EP. We are not aware of any proposal along this line. Menuzzi (1996, 1999) suggests another line of explanation, based on constraint violability and a second constraint derivable from R&R's chain condition, namely *chain visibility*: the head of a chain must be fully specified for φ-features. (Recall that the first constraint is what we called *chain economy*; cf. discussion of (4).)

Given constraint violability, chain visibility will have the following effects: (i) the more specified a bound form is for φ-features, the more it counts as the head of a chain; hence, the less close it needs to be to a c-commanding antecedent; (ii) inversely, the less a bound form is specified for φ-features, the less it counts as the head of a chain; hence, the closer it must be to a c-commanding antecedent. That is, *se*-forms, which are unspecified for φ-features, must establish a relation with a close c-commanding antecedent. Moreover, the approach predicts a parameter of variation for *se*-forms, P3: the distance of binding will vary according to their φ-feature specification—more specified forms can be bound at longer distances than less specified forms.

Now, Tables 18.1 and 18.2 above indicate that *se*-forms must be very much unspecified in $BP_{se/si}$ but not in EP. In $BP_{se/si}$ the pronominal system contains many forms that are *grammatically* 3rd person (though not semantically), and reflexive *se* is used with all semantic persons except the 1st person singular; that is, the only opposition is *se* vs. *me* (Table 18.2). In EP, on the other hand, the reflexive *se* is not used for 1st person, singular and plural, neither for 2nd person singular, and the system opposes *se* to *me*, *nos* and *te* (Table 18.1). We conclude that *se*-forms have very little φ-feature specification in $BP_{se/si}$, hence binding must be very local; but they have more φ-feature specification in EP, supporting binding at longer distances (Menuzzi 1996, 1999).

4. Bound variables in Portuguese

4.1. *Binding of null subjects vs. full pronouns*

Montalbetti (1984) was the first to explore the different anaphoric options of referential and quantificational antecedents in Romance. He identified in Spanish a restriction he called

"Overt Pronoun Constraint" (OPC): where a null argument is available, pronouns cannot be bound by quantificational antecedents like *nadie*:

(15) a. <u>Juan</u> cree que {*pro/él*} es inteligente.   [Spanish]
    b. <u>Nadie</u> cree que {*pro/*él*} es inteligente.
       "*Juan / Nobody* believes that *he* is intelligent."

Montalbetti's example in (16) shows that the contrast disappears where the null argument is unavailable (prepositions do not allow null arguments in Spanish):

(16) <u>Nadie</u> quiere que María hable de {*él/*pro*}.   [Spanish]
      "*Nobody* wants Maria to talk about *him*."

For Portuguese, Negrão and Muller (1996) claimed that similar contrasts between null and overt pronominal subjects should be accounted for in terms of coreference vs. variable binding. Their proposal appeared in the context of the debate concerning null subjects in BP; it was conceived as an alternative to the 1990s prevailing view according to which BP was changing into a non-null subject grammar. Negrão and Muller argued that this would not explain the actual distribution of BP null subjects; in particular, the fact that 3rd person null subjects are quite frequent (see Section 2). In addition, they observed that, except for impersonal null subjects, most 3rd person null subjects are "anaphor-like" in BP: they have an antecedent, often within the same sentence—a property much explored in later literature (see below).

     Under Negrão and Muller's view, BP was not losing null subjects; rather, null subjects and overt pronouns in BP were becoming "specialized": null subjects as "bound forms", and overt pronouns as forms for coreference relations. Though this is not equivalent to Montalbetti's OPC, it correctly predicts that BP will show contrasts similar to (15):

(17) a. <u>João</u> acredita que {<u>pro</u>/<u>ele</u>_{BP}/?<u>ele</u>_{EP}} é inteligente.   (BP/EP)
    b. *<u>Ninguém</u> acredita que* {<u>pro</u>/*<u>ele</u>} *é inteligente.*
      "Nobody believes that he is intelligent."

Basically the same facts are found in EP, though a full pronoun requires "emphasis" or "contrast" to be used in (17a), as in all typical null subject languages; hence, it may be considered a marked option with respect to null subjects (Brito 1991).

     From the mid 1990s on, many studies explored the view that BP is, after all, a null subject language, but one with a highly constrained type of null subject (Ferreira 2009, Modesto 2011 for surveys). Besides the strong tendency for having a linguistic antecedent, this literature has collected a number of other "anaphor-like" properties of BP null subjects: (a) their antecedent must be the closest subject (18); (b) it must c-command the null subject (19); and (c) the null subject is interpreted as a bound variable; hence, strict identity readings seem to be unavailable (20):

(18) *<u>João</u> disse* [*que o Paulo acha* [*que* {<u>ele</u>/*<u>pro</u>_{BP}/??<u>pro</u>_{EP}} *é esperto*]].   (BP/EP)
      "*João* said [Paulo thinks [*he* is smart]]."

(19) [*A mãe do <u>João</u>*] *acha que* {<u>ele</u>/*<u>pro</u>_{BP}/??<u>pro</u>_{EP}} *é esperto.*   (BP/EP)
      "[*João's* mother] thinks *he* is smart".

(20) *<u>João</u> acha que <u>pro</u> vai ganhar a corrida, e <u>a Maria</u> também.*   (BP/EP)
      "*João* thinks *he* will win the race, and *Maria* too
      (thinks <u>she</u> will win the race)."
      #"*João* thinks *he* will win the race, and *Maria* too
      (thinks <u>he</u> will win the race)."

Recently, similar restrictions were observed in EP (Branco 2007), though the requirements imposed on the BP null subject seem to be stronger, and the relevant interpretations available in EP under appropriate discourse conditions (e.g. high topicality of the antecedent; cf. Barbosa, Duarte, and Kato 2005).

Examples like (17)–(20) do suggest that BP null subjects must be bound forms—hence, interpreted as bound variables, as claimed by Negrão and Muller. For EP we should say, perhaps, that they prefer a bound variable interpretation.

And what about the claim that overt pronouns are "specializing as referential expressions" in BP? Negrão and Muller take this to mean that overt pronouns cannot be interpreted as bound variables in BP; they should only enter coreference relations; Muller (1997) illustrates this with (21a); we add (21b, c) for comparison:

(21) a. *Joana confia nela, e Jorge também.* (BP/EP)
       "*Joana* trusts *herself*, and *Jorge* too (trusts *her*)."
       #"*Joana* trusts *herself*, and *Jorge* too (trusts *himself*)."
    b. *Joana confia em si, e Jorge também.* (BP/EP)
       #"*Joana* trusts *herself*, and *Jorge* too (trusts *her*)."
       "*Joana* trusts *herself*, and *Jorge* too (trusts *himself*)."
    c. *Ninguém mais confia {em si/*nele}.* (BP/EP)
       "*Nobody* trusts *himself* anymore."

It does seem difficult to get the bound variable reading in (21a); (21b) shows that this reading is best expressed by reflexive *si*, which, in turn, makes the strict identity reading difficult. (21c) shows a contrast similar to (17): the pronoun is excluded with quantificational "nobody" as an antecedent because there is a better alternative, namely *si*. In EP judgments are similar (Estrela 2006). Thus, full pronouns do seem to be at least disfavored as bound forms—hence, as bound variables—in both BP and EP.

Still, the claim that they cannot be interpreted at all as bound variables seems too strong. First, recall Montalbetti's observation: bound pronouns are constrained in Spanish only where no null pronominal is available. In Portuguese, we find similar effects: e.g., in EP and for some BP speakers, reflexive *si* may be long distance bound; still, such dependencies are often not optimal, and the natural option is a full pronoun:

(22) *Nenhum aluno quis saber se o professor tinha falado mal {dele/?de si}.* (EP/BP$_{se/si}$)
       "*No pupil* wanted to know whether the teacher had spoken ill {of *se*/of-him}"

Second, we do find in the literature on BP examples with pronominal subjects bound by quantificational antecedents; and with full pronouns claimed to be ambiguous between a strict and a sloppy reading. The examples below are from Ferreira (2009):

(23) *Nenhum menino disse que Maria acha que {ele/*pro} é inteligente.*[7]
       no boy said that Mary thinks that {he/pro} is intelligent."
       No boy said that Mary thinks that he is intelligent."

(24) *João acha que ele vai ganhar a corrida; Maria também.*
       "*João* thinks that *he* will win the race; *Maria* too (thinks *he* will win)."
       "*João* thinks that *he* will win the race; *Maria* too (thinks *she* will win)."

In sum: there is some indication that null subjects must be bound forms in BP, and are favored as such in EP. Inversely, full pronouns do seem disfavored as bound forms where a null subject or a form like reflexive *si* is available. But the constraint on pronouns does not seem to be categorical, or "inherent" to them; rather, it depends on the presence of an alternative form—as suggested by Montalbetti's OPC.

4.2. Binding of 3rd person possessives

In EP, both *seu* "his/her/their" and *dele* "of-him" can be used with referential antecedents (25a) (Castro 2001, Estrela 2006);[8] but in spoken BP *seu* is not used at all with 3rd person referential antecedents, and *dele* is the current possessive (25b):

(25) a. *João está procurando {seu irmão/?o irmão dele}.* (EP)
　　 b. *João está procurando {??seu irmão/o irmão dele}.* (BP)
　　　　 "*João* is looking (for) {*his* brother/the brother of *him*}."

Recall that semantic 2nd person *você* "you" is grammatically 3rd person, hence *seu* is used for 2nd person both in EP and BP. In BP, however, this is its main use—hence, by far the preferred reading of *seu* in (25), which is not the case in EP. Because of this, early literature suggested that *seu* in BP had been reanalyzed as corresponding strictly to *você*, and a new series, of *dele* "of-him", had been developed for (semantic) 3rd person (Perini 1985). However, Menuzzi (1996), Negrão and Muller (1996) and Muller (1997) noticed that quantitative studies told a different story (e.g. Silva 1991). Most occurrences of *seu* in spoken language do refer to 2nd person (*você* "you"). But there is also a significant number of 3rd person occurrences, up to about 50 percent in some samples.

Moreover, the distribution of 3rd person *seu* is conditioned by semantics. Antecedents favoring *seu* include those denoting institutions, inanimates, or having generic interpretation. Particularly important is the divide between referential and quantificational antecedents: the former strongly favor *dele* (25); quantified antecedents, on the contrary, favor *seu*—specially in the case of "nobody" antecedents (26); a similar effect was found for EP (Castro 2001):

(26) *Ninguém gosta de falar mal {de sua família/*da família dele}.* (BP/EP)
　　　 "*Nobody* likes of to-speak ill {of *his* family/of the family *of-him*}."

The contrast in (26) is similar to the OPC-like effect we have seen in (17), where the null subject is the best option, and in (21c), where the reflexive *si* is. In (26), it is the availability of the possessive *seu* that triggers the constraint on *dele*.

The effect is not specific to BP; what is specific to BP is that *seu* is not used for referential 3rd person antecedents; rather, *dele* is. This fits Negrão and Muller's suggestion that full pronouns are specialized as expressions for "coreference" in BP, as opposed to null subjects and possessive *seu*, which would be specialized for the bound variable interpretation. But, again, there are reasons to believe this is a too strong claim.

First, as we mentioned, quantitative studies have shown that other semantic properties of antecedents are relevant for the choice of *seu* in BP. And, though some of the relevant properties may be reducible to the idea that *seu* must be interpreted as a bound variable (e.g. genericity, cf. Muller 1997), others cannot (e.g. the fact that institutions and inanimate referents favor *seu*).

Second, Negrão and Muller's proposal entails that sentences like (27) below would only have a strict reading; Muller (1997) claims this is correct, but there are BP speakers who accept sloppy readings for pronouns (as she admits):

(27) A: *Paulo vai arrumar o quarto dele no fim de semana?*
　　　　 "Will *Paulo* tidy *his* room this weekend?"
　　 B: *Não sei. O João vai.*
　　　　 "I don't know. *João* will (tidy *his* room)."

Finally, though quantificational antecedents such as *ninguém* "nobody", *todo mundo* "everybody", *cada um* "each one", *quem* "who" are strongly disfavored as antecedents of the pronoun *dele*, many speakers accept examples like (28), taken from the internet:[9]

(28) a. *Não é qualquer menina que me chama para ir na casa dela.*
    "It is not *any girl* who calls me to go to *her* house."

  b. *Pergunte a qualquer político qual é a relação do partido dele com*
    a realidade da cidade.
    "Ask *any politician* what the relationship of *his* party is with the city's reality."

Like the examples in (22), (23) and note 5, (28) are also counterexamples to the idea that full pronouns cannot be bound by quantificational antecedents. The antecedents in all these sentences are similar in that they have a nominal projection, unlike "bare" quantifiers such as "nobody", "everybody", "each one". Menuzzi (1996, 1999) observed this, and suggested an independent constraint was depressing acceptability of full pronouns in (17b), (21c) and (26) (see section 4.4 below).

In sum: (a) EP possessive *seu* "his" is used for all types of antecedents; hence, it can be either coreferential or bound; *dele* may also be used, but mostly for coreference. (b) In BP, *dele* is used with referential antecedents, and *seu* specially with quantificational antecedents. (c) For many speakers, *dele* may also be bound by quantificational antecedents containing a nominal projection, though, like other occurrences of full pronouns, it is strongly constrained with bare quantificational antecedents, like *ninguém* "nobody" and *todo mundo* "everybody."

4.3. *Bound forms, c-command and almost c-command*

Although by no means straightforward, we do discern some basic tendencies underlying the EP and BP facts discussed so far: null subjects, reflexive *si* and possessive *seu* are alternatives to full pronouns; they prefer or require to have bound readings, and are generally OK with quantificational antecedents; full pronouns may also have bound readings, but sometimes favor coreference and may be constrained with quantificational antecedents (specially, of the "nobody" type).

Now, the forms that alternate with full pronouns share important properties (Menuzzi 2003a,b). First of all, they are morphosyntactically more "economical" than full pronouns, that is, less specified for φ-features. Second, they have "anaphor-like" properties in BP, where they cannot be interpreted deictically (cannot refer to a 3rd person referent), and require a close c-commanding antecedent. These are well-known properties of the reflexive *si*, and are also found with null subjects in BP. Moreover, they are true of possessive *seu* as well, except perhaps for the "closeness" requirement (cf. Menuzzi 1996, Muller 1997, Menuzzi 2003b): deictically, *seu* can only refer to semantic 2nd person (that is, to *você* "you"); and contrasts like (29) show that *seu* must be c-commanded by its antecedent in BP (Menuzzi 2003b):

(29) a. *Quase todo rapaz se preocupa com sua namorada.*
    "*Almost every boy* worries with [about] *his* girlfriend."

  b. **[A mãe de quase todo rapaz] se preocupa com sua namorada.*
    "[*Almost every boy's* mother] worries with [about] *his* girlfriend."

In EP, similar effects are found with some quantificational antecedents but not others (e.g. with "each boy" but not with "any boy").

Following Negrão and Muller (1996) and Muller (1997), we might say null subjects, reflexive *si* and possessive *seu* are "specialized" for bound variable interpretation, and full pronouns are for (co)reference, trying to explain counterexamples away, e.g. by appealing to dialect variation. But we think this approach faces two difficulties.

First, the same forces seem to be acting in all varieties of Portuguese, even if not with the same force. Second, the approach misses an important generalization: in all dialects we find *competition* between the alternants for bound readings. In particular, if some condition plays against forms that favor bound readings (e.g. distance against null subjects and *si*), full pronouns become an option. Indeed, we have a final argument for this view. It comes from the so-called "almost c-command cases": when a quantificational antecedent does not c-command a form, but still can take it in its scope (see Safir 2014 and references cited there). For many speakers of BP, what happens is that null subjects, reflexive *se* and possessive *seu* are excluded—because of their "anaphor-like properties"; and a full pronoun must be used as a bound variable, as shown by the sloppy readings of the sentences (from Menuzzi 2003b):

(30) a. [*A mãe de qualquer garoto*] *diria que* {*ele*/??*pro*} *é um bom menino;*
        só a mãe do João que não.
        "[*Every boy's* mother] would say *he* is a good boy;
        only João's mother wouldn't (say that *he* [=João] is)."

   b. [*A mãe de qualquer garoto*] *confiaria cegamente* {*nele*/*em si*};
        só a mãe do João que não.
        "[*Every boy's* mother] would trust {*him*/*himself*} blindly;
        only João's mother wouldn't (trust *him* [=João] blindly)."

   c. [*A mãe de qualquer garoto*] *se preocuparia com* {*a namorada dele*/
        ??*sua namorada*}; *só a mãe do João que não.*
        "[*Almost every boy's* mother] worries about *his* girlfriend;
        only João's mother wouldn't (worry about *his* [=João's] girlfriend."

Again, EP is a bit different: strong effects are observed only with *si*.

In short: null subjects, reflexive *si* and possessive *seu* may even be favored over full pronouns as bound forms; but in BP they require a c-commanding antecedent; if this requirement is not met, full pronouns are the only available forms for bound variables.

4.4. *Sketch of analysis*

The patterns of anaphoric choices for bound variables in Portuguese are pretty complex; we can only discuss some of the main generalizations:

  (i) null subjects, *si* and *seu* possess "anaphor-like properties" in BP: they cannot have deictic 3rd person interpretation, they need a close c-commanding antecedent and must be interpreted as bound variables;

 (ii) the EP corresponding forms show similar properties, but in general in a less strict way (e.g., null subjects and *seu* may have deictic 3rd person interpretation under appropriate discourse conditions, and *si* can be long-distance bound);

(iii) full pronouns (*ele/dele*) can enter coreference relations in BP, unlike null subjects, *si* and *seu*; in EP, again, the opposition is less strict (null subjects and *seu* do support coreference relations);

(iv) in BP full pronouns occur where null subjects, *si* and *seu* are also acceptable (except with "nobody" antecedents); in EP null subjects are preferred over full pronouns; maybe *si* and *seu* are, too, though this is less clear;

 (v) there is some strong constraint on the use of full pronouns with "nobody" antecedents, equally active in both BP and EP.

We will consider these facts from the perspective of the constraint violability approach sketched in Section 3.3. The chain condition effects we called *chain visibility* and *chain economy* will be instrumental. Recall, in particular: φ-feature unspecified forms violate chain visibility more the farther they are from a c-commanding antecedent; and full pronouns violate chain economy more the closer they are to a c-commanding antecedent. (For detailed discussion, Menuzzi 1996, 1999.)[10]

First of all, we think BP null subjects, *si* and *seu* are "truly [-R]" elements, in the sense that they are very much unspecified for φ-features. We have already pointed out BP *se*-forms, including *si* and *seu*, may be used with most semantic persons (see Table 18.2). The same can be said of BP 3rd person null subjects—most tenses distinguish only two verb forms. Let us assume that null subjects and *se*-forms (*se*, *si* and *seu*) have become so impoverished in φ-feature specification as to be unable to support an independent chain; hence, to be licensed they must enter an anaphoric A-chain.

The properties in (i, iii) now follow. (a) Because of visibility BP φ-feature impoverished forms are unable to head an independent chain and cannot be deictically interpreted. (b) Moreover, their antecedent must be close enough and must c-command them. (c) In order to be in an anaphoric chain, they must be coindexed with the antecedent, hence the bound variable interpretation. Finally, (d) if they must be bound, they cannot receive an independent index, hence cannot (co)refer; only full pronouns can. In this account, null subjects, *si* and *seu* are bound variables in BP, but pronouns are not required to enter only coreference relations.

Consider (iv). Suppose BP φ-feature impoverished forms are so much unspecified as to be an optimal form only in the most local context, where A-movement is possible, i.e. transitive structures. In this context, *se* violates chain visibility the least because it is part of an optimal A-chain, and *ele* violates chain economy the most, by the same reason; hence, *se* wins over bound pronouns in transitive structures in BP (or, rather, BP$_{se/si}$). However, no such optimal chain is available for other φ-impoverished forms: in the case of null subjects, binding crosses CP (17); in the case of *si*, it crosses PP (21c); and in the case of *seu*, DP (26); and all these categories block A-movement. Hence, no optimal chain is possible and these forms incur in visibility violations. By similar reasoning (the chain is not optimal), chain economy has its effects weakened on pronouns. Except for transitive structures, we take visibility effects on BP impoverished forms to be approximately as costly as economy effects on full pronouns—hence, the possibility of having bound full pronouns where null subjects, *si* and *seu* are possible in BP (except for "nobody" antecedents; see below).

Of course, the crucial distinction between EP and BP, as suggested in section 4.3, is in φ-feature specification: EP pronominal forms are more specified than BP's because the number of paradigm oppositions is higher in EP. Now, consider (iv) again: EP φ-feature impoverished forms are more economical than full pronouns; hence, because of chain economy, they are preferred over pronouns when a c-commanding antecedent is close enough for a near-optimal anaphoric chain; and they will be disfavored where this chain becomes less optimal (deixis, no c-command, long distance). With respect to (ii, iii), we assume they are sufficiently φ-feature specified to be more tolerant to visibility violations than BP impoverished forms; thus, they will be more tolerant to locality effects; under appropriate conditions, they will even be able to head their own chains.

Finally, we need to explain (v), the particular effects antecedents like "nobody" trigger on full pronouns. In part, they may have to do with the bound variable interpretation, as suggested by Montalbetti, and Negrão and Muller; in our approach, we do expect some effects, since binding triggers economy effects on pronouns. But this does not explain the contrast between "nobody" antecedents and quantificational antecedents with nominal projection. Menuzzi (1996, 1999) attributes this contrast to *agreement*: "nobody" antecedents do not have gender, favoring φ-feature impoverished forms, which are not specified for gender; antecedents with nominal projections do have gender, being compatible with full pronouns, which are also specified for gender.

5. Concluding remarks

In this chapter we have presented a few of the binding patterns found in BP and EP, focusing on 3rd person dependencies. We tried to show how these patterns may contribute to BT, highlighting some of the concepts that seem crucial: predicate reflexivity, chains, φ-feature specification of anaphoric forms, competition between pronouns and φ-feature impoverished forms, gradual effects of locality. Many aspects of the phenomena discussed were hardly touched on, and deserve further investigation. This is the case of the BP variation concerning lexical operations and classes of verbs that allow or not *se* deletion; and also the case of long-distance bound *si*. Dialect variation related to binding patterns should be studied more systematically: it is an open area in EP, for which we find little discussion in the literature; and for BP, it is still a source of uncertainty (e.g. concerning preposition-governed *si* and binding of full pronouns by different antecedent types). Many other phenomena still need exploration in both EP and BP. These include: the precise use and nature of the emphatic forms *próprio* "own" and *mesmo* "same", which may be relevant for the relation between binding and pragmatics (see n.4); null possessives, which may tell more about economy (see n.9); and the properties of "φ-feature mismatching dependencies", which are relevant to investigate the relation between φ-features and locality effects.[11] Finally, we must also say that the Portuguese phenomena discussed here seem to be relevant for new recent proposals and should be explored from these new perspectives (see note 7).

NOTES

1   We assume the reader is familiar with "Government and Binding" model of grammar (see Carnie 2013); in particular, with its component called "Binding Theory" (BT), and with the main facts motivating it (see Safir 2013). Familiarity with Reinhart and Reuland (1993)'s version of BT is also advisable.

2   SELF forms are lexical elements like *-self* in English, *mesmo* "same" or *próprio* "own" in Portuguese; *se* forms are pronominal elements relatively unspecified for φ-features, such as the reflexives *zich* in Dutch and *se/si* in Portuguese.

3   "EP" here corresponds to the close-to-standard spoken dialects of Lisbon and Central regions of Portugal; in Brazil, to the urban dialect of educated speakers of the southeast region, including São Paulo and Rio de Janeiro; this dialect, to some measure, is also used in other capitals in Brazil.

4   *A gente* is also found in EP (Brito 1999); but it is socially marked, being common for speakers of non-standard varieties (Sória 2013).

5   Portuguese SELF forms—*mesmo* "same" or *próprio* "own"—are not specialized for reflexivity marking, being used to emphasize other anaphoric dependencies as well (Vieira 2014). *Próprio* may behave as a long-distance anaphor, but it is not necessarily subject-oriented (Brito 1990, Branco and Marrafa 1999).

6   On "inherent reflexive and similar verbs", see Reinhart and Siloni (2005), Alexiadou and Schäffer (2014); on verb classes that favor *se* deletion in Portuguese, see Nunes (1990, 1995), Pereira (2007).

7   Similar examples are also easily found on the internet:

(i)   *Eu não chamo <u>nenhuma pessoa</u> de amigo, de amor ou de "fdp" sem que <u>ela</u> seja.*
      "I don't call <u>any person</u> a friend, my love or "SOB" if <u>she</u> is not."
      https://instagram.com/p/x4IZAxvgiQ/

(ii) *<u>Todo político</u> é corrupto até que <u>ele</u> prove o contrário.*
      "<u>Every politician</u> is corrupt until <u>he</u> proves he is not."
      http://politico10honesto.blogspot.com.br/2013/08/todo-politico-e-corrupto-ate-que-ele.html

8   Actually, in EP the best option in (25a) is a *null* possessive (i.e., "the brother"), cf. Lobo (2013). Indeed, the construction has general use in EP, and would compete with *seu* and *dele* in many patterns presented below. The construction is possible in BP, too, but for reasons of space we cannot discuss it here.

9   (14a) is from http://www.wattpad.com/121000862-um-conto-quase-de-fadas-capitulo-2/page/2; (14b), from https://carlostonet.wordpress.com/2012/06/04/licao-de-hoje-como-funcionam-as-aliancas-politicas/.

10   Many of the facts discussed in Sections 4.1 to 4.3 seem to provide support for Safir's (2004) recent proposal for "one true anaphor"; indeed, φ-impoverished forms might be morphological spell-outs of Safir's "D-bound" anaphor. For reasons of space, we cannot compare Safir's approach to ours here.

11   These dependencies include those combining grammatically 3rd person *a gente* "we" (lit. "the people") with 1st person forms like *nos* "us" and *nosso* "ours", whose properties where explored in Menuzzi (1999). In EP, we anticipate similarly interesting phenomena related to dependencies combining grammatically 3rd person *vocês* "you, pl." with the old 2nd person object form *vos* "you, pl.".

REFERENCES

Alexiadou, A. and F. Schäfer (2014). Towards a non-uniform analysis of naturally reflexive verbs. In R. E. Santana-LaBarge (ed.), *Proceedings of the 31st West Coast Conference on Formal Linguistics*, pp. 1–10.

Baauw, S. and D. Delfitto (2005). New views on reflexivity: delay effects in romance. *Probus*, 17, pp. 145–184.

Barbosa, P., M. E. L. Duarte, and M. A. Kato (2005). Null subjects in European and Brazilian Portuguese. *Journal of Portuguese Linguistics*, 4 (2), pp. 11–52.

Bertolino, K. G. (2013). Restrições sobre a interpretação do proforma *ele* com antecedente local em português brasileiro. Masters dissertation, University of São Paulo.

Branco, A. (2007) Null subjects are reflexives, not pronouns. In A. Branco (ed.), *Anaphora: Analysis, Algorithms and Applications*. Berlin: Springer-Verlag, pp. 59–76.

Branco, A. and P. Marrafa (1999). Long-distance reflexives and the binding square of opposition. In G. Webelhuth, J. P. Koenig, and A. Kathol (eds.), *Lexical and Constructional Aspects of Linguistic Explanation*. Standford, CA: CSLI.

Brito, A. M. (1990). *Próprio* as a local and long distance anaphoric expression in Portuguese. In *Workshop sobre a Anáfora*. Lisboa: Colibri, pp. 116–138.

Brito, A. M. (1991). Ligação, co-referência e o princípio evitar pronome. In *Encontro de Homenagem a Óscar Lopes*. Lisboa: Associação Portuguesa de Linguística, pp. 101–121.

Brito, A. M. (1999). Português europeu/ português brasileiro: algumas diferenças sintácticas. *(Pré)Publications*, 168, pp. 12–34.

Brito, A. M., I. Duarte, and G. Matos (2003). Tipologia e distribuição das expressões nominais. In M. H. M. Mateus, A. M. Brito, I. Duarte, and I. Faria (eds.), *Gramática da Língua Portuguesa*, 5th edn. Lisbon: Editorial Caminho, pp. 795–867.

Burzio, L. (1991). The morphological basis of anaphora. *Journal of Linguistics*, 27, pp. 81–105.

Carnie, A. (2013) *Syntax: A Generative Introduction*. 3rd edn. Oxford: Wiley-Blackwell.Castro, A. (2001). Os possessivos em português europeu e português brasileiro: unidade e diversidade. In *Actas do XVI Encontro Nacional da Associação Portuguesa de Linguística*. Lisbon: Associação Portuguesa de Linguística, pp. 599–613.

d'Albuquerque, A. C. R. C. (1984). A perda dos clíticos num dialeto mineiro. *Tempo Brasileiro*, 78/79, pp. 97–121.

Estrela, A. (2006). A Teoria da Ligação: dados do português europeu. Masters dissertation, Universidade Nova de Lisboa.

Ferreira, M. (2009). Null subjects and finite control in Brazilian Portuguese. In J. Nunes (ed.), *Minimalist Essays on Brazilian Portuguese Syntax*. Amsterdam: John Benjamins, pp. 17–49.

Galves, C. (1986). A interpretação "reflexiva" do pronome no português brasileiro. *DELTA*, 2, pp. 249–264.

Grolla, E. (2005). Pronouns as elsewhere elements: implications for language acquisition. Ph.D. dissertation, University of Connecticut.

Grolla, E., and K. Bertolino (2012). O pronome "ele" está sujeito ao princípio B? Uma discussão sobre resultados experimentais. *Revista LinguíStica (UFRJ)*, 8, pp. 86–99.

Hornstein, N. (2001). *Move! A Minimalist Theory of Construal*. Oxford: Blackwell.

Koster, J. and E. Reuland (eds.) (1991). *Long-Distance Anaphora*. Cambridge: Cambridge University Press.

Lara, V. (2015). Los tratamientos de 2pl en Andalucía occidental y Portugal: estudio geo- y sociolingüístico de un proceso de gramaticalización. Ph.D. dissertation, Universidad Autónoma de Madrid.

Lasnik, H. (1989). On the necessity of binding conditions. In H. Lasnik, *Essays on Anaphora*. Dordrecht: Kluwer, pp. 149–167.

Lobo, M. (2013). Dependências referenciais. In E. Raposo, M. F. B. do Nascimento, M. A. Coelho da Mota, L. Seguro, and A. Mendes (eds.), *Gramática do Português*, Vol. 2.. Lisbon: Gulbenkian, pp. 2177–2227.

Menuzzi, S. (1996). 3rd person possessives in Brazilian Portuguese: on the syntax–discourse relation. *UCREL Technical Papers*, 8, pp. 191–210.

Menuzzi, S. (1999). *Binding Theory and Pronominal Anaphora in Brazilian Portuguese*. The Hague: Holland Academic Graphics.

Menuzzi, S. (2003a). Sobre as opções anafóricas para antecedentes genéricos e para variáveis ligadas. *Letras de Hoje*, 38, pp. 125–144.

Menuzzi, S. (2003b). Escopo e variáveis ligadas típicas do português brasileiro. *Revista de Letras*, 61, pp. 213–248.

Modesto, M. (2011). Finite control: where movement goes wrong in Brazilian Portuguese. *Journal of Portuguese Linguistics*, 10, pp. 3–30.

Montalbetti, M. M. (1984). After binding: on the interpretation of pronouns. Ph.D. dissertation, MIT.

Moreira da Silva, S. (1983). Etudes sur la symétrie et l'asymétrie sujet/objet dans le Portugais du Brésil. Ph.D. dissertation, Université Paris VIII.

Müller, A. L. (1997). A gramática das formas possessivas no português do Brasil. Ph.D. dissertation, Unicamp.

Napoli, D. J. (1979). Reflexivization across clause boundaries in Italian. *Journal of Linguistics*, 15, pp. 1–28.

Negrão, E. V. and A. L. Müller (1996). As mudanças no sistema pronominal do português brasileiro. *DELTA*, 12, pp. 125–152.

Neves, M. H. M. (2008). Os pronomes. In R. Ilari and M. H. M. Neves (eds.), *Gramática do Português Culto Falado no Brasil*, vol. III. Campinas: Editora da Unicamp, pp. 507–622.

Nunes, J. M. (1990). O famigerado se: uma análise sincrônica e diacrônica das construções com se apassivador e indeterminador. Masters dissertation, Unicamp.

Nunes, J. M. (1995). Ainda o famigerado *se*. *DELTA*, 11, pp. 201–240.

Pereira, D. C. (2007). Variação e mudança no uso dos pronomes reflexivos no português popular da capital paulista. Ph.D. dissertation, University of São Paulo.

Perini, M. (1985) O surgimento do sistema possessivo do português coloquial: uma abordagem funcional. *DELTA*, 1(1/2), pp.1–16.

Reinhart, T. (1983). *Anaphora and Semantic Interpretation*. London: Croom Helm.

Reinhart, T. and E. Reuland (1993). Reflexivity. *Linguistic Inquiry*, 24, pp. 657–720.

Reinhart, T. and T. Siloni (2005). The lexicon-syntax parameter: reflexivization and other arity operations. *Linguistic Inquiry*, 36, pp. 389–436.

Reuland, E. (1990). Reflexives and beyond: non-local anaphora in Italian revisited. In J. Mascaró and M. Nespor (eds.), *Grammar in Progress*. Dordrecht: Foris, pp. 351–361.

Reuland, E. (2011). Anaphora and Language Design. Cambridge, Mass: MIT Press.

Rodrigues, A. C. S. and D. C. Pereira (2006) Pronomes reflexivos no português popular brasileiro. In *XIV Congresso Internacional da ALFAL, Monterrey*.

Safir, K. (2004). *The Syntax of Anaphora*. Oxford: Oxford University Press.

Safir, K. (2013). Syntax, binding and patterns of anaphora. In M. den Dikken (ed.), *The Cambridge Handbook of Generative Grammar*. Cambridge: Cambridge University Press, pp. 515–576.

Safir, K. (2014). One true anaphor. *Linguistic Inquiry*, 45, pp. 91–124.

Silva, G. M. de O. (1991). Um caso de definitude. *Organon*, 18, pp. 90–108.

Sória, M. (2013). "Nós", "a gente" e o sujeito nulo de primeira pessoa do plural. MA Dissertation. Lisbon: Faculdade de Letras da Universidade de Lisboa.

Vieira, R. C. (2014). A aquisição da proforma "ele mesmo" no português brasileiro. Masters dissertation. São Paulo: Departamento de Linguística, USP.

Zribi-Hertz, A. (1980). Coréférence et pronoms réfléchis: notes sur le contraste *lui /lui-même* en francais. *Lingvisticae Investigationes*, 4, pp. 131–179.

19 The Semantics of DPs

MARCELO BARRA FERREIRA AND CLARA NUNES CORREIA

1. Introduction

This article discusses properties of definite and indefinite DPs (Determiner Phrases) in Portuguese related to their potential to refer to or quantify over entities belonging to a certain universe of discourse. We will limit our attention to DPs introduced by the definite article and a few indefinite determiners and followed by a noun phrase, leaving out other quantifier determiners, as well as personal pronouns. Our focus will be on the interaction between (in)definiteness and other semantic properties, emphasizing theoretically relevant facts and puzzles. The article is organized in three sections: we discuss DPs introduced by the definite article in Section 2, DPs headed by indefinite determiners in Section 3, and the so-called bare nominals (NP/DPs not preceded by any overt determiner) in Section 4.

2. Definites

Portuguese definite article *o*, like its English counterpart *the*, combines with noun phrases (NPs) to form determiner phrases (DPs).[1] From a pragmatic perspective, these definite DPs relate to the retrieval of information previously introduced, explicitly or implicitly, in the universe of discourse. Operating at the referential level, they convey a sense of familiarity. They contrast with indefinite articles, which are used to introduce new discourse referents, conveying a sense of novelty. (1), below, should be enough, to illustrate this general point:[2]

(1) *A Maria comprou um gato. O gato é muito bonito.*
     "Maria bought a cat. The cat is very cute."

Semantically, a definite DP can be taken to denote a contextually salient individual (or group of individuals) that belongs to the NP denotation. A singular definite DP, for instance, conveys that that there is only one such individual, and denotes this unique individual.[3] More explicitly:

(2) A singular DP of the form [*o/a* NP-sg] denotes the unique contextually salient individual that belongs to the denotation of NP-sg, if there is one. If there is none, its denotation is undefined.

The Handbook of Portuguese Linguistics, First Edition. Edited by W. Leo Wetzels, João Costa, and Sergio Menuzzi.
© 2016 John Wiley & Sons, Inc. Published 2020 by John Wiley & Sons, Inc.

Thus, the DP *a presidente do Brasil em 2014* "The president of Brazil in 2014" has a denotation, since there is a unique president of Brazil in 2014, namely Dilma Rousseff. On the other hand, The DP *a rainha do Brasil em 2014* "The queen of Brazil in 2014" has no denotation, since there is no such individual. For NP denotations with larger cardinalities, we must rely on the context dependency alluded to in (2):

(3) *Um brasileiro e um português se encontraram. O brasileiro estava feliz.*
      "A Brazilian and a Portuguese met. The Brazilian was happy."

Plural definites are similar but also a little bit different, since they denote groups of two or more individuals. If we assume that plural NPs have such groups in their denotations, we can have the following:

(4) A plural DP of the form [*os/as* NP-pl] denotes the largest contextually salient group of individuals that belong to the denotation of NP-pl, if there is such a group. If there is none, its denotation is undefined.

Thus, both the DPs "*as presidentes do Brasil em 2014*" and "*as rainhas do Brasil em 2014*" do not have denotations. On the other hand, a DP such as "*os brasileiros*" denotes the largest group of Brazilians that is contextually salient.

  Besides being used to refer to specific individuals (or groups of individuals), definite DPs also have non-specific uses, as when they occur under the scope of a quantified phrase:

(5) *Toda mulher casada levou o (seu) marido pra festa.*
      "Every married woman brought the (her) husband to the party."

In this example, the singular definite DP does not refer to any particular individual. Its denotation can be paraphrased as "*the husband of x*," with x being interpreted as a variable bound by the subject quantifier phrase. Note, however, that the definite article is used because uniqueness is still ensured: whatever the married woman x, (assuming legal western arrangements) x has only a unique husband y, whoever y is.

  With this minimal background in place, we discuss two facts about the use of the definite article in Portuguese that raise some interesting theoretical points.

2.1. Definite article with proper nouns

Most semantic theories treat proper nouns as referential expressions denoting individuals. They differ from common nouns, which are assumed to denote predicates, and need the support of a determiner in order to become a referential expression. According to this perspective, combining a definite article with a proper noun, as in (6) below, would be incoherent, since proper nouns *per se* identify a unique individual as its referent. However, both (6) and (7) are well formed, and their subjects seem to refer to the same individual:[4]

(6) *O Pedro é inteligente.*
      "The Pedro is intelligent."

(7) *Pedro é inteligente.*
      "Pedro is intelligent."

If we stick to the traditional view that proper nouns denote individuals, we are left with no option but to assume that the article in (6) is an expletive determiner, with no semantic content.[5] An alternative is to take proper nouns to denote predicates. The noun "Pedro," for instance, would be interpreted as the predicate *"being Pedro,"* or more explicitly, *"being identical to Pedro."* (6), then, would denote the unique individual that satisfy this predicate, which, of course, is Pedro. Notice that under this view proper nouns will always denote a singleton set, and therefore, always satisfy the definite determiner's uniqueness requirement. As for (7), we need to postulate a null determiner with the same meaning of its overt counterpart.

We remain neutral about which option—postulating an expletive or a null determiner—is better. Either way, the semantic analysis will need to be supplemented with considerations of a more pragmatic nature, since the choice of using or not the determiners usually correlates with atitudes that the speaker has towards the referent of the proper noun. This in turn is subject to considerable sociolinguistic variation. As an illustration, consider European Portuguese, which normally uses the definite article in front of a proper noun. Even in this variety, and especially in formal registers, when the referent of the name is, say, culturally distinguished, the article is dropped:

(8) *Aristóteles foi um grande filósofo.*
     "Aristóteles was a great philosopher."

However, if the name "Aristóteles" refers not to the great Greek philosopher, but to my cat, the article should be used:

(9) *O Aristóteles voltou a fugir.*
     "The Aristóteles has run away again."

Thus, even within a single dialect, the "rules" governing whether or not an article should/can be used in front of a proper noun do not seem to be semantic in nature, and depend on the cultural salience of the referent, as well on the degree of formality required by the context of speech.[6]

2.2. Kind-referring definite DPs

Consider (10) below, which is fine in Brazilian and European Portuguese:

(10) *O urso polar está quase extinto.*   (BP, EP)
      "The polar bear is almost extinct."

(10) does not seem to be about any contextually salient bear. Moreover, "be extinct" is not a predicate that applies to ordinary individuals, but rather to species or natural kinds. A possible analysis for this sentence is to treat *polar bear* as a proper noun (the name of a kind) and see (10)'s subject as just another instance of a definite article preceding a proper noun, as we saw in (5). However, something will have to be said about the grammatical status of examples such as (11), in which there is no article (we will discuss this again in Section 3):

(11) *Urso polar está quase extinto.*   (?BP, *EP)
      "Polar bear is almost extinct."

Although there are speakers of Brazilian Portuguese who accept examples like (11), there are also many speakers who do not. Moreover, even among those who reject (11), there are many who accept (7), in which an ordinary proper noun is used without a definite article. Thus, although treating *polar bear* and related singular nouns/noun phrases as names of kinds seems attractive in face of examples such as (10), additional stipulations would still be needed to account for the limited acceptability of (11).

Consider now the case of plural definites:

(12) *Os ursos polares estão quase extintos.* (BP, EP)
   "The polar bears are almost extinct."

This sentence is fine in both Brazilian and European Portuguese. Treating the plural noun *polar bear* as the name of a kind raises some issues here too with respect to EP, since it cannot stand alone without the article in this language (see Section 3):

(13) *Ursos polares estão quase extintos.* (BP, *EP)
   "Polar bears are almost extinct."

Moreover, if *polar bear* is a proper noun referring to a species, it is not clear what the role of plurality is in this case. One might assign (12) a taxonomic reading, according to which the plural definite refers to the sub-kinds of polar bears. However, although this is certainly a possible reading for (12), it is not the only one, and (12) is fine even if it is assumed that there is only one species of polar bear. Thus, it seems that the best analytic option for EP in this case is to maintain the more conventional view that *polar bears* is just an ordinary plural NP predicate and to assume the existence of an intensional definite determiner (homophonous to its extensional counterpart) that turns properties of individuals (the NP intension) into the corresponding kinds, viewed as intensional pluralities (the plural concept *the polar bears*).[7]

As for BP, both options—kinds as proper nouns and kinds as intensional plural DPs— would be available. Needless to say, more empirical and theoretical research needs to be done to see what (if any) differences in meaning and use there are between (10) and (13) and how they can be accounted for under this double identity of kind denoting DPs.

3. Indefinites

This section discusses indefinite noun phrases introduced by *um* 'a/one' and *algum* 'any', as well as their plural counterparts *uns* and *alguns*.[8] At a very general and intuitive level, what makes them a natural class from a semantic point of view is their existential flavor. By that we mean that a sentence of the form [[(alg)*um*/*uns* NP] VP] can be easily paraphrased as saying that there is/are (an) individual(s) belonging to the class denoted by the NP that also belong(s) to the class denoted by the VP. We take this intuition as our starting point, and treat these indefinites as existential quantifiers over individuals. However, it is important to bear in mind that the study of indefinite noun phrases has played a major role in the development of natural language semantic theories focusing on discourse facts about reference, anaphora and quantification, such as Kamp (1981), Heim (1982), and many others after them. These theories have challenged the inherent quantificational force of indefinites, and have proposed alternatives according to which they simply introduce restricted variables, which get bound by other operators or interpretation procedures.[9]

In what follows we do not discuss this discourse-related aspect of Portuguese indefinites, but rather concentrate on their 'sentential' behavior, for which a quantificational view seems well suited, and which we believe can be integrated one way or another into dynamic theories. We focus on four semantic properties: epistemicity, positive polarity, partitivity, and scope taking. We believe these properties provide a very good illustration of similarities and differences between *um, uns, algum* and *alguns,* as well as the challenges their complex behavior poses for any semantic theory of indefinites.

3.1. *Epistemicity*

Consider the following two sentences:

(14) *O professor está conversando com um aluno.*
      "The professor is talking to a student."

(15) *O professor está conversando com algum aluno.*
      "The professor is talking to some student."

The first point to notice is that both *um* and *algum* are interpreted existentially, and both sentences above convey that there is (at least) one student to whom the professor is talking. However, there is a clear difference between them. (15) suggests that the speaker is not in direct contact with the student, and is not able to identify who he is. For instance, imagine that I am in my office, and the conversation between the student and the professor is taking place in the office right in front of me, where I can see them. Now, suppose the phone in my office rings, I pick it up, and the person who called asks if the professor is available; then, I can answer with (14), but not with (15). (15) would be fine, however, if I were locked in my office and could not see what was happening in the other office, but still could guess the professor is talking to a student, because I can hear his voice and I noticed that he is giving academic advice to a person.[10] Thus, *algum*, but not *um*, conveys an epistemic effect of ignorance of the speaker about the identity of the referent to which the indefinite phrase is connected. One important thing to notice is that this epistemic effect does not seem to be cancelable, unlike what happens with *um* 'a':

(16) ??*O professor está conversando com algum aluno, o Pedro.*
      "The professor is talking to some student, namely, Pedro."

(17) *O professor está conversando com um aluno, o Pedro.*
      "The professor is talking to a student, namely, Pedro."

However, the epistemic effect seems to vanish when the indefinite appears under the scope of certain operators, such as the determiner *todo* "every" or the adverb of quantification *sempre* "always":

(18) *Todo professor reprovou algum aluno.*
      "Every professor rejected some student."

(19) *Todo professor que reprovou algum aluno se arrependeu.*
      "Every professor that rejected some student regretted it."

(20) *Sempre que o professor reprovou algum aluno, ele se arrependeu.*
      "Every time the professor rejected some student, he regretted it."

The first sentence can be followed by a list with names pairing professors and students: professor *X* rejected student *A*, professor *Y* rejected student *B*, ... The second sentence is about professors that rejected students, and it does not suggest that the identity of any of the students is unknown to the speaker or the professor. The third sentence generalizes over the same type of situations, including the ones in which the identity of the student is known. In these examples, replacing *algum* by *um* does not seem to result in any difference in meaning, if the indefinites are interpreted as having narrow scope.

Interestingly, the epistemic effect discussed above with *algum* is not observed with the plural form *alguns*. In fact, both (21) and (22) below could be used in the scenario described above with the speaker in his office watching what was happening in the other office, but with the professor talking to a group of students.

(21) *O professor está conversando com uns alunos.*
  "The professor is talking to some students."

(22) *O professor está conversando com alguns alunos.*
  "The professor is talking to some students."

The situation is puzzling. The facts we presented before contrasting *um* and *algum* suggest a decomposition of *algum* into two pieces, *alg–* and *um*, with the former carrying some semantic ingredient that triggers the epistemic effect. However, this extra component of *alg–* seems to be missing when the plural morpheme *–s* is added, and it is far from obvious what plurality and the ignorance effect have to do with each other.[11] A more precise characterization of the epistemic effect as well as its interaction with plurality and other elements, such as the operators in (18)–(20), is beyond the scope of this paper, and at the moment we are not aware of any unified proposal in this direction. We only want to point out here that epistemic determiners are attested in other languages as well, including Spanish *algún*, Italian *un qualque*, German *ingendein*, and English *some*, all conveying some sort of ignorance about who is the individual satisfying the existential claim, but differing in which type of ignorance they convey.[12]

3.2. Positive polarity

One salient feature of both *algum* and *alguns* is that they cannot be interpreted under the scope of a clause-mate negation:[13]

(23) *O professor não aprovou algum aluno.*   (* neg >> *algum*)
  "The professor did not approve some student."

(24) *O professor não aprovou alguns alunos.*   (* neg >> *alguns*)
  "The professor did not approve some students."

These sentences are never used to convey that the professor did not approve any student. Such a situation would require the negative quantifier *nenhum* "no":

(25) *O professor não aprovou nenhum aluno.*
  The professor not approved no student
  "The professor did not approve any student."

What (23) and (24) express is the existence of students who the professor did not approve. This becomes clear when the indefinites are resumed by a pronominal anaphora, in which case the pronoun refers to the individual(s) whose existence was stated in the previous discourse.

(26) *O professor não aprovou alguns alunos. Eles ficaram decepcionados.*
  "The professor did not approve some students. They were disappointed."

That these facts are connected to negation, and not to some general tendency of out-scoping clause-mate operators, can be seen in examples such as (27):

(27) *Todo professor aprovou algum/alguns alunos.*
  "Every professor approved some student(s)."

In the most salient reading of this sentence the students co-vary with the professors, showing that the indefinite can be interpreted under the scope of the universal quantifier *todo*.

The fact that *algum* and *alguns* cannot occur under the immediate scope of negation makes them members of some class of positive polarity items. The question is what particular class they belong to. Marti (2006) classifies the plural indefinites *uns* and *alguns* (as well as their Spanish counterparts) as items that cannot be interpreted under the immediate scope of a clause-mate anti-additive operator, such as the negation *não*, the preposition *sem* "without" and the negative quantifier *ninguém* "nobody":[14]

(28) *O prefeito não convidou alg(uns) políticos para o seu aniversário.*   (*não>>(alg)uns*)
     "The mayor did not invite some politicians to his birthday party."

(29) *O prefeito celebrou seu aniversário sem (alg)uns políticos.*   (*sem>>(alg)uns*)
     "The mayor celebrated his birthday without some politicians."

(30) *Ninguém conversou com (alg)uns políticos durante a festa.*   (*ninguém>>(alg)uns*)
     "Nobody talked to some politicians during the party."

We agree with Marti and believe that her claims can be extended to the singular indefinite *algum*, always bearing in mind its epistemic component discussed above:

(31) *O prefeito não convidou algum político para o seu aniversário.*   (*não>>algum*)
     "The mayor did not invite some politician to his birthday party."

(32) *O prefeito celebrou seu aniversário sem algum político.*   (*sem>>algum*)
     "The mayor celebrated his birthday without some politician."

(33) *Ninguém conversou com algum político durante a festa.*   (*ninguém>>algum*)
     "Nobody talked to some politician during the party."

Judgments seem more complex with *um*. The counterparts of (28) and (29) sound fine with the indefinite taking narrow scope, as long as we emphasize it:[15]

(34) *O prefeito não convidou UM político para o seu aniversário.*   (OK *não>>um*)
     "The mayor did not invite *UM* politician to his birthday party."

(35) *O prefeito celebrou seu aniversário sem UM político.*   (OK *sem>>um*)
     "The mayor celebrated his birthday without *UM* politician."

This type of emphasis is phonologically similar to the prosodic contour that is used when emphatic words like *único* ("single") or *sequer* ("whatsoever") appear in the noun phrase that accompanies the indefinite:

(36) *O prefeito não convidou um único político para o seu aniversário.*   (OK *não>>um*)
     "The mayor did not invite a single politician to his birthday party."

(37) *O prefeito celebrou seu aniversário sem um político sequer.*   (OK *sem>>um*)
     "The mayor celebrated his birthday with no politician whatsoever."

It is important to bear in mind that neither the emphatic contour nor the co-occurrence with *único* or *sequer* are available to the determiners *uns*, *algum* or *alguns*.

Finally, we notice that the counterpart of (30) with *um* is fine under the relevant interpretation even without emphasis:[16]

(38) *Ninguém conversou com um político durante a festa.*   (OK *ninguém>>um*)
      "Nobody talked to a politician during the party."

We will not attempt to provide an explanation for the polarity/scopal behavior of *um* here, but we believe it is worth pointing out that the word *um* is also the word for the numeral "one." We speculate that this interpretation might be the one targeted by the emphasis or by words like *único* and *sequer*. It could also be responsible for the narrow scope detected in (38), since cardinal noun phrases can easily scope under negative quantifiers:

(39) *Ninguém levou dois parentes para a festa.*   (OK *ninguém>>dois*)
      "Nobody took two relatives to the party."

It might then be possible to generalize to singular *um* and *algum* Marti's claim that the plural indefinites *uns* and *alguns* are polarity items that do not occur under the immediate scope of anti-additive operators. One only needs to bear in mind that the form *um* is also a numeral and can behave as such in certain circumstances.

3.3. Partitivity

We now discuss the behavior of *um*, *uns*, *algum*, and *alguns* in partitive constructions of the form *indefinite* + *de* ("*of*") + *plural definite*, which introduce quantification over a salient group of individuals (denoted by the plural definite). Consider, for instance, the following sentences:

(40) *O professor reprovou algum dos alunos.*
      "The professor rejected ALGUM (some, sg.) of the students."

(41) *O professor reprovou alguns dos alunos.*
      "The professor rejected ALGUNS (some, pl.) of the students."

(42) *O professor reprovou um dos alunos.*
      "The professor rejected UM (one, sg.) of the students."

(43) ??*O professor reprovou uns dos alunos.*
      "The professor rejected UNS (one, pl.) of the students."

While both singular *algum* and its plural counterpart *alguns* are fine in these constructions, singular *um* contrasts with its plural counterpart *uns*, as shown in (42) and (43). Although this might be an idiosyncratic feature of the form *uns*, a different (and one might say, conceptually more interesting) way to look at this paradigm is to attribute the acceptance of (42) to the fact that *um* is also the word for expressing the numeral *one*, as we pointed out in the previous subsection. This behavior of *um* in (42) would then be on a pair with the behavior of other numerals, which are fine in partitive constructions:

(44) *O professor reprovou cinco dos alunos.*
      "The professor rejected five of the students."

Since numerals do not pluralize in Portuguese (*cincos, 'five, pl.'), the form *uns* in (45) is unambiguous—that is, it must be an indefinite quantifier, and not a numeral. This would make it possible to state that the indefinite forms *um*/*uns* do not enter into overt partitive constructions. This could follow from a compositional treatment of these indefinites, if we follow Marti (2006) and assume that *alg–* and *um* are separate morphemes, and the ability to enter into a partitive construction is introduced by *alg–*. Moreover, it would make the contrast between *alguns* and *uns* seen above consistent with what happens in covert partitives, when *de+os* ("of+the") does not appear overtly:

(45) *O professor reprovou alguns alunos. Os outros, ele aprovou.*
      "The professor rejected some students. The others, he approved."

(46) *O professor reprovou uns alunos. ?? Os outros, ele aprovou.*
      "The professor rejected UNS students. The others, he approved."

For many speakers, there is a clear contrast here. The definite *os outros* is totally natural in (45), but its use in (46), if acceptable at all, seems to require some sort of accommodation on the part of the hearer. This would follow if *uns* is not compatible with partitive interpretations. Marti's idea is that *uns* is a plain existential quantifier, and that *alg–* acts as a modifier, leaving the assertive meaning of *uns* intact, but introducing an implicature. For instance, the first sentences in (45) and (46) both mean that there are students who were rejected by the professor. However, due to the presence of *alg–*, (45) implicates that are also students who were not rejected.[17] In other words, only *alguns*, as part of its meaning, would make the complement set of the students immediately salient and available for being picked by *os outros*.

3.4. Scope taking

The last property we would like to consider is scope taking. Indefinites have been reported to be insensitive to scope islands or at least to be more liberal than other quantified phrases in how far from their surface position they can scope. This has been claimed to be the case for English *a/some* and special scopal mechanisms have been proposed to account for this fact.[18] In this respect, both *um* and *algum* do not seem to obey island constraints that are known to limit syntactic movement. Here we provide two cases, adapted from the literature:

(47) *Se (alg)um parente do Pedro morrer, ele herdará uma fortuna.*
      "If some relative of Pedro dies, he inherits a fortune"

(48) *Todos os livros que eu emprestei pra (alg)um aluno sumiram.*
      "All the books that I lent to some student disappeared."

Judgments are delicate in these cases, but it seems that under appropriate discourse circumstances, the indefinites can take matrix scope in these examples. In (47), the indefinite is inside an adverbial *if*-clause. If it scopes inside this clause, the sentence will mean that the death of any relative of Pedro's will yield him inherit a fortune. This reading is certainly possible and, in fact, seems to be the most salient one. The wide (matrix) scope reading in this case would express a situation in which there is a particular relative of Pedro whose death would make Pedro inherits a fortune. In this case, the death of any other relative of his might be irrelevant. Although this reading may not be very salient, it seems to arise in discourses like the following:[19]

(49) *Eu tenho certeza que se (alg)um parente do Pedro morrer, ele herdará uma fortuna. Eu só não me lembro qual parente é esse.*
      "I am sure that if a relative of Pedro dies, he inherits a fortune. I just cannot remember which relative it is."

In sentence (48) the indefinite is inside a relative clause. In this case, the narrow scope reading would mean that no student who borrows a book from me returns it. Once again, this is certainly a possible reading for the sentence. However, the wide scope reading is also possible. In this case, the sentence would mean that there is one particular student such that every book that I lend to him never comes back to me. This reading becomes salient in contexts such as the following:

(50) *Todos os livros que eu emprestei pra um aluno sumiram. Só ele age assim! Todos os outros alunos devolveram os livros que me pediram emprestados.*
"All books I lent to some student disappeared. He is the only one that does that. All other students returned the books that they had borrowed from me."

Replacing *um* by *uns, algum* or *alguns* in the examples above does not seem to affect the judgements, if similar contextual environments are established.

We conclude this section by noticing that scopal freedom contrasts with the previous three properties that we presented before in applying (for some speakers at least) to all four Portuguese indefinites we looked at. This can be taken as indicative that this freedom should not be theoretically tied to any of those other properties. What exactly is behind this peculiar trait of indefinites is still a debatable matter.[20]

4. Bare nominals

Both European and Brazilian Portuguese (EP/BP) allow for bare nominals in argument positions. By bare nominals we mean noun phrases headed by common nouns not preceded by overt functional material such as determiners and numerals, as in the following example:

(51) *Pedro viu estudantes na festa.*
"Pedro saw *students* at the party."

In (51) we have an instance of a bare plural in object position. As we will see below, bare plurals are allowed in both varieties of Portuguese, but their distribution is constrained by different factors, BP being more liberal than EP. Bare singulars, on the other hand, are not allowed with count nouns in EP, but are fine in BP, as shown in (52):[21]

(52) *Pedro viu estudante na festa.* (*EP/✓ BP)
*"Pedro saw *student* at the party."

We start our discussion with the use of bare plurals in both varieties, and then proceed to bare singulars in BP.

4.1. Bare plurals

In episodic sentences such as (52), bare plurals receive an existential interpretation. (52) is true if there are students that Pedro saw at the party, and false otherwise. In this respect, bare plurals can be paraphrased as DPs formed with *uns* or *alguns*:

(53) *Pedro viu uns estudantes na festa.*
"Pedro saw some students at the party."

Despite the similarity in interpretation between (51) and (53), when scope-taking expressions are present in the same clause, the interpretation of bare plurals is different from that of overt indefinites. For instance, they always take scope below a clause-mate negation, whereas this is not the case with overt indefinites, as we saw in the last section:

(54) *Pedro não viu estudantes na festa.* (OK *não* >> ∃; *∃ >> *não*)
"Pedro didn't see students at the party."

(55) *Pedro não viu (alg)uns estudantes na festa.* (* *não* >> ∃; ok ∃ >> não)
"Pedro didn't see some students at the party."

(54) is true if, and only if, Pedro saw no students at the party. The indefinites in (55), on the other hand, are positive polarity items and only allow for the inverse scope reading. The same is true with respect to other clause-mate negative elements:

(56) a. *Ninguém viu estudantes na festa.*
"Nobody saw students at the party."
b. *Pedro consertou a máquina sem ferramentas.*
"Pedro fixed the machine without tools."

Bare plurals are also interpreted with narrow scope when embedded in the complement of intensional verbs:

(57) *Pedro quer encontrar estudantes.*
"Pedro wants to find students."

In (57), Pedro's desire is not directed towards some specific group of students. A continuation such as *Eles estão na casa da Maria*, in which the pronoun refers to a group of five students who are at Maria's house, sounds weird.[22] This would be perfectly fine if we had an overt indefinite, as in (58):

(58) *Pedro quer encontrar (alg)uns estudantes.*
"Pedro wants to find some students."

As for their syntactic distribution in episodic sentences, bare plurals cannot appear in preverbal, subject positions in EP, but are fine in BP:[23]

(59) *Cachorros morderam o Pedro.*   (*EP/✓BP)
"Dogs bit Pedro."

In this regard, BP is like English, whereas EP resembles Spanish and Italian.[24] The same contrast is observed in non-episodic sentences. This includes both generic statements and kind predication:

(60) *Cachorros (normalmente) não mordem os seus donos.*   (*EP/✓BP)
"Dogs (normally) don't bite their owners."

(61) *Dinossauros estão extintos.*   (*EP/✓BP)
"Dinosaurs are extinct."

(60) is a generic statement that assigns to every (normal) dog the property of not biting her owner. Although this is a generic statement about dogs, genericity does not seem to be tied to the presence of a bare plural, but rather to tense and aspect (simple present in Portuguese, as in English, only gives rise to habitual readings with eventive predicates) or an adverb of

quantification. Replacing a bare plural by an overt (singular) indefinite would not change the generic character of the interpretation:

(62) *Um cachorro (normalmente) não morde o seu dono.*
"A dog (normally) doesn't bite his owner"

In (61), we have a predicate that applies to kinds and not to ordinary individuals. The interpretation is that members of the kind ceased to exit. In this context, replacing a bare plural by an overt indefinite is not possible (except, maybe, under a taxonomic interpretation):

(63) *Um dinossauro está extinto.*   (*EP/*BP)
*"A dinosaur is extinct."

Good paraphrases are obtained with an overt definite, as we saw in section 1:

(64) *Os dinossauros estão extintos.*   (EP/BP)
"The dinosaurs are extinct."

Accounting for the distribution of bare plurals has been a challenge for syntactic and semantic theorists working on many languages.[25] As we have just seen, even closely related dialects can impose very different constrains on their distribution. To present and discuss such theories is, of course, beyond the scope of this paper. We just want to point out that the ungrammaticality of bare plurals with kind predicates in EP makes it implausible that they denote kinds in this language. A more plausible alternative is to treat bare plurals as DPs headed by a covert indefinite determiner. Its sensitivity to subject/object asymmetries might then be related to the licensing of empty categories, which is known to be affected by lexical government by verbs and related matters. This is the route taken by Chierchia (1998) for Italian (see also Longobardi 2000). Of course, how the scopal behavior of bare plurals discussed above is to be accounted for by such a theory remains to be spelled out (the same is true for the heaviness constraint mentioned in note 17).

Treating bare plurals as kind-denoting expressions seems more promising for BP (as well as for English), though taking them to denote predicates that can be type-shifted to kinds or existential quantifiers is also an option, as argued for by Pires de Oliveira and Rothstein (2011).

4.2. Bare singulars

BP allows for bare singulars in argument positions. However, their distribution is not the same as the one we have just seen for bare plurals. We start with an example in which a bare singular occurs in the object position of a transitive verb in an episodic sentence.

(65) *Pedro viu estudante na festa.*
"Pedro saw student at the party."

In this sentence, the bare singular receives an existential interpretation. In this respect, it behaves like a bare plural, as we saw in (53) above. Bare singulars also behave like bare plurals with respect to the scopal properties discussed in the previous section. For instance, they can only take scope below a clause mate negation. (66), below, is true if, and only if, there is no student that Pedro saw at the party.[26]

(66) Pedro não viu estudante na festa.
*"Pedro didn't see student at the party

There are differences, however. Whereas (52) conveys that at least two students were seen by Pedro, (64) is neutral in this respect. The existence of a single student seen by Pedro is enough to make the sentence true and felicitous. Moreover, the neutrality observed with bare singulars concerns not only plurality, but also the count / mass distinction. This is illustrated below with the count noun *melancia*.

(67)   *O bebê comeu melancia/melancias.*
       "The baby ate watermelon/watermelons."

The version with a bare singular can be true if the baby ate only some small pieces of a watermelon, or even some kind of sauce made with the fruit. It can also be used in less plausible cases in which a whole watermelon was eaten or in which more than one fruit was eaten by a hungry child. Though grammatical, the version with a bare plural sounds a bit odd at first, because it conveys that at least two watermelons were eaten by the baby.

As for their distribution, bare singulars seem not to be acceptable in the subject position of episodic sentences:[27]

(68)   **Cachorro mordeu o Pedro ontem.*
       *"Dog bit Pedro yesterday."

They are fine, however, in the subject (as well as in the object) position of generic sentences. In these cases, replacing the bare singular by a bare plural results in no obvious difference of interpretation:[28]

(69)   *Cachorro, normalmente, não morde o próprio dono.*
       *"Dog, normally, doesn't bite its owner."

Bare singulars also seem to be fine, at least for some speakers, as subjects of kind predicates in BP:[29]

(70)   *Dinossauro está extinto.*
       *Dinosaur is extinct

Notice that (70) is very close in form to sentences with a kind predicate and a bare mass noun as subject:

(71)   *Petróleo está escasso.*
       Oil is rare

Notice further that bare mass nouns behave like bare singulars in being ungrammatical in the preverbal subject position of episodic predicates, but perfectly fine in generic statements:[30]

(72)   **Vinho vazou no chão da adega.* (cf. *Vazou vinho no chão da adega.*)
       "Wine spilt on the cellar's floor."

(73)   *Vinho vaza quando não é posto em um barril bem vedado.*
       "Wine spills when it is not in a sealed barrel."

Similarities like these have led Pires de Oliveira and Rothstein (2004) to propose that bare singulars and bare mass nouns are semantically alike. This may sound odd at first due to the fact that typical bare singulars such as *cachorro* ('dog') or *estudante* ('student') seem to refer to naturally atomic properties, which apply to individuals or groups of individuals, whereas typical mass nouns such as *vinho* ('wine') or *óleo* ('oil') do not refer to atomic properties and do not apply to individuals. However, the authors point out that several mass nouns are also naturally atomic: *furniture, jewelry, silverware* are some examples. Refuting previous arguments by Schmitt and Munn (1999) against the parallel between bare singulars and bare mass noun phrases based on distributive predication, they present examples such as (74) below in which we see distribution down to atomic individuals with both types of bare noun phrases:

(74) a. *Criança pesa 20 kg nessa idade.*
        "Child weighs 20 kg at this age."
     b. *Bijouteria custa 10 dólares nesta loja.*
        "Jewelry costs 10 dollars at this store."

(75) a. *Tinha brinquedo espalhado por todo quarto.*
        "There was toy scattered all over the room."
     b. *Tinha bijouteria espalhada por todo o balcão.*
        "There was jewelry scattered all over the counter."

Pires de Oliveira and Rothstein (2004) propose to capture these similarities by treating both bare singulars and bare mass nouns as kind-denoting expressions. An issue that deserves further attention before one can fully evaluate this type of proposal is how kind-denoting arguments interact compositionally with their predicates in episodic sentences and why (non-contrasting) bare singulars are not acceptable in preverbal, subject positions of such sentences.[31]

As the above presentation made clear, a comprehensive and detailed analysis of the syntax, semantics, and pragmatics of are singulars in BP remains an open and challenging topic.

NOTES

1 Unlike *the*, the Portuguese definite article inflects for gender (masculine/feminine) and number (singular/plural), giving rise to four different forms: *o* (m.s.), *a* (f.s.), *os* (m.pl.), *as* (f.pl.).
2 See Heim (1983) for a semantic/pragmatic theory of (in)definiteness in which novelty/familiarity plays an important role. See Lyons (1999) for a detailed discussion of the variety of morphological, syntactic, semantic and pragmatic issues connected to the notional category of definiteness.
3 It should be noted that not every theory (most notably Bertrand Russell's) treats definite descriptions as referential expressions. For presentation and discussion of different proposals in this area, see, for instance, Neale (1990), Heim (1991), Abbott (2010), Elbourne (2013). As far as we can see, Portuguese data do not raise any new issues that would help pending for one or the other side in this debate.
4 There are other languages in which a definite article may be found with proper nouns (often subject to dialectal variation), e.g. Modern Greek, Albanian, German, and Western Armenian (see Lyons 1999: 121ff).
5 See, for instance, Longobardi (1994), who postulates a pleonastic determiner for Italian DPs in which a proper noun is preceded by a definite article. He also proposes that article-less proper nouns in Italian occupy (via syntactic movement) the Determiner position that the definite article otherwise occupies.
6 This variability too is not exclusive to Portuguese. Lyons (1999:122), for instance, comments about German that "it is common in colloquial usage to use the article with first names (*die Claudia, der Hans*), and this usually conveys familiarity."

7   See Chierchia (1998) for the idea of kinds as intensional maximal pluralities. See Carlson (1977) for a treatment of English bare plurals as kind-denoting expressions. For excellent overviews of the complex issues surrounding the semantic notion of genericity, including kinds and kind-denoting expression, see Krifka et al. (1995) and Beyssade et al. (2013).

8   These are the masculine forms. The feminine ones are: *uma, alguma, umas, algumas*. Since gender does not play any relevant role in the constructions we discuss, we only employ the masculine forms in our examples.

9   But see Heim (1990) for re-evaluation of some of the data and analysis. We only mention here that typical examples that have motivated a non-existential, unselective binding approach are easy to construct with all these indefinites:

   (i)   *Todo fazendeiro que tem (alg)um burrinho bate nele.*
         "Every farmer who owns a/some donkey beats it."

   (ii) *Todo fazendeiro que tem (alg)uns burrinhos bate neles.*
         "Every farmers who owns some donkeys beats them."

10   Even in this context, some speakers still consider (15) somewhat marked and would prefer to add an overt epistemic modal verb such as *deve* ("must"), as in (i) below:

   (i)   *O professor deve estar conversando com algum aluno.*
         "The professor must be talking to some student."

11   For a concrete proposal for Spanish *algunos*, see Alonso-Ovalle and Menéndez-Benito (2011).

12   For more discussion on Portuguese *algum*, see Silva (2012), for Spanish *algun/algunos*, see Alonso-Ovalle and Menéndez-Benito (2010, 2011). For a cross-linguistic perspective, see Alonso-Ovalle and Menéndez-Benito (2013) and the references therein.

13   The singular form *algum* can also be used after the noun, forming a negative-polarity item:

   (i)   *O professor não aprovou aluno algum.*
         The professor not approved student some
         "The professor did not approve any student (at all)"

   We will not discuss this post-nominal use of *algum* in this paper.

14   Formally, an operator *f* is anti-additive if *f(x or y)* is equivalent to [*f(x) and f(y)*]. (i) illustrates this property for *sem* "without":

   (i)   *Pedro saiu sem Maria ou Sandra = Pedro saiu sem Maria e Pedro saiu sem Sandra.*
         Pedro left without Maria or Sandra = Pedro left without Maria and Pedro left without Sandra.

   For discussion on positive and negative polarity items, see Szabolsci (2004) and the references therein.

15   In European Portuguese (at least for some speakers), adding prosodic emphasis is not enough to get the desired interpretation. Emphatic expressions similar to "a single" or "whatsoever" need to be used, as illustrated in (35) and (36).

16   Although, for many speakers, the use of "*nenhum político*" ("no politician"), instead of "*um político*" ("a politician"), would make the sentence sound more natural.

17   Here is a sketch of Marti's (2006) compositional implementation of this idea (ignoring number):

   (i) $[[\text{um}]] = \lambda P. \lambda Q. \exists x: P(x) \& Q(x)$

   (ii) $[[\text{alg-}]] = \lambda R. \lambda P. \lambda Q. R(P)(Q)$
         implicature: $R(P)(\sim Q)$

   (iii) $[[\text{algum}]] = [[\text{alg-}]]([[\text{um}]]) = \lambda P. \lambda Q. \exists x: P(x) \& Q(x)$
         Implicature: $\exists x: P(x) \& \sim Q(x)$

18 For relevant discussion, see Fodor and Sag (1982), Ruys (1992), Reinhart (1997), and Winter (1997), among many others.

19 For some speakers, this reading is easily available with *um*, but very hard to get with *algum*.

20 However, as observed in note 16, some speakers reject the wide scope reading for *algum*. For such speakers, one might pursue an analysis according to which *algum* turns its NP into an existential quantifier inaccessible for any mechanism for wide-scope readings. For instance, under the choice function approach (Reinhart 1997, Winter 1997) *algum* might block the insertion of a choice function variable that takes the NP as an argument.

21 Judgments are not always crystal clear. A reviewer judged (51) a bit weird out of the blue, but fine under focus:

(i) *Pedro só viu estudante na festa.* (stress on *"estudante"*)
Pedro only saw student at the party

Other speakers, however, find (51) fine, even if the bare NP is unfocused.

22 Matters become more complicated when bare plurals appear under intensional verbs whose subjects are plural. This has been pointed out for English by Partee (1985), as well as for Portuguese by Munn and Schmitt (2005).

(i) *Os estudantes estão procurando artigos de linguística.*
"The students are looking for linguistics articles"

In this example, it seems that the bare plural can take scope above the intensional verb. If it scopes below the subject, then for each student there are (possibly) different articles that (s)he is looking for. If it scopes above the subject, then there must be some particular set of articles that all the students are looking for. We wanted to point out that judgments are subtle and the contrast between (i) and (56) was not obvious to some of the speakers we consulted.

23 Bare plurals in subject positions become grammatical in EP if they are *heavier*, as in (i) below, taken from Oliveira and Muller (2004):

(i) *Amigos de Coimbra partiram ontem.*
"Friends from Coimbra left yesterday"

The same is true in Italian, as reported in Chierchia (1998) and Longobardi (2000).

24 The parallel between English and Brazilian Portuguese breaks up when bare plurals occur in the object position of creation verbs, such as *inventar* ("invent"). In BP (and also in EP), they can only have a taxonomic ("types of") interpretation:

(i) *Os americanos inventaram transistores.* (only taxonomic reading)
The Americans invented transistors.

25 See Carlson (1997), Krifka et al. (1995), Chierchia (1998), Krifka (2004) among others for thorough discussion of English bare plurals.

26 It is not obvious that bare plurals behave differently in situations in which there is only one student that Pedro saw. Many speakers find (i) false in this case:

(i) *Pedro não viu estudantes na festa.*
Pedro did not see students in the party

Moreover, dialogues like (ii) sound coherent to these speakers:

(ii) A: *Havia estudantes na festa?*
Were there students at the party?
B: *Sim. Mas apenas um.*
Yes. But only one

However, conflicting judgments have been reported in the literature (see Muller 2002, for instance). This seems to indicate that there is variation in whether or not bare plurals are inherently plural. For discussion of this issue with respect to English, see Spector (2003) and Zweig (2009).

27   Bare singulars are acceptable in contrasting, list-like environments, as noticed by Schmitt and Munn (1999):

(i)   *Durante a festa, mulher discutiu política, homem discutiu futebol, …*
     During the party, woman discussed politics, man discussed soccer, …

At first sight, bare singulars do not seem to receive an existential interpretation in these cases. In (i), for instance, they seem to refer to the totality of women and the totality of men who were at the party. But this is not necessarily the case, as a reviewer pointed out to us. The reviewer offered the following scenario: someone throws a party in which plenty of lawyers and doctors are present. Lawyers are supposed to be lazy, and doctors too serious to tell jokes; but the party was so crazy that the cook was a lawyer, and the star of the night was a doctor who turned out to be a comedian. With this scenario in mind, the reviewer adds, one can certainly utter (i):

(ii)   *A festa foi realmente louca: advogado cozinhou, médico contou piada, …*
      The party was really crazy: lawyer cooked, doctor told jokes, …

Understanding the role played by contrastiveness in the licensing of these subject bare singulars is a topic that certainly deserves further attention. See Schmitt and Munn (1999) for other cases in which bare singulars can receive this interpretation. See also Dobrovie-Sorin (2010) for discussion and comparison with certain uses of bare plurals in English discussed by Condoravdi (1992, 1994).

28   An overt indefinite *"um cachorro"* ("a dog") would also be fine here (as it would in EP, which does not allow (70)).

29   Muller and Oliveira (2004), however, judge bare singulars unacceptable in kind predication.

30   As a reviewer pointed out, like count bare singulars, bare mass nouns also become fine in episodic sentences, if list-like or contrastive situations of the type discussed in note 21.

31   See Pires de Oliveira and Rothstein (2004) for some preliminary discussion. Also relevant is their observation that even in object position, bare singulars are sometimes constrained in episodic sentences:

(i)   *Maria comeu bolo.*
     Maria ate the cake

(ii)   ??*Maria costurou blusa.*
      Maria sewed the blouse

Although they do not develop an analysis, they suggest the contrast might be related to the way perfective aspect affects non-kind predicates applied to kind arguments. Definitely, more types of NPs and VPs must be studied before any conclusion can be taken.

REFERENCES

Abbott, B. (2006) Definite and indefinite. In K. Brown (ed.), *The Encyclopedia of Language and Linguistics*, 2nd ed., vol. 3. Oxford: Elsevier, pp. 392–399.

Abbott, B. (2010). *Reference*. Oxford: Oxford University Press.

Alonso-Ovalle, L., and P. Menéndez-Benito (2010). Modal Indefinites. *Natural Language Semantics* 18 (1), pp. 1–31.

Alonso-Ovalle, L., and P. Menéndez-Benito (2011). Domain Restrictions, Modal

Implicatures, and Plurality: Spanish Algunos. *Journal of Semantics* 28 (2), pp. 211–240.

Alonso-Ovalle, L., and P. Menéndez-Benito (2013). Epistemic Indefinites: Are We Ignorant about ignorance? In M. Aloni, M. Franke, and F. Roelofsen. (eds.), *Proceedings of the 19th Amsterdam Colloquium*.

Chierchia, G. (1998). Reference to kinds across languages. *Natural Language Semantics* 6 (4), pp. 339–405.

Dobrovie-Sorin, C. (2010). Number Neutral Amounts and Pluralities in Brazilian Portuguese. *Journal of Portuguese Linguistics* 9(1), pp. 53–74.

Elbourne, P. (2013). *Definite Descriptions*. Oxford. Oxford University Press.

Fodor, J., and I. Sag (1982). Referential and Quantificational Indefinites. *Linguistics and Philosophy* 5, pp. 355–400.

Heim, I. (1982). *The Semantics of Definite and Indefinite Noun Phrases*, Ph.D. dissertation, University of Massachusetts at Amherst.

Heim, I. (1983). File change semantics and the familiarity theory of definiteness. In R. Bauerle, C. Schwarze, and A. v. Stechow (eds), *Meaning, Use and the Interpretation of Language*. Berlin: Walter de Gruyter, pp.164–89.

Heim, I. (1990). E-type pronouns and donkey anaphora. *Linguistics and Philosophy* 13 (2), pp. 137–77.

Heim, I. (1991). Artikel und Definitheit. In A. v. Stechow, and D. Wunderlich (eds.), *Handbuch der Semantik*. Berlin: de Gruyter, pp. 487–535 [English Translation]

Kamp, H. (1981). A Theory of Truth and Semantic Representation. In J. Groenendijk, and M. Stokhof (eds.) *Formal Methods in the Study of Language*. Amsterdam: University of Amsterdam pp. 277–322.

Krifka, M. (2004). Bare NPs: kind-referring, indefinites, both, or neither? In R.B.Y. Seattle, and Y. Zhou, (eds.), *Proceedings of Semantics and Linguistic Theory* (SALT) XIII, University of Washington. Cornell: CLC Publications, pp. 1–24.

Krifka, M., F.J., Pelletier, G.N. Carlson, A. ter Meulen, G.Chierchia, and G. Link (1995). Genericity: an introduction. In G.N. Carlson, and F. Pelletier (eds.), *The Generic Book*. Chicago: The University of Chicago Press, pp. 1–124.

Longobardi, G. (2001) How Comparative is Semantics? A Unified Parametric Theory of Bare Nouns and Proper Names. *Natural Language Semantics* 9, pp. 335–369.

Marti, L. (2008) The Semantics of Plural Indefinites in Spanish and Portuguese. *Natural Language Semantics*, 16, 1, pp. 1–37.

Muller, A., (2002). The semantics of generic quantification in Brazilian Portuguese. *PROBUS* 2 (14), pp. 279–298.

Muller, A., and F. Oliveira (2004) Bare Nominals and Number in Brazilian and European Portuguese. *Journal of Portuguese Linguistics*, v. 3, n. 1, pp. 9–36.

Munn, A., and C. Schmitt (2005). Number and indefinites. *Lingua* 115, pp. 821–855.

Partee, B., 1985. Situations, worlds, and contexts. *Linguistics and Philosophy* 8, pp. 53–58.

Pires de Oliveira, R., and S. Rothstein (2011). Bare singular noun phrases are mass in Brazilian Portuguese. *Lingua* 121, pp. 2153–2175.

Reinhart, T. (1997). Quantifier Scope: How Labor is Divided between QR and Choice Functions. *Linguistics and Philosophy* 20: 335–397.

Ruys, E. (1992). *The scope of indefinites*. PhD dissertation., Utrecht: OTS dissertation series.

Schmitt, C., and A. Munn (1999). Against the nominal mapping parameter: bare nouns in Brazilian Portuguese. In: *Proceedings of NELS* 29, pp. 339–353.

Silva, L. L. (2012). *A manifestação das noções de ignorância e de conhecimento no português brasileiro: o caso de algum e (um) certo*. PhD Dissertation, São Paulo: Universidade de São Paulo.

Spector, B. (2003). Plural indefinite DPs as PLURAL-polarity items. In J. Quer, J. Schroten, M. Scorretti, P. Sleeman, and E. Verheugd (eds.), *Romance languages and linguistic theory 2001: Selected papers from 'Going Romance'*. Amsterdam and Philadelphia: J. Benjamins.

Szabolcsi, A. (2004) 'Positive polarity. *Natural Language and Linguistic Theory* 22, pp. 409–452.

Winter, Y. (1997). Choice Functions and the Scopal Semantics of Indefinites. *Linguistics and Philosophy* 20, pp. 399–467.

Zweig, E. (2009). Number Neutral Bare Plurals and the Multiplicity Implicature. *Linguistics and Philosophy* 32 (4), pp. 353–407.

20 Lexical Semantics: Verb Classes and Alternations[1]

MÁRCIA CANÇADO AND ANABELA GONÇALVES

1. Introduction

The first issue to be addressed when dealing with verb classes is to know what are the criteria to establish a verb class. That is, what properties do certain verbs share so that they are classified as a coherent linguistic class and not as a simple grouping of verbs based on incidental similarities of meaning? To answer this question, we follow Fillmore (1970), Levin (1993), Levin and Rappaport Hovav (2005), Grimshaw (2005), Pesetsky (1995), among others, and assume the hypothesis that similarities of meaning components, by themselves, are not enough to classify verbs in a generalized and systematic way. For instance, Pesetsky (1995) shows that there is no kind of syntactic generalization contrasting verbs that denote emission of loud speech (*holler, shout*) with verbs that denote emission of quiet speech (*whisper, murmur*). Conversely, the distinction between English verbs that denote a manner of speaking (*holler, whisper*) and verbs that denote a content of speaking (*say, propose*) seems to be relevant for their selection properties, since only the latter accept sentential complements: *Mary said that she is hungry* is well-formed, but **Mary whispered that she is hungry* is not.

Therefore, in the view adopted here, classifying verbs implies grouping them in clusters that share an array of semantic properties that have impact in their syntactic behavior, such as possible argument realizations, passivization, reflexivization, etc. (See Fillmore 1970, Pinker 1989, Dowty 1991, Levin 1993, Levin and Rappaport Hovav 1995, 2005, Van Valin 2005, Wunderlich 2012, among others.) Thus, the semantic information carried by a verb is not just a list of idiosyncratic meanings, but contains types of meanings that are grammatically relevant. These meanings are encoded in the semantic structure of verbs and can be represented in many different ways.

Levin (2010) points out another important aspect of semantic verb classification: verb classes can be of different sizes depending on the kind and the level of generality of the linguistic phenomena to be accounted for. Verb classes may have different "levels of granularity": they can be "coarse-grained," "medium-grained," or "fine-grained."

The coarse-grained classification can be illustrated by the well-known distinction between internally and externally caused verbs, as proposed by Levin and Rappaport Hovav (1995). The authors claim that verbs denoting an internally caused eventuality show that some property inherent to the their argument is "responsible" for bringing about the eventuality, and verbs denoting an externally caused eventuality inherently

The Handbook of Portuguese Linguistics, First Edition. Edited by W. Leo Wetzels, João Costa, and Sergio Menuzzi.
© 2016 John Wiley & Sons, Inc. Published 2020 by John Wiley & Sons, Inc.

imply the existence of an external cause with immediate control over bringing about the eventuality denoted by them:

(1) *A   menina   dançou   uma   valsa.*   (internally caused verb)
     the girl   danced a   waltz
     "The girl danced a waltz."

(2) *O   furacão   quebrou as   janelas.*   (externally caused verb)
     the hurricane broke   the windows
     "The hurricane broke the windows."

This distinction is grammatically relevant because it determines the syntactic realization and the properties of the verb's arguments. For instance, internally caused verbs only select for cognate or hyponymous objects, as in (1), a restriction that does not apply to externally caused verbs, as in (2), and object alternations are favored in the context of externally caused verbs (e.g., the causative–inchoative alternation and the agent–beneficiary alternation that we will discuss below).

The medium-grained classification can be illustrated by the distinction between change-of-state verbs and *locatum* verbs (or change-of-possession verbs, as proposed by Cançado et al. 2013, since the entity denoted by the object becomes provided with something as a result of the action described by the verb):

(3) *O   sol   derreteu o   gelo.*   (change-of-state verb)
     the sun melted   the ice
     "The sun melted the ice."

(4) *A   cozinheira temperou a   comida.* (change-of-possession verb)
     the cook   spiced   the food
     "The cook spiced the food."

The distinction between change-of-state and change-of-possession verbs is grammatically relevant because it determines, for example, the causative–inchoative verb alternation. Only the first group of verbs allows the alternation, in Brazilian Portuguese (BP) and European Portuguese (EP):

(5) *O   gelo (se) derreteu.* (BP)   / *O   gelo derreteu(-se).*   (EP)
     the ice   (SE) melted   (BP)   / the ice   melted(-SE)   (EP)
     "The ice melted."

(6) **A   comida (se) temperou.*   (BP) / **A   comida temperou(-se).*   (EP)
     the food (SE) spiced   (BP) /   the food   spiced(-SE)   (EP)

Note that this distinction does not divide these verbs into two very broad classes, since they all belong to the class *verbs of change*, which in turn is a subset of externally caused verbs.

The fine-grained classification can be illustrated by psychological verbs of the *preocupar* "worry" type (object experiencer verbs):

(7) *A   filha   preocupa a   mãe.*
     the daughter worries the mother
     "The daughter worries her mother."

In a medium-grained analysis, this verb belongs to the change-of-state class. However, its lexical meaning further specifies a particular psychological state for the internal argument, an information that belongs to the verb's root. As we will see in the next section, the root is the element in the verb's meaning that is not shared with other verbs. Hence, it carries very specific information. Still, the distinction between psychological verbs and other change-of-state verbs is grammatically relevant because it predicts that the former can take sentential subjects, while other change-of-state verbs cannot (Cançado and Franchi 1999):

(8) *Que o   Pedro ainda não tenha chegado preocupa a   Maria.*
     that the Pedro yet   not has   arrived worries the Maria
     "It worries Maria that Pedro hasn't come yet."

(9) **Que o   menino tenha pulado   muito partiu a   mesa.*
     that the boy   has   jumped a-lot broke the table

In sum, semantic verb classes of different grain-sizes may be relevant to grammar, even if in different ways. The choice of one or another level of "granularity" in classification will depend on the topic of research. In any case, we expect that these differences in verb class grain-size ultimately find their source in the lexical semantic representation of the verbal meanings. The issue now is to propose an adequate way of representing this lexical information.

2. Lexical semantic representations

There are many possible approaches to lexical semantic representations. One of the most commonly assumed is the Semantic Role List approach. Semantic or thematic relations (as usually known) are given in a list of labels that represent grammatically relevant aspects of the verb meaning. These labels identify the role played by each of the verb's arguments in the event it denotes:

(10) *limpar* "clean": {Agent, Patient}

(11) *dar* "give": {Agent, Theme, Goal}

Under this approach, sets of roles such as (10) and (11) are the grammatically relevant semantic structures of the verbs; hence, verbs that show the same syntactic behavior, for example projecting arguments in a similar syntactic structure, should have the same semantic structure—the same list of thematic roles. In this way, thematic roles can be used to specify a verb class.

Although still used by many researchers, thematic roles have been very much criticized in the literature. First, their definitions are too vague and often difficult to apply reliably. Moreover, there is a lot of divergence among authors as to which thematic role types should compose the list. Another criticism is that, with some verbs, it seems necessary to assign more than one thematic role to a single argument. (E.g., does *run* assigns an agent or a theme role to the argument in subject position?) Finally, thematic roles do not seem to be the proper tool to deal with levels of granularity in verb classification. On the one hand, coarse-grained classes require very general, and few, roles; on the other hand, fine-grained classes require specific roles, and many in number; but, by assumption, arguments have only one such role. So, which role to choose? Apparently, a unique list of roles is not suitable.

The difficulties in identifying a list of thematic roles and in assigning these roles to certain DPs have made many researchers reject the assumption that thematic roles can be characterized by a cluster of necessary and sufficient conditions. Proposals to overcome these difficulties have appeared in many theoretical frameworks (Jackendoff 1990, Dowty 1991, Levin and Rappaport Hovav 1995, 2005, Van Valin, 2005, Wunderlich 2012, among others). Here, we present the one we use in our analysis of Portuguese verb classes: predicate decomposition. This approach consists of a more structured lexical representation: it not only contains elements that allow for structural distinctions between verb classes of different grain-sizes, but also has other theoretical advantages over the thematic role list approach. Nevertheless, we will keep using thematic role labels in our discussion as a descriptive tool, since they are the most common way of describing semantic relations.

Some semanticists have kept the idea, originated in Generative Semantics, that a verb can be represented in terms of one or more "primitive predicates," chosen to represent meaning components that are recurrent in a grammatically relevant group of verbs; this approach is called "predicate decomposition" (Pinker 1989, Jackendoff 1990, Levin and Rappaport Hovav 1995, 2005, Grimshaw 2005, Van Valin 2005, Wunderlich 2012, among others). Let us illustrate this type of meaning representation with an example from Portuguese:

(12) *derreter* "melt":
    [[X ACT] CAUSE [BECOME [Y <*DERRETIDO* "MELTED">]]]

The structures are always composed of meta-predicates, such as ACT and BECOME, and their arguments, which may be variables, such as X and Y, or semantic constituents, such as [Y <*DERRETIDO*>]. Besides, in the structure (12), there are two sub-events, related to each other by means of the meta-predicate CAUSE, which takes sub-events as arguments.

There is broad consensus in decompositional approaches that the distinction between "root" and "predicate structure" is necessary. Predicate structure is everything but the root in decomposition; it represents the part of the verbal meaning shared by members of the same class. The root is the unitary, idiosyncratic part of verbal meaning, which belongs to a single specific verb, and is represented between angled brackets (e.g., "<*DERRETIDO*>" in (12)). According to Levin and Rappaport Hovav (2005), roots, even though idiosyncratic, may be classified according to ontological categories. Among the ontological categories most frequently used in the literature are STATE, THING, PLACE, and MANNER. In the decomposition predicate structure, these categories can be meta-predicates, arguments or modifiers. For instance, while STATE, in (13), is a monadic meta-predicate, THING and PLACE are arguments of the dyadic meta-predicates WITH and IN, in (14) and (15), and MANNER is a meta-predicate modifier, in (16). The tools provided by predicate decomposition allow us to represent a verb class by a type of schema (Levin and Rappaport Hovav 2005, Cançado et al. 2013):

(13) *Change of state* (e.g., *quebrar* "break," *derreter* "melt," *secar* "dry," etc.)
    [[X ACT] CAUSE [BECOME [Y <*STATE*>]]]

(14) *Change of possession* (e.g., *temperar* "spice," *emoldurar* "frame," *mobilar* "furnish," etc.)
    [[X ACT] CAUSE [BECOME [Y WITH <*THING*>]]]

(15) *Change of place* (e.g., *engarrafar* "bottle," *empacotar* "package," *enjaular* "jail," etc.)
    [[X ACT] CAUSE [BECOME [Y IN <*PLACE*>]]]

(16) *Manner verbs* (e.g., *dançar* "dance," *pular* "jump," *cantar* "sing," etc.)
    [X ACT $_{<MANNER>}$]

It is worth noting that although the structure in (16) represents a single event, with a single semantic argument, X, Levin and Rappaport Hovav (2005) and Grimshaw (2005) argue that this type of "intransitive semantic representation" can also account for the transitive use of the verb, as in *the girl danced a waltz*. The authors claim that, in such cases, the object would actually be an argument of the root MANNER, not an argument of the verb, since it need not be expressed, as in *the girl danced all night*. That is why the object argument does not appear in the verb argument structure represented in (16).

Besides, using these structures to represent verb classes allows us to predict syntactic properties by means of the predicate decomposition. For example, change-of-state verbs present the causative–inchoative alternation (*John broke the window.* / *The window broke*), and the other verb classes do not.

Predicate decomposition structure also provides the means to represent verb classes of different grain-sizes. For instance, the schemas presenting the meta-predicate CAUSE, in (13), (14), and (15), correspond to externally caused verbs and the schema in (16) corresponds to internally caused verbs. Concerning medium-grained classes, one can represent their differences by resorting to slightly different predicate structures; see, for example, the distinction between change of state in (13), change of possession in (14), and change of place in (15). In a fine-grained analysis, since the idiosyncratic meaning of the verb is relevant, predicate decomposition structures may represent it by means of the root as a particular semantic constituent, as in the case of a psychological verb in (17):

(17) *preocupar* "worry":
     [[*X* ACT] CAUSE [BECOME [*Y* <*PREOCUPADO* "worried">]]]

Finally, predicate decomposition is also an articulated representation of events. This allows one to derive information about lexical aspect. For example, manner verbs denote activities and causative verbs denote accomplishments, a distinction that can be derived from representations like (13) to (16), but not from thematic structure representations. Even thematic information itself can be derived from predicate decomposition structures; for instance, the structure [*X* ACT] encodes the thematic role of agent (Cançado et al. 2013, for BP, and Jackendoff 1990, for English).

In the next section, we analyze verb classes and alternations in BP and EP in the framework of predicate decomposition.

3. Verb classes and alternations

In this work, we assume that verb alternation encompasses syntactic and semantic alternate ways of organizing the arguments of a predicate (Levin 1993); moreover, we also assume that each type of alternation encompasses a specific verb class, since we have proposed a strict relation between a verb class and its semantic and syntactic properties. For instance, (18) and (19) illustrate two verb alternations much discussed in the literature:

(18) a. *O sol derreteu o gelo.*
         the sun melted the ice
         "The sun melted the ice."
     b. *O gelo (se) derreteu.* (BP) / *O gelo derreteu-(se).* (EP)
         the ice (*SE*) melted   / the ice melted (*SE*)
         "The ice melted."

(19) a. *As ideias do   adolescente amadureceram.*
         the ideas of-the teenager   ripened
         "The teenager's ideas ripened."
     b. *O tempo amadureceu as   ideias do   adolescente.*
         the time ripened   the ideas of-the teenager
         "Time ripened the teenager's ideas."

Usually, in the literature, these alternations are not distinct, and they are known as "causative alternation," "anticausative alternation" or "causative–inchoative alternation." However, there are differences between (18) and (19), suggesting that two different (although related) types of alternations are involved.

In (18), a causative–transitive sentence alternates with an inchoative–intransitive sentence. The presence of the clitic *se* is optional in (18b), both in EP and BP (the only difference being the position of the clitic). In (19), an intransitive–inchoative sentence alternates with a causative–transitive sentence. In this case, the insertion of the clitic *se* in (19a) is not possible, although the intransitive verb accepts the insertion of a causative argument, as in (19b), in both Portuguese varieties.

According to Haspelmath (1993), in his typological work about inchoative / causative verb alternations, these two types of inchoative / causative verb pairs illustrate the anticausative alternation in (18), and the causative alternation in (19). In the anticausative alternation, the causative variant is basic and the inchoative one is derived. In general, the derived form is marked, what is corroborated by the presence of the clitic *se* in the Portuguese inchoative variant. In the causative alternation, the basic variant is the inchoative and the causative one is derived. In this Portuguese alternation type, neither of the forms is marked, which is also possible, according to the author. Thus, we assume the existence of "basically causative verbs" (18), and "basically inchoative verbs" (19). We can present evidence from BP and EP that the two verb types behave differently, taking into account the presence or the absence of the clitic *se* in the intransitive sentences and the alternations of EP to be presented below.

This kind of alternation is productive in several languages, besides Portuguese, and is much discussed in the literature, so we will not pursue this matter further. Instead, we will introduce in the next sections other types of alternations, which seem to have distinctive properties in Portuguese, and hence are interesting from a comparative perspective.

3.1. *Two types of alternations in BP*

In BP, there are two very productive argument alternations which, though functionally similar to alternations found in other languages (including EP), differ significantly from these in the grammatical tools they resort to. The first alternation involves verbs like *cortar* "cut," *lavar* "wash," *extrair* "extract," *operar* "operate." These verbs have an agent and a patient in their argument structure, and since the agent is usually the most prominent thematic role, it is aligned with the subject position:

(20) O   cabeleireiro cortou o   cabelo do   João.
       the hairdresser cut   the hair of-the João
       "The hairdresser cut João's hair."

Nevertheless, in many languages it is possible to give prominence to the possessor / beneficiary inside the complex patient, and this grammatical operation often makes use of causative verbs (21), morphemes like the reflexive *se* in Romance languages (22), or both elements, as in French (23):

(21) John *had* his hair cut.   (English)

(22) Juan *se* cortó el pelo.   (Spanish)
       Juan *SE* cut   the hair

(23) Jean *s'est fait* couper les cheveux.   (French)
       Jean *SE* made cut   the hair

In BP, the same alternation can be achieved without resorting to causative verbs or morphemes like the clitic *se*. So, the structure [DP1 V [DP2's DP3]] simply alternates with [DP2 V DP3]:

(24) a. *O cabeleireiro   cortou o cabelo do   João.*
      the hairdresser cut   the hair of-the João
      "The hairdresser cut João's hair."
   b. *O João cortou o cabelo.*
      the João cut   the hair
      "João had his hair cut."

The second alternation that will interest us here concerns verbs like *quebrar* "break," *abrir* "open," *estragar* "ruin," *rasgar* "rip":

(25) a. *Alguém   quebrou o   braço do   João.*
      someone broke   the arm of-the João
      "Someone broke João's arm."
   b. *O João quebrou o   braço.*
      the João broke   the arm
      "João broke his arm."

Syntactically, the structure [DP1 V [DP2's DP3]] in (25a) alternates with [DP3 V DP2] in (25b), in the same way as in (24a, b). Based on these examples, one could conclude that the sentences in (24) and (25) illustrate the same alternation. In fact, some studies do argue for this analysis, claiming that in both cases the agent alternates with a possessor in the subject position, which is known as the "possessor raising construction." Levin (1993) shows that sentences like *Carrie broke her arm* and *Sylvia cut her finger* are also possible in English—in an "unintentional interpretation with body-part object," in Levin's words, or in an intentional reading. However, while the sentence interpretation with *break* corresponds to (25b) in BP (in both readings), the sentence interpretation with *cut* is not equivalent to (24b). In fact, although the English sentence means that Sylvia has intentionally or unintentionally injured herself, which is also possible in BP due to *cut* polysemous behavior, the meaning of *cut* in (24b) is slightly different: someone intentionally has cut his own hair, or someone intentionally has his hair cut by someone else. We will only focus on this latter meaning.

Cançado (2010) shows that there are semantic and syntactic properties that distinguish the sentences in (24) and (25). According to the author, the differences are due to lexical properties of the verbs involved, which must be classified into two distinct classes. The goal of the next two sections is to understand the semantic and syntactic properties of these verb classes in BP and to provide an analysis of the relevant semantic structures. The section on EP (3.2) will rely on this analysis.

3.1.1. The agent–beneficiary and the part–whole alternations in BP

As we mentioned before, the first point to observe is that both sentences in (24b) and (25b) can have an agentive interpretation: *João cut / broke his own hair / arm*. This interpretation is not the alternate form of the sentences in (a); it is a reflexive use of the verbs *cut* and *break*. However, these sentences can have another reading, in an alternate form. As shown for English, sentence (25b) can also mean that João has unintentionally injured himself. Nonetheless, the sentence in (24b) cannot have this interpretation, but it can mean that João intentionally had his hair cut by someone else. Cançado (2010) shows that the sentence in (24b), with *cortar* "cut"-type verbs, can have the reading in (26), which is not adequate to *quebrar* "break"-type verbs in (28):

(26) "João had someone cut his hair deliberately."

(27) ? "João had someone break his arm deliberately."

Instead, a good paraphrase of (25b) would be (28):

(28) "João's arm broke."

Empirical evidence can make these distinctions more explicit. The sentence in (24b) only allows an adjunct that denotes control/volition over the event, as in (29), while the sentence in (25b) only accepts an adjunct that implies the opposite, as in (30):

(29) O   João cortou o cabelo   deliberadamente/*acidentalmente.
     the João cut   the hair deliberately/   accidentally
     "João had his hair cut deliberately/*accidentally."

(30) O   João quebrou o   braço acidentalmente/*deliberadamente.
     the João broke   the arm accidentally/   deliberately
     "João broke his arm accidentally/*deliberately."

Besides, sentences with *cortar*-type verbs accept an agent in an adjunct position, which is not permitted for sentences with *quebrar*-type verbs:

(31) O   João cortou o   cabelo com um bom   cabeleireiro.
     the João cut   the hair with a good hairdresser
     "João had his hair cut by a good hairdresser."

(32) *O João quebrou o   braço com alguém.
      the João broke   the arm with someone

Another difference between these two verb classes is that sentences with *cortar*-type verbs cannot have inanimate subjects in the alternate form, but the sentences with *quebrar*-type verbs can:

(33) *A   árvore cortou o   galho.
      the tree   cut   the branch

(34) A   árvore quebrou o   galho.
     the tree   broke   the branch
     "The tree's branch broke."

These data led Cançado (2010) to conclude that the subject of the sentence in (24b), with *cortar* "cut," has some kind of agentivity, and can be interpreted as if an indirect agent licenses another agent to act in his place. This linguistic phenomenon allows both "agents" to be present in the sentence—it is worth observing that this interpretation is not comitative in BP in (31). Differently, the alternate sentence in (25b) shows that the possessor, in subject position, is necessarily associated with the argument in object position, and it can only have an affected reading.

There is a further syntactic difference between these verb classes, related to the causative–inchoative alternation: *cortar*-type verbs do not undergo this alternation; in contrast, *quebrar*-type verbs accept it.

(35) **O cabelo do   João (se) cortou.*
     the hair   of-the João (SE) cut

(36) *O braço do   João (se) quebrou.*
     the arm   of-the João (SE) broke
     "João's arm broke."

Thus, up to here we have shown evidence that we are dealing with two verb classes, which have distinct syntactic and semantic properties. Following Cançado et al. (2013), we call the alternation that occurs with *cortar*-type verbs "the agent–beneficiary alternation," which is highly productive in BP as opposed to other Romance languages (see the comparison with EP in Section 3.2). In (37) to (49), we present some further examples of the agent–beneficiary alternation:

(37) *A Maria lavou   o   carro (com o   rapaz do   escritório).*
     the Maria washed the car   (with the boy   of-the office)
     "Maria had her car washed (by the office boy)."

(38) *O João extraiu   o   dente (com o dentista da   vizinhança).*
     the João extracted the tooth (with the dentist of-the neighborhood)
     "'João had his tooth extracted (by the neighborhood dentist)."

(39) *O João operou   o   nariz (com um médico famoso).*
     the João operated-on the nose (with a   doctor famous)
     "João had his nose operated on (by a famous doctor)."

The agent–beneficiary alternation is frequent in BP: in a collection of data containing 862 verbs (Cançado et al. 2013), 144 accept this alternation. In (40), we present a sample of these verbs:

(40) *afiar* "sharpen," anestesiar *"anesthetize,"* limpar *"clean,"* consertar "fix," decorar
     "decorate (a house)," *demolir* "demolish," *construir* "build," *esterilizar* "sterilize,"
     fotografar "photograph," *gravar* "record," *pintar* "paint," *radiografar* "radiograph,"
     retirar "remove," *remover* "remove"

The second alternation, the one that occurs with *quebrar*-type verbs, is not unusual and is found in many other languages. As we have already mentioned, Levin (1993) calls this alternation type the "unintentional interpretation with body-part object," also possible in English: *John broke his arm*. We find this alternation in EP as well, but it has properties slightly different from those of the BP alternation, as we will show in Section 3.2. Both in English and in EP, it seems that the relation established between the possessor and the possessed element must be a body-part relation, like a relation between a person and his / her arms, legs, etc. In BP, nevertheless, one can find many examples with other part–whole relations, a possibility unavailable in English, and even in EP, as far as we know. Furthermore, in BP, a cause can also appear as an adjunct:

(41) *A árvore quebrou o   galho   (com   a   ventania).*
        the tree broke   the branch (with the wind)
        "The branch of the tree broke because of the wind."

(42) *O   relógio estragou o   ponteiro (com o   tempo).*
        the clock   ruined   the hand   (with the time)
        "The clock's hand ruined with time."

(43) *O   casaco rasgou a   manga (com   a   lavagem).*
        the coat   ripped the sleeve (with the washing)
        "My coat's sleeve ripped from the washing."

In this case, the "possessor" (whole) of an affected object (part) is raised to the subject position of a transitive alternate form of the verb.[2] We call this alternation the "part–whole alternation," following Cançado et al. (2013), who found 230 verbs of this type, in the same collection of data mentioned previously. This shows that, like the agent–beneficiary alternation, the part–whole alternation is productive in BP. We list some verbs that allow it in (44):

(44) *apagar* "switch out," *apodrecer* "rot," *arranhar* "scratch," *arruinar* "ruin," *arrebentar* "burst," *contundir* "bruise," *desbotar* "discolor," *machucar* "hurt," *queimar* "burn," *rasgar* "tear," *torcer* " twist," *trincar* "crack" …

To conclude, the agent–beneficiary alternation and the part–whole alternation in BP are characteristic of two different verb classes, namely *cortar*-type class and *quebrar*-type class. In the next section, we will sketch an analysis of these phenomena, with the aim of determining which semantic properties in the lexical structures of these verbs allow them to enter these alternations.

3.1.2. *Lexical semantic representations and constraints*

In this section, we use the predicate decomposition approach to identify the verb classes that trigger agent–beneficiary and part–whole alternations. As show in Section 2, this type of semantic representation captures coarse, medium and fine-grained distinctions among verb classes, which is crucial for our analysis. Here we follow Cançado et al. (2013) and Cançado and Negrão (2010), who present a deeper analysis of the data, in particular of the semantic and the pragmatic conditions involved.

The agent–beneficiary alternation occurs with agentive transitive verbs from the *cortar*-type class, as illustrated in Section 3.1.1. However, being an agentive transitive verb is a necessary but not a sufficient condition, for there are verbs that satisfy this condition and still do not allow the alternation (the sentences b. below are grammatical only under a comitative reading):

(45) a. *O João pulou   a   cerca do   vizinho.*
          the João jumped the fence of-the neighbor
          "João jumped the neighbor's fence."
       b. **O   vizinho   pulou   a   cerca (com o   João).*
          the neighbor jumped   the fence (with the João)

(46) a. *A   cantora   cantou a   música do   Jobim.*
      the singer   sang   the music of-the Jobim
      "The singer sang Jobim's song."
   b. **O Jobim   cantou a   música (com   a   cantora).*
      the Jobim sang   the music (with   the   singer)

Recall Levin and Rappaport Hovav's (1995) proposal: the external argument of internally caused verbs presents some inherent property that is responsible for bringing about the eventuality; in turn, externally caused verbs entail the existence of an external cause with immediate control on bringing about the eventuality denoted by the verb. Based on this, we observe that the verbs in (45) and (46) denote internally caused events, while verbs in (37) to (39) (*lavar* "wash," *extrair* "extract," *operar* "operate"), which accept the agent–beneficiary alternation, denote externally caused events. Thus, the first constraint on this alternation is that the verbs that participate in the alternation cannot belong to the internally caused verb class. As we have shown before, this is a coarse-grained semantic distinction that can be represented by the verb schema [X ACT $_{<MANNER>}$]. So, we can conclude that verbs which present this semantic predicate structure cannot participate in the agent–beneficiary alternation.

However, Cançado and Negrão (2010) observed that some verbs that meet this "externally caused event" condition still do not permit the alternation. The authors concluded that there is an additional, pragmatic, condition: the alternation is allowed only if the VP refers to a kind of action that one usually asks someone else, an expert, to do for him/her; otherwise, the alternation fails. Consider (47) and (48):

(47) a. *O   João   derrubou   o   vaso do   José.*
      the João   broke down   the pot of-the José
      "João broke down José's pot."
   b. **O José   derrubou   o   vaso com   o   João.*
      the José   broke down   the pot with   the João
      (grammatical under the comitative reading)

(48) a. *Um ótimo pedreiro   derrubou   as   paredes da   casa   do   João.*
      a   great bricklayer broke down the   walls   of-the house of-the João
      "A great bricklayer broke down the walls of João's house."
   b. *O   João   derrubou   as   paredes da   sua casa   com   um ótimo*
      the João   broke down   the   walls   of-the his house with   a   great
      pedreiro.
      bricklayer
      "João had the walls of his house broken down by a great bricklayer."

In both examples, we have the same verb, *derrubar* "break down," which denotes an externally caused event and which, considering only the first condition, should participate in the alternation. Nevertheless, since it is not usual to ask an "expert in breaking down pots" to break down a pot for you, the alternation fails in (47). In contrast, it is usual to ask a bricklayer to do the job of breaking down walls and, consequently, the alternation holds in (48). These examples show that the agent–beneficiary alternation is constrained by both lexical and pragmatic factors.

Regarding the part–whole alternation, the first observable restriction comes from a medium-grained size classification, based on the verbs' schemas proposed in (13), (14), and

(15). Of these three classes, only the first one—verbs that denote change of state—accept the part–whole alternation. Preliminarily, the condition proposed by Cançado et al. (2013) is that for a verb to occur in the part–whole alternation, it must entail a change of state, which is represented by the following semantic structure:

(49) [BECOME [*Y* <*STATE*>]]

It is worth remarking that this alternation applies both to basically causative verbs ((41) to (43)), and to basically inchoative verbs ((50), (51)), in Haspelmath's (1993) terms:

(50) a. *As ideias do adolescente amadureceram.*
  the ideas of-the teenager ripened
  "The teenager's ideas ripened."
  b. *O adolescente amadureceu as ideias.*
  the teenager ripened the ideas
  "The teenager's ideas ripened."

(51) a. *A fechadura do portão enferrujou.*
  the lock of-the front door rusted
  "The front door's lock rusted."
  b. *O portão enferrujou a fechadura.*
  the front door rusted the lock
  "The front door's lock rusted."

However, Cançado et al. (2013) point out that entailing a change of state is a necessary but not a sufficient condition, because there are some verbs in the change-of-state class (basically causative or basically inchoative) that do not accept the part–whole alternation. For example, *preocupar* "worry" and *adoecer* "get sick" are change-of-state verbs; evidence for this fact is that they accept the causative–inchoative or inchoative–causative alternation, which is a typical property of this class, according to the authors:

(52) a. *A conversa aborreceu a Maria.*
  the conversation bored the Maria
  "The conversation bored Maria."
  b. *A Maria (se) aborreceu (com a conversa).*
  the Maria (SE) bored (with the conversation)
  "Maria got bored (with the conversation)."

(53) a. *O bebê adoeceu (com o tempo frio).*
  the baby got sick (with the weather cold)
  "The baby got sick with the cold weather."
  b. *O tempo frio adoeceu o bebê.*
  the weather cold got sick the baby
  "The cold weather made the baby sick."

Nevertheless, these verbs do not accept an argument denoting a part–whole relation in object (causative verbs) or subject position (inchoative verbs), which prevents the alternate sentences in (54b) and (55b):

(54) a. *A conversa   aborreceu a   cabeça da   Maria.
        the conversation bored   the head   of-the Maria
     b. *A Maria aborreceu a   cabeça.
        the Maria bored   the head

(55) a. *O pulmão do   bebê adoeceu (com o   tempo   frio).
        the lung   of-the baby got sick (with the weather cold)
     b. *O bebê adoeceu o   pulmão.
        the baby got sick the lung

Thus, a fine-grained distinction is also necessary: the part–whole alternation is possible only when the verb selects for an object (basically causative verbs), or a subject (basically inchoative verbs) that can denote a part–whole relation, this being a selectional restriction of the verb. The verbs in (54) and (55) do not accept a part–whole argument, and, consequently, the alternation fails. All the 230 verbs examined by Cançado et al. (2013) meet the two conditions proposed.[3]

Having delimited the semantic and pragmatic conditions that constrain the part–whole and the agent–beneficiary alternations in BP, we now examine the corresponding facts of EP.

3.2. Data from European Portuguese

In EP, the pattern [DP1 V [DP2's DP3]] also alternates with [DP2 V DP3]] in the context of *cortar* and *quebrar*-type verbs:

(56) O João cortou o   cabelo.
     the João cut   the hair
     "João had his hair cut."

(57) O João partiu o   braço.[4]
     the João broke the arm
     "João broke his arm."

As in BP, there is empirical evidence to consider (56) and (57) two different kinds of verb alternations in EP: agent–beneficiary and part–whole respectively. In particular, (i) only adjuncts denoting control/volition are allowed in sentences with *cortar*-type verbs, the opposite being observed in sentences with *quebrar*-type verbs (see the BP examples in (29) and (30), which are grammatical in EP, too); (ii) *cortar*-type verbs do not allow for the causative–inchoative alternation, as opposed to *quebrar*-type ones (see the BP examples in (35) and (36); the only difference between BP and EP is the clitic position—proclitic in the former, enclitic in the latter).

However, the two alternations do not have exactly the same properties in EP and BP. Consider first, the part–whole alternation illustrated in (57).

As we have previously showed, in BP the part–whole alternation occurs with change-of-state verbs—that is, verbs that contain the structure [BECOME Y <STATE>] in their semantic representation—provided that these verbs accept an argument denoting a part–whole relation.

However, in EP, this alternation is more severely constrained. First, not all change-of-state verbs enter the alternation, even if they meet the part–whole argument condition:

(58) a. *As ideias do adolescente amadureceram.* (^{OK}BP/^{OK}EP)
the ideas of-the teenager ripened
"The teenager's ideas ripened."
b. *O adolescente amadureceu as ideias (com o tempo).* (^{OK}BP/*EP)
the teenager ripened the ideas (with the time)
"The teenager's ideas ripened (over time)."
(with the meaning that something ripened
the teenager's ideas)

This contrast leads us to the first restriction for EP: only basically causative verbs (Haspelmath 1993) allow the part–whole alternation; basically inchoative verbs preclude it. This accounts for the contrast between (57) and (58a) in that variety.

The restriction on the verb class in nonetheless insufficient. In fact, the alternation is even more restricted in EP: sentences in (59) and (60) below, which are possible in BP, are ungrammatical in EP, in spite of involving basically causative verbs:

(59) *A árvore quebrou o galho.* (BP) / *A árvore partiu o ramo.* (EP)
the tree broke the branch / the tree broke the branch
"The branch of the tree broke."

(60) *O relógio estragou o ponteiro.* (^{OK}BP/*EP)
the clock ruined the hand
"The hand of the clock (was) ruined."

In section 3.1.1, we accounted for the BP data by saying that this language is less restrictive than others with respect to the relation between the (raised) possessor and the possessed element. As we have shown, not only the body–part relation but also other part–whole relations—e.g., between an object and a piece of it—are available for the BP part–whole alternation, which accounts for the grammaticality of (59) and (60). Like other languages, EP is more restrictive than BP in that relations between objects and their parts do not license the part–whole alternation. This fact explains not only the ungrammaticality of (59) and (60), but also the contrast between (61) and (62) in EP ((61) has both the relevant unintentional reading, and an intentional one, too):

(61) *O João queimou a mão.* (^{OK}BP/ ^{OK}EP)
the João burned the hand
"João burnt his hand./João had his hand burnt."

(62) *O carro queimou o motor.* (^{OK}BP/*EP)
the car burned the engine
"The car engine caught fire."

Thus, in EP the part–whole alternation is accepted only if a body-part relation is involved; in BP, all part–whole relations (including the body-part one) are possible. It is worth noting, however, that the body-part relation must be understood in a broad sense in the two varieties. In fact, (63b) below is possible both in EP and in BP with the required interpretation if

João was wearing the coat when the wind ripped it, as if the coat was part of him—this is close to the concept of inalienable possession underlying the body-part relation. Otherwise, an agentive reading of the subject obtains (in which case João need not be wearing the coat), and the causative PP is excluded.

(63) a. O   vento   rasgou   o   casaco   do   João.
         the wind   ripped   the   coat   of-the João
         "The wind ripped João's coat."
    b. O   João   rasgou   o   casaco   (com   o   vento).
         the João   ripped   the coat   (with the wind)
         "João had his coat ripped by the wind."

If the possessor and the possessed element in the complex object do not establish the required (part–whole or body-part) relationship, the part–whole alternation is forbidden, as expected. Thus, (64) below is ungrammatical in both varieties with the relevant reading (the one in which João had his carpet burned—a case of the part–whole alternation), because the carpet can never be viewed as part of João. This contrasts with (63b), in which the coat could somehow be a part of João, as mentioned. Therefore, (64) is interpretable only under an agentive reading of the subject.

(64) *O   João   queimou   o   tapete   (com   um   cigarro).
        the João   burned   the   carpet (with a   cigarette)

The fact that the part–whole alternation is restricted to the context of body-part relations in EP is also responsible for the impossibility of inanimate subjects in this variety. On the contrary, BP accepts that kind of subjects, as long as a part–whole relation holds. Compare (63b), grammatical in both varieties, with (65b), grammatical only in BP:

(65) a. O   vento   rasgou   as   mangas   do   casaco.
         the wind   ripped   the   sleeves of-the coat
         "The wind ripped the sleeves of the coat."
    b. O   casaco rasgou   as   mangas   com   o   vento.   (*EP/^{OK}BP)
         the coat   ripped   the   sleeves with the wind
         "The wind ripped the sleeves of the coat."

To sum up, EP displays the part–whole alternation, but this is constrained by the subtype of change-of-state verbs involved (only basically causative verbs), the relationship between possessor and possessed element (only body-part or a kind of body-part relationship), and consequently the semantic features of the possessor (only animate possessors).[5]

As for the agent–beneficiary alternation in (66) below, there is some fluctuation in the grammaticality judgments of EP speakers. Thus, although (66b) is unanimously accepted with the required interpretation (João asked someone/the hairdresser to do something in his place), (66c) is more problematic, and some speakers even reject it in the relevant interpretation:

(66) a.   O   cabeleireiro   cortou   o   cabelo   do   João.
          the hairdresser cut   the   hair   of-the João
          "The hairdresser cut João's hair."
    b.   O   João   cortou   o   cabelo.
          the João   cut   the   hair
          "John had his hair cut."
    c. ?/*O   João   cortou   o   cabelo   com   o   cabeleireiro.
          the João   cut   the   hair   with the hairdresser
          "John had his hair cut by the hairdresser."

For some EP speakers, the PP in (66c), as well as the PPs in (37) to (39) above, have a comitative reading: the DP subject and the DP inside the PP are a kind of discontinuous agent, and the first does not necessarily denote the possessor of the direct object.

Speakers who accept the agent–beneficiary alternation consider that this possibility is strongly constrained by pragmatic conditions, something we have already noticed for BP. Thus, (38) and (39) are more easily accepted than (37) with the interpretation underlying the agent–beneficiary alternation because we know that teeth are extracted by dentists and nose surgery is performed by doctors. So, knowledge of the world leads to the inference that the action is performed by the entity denoted by the DP inside the PP.

It is worth noting that in EP the agent–beneficiary alternation is widely accepted if the PP is not lexically present. In this case, the sentences are potentially ambiguous: the subject DP may be interpreted as the agent (no alternation being at stake) or the beneficiary (thus illustrating the agent–beneficiary alternation). Again, knowledge of the world may facilitate one of the readings: for instance, in (67) and (68) the subject may correspond either to the agent or to the beneficiary (in the latter case, the agent remains implicit), but in (69) it is preferably interpreted as the beneficiary, because it is hard for people to operate on their own nose.

(67) *A   Maria   lavou   o   carro.*
     the Maria   washed   the   car
     "Maria washed her car." / "Maria had her car washed."

(68) *O   João   arrancou   o   dente.*
     the João   extracted   the   tooth
     "João extracted his tooth." / "João had his tooth extracted."

(69) *O João operou o nariz.*
     the João operated-on the nose
     "João operated on his nose." / "João had his nose operated on."

When allowed, the agent–beneficiary alternation in EP does not hold with internally caused verbs, the same being true for BP (see example (46), repeated in (70); in (70b), the PP only has a comitative reading):

(70) a. *A   cantora   cantou   a   música   do   Jobim.*
        the   singer   sang   the   music   of-the   Jobim
        "The singer sang Jobim's song."
     b. **O   Jobim   cantou   a   música   (com   a   cantora).*
        the   Jobim   sang   the   music   (with   the   singer)

In sum, the agent–beneficiary alternation is less productive in EP than in BP. First, some EP speakers reject it; second, those who accept it still do it only under severely constrained pragmatic conditions.

4. Final considerations

In this chapter, we discussed the properties of a few verb classes and argument alternations in BP and EP. In order to do this, we adopted the predicate decomposition approach, which seems to be adequate for the analysis of two specific alternations found in Portuguese that have received little attention in the literature: the part–whole and the agent–beneficiary alternations. We tried to show that the predicate decomposition approach explains not only the main properties of these alternations, but also the differences between BP and EP: the alternations are present in both varieties of Portuguese, but they are more productive in BP than in EP. In particular, in BP the part–whole alternation occurs with change-of-state verbs provided that they select for an object denoting a part–whole relation, while in EP only change-of-state verbs that are basically causative enter the alternation; in addition, EP only accepts this alternation if a body-part relation is involved, which accounts for the fact that the possessor must be animate. As for the agent–beneficiary alternation, the data show that it is constrained by lexical and pragmatic factors in both varieties of Portuguese: on the one hand, only externally caused verbs enter the construction; on the other hand, it is allowed only if the VP refers to an action that one usually asks someone else (an expert) to do for him. This alternation is much more accepted among BP speakers; in EP, speakers prefer to omit the PP containing the agentive DP, thus avoiding the comitative reading of this PP.

In closing the chapter, we would like to briefly mention some of the research carried out in lexical semantics for BP and EP. Besides the studies already referred, we can point out some other work on the interface between lexical semantics and syntax which investigated the relation between semantic properties and argument realization.

For BP, Whitaker-Franchi (1989) offers a seminal analysis for the causative–inchoative alternation, based on Jackendoff's proposal. Souza (1999) also deals with the causative alternation in BP through a comparison between Hale and Keiser's lexical syntactic approach and Pustejovsky's generative lexical approach. Camacho (2003) aims at providing formal, semantic and typological evidence in order to postulate a distinction between middle and reflexive–reciprocal constructions, the causative–inchoative alternation being included in the middle construction. Finally, it is worth mentioning Ribeiro (2010), who investigates the distribution of the clitic *se* in the causative alternation in BP.

For EP, the causative–inchoative alternation is also the focus of several works, both from a syntactic and a (lexical) semantic viewpoint. Eliseu (1984) focuses on the syntax of Portuguese unaccusative verbs, and analyzes that alternation in two constructions: AVB/BV pairs and constructions with unaccusative (ergative) *se*. This study was developed within the Government and Binding Theory and tests the unaccusativity hypothesis. More recently, the causative–inchoative alternation has been described in Matos (1999), in a wider work on causative constructions in Portuguese, and analyzed in accordance to Levin and Rappaport Hovav's work. Mendes (2004) deals with the causative–inchoative alternation, in particular with psychological verbs. See also Duarte (2013) for a general description of this alternation in EP.

Obviously, the list of authors dealing with this phenomenon in BP and EP does not end with the references above. In any case, as far as we know, the two kinds of alternations we discussed in this work have not been explored for EP previously.

NOTES

1   The authors thank Luana Amaral for helpful comments, the EP speakers who helped us with their judgments, and the editor Sérgio Menuzzi for the detailed revision and very helpful suggestions. The work was supported by CNPq and FAPEMIG (Márcia Cançado), and Centro de Linguística da Universidade de Lisboa - PEst-OE/LIN/UI0214/2013 (Anabela Gonçalves).

2   Actually, the possessor is a non-canonical subject in this construction. This is known as the "subject topics phenomenon", which consists of the movement of a genitive into subject position, and is considered as a subtype of topicalization by many authors.

3   There is another type of verb that accepts this alternation (Levin 1993): *The girl hit her head in the door*. This sentence is also grammatical in Portuguese, although *hit* is not a change-of-state verb. Therefore, the conclusion is that if the verb belongs to a change-of-state class, it will accept the part–whole alternation, although there are other classes that accept it too. However, the fine-grained distinction— the verb accepting a part–whole object—still holds for the alternation with these other verb classes.

4   In this context, EP uses the verb *partir* with the same meaning as *quebrar*.
5   The fact that BP is less restrictive than EP with respect to the part–whole alternation may be related to the possibility of subject topics in that variety, a phenomenon that is not available in EP. In this case, we should emphasize that raising the possessor to the subject position is a generalized strategy in BP, considering possession in a broad sense (a part–whole relation). In EP, only human possessors involved in body-part relationships (a kind of inalienable possession) can surface as the subject of a possessor-raised sentence.

REFERENCES

Camacho, R. (2003). Em defesa da categoria de voz média no português. *DELTA*, 19 (1), pp. 91–122.

Cançado, M. (2010). Verbal alternations in Brazilian Portuguese: a lexical semantic approach. *Studies in Hispanic and Lusophone Linguistics*, 3 (1), pp. 77–111.

Cançado, M. and C. Franchi (1999). Exceptional binding with psych verbs? *Linguistic Inquiry*, 30 (1), pp. 133–143.

Cançado, M., L. Godoy, and L. Amaral (2013). *Catálogo de verbos do português brasileiro: classificação verbal segundo a decomposição de predicados* (Vol. I – Verbos de mudança). Belo Horizonte: Editora UFMG.

Cançado, M. and E. Negrão (2010). Two possessor raising constructions in Brazilian Portuguese. *VIII Workshop on Formal Linguistics / USP*.

Dowty, D. (1991). Thematic proto-roles and argument selection. *Language*, 67 (3), pp. 547–619.

Duarte, I. (2013). Construções ativas, passivas, incoativas e médias. In E. Raposo, M. F. Bacelar, M. A. Mota, L. Segura, and A. Mendes (eds.), *Gramática do Português*. Lisbon: Fundação Calouste Gulbenkian, pp. 429–458.

Eliseu, A. (1984). *Verbos Ergativos do Português: Descrição e Análise*. Masters dissertation, Universidade de Lisboa.

Fillmore, C. (1970). The grammar of hitting and breaking. In R. Jacobs and P. Rosenbaum, *Readings in English Transformational Grammar*. Waltham, MA: Ginn, pp. 120–133.

Grimshaw, J. (2005). *Words and Structure*. Stanford, CA: CSLI Publications.

Haspelmath, M. (1993). More on the typology of inchoative/causative verb alternations. In B. Comrie and M. Polinsky, *Causatives and transitivity*. Amsterdam: John Benjamins, pp. 87–120.

Jackendoff, R. (1990). *Semantic Structures*. Cambridge, MA: MIT Press.

Levin, B. (1993). *English Verb Classes and Alternations: A Preliminary Investigation*. Chicago: University of Chicago Press.

Levin, B. (2010). What is the best grain-size for defining verb classes? Conference on Word Classes: Nature, Typology, Computational Representations, Second TRIPLE International Conference, Università Roma Tre, Rome, March 24–26.

Levin, B. and M. Rappaport Hovav (1995). *Unaccusativity: At the Syntax Lexical Semantics Interface*. Cambridge, MA: MIT Press.

Levin, B. and M. Rappaport Hovav (2005). *Argument Realization*. Cambridge: Cambridge University Press.

Matos, G. (1999). Desvio e Conhecimento Linguístico em Construções Causativas do Português Europeu. In I. H. Faria (ed.), *Lindley Cintra. Homenagem ao Homem, ao Mestre e ao Cidadão*. Lisbon: Edições Cosmos, pp. 541–564.

Mendes, A. (2004). *Predicados Verbais Psicológicos do Português. Um Contributo para o Estudo da Polissemia Verbal*. Lisbon: Fundação Calouste Gulbenkian.

Pesetsky, D. (1995). *Zero Syntax*. Cambridge, MA: MIT Press.

Pinker, S. (1989). *Learnability and Cognition: The Acquisition of Argument Structure*. Cambridge, MA: MIT Press.

Ribeiro, P. (2010). A alternância causativa no português do Brasil: a distribuição do clítico se. Masters dissertation, Universidade Federal de Ciências da Saúde de Porto Alegre.

Souza, P. (1999). *A alternância causativa no português do Brasil: defaults num léxico gerativo*. Ph.D. dissertation, University of São Paulo.

Van Valin, R. (2005). *Exploring the Syntax-Semantics Interface*. Cambridge: Cambridge University Press.

Whitaker-Franchi, R. (1989). As construções ergativas: um estudo sintático e semântico. Masters dissertation, Unicamp.

Wunderlich, D. (2012). Lexical decomposition in grammar. In M. Werning, W. Hinzen, and E. Machery (eds.), *The Oxford Handbook of Compositionality*. Oxford: Oxford University Press, pp. 307–327.

21 Tense and Aspect: A Survey

RODOLFO ILARI, MARIA FÁTIMA OLIVEIRA, AND RENATO MIGUEL BASSO

In Portuguese, as in most Romance languages, the word that means tense also means time. For the first grammarians of Portuguese (e.g. Fernão de Oliveira, João de Barros, Contador de Argote, amongst others), speaking about tenses was the same as speaking about time, i.e. locating events in present, past or future time. In that framework, tenses were considered as divisions of moods, and the Indicative was said to have in all six "simple" tenses: (1) present –*canto* "I sing"; (2) imperfect—*cantava* "I used to sing/was singing"; (3) perfect—*cantei* "I sang"; (4) pluperfect—*cantara* "I had sung"; (5) future— *cantarei* "I will sing"; (6) conditional—*cantaria* "I would sing";[1] and four "compound" tenses: (7) compound preterit (henceforth PPC, from "pretérito perfeito composto")—*eu tenho cantado*, literally "I have sung"; (8) compound pluperfect—*eu tinha cantado*, "I had sung"; (9) compound future—*eu terei cantado*, "I will have sung"; (10) past conditional— *eu teria cantado* "I would have sung." This array of tenses is still described as the "paradigm" of verb inflection for the Indicative.

From a linguistic perspective, things are not that clear: both in European and Brazilian Portuguese (henceforth EP and BP), the simple pluperfect in (4) above is rarely used,[2] and neither is the simple future (6), as oncoming events are most usually referred to in the present or in a construction containing *ir* ("to go") plus a main verb.[3] But *ir* is only one among the auxiliary or semi-auxiliary verbs that enter compound forms with the infinitive, the past participle or the gerund of a main verb.[4] These compound forms are pervasive both in EP and BP, in spoken and written language, in environments where simple forms were mandatory in past centuries and still are in other Romance languages, and this raises a question about the boundaries of the verb paradigm. Assuming that the auxiliaries exert the function of the old morphemes, we could include in an "enlarged" paradigm of the Portuguese verb periphrastic forms like *estou* $_{EP}$ *a procurar/* $_{BP}$*procurando* "I am looking for/ searching," $_{EP,BP}$ *vou procurar* "I will look for/search," and $_{EP,BP}$ *acabo de encontrar* "I have just found," to quote just a few.[5]

The aim of this chapter is to account for time and aspect contents of Portuguese sentences, and so the first obvious thing to do is to look at tenses. But Portuguese grammar puts tenses to many other uses, as illustrated by the following examples:

(1) *Agora eu <u>era</u> o herói e meu cavalo só <u>falava</u> inglês.*
 "Now I <u>was</u> the hero, and my horse <u>spoke</u> English only."

(2) *Se eu fosse um peixinho e soubesse nadar, <u>levava</u> você para o fundo do mar.*
 "If I were a little fish and I could swim, <u>I would take</u> you to the bottom of the sea."

The Handbook of Portuguese Linguistics, First Edition. Edited by W. Leo Wetzels, João Costa, and Sergio Menuzzi.
© 2016 John Wiley & Sons, Inc. Published 2020 by John Wiley & Sons, Inc.

In (1), from a song by Brazilian composer Chico Buarque de Hollanda, a boy invites his girl playmate to imagine a fantasy world where he is a hero. Here, imperfects do not denote past events; rather, they introduce a fairytale world. Similarly, in the nursery rhyme (2), *fosse*, *soubesse* and *levava* inform that the events evoked in both sentences are unreal.[6] These modal usages of imperfect don't seem to have anything to do with time.[7]

It would be a mistake to ask simply what time or aspect information is given by tenses *per se*, because tenses are just one of the building blocks of the time and aspect information given by sentences. In the semantics of sentences, contents provided by tenses interact in many ways with many other factors, the most relevant ones being: (1) the lexical content of predicates, (2) auxiliaries and semi-auxiliaries, (3) adjuncts, and (4) the semantic nature (e.g. count vs. non-count) and quantificational properties of the arguments of the verb. In order to deal with these factors, we need to answer the following questions:

- What happens when such and such tense is associated with such and such predicate?
- What happens when a particular auxiliary is introduced in the sentence?
- What is the point of combining tenses and adjuncts?
- To what extent can the quantification of NPs modify the aspectual information given by the verb?

1. Time

In this section, only temporal usages will be considered.

1.1. Time and tenses

Time is usually represented as a line oriented from left to right, which corresponds to past-to-future orientation. In this line, the information given by tenses is represented by the relative location of different points or intervals. Although present, past and future are naturally associated to events located *at* speech time, *before* speech time or *after* speech time, as shown in Figure 21.1a–c, a third moment is required for the interpretation of pluperfects and conditionals used as futures relatively to a past time and for most uses of imperfect, as in Figure 21.1d–f ("ST" stands for "speech time" in the figure; and "ET" for "event time"). This third moment, called reference time, is identified by several means, including adjuncts (as in (3)), subordinate clauses and the chronological information given by the context (as in (4)). Contextual retrieval is crucial for the interpretation of these tenses, and gives them an anaphoric nature.

(3) *Na manhã do dia 25 de agosto, os jornais noticiaram que o presidente tinha-se suicidado às 23 horas da véspera.*
    "In the morning of August 25, the newspapers broadcast that the president had committed suicide at 11 p.m. the night before."

(4) *Maria entrou no quarto. O gato dormia no sofá. Tinham deixado um envelope sobre a mesa, onde encontraria algum dinheiro.*
    "Mary entered the room. The cat was sleeping on the couch. Somebody had left on the table an envelope in which she would find some cash."

The "Reichenbach diagrams" of Figure 21.1 show the time relations just described:[8]

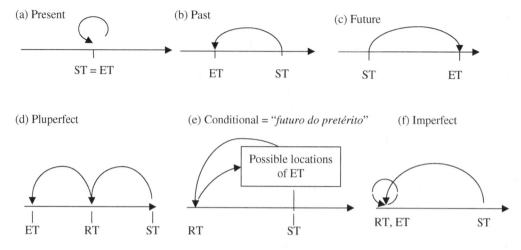

Figure 21.1   "Reichenbach diagrams" showing time relations.

1.2. *Time adjuncts*

Portuguese, as most natural languages, has a large variety of time adjuncts: some of them locate events on the time line, others measure durations and still others refer to repetitions (quantifications over times or events) occurring within an interval. Adjuncts locating events in time can identify either an ET or RT (for instance, in (3), "in the morning of August 25" is the ET of "*noticiaram*" and the RT of "*tinha-se suicidado*").

As time adjuncts locate events in the past, present or future, much like tenses do, one could ask which adjuncts can co-occur with which tenses: mismatches as the one illustrated in (6) below should be pervasive if any adjunct could occur with any tense. This is probably avoided by some general restriction stating, for instance, that ET, as expressed by adjuncts, should be temporally aligned to time as expressed by verbal tense—an adjunct denoting a past ET, for example, would not be temporally aligned to present tense or future tense, resulting in the mismatch shown in (6) (cf. Hornstein 1993).

(5) *Ontem João correu/corria.*
   "Yesterday John ran/was running."

(6) **Ontem João corre/vai correr/correrá.*
   "Yesterday John runs/is going to run/will run."

Nevertheless, some mismatches do occur, as in (7) and (8) below, yielding the constructions known respectively as "*presente histórico*" (historical present) and "*presente futuro*" (i.e., present tense talking about future events). In these cases, language takes advantage of a mismatch to yield new meaning effects.[9]

(7) *Em 1808, o rei de Portugal muda-se com a corte para o Brasil.*
   "In 1808, the king of Portugal moves with his court to Brazil."

(8) (a) _{EP/BP} *Viajo amanhã para Lisboa.*
"I am leaving tomorrow for Lisbon."

   (b) _{BP/*EP} *Estou viajando amanhã para Lisboa.*
"I am leaving tomorrow for Lisbon."

1.3. Time auxiliaries

While the present participle is no longer productive in Portuguese,[10]an infinitive, a gerund or a past participle can be derived from any verbal stem. Although these forms are exceptional as main verbs of independent sentences,[11] they are important because of the compound tenses they produce in association with (semi-) auxiliaries *estar, ter, haver,* [12] *ir, acabar de,*[13] *ficar,* etc., as exemplified in (9)–(11):

(9) *Quando me aposentei, (já) tinha/havia viajado muito.*
"When I retired, I had (already) traveled a lot."

(10) *Quando me aposentar, vou viajar muito.*
"When I retire, I will travel a lot."

(11) *Acabo de ler o relatório.*
"I have just finished reading the report."

Ter, ir and *acabar de* are *time* operators in sentences like (9)–(11) because they trigger the following calculus:

(a) Look for the *event* time that would apply to the tense *of the auxiliary;*
(b) Consider it as the *reference time* for the compound tense (auxiliary + main verb);
(c) Place the ET of the compound tense:
   (i) earlier than RT for "*ter, haver* + past participle";
   (ii) after RT for "*ir* + infinitive";
   (iii) in a previous and recent time vis-à-vis the RT for "*acabar de* + infinitive."

For instance, in (9) above:

- by (a) the ET for imperfect *tinha* ("had", imperfect), taken in isolation, would be "earlier than ST";
- by (b) the compound tense will have a RT earlier than ST (RT is the event of the speaker's retiring);
- by (c.i) the ET of the compound verb will be earlier than RT, that is, the speaker's travels happen before his/her retirement.

Notice that this calculus doesn't apply to Portuguese PPC (see Section 2.2.3 below).

2. Aspect

"Aspect" as a general term covers a set of related facts, rather than a single well delimited phenomenon. For this reason, instead of starting this section by a strict definition, we comment on two intuitions usually found in its treatments: (a) aspect is a "way of looking into" predicates; (b) aspect operates *inside* predicate structure.

In order to illustrate the first perspective we refer to a well-known fact: Portuguese has two copular verbs that occur in the same environments but have different meanings. This is shown in (12)–(14):

(12) $_{BP}$*Você é bobo/*$_{EP}$*Tu és parvo.*
       "You are foolish."

(13) $_{BP}$*Você está bobo hoje/*$_{EP}$*Tu estás parvo hoje.*
       "You are foolish today."

(14) $_{EP}$*Você está sendo bobo/*$_{EP}$*Tu estás a ser parvo.*
       "*You are being foolish.*"

As most sentences used for calling names, (12) represents stupidity as an individual level property of the hearer; in (13), stupidity is a stage level property; (14) refers to a particular occurrence of stupidity (again a stage level property)—the addressee is said to be acting foolishly *on the particular occasion* reported in (14). In these sentences, *ser, estar* and *estar sendo* encode alternative ways of looking at the same property, and this is essentially what aspect does. Taking advantage from the etymology of the word *aspect* itself, which contains the same root as Latin *spectare* "look at," and English *perspective* (Castilho 1968: 14, 2000: 17), we can define aspect as the set of perspectives that can be applied to a predicate.

As for the point of view in (b) above, we may assume that "perspectivizing a predicate" is an operation affecting its internal time structure. If we adopt this view, we must conclude that the research on aspect for a particular language is committed to establishing a complete inventory, for that language, of the ways of operating on the internal time structure of predicates.

Notice that although some notion of time is needed to understand the semantics of aspect (time intervenes indirectly in the distinction between stage level and individual level predicates) this notion is not the same as we used in 1.1. to "locate events in time." Location of events in time is always relative to ST or to some RT provided by context. No such dependency holds for aspect. This is why some authors say that linguistic time is *deictic* (or *anaphoric*) while aspect is not (see Castilho 2010: 418).

2.1. Aspect vs. aspectual calculus: verbs and action classes

We have assumed that aspect is a property of sentences, worked out through a compositional calculus involving several factors. The present section will describe some of these factors and how they interact in the aspectual calculus.

Verbs are a crucial ingredient of aspectual calculus, due to the information given by their morphology (see 2.3.4), and to the lexical information they carry. In order to deal with the latter, it has been usual since Vendler (1967)[14] to sort verbs into "action classes." According to Oliveira (2006), five such classes are needed for Portuguese, namely *processes, culminating processes, culminations, points* and *states*. These classes are based on linguistic criteria, such as compatibility with specific kinds of adjuncts and entailment patterns, and are themselves the result of combining five underlying features: ±dynamic, ±telic, ±dura-tive, ±capable of bringing about a new state, ±homogeneous. For ease of exposition, we give the scheme by means of which Oliveira (2006) associates classes to the underlying aspectual features in Table 21.1; then, we comment a few examples of each class, pointing to their distinctive properties.

Table 21.1   Temporal schemata for Portuguese predicates.

	Dynamic	*Telic*	*Durative*	*Resulting state*	*Homo-geneous*
States	–	–	–	–	+
Processes	+	–	+	–	+
Culminating Processes	+	+	+	+	–
Culminations	+	+	–	+	–
Points	–	(–)	–	–	–

(i)   As an example of a *state*, consider the following sentence:

   (15)   *Lisboa <u>é a capital de Portugal</u>.*
      "Lisbon is the capital of Portugal."

   The property of being the capital of a country can hold for centuries, and is coded linguistically as lasting indefinitely (that's why *ser* rather than *estar* was used as the copula in (15)). No result is expected or triggered, and any subpart of Lisbon's being the capital is still a part of Lisbon's being the capital (this is "homogeneity"). Questions that can be asked about (15) are *"Desde quando?"* *"Há quanto tempo?"* ("Since when…?", "For how long?"); a pointless question would be *"*Em quanto tempo?"* ("How long did it take to…?").

(ii)   A good example of a *process* is *nadar* "to swim," as in (16):

   (16)   *A Maria nadou.*
      "Mary swam/has swum."

   Swimming is a time-consuming activity, and no result is coded by the verb *nadar* as a part of this activity (atelicity); moreover, each subpart of a swimming activity is still swimming (homogeneity). Good questions to be asked for (16) are about duration, such as *"Por quanto tempo?"* ("For how long?"); pointless questions are, for instance, the ones about the amount of time required for accomplishing the event, for example *"*Em quanto tempo ela nadou?"* ("*In how much time did she swim?").

(iii)   *Culminating processes* can be illustrated by (17):

   (17)   *A Maria <u>cozinhou o bolo</u>.*
      "Mary baked/has baked the cake."

   Baking a cake involves dynamism, takes some time, and yields a result (telicity) after a "preparatory" stage; preparation and result are different in nature, which precludes homogeneity. Questions to be asked about Mary's baking the cake are *"Em quanto tempo?"* or *"Quanto tempo levou para…?"* (literally, "In how much time?", "How long did it take for…?").

(iv)   The predicates in (18) exemplify *culminations*:

   (18)   PE *ganhar*/PB *tirar a sorte grande na loteria* ("to win the big prize in the lottery")
      PE *encontrar*/PB *achar as chaves* ("to find the keys")
      Cruzar a linha de chegada ("to cross the finish line")

   Winning the lottery takes just a moment, and brings about a new state—the winner becomes rich(er). For winning, some conditions must be fulfilled (for instance buying the right ticket), but they are not coded as a part of the meaning of *tirar/ganhar a sorte grande*; in other words, we talk about winning independently from its preparation, and this distinguishes culminations from culminating processes. Good questions about such processes aim at identifying the moment the culmination happened, like *"Quando (exatamente)?"* ("When (exactly)?"); questions about the duration of the process, or of the resulting state would be senseless; e.g. *"Por quanto tempo?"* ("For how long?").

(v)   Finally, Oliveira (2006) calls *points* those momentary events that don't bring about a new state, such as the one described in (19).

(19)   *A Maria espirrou.*
       "Mary sneezed."

The questions to be asked about points are similar to the ones about culminations, with the exception of those relating to the result of the event—since there are no results for "points."

2.2. *Further ingredients of the aspectual calculus*

2.2.1. *Object NPs*

The information given by the root of the verb can change when the predicate contains other constituents, and indeed, in sentences (20a)–(20d) below the culminating verb *vender*, "to sell," is turned into an atelic predicate by associating with *vinho, azeite/casas* ("wine, oil, houses"), or with semi-auxiliary *tentar*, "to try." (In these examples, we have included adjuncts as an evidence for classifying the predicates into the action classes described in 2.2.).

(20)   a.   *O João *vendeu uma casa* $_{BP}$ *por/* $_{EP}$ *durante cinco anos.*
             "João sold a house for five years."
        b.   *O João vendeu uma casa em dois meses.*
             "João sold a house in two months."
        c.   *O João vendeu vinho/azeite/casas* $_{BP}$ *por/* $_{EP}$ *durante cinco anos.*
             "João sold wine/oil/houses for five years."
        d.   *O João tentou vender sua casa durante cinco anos.*
             "João sold houses/tried to sell his house for five years."

Many of the phenomena occurring in this area are found cross-linguistically, and were mapped during the last decades (see, for example, Comrie 1976). As for nominal quantification, it is now well established that bare plurals and mass nouns in object position of telic verbs yield atelic predicates, while singular count nouns and determined plurals preserve the telic nature of the verb (Basso 2007, 2011; Santos 1996).

2.2.2. *Adjuncts*

Further action class shifts can be triggered by other sentential components, such as adjuncts/adverbials, auxiliaries, and tenses. For instance, a (non-culminating) process verb like *caminhar* ("to walk") yields a culminating process in *caminhar até à estação* ("to walk to the station"), as is confirmed in (21 a–d) by the (un)acceptability of the adjuncts *em/por quatro horas* ("in/for four hours"):

(21)   a.   *João caminhou por quatro horas.*
             "João walked for four hours."
        b.   **João caminhou em quatro horas.*
             "João walked in four hours."
        c.   **João caminhou* $_{BP}$ *até a/* $_{EP}$ *até à estação por quatro horas.*
             "João walked to/until the station for four hours."
        d.   *João caminhou até a/até à estação em quatro horas.*
             "João walked to/until the station in four hours."

In principle, not any adjunct is suitable for any action class, and one could expect—once again—that mismatches would be avoided. However, again this expectation is not fulfilled: Portuguese makes an extensive use of adjuncts that, in principle, would be in contrast with the action class of the verb, as a device to create new meanings without "inflating" the lexicon. This is seen, for instance, in (22)–(23):

(22) a. *A criança dormiu* $_{BP}$ *por/*$_{EP}$ *durante oito horas.*
           "The child slept eight hours."
      b. $_{BP}$ *A criança dormiu às oito horas.*
           Literally: "The child slept at eight."
           meaning "The child fell asleep at eight."

(23) *O João saiu por./.durante duas horas.*
       Literally: "John went out for two hours."

As *dormir* ("to sleep") is an atelic process, a natural question about *dormiu* would be "for how long?", and this question would get a well-behaved answer in (22a). The time location adjunct *às oito horas* ("at eight o' clock") would seem to be incompatible for this sort of predicate, but (22b) is a fully acceptable BP sentence[15] which focuses on the starting point of the process, instead of the process as a whole: *dormir* is then interpreted as its "inchoative" cognate, *adormecer* ("Fall asleep," cf. Italian *dormire* vs. *addormentarsi*). In (23), another "clashing" adjunct, *por duas horas* ("for two hours") measures the duration of the state that results from João's going out. Finally, consider one more example, (24) below:

(24) *A criança tossiu por meia hora/a noite toda.*
       "The child coughed for half an hour/all night long."

It could seem a transgression to apply a duration adjunct to a punctual verb like *tossir* ("to cough"); but this "transgression" yields the reading that the child coughed over and over during the night. This is not exceptional: point verbs, when they are associated with a duration adjunct, yield iterative readings.[16]

2.2.3. *Auxiliaries*

The PPC (again, *pretérito perfeito composto*, lit. "compound perfect past") and the meaning of *ser* and *estar* in copular sentences have long been identified as major semantic puzzles in Portuguese. Both are aspectual in nature.

(a) *Tenho dito, tenho feito*: The Portuguese PPC
As most Romance languages, Portuguese has a Latin-inherited simple past and a Romance-born compound past. Benveniste (1959) explained away this "redundancy" for French by associating the choice between *je chantai* vs. *j' ai chanté* to the relevance of the reported events at speech time: according to his explanation, French speakers employ the compound past for events with which they are still concerned and the simple past for unconcerning events. In Portuguese, this division of labor does not exist. All past events are referred to by means of the simple past, irrespective of their being recent or remote, and highly or poorly relevant at ST, so that a sentence like *"Perdi a carteira"* can be part of very different texts, such as (25) and (26):

(25) *Meu Deus! Perdi a carteira. E agora?*
       "Gosh! I've lost my wallet! What can I do now?"

(26) *Perdi a carteira pela primeira vez há quarenta anos.*
       "I lost my wallet for the first time forty years ago."

Moreover, and more important, the PPC conveys an idea of repetition, so that *tenho perdido a chave* (literally: "I have lost my key") never reports a single episode.[17] But this is just one of the vagaries of the PPC. (27)–(36) illustrate more conditions under which it is used:

(27) *Abra, rápido, o carteiro já tocou/*tem tocado a campainha três vezes.*
       "Go and open the door quickly, the mailman has already rung the doorbell three times."

(28) *O José visitou-nos/*Tem nos visitado ontem.*
       "José visited us yesterday."

(29) *O José viaja muito. Tem estado muito em Paris.*
       "José travels a lot. He has been (often) to Paris."

(30) *Desde que o pai adoeceu, o médico nos visitou/*tem-nos visitado 9 vezes ao todo.*
       "Since our father got sick, the doctor visited us nine times in all."

(31) *Desde que o pai adoeceu, o médico tem-nos visitado/nos visita três vezes por semana.*
       "After Dad got ill, the doctor has been visiting us three times a week / visits us three times a week."

(32) *Durante a última copa os torcedores *têm usado/usaram o metrô como transporte.*
       "During the last soccer cup, the fans have used / used the subway for transportation."

(33) *Muitos imigrantes têm vindo ultimamente do Haiti.*
       "Many immigrants have come lately from Haiti."

(34) *A Maria morreu/*tem morrido ontem.*
       "Maria died / has died yesterday."

(35) *Morremos/temos morrido de medo sempre que ouvimos as sirenes da polícia.*
       "We are / have been scared to death every time we hear the police sirens."

(36) *Muitas pessoas têm morrido todos os dias no trânsito de S. Paulo.*
       "Many people have died every day in São Paulo's traffic."

Examples (27) and (28) show that the PPC is not a "recent past"; (29) and (32) show that it refers to a period that is "still open" when the sentence is uttered (*têm vindo* is unacceptable in (32) precisely because the soccer cup is over). (34) and (35) are evidence that only events that can be repeated can be rendered by the PPC:[18] anyone can go several times through the experience of *morrer de medo* (lit. "to die of fear," meaning "to be scared to death"), not so for *morrer* ("to die"). (36), where the predicate is also *morrer*, is acceptable because the subject is plural (*many people*), allowing event repetition. (30) and (31) show that numerals are not allowed in PPC context. Our explanation for this phenomenon lies in the aspectual operation carried out by this tense: the PPC creates a process built on an undetermined number of repetitions (Oliveira and Leal 2012; Molsing 2010).[19] Nevertheless, (31) is acceptable and the reason is that the undetermined iteration is obtained by *por semana* ("a week") and not by *três vezes*, "three times."

To conclude our discussion of the Portuguese PPC, we insist on two of its consequences: (1) the PPC belongs to the paradigm of compound tenses morphologically but not semantically (the PPC is the only tense featuring *ter* that denotes repetition, its RT is a time span, not a moment, and it obligatorily includes speech time); (2) it is not equivalent to its Romance analogs.[20]

(b)   *Esta casa está alugada/esta casa é alugada/Aluga-se esta casa*: *ser*/*estar* + past participle
In addition to the constructions where they occur with adjectives, *ser* and *estar* co-occur also with past participles (*A ameaça está afastada, A confusão está formada, A casa é alugada* "The threat is removed, Havoc is established, The house is a rental house") and with gerunds (*A ameaça está sendo afastada, O calor está formando nuvens, Ainda estamos pagando a casa*, "The threat is being removed, The heat is forming clouds, We are still paying for the house").

Although it can be difficult to distinguish past participles from adjectives when they occur with *estar* (many present day adjectives are ancient past participles) there is a good aspectual reason for keeping apart the two constructions: when *estar* and a past participle are joined into a predicate, this predicate is often intended to describe the result of a past action. If so, *estar* + past participle conveys a twofold information: (1) a certain action was accomplished in the past, and (2) a state holds ever since. Indeed, (37)–(38) and (39)–(40) are equivalent ways of announcing the end of a car wash or the clearance from a mortgage:

(37) *Pronto, o carro está lavado.* ("Here you go, the car is washed/the car is clean.")

(38) *Finalmente, a casa está paga.* ("At last, the house is paid for.")

(39) *Pronto, lavei o carro.* (Literally "Here you go, I've washed the car.")

(40) *Finalmente, pagamos a casa.* ("At last, we've paid for the house.")

More research would be needed to establish how the different pieces of information (past action and resulting state) given by (37) and (38) depend on the auxiliary and the past participle, and whether they are parts of the core meaning of the construction, or some kind of implicature. For now, suffice it to acknowledge that in (37)–(38) *estar* is once again associated with a stage level property. The stage level vs. individual level distinction can be applied to past participles, as shown in (41)–(42), *estar* and *ser* apply to the same predicate ("alugar"):

(41)   *A casa que você achou bonita está alugada.*
        (Literally "The house you found nice *is* rented." Meaning "Someone is renting the house you've found nice.")

(42)   *A casa que você achou bonita é alugada*
        ("The house you found nice *is* rented." Meaning "The house you've found nice is a rental house/for renting."

Notice that, contrary to the opinion found in school grammars, it would be a mistake to interpret (42) as the passive voice of *Alugam a casa que você achou bonita.* (Ali 1966; Duarte and Oliveira 2010a, b). At least in Brazilian Portuguese, in order to express the passive of *alugar* in the present, one should use the progressive form: ??*A casa que você achou bonita é alugada pelo João* ("The house you found nice is rented by João"), but *A casa que você achou bonita está sendo alugada pelo João* ("The house you found nice is being rented by João").

2.2.4. Tenses

The application of tenses to predicates of different action classes yields different results for the acceptability and the interpretation of sentences. To illustrate this, consider the following example:

(43) *Meu avô foi português de origem.*
      "My grandfather was of Portuguese descent."

As having a Portuguese ancestry is a permanent property (therefore a state, according to 2.2.), the use of perfect *foi* triggers the implicature that the grandfather is dead at ST. No such implicature would be expected with predicates such as *foi até Macau* or *enriqueceu* ("went as far as Macau," "grew rich"), which denote a process and a culminating event, respectively.

The point of these examples is that tense and aspect interact in a complex way, and only a detailed analysis could account for them thoroughly.[21] Keeping in mind this fact as a warning against hasty generalizations, we claim that the two major aspectual alternatives coded by tenses in Portuguese are *semelfactivity vs. repetition* and *perfectivity vs. imperfectivity*.

Semelfactivity, habituality and repetition

We consider repetition as an important grammatical option[22] of Portuguese because some Portuguese tenses that had originally a semelfactive meaning have acquired during the last centuries an iterative or habitual one. We consider "semelfactive" events as the ones which happen only once, such as João's having lunch in a sentence like *João está almoçando (agora)* ("João is having lunch (now)"); iteratives, habituals, and repetitions are opposed to semelfactives because they involve more than one occurrence of an event. What we consider important to notice in this section is that some verbs (and some tenses) can have a semelfactive interpretation or an iterative/repetitive one depending on the sentential context.

Both a semelfactive and a repetitive meaning are available for some tenses (we say that these tenses are neutral for this option), as is the case for the simple past: that is why (44), uttered by the physician during a medical interview aimed at evaluating past habits of a senior female patient, can get answers as different as (45) and (46):

(44) *A senhora já fumou?*
      Literally "Did you already smoke?" Meaning either "Have you ever smoked?" or "Were you ever a smoker?"

(45) *Sim, já fumei e me embrulhou o estômago.*
      Literally "Yes, I have, and I felt sick."

(46) *Sim, fumei desde os 15 anos, até um ano atrás.*
      Literally "Yes, I've smoked from 15 years, until a year ago." Meaning "Yes, I started smoking when I was fifteen and I quit a year ago."

Although they are both grammatically acceptable, (44) and (45) do not form a felicitous dialogue in the context described above, because the doctor is asking for habits, and by uttering (45) the patient recalls an isolated experience; (44) and (46), on the other hand, would be a good dialogue under the same circumstances. As we can see, depending on the sentential context, the same verb and tense can be interpreted either as a semelfactive or as a repetition, which can then result in a coherent or in an incoherent conversation.

Only a habitual[23] reading is available for some other tenses, and this is the case for *toma* "takes" in (47):

(47) *João toma o trem para ir ao trabalho.*   (iterative/habitual)
      "João takes the train to go to work."

This verb describes a daily habit (it answers questions like *Como é a rotina matinal do João?* "What is João's morning routine?"), and this is no exception: semelfactive readings are very rare for the indicative present and imperfect in modern Portuguese,[24] as the expression of semelfactivity was taken over gradually in EP by the construction *estar a* + Infinitive, and in BP by the construction *estar* + Gerund:

(48) _{EP} *O João está a tomar o comboio para o trabalho.* (semelfactive)

(49) _{BP} *João está tomando o trem para o trabalho.* (semelfactive)
      "João is boarding the train to his working place."[25]

Perfectivity vs. imperfectivity
The main aspectual difference correlated to tenses, in Portuguese as well as in many other languages, is imperfective vs. perfective. Among the tenses of Indicative, present, imperfect and future are imperfective; perfect and most compound tenses are perfective; and the PPC has a special status.

As should be expected, the opposition "perfective vs. imperfective" is best illustrated by comparing sentences with "imperfect" and "perfect" past tense. Take for instance (50)–(53), where the imperfects are underlined and the perfects are double underlined.

(50) *Quando João <u>voltou</u> ao Rio, no lugar da antiga selaria <u>havia</u> uma lotérica.*
      "When John returned to Rio, in the place of the old saddler there was a Lotto retailer."

(51) *Enquanto a televisão <u>transmitia</u> as notícias, <u>faltou</u> a luz.*
      "While the TV broadcast the news, the light went off."

(52) *??Quando João <u>voltava</u> ao Rio, no lugar da antiga selaria <u>houve</u> uma lotérica.*
      "When John returned to Rio, in the place of the old saddler there was a Lotto retailer"

(53) *?Enquanto a televisão <u>transmitiu</u> o noticiário, <u>faltava</u> a luz.*
      "While the TV broadcast the news, the light went off."

While (50) and (51) are acceptable, (52) and (53), where the tenses were reversed, are awkward (or maybe they tell different stories), showing that there is more to tenses than time location. In (50), this extra meaning is that the saddler was there before and after John put his feet back in Rio, and in (51), that the news broadcasting extended before and after the electricity blackout. This is typically an aspectual difference, as the event is taken as a whole, i.e., perfectively, in *voltou* and *faltou a luz*, but is seen at an intermediate stage (i.e. imperfective aspect) in *havia* and *transmitia*.

In a more intuitive but equivalent account of what distinguishes perfective and imperfective aspect, it has been said that perfective "packages" events, while imperfective "unpackages" their internal temporal structure. For culminated processes, this means that imperfects will locate event time in their preparation, with no guarantee that the culmination will be attained. By (54) below, where a chronological link is established between João's going to school (imperfective) and the beginning of the rain (perfective), we know that the rain started while John was on his way to school, but we don't know what happened next: maybe he kept walking and arrived in school (which is the culmination of *ir para a escola* "go to school"), maybe he went back home. On the other hand, the only possible readings for (55) are (1) that John's leaving for school and the beginning of the rain were close in time, or (2) that it started raining and then he left for school. In both cases, the two events are viewed as "packaged."

(54) *João estava indo/ia para a escola, quando começou a chover.*
"João was going/went to school, when it started raining."

(55) *João foi para a escola quando começou a chover.*
"João went to school when it started raining."

As a last example of the "packaging" effect of perfective, consider (56) and (57):

(56) *Meu avô tinha três esposas.*
"My grandfather had (imperfect) three wives."

(57) *Meu avô teve três esposas.*
"My grandfather had (perfect) three wives."

While (57) says that grandpa had three wives in all (maybe he married three times in his lifetime), the reading expected for (56) is that at a certain moment of his life (to be retrieved anaphorically from the context) he was married simultaneously to three different wives.[26]

3. Epilogue

Time and aspect entered Portuguese grammarians' agenda at different moments: while time was already a topic of the first Portuguese grammars (and their Latin models), aspect had to wait until the late sixties of the twentieth century to be recognized as an independent research area in Portuguese linguistics; during the last five decades, intensive research has been going on in this area, both in Portugal and in Brazil. Many problems were detected and different accounts were argued for.

In this chapter, we have claimed that, in order to work out the information that sentences give about time and aspect, language users perform a calculus that starts from the action properties of verbs/predicates and goes on by taking into account modifications due to the nature and quantification of argument NPs, adjuncts, auxiliaries and tenses. We have focused on time and aspect phenomena that can be considered basic, or typical, for Portuguese, giving them an informal description. Having worked both on EP and BP, we can say that the two main varieties of Portuguese are very close insofar as the expression of time and aspect is concerned, but we have also noticed a few differences that could signal diverging drifts.[27]We hope this chapter will help our readers to map the area and the technical literature written on it during the last decades.

NOTES

1   We call conditional the tense containing the morpheme *–ria*. This tense has in fact two main roles: (1) talking about facts that depend on a condition (*Eu mudaria para Londres se fosse rico*, "I would move to London if I were rich"), and (2) locating facts in a time viewed as future relative to some moment in the past (*Ele disse ontem que iria para Londres hoje*, "He said yesterday he would leave for London today").
2   This usage is found in EP newspapers and in EP/BP literature.
3   Having lost its time value, the future tense survives nevertheless in modal usages. For BP, see Josane Oliveira (2011), Silva (2011).

4 By "gerund" we mean all the forms derived from a verbal stem by adding the ending *–ndo*, as in *cantando* ("singing"), *correndo* ("running"), *sorrindo* ("smiling"). These forms occur in constructions like *Ele ganha a vida cantando, Vi um menino correndo, A menina estava sorrindo* ("He makes a living singing", "I saw a boy running", "The girl was smiling").

5 For different treatments of auxiliaries in EP and BP, see Oliveira, Cunha, and Gonçalves (2004) for EP; Lobato (1973), Perini (2002: 155–163) and Ilari and Basso (2014: 77–86) for BP.

6 This interpretation of the imperfect is quite common in EP (in sentences such as *Eu agora tomava um cafezinho*, "I'd like to have a coffee now").

7 However, recent works on the semantics of tenses in conditional sentences do claim that tenses preserve their time values in this context. See, for example, Kaufmann (2005) for English.

8 In diagrams (a–f), ST, RT and ET stand for "speech time," "reference time," and "event time." These diagrams are based on Reichenbach (1947) but some of the intuitions on which they rely were already in Barbosa (1802).

9 For a different account of historical present, see Givón (1993: 167).

10 *Amante* ("lover"), *temente* ("afraid of") and $_{BP}$ *concluinte* ("student in the last stage of a degree") are connected historically to *amar* ("to love"), *temer* ("to fear") and *concluir* ("to conclude, to finish"), but are no longer recognized as forms of these verbs. $_{BP}$ *Ficante* (as in *Ele não é meu namorado, é só meu ficante*, "He is not my boyfriend, he is just my casual date") is obviously a noun, and newly created verbs, like *deletar* (cf. English *to delete*) do not take *–nte* endings.

11 *Andando!* Literally, "Marching!" can be used as an imperative.

12 The view found in school grammars that *ter* and *haver* can be used indifferently in compound tenses is incorrect, as compound tenses like *hei feito, haverei feito* and *haveria feito* are awkward both in EP and BP.

13 *Acabar* de can be used as an auxiliary in EP either with a temporal or an aspectual meaning. It is temporal with predicates lacking an internal duration (*Ele acaba de chegar* means "He has just arrived"), and aspectual with durative predicates (*Ele acabou de ler o livro* means "He *has finished* reading the book"). In BP, two different auxiliaries, *acabar* and *terminar* account for these two functions (Dascal, 1982).

14 Most authors working on Portuguese aspect during the last decades of the past century were strongly influenced by Vendler's ideas and some of them tried to adapt to Portuguese the classification he had proposed for English. Although Vendler's ideas remain influential, a tendency can be observed more recently to look for "Portuguese aspectual classifications" and for phenomena that "subvert" Vendler's classifications or introduce new subcategories (e.g. Santos, 1996; Cunha, 2013; Basso, 2007).

15 *Adormecer* is mandatory in EP for this reading.

16 A similar effect of repetition is obtained by associating point predicates with the progressive periphrasis, *estar* + gerund in BP) and *estar* + *a* + infinitive in EP: *A Mariazinha está* $_{BP}$ *espirrando/* $_{EP}$ *a espirrar* describes a repetition of sneezings.

17 EP has sentences like *Quando a Ana voltar da Itália, já a Rita tem terminado a tese/tem deixado Lisboa* ("When Ana returns(future) from Italy, Rita has already finished writing her thesis/has already left from Lisbon"), where the PPC has a strictly temporal reading. BP lacks this usage.

18 Nevertheless, when combined with a state predicate, PPC conveys the information that this state started in the past and is still true at ST.

19 This explanation takes advantage of recent treatments of plural and event quantification and overrides older accounts based on the nature of what used to be called "plurality of events." During the first half of the twentieth century, a long-lasting polemic on this subject opposed the partisans of two competing accounts, based respectively on repetition (Viana 1903), and duration (Boléo 1937). Ilari (2000) argued the PPC and duration adjuncts exert a similar role, insofar as their association with non stative predicates triggers a repetition reading.

20 The auxiliary of these constructions is *ter*, not *haver*, another point where Portuguese contrasts with its Romance siblings. It is worth observing that in this respect the PPC differs from the compound plus-*que*-perfect, which can be built with *haver* in formal register.

21 An attempt at such an analysis is found in Oliveira (2013).

22 Some researchers (e.g. Castilho, 1968 and Travaglia, 1981), noticed pairs of verbs such as *saltar/ saltitar, beber/bebericar*, where the longer form involves repetition of the action described by the

shorter one (*saltar* and *saltitar* refer respectively to a single "jump" and to a sequence of small jumps; *bebericar*, as opposed to *beber* involves the idea of a repetition of small sips), and argued for an aspectual explanation of this fact. We consider this a lexical phenomenon.

23   We use "repetition" and "habit" as synonyms in this chapter.

24   For eventive verbs in the indicative present, a semelfactive reading occurs only in some very specific kinds of texts, such as performatives (*Prometo vir* ("I promise to come")), or running commentaries in sport matches.

25   As far as EP is concerned, there is a clear distinction between habitual (46) and semelfactive (47); in BP, (48), usually semelfactive, could as well describe a recently acquired or temporary habit, cf. *Esse homem está indo de trem para o trabalho por causa das obras da rodovia* ("This man is going by train to work, because or the works in the highway").

26   For more on perfective and imperfective, see Ilari and Basso (2014).

27   For instance, BP makes a larger use of "clashing" adjuncts than EP, and several differences were noticed in the meaning of (semi-)auxiliaries.

REFERENCES

Barbosa, J. S. (1802). *Grammatica Philosophica*. Lisbon: Academia Real das Sciencias.

Basso, R. M. (2007). Telicidade e detelicização: semântica e pragmática do domínio tempo-aspectual. Masters dissertation, Campinas. http://www.bibliotecadigital.unicamp.br/, accessed November 4, 2015.

Basso, R. M. (2011). Uma proposta para a semântica dos adjuntos "em X tempo" e "por X tempo." *Alfa*, 55 (1), pp. 113–134.

Benveniste, É. (1959). Les relations de temps dans le verbe français. In *Problèmes de Linguistique Générale*. Paris: Gallimard, pp. 238–250.

Boléo, M. de P. (1937). *O pretérito e o perfeito em Português, em confronto com as outras línguas românicas*. Coimbra: Imprensa da Universidade.

Castilho, A. T. (1968). *Introdução ao Estudo do Aspecto Verbal na Língua Portuguesa*. Marília: Faculdade de Filosofia, Ciência e Letras de Marília.

Castilho, A. T. (2000). Problemas do aspecto no Português falado no Brasil. In E. Gärtner, C. Hundt, and A. Schönberger (eds.), *Estudos de Gramática Portuguesa, III*. Frankfurt am Main: TFM, pp. 17–46.

Castilho, A. T. (2010). *Nova Gramática do Português Brasileiro*. São Paulo: Contexto.

Comrie, B. (1976). *Aspect*. Cambridge: Cambridge University Press.

Cunha, L. F. (2013). Aspecto. In E. B. P. Raposo, M. F. Bacelar do Nascimento, M. A. Coelho da Mota, L. Segura, and A. Mendes (eds.), *Gramática do Português*. Lisbon: Fundação Calouste Gulbenkian, pp. 585–624.

Dascal, M. (1982). Comecemos a acabar de começar? Prolegômenos para uma análise semântica de algumas perífrases verbais indicadoras de fase, em português. *Cadernos de Estudos Linguísticos*, 3, pp. 123–186.

Duarte, I. and F. Oliveira (2010a). Particípios resultativos. In A. Brito, F. Silva, I. Veloso, and A. Fiéis (eds.), *Textos selecionados do XXV Encontro da APL*, pp. 397–408.

Duarte, I. and F. Oliveira (2010b). Sobre particípios e construções resultativas em português. In P. Cano Lopez and S. Cortiñas (eds.), *Actas do XLIX Encontro Internacional de la Sociedad Española de Lingüística (SEL)*, disponível em CD, *Seção Gramática*, Santiago de Compostela.

Givón, T. (1993). *English Grammar*, vol.1. Amsterdam: John Benjamins.

Hornstein, N. (1993). *As Time Goes By*. Cambridge, MA: MIT Press.

Ilari, R. (2000). Notas para a semântica do passado composto em português. *Actas do Congresso Internacional organizado por motivo dos 20 anos de português no ensino superior*. Budapest: Eötvös Loránd University, pp. 224–247.

Ilari, R. and R. Basso (2014). O verbo. In R. Ilari (ed.), *Gramática do Português Culto Falado no Brasil*. São Paulo: Contexto.

Kaufmann, S. (2005). Conditional truth and future reference. *Journal of Semantics*, 22 (3), pp. 231–280.

Lobato, L. (1973). L'auxiliarité en langue Portugaise. Ph.D. dissertation, Université de Paris III.

Molsing, K. V. (2010). The present perfect: an exercise in the study of events, plurality and aspect. Ph.D. dissertation, Pontifícia Universidade Católica do Rio Grande do Sul.

Oliveira, F. (2006). Tempo e aspecto. In M. H. Mateus, A. M. Brito, I. Duarte, I. Faria, S. Frota, G. Matos, F. Oliveira, M. Vigário, and A. Villalva (eds.), *Gramática da língua portuguesa*, 7th edn. Lisbon: Caminho, pp. 127–178.

Oliveira, F. (2013). Tempo verbal. In E. B. P. Raposo, M. F. Bacelar do Nascimento, M. A. Coelho da Mota, L. Segura, and A. Mendes (eds.), *Gramática do Português*. Lisbon: Fundação Calouste Gulbenkian), pp. 510–556.

Oliveira, F., L. F. Cunha, and A. Gonçalves (2004). Aspectual verbs in European and Brazilian Portuguese. *Journal of Portuguese Linguistics*, 3 (1), pp. 141–173.

Oliveira, F. and A. Leal (2012). Sobre a iteração do pretérito Perfeito Composto em Português Europeu. *Revista de Estudos Linguísticos da Universidade do Porto*, 7, pp. 65–88.

Oliveira, J. (2011). A expressão variável do futuro verbal na escrita: Brasil e Portugal em confronto. *Revista da Abralin*, special issue, 1, pp. 367–383.

Perini, M. (2002). *Modern Portuguese, a Reference Grammar*. New Haven, CT: Yale University Press.

Reichenbach, H. (1947). *Elements of Symbolic Logic*. New York: Free Press.

Santos, D. (1996). Uma classificação aspectual portuguesa do português. *Actas do XII Encontro da Associação Portuguesa de Linguística*, Braga, October 1–3, 1996, pp. 299–315.

Silva, R. P. da (2011). A representação do tempo futuro em textos escritos: uma análise diacrônica. *Revista da Abralin*, special issue, 1, pp. 395–429.

Travaglia, L. (1981). *O aspecto verbal no português*. Uberlândia: Universidade Federal de Uberlândia.

Vendler, Zeno (1967), *Linguistics in Philosophy*. Ithaca, NY: Cornell University Press.

Viana, A. R. G. (1903). *Le Portugais: Phonétique et Phonologie: Morphologie: Textes*. Leipzig: Teubner.

22 Mood and Modality

RUI MARQUES AND ROBERTA PIRES DE OLIVEIRA

"Hypotheticals, 'imaginaries', conditionals, the syntax of counterfactuality and contingency may well be the generative centres of human speech"

(George Steiner, *After Babel* (1998), 226)

1. This chapter

Mood and modality are closely intermingled and play a fundamental role in our lives: through them we express knowledge, and beliefs, about the world, as well as desires, conjectures, etc. These are important tools for surviving, as Hockett (1960) stressed. Languages vary greatly with respect to the ways they express the relations to the factual, the hypothetical, the counterfactual. This is a vast territory. In this chapter, our aim is twofold: empirically, we want to compare European Portuguese (EP) and Brazilian Portuguese (BP) with respect to mood and modality and show some of their differences; and we want to show that the relevant properties of Portuguese can be insightfully discussed with the tools provided by possible world semantics, in which semantic accounts of mood have appeared for different languages (cf. e.g., Farkas 1992, Portner 1993, Marques 2009, Giannakidou 2013).[1]

We begin with mood in Portuguese, that is, the verb inflectional category associated with the expression of an attitude towards the proposition. Empirically, we will show that BP and EP differ with respect to the complement of some evaluative expressions, and of fiction verbs like *imaginar* ("to imagine"); moreover, we will show that the "future in the past" (*futuro do pretérito* in BP grammatical terminology, and *condicional* in EP terminology) do not have the same interpretation in the two varieties. We also discuss why some tenses traditionally taken to belong to the indicative mood seem problematic under this classification: the *futuro do pretérito/condicional* itself, the *pretérito imperfeito* ("imperfect past"), and the *futuro do presente* ("simple future").

In Section 3 we apply Kratzer's seminal proposals (2013) to Portuguese modal auxiliaries, such as *poder* ("can") and *dever* ("must").[2] Modals are quantifiers that relate an ordered modal basis and a proposition. In this section we also discuss very briefly the contribution of the *pretérito imperfeito do indicativo* ("indicative imperfect past") to the interpretation of the modal auxiliaries.

The *imperfeito* ties together mood and modality, the topic of Section 4, where we argue that the *imperfeito* does belong to the indicative mood, although, in some cases, it seems to involve

The Handbook of Portuguese Linguistics, First Edition. Edited by W. Leo Wetzels, João Costa, and Sergio Menuzzi.
© 2016 John Wiley & Sons, Inc. Published 2020 by John Wiley & Sons, Inc.

counterfactuality. Concerning the main moods of Portuguese—the indicative and the subjunctive—we argue that the selection among them is conditioned by the worlds that are taken into consideration: the indicative requires that the proposition is true in every considered possible world; and the denotation of a subjunctive proposition includes at least one world in which the proposition is not true. We propose that the *imperfeito* and the *futuro do pretérito/condicional* do not select for an ordering source, whereas other indicative tenses select for "normality." Moreover, we suggest that the difference between EP and BP with respect to the combination of evaluative predicates and fiction verbs is due to different constraints on the indicative: in EP the indicative imposes no restrictions concerning the world of evaluation; in BP, some predicates suggest an association between the real world and the indicative.

This chapter is just a glimpse into mood and modality in Portuguese. The hypotheses we raise here surely need to be further investigated. Moreover, there is a lot to be studied that we cannot but mention: imperatives, exclamatives, conditionals, and infinitive clauses, constructions whose meaning and use also depend on the semantics of mood and modality.

2. Mood in Portuguese

Not only there are no uniform criteria for the identification of moods in Portuguese in traditional grammars, but their definition is often left unclear. The European Portuguese grammatical terminology considers four moods: indicative, subjunctive, imperative, and conditional. The Brazilian terminology understands that there are three: indicative, subjunctive, and imperative. Usually, mood is said to indicate the speaker's evaluation of the *dictum*, of what is said; the evaluation might be one of certitude, doubt, supposition, ordering, etc. This section concentrates on the subjunctive and the indicative, the best studied moods in Portuguese. In particular, we show that the traditional view—according to which the indicative expresses reality, and the subjunctive, non-reality—is inadequate.

Traditional grammars consider the indicative the "default" mood, in opposition to the subjunctive, which is considered the "marked" one. The subjunctive is often described as the mood of subordination, for it occurs mainly in subordinated clauses.[3] This suggests that the subjunctive requires the scope of certain types of operators. Indeed, a large amount of literature has been devoted to finding out what distinguishes the relevant contexts.

The first observation is that some predicates select either the indicative or the subjunctive, exclusively, as in (1), whereas in other cases both moods are allowed—but with different interpretations, as in (2):

(1) a. *Nós sabemos que ela cant-a   / *cant-e.*[4]
      We know that she sing-prs.ind / *sing-prs.subj
      "We know that she sings."
   b. *Nós queremos que ela cant-e   / *cant-a.*
      We want that she   sing-prs.subj / *sing-prs.ind
      "We want her to sing."

(2) *Ele quer comprar uma casa que tem   / tenh-a   canil.*
    he wants to-buy a house that have.prs.ind / have.prs.subj kennel
    "He wants to buy a house that has a kennel."

The indicative in the relative clause in (2) is felicitous in a context where there is a certain house with kennel which someone wants to buy. With the subjunctive, the sentence does not refer to any particular house (only the non-specific, *de dicto*, reading of "a house" is available).

Syntactically, it is important to characterize the structures in which one but not the other mood is grammatical—as in (1)—and those in which both moods are allowed, as in (2), where the difference in meaning cannot be ignored. Semantically, one wants to have a better understanding of what distinguishes the meaning of the subjunctive and the indicative structures. Though in this chapter the focus is on the semantic side, it is a fact that meaning is syntactically encoded in natural languages.

At the syntax–semantics interface, one may wonder whether the subjunctive and indicative morphemes are semantic operators, contributing to the meaning of the sentence, or whether they signal the presence of a certain semantic value in the context where they occur, parallel to what is seen with negative polarity items, which do not convey negation, but only occur in contexts with a certain semantic value. An intermediary position considers that the subjunctive has a semantic value in cases where the substitution for the indicative is grammatical, though with meaning change, as in (2); and the subjunctive is empty of meaning in syntactic structures where it cannot be substituted for the indicative, as in (1). However, it would be good to understand why one cannot use the subjunctive in (1a), but may in (1b).

The literature on mood has also paid attention to the dimension of use. In the next sections, we summarize the main lines that were explored in order to explain the distribution of the indicative and the subjunctive in Portuguese.

2.1. *The relation between mood and truth value*

The hypothesis, widely explored in traditional grammars, that the opposition between the subjunctive and the indicative is related to the opposition between *realis* and *irrealis* explains a vast number of cases. However, it cannot account for the obligatoriness, in EP, of the subjunctive in many kinds of sentences that describe facts: complement clauses of factive-emotive (or "evaluative") predicates (3a); complement clauses of causatives (3b); concessive clauses introduced by *embora* ("although") (3c). (For BP, see Section 2.4 below.) And it cannot account, in EP, for the mandatoriness of the indicative in clauses embedded under verbs or other expressions that introduce a fictional context, such as *sonhar* ("to dream"), *fingir* ("to pretend"), or *fazer de conta* ("to pretend") (3d) (for BP, see 2.4 below, again):

(3) a. *Lamento que ela   est-eja   desempregada.*
       regret that she   be-prs.subj unemployed
       "I regret that she is unemployed."
   b. *O governo deixou que a situação   chega-sse   a este ponto.*
       The government allowed that the situation reach-impf.subj at this point
       "The government allowed that the situation reached this point."
   c. *Embora ele   fo-sse   um bom jogador, era raramente utilizado.*
       Although he was-impf.subj a good player, was rarely used.
       "Although he was a good player, he was rarely used."
   d. *Sonhei que ele   ganh-ou   o prémio Nobel.*
       dreamed that he win-perf.ind the Nobel Prize.
       "I dreamt that he won the Nobel Prize."

The one-to-one correspondence between *realis* and indicative, and *irrealis* and subjunctive, also faces difficulties to explain the possibility of the indicative in the antecedent of counterfactual (4a) and hypothetical conditionals (4b):

(4) a. *Se ele cheg-a*　　　*dez minutos mais tarde, não encontrava*　　　*a filha!*
　　　If he arrive-prs.ind ten minutes more late, not　　find-impf.ind　the daughter.
　　　"If he'd arrived ten minutes later, he wouldn't have met his daughter."
　　b. *Se eu descubr-o que eles me*　　　*enganar-am, bem podem fugir!*
　　　If I find-prs.ind that they me cheat-perf.ind, well can run.
　　　"If I find out that they cheated me, they may well run away."

Concerning fictional contexts, the selection of the indicative is accounted for if the concept of *realis* is replaced by Farkas (1992)'s concept of extensional anchoring, or Giannakidou (1999)'s concept of "relativized vericadility" (or "subjective (non)veridicality"). According to Giannakidou's concept, a sentence is veridical if it is taken to be true by someone in the relevant model (the dream model, in the case of complement clauses of *dream;* someone's beliefs' model, in the case of complement clauses of *think,* etc.), independently of its truth value in the real world. Giannakidou shows that in Modern Greek the subjunctive can only occur in non-veridical contexts and, according to Farkas (1992), the same is true in Romanian. Fiction predicates do not require the subjunctive because they are veridical. However, in Portuguese (as in other Romance languages), non-veridicality is not a sufficient condition for the selection of the subjunctive, since this mood may occur in veridical contexts, as shown in (3a) to (3c) above.

2.2. *The relation between the mood and the illocutionary force*

The functionalist tradition has explored the idea that the indicative mood occurs in assertive utterances whereas the subjunctive is restricted to non-assertive utterances (cf., e.g., Hooper 1975). Simplifying, the idea is that the indicative allows emphasis in the information expressed by the sentence, ascribing to it more relevance than if the subjunctive is used. Such an analysis explains the fact that with factive predicates such as *lamentar* ("to regret") or *ser (uma) pena* ("to be (a) pity") the subjunctive is obligatory in EP, since the dependent clause is taken to convey information that is already known by the listener—hence, contextually presupposed. But this approach cannot explain why in BP some of these predicates (e.g., *ser (uma) pena / ser bom;* "to be a pity/to be good") seem to preferably select the indicative: *Que bom que está chovendo* ("how nice that it be.pres-ind raining") seems more natural in colloquial BP than *Que bom que esteja chovendo* ("how nice that it be.pres-subj raining"). And, at least in some varieties of BP, predicates like *lamentar* also seem to accept both forms: in such varieties, not only (3a) is fine, but also *Lamento que ela está desempregada* "I regret that she be.pres.ind unemployed." Moreover, although a relation between indicative/subjunctive and assertion/non-assertion is widely observed in the literature, an issue this approach must face is that of defining "assertion" (and similar terms, such as "affirmative utterance," etc.), as Palmer 1986 observes.

In Speech Acts Theory (Austin 1962, Searle 1969), an utterance is assertive if the utterer's goal is to express his belief in the truth of the uttered proposition. But if the selection of the indicative depends on the conveying a belief in the proposition, we meet basically the same problems raised against the hypothesis that relates the selection of mood to the truth value attributed to the sentence. Moreover, if we adopt Stalnaker's (1979) concept of assertion, according to which to assert an utterance is to introduce new information into the discourse, we also have problems, since an utterance in the subjunctive may introduce new information, as in (5):

(5) *A derrota da seleção*　　　*não imped-iu*
　　The defeat of-the team not prevent-perf.ind
　　que os adeptos festeja-ssem　　　*a noite toda.*
　　that the fans　celebrate-impf.subj the night all
　　"The team's defeat didn't prevent the fans celebrating all night long."

Sentence (5) may be uttered in a context where the fact that the fans celebrated all night is not known. Moreover, it may also be the case that an indicative utterance does not introduce new information into the discourse:

(6) *Já   sabíamos   que ele   era   candidato,*
Already know-perf.ind that he   be.impf.ind candidate,
a novidade é que vai concorrer contra a própria mulher.
the novelty is that will compete against his own wife.
"We knew that he was a candidate, the news is that he will compete against his wife."

One may relate assertion (or affirmative force) to the relevance one gives to the information introduced by the utterance (Santos 2003). This may explain some cases where the speaker has the option for the indicative or the subjunctive, with the corresponding difference in meaning, as in (7a), and also cases in which the speaker uses the indicative to make the information expressed by the sentence salient in contexts where the subjunctive is allegedly obligatory, as in (7b). It is not the case, however, that the speaker always uses the indicative when he wants to make the proposition expressed by the utterance salient, as in (8):

(7) a. *Insisto em que ele   vem   / venh-a.*
(I) insist in that he   come.prs.ind / come.prs.subj
"I maintain that he will come."
  b. *Ninguém me abriu a porta, embora eu   sei   que ele estava em casa!*[5]
Nobody me opened the door, although I know.prs.ind that he was.ind in house
"Nobody opened the door, although I knew he was home."

(8) *Espero que amanhã só   chov-a   / *chov-e!*
Hope that tomorrow only rain.prs.ind   / rain.prs.subj
"I hope it rains the whole day tomorrow."

2.3. *The relation between mood and propositional attitudes*

Another approach to mood distribution in Portuguese explores the idea that the indicative is selected when the proposition is taken to be true *and* the attitude expressed with respect to this proposition is epistemic or doxastic (i.e., an attitude of knowledge or belief); otherwise the subjunctive being selected (cf. Marques 1995). In other words, the indicative is selected when an attitude of knowledge or of positive belief towards the proposition is expressed, and the subjunctive is the default mood, that occurs in all the other cases (i.e., cases in which the proposition is not taken to be true, as in, e.g., complement clauses of "to doubt," as well as cases where the attitude towards the proposition is not epistemic or doxastic, as in the complement clauses of "to regret").

This hypothesis explains why all non-veridical verbs (in Giannakidou's sense of non-veridicality) select the subjunctive, and why some veridical predicates are indicative rulers and others subjunctive rulers: the ones that in EP select and in BP accept the subjunctive, such as "to be good," express an attitude of evaluation of the fact described by the subordinated clause, while indicative rulers such as "to know" or "to discover" express an epistemic attitude. Hence, the cases that were observed to be problematic for the idea that mood distribution is related to the (acceptance) of the truth of the proposition are accounted for by this hypothesis: the indicative does not merely signal that the proposition is taken to be true, it signals that the attitude towards the proposition is of epistemic or doxastic nature, that is, of knowledge or positive belief.

This approach to mood in Portuguese also accounts for the facts that are problematic for the (non)assertion approach, since it grounds mood selection on the meaning of the construction, not on the communicative intention. This is compatible with the observation that the indicative is the only mood allowed in simple declarative clauses like *O homem chegou à lua* ("Mankind has reached the moon"), which can obviously be assertions, whatever the concept of assertion one has. By asserting the sentence, the speaker expresses his belief that the sentence is true; the attitude expressed towards the proposition is of doxastic nature, hence the selection of the indicative.

However, the idea that the indicative is related to the expression of an attitude of knowledge or (positive) belief is problematic if we take into consideration the sentences below: (9a) conveys a desire, not a state of knowledge or belief, and the verb carries morphology corresponding to the indicative imperfect past; (9b) shows that the *futuro do indicativo* ("indicative future") may express uncertainty (hence, (9b) does not allow the inference that "the population is around 3 million" is true); and (9c) shows the same with respect to the *futuro do pretérito/condicional*:

(9) a. *Por mim, João casa-va   e   fica-va   tudo bem.*
    For me, João marry-impf.ind and become-impf.ind everything fine
    "For me, João could marry and everything would be fine."
  b. *Atualmente, a população   será   (talvez) de uns três milhões.*
    Nowadays, the population be.cond/fut.ind (perhaps) of some three millions
    "Nowadays, the population will be (perhaps) around three millions."
  c. *O presidente esta-ria   (supostamente)   a preparar um documento.*
    the president be-fut.pret.ind (supposedly)   at preparing a document.
    "The president would be preparing a document."

We come back to this issue in Section 4. In the next subsection, we compare BP and EP.

2.4. *Variation in mood in EP and in BP*

In most contexts, European and Brazilian Portuguese do not show differences regarding the selection of mood. However, there are cases where they contrast. These differences are found mainly in complement clauses, and in a particular kind of main clause. Concerning complement clauses, in some the selection of the subjunctive is obligatory in EP, but in BP the indicative might occur, as with some evaluative predicates, such as *ser bom / ser pena* ("to be good"/"to be a pity"), as in (10). In other complement clauses, the opposite situation obtains: the indicative is obligatory in EP, while in BP the subjunctive may occur, as in complement clauses of fiction verbs, like *imaginar* ("to imagine"), as in (11):[6]

(10) a. *Que pena que ela   est-eja   desempregada.*   (BP/EP)
      he regrets that she be-prs.subj unemployed
      "He regrets that she is unemployed."
   b. *Que pena que ela   está   desempregada.*   (BP/*EP)
      he regrets that she be.prs.ind unemployed
      "He regrets that she is unemployed."

(11) a. *Imagine que todos os computadores deixa-ssem   de funcionar.*   (BP/*EP)
      Imagine that all the computers   stop-impf.subj of functioning.
   b. *Imagine que todos os computadores deixa-vam   de funcionar.*   (BP/EP)
      Imagine that all the computers   stop- impf.ind of functioning
      "Imagine that all the computers stopped functioning."

These facts suggest that mood distribution in BP is more sensitive to the *actual/non-actual* or *realis/irrealis* distinction than in EP. In EP the indicative is selected if the sentence is taken to be true in the relevant model, otherwise the subjunctive is selected; in BP the indicative might be selected if the state of affairs described by the sentence is verified in the actual world; if it is verified in some possible world, but not necessarily in the actual world, the subjunctive is preferred: (11a) seems better than (11b).

The interpretation of the *condicional* ("conditional," European grammatical terminology) or the *futuro do pretérito* ("future in the past," Brazilian terminology) with a purely modal value is another difference between between the two varieties of Portuguese. In sentences like (12), where the embedded proposition expresses uncertainty on the part of the speaker, the *futuro do pretérito/condicional* is acceptable in BP, but not in EP:

(12) *Os dados que recolhi sugerem que o livro   ter-ia*
      the data that I collected suggest that the book have-cond/fut.pret.ind
      sido   escrito antes de 1500.   (BP/*EP)
      be.past.part   written before 1500
      "The data that I collected suggest that the book will have been written before 1500."

A proposal to account for these differences is the topic of Section 4. In the next section, we turn to modality.

3. Modals in Portuguese

Aristotle was the first to relate modality to the truth value of propositions. His interest was the "alethic" modality, which expresses logical necessity or possibility:

(13) *Necessariamente, Platão saiu ou Platão não saiu.*
      "Necessarily, either Plato left or Plato didn't leave."

(13) is a tautology. The truth of the disjunction requires that at least one of the sentences is true. Since there are only two possibilities with respect to Plato's having left—either he did or he didn't—the coordination is necessarily a true sentence.

However, necessity and possibility are relevant in other domains, which are not regulated by the same deductive rules. Consider the sentences in (14):

(14) a. *Obrigatoriamente, Platão está preso.*
          "Obligatorily, Plato is in jail."
      b. *Platão está preso.*
          "Plato is in jail."

In the domain of the laws and regulations, the deontic domain, the inference of (14b) from (14a) is not valid. (14a) establishes what the law states, according to which Plato is arrested, but the actual world may not conform to the law. Imagine that according to the laws, anyone who stole something is arrested. Suppose that Plato has stolen something. This fact together with the set of laws does not warrant that Plato is arrested. Indeed, in reality not all cases of robbery end with the burglar in prison. The actual world is not a perfect moral world. (13) and (14) exemplify different "shades" of modality.

3.1. Shades of modality

There is no consensus on what the types of modality are, nor on how to account for those that have been established. Classically, one finds the distinction between alethic, epistemic, and deontic modalities. Epistemic modality is associated with knowledge; deontic modality with laws and regulations, obligation and permission; and alethic modality with logical necessity/possibility. However, the literature also refers to doxastic modality, frequently associated with epistemic modality, since it deals with beliefs; volitional (or bouletic) modality, associated with desires; evaluative modality, which expresses evaluation of facts; and teleological modality, which has to do with aims and goals. Mainly in the syntactic literature, one finds the distinction between epistemic and root modalities, where epistemic covers knowledge and beliefs, and root designates all the other types of modality: deontic, volitional, etc. The syntactic distinction relies on important properties of the items that express modality in natural languages, such as adverbs and auxiliaries. Let us illustrate this with the auxiliaries *dever* ("must") and *poder* ("can"):

(15) *Ele deve   poder   sair.*
      he must.prs.ind   to can to leave
      "He must be able to leave."

(15) cannot but be interpreted as follows: it is probably the case that he has permission (or the capacity) to leave. The finite modal cannot be interpreted as a deontic, it must be epistemic, and the embedded modal, in the infinitive, must be non-epistemic (expressing root modality, which includes permission, capacity, among others). Thus, there are constraints on the interpretation of modals: the deontic interpretation cannot prevail over the epistemic one. Cinque (2006) explores this important finding in his hierarchy of functional categories, and Hacquard (2006) in the interpretation of Kratzer's distinction between epistemic and circumstantial modal bases.

3.2. Expressing modality in Portuguese

There are several linguistic means of expressing modality. Indeed, a cross-linguistic inventory of all these possibilities is one of the aims in this area of study. In Portuguese, modality can be expressed via modal auxiliaries—*poder* ("can"), *dever* ("must"), *ter de/que* ("to have to"); Oliveira and Mendes (2013) also mention *haver de* (also "to have to") and *ser capaz de* ("to be able to")—, and plain verbs—*saber* ("to know") and *crer* ("to believe") —are full verbs that express the epistemic and the doxastic modality, respectively. If modality covers also the expression of propositional attitudes, then *querer* ("to want") and *esperar* ("to expect, to hope") are associated with volitional modality; and verbs like *lamentar* ("to regret") and *apreciar* ("to appreciate") express evaluative modality. Other lexical classes may express modality: nouns (*certeza* "certainty," *possibilidade* "possibility"), adjectives (*obrigatório* "obligatory," *possível* "possible"), adverbs (*talvez* "maybe," *possivelmente* "possibly," *certamente* "certainly"). Morphologically, there are sufixes with modal value, like *–vel* in *lavável* ("washable") and *louvável* ("laudable") (see Costa Moreira 2014). (9b) above shows that the *futuro do indicativo* ("indicative future") expresses a high probability but not certainty (the so-called "epistemic future"); thus, verbal tenses may have modal values. The *presente do indicativo* ("indicative present") in (16) expresses an ability/capacity, hence a modality:

(16) *Esse carro faz 200 km/h.*
      "This car does 200 km/h."

Syntactically, several phrases show modal values: *com certeza* ("for sure"), *o mais provável* ("the most probable"), etc. Infinite phrases may also have a modal meaning, as in (17) below, which might convey the same meaning as "there are mountains that we need to climb and rivers that we must cross":[7]

(17) *Há montanhas a subir e rios a atravessar.*
　　 "There are mountains to climb and rivers to cross."

If modality conveys an attitude towards a proposition, then intonation may also be a means of expressing it.[8]

Most of the contemporary research on modality concentrates on modal verbs / auxiliaries, which are the topic of the next section.

3.3. *Modal verbs/auxiliaries in Portuguese*

Syntactically, auxiliaries do not c-select categories other than VPs (and their extended projections). This property seems to be tied to the type of modality the modal expresses. Although epistemic *poder* does not seem to select for the external argument, the deontic one seems to select for an agent; (18) does not convey that the stone has permission to fall:[9]

(18) *A pedra pode cair.*　　　Epistemic/*Deontic.
　　 "The stone may fall."

Pontes (1973) distinguishes three verbs *poder* ("may/can/is able to"): permission, possibility, and capacity. According to her, only *poder* of possibility is an auxiliary. For other authors, all modal verbs are auxiliaries (Miranda 1975). Finally, some authors see the issue of identifying a class of "auxiliaries" in Portuguese more in terms of a "scale of auxiliarity" than in terms of a categorical distinction "auxiliary" vs. "lexical verbs." For example, Gonçalves (1992) argues for such a position for EP verbs (cf. Mateus *et al.* 2003), claiming that modal verbs are "semi-auxiliaries" in this variety: they would have some properties of auxiliaries, but not as many as a prototypical auxiliary, such as the verb *ter* "to have" in "compound tenses" (e.g., the compound pluperfect in *João tinha partido* "John had left"). For a recent similar proposal for modals in BP, see Rech (2011).

Semantically, according to Kratzer (2013), modal verbs are quantifiers that relate an ordered modal base and the proposition expressed by the embedded sentence. In a very intuitive and informal way, the modal base corresponds to the information—conceived as a set of worlds—that the speaker relies on to assert the modalized sentence. For example, (18) expresses that there is at least one among the relevant worlds—those compatible with the epistemic base of (18), that is, with what is known about the situation in which (18) is uttered—in which the stone falls.

The modal base of an utterance (the relevant body of information relative to which the truth of the utterance is evaluated) may be explicitly given, as in (19) below, or it may be recovered from the context, as in (20). (20) may have different interpretations precisely because the modal base is not explicit: it may have an epistemic reading ("maybe / for sure, she marries"), or a deontic one ("she is obliged to marry"). In (19), on the other hand, the modal base is linguistically conveyed, and the only reading is epistemic ("it is likely that she marries"):

(19) *De acordo com o que se sabe, a Ana deve casar.*
　　 "According to what is known, Maria shall marry."

(20) *A Ana deve casar.*
     "Ana must marry."

In Kratzer's quantificational approach, the auxiliary lexically conveys the quantificational force of the utterance: thus, *poder* ("may/can") conveys existential force, that is, there is at least one alternative which is compatible with the background; *dever* ("must"), on the other hand, would express universal force, that is, that all alternatives verify the claim. If *dever* expresses universal quantification, and if the modal basis is realistic, that is, it includes the actual world, then both (19) and (20) entail (21):

(21) *A Ana vai casar/casa-rá.*
     "Ana will marry."

But according to our intuitions, (19) and (20) may be true without it being the case that Ana actually comes to marry. How do we account for our intuitions? Kratzer explains this pattern of inference in natural languages by building an "ordered semantics": the set of worlds in the modal base are ordered according to some set of propositions, also provided by the context, which establishes the "ideal" worlds—ideal according to the laws, or to what is normal, or to the speaker's desires, etc. The worlds in a modal base are ordered according to the proximity to this ideal. Thus, (19) and (20) say that, according to what is known, and taking into consideration the normal course of events, in all the normal worlds, Ana will marry. It does not entail that she will actually marry in the actual world, because the actual world may be not a normal world. Kratzer's proposal also accounts for the fact that modality is gradable: *é pouco provável* ("it is not very likely"), *é bem possível* ("it is highly possible"), etc.

In sum, for Kratzer modality has three ingredients: the force (possibility, necessity), the modal basis (the body of information—conceived as a set of worlds—against which the proposition is interpreted), and the ordering source (the ordering of worlds concerning their proximity to normality, or to what the law provides, etc). Modal force is the only information that is carried by the modal verbs in Portuguese (*poder* "can" conveys possibility, *ter de/que* "have to," necessity); the other ingredients—the modal basis and the ordering relation—come from other sources (e.g., by context, as in (20), or by compositional means, as in (19)). This division of labor is not necessary for all languages. Rullmann, Matthewson, and Davis (2008) show that in the Salishan languages, the force is contextually given, while the modal basis is part of the lexical meaning.

3.4. Tense, aspect and modality

The interaction of modal verbs with tense, aspect, and mood raises issues that can only be mentioned here in passing. Condoravit (2002) distinguishes between the temporal perspective, which is the time when the body of information is taken into consideration, and the time of the event. Consider (20): the temporal perspective is present, since the speaker is invoking what is known at the speech time; but the time of the event is future, the event of Ana's marriage is after the speech time. With (22), the speaker conveys that, given the information that he has at speech time—the temporal perspective—he believes that the event denoted by the embedded sentence has happened—the compound form (*ter casado*, "have married") conveys that the time of the event is past:

(22) *Ela deve   ter casado.*
     she *dever*.prs.ind to have married.
     "She must have married."

However, if *deve* is substituted for the imperfect past *devia*, an interpretation of desire pops up, particularly if we add an exclamative contour:

(23) *Ela devia   ter casado.*
    she *dever*.impf.ind to have married
    "She should have married."

(23) is ambiguous: (i) Suppose that for all the speaker knows, Ana was planning her marriage, but this is the most information that the speaker has; he is not sure whether she actually married; in this case the temporal perspective is past (given the information that the speaker had at some point in the past), and the time of the event is past with respect to the temporal perspective; (ii) the speaker is not wondering about the event, since he knows what happened, the temporal perspective is present; he is rather commenting on something that he takes for granted that has *not* happened (the person referred to in (23) did *not* marry). Thus, the speaker knows what happened—she has not married—and is regretting the course of events. Ana prepared herself to marry, everything was ready for the marriage, but it has not happen (because she is too perfectionist and postponed it, or for any other reason). The speaker is conjecturing about what is not the case, but could have happened—a counterfactual reasoning. This counterfactual reading only happens with the imperfective.

The difference between indicative present and imperfect past also shows in the following pair of sentences:

(24) a. *O João deve   casar em março.*   Epistemic/*Desire
        the João *dever*.prs.ind to marry in March
        "João will probably marry in March."
    b. *O João devia   casar em março.*   ?? Epistemic/Desire
        the João *dever*.impf.ind to-marry in March.
        "João should marry in March."

In parallel with the readings available for (23) but not for (22), only (24b) can be used in two scenarios: (i) one where we know that João married, but not in March (in which (24b) might be followed by "but he did only in April"); or (ii) in a context, previous to March (say, (24b) being uttered in January), where the speaker knows that João has not married yet and wishes he does that in next March. (24a) can only be used in the context where one knows that João has not married yet. In a context where the temporal perspective is the speech time, and the event is future oriented, only the imperfect past conveys uncertainty, desire, etc.

Moreover, when the temporal perspective point is speech time, the imperfect is hardly interpreted as expressing epistemic modality. Suppose the speaker is closed into a room without windows, but he sees people arriving wet, with wet umbrellas. In such a situation, the imperfective form is not felicitous:

(25) *Deve   /#Dev-ia estar chovendo.*[10]
    Dever.prs.ind/impf.ind to be raining.

The same contrasts and constraints appear with *poder* ("can"): only (26a) answers the question "Do you believe there is water on Mars?":

(26) a. *Marte pode   ter água.*
        Mars *poder*.prs.ind to have water
    b. *Marte podia   ter água.*
        Mars *poder*.impf.ind to have water
        "Mars may/could have water."

With the present form, the speaker entertains the possibility that Mars has water, whereas with the imperfect he may convey his desire that Mars has water.[11]

Other issues enter into the discussion if we consider the perfect past *pôde* ("was able to"):

(27) a. *Ele pôde   levantar a mesa.*
       he *poder*.perf.ind to lift the table.
   b. *Ele levantou   a mesa.*
       He lift.perf the table.

Hacquard (2006) argues that the French counterpart of *pôde* is a veridical operator, it entails that the proposition under its scope is true. Does (27a) entail (27b)? We believe it does, but we will not discuss this case here.

In the next section, we aim to shed some light on ways of integrating mood and modality. In order to do this, we will argue that there is something in common between the modal properties of the imperfect discussed in this section and our previous observations about mood in Portuguese—and this is precisely what requires an integrated account of mood and modality.

4. Towards an integrated analysis of mood and modality

Over the last decades, an increasing amount of work in semantics has been devoted to formal analyses of mood and modality in different languages. In this section, we briefly outline how a treatment of mood and modality can be achieved within possible worlds semantics. As seen above, Kratzer"s model allows for the description of the semantics of modal operators, in particular modal verbs. Unsurprisingly, many of the concepts designed to account for modals have also been used for the semantics of mood. In particular, central to the formal analysis of both modality and mood is the notion of possible world (or possible situation, cf. Kratzer 2013).[12] The analysis of the semantics of modal verbs was sketched above. Other modal operators in Portuguese (such as modal adverbs, epistemic adjuncts like *com certeza*, and so on) have not been studied with the same depth. Our aim in Section 3 was to highlight the interaction between aspect, the *imperfeito*, and modal verbs: it shows that the imperfect allows for desire interpretations, and counterfactual readings.

As for mood, the hypothesis sketched in Section 2 was that in EP the indicative occurs in veridical epistemic contexts. This hypothesis can be formalized along the following lines (cf. Marques 2009): if only p-worlds (i.e., worlds where the state of affairs described by the proposition is verified) are considered, the indicative is selected; if at least one non p-world is taken into consideration, the subjunctive occurs. This explains why the indicative is obligatorily selected by verbs that point to an entity's knowledge or belief state and why the subjunctive is selected by non-veridical verbs (considering Giannakidou's definition of veridicality). As for veridical verbs that select the subjunctive, namely, evaluative predicates like *lamentar* ("to regret") and causative predicates like *fazer* ("to make"),[13] if one accepts that their meaning involves counterfactual reasoning, then their meaning also involves the consideration of non-p worlds.

Heim (1992) defends the idea that evaluative predicates involve counterfactual reasoning. She proposes that the meaning of "John regrets that it is raining" is, informally, the following: it is raining and, for John, it would have been better if it were not raining. Conversely, "John is glad that it is raining" means that it is raining and, for John, this is better than if it were not raining. As for causative predicates, the hypothesis that their meaning also involves the consideration of non-p worlds is supported by the assumption that the notion of causality involves counterfactual reasoning, as defended by Salmon (1998). In simple terms, he proposes that "Ice on the road caused the accident" means that if there were no ice on the road (all the rest being equal to the actual world), the accident would not have happened. Given that predicates like *fazer* "to make" involve causality, then accepting Salmon's proposal amounts to claim that such predicates also involve counterfactual reasoning (and, hence, consideration of non p-worlds).

As for BP, a large scale empirical survey is still in need. As far as we could detect, some evaluative predicates like *ser bom* ("to be good") preferably select the indicative like in other languages cited above, *lamentar* ("to regret") seems to combine with both moods, and fiction verbs as *imaginar* ("to imagine") accept the subjunctive. This data may suggest the tendency to select the indicative if the proposition is presupposed, i.e. if it is taken to be true in the actual world.

Now, we observe that (28), with the imperfect, is problematic for the hypothesis that the indicative occurs in epistemic veridical environments:

(28) *Por mim, o João   casa-va.*
     For me,   the João marry-impf.ind
     "In my opinion, João should marry."

This sentence expresses a desire, not a belief. So its meaning is not that John gets (or has got) married in every world compatible with what the speaker assumes; instead, it means that John gets married in every desire-world of the speaker. That is, (31) involves a bouletic ordering source. Moreover, (28) may be felicitously asserted in a context where João's getting married is an available possibility, as well as in a context where it isn't. As seen above, the same effects appear when a modal verb is associated with the imperfect.

Given this, there are two choices. One is to assume that the indicative mood selects an epistemic modal base and involves the consideration of only p-worlds, and that the *imperfeito* does not belong to the indicative. However, the syntactic criterion for the indicative is the fact that the verbal form can be used in independent clauses without any (open) modal operator. With respect to this criterion, the imperfect is an indicative tense. Thus, let's assume the second choice and stick to the idea that the indicative involves the consideration of only p-worlds, the distinction between the indicative and the subjunctive being that the latter occurs in contexts where there is at least one non-p world. Let's also assume that the modal basis in cases like (28) is epistemic, in the sense that it deals with empirical evidence, with a body of information conversationally accessible. We can now account for this information using the ordering source, as suggested by Kratzer. This line of reasoning would allow for the *imperfeito* to be a tense of the indicative, but it requires that different tenses be specified for the kind of ordering source they select. Most tenses of the indicative would require a normality ordering source; but the *imperfeito* would accept any kind of ordering. In (28) the modal base would be epistemic and the ordering source bouletic. The information is conveyed that in all worlds (compatible with what is known) that conform to the speaker's desires, John gets married.

Similar considerations are relevant for the *futuro do presente* ("simple future") and the *futuro do pretérito/condicional* ("future in the past/conditional"). As seen above, in sentences as (9b), the *futuro do presente* expresses uncertainty, and in BP the same value is expressed by the *futuro do pretérito/condicional*, as shown by (12). These tenses may also have a reportative reading, which also does not convey certainty on the part of the speaker:

(29) *De acordo com o jornal, o assaltante*   *ter-ia /ter-á*
    According to the newspaper, the burglar   have-cond/fut.pret.ind /fut.ind
     usado explosivos.
     used explosives.
    "According to the newspaper, the burglar would have used explosives."
    … *mas eu não acredito / veremos se é verdade.*
    … "but I don't believe / we shall see whether it is true."

In either reading, they differ from other tenses of the indicative in the fact that they do not convey that the proposition is verified in every world compatible with what is known (in other words, they express some degree of doubt). Thus, one choice is, again, to claim that they do not belong to the indicative mood. Another choice is to assume that they are tenses of the indicative that select particular epistemic modal bases. In the reportative reading, the modal base will be relativized to the source of information. In the "uncertainty" reading, the modal base would be the set of worlds compatible with the partial information available to the speaker, and, once again, we can keep the idea that the indicative involves the consideration of only p-worlds. The value of uncertainty associated with these tenses would follow from the fact that the speaker is relying on partial information or, in the case of the reportative reading, on information (or beliefs) that he might not share, but the ordering source would still be normality.

    The *futuro do pretérito/condicional*, just as the *imperfeito*, may also convey desire and counterfactuality:

(30) *Ele casa-ria/cas-ava*   *com ela, se fosse possível.*
    he marry-cond/IMperf with her if it were possible
    "He would marry her, if it were possible"

It is not surprising that these tenses are in variation. If these tenses are not marked for the ordering source, they allow for different interpretations.

5. Other issues to be explored

As speculative as the answers we provided may be, they were meant to highlight the intricate relations between mood and modality, and the need for further investigation. But other connected issues, which have not even been mentioned here, also require exploration. What follows is obviously a non-exhaustive inventory.

    Imperatives should be better understood. Exclamative clauses in Portuguese have not been semantically studied yet, as far as we know. The semantics of infinitive clauses in Portuguese has been less explored than the semantics of finite clauses. In some cases, no clear semantic difference is associated with the infinitive *vs.* a finite mood, although even in such contexts, there may be still be subtle differences, as in (31):

(31) *Isso não impediu*   *[que a Ana saí-sse]*   */ [a Ana de sai-r].*
    That not prevented [that the Ana leave-imp.subj] / [Ana of leave-inf]
    "This didn't stop Ana from leaving."

The subjunctive form seems to convey that Ana has left, whereas the infinitive may imply that she has left, but is also compatible with a situation where she could have left, though she did not. A semantic contrast between finite and infinitive clauses is stronger in temporal clauses with *até* ("until") or *antes* ("before"):

(32) *Platão ficou na rua até   começa-r   a chover / até que   começa-sse   a chover.*
  Plato waited until   start-inf at to-rain / until that start-impf.subj at to rain
  "Plato waited until it started raining."

(33) *Platão entrou antes de   começa-r a chover / que começa-sse   a chover.*
  Plato entered before of start-inf at to-rain / that start-impf.subj at to-rain
  "Plato went in before it started raining / would start raining."

Both in (32) as in (33), if the subjunctive is chosen, there is an inference that Plato expected rain, while with the infinitive this information is not necessarily conveyed. By asserting the sentences and choosing the infinitive, the speaker takes his/her own knowledge at speech time and describes two situations temporally ordered. In contrast, by choosing the subjunctive, the situations are presented following Plato's perspective at the relevant time (when he decided to stay out, in (32), and when he decided to go in, in (33)) (cf. Marques and Alves 2013 for constructions such as in (33)). Other constructions where the infinitive is an alternative to a finite mood may also show similar semantic differences.

Conditional clauses in Portuguese are another topic that deserves further attention. In particular in the literature in philosophy, the relation between mood and conditionals is the criterion to distinguish two types of conditionals:

(34) a. *Se João sai-u,   a Maria   cozinh-ou.*
      If João leave-perf.ind, the Maria cook-perf.ind
      "If João has left, Maria has cooked."
   b. *Se João saí-sse,   a Maria cozinha-va   / cozinha-ria.*
      If João leave-impf.subj, the Maria cook-impf.ind / fut.pret.ind
      "If João would leave, Maria would cook."

The *futuro do pretérito/conditional* are the verbal forms that appear in the main clause of the so-called "counterfactual conditionals," as (34b) (in which the *imperfeito* seems to be more informal than the *conditional*). And they are precisely those forms that seem problematic if classified as indicative forms (see the previous section). Thus, a better understanding of conditionals may help us understand these tenses.

In this chapter, our aim was to provide an introductory and concise view of the state of the art in the study of mood and modality via an analysis of various facts in contemporary Portuguese. We argued that the indicative mood signals that only p-worlds are considered. This is even the case for the *futuro do presente*, the uncertainty being associated with partial knowledge. The *futuro do pretérito/condicional* and the *imperfeito* belong to the indicative mood, but they do not select for an ordering source, while with other indicative tenses the set of worlds is ordered by normality. We also advanced a hypothesis to explain some of the mood contrasts between EP and BP: some data point to the tendency for the indicative in BP to carry an assumption of factuality. Most of the issues addressed were barely studied or not studied at all; moreover, we showed that they seem to be related to other issues which also demand further investigation. These topics only recently began to be considered in fields as language teaching, language acquisition or corpora annotation. But clearly, not only in Portuguese, these are flourishing subjects of research.

NOTES

1   The notion of possible world has a long tradition in philosophy. The real world is one of an infinity of possible worlds. A proposition is the set of possible worlds in which the state of affairs described by such proposition is verified. See Portner (2009) for an introduction to modal logic and modality in natural languages.

2   Kratzer (2013) collects in a unique volume a series of papers from the end of the 1970s and beginning of the 1980s which established the background of the contemporary formal view on Mood and Modality.

3   In non-subordinated clauses, the subjunctive occurs in: imperative clauses, as in (i); in (semi-)-formulaic constructions, as in (ii); and under the scope of *talvez* ("maybe") or *oxalá* ("God wishes"), as in (iii)–(iv):

   (i)   *Saiam!*
         "(You) Leave!"
   (ii) *Deus queira!*
         "God wishes!"
   (iii) *Oxalá não chova.*
         "Wish it doesn't rain."
   (iv) *Talvez ele venha.*
         "Maybe he comes."

4   The glosses focus exclusively on the verb inflection that is under our investigation. The following abbreviations are adopted: prs = Present; ind = Indicative; subj = Subjunctive; impf = Imperfect; perf = Perfect.

5   Sergio Menuzzi (p.c.) observes that these cases might be due to some tense and mood harmony within the complement clauses of *embora* and of the embedded predicate: use of *saiba* "know-prs. subj" would call for the subjunctive in the complement of "know," that is, for *estivesse* "was.subj"; but "to know" is not used with subjunctive complements, normally. We thank him for the observation.

6   In EP, the complement clause of *imagine* may also be in the subjunctive, but only in the epistemic reading of the verb (in which it is roughly equivalent to *believe*) and if a low degree of belief is expressed.

7   Infinitive clauses with modal meaning are at the heart of the studies on covert modality (e.g., Bhatt 2006, Abraham and Leiss 2012).

8   See Pessotto and Teixeira (2011).

9   In cases like *Quando acordei, devia estar chovendo*, the sentence with the imperfective form is acceptable, but the temporal perspective is not the speech time.

10 The use of (18) in a context where a director orders someone to let the stone fall reinforces the claim that the deontic use seems to require an agent.

11 See Pires de Oliveira and Pessotto (2010).

12 See Mortari and Pires de Oliveira (2014) for an introduction to Kratzer's formal apparatus.

13 Unlike English causative "to make," *fazer* does accept full (subjunctive) clauses, as in (i) below:

   (i)   *O João fez com que a Maria partisse.*
         the João made with that the Maria leave.impf.subj
         "João made Maria leave."

REFERENCES

Abraham, W. and E. Leiss (eds.) (2012). *Covert Patterns of Modality*. Newcastle upon Tyne: Cambridge Scholars Publishing.

Austin, J. L. (1962). *How to Do Things with Words*. Oxford: Clarendon Press. (Reimp. 1980, Oxford University Press).

Bhatt, R. (2006). *Covert Modality in Non-Finite Contexts*. Berlin: de Gruyter.

Cinque, G. (2006). Restructuring and functional structure. In G. Cinque, *Restructuring and Functional Heads: The Cartography of Syntactic Structures*. vol. 4. New York: Oxford University Press, pp. 11–63.

Condoravit, C. (2002). Temporal interpretation of modals: modals for the present and for the past. In D. Beaver, S, Kaufmann, B. Clark, and L. Casillas (eds.), *The Construction of Meaning*. Sanford, CA: CSLI Publications, pp. 59–88.

Costa Moreira, B. E. (2014). Two types of dispositional adjectives. *ReVEL*, special issue, 8, pp. 186–196.

Farkas, D. (1992). On the semantics of subjunctive complements. In P. Hirschbühler (ed.), *Romance Languages and Modern Linguistic Theory*. Amsterdam: John Benjamins, pp. 69–105.

Giannakidou, A. (1999). Affective dependencies. *Linguistics and Philosophy*, 22 (4), pp. 367–421.

Giannakidou, A. (2013). (Non)veridicality, evaluation, and event actualization: evidence from the subjunctive in relative clauses. In M. Taboada and R. Tvranc (eds.), *Nonveridicality, Perspective, and Discourse Coherence*. Brill, Studies in Pragmatics Series.

Gonçalves, A. (1992). Para uma Sintaxe dos Verbos Auxiliares em Português Europeu. Masters dissertation, University of Lisbon.

Hacquard, V. (2006). Aspects of modality. Ph.D. dissertation, MIT.

Heim, I. (1992). Presupposition projection and the semantics of attitude verbs. *Journal of Semantics*, 9 (3), pp. 183–221.

Hockett, C. F. (1960). The origin of speech. *Scientific American*, 203, pp. 89–96.

Hooper, J. B. (1975). On assertive predicates. In J. P. Kimball (ed.), *Syntax and Semantics 4*. New York: Academic Press, pp. 91–124.

Kratzer, A. (2013). *Modals and Conditionals*. Oxford: Oxford University Press.

Marques, R. (1995). Sobre o valor dos modos conjuntivo e indicativo em português. Masters dissertation, University of Lisbon.

Marques, R. (2009). On the selection of mood in complement clauses. In L. Hogeweg, H. de Hoop, and A. Malchukov (eds.), *Cross-linguistic Semantics of Tense, Aspect, and Modality*. Amsterdam: John Benjamins, pp. 179–204.

Marques, R. and A. T. Alves (2013). Sobre as variações de modo nas frases subordinadas temporais com *antes*. In A. Moreno, F. Silva, I. Falé, I. Pereira, and J. Veloso (eds.), *XXIX Encontro Nacional da Associação Portuguesa de Linguística: Textos Selecionados*. Porto: Associação Portuguesa de Linguística, pp. 333–343.

Mateus, M. H. M., A. M. Brito, I. Duarte, and I. H. Faria (2003). *Gramática da Língua Portuguesa*. Lisbon: Caminho.

Miranda, Z. B. de A. G. (1975). Aspectos do comportamento sintático dos modais "dever" e "poder." Masters dissertation, Universidade Estadual de Campinas.

Mortari, C. and R. Pires de Oliveira (2014). Operadores modais: sistemas formais e línguas naturais. *ReVEL*, special issue, 8, pp. 159–185.

Oliveira, F. and A. Mendes (2013). Modalidade. In Eduardo Paiva Raposo, M. F. Bacelar do Nascimento, M. A. C. da Mota, L. Segura, and A. Mendes (eds.), *Gramática do Português*. Lisbon: Fundação Calouste Gulbenkian, pp. 623–669.

Palmer, F. R. (1986). *Mood and Modality*. Cambridge: Cambridge University Press.

Pessotto, A. L. and L. R. Teixeira (2011). A contribuição da prosódia para a interpretação do item "podia." *Working Papers em Linguística (Online)*, 12, pp. 27–52.

Pires de Oliveira, R. and A. L. Pessotto (2010). Wishing it were: *podia* and the implicature of desire in Brazilian Portuguese. In S. Lima (ed.), *Proceedings of SULA 5: Semantics of Under-Represented Languages in the Americas, 1*. Amherst, MA: GLSA Publications, pp. 189–204.

Pontes, E. (1973). *Verbos Auxiliares em Português*. Petrópolis: Vozes.

Portner, P. (1993). The semantics of mood, complementation, and conversational force. Natural Language Semantics, 5, pp. 167–212.

Portner, P. (2009). *Modality*. Oxford: Oxford University Press.

Rech, N. F. (2011). Hierarquia dos núcleos funcionais no português brasileiro. *Revista da Anpoll*, 31 (1), pp. 207–225.

Rullmann, H., L. Matthewson, and H. Davis (2008). Modals as distributive indefinites. *Natural Language Semantics*, 16 (4), pp. 317–357.

Salmon, W. C. (1998). *Causality and Explanation*. Oxford: Oxford University Press.

Santos, M. J. V. (2003). Os usos do conjuntivo em Língua Portuguesa: uma proposta de análise sintáctica e semântico-pragmática. Ph.D. dissertation, University of Coimbra.

Searle, J. R. (1969). *Speech Acts: An Essay in the Philosophy of Language*. Cambridge: Cambridge University Press.

Stalnaker, R. (1979). Assertion. In P. Cole (ed.), *Syntax and Semantics*, vol. 9. New York: Academic Press, pp. 315–332.

23 Some Issues in Negation in Portuguese

SCOTT A. SCHWENTER

1. Introduction

Negation in Portuguese shares many properties with negation in other Romance languages, but also displays some unique characteristics, especially when we take into account the wider range of negation strategies found in varieties of spoken Brazilian Portuguese (BP).[1] Because of parallelisms between certain structures and uses of negation and those of non-negative elements, it would also be necessary to situate negation in the broader perspective of polarity-related phenomena, such as in the work of Martins (2013) on European Portuguese (EP). However, space limitations prevent me from doing that in detail here, and from providing a comprehensive view of negation and all its intricacies at the sentential, constituent, and other levels. Luckily, this has been done quite recently by Peres (2013), albeit with a near-exclusive focus on EP.

In addition to links between negation and other polarity-related structures, the interactions of negation with other grammatical phenomena are legion. While those found in Portuguese may not be as striking as in, e.g., English, they still may effect profound changes in linguistic structure. To cite just one of these structural phenomena, consider clitic pronoun placement in EP (Washington forthcoming). As is well-known, in finite clauses EP clitics tend to appear in enclitic position (1a). But in the presence of certain triggers, such as complementizer *que* "that," adverbs like *já* "already" or *também* "also/too," or WH-questions with a *qu-* word, the clitic instead occurs in proclitic position. Negative words constitute one class of such triggers, as the examples with *não* "not" and *nunca* "never" show in (1b, c), where the proclitic position of the clitic *te* "you" contrasts with its enclitic placement in the affirmative example (1a).

(1a) *Vi-te na escola do meu filho.*
 "I saw you at my son's school."
(1b) ***Não** te vi na escola do meu filho.*
 "I didn't see you at my son's school."
(1c) ***Nunca** te vejo na escola do meu filho.*
 "I never see you at my son's school."

The pattern in (1) is described and at least implicitly prescribed by Portuguese grammars (e.g. Cunha and Cintra 1985) and formal analyses (e.g. Martins 1995). Recent research on naturally-occurring data (Washington forthcoming) shows however that individual members of the class of proclitic triggers actually demonstrate differences regarding how

The Handbook of Portuguese Linguistics, First Edition. Edited by W. Leo Wetzels, João Costa, and Sergio Menuzzi.
© 2016 John Wiley & Sons, Inc. Published 2020 by John Wiley & Sons, Inc.

often they lead to proclisis in speech or writing. The important point for this chapter is that negative elements can have important interactions with syntactic phenomena, and therefore that negation makes up a core morphosyntactic process, fully integrated into grammatical structure.

The rest of this chapter is organized as follows. In Section 2 I discuss "canonical" sentence negation in Portuguese, and explain what that label entails. Section 3 deals with the best-known "non-canonical" negative in Portuguese, mainly in BP, the so-called *dupla negação* or NEG2. It also describes differences between NEG2 and other non-canonical negators, such as strictly postverbal *não* or NEG3. Section 4 presents negative concord in Portuguese, and suggests as worthy of further research some possible changes underway in BP. Section 5 discusses metalinguistic negation (Horn 1985) and points out important distinctions for examining this notion in Portuguese. Section 6 provides concluding remarks.

Throughout the discussion, I attempt to be as theory-neutral as possible, both for readers who may not know a given theory, and also due to the strong bias in Lusophone linguistics toward generative / minimalist theories, and a comparative lack of analyses in other frameworks. Indeed, one goal for this chapter is to foment future research on Portuguese negation from a diverse set of theoretical perspectives, not only in syntax, but also semantics and pragmatics.[2] I also hope it will spur more research on negation in EP, where little investigation into this corner of the grammar has been carried out.

2. Canonical or "standard" negation

According to Dahl (2010: 10), "there has been a strong tendency for typological studies to concentrate on what has been seen as the basic negation constructions in [individual] languages." Along these lines, and following typological studies by Miestamo (2005) and Bond (2013), it is first useful to distinguish between canonical and non-canonical negation in Portuguese. The canonical form, which has been termed "standard negation" by Miestamo (2005) and Payne (1985), provides a basis for comparison for all other forms. The latter can diverge from the canonical expression in both morphosyntactic and semantic / pragmatic terms, for instance by containing extra or distinct morphological material, requiring a specific word order not found with the canonical negative construction, or being constrained by/to a set of particular discourse-contextual circumstances. Payne (1985:198) defines "standard" negation this way in his typological overview of the phenomenon:

> By "standard" negation we understand that type of negation that can apply to the most minimal and basic sentences. Such sentences are characteristically main clauses, and consist of a single predicate with as few noun phrases and adverbial modifiers as possible.

One must be careful however not to associate "standard" with social evaluation of the negative form, since there is no necessary connection between a language's canonical negator and its social acceptance or rejection.[3] Indeed, over time, what was the canonical form in a language can become a non-canonical form due to linguistic change, which always occurs embedded in a social context. It is for this reason that I will prefer the label "canonical" to "standard" in the rest of this chapter. In Portuguese, the form that fits the bill of the canonical negator is the negative morpheme *não* in preverbal position in simple declarative main clauses such as in (2a, b):

(2a) *A Patrícia **não** dorme.*
    The   P.   not   sleep:3sg
    "Patricia does not sleep."

(2b)   *A Patrícia **não** come carne.*
   "Patricia does not eat meat."

The semantic function of canonical or "standard" negation is to take an affirmative proposition *p* and convert it into a negated proposition *~p*. Thus, in (2a), *não* reverses the polarity of the affirmative proposition "Patricia sleeps," i.e. changes the truth value of that proposition from T to F, "Patricia does not sleep."

According to Perini (2006: 86) there are two sentential negative morphemes in Portuguese. In addition to the canonical negator *não*, the adverb *mal* "barely, hardly" should also be considered a sentential negator when in preverbal position. He provides the following example (3) to illustrate:

(3)   *A noiva **mal** chegou a tempo para o casório.*
   "The bride barely arrived on time for the wedding."

(3′)   *A noiva chegou a tempo para o casório.*
   "The bride arrived on time for the wedding."

It is debatable whether this use of *mal* should be considered a sentential negative, or one that is on a par with canonical *não*. In fact, one of the entailments of (3) is (3′), i.e. that the bride actually *did* arrive on time, with the caveat that she was close to *not* arriving on time (cf. Amaral 2007). In this use, *mal* is considered an approximative adverb with two meaning components (cf. Horn 2002), an entailed, but non-asserted, polar component (the proposition is entailed to be true), and an asserted proximal component, which in (3) asserts closeness to the non-realization of the bride's arrival (cp. *quase*, whose polar and proximal components are the opposite of *mal*). Thus, while *mal* has an evaluatively negative meaning in (3), it is not commutable with *não*. There are other uses of *mal* in EP, especially, where a negative polar meaning is conveyed (like some uses of preverbal *hardly* in English), but these all occur in specific construction with an epistemic stative verb (e.g. *saber* "to know") expressing imperfective aspect, typically with a postposed subject, and introducing a sentential complement (4).

(4)   *Mal sabia eu que estava perdido.*
   "Little did I know that I was lost."

Such uses require a specific information-structural configuration in the discourse context in order to be felicitously licensed; they cannot be uttered in discourse-initial position (for detailed discussion, see Amaral and Schwenter 2009). In sum, these particular properties of *mal* when it expresses a negative polar meaning actually make it a clear instance of a non-canonical negative form, and evince the polysemy of *mal* as both an approximative (3) and as a non-canonical negator (4).[4]

3. Non-canonical sentence negation: NEG2 (*dupla negação*) and NEG3

One of the most well-known properties of sentential negation in Portuguese is that there exists the option of "doubling" the negative morpheme *não* in a single sentence. Structurally, this kind of sentence consists of a preverbal negative and a postverbal negative "copy" that occurs in sentence- or utterance-final position. While the second negative is often represented orthographically after a comma, in speech there is rarely a pause before the second instance of *não*, and prosodically it is contained within the intonational contour of the whole sentence. In addition to the *dupla negação*, there also exists in BP the option of a postverbal negative without a corresponding preverbal negator. These structures are illustrated in (5b, c), and labeled, as is now typical, as NEG2 and NEG3, respectively, along with the canonical NEG1 (5a):

(5a) **Não** *vai muito para a universidade.*   (NEG1)
      "She doesn't go much to the university"
(5b) **Não** *vai muito para a universidade* **não.**   (NEG2)
(5c) *Vai muito para a universidade* **não.**   (NEG3)

(5b, c) express the same propositional content as the corresponding canonical NEG1 (5a). Where the two non-canonical negatives differ from NEG1, is in their information-structural constraints: only NEG1 can "surface in simple, unmarked declaratives" (Cyrino and Biberauer 2009) that introduce new information into the discourse. While this phenomenon is typically associated with BP, NEG2 is also found less frequently in EP (Hagemeijer 2003; Peres 2013; Nunes 2014), although its precise characteristics in Portugal remain to be described in detail. Some scholars have attributed this construction in BP to a process of creolization, since many African languages whose speakers were taken to Brazil for slavery have double negation constructions. However, its roots (like other phenomena with purported creole origin in BP) appear to lie in a similar structure that has been available to EP speakers for centuries, and appears, for instance, in sixteenth-century plays by Gil Vicente (Cyrino and Biberauer 2009). Note also that speakers of closely-related Romance languages like Spanish allow *no*-doubling in all varieties, despite greater frequency in Caribbean dialects (cf. Schwegler 1996).

In some grammars (e.g. Thomas 1969), the availablity of doubling negatives is linked to the presence of a preverbal *não*, but in reality the preverbal neg-word does not have to be *não* specifically, but rather can be drawn from any of the class of neg-words, and *não* cannot co-occur preverbally with another of these neg-words (in contrast to, e.g., standard varieties of Catalan, where combining preverbal neg-words with sentential negation is grammatical):

(6a) *A sua mãe nunca (*não) comeu em casa com a gente não.*
      "Your mother never ate with us at home."
(6b) *Ninguém (*não) pensa que vá chegar na hora não.*
      "Nobody thinks that she's going to arrive on time."

This kind of doubling construction is not, however, unique to negative sentences in Portuguese; it is also possible to find doubling of adverbs such as *já* "already." For instance, a possible retort challenging the truth validity of a negative assertion could be as in (7):

(7) João: *A sua mãe nunca comeu na minha casa.*
             "Your mom has never eaten at my house."
     Maria: *Ela* **já** *comeu* **já.**
             "She ate [there] already."

More generally, utterance-final postverbal position can be seen as a host for polarity-reversing items ("emphatic polarity"; Martins 2013), which often challenge the truth of a proposition derivable from a prior utterance, as in (8), where the postverbal reinforcement of the affirmative with *sim* targets the truth of the proposition derivable from João's prior turn:

(8) João: *A sua mãe nunca comeu na minha casa.*
             "Your mom has never eaten at my house."
     Maria: *Ela (já) comeu* **sim!**
             "Yes she has eaten there!"

Such reinforcement with *sim* is extremely common in both BP and EP (Martins 2013). It occurs most often in dialogic contexts such as (8), where one speaker is attempting to refute a prior assertion by their interlocutor, or in adversative clauses after a conjunction like *mas*, where it can be used in ellipsis to reverse the polarity of the prior clause (*A Maria não come farofa, mas o João sim*, "Maria doesn't eat farofa, but João does"). But the broader strategy of reinforcement through repetition of polarity goes beyond the use of the polarity particles themselves. For instance, in EP especially it is also common to use reduplication of the verb in a context like (9), as discussed by Martins (2013):

(9) João: *A sua mãe nunca comeu na minha casa.*
             "Your mom has never eaten at my house."
    Maria: *Comeu comeu!*
             "Yes she has eaten there!"

In all cases, the additional material functions to overcome the metaphorical obstacle posed by the opposing interlocutor's viewpoint. It is in this sense that NEG2 or any doubling construction can be considered intuitively "emphatic" (cf. Furtado da Cunha 2007:1650), since they often deny a previous asserted viewpoint—typically an interlocutor's immediately prior utterance—accessible in the discourse situation.

For Perini (2002: 436), the "double negative must be learned, because it is one of the important patterns of the language and is extremely common in Brazilian speech," a position not held by many grammarians, since few, if any, other grammars even mention the existence of the construction. Instead, many discussions of the NEG2 (and also NEG3, see below) structures in BP have been contextualized in the rubric of what has come to be known (Dahl 1979) as "Jespersen's Cycle," following the original formulation by Otto Jespersen (1917). This is the cyclical process by which sentential negatives are renewed via postverbal negative "strengtheners," as occurred, most famously, in French. While the exact number of stages can vary, a typical characterization of the French case, where the postverbal reinforcer *pas* (< "step") has been reanalyzed as the main exponent of sentential negation, is in (10) (cf. Cyrino and Biberauer 2009):

(10) French
    Stage 1   *Je ne mange*   "I don't eat"
    Stage 2   *Je ne mange (pas)*
    Stage 3   *Je ne mange pas*
    Stage 4   *Je (ne) mange pas*
    Stage 5   *Je mange pas*

While some have recently either questioned a single characterization of the Cycle (Larrivée 2011), or have attempted to define multiple variants of the Cycle (van der Auwera 2009), it remains a useful generalization of a pattern for cross-linguistic comparison. In Jespersen's Cycle negative constructions move from being strictly preverbal, i.e. of the NEG1 type, to being reinforced by a postverbal element in an "embracing" negative construction, i.e. of the NEG2 type, and then strictly post-verbal, of the NEG3 type, with variation typical of the intermediate stages. French and English are the most well-known cases of languages that have gone through this Cycle, although modern-day spoken European French still allows for variation between Stages 4 and 5, and additional changes to the English grammatical system, such as the introduction of *do*-support, complicate comparisons. What differentiates cases like these from that of Portuguese is that, first, as discussed below, NEG1 is still overwhelmingly more frequent than either NEG2 or NEG3 in any variety, and in French and English the original NEG1 construction was lost. Second, the cases that Jespersen (1917) and others have used as models for the Cycle do not contain a repetition of the pre-verbal negator in postverbal position, but rather a minimizing element (French *pas* "step") or a negative indefinite (English *not* < *naught* "nothing"), that later becomes the canonical sentential negator.

While not wholly discarding the diachrony of the Portuguese system, greater attention has been focused on the synchronic conditions licensing NEG2. Schwenter (2005, 2006) offered an explanation for the use of NEG2 in BP based on information structure (cf. Birner 2006; Prince 1992), taking into account the contrast between activated and non-activated propositions in discourse (Dryer 1996). NEG2 or *dupla negação* is pragmatically felicitous precisely in those cases where the proposition it is negating is one that has been activated in previous discourse, including via implicature; it is infelicitous in contexts without activation. An example that illustrates this difference, and the non-canonical nature of NEG2 versus the canonical NEG1, can be seen in (11). Imagine a scenario in which the speaker leaves home and remembers that she forgot to turn off the stove. She is walking along the street with her friend when she suddenly realizes this mistake. Crucially, when verbalizing this state of affairs, which is information being newly added into the discourse model, NEG1 is felicitous, while NEG2 is not:

(11) *Nossa, não desliguei o fogão (#não)!!!*
      "Damn, I didn't turn off the stove!!!"

The importance of the activation of the proposition becomes apparent once it is accessible in the discourse context. Suppose the speaker's friend asks her whether or not she turned off the stove. In this case, NEG2 would become felicitous in the context (with ellipsis of the direct object), and NEG1, being the canonical form without information-structural restrictions on its occurrence, would remain felicitous.

(12) A: *Você desligou o fogão?*
           "Did you turn off the stove?"
      B: *Nossa, não desliguei [o fogão] (não)!!!*
           "Damn, I didn't turn off the stove!!!"

What the difference in felicity between (11) and (12) illustrates is that NEG2 is sensitive to the discourse activation of the proposition it negates. While others have seen this as a sensitivity to (pragmatic) presuppositions (Schwegler 1991), the last example illustrates that this is not the case, since the proposition derivable from A's question is neither presupposed nor necessarily believed to be true when it is asked.

One important advantage of this account over others that posit pragmatic presupposition or vague notions like "emphasis" as the keys to the felicity of NEG2 is that it can also account for examples where the doubling of negation occurs in contexts of **agreement** between two interlocutors, instead of disagreement and denial.

(13) A: *A Maria não vai para a escola hoje.*
           "Maria isn't going to school today."
      B: *É. Não vai não.*
           "Yes. She's not going."

Such contexts are extremely difficult for an emphasis-based account to deal with, since it would be unclear what was being emphasized, or why agreement with NEG2 should be different from that with NEG1. On the information-structural account, this case is treated like any other: NEG2 is licensed by the occurrence in the prior discourse of an activated proposition ("Maria is not going to school today"), which is "re-negated" by NEG2. No special explanation is needed for cases such as (13) where there is no denial of a prior affirmative proposition, but instead agreement with a prior negative proposition (cf. De Cuypere 2008: 235–6, who analyzes BP NEG2 as "emphatic"). Research on the diachronic development of French and Italian negation (Hansen and Visconti 2009) has since corroborated the usefulness of information-structural notions for explaining the rise of and motivation for non-canonical negatives.

Like much research in information structure (e.g. Birner and Ward 1998), this analysis has provided an account of a sufficient licensing condition for NEG2 in BP, but not an explanation for why speakers employ NEG2 at certain points in discourse but not others. More recent research on BP has corroborated and refined Schwenter's (2005) analysis, and identified different types of NEG2. Working with data from the state of Rio Grande do Sul, in far southern Brazil, Goldnadel and Lima (2014) have argued that NEG2 usage can be differentiated pragmatically into "emphatic" uses that correct misguided prior assumptions in discourse, and "topic maintenance" uses that signal that the current discourse topic will be continued by the speaker. Nunes (2014) has recently found the same distinction to hold for NEG2 in Lisbon Portuguese, in analyses of data from naturally occurring speech and perception tests. These two types are prosodically distinct: "emphatic" uses contain a tonic pitch accent on the postverbal negative, while "topic maintenance" uses do not. This distinction is crucial for providing independent evidence for the two uses, instead of assuming that NEG2 (or any repeated negative) constitutes an inherently emphatic usage. In essence, this work has taken a complementary tack to that of Schwenter, by focusing on the forward-looking functions of NEG2 as opposed to the backwards-looking contextual-licensing requirements. Together, both kinds of approaches will combine to provide a more comprehensive view of the meaning and discourse-pragmatic function of NEG2.

How do NEG2, the *dupla negação*, and NEG3, the strictly postverbal negative, differ? For Schwenter (2005), NEG3 is found in a proper subset of contexts where NEG2 can be found. The main discourse-pragmatic licensing difference resides in the accessibility of the negated proposition: NEG2 is felicitous with inferrable propositions, while NEG3 requires that the proposition it targets be explicitly activated in the preceding discourse. Thus, while both structures are felicitous in (14a), where the reply targets the "liking" proposition from A's utterance, only NEG2 is felicitous in (14b), where B is targeting an inferred proposition that she believes A must believe to be true given the question:

(14a) A: *Você gostou do filme?*
          "Did you like the movie?"
       B: *(Não) gostei não.*   [Both NEG2 and NEG3 possible]
          "I didn't like it."

(14b) [A assumes that B went to see the movie]
       A: *Você gostou do filme?*
          "Did you like the movie?"
       B: *Ah, #(não) fui não*   [Only NEG2 possible]
          "Ah, I didn't go."

Other important differences between the two forms relate to frequency: NEG2 is considerably more frequent in any variety of Portuguese where both NEG2 and NEG3 are found, and indeed, as noted by Goldnadel and Lima (2014) there are varieties in the far southern region of Brazil (e.g. Curitiba, Florianópolis, and Porto Alegre) where NEG3 is extremely rare, if used at all. Even in northern and northeastern Brazil, where the popular view holds that NEG3 is common, the frequency of NEG3 is low even in spontaneous conversation: only 13.3 percent of 466 negative tokens in the Natal data reported in Furtado da Cunha (2007) are NEG3 versus 20.6 percent NEG2 and 66 percent NEG1.

Finally, recent work by Teixeira de Sousa (2011) and Cyrino and Biberauer (2009) has brought to light a number of structural differences between NEG2 and NEG3 that suggest that NEG3 is not merely a "reduced" version of NEG2 whose preverbal negative has been "dropped" (cf. Furtado da Cunha 2007; Schwegler 1991).[5] Among these differences are the fact that only NEG2, not NEG3, is found in subordinate clauses and that

NEG3 is possible in metalinguistic negation, while NEG2 is barred from such contexts (Schwenter 2005; Teixeira de Sousa 2011). As an alternative to the view that sees NEG3 as a "reduced" version of NEG2, Cyrino and Biberauer (2009) advance convincing arguments that NEG3 derives historically from responses to yes–no questions (a context where it is still used), while the postverbal *não* in NEG2 comes from a different source, namely from an originally right-dislocated negative that has been incorporated into sentential structure.

3.1. *Changes in progress in BP?*

One of the most fascinating aspects of BP negation is its variability between NEG1, NEG2, and NEG3 structures. An important question that arises with respect to these different structural options is whether they are stable in time or whether they represent distinct synchronic stages in a larger diachronic process that is changing the expression of negation in this variety (or in some subset of BP varieties). For some authors (e.g. Furtado da Cunha 2007; Schwegler 1991), the variation between the different sentence negation constructions constitutes a case of grammaticalization and change in progress, where the endpoint of this Jespersen Cycle-style process is a new system of negation where NEG2 (and ultimately NEG3) is the unmarked member.

In the discussion above, I have cast doubt on the view that derives NEG3 from NEG2 in the same way that French [V *pas*] derives from [*ne* V *pas*], by primarily basing the discussion on discourse-pragmatic constraints. But also problematic with this position is the fact that there is little evidence, neither from apparent-time data nor from real-time diachronic data, of change either occurring or having occurred. From a structural perspective, it is not the case that the postverbal *não* has become grammatically obligatory in the sentential negation construction, in the way that *pas* has in French; rather, it remains optional in all contexts. From a social perspective, one would also expect to see, for instance, greater use of NEG2 and/or NEG3 among younger generations when compared to older generations, as well as reasons for believing that these patterns are revealing more than age-grading between the generations. To my knowledge, however, such patterns have not yet been discovered in BP. There are clear indications, nevertheless, of regional differences. Brazilian speakers' intuitions that *nordestinos* use more NEG2 and NEG3 appear to be borne about by the empirical facts (cf. Souza 2004), while speakers in the extreme south, such as in Rio Grande do Sul, use NEG2 much less frequently and use NEG3 very rarely, if ever (Goldnadel and Lima 2014).

Cavalcante (2009) shows that in isolated Afro-Brazilian communities in northeast Brazil there is lower use of NEG1, and higher use of NEG2/3, than in other communities in the region that have a more mixed ethnic and demographic history, such as Fortaleza and Natal. Nevertheless, his data from these Afro-Brazilian communities shows that there is stability in the usage patterns of the three variants. In fact, it is the *oldest* group (> 60 years of age) of speakers that uses the most NEG2 and NEG3, while the two younger groups in his study (40–60 and 20–40 years of age) both use more NEG1 than the oldest speakers. Thus, even in what might be considered extreme non-standard varieties of BP, stable variation between the three negative forms reigns (Cavalcante 2009: 266). In conclusion, there is no clear evidence from any BP variety of change in progress of the type NEG1 > NEG2 > NEG3. Rather, there is stability in the system whereby canonical NEG1 is the overwhelmingly preferred form in any variety, despite frequency differences, while NEG2 and NEG3 are discourse-pragmatically marked variants with specific licensing constraints.

4. Negative concord and negative indefinites

Like its Romance sisters Spanish and Italian, Portuguese is a negative concord language that requires that polarity-sensitive words in a sentence agree with each other, specifically, a negative indefinite (like *nada, nunca, ninguém*) in postverbal position requires that there be another negative in preverbal position to license the postverbal indefinite. The co-occurrence of these negative words in the same sentence does not result in a semantically positive interpretation (as it might, for instance, in prescriptive English, where pedants stress that "two negatives make a positive," despite the absurdity of this rule and the fact that it is frequently disregarded in many varieties of English). Thus for instance, while (15a) is grammatical with *não* and the negative indefinite *nunca*, (15b) is not, since there is a lack of agreement between the negative word *não* and the temporal adverbial *alguma vez*, which is a positive polarity item incompatible with a co-occurring negative in preverbal position:

(15a) *A Maria não vem nunca às festas.*
    "Maria never comes to the parties."
(15b) **A Maria não vem alguma vez às festas.*
    "Maria doesn't come sometimes to the parties."

As the gloss for (15a) makes clear, the two negative words *não* and *nunca* lead to a single negative interpretation, not the negative-canceling (i.e. positive) interpretation. When negative indefinites in Portuguese appear in preverbal position, they do not need another preverbal trigger in order to be licensed and in fact cannot co-occur with one, but in postverbal position, they require a negative trigger, as can be seen by the contrast in grammaticality between (15a) above and (16b) below:

(16a) *A Maria nunca (*não) vem às festas.*
    "Maria never comes to the parties."
(16b) **A Maria vem nunca às festas.*

It is typically assumed implicitly or explicitly that the preverbal negative licensor in such cases is the canonical negator *não*. But as (16a) shows, this is not the case, since the requirement is just that some negative word must appear in preverbal position in order to provide the polarity agreement on each side of the verb that is characteristic of negative concord. Another way to formulate this generalization, as Thomas (1969: 287) points out, is that in any negative clause that has a verb in it, at least one negative word must occur in preverbal position. As we will see below, however, there exist some seemingly recent exceptions in the class of negative sentences in BP that offer evidence to modify this position somewhat.[6]

    Haspelmath (1997, 2013) distinguishes between three types of systems of negative indefinites typologically, as below. While the first type is the most frequent cross-linguistically, among the Romance languages the most common pattern is as found in Portuguese, Spanish, and Italian, where there is a mixed behavior depending on pre- vs. postverbal syntactic position.

1. NIs that *always* co-occur with predicate negation (e.g. Russian)
2. NIs that *never* co-occur with predicate negation (e.g. standard German)
3. NIs that show a *mixed* behavior:
   - Different sets of NIs (e.g. standard English, Swedish)
   - NIs with different behavior due to syntactic position (e.g. Spanish, Portuguese)
   - Languages with bipartite negators wherein one part is precluded when co-occurring with NIs

Within Romance, distinct varieties are classified as "strict" or "non-strict" negative concord languages: Romanian and Standard French are examples of the former, while Spanish, Portuguese, and Italian are examples of the latter (Catalan is optionally strict, since neg-words may occur in preverbal position with or without negation). This means that negative indefinites appearing in preverbal position either do ("strict") or do not ("non-strict") co-occur with predicate negation. Thus, in Standard French *personne* "no one" co-occurs with *ne* "not" (17a), but in Portuguese *ninguém* cannot co-occur with *não* when in preverbal position (17b).

(17a) *Personne n'est venu.*
        "No one came."   (Standard French)
(17b) *Ninguém (*não) veio.*
        "No one came."   (Portuguese)

Again, however, when the neg-word appears postverbally this picture changes: the postverbal version of (17b) without a preverbal negator is ungrammatical (*Veio ninguém) but grammatical with the preverbal negator (*Não veio ninguém*). This behavior warrants the inclusion of Portuguese in the mixed behavior class of negative indefinite languages in Haspelmath's typology.

However, the case of the negative indefinites appears somewhat more complex in Brazilian Portuguese than in European Portuguese, despite a near-complete lack of attention to this dialectal difference in the existing literature (cf. Fonseca 2004). When neg-words appear in postverbal position, they purportedly require, as noted above, another negative in preverbal position to be licensed. However, examples of negative indefinites in postverbal position in colloquial BP *without* a preverbal negative trigger are nowadays easy to find, especially on social media, as in the headline from a website for crowdsourcing questions and answers (18a), from the community help pages of Facebook in (18b), or from an example posted to Twitter (18c):

(18a) *Minha mulher me deixou e eu fiz nada, como faço pra superar?*
        "My wife left me and I did nothing, what do I do to overcome [this situation]?"
                [http://br.answers.yahoo.com/question/index?qid=20110530175135AAFTAu3]
(18b) *vocês podem me ajuda desbloquiar eu fiz nada pra ser bloqueado*[7]
        "Can you guys help me get unblocked I did nothing to be blocked."
                [https://www.facebook.com/help/community/question/?id=234721516691987]
(18c) *Última vez que ele fez isso o radiador tava furado e ele falou nada.*
        "Last time he did that the radiator was pierced and he said nothing."
                                                        [Twitter, 14 Dec. 2013]

It is probably no coincidence that these examples (a) come from a colloquial, and perhaps even "oral" style such as that found on social media like Facebook or Twitter (where there are thousands of BP examples of *eu fiz nada* "I did nothing," but also many with other negative indefinites). Informal queries of native speakers who variably employ this form call it "informal" as well as "not something I would use in formal writing," suggesting a style distinction between the grammar of negative concord, on the one hand, and postverbal negative indefinites that appear without preverbal negative triggering, on the other hand.[8] At the same time, however, it is striking that this possibility exists in BP, where word order has also been shown to be becoming much more fixed in SVX order and where overt pronominal subjects are becoming more and more frequent (Tarallo 1996). In other languages where word order has become fixed as SVX and overt subjects have become the norm, such as French or English, the possibility of using negative indefinites in postverbal position without a preverbal trigger not only exists, but is the preferred pattern, at least in the standard language (compare Standard English *I saw nothing* vs. Non-Standard *I didn't see nothing*).

An additional clue to this further development in the system of negative indefinites in BP comes from Martins (1997, 2000), who notes that, unlike their Spanish or Italian counterparts, which can still appear in certain non-negative contexts present-day Portuguese negative indefinites are strong negatives that cannot appear in any non-negative contexts (e.g. modals or conditionals, or with predicates of doubt), even though they could in medieval and classical Portuguese. The examples in (18), then, would represent a logical next step in the process of development, whereby negative indefinites are now fully inherently negative and do not require preverbal negative triggering to be grammatical. This would lead to BP being classified as a different kind of mixed system than those in Haspelmath's classification: negative indefinites in postverbal position such as those in (18) may occur variably without preverbal negative licensing, just as they occur bare in preverbal position. This phenomenon, of course, is reminiscent of Jespersen's Cycle, where postverbal elements that were not (fully) negative are reinterpreted as such, except in this case the change is not affecting the canonical expression of sentential negation (as it did in French or English), which as argued above is stable and dominated by NEG1 in Portuguese, but rather the system of negative concord and the licensing of postverbal negative indefinites.

5. Metalinguistic negation

In a now-classic article, Horn (1985) introduced into the linguistic world the concept of "metalinguistic" negation, a particular use of negatives that does not affect the propositional content of the negated sentence, but rather targets other aspects of it, such as its presuppositions, the conversational implicatures associated with it, aspects of its pronunciation, etc. Portuguese examples of each using the canonical negator *não* are given in (19):

(19a) *Ele **não** deixou de fumar, ele nunca fumou.*   [presupposition-canceling]
   "He didn't stop smoking, he never smoked."
(19b) *Ela **não** é alta, é altíssima!*   [scalar implicature-canceling]
   "She's not tall, she super-tall!"
(19c) A: *Eu [trusi] o feijão.*   [pronunciation-objecting]
   "I brung the beans."
   ["incorrect" pronunciation]
   B: *Você **não** "[trusi]" o feijão, você "[trowsi]" o feijão.*
   "You didn't *brung* the beans, you *brought* the beans."
   ["correct" pronunciation]

In (19a), the presupposition of the verbal construction *deixar de* + INF is that the subject of the sentence engaged in the action described by the infinitive in the past. The metalinguistic negation in (19a) does not deny the truth of the asserted proposition "He doesn't smoke [now]" but rather the presupposition that he smoked in the past. In (19b), the assertion that the woman in question is *alta* can, and typically will, invite the inference that she is no more than *alta*, i.e. that there is no stronger term on a scale of "tallness" that can be applied to her appropriately. The metalinguistic negation here does not deny her tallness, but rather objects to the upper scalar bound put in place by the adjective *alta*, and corrects it to a stronger scalar term using the superlative *altíssima*. Finally, in (19c), the negation does not make reference to the propositional content ("A brought the beans"), but rather targets A's pronunciation of the verb *trouxe*, which in non-standard Brazilian varieties is often "incorrectly" produced as [trusi]. The ensuing sentence provides what B considers to be the "correct" pronunciation, i.e. [trowsi].

These examples illustrate what seems to be a universal property of canonical negation across languages: the canonical negator in a given language can always be used to convey metalinguistic negation. Other, non-canonical negators are more restricted in their range of functions, as their name suggests, and one of their limitations is precisely the ability to be employed in contexts of metalinguistic negation. For BP, Teixeira de Sousa (2011, 2013) notes that one characteristic for distinguishing between NEG2 and NEG3 is precisely that only the latter can be employed in contexts of metalinguistic negation: for instance, NEG2 would be infelicitous in the examples in (19) above, while NEG3 would be fine. Following Martins (2010), she notes that metalinguistic negation cannot occur in subordinate clauses, and neither can NEG3, while both NEG1 and NEG2 are acceptable in such contexts.

Martins (2010, 2014), for her part, describes three metalinguistic negation markers in EP: *lá*, *cá*, and *agora*, and distinguishes on syntactic grounds between "peripheral" (*agora*) and "internal" (*lá, cá*) metalinguistic negation. Among other properties, "peripheral" makers can be employed as stand-alone negative responses, but "internal" markers cannot. She exemplifies all three in the following short discourse sequence, and includes the example with the canonical negator *não* for comparative purposes, since, as we have already seen, it can also be used for metalinguistic negation.

(20) A: *Tu estás um pouco preocupado, não estás?*
            "You're a little worried, aren't you?"
      B1: *Eu **não** estou um pouco preocupado.* Estou morto de preocupação.
      B2: *Eu estou {**lá**/**cá**/**agora**} um pouco preocupado.* Estou morto de preocupação.
            "I'm not a little worried. I'm dying of worry."

The function of these markers in (20) is again to object to the potential scalar bound that "a little worried" could impose on interpretation. But in spite of the claim (Martins 2014: 638) that these are "unambiguous M[etalinguistic] N[egation] markers," none of them perform the metalinguistic denial on their own; the negation is only understood to be metalinguistic once the second sentence with the upward scalar correction is uttered or written. Indeed, Martins (2014: 660–61) provides other examples where all three of these markers are used as descriptive negation that deny explicitly expressed propositional content (the English glosses in [21] and [22] are from Martins). Since there is no phrase added to rectify the negated proposition, as there is (20) above, all three negative markers are necessarily understood as carrying out denials of propositional content and therefore classified as instances of descriptive negation:[9]

(21) A: *O hamster bateu a bota.*
            "The hamster died."
      B: *Bateu {lá/cá/agora} a bota.*
            "No way it died."   [i.e. it is still alive]

(22) A: *Tu sabes! Conta-me tudo.*
            "You know! Tell me everything."
      B: *Sei {lá/cá/agora}.*
            "Like hell I know."

The general point here is that objections to prior assertions, as long as they target a proposition derivable or inferrable from an assertion, are not necessarily a case of metalinguistic negation, even though they are all construable as "denials" (Geurts 1998). As Horn (1985, 1989) pointed out, an objection to a prior utterance is a necessary but not sufficient condition for identifying metalinguistic negation. Horn (2002) expands on this idea, utilizing the four-part typology of denials proposed by Geurts (1998), and arguing that what binds together the different metalinguistic uses of negation cross-linguistically is that they target *non-asserted* material (Horn 2002:78–9). Crucially, then, in order for an individual instance of negation to be understood as metalinguistic in a stricter sense it must also be understood as not targeting the asserted propositional content of that prior utterance; the negatives in both (21) and (22) target explicitly-asserted propositions derived from speaker A's utterances, yet all three EP "metalinguistic" markers are possible in these contexts. It remains to be seen whether Portuguese, or any other language, has negative words or morphemes that are wholly barred from targeting explicitly asserted propositional content. The converse situation, however, seems to be uncontroversially true. Existing research (Schwenter 2005; Teixeira de Sousa 2013) has already shown that NEG2 in BP, and presumably in EP as well, is a primarily echoic form that targets the propositional content derivable or inferrable from a prior assertion, but which cannot be employed in contexts of metalinguistic negation as understood in stricter fashion as denials of non-propositional content. Thus, while negators that are only compatible with propositional or descriptive negation are possible, negators that are only compatible with metalinguistic negation in the revised (Horn 2002) sense being argued for here are not. Future research on Portuguese will need to sort out these issues from both structural and discourse-functional perspectives.

6. Conclusion

In this chapter, I have provided a brief overview of some of the most interesting recent research in the realm of negation in Portuguese. As I have tried to emphasize throughout, there are many sites in the landscape of negation and polarity more generally that are currently in flux, especially in the diverse varieties of spoken BP. It is my hope that the discussion here will help generate considerable future research on negation in Portuguese, most especially on EP, where our knowledge of negation is actually much more rudimentary than in BP.

I have suggested implicitly that most of the "action" in Portuguese negation is to be found in the non-canonical negative forms and constructions. Not only do I believe this to be correct for Portuguese, I think it holds true regardless of the language of study, since their examination reveals more about the motivations behind negation and how markedness relations among negative forms and constructions are organized. Some of the non-canonical negatives that I have not dealt with here due to space reasons deserve their own detailed analysis: scalar additive negatives like *nem* (cf. Amaral 2013), negative-polarity items, both individually and as a group (cf. Martins 2000), additive negators like *também não* (cf. Schwenter 2003 on Spanish *tampoco*), to name just a few. And as is typically the case when dealing with grammatical phenomena, the differences between BP and EP are usually anecdotal, at best, and remain to be fully investigated and explained.

NOTES

1 For feedback, intuitions, and bibliographical pointers, I am very grateful to Patrícia Amaral, Sonia Cyrino, Maj-Britt Mosegaard Hansen, Larry Horn, Mary Johnson, Tammy Jones, Luana Lima, Luana Nunes, Lílian Teixeira de Sousa, and Hannah Washington. As Larry would say, needless to say…

2 I believe it is fair to say that this bias extends well beyond negation to other grammatical phenomena in Portuguese. The construction-based and probabilistic syntactic approaches that have proven to be very enriching alternatives to mainstream generative theories in recent years are essentially absent from research on Portuguese.

3 Even if preverbal *não* is considered the "standard" negator, there are other ways of pronouncing or writing it that might be considered "substandard." For instance, in BP it is often rendered in speech

as *num* or *nu*, and recent studies have shown this to be a very frequent pronunciation (Ramos 2002; Teixiera de Sousa and Vitral 2010), albeit with stratification by both age and education level.

4   Matos (2003) also mentions *sem* and *nem* as basic negators in Portuguese, presumably due to the fact that neither needs to be licensed by another negative to be grammatical. However, these forms also show clear differences when compared to canonical preverbal *não*. In the first case, *sem* is a preposition that cannot negate a finite verb, and in the second, *nem* is either part of a negative coordination structure (corresponding to English *neither… nor…*) or, if not, a scalar additive negator whose focus is an extreme negated value in a scalar model (e.g. *Nem o mais rico pode comprar isso* "Not even the richest person can buy that").

5   Teixeira de Sousa (2011) also discusses some uses of NEG3 in Northeastern BP that are not possible in other varieties.

6   Another phenomenon involving negation that is sensitive to preverbal vs. postverbal placement in BP is the ordering of quantifier plus negative indefinite, e.g. *mais nada* vs. *nada mais* "nothing more." As Peake and Schwenter (2014) show using naturally occurring corpus data, the former, preposed quantifier variant is much more frequent in postverbal position with a co-occurring preverbal negative, while the latter, postposed quantifier variant is heavily preferred in preverbal position without a co-occurring negative.

7   For example, examples like **O João contou nada ao Pedro* "João didn't tell Pedro anything" are considered wholly ungrammatical in grammars (e.g. Matos 2003:787), and probably rightly so in EP.

8   Speakers from far southern Brazil (e.g. Porto Alegre) in general rarely employ strictly postverbal negation (NEG3), as Goldnadel and Lima (2014) have shown. However, in a recent study of the acceptability of the lack of negative concord in BP (Agostini and Schwenter 2015), no significant differences were found for respondents from Porto Alegre when compared to respondents from São Paulo (who by contrast employ NEG3 regularly), thereby suggesting that NEG3 and lack of negative concord are at least partially independent phenomena.

9   Other research (e.g. Peres 2013: 465) also fails to distinguish between dialogic metalinguistic negation targeting non-asserted content and dialogic negation that applies to asserted propositional content, which would be considered non-metalinguistic descriptive negation following Horn's (2002) revised schema.

REFERENCES

Agostini, T. and S. A. Schwenter (2015). Variability in negative concord in Brazilian Portuguese. Paper presented at the Buckeye Language Network Symposium, Columbus.

Amaral, P. M. (2007). The meaning of approximative adverbs: evidence from European Portuguese. Ph.D. dissertation, Ohio State University.

Amaral, P. M. (2013). "Smart as a fox": Scalar negation and comparative constructions in Brazilian Portuguese. Paper presented at ICL 19, Geneva.

Amaral, P. M. and S. A. Schwenter (2009). Discourse and scalar structure in non-canonical negation. *Proceedings of the Annual Meeting of the Berkeley Linguistics Society*, 35, pp. 367–378.

Birner, B. J. (2006). Inferential relations and noncanonical word order. In B. J. Birner and G. Ward (eds.), *Drawing the Boundaries of Meaning*. Amsterdam: John Benjamins, pp. 31–51.

Birner, B. J. and G. Ward (1998). *Information Status and Noncanonical Word Order in English*. Amsterdam: John Benjamins.

Bond, O. (2013). A base for canonical negation. In D. Brown, M. Chumakina, and G. G. Corbett (eds.), *Canonical Morphology and Syntax*. Oxford: Oxford University Press, pp. 20–47.

Cavalcante, R. (2009). A negação sentencial. In D. Lucchesi, A. N. Baxter, and I. Ribeiro (eds.), *O português afro-brasileiro*. Salvador: EDUFBA, pp. 251–267.

Cunha, C. and L. F. L. Cintra (1985). *Nova Gramática do Português Contemporâneo*. Rio de Janeiro: Nova Fronteira.

Cyrino, S. and T. Biberauer (2009). Appearances are deceptive: Jespersen's Cycle from the perspective of the Romania Nova and Romance-based creoles. Paper presented at Going Romance 23, Nice.

Dahl, Ö. (1979). Typology of sentence negation. *Linguistics*, 17, pp. 79–106.

Dahl, Ö. (2010). Typology of negation. In Laurence R. Horn (ed.), *The expression of negation*. Berlin: Mouton de Gruyter, pp. 9–38.

De Cuypere, L. (2008). *Limiting the Iconic*. Amsterdam: John Benjamins.

Dryer, M. S. (1996). Focus, pragmatic presupposition, and activated propositions. *Journal of Pragmatics*, 26, pp. 475–523.

Fonseca, H. D. C. da (2004). Marcador negativo final no português brasileiro. *Cadernos de Estudos Linguísticos*, 46, pp. 5–19.

Furtado da Cunha, M. A. (2007). Grammaticalization of the strategies of negation in Brazilian Portuguese. *Journal of Pragmatics*, 9, pp. 1638–1653.

Geurts, B. (1998). The mechanisms of denial. *Language*, 74, pp. 274–307.

Goldnadel, M. and L. S. de Lima (2014). Topic maintenance as the pragmatic motivation for the rise of double negative utterances in spoken Brazilian Portuguese. Paper presented at AMPRA 2, Los Angeles.

Hagemeijer, Tjerk. 2003. Elementos polares na periferia direita: negação aparentemente descontínua, afirmação enfática e tags. Paper presented at the XIX Encontro Nacional da Associação Portuguesa de Linguística, Lisbon.

Hansen, M.-B. M. and J. Visconti (2009). On the diachrony of "reinforced" negation in French and Italian. In C. Rossari, C. Ricci, and A. Spiridon (eds.), *Grammaticalization and Pragmatics*. Bingley: Emerald, pp. 137–171.

Haspelmath, M. S. (1997). *Indefinite Pronouns*. Oxford: Oxford University Press.

Haspelmath, M. S. (2013). Indefinite pronouns. In M. S. Dryer and M. Haspelmath (eds.), *The World Atlas of Language Structures Online*, Leipzig: Max Planck Institute for Evolutionary Anthropology. Available online at http://wals.info/chapter/46.

Horn, L. R. (1985). Metalinguistic negation and pragmatic ambiguity. *Language*, 61, pp. 121–174.

Horn, L. R. (1989). *A Natural History of Negation*. Chicago: University of Chicago Press.

Horn, L. R. (2002). Assertoric inertia and NPI licensing. *Proceedings of the Annual Meeting of the Chicago Linguistic Society. Volume 38, Part Two: The Panels*, pp. 55–82.

Jespersen, O. A. (1917). *Negation in English and Other Languages*. Copenhagen: A.F. Høst & Son.

Larrivée, P. (2011). Is there a Jespersen Cycle? In Pierre Larrivée and Richard Ingham (eds.), *The Evolution of Negation: Beyond the Jespersen Cycle*. Berlin: de Gruyter, 1–21.

Martins, A. M. (1995). Clitic placement from Old to Modern European Portuguese. In H. Andersen (ed.), *Historical Linguistics 1993: Selected Papers from the 11th International Conference on Historical Linguistics*. Amsterdam: John Benjamins, pp. 295–307.

Martins, A. M. (1997). Aspectos da negação na história das línguas românicas. *Actas do XII Encontro da Associação Portuguesa de Linguística*, vol. II. Lisboa: Associação Portuguesa de Linguística, pp. 179–210.

Martins, A. M. (2000). Polarity items in Romance: underspecification and lexical change. In S. Pintzuk, G. Tsoulas, and A. Warner (eds.), *Diachronic Syntax: Models and Mechanisms*. Oxford: Oxford University Press, pp. 191–219.

Martins, A. M. (2010). Negação metalinguística (*lá, cá, agora*). In A. M. Brito, F. Silva, J. Veloso, and A. Fiéis (eds.), *Actas do XXV Encontro da Associação Portuguesa de Linguística*. Lisbon: Associação Portuguesa de Linguística.

Martins, A. M. (2013). Emphatic polarity in European Portuguese and beyond. *Lingua*, 128, pp. 95–123.

Martins, A. M. (2014). How much syntax is there in metalinguistic negation? *Natural Language and Linguistic Theory*, 32, 635–672.

Matos, G. (2003). Aspectos sintácticos da negação. In M. H. M. Mateus, I. Duarte, and I. H. Faria (eds.), *Gramática da língua Portuguesa*. Lisbon: Editorial Caminho, pp. 767–793.

Miestamo, M. (2005). *Standard Negation: The Negation of Declarative Verbal Main Clauses in a Typological Perspective*. Berlin: de Gruyter.

Nunes, L. L. (2014). Motivações pragmáticas para o uso de dupla negação: um estudo do fenômeno em português europeu. Bachelor dissertation, Universidade Federal do Rio Grande do Sul.

Payne, J. R. (1985). Negation. In T. Shopen (ed.), *Language Typology and Syntactic Description, vol. 1: Clause Structure*. Cambridge: Cambridge University Press, pp. 197–241.

Peake, J. and S. Schwenter (2014). *Nada mais* variation in Brazilian Portuguese, *mais nada*. Paper presented at NWAV 43, Chicago.

Peres, J. A. (2013). Negação. In E. B. P. Raposo, M. F. B. do Nascimento, M. A. C. da Mota, L. Segura, and A. Mendes (eds.), *Gramática do Português*, vol. 1. Lisbon: Fundação Calouste Gulbenkian, pp. 459–498.

Perini, M. A. (2002). *Modern Portuguese: A Reference Grammar*. New Haven, CT: Yale University Press.

Perini, M. A. (2006). *Gramática descritiva do português*. São Paulo: Editora Ática.

Prince, E. F. (1992). The ZPG letter: subjects, definiteness, and information status. In S. A. Thompson and W. Mann (eds.), *Discourse Description: Diverse Analyses of a Fundraising Text*. Amsterdam: John Benjamins, pp. 295–325.

Ramos, J. M. (2002). A alternância entre "não" e "num" no dialeto mineiro: um caso de mudança lingüística. In M. A. A. M. Cohen and J. M. Ramos (eds.), *Dialeto Mineiro e Outras Falas: Estudos de Variação e Mudança Lingüística*. Belo Horizonte: UFMG, pp. 155–167.

Schwegler, A. (1991). Predicate negation in contemporary Brazilian Portuguese: a change in progress. *Orbis*, 34, pp. 187–214.

Schwegler, A. (1996). La doble negación dominicana y la génesis del español caribeño. *Hispanic Linguistics*, 8, pp. 247–315.

Schwenter, S. A. (2003). *No* and *tampoco*: a pragmatic distinction in Spanish negation. *Journal of Pragmatics*, 35, pp. 999–1030.

Schwenter, S. A. (2005). The pragmatics of negation in Brazilian Portuguese. *Lingua*, 115, pp. 1427–1456.

Schwenter, S. A. (2006). Fine-tuning Jespersen's Cycle. In B. J. Birner and G. Ward (eds.), *Drawing the Boundaries of Meaning: Neo-Gricean Studies in Honor of Laurence R. Horn*. Amsterdam: John Benjamins, pp. 327–344.

Souza, A. S. de. (2004). As estruturas de negação em uma comunidade rural afro-brasileira: Helvécia-BA. Online at http://www.hyperion.ufba.br/_texts/2004-2/arivaldosouza.doc (accessed November 24, 2015).

Tarallo, F. (1996). Turning different at the turn of the century: 19th century Brazilian Portuguese. In G. R. Guy, C. Feagin, D. Schiffrin, and J. Baugh (eds.), *Towards a Social Science of Language: Papers in Honor of William Labov*, vol. 1. Amsterdam: John Benjamins, pp. 199–220.

Teixeira de Sousa, L. (2011). Sentential negation in Brazilian Portuguese: pragmatics and syntax. *JournaLipp*, 1, pp. 89–103.

Teixeira de Sousa, L. (2013). Sentential negation at the syntax-prosody interface. *Veredas*, 17, pp. 1–19.

Teixeira de Sousa, L. and L. Vitral (2010). Formas reduzidas da forma "não" no português brasileiro. In L. Vitral and S. Coelho (eds.), *Estudos de Processos de Gramaticalização em Português*. Campinas: Mercado de Letras, pp. 229–254.

Thomas, E. W. (1969). *The Syntax of Spoken Brazilian Portuguese*. Nashville: Vanderbilt University Press.

van der Auwera, J. (2009). The Jespersen Cycles. In E. van Gelderen (ed.), *Cyclical Change*. Amsterdam: Benjamins, pp. 35–71.

Washington, H. (forthcoming). Lexical frequency and language change: object clitic placement in European Portuguese. *Estudos Linguísticos/Linguistic Studies*.

24 Discourse Markers

ANA CRISTINA MACÁRIO LOPES

1. Introduction

The concept of Discourse Markers (henceforth DMs) is far from being settled in the linguistic community. Furthermore, there is a range of alternative expressions competing with it, such as pragmatic markers (Fraser 1990, Brinton 1996), discourse particles (Shourup 1985, Fisher 2006), discourse connectives (Blakemore 1987), cue phrases (Knott and Dale 1994), discourse operators (Redecker 2006), among others. Although there is no definition of DMs that is universally accepted, specially because of the wide range of linguistic approaches grounded in different theoretical frameworks,[1] there are two main subsets of linguistic expressions that are usually labeled by the term: on the one hand, expressions that index the utterances to the speaker and/or the hearer, enabling joint coordination of interaction; on the other hand, expressions that signal a relation between two discourse segments, guiding hearers in the interpretation process.

Pervasive in spontaneous, informal and unplanned conversations, expressions belonging to the first subset are devices to manage the interaction (signaling turn-taking, turn-holding and turn-yielding, marking back-channel feedback, pointing out hesitations in on-line discourse planning) and to smooth interpersonal relations through politeness discourse strategies. Some examples of these DMs, in Portuguese, are *olha, ouve lá* ("look"), *percebes* ("you see"), *não é, né?, certo?* ("right?"), *pronto* ("ok"), *tás a ver* ("you know"), *pois, claro* ("yeah," "sure," "right"), *bem* ("well"), *por favor* ("please"). Conversational Markers would be a transparent label to refer to this subset of DMs. Conversation Analysis and Politeness Theory provide relevant tools to describe and explain the interactional functions of this subset of items.[2] The second set of expressions is not restricted to oral interactions and its function is to contribute to discourse coherence; examples in Portuguese are: *contudo* ("however"), *além disso* ("furthermore"), *de facto* ("in fact"), *ao invés, pelo contrário* ("on the contrary"), *portanto* ("so"), *quer dizer* ("that is"), *"de qualquer modo* ("anyway"), *já* ("whereas"). Being discourse connectives, they are two-place operators, giving instructions on how to relate their host unit with a previous discourse segment, thus guiding discourse interpretation. The two subsets of expressions share a common property: both require pragmatic descriptions, since both operate at different levels of discourse structure.

In this chapter, the label DMs will be used to refer to the second subset of expressions. It will be assumed that DMs are relevant in the recognition of discourse relations,[3] that is, relations that hold together different segments of a discourse, building up its coherence. The recognition of discourse relations by the hearer or the reader enables them to construct a

The Handbook of Portuguese Linguistics, First Edition. Edited by W. Leo Wetzels, João Costa, and Sergio Menuzzi.
© 2016 John Wiley & Sons, Inc. Published 2020 by John Wiley & Sons, Inc.

coherent mental representation of the whole discourse, and there is experimental evidence that DMs play an important role in this process. It will also be assumed that DMs link utterances, i.e., discourse units, and not clauses within a complex sentence. The aim of this chapter is not to provide the reader with an exhaustive list of Portuguese DMs, but rather to sketch a synthesis of the most widely discussed properties of DMs, drawing on current scholarly debates, to relate classes of DMs with discourse relations, through clear examples from the Portuguese language, and to outline future research in the area.

The empirical data used in this chapter involve constructed examples as well as data collected from corpora.[4] The latter are presented between quotation marks. All the examples are from contemporary European Portuguese.[5]

2. Properties of DMs

In spite of the impressive diversity of perspectives on DMs, it is still possible to draw up a cluster of properties generally discussed by researchers in the area. First of all, DMs are a syntactically heterogeneous class of linguistic expressions that include conjunctions (*mas, e...*), adverbs (*agora, então, já...*), prepositional phrases (*de qualquer modo, por conseguinte, no entanto...*), and other fixed phrases involving verbs (*isto é, quer dizer...*); thus, DMs can only be defined in pragmatic or functional terms, i.e., taking into account their connective function in discourse. Typically, they articulate two adjacent discourse segments, as is shown in example (1), but they can also relate their host segment with several previous segments, as (2) illustrates:

(1) *O Rui fuma muito.* <u>No entanto</u>, *não tem problemas de saúde.*
     "Rui is a heavy smoker. *However*, he is healthy."

(2) *Aprendeu a língua do país de acolhimento e conseguiu um emprego. Fez amigos.* <u>*Enfim*</u>, *integrou-se.*
     "He has learned the language of his host country and got a job. He has made friends. *To sum up*, he has adapted."

Another issue widely discussed in the literature on DMs is related to their meaning. It is acknowledged that DMs do not contribute to the propositional content of their host utterance,[6] since they do not have conceptual or representational meaning. Their core meaning is procedural, i.e., they encode instructions on how the segment they typically introduce is to be interpreted relative to prior discourse.[7] Therefore, they provide clues for the hearer/reader "on how to integrate their host utterance into a coherent mental representation of discourse." (Hansen 1998: 358). Given their procedural meaning, DMs are crucial devices constraining the process of discourse interpretation, hence playing a decisive role in the building up of discourse or text coherence. This can be illustrated by (3), where the DM *portanto* signals that the second utterance is to be interpreted as a conclusion derived from the previous one:

(3) *O carro está na garagem.* <u>*Portanto*</u>, *o Rui está em casa.*
     "The car is in the garage. *Therefore*, Rui is at home."

Another relevant issue concerning DMs is their distribution. Typically, they occur in utterance initial position, as in (3). But many of them may float, which means that they may also occur in medial or final position in the utterance, as is shown in the following examples:

(3a) *O carro está na garagem. O Rui,* <u>*portanto*</u>, *está em casa.*

(3b) *O carro está na garagem. O Rui está,* <u>*portanto*</u>, *em casa.*

(3c) *O carro está na garagem. O Rui está em casa,* <u>*portanto*</u>.

Thus, contrary to conjunctions that relate clauses within a complex sentence, which have a fixed initial position, a large number of DMs display a certain mobility within their host utterance. It is worth noticing that, when they are interpolated or parenthetical, they can occur between the subject and the predicate (3a) or between the constituents of the verb phrase (3b), but they cannot be more embedded than this. Hence, they cannot occur within noun phrases or prepositional phrases (cf. 3d, 3e):

(3d) *O carro está na garagem. *O, portanto, Rui está em casa.*
(3e) *O carro está na garage. *O Rui está em, portanto, casa.*

In terms of morphological properties, DMs are invariable units. When they are formed by more than one lexical item, they behave as frozen phrases, and have to be analyzed as a single lexical entry. See the contrast between (4) and (5):

(4) *Eles não tomam calmantes. <u>Quer dizer</u>, tomam muito raramente.*
     They don't take tranquilisers. Wants to-say, they take them very rarely.
     "They don't take tranquilisers. *I mean*, it's rare."

(5) *Eles <u>querem dizer</u> que só raramente tomam anseolíticos.*
     "They want to say that it is rare for them to take tranquilisers."

In (4), *quer dizer* is a reformulative DM, and therefore verbal inflection is totally excluded, whereas in (5) *querem dizer* is as a syntactic combination, constrained by the rules of verbal agreement. The fact that DMs with more than one item behave as frozen fused phrases with a connective function may be seen as the outcome of a grammaticalization process.[8] In fact, many DMs have developed from free syntactic and semantic word combinations, namely prepositional phrases (*em todo o caso* "in any case," *de qualquer modo* "anyway," *ao invés* "on the contrary"). This means that they have "derived from terms that served primarily contentful rather than procedural functions" (Traugott and Dasher 2002: 153), undergoing a process involving decategorization and reanalysis, and there is empirical evidence that this process is replicated cross-linguistically (Traugott 1995, Traugott and Dasher 2002, a.o.). Fused expressions that in contemporary Portuguese behave, in certain contexts, as DMs still occur in other contexts as verbal adjuncts or adverbials, with different semantic functions within the proposition, according to their basic semantic value. This phenomenon, known as "layering" and also attested in other languages, shows that the emergence of new meanings and functions may coexist with old ones, reflecting different stages of the grammaticalization process.[9]

Concerning their prosodic behaviour, some authors argue that prototypical DMs are a tone unit, with a parenthetical intonation contour, i.e., separated by pauses from the segments they connect. In written texts, these pauses are signaled by punctuation (comas, semicolon and coma, or period and coma). But no strong generalization can be made, since there are DMs like *e* ("and") that do not fit this pattern.

Finally, a property usually refered to as inherent to DMs is their polyfunctionality.[10] In fact, many descriptive studies of DMs, in different languages, confirm that a single item may fulfill more than one function. Let us give an example in Portuguese, namely the DM *enfim*:[11]

(6) *E o sucesso desta novela (…) prende-se com pontos tão inequívocos como a boa direcção de actores, a utilização de uma história portuguesa, o aproveitamento do passado recente para uma série de ficção, <u>enfim</u>, a introdução de um ritmo de trabalho espartano.*
     "And the success of this soap opera is the outcome of the director's role concerning the actors, the choice of a Portuguese story, the use of the recent past in a fictional series, *and, finally*, the introduction of a spartan rhythm of work."

(7)   *Carrego água para o gado, trato do gado, trabalho com o tractor, enfim, faço tudo o que é preciso fazer.*
"I feed and water the cattle, work with the tractor, *well/to sum up*, I do everything necessary."

In (6), *enfim* signals the end of an enumeration, whereas in (7) it signals that the next utterance summarizes and concludes the speaker's intervention.

In short, there are three competing perspectives on the issue of DMs polyfunctionality. The homonymic approach postulates that if a given form has different uses, then these uses are taken to represent separate lexical entries. This approach is unable to address the common intuition among native speakers that "homonyms" are somehow semantically related, and thus it is rather unsatisfying. The monosemic perspective, which aims to simplify semantic descriptions and avoid an unnecessary proliferation of lexical entries, strives to circumsbribe an invariant core meaning underlying the different uses of a DM, and explains the different modulations of meaning attested as the outcome of contextual linguistic constraints. In descriptive terms, this approach is not without problems, mainly because the formulation of the invariant core meaning may end up being so general and abstract that it risks becoming onomasiologically non-distinctive. Finally, the polysemic approach defends that there is a basic meaning from which all others have developed, triggered by cognitive or pragmatic factors. In this perspective, it is is possible to relate different meanings in a motivated way, emphasizing their family resemblances. When the polysemic approach is complemented with historical research (Traugott and Dasher 2002, a.o.), the interdependency between synchronic usages and diachronic change is highlighted and gives rise to fruitful hypotheses on the development of DMs.

Any attempt to delimit classes of DMs has to cope with the polyfunctionality of these versatile items. Being aware of the difficulty to establish clear-cut classes of DMs, I will address, in the next section, the possibility of grounding some general classes of DMs on the discourse relations they may signal. The interaction with the linguistic context of occurrence, as well as the discourse type in which it occurs, may be responsible for a more fine-grained specification of the functions of each DM.

3. Classes of DMs

The classes of DMs which will be discussed in this section are a simple, and by no means exhaustive, contribution for the description of the functional spectrum of DMs, based on Portuguese data.[12] The challenge is to verify if there is a match between discourse relations and (some) classes of DMs.[13] As the set of discourse relations is not definite or closed, and the terms used to identify and to define them are not convergent in the different theoretical frameworks focused on discourse or text coherence[14], the option taken in this section was to choose the more transparent labels available in the literature and to provide a simple and intuitive characterization of each relation at stake. Moreover, this section also questions how to categorize DMs whose function cannot be directly explained within the framework of discourse relations.

3.1. *Elaborative DMs*

This broad class includes DMs which typically introduce utterances providing additional information about the situation described in the previous utterance (or some aspect of it).[15] This basic additive value may encompass an exemplification or a specification. The following sequence illustrates an elaboration through specification:

(8) *Estas medidas visam uma maior abertura do Estado e o estabelecimento de transparência na relação Estado-cidadão. Mais concretamente, as medidas propostas pretendem acelerar a educação para a sociedade da informação e disponibilização de meios de base e de recursos às escolas, às associações, às bibliotecas (J64267).*

"These measures are intended to establish a greater transparency in the relationship between the State and the citizens. *More concretely* ("in particular"), the measures are intended to speed up the process of educating for the information society and to provide the schools, the associations and the libraries with the basic resources"

Other Portuguese DMs belonging to this class are *por exemplo* "for example," *nomeadamente* "namely," *designadamente* "particularly," *em particular* "in particular," *especificamente* "specifically," *a saber* (literally"to know," meaning "namely"). The latter is predominantly used to signal that an enumeration will specify what has just been stated:

(9) *É necessário percorrer diversas etapas, a saber: levantar o formulário na repartição de finanças, preenchê-lo, devolvê-lo acompanhado de fotocópia do BI e do cartão de contribuinte.*

"It is necessary to go through different steps, *to know* ("namely"): get the application form in the tax office, fill it out, hand it in with a photocopy of your identity card and the taxpayer's card."

DMs like *de facto* "in fact," *com efeito* (literally "with effect," meaning "in fact, indeed"), *efectivamente* (literally "effectively," meaning "indeed"), *na verdade* (literally "in the truth," meaning "as a matter of fact"), *na realidade* (literally "in the reality," meaning "actually") may also be included in this class, since their main function is to elaborate, and consequently expand, the content of the previous utterance, in order to make it more precise or detailed:

(10) *A televisão (…) exerce com vantagens a função de integração cultural. De facto, a televisão é bem o instrumento privilegiado de veiculação e de imposição aos que se encontram ainda à margem do sistema das maneiras de pensar, de sentir e de agir mais consentâneas aos códigos culturais da sociedade industrial.*

"Television has advantages in terms of cultural integration. *In fact*, television is the ultimate tool to convey and impose ways of thinking, feeling and acting, which correspond to the cultural codes of industrial society, on those who remain on its margins."

The correlative DM *por um lado… por outro…* "on the one hand…on the other hand," in many contexts, pinpoints the same discourse relation, since the segments it introduces instantiate previous information. But it is worth noticing that it also draws a contrast between the two segments it joins in the elaboration, as is shown in (11):

(11) *Havia na sua personalidade contradições insolúveis. Por um lado, um egoísmo desumano e cego; por outro, a mais espontânea disponibilidade para servir o semelhante.*

"His personality was irremediably contradictory: *one the one hand*, a blind and inhuman selfishness; *on the other hand*, the most spontaneous availability to serve others."

As has already been pointed out, the polyfunctionality of DMs makes it rather difficult to assign a single function to many (if not to the majority) of them. In fact, elaborative DMs may be used, in certain discourse types, namely in argumentative discourse, to instruct the hearer/reader that the next segment is to be processed as additional information leading to a conclusion which could already be derived from the previous utterance. In other words, they may relate two utterances with a similar argumentative orientation, thus reinforcing or strengthening the speaker's / writer's standpoint and bolstering the hearer's acceptance of it. The following example illustrates our point:

(12)   *O local onde vamos intervir é, actualmente, pasto de marginais. Trata-se de uma área que funciona como reduto de toxicodependentes. <u>Além do mais</u>, dado o seu estado de abandono, existem enormes quantidades de silvas que, no verão, provocam inúmeros incêndios. (…) É um autêntico "câncro" na cidade.*
       "The place where works are planned is full of those living on the margins of society. It is an area where drug addicts hang around. *Furthermore*, given its abandoned state, it is full of brambles, which, in the summer, give rise to lots of fires. It is a real "cancer" on the city."

Empirical data like (12) raise some questions, both in theoretical and in descriptive terms: is the marking of an elaborative relation somehow backgrounded by the marking of a supplementary supporting argument for an identical claim? Do the two functions overlap, one of them characterized in relation to the content domain (elaboration), and the other one in relation with the pragmatic domain (evidence)? Do argumentative discourse types coerce elaborative DMs to signal *supplementary evidence*? It seems plausible that extensive and cross-linguistic data-driven research on DMs, focused on different discourse types, may refine discourse relations' taxonomies and shed further light on regular correspondences between the content and the pragmatic or rhetorical domains of discourse structure.

In Portuguese, there are other DMs which typically behave like elaborative ones: *além do mais* (literally "beyond anything else," meaning "besides"), *mais (ainda)* "(even) further," *para mais* (literally "for more," meaning "moreover"), *de mais a mais* (literally"from more to more," meaning "moreover"), *além disso* (literally "beyond this," meaning "furthermore"), *adicionalmente* "in addition," *inclusive* (literally "inclusively," meaning "furthermore, besides"), *sobretudo* (literally "above all," meaning "mainly"), *ainda por cima* (literally "yet above the top," meaning "on top of this"), *acima de tudo* "above all," *para cúmulo* "to top it all." But it is worth noticing that they are not totally equivalent and, thus, not interchangeable in all contexts of use. A more fine-grained analysis shows that, for example, *ainda por cima* and *para cúmulo*, unlike *além disso* or *adicionalmente*, occur in argumentative discourses where an implicit evaluative scale is activated in the interpretation process. The segments introduced by the DM's *ainda por cima* and *para cúmulo* must follow the same argumentative orientation as the previous ones, with the extra requirement of adding a final stronger point for an intended conclusion. In example (13a) below, the fact that the houses are expensive is presented as even worse than all the other negative aspects previously mentioned:

(13a) *As canalizações rebentam, as portas não têm todas o mesmo tamanho, as paredes são tortas e feitas de blocos de cimento (…)—<u>e ainda por cima</u> são caras.*
       "The plumbing bursts, the doors are different sizes, the walls aren't straight and are made of cinderblocks (…)—*and on top of that*, the houses are expensive."

Whereas (13a) is totally coherent, (13b) is perceived as incoherent or unacceptable, because its last utterance flouts the constraints imposed by the DM. Indeed, instead of following and reinforcing the orientation of the previous segments, the last utterance adds a point for an opposite conclusion:[16] it's oriented to a positive pole, flouting the constraints imposed by the DM:

(13b)   # *Rebentam as canalizações, as portas não têm todas o mesmo tamanho, as paredes são tortas e feitas de blocos de cimento (…)—e ainda por cima são baratas.*
"# The plumbing bursts, the doors are different sizes, the walls aren't straight and are made of cinderblocks (…)—*and on top of this*, the houses are cheap."

To sum up, when considering the class of elaborative DMs, two promising lines for future research have emerged: the interactions between the connectives and specific discourse types, and the need to clearly define what the specific constraints are that each DM imposes on its linguistic environment.

3.2. *Contrastive DMs*

This broad category, pervasive in the literature, is not easy to define within the framework of discourse coherence, since there is no consensus in the linguistic community on the definition of the discourse relation "Contrast." My attempt is to fine-tune it, showing that it encompasses two distinct discourse relations: counterargument,[17] on the one hand, and contrast between two comparable situations, on the other. To tackle the issue, two main subclasses of DMs will be delimited in this subsection: counterargumentative DMs and contrastive–comparative ones.

3.2.1. *Counterargumentative DMs*

This first subclass includes, in Portuguese, *porém* "however," *contudo* (literally "with-all," meaning "however"), *todavia* (literally"all-the-way," meaning "nonetheless, nevertheless"), *no entanto* (literally "in-the- meanwhile," meaning "nonetheless, nevertheless"), *não obstante* "notwithstanding." These DMs typically introduce an utterance that suppresses an inference triggered by the previous discourse segment. See the following example:

(14)   *A Maria fuma muito.* <u>Contudo</u>, *não tem problemas de saúde.*
"Maria is a heavy smoker. *However*, she does not have health problems."

In (14), *contudo* instructs the hearer / reader to process the content of the second segment (*A Maria não tem problemas de saúde*) as contrasting with an expected inference (*A Maria tem problemas de saúde* "Maria has health problems"), activated by the content of the first segment (*A Maria fuma muito*). The expected inference is warranted by a pragmatic presupposition, based on shared world knowledge (that usually, heavy smokers have health problems). Therefore, in (14), the speaker states that Maria is a heavy smoker and she does not have health problems, and implies that the second situation is unexpected, given the information expressed in the first utterance.

The DM *contudo* may, in general, be replaced by: *porém, todavia, no entanto, não obstante* and *mas*. However, *mas* may co-occur with the other DMs (*mas, contudo…/mas, todavia…/mas, no entanto…*) This co-occurence with *mas* ("but"), being redundant, has an emphatic effect, stressing the intended instruction. Contrary to *mas*, with a fixed initial position, the other contrastive DMs have a certain mobility within their host utterance, as the following examples illustrate:

(14a)   *A Maria fuma muito; não tem, <u>no entanto</u>/<u>contudo</u>, problemas de saúde.*
(14b)   *A Maria fuma muito; não tem problemas de saúde, <u>no entanto</u>/<u>contudo</u>.*

Empirical data provide evidence that the same set of Portuguese DMs may often be found in quite different discourse configurations, paradigmatically illustrated by (15):

(15)   *O João é criativo; <u>no entanto</u>, não é responsável.*
"João is creative; *nevertheless*, he is not responsible."

What differentiates (14) from (15) is the fact that in (15) the second utterance does not suppress an inference activated by the former one. In fact, the first statement does not trigger the inference that João is not a responsible person, since there is no pragmatic presupposition that warrants this inference. Still, the procedural meaning of *no entanto* involves the search for a contrast, in the interpretation process. The relevant question to ask, in this case is, in which context is it appropriate to utter (15)? Imagine a context where the discourse topic is João's chances of getting a job. In such a context, the first segment may trigger the inference that he will get it, but the second segment triggers the opposite inference, that is, he will not get it. This second inference is presented as the one that should prevail, thus constraining the continuation of discourse.[18] Using Ducrot's terminology, the two segments in (15) are argumentatively anti-oriented, i.e., each one is an argument for opposite conclusions, and the second segment has a stronger argumentative weight. Thus the target of the contrast signalled by the DM involves the inferences activated by the two related segments, given the appropriate discourse context.

In any case, counterargumentative DMs always encode an instruction of contrast: either a contrast between an inference read off from the first segment and the propositional content of the second segment, as in (13), or a contrast between the inferences triggered by the two related discourse segments, as in (14).[19]

3.2.2. *Contrastive–comparative DMs*

This second subset involves DMs like *ao invés* (literally "on the reverse," meaning "on the contrary"), *ao contrário* ("on the contrary"), *pelo contrário* (literally "by the contrary," meaning "quite the contrary"),[20] *já* (literally "already," meaning"whereas"), *enquanto que* "while," *ao passo que* "whereas," which signal an antithetical contrast between two comparable situations, as is shown in (16) and (17):

(16)   *O João é baixo. <u>Ao invés</u>,/<u>Pelo contrário</u>,/<u>Já</u> o irmão é alto.*
"João is short. *In contrast*, his brother is tall."

(17)   *Pior sorte teve o brigadeiro da Força Aérea Lami Dozo, que viu a sua pena de oito anos agravada para doze. <u>Ao invés</u>, o almirante Jorge Anaya viu a sua reduzida de 14 para 12 anos.*
"The airforce officer Lami Dozo was not so lucky as his sentence was increased from eight years to twelve. *In contrast*, the admiral Jorge Anayu had his sentence reduced from fourteen to twelve years."

In (16) and (17), the speaker compares two individuals, highlighting their dissimilarities. Notice that the predicates of the two segments related by the connective have to belong to the same conceptual domain, i.e., they have to encode opposite values of the same underlying property. The relevance of this restriction becomes clear if we compare the unacceptability of (18) with the full acceptability of (16):

(18)   # *A Inês é alta. O irmão, <u>ao invés</u>, é inteligente.*
"# Inês is tall. Her brother, *on the contrary*, is clever."

The fact that *baixo* and *alto* specify opposite values of a more abstract property (the gradable property "height") licenses the occurrence of *ao invés/pelo contrário/já* in (16); example (18) is odd because there is no single scale underlying *baixa* ("short") and *inteligente* ("clever").

It is thus clear that these DMs impose strong semantic constraints on their environement. Typically, they are appropriate in contexts where two individuals are associated with two opposite predicates, lexically marked as contrary or contradictory. But it is worth noticing that other peripheral contexts of use are also acceptable, as is shown in the following example:[21]

(19) *A Ana foi fazer ski. Ao invés, o irmão foi ao cinema.*
"Ana went skiing, *whereas* her brother went to the cinema."

(19) is appropriate in a context where only two possibilities, in exclusive disjunction, are taken into consideration: skiing or going to the cinema, two possible specifications of a more abstract predicate, related with free-time activities. Such a context licenses the interpretation of skiing and going to the movies as contradictory terms, and, consequently, the contrastive comparison reading may be preserved. Therefore, if the constraints imposed by the connective are compatible or, at least, not inconsistent with world knowledge or background assumptions, the construction is still acceptable in Portuguese.

3.3. Conclusive DMs

The Portuguese DMs *logo* "therefore," *portanto* "so," *por conseguinte* "consequently," *por consequência* "in consequence," *então* "then," *assim* (literally "in this way," meaning"hence," "thus") signal that the segment they typically introduce is to be read as a conclusion (or a logical consequence) inferred from what was previously said. In other words, the first utterance provides grounds for drawing the conclusion expressed in the second one:[22]

(20) *O carro está estacionado em frente da garagem; portanto/logo/por conseguinte, a Maria está em casa.*
"The car is parked in front of the garage. *Therefore*, Maria is at home."

However, free commutation is not possible with all the DMs mentioned above, as the dialogical exchange in (21) illustrates:

(21) A: *O carro está estacionado em frente da garagem.*
B: *Então/# Portanto, deve estar alguém em casa.*

Então is acceptable in dialogical contexts like (21), where speaker B does not commit him- / herself to the truth of A's statement. *Então* signals that the conclusion drawn by B is based on a hypothetic premiss (if the car is parked, then...), contrary to what happens in (20), where the speaker commits him-/herself to the truth of what he/she says in his/her intervention: it is because he / she knows that the car is parked in front of the garage that he / she deduces that Maria is at home. Therefore, *portanto* introduces a conclusion based on a fact, whereas *então* introduces a conclusion based on a conditional premiss. That is why *então* is the Portuguese connective selected to introduce the apodosis of conditional constructions (22):

(22) *Se x for sinónimo de y, então/*portanto y é sinónimo de x.*
"If x is a synonym of y, *then* y is synonymous with x"

Conclusive DMs can be fully characterized within the theoretical framework of discourse relations. But this brief discussion on the restrictions of use of *portanto* and *então* emphasizes the fact that research on the specific constraints each one imposes on the semantic profile of the utterances they connect has to be carried out to fully describe the appropriate use of each conclusive DM.[23]

3.4. *Justificative DMs*

Pois "for," *porque* "for, because," and *que* "for, because" are the prototypical DMs which in Portuguese introduce an utterance providing a justification as to why the speaker has uttered the first segment, but *visto que, dado que,* and *uma vez que* "since, given that" may also fulfil the same function. See the following example:

(23) *Deve estar gente em casa, pois/visto que as luzes estão acesas.*
    "There must be someone at home, *for/since* the lights are on."

In (23), the first segment is a deduced assertion, clearly marked by the modal verb *dever*, and the second segment expresses the evidence on which the deduction was based. The speaker advances the second discourse segment as an attempt to justify his / her first claim, in order to convince the listener of its credibility. Constructions with justificative DMs mirror constructions with conclusive ones. In fact, both (20) and (23) express an inferential reasoning and both involve two assertive speech acts with different, though interdependent functions: in (20), the first act expresses the evidence and the second one the claim drawn from it; in (23), the first act expresses the speaker's claim, and the second one, designed to justify that claim, provides the evidence that supports it. Justificative DMs may also introduce an utterance that justifies an order, or a question, as the following examples illustrate:

(24) *Despacha-te, que são horas de ires para a escola!*
    "Hurry up, *because* it's time to go to school!"

(25) *Estás com muita pressa? É que preciso urgentemente de falar contigo.*
    "Are you in a hurry? *Because* I need to talk to you, urgently."

In Portuguese, the illocutionary status of the first discourse segment constrains the choice of the justificative DM: *que* is typically used after an order while *é que* is used after a question.

3.5. *Reformulative DMs*

Reformulation is a metadiscourse relation (Roulet 1987, Rossari 1994, a.o.), by which the speaker rephrases an utterance in order to facilitate the understanding of what s/he actually means, to reduce possible communicative misunderstandings or even to correct what s/he has said. This definition is focused on cases of self-reformulation, but there are also cases of hetero-reformulation, in dialogical discourse, when the hearer restates a previous intervention (or part of it) on behalf of the original speaker, always with a cooperative intention and typically to confirm comprehension. Cases of hetero-reformulation will not be considered in this chapter.

Within the class of reformulative DMs, a more fine-grained subtypology is required: some of them signal, roughly speaking, an equivalence between the original utterance and the restated one (paraphrastic reformulative DMs); others signal a dissociation between the two utterances, showing that the speaker fully reconsiders his/her first formulation and substitutes it by a new one (non-paraphrastic reformulative DMs, here labeled corrective DMs).[24] The issue of whether summary DMs like *em suma* "in sum, to sum up," *em síntese* "in short," *numa palavra* "in a word," *enfim* (literally "at last," meaning "in short," "briefly," "to sum up") may indeed be characterized as reformulative DMs, as claimed by some authors (Roulet 2006, Zorraquino and Portolés 1999), will be discussed at the end of this section.

3.5.1. *Paraphrastic reformulative DMs*

In Portuguese, the main paraphrastic reformulative DMs are *ou seja* (literally "or be Subj," meaning "that is"), *quer dizer* (literally "(one) wants to-say," meaning "I mean"), *isto é*, "that is"; but this subclass also includes expressions like *por outras palavras* (literally "by other words," meaning "in other words"), *noutros termos* (literally "in other terms," meaning "in other words"). The core meaning, or the instruction, encoded by this set of DMs, may be roughly glossed by "interpret the following utterance as a better alternative formulation of the preceding one."

Let us see two examples where paraphrastic reformulative DMs occur:

(26) *Até já se consegue fazer ali vida de cidade, <u>quer dizer</u>, já há o anonimato que há nas cidades.*
"You can even have the same life there as in the city, *that is*, there is already the same anonymity that there is in the cities."

(27) *(…) uma sondagem deve ser feita junto de uma amostra representativa da população, <u>isto é</u>, a proporção de homens e mulheres na amostra deve ser idêntica à que se regista a nível nacional.*
"A survey should be done with a sample that is representative of the population, *in other words*, the proportion of men and women in the sample should be identical to that of the national population."

As the examples show, the segment introduced by the DMs does not repeat, in exactly the same way, the content of the first segment, which means that strict semantic equivalence is hardly ever the case. It only occurs in contexts of translation, definition or gloss. In the vast majority of cases, these DMs head a restatement whose role is to facilitate the hearer's understanding of the original, and this goal is achieved through the clarification of the content of the previous utterance.

3.5.2. Corrective DMs

This subclass involves DMs which encode a corrective or rectificative instruction, thus signalling that the speaker intends to correct some aspect of his / her previous utterance. In these cases, the rephrased content is taken by the speaker as the only valid information for the continuation of discourse. The Portuguese DMs that prototypically encode this instruction are (*ou*) *melhor* "or better," *ou antes* "or rather," (*ou*) *mais exactamente*, (*ou*) *mais correctamente*, (*ou*) *mais precisamente* "(or) more exactly / correctly / precisely," *aliás* (from Latin *alias* "in another way," meaning "or better"). But *quer dizer*, *ou seja* and *isto é*, mentioned in the previous subsection, may also fill this function: their polyfunctionality depends on the propositional content of the two related segments. Examples are provided below:

(28) *Toda a gente toma calmantes. Eu devo dizer que não tomo! <u>Ou antes</u>, tomo raríssimas vezes.*
"Everybody takes tranquilizers. I never do. *Or rather*, it's very rare."

(29) *A pornografia é uma invenção masculina. A prostituição é uma coisa masculina, não há pornografia ou prostituição para as mulheres. <u>Quer dizer</u>, só há para uma minoria.*
"Pornography is a masculine invention. Prostitution is a masculine thing, there is no pornography or prostitution for women. *That is to say* ('or rather'), there is only for a minority."

3.6. Summary DMs

DMs like *em suma* "to sum up," *em resumo, em síntese* "in short," *enfim* "briefly," *numa palavra* "in a word" signal that the next utterance is to be read as a summary of the information expressed in previous utterances. If we consider that a summary involves a shorter restatement or reformulation of the content of previous discourse units, then the markers that encode an instruction of summary may be included as a subclass in the broad class of reformulative DMs.[25] Furthermore, it is relevant to note that these DMs, unlike the paraphrastic and corrective ones, display an extra function: in fact, they also signal that the next utterance is the final part of a discourse sequence on a common topic. Therefore, they could also be included in the class of discourse-structuring DMs, discussed in the next subsection. The overlapping of the two functions proves, once again, the polyfunctionality of DMs, which is a real obstacle to discrete class definitions.

3.7. *Discourse-structuring DMs*

According to the main criterion adopted in this chapter to delimit DMs classes, it is hardly tenable to postulate a class of discourse-structuring DMs, since none of the more relevant theoretical frameworks on discourse relations contemplate the material structure of discourse or text. In fact, there is a quite consensual distinction between semantic (content-level or subject-matter) discourse relations and pragmatic (illocutionary-level or presentational) ones, but discourse coherence as such does not seem dependent on instructions about the speaker's strategy of discourse planning. However, it is undeniable that there are items, usually referred to as DMs, which occur typically in written texts and in in formal and public oral genres, that have a relevant function in terms of structuring the information throughout the discourse: *para começar* "to begin with" opens a discourse sequence, *depois* "then" signals continuity, *por fim* "lastly / finally" marks the end of the sequence. Other items with similar functions are: *em primeiro lugar, primeiro* "firstly," *em segundo/terceiro… lugar, segundo/terceiro* "secondly," "thirdly"…, *a seguir* "then," *em último lugar, por último, finalmente* "and finally," *para concluir* "to conclude." Here is an example:

(30) *Pensei falar <u>em primeiro lugar</u> sobre Portugal e a construção da Europa; <u>a seguir</u>, sobre o papel do Estado e dos agentes económicos e sociais; <u>depois</u>, sobre a educação e os recursos humanos; <u>finalmente</u>, sobre a responsabilidade dos cristãos na construção da Europa.*
"*Firstly*, I will speak about Portugal and the construction of Europe; *then*, about the role of the state and the economic and social agents; *afterwards*, about education and human resources *and finally*, about the responsibility of Christians in the construction of Europe."

The same items are also quite productive in ordering arguments supporting the same claim, within an argumentative discourse sequence (31):

(31) *Não faz sentido acusar a reforma de ser uma cedência do "português" ao "brasileiro": <u>primeiro</u>, porque o Brasil é de longe o principal "dono" da língua; <u>depois</u>, porque as mudanças são bilaterais; <u>por último</u>, porque na falta de unificação ortográfica será a norma brasileira a impor-se, dado o maior peso populacional do país.*
"It makes no sense to say that the reform is a capitulation of "European Portuguese" to "Brazilian Portuguese": *firstly*, because Brazil is by far the principal "owner" of the language, *secondly*, because the changes are bilateral *and finally*, because in the absence of a joint orthography the Brazilian norm will triumph, given the greater critical mass of the country's population."

Even though they do not signal any semantic or pragmatic discourse relation, they still have a role in the construction of discourse, providing some kind of connection in the domain of the material structure of text or discourse, organizing and ordering the discourse constituents. In line with Redecker (2006) and Pons Bordería (2006), I assume that another level of discourse has to be taken into consideration to encompass the functions of this subset of DMs. Therefore, I argue that they operate on the sequential structure of discourse, marking the beginning, the continuation or the end of a sequence—in a word,"displaying" the processes of text or discourse presentation.

4. Final remarks

In this chapter it has been assumed that DMs are discourse connectives and that they signal a relation between discourse utterances or segments, thus giving instructions to the hearer / reader on how to integrate them coherently into the mental representation of the discourse, in the incremental interpretation process. In other words, DMs were analyzed taking into consideration the role that the utterance they typically preface plays in the discourse context. The discussion on some classes of DMs was guided by the hypothesis that it should be possible to establish correlations between DMs and discourse or rhetorical relations. To some extent, this has proved to be tenable. Our data also validate the distinction between semantic and pragmatic discourse relations, i.e., relations which articulate the propositional content of utterances (for instance, elaboration) and relations which operate at the illocutionary level of discourse organisation, relating speech acts (for instance, justification).

However, the discussion about discourse-structuring DMs clearly showed the need to consider the organizational aspects of discourse connection, a domain that is not captured within the frameworks dealing with semantic and pragmatic discourse coherence. In this way, discourse relations may be valuable tools to delimit prototypical classes of DMs; nevertheless, there is at least one peripheral subset of DMs, the discourse structuring ones, that cannot be accounted for within theoretical frameworks focused on discourse coherence. A more thorough and accurate description and explanation of the role of DMs in the building of discourse is, in my view, highly dependent on further research on hierarchical or modular models of discourse organisation, both in monological and dialogical discourses (Roulet 2006, Pons Bordería 2006). This line of research would help to address and clarify issues related with markers whose function is to introduce a (new) topic, to signal topic shifts and digressions, issues which are not contemplated in this chapter.

Another challenging direction for future research involves the identification and characterization of discourse relations that are created exclusively by the use of a specific (subset of) DM(s), thus not inferable in its absence. *De qualquer modo* "anyway," for instance, is a paradigmatic example of a DM which articulates two discourse spans, imposing an interpretation that is never available in its absence. Further, the question of whether there is a relevant correlation between types of discourse, discourse genders and specific sets of DMs remains to be answered.

Concerning future research focused on Portuguese data, a systematic fine-grained study of the constraints that each Portuguese DM imposes on its linguistic environment is needed. As was mentioned before, within each broad class of DMs there are specificities related to the appropriate conditions of use of each DM, and this heuristic study is far from being concluded.

Finally, a contrastive study of DMs between Portuguese and other Romance languages is a direction of research that should not be dismissed.

NOTES

1 See Jucker and Ziv (1998), Fraser (1999), and Fisher (2006) for a thorough perspective on the wide and heterogeneous spectrum of approaches to DMs.

2 Schiffrin (1987) is a groundbreaking work which inspired many of the subsequent studies on the functions DMs may fulfil in the management of a conversation. On conversational markers in Portuguese, see, a.o., Marcuschi (1989), Risso et al. (1996), Rodrigues (1998).

3 Also refered to in the literature as rhetorical relations (Mann and Thompson (1988), Asher and Lascarides (2003)), or coherence relations (Knott and Sanders (1998), (Sanders, Spooren and Nordmann (1992)).

4 CETEMPúblico (www.linguateca.pt) and Corpus de Referência do Português Contemporâneo (CRPC) (www.clul.ul.pt).
5 The two following sections build upon Lopes and Carrilho (forthcoming).
6 Needless to say that this property implies that DMs are external elements concerning the syntactic structure of the sentence.
7 Within the Relevance Theory framework (Blakemore 1987), procedural meaning is defined as an instruction on how to compute conceptual representations. As discourse connectives specify the ways in which information conveyed by an utterance can be contextually relevant, their meaning can be characterized as procedural.
8 Cf. studies on grammaticalization of Portuguese DMs: Martelotta (2008), Lima (2002), a.o.
9 A similar process of grammaticalization undergoes the developement of DMs from adverbs.
10 See Fisher (2006) for a relevant theoretical discussion on this issue.
11 For a more comprehensive analysis of the multiple uses of *enfim*, see Lopes (2008). See also Lopes, Pezatti and Novaes (2001) on the multifunctionality of *portanto* in Portuguese.
12 A similar typology is adopted in Lopes and Carrilho (forthcoming). There are different typologies of DMs competing in the literature. See, a.o., Martín Zorraquino and Portolés (1999), Bazanella (1995).
13 Taboada (2006).
14 Mann and Thompson (1988), Asher and Lascarides (2003), Sanders et al.(1992) are relevant references in the field. See Taboada (2006) for an empirical study on discourse realations and DMs. See also Taboada and Mann (2006) for a comprehensive overview of different approaches to discourse relations.
15 Elaboration is a content or semantic discourse relation ("subject-matter" in Mann and Thompson 1988's terminology), in the sense that it relates propositions extensionally interpreted.
16 Indeed, the best choice in (13b) would be *mas* ("but"), which shows that the text requires a marker of contrast to be coherent.
17 Violation (or Denial) of Expectation is another expression used by some researchers to label this discourse relation.
18 See the unacceptability or the oddness of the following discourse continuation: # *O João é esperto. No entanto, não é trabalhador. Vai conseguir entrar na Universidade* [# "João is smart. However, he does not work hard. He will get into university."]
19 *Agora* "Now" may also function, in Portuguese, as a counterargumentative DM (Lopes 1998).
20 The DM *pelo contrário* may also signal a different discourse relation in Portuguese, in distinct discourse configurations. In fact, in dialogues and, more precisely, in reactive refutation moves, the speaker may express his/her disagreement with his/her interlocutor, rejecting a previous utterance (or part of it), on the grounds of its falsity or inappropriateness, and adding a segment introduced by *pelo contrário* that corrects the target of refutation:

A: *A situação está a melhorar.* [The situation is improving.]
B: *A situação não está a melhorar.* Pelo contrário, *a situação está cada vez pior!*

"The situation is not improving. *On the contrary*, it is getting worse."

See Lopes and Sousa (2014) for a thorough analysis of *pelo contrário* in Portuguese.
21 Example adapted from Rossari (2000).
22 It is worth stressing that implicit information generally has to be added to the content of the first segment so that the inference is deduced soundly (Lopes 2009). Details will not be discussed here.
23 Conclusive DMs may also introduce an order, since it is still possible to retrieve the inferential reasoning that underlies the connection: *São horas de ir para a escola.* Portanto, *toca a levantar!* "It is time to go to school. *So*, get out of bed!"
24 Some researchers (Zorraquino and Portolés 1999, Rossari 1994, Roulet 2006, a.o.) include in the class of reformulative DMs expressions equivalent to the following Portuguese connectives: *de qualquer modo* (literally "of any way," meaning "anyway"), *de qualquer maneira* (literally "of any manner," meaning "anyway"), *em todo o caso* "in any case," *seja como for* (literally "be-Subj (it) as (it) will-be-Subj," meaning "be that as it may, anyway"). Given the definition of reformulation outlined above, it is hardly consistent to follow their proposal. In fact, these DMs signal that the speaker distances him- / herself from what was previously said and invites the hearer to focus

his / her attention on the discourse segment they introduce, the one which he / she considers to be really relevant for the continuation of the discourse. The instruction encoded could be roughly paraphrased by "dismiss what has been said and read the next utterance as the one which is actually relevant for discourse continuity." Using these DMs, the speaker reorients his / her discourse, foregrounding the information of the segment which hosts them and disqualifying previous information. See Lopes (2012) for a more detailed description of the DM *de qualquer modo* in Portuguese. As far as I know, none of the current typologies of discourse relations incorporates the one which is encoded by this subset of DMs.

25 Calling upon Mann and Thompson's taxonomy, these DMs signal two discourse relations, Restatement (labeled Reformulation in this chapter) and Summary.

REFERENCES

Asher, N. and A. Lascarides (2003). *Logics of Conversation*. Cambridge: Cambridge University Press.

Bazzanella, C. (1995). I signali discorsivi. In L. Renzi, G. Salvi, and A. Cardinaletti (eds.), *Grande Grammatical Italiana de Consultazione*, vol. 3. Bologna: Il Mulino, pp. 225–257.

Blakemore, D. (1987). *Semantic Constraints on Relevance*. Oxford: Blackwell.

Brinton, L. (1996). *Pragmatic Markers in English. Grammaticalization and Discourse Function*. Berlin: de Gruyter.

Fisher, K. (ed.) (2006). *Approach to Discourse Particles*. Amsterdam: Elsevier.

Fraser, B. (1999). What are discourse markers? *Journal of Pragmatics*, 31, pp. 931–952.

Fraser, B. (1990). An approach to discourse markers. *Journal of Pragmatics* 14, pp. 383–395.

Hansen, M.-B. M. (1998). *The Functions of Discourse Particles. A Study with Special Reference to Spoken French*. Amsterdam: John Benjamins.

Jucker, A. and Y. Ziv (1998). *Discourse Markers: Descriptions and Theory*. Amsterdam: John Benjamins.

Knott, A. and R. Dale (1994). Using linguistic phenomena to motivate a set of coherence relations. *Discourse Processes*, 18, pp. 35–62.

Knott, A. and T. Sanders (1998). The classification of coherence relations and their linguistic markers: an exploration of two languages. *Journal of Pragmatics*, 30, pp. 135–175.

Lima, J. P. de (2002). Grammaticalization, subjectivation and the origin of phatic markers. In I. Wischer and G. Diewald (eds.), *New Reflections on Grammaticalization*. Amsterdam: John Benjamins, pp. 363–378.

Lopes, A. C. M. (1998). Contribuição para o estudo semântico-pragmático de *agora*. *Revista Portuguesa de Filologia*, vol. XXII, pp. 363–376.

Lopes, A. C. M. (2008). Enfim. *Estudos Linguísticos/Linguistic Studies*, 2, pp. 61–76.

Lopes, A. C. M. (2009). Justification: a coherence relation. *Pragmatics*, 19 (2), pp. 223–239.

Lopes, A. C. M. (2012). A polifuncionalidade das expressões *de qualquer modo e de outro modo* em PEC. In A. Costa and I. Duarte (eds.), *Nada na Linguagem lhe é Estranho. Estudos de Homenagem a Isabel Hub Faria*. Porto: Edições Afrontamento, pp. 79–92.

Lopes, A. C. M., E. Pezatti, and N. Novaes (2001). As construções com *portanto* no Português Europeu e no Português Brasileiro. *Scripta*, 5 (9), pp. 203–218.

Lopes, A. C. M. and E. Carrilho (forthcoming) Discurso e marcadores discursivos. In E. P. Raposo, M. F. B. do Nascimento, M. A. C. da Mota, L. Seguro, and A. Mendes (eds.), *Gramática do Português*, vol. 3. Lisbon: Fundação Calouste Gulbenkian.

Lopes, A. C. M. and S. Sousa (2014). The discourse connectives *ao invés* and *pelo contrário* in European Contemporary Portuguese. *Journal of Portuguese Linguistics*, 13 (1), pp. 3–28.

Mann, W. and S. Thompson (1988). Rhetorical structure theory: towards a functional theory of text organization. *Text*, 8, pp. 243–281.

Marcuschi, L. A. (1989). Marcadores conversacionais no português brasileiro: formas, posições e funções. In A. T. Castilho (ed.), *Português Falado Culto no Brasil*. Campinas: Editora da Unicamp, pp. 281–322.

Martelotta, M. (2008). Gramaticalização de conectivos portugueses: uma trajetória do espaço para o texto. *Estudos Linguísticos/Linguistic Studies*, 2, pp. 41–60.

Martín Zorraquino, M. A. and J. Portolés (1999). Los marcadores del discurso. In I. Bosque and V. Demonte (eds.), *Gramática Descriptiva de la*

Lengua Española, vol. 3. Madrid: Espasa Calpe, pp. 4051–4203.

Pons Bordería, S. (2006). A functional approach to the study of discourse markers. In K. Fisher (ed.), *Approaches to Discourse Particles*. Amsterdam: Elsevier, pp. 77–100.

Redecker, G. (2006). Discourse markers as attentional cues at discourse transitions. In K. Fisher (ed.), *Approaches to Discourse Particles*. Amsterdam: Elsevier, pp. 339–358.

Risso, M. S., G. O. Silva, and H. Urbano (1996). Marcadores discursivos: traços definidores. In I. Koch (ed.), *Gramática do Português Falado*, vol. VI. Campinas: Editora da Unicamp, pp. 21–61.

Rodrigues, I. (1998). *Sinais Conversacionais de Alternância de Vez*. Porto: Granito Editores e Livreiros.

Rossari, C. (1994). *Les Opérations de Reformulation*. Bern: Peter Lang.

Rossari, C. 2000 *Connecteurs et relations de discours: des liens entre cognition et signification*. Nancy: Presses Universitaires de Nancy.

Rossari, C. (2006). Formal properties of a subset of discourse markers: connectives. In K. Fisher (ed.), *Approaches to Discourse Particles*. Amsterdam: Elsevier, pp. 299–314.

Roulet, E. 1987 L'intégration des mouvements discursifs et le rôle des connecteurs interactifs dans une approche dynamique de la construction du discours monologique. *Modèles linguistiques*, 9, pp. 19–31.

Roulet, E. (2006). The description of text relation markers in the Geneva model of discourse organization. In K. Fisher (ed), *Approach to Discourse Particles*. Amsterdam: Elsevier, pp. 115–132.

Roulet, E., A. Auchlin, J. Moeschler, C. Rubattel, and M. Schelling (eds.) (1985). *L'articulation du Discours en Français Contemporain*. Bern: Peter Lang.

Sanders, T., W. Spooren, and L. Noordman (1992). Towards a taxonomy of coherence relations. *Discourse Processes*, 15, pp. 1–35.

Schiffrin, D. (1987). *Discourse Markers*. Cambridge: Cambridge University Press.

Schorup, L. 1985 *Common discourse particles in English conversation: like, well, y'know*. New York: Garland.

Taboada, M. (2006). Discourse markers as signals (or not) of rhetorical relations. *Journal of Pragmatics*, 38, pp. 576–592.

Taboada, M. and W. Mann (2006). Rhetorical structure theory: looking back and moving ahead. *Discourse Studies*, 8 (6), pp. 423–459.

Traugott, E. (1995). The role of the development of discourse markers in a theory of grammaticalization. http://citeseerx.ist.psu.edu/viewdoc/download;jsessionid=19AD7FC49EB38EF428953EA892BFC96A?doi=10.1.1.89.2536&rep=rep1&type=pdf .

Traugott, E. and R. Dasher (2002). *Regularity in Semantic Change*. Cambridge: Cambridge University Press.

Zorraquino, M. and Portolés, J. (1999). Los marcadores del discurso. In I. Bosque and V. Demonte (eds.) *Gramática descriptiva de la lengua española*. Tmo III, Madrid: Espasa Calpe.

25 From Latin to Portuguese: Main Phonological Changes

D. ERIC HOLT

1. Introduction

The present chapter explores the main phonological changes that characterize the linguistic evolution of Portuguese from Latin, with special attention to those that distinguish it from its neighbors, although as a descendant of Latin, Portuguese shares many traits with its Romance language sisters, particularly in the Iberian Peninsula.

The chapter is organized as follows: Section 2 treats various issues related to the evolution of syllable structure from Late Spoken Latin through Hispano-Romance to Modern Portuguese. This will include treatment of (inter-)related phenomena that affect segments, both individually and in combination, of vowels and consonants, including some that occur only sporadically. Section 3 further addresses salient characteristics of the vocalic system. Section 4 treats morphophonological issues of grammaticalization, contraction and prosody that characterize Portuguese in contrast to other Romance varieties. Section 5 offers a brief conclusion.

2. Syllable structure, sonority and moras: Their interaction in Latin, Hispano-Romance and Galician/Portuguese, and consequences for consonantal inventories

Arguably, changes related to syllable structure that affect Late Spoken Latin drive most other phonological changes in Hispano-Romance and Galician/Portuguese.[1] Specifically, under a moraic approach to the syllable (Hayes 1989), and by understanding both the role of sonority in syllable structure (Clements 1990) and the relationship between the sonority of a segment and its mora-bearing status (Zec 1995), the shape of the syllable and the behavior of its constituents (particularly in the rime, or intervocalically) may be analyzed as intimately interconnected.

The most sonorous elements of the syllable are vowels, which occupy the nuclear position. They are prototypical mora-bearing elements, with simple vowels monomoraic, and long vowels bimoraic. Latin vowels occurred with one of five qualities and one of two weights, that is short and long /i e a o u/. At first, phonological weight was realized by means of longer or shorter duration, and any articulatory differences were negligible, with the short : long opposition stable. Subsequently, subtle articulatory differences eventually grow and

The Handbook of Portuguese Linguistics, First Edition. Edited by W. Leo Wetzels, João Costa, and Sergio Menuzzi.
© 2016 John Wiley & Sons, Inc. Published 2020 by John Wiley & Sons, Inc.

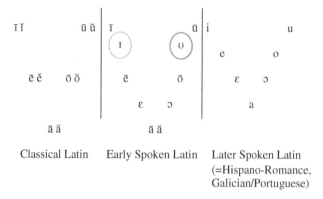

Classical Latin   Early Spoken Latin   Later Spoken Latin
(=Hispano-Romance,
Galician/Portuguese)

Figure 25.1   Evolution of vowel length from Latin to Hispano-Romance and Galician/Portuguese.

lead to the abandonment of length, and reanalysis of vocal contrast is shifted solely to quality rather than both quality and quantity (Pulgram 1975); specifically, the phonetic manifestation of weight as length came to include differences in tongue height and tenseness, and quite early on, /ī, ū/ began to differ from /ĭ, ŭ/ articulatorily, as did /ē, ō/ from /ĕ, ŏ/. The long vowels were stable, but the short vowels came to be realized lower and laxer, with the result that /ĭ, ŭ/ opened to [ɪ, ʊ], and /ĕ, ŏ/ opened to [ɛ, ɔ]. The eventual result is the merger of Latin /ĭ, ŭ/ and /ē, ō/, since their phonological contrast is now realized sufficiently be their distinct vowel quality, which would be easier to articulate and perceive than vowel duration (summarized from Lloyd 1987: 71–75, 110–111, and Holt 2003: §1).

This abandonment of weight (mono- vs. bimoraic status) as a phonologically independent feature of vowels yields the vocalic inventory of Hispano-Romance, which persists in Galician/Portuguese and Modern Portuguese, /i, e, ɛ, a, o, ɔ, u/. (Other characteristics of the vocalic system are treated in Section 3.) And, as discussed below, there are profound consequences for the consonantal system, which leads to the emergence of various identifying characteristics of Galician/Portuguese.

Specifically, the lack of phonologically long vowels in Hispano-Romance suggests that long consonants may likewise be disfavored, as these are less sonorous elements (see Zec 1995, pursued in Holt 1997, 1999 et seq.). Systemic parity or balance in this regard is recovered by the gradual elimination of the moraic status of consonants, which took place according to the sonority of the segment in question. Consequently, Latin geminate obstruents (including secondary ones that resulted from total assimilation; see below) and syllable-final velars are eroded and simplified. The Western Romance term *lenition* includes some of these changes, though it usually does not imply necessary changes in syllable-final (nongeminate) consonants, which are integral to the analysis presented here that links mora-bearing status in general with sonority.

The host of changes subsumed by the term *lenition* are all forms of weakening, in the sense of becoming less consonantal and more sonorous, that is, acquiring more features that characterize vowels, [+voice], [+continuant], [+sonorant]. These include degemination (by loss of mora) of intervocalic/geminate ("long") consonants (/pp tt kk ss; (rare, bb dd gg ff)/) (e.g., CUPPAM, CATTUS, SICCUM, CASSAM > *copa* "cup," *gato* "cat," *seco* "dry," *cassa* "empty"); voicing of obstruents (/p t k f s/, e.g., LUPUM, ROTAM, LACUM, AURIFICEM, CASAM > *lobo* "wolf," *roda* "wheel," *lago* "lake," *ourives* "goldsmith," *casa* "house"); and, spirantization (with not infrequent loss) of voiced obstruents (/b d g/, e.g., IBA, PEDEM, REGEM > *ia* "was going (3p.sg.)," *pé* "foot," *rei* "king"). Instead of viewing this constellation of changes as sequential (either as a traditional "push"- or "pull"-chain), they may instead be n > Ø (MANUM > *mão* "hand")   nn > n (ANNUM > *ano* "year")

l > Ø (CAELUM > *céu* "heaven")   ll > l (BELLO > *belo* "beautiful")

Figure 25.2 Evolution of Latin short /n, l/ and long /nn, ll/.

viewed as co-occurring.[2] That is, the entire consonantal system may be seen to react to the reanalysis of vowel quality and length.

In the case of Galician/Portuguese, the effacement of voiced intervocalic single consonants, which are targeted due to their [−cont] status, applies as well to /n, l/. In the case of the nasal, the so-called nasal vowels result (e.g., MANU > *mão* "hand"; see also Section 3),[3] and in the case of the lateral, there is total loss between vowels (e.g., CAELUM > *céu* "sky").[4] Syllable-finally, the (nongeminate) dorsal consonants /k, g/ are similarly affected—these segments undergo featural changes that prolong their ability to bear a mora and occur independently in the coda (that is, without assimilation to a following onset consonant). The result is the formation of higher-sonority glides, either palatal [j] or labio-velar [w], depending on the nature of the surrounding segments (e.g., OCTO, ACTOR, INTEGRU > *oito* "eight," *autor* "author," *enteiro* "whole").[5] Similarly, while not an obstruent, lateral [l] likewise vocalizes in coda position due to its [−cont] status (e.g., MULTU > *muito* "many"; ALTERU > *outro* "other," with raising of [a]).

Remaining syllable-final consonants lose their independence as well, and geminate obstruents result from assimilation to the following consonant (e.g., URSUM, IPSE, CAPTUS > osso "bear," ISSE "self," CATTUS "siezed, caught"). These segments undergo not featural change, *per se*, but structural change (total assimilation, thus being licensed in syllable-final position due to their concomitant onset position) to persist in the language, though these secondary geminates likewise simplified along with the Latin primary geminates. When such accommodating changes are not possible, like word-finally, segments are typically lost, e.g., the morphological endings *–m* and *–t*.

The more sonorous geminates /nn, ll/ endured longer, but eventually lose their moraic status as well, and with no imperative to avoid merger with /-n-, -l-/, since these have been previously lost (in contrast with the case of Old Spanish; see Holt 2003), result in singleton *n, l* (e.g., ANNUM > *ano* "year," BELLO > *belo* "beautiful"). Thus, noncontinuants are no longer permitted syllable-finally or as geminates in intervocalic position, as these both require moraic status. In the end, the drive to eliminate consonantal moraicity in its entirety has reshaped the consonantal system, and the result of these leniting processes is a consonantal inventory that no longer shows an imbalance of mora-bearing segments.

Additional changes in syllable structure occur that lead to a more symmetrically dispersed inventory of consonants. The loss of moraic consonants means that the number and type of consonant-consonant sequences is reduced, as there are no longer geminates, and syllable-final consonants have been eroded as well. Other cases of CC are likewise affected and reduced or simplified.[6] Specifically, in onset position, a new palatal series emerges (/ɲ ʎ ʃ ʒ/), resulting indirectly from a change in accent type with loss of hiatus that leads to formation of a glide ("yod") from Latin (now asyllabic) /i, e/; this yod then influences the articulation of a preceding consonant, yielding palatalization, and a simpler onset to the syllable: nasal /ɲ/ (e.g., SENIOREM "older" > senjor > *senhor* "lord, mister"; VINEA > vinia > vinja > *vinha* "vine(yard)"); lateral /ʎ/ (e.g., ALLIUM > aljo > *alho* "garlic"; MULIEREM > muljer > *mulher* "woman"; FOLIA > folja > *folha* "leaf, sheet"; see further below for an additional source of /ʎ/); (alveo-)palatal /ʃ/ (e.g., BASSIUM > baixo "low"; PASSIONEM > *paixão* "passion"), and along with the lenition as described above, /ʒ/ (e.g., BASIUM > *beijo* "kiss"; CASEUM > *queijo* "cheese"); additional cases of /ʒ/ come from the effect of yod on /d/ and /g/: HODIE > *hoje* "today," VIDEO > *vejo* "see (1p.sg.)"; FUGIO > *fujo* "flee (1p.sg.)." Yod affects the voiceless

/ɲ/ (<[nj])

/ʎ/ (<[lj])

/ʃ/ (<[sj])

/ʒ/ (<[sj] in leniting/voicing contexts; also < /d/, /g/ + yod)

/ts/ (</t, k/ + yod)

/dz/ (</t, k/ + yod in leniting/voicing contexts)

Figure 25.3 Emergence of new palatal series (/ɲ ʎ ʃ ʒ/) and affricates (/ts, dz/).

stops /t, k/ by assibilating them to /ts/ (e.g., FORTIAM > *força* "force," TERTIARIUM > *terceiro* "third," BRACCHIUM > *braço* "arm"), which in leniting contexts yields expected /dz/ (e.g., RATIONEM > *razão* "reason," JUDICIUM > *juizo* "judge"). (Most examples from Williams 1962.)

While onset coronals and velars underwent palatalization rather easily and apparently earlier, labials did not, or at least, the greater markedness of these sounds seems to have led to their later creation and then differential resolution and simplification, often involving metathesis (which also affected *s, r*; see also discussion of sporadic sound changes further below). Examples include SAPIAT > *saiba* "know (subjunctive, 1, 3p.sg.)"; RABIAM > *raiva* "rage," with attested *ravha* seemingly indicating an intermediate palatalized form; and there are attestations of forms such as *cambhar* "to change," *limpho* "clean," *mho/a(s)* "my." (See Pensado Ruiz 1986 for exhaustive discussion, as well as Holt 2004.)

An additional case of onset simplification comes from that of voiceless consonant+*l* (the so-called *muta cum liquida* clusters), which also frequently yield palatals, usually /ʎ/ medially (e.g., OCULUM > *olho* "eye," AURICULAM > *orelha* "ear," APICULAM > *abelha* "bee," REGULAM > *relha* "plowshare"), as well as /tʃ/ word-initially (e.g., PLORARE > *chorar* "to cry," FLAMMAM > *chama* "flame," CLAUEM > *chave* "key") or medially following a consonant (e.g., INFLARE > *encher* "inflate," MA(N)CULA > *mancha* "stain," SARCULARE > *sachar* "to hoe," MASCULUM > *macho* "male, macho"). The processes by which these changes take place are as follows: first, it is in the *c+l* sequences (and less frequently, *g+l* sequences) where the changes are thought to have initiated, that is, the /l/ comes to retract its articulation toward the velar region where /k, g/ are produced, and this assimilation yields [kʎ], and more variably, [gʎ] (e.g., SPECULUM > *espelho* "mirror," TEGULA > *telha* "tile," vs. GLATTIRE > *latir* "beat"). This palatal realization of *l* is then generalized by analogy to labial+*l* sequences (e.g., SCOPULUM > *escôlho* "cliff, crag," TRIBULUM > *trilho* "rail").

This assimilation may be understood as a giving up of independence of the liquid; that is, the *l* in these sequences approximates the place of articulation of the velar, in some sense simplifying the sequence, and the spread by analogy to other consonants also represents a simplification or reduction of the possible realizations of *C+l* sequences. While the sequencing is simplified, the articulatory result is complex, and subsequently the initial consonant is lost, yielding /ʎ/, and this is what we find in the written record (*olho* "eye," *coalho* "curd," etc.).

In strong positions, the evolution follows a slightly different path. That is, both word-initially and medially after a consonant (where that consonant has assimilated to the C, further anchoring it and shielding it from simplification), the /Cʎ/ undergoes additional assimilatory changes, with the voicelessness of the C coming to devoice the now-palatal *l*; the phonetic result is a sequence that is very similar acoustically to [tʃ], and which is then reanalyzed as *ch*, which occurs in the earliest written records (e.g., *chorar* "to cry," *chama* "flame," *chave* "key"; *encher* "to inflate," *mancha* "stain"; also medial in Spanish *hinchar, mancha*, but cf. initial *llorar, llama, llave*). (See Holt 1998, 2000, 2007 for fuller analysis and additional references.) The HR and GP sibilants subsequently underwent a host of changes

Table 25.1   Hispano-Romance and Galician/Portuguese consonantal phoneme inventory.

	Bilabial		*Labio-dental*		*Dental/alveolar*		*Palatal*		*Velar*	
Plosive	p	b			t	d			k	g
Nasal	m				n		ɲ			
Fricative			f	v	s	z	ʃ	ʒ		
Affricate					<u>ts</u>	<u>dz</u>	tʃ			
Lateral					l		ʎ			
Rhotic					ɾ					
					r					

Key: <u>new affricates</u>; *new voiced fricatives*; **new palatals**

(see Williams 1962: 63, 79–80, Penny 1991: 22–23), providing a further example of simplification or reduction of complexity: *ch* deaffricated to /ʃ/ around 1700 (yielding the current pronunciation of words like *chave* as [ʃave]), and (by 1500) /ts/ and /dz/ become /s/ and /z/ (e.g., *força* "force," *razão* "reason").

A change that further improves the sonority cycle of the syllable (see Clements 1990) by maximizing the cline from onset to nucleus is that of the strengthening of initial asyllabic *i, u,* that is, the glides [j, w]. In initial position, /j/ becomes *j* (/(d)ʒ/, e.g., IUSTUM > *justo* "just," CUIUM > *cujo* "whose." IANUARIUM > *janeiro* "January"), and /w/ becomes *v* (e.g., UACCA > *vaca* "cow," UINUM > *vinho* "wine," VIDERE > *ver* "to see"), and this makes them more consonant-like, and therefore serve better in the role of onset to the syllable as the dispersion in sonority is greater.

The result of this host of changes is the following segmental inventory of consonants, which shows greater balance and complementarity among consonant types.

A final example of simplification of syllable structure comes from *s+C* sequences. Just as many other CC sequences have been altered (e.g., CT > *it*; NI > *nh*; LI > *nh*; CL > *lh* or *ch*, etc.), sC likewise undergoes modification (and likely very early on) in such a way as to simplify syllable structure, again in this case reducing the complexity of the syllable onset. In earlier Latin these form an onset cluster, but as with other clusters that come to be seen as difficult to produce, the *s* in combination comes to be viewed as "impure" (see Lloyd 1987: 148–150, Penny 1991: 36, and Williams 1962: 6, among many others), and a short *i* (which later developed to *e*) is introduced to support the *s* in the coda of a newly-formed preceding syllable (e.g., STARE > *estar*). The result is that the original C becomes the sole member of the onset. Furthermore, sonority considerations favor this outcome as well, as this maximizes the sonority cline of the syllable onset, since an onset sC– presents an anomalous sonority reversal given the higher sonority of [s] followed by a lower sonority consonant preceding the sonority peak of the vocalic nucleus. In similar fashion, it is possible that the higher sonority of [s] (compared to the following consonant) led speakers to analyze it as part of an anomalous "semi-syllable" (Penny 1991: 36), and as syllables are headed by a vowel, epenthesis occurs to solidify the well-formedness of the syllable (see also Lloyd 1987: 149).

Several sporadic sounds changes also affect Hispano-Romance, and these result from situations of phonotactic distress as well. These include dissimilation, consonantal epenthesis, progressive nasalization, and metathesis. (See Williams 1962: 102–115 for further discussion of these and other sporadic changes.)

Cases of dissimilation of consonants include LOCALE > *lugar̠* "place," ANIMAM > anma > a̱lma "soul," MEMORARE > ̠nembrar > ̱lembrar "to remember," and SIMILARE > semlar > *sembr̠ar* "to resemble" (cf. *semelhar*, from unattested *SIMILIARE). These final two also show consonantal epenthesis, the result of reanalysis following an articulatory mis-timing between the nasal and following liquid that leads to the perception of an "intrusive" segment,[7] which has the effect of strengthening the syllable onset. This is also seen in cases like HUMERUM > omro > *ombro* "shoulder," HONORARE > *ondrar* "to honor" (old [cf. modern *honrar*], though perhaps a borrowing from Spanish, where intrusive *d* is more common, e.g., Sp. *pondrá* vs. GP *porá* "will put (3p.sg.)"). A different type of epenthesis occurs when certain vowels are in hiatus, and an onset consonant develops that adopts characteristics of neighboring sounds: AUDIRE > *ouvir* "to hear," LAUDAT > *louva* "praise (3p.sg.)"; SEDEAT > *seja* "be (subjunctive, 1,3p.sg.)," UNAM > ũa > *uma* "one (fem.)"; VINUM > vĩo > *vinho* "wine," MEAM > mia > mĩa > *minha* "my, mine (fem.)."[8] These last examples show progressive nasalization, which is also seen in MATREM > *mãe* "mother," AD NOCTE > *ontem* "yesterday." Metathesis involves the reversal of sounds, including of vowels (e.g., GENUCULUM > *geolho* > *joelho* "knee") or a vowel and a consonant (e.g., INTER > *entre* "between," INODIUM > *enojo* > *enjôo* "sickness, boredom"), though more typically of a consonant and a glide (e.g., SAPIAT > *saiba* "know (subjunctive, 1,3p.sg.)," RABIAM > *raiva* "rage," PRIMARIU > *primeiro* "first" (with raising of *a* to *e*)), or of two consonants, either in contact (e.g., SIB(I)LARE > *silvar* "to whistle"), or at a distance (e.g., PARABOLA > *palavra* "word").

Two other noteworthy characteristics of the consonants of Modern Portuguese emerge in the Renaissance period, in addition to the simplification of the sibilant system discussed above: the heavy velarization of syllable-final /-l/ ([ɫ]) and the retraction and frication of trilled /r/ in most regions to uvular /ʁ/.

Dissimilation:

> l > r (LOCALE > *lugar* "place")

> n > l (ANIMAM > anma > *alma* "soul")

> m > l (MEMORARE > *nembrar* > *lembrar* "to remember")

Consonantal epenthesis:

> mr > mbr (HUMERUM > omro > *ombro* "shoulder")

> nr > ndr (HONORARE > *ondrar* "to honor")

Anti-hiatic epenthesis:

> v (AUDIRE > *ouvir* "to hear")

> m (UNAM > uã > *uma* "one (fem.)")

> j (SEDEAT > *seja* "be (subjunctive, 1,3p.sg.)")

> ɲ (VINUM > vĩo > *vinho* "wine")

Progressive nasalization (MATREM > *mãe* "mother")

Metathesis of

> vowels (GENUCULUM > *geolho* > *joelho* "knee")

> vowel + consonant (INTER > *entre* "between")

> consonant + glide (RABIAM > *raiva* "rage")

> two consonants

>> in contact (SIB(I)LARE > *silvar* "to whistle")

>> at distance (PARABOLA > *palavra* "word")

Figure 25.4 Some sporadic sound changes from Latin to Galician/Portuguese.

3. More on the vocalic system: Oral and nasal vowels and diphthongs, reduction and metaphony

Returning to vowels, the shared Hispano-Romance vocalic inventory persists in Galician/Portuguese and Modern Portuguese: /i, e, ɛ, a, o, ɔ, u/ occur in stressed position, but in unstressed position /ɛ, ɔ/ are lacking, and word-finally, only /e, a, u/ are common.

This system contrasts with that of Old Spanish in the lack of diphthongized reflexes of Latin short /e, o/ (/je, we/). This appears to be due to differential Germanic influence in these two Romance varieties (Meillet 1970: 38). The new intensified stress accent characteristic of Late Spoken Latin and Hispano-Romance in the period of Germanic contact and conquest seems to have occurred later and more slowly in the more remote territory of GP. Additional phenomena that support this weaker accent (see Williams 1962: 11–13, 53, 56–57, 78, 87–88) include fewer cases of syncope (cf. GP *–ável* / *–ível* vs. Sp. *–able* / *–ible*, NEBULAM > *névoa* vs. Sp. *niebla* "mist, fog," DUBITAM > *dúvida* vs. Sp. *deuda* "debt," CAPITALEM > *cabedal* vs. Sp. *caudal* "wealth," etc.), slower formation of yod and wau (which allows for more occurrence of inter-vocalic voicing, e.g., *saiba* vs. Sp. *sepa*, SEPIAM > *siba* "cuttlefish," etc.), and longer retention of hiatus (e.g., from versification in the *Cancioneiro Geral* (1516), the syllabic value of *e* in forms like *côdea* "bark," *fêmea* "female").

There is an extensive system of diphthongs in GP, however, and these come from several sources, such as the loss of Latin hiatus (e.g., DEUS > *deus* "god," FUIT > *foi* "was (1p.sg.)," MEAM > *mia* (later, *minha* "my, mine (fem.)").[9] We saw above that the yod formed in these cases often has a palatalizing or assibilating effect on the preceding consonant: SENIOREM "older" > *senhor* "lord, mister," MULIEREM > *mulher* "woman"; BASSIUM > *baixo* "low," BASIUM > *beijo* "kiss," VIDEO > *vejo* "see (1p.sg.)," FUGIO > *fujo* "flee (1p.sg.)"; and, FORTIAM > *força* "strength," RATIONEM > *razão* "reason." The loss of a consonant (due to lenition) can also lead to vowels in contact with resolution into a diphthong, either syllable-finally (e.g., ALTERUM > *outro* "other," NOCTEM > *noite* "night") or intervocalically (e.g., VADO > vao > *vou* "go (1p. sg.)," MALU > *mau* "bad," CAELU > *céu* "sky," MAGIS > *mais* "more"), and this likewise occurs when the consonant is lost in the pre-Modern period: *faciles* > *facees* > *fáceis* "easy (pl.)," *sabedes* > *sabees* > *sabéis* "know (2 p.pl.)."

The existence of nasal diphthongs ([ɐ̃j̃, õj̃, ũj̃, ẽw̃]) results from the loss (due to lenition) of /-n-/ or from consonantal loss with progressive nasalization (e.g., MATER > *mãe* "mother," PONET > *põe* "put (3p.sg.)," MULTUM > *muito* "many, much," MANUM > *mão* "hand").[10] The GP nasal vowels ([ĩ, ẽ, ɛ̃, õ, ũ]) likewise result from loss of a nasal (e.g., FINE > *fĩe > *fĩi* > *fim* "end," BENE > *bem* "well, good," BONUM > *bõo* > *bom* "good," GERMANA > *irmã* "sister," UNUM > *ũu* > *um* "one (masc.)"). (These, especially [ẽ], may be phonetically diphthongized, especially in final position.)[11]

Metaphony (also known as umlaut, inflection, and vowel harmony) is another salient characteristic of the vocalic system of GP.[12] Not all examples of Latin vowels evolved the

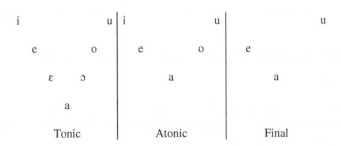

Figure 25.5 Inventories of vowels in Galician/Portuguese by position.

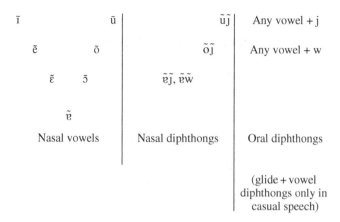

Figure 25.6   Inventory of nasal vowels and nasal and oral diphthongs in Galician/Portuguese.

LACTEM > [lajte] > *leite* 'milk'; ALTERUM > [awtɾo] > *outro* 'other'

Figure 25.7   Results of assimilatory vowel raising in Galician/Portuguese.

same way, and this is due to the effect of some neighboring sound. For example, when the mid vowels /ɛ, ɔ/ precede a nasal, they become close (e.g., TEMPUS > *tempos* "time," QUEM > *quem* "who," with [ẽ] rather than [ɛ̃], and PONTEM > *ponte* "bridge," with [õ] rather than [ɔ̃]), and pre-tonic /e, o/ fail to raise in *sentir* "to feel," *vontade* "will." Another example is the raising effect of wau (e.g., ALTERUM > [awtɾo] > *outro*, reduced in the sixteenth century to [o]) and of yod (e.g., LACTEM > [lajte] > *leite* "milk," –ARIU > [ajro] > *–eiro*) or other palatal (e.g., TENEO > *tenho* "have (1p.sg.)," FOLIA > *folha* "leaf, sheet," SEDEAT > *seja* "be (subjunctive, 1,3p. sg.)"). This vocalic interchange ([e~ɛ], [o~ɔ]) is also seen in several morphophonemic alternations, serving to enhance alternations in number (e.g., *ovo/ovos* "egg(s)"[ovu/ɔvus]) and gender (e.g., *novo/nova* "new (masc./fem.)" [no.vu/nɔ.va]). (See Nunes 1989, *inter alia*).

Other vocalic changes occur during the Renaissance period, when a greatly intensified stress accent developed (Williams 1962: 52–58) that particularly affected unstressed vowels. This prosodic change leads to the raising of pre-tonic vowels, such that /a/ > [ɐ], o > [u] and /e/ > [i], and more extreme reduction, especially with devoicing of final unstressed vowels, makes them often scarcely perceptible and leads to deletion (e.g., *sáb(a)do* "Saturday," *côm(o) do* "comfortable," *pêss(e)go* "peach," *poder(o)so* "powerful," *c(o)rôa* "crown," *p(a)ra* "for," *cidad(e)* "city," etc.) This promotes a general tolerance for syllable-final consonants.

4. Morphophonology: Contraction, grammaticalization and prosody

In this section several structural characteristics of Portuguese are treated that interleave matters of phonology and morphology. (See also Ferreira and Holt 2014, as well as Williams 1962 and Mattoso Camara 1972.)

Table 25.2 Contractions of prepositions *a, de, em, por* + articles.

	a "to"	*de* "from"	*em* "in"	*por* "for, through"
o "the (masc.); sg./pl."	ao(s)	do	no(s)	pelo[a]
a "the (fem.); sg./pl."	à(s)	da(s)	na(s)	pela(s)
um "a/one (masc.); sg./pl."		dum (duns)	num (nuns)	
uma "a/one (fem.); sg./pl."		duma(s)	numa(s)	

[a] The use of the Latin prepositions PER "through" and PRO "in front of" (both with metaphorical extensions) evolves over time. Portuguese *por* (< PRO) comes to take over functions of *per*, except in these cases of *per* + *lo* > *pelo*, etc., but cf. the alternative archaic forms *polo*, etc. in Table 25.4. See Mattoso Camara 1972: 154–156 for discussion.

First, compared to its Iberian neighbor, in GP (and other related dialects) there is large-scale contraction of prepositions with other words. This occurs most frequently with articles of both genders and numbers with the prepositions *a* "to," *de* "from," *em* "in" and *por* "for, through" (see Table 25.2); and for *de* and *em*, also occurs with demonstratives, pronouns, adverbs and other forms. (See Table 25.3. Additional archaic contractions are given in Table 25.4.)

The writing as a single form indicates that these are fused in pronunciation and may be interpreted as a complex morpheme, and is the result of prosodic merger of the two items. Segmentally, we observe several of the same phonological adjustments as seen in other areas of GP phonology and grammar. For instance, *do* and *ao* result from the loss of intervocalic /-l-/ in *lo* (the archaic article form that emerges historically in Hispano-Romance from the Latin demonstratives) with subsequent loss of final unstressed vowels before a vowel-initial word: *de* + *lo* > *de o* > *do*; *a* + *lo* > *a o* > *ao*; similarly for *a* + *la(s)* > *a a(s)* > *à(s)*, with merger of identical vowels (like SEDERE > *seer* > *ser* "to be"). (There are also archaic forms such as *mo* < *me lo*.)

For forms with *em* and *por*, there is assimilation (*n*+*l* > *nn*, *r*+*l* > *ll*) and simplification, consistent with the discussion of lenition in Section 2. (See Elsman and Holt 2009 for related discussion and formal analysis.) Additionally, the forms based on *em* come to lose their initial vowel (a similar aphaeresis as occurs in APOTHECA "storeroom (esp. for wine)" > *bodega* "bar, tavern"), and in opposition to the plain article *o, a, n-* is reanalyzed as a variant of *em*, and combines widely. Historically, a form like *nesto* is doubly contracted: *em esto* [ẽ esto] gives attested *éésto* (with accent indicating nasality), and *em* is reintroduced (around 1300), and with subsequent loss of initial *e*, becomes *nesto* (Williams 1962: 146–147).

The archaic article forms (or an assimilated variant) do persist in other cases where *l* was not intervocalic, such as when the pronoun follows a verbal form that ends in a consonant or nasal sound, and is the source of the modern pronominal endings *–lo, –no* and their inflected variants. (See Table 25.5.)

A second issue of morphophonology is the evolution of the verbal system of Romance, where new constructions emerge to express the future tense and conditional mood. These are based on the use of the infinitival form of a verb along with a present tense form of auxiliary HABERE "to have" (eventual future) or an imperfect aspect form of IRE "to go" (eventual conditional), such that *comer* + *he* ("to eat I have") > *comerei* ("I have to eat," with semantic bleaching of obligation but retention of implied futurity to "I will eat"); similarly for *comer* + *ia* ("to eat I was going" > *comeria* ("I was going to eat," still used as a future of the past in the sequencing of tenses, as well as with semantic shift to conditional meaning,

Table 25.3 Contractions of *a, de, em* + demonstratives, pronouns, adverbs and other forms.

	a "to"	*de* "from"	*em* "in"
este[a] "this (masc.); (sg./pl.)"		deste(s)	neste(s)
esta "this (fem.); (sg./pl.)"		desta(s)	nesta(s)
esse "that (masc.); (sg./pl.)"		desse(s)	nesse(s)
essa "that (fem.); (sg./pl.)"		dessa(s)	nessa(s)
aquele	àquela(s)	daquele(s)	naquel(e)(s)
aquela	àquele(s)	daquela(s)	naquela(s)
isto "this" (neuter)		disto	nisto
isso "that" (neuter)		disso	nisso
aquilo "that, those" (neuter)	àquilo	daquilo	naquilo
ele "he; they (masc.)"		dele(s)	nele(s)
ela "she; they (fem.)"		dela(s)	nela(s)
aqui "here"		daqui	
aí "there (near)"		daí	
ali "(over) there"		dali	
acolá "(way over) there"		dacolá	
além "beyond"		dalém	
aquém "this side"		daquém	
algures "somewhere"		dalgures	
antes "before"		dantes	
onde "where"		donde	
outro "other (masc.); sg./pl."		doutro(s)	noutro(s)
outra "other (fem.); sg./pl."		doutra(s)	noutra(s)
outrem "somebody else"		doutrem	noutrem
algum "some" (masc.); sg./pl."		dalgum (dalguns)	nalgum (nalguns)
alguma "some (fem.); sg./pl."		dalguma(s)	nalguma(s)
algo "some"			nalgo
alguém "somebody"			nalguém

[a] These forms also combine with *outro*, yielding archaic *estoutra, essoutros*, where only the final contributing form inflects for feminine gender and plural number. See Williams 1962: 158–159.

Table 25.4 Additional archaic contractions (*a, com, por*).

	a "to"	*com* "with"			*por* "for, through"
o "the (masc.); sg./pl."	ò(s)[a]	co(s)	cò(s)	cono(s)	polo(s)
a "the (fem.); sg./pl."		coa(s)[b]	cà(s)	cona(s)	pola(s)

[a] The grave accent of *ò* and *à* indicates a lowered pronunciation. In European Portuguese, *à* = [a], and *a* = slightly raised [ɐ]. In the archaic language, *a* + *o* = [ɔ]; later, the contraction adopted is *ao* [aw]. See Mattoso Camara 1972: 156–157.

[b] Forms like *coa* show loss of nasality in hiatus as likewise occurs in ARENA > *arẽa > *areia* "sand."

Table 25.5 Contractions of articles after a consonant.

amá-lo "to love it/him"(< *amar*)
amam-na "they love it/her"
põe-nas "they put them (fem.)"
quere-la "want it/her" (< *queres*) (classical)
qué-los "want them (masc.)" (< *quer*) (classical)

dar te lo ei, dar te lo ia
Possible in Hispano-Romance, early Galician/Portuguese and European Portuguese

te lo daré, te lo daría
Only possibility in Modern Spanish (similarly in most spoken Galician/Portuguese)

Figure 25.8 Medioclisis/separability of future and conditional endings.

"I would eat"). The morphological and prosodic status of these forms, however, has evolved over time, and still show a certain ambiguity given the continued separability of the main verb from these "endings." For instance, there are ample attestations of so-called *medioclisis* or *mesóclise*, with weak object pronouns between the verbal forms: e.g., *dar te lo ei* "give to you it I will," *dar te lo ia* "give to you it I was going." While parallel forms fell from use from Old to Modern Spanish, they still obtain in European Portuguese. (See also Ferreira and Holt 2014 and Holt 2004.)

Regarding a final issue that involves prosodic independence, as mentioned in passing above, the Latin demonstratives develop into the definite articles and the object pronouns *o(s)*, *a(s)*. The Latin forms are strong, that is, bear stress, but in their new grammaticalized function, the Hispano-Romance forms are prosodically weak, depending on neighboring words,[13] with phonology interacting with syntax to determine their placement. This is more restricted in GP than in neighboring Spanish, and a prominent condition is that these forms not appear in initial position, and as such are enclitic in most syntactic contexts: *Eu esperava ver-te* "I hoped to see you," *Ela manda-lhe um livro* "She sends him/her a book," *Ele vai levar-nos* "He is going to take us." Proclisis is triggered by negation (*não o vejo* "I don't see it/him"), quantifiers (*ninguém me compreende* "nobody understands me," *alguém a ama* "somebody loves me"), *wh*-phrases (*Quem te deu esse relógio?* "Who gave you that watch?"), contrastive focus (*só nós a escrevemos* "only we write it (fem.)") and certain adverbs (*Maria sempre os compra* "Maria always buys them"). (See Ferreira and Holt for limited additional discussion, as well as references to formal approaches to these and related phenomena in Hispano-Romance. See Perini 2002: §29, the source of many of these examples, for additional discussion.)

5. Conclusion

In this chapter, the major phonological changes from Latin to Portuguese were discussed, highlighting the initial significance of the evolution of syllable structure, including the loss of contrastive vowel length and the concomitant loss of geminate and many syllable-final consonants. A series of inter-related phenomena ensue that leads to further changes in the vocalic and consonantal systems, including interactions between the two (e.g., loss of hiatus and resulting palatalization, the loss of various consonants and resulting vocalic modifications). We also saw that in the early Modern period, several additional changes occur that yield other of the salient characteristics of GP (e.g., deaffrication of *ch*, atonic vowel reduction). The final section looked at issues of grammaticalization, contraction and prosody of a morphophonological nature that characterize Portuguese in contrast to other Romance varieties. While the treatment here has been brief, it is hoped that the reader will be inspired to investigate further.

Acknowledgments

The author would link to thank Leo Wetzels for his comments and suggestions on this chapter as well as for his editorial guidance.

NOTES

1   In this work I employ the abbreviations HR (Hispano-Romance) and GP (Galician/Portuguese), which variably indicates that some feature is shared by Galician and Portuguese, or refers to the historical stage when they were unitary. The present chapter is necessarily brief; for general over-views of the evolution of GP, the interested reader is referred to the references cited in the text, as well as Castro 2004, Parkinson 1988, Silva Neto 1988, *inter alia*.

2   For one approach along these lines using a dispersion-theoretic optimality-theoretic approach, see Baker 2007.

3   By definition, [−cont] means no oral airflow; nasal consonants bear this feature because the airflow is through the nasal cavity. The marked configuration [nasal, +cont] that would result from lenition is disfavored (see discussion and references in Holt 2002), and /n/ comes to lose its consonantal status; that is, nasal(ized) vowels result. See also Morales-Front and Holt 1997.

4   See Holt 2002 for discussion of the doubly-articulated structure of laterals. Briefly, /l/ is [-cont] at its primary coronal articulation, and [+cont] at its secondary dorsal articulation. When the primary [−cont] is changed, /l/ becomes a glide, and this higher sonority status licenses it to occur in the coda. This option is not possible in onset position, and in that position, intervocalic (nonmoraic) /l/ is lost.

5   The change is first one of [continuant] (k > x; g > ɣ), then of [sonorant] (> [j]).

6   We could conceptualize this in optimality-theoretic terms as due to increasing dominance of a con-straint NoCOMPLEX.

7   For theoretical analyses, see Holt 2004 and discussion and references therein.

8   See Holt 1993 for discussion in autosegmental terms of this and related phenomena in several Romance varieties.

9   However, when a high vowel precedes a non-high vowel, e.g. *viagem* "travel, journey," *sueco* "Swede," *suave* "smooth," *sour* "sweat," hiatus remains (cf. diphthong formation in Spanish in *viaje, suave*, etc.), such that phonologically there are no rising diphthongs (glide+vowel) in GP. (Agard 1984: 189.)

10   The phonological status of these has been long debated, see, e.g., the discussion and references in Morales-Front and Holt 1997.

11   The occurrence and alternations of nasalization in plural formation in Galician and Portuguese varieties (e.g. *irmão(s)* "brother(s)," *irmã(s)* "sister(s)"; *razão* ~ *razões* "reason(s)"; *pão* ~ *pães* "bread(s)") is a much-treated phenomenon. See Colina 2011, Ferreira and Holt 2014, Holt 2002, and Morales-Front and Holt 1997, among very many others.

12   See Williams 1962: §100 for further discussion, as well as Penny 2009.

13   One indication of this is that they are stress-neutral, cf. *falávamos / falávamos-lhe* "we used to talk (to him/her)," where stress comes to fall before the so-called three-syllable window.

REFERENCES

Agard, F. B. (1984). *A Course in Romance Linguistics. Volume 1: A Synchronic View. Volume 2: A Diachronic View*. Washington, DC: Georgetown University Press.

Baker, G. K. (2007). Duration, voice, and dispersion in stop contrasts from Latin to Spanish. In F. Martínez-Gil and S. Colina (eds.), *Optimality-Theoretic Studies in Spanish Phonology*. Amsterdam: John Benjamins, pp. 399–423.

Castro, I. (2004). *Introdução à História do Português. Geografia da Língua Portuguesa Antiga*. Lisbon: Colibri.

Clements, G. N. (1990). The role of the sonority cycle in core syllabification. *Papers in Laboratory Phonology*, 1, pp. 283–333.

Colina, S. (2011). Plural formation in Galician. In J. Herschensohn (ed.), *Selected Proceedings from the 40th Linguistic Symposium on Romance Languages*. Amsterdam: John Benjamins, pp. 79–98.

Elsman, M. M. and D. E. Holt (2009). When small words collide: morphological reduction and phonological compensation in Old Leonese contractions. In R. Leow, H. Campos, and D. Lardiere (eds.), *Little Words: Their History, Phonology, Syntax, Semantics, Pragmatics, and Acquisition*. Washington, DC: Georgetown University Press, pp. 21–33.

Ferreira, L. and D. E. Holt (2014). On the partially divergent phonology of Spanish, Portuguese and points in between. In P. Amaral and A. M. Carvalho (eds.), *Portuguese/Spanish Interfaces: Diachrony, Synchrony, and Contact*. Amsterdam: John Benjamins, pp. 123–150.

Hayes, B. (1989). Compensatory lengthening in moraic phonology. *Linguistic Inquiry*, 20, pp. 253–306.

Holt, D. E. (1993). Anti-hiatic insertion and spreading processes in Hispano-Romance. *Aleph*, 8 (2), pp. 84–98.

Holt, D. E. (1997). The role of the listener in the historical phonology of Spanish and Portuguese: an optimality-theoretic account. Ph.D. dissertation, Georgetown University.

Holt, D. E. (1998). The role of comprehension, reinterpretation and the Uniformity Condition in historical change: the case of the development of *Cl* clusters from Latin to Hispano-Romance. In V. Samiian (ed.), *Proceedings of the Twenty-Sixth Western Conference on Linguistics*. Fresno, CA: Department of Linguistics, California State University, pp. 133–148.

Holt, D. E. (1999). The moraic status of consonants from Latin to Hispano-Romance: The case of obstruents. In J. Gutiérrez-Rexach and F. Martínez-Gil (eds.), *Advances in Hispanic Linguistics: Papers from the Second Hispanic Linguistics Symposium*. Somerville, MA: Cascadilla Press, pp. 166-181.

Holt, D. E. (2000). Comparative optimality-theoretic dialectology: singular/plural nasal alternations in Galician, Mirandese (Leonese) and Spanish. In H. Campos, E. Herburger, A. Morales-Front, and T. J. Walsh (eds.), *Papers from the Third Hispanic Linguistics Symposium*. Somerville, MA: Cascadilla Press, pp. 125–143.

Holt, D. E. (2002). The articulator group and liquid geometry: implications for Spanish phonology present and past. In C. Wiltshire and J. Camps (eds.), *Romance Phonology and Variation*. Amsterdam: John Benjamins, pp. 85–99.

Holt, D. E. (2003). The emergence of palatal sonorants and alternating diphthongs in Hispano-Romance. In D. E. Holt (ed.), *Optimality Theory and Language Change*. Dordrecht: Kluwer Academic, pp. 285–305.

Holt, D. E. (2004). Optimization of syllable contact in Old Spanish via the sporadic sound change metathesis. *Probus: International Journal of Latin and Romance Linguistics*, 16, pp. 43–61.

Holt, D. E. (2007). Optimality theory and language change in Spanish. In F. Martínez-Gil and S. Colina (eds.), *Optimality-Theoretic Advances in Spanish Phonology*. Amsterdam: John Benjamins, pp. 378–396.

Lloyd, P. M. (1987). *From Latin to Spanish. Volume I: Historical Phonology and Morphology of the Spanish Language*. Philadelphia, PA: The American Philosophical Society.

Mattoso Camara, J. (1972). *The Portuguese Language*. Translated by A. J. Naro. Chicago: University of Chicago Press.

Meillet, A. (1970). *General Characteristics of the Germanic Languages*. Translated by W. P. Dismukes. Coral Gables, FL: University of Miami Press.

Morales-Front, A. and D. E. Holt (1997). On the interplay of morphology, prosody and faithfulness in Portuguese pluralization.

In F. Martínez-Gil and A. Morales-Front (eds.), *Issues in the Phonology and Morphology of the Major Iberian Languages*. Washington, DC: Georgetown University Press, pp. 393–437.

Nunes, J. J. (1989). *Compêndio de Gramática Histórica Portuguesa: Fonética e Morfologia*, 9th edn. Lisbon: Livraria Clássica Editora.

Parkinson, S. (1988). Portuguese. In M. Harris and N. Vincent (eds.), *The Romance Languages*. New York: Oxford University Press, pp. 131–169.

Penny, R. (1991). *A History of the Spanish Language*. Cambridge: Cambridge University Press.

Penny, R. (2009). Vowel harmony and metaphony in Iberia: a revised analysis. *Estudos de Lingüística Galega*, 1, pp. 113–124.

Pensado Ruiz, C. (1986). *Comha, ravha*, y otras grafías similares en portugués medieval. *Verba: Anuario Galego de Filoloxia*, 13, pp. 329–340.

Perini, M. A. (2002). *Modern Portuguese: A Reference Grammar*. New Haven, CT: Yale University Press.

Pulgram, E. (1975). *Latin-Romance Phonology: Prosodics and Metrics*. Munich: Wilhelm Fink.

Silva Neto, S. (1988). *História da Língua Portuguesa*, 5th edn. Rio de Janeiro: Presença.

Williams, E. B. (1962). *From Latin to Portuguese: Historical Phonology and Morphology of the Portuguese Language*. Philadelphia, PA: University of Pennsylvania Press.

Zec, D. (1995). Sonority constraints on syllable structure. *Phonology*, 12, pp. 85–129.

26 Main Morphosyntactic Changes and Grammaticalization Processes

CÉLIA REGINA DOS SANTOS LOPES
AND MARIA TERESA BROCARDO

1. Introduction

This chapter discusses some morphosyntactic changes, in the history of Portuguese, based on the broad concept of grammaticalization, here understood as a process by which lexical items in particular constructions assume, in certain linguistic contexts, a new status as grammatical forms.

The grammaticalization processes often involve not only maintenance of previous features, but also the loss and the gain of grammatical properties, such as change in the original meaning (*bleaching*) and in morphosyntactic features as well as extension of use to news contexts (Heine 2003: 579). Eventually, but not mandatorily, there can be phonetic reduction. Typical examples of grammaticalization in Romance languages include the evolution of the Latin verbal construction formed by an infinitive verb and the auxiliary *habere* "have" (*amare habeo* "love (I) have") into the simple future, and the morphologization of the Latin noun *mente* "mind" into an adverbial suffix (cf. Hopper and Traugott 2003: 9, 140–141, among others).

In the following sections, we will describe some instances of grammaticalization processes that occurred in the history of Portuguese focusing mainly on the principles of *persistence* and *decategorialization* (Hopper 1991; Heine 2003).[1] The *persistence* principle allows us to assume that some original meanings will tend to survive in the new grammaticalized form. According to the principle of *decategorialization*, grammaticalized constructions tend to lose the morphosyntactic properties of the source forms, such as their syntactic freedom and independence as autonomous forms (Heine and Kuteva 2007: 40). In Section 2, we discuss the development of some verbal forms and constructions. Section 3 focuses on the grammaticalization of nominal and pronominal categories.

2. Grammaticalization of verb forms and constructions

2.1. Forms and constructions expressing futurity[2]

The Portuguese synthetic future (*amarei, amaremos*, etc. "(I) will sing," (we) will sing"), as well as cognate forms in other Romance languages, are the result of morphologization of the Latin auxiliary *habere* "have" into a marker of future tense. The Latin periphrastic construction

The Handbook of Portuguese Linguistics, First Edition. Edited by W. Leo Wetzels, João Costa, and Sergio Menuzzi.
© 2016 John Wiley & Sons, Inc. Published 2020 by John Wiley & Sons, Inc.

was formed by a verb in the infinitive and *habere*: *amare habemus* or *habemus amare* (love-inf have-1pl, "We have to love"). For Adams (1991), the order *habemus* + inf was unmarked and interpreted as a modal construction, expressing possibility in the period of later Latin. From the early Empire onwards, examples expressing necessity/obligation or related values began to appear mainly, but not exclusively, in the marked order *inf* + *habemus*. The author points out that the periphrasis (*amare habemus*) with a future meaning is only attested from the second to the third century CE. The trigger to mark the future was developed from the obligation/necessity value. Portuguese forms such as *amaremos* "(we) will love," *amareis* (Old Port. *amaredes*) "(you.pl) will love," etc., show phonetic reduction of the (original) auxiliary, in contrast with the periphrastic construction which also persisted in Portuguese: *havemos, haveis* (Old Port. *havedes*) *de amar* "we, you.pl have to love." Since the most ancient written Portuguese records the competition between the synthetic future and the *haver* (preposition) + *inf* periphrasis is attested, apparently opposing tense and modal values (Brocardo 2013). The *persistence principle* is observed in some word-like properties of the current future tense markers: in Portuguese, the clitic pronoun can still appear in medial position, that is, between the ancient main verb and the auxiliary verb (Posner 1996: 178): *encontrar-te-emos* "find-inf-you-fut.suf" = "we will find you"; *pagá-lo-íamos* "pay-inf-it-fut.suf" = "we would pay it." These possibilities only occur with the simple future (*amaremos* "we will love") and the future in the past or conditional (*amaríamos* "we would love"), precisely the two verbal tenses that originated from the periphrastic construction with *habere* (*infinitive*-V + *habere*-Aux).

Currently, a common alternative construction for future reference is the "periphrastic future," a construction with the auxiliary *ir* "go" + *inf* (e.g., *Ele vai acabar o curso (no próximo ano)* "He will (is going to) graduate (next year)"). This is a case of the recurrent grammaticalization path of (movement in) space > (movement in) time (cf. Heine 2003: 586, among others). Note that the construction remains periphrastic, with no phonetic reduction, which probably indicates that it has grammaticalized rather late in the history of the language. According to Lima (2001: 125), from the thirteenth to the sixteenth century, this construction remained quite stable, preserving the three features of "motion," "intention" and "future": "motion" and "intention" being part of the meaning of *ir* "go," while "future" appears as a result of pragmatic inference. A contrastive analysis of occurrences of *ir* + *inf* and of the synthetic future in fifteenth century testimonies shows that the periphrasis is not fully grammaticalized around this period: even though it can have a future time reference, it occurs mainly in contexts where "motion" is presupposed (Brocardo 2013). In Contemporary Portuguese, some constraints apparently still restrict the use of this "go" future: in some varieties, the periphrasis cannot be used with lexical *ir*, resulting in contrasts like: *Amanhã vou trabalhar/(*)ir ao cinema* "Tomorrow I'm going to work/(*)go to the cinema."

2.2. *Progressive periphrases with* ir *"go,"* andar *"walk" and* estar *"be"* + *gerund*

In aspectual periphrases with *estar* ("be" < Latin *stare* "stand") and *andar* ("walk" < Latin *ambulare* "walk"), BP and EP contrast in the use of constructions with gerund or with the preposition *a* "to, at" + inf (BP *Ele está/anda trabalhando* [be/walk.pres.3sg work.ger] *demais*, EP *Ele está/anda a trabalhar* [be/walk.pres.3sg prep work.inf] *demais* "He is working too much"). The BP alternative is diachronically more conservative since it corresponds to the type of construction attested in Portuguese ancient texts. This formal variation does not, however, occur in the parallel construction with *ir* "go," in which EP also preserves the gerund periphrasis for the expression of progressive (e.g., BP, EP *O tempo vai passando* [go.pres.3sg pass.ger] "Time is passing").[3] The analysis of extant written records from Old and Middle Portuguese (thirteenth to mid-sixteenth century) shows grammaticalization of the aspectual periphrasis *ir* + ger: in many occurrences we find the bleaching of *ir*, with loss of its literal "motion" value, and it can occur with non-animate subjects (Mattos e Silva 1989: 45), as in:

(1) *A caentura da carne*   ***vai***   *escaecendo e*   ***morrendo***   *no homen*
    The warmth of the flesh   go.pres.3sg forget.ger and die.ger   in the man
    "The warmth of the flesh progressively forgets and dies in the man (men progressively lose desire as they grow old)"[4]
    (*Diálogos de São Gregório*, fourteenth century)

By contrast, during the same periods, constructions with *andar* still allow a (literal) "motion" reading, or are of ambiguous interpretation, apparently showing a grammaticalization process still in progress. We find evidence of full grammaticalization of progressive periphrases with *andar* only in later testimonies, which indicates that the grammaticalization processes involving the two periphrases were diachronically distinct. Comparing occurrences of *ir* and *andar*+ger in the same period, we conclude that the values of the two constructions overlap only in the marking of iteration. When *andar/ir* occur in similar contexts, it is clear that only *ir* periphrases denote an "incremental" value (Laca 2005: 7) or, in a different formulation, "a situation in which every instant of the given interval is conceived of as a possible vantage point for the evaluation of the event" (Bertinetto 2000: 576). This can be observed comparing examples such as (2) and (3): *andar*+ger denotes a more "static" situation, with a value similar to the one expressed by the *estar*+ger periphrasis, while *ir*+ger induces a "dynamic" reading of the situation:

(2) *uirõ (…)*   *que a az da coynha*   ***andaua***   ***destroindo*** *ẽ eles*
    see.PPS.3pl that the battle formation walk.imperf.3sg destroy.ger in they
    "they noticed (…) that the battle formation was doing them damage"
    (*Livro de Linhagens do Conde D. Pedro*, late fourteenth century)

(3) *ali*   *foy*   *a morte deles*   *grande*   *porque*   *os castelaãos*
    there be.PPS.3sg the death their great because   the Castilians
    os   *leuauã ẽ encalço*   *e*   ***hyã***   ***ferĩ do***   *e*
    they.acc pursue.imperf.3pl and go. imperf.3pl injure.ger and
    deribãdo   *ẽ eles*
    make fall.ger in they
    "many of them died there because the Castilians were pursuing them and they were injuring them and making them fall (more and more)"
    (*idem*)

In fact, only *ir* periphrases denote a value characterizable as "a gradual and durative process tending towards the telos" (Squartini 1998: 257), as in:

(4) *mostrãdolho*   *pelas*   *scripturas per que temã*   *Deus*
    show.ger he.dat it.acc by the scriptures so that fear.pres.subj.3pl God
    e   *per que* *sse*   *uãa*   *quitando* *daquelle*   *erro*
    and so that they. refl go. pres.subj.3pl depart.ger from that fault
    "showing it to them by the scriptures in such a way that they fear God and that they progressively leave that fault"
    (*Primeira Partida de Afonso X*, fourteenth century)

In testimonies from the fifteenth century onward, we also find occurrences of *ir* constructions denoting an "inceptive" interpretation (in the expression of Bertinetto 2000: 679 for Spanish), which also corresponds to one of its values in Contemporary Portuguese:

(5) *Pareceme*   (...) *que*   *ia*   *estes* *nossos* *pouco*   *amigos*
    Seem.pres.3sg I.dat (...) that   already these our   not much friends
    uaão   *conhecendo* *o que* *teẽ*   *em* *nos*
    go.pres.3pl know.ger   what   have.pres.3pl in   us
    "It seems to me (...) that already these not much friends of ours begin to understand
    what they have in us (are to expect from us)"
    (*Crónica do Conde D. Duarte de Meneses* de Gomes Eanes de Zurara, late fifteenth century)

Note that the coexistence of two constructions with "motion" verbs (*ir*, denoting oriented motion, and *andar*, denoting non-oriented motion) is a distinctive feature of Portuguese (and Spanish) in the Romance context (Squartini 1998; Laca 2005, among others). The observed semantic differences between the two constructions may be interpreted, from the perspective of grammaticalization, as the result of persistence of original lexical values inherent to *ir* and *andar* as non-auxiliaries (cf. Squartini 1998: 255, ff.). It is clear that distinct values were already marked by periphrases with the two verbs in past stages of Portuguese, and that there is persistence of the feature of "directionality" or "telicity" in the case of *ir*+ger constructions. The fact that the two periphrases followed distinct diachronic paths and, in particular, the fact that the progressive construction with *ir* appears to have grammaticalized earlier, allow us to hypothesize that the values for the constructions with *ir* were already clearly defined when the constructions with *andar* began to grammaticalize. This may have prevented the merger of the two constructions, a hypothesis put forward by Brocardo and Correia (2012).

In Contemporary Portuguese there is also a progressive construction with yet another motion verb, *vir* "come," as in ***Vem aumentando*** [come.pres.3sg increase.ger] *o número de pessoas descontentes* ["The number of discontent people is increasing (more and more)"]. The grammaticalization of this type of construction seems to have occurred rather late in the history of Portuguese. In fact, we do find attestation of *vir*+ger in fifteenth-century testimonies, but the "deictic orientation" (Squartini 1998, among others) typical of these constructions is still of a locative nature, as in:

(6) *Mas os mouros*   *como uyrã*   *que*   *os*   *nossos* *começauõ*
    But the Moors as   see.PPS.3pl that   the   our   start.imperf.3pl
    aquelle   *trabalho,* *uyeronse*   *chegando*
    that   fight   come.PPS.3pl   approach.ger
    "But the Moors, as they saw that our men were starting that fight, came approaching"
    (*Crónica do Conde D. Pedro de Meneses* de Gomes Eanes de Zurara, late fifteenth century)

The evolution of *vir*+ger would then follow the typical (unidirectional) trend: (movement in) space > (movement in) time. However, we have found that these periphrases have a relatively low frequency in the data from past stages; hence, it is not clear yet how the diachronic process really developed, except that the grammaticalization of *vir*+ger is late.

The "state" counterpart of these periphrases is expressed in Contemporary Portuguese with *estar*, corresponding to the sole syntactic context where *ser* and *estar* cannot alternate (*Ele *é/está trabalhando/a trabalhar* "He is working").[5] It should, however, be noted that the contemporary paradigm of *ser* is suppletive, with forms from Latin *esse* "be" and *sedere* "sit." In past stages some occurrences of forms from *sedere* still show the preservation of their etymological "postural" value, while the lexical original value of *estar* "stand" seems to have bleached earlier. Except for, perhaps, a few residual cases (Mattos e Silva 1989: 455–457), periphrases with *estar*+ger show full grammaticalization, as in:

(7) *e*   **esteue**   *hũa gram peça* **pensando** *nas*   *palauras*
and be(stand).PPS.3sg a long time think.ger on the words
"And for a long time he was thinking about those words"
(*Livro de Linhagens do Conde D. Pedro*, late fourteenth century)

This is never the case with *ser*: when it occurs in constructions with the gerund, it has a lexical "postural" value, as in (8), and we have found no evidence for a grammaticalization process affecting the construction for the expression of the progressive aspect (this coincides with the description made by Mattos e Silva 1989: 450–451).[6]

(8) *E ...* **seendo**   *comẽdo filhou*   *dõ gonçalo*   *sa molher*
And be(sit).ger eat.ger grabb.PPS.3sg don gonçalo his wife
"And while he was sitting eating Don Gonçalo grabbed his wife"
(*idem*)

To sum up, the Portuguese aspectual periphrases discussed in this section followed distinct diachronic paths: both "state" progressive *estar*+ger and "motion" progressive *ir*+ger appear to have achieved full grammaticalization early; data from Old Portuguese appear to show a similar process for *andar*+ger, but this process was still in progress by the late fourteenth century; *vir*+ger, the less frequent, appears to have grammaticalized much later, since we have found no clear examples of the bleaching of *vir* "come" in this construction until the late fifteenth century. The different values conveyed by "motion" periphrases can be interpreted as a consequence of the persistence of original lexical values inherent to *ir* ("oriented motion") vs. *andar* ("non-oriented motion"). The latter, once grammaticalized, came to compete with the (earlier grammaticalized) construction with *estar*, resulting in a somewhat subtle opposition of semantic values. The opposition appears to be productive already in past stages, as shown in the examples (9) and (10), where *andar* adds iterativity to the process expressed by the main verb, while *estar* simply marks its durative aspect:

(9) *Jsto*   *entenderom*   *muytos* *em sua*   *contenẽça*
This understand.PPS.3pl many by his expression
quando **estaua**   **sguardando** *a*   *grandeza da cidade*
when be.imperf.3sg observe.ger the greatness of the city
"Many of them understood this by his expression while he was observing the greatness of the city"
(*Crónica do Conde D. Duarte de Meneses* de Gomes Eanes de Zurara, late fifteenth century)

(10) *e*   *nojarã-se*   *muito*   *por ello, pello quall* *a*
And upset.PPS.3pl them very much by that by what the
gemte   *miuda* **amdava**   *rrazoãdo* *mall* *do*   *comde*
people small walk. imperf.3sg say.ger bad of the count
"And they were very upset about that, the reason why the people were (repeatedly) saying bad things about the count"
(*idem*)

2.3. *Emergence of compound tenses and persistence of synthetic verb forms*

In Contemporary Portuguese, the *pretérito perfeito composto* (PPC) "compound past perfect" expresses values that are clearly distinct from those expressed by the large majority of other Romance compound tenses originated from the same sources.[7] The Portuguese PPC either denotes a durative situation, starting in the past and continuing up to the present (e.g., *Ele tem sido* [have.pres.3sg be.PP] *um bom rapaz* "He has been [and still is] a good boy"), or denotes iteration (e.g., *Ele tem feito* [have.pres.3sg do.PP] *os trabalhos de casa* "He has done/has been doing his homework"), depending on the verb or the context. The contrast between the PPC and the *pretérito perfeito simples* (PPS) "simple past perfect" is thus very clearly marked (*Ele foi* [be.PPS.3sg] *um bom rapaz* "He was a good boy"; *Ele fez* [do. PPS.3sg] *os trabalhos de casa* "He has done / did his homework"; see Campos 1997 for a detailed description). This type of distinction is not, however, noticeable in past stages of Portuguese.

We should begin by noting that, in Old and Middle Portuguese, compound forms of unaccusative verbs (e.g., *partir(-se)* "leave," *chegar* "arrive," *tornar* "return," *vir* "come"), including originally deponent verbs (*morrer* "die," *nascer* "be born"[8]), occur with the auxiliary *ser* "be" (< Latin *esse* "be"), alternatively to the PPS.[9] This is shown in:

(11) *E esto   he   que   o   velho   que   ally   estaa*
      And this   be.pres.3sg   that   the   old man   who   there   be.pres.3sg
      por   capitão   he   partido   pera   o   seu   rregno
      as   captain   be.pres   leave.PP   to   the   his   country
      "And the fact is that the old man who is there as captain has left to his country"
      (*Crónica do Conde D. Pedro de Meneses* de Gomes Eanes de Zurara, late fifteenth century)

The different selection of the auxiliary did not persist in Portuguese, contrary to other Romance areas (as in French, for instance, in which *être* is still used with unaccusatives, and *avoir* with other verbs). The loss of this "be" construction appears to have occurred after the full grammaticalization of the periphrases with *haver* and especially *ter* "have"+PP, a process that may have been favored precisely by the analogy with the preexisting "be"+PP structure (see Ledgeway 2011: 455–456 for a detailed proposal on this relation).

Many occurrences of "have" (*haver* or *ter*)+PP in early testimonies do not allow a compound tense reading (or are ambiguous), and correspond to the type of construction usually described as "resultative" (Squartini and Bertinetto 2000: 405): there is no obligatory coincidence between the subject of *haver/ter* and the subject of the PP, which has a predicative function related to the object of *haver/ter*; hence, there is gender and number agreement between the PP and the object, as shown in (13).[10] In such occurrences, "have" does not yet correspond to an auxiliary, but preserves its lexical meaning; concomitantly, adjacency and relative order of the verbs are also less restricted, as shown in (12) and (14).

(12) *E   por   istes   tortos   que   li   feçerũ*
      And   for   these   wrong things   which   he.dat   do.PPS.3pl
      tem   qua   a   seu   plazo   quebrãtado
      have.pres.3sg   that   have.pres.3sg   his   pact   break.PP
      "And because of these wrong things that they have done to him he considers that he (literally) has his pact broken (the pact is broken)"
      (*Noticia de Torto*, 1214?)

(13) *Dizemos   que   os   iudeus   bẽ   possā   guardar*
  Say.1pl that the Jews well may.pres.subj.3pl respect
  seus   sabados (…)   e   que   usẽ   todas   as   outras cousas
  their Sabbath.pl (…) and that use.pres.subj.3pl every the other things
  *que   **han**   **outorgadas**   per   Sancta Eygreya.*
  that have.pres.3pl authorize.PP.fem.pl by Holy Church
  "We say that Jews may respect their Sabbath (…) and that they may use all those other
  things that they have that were authorized by the Holy Church"
  (*Foro Real*, late thirteenth century)

(14) *e   diselhi   senhor   leuātadeuos*
  and say.PPS.3sg-he.dat sir stand up.imp.2pl-you.2pl.refl
  *di (…)   ca   **adubado**   o   **teedes**.*
  from there (…) because prepare.PP it.acc have.pres.2pl
  "And he said to him sir stand up from there (…) because (literally) you have it
  (the food) prepared (the food is prepared)"
  (*Livro de Linhagens do Conde D. Pedro*, late fourteenth century)

Although several earlier examples have been pointed out (Cardoso and Pereira 2003), the frequency of the construction "have"+PP as the fully grammaticalized PPC increases especially from the fifteenth century on in the extant written records. The grammaticalization process entails the semantic bleaching of the lexical meaning inherent to *haver* and *ter*, which obviously implies the loss of the (possible) semantic contrast between the two verbs (see Chapter 1, History and Current Setting, Section 4.2). In an initial stage the verb most likely to grammaticalize as an auxiliary probably was *haver*, since its meaning was more general. In fact, our investigation of earlier attestations of the grammaticalized PPC indicates that constructions with *haver* were apparently more frequent. Below we provide an early occurrence:

(15) *E   forõ   cõ   el   na busca   da   uera cruz*
  And go.PPS.3pl with he in the quest for the holy cross
  por saluamēto   da   fe   de iesu cristo (…)
  for salvation of the faith of Jesus Christ (…)
  *asi como   **auemos**   **mostrado**.*
  as how have.pres.1pl show.PP
  "And they went with him in quest for the holy cross for the salvation of Jesus Christ's
  faith (…) as we have shown"
  (*idem*)

But the generalization of the meaning of *ter* (that also dictated its prevalence over *haver* as a main verb) would soon reverse the initial trend. In the fifteenth century (but also earlier), *ter* is already the auxiliary in many PPC examples:

(16) *E vos (…)   fazey   registar   esta carta   no liuro uosso (…)*
  And you.pl (…) make.imp.2pl register this document in the book your (…)
  *por   se saber   como isto   **temos**   **dado**   ao dito Dõ Duarte*
  so that know how this have.pres.1pl give.PP to the mentioned D.D.
  "And you (…) register this document in your book (…) so that it is known that we
  have given this to the mentioned Don Duarte."
  (*Crónica do Conde D. Duarte de Meneses* de Gomes Eanes de Zurara, late fifteenth
  century)

(17) *Ate'quy   nõ   temos   feita   nenhũa cousa*
Until now   not   have.pres.1pl   do.PP.fem   anything
(...) per que   devamos   ser   prezados
(...) by which   must.pres.subj.1pl   be.inf   praise.PP.pl
"Until now we haven't done anything (...) by which we should be praised"
(*Crónica do Conde D. Pedro de Meneses* de Gomes Eanes de Zurara, late fifteenth century)

(18) *E   faço   fim   de meu rrazoado   emcomemdãdo-vos*
And   make.pres.1sg   end   of my words   recommend.ger you. dat.pl
todo   o   que dito   tenho
everything   that   have.PP   say.pres.1sg
"And I finish my words recommending everything that I have said"
(*idem*)

Examples like these, where a "single occurrence" (Campos 2000: 58) of the event is expressed, show a value of the PPC still clearly distinct from the one in Contemporary Portuguese (in which the PPC denotes iteration with the above types of verb). This allows us to conclude that the specificity of its functioning in Portuguese emerged later than the formal innovation—that is, the replacement of *haver* by *ter*. Also note that overt agreement with the object (17) and a verb-auxiliary order (18) persist in many examples of grammaticalized PPC. There is no consensus on the chronology of the semantic drift that would lead to the specificity of the Portuguese PPC. Examples from seventeenth-century texts were cited where the PPC supposedly still persists with non-iterative or non-durative values, but the same data have been interpreted differently by other scholars, according to Squartini and Bertinetto (2000: 419).[11]

As we said, the mentioned semantic innovation cannot be attributed to the specificity of the auxiliary (originated from *tenere*, and not from *habere*, which was the source of the auxiliary in most Romance languages). We believe it is more likely to be a result of the persistence of the PPS, whose frequency never decreased, contrary to what happened in other Romance areas where the compound tense came to express at least part of the values originally expressed by the simple past (see Squartini and Bertinetto 2000: 408–410 for discussion). This may have been a decisive factor, favoring the meaning differentiation between the simple and the compound tenses. The grammaticalization of resultative constructions as a compound tense led to a situation of competition between the PPS and the PPC for the expression of identical, or at least closely related, values. The result of this competition, in most areas of Romance, was that the compound tense assumed (part of) the values once restricted to the PPS; but in Portuguese it led instead to a differentiation of the two forms, with the development of "new" values for the PPC.

Another instance of competition between simple and compound verb forms occurred in the history of Portuguese with the pluperfect, but the result was different. Similarly to what happened with the PPC, not only the construction "have"(*haver/ter*) imperf+PP (e.g., *Ele havia/tinha feito* "He had done") grammaticalized as a compound pluperfect, but also "be" (*ser*) imperf+PP (of unaccusative verbs) constructions are found in the initial stages of the process (e.g., *Ele era* [be.imperf] *partido* [leave.PP]"He had left").[12] The synthetic pluperfect (e.g., *fizera, partira*) lost the potential it had in past stages to express modal values, in particular when used with inherently modal verbs and in conditional constructions; in Portuguese it retained only its temporal "past in the past" meaning.[13] Even if it is still productive in more formal styles and in written language in Contemporary Portuguese, its use clearly decreased in favor of the periphrastic form, a tendency to which the syncretism between 3rd person plural forms of the simple pluperfect and of the PPS may also have contributed (see Chapter 1, History and Current Setting, Section 2.2). In any event, there seems to be no clear semantic differentiation between the simple and the compound pluperfect in Contemporary Portuguese (but see Campos 2000; and also the discussion in Brocardo 2010).

3. Grammaticalization of nominal and pronominal categories

The "pronominalization process" or, more precisely, the grammaticalization of nouns (or noun phrases) into personal pronouns, is a quite common process of language change (see details in Heine and Song 2011). In Portuguese, there are some illustrative cases. The form *homẽ* "one, someone"—which originated from the Latin noun *homo* in its accusative form *hominem* "person, man"—was used as an indefinite pronoun in the medieval period (until the sixteenth century): *que nunca* homem *viu na gram bretanha* literally, "that never *anyone* saw in Great Britain" (Reinhard Stoettner 1887: 43). Although this use disappeared in Portuguese, it was maintained, for example, in French; at first, as an impersonal pronoun *on* "one," and then as a personal pronoun of the 1st person plural, *on* "we." In Portuguese, however, this gap has been filled by another noun phrase: *a gente* "the people," which was also used as an indefinite pronoun before it became a personal pronoun (*a gente* "we"). A possible pathway for this grammaticalization process appears to be the following: *a gente*, literally "the people" [generic noun] > *a gente* "anyone" [indefinite pronoun] > *a gente* "we" [1st person plural pronoun]. Nowadays, both in EP and BP, the new pronoun *a gente* "we" occurs in variation with the old pronoun *nós* "we" to refer to the 1st person plural (Lopes 2003; Marcotulio, Vianna and Lopes 2013). Portuguese has another canonic case of grammaticalization from noun phrase to pronoun: the nominal possessive construction *Vossa Mercê* "Your Grace/Mercy" has grammaticalized into a 2nd person pronoun *você* "you."

3.1. From gente *to* a gente: *changes in semantic and formal features*

The change process from the noun *gente* "people" to the pronoun *a gente* "we" was possible because of the inherent value of the original form (Lopes 2003; Zilles 2005). The source noun *gente* presupposes "a group of people," and the speaker is necessarily a "person." Hence, in certain contexts this form could have either an "inclusive" interpretation ("a group of people including me"), or an "exclusive" reading ("a group of people excluding me"). The example below illustrates this ambiguity:

(19) *E   os   tigres, em tanta cantidade   (por   não haver   descampados),*
    And   the tigers, in so great amount   (because   not have.inf   open fields),
    que,   em se metendo a rês   no mato,   não sae,   e o mesmo
    that,   in entering   the neat   in the bushes,   not go out.pres.3sg   and the same
    risco corre   a gente,   se não anda acompanhada
    risk suffer.pres.3sg   we/the people, if   not be/walk pres.3sg   accompanied
    "And the tigers, in such great amount (due to lack of open fields), that, when the neat enters in the bushes, it doesn't go out, and we/the people run the same risk, if not accompanied"
    (*Noticiário Maranhense*, eighteenth century. In Marcotulio, Vianna, and Lopes 2013:126)

Although in (19) the noun *a gente* can be interpreted as "the people, everybody," the reading "including the speaker" is available, because "any person is in danger in the bush with tigers, including the first person." These meaning properties of *a gente* certainly interacted with the pronominal concept of 1st person plural expressed by the pronoun *nós* "we," which presupposes "an amplified first person," that is, it includes the speaker and one or more non-speakers (Benveniste 1988). In particular, *nós* "we" can refer either to a determined group (the speaker+you/he), as in (20), or to an indeterminate group (the speaker+everybody/a group of people), as in (21). This last case, of course, approximates the use of the pronoun *nós* and uses of *a gente* like (19)—hence, the similarity of (19) and (21) may have given rise to the use *a gente* as a 1st person plural pronoun.

(20) **Nós**, *meu irmão e eu, gostávamos*   *de brincar*   *no quintal.*
  We, my brother and I, like.imperf.1pl   to play   in the backyard.
  "We, my brother and I, liked to play in the backyard."

(21) **Nós** *cidadãos precisamos*   *resolver o problema*   *da educação.*
  We   citizens   need.pres.1pl   to solve the problem   of education."
  "We citizens need to solve the problem of education."

This grammaticalization process involving the incorporation of *a gente* into the pronominal system of Portuguese can be attested in the eighteenth century but its gradual diffusion occurred from the nineteenth century on, and it was faster in Brazil than in Portugal. It resulted first in a change in the number features of the noun and, after, in a change in the semantic features of gender of the new pronoun. That is, the pronoun *a gente* acquired some intrinsic properties of the personal pronouns. However, it maintained some historical morphosyntactic features of the noun *gente* (*persistence* principle).

Regarding person and number features, the pronoun *a gente* is mixed: it is grammatically specified for 3sg and semantically for 1pl. The 3rd singular verbal agreement, which originated from the agreement properties of the noun phrase *a gente* "the people," has been retained, even though the new pronoun acquired the 1st person plural interpretation. The example (22a) shows the 3sg verb agreement, and at the same time the 1pl interpretation, reflected in the anaphoric relation between *a gente* and the possessive *nossa* "our"—that belongs to the paradigm of *nós* "we" in Portuguese. One also frequently finds, mainly among less educated speakers, a non-standard verb agreement in which the morphology of 1pl appears in the verbal ending, as in (22b) (see Chapter 31, Main Current Processes of Morphosyntactic Variation).

(22) a. **A gente**$_i$ *andava*   *de bicicleta, era*   *o esporte preferido*   **nosso**$_i$
    We   ride.imperf.**3sg**$_i$ a bike   was the sport favorite   our$_i$.1pl
    "We used to ride a bike, it was our favorite sport"
  b. **A gente**   **andamos**   *de bicicleta*
    We   ride.pres.1pl   a bike
    "We ride a bike"

The *decategorialization*, principle can be illustrated in patterns of gender agreement in predicative structures with *a gente* "we" in Portuguese (Menuzzi 2000; Menuzzi 1995; Lopes and Rumeu 2007; Costa and Pereira 2012, among others). Unlike the feminine noun phrase *a gente*, the pronoun *a gente* lost its formal specification for gender, assuming the peculiar behavior of the 1st and 2nd personal pronouns, which do not show formal gender (*eu, tu/ você, nós, vós/vocês* "I, you.sg, we, you.pl"). In predicative constructions, however, gender agreement (masculine or feminine) is a reflex of the referent's gender, that is, it depends on the sex of the speaker. In predicative structures, the co-occurrence with feminine singular and/or plural is restrictive. In the singular, the referent is a woman (female); in the plural, the referent is more than one woman. The masculine, on the other hand, leads to a neuter interpretation: singular (group of men, mixed group or generic referent); plural (group of men and mixed group).

(23) a. *Eu   estou   velha.*
        I   am   old.fem.sg (Women-exclusive, i.e, the speaker is a woman)
    b. *Eu   estou   velho.*
        I   am   old.masc.sg" (Men-exclusive, i.e., the speaker is a man)
        "I am old"

(24) a. **A gente**   está velha.
        We   are   **old.fem.sg** (Women-exclusive)
    b. **A gente**   está velho.
        We   are   **old.masc.sg** (The speaker is probably a man)
        "We are old (fem/masc)."

(25) a. *A gente   está cansadas.*
        We   are tired.fem.pl (Women-exclusive, a group of women)
    b. *A gente   está cansados.*
        We   are tired.masc.pl (Men-not exclusive, a group of men or mixed)
        "We are tired (fem/masc)."

As further evidence of the action of the decategorialization principle, we point out that pronominal *a gente* has lost its syntactic privileges of noun phrase. As a noun, *gente* may have different determiners (*esta/pouca gente* "these/few people") and can be modified by adjectives (*gente bonita* "beautiful people"). Personal pronouns, however, are almost categorically composed by an isolated head and the presence of a modifier would be ungrammatical: *Eu cantei; *O eu cantei;*Eu bonita cantei* "I sang; *the I sang; *I nice sang"). Pronominal *a gente* cannot be used with other, or additional, determiners, nor can it be modified by adjectives (*esta/pouca gente* "these/few people" and *gente bonita* "beautiful people" have no reading related to 1st person plural).

3.2. *From* Vossa Mercê *to* você

The grammaticalization of the nominal form *Vossa Mercê* emerges with the semantic-pragmatic bleaching of the polite pronoun *Vós* "you-pl," which was used with a singular addressee (the king, a noble) to express respect, reverence, etc.

In the fourteenth century, *Vossa Mercê* was an ordinary noun phrase with a possessive pronoun that corresponded to *vossa vontade* "your will":

(26) *se for   **vossa mercee**, quero   seer   vosso vassallo*
     if be.subj   your mercy   want.pres.1sg be.inf   your vassal
    "if it is your mercy, I want to be your vassal"
    (*Crónica Geral de Espanha de 1344*)

The noun phrase was reanalyzed as a pronoun during the fifteenth century. The reanalysis was due to the metonymic relationship between the 2nd person feature of the possessive *vossa* "your" and the semantic value of the noun *mercê* "mercy."

The construction *Vossa Mercê*, initially used as a nominal form of address, became widespread as a 2nd person polite pronoun in Old Portuguese. From the fifteenth century on, *Vossa Mercê* was used, alongside with *vós* (you.pl for 2sg), to show deference to the king. Similarly to what happened to the pronoun *Vós*, the nominal form of address began to be used also to address other social positions, which triggered a process of semantic bleaching and, eventually, the use of new forms, such as *Vossa Senhoria* "Your Lordship" and *Vossa Alteza* "Your Highness." As the use of the form generalized, it suffered phonetic erosion, until the modern form *você* was born (*Vossa Mercê>vosmecê>você*).

In extant texts of the seventeenth century, *Vossa Mercê* and its written variants *vosmecê*, *mecêa*, *vosse*, *você* were used in asymmetrical relations, co-existing in the same contexts as variant forms. The following examples, from a play written in the eighteenth century, show the same character (Don Quixote) using both forms (*Vossa Mercê* or *Você*) to address the same person, in this case, the barber (Lopes and Duarte 2003):

(27) *Senhor   mestre barbeiro,   veja   **vossa mercê***
     Sir   master barber,   see.imp Your Mercy
     como me   pega   nestas   barbas
     how   me.dat handle.inf in these   beards
     "Sir master barber, see Your Mercy how do you handle my beards"
     (*A Vida de Don Quixote*, p. 42)

(28) *Ora,   sô Mestre,   **você** bem   sabe*
     Well, Sir master,   you   well   know.pres.3sg
     que   é obrigação dos de   seu ofício
     that   is duty   of the ones of   your profession
     "Well, Your Master, you know that it is the duty of your profession"
     (*Idem*, p. 45)

From the mid-eighteenth century onwards, *Vossa Mercê* and the variant form *você* become functionally divergent. The first one continued to be used in ascendant asymmetrical relations (from inferior to superior), whereas the new form was also frequent in descendant relations (from superior to inferior).

In the nineteenth century, studies based on Brazilian manuscript letters show a further step in the process, not attested for European Portuguese. The grammaticalized pronoun *você* presented a hybrid and unstable behavior, quite typical of change in process: it had its contexts of use extended and became quite variable in its values. It could be used as an addressing pronoun by the Brazilian elite with some feature of politeness; at the same time, it also circulated as a variant of the original pronoun *tu* "you.sg" to indicate proximity and intimacy. The example (29) below shows this second use in the letter written in 1885 by a grandmother to her grandson: to address him, she uses both the new pronoun *você* and the old pronoun *tu*, expressed in the example by the verbal morphology:

(29) *Estimei   muito as   boas noticias   que tive*
     Esteemed.1sg very much the good news that had.1sg
     *que **voce** está muito estudiozo.*
     that you   are   very studious.
     Continue   para   nos   dar   muito gostos
     Continue.3sg to   us.dat give.inf   much happiness
     *e   a   sua   Mae   aquem   **abraçarás**   por mim!*
     and   to your   mother   to-whom   embrace.fut.2sg   for me
     "I esteemed greatly the good news that I had that you are very studious. Continue to give us much happiness and for your mother whom you will embrace for me."
     (*Missive written by Barbara Ottoni for Mizael*, nineteenth century. In Lopes 2005: 251)

Though becoming a variant of symmetrical *tu* and diverging from the original form *Vossa Mercê*, the grammaticalized pronoun *você* still preserves some of its original semantic values in BP. Studies based on synchronic data (e.g., Lopes et al. 2009) have demonstrated that the old pronoun *tu* "you-sg" is increasingly frequent in directive acts to indicate proximity and social identity, especially among younger men in some urban areas in Brazil, such as Rio de Janeiro. Opposed to this, the new pronoun *você* can be used as a neutral and "less-marked" form, because it is felt to be less directive, less invasive and less "threatening to the hearer's face." Somehow, it has kept a level of "abstraction of politeness" that seems to be a property inherited from *Vossa Mercê* (Koch 2008: 59).

Moreover, although the new grammaticalized pronoun *você* is interpreted as a 2nd person singular, some of its grammatical features go further back, having as a source the original noun phrase with the possessive pronoun—one more example of the action of the persistence principle. Taking into consideration its person and number features, the pronoun *você* is mixed: it is grammatically specified for 3sg and semantically for 2sg. Hence, as far as verbal agreement is concerned, it patterns with the 3rd person pronouns (Rumeu 2013).

The functional overlap between *você* and the old 2nd person *tu* has led to a complex pronominal paradigm in BP. In particular, the new form *você* has not been implemented with the same level of success in the whole pronominal paradigm, and there are contexts of resistance of forms of the old 2nd person (Lopes and Cavalcante 2011). For example, the clitic *te* "you.acc/dat" has been preserved as an object form for 2nd person, alongside with *você* and *lhe* (this last form being the old 3rd person clitic for indirect objects). Similarly, the possessive forms of *tu* (*teu* "your" and its feminine and plural forms) are also used as an alternative to the old 3rd person possessive *seu*. All these options are illustrated in (30) below.

(30) **Você**₍ᵢ₎ *quer que eu* **lhe/te**₍ᵢ₎   *encontre (**você**₍ᵢ₎) na escola*
   You   want that I   you.3sg/you.2sg   meet   (you)   at school
   para   entregar   seu/teu₍ᵢ₎   *livro?*
   to   give back   your.3sg/your.2sg   book
   "Do you want me to meet you at school to give your book back?"

The differences between BP and EP are at the level of the spreading of the new pronominal form (faster in Brazil than in Portugal). Probably up until the nineteenth century, the pronominal system underwent the same changes in both varieties. From the twentieth century on, however, the spread of the new form *você* in both territories followed different pathways. In BP, there was a progressive increase in the use of *você* in competition with *tu*. In EP, however, the old pronoun *tu* not only continued to be the predominant form, but its frequency increased over the past century. *Você*, in this variety, is still pragmatically different from *tu*.

NOTES

1   We assume a gradient view of grammatical categories, such that less prototypical exemplars of the category may not have some of the category's optimal properties.
2   The following abbreviations are used in this chapter: 1, 2, 3 = 1st, 2nd, 3rd person; acc = accusative; aux = auxiliary verb; BP = Brazilian Portuguese; dat = dative; EP = European Portuguese; fem = feminine; fut = future; gen = genitive; ger = gerund; imp = imperative; imperf = imperfect; inf = infinitive; masc = masculine; nom = nominative; obl = oblique; pl = plural; PP = past participle; prep = preposition; pres = present; PPC = *pretérito perfeito composto* "compound past perfect"; PPS = *pretérito perfeito simples* "simple past perfect"; sg = singular; refl = reflexive; subj = subjunctive; suf = suffix; V = verb.

3   Note that the alternative periphrasis with *ir* followed by *a* + infinitive also occurs in EP, but in a distinct construction, characterizable as "perambulative" (Bertinetto 2000: n.18): in this construction, *ir* "go" denotes motion, thus corresponding to a less, or non, grammaticalized use of the verb (e.g., *Ele foi a cantar/cantando* [go.PPS.3sg prep sing.inf/sing.ger] *pelo caminho* "He went singing along the way").

4   These grammaticalized uses of *ir*+GER obviously also co-occur with perambulative constructions in past stages, e.g., *e uã* [go.pres.3pl] *per terras alheas* **lazerando** [hurt.ger] *os corpos e* **despendendo** [spend.ger] *os aueres*. (*Primeira Partida*, fourteenth century) "and they go through foreign lands hurting their bodies and spending their goods."

5   We use here a simplified opposition between constructions with verbs that originally had a "state" or "postural" meaning (as Latin *esse* "be," *sedere* "stand," *stare* "sit") and constructions with verbs that originally expressed "motion" meanings (as Latin *ire* "go," *ambulare* "walk," *venire* "come"). Note that in Portuguese past stages the use of *ser* was semantically less restricted, and it could alternate with *estar* in contexts where, in Contemporary Portuguese, only the later can occur. For example it could express a transitory or non-inherent state, in examples such as *Os cristãaos* **erã** [be. imperf.3pl] *tã fora de força* (*Livro de Linhagens do Conde D. Pedro*, late fourteenth century) "The Christians were (literally) so out of force (very tired)," while in Contemporary Portuguese in this type of contexts only *estar* is possible.

6   Yet another postural verb, *jazer* "lay" (< Latin *iacere* "lay") occurred in Portuguese past stages, but in constructions with ger it also shows the preservation of its lexical meaning, as in late fifteenth century examples such as *Jazia* [lay.imperf.1sg] *dormindo* [sleep.ger] "I was lying down sleeping."

7   Note that the Portuguese PPC, as other Romance compound pasts, originated from Latin *habere* "have"+ past participle, corresponds in form to the English present perfect; but the semantic values expressed by these tenses do not overlap totally. We here use the more usual designation for the Portuguese grammatical form, given that there is no unified terminology in the Romance context (cf. Squartini and Bertinetto 2000: 403).

8   Latin deponent verbs are usually described as verbs with "passive forms" or "passive morphology" but with non-passive meanings.

9   But this does not mean that the two forms could freely alternate in all contexts.

10   Note that in Contemporary Portuguese, resultative constructions (with a structure similar to the presented examples) also occur with or without co-reference of the subject of *ter* and the subject of the past participle. An example such as *Tenho a casa limpa* "(literally) (I) have the house cleaned" ("The house is clean") can, out of a precise context, be ambiguous, since the subjects of *have* and of *clean* may be co-referents or not.

11   Expressions such as *Tenho dito* "(I) have said" sporadically occur with non-iterative meaning in Contemporary Portuguese in specific (formal) contexts. They seem to be relics of the old perfective value of the PPC.

12   The earliest, but still sporadic, attestations of the compound pluperfect with verbs like *partir* "leave" and *chegar* "arrive" co-occurring with the auxiliaries *haver* / *ter* were found in late fifteenth-century and early sixteenth-century testimonies (Brocardo 2010).

13   Contrary to what happened in Spanish, where it lost its temporal value and turned into a (past) subjunctive (Becker 2008, among others).

REFERENCES

Adams, J. N. (1991). Some neglected evidence for Latin *Habeo* with infinitive: The order of the constituents. *Transactions of the Philological Society*, 89.2, pp. 131–96.

Becker, M. G. (2008). From temporal to modal: divergent fates of the Latin synthetic pluperfect in Spanish and Portuguese. In U. Detges and R. Waltereit (eds.), *The Paradox of Grammatical*

Change. Perspectives from Romance. Amsterdam: John Benjamins, pp. 147–179.

Benveniste, E. (1988). *Problemas de lingüística geral I*. Campinas: Pontes/Editora da Unicamp.

Bertinetto, P. M. (2000). The progressive in Romance, as compared with English. In Ö. Dahl (ed.), *Tense and Aspect in the Languages of Europe*. Berlin: de Gruyter, pp. 559–604.

Brocardo, M. T. (2010). Portuguese pluperfect: elements for a diachronic approach. *Estudos Linguísticos/Linguistic Studies*, 5, pp. 117–130.

Brocardo, M. T. (2013). Sobre o *futuro*—formas e construções marcadoras de posterioridade em textos portugueses dos séculos XIII a XV. In R. Álvarez, A. M. Martins, H. Monteagudo, and M.A. Ramos (eds.), *Ao sabor do texto. Estudos dedicados a Ivo Castro*. Santiago de Compostela: Universidade de Santiago de Compostela, Servizo de Publicacións e Intercambio Científico, pp. 7790.

Brocardo, M. T. and C. N. Correia (2012). *Ir* + gerúndio em português—aspetos sincrónicos e diacrónicos. In A. Costa, C. Flores, and N. Alexandre (eds.), *Textos Selecionados. XXVII Encontro Nacional da Associação Portuguesa de Linguística*. Lisbon: Associação Portuguesa de Linguística, pp. 121–135.

Campos, M. H. C. (1997). Pretérito perfeito simples/pretérito perfeito composto: uma oposição aspectual e temporal. In M. H. C. Campos, *Tempo, Aspecto e Modalidade. Estudos de Linguística Portuguesa*. Porto: Porto Editora: pp. 9–51.

Campos, M. H. C. (2000). Sur les formes composées du prétérit en portugais. In A. Englebert, M. Pierrard, L. Rosier, and D. van Raemdonck (eds.), *Actes du XXIIe Congrès International de Linguistique et Philologie Romanes*, II, pp. 57–63.

Cardoso, A. and S. Pereira (2003). Contributos para o estudo da emergência do tempo composto em português. *Revista da ABRALIN, II* (2), pp. 159–181.

Costa, J. and S. Pereira (2012). "A gente": revisitando o estatuto pronominal e a concordância. In A. P. Sedrins (ed.), *Por amor à Linguística: Miscelânea de Estudos Linguísticos Dedicados à Denilda Moura*. Maceió: EDUFAL, pp. 101–119.

Hopper, P. J. (1991). On some principles of grammaticalization. In E. C. Traugott and B. Heine (eds.), *Approaches to Grammaticalization*, vol. I. Amsterdam: John Benjamins, pp. 17–36.

Hopper, P. J. and E. C. Traugott (2003). *Grammaticalization*, 2nd edn. Cambridge: Cambridge University Press.

Heine, B. (2003). Grammaticalization. In B. D. Joseph and R. D. Janda (eds.), *The Handbook of Historical Linguistics*. Cambridge, MA: Blackwell, pp. 575–601.

Heine, B. and T. Kuteva (2007). *The Genesis of Grammar: A Reconstruction*. Oxford: Oxford University Press.

Heine, B. and K. Song (2011). On the grammaticalization of personal pronouns. *Journal of Linguistics*, 27, pp. 587–630.

Koch, P. (2008). Tradiciones discursivas y cambio linguístico: el ejemplo del tratamiento vuestra merced en español. In J. Kabatek (ed.). *Sintaxis histórica del español y cambio linguístico: nuevas perspectivas desde las Tradiciones Discursivas*. Madrid: Iberoamericana, pp. 53–88.

Laca, B. (2005). Indefinites, quantifiers, and pluractionals. What scope effects tell us about event pluralities. In S. Vogeleer and L. Tasmowski (eds.), *Non-Definiteness and Plurality*. Amsterdam: John Benjamins. http://halshs.archives-ouvertes.fr/docs/00/10/46/43/PDF/LacaIndPlurac.fin.pdf, accessed November 6, 2015.

Ledgeway, A. (2011). Syntactic and morphosyntactic typology and change. In M. Maiden, J. C. Smith, and A. Ledgeway (eds.), *The Cambridge History of The Romance Languages, vol. I Structures*. Cambridge: Cambridge University Press, pp. 382–471.

Lima, J. P. de (2001). Sobre a génese e a evolução do futuro com ir em português. In A.S. da Silva (ed.), *Linguagem e Cognição. A Perspectiva da Linguística Cognitiva*. Braga: Associação Portuguesa de Linguística, pp. 119–145.

Lopes, C. R. S. (2003). *A Inserção de "a Gente" no Quadro Pronominal do Português*. Frankfurt am Main: Vervuert.

Lopes, C. R. S. (ed.) (2005). *A Norma Brasileira em Construção: Fatos Lingüísticos em Cartas Pessoais do Século XIX*. Rio de Janeiro: Pós-Graduação em Letras Vernáculas/FAPERJ.

Lopes, C. R. S. and S. R. Cavalcante (2011). A cronologia do voceamento no português brasileiro: expansão de você-sujeito e retenção do clítico-te. *Lingüística (Madrid)*, 25, pp. 30–65.

Lopes, C. R. S. and M. E. L. Duarte (2003). De vossa mercê a você: análise da pronominalização de nominais em peças brasileiras e portuguesas setecentistas e oitocentistas. In S. F. Brandão and M. A. Mota (eds.), *Análise Contrastiva de Variedades do Português: Primeiros Estudos*. Rio de Janeiro: In-Fólio, pp. 61–76.

Lopes, C. R. S., L. Marcotulio, V. Santos, and A. Silva (2009). Quem está do outro lado do túnel? Tu ou você na cena urbana carioca. In U. Reich and C. Lopes (eds.), *Neue Romania*, vol. 39. Berlin: Instituts für Romanische Philologie der FU, pp. 49–66.

Lopes, C. R. S. and M. C. B. Rumeu (2007). O quadro de pronomes pessoais do português: as mudanças na especificação dos traços intrínsecos. In A. de Castilho, M. A. T. Morais, R. E. V. Lopes, and S. M. L. Cyrino (eds.), *Descrição, história e aquisição do português brasileiro*. São Paulo: FAPESP, pp. 419–436.

Marcotulio, L., J. Vianna, C. and Lopes (2013). Agreement patterns with "a gente" in Portuguese. *Journal of Portuguese Linguistics*, 12, pp. 125–149.

Mattos e Silva, R. V. M. (1989). *Estruturas Trecentistas. Elementos para uma gramática do Português Arcaico*. Lisbon: IN-CM.

Menuzzi, S. M. (1995). 1st person plural anaphora In Brazilian Portuguese and chains. In M. den Dikken and K. Hengeveld (eds.), *Linguistics in the Netherlands*. Amsterdam: John Benjamins, pp. 151–162.

Menuzzi, S. M. (2000). 1st person plural anaphora in Brazilian Portuguese, chains and constraint interaction in Binding Theory. In J. Costa (ed.), *Portuguese Syntax: New Comparative Studies*. Oxford: Oxford University Press, pp. 191–240.

Posner, R. (1996). *The Romance Languages*. Cambridge: Cambridge University Press.

Reinhard Stoettner, K. von (1887). *A História dos Cavalleiros da Mesa Redonda e da Demanda do Santo Graal*, Berlin: Druck und Verlag von A. Haack.

Rumeu, M. C. B. (2013). *A implementação do '"Você" no Português Brasileiro Oitocentista e Novecentista: um estudo de painel*. Rio de Janeiro: Ítaca.

Squartini, M. (1998). *Verbal Periphrases in Romance. Aspect, Actionality and Grammaticalization*. Berlin: de Gruyter.

Squartini, M. and P. M. Bertinetto (2000). The simple and compound past in Romance languages. In Ö. Dahl (ed.), *Tense and Aspect in the Languages of Europe*. Berlin: de Gruyter, pp. 403–439.

Zilles, A. M. S. (2005). The development of a new pronoun: the linguistic and social embedding of *"a gente"* in Brazilian Portuguese. *Language Variation and Change*, 17, pp. 19–53.

27 Main Syntactic Changes from a Principle-and-Parameters View

CHARLOTTE GALVES AND ANTHONY KROCH

1. Introduction

Although the first available documents written in Portuguese are more recent than is the case for many other European languages and although, when the language first appears in texts, (Old) Portuguese already looks much closer to its modern descendant than Old French or Old English do, the language born in the northwest of the Iberian Peninsula still offers, in its development, a very useful case study for students of language change. In this chapter, we will propose a description and analysis, framed in the principle-and-parameters framework of generative grammar, of the major syntactic changes found in Portuguese from the first texts of the late twelfth century to the modern grammars of its two most widely spoken current varieties, Modern European Portuguese and Modern Brazilian Portuguese. In discussing these changes, we will depart from the traditional historical point of view and, rather than considering the surviving texts of the older language as our objects of inquiry, we will treat them as evidence, necessarily indirect, of the grammars of their authors. This move from observable data to the underlying grammatical system that guided the production of that data is inspired by the shift proposed by Chomsky (1986) from E-Language to I-Language. By E-language Chomsky intended to evoke External and Extensional language, that is, observable data, and by I-Language he meant Internal and Intensional language, that is, the system of grammatical knowledge by virtue of which people can be speakers of a given language. I-Languages constitute the knowledge attained by children in the course of language acquisition. They correspond, therefore, to parametrizations of the faculty of language in which the choice points that allow for cross-linguistic variability are given fixed values. In what follows, we further adopt the approach to the theory of parameters originally proposed by Hagit Borer, the so-called "Borer–Chomsky" conjecture, according to which the loci of parametric variability in grammar are the grammatical feature contents of the functional projections (Tense, Aspect, Definiteness, etc.) that control syntactic structure. Our aim in this essay will be to describe the successive I-languages that underlie the Portuguese E-languages as manifested in the written texts that constitute its historical record. The succession of I-languages that we will present are defined by a specific sequence of parametric changes and the texts we examine contain our evidence for the character of the grammatical parameters involved and the timing of the changes in their settings.

One important aspect of our approach is that there is no necessary one-to-one connection between texts and grammars. A text can be a locus where more than one grammar is expressed, hence diglossic, and in the course of a change such diglossic variation

The Handbook of Portuguese Linguistics, First Edition. Edited by W. Leo Wetzels, João Costa, and Sergio Menuzzi.
© 2016 John Wiley & Sons, Inc. Published 2020 by John Wiley & Sons, Inc.

can characterize a body of texts over an extended period of time. To be precise, a particular instance of variation in morphosyntactic form found in texts can have two sources. On the one hand, it can be produced by a single grammar, as when authors vary between the active and the passive voice or between canonical word order and the topicalized or scrambled placement of verbal complements. On the other hand, the observed variation may reflect the competition between two grammars, that is, two different parameter settings. Among other advantages, the notion of grammar competition (cf. Kroch 2001) allows us to reconcile the point of view that grammatical changes must be abrupt, since they arise in the individual when language acquirers change the setting of some parameter, with the fact that such changes, as manifested in texts, normally exhibit text-internal variation and take several generations to go to completion.

Our chapter is organized as follows. Section 2 reformulates the traditional periodization of European Portuguese on the basis of the shift in perspective from E-language to I-language. We then propose that the main syntactic features of the grammatical evolution of Portuguese from the first written texts to modern European Portuguese can be accounted for as a succession of three different grammars and we discuss the parameters involved in this succession. In Section 3 we describe the main changes that characterize the syntactic history of Brazilian Portuguese as it diverges from European Portuguese and discuss what parameters will best account for the changes. In Section 4, we summarize our findings and make some concluding remarks.

2. Parametric changes in European Portuguese

2.1. *How many stages are there in the history of Portuguese?*

The traditional periodization of Portuguese (see Mattos e Silva 1994 for a survey) acknowledges three main periods: *Old Portuguese* (henceforth OP), from the first remaining manuscripts of the beginning of the twelfth century to the first half of the sixteenth century, *Classical Portuguese* (henceforth ClP), up to the eighteenth century and *Modern European Portuguese* (henceforth EP) from 1800 on. In addition, several scholars divide OP into *Galego-Portuguese* (GP), up to the end of the fourteenth century, and *Middle Portuguese* (henceforth MP), from roughly 1400 to the first half of the sixteenth century. The basis for this division is primarily sociohistorical but is also grounded in linguistic characteristics, mostly phonological and morphological, since these two levels sharply differentiate GP and part of MP from the subsequent periods (see Chapter 1, History and Current Setting). MP can be thought of as the period in which the peculiarities of OP gradually disappear from texts.

When we turn to the syntax, given our perspective, we have two tasks: first to discover the grammars that underlie the texts and then to determine how the parameter settings defining them change over time. Note that, since we believe that grammar change occurs abruptly and then spreads, we should define periods not by the disappearance of archaic phenomena but by the appearance of innovations, since the latter signal the emergence of a new grammar. Along these lines, Galves, Namiuti, and Paixão de Sousa (2006) proposed that the history of European Portuguese has three grammatical stages.[1] It begins with the grammar that underlies the Old (or Galego-) Portuguese texts. Then, at a certain point, a new grammar appears, giving rise to a long period of morphosyntactic variation, the period traditionally known as as Middle Portuguese. The purest expression of this new grammar is found in the texts of the following Classical Portuguese (ClP) period, by which time the OP grammar has died out. The final stage begins when a further new grammar emerges, yielding a new competition. This grammar is the one underlying Modern European Portuguese (EP).

The main difference between our periodization and the traditional one, which also recognizes three periods, is that MP is no longer to be thought of as "late" OP and becomes instead "early" ClP because MP is now analyzed as exhibiting a competition between the grammar of OP and the new ClP grammar. In our view, the latter is probably already the grammar of the vernacular language when variation first appears in texts. We should note that, since we consider MP to be nothing but a competition in use between the grammars of OP and ClP, the latter must, for us, begin to manifest itself in texts much sooner than claimed by the tradition. For the subsequent transition from ClP to EP, the surviving data are much more extensive than for the earlier period and several recent studies based on the Tycho Brahe Corpus show clearly that EP first emerges in the writings of authors born after 1700 (Galves et al. 2005a; Antonelli 2011; among others). We discuss the evolution of this stage in Section 2.3 below.

2.2. *The changes from OP to ClP*

In discussing the development from OP to ClP, we concentrate on word-order evidence, specifically clitic placement, scrambling, and the position of the verb, since those phenomena have been well studied, both empirically and theoretically.[2]

With regard to clitic placement, it is important to remember that certain aspects of the phenomenon remain constant, at least on the surface, throughout the history of Portuguese on the European continent. For one thing, clitics may never appear as proclitics on a verb in first position in a root sentence. On the other hand, there are contexts of obligatory proclisis which never change or vary (see Chapter 12, Clitics: Phonology, Morphology and Syntax), for example in tensed subordinate clauses. Non-V1 main clauses, unless the sentence contains preverbal elements that force proclisis, are the main context of historical variation. There clitics are predominantly postverbal in OP, as in example (1), and predominantly preverbal in ClP, as in example (2) below.

(1) *é   Móór eanes obligouse a dar   os filhus   a outorga* (NO, 1273)
and Moor Eanes obliged-*se* to give to.the sons the donation
(Martins 1994: 60, ex. 25)

(2) *O brâmene   lhe deu por isso seus agradecimentos,*
The braman   to.him **gave** for that his thanks,
"The Brahmin thanked him for that," (Pinto, born1510)

Additionally, in a phenomenon known as "interpolation," we find in older Portuguese that embedded-clause preverbal clitics can be separated from the verb by intervening phrases. In OP the phrase can be of any syntactic function, including the subject (example (3)) but by the time of ClP only negation survives as an interpolatable element (example (4)).

(3) *assy como vola   os ditos Moesteyros derõ e outorgarõ* (NO, 1285)
as well as to.you.it the said Monasteries gave and donate
(Martins 1994: 172, ex. 192)

(4) *disse que llj nõ enbargava a meyadade* (NO, 1289)
(Martins 1994: 162, ex. 3)
said that to.him not seized the half

Although we do find isolated examples of interpolation of other elements as late as the sixteenth century, late examples are probably remnants of the competition between OP and

ClP in the texts. Some examples may reflect a third type of interpolation, restricted to pronouns and a few adverbs (cf. Magro 2008), which lasted until the twentieth century in dialectal Portuguese. Significantly, interpolation in OP is possible only in clauses where proclisis is obligatory, while in ClP the interpolation of negation is possible in any non-V1 clause (Namiuti 2008):

(5) *Dom Manoel de Lima o <u>não</u> quiz ouvir naquele negócio* (Couto, born1542)
     Dom Manoel de Lima him not wanted to hear in that business

Note also that, OP exhibits scrambling, a word-order effect under which the (nominal, clausal or verbal) complement of a main verb is displaced to the verb's left, as illustrated in (6). Such scrambling is always optional (compare (6) and (7)). Here are examples from thirteenth-century legal documents (Martins 2005: 182):

(6) *sse pela uĕtujra uos alguĕ <u>a dita vỹa</u> enbargar*
     if by chance you-dat someone *the mentioned vineyard* blocks

(7) *sse pela uĕtujra uos alguĕ enbargar <u>a dita vỹa</u>*
     if by chance you-dat someone blocks *the mentioned vineyard*
     "and if by chance someone blocks the vineyard from you"

Following work on clitic placement in other medieval Romance languages (cf. Cardinaletti and Roberts 2003 among others),[3] Martins (1994, 2005) proposes that in OP, the enclitic position of the pronoun is derived by movement of the verb across the position that hosts the clitic. She argues that the verb moves to a high functional category, Sigma (Σ), which encodes polarity. According to this author, Σ is strong in OP and, as such, must be lexicalized. When C or NEG or some polarity marking item is not present, the verb fulfills this requirement by moving to Σ, leaving the clitic in a string-wise postverbal position.

In discussing the structural position of clitics, Martins asserts that they land in the specifier of AgrSP, which in OP carries an EPP feature and allows multiple Specs. It is this multiple spec property that licenses interpolation in cases like (3) and (4) above. "Because clitics are minimal/maximal entities (Chomsky 1994, 1995), clitic movement may target either a head or a Spec position. If the latter option is taken, clitics move into the same domain as non-clitic scrambled objects, that is Spec of AgrS. (...) [I]nterpolation (i.e. non adjacency between the clitic and the verb) is derived with the clitic placed in the outer Spec,AgrSP while scrambled objects or the subject occupy "embedded" Spec positions in the AgrS domain" (Martins 2005: 176).[4] Martins (1994) points out that as early as the thirteenth century, some cases of proclisis are found in the absence of any polarity sensitive element, the phenomenon that becomes dominant in the ClP period. This option, she claims, is be to explained by the clitic's ability to head-adjoin to Σ when the latter hosts the verb.

The dual nature of clitics as heads and as maximal projections explains another sort of variation in OP: the optionality of interpolation, as illustrated by the existence of sentences like (8), to be compared with (3) above:

(8) *ca   <u>elle</u> o   octorgava* (NO, 1277)
     because he   cl.acc.3 donated
     "because he donated it"
     (Martins 1994: 191, ex. 329)

In both (8) and (3), according to Martins, Σ is occupied by a conjunction (*"ca"* and *"sse,"* respectively) and the verb is in AgrS. But while the clitic is adjoined as a head to AgrS in (8), it moves as a phrase to the edge of Spec,AgrS in (3). According to the analysis presented above, interpolation and scrambling are lost together because "AgrS loses the ability to select multiple Specs" (Martins 2005: 186).

The decline of enclisis in ClP cannot be derived from the loss of V-to-Σ since the verb continues to move to a high position (see Section 2.3 below). The fact that proclisis becomes more and more frequent in contexts where enclisis had been dominant indicates that in ClP enclisis is no longer ever a consequence of V-movement. Since enclisis does not disappear from European Portuguese, in contrast to the other Romance languages (see, for example, Fontana 1993 for Spanish), the grammars underlying both OP and ClP produce both enclisis and proclisis, but they do so partially by different means and at different rates in usage, which are detectable in texts. In both OP and ClP, a prosodic requirement, the so-called Tobler–Mussafia Law (Salvi 1991; Galves et al. 2005a; Galves and Sandalo 2012), bars clitics from appearing at the left edge of an Intonational Phrase and forces enclisis in V1 root sentences.[5] In OP, however, enclisis is characteristic even in non-V1 sentences and thus must result largely from verb movement to a high position. In ClP, on the other hand, enclisis serves only to fulfill the prosodic requirement.

To locate the verb in a high enough position in root clauses in OP to account for the dominance of enclitic placement, Martins places it in Σ but other researchers have argued that its position is just C, and, therefore, that OP is a kind of V2 language (Salvi 1991; Ribeiro 1995). Their claim is supported by the high frequency of sentences in which a non-subject precedes the verb, with the subject either following the verb or being null (Ribeiro 1995: 99). Sentences (9) and (10) illustrate the orders OVS and XVSO, orders typical of V2 languages. In addition, the adverb in (9) follows the subject, suggesting that the postverbal subject, and consequently the verb to its left, are in a high position (cf. the discussion in Section 2.3 below):

(9) *E esta vertude de paceença ouve este santo monge Libertino mui compridamente* (DSG 1.5.5)
and this virtue of patience had this holy monk Libertino very fully

(10) *Com estas e outras taaes rrazoões arrefeçeo el-rrei de sua brava sanha*
For these and other such reasons cooled-down the King from his brave fierceness
(CDP.7.62–63)
(Ribeiro (1995: 100, ex. h,q)

A significant problem for a V2 analysis of OP, however, is that the texts contain large numbers of V1 and V3 sentences along with the expected V2 cases (cf. Sitaridou 2012 among others). Indeed, in root clauses, Ribeiro herself reports about 20 percent V1 clauses and 15 percent V2 clauses in her thirteenth- and fourteenth-century texts. Still, since V-to-C, even in the Germanic languages, can be grammatically independent of the movement of a phrase to Spec, CP, the data remain consistent with a V-to-C requirement or at least with a required movement to a position higher than Tense.[6] We will see in the next section that some such movement requirement must have survived into ClP.

Summarizing the discussion to this point, the changes in word order from OP to ClP can be said to follow from a parametric change in the properties of the functional head AgrS, which loses its capacity to license multiple Specs. Hence, a single parameter change explains the loss both of scrambling and of interpolation. Moreover, the evolution of clitic placement is a by-product of this change, given the plausible assumption that interpolation was the main evidence for learners of the movement of clitics as phrases to the edge of AgrSP. As the surface position of clitics becomes more and more frequently compatible with ordinary head movement, the way opens for learners to reanalyze both proclisis and enclisis as outputs of a postsyntactic (that is, morphological) rule governing the placement of the clitic at the left versus right edge of the verb, independently of the verb's syntactic position. Enclisis remains in the language as a morphophonogical requirement, the Tobler–Mussafia law, which bars clitics in first position in an intonational phrase. We see this result clearly in ClP, where, in non-V1 sentences, enclisis is frequent only when the constituent preceding the verb is prosodically heavy enough to form a separate intonational phrase, a dependent clause or a conjoined phrase (cf. Galves et al. 2005a),[7] being marginal when preverbal phrases are subjects (cf. Figure 27.1), adverbs or simple PPs. Some exceptions can be found, as in the case of Vieira's *Sermons*, where enclisis reaches 52 percent of the cases. The fact that in all such enclitic sentences in the sermons, the preverbal phrase receives the interpretation of a contrastive topic (Galves 2002) reinforces the idea that clitic-placement is sensitive to prosody, since contrastive topics tend to be associated with an independent prosodic contour (cf. Frascarelli and Hinterholzl 2007).

2.3. *The changes from ClP to EP*

We consider that three main syntactic changes constitute the transition from ClP to EP.[8] The first again concerns clitic placement. As shown by Galves et al. (2005a), in the same contexts where proclisis replaces enclisis from OP to ClP, enclisis replaces proclisis from ClP to EP, in a gradual evolution beginning in texts written by authors born in the first quarter of the eighteenth century and arriving at completion one and a half centuries later. The second change affects the position of subjects and begins with the same generation of authors, whose texts manifest an abrupt drop in the frequency of VS word order (Galves and Paixão de Sousa 2013). Figure 27.1 traces the evolution of the two changes.

Figure 27.1 shows the rise of enclisis with preverbal subjects (black diamonds) and the decline of VS word order (grey triangles) in 16 authors born from 1502 to 1836, with each point corresponding to the author's birth date.[9] Before 1700, the frequency of enclisis with preverbal subjects ranges from 0 to 18 percent, with an overall mean of 6 percent for the sixteenth and seventeenth centuries combined. These figures ignore its high frequency (52 percent) in the sermons of Padre Vieira, which we believe to be a consequence of his

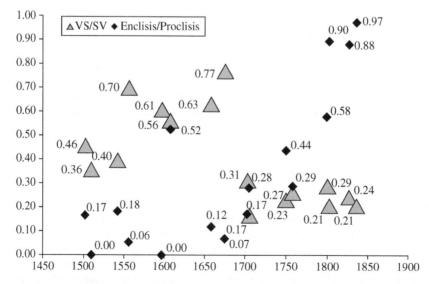

Figure 27.1   Comparative evolution of VS order (vs. SV order) and of enclisis with preverbal subjects, i.e., S-Vcl (vs. S-clV) (Galves and Paixao de Sousa 2013).

special style (see above). Over the same time span, VS appears with a frequency ranging from 36 percent to 77 percent, with an overall mean of 56 percent for the same two centuries. After 1700, the frequency of enclisis with preverbal subjects gradually increases, reaching 97 percent by the middle of the nineteenth century, while the frequency of VS drops abruptly to a stable mean of approximately 25 percent for the entire course of the eighteenth and nineteenth centuries.

With regard to the change in the position of subjects, we observe changes not only in the frequency of VS, but also in its interpretation. Galves and Gibrail (forthcoming) show that in ClP texts, in contrast to EP (cf. Costa 2004), postverbal subjects may receive a non-focal interpretation, as illustrated in (11):

(11) *e sendo este negócio dos maiores, que podia ter uma Monarquia, <u>o fiou</u>*
     and being this deal of the greatest, that could have a Monarchy, *it entrusted*
     <u>o animoso Rei</u> <u>inteiramente</u> *da intelligência e indústria de um só homem*
     the brave king entirely to the intelligence and industry of a only man
     "and being among the greatest of deals which could have a Monarchy, the brave
     king entrusted it entirely to the intelligence and industry of just one man"

Here the focus of the sentence is "*da intelligência e indústria de um só homem,*" while the postverbal subject receives a "familiar topic" interpretation, since the king has already been mentioned several times and is one of the established characters in the narrative. This usage, which is extremely frequent in texts written by authors born in the sixteenth and seventeenth centuries, suggests that postverbal subjects in ClP can occupy a high position in the clause, to the left of the right peripheral domain associated with normal focus assignment. This behavior is accounted for if we adopt the hypothesis, put forward by several scholars (cf. Antonelli 2011, among others), that in ClP the verb raises to the C domain in main clauses, leaving the subject behind it in the specifier of Tense. This analysis is supported by the fact postverbal subjects can precede manner and other VP peripheral adverbs, as in the Germanic languages. Example (11) above illustrates this phenomenon in the placement of the adverb "*inteiramente.*"

Our analysis assigns to ClP a syntactic property typical of V2 languages, namely leftward movement of the verb to a position in the C domain. However, as in OP, verb movement to C in ClP is not always accompanied by the movement of any phrase to Spec,CP. Galves and Paixão de Sousa (2013) argue that Portuguese, unlike the Germanic V2 languages, allows Spec,CP to remain empty. In the Germanic V2 languages, movement to Spec,CP derives from two different sources: one is the presence of a formal feature in C that forces movement as a last resort in every matrix declarative clause and the other is a discourse-related feature that triggers movement under certain information structural conditions (Light 2012). In ClP and arguably in OP, the only licensor of XP-movement to Spec,CP is the discourse-related feature. In the absence of a discourse motivation, no phrase moves to the preverbal position and the verb remains initial. If our analysis is on the right track, the observed decline of VS in the transition from from ClP to EP must reflect the loss of V-to-C, as it is clear that the modern language lacks general V-to-C movement.

Another innovation in EP appears at the end of the eighteenth century (Andrade, 2015). It is illustrated in (12) and (13) and concerns what Raposo (2004) calls "null object constructions." It consists in the option for a definite pronominal object to be replaced by a null category, both in clauses with canonical word order (12b) and in topic-first sentences (13b). The latter case is so-called "Topicalization," whose existence distinguishes EP from the other Romance languages, where null objects are restricted to indefinite or generic interpretations and where fronted objects not doubled by clitics are interpreted as foci and not as topics.

(12) a. *Eu só o encontrei na FNAC.*
        I only it found in-the FNAC.
     b. *Eu só encontrei __ na FNAC.*
        I only found __ at the FNAC.

(13) a. *Esse livro, eu só o encontrei na FNAC.*
        this book, I only it found in-the FNAC.
     b. *Esse livro, eu só encontrei __ na FNAC.*
        this book, I only found __ at the FNAC.

Andrade (2015) claims that the rise of Topicalization in EP is another consequence of the loss of V-to-C. He shows that from an information structural perspective, the construction continues the Germanic-style discourse-related V2 construction of ClP. Both alternate with Clitic Left-Dislocation and do so at the same rate. He concludes that the loss of V-to-C movement simply replaced *TOP V S* with *TOP S V*. As for null objects, according to Raposo (1986), they are bound by a null topic at the left edge of the sentence. It is tempting, therefore, to also derive the fronting of null objects in EP from the loss of V-to-C. Such a connection would account for the fact that no cases of null topics, i.e null objects, have so far been found in texts of the ClP period. This property, however, cannot be straightforwardly imputed to V2 topicalization, since the V2 Germanic languages often do allow for null topics with definite reference. Additionally, English, which is not a V2 language, allows Topicalization but does not license null topics, showing that the correlation does not obtain in the other direction either. We leave this interesting issue for further research.

Thus, it is clear that the most important parametric difference between ClP and EP is the loss of V-to-C in declarative sentences. At the same time, the change in clitic placement between ClP and EP cannot be said to follow from this parameter difference, since, as we have said, enclisis in ClP reflects only a prosodic constraint (the Tobler–Mussafia Law), and is independent of verb movement. Galves et al. (2005a) and Galves and Sandalo (2012) argue that the prosodic constraint no longer holds in EP. One clear piece of evidence for this change in the character of the constraint governing enclisis is a loss in sensitivity to the length of preverbal clauses in sentences in which the verb immediately follows a dependent clause. Before 1700, short preverbal clauses, those less likely to constitute independent Intonational Phrases, are somewhat less likely to co-occur with enclitic placement than longer clauses, a difference that plausibly reflects a Tobler–Mussafia type prosodic effect. After 1700, however, there is no appreciable difference in the likelihood of enclisis associated with the length of a preverbal clause (see the bottom row in Table 27.1, taken from Galves and Kroch 2014).

Working within the framework of Distributed Morphology, Galves and Sandalo (2012) propose that this loss of sensitivity to prosody results from a change in the domain of

Table 27.1   Effect of preposed clause length on frequency of enclisis by period.

	Clauses > 8 words	*Clauses ≤ 8 words*	*Percent long minus short*
Before 1700			
Number	70	209	
Percent enclisis	60	47	13
After 1700			
Number	59	148	
Percent enclisis	71	68	3

application of the restriction against Clitic-First. In ClP, the domain is prosodic (IntP), and the rule is Prosodic Inversion, which applies after the structure is linearized. In EP, the domain is syntactic (the local phase), and the rule is Lowering, which has access to syntactic structure but not to prosody.

3. Syntactic changes from European to Brazilian Portuguese

According to the grammatical periodization we have proposed, there can be little doubt that the version of Portuguese transplanted to Brazil was ClP. Although at the very beginning of the colonization, the Portuguese of the settlers was often a minority dialect in comparison to lingua franca versions of Tupi languages, it eventually came to dominate throughout the country due to the joint effect of the permanent arrival of new Portuguese settlers and of the widespread acquisition of Portuguese as a second language, mainly by African slaves, who transmitted it as both a first and as a second language during the three centuries of the slave trade. In the following discussion, we will present the most salient morphosyntactic differences between Modern Brazilian Portuguese (henceforth BP) and both ClP and EP. In Section 3.4, we will address the issue of the parameter changes responsible for these differences, which will lead us to introduce other significant features of Brazilian Portuguese.

3.1. Less and more agreement

As described in Chapter 31, Main Current Processes of Morphosyntactic Variation, BP displays variable verbal and nominal agreement in contexts where it is categorical in European Portuguese, a phenomenon that has led some to argue that BP went through a phase of creolization (Guy 1981). The variability of verbal agreement affects both number and person and in most regions of Brazil, the 2nd person singular inflection is no longer part of the verbal paradigm.[10]

Less well analyzed until recently are the agreement facts correlated with the "topic-oriented" properties of BP, first described by Pontes (1987). Pontes showed that, as in "topic-oriented" languages like Chinese, BP has sentences in which the first constituent DP is not the subject but some locative or genitive argument, immediately followed by the verb and its internal argument(s), as in (14) and (15):[11]

(14) *A   Sarinha   nasceu   dois   dentes*
     the Sarinha   was-born.sg   two   teeth
     "Sarinha has got two teeth."

(15) *Estas   casas   batem   muito   sol*
     these   houses   strike.pl   much   sun
     "There is too much sun on this house"

The possibility of agreement between the verb and the preverbal DP in such constructions sharply distinguishes BP from both ClP and EP, where it is completely impossible (cf. Costa 2010). This sort of agreement is also found in the Portuguese spoken as a second language in Mozambique (Gonçalves, 2010), suggesting that it is an result of contact with African languages.

3.2. *A new pronominal system*

The core facts of the BP pronominal paradigm and syntax are as follows (cf. Chapters 31 Main Current Processes of Morphosyntactic Variation and 13 The Null Subject Parameter and the Structure of the Clause):

- Accusative and dative clitic pronouns vary with strong pronouns (16).
- Null objects tend to replace 3rd person accusative clitics (17).
- The clitic pronouns *"lhe"* and *"te"* and accordingly possessive pronouns *"teu"* and *"seu,"* vary freely in referring to the 2nd person (respectively (18) and (19)).

(16) a. *Eu   não   te   vi   ontem*
       I   not   cl2   saw   yesterday
   b. *Eu   não   vi   você   ontem*
       I   not   saw   you   yesterday
      "I did not see you yesterday"

(17) *%Eu   não   (o)   vi*
     I   not   cl3Sg   saw
   "I did not see him"

(18) *Eu   te/lhe   dei   esse   livro*
    I   cl 2/3.dat   gave   this   book
   "I gave you this book"

(19) *Você   trouxe   teu/seu   livro?*
   you   brought   POS2/3   book
   "Did you bring your book?"

Examples (16)–(19) show that clitics with 3rd person reference disappear from the spoken language and that, consistent with the absence of the 2nd person in the verbal paradigm, the 2nd and the 3rd person forms no longer bear distinct pronominal features. Furthermore, tonic pronouns apparently bear no morphological case features, since they appear in all positions with the same form and since, in colloquial spoken BP, clitic doubling occurs between an object clitic and a strong form pronoun that is nominative in EP:

(20) *Me   leva eu   contigo*
   1pcl   take I   with-you
   "Take me with you"

It is especially noteworthy that BP differs from ClP/EP in its clitic placement grammar. Clitics in BP can occur in absolute first position, contrasting with what is observed in all periods of the European language. Furthermore, the category to which clitics attach is different. In ClP/EP, they adjoin to the tensed verbal form, whether an auxiliary or the thematic verb, while in BP they are proclitic on the thematic verb, whether tensed or not (cf. Galves et al. 2005b. and Chapter 2 The Main Varieties of Portuguese: An Overview).

3.3. *Fewer null subjects and more null objects*

EP and BP are both null subject and null object languages, but they differ in the grammar of these properties. Null objects are less constrained in BP than in EP, since they can be used inside syntactic islands, and are the most frequent strategy to refer back to an antecedent in discourse (Duarte 1989). Null subjects, on the other hand, are more constrained in BP than in EP, leading many researchers to argue that BP is only a Partial Null Subject language (henceforth PNS, cf. Chapter 13 The Null Subject Parameter and the Structure of the Clause). One of the characteristic properties of such PNS languages is the possibility of interpreting the null subject of a tensed clause as indeterminate in reference. This usage occurs in BP, as illustrated in the following dialogue drawn from a comic strip:

(21) a. Q: *Onde   está   minha   cueca   de   dinossauro?*
             Where is   my   pants   of   dinosaurs
             "Where are my pants with the dinosaurs?"
     b. A: *Está   lavando*
             is   washing
             (i) "Somebody is washing them"
             (ii) "They are being washed"

Two interpretations are available for (21)b. Either the null subject is indeterminate and the null object refers to the discourse topic (i) or the null subject is interpreted as the topic itself and the sentence is a kind of passive (ii). This ambiguity is even more evident in the following example, drawn from an advertisement, where the topic (*"Tapete de Madeira"* Carpet of Wood) is both the thematic subject of the unergative verb *"encolhe"* (*shrink*) in b., and the thematic object of the transitive verb *"encera"* (*polish*) in c.

(22) a. [*Tapete   de   Madeira*]$_i$
          carpet   of   wood
     b. [*e*]$_i$ *Não   encolhe*
          not   shrinks
     c. *Não   encera* [*e*]$_i$
          not   polishes
          "Wood carpet"
          "It does not shrink"
          "One does not need to polish it"/"It does not need to be polished"

In EP, (22c) would require the presence of indefinite/passivizing *se*: *"Não se encera."* Indeterminate *se*-constructions, as well, usually occur without *"se"* in spoken BP, an option that is impossible in EP.

(23) a. *Aqui   conserta   sapatos* (BP)
          here   repair.3sg   shoes
     b. *Aqui   conserta(m)-se*   *sapatos* (ClP/EP)
          here   repair.3sg(pl)-refl   shoes
          Here shoes are repaired

The examples in (21b), (22c) and (23a) are all consistent with the characterization of BP as a PNS language.

To sum up, in the process of developing in the New World, BP lost morphology: it lost the 2nd/3rd person distinction, it lost obligatory plural agreement on nouns, and person/number agreement became variable on verbs. The language also came to avoid 3rd person clitics and non-reflexive *se*-constructions. Thus, BP has less morphology than EP and has syntactic characteristics distinct from the whole Romance family, including as it does, agreement processes typical of other families of languages, in particular Niger–Congo languages, that systematically display agreement with "non-subject" preverbal phrases (Baker 2008). Still, it retains, in contrast to Creole languages, a substantial amount of flexional morphology. Given this complex situation, even if BP was never precisely a creole, we can suppose that the intimate processes of contact that Portuguese underwent in Brazil deeply affected its syntax.[12] In the next section, we shall see that this reflects in the nature of the parametric changes that occurred from ClP to BP.

3.4. *The parametric changes from ClP to BP*

The properties described above raise challenging questions for Parameter Theory. Following Pontes" typologically based analysis, several researchers have argued that BP is a topic-oriented language (Galves 1993; Negrão 1999; Negrão e Viotti 2000). From a Borer–Chomsky-type principles and parameters perspective, this characterization must be formulated in terms of feature properties of one or more functional heads. Several proposals have been made along these lines, attributing new characteristics to Tense or Agreement or both. One idea is that the features of the head of a clause are in some sense weak in BP, which would explain not only the variability in the morphological realization of Agreement but also the pronominal paradigm, in which the 2nd and 3rd person are non-distinct, as well as the peculiar properties of null subjects.[13] A third property that can be accounted for in this way is the fact that, for many speakers, the subject position of tensed clauses seems to allow A-extraction, as evidenced by the grammaticality of hyper-raising, as in (24):

(24)   *Os meninos_i parecem que t_i fizeram a tarefa*
        the boys seem.3pl that _ did.3pl the homework

Ferreira (2009) derives both hyper-raising and the properties of null subjects in BP from incompleteness in the phi-features of Tense, which makes finite T behave like non-finite T in that it "is unable to eliminate [i.e., check] the Case feature of the moved element" (Ferreira 2009: 29), forcing the subject to move further. For him, null subjects in BP are, in general, not null pronouns but rather traces of displaced subjects, as in hyper-raising.

The idea that referential null subjects in BP are not null pronouns but anaphors (i.e., A-bound empty categories), or variables (i.e., A-bar bound empty categories), goes back to Figueiredo Silva (1996), and was developed in different ways by Modesto (2004) and Rodrigues (2004). For the former, null subjects are not derived by movement but are base-generated as parts of a topic chain, a behavior that would be correlated with the fact that BP is a topic-oriented language; in particular, BP would have a special position for topics always projected in the CP layer. Rodrigues (2004) argues that 1st person null pronouns move to such a topic position and are then deleted, while 3rd person definite null pronouns, found only in embedded clauses, are traces of movement to the subject position.[14]

For all of the authors mentioned, the fact that BP null subjects behave differently from those of other Romance pro-drop languages is correlated with the weakening of the verbal morphology, which reflects some deficiency of T/Agr. However, instead of losing pro-drop, as French did, BP became a PNS language, perhaps because of widespread diglossia between the spoken vernacular and the EP-based language of the elite. In some analyses (for example those of Modesto and Rodrigues), this development is explicitly correlated with the topic-oriented properties of the language. Going a step further, Negrão and Viotti (2000) argue that BP restrictions on the use of null subjects do not derive from weakening of the inflectional morphology, but as a consequence of the discourse-oriented properties of the language, which entail that "the recoverability of empty categories occurs via discourse prominence" (Negrão and Viotti 2000: 109).

It is clear that more than one parameter is at stake in the differences between BP and both ClP and EP. The facts that led Pontes to claim that BP was a topic-oriented language (cf. examples (14)–(15) above) do not derive straightforwardly from the deficiency of T/Agr, nor does the use of strong pronouns instead of clitics (cf. (16)) or the special position of the latter. Avelar and Galves (2011) derive the topic-oriented properties of BP by adopting the claim of Holmberg (2010) that in some languages (e.g., Icelandic) the EPP features of T are phi-independent, in the sense that the attraction of some DP to the specifier of T is independent of the agreement processes induced by phi-features. Relying on a recent version of the minimalist framework, the authors then propose that in BP the EPP features of Tense are satisfied before T is merged with C and inherits its features from C. Given Chomsky's (2008) definition of A and A-bar positions, it follows from this analysis that Spec/T counts as an A-bar position, which explains why extraction is possible from the subject position of tensed sentences in hyper-raising constructions: hyper-raising movement can then go through Spec/C, an undoubted A-bar position, to the subject position of the matrix clause, which is now also an A-bar position.

There is another question raised by sentences like (14)–(15): What is the source of case for the postverbal DP? Avelar and Galves (2011) answer that DPs in BP can be inserted into the derivation without a case feature.[15] This possibility also accounts for the invariability of tonic pronouns in subject and object position (cf. (16)). Moreover, given the relationship between case and agreement in Chomsky (2008), the variability of subject–verb agreement can be explained in a similar way: Only when the DP enters the derivation with Case-features is agreement instantiated.[16]

Finally, consider the innovative clitic placement in BP by which the clitic is affixed to the non-inflected form of the thematic verb, in contrast with EP, where the clitic must raise to the inflected auxiliary. We can assume that lack of syntactic movement to Inflection is indeed due to the weakness of T/Agr. Given this, in accord with the morphological constraint that yields proclisis, clitics are moved by local dislocation to the left of V in the post-syntactic component of the grammar. From this point of view, they can be considered as allomorphs of the tonic pronouns, differing from them phonologically with respect to the clitic feature, and additionally, if we follow Avelar and Galves (2011) with respect to the case feature.

4. Concluding remarks

The analyses we have discussed are summarized in Table 27.2, where the values in boldface indicate changes relative to the values in prior historical stages of the language.

From Table 27.2 and the discussion that it summarizes we can see that there has been large-scale surface variation throughout the history of the Portuguese E-language(s). Nonetheless, we find that the grammatical parameters needed to account for the changes we have tracked, not only the internal ones but also those associated with language contact in Brazil, are limited in number. It is even possible, though beyond the scope of this paper to investigate, that some of the parameters that distinguish BP from EP could be merged into a single one via the weakening of morphological marking. Perhaps more likely is the possibility that such weakening, arising out of language contact, affected several grammatical parameters simultaneously via language acquisition, by reducing the evidence for various syntactic properties which then revert to default values.

There is, of course, much uncertainty regarding the details both of Portuguese grammar and of linguistic theory, so that the results we have presented can only be considered

Table 27.2   Evolving parameters in the history of Portuguese.

	OP	*ClP*	*EP*	*BP*
Multiple AgrS specifiers	yes	**no**	no	no
C attracts V	yes	yes	**no**	no
Phi-dependent EPP in T	yes	yes	yes	**no**
Deficient T/Agr	no	no	no	**yes**
Obligatory case feature on DP	yes	yes	yes	**no**
Restriction against Cl1	yes: prosodic	yes: prosodic	yes: **morphosyntactic**	**no**

tentative, though we think it unlikely that future discoveries will undermine our general parametric approach. In one domain, however, recent theoretical developments have had a large effect on the sort of analysis we think most promising: the domain of the evolution of clitic placement. Here we have followed several recent studies in claiming that the alternation between enclisis and proclisis is governed in part by the morphological component of the grammar, relying on operations defined by the theory of Distributed Morphology. If this approach is sound, it means that there are linguistic phenomena, in our case clitic placement, whose historical evolution undergoes a change in the grammatical module governing them. Since the morphological component of grammar is independent of the narrow syntax, allowing both modules to affect clitic placement implies the possibility of greater surface variability than a purely syntactic approach would lead one to expect. The actual history of Portuguese seems to require this extra flexibility and we hope to have shown that it allows us not only to describe the grammatical systems involved but also to account in an insightful way for the transitions between them.

NOTES

This research was partially funded by the Fapesp grant 2012/06078-9 and the CNPq grant 309764/2014–9.

1   Against Martins (1994) who argues that the language changes directly from OP to EP.
2   Other changes include the loss of features typical of Gallo-Romance syntax like *"ende,"* auxiliary shift, agreement with objects (see Mattos e Silva 1994). As far as we know, there is nothing about the diachronic evolution of these phenomena in the generative literature.
3   For Cardinaletti and Roberts, the movement of the verb is a last resort process that prevents the clitic from being in first position in the C domain. Their analysis, however, only accounts for enclisis with verbs in absolute first position and fails to explain the high frequency of enclisis with V2 in OP.
4   In order for her analysis to derive the right word order of interpolation, Martins adopts the Edge Principle proposed by Raposo, which requires that clitics always appear on the edge of the category to which they adjoin.
5   Adopting Martins' analysis of proclisis in main clauses forces us to assume that the Tobler–Mussafia Law is already operative in OP. Otherwise, we would expect proclisis to be possible in V1 sentences when the clitic raises to C as a head attached to the verb.
6   The question remains of deciding whether this functional category is part of the IP layer or the CP layer. We will assume the minimal hypothesis that there is no functional category above T in the IP layer.
7   Note that the frequency of enclisis in such cases varies widely from author to author (cf. Galves et al. 2005a).
8   The data in this section are drawn from the Tycho Brahe Corpus of Historical Portuguese (TBC). cf. http://www.tycho.iel.unicamp.br/~tycho/corpus.

9   Figure 27.1 is based on data drawn from 16 syntactically-parsed texts written by authors born from 1502 to 1836. The data were extracted from non-dependent clauses, and concern all the verbs except *ser* "to be."

10   It is important to note that agreement is variable in all social classes (cf. Chapter 31).

11   For generative analyses of this phenomenon, see Galves (1998); Avelar and Galves (2011), Munhoz and Naves (2012); Andrade and Galves (2014), among others.

12   In the terms of Holm (2004), BP is a "restructured language."

13   The weakness of T/Agr can also explain the properties of verb-movement in BP, as argued by Galves 1993.

14   This analysis relies on a revision of the theory of thematic roles under which theta roles are features to be valued.

15   This exotic feature of BP could be due again to contact with African languages. For evidence in favor of the absence of case features in Bantu languages, see Diercks (2012).

16   This approach entails that T should bear phi-features when agreement is instantiated. Avelar and Galves (2011) do not address this question.

REFERENCES

Andrade, A. (forthcoming). On the emergence of topicalization in Modern European Portuguese: a study at the syntax-information structure interface. *Estudos Linguísticos*, CLUNL.

Andrade, A. and C. Galves (2014). A unified analysis for subject topics in Brazilian Portuguese. *Journal of Portuguese Linguistics*, 13 (1), pp. 117–148.

Antonelli, A. (2011). Sintaxe de posição do verbo e mudança gramatical na história do português europeu. Ph.D. dissertation, University of Campinas.

Avelar, J. and C. Galves (2011). Tópico e concordância em português brasileiro e português europeu. In A. Costa, I. Falé, and P. Barbosa (eds.), *Textos Seleccionados: Actas do XXVI Encontro Nacional da Associação Portuguesa de Linguística*, pp. 49–65.

Baker, M. (2008). *The Syntax of Agreement and Concord*. Cambridge: Cambridge University Press.

Cardinaletti, A. and I. Roberts (2003). Clause structure and X-Second. In G. Cinque (ed.), *Functional Structure in DP and IP. The Cartography of Syntactic Structures*, vol. 1. Oxford: Oxford University Press, pp. 123–166.

Chomsky, N. (1986). *Knowledge of Language: Its Nature, Origin, and Use*. New York: Praeger.

Chomsky, N. (1994). Bare Phase Structure. MIT Working Papers, Cambridge, MA: MIT.

Chomsky, N. (1995). *The Minimalist Program*, Cambridge, MA: MIT Press.

Chomsky, N. (2008). On phases. In R. Freidin, C. Otero, and M. L. Zubizarreta (eds.), *Foundational Issues in Linguistic Theory*. Cambridge, MA: MIT Press, pp. 133–166.

Costa, J. (2004). *Subject Positions and Interfaces: The Case of European Portuguese*. Amsterdam: de Gruyter.

Costa, J. (2010). PB e PE: orientação para o discurso importa? *Estudos da Lingua(gem)*, 8 (1), pp. 123–144.

Diercks, M. (2012). Parameterizing Case: Evidence from Bantu. *Syntax*, 15 (3), pp. 253–286.

Duarte, M. E. (1989). Clítico acusativo, pronome lexical e categoria vazia no português do Brasil. In F. Tarallo (ed.), *Fotografias Sociolinguísticas*. Campinas: Editora da Unicamp, pp. 19–34.

Ferreira, M. (2009). Null subject and finite control in Brazilian Portuguese. In J. Nunes (ed.), *Minimalist Essays on Brazilian Portuguese Syntax*. Amsterdam: John Benjamins, pp. 17–49.

Figueiredo Silva, C. (1996). *A Posição Sujeito Em Português Brasileiro – Frases Finitas e Infinitivas*. Campinas: Editora da Unicamp.

Fontana, J. (1993). Phrase-structure and the syntax of clitics in the history of Spanish. Ph.D. dissertation, University of Pennsylvania.

Frascarelli, M. and R. Hinterholzl (2007). Types of topics in German and Italian. In S. Winkler and K. Schwabe (eds.), *On Information Structure, Meaning and Form*. Amsterdam: John Benjamins, pp. 87–116.

Galves, C. (1993). O enfraquecimento da concordância no português brasileiro. In M. Kato and I. Roberts (eds.), *Português Brasileiro: Uma Viagem Diacrônica*. Campinas: Editora da Unicamp, pp. 387–403.

Galves, C. (1998). Tópicos, sujeitos, pronomes e concordância no português brasileiro. *Caderno de Estudos Linguísticos*, 34, pp. 7–21.

Galves, C. (2002). Syntax and style: clitic-placement in Padre Antonio Vieira. *Santa Barbara Portuguese Studies*, 6, pp. 387–403.

Galves, C., H. Britto, and M. C. Paixão de Sousa (2005). [Galves et al. 2005a] The change in clitic placement from Classical to Modern European Portuguese: results from the Tycho Brahe Corpus. *Journal of Portuguese Linguistics*, 4 (1), pp. 39–68.

Galves, C. and A. Gibrail (forthcoming). Subject inversion in transitive sentences from Classical to Modern European Portuguese: a corpus-based study. To appear in A. Cardoso and A. M. Martins (eds.), *Word Order Change*. Oxford: Oxford University Press.

Galves, C. and A. Kroch (2014). Syntactic changes in the history of Portuguese: a corpus-based approach. Paper presented at the *Linguistics Department Colloquium Series*, York University. http://www.tycho.iel. unicamp.br/~tycho/pesquisa/, accessed November 6, 2015.

Galves, C., C. Namiuti, and M . C. Paixão de Sousa (2006). Novas perguntas para antigas questões: a periodização do português revisitada. In A. Endruschat, R. Kemmler, and B. Schäfer-Prie (eds.), *Grammatische Strukturen des Europäischen Portugiesisch*. Tubingen: Calapinus Verlag, pp. 45–75.

Galves, C. and M. C. Paixão de Sousa (2013). The loss of verb-second in the history of Portuguese: subject position, clitic placement and prosody. Revised version of the paper presented at DIGs 12, Cambridge. http:// www.tycho.iel.unicamp.br/~tycho/pesquisa/, accessed November 6, 2015.

Galves, C., I. Ribeiro, and M. A. Torres Moraes (2005). [Galves et al. 2005b] Syntax and morphology in the placement of clitics in European and Brazilian Portuguese. *Journal of Portuguese Linguistics*, 4 (2), pp. 143–177.

Galves, C. and F. Sandalo (2012). From intonational phrase to syntactic phase: the grammaticalization of enclisis in the history of Portuguese. *Lingua*, 122 (8), pp. 952–974.

Gonçalves, P. (2010). *A Gênese do Português de Moçambique*. Lisbon: INCM.

Guy, G. (1981). Linguistic variation in Brazilian Portuguese: aspects of phonology, syntax and language history. Ph.D. dissertation, University of Pennsylvania.

Holm, J. (2004). *Languages in Contact. The Partial Restructuring of Vernaculars*. Cambridge: Cambridge University Press.

Holmberg, A. (2010). Null subject parameters. In T. Biberauer, A. Holmberg, I. Roberts, and M. Sheehan (eds.), *Parametric Variation: Null subjects in Minimalist Theory*. Cambridge: Cambridge University Press, pp. 88–124.

Kroch, A. (2001). Syntactic change. In M. Baltin and C. Collins (eds.), *The Handbook of Contemporary Syntactic Theory*. Oxford: Blackwell, pp. 699–729.

Light, C. (2012). The syntax and pragmatics of fronting in Germanic. Ph.D. dissertation, University of Pennsylvania.

Magro, C. (2008). Clíticos: variação sobre o tema. Ph.D. dissertation, University of Lisbon.

Martins, A. M. (1994). Clíticos na história do português. Ph.D. dissertation, University of Lisbon.

Martins, A. M. (2005). Clitic placement, VP-ellipsis and scrambling in romance. In M. Batllori, M.-L. Hernanz, C. Picallo, and F. Roca (eds.), *Grammaticalization and Parametric Change*. Oxford: Oxford University Press, pp. 175–193.

Mattos e Silva, R. V. (1994). Para uma caracterização do período arcaico do português. *D.E.L.T.A*, 10, pp. 247–276.

Modesto, M. (2004). Sujeitos nulos em línguas de tópico proeminente. *Revista da Abralin*, 3 (1–2), pp. 121–148.

Munhoz, A. and R. Naves (2012). Construções de tópico-sujeito: uma proposta em termos de estrutura argumental e de transferência de traços de C. *Signum*, 15, pp. 245–265.

Namiuti, C. (2008). Aspectos da história gramatical do português. Interpolação, negação e mudança. Ph.D. dissertation, University of Campinas.

Negrão, E. (1999). Português brasileiro: Uma língua voltada para o discurso. Ph.D. dissertation, University of São Paulo.

Negrão, E. and E. Viotti (2000). Brazilian Portuguese as a discourse-oriented language. In M. Kato and E. Negrão (eds.), *Brazilian Portuguese and the Null Subject Parameter*. Frankfurt: Vervuert Verlag, pp. 105–125.

Pontes, E. (1987). *O Tópico no Português do Brasil*. Campinas: Pontes.

Raposo, E. (1986). On the null object construction in European Portuguese. In O. Jaeggli and C. Silva-Corvalan (eds.) *Studies in Romance Linguistics*, Dordrecht: Foris, pp. 373–390.

Raposo, E. (2000). Clitic Positions and Verb Movement. In J. Costa (ed.) Portuguese Syntax: New Comparative Studies. Oxford University Press, Oxford, pp. 266–297.

Raposo, E. (2004). Objetos nulos e CLLD: uma teoria unificada. *Revista da Abralin*, 3 (1–2), pp. 41–73.

Ribeiro, I. (1995). A sintaxe da ordem no português arcaico; o efeito V2. Ph.D. dissertation, University of Campinas.

Rodrigues, C. (2004). Impoverished morphology and A-movement out of case domains. Ph.D. dissertation, University of Maryland.

Salvi, G. (1991). La sopravvivenza della legge di Wackernagel nei dialettioccidentali della peninsola iberica. *Medioevo Romanzo*, 15, pp. 177–210.

Sitaridou, J. (2012). A comparative study of word order in Old Romance. *Folia Linguistica*, 46 (2), pp. 553–604.

28 Main Current Processes of Phonological Variation

CELESTE RODRIGUES AND DERMEVAL DA HORA

1. Introduction

Variation studies in Brazil predominantly have a sociolinguistic orientation, with as their main methodological foundation the pioneering work of William Labov (Labov, 1966, 1972; Weinreich, Labov, and Herzog, 1968). The 1970s saw the first sociolinguistic projects with a focus on variable phonological processes identified in different spoken-language corpora. This type of research started at the Universidade Federal do Rio de Janeiro with a group of researchers coordinated by Anthony Naro. Since then, several research groups in different regions have been formed, whose work has significantly increased our knowledge of phonological variation in the different variants of spoken Brazilian Portuguese (BP).

Along with the variationist studies, extensive dialectal studies have been carried out, culminating in the ongoing project of the Linguistic Atlas of Brazil (*Atlas Linguístico do Brasil*—AliB), of national significance, supervised by Suzana Cardoso.

Unlike the case in Brazil, sociolinguistic variation in Portugal has not yet received much attention, although a few sociolinguistic studies with different theoretical orientations have been carried out during the last decades, which will be discussed in this chapter. Instead, variation studies in Portugal cover, above all, regional differences, especially those between the northern and the central-southern dialects. These two broad dialect areas of Portugal are distinguished on the basis of the isoglosses involving the coronal and labial fricatives in the syllable onset. The fricatives /s z/ emerge in the central-southern region (including the dialect of the Lisbon urban area, which is considered the standard dialect of European Portuguese (EP)), whereas the more conservative apical pronunciation /ʂ ʐ/ is typical of the north, though some areas preserve a complex system of four sibilants (two apical and two dento-alveolar) (Segura, 2013). Also, the bilabial fricative /β/ characteristic of the northern dialects corresponds with the labio-dental fricative /v/ in all the central-southern dialects. As a matter of fact, most consonantal isoglosses concur in defining these two major dialects in EP. Within the two main areas several subareas are often identified, which differ mainly in their vowel systems (all the geographical areas mentioned are included in the dialectal map presented in the following section).

This chapter aims to treat the more significant variable phonological processes of Brazilian and European Portuguese. In our exposition of the data we will first discuss the variation in the vocalic sounds, for both varieties, after which we turn to the consonantal variation.

The Handbook of Portuguese Linguistics, First Edition. Edited by W. Leo Wetzels, João Costa, and Sergio Menuzzi.
© 2016 John Wiley & Sons, Inc. Published 2020 by John Wiley & Sons, Inc.

2. Vowel variation

Both EP and BP realize a symmetrical seven-vowel system under stress: /i, e, ɛ, a, u, o, ɔ/. Table 28.1 presents the distinctive feature definition of the vowel phonemes in Portuguese that will be used throughout this chapter, without any strong commitment regarding the way in which the distinction between upper and lower mid-vowels is defined. Unlike some other scholars, we assign the low vowel to a separate aperture class (see Mateus and Andrade (2000) and Wetzels (2011) for discussion of the question of aperture distinctions in Portuguese[1]).

Some scholars consider [ɐ] a phonological vowel of the EP vowel system (see Veloso, 2012 for discussion). In EP, [ɐ] is the typical unstressed allophone of /a/. In addition to that, [ɐ] emerges in two other contexts: as the allophone of the stressed verbal theme vowel /a/ before the nasal consonant of the 1pl present suffix –*mos* in forms such as *amamos* [ɐmɐmuʃ] "we love" or *ficamos* [fikɐmuʃ] "we stay," or as the allophone of the front mid-vowels /e/ or /ɛ/ before palatal sounds: *abelha* [ɐbɐ́ʎɐ] "bee," also when unstressed: *coelhinho* [kwɐʎíɲu] "little rabbit." The 1pl present forms contrast with the corresponding 1pl past forms, which have [a] instead of [ɐ]: *ficámos* [fikámuʃ], *falámos* [fɐlámuʃ] in the southern dialects of EP (including the standard one).[2] The northern dialects merge the present and past forms, which all show stressed [ɐ], whereas the central-southern dialects still maintain the contrast.

2.1. The stressed vowel system: dialectal variation in EP

Following Cintra (1971), Segura (2013) recognizes two main dialectal areas in the Portuguese mainland,[3] both of them containing subareas with some characteristic features of their own. Figure 28.1 shows the dialectal areas and subareas that are relevant for the discussion in this chapter.[4]

The extreme southwest (Barlavento of Algarve) as well as the interior part of central Portugal show some typical features within the central-southern region and so does the northwest within the northern dialect area. These subareas have different vowel inventories, which are still in need of a detailed analysis. The phonological status of some vowel sounds remains as yet unclear (Brissos and Rodrigues, forthcoming). We will therefore not comment on the specificities of the segments that are proposed as part of the vowel systems, since the differences with the standard Lisbon vowel inventory have not been made sufficiently clear as yet.

Dialectologists have identified the following three vowel systems:

1. Within the central-southern dialects, one finds in the interior of Alto Alentejo and of Beira Baixa the system /i e ɛ ə a ɔ o o ɵ ʉ/ (Brissos, 2012, 2014a).
2. The southwestern part of Portugal, which roughly coincides with the Algarve region has the system: /i e ɛ æ ɒ ɔ o y/ (Segura, 2013).
3. The northwestern part of Portugal, comprising Minho and the Douro coastal region, diverges from the standard language for having replaced a number of vowels with diphthongs (Brissos and Rodrigues, forthcoming).

Table 28.1   Stressed vowel system of BP and EP.

	Coronal	*Dorsal*	*Labial*
High	i		u
Upper Mid	e		o
Lower Mid	ɛ		ɔ
Low		a	

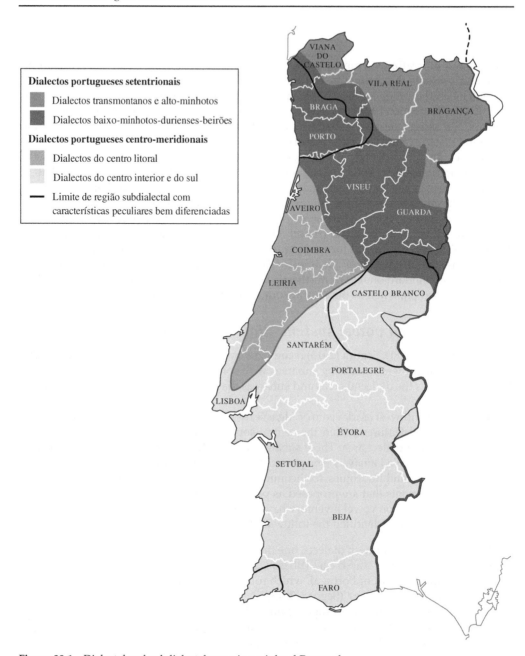

Figure 28.1   Dialectal and subdialectal areas in mainland Portugal.

Recently, different local inventories of stressed vowels were found as part of a broad dialectal research based on data extracted from the ALEPG corpus—*Atlas Linguístico e Etnográfico de Portugal e da Galiza*—through the Acoustic Atlas of Portuguese Stressed Vowels (AVOC) (Brissos, 2014a, b; Brissos and Saramago, 2014). AVOC provides an acoustic analysis of the vowel systems encountered, which will soon be available online. These studies show that the dialects of the center and the south are more heterogeneous than was suggested by earlier impressionistic descriptions (Cintra, 1971).

In the standard language as well as in the dialects of the north, the coronal mid-vowels /e/ and /ɛ/ undergo a process of centralization before a palatal sound. Before tautosyllabic [j], these vowels are centralized independently of being stressed or unstressed, whereas before the hetero-syllabic consonants [ʃ], [ʒ], [ʎ], [ɲ] centralization of coronal mid-vowels only occurs under stress. This process is illustrated with the words in (1) and (2) below.[5] In the standard and northern dialects, the words in (2) may also surface with an epenthetic palatal glide: [ɐj].

(1) Tautosyllabic centralization

leite	[lɐ̃j.tɨ]	"milk"	*leiteiro*	[lɐj.tɐ̃j.ɾu]	"milkman"
lei	[lɐ̃j]	"law"	*respeitar*	[ʀiʃ.pɐj.táɾ]	"respect"
areia	[ɐ.ɾɐ̃j.ɐ]	"sand"	*europeizar*	[ew.ɾupɐj.záɾ]	"europeanize"
anéis	[ɐ.nɐ̃jʃ]	"ring-pl"	*bebeis*	[bɨ.bɐ̃jʃ]	"drink-2pl pres.ind."

(2) Heterosyllabic centralization

cereja	[siɾɐ̃ʒɐ]	"cherry"	*inveja*	[ĩvɐ̃ʒɐ]	"envy"
fecha	[fɐ̃ʃɐ]	"close-3sg pres.ind."	*telha*	[tɐ̃ʎɐ]	"tile"
senha	[sɐ̃ɲɐ]	"ticket"	*Tejo*	[tɐ̃ʒu]	"Tejo"

With the exception of the standard dialect, centralization of the coronal mid-vowels in the central-southern dialects of EP does not occur in the speech of older speakers.[6] Instead, centralization and epenthesis is typical for the speech of the younger generations, as a consequence of education and linguistic standardization. A systematic sociolinguistic study remains to be done. The central-southern dialects diverge furthermore from the standard due to a process of coronal glide deletion in words such as *leite* [léti] "milk," *leiteiro* [letéɾu] "milkman," but not in *areia* [ɐɾéjɐ] "sand," *bebeis* [bibéjʃ] "drink" 2p pl. or *lei* [léj] "law." The words in which the glide is preserved show no centralization, that is, they surface as [ej] in these dialects. So, at least in the speech of the elderly, /e/ and / ɛ/ are systematically realized as [e] and [ɛ] in stressed syllables (*velho* [véʎu] "old," *anel* [ɐnéɫ] "ring").

Although centralization of coronal mid-vowels is common in the standard dialect, there also are exceptions, such as the word *Beja* (toponym) which is pronounced as [bέʒɐ] or [béʒɐ]. The process of glide insertion that creates the phonetic diphthong [ɐj] in the words of (2) in standard EP and the northern dialects is variable. Some dialects of the northern areas allow this insertion also before sonorants *telha* [tɐ̃(j)ʎɐ] "tile," *senha* [sɐ̃(j)ɲɐ] "ticket," unlike the standard language.

According to Barros (1994), glide insertion in Lisbon occurs in syllables with /e/ and /ɛ/ before both tauto- and hetero-syllabic palatal consonants. On the other hand, branching /eI/[7] nuclei may lose the glide not only before hetero-syllabic /ɾ/ *cadeira* [kɐdéɾɐ] "chair," where it is most frequent, but also before /ʒ/: *beijo* [béʒu] "kiss," showing that the rule is targeting new contexts. The variants which preserve the glide are prestige variants, produced by highly-educated speakers, as shown by Barros (1994:180–184). The same type of variation described by Barros for Lisbon was later studied by Rodrigues (2003) for speakers of both Lisbon and Braga, the latter city belonging to the Northern dialect. The underlying diphthong /ɛI/ surfaces as [ɐj] or [ɛj] (*ideia* [idɐ̃j.ɐ]~[idɛj.ɐ] "idea"), with a small preference (60 percent) of the first variant over the second in Lisbon, while the diphthong /eI/ is almost systematic (90 percent) in the two cities (*beijo* [béʒu]~[béʒu] "kiss"). Non-branching /ɛ/ is always pronounced as [ɛ] by Braga speakers in all contexts, but it is diphthongized by Lisbon speakers, particularly before syllable-initial /ʃ/ or /ʒ/ (*inveja* [ĩvɐ̃ʒɐ]~[ĩvɛ̃ʒɐ]~[ĩvéjʒɐ] "envy"). Nevertheless, [ɛ] prevails over the centralized variants in Lisbon. Upper mid /e/ exhibits more contextual variation: in both cities, [e] is preferred before the coda coronal fricative, with [ɐ] being used elsewhere. The coronal fricative in the prefixes *extra-*, *ex-* as well as in words like *texto* "text," *sexto* "sixth" may undergo centralization and epenthesis, different from similar words like *cesto* [séʃtu] "basket" which do not undergo either of these processes.

Unlike EP, BP does not show noticeable variation in the quality of stressed vowels. BP realizes the stressed vowel system in Table 28.1, illustrated by the examples in (3), without any important dialectal or sociolinguistic variation.

(3)

mapa	['mapa]	"map"
tipo	['tʃipu]	"type"
tudo	['tudu]	"everything"
mesa	['meza]	"table"
tela	['tɛla]	"screen"
moço	['mosu]	"boy"
bola	['bɔla]	"ball"

2.2. *Unstressed vowels in EP*

2.2.1. *Unstressed vowel neutralization*

Except for the high vowels /i/ and /u/, unstressed vowels are raised in all the dialects of EP. For the coronal vowels, the aperture distinctions are neutralized word-initially so that [i] is the only representative of this vowel class in this position. In all other unstressed contexts, coronal mid-vowels are not only raised but also centralized as [i]. The low vowel /a/ surfaces as upper mid [ɐ]. In the standard dialect, unstressed labial mid-vowels /o/ and /ɔ/ either remain unchanged word-initially or their aperture contrast is neutralized by the lowering of /o/, as in *ocasião* [ɔkɐzjɐ̃w] "occasion," especially for young speakers. Apart from this tendency, which is typical for standard EP, the central-southern dialects generally preserve the phonological contrast between the three unstressed labio-dorsal vowels word-initially. On the other hand, in some of the northern dialects neutralization may also affect this vowel class, which is consequently only represented by the high vowel [u]: *ocasião* [ukɐzjɐ̃w] "occasion." This word-initial neutralization of labial vowels was observed for the Braga region by Rodrigues (2003), who found this variant typically in the speech of middle-aged male speakers with a low education level. Except word-initially, the aperture distinctions among labial vowels are neutralized by raising to [u] in all other unstressed positions in all regional variants of EP.

2.2.2. *Unstressed vowel reduction/deletion*

Neutralized unstressed vowels [i ɐ u] may either be produced as such, they can be devoiced, or deleted, depending on linguistic and non-linguistic factors, such as vowel class, syllable structure, dialect, speech style, or social profile of the speaker, with the exception of [ɐ] which can only be devoiced, not deleted. Examples are provided in (4).

(4) Devoicing and deletion in EP

feito	[fɐ̃jtu]	[fɐ̃jtu̥]	[fɐ̃jt]	"done"
leite	[lɐ̃jti]	[lɐ̃jti̥]	[lɐ̃jt]	"milk"
laca	[lákɐ]	[lákɐ̥]		"hair spray"

Devoicing and deletion can be viewed as weakening (or reduction) processes. These rules apply in all syllable types and in all positions within the word, with varying frequency (devoicing is more common word-finally).

Lexical unstressed /i/ and /u/ are produced as [i] and [u] in EP, with the exception of word-final unstressed /i/, which is realized as [i]. The deletion rates for lexical high vowels tends to be lower than those derived from underlying mid-vowels.

In the following paragraphs, we discuss the variable deletion of coronal and labial vowels. We will not discuss devoicing any further, since there is no in-depth analysis available of this process in EP.

The deletion of unstressed coronal vowels

There are very few variation studies dealing with variable unstressed vowel deletion in EP. Our account of the facts is therefore limited by the scarcity of available reports. Rodrigues (2003) analyzes and compares two speech samples, one from the standard Lisbon dialect and the other one from the Braga city dialect, which belongs to the northern dialect region.

As observed above, in word-internal and word-final unstressed syllables, /e/ and /ɛ/ neutralize to [ɨ], a high, unrounded, back vowel.[8] Word-final unstressed /i/ is also centralized to [ɨ]. The probability of deletion of all instances of [ɨ] is related to the structure of the syllable, such that deletion affects vowels in open syllables more often than in closed syllables (Rodrigues, 2003). The frequency of deletion depends moreover on the underlying vowel quality. The [ɨ] sound representing underlying /e/ is deleted more often than all the others.

A word must be said about word-initial clusters such as exemplified in (5). Unlike in the Lisbon dialect, in the northern dialects these words start with an initial [i] (Rodrigues (2003: 209). We analyze [i] in these dialects as the result of an insertion rule, whereas in the Lisbon dialects the same words begin with an empty nucleus.

(5)

	Lisbon	Braga	
escola	[ʃkɔ́lɐ]	[iʃkɔ́lɐ]	"school'
estreito	[ʃtréjtu]	[iʃtréjtu]	"narrow"
esguio	[ʒgíw]	[iʒgíju]	slender"
esboço	[ʒbósu]	[iʒbósu]	"sketch"

Deletion of unstressed labial vowels

While one would expect that all the underlying labial vowels /u, o, ɔ/, once they are raised to [u], act as a single class with regard to the deletion process, this expectation is not borne out by the facts, with the exception of the northern dialects, where some speakers delete [u] uniformly, independently of their lexical source.

Word-initially, unstressed lexical /u/ is invariably produced as [u] (*usura* [uzúɾɐ] "usury") in all dialects. Initial /o/ is normally produced as [o], although, as discussed above, it is also realized as [ɔ] in some dialects, including the standard Lisbon dialect. In a comparative study of the speech of 20- to 24-year-old university students in the cities of Lisbon and Oporto, Mascarenhas (1996) observed for both cities that young speakers prefer [ɔ] to [o]. Initial /ɔ/ is always produced as [ɔ]. Rodrigues (2003) further noticed that both unstressed /o/ and the diphthong /oU/ are pronounced alike in word-initial position by Lisbon speakers, who produce the sounds variably as [o] or [ɔ] (*ovinho* [ovíɲu]/[ɔvíɲu] "little egg," *ouvir* [ovíɾ]/[ɔvíɾ] "listen"), depending on age, education profile, and geographical origin of the speakers. Thus, the deletion of labial unstressed vowels is blocked in word-initial position.

Word-internally, the contrast between /u/, /o/ and /ɔ/ is neutralized to [u], where it is subject to deletion, irrespective of its lexical origin, although its underlying quality influences the frequency of deletion. Rodrigues (2003) observed that the deletion of [u] from /u/ is less common than the deletion of [u] from /o/ and /ɔ/, and that the latter is deleted more often in Lisbon (14.9 percent) than in Braga (12.2 percent). Moreover, deletion is conditioned by syllable structure in both cities. It is more common in CV syllables (20 percent in Lisbon, against 14 percent in Braga), than in CCV- or CVC-syllables (less than 5 percent in both cities). The sociolinguistic profile of speakers is also a factor contributing to the variation. Young Lisbon speakers with a low education level delete more often than their peers with higher education levels (35 percent vs. 21 percent). Also, men delete more than women (35 percent vs. 26 percent). For Braga speakers, deletion is correlated with education and age (higher values were found in younger speakers with higher education), while gender plays no role. From these data, Rodrigues concluded that, since female speakers of the standard dialect delete less than men, the deletion rate is not correlated with prestige. As a consequence, deletion spreads faster among the younger speakers of Braga than among the older ones, with no clear difference between men and women.

The vowels /o/ and /ɔ/, neutralized as [u], often undergo deletion word-internally. Unstressed vowel deletion is not only constrained by phonological contexts, part of it is conditioned by socio-linguistic factors. Lisbon young male speakers more frequently delete [u] from unstressed /o/ and /ɔ/ in word-internal CV syllables than female speakers do (28.7 percent, against 22.4 percent, respectively). Results from the city of Braga (14.4 percent in male speakers and 15.4 percent in female speakers) show that the deletion process is spreading faster among young speakers than among speakers of the older generation (18.3 percent vs. 9.3 percent). The situation is identical in Lisbon (36.9 percent vs. 21 percent), even though deletion does not seem to be a highly valued feature. In fact, young males lead the change in Lisbon over young females.

Word-final unstressed /o/, which is regularly raised to [u], often suffers deletion (*pato* [pátu]/[pát] "duck"). Rodrigues (2003: 138–153) found that deletion affects 53.3 percent of the words ending in unstressed /o/ in Lisbon, while 42.3 percent of these vowels are deleted in Braga. The variability of deletion is co-conditioned by the phonological properties of the following context. It is common before a pause (36.8 percent in Lisbon and 26.8 percent in Braga), more frequent before consonants (65.1 percent in Lisbon and 55 percent in Braga) and most frequent before vowels (81.2 percent in Lisbon and 81.1 percent in Braga). The deletion rate is also conditioned by non-linguistic parameters like age, with deletion being more frequent among young speakers than in speakers over 40 years old. In the Lisbon dialect, deletion is frequent among speakers of all ages, while in the Braga dialect it is relatively rare in the speech of the elderly (15 percent).

In final unstressed CVC-syllables, normally /CoS/,[9] the [u] (from underlying /o/) deletes more often when the coda-fricative is voiced as opposed to voiceless (71.3 vs. 54.4 percent in Lisbon and 53.7 vs. 39.7 percent in Braga). The rate of deletion of unstressed /o/ in final syllables with /oS/ is higher in Lisbon than in Braga (62.1 percent vs. 46.1 percent). This deletion occurs with varying frequency in examples such as: *comemos uma* [kumémzúmɐ] "we eat one," *perfeitos* [pirfɐ̃jtʃ] "perfect-pl"

2.3. *Unstressed vowels in BP: pretonic mid-vowels*

Pretonic mid-vowels have roused the interest of many scholars in Brazil, who have produced conjointly a detailed picture of their use in many regions of the Brazilian territory. In Nascentes' (1922) view, the quality of the pretonic mid-vowels divides Brazil in two parts: the northern dialects are claimed to prefer the lower mid-vowels while the upper mid-vowels are typical of the southern dialects.[10] Indeed, the preference for one or the other of the unstressed five-vowel systems /i, {e, ɛ}, a, {o, ɔ}, u/ changes from one region to the other, as is well-demonstrated in studies of such authors as Bisol (1981), for the State of Rio Grande do Sul; Maia (1986), for the State of Rio Grande do Norte; Silva (1989), for the State of Bahia; Viegas (2001) for the State of Minas Gerais; Pereira (1997), for the State of Paraíba; Callou, Leite and Coutinho (2001), for the State of Rio de Janeiro; Silva (2009) for the State of Piauí. As it appears, the dialectal split based on the unstressed vowel systems is not as clear-cut as Nascentes asserts in his early publication.

A team of scholars, collaborators in the *Atlas Linguístico do Brasil* (*Linguistic Atlas of Brazil*),[11] have described the distribution of coronal mid-vowels in pretonic position as displayed in Figure 28.2, showing a concentration of upper-mid qualities in the south and the southeast

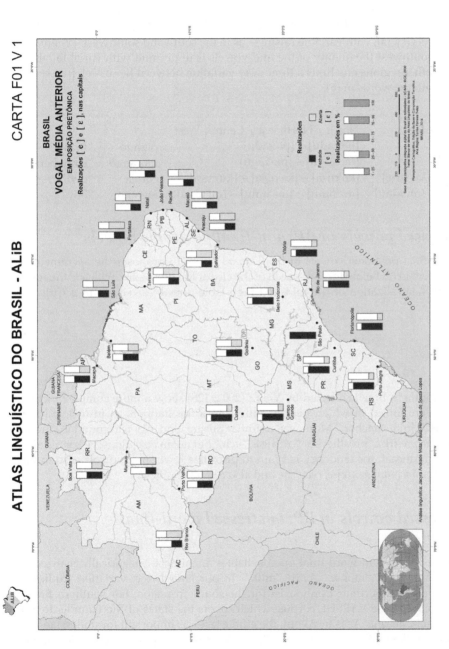

Figure 28.2 Distribution of coronal mid-vowels in pretonic position. Abbreviations in the map refer to the names of states, as follows: In the Northern Region: AC = Acre, RO = Rondônia, AM = Amazonas, RR = Roraima, AP = Amapá, PA = Pará, TO = Tocantins; In the Northeastern Region: MA = Maranhão, PI = Piauí, CE = Ceará, RN = Rio Grande do Norte; PB = Paraíba, PE = Pernambuco, AL = Alagoas, SE = Sergipe, BA = Bahia; In the Southeastern Region: ES = Espírito Santo, MG = Minas Gerais, RJ = Rio de Janeiro, SP = São Paulo; In the Mid-Western Region: GO = Goiás, MT = Mato Grosso, MS = Mato Grosso do Sul; In the Southern Region: PR = Paraná, SC = Santa Catarina, RS = Rio Grande do Sul.

as well as in the central-west. In the northeast, the lower mid quality [ɛ] is clearly predominant, more so than in the north.

Studies on the same topic have found that the pretonic vowel systems are distributed geographically as follows: (a) the south and southeast show a remarkable predominance of upper mid-vowels [e], [o], which are subject to a variable rule of raising to [i], [u], respectively; (b) the northeast, central-west and north regions, witness a clear predominance of the lower mid-vowels [ɛ], [ɔ], with variable raising—as in the south and southwest. Whereas in the south and southwest the quality of the mid-vowels is upper-mid with variable raising to high, in the other regions one finds a three-way variation between [i ~ e ~ ɛ], [u ~ o ~ ɔ], as illustrated with the words in (6).

(6)

South / Southeast	North / Northeast / Central-West		
[pe'zadu]	[pe'zadu] ~ [pɛ'zadu]	pesado	"heavy"
[mo'rãgu]	[mo'rãgu] ~ [mɔ'rãgu]	morango	"strawberry"
[ko'ruʒa] ~ [ku'ruʒɐ]	[ko'ruʒa] ~ [kɔ'ruʒa] ~ [ku'ruʒa]	coruja	"owl"
[me'ninu] ~ [mi'ninu]	[me'ninu] ~ [mɛ'ninu] ~ [mi'ninu]	menino	"boy"

2.4. *Unstressed vowels in BP: non-final posttonic vowels*

As for the non-final posttonic vowels in BP, Câmara Jr. (1970) proposes the asymmetrical four-vowel system in (7) below for the speech of the city of Rio de Janeiro, which is the result of a process of neutralization of the mid and high labio-dorsal vowels, as in *pér*[u]*la* for *pér*[o]*la* "pearl."

(7) High   /i/   /u/
    Mid   /e/   /../
    Low   /a/

Data from southern Brazil collected by Vieira (2002: 128) show a more complex picture. Many words were found in which neutralization does not happen, as in *(de) cóc*[o]*ras* "squatting" or *ânc*[o]*ra* "anchor." Moreover, a similar raising tendency was found in coronal mid-vowels, as in *prót*[i]*se* "prosthesis," "*cóc*[i]*gas* "itch," but not in *vésp*[e]*ra* "eve" or *cát*[e]*dra* "chair." In the northeast, the tendency is again to prioritize lower mid-vowels, also in this context: *cóc*[ɔ]*ras*, *ânc*[ɔ]*ra*, *prót*[ɛ]*se*, *cóc*[ɛ]*ga*, and also *vésp*[ɛ]*ra*, *cát*[ɛ]*dra*.

2.5. *Unstressed vowels in BP: unstressed word-final open syllables*

In BP, unstressed vowels in word-final open syllables are almost categorically realized as high vowels, as in *rat*[u] "mouse," *leit*[i] "milk." To our knowledge, variation studies of unstressed vowels in this context only exist for the southern region. For southern Brazil, Vieira (1994) analyzed the VARSUL corpus, which covers the states of Rio Grande do Sul, Paraná, and Santa Catarina. As is turns out, the ethnic factor is important for understanding the distribution of the mid-vowels [e, o] vs. the high vowels [i, e] in the different communities of the southern states.

As is obvious from the results shown in Table 28.2, the variation in the application of word-final vowel raising varies greatly within each state. In RS, the application of the rule is most productive in the state capital of Porto Alegre (0.99) and least productive in Flores da Cunha (0.22), a city colonized by Italians (0.22). For the state of Paraná, the city of Blumenau

Table 28.2 Geographical distribution of the quality of word-final unstressed vowels in southern Brazil.

State	Factor	High vowels / total	Percent	Relative weight
Rio Grande do Sul (RS)	Porto Alegre	48/59	81	0.99
	Parnambi	10/43	23	0.29
	São Borja	33/82	40	.044
	Flores da Cunha	21/115	18	0.22
Santa Catarina (SC)	Florianópolis	35/61	57	0.66
	Blumenau	48/77	62	0.72
	Chapecó	27/107	25	0.25
	Lages	11/44	23	0.29
Paraná (PR)	Curitiba	37/100	37	0.45
	Pato Branco	40/57	70	0.81
	Irati	16/76	21	0.25
	Londrina	25/56	45	0.48

Input: 0.34; Significance: 0.00
Vieira 1994: 153.

(0.72), with a high population of German immigrants, has the highest application index for the raising rule, followed by the state capital of Florianópolis (0.66). In Paraná, raising is most frequent in Pato Branco (0.81), least frequent in Irati. The results for the state capital of Curitiba together with Londrina are close to the neutral application point.

Considering the fact that elsewhere in Brazil the absence of mid-vowels in unstressed word-final open syllables is almost categorical, we may conjecture that the variability found in the southern states is due to the predominant presence in this part of Brazil of Italian, Spanish, and German immigrants.

3. Consonant Variation

3.1. *Onset consonants in EP*

The system of consonantal phonemes, as provided in Table 28.3, is identical for EP and BP.[12]

The subareas within the northern dialects of EP show different subsets of fricative phonemes in the syllable onset. Dialectologists agree on the existence of two main areas marked by the use of different fricatives in this position.

(i) Trás-os-Montes and Alto Minho preserve both /s, z/ (for instance: *cedo* "early," *praça* "square" / *zarpar* "set off") and /ş, ʐ/ (*sol* "sun," *passo* "step," *caso* "case").
(ii) Baixo-Minho, Douro and Beiras only have /ş, ʐ/ for all the words exemplified in (i).

The dialect of Trás-os-Montes and Alto Minho also preserves the ancient contrast between the fricative /ʃ/ and the palatal affricate / t͡ʃ/, which got lost in standard EP (*chapéu* [ʃɐpέw] "hat" and *xarope* [ʃɐɾɔpɨ] "syrup"). This contrast corresponds, in this geographical area, with the different spellings <ch> and <x> (*chapéu* [t͡ʃɐpέw] "hat" vs. *xarope* [ʃɐɾɔpɨ] "syrup").

All the northern dialects are known to preserve the non-strident labial fricative /β/, instead of the strident /v/, which is a stereotype feature of this linguistic area. In these dialects, speakers use [β] or [b] (more or less interchangeably, depending on dialects and

Table 28.3   Consonantal phonemes of EP and BP.

	Labial	Coronal		Dorsal
		+ anterior	− anterior	
Stops	p b	t d		k g
Fricatives	f v	s z	ʃ ʒ	
Rhotics		ɾ		
Laterals		l	ʎ	
Nasals	m	n	ɲ	

contexts) among peers and some percentage of [v], when they interact with speakers from other geographical origins.

The variation described in (i) and (ii) above has not been studied yet from a sociolinguistic perspective. Rodrigues (2003) found a categorical use of /v/ in standard EP and observed the reported variation associated with /β/ in the northern dialect of Braga. /β/ was produced by native Braga speakers in semi-spontaneous conversation (involving also a speaker of the central-southern dialect) as: [v] (66.3percent), [β] (32.4 percent) or [b] (1.3 percent). The [b] allophone emerges utterance-initially. The use of [v] depends on the social profile of the speakers (education and age) and the speech style. The [v] variant is increasingly used by speakers with an academic degree, particularly the younger ones in formal reading-aloud tasks, which were part of the sociolinguistic interview applied.

3.2. *Coronal onset stops in BP*

Through the influence of the high vowel [i] or the glide [y], the coronal stops /t, d/ are affricated in BP, becoming [tʃ] and [dʒ]. The affrication rule is productive in most parts of Brazil and has been studied by several researchers.[13] Examples are given in (8).

(8) Lexical high vowels   Derived high vowels
   /di/tado ~ [dʒi]tado   "saying"   po/te/ > po[ti] ~po[tʃi]   "pot"
   re/ti/ro ~ re[tʃi]ro   "retreat"   d/eʃ/tino > [diʃ]tino ~ [dʒiʃ]tino   "destiny"
   po/ti/ ~ po[tʃi]   "shrimp"

Bisol (1985) studied the affrication of coronal stops in the speech of "four cohorts of socio-culturally different individuals, representative of the Portuguese variety spoken in Rio Grande do Sul." The sample comprised 15 monolingual speakers from Porto Alegre, 15 speakers from the frontier area, 15 bilingual subjects of German descent and 15 speakers from Italian descent. All of them had received elementary school education only. A control sample consisted of 15 speakers from Porto Alegre, with a university degree.

The study found a number of linguistic factors that favor or disfavor the affrication process. A coronal fricative preceding or following the coronal stop appears to disfavor affrication: *in*[sti]*tuto* ~ *in*[stʃi]*tuto* "institute," *pare*[dis] ~ *pare*[dʒis] "walls." Affrication is also sensitive to stress. The process occurs more easily in stressed vowels, less frequently in pretonic syllables, and least in posttonic syllables: *an*['tʃi]*go* "ancient," [dʒi]'*lema* "dilemma" and '*vin*[tʃi] "twenty." The prefixes *de-*, *des-* and *dis-* resist affrication, unlike the clitics *de* "of" and *te* "you," which undergo the rule. Bisol observed a relation between the frequency of mid-vowel raising, especially /e/ > [i] and the rate of affrication. Especially the members of the German cohort were found not to apply /e/-raising[14] and consequently applied affrication in the context of underlying /i/ only. On the other hand, the descendants of Italian immigrants not only resisted against vowel raising but failed to apply affrication also in the context of lexical /i/.

Another study on the variable application of affrication was conducted by Hora (1990) in the community of Alagoinhas in the state of Bahia. The linguistic variables that were controlled were identical to the ones studied by Bisol (1985) and showed a similar favoring or disfavoring impact on the productivity of the rule. The number of non-linguistic parameters in Hora's study was different: social class, gender, age, and style. Hora found that the use of affrication is most frequent in the speech of the upper and middle classes, especially in the 15-47 year age range, regardless of gender, as well as in the more formal styles, as in reading. He also concludes that affrication is a marker of prestige, since it is more used in formal styles and by speakers with greater purchasing power and a higher level of education.

Both studies characterize affrication as a variable process, of which the variability is influenced by linguistic and non-linguistic factors.

There is another affrication process that targets the coronal stops, which does not occur in the south but is common in the northeast. This affrication results from progressive assimilation in a sequence [jt/dV], exemplified in (9), where V is not a high coronal vowel.

(9) ['ojtu] ~ ['otʃu]   "eight"
    ['ʒejtu] ~ ['ʒetʃu]   "way"
    [lej'tura] ~ [le'tʃurɐ] "reading"
    ['dojda] ~ ['dodʒa]   "crazy"
    ['gɔʃtu] ~ ['gɔʃtʃu]   "like-1sg pres. ind."

In this process, the trigger for affrication of /t, d/ is not a following high vowel, which in fact prevents the process from applying, as in *noite* 'night', obligatorily pronounced as ['nojti]. As the examples in (9) show, the process is triggered by a preceding coronal glide. Affrication moreover occurs after a (obligatory palatal) fricative in the coda preceding the coronal stop, as in *go[ʃt]o* "taste," optionally pronounced as *go[ʃtʃ]o*. In general, in the communities of northeastern Brazil where progressive palatalization cum affrication is productive, the plain and affricated pronunciations of coronal stops coexist.

3.3. Coda Consonants in EP

3.3.1. The lateral /l/

In EP, /l/ is velarized in all contexts, although velarization is stronger syllable-finally (Andrade, 1998, 1999; Marques, 2010). Usually, the onset lateral is represented as [l], the strongly velarized lateral as [ɫ]. The syllable affiliation of [ɫ] is controversial. It is syllabified by some scholars as a coda segment (Mateus and Andrade, 2000; Rodrigues, 2003), by others as part of the nucleus (Freitas, 1997; Gonzalez, 2008). The former group of authors assumes that the consonantal nature of the lateral is sufficient reason to justify its affiliation with the coda in EP. On the other hand, Freitas (1997) argues on the basis of language acquisition data that the lateral is syllabified in the nucleus, which would explain why it is acquired earlier than the other coda consonants. Most scholars, ourselves included, describe the lateral sonorant in EP as a coronal coda consonant with a secondary dorsal articulation, in contrast with BP, where it is produced as a glide and therefore associated with the syllable nucleus.

3.3.2. The rhotic /ɾ/

In the coda, /ɾ/ (> [ɾ]) contrasts with the consonants /l/ and /S/. In EP, word-final codas may variably delete. Postlexical restructuring as a syllable onset saves word-final /ɾ/ from deletion in connected speech as in the example sentences in (10). Conversely, the presence of a following consonant favors /ɾ/ deletion.

(10)   /ɾ/ in coda

Vou ler o livro.	[vólɛɾulívɾu]	"I"m going to read the book."
A flor é amarela.	[ɐflóɾɛɐmɐɾɛlɐ]	"The flower is yellow."
Vou comer fruta.	[vókuméfɾútɐ]	"I"m going to eat fruit."
Eu tenho medo do mar.	[éwtɐ̃ɲumédumáɾi]	"I"m afraid of the sea."
Ele não quer falar.	[élinɐ̃ẃkɛɾfɐláɾ]	"He doesn"t want to talk."

In the last two examples in (10), [ɾ] is located at the end of an intonational phrase, where it is usually maintained, either as such, or followed by an epenthetic [i]. The insertion of [i] in this context is used as a strategy to preserve word-final /ɾ/ and to signal the intonational boundary, which is particularly noticeable in turn-taking situations. Southern dialects within the Alentejo region may insert either [i] or [ɨ] in this context, while the standard dialect and northern dialects only insert [i].

In Rodrigues' (2003) study of the Lisbon and Braga varieties, deletion of [ɾ] is close to 30 percent, varying more in function of the phonological context than for regional or sociocultural reasons. As mentioned, the presence of a consonant following /ɾ/ favors deletion (58 percent before sonorants and 55 percent before non-sonorants in Lisbon; 53 percent before sonorants and 59 percent before non-sonorants in Braga). Only 10–15 percent of /ɾ/ deletion is registered utterance-finally and before a vowel. The frequency of [i] insertion after /ɾ/ in Braga is higher than in Lisbon (11.1 percent in Lisbon, against 30.2 percent in Braga).

Mateus and Rodrigues (2003) compared data from interactions in TV and radio interviews for Lisbon and Braga speakers. The data show that in both cities speakers have a slight preference for deletion in verbs over deletion in non-verbs, although this difference may also be a consequence of prosodic factors (namely phrasing and intonation). These authors also observe that speakers delete more often in radio interactions than in television programs.

3.3.3. *The fricative /S/*

The fricative consonant /S/ is produced as [ʃ] or [ʒ] in the syllable coda, depending on the voice specification of the following consonant within the prosodic word, as exemplified in (11) below. When /S/ is resyllabified with a following vowel as a syllable onset, it surfaces as alveolar and voiced [z].

(11)   /S/ in EP

Festa	[féʃtɐ]	"party"	
As festas	[féʃtɐʃ]	"the parties"	
Asno	[áʒnu]	"donkey"	
Os dias	[uʒdíɐʃ]	"the days"	
Os amigos	[uzɐmíguʃ]	"the friends"	
Desunir	[dizunír]	"separate"	(/deS+uniɾ/)

Word-final /S/ before a pause signaling a prosodic boundary surfaces as [ʃ]. Its place of articulation is consequently always predictably palatal in coda position. However, derived sequences of coda–/S/+coronal fricative may have separate articulations in careful speech in the standard dialect, whereas in more rapid speech the sequences are realized as a single consonant, either alveolar or palatal, as in the examples in (11) below. The palatal variant emerges often in southern dialects and also in some dialects of the northern area, especially among the young speakers. Older speakers of the northern dialects realize mainly the (onset) right fricative [s] or [z] from underlying sequences /S.s/ and /S.z/, showing a preference for coda deletion, even though some speakers produce the palatal articulation typical of the coda position.

(12) /S/ + fricatives

descida	[diʃsídɐ]~[diʃídɐ]~[disídɐ]	"downhill"
deszincar	[diʒzĩkáɾ]~[diʒĩkáɾ]~[dizĩkáɾ]	"unzinc"
disjunto	[diʒʒũtu]~[diʒũtu]	"disjunct"
fez sumo	[féʃsúmu]~[féʃúmu]	"made juice-3sg"
tens chaves	[tẽjʃʃáviʃ]~[tẽjʃáviʃ]	"you"ve got keys"
os zumbidos	[uʒzũbíduʃ]~[uʒũbíduʃ]	"the buzzes"

Young speakers of the southern dialects pronounce [ʒ], even when /S/ is re-syllabified in the onset before a vowel-initial word: *os amigos* [uʒɐmíguʃ] "the friends," *os olhos* [uʒɔ́ʎuʃ] "the eyes" (Rodrigues, 2012). In these productions, the underlying unspecified /S/ is spelled out as palatal in the coda and subsequently resyllabified in the onset. This phenomenon is spreading fast all over the country in informal speech styles, although it is still rare in the data gathered by Rodrigues (2003), representing less than 3 percent of the cases, both in Lisbon and Braga.

3.4. Coda Consonants in BP

The BP coda can only be filled by one of the consonants /l, R, S, N/, according to Camara Jr. (1970). Leaving aside the variation observed in the realization of underlying /N/,[15] their occurrence in word-internal and word-final positions is illustrated in (13).

(13)

/l/	/R/	/S/
Word-internal	Word-internal	Word-internal
fal.ta "lack"	*car.ta* "card"	*pas.ta* "pasta"
Word-final	Word-final	Word-final
jor.nal "newspaper"	*tu.mor* "tumor"	*mas* "but"

3.4.1. The rhotic /R/

The coda rhotic in BP is phonetically represented by a wide range of sounds, as illustrated in (14). The variants [r], [ɾ], [ɽ], [w], [j] are relatively infrequent throughout Brazil. In final position, the glottal fricative is the most productive of all. When word-final /R/ moves from the coda to the onset in connected speech, as in *mar abaixo* > *ma.ra.bai.xo* "sea below," it is pronounced as a tap [maraˈbajʃu].

(14) phonetic variation in the realization of the syllable-final rhotic

[r]	Word-internal	ca[r].ta	ga[r].fo	Word-final	ma[r]	can.ta[r]
[ɾ]	---	ca[ɾ].ta	ga[ɾ].fo	---	ma[ɾ]	can.ta[ɾ]
[x]	---	ca[x].ta	ga[x].fo	---	ma[x]	can.ta[x]
[ɽ]	---	ca[ɽ].ta	ga[ɽ].fo	---	ma[ɽ]	canta[ɽ]
[h]	---	ca[h].ta	ga[h]fo	---	ma[h]	can.ta[h]
[ø]	---	*ca[ø].ta	ga[ø].fo	---	ma[ø]	can.ta[ø]
[j]/[w]	---	ca[j].ta	ga[w].fo	---	*ma[j/w]	*canta[j/w]
		"card"	"fork"		"sea"	"sing"

In the speech of João Pessoa, the state capital of Paraíba, as well as in other cities of the northeast, the zero [ø] realization of /R/ only occurs before a fricative consonant, alternating with the glottal fricative [h] elsewhere in the syllable coda.

(15)

força	[ˈfosa]	"strength"
várzea	[ˈvazɛa]	"lowland"
garfo	[ˈgafu]	"fork"
cerveja	[seˈveʒa]	"beer"
marcha	[ˈmaʃa]	"march"
gorjeta	[goˈʒeta]	"tip"

In her study of the allophones of the rhotic consonant in the state of Rio Grande do Sul, Monaretto (1992) found that the [ø] variant is more frequent in verbs than in nouns. This difference was not encountered in the speech of João Pessoa and Rio de Janeiro (see Votre (1978), Callou, Moraes, and Leite (1994)).

Figure 28.3 provides an overview of the distribution of four frequent allophones of /R/, in the word-final coda of infinitives for the state capitals of Brazil. As is partially shown on the map, a relatively productive allophone of /R/ is the retroflex [ɻ], although it is geographically limited to the interior of the states of São Paulo, Paraná, and Mato Grosso do Sul, and to the southern part of the states of Goiás, Mato Grosso, and Minas Gerais (Aguilera 2011: 125). In this broad region, the retroflex variant is realized both word-internally and word-finally.

3.4.2. The lateral /l/

In BP, the most frequent variants of the lateral consonant in the coda position are [w], [ɫ] and [ø]. Other possibilities exist. In popular speech, for example, it is not unusual for [ɫ] to alternate with a glottal fricative derived from /R/, as in fa[w]ta ~ fa[h]ta (< /farta/). Here we will concentrate on the variants [w], [ɫ], [ø], exemplified in (16), which are the most recurrent variants of /R/ found in Brazil.

(16)

Word-internal coda			Word-final coda		
[w]	[ɫ]	[ø]	[w]	[ɫ]	[ø]
de[w].ta	de[ɫ]ta	*de[ø]ta	pape[w]	pape[ɫ]	pape[ø]
delta "delta"			*papel* "paper"		
fo[w]ga	fo[ɫ]ga	fo[ø]ga	so[w]	so[ɫ]	so[ø]
folga "rest"			*sol* "sun"		
cu[w]pa	cu[ɫ]pa	cu[ø]pa	azu[w]	azu[ɫ]	azu[ø]
culpa "guilt"			*azul* "blue"		

The glide [w] is the most frequent variant of the lateral consonant in Brazil, both word-internally and word-finally. It is found all over the Brazilian territory without any clear sociocultural bias. Word-internally, when following a labiodorsal vowel, especially when high, the vocalization of the lateral takes place more easily than after other vowels. The emerging sequence of labiodorsal vocoids is often simplified by the deletion of the glide. Deletion of the glide never happens after a non-labial vowel

Studies conducted in the southern region show a relatively high incidence of the velarized alveolar [ɫ], mainly in the interior of the state of Rio Grande do Sul, where its use is strongly correlated with age, with a higher incidence in the speech of older speakers (Quednau, 1993; Tasca, 1999; Espiga, 2001). In a study conducted by Hora (2006) in the city of João Pessoa, this variant is poorly represented. When it occurs, it is again found most often in the speech of the elderly.

In the dialect of João Pessoa, the word-final deletion of the lateral is favored by a number of factors, linguistic and non-linguistic. Its frequent deletion is typical of speakers with a low school education. Furthermore, similar to what happens after /u/ word-internally, the deletion of /l/ is nearly categorical after /u/ word-finally, as in the word *azul* "bleu," among

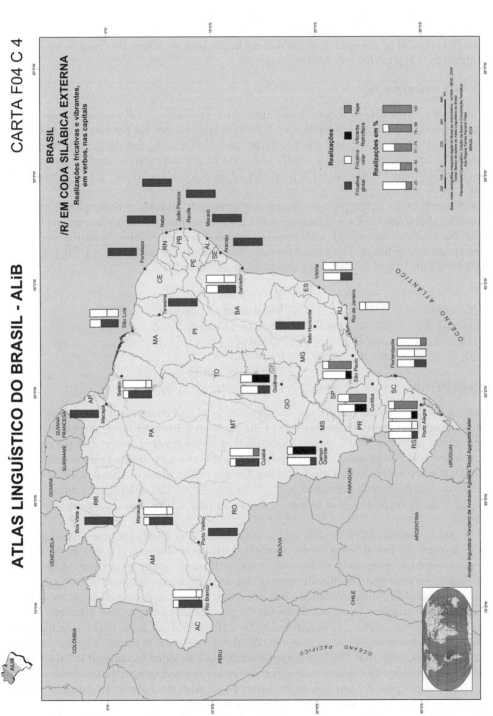

Figure 28.3 Distribution of the allophones of the rhotic consonant verb-finally in the state capitals of Brazil.

all speakers (Hora, 2006). The surveys conducted in the state of Rio Grande do Sul found no sign of deletion of the lateral in any position (Quednau, 1993, Tasca, 1999, Espiga, 2001).

From the available surveys of the variable realization of the lateral consonant in Brazil we conclude that the vocalized form is the most productive in all parts of the country. The variant [ɫ] is typical of the speech of the elderly in the regions where it occurs, whereas the [ø] realization is typical for low education classes.

3.4.3. The fricative /S/

Syllable-final s/z must have acquired its palatal pronunciation in EP around the sixteenth century, as was first suggested by Verney (1746). Palatalization did not become general in the northern dialects of EP, and neither in BP and Galician. In the dialects of Northern Portugal the apico-alveolar pronunciation of coda [s,z] predominates and in the speech varieties of Northeast Portugal, [s] is pronounced as apico-alveolar and [z] as a predorsal dental.

In most parts of Brazil, the pronunciation is predominantly alveolar, with the palatal pronunciation being characteristic of some varieties, such as the city dialects of Rio de Janeiro and Belém.

Like the rhotics, the voiced and voiceless coronal fricatives have been the object of numerous studies in Brazil. Their most frequent realizations are [s], [ʃ], [z], [ʒ], [h], [ø]. Their word-internal and word-final distributions are presented in (17):

(17)

Variants			Word-internal position
[s] ~ [ʃ]	*casca*	"peel"	[ˈkasca] ~ [ˈkaʃkɐ]
[z] ~ [ʒ] ~ [h]	*desde*	"since"	[ˈdezdʒi] ~ [ˈdeʒdʒi] ~ [ˈdehdʒi]
[ø]	*mesmo*	"same"	[ˈmeømu]
			Word-final position
[s] ~ [ʃ] ~ [h]	*lapis*	"pencil"	[ˈlapis] ~ [ˈlapiʃ] ~ [ˈlapiø]

Among the six variants considered, the alveolar [s,z] and palatal [ʃ,ʒ] ones are the most frequent word-internal realizations of /S/. The study of Callou, Moraes, and Leite (1994), based on data from the NURC project,[16] shows that alveolars are preferred in the cities of Porto Alegre, São Paulo, and Salvador, whereas in the cities of Rio de Janeiro and Recife the palatals are preferred. In a study on the speech of the State of Paraíba, Hora (2003) observes that, although the alveolar realization represents the default for coronal fricatives, the palatal variants occur before /t,d/, as in *leste* le[ʃ]te "east" and *desde* de[ʒ]de "since."

In his study conducted in the city of Rio de Janeiro, Guy (1981) proposes two separate rules to account for the absence of the word-final fricative: one rule is active in the plural noun phrase, which operates in such a way that not all words are necessarily marked by the plural suffix. For example, the pluralization of the noun phrase *a casa grande* "the big house" may contain different plural markings, such as *as casas grandes, as casas grande, as casa grande*, with the definite article *as* being marked with the plural suffix categorically. Another rule is phonological, which deletes /S/ word-finally, be it the plural suffix, as in *casas*, or the final segment of a lexical morpheme, as in *menos*. Word-final deletion is sensitive to the position of the main stress, such that /S/ is more resistant against deletion in stressed syllables than in unstressed syllables. For example, /S/ is more easily deleted in words like *ônibus ~ ônibu* "bus," *lápis ~ lápi* "pencil," but less so in *ra'paz* "boy," with final stress. Deletion of /S/ is moreover less frequent in female speech than in male speech.

Word-finally, the voiceless alveolar variants [s, ʃ] are always preferred. Here also, the preference for the alveolar or palatal articulations shows the same geographical distribution as the one observed word-internally. The complete deletion of the word-final fricative is

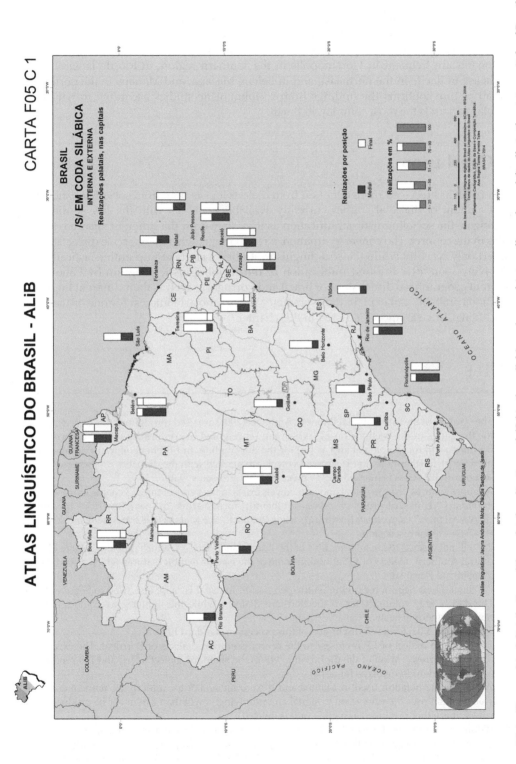

Figure 28.4 Geographical distribution of the palatal realizations of /S/ in the syllable coda word-internally and word-finally in the state capitals of Brazil.

relatively frequent, both in words representing lexical morphemes, as in *menos* "minus" or when the fricative functions as the exponence of plurality, as in *casa+s*, "house-pl."

The global dialectal distribution of the palatal variants is shown in Figure 28.4. Palatal consonants are frequent in Florianópolis in the southern region, in Rio de Janeiro in the southeast, in Recife in the northeast, and in Belém, Macapá, and Manaus in the north. The overall picture confirms the findings from sociolinguistic studies according to which the alveolar variant is the most common in Brazil.

4. Conclusion

Modern EP has received more attention from dialectologists than from sociolinguistics. The great amount of dialectal studies currently available contrasts with the few studies that investigate the sociolinguistic stratification as it exists within the different speech communities in the country. The converse situation exists in Brazil, where large-scale dialect studies started only recently while the sociolinguistic studies were taken up enthusiastically and massively soon after the first publication of the sociolinguistic program by Labov. The different geographical dimensions of Brazil and Portugal as well as their different linguistic traditions probably can explain the asymmetry in the scholarly interest for one or the other type of linguistic variation discussed in this chapter.

NOTES

1   The symbols of the International Phonetic Alphabet (2005) are used throughout this chapter, except for the glides in the sections on EP, which are represented in conformity with the Portuguese tradition as [j] for the palatal and as [w] for the dorsal glide. In BP phonetic transcriptions, [r] is used for [ɾ]. Furthermore, in EP, stressed vowels are marked with the diacritic " ´ " , whereas in the sections on BP, stress is marked as " ' " preceding the stressed syllable.

2   A similar contrast between nasal and oral vowels exists in the verbs of the 2/3 conjugations: *bebemos* [bibému∫] "drink-2pl pres." *vs. bebemos* [bibému∫] form "drink-2pl past," *partimos* [pɐrtímu∫] "leave-2pl pres." vs. *partimos* [pɐrtĩmu∫] "leave-2pl past." See Mateus (1982: 165–166) and Andrade (1977: 60–76) for discussion.

3   We will not discuss the insular regions of the Azores and Madeira, which globally behave like the central-southern dialects of EP, although some of the islands exhibit features which are unknown in mainland Portugal.

4   We thank Luísa Segura for giving us the permission to use this map, also used in Segura (2013). The darker gray colours refer to the northern dialects, while the lighter gray colours indicate central-southern dialects.

5   See Vigário (2003) for a full discussion of this process in standard EP.

6   The standard dialect of EP is closest to the central-southern dialects of Portugal. The exceptions concern the preservation of the diphthong /eI/ in the standard dialect as [ɐj] and the production of the coronal mid-vowels as [ɐ] or [ɐj].

7   We follow the notation used in Mateus and d'Andrade (2000) for underlying branching nuclei. This notation uses the uppercase to signal an underlying vowel than can never be produced as a vowel (it is either produced as a glide or it is deleted).

8   Within the central-southern dialects, speakers of the Lisbon dialect may raise the upper mid-vowel /e/ to [i] word-initially, without dorsalization: *elevador* [ilivɐdór] "lift," *ermida* [irmídɐ] "hermit-age." The raising of word-initial unstressed /e/ to [i] in Lisbon is probably an innovation, as one concludes from Mascarenhas (1996), who pointed out that among Lisbon speakers there was still variation between [e] and [i] at the end of the twentieth century.

9   /S/ is the coda-fricative of Portuguese. We assume that this consonant is unspecified both for voice and place of articulation. In EP, this consonant has the variants [ʃ] and [ʒ] in the syllable coda and [z] or [ʒ] when it is resyllabified as an onset, as we will discuss below.

10 Antenor Nascentes futher divides the dialect of the north into two areas, 1. the Amazonian region (*amazônico*), comprising the states of Acre, Amazonas, Pará and part of Goiás and 2. the northeastern region (*nordestino*), which comprises the states of Maranhão, Piauí, Ceará, Rio Grande do Norte, Paraíba, Pernambuco and part of Goiás. The southern dialect is subdivided into four regions: 1. The Bahia region (*baiano*), including the states of Sergipe, Bahia, part of Minas Gerais, and part of Goiás; 2. the Rio de Janeiro region (*fluminense*), comprising the states of Espírito Santo, Rio de Janeiro, Distrito Federal and part of Minas Gerais; 3. The region of Minas Gerais (*mineiro*), comprising the central, western and some of the eastern regions of Minas Gerais; 4. The southern region (*sulista*), comprising the States of São Paulo, Paraná, Santa Catarina, Rio Grande do Sul, the southern part of Minas Gerais plus the region known as the "Triângulo Mineiro," the south of Goiás, and Mato Grosso.

11 All the BP dialect maps used in this chapter are taken from Cardoso et al. (2014).

12 Some disagreement exists regarding the lexical definition of the rhotic in BP and about the interpretation of [gw]/[kw] (*água* "water," *quando* "when") as a sequence of phonemes /ku, gu/ or as a single phoneme /kʷ, gʷ/. For discussion, see Chapter 4, A Comparative Study of the Sounds of European and Brazilian Portuguese: Phonemes and Allophones.

13 Lopez (1979) analyzed the dialect of the city of Rio de Janeiro, Bisol (1985) worked with speech data collected in different communities in the state of Rio Grande do Sul (RS). Other studies in RS were carried out more recently (Almeida, 2000; Dutra, 2007; Battisti et al. 2007). Hora (1990) analyzed palatalization in the community of Alagoinhas (state of Bahia). Macedo (2004) studied several communities in the city of Rio de Janeiro, and Pagotto (2004) surveyed some communities in Florianópolis (state of Santa Catarina).

14 Observe that the unproductivity of unstressed word-final vowel raising observed by Bisol in the speech of speakers of German descent living in the state of RS contrasts with the findings of Vieira in the city of Blumenau discussed earlier (see Table 28.2 and related discussion).

15 See Chapter 4, A Comparative Study of the Sounds of European and Brazilian Portuguese: Phonemes and Allophones, and Chapter 6, The Syllable, for extensive discussion of the variation in the realization of the nasal mora.

16 The abbreviation NURC stands for the (*Projeto de Estudo da*) *Norma Linguística Urbana Culta*, literally "Cultured Linguistic Urban Norm." This sociolinguistic project, which was started in 1969, was carried out by research groups form the public universities in the cities of São Paulo, Rio de Janeiro, Porto Alegre, Salvador, and Recife.

REFERENCES

Aguilera, V. A. (2011). Dois momentos do /r/ retroflexo em Lavras MG: no Atlas linguístico de Minas Gerais e nos dados do projeto do Atlas linguístico do Brasil. *Diadorim*, 8, pp. 125–142.

Andrade, E. (1977). *Aspects de la Phonologie (Générative) du Portugais*. Lisbon: INIC.

Andrade, A. (1998). Variação fonética de /l/ em ataque silábico em Português europeu. In *Actas do XIII Encontro Nacional da Associação Portuguesa de Linguística, October, 1997*. Lisbon: Associação Portuguesa de Linguística, pp. 55–76.

Andrade, A. (1999). On /l/ velarization in European Portuguese. In J. Ohala, Y. Hasegawa, M. Ohala, D. Granville, and

A. Bailey (eds.), *Proceedings of the 14th International Congress of Phonetic Sciences*, San Francisco, 1999, pp. 543–546.

AVOC – Acoustic Atlas of Portuguese Stressed Vowels. http://www.clul.ul.pt/en/research-teams/538-avoc-acoustic-atlas-of-portuguese-stressed-vowels, accessed November 9, 2015.

Barros, R. (1994). *Contributo para uma análise sociolinguística do português de Lisboa: variantes de /e/ e /ɛ/ em contexto pre-palatal*. MA thesis, University of Lisbon.

Battisti, E., A. A. Dornelles Filho, J. I. P. Lucas, and N. M. P. Bovo (2007). Palatalização das oclusivas alveolares e a rede social dos informantes. *ReVEL*, 5 (9), pp. 1–29.

Bisol, L. (1981). *Harmonização vocálica: uma regra variável.* Ph.D. dissertation, Federal University of Rio de Janeiro.

Bisol, L. (1985). *A palatalização e sua restrição variável.* Unpublished research report, Universidade Federal do Rio Grande do Sul.

Brescancini, C. R. (2002). *A fricativa palatoalveolar e sua complexidade: uma regra variável.* Ph.D. dissertation, Pontifícia Universidade Católica do Rio Grande do Sul.

Brissos, F. (2012). *Linguagem do Sueste da Beira no Tempo e no Espaço.* Lisbon: Centro de Linguística da Universidade de Lisboa.

Brissos, F. (2014a). New insights into Portuguese central-southern dialects: understanding their present and past forms through acoustic data from stressed vowels. *Journal of Portuguese Linguistics,* 13 (1), pp. 63–115.

Brissos, F. (2014b). A vogal *u,* os dialectos do Centro-Sul português e a dialectologia acústica. In *Textos Selecionados, XXIX Encontro Nacional da Associação Portuguesa de Linguística.* Porto: Associação Portuguesa de Linguística, pp. 85–102.

Brissos, F. and J. Saramago (2014). O problema da diversidade dialectal do Centro-Sul português: informação perceptiva *versus* informação acústica. *Estudos de Linguística Galega,* 6, pp. 53–80. http://www.usc.es/revistas/index.php/elg, accessed November 9, 2015.

Brissos, F. and C. Rodrigues (forthcoming). Vocalismo acentuado do Noroeste português – descrição acústica, variação dialectal e representação fonológica. *Revue Romane.*

Camara Jr., J. M. (1970). *Estrutura da Língua Portuguesa.* Petrópolis: Vozes.

Callou, D., J. Moraes, and Y. Leite (1994). *A variação de /s,r/ em posição final de sílaba e os dialetos brasileiros.* Manuscript.

Callou, D., Y. Leite, and L. Coutinho (2001). Elevação e abaixamento das vogais pretônicas no dialeto do Rio de Janeiro. *Organon,* 5, pp. 71–78.

Cardoso, S. A. M., J. A. Mota, V. de A. Aguilera, M. do S. Silva de Aragão, A. N. Isquerdo, A. Razky, F. W. Margotti, and C. V. Altenhofen (2014). *Atlas Linguístico do Brasil.* Londrina: Editora da Universidade Estadual de Londrina.

Cintra, L. F. L. (1971). Nova proposta de classificação dos dialectos galego-portugueses, *Boletim de Filologia,* XXII, pp. 81–116.

Dutra, E. de O. (2007). A palatização das oclusivas dentais /t/ e /d/ no município de Chuí, Rio Grande do Sul. Masters dissertation, Pontifícia Universidade Católica do Rio Grande do Sul.

Espiga, J. (2001). O Português dos Campos Neutrais. Um estudo sociolingüístico da lateral pósvocálica nos dialetos fronteiriços de Chuí e Santa Vitória do Palmar. Ph.D. dissertation, Pontifícia Universidade Católica do Rio Grande do Sul.

Freitas, M. J. (1997). *Aquisição da Estrutura Silábica do Português Europeu.* Ph.D. dissertation, University of Lisbon.

Gonzalez, M. (2008). *Português Europeu e Galego: Estudo Fonético e Fonológico das Consoantes em Rima Medial.* MA thesis, University of Lisbon.

Guy, G. R. (1981). *Linguistic variation in Brazilian Portuguese: aspects of the phonology, syntax, and language history.* Ph.D. dissertation, University of Pennsylvania.

Hora, D. da (1990). *A palatalização das oclusivas coronais: variação e representação nao-linear.* Ph.D. dissertation, Pontifícia Universidade Católica do Rio Grande do Sul.

Hora, D. da (2003). Reanálise da consoante em final de palavra: coda ou ataque de núcleo vazio? In C. Roncarati and J. Abraçado (eds.), *Português Brasileiro II: Contato Lingüístico, Heterogeneidade e História.* Rio de Janeiro: EDUFF, pp. 79–92.

Hora, D. da (2006). Vocalização da lateral /l/: correlação entre restrições sociais e estruturais. *Scripta,* 9, pp. 31–46.

International Phonetic Alphabet. (2005). International Phonetic Association. http://internationalphoneticassociation.org/, accessed November 9, 2015.

Labov, W. (1966). *The Social Stratification of English in New York City.* Washington, DC: Center for Applied Linguistics.

Labov, W. (1972). *Sociolinguistic Patterns.* Philadelphia, PA: University of Pennsylvania Press.

Lopez, B. S. (1979). *The sound pattern of Brazilian Portuguese.* Ph.D. dissertation, University of California.

Maia, V. L. M. (1986). Vogais pretônicas médias na fala de Natal. *Estudos Linguísticos e Literários,* 5, pp. 35–47.

Macedo, A. V. T. de (2004). Linguagem e contexto. In M. C. Mollica and M. L. Braga (eds.), *Introdução à Sociolingüística: O Tratamento da Variação,* 2nd edn. São Paulo: Contexto, pp. 59–66.

Marques, I. (2010). *Variação Fonética da Lateral Alveolar no Português Europeu.* Masters dissertation, University of Aveiro.

Mattos e Silva, R. V. (1996). Sobre desencontros e reencontros: Filologia e Lingüística no Brasil no século XX. In *XI Encontro Nacional da ANPOLL*, pp. 32–45.

Mascarenhas, I. (1996). *Estudo da Variação dialectal entre Lisboa e Porto das vogais átonas [−rec] e [+arr] em contexto inicial*. MA thesis, University of Lisbon.

Mateus, M. H. (1982). *Aspectos da Fonologia Portuguesa*. Textos de Linguística 6. Lisbon: INIC.

Mateus, M. H. and E. Andrade (2000). *The Phonology of Portuguese*. Oxford: Oxford University Press.

Mateus, M.H. and Rodrigues, C. (2003). A vibrante em coda no Português Europeu. In D. Hora and G. Collischonn (eds.), *Teoria Linguistica Fonologia e outros Temas*. Editora Universitária da Universidade Federal da Paraíba, João Pessoa, pp. 181–199.

Monaretto, Va de O. (1992). *A vibrante: representação e análise sociolingüística*. MA thesis, Pontifícia Universidade Católica do Rio Grande do Sul.

Nascentes, A. (1953 [1922]). *O Linguajar Carioca*. Rio de Janeiro: Organizações Simões.

Pereira, R. C. M. (1997). *As vogais médias pretônicas na fala dos pessoenses urbanos*. MA thesis, Universidade Federal da Paraíba.

Pagotto, E. G. (2004). *Variação e Identidade*. Maceió: EDUFAL.

Quednau, L. (1993). *A lateral pós-vocálica no português gaúcho: análise variacionista e representação nao-linerar*. MA thesis, Pontifícia Universidade Católica do Rio Grande do Sul.

Rodrigues, C. (2003). *Lisboa e Braga: Fonologia e Variação*. Ph.D. dissertation, University of Lisbon.

Rodrigues, C. (2012). Todas as codas São Frágeis em Português Europeu? *LinguíStica*, 8 (1), pp. 211–227.

Segura, L. (2013). Variedades dialetais do Português Europeu. In E. Raposo, M. F. B. do Nascimento, M. A. C. da Mota, L. Seguro, and A. Mendes (eds.), *Gramática do Português*, vol. I. Lisbon: Fundação Calouste Gulbenkian, pp. 85–122.

Silva, A. do N. (2009). As pretônicas no falar teresinense. Ph.D. dissertation, Pontifícia Universidade Católica do Rio Grande do Sul.

Silva, M. B. da (1989). *As pretônicas no falar baiano*. Ph.D. dissertation, Federal University of Rio de Janeiro.

Tasca, M. (1999). *A lateral em coda silábica no sul do Brasil*. Ph.D. dissertation, Pontifícia Universidade Católica do Rio Grande do Sul.

Veloso, J. (2012). Vogais centrais do português europeu contemporâneo: uma proposta de análise à luz da fonologia dos elementos. *Letras de Hoje*, 47 (3), pp. 234–243.

Viegas, M. do C. (2001). *O alçamento de vogais e itens lexicais*. Ph.D. dissertation, Universidade Federal de Minas Gerais.

Vieira, M. J. B. (2002). As vogais médias postônicas: uma análise varicionista. In L. Bisol and C. Brescancini (eds.), *Fonologia e Variação: Recortes do Português Brasileiro*. Porto Alegre: EDIPUCRS, pp. 127–160.

Vigário, M. (2003). *The Prosodic Word in European Portuguese*. Interface Explorations Series, 6. Berlin: de Gruyter.

Votre, S. J. (1978). *Variação fonológica no Rio de Janeiro*. Ph.D. dissertation, Pontifícia Universidade Católica do Rio de Janeiro.

Weinreich, U., W. Labov, and M. Herzog (1968). Empirical foundations for a theory of language change. In W. Lehmann and Y. Malkiel (eds.), *Directions for Historical Linguistics*. Austin: University of Texas.

Wetzels, W. L. (2011). The representation of vowel height and vowel height neutralization in Brazilian Portuguese. In E. Hume, J. Goldsmith, and W. L. Wetzels (eds.), *Tones and Features*. Berlin: de Gruyter, pp. 331–359.

29 Main Current Processes of Morphosyntactic Variation

MARIA MARTA PEREIRA SCHERRE AND MARIA EUGÊNIA LAMMOGLIA DUARTE

1. Introduction

Morphosyntactic variation has been a central issue in the research carried out in Brazil ever since Anthony J. Naro introduced Variationist Sociolinguistics in the early 1970s. The results from such studies have brought solid empirical foundations to build a reliable description of the grammar of Brazilian Portuguese (BP) and to understand variation and change in progress. In Portugal, the focus of interest has been in Historical Linguistics, in Dialectology and in formal descriptions of contemporary grammar. Only around the turn of the twentieth century, with the development of cooperation projects carried out by Brazilian and Portuguese linguists, did sociolinguistic research entered the agenda of linguistic studies of variation in European Portuguese (EP). Nevertheless, it is possible to explore advances in variationist studies here and there. This chapter explores two main issues: variable concord (VC) and variation in the pronominal systems in BP and EP.

In Section 2 we will concentrate our description on Subject–Verb Concord (SVC), which raises interesting comparisons. Noun Phrase Concord (NPC), involving gender and number agreement between a noun and its modifiers, is practically invariant in EP. Thus, this phenomenon will be only briefly illustrated in Section 2 and resumed in our final remarks in order to point out some common features this process shares with variation in SVC. We will approach SVC from the social and structural dimensions, considering 3rd person and 1st person plural concord. As for this last case, variation arises because 1st person plural can be expressed by the pronoun *nós* (we) and by the new pronoun *a gente*, derived from a collective NP (literally meaning "the people") and fully grammaticalized in BP.

Section 3 is dedicated to the pronominal system and will focus on variation related to variable use of 2nd person singular and 1st person plural nominative pronouns and to overt or null pronominal subjects in each variety. Variation associated with pronominal clitic complements and competing strategies will also be addressed. Unlike what we see for variable concord, variation in the pronominal system is not subject to stigma and, except for 2nd person reference, which is geographically constrained, age has been the most important social factor group in a number of studies. This section stresses its relevance associated with structural factors in the processes analyzed.

The Handbook of Portuguese Linguistics, First Edition. Edited by W. Leo Wetzels, João Costa, and Sergio Menuzzi.
© 2016 John Wiley & Sons, Inc. Published 2020 by John Wiley & Sons, Inc.

2. Variable concord in Portuguese

2.1. Preliminaries

Variable Concord (VC) in Portuguese is a remarkable phenomenon, particularly in Brazil. It has been historically analyzed as a consequence of a process of creolization, resulting from contact of languages during colonization. The hypothesis persists in a relativized view, according to which it is a result of irregular transmission during the acquisition of Portuguese as second language (Lucchesi, Baxter, and Ribeiro 2009). Equally challenging is the fact that VC presents ordered heterogeneity, revealed by the social and structural constraints that govern it. This has led Naro and Scherre (2000, 2007) to emphasize the existence of a *confluence* of motivations for variation in BP, including contact, but without linguistic rupture in its *origin*.

Seminal sociolinguistics studies carried out since the early 1970s observed the fundamental constraints on VC (Lemle and Naro 1977; Naro 1981; Naro, Görski and Fernandes 1999), which remained prominent in subsequent literature (Naro and Scherre 2000; Scherre et al. 2014; Scherre and Naro 2014). From 2000 on, especially for SVC, the studies advanced with comparative analyses based on samples from BP, EP and African Portuguese (AP) (Monguilhott 2009; Monte 2012; Rubio 2012; Vieira and Bazenga 2013; Barreto 2014).

Examples of variable 3rd person SVC in BP are in (1): in (1a) we see that both standard (*merecem*) and non-standard concord (*ganharu* instead of standard *ganharam*) are used side by side; and in (1b) we see no concord (non-standard)—the default 3rd person singular verb form with a plural postverbal subject.

(1) SVC—3rd person plural:
   a. *Elas ganharu e elas merecem isso*
      they won.3ppl and they deserve.3ppl it
      "They won it and deserve it"
   b. *Ganhou essas duas meninas aí.*
      won3.psg these two girls there
      "These two girls won it"

In (2) and (3), we show standard vs. non-standard SVC with 1st person plural pronoun *nós* ("we") and with gramatically 3rd person singular *a gente* ("we," literally "the people"), respectively; in (4) we illustrate variable NPC.

(2) SVC—1st person plural *nós*:
   a. *Nós   conversamos   muito*   [standard]
      we.1ppl talk.1ppl.pres a lot
      "we talk a lot"
   b. *Nós   conversa   muito*   [non-standard]
      we.1p.pl talk.1psg.pres a lot
      "we talk a lot"

(3) SVC—1st person plural "*a gente*":
   a. *A gente   fez   bolo*   [standard]
      we.1psg made.3psg cake
      "we made cake"
   b. *A gente   fizemos   bolo*   [non-standard]
      we.1psg made.1ppl cake
      "we made cake"

(4) NPC:
   a. *As   boas   ações*   [standard]
      the.pl. good.pl actions.pl
      "The good actions"
   b. *As   porta   aberta*   [non-standard]
      the.pl doors.sg open.sg
      "The open doors"

Even though SVC variation with 3rd person is more frequent in BP than in EP, both varieties present similar patterns, amplified or intensified in contexts of social rupture (Naro and Scherre 2007). NPC and SVC with the pronoun *nós* are categorical under the standard form in EP (Brandão and Vieira 2012), but variable in BP. However, SVC with the new pronoun *a gente* shows more variation in EP than in BP. The social constraints on variable SVC include the role of years of schooling, age and gender. Among the linguistic constraints, we emphasize the relative position and animacy of the subject, besides verbal tense.

2.2. Social dimensions of variation in Brazil and Portugal

2.2.1. SVC concord with 3rd person plural

Brazil has continental dimensions, with more than 200 million inhabitants, and still has strong social contrasts. This led Bortoni-Ricardo (1998) to stress the importance of analyzing variation in BP along three different continua: literacy, the rural–urban parameter, and style or speech monitoring. One could then hypothesize a direct correlation between [–literacy], [–urban], [–monitoring] and fewer use of standard Overt Concord (OC), on the one hand; and [+literacy], [+urban], [+monitoring] and more OC, on the other hand. However, VC in BP is more complex than that.

Naro (1981), the first to use variationist sociolinguistics in the early 1970s, showed that 17 semi-illiterate speakers presented rates of overt SVC ranging from 23.8 percent through 80.5 percent. He argued that this result was better understood in the light of an alternative social variable—contact with TV. He proposed a variable he called *cultural orientation*, which might be "vicarious" or "experiential," according to the kind of TV program watched. Vicarious orientation, associated with soap opera watching, favors standard OC. Brazilian soap operas convey predominantly cultural and economic concerns of the higher classes, and the speech of their characters contains a high frequency of OC, an overt symbol of prestige.

However, the effect of years of schooling is unquestionable and it is increasing in urban areas. In a trend study based on two random samples of the community of Rio de Janeiro (sociolinguistic interviews recorded in 1980 and 2000), Scherre and Naro (2014) found an increase in the rates of OC (from 73 percent through 83 percent) and also a robust increase in the effect of schooling. This is indicated in Table 29.1 by the ranges, which go from 12 through 56.[1] Thus, the effect of schooling expands and appears as a watershed in VC in Brazil, especially in the more monitored styles captured by sociolinguistic interviews.[2] In fact, the number of years of schooling has a regular effect in other urban areas of Brazil (Table 29.1). The range is broader (76) when the sample includes illiterate speakers, as is the case of Monte's analysis for an small town in the State of São Paulo. Vieira and Bazenga (2013: 25) show similar results for two neighborhoods in Rio de Janeiro.

Brandão and Vieira (2012) and Vieira and Bazenga (2013) discuss the status of VC in recent samples of BP, EP and AP, adopting Labov's typology of linguistic rules according to frequency: a rule is "categorical" if it applies in 100 percent of the cases; it is a "semi-categorical" if it applies from 95 percent to 99 percent of the cases; and it is a "variable rule" if it applies from 5 percent to 95 percent of the cases. As shown in Tables 29.1 and 29.2, only speakers

Table 29.1   Subject–Verb Concord of 3rd person according to years of schooling in BP: samples of Rio de Janeiro (RJ) and São Paulo (SP).

Samples	*Scherre and Naro (2014: 336; 341)*				*Rubio (2012: 347)*		*Monte (2012: 135)*	
	Rio de Janeiro-RJ 1980		*Rio de Janeiro-RJ 2000*		*São José do Rio Preto-SP*		*São Carlos-SP*	
Years of schooling	*RW*	*%*	*RW*	*%*	*RW*	*%*	*RW*	*%*
Illiterate	–	–	–	–	–	–	.15	19%
1–4	.43	63%	.26	78%	.22	52%	.35	40%
5–8	.55	78%	.50	85%	.41	66%	.91	85%
9–11	.54	82%	.82	95%	.52	77%	–	–
>11	–	–	–	–	.71	88%	–	–
Range	12		56		57		76	
% Overall		73%		83%		73%		48%
N	4660		2069		2699		1422	

Table 29.2   Subject–Verb Concord of 3rd person according to years of schooling in BP, AP and EP: samples of 2010 Luso-Brazilian Project.

Samples	*Vieira and Bazenga (2013: 25)*				*Barreto (2014: 93)*	
	BP: Copacabana Rio de Janeiro—Brazil		*AP: São Tomé São Tome e Príncipe—Central Africa*		*EP: Funchal Island of Madeira—Portugal*	
Years of schooling	*RW*	*%*	*RW*	*%*	*RW*	*%*
5–8	.17	73%	.14	83%	.16	90%
9–11	.41	89%	.49	93%	.47	96%
>11	.79	98%	.81	98%	.73	96%
Range	62		67		57	
% Overall		88%		92%		91%
N	1395		737		1226	

with 9–11 years or more of schooling from Rio de Janeiro 2000/2010, from São Tomé (Africa), and from Funchal (non-continental EP) exhibit a semi-categorical rule or are close to this.

In contrast, recent data for Continental EP show (close-to) semi-categorical OC for all groups. Vieira and Bazenga (2013: 12), analyzing two comparable neighborhoods in the capital of Portugal, Lisbon, found high frequencies of OC, ranging from 95 percent through 99.1 percent; Monte (2012) shows that even illiterate speakers from Évora exhibit 91.2 percent of OC. Illiterate Brazilians from cities in the State of São Paulo located far from the capital show only 19 percent of overt SVC.

Thus, percentages of overt SVC in EP can be much higher than those found for BP; still, according to the Labovian typology, it can be characterized as a variable rule. And, indeed, it does show schooling effects, as revealed by Monguilhott (2009). She has analyzed four

Table 29.3   Subject–Verb Concord of 3rd person according to years of schooling and age: samples from of Lisbon, Portugal and Florianópolis, Brazil (Monguilhot 2009: 132, 156).

Samples		Florianópolis-BP		Lisbon-EP	
Years of schooling	Age	RW	%	RW	%
5–8	15–36	.32	72%	.30	89%
5–8	48–74	.28	67%	.49	90%
>11	22–33	.74	89%	.61	94%
>11	45–76	.52	88%	.59	92%
Range		46		31	
% Overall			80%		91%
N		794		807	

localities in Lisbon and four localities in Florianópolis, the capital of Santa Catarina, South of Brazil, considering two school levels and two age groups (Table 29.3). Schooling is, again, significant for BP; moreover, it shows a stronger effect in Continental EP: all groups analyzed present a variable rule for 3rd person SVC, and RWs for speakers with 5–8 years of schooling disfavor OC when compared to those with more than 11 years of schooling.

It must also be noticed that the younger group with higher school levels favors OC in BP. This is in accordance with Naro and Scherre's (2013) results that show an increase in OC among younger speakers in the PEUL 2000 sample, and supports Naro's (1981) speculation of a possible reversal in the direction towards the elimination of agreement marks. This also provides an additional evidence for the model of flows and counterflows sketched by Naro and Scherre (2013) for variable number concord in Brazil. The model claims that conflicting trends should be natural in stigmatized linguistic phenomena strongly embedded in the language.

2.2.2. SVC concord with nós and a gente

As we have seen in Section 2.2.1, there is evidence for an increase in SVC concord with 3rd person plural according to schooling and age, with younger speakers leading concord in the 2000 sample for Rio de Janeiro. However, Mattos (2013) notices opposite effect of age group for SVC with 1st person plural pronoun *nós* "we" (examples (2a, b)) in the speech of Goiás, center-west of Brazil, with data from speakers with over nine years of schooling: younger speakers show lower rates of OC with *nós* "we," although lack of OC with *nós* usually receives strong stigma in urban areas. Mattos interprets this as an index of local identity, because of the increasing prestige associated to rural areas in the center-west of Brazil. Still another picture emerges from Rubio's (2012) analysis of data from speakers with 1 to 12 years of schooling in inner São Paulo: the pattern is curvilinear for age groups, suggesting stable variation in which intermediate age groups, usually inserted in the labor market, change their linguistic performance. We can see these conflicting trends again in the light of the model of flows and counterflows, though both studies of variable concord with *nós* also relate more OC to higher school level, reflecting the prestige associated to standard OC in Portuguese.

In EP, SVC with *nós* is not variable. However, SVC with the 3rd person singular *a gente* (lit. "the people," but meaning "we") is more variable in EP than in BP (Table 29.4). As in (3a), the 3rd person singular verb form with *a gente* indicates standard concord; as in (3b), the 1st person plural form indicates lack of grammatical concord, a non-standard, strongly

Table 29.4 Subject–Verb Concord with *a gente* according social constraints: samples from BP (ALIP) and EP (CRPC) (Rubio 2012: 301, 302, 305).

Samples	São José do Rio Preto, São Paulo-BP		EP	
Constraints	RW	%	RW	%
Age				
16–25	.61	96%	.35	58%
26–35	.30	90%	.55	77%
36–55	.49	94%	.58	77%
>55	.60	96%	.70	97%
Range	31		35	
Years of schooling				
1–4	94%	–	.39	69%
5–8	92%	–	.54	81%
9–11	96%	–	.66	85%
>11	95%	–	.70	95%
Range			31	
Gender				
Male	93%	–	.36	71%
Female	95%	–	.87	84%
Range			51	
% Overall	93%			76%
N	1602			200

stigmatized, construction in urban BP. Rubio's results in Table 29.4 reveal that concord reaches 93 percent in BP, and 76 percent in EP. In this case, BP exhibits more standard forms than EP.

Other results for BP confirm overall percentages in Table 29.4 (Naro, Görski, and Fernandes 1999, Mattos 2013). Otherwise, the 76 percent of concord shows that SVC with *a gente* is a variable rule in EP, and the RWs show strong social constraints: female and older speakers, as well as speakers with more years of schooling, favor standard concord. As for BP, the only factor statistically significant is age, with younger groups reversing the path and favoring standard concord. We speculate that non-standard concord in EP is related to the fact that lexical *a gente* has not been fully integrated into the pronominal system in EP, having an uncertain status, hence being more susceptible to semantic agreement with its plural meaning (cf. Section 3.1).

2.3. *Linguistic dimensions of variation in Brazil and Portugal*

2.3.1. *SVC with 3rd person plural*

SVC variation in BP and EP shows differences and similarities related not only to social but also to linguistic constraints. On the one hand, phonic salience in the opposition singular/plural of 3rd person verb forms seems to be remarkable only in BP (Naro 1981); on the other, verb transitivity constrains variable SVC only in EP (Monguilhot 2009; Monte 2012). These are interesting differences, requiring further research. Still, SVC variation in the two varieties does show similarities, such as with respect to subject position and animacy.

Table 29.5 shows that preverbal subjects tend to favor OC, whereas postverbal subjects tend to disfavor it. Barreto (2014) and Rubio (2012) found similar results for other Brazilian and European samples.

Table 29.6 shows that [+animate] subjects favor OC; [-animate] subjects disfavor it, in both varieties. There are further results pointing in the same direction.

The regularity of such linguistic effects resulting from different samples of Portuguese is really striking. They have also been attested in texts of Archaic Portuguese, and in data collected in Portuguese Dialectology (Naro and Scherre 2000; 2007). This indicates persistent constraints in the varieties analyzed, with very regular oppositions, signaling a deep linguistic embedding of Variable Concord in spite of undeniable differences. Preverbal subjects and [+animate] referents promote more overt plural marks because they are more salient in a broader sense. As Naro (1981: 97) claims, "salience is a general property of the linguistic system." (See also Labov 1994: 560–568.)

Table 29.5   SVC of 3rd person verb forms according to subject position in Brazilian and European Portuguese.

Samples	Scherre and Naro (2014) Personal archive				Monguilhott (2009: 146)		Monte (2012: 91)	
	1980-RJ-Brazil		2000-RJ-Brazil		Lisbon-Portugal		Évora-Portugal	
Position of subject	RW	%	RW	%	RW	%	RW	%
Preverbal	.54	78%	.52	85%	.56	92%	.58	95%
Postverbal	.09	26%	.17	53%	.18	59%	.24	77%
Range	45		34	34	38		34	
% Overall		75%		88%		88%		91%
N	3253		1436		453		914	

Table 29.6   SVC of 3rd person verb forms according subject animacity in Brazilian and European Portuguese.

Samples	Scherre and Naro (2014) Personal archive				Monguilhott (2009: 145)		Barreto (2014: 97)	
	1980-RJ		2000-RJ		Lisbon-Portugal		Funchal, Island of Madeira-Portugal	
Animacy of subject	RW	%	RW	%	RW	%	RW	%
+animate	.54	76%	.52	84%	.61	96%	.58	97%
−animate	.31	54%	.32	75%	.11	71%	.25	83%
Range	23		35		50		33	
% Overall		73%		83%		92%		95%
N	4660		2059		807		1226	

2.3.2. *SVC concord with* a gente *and* nós

Rubio's (2012) analysis reveals that one of the main structural variables in SVC with *a gente* in EP is the verb tense (in the indicative mood): preterite favors non-standard usage of overt 1st person inflection *–mos* with *a gente* (example (3b)). In BP, preterite is also decisive for the presence of the inflection *–mos*, in particular with the plural pronoun *nós*, the standard concord. Naro, Görski and Fernandes (1999), studying the speech of speakers with low level of schooling, found 97.6 percent of inflection *–mos* with *nós* in the preterite; but only 35.8 percent in the present. The authors suggest that, in some speech communities, *–mos* may tend to become a mark of preterit, and its absence a mark of the present.

Indeed, this is the pattern found in rural speech of Santa Leopoldina, State of Espírito Santo, Southeast of Brazil (Scherre *et al.* 2014): 99.4 percent of the preterite forms show *–mos* when preterite and present have the same form in the standard paradigm; but only 7 percent of the present forms show *–mos*. That is, in this variety the presence of *–mos* distinguishes preterite and present forms for verbs that, in standard language, have one and the same form for both tenses: *Nós* **conversamos** *muito* can mean either "we *talked* a lot" or "we *talk* a lot." In the relevant varieties, *Nós* **conversa** *muito* "we *talk*.∅ a lot" would oppose to *Nós* **conversamos** *muito* "we *talked*.1ppl a lot." Interestingly, the opposition is much weaker when the verb has different forms for preterite and present. In the same sample, 100 percent of preterite forms show *–mos* when there is no syncretism (as with irregular *ir* "to go": *Nós fomos* "we went.1ppl" vs. *nós vamos* "we go.1ppl"); and almost 70 percent of present forms also show *–mos*—that is, 30 percent show no concord—under the same circumstances. In these cases, there is no possibility of ambiguity. The main principle working here is the phonic salience of singular/plural opposition (Naro, Görski, and Fernandes 1999).

In Brazil, SVC with *nós* is deeply embedded in the linguistic system. Besides the resolution of paradigm ambiguities, one should consider the cognitive aspects underlying the effect of phonic salience. Moreover, we can also see effects of old structural diachronic tendencies. For example, the rare presence of *–mos* with imperfect forms may be a result of the tendency to avoid antepenultimate stress (*Nós conversava* "We used-to-talk.∅," as opposed to the standard *Nós conversávamos* "We used-to-talk.1ppl"), a major trend from Latin to Iberian Romance.

3. Variation related to the pronominal system

3.1. *Variation in subject forms in EP and BP*

In Table 29.7 we show the set of nominative pronouns in EP and BP. The 2nd person plural *vós* (in bold) is absent in spoken BP, and though it is rare in EP, it can still occur as a clitic, an oblique or a possessive form (*vos* "you," *convosco* "with you," *vosso* "yours") in combination with 2nd person plural *vocês*. As for the underlined forms, Raposo (2013: 897–900) suggests they do not belong to the canonical set of nominative pronouns in EP, because with these forms semantic person does not match grammatical person. That is, for Raposo only the pronouns that trigger their own person concord should be incorporated to the canonical set. In this view, *você(s)* and *a gente*, which combine with unmarked 3rd person verb form, deserve especial treatment. In this connection, it is important to recall these forms have a *nominal* origin, *você* deriving from the address form *Vossa Mercê* "your mercy," and *a gente* (literally "the people") being a grammaticalization of the corresponding collective NP (see Chapter 28, Main Morphosyntactic Changes and Gramaticalization Processes).

Indeed, *você* and *a gente* do not seem so fully grammaticalized in EP as they are in BP. In EP, *tu* and *você* are in complementary distribution: *tu* is a familiar form of address; *você*, usually null in the singular, indicates different degrees of social distance between interlocutors and

Table 29.7   Nominative Pronouns in EP and BP and the inflectional paradigm for the verb *estudar* ("to study") in the Indicative Present.

Person	Nominative pronouns	European Portuguese	Brazilian Portuguese
1ps	*eu*	*estud<u>o</u>*	*estud<u>o</u>*
1pp	*nós*	*estuda(<u>mos</u>)*	*estuda(<u>mos</u>)*
	<u>a gente</u>	*estuda(mos)*	*estuda(mos)*
2ps	*tu*	*estuda<u>s</u>*	*estuda(<u>s</u>)*
	<u>você</u>	*estuda*	*estuda*
2pp	**vós**	*estuda<u>is</u>*	....
	<u>vocês</u>	*estuda<u>m</u>*	*estuda(<u>m</u>)*
3ps	*ele, ela*	*estuda*	*estuda*
3pp	*eles, elas*	*estuda<u>m</u>*	*estuda(<u>m</u>)*

is in variation with proper names as well as with other forms of address that express higher degrees of courtesy, such as *o senhor* ("the lord"), as in (5).

(5) *A Maria/o senhor deseja mais alguma coisa?*
   the Mary/the lord wish.3ps anything else?
   "Do you (Mary)/you (Sir) wish anything else?"

In Brazil, *você* is in variation with *tu* in many regions, with the predominance of one or the other. A similar difference is true for the pronominal 1st person plural *a gente*, which is less frequent than the canonical pronoun *nós* in EP. A reflex of this slower implementation in the pronominal system is the persistence of its nominal use, as shown in (6):

(6) [$_{NP}$ *A gente que se encontra neste recinto*] *corre um grave perigo.* (Raposo 2013: 900)
   the people who is.3ps in this place runs.3ps a serious risk
   "[$_{NP}$ The people who are in this place] run a serious risk"

In BP, the noun *gente* "people" has very restricted use, appearing just in a few combinations with quantifiers (*muita/pouca gente* "a lot of/few people"). For (6), BP would resort to the plural noun *as pessoas* (literally "the persons"). This reinforces the conclusion that in BP *a gente* basically has lost its nominal use and is fully inserted in the pronominal system, as attested by its preference over *nós*, either with definite 1st person plural or generic interpretation, as will be shown.

As a consequence of these differences, BP does show fewer verb oppositions, that is, its verb paradigm is more reduced than the EP. This should be, at least in part, responsible for the tendency to use more overt nominative pronouns in BP. In the remaining parts of this section we will focus on some social and structural constraints related to the variable use of *tu/você, nós/a gente*, overt/null pronominal subjects, but we will also briefly comment on the variation related to clitic complements, comparing BP and EP whenever possible.

3.1.1. The alternation tu/você in BP

Contrary to what happens in EP (Section 3.1), where there is no competition between *tu/você* but complementary distribution determined by interactional relations, the variation between the two forms (including *você*'s reduced forms, *cê* and *ocê*) is remarkable in BP.

First, the alternation *tu/você* is a system of diatopic variation in BP. Scherre et al. (2015) reviewed a representative number of studies using different methods of data collecting, covering approximately 60 samples and 29,000 tokens. The analysis of these data indicates the existence of six sub-systems for 2nd person reference, characterized by the following factors: the possible presence of *tu*, the frequency of *tu*, the presence or absence of use of the canonical verb inflection –*s* and, finally, the average rate of OC with *tu*. The geographic distribution of these subsystems does not coincide with the current political division of the country in 26 states; rather, it may reflect different moments of colonization and different flows of immigration and migration.

Another remarkable feature of the system is non-overt OC, that is, the lack of the overt 2nd person singular canonical agreement mark –*s* has no significant stigma associated to it.

Moreover, as regards the pronominal system in BP, besides the variation *tu/você*, only the variable use of the reflexive clitic pronouns shows significant *geographic* influence. For all other phenomena to be presented in this section, the distribution of variants is very regular across the different regions in Brazil. And, differently from variable concord, the social restriction most frequently co-related to variation in the pronominal system, at least in the urban areas, is age group; the influence of years of schooling is rarer.

3.1.2. *The alternation* nós/a gente *in BP*

The process of replacement of *nós* by *a gente* in BP has been largely investigated in the past 25 years, since Omena's (1986) analysis of the speech of Rio de Janeiro using the PEUL Project 1980 sample (see note 2). Omena studied the variation in apparent time (i.e. across age groups) and the results suggested change in progress. A trend study, comparing the 1980 data with a new sample of the same community, confirmed this initial hypothesis, as shown in Table 29.8.

We can see that the two synchronies reveal the age pattern of variation and change in the community. First, the younger groups show higher rates of use of *a gente* than the older groups. Moreover, when we move from the 1980 sample to the 2000, we see a regular increase of use of the innovative pronoun for all age groups, the increase being again higher for younger groups. Since the process is already very advanced, the picture is consistent with an S-shaped curve, which predicts a reduction in the speed of a change process as it reaches completion.[3]

Vianna and Lopes (2015) present a thorough mapping of the phenomenon in Brazil, reviewing 22 studies carried out in 11 states of the Federation, including capitals and other cities, some considered important industrial areas whereas other are more isolated. All the studies confirm Omena's results, even though change seems to progress faster in capitals and larger cities. Age always shows statistical significance, suggesting generational change (Labov 1994: 83–84; 112). The fact that the use of *a gente* in speech is not subject to stigma may be responsible for its impressive spread in Brazil. The same does not happen in Portugal, as shown by Vianna and Lopes (2013, Table 29.9), based on recent comparable samples of EP and BP.

Table 29.8   Use of *a gente* (vs *nós*) according to age group: two samples of a community in Rio de Janeiro (Omena 2003: 66).

Samples	1980		2000	
Age group	*RW*	*%*	*RW*	*%*
7–14	.79	89%	.84	94%
15–25	.70	87%	.84	93%
26–49	.34	73%	.43	83%
>50	.20	58%	.22	65%
Range	59		62	
% Overall		77%		79%
N	1295		968	

Table 29.9   Use of *a gente* (vs *nós*): samples from Rio de Janeiro and Lisbon (Lopes and Vianna 2013: 83).

Nova Iguaçu, RJ		Copacabana, RJ		Cacém, Lisbon		Oeiras, Lisbon	
n/N	%	n/N	%	n/N	%	n/N	%
513/664	77%	628/768	82%	152/691	22%	68/787	9%

As mentioned in Section 3.1, the NP *a gente*, with fully compositional syntax and semantics, is still common in EP, which indicates its slower process of grammaticalization as a pronominal element. In BP, the large preference for *a gente* over the old pronoun *nós* shows its integration into the pronominal system.

3.1.3. The alternation overt/null subjects

The variation *tu/você*—which induces the loss of *–s* as the verb inflection for 2nd person singular—and the replacement of *nós* by *a gente* are both changes that lead to the use of the unmarked verb form, the 3rd person singular, instead of other specific verb forms for person (see Table 29.8). This is certainly the source of the significant reduction in the number of oppositions in BP inflectional paradigm mentioned before. It would be counter-intuitive to postulate the inverse process, that is, to claim that the loss of verb inflection started before the emergence of the new pronominal forms: the use of the 3rd person singular verb form, unmarked for inflection, is a consequence of the nominal origins of the new pronouns (*você* and *a gente*). Moreover, the reduction in the verb oppositions has been related to the well-known tendency to use overt nominative pronouns in BP. This makes sense, since the new generalized verb form is not able to distinguish discourse persons by itself anymore. Licensing and identification of null subjects in BP today are no longer related to inflection.

Empirical evidence for this comes from Duarte's (1993, 2000) study of popular theater plays of the nineteenth and twentieth century. Before the neutralization of *tu/você*, i.e. when the pronouns were in complementary distribution as they still are in EP, and before the propagation of *a gente*, the inflectional verb paradigm exhibited five or six different forms; concomitantly, null subjects were much more frequent than overt subjects. Duarte's results for a play written in 1992, the last across seven synchronies, reveal an impressive similarity with those found by Duarte (1995) for a speech sample recorded in 1992 with university graduates. In the same study, Duarte analyzed a sample of spoken EP taken from CRPC (see note 2); speakers were distributed according to the same social stratification used for BP sample. Table 29.10 shows a clear case of change in apparent time for BP; age was, in fact, the only social factor to show statistical significance for BP. For EP, age was not significant—all age groups prefer null subjects.[4]

Among the structural variables considered by Duarte (1995; 2000), only coreference with the subject of the previous matrix clause (Table 29.11) and animacy of 3rd person subjects (Table 29.12) showed statistical significance for both BP and EP.

The RWs, with the same virtual range for BP and EP, confirm the effect of coreference in the realization of a pronominal subject *in languages which have a null subject as an option*. The percentage differences, however, show that even if the conditioning is similar, the two varieties are still pretty different systems: in the most unfavorable context for a null subject, i.e., a non-coreferential antecedent, BP reaches 88 percent of overt pronouns, whereas EP shows 51 percent; and in the most favorable contexts, a coreferential antecedent, BP already shows 68 percent of overt pronouns, but EP only 9 percent. Considering these results in the light of the Null Subject Parameter, it is clear that EP behaves like a stable system of null subjects, whereas BP exhibits overt pronouns even when there is a coreferential antecedent. This indicates that BP is becoming a non-null subject language (cf. Duarte 1995, 2000, Barbosa, Duarte, and Kato 2005, inter alia).

Table 29.10   Overt (vs null) subjects in BP and EP according to age group.

Samples	BP		EP
Age group	RW	%	%
25–35	.59	78%	35%
36–45	.54	73%	25%
>46	.38	61%	25%
Range	21		
% Overall		71%	28%
N	1009/1424		144/508

Table 29.11   Overt (vs null) subjects in BP and EP according to coreference with previous subject.

Samples	BP		EP	
Coreference	RW	%	RW	%
No	.64	88%	.75	51%
Yes	.38	68%	.46	9%
Range	26		29	
% Overall		77%		29%
N	313/405		51/174	

Table 29.12   Overt (vs null) subjects in BP and EP according to animacy of the referent.

Samples	BP		EP	
Animacy	RW	%	RW	%
[+animate]	.59	68%	.78	39%
[–animate]	.39	56%	.25	6%
[generic]	.29	44%	.29	4%
Range	30		53	
% Overall		62%		21%
N	337/546		43/209	

As for the animacy of the referent, once again there are important differences between BP and EP, shown in Table 29.12.

Though the feature [+animate] (*Mary, the boy, my daughter*) favors overt pronouns in both varieties, as shown by RWs, percentages are again very different for each variety, which is consistent with the results for the other factors. With features [–animate] (*the house, Rio de Janeiro*) and [generic] (*a man, men, a house, houses*), we see that EP avoids overt pronouns, which is also consistent with the behavior of Romance Null Subject Languages. In BP, these features are more resistant to overt pronouns; however, percentages are still expressive. If one considers that variation is a condition to change, it is impossible not to interpret the preference for overt referential pronominal subjects in BP as an evidence of change in progress. A number of analyses focusing on the expression of pronominal subjects confirm the role of coreference and of animacy in the change underway in BP (Barbosa, Duarte, and Kato 2005).

3.2. *Variation in complement forms*

In the set of clitic pronouns (Table 29.13), we underline forms that have disappeared or are almost extinct in spoken BP, regardless of school level (see references in Duarte and Ramos 2015).

Only 1st and 2nd person singular clitics (*me*, *te*) are consistently used in BP. 2nd person plural *vos* as well as nominative pronoun *vós* (Table 29.7) have completely disappeared. 1st person plural clitic *nos*, due to the obsolescence of nominative *nós* (Section 3.1.2), is rare in spontaneous speech in urban areas, even among older people (Duarte 1995, inter alia). Accusative *o(s)*, *a(s)* and dative *lhe(s)*—originally 3rd person, but also used with *você*—are even rarer in spoken BP. And other forms of address are very rare in speech. A consequence of this—and at the same time an important evidence of the full insertion of *você* in BP pronominal system (Section 3.1)—is the combination of nominative *você* with the dative or acusative clitic *te*, originally belonging to the paradigm of nominative *tu*:[5]

(7) *Eu não te dei o livro porque você não veio à escola*
     I not *te* (to you) gave the book because *você* (you) not came to-the school
     "I didn't give you the book because you didn't come to school"

This combination is not attested in EP, which supports the idea that in EP *tu*/*você* are complementary in EP, and *você* has a lower degree of grammaticalization. The combination noticed in EP is the use of nominative *vocês* (2nd person plural) with the clitic *vos* belonging to the nominative *vós* paradigm (Raposo 2013).

The only group of clitics subject to regional variation in Brazil belongs to the reflexive system: in most regions investigated, they are very stable (8a), (9a); but in the South-East region, especially in the State of Minas Gerais, they are preferably null, regardless of their argumental status (8b), (9b).[6]

Table 29.13   System of clitics in EP and BP.

Person	Reflexive Clitics	Accusative Clitics	Dative Clitics	Indefinite Clitic
1ps	*me*	*me*	*me*	
1pp	*nos*	*nos*	*nos*	
2ps	*te*	*te*	*te*	
	se	*o,a, lhe,te*	*lhe, te*	*se*
2pp	*vos*	*vos*	*vos*	
	se	*os, as*	*lhes*	
3ps	*Se*	*o, a*	*lhe*	
3pp	*Se*	*os, as*	*lhes*	

(8) a. *Eu me formei em 1970.*
  I me (myself) graduated in 1970
 b. *Eu formei em 1970.*
  "I graduated in 1970"

(9) a. *Ele se suicidou.*
  He *se* (himself) killed
 b. *Ele suicidou.*
  "He committed suicide"

Variation affecting 3rd person accusative and dative clitics has a regular distribution all over Brazil. A comparative analysis of variable use of 3rd person accusative clitics in BP and EP was carried out by Freire (2000), based on data from NURC-RJ for BP and CRPC for EP. Four strategies were attested (all sentences may be an answer to "Have you seen João lately?"):

(10) a. *Eu o vi ontem* (written standard BP)/*(Eu) vi-o ontem* (EP)
  I *him* saw yesterday/(I) saw-*him* yesterday
 b. *Eu vi ele ontem* (spoken BP)[7]
  I saw *he* yesterday
 c. *Eu vi o João/o cara ontem* (BP/EP)
  I saw *the João/the guy* yesterday
 d. *Eu vi ontem* (BP/EP)
  I saw [ø] yesterday
  "I saw him yesterday"

Table 29.14 summarizes Freire's results:

Freire's comparison shows that 3rd person accusative clitic is almost absent in the speech of university graduated speakers of BP (3 percent), with preference for the anaphoric NP and the null object. EP, on the other hand, exhibits an expressive rate of 3rd person accusative clitic in speech (44 percent)—the same rate university graduated Brazilians exhibit in writing—but also shows a significant use of null objects. However, the literature reports that constraints on null objects are more restrict in EP (see Chapter 17, Null Objects and VP Ellipsis).

Examples in (11) show the clitic *lhe* and two variant strategies (sentences may be an answer to "What did you give Mary for her birthday?"):

(11) a. *Eu dei-lhe um livro* (EP)
  I gave-*lhe* (her) a book
 b. *Eu dei um livro pra ela* (BP)/*Eu dei um livro a ela* (EP)
  I gave a book to her (to=*para, pra*/to=*a*)
 c. *Eu dei um livro* (EP/BP)
  I gave a book [ø]
  "I gave her a book/a book to her"

Table 29.14 The accusative 3rd person clitic and its variants (Freire 2000).

Samples	*BP*		*EP*	
Variants	*n/N*	*%*	*n/N*	*%*
Clitic *o(s)/a(s)*	4/117	3%	48/109	44%
Nominative pronoun	5/117	4%	–	–
Anaphoric NP	40/117	34%	27/109	25%
Null object	68/117	59%	34/109	31%

Freire's (2000) results on clitic *lhe* and its variants are shown in Table 29.15. Though the sample has a small number of tokens, it is clear that dative *lhe* as a 3rd person form is absent in BP and productive in EP.

Other studies on BP samples, including popular speech, confirm the absence of *lhe* for 3rd person reference in spoken BP.[8] In standard writing it reaches about 30 percent.

Finally, we have the standard indefinite *se*, which suspends the external argument in active and passive structures. It is also almost extinct in spoken BP; alternative strategies come from nominative pronouns, particularly *você* and *a gente*, used to convey generic meaning.[9]

(12)   a. *Não se vê mais chapéu* (?BP/EP)
           not *se*.cl see.3ps more hat
       b. *Você não vê mais chapéu* (BP)
           you not see more hat
       c. *Não vê mais chapéu* (BP)
           not see.3ps more hat
       d. *A gente não vê mais chapéu* (BP/?EP)
           the people not see.3ps more hat
       e. *Nós não vemos mais chapéu* (?BP/EP)
           we not see.1pp more hat
           "One doesn't see hats any more," "Hats are not seen any more"

The use of *você* in BP reaches the same rate attested for clitic *se* in EP (Table 29.16). The second strategy in BP—the 3rd person singular verb form with *no other mark*—is used to convey genericity (12c), and also necessity. This strategy is completely absent in EP.

Table 29.15   The 3rd person dative clitic and its variants (Freire 2000).

Samples	*BP*		*EP*	
Variants	*n/N*	*%*	*n/N*	*%*
Clitic *lhe*(s)	–	–	29/33	88%
Anaphoric PP	9/14	64%	1/33	3%
Null dative	5/14	36%	3/33	9%

Table 29.16   The indefinite *se* and its variants (Duarte 2000).

Samples	*BP*		*EP*	
Variants	*n/N*	*%*	*n/N*	*%*
clitic *se*	26	9%	36	51%
Você	140	52%	5	7%
Ø+3ps	56	21%	–	–
a gente	41	15%	18	25%
Nós	8	3%	12	17%
	271		71	

In sum, with respect to clitics, EP shows a more stable paradigm than BP, particularly for 3rd person. BP resorts to nominative pronouns or null categories for pronominal anaphora with accusatives and datives. This system is established in spontaneous speech for all age groups and in all areas studied. The extremely low rates of clitics in the speech of university graduates show that they do not carry to their speech the forms learned through schooling. Moreover, the innovative colloquial variants are already being implemented in written language.

4. Final remarks

As we have seen, analyses of urban sociolinguistic data in Brazil have captured social constraints such as years of schooling, age and gender, and, in the case of samples collected in other speech communities, contact with urban areas also has statistical significance. Thus, people who produce more OC are those with higher schooling level, in more contact with urban areas, more exposed to situations of linguistic sensibility and occupying higher positions in the work market. This is an expected direction for phenomena subject to social stigma. Even so, we emphasize that variable concord is common in Brazil even among highly educated people in spontaneous speech. A brief survey of data from natural interactions (Pereira and Scherre 1995 apud Scherre and Naro 2014, 349) reveals that one speaker with over 11 years of schooling shows 98 percent, 91 percent and 24 percent of 3rd person overt SVC when interacting with the boss, the wife or the employees, respectively. Indeed the type of interaction or stylistic dimension for SVC and NPC has to be further explored in Portuguese.

As regards structural conditioning of number concord, we know phonic salience of the verb operates systematically in SVC and in NPC in BP. In EP, the type of verb according to transitivity is effective. However, in BP the statistical relevance of the type of the verb emerged only when Monguilhott (2009: 128–130) excluded the factors subject position and animacy from the quantitative analysis. In BP, the type of verb is relevant for the order of the subject (unaccusative verbs really favor VS), but, as far as we know, not for SVC concord: its effect is indirect. These three aspects deserve further examination in future research.

As for pronouns, EP shows a more stable system, very close to the standard system described in normative grammars still inspiring Brazilian formal education. The BP native system, however, has moved away from the standard. With respect to subject form, it shows full grammaticalization of *você* and *a gente*, forms that take the unmarked 3rd person singular verb form, and an intricate regional variation between *tu*/*você* for 2nd person singular reference. Because of these and other facts (for 3rd person plural, there is also variation in concord, cf. *Eles comem/Eles come* "They eat.pl/They eat.sg" are found), one can say that BP verb paradigm is extremely reduced in number of oppositions. This must be related to the strong tendency to avoid null definite and arbitrary subjects.

With respect to the clitic complements, BP also reveals a remarkable reduction in the 3rd person set. Though such almost extinct forms are partially recovered by school action, they remain almost completely absent in spontaneous speech, even for speakers with longer permanence in school and frequent contact with reading. In monitored styles, rates of 3rd person clitics can be a little higher but they cannot be considered expressive. The oblique pronoun set also attests innovations in BP, with a large use of nominative forms preceded by prepositions. The reduction attested in the clitic and the oblique paradigms is certainly embedded in a social matrix and surely deserves further investigation. The non-salience of null categories in complement function may explain the absence of stigma and the remarkable propagation of null objects. Conversely, the salience of nominative pronouns in accusative function, even though much rarer than null objects, may explain the stigma against these forms instigated by grammarians and some teachers.

In sum, this chapter presented two main areas of current morphosyntactic variation in Portuguese. With respect to number concord, we can see differences, but also similarities, in the variation found in BP and EP, both in the linguistic and the social aspects. With respect to the pronominal system, the two varieties seem really to diverge, with BP showing expressive variation and change, unlike EP. Both processes of variation still need further investigation, since important social changes in course in the present can affect the picture shown here in the future.

NOTES

1   The *range* measures the difference between the lower and higher relative weights associated to the factors in each group, showing the strength of a given constraint. Relative weights (RW) are values projected by appropriate statistical programs and reveal abstract properties; through corrected frequencies, they show the real effects of factors of each independent variables (Naro 1981; Scherre and Naro 2014).

2   The samples come from *corpora* of the following sources: PEUL (Programa de Estudos sobre o Uso da Língua, www.letras.ufrj.br/peul); NURC (Norma Urbana Culta, www.letras.ufrj.br/nurc-rj); ALIP (Amostra Linguística do Interior Paulista, www.iboruna.ibilce.unesp.br); CRPC (*Corpus de Referência do Português Contemporâneo*, for EP, in Nascimento et al. 1987); Luso-Brazilian Project (www.concordancia.letras.ufrj.br).

3   Unlike a curvilinear pattern, an S-shaped curve shows the course of change in progress: it starts slowly, then it tends to accelerate, to finally show reduced speed as the process reaches completion with a new form replacing an old variant (Paiva and Duarte 2003).

4   The results for BP in Tables 29.10, 29.11 and 29.12 are adapted from Duarte (1995); those for EP have been reviewed for the present chapter.

5   A related innovation is the increasing use of *lhe* in accusative function in variation with *te*; see note 8. As we said, *lhe* is rare for 3rd person reference; actually, it has not been attested in the studies carried out so far.

6   *Oblique* reflexives also deserve mention: whereas EP preserves the complete paradigm (*mim mesmo* "myself," *ti mesmo* "yourself)," *si mesmo* "himself," etc.), BP prefers the nominative forms + *mesmo* ("self"), already implemented even in writing.

7   Though the use of nominative *ele(s)/ela(s)* in object position in BP is often observed in the descriptive literature, sociolinguistic studies show they have low frequency (4 percent to 15 percent in spontaneous speech), depending on the level of education. Such studies also point out the use of 1st and 2nd nominative pronouns in accusative functions. In BP all nominative pronouns can appear as complements (direct, indirect, oblique), though 1st and 2nd person are more socially constrained. However, rates are significantly higher when the pronoun appears in "exceptional Case marking structures": *Eu fiz ela sair* lit. "I made she leave"; *Ela acha eu legal* literally "She finds I nice."

8   Interestingly, the obsolescent 3rd person dative *lhe* appears as an accusative with 2nd person reference in variation with *te*, a process which started in the northeast of the country but reaches Rio de Janeiro, in the southeast (see references in Duarte and Ramos 2015):

Eu te/lhe vi ontem
I you saw yesterday
"I saw you yesterday."

9   Table 29.16 does not include another strategy for arbitrary subjects, namely, the 3rd person plural verb form, which usually excludes the speaker. BP shows variation between overt pronoun and null category, whereas EP only shows a null category: *(Eles) estão roubando carro(s) no campus* "They are stealing cars in the campus" (see Duarte 1995; 2000).

REFERENCES

Barbosa, P., M. E. L. Duarte, and M. A. Kato (2005). Null subjects in European and Brazilian Portuguese. *Journal of Portuguese Linguistics*, 4 (2), pp. 11–52.

Bortoni-Ricardo, S. M. (1998). A análise do português brasileiro em três *continua*: o *continuum* rural-urbano, o *continuum* de oralidade-letramento, o *continuum* de monitoração estilística. In S. GroBe and K. Zimmermann (eds.), *"Substandard" e mudança no português do Brasil*. Frankfurt am Main: Teo Ferrer de Mesquita, pp. 101–118.

Barreto, F. V. V. (2014). A concordância verbal de 3ª. Pessoa do plural no português brasileiro. Ph.D. dissertation, Federal University of Rio de Janeiro.

Brandão, S. F. and S. R. Vieira (2012). Concordância nominal e verbal: contribuições para o debate sobre o estatuto da variação em três variedades urbanas do português. *Alfa*, 56 (3), pp. 1035–1064.

Duarte, M. E. L. (1993). Do pronome nulo ao pronome pleno: a trajetória do sujeito no português do Brasil. In I. Roberts and M. A. Kato (eds.), *Português Brasileiro: Uma Viagem Diacrônica*. Campinas: Editora da Unicamp, pp. 107–128.

Duarte, M. E. L. (1995). A perda do princípio "Evite Pronome" no português brasileiro. Ph.D. dissertation, Universidade Estadual de Campinas.

Duarte, M. E. L. (2000). The loss of the Avoid Pronoun principle in Brazilian Portuguese. In M. A. Kato and E. V. Negrão (eds.), *Brazilian Portuguese and the Null Subject Parameter*. Frankfurt: Vervuert, pp. 17–36.

Duarte, M. E. L and J. Ramos (2015). Variação nas funções acusativa, dativa e reflexiva. In M. A. Martins and J. Abraçado (eds.), *Mapeamento Sociolinguístico do Português Brasileiro*. São Paulo: Contexto, pp. 173–195.

Freire, G. (2000). Os clíticos de terceira pessoa e as estratégias para sua substituição na fala culta brasileira e lusitana. Masters dissertation, Federal University of Rio de Janeiro.

Labov, W. (1994). *Principles of Linguistic Change – Internal Factors*. Cambridge: Blackwell.

Lemle, M.; Naro, A. J. (1977). Competências básicas do português. Rio de Janeiro: Mobral/MEC, Ford Foundation. Unpublished manuscript.

Lopes, C., Vianna, J. S. (2013). A gramaticalização de "a gente" no PB e no PE: como explicar as diferenças nos dois espaços geográficos? In M. M. Cezário and M. A. Furtado (eds.) Linguística centrada no uso: homenagem a Mário Martelotta. Rio de Janeiro: Mauad, pp. 81–96.

Lucchesi, D., A. Baxter, and I. Ribeiro (eds.) (2009). *O Português Afro-Brasileiro*. Salvador: Editora da Universidade Federal da Bahia.

Mattos, S. E. R. (2013). Goiás na primeira pessoa do plural. Ph.D. dissertation, Universidade de Brasília.

Monguilhott, I. (2009). Estudo sincrônico e diacrônico da concordância verbal de terceira pessoa do plural no PB e no PE. Ph.D. dissertation, Universidade Federal de Santa Catarina.

Monte, A. (2012). Concordância verbal e variação: um estudo descritivo-comparativo do português brasileiro e do português europeu. Ph.D. dissertation, Universidade Estadual Paulista em Araraquara.

Naro, A. J. (1981). The social and structural dimensions of a syntactic change. *Language*, 57, pp. 63–98.

Naro, A. J., E. Görski, and E. Fernandes (1999). Change without change. *Language Variation and Change*, 11, pp. 197–211.

Naro, A. J. and M. M. P. Scherre (2000). Variable concord in Portuguese: the situation in Brazil and Portugal. In J. McWhorter (ed.), *Language Change and Language Contact in Pidgins and Creoles*. Amsterdam: John Benjamins, pp. 235–255.

Naro, A. J. and M. M. P. Scherre (2007). *Origens do Português Brasileiro*. São Paulo: Parábola.

Naro, A. J. and M. M. P. Scherre (2013). Remodeling the age variable: number concord in Brazilian Portuguese. *Language Variation and Change*, 25 (1), pp. 1–15.

Nascimento, M. F. B. do, M. L. G. Marques, and M. L. S. da Cruz (1987). *Português Fundamental: Volume Segundo. Métodos e Documentos: Tomo Primeiro. Inquérito de Frequência*. Libon: Instituto Nacional de Investigação Científica. Centro de Lingüística da Universidade de Lisboa.

Omena, N. P. de (1986). A referência à primeira pessoa do plural. In A. J. Naro et al. (eds.), *Relatório Final de Pesquisa: Projeto Subsídios do Projeto Censo à Educação*, vol II. Rio de Janeiro: UFRJ, pp. 286–319.

Omena, N. P. de (2003). A referência à primeira pessoa do plural: variação ou mudança? In: M. C. Paiva and M. E. L. Duarte (eds.), *Mudança Linguística em Tempo Real*. Rio de Janeiro: ContraCapa, pp. 63–80.

Paiva, M. C. and M. E. L. Duarte (eds.) (2003). *Mudança Linguística em Tempo Real*. Rio de Janeiro: ContraCapa.

Raposo, E. B. P. (2013). Pronomes pessoais. In E. B. P. Raposo, M. F. B. do Nascimento, M. A. C. da Mota, L. Seguro, and A. Mendes (eds.), *Gramática do Português*, vol I. Coimbra: Fundação Calouste Gulbenkian, pp. 883–920.

Rubio, C. F. (2012). Padrões de concordância verbal e de alternância pronominal no português brasileiro e europeu: estudo sociolinguístico comparativo. Ph.D. dissertation, Universidade Estadual Paulista em São José do Rio Preto.

Scherre, M. M. P. and A. J. Naro (2014). Sociolinguistic correlates of negative evaluation: variable concord in Rio de Janeiro. *Language Variation and Change*, 26 (3), pp. 331–357.

Scherre, M. M. P., A. J. Naro, S. E. R. Mattos, C. C. Foeger, and S. de A. Benfica (2014). Concord without concord: 1st. plural pronoun *nós* "we" in Brazilian Portuguese. Paper presented at *New Ways of Analyzing Variation (NWAV) 43*. University of Illinois at Urban-Champaign and University of Illinois at Chicago, October 23–26.

Scherre, M. M. P., E. P. Dias, C. Q. Andrade, and G. F. Martins (2015). Variação dos pronomes TU e VOCÊ. In M. A. Martins and J. Abraçado (eds.), *Mapeamento Sociolinguístico do Português Brasileiro*. São Paulo: Contexto, pp. 133–155.

Vianna, J. and C. Lopes (2015). Variação dos pronomes NÓS e A GENTE. In M. A. Martins and J. Abraçado (eds.), *Mapeamento Sociolinguístico do Português Brasileiro*. São Paulo: Contexto, 109–131.

Vieira, S. R. and A. Bazenga (2013). Patterns of third person plural verbal agreement. *Journal of Portuguese Linguistics*, 12 (2), pp. 7–50.

30 Acquisition of Phonology

GIOVANA FERREIRA-GONÇALVES
AND MARIA JOÃO FREITAS[1]

1. Introduction

The advent of studies on the acquisition of Portuguese phonology is closely related to the field of Clinical Phonology. The evaluation of Brazilian children showing an atypical phonological development started in the early 1980s. Since then, a very productive interdisciplinary cooperation has developed between linguists and speech therapists, showing the relevance of phonology-based models to improve the accuracy of the diagnosis and the efficiency of the clinical intervention. The interchanges between the two professional groups thus triggered the production of research on normally developing children acquiring Brazilian Portuguese (BP) and European Portuguese (EP). The main purpose was to establish the natural acquisition patterns, which are crucial for the study of atypical development.

The research on phonological acquisition in BP and in EP followed the theoretical models in vogue at their time. The studies by Lamprecht (1986) and Yavas and Lamprecht (1988) were inspired by the principles of rule naturalness and (lack of) abstraction of underlying structures within the Natural Generative Phonology framework. Matzenauer-Hernandorena (1988; 1990) explored the adequacy of the feature theory proposed by Chomsky and Halle (1968) to account for the setting of segmental contrasts in child development. From the 1990s on, different nonlinear models were used to describe the phonological acquisition of BP and EP. Some scholars used Syllable Theory, in some cases associated with the Principles and Parameters framework, in order to study the acquisition of syllable structure. This was the case of Freitas (1997) and Mezzomo (2004), who described the acquisition of syllable structure in normally developing Portuguese and Brazilian children, and of Ramos (1996), who described the systems of phonologically disordered children. Mota (1996) based her research on feature organization as modeled in Feature Geometry (Clements and Hume 1995); this was also the case in Costa (2010) for EP. In the field of Clinical Phonology, Keske-Soares (2001) and Lazzarotto-Volcão (2009) followed the theoretical and methodological pathway set out by Mota (1996) and Ramos (1996), while Bonilha (2000), among others, used the Optimality Theory framework to account for the developmental patterns exhibited by both typically and atypically developing children. Speech produced by children with typical and atypical phonological profiles was also studied from the perspective of the Articulatory Phonology framework, as reported in Berti and Albano (2008).

In order to master the phonology of a language, a child must acquire the segment inventory of the language, the way phonological segments combine to create well-formed words, the phonological processes constraining the output forms of underlying sequences

The Handbook of Portuguese Linguistics, First Edition. Edited by W. Leo Wetzels, João Costa, and Sergio Menuzzi.
© 2016 John Wiley & Sons, Inc. Published 2020 by John Wiley & Sons, Inc.

and the restrictions on the prosodic shape of words or sequences of words. In this chapter we focus on the acquisition of segmental and prosodic constituents by Brazilian and Portuguese children.

2. Segments and phonological processes

In the history of the research on phonological acquisition, scholars' attention was first directed towards the development of the segment inventory (Bernhardt and Stemberger 1998). Segmental development is related to motor skills (the ability to articulate the target segments accurately) and to cognitive processing (the setting of phonological categories despite the dynamic nature of speech). In this chapter, we will focus mainly on the latter issue.

The acquisition of phonological contrasts is normally captured in terms of feature setting. The *vowel/consonant* contrast, which may be expressed as [±vocoid], is available from the onset of phonological development (Jakobson 1941/68; Bernhardt and Stemberger 1998). It is commonly assumed that vocalic segments become stable by the end of the second year of life; on the contrary, the consonantal inventory is gradually set during the first 5–6 years of life in typically developing children. Regarding the acquisition of the vowel inventory, research on BP showed that /a, i, u/ tend to be acquired before /e, o/; as for /ɛ, ɔ/, these are described as the last vowels to become stable (Rangel 2002; Bonilha 2004). As for EP, no studies on the order of acquisition of vowels were systematically performed so far, although some partial information involving this segment class is already available (see information below).

As for consonants, the stable appearance of the different sound classes follows a cross-linguistic trend. In terms of manner of articulation (MoA), the *sonorant / obstruent* contrast ([±sonorant]), one of the most robust contrasts in the languages of the world (see Clements 2009), is reported as being early mastered by both Brazilian and Portuguese children (Matzenauer-Hernandorena 1990; Mota 1996; Freitas 1997; Lamprecht et al. 2004; Lazzarotto-Volcão 2009; Costa 2010; Almeida 2011; Amorim 2014). This implies an early mastery of oral and nasal stops. The next contrast that is set involves the feature [±continuant] within the class of obstruents ([–sonorant]), giving rise to the regular appearance of fricatives; finally, the setting of the same contrast in the class of sonorant consonants occurs, witnessed by the appearance of liquids, normally the last class of segments to become stable in Portuguese.[2] As for place of articulation (PoA), children tend to first acquire anterior consonants, therefore, [labial] and [coronal, +anterior] PoAs become stable before non-anterior ones, such as [coronal, –anterior] and [dorsal] (Matzenauer-Hernandorena 1990, Costa 2010, Amorim 2014).

The use of distinctive features to represent the developing of phonological knowledge led scholars to propose a gradual setting of feature combinations, based on the description of errors in child production data. These feature combinations allow for the representation of the interactions between MoA and PoA properties. For instance, not all anterior coronal consonants show an early emergence across manner classes; some studies suggest that this type of consonants first emerge within the class of stops, as the result of the early setting of [coronal, +anterior; –sonorant; –continuant]; however, within the class of sonorant consonants, studies have reported the acquisition of posterior PoAs before the anterior ones (/ʀ/ >> /ɾ/; /ʎ/>>/l/). This argues for the relevance of specific feature combinations for the study of child phonology (Matzenauer-Herandorena 1999; Lamprecht et al. 2004; Lazzarotto-Volcão 2009; Costa 2010; Amorim 2014).

The setting of specific MoA and PoA feature combinations may differ in BP and EP. Research on fricatives show that alveolars are acquired before palatals in BP but not in EP

(Lamprecht et al. 2004; Amorim 2014). According to Bernhardt and Stemberger (1998), the acquisition pattern where /s/ is set before /ʃ/ may not be considered universal; palatal consonants precede alveolar consonants in some acquisition paths. The role of BP and EP target properties in the children's different behavior is yet to be explored (Amorim 2014).

Another example showing the importance of feature co-occurrence comes from the interaction between MoA and voicing. In BP, voiced fricatives emerge before voiceless ones (according to Lamprecht et al. 2004, the order of acquisition in non branching onsets is: /v/ >> /f/ >> /z/ >> /s/ >> /ʒ/ >> /ʃ/); this is not attested for plosives, in which category [−voice] is mastered before [+voiced] (Lamprecht et al. 2004). As for EP, a general preference for early voiceless plosives and fricatives over voiced ones was observed (Mendes et al. 2009, Costa 2010 and Amorim 2014). A comparison between BP and EP shows different tendencies for the interaction between MoA and [voice], for both plosives and fricatives. Further research is needed to confirm the patterns identified so far and to understand the reasons underlying the children's dissimilar behavior.

Although linguists commonly think of segments as hierarchically organized sets of distinctive features, most professionals dealing with language assessment and language training often conceive of segments as indivisible phonological units. This led researchers to publish ordered lists of segments representing the general segmental profile of children in the process of acquisition. This was done in Lamprecht et al. (2004) for BP, based on data from about 400 children (see Table 30.1), and in Mendes et al. (2009), based on data from over 700 children (see Table 30.2). The information in the tables relates to segments in simple onset position; in contexts other than the syllable onset, the same segments may be acquired at ages different from those mentioned in Tables 30.1 and 30.2 (see Section 3 in this chapter).[3]

Phonological processes are used by phonologists as generalizations over segments displaying a predictable behavior in specific contexts. The literature on phonological acquisition, however, exhibits two definitions of the concept of *phonological process* (Kiparsky and Menn 1977; Fikkert 2007): (1) phonological processes refer to the children's repair strategies when processing complex adult targets (*velar fronting, stopping,* among others); Kiparsky and Menn (1977) use the term *invented rules* to name these child-specific rules, which are to be gradually abandoned by children in the acquisition process; (2) phonological processes are generalizations over the output form of segments in the adult grammar, which are to be acquired on the basis of positive evidence in the input.

The rule concept as defined in (1) is familiar among speech therapists evaluating a child's phonological development (see AFI[4] for BP and ALPE[5] for EP). The question one might raise

Table 30.1 Acquisition of BP segments in simple onset (years.months; data from Lamprecht et al. 2004).

1.0–1.6	1.6–2.0	2.0–2.6	2.6–3.0	3.0–3.6	3.6–4.0	4.0–4.6
/p, b, t, d, m, n, N/	/k, g, f, v, z/	/s, ʒ/	/ʃ, l/	/ʀ/	/ʎ/	/ɾ/

Table 30.2 Acquisition of EP segments in simple onset (years.months; data from Mendes et al. 2009 and Costa 2010).

1.0–1.6	1.6–2.0	2.0–2.6	2.6–3.0	3.0–3.6	3.6–4.0	4.0–4.6
/p, m/	/d, b, n, t/	/k/	/v, f, g/	/ɲ, s, ʃ, ʀ/	/l, ʎ/	/z, ʒ, ɾ/

concerning the use of phonological processes as child-specific rules is how adequate it is as a tool to achieve an accurate description of the phonological acquisition process. Assuming that language acquisition is a process aiming at the discovery of the adult system, is it necessary to assume the existence of child-specific rules that are subsequently eliminated? Children generally go from simple to complex structures and the production patterns they exhibit may be viewed, not as the outcome of transitory child-specific rules, but as resulting from the lack of specific adult grammar structures in the child's system, which will gradually develop in the course of their linguistic development.

The rule concept as presented in (2) above (*phonological processes are generalizations over the output form of segments in the adult grammar*) is the one commonly used among phonologists. The acquisition of these phonological processes that are part of the target grammar is rarely investigated. However, the description of how children acquire the allophonic variants associated to the target phonological processes provides relevant empirical evidence to discuss the nature of phonological representations on the route of language development. On the assumption that allophony shows the activity of phonological features and that allophonic variants are represented as phonetic outputs of a single phonological unit, the way children master these variants constitutes an important research area that will reveal the way in which they gradually store segmental information as part of phonological representations (Fikkert 2007). We will end this section by discussing some of the few studies that have been undertaken in this area.

The Portuguese vowel system is particularly rich in terms of allophonic and allomorphic variation, thus entailing the activation of different phonological processes. The stressed vowel [ɐ] has different phonological sources and exclusively emerges in the following contexts:

(i) as an allophone of /a/ when followed by a nasal consonant (/m, n, ɲ/, as in c*a*ma ['kɐmɐ] "bed");
(ii) as an allophone of /e/ when followed by a palatal segment (/ʃ, ʒ, ɲ, ʎ, j/, as in ab*e*lha [ɐ'bɐʎɐ] "bee").

The different unstressed realizations of this stressed [ɐ] in the two contexts are used as arguments to propose different phonological forms for the vowel:

(i) [ɐ] is the unstressed output form of the vowel in the nasal context (c*a*minha [kɐ'miɲɐ] "bed" *diminutive*);
(ii) [i] is the untressed output form of the vowel in the palatal context (ab*e*lhinha [ɐbi'ʎiɲɐ] "bee" *diminutive*).

EP unstressed vowel reduction yields [ɐ] as the output form of /a/ (m*a*la ['malɐ] "bag"; m*a*linha [mɐ'liɲɐ] "bag" *diminutive*) while [i] is the output form of /e/ (m*e*sa [mézɐ] "table"; m*e*sinha [miziɲɐ] "table" *diminutive*[6]). Based on the /e/ ←[i] and /a/ ←[ɐ] relationships in the vowel reduction process in EP, it is assumed that unstressed [ɐ], in the nasal context, is the output form of /a/ and that the unstressed [i], in the palatal context, is the output form of /e/ (Mateus and Andrade, 2000).

Fikkert and Freitas (2006) examined data from seven Portuguese children aged 0.11 to 3.7 in order to explore the production of lexical items exhibiting the structures just mentioned. The results showed that, when faced with stressed [ɐ], Portuguese children are able to distinguish the different phonological sources of the vowel: in the nasal context mostly dorsal variants were attested, while, in the palatal context, both dorsal and coronal variants appeared (Table 30.3).

Table 30.3 Production data for target stressed [ɐ] (Fikkert and Freitas 2006).

Processes	Production data	
	Dorsal	*Coronal*
V+nasal consonant context	99%	1%
	(88% [ɐ]; 11% [a])	([e])
V+palatal segment context	56%	44%
	(55% [ɐ]; 1% [a])	(26% [e]; 17% [ɛ]; 1% [i])

Variants in the nasal context are consistent with the dorsal nature of the phonological vowel /a/. However, in 44 percent of the cases, variants in the palatal context mirror the coronal nature of the phonological vowel /e/. The data showed that the /a/ → [ɐ] raising process was mastered before the /e/ → [ɐ] process, which involves a change of both aperture and V-place features. The children's behavior was interpreted as the proof of early sensitivity to allophonic and allomorphic variation in the target system, showing the relevance of studying the acquisition of target phonological processes for our understanding of how children gradually store phonological information in the lexicon.

Another example of the acquisition of phonological processes relates to the use of [i] in EP (Freitas 2004). This vowel may be the result of a neutralization process in unstressed syllables involving /e, ɛ/, thus affecting aperture as well as V-place features (*mesa* ['mezɐ] "table" and *mesinha* [mi'ziɲɐ] "table" *diminutive*; *terra* ['tɛʀɐ] "earth" and *terreno* [ti'ʀenu] "land"). The vowel [i] is also used as a prosodic filler in EP, in cases where segments in unlicensed syllable positions are rescued by epenthesis (*pneu* [p'new]/[pi'new] "tyre"; *mar* ['maɾ]/ ['maɾi] "sea") (Mateus and d'Andrade 2000). Again, the data showed that children are able to discriminate between the product of neutralization and epenthesis, despite the similar phonetic shape of the vowel [i] in both contexts:

(i)   the target neutralized [ɨ] showed different phonetic forms in child data, [i] and [ɨ] being the preferred variants; the vowel was not available at the onset of speech;

(ii) the prosodic filler [i] was available at the onset of speech and consistently surfaced with the target format; in the developmental process, it was often used to match the available syllable or word shapes in the child's system: at the left edge of words, in early productions (*pé* [i'pɛ] "foot" Inês: 1.5.11; *dá* [i'da] "give (me)" Inês: 1.4.9); in the acquisition of sC clusters (*estrela* [iʃ'tɛlɐ] "star" Marta:1.8.18); at the right edge of words with final liquid (*flor* ['ʃowi] "flower" Marta: 1.2.0); in the acquisition of branching onsets (*três* [ti'ʀeʃ] "three" Laura: 2.2.30).

These facts showed that children may be sensitive early to the different phonological sources of similar phonetic segments.

The vowel inventory in unstressed position clearly distinguishes BP and EP. In the case of EP, the acquisition of /a/ → [ɐ] and /ɛ, e/ → [i] in unstressed position was observed in Freitas (2007). The results showed that /a/ → [ɐ] is acquired before /ɛ, e/ → [i]. This outcome was interpreted as an effect of feature activity: the former process only affects aperture features, while the latter involves both aperture and V-place features. Moreover, and considering the morphological distribution of the two vowels, the class markers [i] and [ɐ] were acquired before their lexical counterparts in the stem; this was interpreted as the result of the phonology–morphology interface, which may bootstrap the acquisition of specific structures in EP (Freitas, Miguel, and Faria 2001).

3. Syllables

Prosodic constituency is assumed to play a crucial role both in phonological processing and in language development. Under this perspective, research on bootstrapping from speech to grammar in early developmental stages became popular since the late eighties. The syllable was the first prosodic structure to be described in the studies on the acquisition of Portuguese phonology. Research based on both longitudinal and cross-sectional data revealed important information on the acquisition of syllable patterns in Portuguese.

The results available so far show that Portuguese and Brazilian children start with both CV and V patterns (Freitas 1997 for EP; Scarpa 1999 for BP), despite the claims made by Jakobson (1941/68) and followers, according to which the universal CV pattern is the only template available at the onset of speech, with the aim of establishing a relation between typological markedness and the order of acquisition. This is different for languages such as Dutch or English (Fikkert 1994), where only CV is possible at the onset of speech. The properties of the target languages are certainly underlying the different behaviours exhibited by the children observed so far, although no consistent explanation accounting for this cross-linguistic asymmetry is available in the literature. The presence of the V pattern at the onset of speech is also attested in the frequent production of a word-initial vowel (/dá/ [ɐ'da]/['da] "give (me)" Inês: 1.1), interpreted either as a prosodic filler or as a proto-morpheme (Scarpa 1999; Freitas 1997).

After an initial state where only CV and V are possible, Portuguese and Brazilian children display a different behaviour. Portuguese children develop the (C)VC pattern; however, at this second stage, only coda fricatives are licensed. Subsequently, Portuguese child speech shows liquids in syllable-final position (Freitas 1997). Correia (2004) and Amorim (2014) found the same order of acquisition: (C)VC$_{fricative}$ >> (C)VC$_{liquid}$. The setting of syllable-final liquids occurs by the time branching nuclei (falling diphthongs) become stable. Until that moment, children are able to produce both V and VG, although the two structures may alternate for a single target, vowel or diphthong, showing that the structure is not yet mastered (/ʃɐ'pɛw/ [ʃɐ'pe] "hat" Inês: 1.7; /'ladu/ ['ajdu] "side" Inês: 1.10; /dinɔ'sawɾu/ [dinɔ'saɾ] "dinosaur" Pedro: 3.7). A similar behavior was attested for Dutch concerning the short / long vowel contrast and the emergence of syllable-final liquids (Fikkert 1994). Following Fikkert's proposal, Freitas (1997) proposed that both VG and VC$_{liquid}$ structures were processed as branching nuclei, which would account for the late mastery of syllable-final liquids.

As for BP, for the second stage of syllable development two different analyses were proposed: the early emergence of [(C)VG] structures were interpreted by different scholars as either the setting of /(C)VV/ or as the setting of /(C)VC/. Bonilha (2000) claims that this second stage corresponds with the mastery of the /(C)VV/ pattern, assuming that the first glides to emerge are represented in a complex nucleus (as is claimed for the adult grammar by scholars like Câmara Jr. 1977). Just after this stage the [CVC] structure would emerge. However, Mezzomo (2004) claims that the glide in early VG structures is processed as a coda, in agreement with adult grammar analyses such as proposed by Collischonn (1997). In this analysis, there are no branching nuclei in the Brazilian Portuguese phonological system.

As for branching onsets, it has been reported that this is the last complex structure to develop in Portuguese and Brazilian children (Freitas 1997; Lamprecht et al. 2004). However, recent data from Mendes et al. (2009) and Amorim (2014) showed that Portuguese children may acquire CCV syllables before CVC$_{lateral}$ ones, although no explanation for these divergent findings was yet proposed. One crucial difference between BP and EP is the use of vowel epenthesis by Portuguese children (*cobra* ['kɔbiɾɐ] "snake" Pedro: 3.5) before the setting of CCV, which is not reported for Brazilian children.

Table 30.4 Order of acquisition for syllable structure in EP.

Stage 1	Non-branching onsets + non-branching rhymes: CV/V	
Stage 2	Branching rhymes: (C)VC$_{fricative}$	
Stage 3	Branching nuclei: (C)VG/(C)VC$_{liquid}$	Branching onsets: CCV
Stage 4	Branching onsets: CCV	Branching nuclei: (C)VC$_{liquid}$ [a]

[a] The relationship between this path and the setting of VG structures was not studied.

Table 30.5 Order of acquisition for syllable structure in BP.

Stage 1	Non-branching onsets + non-branching rhymes: CV/V
Stage 2	Branching nucleus: (C)VG
Stage 3	Branching rhymes: (C)VC$_{lateral\ liquid}$
Stage 4	Branching rhymes: (C)VC$_{nasal}$
Stage 5	Branching rhymes: (C)VC$_{fricative}$
Stage 6	Branching rhymes: (C)VC$_{non\text{-}lateral\ liquid}$
Stage 7	Branching onsets: CCV

To sum up, the research results discussed above lead to the identification of the following order(s) of acquisition in EP: CV/V >> CVC$_{fricative}$ >> CVG/CVC$_{liquid}$ >> CCV (CVC$_{lateral}$). (See Table 30.4.)

As for BP, the following order of acquisition was found (Lamprecht et al. 2004): CV / V >> CVG >> CVC$_{lateral\ liquid}$ >> CVC$_{nasal}$[7] >> CVC$_{fricative}$ >> CVC$_{non\ lateral\ liquid}$ >> CCV. (See Table 30.5.)

As for the acquisition of the more complex syllable structures of BP, in which the rhyme contains three contrastive positions, such as CVVC as in, for example, *seus* ['sews] "yours," a study conducted by Bonilha (2000), based on data from 86 monolingual children between age 1.0 and 2.5, found that only 28 out of the 48 possible /CVVC/ targets were produced accurately as [CVGC] (58.3 percent) The remaining productions showed 30 percent instances of [CVG] or [CVC]. Considering the fact that children had already acquired complex nuclei and codas, the production of target /CVVC/ was to be expected. The late acquisition of this type of structure was also found in other studies, as in Fikkert and Freitas (1998) for Dutch and EP and for English by Bernhardt and Stemberger (1998). This result shows that the complexity of the rhyme is not mastered early, as suggested by Fikkert (1994).

An interesting fact about the developmental syllable patterns concerns the interaction between complex syllable constituents and their preference for specific segments or segment sequences.

In the acquisition of (C)VG, different developmental stages can be distinguished relating to the sonority difference between the vocoids that constitute falling diphthongs, as well as their degree of homorganicity (Bonilha 2000). The acquisition of tautosyllabic VG sequences appears to start with /aw/, of which both the composing vocoids share the same dorsal PoA: the production of [aw] (as in *auau* [awaw] "dog") goes beyond 80 percent in the early age groups, while high production rates are sustained in all age groups. Soon after, the acquisition of [aj] (*papai* [papaj] "daddy") takes place. In this case, the low vowel and the glide have different PoAs. What both sequences have in common is the relatively sharp sonority contrast between nucleus and margin. It thus appears that children first acquire diphthongs of which the low vowel and the glide share their PoA, as in [aw]. In a later stage, children learn to assign different PoA features to VG sequences, as in [aj]. Diphthongs exhibiting mid or high vowels are acquired at later stages of acquisition in BP: *seu* [sew] "your"; *rei* [xej] "king"; *boi* [boj] "ox."*fui* [fuj] "(I) went."

As will be shown below, the interaction between syllables and segments in phonological development provides important information both for assessment and intervention in a clinical context and for language training in educational settings: success rates for the production of a specific segment should not be calculated exclusively on the basis of its global accuracy; a more adequate evaluation takes into account the child's performance of a given target segment in a specific syllable position.

Not all segments are possible in all syllable positions: for example, in Portuguese, the segments that may appear in the coda (/s, l, ɾ, (n)[8]/) constitute a small subset of the segments occurring in the syllable onset. The liquids /l, ɾ/ may occur in three syllable positions: in a non-branching onset (*amarelo* "yellow"), as the second consonant in a branching onset (*prato* "dish," *flor* "flower") and in the syllable coda[9] (*mar* "sea"; *mel* "honey"). The fact that a given segment shows a limited distribution in child speech may be directly linked to the degree in which syllable complexity is part of the child's phonological system. In the examples below, the child accurately produces [l] in onset position; its absence in the branching onset and in the coda is due, not to problems with processing the alveolar lateral, but to the fact that branching onsets and codas are not yet available (See Table 30.6).

Lamprecht (1986) and Miranda (1996) show for BP that the position of a segment in the syllable is crucial for the evaluation of the child's ability to produce that segment. From an analysis of cross-sectional data from 110 children aged between 2.0 and 3.9, Miranda (1996) was able to show that the position of /ɾ/ within the syllable and the word were the most important factors that accounted for its acquisition. According to the author, the rhotic is first acquired in coda position, then as a simple onset and finally as part of a branching onset. The early acquisition of this consonant in word-final codas was interpreted as the result of the phonetic salience of segments in that position. The salience of word-final /l, ɾ/ was also attested for EP (Freitas 1997; Correia 2004), where these segments appear to be processed early: (i) they tend to emerge by the time /l, ɾ/ are available as simple onsets and (ii) their production consistently triggers vowel epenthesis (Marta: *colar* [kɐˈlalɐ] "necklace" (1.5); *urso* [ˈusu] "bear" (2.2)

Another example showing that segments may emerge gradually depending on aspects other than segmental information relates to coda fricatives in EP, which also show a word-edge effect: these consonants first emerge in the coda of word-final syllables (mostly unstressed, due to the language's preference for the trochaic pattern). This behaviour is unexpected, since word-final unstressed syllables are considered acoustically non-salient in EP. The examples in Table 30.7 were taken from the child Inês at 1.9/1.10.

Table 30.6 Syllable–segments interaction (EP data from Luís).

non-branching onset	*amarelo*	[mɐˈɾɛw]	"yellow"	1.9
coda	*barco*	[ˈbaku]	"boat"	1.9
branching onset	*frente*	[ˈfẽti]	"front"	1.11

Table 30.7 Data on the emergence of Coda fricatives.

stressed/word-medial/lexical	*festa* "party"	[ˈtɛtɐ]	1.9
✓ stressed/word-final/morphological	*meus* "mine"	[ˈmewʃ]	1.9
stressed/word-final/lexical	*nariz* "nose"	[ɐˈgiɐ]	1.9
unstressed/word-medial/lexical	*buscar* "to get"	[βuˈka]	1.10
✓ unstressed/word-final/morphological	*bolos* "cakes"	[ˈboloʃ]	1.9
unstressed/word-final/lexical	*lápis* "pencil"	[ˈpatu]	1.9

The early emergence of word-final coda fricatives in EP was interpreted in Freitas et al. (2001) as due to the fact that this structure often encodes plural marking in nouns. Lamprecht et al. (2004) also report that word-final coda fricatives emerge before word-medial ones in BP. Mezzomo et al. (2010) specifically study word-final fricatives; they observe that word-final lexical fricatives are acquired before morphological ones in nouns. The asymmetry attested for nouns is consistent with the different distribution of the plural morpheme in the target language: Portuguese children produce word-final morphological fricatives in nouns because number agreement in EP requires the presence of the plural morpheme in both the determiner and the head of the nominal phrase; Brazilian children, on the contrary, produce the number feature overtly only in the determiner, not in the noun, matching the adults' behavior in BP.

Although morphological factors may stimulate the acquisition of segments, as shown in the case of coda fricatives (Freitas *et al.* 2001) and class markers (Freitas 2007) in EP, they may hinder it in other contexts. The irregular plural forms of words with word-final nasal diphthongs (*cão/cães* "dog(s)," *limão/limões* "lemon(s)," *mão/mãos* "hand(s)") and of words with word-final laterals (*animal/animais* "animal(s)") showed success rates above 50 percent only at age 5.0, despite the early acquisition of the EP plural marker, which is normally mastered before 2.0 (Ramalho and Freitas 2012; Freitas and Afonso (in press)). These opposite tendencies call for further investigation on the effect of the phonology/morphology interface in language acquisition, which is not systematically explored in the literature on language development.

4. Stress

Over the past three decades, the prosodic unit that has received most attention from acquisition researchers in Brazil has been the syllable. There have been specific studies focusing on the syllable and its constituents in normal acquisition as well as in clinical studies, besides those, already discussed in Section 3, in which segmental acquisition was studied in relation with syllable structure.

Much less attention has been given to another prosodic entity, the foot as a domain for stress. There are still few studies that deal with the acquisition of this prosodic unit. In Brazil, the most important contributions to this area of acquisition research are Santos (2001, 2007), Bonilha (2004), Baia (2008), and Ferreira-Gonçalves and Brum-de-Paula (2011). For European Portuguese stress, the main reference is Correia (2009). These authors used different theoretical models, from the Principles and Parameters model (Santos 2001) and Metrical Phonology (Baia 2008; Correia 2009) to Optimality Theory (Bonilha 2004). In addition to searching for general trends in the acquisition of primary stress in Portuguese, these studies try to find arguments allowing to evaluate the proposals put forward to explain the stress patterns of the adult grammar, such as Bisol (1992), Pereira (1999), Wetzels (2006), and Lee (2007).

For Bisol (1992), Portuguese stress is rhythmic, assigned to nouns and verbs by way of a single rule. The stress foot is defined as a binary constituent, left-headed, and sensitive to syllable weight in non-verbs, in which category the rule applies cyclically. Non-verbs with a final light syllable, e.g. *vidro* "glass," *sala* "room," etc. receive stress on the penultimate syllable, while words of this class with a final heavy syllable receive final stress, e.g. *pomar* "orchard," *valor* "value," etc. To account for irregular nouns like *úti<l>* "useful" and *fósfo<ro>* "match," the author marks the final consonant and final syllable as extrametrical, as indicated with the angled brackets. Words with stress on the final open syllable, such as *café* "coffee," *jacaré* "cayman," etc. are lexicalized with an abstract morpheme-final consonant (catalexis). In verbs, the stress rule applies non-cyclically at the word-level. The final syllable of the 1/2pl forms of the indicative and subjunctive imperfect as well as all final consonants that function as suffixes are made extrametrical, such as in *gostáva<mos>* and *cantásse<mos>*.

Pereira (1999) considers that, in Portuguese, stress is morphological in nature, both in nouns and verbs. The domain within which the stress rule applies is the root for non-verbs and the lexical word for verbs. In non-verbs an iambic foot is constructed, originating from the placement of stress on the last vowel of the root, which yields surface stress on the penultimate syllable in words with a class marker, as in *punho* "fist," but on the last syllable in athematic words, like *café* "coffee" or *pomar* "orchard." In verbs, the stress rule creates syllabic trochees. Unstressed inflectional morphemes are irrelevant for the process of stress distribution. The author takes the position that syllable weight is completely irrelevant for stress in EP, also because there is no independent evidence for its function in other areas of the phonology of Portuguese.

Wetzels (2006) presents a proposal closer to that of Bisol (op.cit.) by taking the position that stress in non-verbs, which applies at the word level, is weight-sensitive. The unmarked stress pattern, which emerges for example in the creation of new words, such as acronyms, is penultimate when the final syllable is light, but final in words ending in a heavy syllable. According to this author, syllable weight in Portuguese is not only relevant for the distribution of main stress, but also conditions segmental rules, such as the rule that neutralizes the contrast between upper and lower mid vowels in words with a final heavy syllable (*pr[ɔ]ton* "proton," *d[ɔ]lar* "dollar"). The lack of proparoxytonic words with a heavy penultimate syllable (*aberto*, **abérto* "open") and the recurrent emergence of final stress in newly created words with a final heavy syllable are good arguments in favor of syllable weight as a relevant concept in Portuguese phonology. In Wetzels' proposal, antepenultimate stress, stress on a word-final light syllables and penultimate stress in words with a final heavy syllable is lexicalized. Verb stress is distributed on the basis of the tense categories, "present," "past," and "future."

Lee (2007) proposes a unified analysis of Portuguese stress for nouns and verbs. In his analysis, framed in Optimality Theory, stress patterns emerge from the interaction between prosodic and morphological constraints. Importantly, morphological constraints—such as Rooting, Paradigm Uniformity and Align[10]—dominate metrical constraints in the constraint hierarchy proposed, which fact highlights the key role of morphology in the stress system of Portuguese. The domains for foot formation are the derivational root for non-verbs and the lexical word for verbs. Consequently, it is the morphology that determines whether the outputs that are selected as optimal are iambs or trochees, because stress falls on the last syllable of the stem as in *ja(caré)* "cayman," with the formation of an iamb, but in *bo(níto)* "pretty," with the formation of a trochee. For heavy paroxytones and proparoxytones, the stress is considered lexical. According to the author, an important fact supporting the idea that the Portuguese stress rules are morphologically conditioned is its distinctiveness, as shown by the words *sábia* "wise-fem.," *sabía* "knew-3sg," *sabiá* "bird species."

The first more comprehensive study of the acquisition of primary stress in Portuguese was done by Santos (2001). Based on longitudinal data of two children between 1.0 and 3.0 years, the author developed her analysis within the theory of Principles and Parameters. Santos observed that children show no errors in the production of primary stress from an early age. She emphasizes, however, that the stress prominence heard and reproduced by the child refers actually to the stress of the phonological phrase, not of the word. In her attempt to determine when the child starts making use of the primary stress algorithm and to evaluate the different theoretical proposals, she concludes that Portuguese is not sensitive to weight, in agreement with the proposal of Lee (1994), because the subjects never presented any proof for syllable weight as a relevant parameter in the acquisition of stress. As for the role of extrametricality, she points out that the data neither corroborate nor contradict the proposals by Bisol (1992) and Lee (1994).

In later work, Santos (2007) argues, based on findings from two children from 1.3 to 3.6, that the initial and recurrent iambic productions already bear witness to the mastery of a specific stress pattern. Consequently, according to the author, the research results again point to the correctness of the proposals presented by Lee (1994) and Pereira (1999) for the Portuguese adult stress system. Three arguments are advanced to support this conclusion: (i) the iambic pattern is maintained even when the child produces the final heavy syllable as a light syllable (*balão* as [ba.ˈa]"balloon"), (ii) the recurrence of iambs in lexical items created by the children, (iii) the fact that repair strategies produce iambic outputs.

In this manner, the difficulties in producing trochees are explained by the interaction with morphology, because trochaic nouns, not iambic ones, carry a final word marker. The trochaic words are produced, therefore, when the child is capable of producing morphological contrasts, like gender.

The acquisition of stress in European Portuguese is studied in Correia (2009). From the productions of five children, the author observes a preference for early iambic structures, but argues that this may be a misapprehension of the facts, because the iambic pattern emerges as the result of reduplication and epenthesis. Portuguese children initially produce monosyllables, with the possible presence of one syllable to the left. According to Correia, for this type of production, the question of the metrical foot is irrelevant. Only later trochaic and iambic forms emerge, followed by a stage in which the trochaic pattern prevails and iambs are truncated to become monosyllables while trisyllables become bisyllabic trochees. The author equally found in her data evidence for the role of syllable weight and also could not rule out the interaction of the stress system with morphology. Another interesting fact in Correia's study is her use of acoustic analyses of the speech data in order to verify possible shifts in the location of stress. She found that the phonetic parameters responsible for stress prominence, i.e., fundamental frequency, intensity, and duration, were not mastered before age 2.0, showing great variability in the words produced by the children.

Bonilha (2004) found light paroxytones (*peixe* [ˈpe.ʃi] "fish," 1.3.10; *carro* [ˈka.xu] "car," 1.5.7), light oxytones (*aqui* [aˈki] "here," 1.1.22; *alô* [a.ˈo] "hello," 1.3.10), and monosyllables (*mãe* [ˈmãj] "mother," 1.5.7) in an early stage of acquisition in data obtained from a longitudinal study of a Brazilian Portuguese child, aged between 1.1 and 4.6. Of these patterns, the percentage of iambic productions was highest, especially when considering the productions resulting from truncation of the final syllable in trisyllabic trochaic targets which are produced in conformity with the target form only around 1.6 (*sapato* [paˈpa] "shoe," 1.1.22; *coroa* [koˈo] "old woman," 1.3.10; *pescoço* [piˈko] "neck," cavalo [kaˈva] horse—1.5.20). Santos (2001) also points out the emergence of iambic forms as truncation outputs, especially at early stages.

Trochaic forms are also produced correctly. Consequently, only heavy paroxytones and proparoxytones show a late appearance. Bonilha (2004) notes that the errors in the production of paroxytones are basically related to segmental emergence. The oxytonic words that are used are either reduplicated target forms, such as *papa* "daddy" and *cocô* "excrement," for example, but there are also productions for which the target is not a reduplicated form, such as *aqui* "here" and *alô* "hello."

Truncation processes systematically preserve the tonic and initial syllables, yielding iambic sequences. Other patterns also are attested, such as those resulting from the reduction of heavy disyllables with the preservation of the initial unstressed syllable, [ˈpa] *papai* "daddy," [ˈba] *balão* "balloon" and [ˈmã] *mamãe* "mammy," or the reduction of light disyllables with preservation of the initial tonic syllable, [ˈga] *gato* "cat." The reduction of trisyllables yields two different patterns: (i) preservation of the tonic syllable and the initial atonic syllable, which causes the emergence of iambs, and (ii) the preservation of the tonic syllable and the initial or final atonic syllable, which may lead to the emergence of trochees. This pattern, however, is attested at later stages, as from 1.5.

According to Ferreira-Gonçalves and Brum-de-Paula (2011), the early production of oxytonic forms, not necessarily related to reduplication, shows the productivity of the iambic pattern at the start of Brazilian Portuguese acquisition. The words resulting from processes of trisyllable truncation, with preservation of the initial and stressed syllables would also confirm that productivity.

As we have mentioned earlier, for Correia (2009) the initial iambic pattern observed in Portuguese acquisition is only apparent, because it is fundamentally driven by reduplication processes. Data from Inês, for example, shown in Table 30.8, demonstrate that, up to session 8, which corresponds to the age of 1.7.2, productions due to the truncation of trisyllabic paroxytonic targets either consist of iambic disyllables, with the preservation of the initial and the tonic syllables or monosyllables. The remaining *ws* outputs are due to epenthesis. It is also observed that trochaic outputs become more frequent as from Session 9, confirming the pattern found in Brazilian Portuguese data, with first trisyllables being truncated as oxytonic disyllables, and, at a subsequent stage, as paroxytonic disyllables.

Data from Brazilian and Portuguese children seem to confirm the stages proposed in Bonilha (2004) regarding the acquisition of the different stress patterns, even if the initial *ws* pattern can be interpreted as the preservation of the initial and the tonic syllables for iambic disyllabic targets (Bonilha 2004; Santos 2007), as truncated forms for *wsw* targets, or as the result of epenthesis and reduplication (Correia 2009). Bonilha (2004), in an Optimality Theory analysis, proposes that from 1.1.22 until 1.5.7, when iambs are produced, there is the pressure of positional faithfulness constraints in the child's grammar such as MAX I/O σ_1 and MAX I/O σ',[11] responsible for the preservation of the initial and tonic syllables, and, as from 1.6, metrical constraints, such as Align (Σ, L, H (Σ), L) and Align (Σ, R, H (Σ), R),[12] are being activated by the inputs from the target language. According to the author, from 1.5.20, the preference for trochees as outputs from the truncation process is due to the ranking Align (Σ, L, H (Σ), L) >> Align (Σ, R, H (Σ), R), triggered by the frequency of inputs and by the demotion of the constraints related to segmental features below the MAX I/O constraint.

One possible explanation for the initial iambic forms is to interpret these as manifestations of the regular Portuguese adult stress pattern, as done by Santos (2007) in accordance with the iambic feet proposed in Lee (1994, 2007) and Pereira (1999). Another possibility, however, is to associate the early emergence of iambs to the frequency of oxytonic words in the language (Ferreira-Goncalves and Brum de Paula 2011).

Table 30.8   Ines—truncation in /WSW/ ([WS], [SW] and [S]) (Correia 2009: 216).

	Orthogr.	Gloss	Target	Output	Age
	chupeta	'pacifier'	/ʃuˈpetɐ/	[ɐˈpe]	1;1.30 (S3)
	babete	'bib'	/bɐˈbeti/	[baˈβæ]	1;3.6 (S4)
	sapato	'shoe'	/sɐˈpatu/	[pɐˈpɐ]	1;4.9 (S5)
[WS]	vestido	'dress'	/viʃˈtidu/	[tʲiˈtʲi]	1;5.11 (S6)
	chupeta	'pacifier'	/ʃuˈpetɐ/	[beˈbe]	1;6.11 (S7)
	cadeira	'chair'	/kɐˈdɐjɾɐ/	[ɣeˈɣe]	1;7.2 (S8)
	boneca	'doll'	/buˈnɛkɐ/	[meˈɲɛ]	1;9.19 (S10)
	chupeta	'pacifier'	/ʃuˈpetɐ/	[ˈpe]	1;1.30 (S3)
	cabelo	'hair'	/kɐˈbelu/	[ˈpeː]	1;3.6 (S4)
[S]	boneca	'doll'	/buˈnɛkɐ/	[ˈɲɐ]	1;5.11 (S6)
	girafa	'giraffe'	/ʒiˈɾafɐ/	[ˈɣa]	1;6.11 (S7)
	cadeira	'chair'	/kɐˈdɐjɾɐ/	[ˈge]	1;7.2 (S8)
	vestida	'dressed'	/viʃˈtidɐ/	[ˈbitɐ]	
[SW]	umbigo	'belly button'	/ũˈbigu/	[ˈbidu]	1;8.2 (S9)
	barulho	'noise'	/bɐˈruʎu/	[ˈbuju]	

Table 30.9 Frequency of use of the different stress patterns of Brazilian Portuguese (Araújo, et al. 2007).

Stress pattern	Relative Frequency			
	Rare	*Uncommon*	*Common*	*Frequent*
Complete database	27.5%	26%	23.7%	22.6%
Monosyllable	0%	0.2%	4.4%	95.4%
Oxytone	21.1%	27.2%	26.1%	25.6%
Paroxytone	26.3%	26.4%	24.2%	23.1%
Proparoxitone	47.5%	24.8%	16.4%	11.4%

As Albano (2001) shows based on a categorization of the words contained in the *Aurélio Mini Dictionary*, paroxytonic words outnumber the oxytonic ones in Portuguese: 53 percent vs. 35 percent. However, the results are different if only the most frequent words are considered, as shown in Table 30.9.

According to the percentages displayed in Table 30.9, calculated over the Portuguese pages available in Google, the penultimate and final stress patterns show similar percentages for the categories "common" and "frequent." One could therefore draw a parallel between the emergence of the iambic pattern in the early productions of Portuguese children and the high frequency of the oxytonic pattern in these categories, especially when taking into account that these percentages could be even higher in the speech directed to children during the early acquisition stage.

Another interesting point worth emphasizing are Correia's (2009) findings regarding the instability of the acoustic parameters related to the phonetic realization of stress. As was already mentioned, the author points out that these parameters are stable only in the productions of children from age 2.0. This raises the question whether it is well-advised to discuss the acquisition of Portuguese stress for the period when the relevant acoustic parameters are unstable. Furthermore, one could raise the question whether the stabilization of the acoustic parameters around age 2.0 corroborate the role of morphology in stress assignment. It was observed by Correia, that stress shifts are not found during the earlier acquisition stages, although data were collected form as early as age (0.11), for example in the case of Inês. In Joana and Luma, stress shifts are reported after 24 months, a phase in which the production of different stress patterns are being reported. One possibility, perhaps, is to consider the hypothesis that stress shifts during the acquisition of stress are indicative of the activity of other aspects of acquisition, for example the acquisition of morphology.

As for the available theoretical descriptions of the Portuguese adult stress system, in conformity with the proposals made by Bisol (1992) and Wetzels (2006), the acquisition data are apt to explain the early acquisition of paroxytones (moraic or syllabic trochees) of heavy oxytones (moraic trochees) and the late acquisition of proparoxytones and heavy paroxytones (extrametricality or lexical stress). There is, however, no obvious explanation for the early emergence of oxytones.

If morphology is considered as the basis for stress assignment in non-verbs, as proposed by Pereira (1999) and Lee (2007), the early acquisition of final stress on the last vowel of words that have no class or gender marker, such as *aqui* "here," the early acquisition of heavy oxytones, such as *trator* "tractor," as well as of proparoxytones, such as *médico* "physician," and heavy paroxytones, such as *fácil* "easy" (words in which the last vowel of the stem is marked as unstressed) seem to corroborate the role of morphology in the placement of stress. On the other hand, the production of accurate trochaic forms, mainly from age 1.6, casts doubt on the hypothesis of Santos (2007) according to which the early non-acquisition of trochees is due to the role of morphology.

According to Ferreira-Gonçalves and Brum-de-Paula (2011), the early emergence of iambic forms could possibly be related to the frequency of iambs in the Portuguese lexicon and particularly in the speech directed to children during acquisition. The stress pattern extracted by the learner would be rhythm-based at that moment, undergoing changes with the acquisition of morphological structures, giving rise to a reanalysis of the foot type for Portuguese.

5. Conclusion

Over the last three decades, starting with studies mainly focusing on atypical phonological acquisition of the sound patterns of Brazilian Portuguese, several acquisition studies were undertaken from different theoretical perspectives.

Albeit with an emphasis on generative phonology, research has been conducted from several theoretical perspectives, involving the acquisition of segments, syllable structure, and stress in European and Brazilian Portuguese. The study of these areas as autonomous fields of research or from the perspective of their interaction have greatly increased our understanding of the developmental routes typical for the phonological acquisition of Portuguese. We have discussed the added value of research directed towards the acquisition of segments and segmental contrasts simultaneously taking into account the different affiliations of these segments with specific syllable positions. Whereas the emergence of the different subsyllabic constituents is correlated with the emergence of the type of segment with which they can be associated, the activity of concepts such as syllable weight can only be demonstrated once complex rhymes have developed. We have also tried to relate the emergence and development of stress pattern in child language with the available proposals that claim to account for the productive and unproductive stress patterns in adult speech. For the time being, no strong conclusions can be drawn, especially with regard to the role of morphology vs. syllable weight in stress attribution. Different interpretations can be given to the findings that have become available until now.

Researchers are currently using profitably such tools as ultrasound and eye tracking equipment, which allow for a more detailed investigation of acquisition data. The systematic use of acoustic analysis of speech data from child language has opened a new line of research searching for details in children's productions revealing the presence of covert contrasts (Scobbie et al. 1997), still poorly described for the speech of Portuguese children. Similarly, other theories particularly interested in the use and functioning of phonetic detail, such as the Phonology of Use and Articulatory Phonology, represent promising lines of research that could provide new insights in the complex process of language acquisition.

NOTES

1   We thank Leo Wetzels for his comments on a previous version of this chapter.
2   Notice that we are referring to general tendencies and not to specific segments. In the case of the lateral /l/, although liquids in general tend to be the last class to be acquired, its acquisition in simple onset position in EP and in BP (and also in the word-final coda in BP) may emerge at early stages and it may even precede the acquisition of some coronal fricatives (Lamprecht et al. 2004 for BP; Mendes et al. 2009 for EP).
3   Lamprecht et al. (2004) provide data for word-initial and word-initial onset position; we consider, in Table 30.1, the first age of acquisition in one of the two positions.

4 Yavas, Hernandorena, and Lamprecht (1991), used by Brazilian speech therapists.
5 Mendes et al. (2009), used by Portuguese speech therapists.
6 According to Mateus and Andrade (2000), although the output form of unstressed /ɛ/ is also [i], this vowel is not produced as stressed [ɐ] in the focused palatal context. Therefore, /e/ is assumed to be the phonological vowel for stressed [ɐ] in the palatal context.
7 In BP, "contrastive" nasal vowels are assumed to derive from a nasal mora (Wetzels 1997), or from a consonantal root node. In EP, Mateus and d'Andrade (2000) assume that this nasality is phonologically represented as a [nasal] autosegment associated with the nucleus node. The different theoretical approaches correspond with the way in which the child data are interpreted: in BP, the setting of nasal vowels is interpreted as the result of the mastery of nasal codas; in EP, it is interpreted as the result of the mastery of the nasal autosegment. In both languages, the structure is early acquired.
8 See note to Table 30.4.
9 Or branching nucleus, depending on the analysis (cf. Freitas, 1997).
10 Rooting (Lx = PrWd): lexical words must be stressed; Align (Stem, Right, Head, Right): the right side of the derivational root coincides with the right side of the head of the foot; Paradigm Uniformity: stress the thematic vowel in the past tense of verb forms (Lee 2007: 129, 134, 139).
11 MAX I/O σ_1: segments belonging to the initial syllable must be preserved; MAX I/O σ´: segments belonging to the stressed syllable must be preserved.
12 Align (Σ, L, H (Σ), L): feet are left-headed; Align (Σ, R, H (Σ), R): feet are right-headed (Bonilha 2004: 264).

REFERENCES

Almeida, L. (2011). *Acquisition de la Structure Syllabique en contexte de Bilinguisme Simultané Portugais-Français*. Ph.D. dissertation, Faculdade de Letras da Universidade de Lisboa.

Albano, E. (2001). *Os Gestos e Suas Bordas – Esboço de Fonologia Acústico-Articulatória do Português Brasileiro*. Campinas: Mercado de Letras/ALB.

Amorim, C. (2014). *Padrão de Aquisição de Contrastes do PE: a interação entre traços, segmentos e sílabas*. Ph.D. dissertation, Faculdade de Letras da Universidade do Porto.

Araújo, G. A., Z. O. Guimarães-Filho, L. Oliveira, and M. Viaro (2007). As proparoxítonas e o sistema acentual do português. In G. A. de Araújo (ed.), *O Acento em Português – Abordagens Fonológicas*. São Paulo: Parábola Editorial.

Baia, M. F. A. (2008). O modelo prosódico inicial do português brasileiro: uma questão metodológica? Masters dissertation, University of São Paulo.

Bernhardt, B. and J. Stemberger (1998). *Handbook of phonological development from the perspective of constraint-based nonlinear phonology*. San Diego: Academic Press.

Berti, L. and E. Albano (2008). Revisiting phonological disorders: an analysis of production and perception. *Studies in Language*, 44, pp. 22–32.

Bisol, L. (1992). O acento e o pé métrico binário. *Cadernos de Estudos Linguísticos*, 23, pp. 83–101.

Bonilha, G. (2000). *Aquisição dos Ditongos Orais Decrescentes: uma Análise à luz da Teoria da Otimidade*. MA thesis, Universidade Católica de Pelotas.

Bonilha, G. (2004). *Aquisição fonológica do português brasileiro: uma abordagem conexionista da Teoria da Otimidade*. Ph.D. dissertation, Pontifícia Universidade Católica do Rio Grande do Sul.

Câmara Jr., M. J. (1977). *Estrutura da Língua Portuguesa*. Petrópolis: Vozes.

Chomsky, N. and M. Halle (1968). *The Sound Pattern of English*. New York: Harper & Row.

Clements, N. (2009). The role of features in phonological inventories. In E. Raimy and C. Cairns (eds.), *Contemporary Views on Architecture and Representations in Phonology*. Cambridge, MA: MIT Press, pp. 19–68.

Clements, G. and E. Hume (1995). The internal organization of speech sounds. In J. Goldsmith (ed.), *The Handbook of Phonological Theory*. Cambridge: Blackwell, pp. 245–306.

Collischonn, G. (1997). Análise prosódica da sílaba em Português. Ph.D. dissertation, Pontifícia Universidade Católica do Rio Grande do Sul.

Correia, S. (2004). *A Aquisição da Rima em Português Europeu - ditongos e consoantes em final de sílaba*. Masters dissertation, University of Lisbon.

Correia, S. (2009). *The acquisition of primary word stress in European Portuguese*. Ph.D. dissertation, University of Lisbon.

Costa, T. (2010). *The acquisition of the consonantal system in European Portuguese: focus on place and manner features*. Ph.D. dissertation, University of Lisbon.

Ferreira-Gonçalves, G. and M. R. Brum-de-Paula (2011). A emergência do padrão acentual do português: desdobramentos. In G. Ferreira-Gonçalves, M. Brum-de-Paula, and M. Keske-Soares (eds.), *Estudos em Aquisição Fonológica*, vol. 2. Santa Maria: Pallotti.

Fikkert, P. (1994). *On the acquisition of prosodic structure*. Ph.D. dissertation, University of Leiden.

Fikkert, P. (2007). Acquiring phonology. In P. de Lacy (ed.), *Handbook of Phonological Theory*. Cambridge: Cambridge University Press, pp. 537–554.

Fikkert, P. and M. J. Freitas (1998). Acquisition of syllable structure constraints: evidence from Dutch and Portuguese. In A. Sorace, C. Heycock, and R. Shillcock (eds.), *Proceedings of the GALA 1997 Conference on Language Acquisition*. Edinburgh: University of Edinburgh, pp. 217–222.

Fikkert, P. and M. J. Freitas (2006). Allophony and allomorphy cue phonological development: evidence from the European Portuguese vowel system. *Journal of Catalan Linguistics*, 5, pp. 83–108.

Freitas, M. J. (1997). *Aquisição da Estrutura Silábica do Português Europeu*. Ph.D. dissertation, University of Lisbon.

Freitas, M. J. (2004). The vowel [i] in the acquisition of European Portuguese. In J. van Kampen and S. Baauw (eds.), *Proceedings of GALA 2003*, vol. 1. Utrecht: LOT, pp. 163–174.

Freitas, M. J. (2007). On the effect of (morpho) phonological complexity in the early acquisition of unstressed vowels in European Portuguese. In P. Prieto, J. Mascaró, and M. Solé (eds.), *Segmental and Prosodic Issues in Romance Phonology*. Amsterdam: John Benjamins, pp. 179–197.

Freitas, M. J., M. Miguel, and I. Faria (2001). Interaction between prosody and morphosyntax: plurals within codas in the acquisition of European Portuguese. In B. Hoehle and J. Weissenborn (eds.), *Approaches to Bootstrapping. Phonological, Lexical, Syntactic and Neurological Aspects of Early Language Acquisition*, vol. 2. Amsterdam: John Benjamins, pp. 45–58.

Freitas, M. J. and C. Afonso (in press). "Os caracoles são azuis? Dados espontâneos e experimentais sobre a aquisição dos plurais das palavras com lateral final". In Ferreira-Gonçalves, G., M. Brum-de-Paula and M. Keske-Soares (eds) *Estudos em Aquisição Fonológica*. Volume IV. Pelotas: Universidade Federal de Pelotas.

Jackobson, R. (1941/1968). *Child Language, Aphasia and Phonological Universals*. The Hague: Mouton.

Keske-Soares, M. (2001). *Terapia Fonoaudiológica Fundamentada na Hierarquia Implicacional dos Traços Distintivos Aplicada em Crianças com Desvios Fonológicos*. Ph.D. dissertation, Pontifícia Universidade Católica do Rio Grande do Sul.

Kiparsky, P. and L. Menn (1977). On the acquisition of phonology. In J. MacNamara (ed.) *Language Learning and Thought*. New York: Academic Press.

Lamprecht, R. (1986). *Os Processos nos Desvios Fonológicos Evolutivos*. MA thesis, Pontifícia Universidade Católica do Rio Grande do Sul.

Lamprecht, R. R., G. Bonilha, G. Freitas, C. Matzenauer, C. Mezzomo, C. Oliveira, and L. Ribas (2004). *Aquisição Fonológica do Português. Perfil de Desenvolvimento e Subsídio Para Terapia*. Porto Alegre: Artmed.

Lazzarotto-Volcão, C. (2009). *Modelo Padrão de Aquisição de Contrastes: uma Proposta de Avaliação e Classificação dos Desvios Fonológicos*. Ph.D. dissertation, Universidade Católica de Pelotas.

Lee, S. H. (1994). A regra do acento do português: outra alternativa. *Letras de Hoje*, 98, pp. 37–42.

Lee, S. H. (2007). O acento primário no português: uma análise unificada na teoria da otimalidade. In G. A. Araújo (ed.), *O Acento em Português: Abordagens Fonológicas*. São Paulo: Parábola.

Mateus, M. H. and E. d'Andrade (2000). *The Phonology of Portuguese*. Oxford: Oxford University Press.

Matzenauer-Hernandorena, C. (1988). *Análise de Desvios Fonológicos através dos Traços Distintivos*. MA thesis, Pontifícia Universidade Católica do Rio Grande do Sul.

Matzenauer-Hernandorena, C. (1990). *Aquisição da Fonologia do Português. Estabelecimento de Padrões com base em Traços Distintivos*. Ph.D. dissertation, Pontifícia Universidade Católica do Rio Grande do Sul.

Matzenauer-Hernandorena, C. (1999). Aquisição da fonologia e implicações teóricas: um estudo sobre as soantes palatais. In R. Lamprecht (ed.), *Aquisição da Linguagem*. Porto Alegre: EDIPUCRS.

Mendes, A., E. Afonso, M. Lousada, and F. Andrade (2009). *Teste Fonético Fonológico – Avaliação da Linguagem Pré-Escolar (TFF-ALPE)*. Aveiro: Universidade de Aveiro.

Mezzomo, C. (2004). Sobre a aquisição das codas. In R. Lamprecht (ed.), *Aquisição Fonológica do Português: Perfil de Desenvolvimento e Subsídios para a Terapia*. Porto Alegre: Artmed, pp. 129–150.

Mezzomo, C. L., H. Mota, R. Dias, and V. Giacchini (2010). Fatores relevantes para a aquisição da coda lexical e morfológica no PB. *Revista CEFAC*, 12 (3), pp. 412–420.

Miranda, A. (1996). *A aquisição do "r": uma contribuição à discussão sobre seu status fonológico*. MA thesis, Pontifícia Universidade Católica do Rio Grande do Sul.

Mota, H. (1996). *Aquisição segmental do Português: um modelo implicacional de complexidade de traços*. PhD. dissertation, Pontifícia Universidade Católica do Rio Grande do Sul.

Pereira, I. (1999). *O Acento de Palavra em Português. Uma Análise Métrica*. Ph.D. dissertation, University of Coimbra.

Ramalho, M. and M. J. Freitas (2012). Morphophonological complexity in the acquisition of EP: the case of nominal plural forms with final nasal diphthongs. In S. Ferré, P. Prévost, L. Tuller, and R. Zebib (eds.), *Selected Proceedings of the Romance Turn IV Workshop on the Acquisition of Romance Languages*. Newcastle: Cambridge Scholars.

Ramos, A. (1996). *Processos de Estrutura Silábica em Crianças com Desvios Fonológicos: uma Abordagem Não-Linear*. Ph.D. dissertation, Pontifícia Universidade Católica do Rio Grande do Sul.

Rangel, G. (2002). *Aquisição do Sistema Vocálico do PB*. Ph.D. dissertation, Pontifícia Universidade Católica do Rio Grande do Sul.

Santos, R. (2001). *A aquisição do acento de palavra no Português Brasileiro*. Ph.D. dissertation, Unicamp.

Santos, R. S. (2007). *A Aquisição Prosódica do Português Brasileiro de 1 a 3 anos: Padrões de Palavra e Processos de Sândi Externo*. Ph.D. dissertation, University of São Paulo.

Scarpa, E. (1999). Sons preenchedores e guardadores de lugar: relações entre fatos sintáticos e prosódicos. In E. Scarpa (ed.), *Estudos em Prosódia*. São Paulo: Editora da Unicamp, pp. 253–284.

Scobbie, J. M., F. Gibbon, W. J. Hardcastle, and P. Fletcher (1997). Covert contrast and the acquisition of phonetics and phonology. In W. Ziegler and K. Deger (eds.), *Clinical Phonetics and Linguistics*. London: Whurr, pp. 147–156.

Wetzels, W. L. (1997). The lexical representation of nasality in Brazilian Portuguese. *Probus*, 9 (2), pp. 203–232.

Wetzels, W. L. (2006). Primary word stress in Brazilian Portuguese and the weight parameter. *Journal of Portuguese Linguistics*, 5 (2), pp. 9–58.

Yavas, M. and Lamprecht, R. (1988). Processes and intelligibility in disordered phonology. *Clinical Linguistics and Phonetics*, 2 (4), pp. 329–45.

Yavas, M., C. Hernandorena, and R. Lamprecht (1991). *Avaliação Fonológica da Criança*. Porto Alegre: Artes Médicas.

31 Acquisition of Portuguese Syntax

JOÃO COSTA AND RUTH E. V. LOPES

1. Introduction

Acquiring the syntax of a language implies achieving adult performance on the production and comprehension of at least the following domains: clause structure, movement and referential dependencies. For these domains, a child must find out the language-particular aspects of the language she is acquiring. Most research on the acquisition of syntax based on a generative background convincingly shows that children are quite precocious in all tasks regarding the acquisition of syntax.

In this chapter we focus on results on the acquisition of Portuguese, concentrating on those aspects of the syntax of the language that are not common to other languages. For the sake of providing a comprehensive state of the art, we focus on the results achieved by the several studies we report on, and refer the reader to the original works for methodological issues or for details on the participants.

The chapter is organized as follows: Section 2 addresses results on the acquisition of word order, clause structure and on the acquisition of the DP. Section 3 reports on findings regarding the acquisition of movement dependencies. Finally, Section 4 addresses referential dependencies and the mastery of constructions involving null categories.

2. Word order, clause structure and the structure of the DP

Acquiring Portuguese word order involves acquiring V-to-I movement. European Portuguese further has I-to-C movement in specific constructions, such as *wh*-questions. The analysis of spontaneous speech data indicates that children master V-to-I movement from very early on. Soares (1998) and Santos (2006), for European Portuguese (EP), and Lopes (2003b, 2009), for Brazilian Portuguese (BP), argue that children move the verb to I since their earliest stages of multiword production. A crucial piece of evidence in favor of this claim comes from Santos's work on VP ellipsis and Lopes's (2009) on null objects. It is important to have in mind that VP-ellipsis involves V-to-I movement in Portuguese (cf. Chapter 16 here). In answers to yes–no questions, Portuguese has the option of using the verb in a VP-ellipsis context instead of the word *sim* "yes." Santos (2006) and Lopes (2009) show that one of

The Handbook of Portuguese Linguistics, First Edition. Edited by W. Leo Wetzels, João Costa, and Sergio Menuzzi.
© 2016 John Wiley & Sons, Inc. Published 2020 by John Wiley & Sons, Inc.

children's first answers are instances of VP-ellipsis, as shown in the following examples for EP and BP, respectively:

(1) Adult: *tu gostas de brincar com caricas?*
          you like PREP play with caps
          "Do you like to play with caps?"
     Child: *(g)o(s)to.*   (Tomás 1.6.18)
          like[1sg]
          "(Yes,) I do."

(2) Adult: *Tomou remédio também?*
          Took medicine too?
          "Did he take some medicine too?"
     Child: *Tomou*   (AC 2.1)
          Took
          "(Yes,) he did."

   Further evidence for an early acquisition of V-to-I comes from repetition tests run by Friedmann and Costa (2010b), who show that children are able to perform V-to-I whenever required. This study further confirms previous findings on the literature with evidence for an early distinction between verb classes: children successfully repeat SV and VS orders with unaccusative verbs, but fail to repeat VS orders with unergative verbs. (3) presents a sample of the sentences tested:

(3) a. Unaccusative verbs SV/VS
         O balão rebentou. / Rebentou o balão.
         the balloon popped / popped the balloon
         "The balloon popped."
     b. Unergative verbs SV/VS
         O rapaz correu. / Correu o rapaz.
         the boy ran / ran the boy
         "The boy ran."

BP does not have the SV/VS order alternation with unergative and transitive verbs but preserves it for unaccusative verbs. Palmiere (2002), analyzing the spontaneous speech of two children from 2.0 to 4.0, shows that all the utterances with unergative verbs are SV (4), as expected, but in the case of unaccusatives, in 76 percent of the cases the children prefer a VS order since the onset (5):

(4) *A beéquinha (= bonequinha) anda.*   (N 2.1.13)
     the doll-little walks
     "The little doll walks."

(5) *Caiu a cade(i)rona!*   (N 2.7.2)
     fell the chair-big
     "The big chair fell!"

   As for I-to-C, available in EP only, Soares (1998, 2003, 2006) show that children fail to fill in the C position with the verb, uttering *wh*-questions of the type in (6):

(6) *O que tu tens aqui na mala?*   (Sandra 2.6.3)
     what you have here in the handbag
     "What do you have in your handbag?"

This asymmetry between an early setting of V-to-I and a later mastery of I-to-C has been argued to be an argument for the key role morphology plays as a clue in parameter setting (Costa and Loureiro 2006). The idea is that when a movement strongly correlates with inflection, the morphology is a strong cue. This is the case in V-to-I, but not in I-to-C contexts. Actually, as shown in Gonçalves (2004), just as in other Romance languages, there is sound evidence that Portuguese children master agreement morphology from very early on, which accounts for the fact that other inflection-related parameters, like the null subject parameter, are set early as well. The same is shown for Brazilian Portuguese in Lopes (2003b) and Magalhães (2006).

Note that, as in other languages, the evidence available is for an early acquisition of the functional domain of the clause. Children are able to perform V-to-I, as just shown, and there is robust evidence for the projection of the left-periphery, as shown by the early availability of *wh*-questions and topic constructions in the case of BP (for EP, Faria et al. 1997, Soares 1998, 2003, 2006; for BP, Grolla 2000).

The same can be argued for the DP. As in other languages, there is some evidence for the early availability of the D head, which is attested by the emergence of proto-determiners (Soares 1998, Faria et al. 1997). These are taken to be prosodic placeholders by Costa and Freitas (2001), although, as far as BP is concerned, it has been claimed that they are prosodic filler sounds instead (see Santos, 2001, 2005, a.o.).

Freitas and Miguel (1998) argue that the early emergence of functional structure in the DP correlates with the prosodic salience of plural codas, arguing for a morphophonological bootstrapping effect in the DP domain. Interestingly, as argued by Corrêa et al. (2005) and Castro and Ferrari-Neto (2007), not only D is available from the onset, but it plays a crucial role in the acquisition of referentiality. These authors show that, in the identification of number, children of 18 to 30 months rely on the marking on determiners more than they do on marking on nouns. This is achieved by comparing children's interpretation of plurality in the two varieties of Portuguese. The test consisted of two grammatical and two ungrammatical DPs in the target grammars composed with novel nouns and invented object entities to which the nouns referred. Children should point to one (singular) or more than one entity (plural) when prompted with the linguistic stimuli:

(7) a. *Mostra [os dabos] pro Dedé.*
Show the-pl *dabo*-pl to-the puppet.
   b. *Mostra [os dabo]…*
Show the-pl dabo …

(8) a. *Mostra [o dabos] …*
Show the dabo-pl …
   b. *Mostra [o dasbo] …*
Show the da-*infix*-bo

The pairs in (7) are grammatical in BP, the difference being that (a) is the standard form and (b) the non-standard form; therefore, arguably children are exposed to both. That is not the case in EP, where only (7a) is found (see Chapter 14, The Structure of DPs, for an overview of the DP-internal agreement patterns). The DPs in (8) are ungrammatical in both varieties, although possible in other languages. In (8a) the plural marking appears in the noun only, while in (8b) it would be an infix. It is also possible to interpret these DPs as singular in the language, since there are singular nouns ending in *–s* or having *–s–* as a coda in the first syllable (respectively, *pires* "saucer" and *casca* "peel").

The authors' overall results show that the Portuguese children recognized the plural condition in a rate of over 76 percent, for (7a), while the Brazilian ones ranged from 57 percent for (7a) to 64 percent for (7b) as expected. These results, together with the fact that the conditions in (8) were not significantly interpreted as plurals, indicate that the number features in

D are being computed. However, Brazilian children also accepted the (8a) condition 33 percent of the times as plural. This is rather interesting when such results are compared to spontaneous production data.

Lopes (2006) and Simioni (2007) show that although an "NP-only stage" is not found in BP, one in which children would drop determiners where they should be present, plural DPs take a while to be produced, starting around their second birthday. But the crucial fact is that the grammatical forms as in (7) are not to be found from the onset. Examining spontaneous production data from five children, the authors found that they exhibit, during a very brief period of time, a pattern close to (8a), marking the plural morphology on the noun and not on the determiner:

(9) *a hienas* (C. 2.4)
     the-sg hyena-pl
     "the hyenas"

These forms soon co-occur with the grammatical patterns but will not disappear entirely from the grammar until past a child's third birthday.

As far as gender is concerned, no mismatches between the gender features in D and the noun were found in children's spontaneous productions in Lopes (2006). In reality, Name (2002) had already shown that very young children are sensitive to the morphological marking of gender in the determiner ascribing it to the noun in an agreement fashion.

3. Acquisition of movement dependencies

As mentioned in the previous section, there is robust evidence for the claim that children acquiring Portuguese perform movement operations from very early on. As remarked, head movement is available in children's earliest production, and the same holds for XP movement. Let us consider several examples attested in the literature.

Several studies report that children do not have troubles with A-movement. Adragão and Costa (2004) and Costa and Friedmann (2012) argue that children's SV utterances with different verbal classes provide evidence for DP-movement from Spec,VP to Spec,TP. The same is true for BP, except that there is an initial asymmetry observed when unaccusative verbs are examined: Lexical DPs tend to be found post-verbally while pronominal ones will always appear pre-verbally, as shown in Lopes (1999, 2003a) and Palmiere (2002). Compare example (5), previously discussed, with (10):

(10) *Eu caí no chão.*   (N 2.8.4)
      I fell on-the floor
      "I fell down."

A central topic of research in the study of the availability of A-movement is the passive. Sim-Sim (1998), Correia (2003), Gabriel (2001) and Estrela (2013) all converge in showing that children acquiring Portuguese produce and comprehend passives. The usual asymmetries between short and long passives and between agentive and non-agentive passives are reported in Sim-Sim (1998), for EP, and Rubin (2004) and Lima Jr. (2012), for BP.

Another interesting result comes from Correia's (2003) work, which reports that children's worst performances are found in SE-passives of the type in (11), only found in EP. Crucially, in these passives the DP object is not A-moved from the object position:

(11) *Comeram-se muitas maçãs.*
      Ate-pl *se* many apples
      "Many apples were eaten."

According to these results, thus, just as in other languages, children do not have problems with A-movement. The same holds for A-bar movement, although some asymmetries internal to A-bar dependencies are worth mentioning.

It has been known at least since Corrêa (1982) that the usual subject-object asymmetries found in the production and comprehension of A-bar dependencies are found in Portuguese as well. As in other languages, subject relatives are easier to comprehend and produce than object relatives (see also Vasconcelos 1991, Costa, Lobo and Silva 2011, for EP, and Perroni, 2001, Lessa de Oliveira 2008, for BP). The fact that subject dependencies are spared in production and comprehension is the relevant piece of evidence indicating that there is no problem with A-bar movement. Children are able to perform it, and have access to the top layers of the clausal structure. Confirming predictions made by Grillo (2008) and Friedmann, Belletti, and Rizzi (2009), the data elicited for Portuguese confirm the idea that children's difficulties with movement dependencies stem from intervention configurations of the type depicted in (12):

(12) $X \dots Y \dots ec_x$

If X and Y share features, Y may act as an intervener for the establishment of the dependency between X and the empty category relating to it. What counts as an intervener is not fully established, but some facts are known. First, X and Y have to be lexically restricted, that is the constituent must contain a noun. There are asymmetries between the comprehension of headed relatives (13a) and free relatives (13b), and between D-linked *wh*-questions (14a) and bare *wh*-questions (14b):

(13)   a. *Mostra-me a menina que a mãe abraça.*
           Show me the girl that the mother hugs
       b. *Mostra-me quem a mãe abraça.*
           Show me who the mother hugs

(14)   a. *Que menina é que a mãe abraça?*
           Which girl is that the mother hugs?
       b. *Quem é que a mãe abraça?*
           Who is that the mother hugs

Costa, Grillo, and Lobo (2012) tested the comprehension of free and headed *wh*-dependencies, showing that free object relatives (13b) are comprehended more easily than headed object relatives (13a). Lessa de Oliveira (2008) also shows that free relatives are produced quite early as well. These findings confirm Cerejeira's (2009) observation that children aged between 3 and 6 have a better comprehension of bare object *wh*-question (14b) than they do for D-linked object questions (14a). This type of asymmetry signals that it is the intervention configuration rather than the mere alternation of canonical order that acts as the source of difficulties for children.

The exact nature of what counts as an intervener remains to be found. In a recent study on the production and comprehension of relative clauses with a relativized constituent with a preposition, as in (15), Costa et al. (2014) found that the two XPs in the relevant configuration may be categorically distinct.

(15)   *Mostra-me a menina com que a mãe sonha.*
       Show me the girl with whom the mother dreams.

Costa et al. (2014) show that children's comprehension and production of PP relatives is similar to their performance with object relatives, which indicates that intervention configurations arise even in the absence of total feature similarity.

These findings support the evidence discussed in Vasconcelos (1991) according to which the presence of a preposition in relative dependencies is a further source of difficulty, but this does not mean that PP relatives are much different from object relatives. (See also Valente 2008 and Fontes 2008 for further data on the acquisition of PP relatives.)

The picture is slightly different in BP, though. PP relatives, especially pied-piped ones as in (15), are extremely rare in production and appear later in development, according to Lessa de Oliveira (2008). Since relatives with resumptive pronouns as in (16) are also rare, as shown by Perroni (2001), children resort to the non-standard (but much more common in BP) option illustrated in (17), in which the preposition is dropped, a strategy also found in topicalization structures as in (18) (example from Grolla, 2000):

(16) *Eu vô no seu colo, porque lá tem aquela cobrinha que as muler (= mulher) dança nela.* (N 3.1)
I go in-the your lap because there has that snake-diminutive that the-pl woman
    dance-sg on-it.
"I'll go in your lap because there is that little snake there in which the women dance."

(17) *Mostra pra mim a menina que a mãe sonha.*
Show to me the girl that the mother dreams.

(18) *Essa boneca eu vou brincar o dia inteiro.* (N 3.10)
This doll I go play-inf the day long
"I'll play with this doll all day long."

Research on other types of A-bar dependencies confirms that A-bar movement is not problematic per se, and that intervention configurations are a source of difficulty. Abalada (2012) found that object topicalization structures are harder to comprehend than canonical word orders in EP. Lobo, Santos, and Soares (2012) studied the production and comprehension of different types of clefts in European Portuguese, and found that object clefts are harder to comprehend than subject clefts.

In BP, children produce subject clefts very early (19), before relative clauses are attested (see Perroni 2001); on the other hand, object topicalization structures (20), together with the topicalization of other functions, are also productively produced since a very early age (see Grolla, 2000):

(19) *O papai que jogô(u) fora no lixo aqui.* (N 2.6)
The dad that threw away in-the trash bin here.
"It was dad who threw (something) in the trash bin here."

(20) *Tudo você tem.* (N 2.5)
Everything you have
"You have everything."

There is further evidence for the claim that movement is not the source of the problems with A-bar dependencies for young children: similar intervention effects are found in the absence of movement as well, provided the same intervention configuration obtains. This has been reported for the comprehension of coordinations with a gap of the type illustrated in (21) (Friedmann and Costa 2010a), and for the comprehension of prepositional infinitival constructions of the type illustrated in (22) (Costa, Fernandes, Vaz, and Grillo, forthcoming):

(21) *O João viu o Pedro e ___ sorriu.*
The João saw the Pedro and ___ smiled.
"João saw Pedro and smiled."

(22)   *O João viu o filho do médico a sorrir.*
        The João saw the son of the doctor P smile-inf
        "João saw the doctor's son smiling."

The comparison between the different types of configuration led Costa and Lobo (2014) to investigate the relevance of c-command for intervention and they found that intervention effects crucially involve a c-commanding intervener.

In both studies cited, it is shown that, even in the absence of movement, the identification of the subject of the second coordinate in (21) or the antecedent of the subject of the infinitival clause in (22) is affected by the intervening DP. Independent evidence for the intervention effect comes from Freire (2013), who tested the comprehension of perception verbs with infinitival constructions in 4- to 9-year-old children. Even the youngest groups performed at ceiling in sentences such as (23) where they did not have to compute the first subject since its features and that of the object were non-coincident:

(23)   *Você viu o Pedro pintar a casa de verde?*
        You saw the Pedro paint-inf the house of green
        "Did you see Pedro paint the house green?"

Interestingly, it may be shown that some of these effects are found in adults as well, which indicates that the difficulties with object dependencies in the presence of intervention configurations are not subject to maturation or to some kind of language growth. Instead, it is very likely that the computation of these configurations is costly, and the differences between adult and children have to do with the ease to deal with costly computations.

Another argument showing that movement is not necessarily difficult for children comes from the analysis of the comprehension of scrambling in EP. In Costa and Szendroi (2006), the comprehension of the interpretative effects associated with scrambling in ditransitive constructions is compared with the comprehension of the effects of stress shift. The relevant piece of data comes from the readings children associate with the focus adverb *só* "only." Although, as Santos (2006/2009) points out, there are issues children must deal with in order to achieve adult performance with focus adverbs, Costa and Szendroi show that there are no deviances in the comprehension of the interpretation of scrambling. In other words, children do not have troubles understanding the effects of scrambling. This is an interesting result, since it indicates that children experience no trouble in the interpretation of certain discourse-related movement operations.

Clear cases of development can, however, be found in movement dependencies. Vaz (2012) and Lobo and Vaz (2012) studied the acquisition of exhaustivity in quantificational structures and in the comprehension of multiple *wh*-questions in EP. In this language, an answer to a multiple *wh*-question is necessarily exhaustive, unlike what happens to single *wh*-questions. Vaz (2012) and Lobo and Vaz (2012) show that until the age of 5, children fail to understand this exhaustivity requirement. This finding attests the presence of certain features in specific structures that may undergo development.

Altogether, these results on the acquisition of movement in Portuguese point into one direction: movement is acquired very early. As a matter of fact, even when given an option, children prefer to move elements rather than not to move them. BP is an optional *wh*-movement language, having both moved and in-situ *wh*-constructions. Grolla (2000, 2005) shows that no *wh* in-situ is attested in children's production until almost their fourth birthday (see (25)):

(24)   a.   *Que é isso aqui?*   (N 2.2)
            "What is this here?"
        b.   *Por que você tá fazendu assim?*   (N 2.6)
            Why you are doing like-that
            "Why are you doing (something) like that?"

(25) a. *P(r)á í(r) aonde?*   (N 3.9)
     Prep go-inf where?
     "Where (will we) have to go?"
   b. *Eu quero brincar com que?*   (N 3.11)
     I want play-inf with what
     "What do I want to play with?"

Comparison with populations with language impairments confirm the robustness of these findings, since generalized difficulties with movement can be found with specific populations (see Ferreira 2008, José 2011, Corrêa and Augusto 2011a, 2011b for Specific Language Impairment; Cerdeira 2006, Lima et al. 2009 for agrammatism; Friedmann and Costa 2011 for hearing impairment; and Rubin, 2004 for Down Syndrome, a.o.).

4. Acquisition of referential dependencies

The acquisition of pronouns and referential dependencies has received major attention over the last three decades. This is an excellent area of comparison between Portuguese and other languages, and between varieties of Portuguese, since these languages differ in curious ways with respect to the behavior of pronominal forms. Here, we focus on the results available in the literature regarding (1) the production of pronouns and clitic placement, (2) the interpretation of pronouns, and (3) the comprehension of null categories.

4.1. *The production of pronouns*

Let us start with the production of pronouns. It is known that, in many languages, children omit clitics in their early productions. This has been tested for many clitic languages, and most findings converge in the observation that clitic omission tends to affect 3rd person accusative clitics. Costa and Lobo (2006) tested clitic production in European Portuguese, in particular trying to differentiate (target deviant) omission from target null objects of the type illustrated in (26):

(26) A: *E o meu carro?*
     And the my car
     "What about my car?"
  B: *Deixei ___ na garagem.*
     Left in the garage
     "I left it in the garage."

Null objects are optional in contexts like in (26); hence, omission in such contexts may look like adult performance. For this reason, Costa and Lobo tried to elicit pronouns in strong islands—a context in which null objects are ruled out in EP, as shown in Raposo (1986). They found that children omit pronouns across the board—both in root contexts and in islands.

This result could still be interpreted in two ways: omission of accusative clitics in more than one context or a generalization of the null object construction. In order to decide between these two options, Costa and Lobo (2007), Silva (2008) and Costa, Lobo, and Silva (2009, 2012) tried to elicit the production of clitics that do not freely alternate with null objects. This allowed for testing whether children overgeneralized the null object construction. They found that, indeed, children omitted 1st and 2nd person clitics, as well as reflexive clitics—all these are not legitimate null objects in adult grammar. On the basis of this result, they formulated the hypothesis that children overextend the null object option to all types of clitic pronouns.

If this hypothesis is on the right track, this means that children know that the language has null objects. This has been confirmed on independent grounds for EP and for BP. For EP, Costa and Lobo (2009) tested the comprehension of sentences containing a verb that could be either transitive or intransitive (e.g. *acordar* / wake up), and checked whether children could assign transitive readings to a verb that is not followed by an overt complement. They found that they can do it, but that they overaccept transitive readings in reflexive contexts and in islands. Interestingly, this is coherent with what was found in the production experiments. Children overuse null objects in production, and they overaccept null objects in comprehension.

BP no longer has 3rd person clitics, and null objects occur quite freely, even within islands, if the antecedent is inanimate. Animate antecedents are recovered with strong pronouns if they are specific. Null objects can also be deictic, with no linguistic antecedent, or anaphoric, with a linguistic antecedent in the previous discourse (see Chapter 16 on null objects in Portuguese).

Null objects are to be found in the Brazilian children's initial utterances. However, as Lopes (2009) has shown, those are instances of deictic null objects. Children also make massive use of lexicalized DPs in object position, especially when they want to establish anaphoric relations (see (27) below). Anaphoric null objects, as well as the use of pronouns, will only be attested in spontaneous production data some time later, after a child's second birthday.

(27) *Agora eu vou botar minha massinha n[o meu forno], porque eu tenho [o meu forno].* (AC 2.8)
      Now I go put_inf my dough_diminutive in+[the my oven], because I have
      [the my oven].
      "I'll put the dough in my oven now, because I have my oven."

But, as is the case with EP, Casagrande (2010) also shows that young children tend to overuse null objects. In an elicited production task with verbs that can be used as accomplishment or activity (such as *pintar* "paint"), the author shows that 3 and 4 year-olds tend to use the null object in almost 80 percent of the time, while adult rates were as low as 33 percent. In a different test, with specific animate antecedents, where the use of pronouns is expected, Casagrande also shows that children tend to avoid their use, overusing the null option or using a lexicalized DP, instead. Only the 6-year-old group displayed adult-like results recovering animate antecedents by means of strong pronouns.

Returning to clitics, it is known that in EP they can appear in proclitic and enclitic environments. This might be argued to be the source of the problems in clitic production. One might think that children avoid clitics because, say, their positional possibilities indetermine their morphophonological status. However, this turns out not to be the case. Duarte et al. (1995) and Duarte and Matos (2000) report that children acquiring EP generalize enclisis, as in the examples in (28):

(28) a. *Não chama-se nada.*   (M 20 months)
          Not call-refl nothing
          "It is not called that."
      b. *Porque é que foste-me interromper?*   (R., 29 months)
          Why is that go-me interrupt-inf
          "Why is it that you interrupted me?"

There are two reasons to dissociate issues related to clitic placement from the generalization of null objects. Costa, Fiéis, and Lobo (2014) show that problems with clitic placement arise even with those clitics that are not as easily omitted, in particular the clitic *se*. Morever, they also show that the generalization of enclisis lasts longer than the period during which, according to Silva (2008)'s findings, children generalize null objects. There is, thus, no correlation between the two phenomena. One interesting aspect of the generalization of enclisis, reported in Costa, Fiéis, and Lobo (2013), is that it is context-sensitive. The authors show that proclisis is acquired in accordance with the following scale:

(29) Negation > Negative Subjects, Subjunctive complements > Proclisis triggering
       adverbs > Adverbial clauses, Quantified subjects

This scale of development relates with input variability and with the inherent properties of each of these contexts: e.g., if one compares negation with adverbs, we can see that negation is a categorical context for proclisis, whereas children must find out which preverbal adverbs trigger proclisis, and which adverbs do not. For instance, for a pair like the one in (30), children will have to learn that only the adverb *já* "already" triggers proclisis, which involves a combination of syntactic and lexical knowledge, differently from what happens with negation:

(30) a. *Eu ontem vi-te.*
          I yesterday saw you$_{cl}$
      b. *Eu já te vi.*
          I already you$_{cl}$ saw

In a sense, proclisis with negation involves only syntactic knowledge, whereas proclisis with adverbs involves syntactic and lexical knowledge.

These data lead to the conclusion that pronoun omission is not a side effect of difficulties with clitic placement in EP.

4.2. *The comprehension of pronouns*

A well-known fact about the acquisition of pronouns is that there is a cross-linguistic difference between languages with clitic pronouns and languages with strong pronouns (Chien and Wexler 1990, McKee 1992, among others). It is known that, until the age of 5, children may assign reflexive readings to strong pronouns, as in English sentences like (31):

(31) Bill washed him.

They do not misinterpret anaphors (*self* forms). It is also known that these interpretation problems do not show up when the pronoun is a clitic. This strong pronoun–clitic asymmetry is interesting, because the acquisition of the varieties of Portuguese provides a good testing ground for the idea that this difference is crucial (recall that BP no longer has 3rd person clitics). Grolla (2010) assessed the comprehension of pronouns by children acquiring BP, and found that there are problems in the interpretation of pronouns. This is different from what was found for EP in Cristóvão (2006) and Silva (2012): in EP, children performed basically at adult levels in the interpretation of pronouns. Crucially, the test items contained strong pronouns in BP and clitics in EP:

(32) a. *O dragão está coçando ele*   BP
          the dragon is scratching him
      b. *A mãe lava-a?*   EP
          the mother washes her$_{cl}$

This asymmetry between clitics and strong pronouns, and the observation that only the interpretation of strong pronouns is affected, led Costa and Ambulate (2010) and Silva (2015) to test the relevance of strong pronouns within one and the same variety of Portuguese.

Costa and Ambulate (2010) tested the comprehension of strong pronouns in embedded contexts, in sentences like (33) in EP:

(33)   *O Shrek disse ao Noddy que ele tem fome.*
       The Shrek told the Noddy that he has hunger
       "Shrek told Noddy that he is hungry."

This is a context in which disjoint reference with the matrix subject is preferred by adults. However, children performed at chance. In order to test cases in which strong pronouns alternate with anaphors, Silva (2012, 2015) tested contexts of binding into prepositional phrases, comparing children's interpretation of strong pronouns, as in (34a), with the interpretation of reflexives, as in (34b):

(34)   a. *A Maria gosta dela.*
           The Maria likes of her
       b. *A Maria gosta de si.*
           The Maria likes of self

Silva found that there is a cumulative effect of the type of pronoun with the disjoint reference. Anaphors are easier to interpret than pronouns, and the weakest forms are easier to interpret than strong pronouns. But contexts such as those in (34a) cannot be compared to those in (32a) either. Bertolino (2013) and Vieira (2014) have shown that Brazilian children, as well as adults, will accept a local antecedent if the pronoun is embedded under a preposition, especially if the predicate has a reflexive flavor.

4.3. *The comprehension of null categories*

We have just seen that the weakest forms (clitics and null) are easier to comprehend in the acquisition of Portuguese. Accordingly, it is expected that null forms are the easiest type. This is partly true, and it depends on the type of empty category to be acquired.

Let us compare different types of null forms, starting with the null subject. As previously mentioned, children experience difficulties in the comprehension of strong pronouns in embedded subject positions. The same does not hold for null embedded subject positions. Both Costa and Ambulate (2010) and Silva (2012, 2015) observe that children behave in an adult-like way in the interpretation of embedded null subjects of the type in (35):

(35)   *O Shrek disse ao Noddy que ___ tem fome.*
       The Shrek told to Noddy that ___ has hunger
       "Shrek told Noddy that he is hungry."

However, not all properties of null subjects have been acquired by the age of 6. In Costa and Lobo (2011), the authors ask the following question: do children acquiring EP know that the embedded null subject is *pro*? In order to answer this question, they tested children's knowledge on the assignment of strict readings to *pro*. Following Miyagawa (2010), who shows that *pro* induces strict readings in sentences like (36), Costa and Lobo tested children's interpretation of this type of utterances:

(36)   *O João disse que os pais estão sentados e o Pedro disse que <u>pro</u> têm chapéu.*
       The João said that the parents are sitting and the Pedro said that *pro* have hat.
       "João said that his parent are sitting, and Pedro said that they wear a hat."

            pro = João's parents (strict reading—available)
            pro = Pedro's parents (sloppy reading—unavailable)

Costa and Lobo found that children are not sensitive to this property of *pro*, and assign sloppy readings to it. This indicates that not all properties of null subjects are acquired yet. Interestingly, this is an area of variation between European and Brazilian Portuguese, since, according to some descriptions, sloppy readings emerge with null subjects in BP only. Costa, Grolla, and Lobo (2013) tested Portuguese and Brazilian children with the same task, and no clear differences emerged, which may indicate that the properties of null categories are acquired late in EP, but are adult-like in BP.

Costa, Grolla and Lobo's test was run in order to compare null subjects and null objects. Unlike null subjects, null objects permit sloppy readings, which is illustrated in (37) ("NO" abbreviates "null object"):

(37) *O Pedro abraça os pais, mas o João beija.*
        The Pedro hugs the parents, but the João kisses NO.
        "Pedro hugs his parents, but João kisses (them = his parents)."

            NO = Pedro's parents (strict reading—available)
            NO = João's parents (sloppy reading—available)

Again, children experienced some difficulties with these data, both in EP and in BP. It should be considered, though, that in BP results might have to do with the fact that the antecedent is animate and, therefore, the null object is not a natural option in such context for the target grammar as well. However, if a pronoun were used, then only a strict reading would be obtained.

There is, nevertheless, no reason to think that there is a generalized difficulty with null categories, since in some well documented cases children perform adult-like in the comprehension of null categories.

We can first consider the acquisition of nominal ellipsis, as in (38):

(38) *Eu vi o urso castanho e tu o ec preto.*
        I saw the bear brown and you the __ black.
        "I saw the brown bear, and you the black one."

Clara (2008) and Lobo and Clara (2009) show that 2-year-old children produce and comprehend nominal ellipsis, and are able to retrieve the antecedent in structures like (38). These authors argue that the gender and number morphology on determiners and adjectives are important clues to the retrieval of the antecedents. Although there is a developmental effect in comprehension, the results presented by Clara (2008) show that children's performance with nominal ellipsis is quite good.

Similar good results emerge in the comprehension of VP ellipsis. Both varieties of Portuguese license VP ellipsis with auxiliaries, modal or main verbs (see Chapter 16 for details).

Santos (2006/2009) tested the comprehension of VP ellipsis in EP in order to check whether 4- to 6-year-old children were able to interpret elided material in an adult-like manner, indicating a target syntactic analysis to VP ellipsis structures as well as adult-like interpretive conditions. Her results show that children perform at ceiling when given a chance, in truth-value judgment tasks, to interpret the elliptical site as identical to the antecedent VP, therefore showing that they preserve the identity requirement on ellipses. Santos's experiment was replicated with Brazilian children. Lopes and Santos (2014) found similar results for the Brazilian children as well. The comprehension data obtained, therefore, shows that children perform at adult levels when they can recover a matching antecedent for an ellipsis site. Since ellipses are subject to both recoverability and licensing conditions, their comprehension involves the ability to recover elided material from a discourse antecedent as well as knowledge of the language-specific syntactic licensing conditions. Therefore, in order to achieve adult-like levels of performance, children have to operate as adults as far as their knowledge of the syntax-discourse interface is concerned.

As previously discussed with respect to movement and the syntax-discourse interface, it seems that, once again, results point in the direction that children can deal with evasive linguistic categories, even when they are silent.

REFERENCES

Abalada, S. (2012). Acquisition of the left and right peripheries in European Portuguese. In S. Stavrakaki, P. Konstatinopoulou, and M. Lalioti (eds.), *Advances in Language Acquisition: Proceedings of GALA 2011*. Cambridge: Cambridge Scholars.

Adragão, M. M. and J. Costa (2004). On the status of preverbal subjects in null subject languages: evidence from acquisition. In J. van Kampen and S. Baauw (eds.), *Proceedings of GALA 2003*. Utrecht: LOT Occasional Series.

Bertolino, K. G. (2013). Restrições sobre a interpretação da proforma "ele" com antecedente local em português brasileiro: um estudo experimental. Master dissertation, Universidade de São Paulo.

Casagrande, S. (2010). A correlação entre objeto e aspecto no português brasileiro: uma análise sintático-aquisicionista. Ph.D. dissertation, University of Campinas.

Castro, A. and J. Ferrari-Neto (2007). Um estudo contrastivo do PE e do PB com relação à identificaçãode informação de número no DP. *Letras de Hoje*, 42 (1), pp. 65–76.

Cerdeira, A. M. (2006). Flexão verbal e categorias funcionais no agramatismo. Master dissertation, Faculdade de Ciências Sociais e Humanas, Universidade Nova de Lisboa.

Cerejeira, J. (2009). Aquisição de interrogativas de sujeito e de objecto em português europeu. Master dissertation, Faculdade de Ciências Sociais e Humanas, Universidade Nova de Lisboa.

Chien, Y.-C. and K. Wexler (1990). Children's knowledge of locality conditions in binding as evidence for the modularity of syntax and pragmatics. *Language Acquisition*, 1, pp. 225–295.

Clara, D. (2008). A aquisição da elipse nominal em português europeu – produção e compreensão. Master dissertation, Faculdade de Ciências Sociais e Humanas, Universidade Nova de Lisboa.

Corrêa, L. M. S. (1982). Strategies in the acquisition of relative clauses. In J. Aitchison and N. Harvey (eds.), *Working Papers of the London Psycholinguistic Research Group*, 4, pp. 37–49.

Corrêa, L. M. S. and M. R. A. Augusto (2011a). Possible loci of SLI from a both linguistic and psycholinguistic perspective. *Lingua*, 121, p. 476–486.

Corrêa, L. M. S. and M. R. A. Augusto (2011b). Custo de processamento e comprometimento da linguagem: movimento sintático na computação on-line e minimalidade relativizada em orações relativas e perguntas-QU. *Anais do VII Congresso Internacional da ABRALIN*, pp. 2364–2378.

Corrêa, L. S., M. Augusto, and J. Ferrari-Neto (2005). The early processing of number agreement in the DP: evidence from the acquisition of Brazilian Portuguese. Poster presented at the 30th Boston University Conference On Language Development.

Correia, D. (2003). Passivas e Pseudo-Passivas em Português Europeu – Produção Provocada e Compreensão. Master dissertation, University of Lisbon.

Costa, J. and J. Ambulate (2010). The acquisition of embedded subject pronouns in European Portuguese. In M. Iverson, I. Ivanov, T. Judy, J. Rothman, R. Slabakova, and M. Tryzna (eds.), *Proceedings of the 2009 Mind/Context Divide Workshop*. Sommerville, MA: Cascadilla Press, pp. 1–12.

Costa, J., A. Fiéis, and M. Lobo (2014). Input variability and late acquisition: clitic misplacement in European Portuguese. *Lingua*, 161, pp. 10–26.

Costa, J. and M. J. Freitas (2001). Morphological and/or prosodic place holders. In *Statistical Physics, Pattern Identification and Language Change, ZIF – Bielefeld*.

Costa, J. and N. Friedmann (2012). Children acquire unaccusatives and A-movement very early. In M. Everaert, M. Marelj, and T. Siloni (eds.), *Theta System*. New York: Oxford University Press, pp. 354–378.

Costa, J., N. Friedmann, C. Silva, and M. Yachini (2014). The boy that the chef cooked: the acquisition of PP relatives in Portuguese and Hebrew. *Lingua*, 150, pp. 386–409.

Costa, J., N. Grillo, and M. Lobo (2012). Minimality beyond lexical restrictions: processing and acquisition of free relatives in European Portuguese. *Revue Roumaine de Linguistique/Roumanian Review of Linguistics*, LVII (2), pp. 143–160.

Costa, J., B. Fernandes, S. Vaz, and N. Grillo (forthcoming). (Pseudo-) Relatives and Prepositional Infinitival Constructions in the Acquisition of European Portuguese. *Probus*.

Costa, J., E. Grolla, and M. Lobo (2013). The acquisition of microvariation in silent categories. Paper presented at GALA 2013, University of Oldenburg.

Costa, J. and M. Lobo (2006). A aquisição de clíticos em PE: Omissão de Clíticos ou Objectos Nulos? *Textos Seleccionados do XXI Encontro Nacional da Associação Portuguesa de Linguística*. Lisbon: Associação Portuguesa de Linguística, pp. 285–293.

Costa, J. and M. Lobo (2007). Clitic omission, null objects or both in the acquisition of European Portuguese? In S. Baauw, F. Drijkoningen, and M. Pinto (eds.), *Romance Languages and Linguistic Theory 2005*. Amsterdam: John Benjamins, pp. 59–71.

Costa, J. and M. Lobo (2009). Clitic omission in the acquisition of European Portuguese: data from comprehension. In A. Pires and J. Rothman (eds.), *Minimalist Inquiries into Child and Adult Language Acquisition: Case Studies across Portuguese*. Berlin: de Gruyter, pp. 63–84.

Costa, J. and M. Lobo (2011) Objeto nulo na aquisição do português europeu: pro ou variável? *XXVI Encontro Nacional da Associação Portuguesa de Linguística. Textos Seleccionados*, pp. 197–207. http://www.apl.org.pt/apl-actas/xxvi-encontro-nacional-da-associacao-portuguesa-de-linguistica.html , accessed November 17, 2015.

Costa, J. and M. Lobo (2014). Testing relativized minimality in intervention effects: the comprehension of relative clauses with complex DPs in European Portuguese. Paper presented at The Romance Turn, Palma de Mallorca.

Costa, J., M. Lobo, and C. Silva (2009). Null objects and early pragmatics in the acquisition of European Portuguese. *Probus*, 21, pp. 143–162.

Costa, J., M. Lobo, and C. Silva (2011). Subject-object asymmetries in the acquisition of Portuguese relative clauses: adults vs. children. *Lingua*, 121 (6), pp. 987–1158.

Costa, J., M. Lobo, and C. Silva (2012). Which category replaces an omitted clitic? The case of European Portuguese. In P. Guijarro-Fuentes and M. P. Larrañaga (eds.), *Pronouns and Clitics in Early Acquisition*. Berlin: de Gruyter, pp. 105–130.

Costa, J. and J. Loureiro (2006). Morphology vs. word order in the acquisition of V-to-I. *Catalan Journal of Linguistics*, 5, pp. 45–58.

Costa, J. and K. Szendroi (2006). Acquisition of focus marking in European Portuguese – evidence for a unified approach to focus. In V. Torrens and L. Escobar (eds.), *The Acquisition of Syntax in Romance Languages*. Amsterdam: John Benjamins, pp. 319–329.

Cristóvão, S. (2006). A co-referência nos pronomes objecto directo na aquisição do português europeu. Master dissertation, Faculdade de Ciências Sociais e Humanas, Universidade Nova de Lisboa.

Duarte, I. and G. Matos (2000). Romance clitics and the minimalist program. In J. Costa (ed.), *Portuguese Syntax. New Comparative Studies*. Oxford: Oxford University Press, pp. 116–142.

Duarte, I., G. Matos, and I. Faria (1995). Specificity of European Portuguese clitics in Romance. In I. Faria and M. J. Freitas (eds.), *Studies on the Acquisition of Portuguese*. Lisbon: Colibri, pp. 129–154.

Estrela, A. (2013). A aquisição da estrutura passiva em português europeu. Ph.D. dissertation, Faculdade de Ciências Sociais e Humanas, Universidade Nova de Lisboa.

Faria, I., G. Matos, M. Miguel, and M. J. Freitas (1997). Functional categories in early acquisition of European Portuguese. In A. Sorace, C. Heycock, and R. Shillcock (eds.), *Proceedings of GALA 1997 (Generative Approaches to Language Acquisition)*. Edinburgh: University of Edinburgh, pp. 115–120.

Ferreira, E. (2008). Compreensão e produção de frases relativas por crianças com perturbação específica do desenvolvimento da linguagem e por adultos com agramatismo. Master dissertation, Faculdade de Ciências Sociais e Humanas, Universidade Nova de Lisboa.

Freitas, M. J. and M. Miguel (1998). Prosodic and syntactic interaction: the acquisition of NP functional projections in European Portuguese. In T. Cambier-Langeveld, A. Liptak, and M. Redford (eds.), *Proceedings of ConSole VI*, pp. 27–44.

Friedmann, N., A. Belletti, and L. Rizzi (2009). Relativized relatives: types of intervention in the acquisition of A-bar dependencies. *Lingua*, 119, pp. 67–88.

Friedmann, N. and J. Costa (2010a). The child heard a coordinated sentence and wondered: on children's difficulty in understanding coordination and relative clauses with crossing dependencies. *Lingua*, 120 (6), pp. 1502–1515.

Friedmann, N. and J. Costa (2010b). Acquisition of SV and VS Order in Hebrew, European Portuguese, Palestinian Arabic, and Spanish. *Language Acquisition*, 18 (1), pp. 1–38.

Friedmann, N. and J. Costa (2011). Last resort or no resort: resumptive pronouns in Hebrew and Palestinian Arabic hearing impairment. In A. Rouveret (ed.), *Resumptive Pronouns at the Interfaces*. Amsterdam: John Benjamins, pp. 223–239.

Fontes, E. (2008). A produção de frases relativas restritivas no final do 1° e 2° Ciclos do ensino básico. Master dissertation, University of Lisbon.

Freire, G. A. N. (2013). Aquisição de verbos perceptivos e causativos e a Teoria da Mente. Ph.D. dissertation, University of Campinas.

Gabriel, R. (2001). A Aquisiçao das Construçoões Passivas em Português e Inglês: Um Estudo Translinguístico. Ph.D. dissertation, Pontifícia Universidade Católica do Rio Grande do Sul.

Gonçalves, F. (2004). Riqueza morfológica e aquisição da sintaxe. Ph.D. dissertation, Universidade de Évora.

Grillo, N. (2008). *Generalized Minimality: Syntactic Underspecification in Broca's Aphasia*. Utrech: LOT.

Grolla, E. (2000). A aquisição da periferia esquerda da sentença em português brasileiro. Master dissertation, University of Campinas.

Grolla, E. (2005). Sobre a aquisição tardia de Qu In Situ em Português Brasileiro. *D.E.L.T.A.*, 21 (1), pp. 57–73.

Grolla, E. (2010). *Pronouns as Elsewhere Elements: Implications for Language Acquisition*. Newcastle: Cambridge Scholars.

José, C. (2011). A produção e compreensão de interrogativas por crianças com Perturbação Específica do Desenvolvimento da Linguagem. Master dissertation, Faculdade de Ciências Sociais e Humanas, Universidade Nova de Lisboa.

Lima, R. J., L. M. S. Corrêa, and M. R. A. Augusto (2009). Padrões de seletividade na produção agramática e distinção entre movimentos sintáticos na computação on-line. *Revista da ABRALIN*, 8, pp. 139–167.

Lima Jr., J. C. de (2012). Revisitando a aquisição de sentenças passivas do português brasileiro:

uma investigação experimental com foco na compreensão. Master dissertation, Pontifícia Universidade Católica do Rio de Janeiro.

Lessa de Oliveira, A. (2008). As sentenças relativas em português brasileiro: aspectos sintáticos e fatos de aquisição. Ph.D. dissertation. University of Campinas.

Lobo, M. and D. Clara (2009). Comprehension of nominal ellipsis in the acquisition of European Portuguese. Poster presented at Theoretical Syntax and (a)Typical Child Language Acquisition, Workshop in tribute to Celia Jakubowicz, University of Paris 8.

Lobo, M., A. L. Santos, and C. Soares (2012). Aquisição de estruturas clivadas no português europeu: produção espontânea e induzida. In A. Costa, C. Flores, and N. Alexandre (eds.), *Textos Selecionados do XXVII Encontro Nacional da Associação Portuguesa de Linguística*. Lisbon: Associação Portuguesa de Linguística, pp. 319–339.

Lobo, M. and S. D. Vaz (2012). Aquisição de exaustividade em estruturas interrogativas e clivadas do português europeu: desenvolvimento pragmático ou gramatical? In A. Costa and I. Duarte (eds.), *Nada na linguagem lhe é estranho. Estudos em homenagem a Isabel Hub Faria*. Porto: Edições Afrontamento.

Lopes, R. E. V. (1999). Uma proposta minimalista para o processo de aquisição da linguagem: relações locais. Ph.D. dissertation, University of Campinas.

Lopes, R. E. V. (2003a). "Command" and the acquisition of subject and object in Brazilian Portuguese. In S. Montrul and F. Ordóñez (eds.), *Linguistic Theory and Language Development in Hispanic Languages*. Somerville, MA: Cascadilla Press, pp. 317–335.

Lopes, R. E. V. (2003b). The production of subject and object in Brazilian Portuguese by a young child. *Probus*, 15, pp. 123–146.

Lopes, R. E. V. (2006). Bare nouns and DP number agreement in the acquisition of Brazilian Portuguese. In N. Sagarra and J. T. Almeida (eds.), *Selected Proceedings of the 9th Hispanic Linguistics Symposium*. Sommerville, MA: Cascadilla Press, pp. 252–262.

Lopes, R. E. V. (2009). Aspect and the acquisition of null objects in Brazilian Portuguese. In A. Pires and J. Rothman (eds.), *Minimalist Inquiries into Child and Adult Language Acquisition*. Berlin: de Gruyter, pp. 105–128.

Lopes, R. E. V. and A. L. Santos (2014). VP-ellipsis comprehension in European and Brazilian Portuguese. In J. Costa, A. Fiéis, M. J. Freitas,

M. Lobo, and A. L. Santos (eds.), *New Directions in the Acquisition of Romance Languages: Selected Proceedings of The Romance Turn V*. Newcastle: Cambridge Scholars, pp. 181–201.

Magalhães, T. (2006). O sistema pronominal sujeito e objeto na aquisição do português europeu e do português brasileiro. Ph.D. dissertation, University of Campinas.

McKee, C. (1992). A comparison of pronouns and anaphors in Italian and English acquisition. *Language Acquisition*, 2, pp. 21–54.

Miyagawa, S. (2010). *Why agree? Why move? Unifying Agreement-based and Discourse Configurational Languages*. Linguistic Inquiry Monograph 54. Cambridge,MA: MIT Press.

Name, M. C. L. (2002). Habilidades Perceptuais e Lingüísticas no Processo de Aquisição do Sistema de Gênero no Português. Ph.D. dissertation, Pontifícia Universidade Católica do Rio de Janeiro.

Palmiere, D. T. L. (2002). A inacusatividade na aquisição da linguagem. Ph.D. dissertation, University of Campinas.

Perroni, M. C. (2001). As relativas que são fáceis na aquisição do português brasileiro. *D.E.L.T.A.*, 17 (1), pp. 59–79.

Raposo, E. (1986). On the null object in European Portuguese. In O. Jaeggli and C. Silva Corvalán (eds.), *Studies in Romance Linguistics*. Dordrecht: Foris, pp. 373–390.

Rubin, M. (2004). A passiva na Síndrome de Down. Ph.D. dissertation, Universidade Federal do Paraná.

Santos, A. L. (2006/2009). *Minimal Answers. Ellipsis, syntax and discourse in the acquisition of European Portuguese*. Amsterdam: John Benjamins.

Santos, R. S. (2001). A aquisição do acento primário no português brasileiro. Ph.D. dissertation, University of Campinas.

Santos, R. S. (2005). Strategies for word stress acquisition in Brazilian Portuguese. In M. Tzakosta, C. Levelt, and J. van de Weijer (eds.), *Developmental Paths in Phonological Acquisition*. Special Issue of *Leiden Papers in Linguistics*, 2 (1), pp. 71–91.

Silva, C. (2008). Assimetrias na aquisição de clíticos diferenciados em português europeu. Master dissertation, Faculdade de Ciências

Sociais e Humanas, Universidade Nova de Lisboa.

Silva, C. (2012). Interpretação de sujeitos pronominais nulos e lexicais encaixados na aquisição do português europeu. In A. Costa, C. Flores, and N. Alexandre (eds.), *Textos Selecionados do XXVII Encontro Nacional da Associação Portuguesa de Linguística*. Lisbon: Associação Portuguesa de Linguística, pp. 567–586.

Silva, C. (2015). Interpretation of clitic, strong and null pronouns in the acquisition of European Portuguese. PhD dissertation, FCSH-Universidade Nova de Lisboa

Sim-Sim, I. (1998). Linguagem e cognição. Um olhar sobre teorias explicativas. In I. Sim-Sim (ed.), *Desenvolvimento da Linguagem*. Lisbon: Universidade Aberta, pp. 291–338.

Simioni, L. (2007). A aquisição da concordância nominal de número no português brasileiro: um parâmetro para a concordância nominal. Master dissertation, Universidade Federal de Santa Catarina.

Soares, C. (1998). As categorias funcionais no processo de aquisição do português europeu. Master dissertation, University of Lisbon.

Soares, C. (2003). The C-domain and the acquisition of European Portuguese: the case of wh-questions. *Probus*, 15, pp. 147–176.

Soares, C. (2006). La syntaxe de la périphérie gauche et son acquisition en Portugais Européen. Ph.D. dissertation, University of Paris 8.

Valente, P. (2008). A produção de frases relativas restritivas no final do 3º Ciclo e do Secundário. Master dissertation, University of Lisbon.

Vasconcelos, M. (1991). Compreensão e produção de frases com orações relativas: um estudo experimental com crianças dos três anos e meio aos oito anos e meio. Master dissertation, University of Lisbon.

Vaz, S. D. (2012). Aquisição de exaustividade em crianças falantes de português europeu. Master dissertation, Faculdade de Ciências Sociais e Humanas, Universidade Nova de Lisboa.

Vieira, R. C. (2014). Aquisição da proforma contrastiva "ele mesmo" no português brasileiro. Master dissertation, University of São Paulo.

32 Second Language Acquisition

ANA MADEIRA

1. Introduction

The goal of this chapter is to present a brief overview of some of the research issues and topics which have been the object of current research on the acquisition of European and Brazilian Portuguese (EP and BP, respectively) as a second language (L2). For reasons of space, I will restrict the focus of this synopsis to work which has been conducted within a generative framework.

The chapter is divided into three sections. The second section provides a brief introduction to some of the research questions which have dominated recent L2 acquisition research, thus setting the stage for the review of studies on L2 Portuguese in the third section. The chapter concludes with a brief balance of what these studies have taught us and of the questions which they raise for future research.

2. Generative second language acquisition

In general, the problem of language acquisition may be argued to be the same for all language acquisition, namely: how does an individual build a mental grammar on the basis of the primary linguistic data he or she is exposed to? There are, of course, important differences between a child's acquisition of one or more first languages and the acquisition of a second language by an adult. Unlike children, for example, adults have a degree of cognitive maturity which allows them to resort to a wider range of learning strategies in the course of acquiring a second language; they already have knowledge of at least one language; and they are unlikely to attain native competence—we know that near-native competence is possible is certain language domains but unlikely to develop in others (e.g., Birdsong 1992), and that interlanguage grammars are prone to fossilization (Selinker 1972; Lardiere 2007), that is, to stabilize at non-native levels. In the face of these differences, and particularly of the fact that the end result of the acquisition process tends to be very different in first and second language acquisition, it has often been assumed that they are qualitatively different processes.

However, in spite of all these obvious differences between L1 and L2, the two processes have certain aspects in common: for example, it is known that, like child first language acquisition, adult second language acquisition is also characterized by systematic developmental sequences, which, in many cases, are similar to those observed in L1 acquisition, which may explain why many of the mistakes produced by adult L2 learners are identical to

The Handbook of Portuguese Linguistics, First Edition. Edited by W. Leo Wetzels, João Costa, and Sergio Menuzzi.
© 2016 John Wiley & Sons, Inc. Published 2020 by John Wiley & Sons, Inc.

those produced by L1 children. Hence, every theory of L2 acquisition must aim to answer (at least) the following questions: (1) What is the nature of the process of second language acquisition? (2) How does second language knowledge develop from the initial state to the steady state? (3) How can we explain the different levels of success in L1 and L2 acquisition, on the one hand, and the similarities between the two processes, on the other?

In the case of the L1, it is suggested, on the basis of the observation that the language environment does not make available to the child enough information to explain the rich and complex knowledge system which he or she ends up developing—the so-called "poverty of the stimulus argument" (Chomsky 1987)—that children are genetically endowed with an innate language faculty, which includes a Universal Grammar (UG), which specifies a set of principles and parameterized options that guide the children in the process of language acquisition, helping them filter and structure the primary linguistic data.

As with L1 acquisition, generative approaches to adult second language acquisition have sought to take into account the roles played by cognitive mechanisms and language input (as well as the learner's L1) in order to explain how learners build their mental representations of the L2 grammar. Hence, the central question behind generative research on L2 acquisition has been whether it is guided by the same principles as L1 acquisition.

In attempting to answer this question, several approaches have arisen. On the one hand, the "No Access" approaches argue that L1 acquisition and L2 learning are two fundamentally different processes; hence, interlanguage grammars may end up displaying properties which are not found in natural languages. Under this view, UG becomes inactive (or inaccessible) beyond the critical period and does not play any role in the learning of an L2 (e.g., Bley-Vroman 1989). Parameter resetting should, therefore, not be possible. On the other hand, the "Full Access" approaches argue for the full availability of UG throughout the acquisition process and, hence, predict parameter resetting, although they may differ as to the role attributed to the L1 at the initial state (e.g., Vainikka and Young-Scholten's 1996 Minimal Trees Hypothesis; Schwartz and Sprouse's 1996 Full Transfer/Full Access Hypothesis). In between the two extremes, we find the "Partial Access" approaches, which assume that no new functional features may be acquired in the L2 (e.g., Hawkins and Chan 1997) or, alternatively, that only certain functional features not instantiated in the learner's L1 remain available for L2 acquisition and, therefore, only some parametric options may be reset (e.g., Tsimpli and Dimitrakopoulou's 2007 Interpretability Hypothesis, which proposes that only uninterpretable features are no longer accessible for the adult L2 learner).

How can one decide among these different approaches? According to Schwartz and Sprouse (2000) (see also White 2003), arguments for Full Access are provided by a large body of empirical evidence suggesting that there is a poverty of the stimulus argument for L2, in that it shows that L2 learners may develop specifically linguistic knowledge which cannot be derived either from the L1 or from the language input available to the learner.

A different line of research which has emerged in recent years centers on the status of different grammatical phenomena for acquisition. A great deal of empirical evidence suggests that what is difficult in acquisition are not syntactic properties, but rather properties which are at the interface between syntax and other language modules or cognitive domains. The syntax–semantics and syntax–discourse interfaces, in particular, have been the focus of much recent research, with various studies suggesting that properties which involve an interface between the syntax and other cognitive domains are subject to developmental delays, tend to exhibit residual optionality effects and are more susceptible to cross-linguistic influence and fossilization, even at the most advanced stages (not only in L2 acquisition but also in other domains such as bilingual L1 acquisition, language attrition, and language change). This observation gave rise to an hypothesis, known as the Interface Hypothesis (Sorace and Filiaci 2006), which states that properties at the interface between the syntax and other domains may never be completely acquired, in contrast to strictly syntactic properties, which are fully acquirable. This greater vulnerability of interface properties has been attributed either to representational deficits or to inadequate processing strategies.

However, it is open to debate whether all interface properties are equally hard to acquire. It has been claimed, for example, that properties at the interface between the grammar and discourse may be more difficult than properties at the syntax–semantics interface (e.g., Tsimpli and Sorace 2006). Hence, for instance, while the discourse conditions which determine the distribution of overt and null pronominal subjects have been shown to develop later than the morphosyntactic properties which make null subjects possible, and are often not fully acquired, even by near-native learners (e.g., Montrul and Rodríguez Louro 2006), much recent work focusing on L2 learners of Romance languages has shown that knowledge of grammatical aspectual distinctions (relevant to the syntax–semantics interface) can be acquired, even by learners whose L1 lacks such distinctions (e.g., Montrul and Slabakova 2003). This has led to a more recent formulation of the Interface Hypothesis, which proposes that the interfaces which are external to the grammar (e.g., grammar–discourse) may present more difficulties in acquisition that those which are internal to the grammar (e.g., syntax–semantics) (Sorace 2011), as they require the integration of linguistic and non-linguistic information, thus being more costly in terms of the cognitive load which they place on the learner.

These issues provide the background for the research on the L2 acquisition of Portuguese which is discussed below.

3. Central issues

In the previous section, we considered some of the research questions which have been addressed within the generative paradigm. In this section, I will provide an overview of some of the topics which have been investigated in research on the L2 acquisition of Portuguese and which are relevant to these issues. I will concentrate on five topics which have received some attention in recent literature: pronominal clitic and null objects, inflected infinitives, aspect, verb movement, and pronominal subjects.

The recent literature on the acquisition of Portuguese has also revealed a growing interest in heritage language and third language (L3) acquisition, following a trend which has been observed for other languages. An examination of this research falls outside the scope of this chapter, although I may refer to some of the studies, given that there is some overlap with respect to the topics investigated.

3.1. Parameter resetting

In this section, we will consider studies on the acquisition of morphosyntactic properties, with the aim of drawing conclusions regarding the possibility of L2 parameter resetting.

One grammatical phenomenon which can help us understand how these properties are acquired is clitic placement: given that clitics are standardly assumed to be associated with functional projections in the clause structure, and considering the distinctive placement patterns which they display in EP, an understanding of how they are acquired may lead us to a better understanding of how syntactic knowledge develops in interlanguage grammars. Madeira and Xavier (2009) address the question of how knowledge of the syntactic distribution of clitics develops in L2 EP. Assuming a Full Access approach, the study tests the different predictions made by two theoretical hypotheses: Schwartz and Sprouse's (1996) Full Transfer/Full Access, which assumes that functional categories may be available at the initial state by transfer from the learner's L1, with their specific properties developing gradually— hence, different developmental paths are predicted depending on the learner's L1;

and Vainikka and Young-Scholten's (1996) Minimal Trees, which argues for the initial unavailability of functional categories, with these emerging gradually (and, hence, identical developmental paths are expected for all learners).

Based on an analysis of spontaneous production data from elementary, intermediate, and advanced learners, as well as on a grammaticality judgment task (administered only to elementary learners), the study compares native speakers of clitic and non clitic languages, and arrives at the following conclusions: (1) clitics are produced from the early stages; (2) learners develop early knowledge of the syntactic properties of clitics, excluding them from positions in which only strong pronouns are allowed; (3) knowledge of placement patterns develops gradually (unlike what has been found for other Romance languages, in which no difficulties with clitic placement have been reported): there is an initial overgeneralization of enclisis (which, in EP, is only allowed in the absence of a proclisis trigger, such as, for example, negation or certain preverbal adverbs and quantifiers), followed by gradual acquisition of the conditions which determine proclisis, starting with negation. Although no advanced learners participated in the study, the results from the intermediate learners indicate that the syntactic properties of clitics may be fully acquired. Hence, the results favor a weak continuity approach (as instantiated by the Minimal Trees Hypothesis): L2 learners acquire the morphosyntactic properties of clitics gradually, following a common developmental path, independently of their L1. This path appears to be similar to that found in the L1 acquisition of EP (Costa, Fiéis, and Lobo 2014).

Despite the misplacement errors produced by L2 learners, there is some evidence indicating that they may be more sensitive to the distinction between enclisis and proclisis than it would appear. An acceptability judgment task used in Fiéis, Madeira, and Xavier's (2013) study on clitic climbing (see section 3.2.), which tested, among other things, for knowledge of enclisis and proclisis in negation contexts, revealed that, although the elementary and intermediate learners did not evidence knowledge of the conditions governing enclisis and proclisis, exhibiting great variability, they were sensitive to the distinction and were aware of the status of negation as a proclisis trigger. Hence, the results of this study showed an asymmetry between clitic climbing contexts with and without negation in the matrix domain—similarly to the native control group, L2 learners displayed higher rates of acceptance of clitic climbing in the presence of negation in the higher clause (hence, (1a) is judged to be more acceptable than (1b)).

(1) a. *O   João não o   vai   ver.*
   the João not him-cl goes see-inf
   "João is not going to see him."

  b. *O   João vai- o   ver.*
   the João goes him-cl see-inf
   "João is going to see him."

The production data analyzed in Madeira and Xavier's (2009) study showed indications that learners occasionally resort to strategies in order to avoid the use of clitics: substitution of a strong pronoun or a full determiner phrase for the clitic, or, more significantly, clitic omission. The latter is a phenomenon which has also been observed to occur in the L1 acquisition of EP (Costa and Lobo 2009) and has been linked to the availability of null objects in the language. Fiéis and Madeira (2014) conducted a study with adult intermediate learners of EP, speakers of English (which has neither clitics nor null objects), Spanish (which has clitics but no null objects in specific contexts) and Chinese (which has null objects but no clitics). Based on production and comprehension data, it was shown that, although all the groups produced and accepted clitics, there was a clear asymmetry between the performance of the Chinese group, which exhibited high rates of (acceptance of) omission, and that of the other two groups. At least in production, the omission decreased in island contexts, which suggested that clitic drop actually corresponded to null objects. Although the rates of omission observed are lower than those reported for L1 EP, they appear to be significantly higher than those found in the adult L2 acquisition of other Romance languages (see, e.g., Arche and Domínguez's 2011 study on Spanish).

Another phenomenon which has been argued to confirm that parameter resetting is possible in L2 acquisition is the inflected infinitive. With the goal of testing the predictions of two different approaches—Full Access and Partial Access (namely, Hawkins and Chan's 1997 Failed Functional Features Hypothesis, according to which L2 morphosyntactic features which are not available in the learners' L1 grammar may not be acquired)—Rothman and Iverson (2007) investigated the acquisition of inflected infinitives in BP by seventeen English and eight Spanish/English bilingual adult learners placed at an advanced level. Assuming Raposo's (1987) analysis of the inflected infinitive as involving two parameters, namely, the Null Subject Parameter and the Inflection Parameter (a morphological parameter), the learning task is assumed to differ for the two groups: whereas the monolingual English group must reset both parameters, the bilingual Spanish/English group only has to reset the Inflection Parameter. Rothman and Iverson (2007) used a grammaticality judgment task to test for knowledge of the syntactic distribution of inflected infinitives (namely, knowledge that they are allowed in certain contexts, such as complements to declarative and factive verbs, but not in others, such as interrogative and relative clauses, as well as finite contexts). They also tested for knowledge of the different properties of inflected and non-inflected infinitives with respect to control properties, which give rise to different semantic interpretations: unlike uninflected infinitival clauses, the subject of inflected infinitival clauses does not require a local c-commanding antecedent (2) and allows split antecedents (3); moreover, inflected infinitives allow a strict interpretation under ellipsis (4).

(2) Eu_i *lamento [-]_j   termos   mentido.*
    I   regret-1sg   have-inf-1pl   lied
    "I regret that we lied."

(3) Eu_i *convenci   o   João_j a [-]_{i+j} irmos   ao   cinema.*
    I   convinced-1sg   the João   to go-inf-1pl to-the cinema
    "I convinced João that we should go to the cinema."

(4) Eu_i *fiquei   feliz   por [-]_j teres   conseguido o   emprego e a Joana também [-].*
    I   was-1sg happy for   have-inf-2sg got the job and the Joana also
    "I was happy that you got the job and Joana was too." (= Joana was happy that you got the job.)

On the basis of the results of a context match task, Rothman and Iverson (2007) conclude that their L2 learners display native-like knowledge of these interpretative restrictions on the inflected infinitive. These results are argued to support Full Access, as no significant differences were found between the results of the two groups and those of the native control group, which indicates that learners have developed native-like knowledge of the morphological and syntactic properties of the inflected infinitive, as well as of the interpretative properties which are derived from their control properties.

Given that the learners in this study were advanced learners, it is possible to reach a conclusion regarding the acquisition of the properties of the inflected infinitive, but not regarding the way in which these properties develop and whether they all develop simultaneously.

Using three experimental tasks (an adapted version of Pires and Rothman's (2009) morphological recognition task, a syntactic distribution task and an interpretation task), Madeira and Xavier (2012) tested adult elementary and advanced Chinese- and Spanish-speaking learners of L2 EP for knowledge both of the morphosyntactic properties of the inflected infinitive and of those control properties which are relevant for the interpretation. The results confirmed Rothman and Iverson's (2007) findings for BP, providing further evidence for Full Access: the advanced learners were found to have developed knowledge of the morphological and syntactic properties of the inflected infinitive, thus showing that successful acquisition is indeed possible for all learners, independently of their L1. However, this knowledge appears to develop gradually, as the elementary groups performed in a significantly different manner both from the advanced groups and from the native controls in the study.

In a different study, Rothman (2009) further tests the predictions of Full Access and Partial Access approaches, this time investigating the acquisition, by twenty-one advanced English learners of L2 BP, of a syntactic asymmetry displayed by inflected and uninflected infinitives. As first noted in Quicoli (1988), inflected infinitival subjects may only undergo movement from A'-positions, whereas uninflected infinitives only allow subject extraction from an A-position (see (5–6)).

(5) *As meninas parecem   gostar(*em)   do   filme.*
     the girls   appear-3pl like-inf-(*3pl) of-the   film
     "The girls appear to like the film."
     (Rothman 2009: 126)

(6) *Que   meninos você acha   ser*(em)   os mais inteligentes do   grupo?*
     which boys   you   think-3sg be-inf-*(3pl) the most intelligent of-the group
     "Which boys do you think are the most intelligent from the group?"
     (Rothman 2009: 127)

A comparison between the results obtained by the L2 learners in a grammaticality judgment task with correction and those of a native control group shows that the L2 learners exhibit target-like behavior with respect to the distinction between inflected and uninflected infinitives with embedded subject movement. Again, this constitutes further evidence for parameter resetting and, hence, for Full Access.

Another morphosyntactic phenomenon which has been investigated is verb movement. In a paper which seeks to determine whether there are any similarities between heritage speakers and L2 learners, Santos and Flores (2013) examine the acquisition of V-to-I movement, by twenty-one adult intermediate learners of EP, who are native speakers of German, comparing them both to child Portuguese–German heritage speakers and to child and adult monolingual EP speakers. Verb raising is a core syntactic property, which determines, amongst other phenomena, the relative order of the verb and low adverbs (7).

(7) *A   Sara pintou   completamente a   parede.*
     the   Sara painted-3sg completely   the   wall
     "Sara painted the wall completely."
     (Santos and Flores 2013: 567)

Although the L2 learners were learning Portuguese in a formal instructional setting, adverb placement was not explicitly taught in class. On the basis of the findings from two experimental tasks (a production task and a grammaticality judgment task), it is shown that the L2 learners do not show any significant differences from the control groups, show a preference for V-Adv order, which confirms that they have acquired V-to-I movement, and show no effects of influence of their L1 V2 grammar, which provides evidence for parameter resetting.

To conclude this section, we consider null subjects. Madeira, Xavier, and Crispim (2009) examine how knowledge of the morphosyntactic properties associated with a positive value of the null subject parameter develops in the grammars of L2 learners of EP at different levels of proficiency. The results of the study, which is based on production data and on data from a preference judgment task, indicate that these properties are acquired early, although some differences are observed between speakers of different L1s, not with respect to the path of acquisition which they follow, but in their pace of development. This confirms the conclusions of an earlier study on the development of null subject properties in the grammars of Spanish-speaking learners of EP, which showed that the null subject L1 grammar of the learners did not appear to influence the developmental path of these properties, with the parametric properties emerging gradually (Mendes 2007).

Although BP displays different properties regarding the availability of null subjects, allowing a reduced use of null subjects and displaying a preference for overt pronominal subjects in many contexts (it has been argued that BP has undergone a change from a full pro-drop to a semi-pro-drop language - see, e.g., Duarte 1995), it appears that the relevant properties are also acquired early by L2 learners of BP; furthermore, their development does not exhibit significant L1 effects and it follows a fixed path (Xavier 2006; Montrul, Dias, and Thomé-Williams 2009; Molsing 2011).

3.2. Interfaces

In this section, we will describe a few studies which aim to determine whether there is selectivity in the acquisition of different types of phenomena, as has been argued under the Interface Hypothesis (see Section 2, Generative second language acquisition).

We start by returning to a construction which was mentioned in the previous section, namely clitic climbing. This is a phenomenon which is found in restructuring contexts and whose acquisition requires developing different types of knowledge: syntactic knowledge, as learners need to develop knowledge of the functional properties of clitics, and lexical knowledge, as they also need to learn which particular verbs allow restructuring. Hence, whether clitic climbing is obligatory or not depends on the degree of functional defectiveness of the complement selected by the verb (see (8) and (9) below).

(8) *Tinham telefonado-te /   Tinham-te   telefonado.*
     had-3pl phoned-pp you-cl / had-3pl you-cl phoned-pp
     "I had phoned you."

(9) *Quero   telefonar- te /   Quero-   te   telefonar.*
     want-1sg phone-inf you-cl / want-1sg you-cl phone-inf
     "I want to phone you."

Clitic climbing was investigated in a study by Fiéis, Madeira, and Xavier (2013). Forty elementary and intermediate Spanish- and German-speaking university students on study-abroad programs in Portugal, as well as ten native controls, participated in the study. The choice of these language groups was determined by the characteristics of each language with respect to the relevant properties: hence, Spanish has both restructuring and clitic climbing, whereas German only exhibits restructuring. The study sought to address the following research questions: (1) How early does clitic climbing develop in the acquisition of L2 EP? (2) Does knowledge of the verbs which disfavor or trigger (obligatory or optional) clitic climbing develop early? and (3) does the L1 play a role in the acquisition of clitic climbing? The results of an acceptability judgement task showed that only the intermediate Spanish-speaking learners performed systematically on a par with the native control group. Clitic climbing was shown to emerge early, independently of the learners' L1, which indicates early availability of the relevant functional positions in the clause structure. Nevertheless, the fact that the performance of the elementary Spanish-speaking group consistently differed from that of the intermediate group with respect to the distinctions established among the different verbs tested showed a clear proficiency effect for this L1 group. The near-target-like behavior of the intermediate group indicates that, at least for some L1 groups, the development of lexicon–syntax interface properties is not delayed. No differences were found between the two German-speaking groups, and the two intermediate groups consistently exhibited different behaviors, which suggests that the L1 may play a facilitating role in the acquisition of these types of properties.

In another study on L2 BP inflected infinitives, Iverson and Rothman (2008) investigated knowledge of the genericity effects which characterize eventive verbs in the inflected infinitival complements of propositional verbs (Ambar 1998). Whereas the inflected infinitive in (10) is impossible with a single event reading, the generic reading forced by the bare plural direct object and by the adverbial in (11) makes the sentence grammatical.

(10) *Penso   lerem   o jornal.*
     think-1sg read-inf-3pl the newspaper
     "I think that they read the newspaper."

(11) *Penso   lerem   jornais   todos os dias.*
     think-1sg read-inf-3pl newspapers all   the days
     "I think that they read newspapers every day."

Assuming that, although knowledge at the interface between syntax and semantics may be harder to acquire than syntactic knowledge, it is, nevertheless, acquirable, Iverson and Rothman (2008) predict convergence on the relevant properties. These predictions are confirmed: the results of a truth value judgment task reveal no significant differences between their advanced English-speaking learners and the native controls, showing that syntax–semantics interface knowledge may indeed be fully acquired.

A similar conclusion is reached regarding the acquisition of aspectual contrasts in BP. In a series of studies investigating L2 learners' knowledge of semantic contrasts associated with the Preterite/Imperfect distinction (e.g., Goodin-Mayeda and Rothman 2007; Rothman and Iverson 2008), it is shown that advanced English learners perform target-like with respect to the interpretation of these contrasts. Rothman and Iverson (2008) argue that even the group of intermediate learners included in their study, although differing from the native controls, still manage to establish a distinction between the Preterite and the Imperfect. It appears, therefore, that knowledge of these properties is not necessarily delayed (despite the deficits in the production of the associated verbal morphology noted in the literature—see, e.g., Lardiere 2007).

Returning to Santos and Flores (2013) (see section 3.1.), another property investigated in their study, which has also been shown to be related to verb movement, is VP-ellipsis. Unlike adverb placement, VP-ellipsis involves knowledge of discourse constraints, as the elided material must be identified by the preceding discourse (12).

(12) *A Teresa tinha oferecido flores à mãe e a Ana também tinha [oferecido flores à mãe].*
     the Teresa had -3sg offered flowers to-the mother and the Ana also had -3sg
     [offered flowers to-the mother]
     "Teresa had offered flowers to her mother and so had Ana."
                         (Santos and Flores 2013: 568)

Using an elicited production task, Santos and Flores (2013) show that all their groups produce VP-ellipsis. However, unlike what was found for adverb placement, the behavior of the L2 group with respect to this property is argued to differ significantly from that of the adult L1 controls, exhibiting significantly lower production rates. Hence, a comparison of these results with those obtained for adverb placement reveals a delayed development of knowledge of VP-ellipsis. This differs from what is known about VP-ellipsis in L1 EP, where it has been shown to be acquired early (Santos 2009).

Another phenomenon which is relevant to the syntax–discourse interface is the distribution of pronominal subjects. Madeira, Xavier, and Crispim (2009) also considered learners' performance with respect to the discourse properties which determine the distribution of null and overt pronominal subjects. The results show a delay in the acquisition of these properties, particularly for speakers of non-pro-drop languages. In a further study (Madeira, Xavier, and Crispim 2012), which examines the preferences of elementary and advanced Italian- and Chinese-speaking learners of EP regarding the interpretation of null and overt pronominal subjects, a clear asymmetry between the Italian and the Chinese learners was revealed. Hence, whereas the Italian learners displayed target-like preferences with both overt and null subjects, the Chinese learners only showed target-like preferences with null subjects, revealing difficulties in the interpretation of overt pronominal subjects. This appears to confirm that there is an L1 effect in the acquisition of the interpretation bias which characterizes (at least, overt) pronominal subjects.

4. Concluding remarks

We have considered the theoretical issues discussed in the introduction to the framework above (see Section 2, Generative second language acquisition) in the light of research conducted in recent years on the L2 acquisition of EP and BP. Some of the constructions which have been investigated present features which, within the context of Romance languages, are specific to Portuguese (e.g., clitic placement patterns, null objects and inflected infinitives), whereas others are also found in some of the other Romance languages (e.g., verb raising or the Preterite/Imperfect distinction). Furthermore, while the two varieties of Portuguese considered here share some of the properties discussed above (e.g., the Preterite/ Imperfect distinction), other properties differ in the two languages (e.g., the distribution of null subjects) and, in other cases, although they display identical characteristics and distribution, they present different degrees of productivity (e.g., inflected infinitives). Nevertheless, the results obtained in the studies which focus on BP and those focusing on EP appear to lead to similar conclusions; and, moreover, the overall conclusions that we reach when we consider the various studies described in this chapter corroborate those reached by research on other languages.

With respect to morphosyntactic phenomena such as clitic placement, inflected infinitives, verb movement and null subjects, the general conclusion appears to be that they tend to be acquired fairly early (with knowledge of clitic placement and inflected infinitives appearing to develop more slowly than knowledge of verb movement and null subjects). Moreover, it appears that, at least for some of the properties (e.g., clitic placement), there is a common developmental path which is not influenced by the learner's L1 and which, for some phenomena, might be similar to the one observed in the L1 acquisition of Portuguese. Taken together, these conclusions support Full Access approaches, confirming that parameter resetting is indeed possible.

Regarding interface properties, we considered different types of properties. Clitic climbing, which requires the integration of syntactic and lexical knowledge, appears to be delayed, but nevertheless acquirable. On the other hand, the genericity restrictions on inflected infinitival complements to propositional verbs and the semantic contrasts associated with the Preterite/ Imperfect distinction, which also involve integration of different types of knowledge (syntactic and semantic knowledge, in the former case, and morphological and semantic in the latter), may also be delayed, but they were shown to have been fully acquired by learners at the advanced level, who displayed target-like knowledge of these properties. Finally, the results regarding VP-ellipsis and pronominal subjects reveal that learners have difficulties with properties which require the integration of syntactic and contextual information. Considered together, these findings appear indeed to confirm Sorace's (2011) formulation of the Interface Hypothesis—external interface properties present more difficulties for L2 learners and appear to be developmentally delayed, when compared to internal interface properties.

There are still many open questions regarding the status of different properties in L2 acquisition. For example, why is knowledge of some morphosyntactic properties delayed when compared to other properties of the same type? It is probably not accidental that the two properties which appear to be delayed in the studies surveyed above are clitic placement (in EP) and inflected infinitives (in both varieties), which are properties which set Portuguese apart from other Romance languages. Could there be a complexity factor at play here? Regarding the interface properties we examined, and which also appear to differ among themselves with regard to timing of acquisition, it has to be noted that not all the learners in the different studies were at the same level of proficiency. In order to reach firmer conclusions on whether there are in fact any asymmetries among different properties, it is necessary to conduct further studies, ensuring homogeneity with respect to the participants' levels of proficiency.

Cross-linguistic influence appears to be stronger with interface properties (in the case of morphosyntactic properties, clear L1 effects are observed only with respect to clitic omission). However, not all knowledge of interface properties shows evidence of cross-linguistic influence: this is visible with respect to the syntax–discourse interface properties (VP-ellipsis and pronominal subjects) as well as with clitic climbing. It is therefore not clear yet why some phenomena are more susceptible to cross-linguistic influence than others.

Regarding VP-ellipsis, Santos and Flores (2013) claim that at least some of their L2 learners tend to avoid VP-ellipsis preferring to resort to alternative strategies which are available in German (and also possible in Portuguese), namely, pseudo-stripping and use of pronouns and adverbs. Hence, in this case, L1 influence would determine a preference for one particular strategy in a situation in which more than one strategy is available.

As for the role of the input and, in particular, of explicit instruction, in general, all the L2 learners in the studies discussed in this chapter had learnt Portuguese formally and many were either on study-abroad programs at the time of the study or had spent some time in a Portuguese-speaking country. Nevertheless, not all the properties investigated and which were argued to have been acquired are taught explicitly in the classroom (this is the case, for example, of some of the interpretative contrasts associated with the Preterite/Imperfect distinction or the genericity constraints found with the inflected infinitive). Moreover, in the case of properties which are explicitly taught, such as clitic placement, the order of acquisition observed does not necessarily coincide with the order in which these constructions are taught. Hence, there are still many questions regarding the effect of explicit instruction on the acquisition of different types of grammatical properties. In particular, it would be interesting to conduct more studies on naturalistic L2 learners in order to understand whether there are any significant differences with regard to the acquisition of different types of properties.

Finally, some of the differences between EP and BP relate to the degree of productivity of grammatical structures. For instance, whereas inflected infinitives are highly productive in all registers of EP (particularly in certain contexts, such as, e.g., adverbial clauses), it is claimed that in colloquial BP the inflected infinitive is no longer a productive option (see, for example, Pires and Rothman 2009, who argue that the inflected infinitive is acquired through schooling). This would be a case where it would be interesting to compare formal and informal learners, and to conduct studies which allowed us to compare informal learners of EP and BP. In general, there are not enough studies which compare the two varieties in the domain of L2 acquisition. This is clearly an area where a lot of work remains to be done.

REFERENCES

Ambar, M. (1998). Inflected infinitives revisited: genericity and single event. *The Canadian Journal of Linguistics/La Revue Canadienne de Linguistique*, 43, pp. 5–36.

Arche, M. and L. Domínguez (2011). Morphology and syntax dissociation in SLA: a study on clitic acquisition in Spanish. In A. Galani, G. Hicks, and G. Tsoulas (eds.), *Morphology and its Interfaces*. Amsterdam: John Benjamins, pp. 291–320.

Birdsong, D. (1992). Ultimate attainment in second language acquisition. *Language*, 68, pp. 706–755.

Bley-Vroman, R. (1989). What is the logical problem of foreign language learning? In S. Gass and J. Schachter (eds.), *Linguistic Perspectives on Second Language Acquisition*. Cambridge: Cambridge University Press, pp. 41–68.

Chomsky, N. (1987). *Language and Problems of Knowledge. The Managua Lectures*. Cambridge, MA: MIT Press.

Costa, J. and M. Lobo (2009). Clitic omission in the acquisition of European Portuguese: data from comprehension. In A. Pires and J. Rothman (eds.), *Minimalist Inquiries into Child and Adult Language Acquisition: Case Studies across Portuguese*. Berlin: de Gruyter, pp. 63–84.

Costa, J., A. Fiéis, and M. Lobo (2014). Input variability and late acquisition: clitic misplacement in European Portuguese. *Lingua*, 2191, pp. 1–17.

Duarte, M. E. L. (1995). A perda do princípio "Evite Pronome" no português brasileiro. Ph.D. dissertation, Universidade Estadual de Campinas.

Fiéis, A. and A. Madeira (2014). Clíticos e Objetos Nulos na Aquisição de Português L2. Paper presented at XXIX Encontro Nacional da Associação Portuguesa de Linguística, Universidade de Coimbra.

Fiéis, A., A. Madeira, and M. F. Xavier (2013). Clitic climbing in L2 Portuguese. In J. Cabrelli Amaro, T. Judy, and D. Pascual y Cabo (eds.), *Proceedings of the 12th Generative Approaches to Second Language Acquisition Conference (GASLA 2013)*. Somerville, MA: Cascadilla Proceedings Project, pp. 39–49.

Goodin-Mayeda, C. E. and J. Rothman (2007). The acquisition of aspect in L2 Portuguese and Spanish: exploring native/non-native performance differences. In S. Baauw, F. Dirjkoningen, and M. Pinto (eds.), *Romance Languages and Linguistic Theory 2005*. Amsterdam: John Benjamins, pp. 131–148.

Hawkins, R. and C. Y.-H. Chan (1997). The partial availability of universal grammar in second language acquisition: the "failed functional features hypothesis." *Second Language Research*, 13, pp. 187–226.

Iverson, M. and J. Rothman (2008). The syntax–semantics interface in L2 acquisition: genericity and inflected infinitive complements in non-native Portuguese. In J. Bruhn de Garavito and E. Valenzuela (eds.), *Selected Proceedings of the 10th Hispanic Linguistics Symposium*. Somerville, MA: Cascadilla Proceedings Project, pp. 78–92.

Lardiere, D. (2007). *Ultimate Attainment in Second Language Acquisition: A Case Study*. Mahwah, NJ: Lawrence Erlbaum.

Madeira, A. and M. F. Xavier (2009). The acquisition of clitic pronouns in L2 European Portuguese. In A. Pires and J. Rothman (eds.), *Minimalist Inquiries into Child and Adult Language Acquisition: Case Studies across Portuguese*. Berlin: de Gruyter, pp. 273–300.

Madeira, A. and M. F. Xavier (2012). The acquisition of the inflected infinitive by speakers of Chinese, Italian and Spanish. Paper presented at the Workshop on Crosslinguistic Influence in L2, Universidade Nova de Lisboa.

Madeira, A., M. F. Xavier, and M. L. Crispim (2009). A Aquisição de Sujeitos Nulos em Português L2. *Estudos da Língua(gem)*, 7 (2), pp. 163–198.

Madeira, A., M. F. Xavier, and M. L. Crispim (2012). Uso e interpretação de sujeitos pronominais em português L2. In A. Costa, C. Flores, and N. Alexandre (eds.), *Textos Selecionados do XXVII Encontro da Associação Portuguesa de Linguística*. Lisbon: Associação Portuguesa de Linguística, pp. 376–397.

Mendes, C. (2007). ¿Acceso a la GU en la Adquisición de L2? Cuando las L1 y L2 comparten el Mismo Parámetro (pro-drop). Master dissertation, Universidad Simón Bolívar.

Molsing, K. (2011). Sobre a Aquisição de uma Língua Semi-Pro-Drop como L2. *Letras de Hoje*, 46 (3), pp. 44–58.

Montrul, S., R. Dias, and A. Thomé-Williams (2009). Subject expression in the non-native acquisition of Brazilian Portuguese. In A. Pires and J. Rothman (eds.), *Minimalist Inquiries into Child and Adult Language Acquisition: Case Studies across Portuguese*. Berlin: de Gruyter, pp. 301–325.

Montrul, S. and C. Rodríguez Louro (2006). Beyond the syntax of the null subject parameter: a look at the discourse-pragmatic distribution of null and overt subjects by L2 learners of Spanish. In V. Torrens and L. Escobar (eds.), *The Acquisition of Syntax in Romance Languages*. Amsterdam: John Benjamins, pp. 401–418.

Montrul, S. and R. Slabakova (2003). Competence similarities between natives and near-native speakers: an investigation of the preterit/imperfect contrast in Spanish. *Studies in Second Language Acquisition*, 25, pp. 351–398.

Pires, A. and J. Rothman (2009). Acquisition of Brazilian Portuguese in late childhood: implications for syntactic theory and language change In A. Pires and J. Rothman

(eds.), *Minimalist Inquiries into Child and Adult Language Acquisition: Case Studies across Portuguese*. Berlin: de Gruyter, pp. 130–153.

Quicoli, C. (1988). *Inflection and parametric variation: Portuguese vs. Spanish*. Manuscript, University of California.

Raposo, E. (1987). Case theory and infl-to-comp: the inflected infinitive in European Portuguese. *Linguistic Inquiry*, 18, pp. 85–109.

Rothman, J. (2009). Knowledge of A/A'-dependencies on subject extraction with two types of infinitives in non-native Portuguese adult bilingualism. *International Journal of Bilingualism*, 13 (1), pp. 111–140.

Rothman, J. and M. Iverson (2007). To inflect or not to inflect is the question indeed: infinitives in second language (L2) Portuguese. *Journal of Portuguese Linguistics*, 6 (2), pp. 3–28.

Rothman, J. and M. Iverson (2008). Poverty-of-the-stimulus and SLA epistemology: considering L2 knowledge of aspectual phrasal semantics. *Language Acquisition*, 15 (4), pp. 270–314.

Santos, A. L. (2009). *Minimal Answers: Ellipsis, Syntax and Discourse in the Acquisition of European Portuguese*. Amsterdam: John Benjamins.

Santos, A. L. and C. Flores (2013). Elipse do SV e Distribuição de Advérbios em Português Língua de Herança e L2. *Textos Selecionados do XXVIII Encontro Nacional da Associação Portuguesa de Linguística*. Coimbra: Associação Portuguesa de Linguística, pp. 563–584.

Schwartz, B. and R. Sprouse (1996). L2 cognitive states and the full transfer/full access model. *Second Language Research*, 12, pp. 40–72.

Schwartz, B. and R. Sprouse (2000). When syntactic theories evolve: consequences for L2 acquisition research. In J. Archibald (ed.), *Second Language Acquisition and Linguistic Theory*. Oxford: Blackwell, pp. 156–186.

Selinker, L. (1972). Interlanguage. *International Review of Applied Linguistics in Language Teaching*, 10, pp. 209–232.

Sorace, A. (2011). Pinning down the concept of "interface" in bilingualism. *Linguistic Approaches to Bilingualism*, 1, pp. 1–33.

Sorace, A. and F. Filiaci (2006). Anaphora resolution in near-native speakers of Italian. *Second Language Research*, 22 (3), pp. 339–368.

Tsimpli, I. M. and M. Dimitrakopoulou (2007). The interpretability hypothesis: evidence from wh-interrogatives in second language acquisition. *Second Language Research*, 23, pp. 215–242.

Tsimpli, I. M. and A. Sorace (2006). Differentiating interfaces: L2 performance in syntax–semantics and syntax–discourse phenomena. In D. Bamman, T. Magnitskaia, and C. Zaller (eds.), *Proceedings of the 30th Annual Boston University Conference on Language Development*. Somerville, MA: Cascadilla Press, pp. 653–664.

Vainikka, A. and M. Young-Scholten (1996). Gradual development of L2 phrase structure. *Second Language Research*, 12, pp. 7–39.

White, L. (2003). *Second Language Acquisition and Universal Grammar*. Cambridge: Cambridge University Press.

Xavier, G. (2006). Português Brasileiro como Segunda Língua: Um Estudo sobre o Sujeito Nulo. Ph.D. dissertation, Universidade Estadual de Campinas.

Index